ENCYCLOPEDIA
OF
ASIAN
HISTORY

ENCYCLOPEDIA
OF
ASIAN
HISTORY

Prepared under the auspices of
The Asia Society

Ainslie T. Embree

EDITOR IN CHIEF

Volume 3

Charles Scribner's Sons
New York

Collier Macmillan Publishers
London

Charles Scribner's Sons
Macmillan Publishing Company
866 Third Avenue, New York, N.Y. 10022

Collier Macmillan Canada, Inc.

Library of Congress Catalog Card Number: 87–9891

Library of Congress Cataloging-in-Publication Data

Encyclopedia of Asian History

Includes bibliographies and index
1. Asia—History—Dictionaries   I. Embree, Ainslie Thomas
DS31.E53   1988   950   87-9891
ISBN 0–684–18619–5 (set)
ISBN 0–684–18900–3 (v. 3)

Acknowledgments of permissions to reproduce photographs
are gratefully made in a special listing in volume 4.

Printed in the United States of America

printing number

2 3 4 5 6 7 8 9 10

ENCYCLOPEDIA
OF
ASIAN
HISTORY

M

(CONTINUED)

MIN, QUEEN (1851–1895), wife of the twenty-sixth Yi monarch, Kojong (r. 1864–1907), and leader of the most powerful political faction in Korean politics between 1874 and her death in 1895. She was chosen as queen in 1866 from an obscure lineage (Yŏhŭng Min) because Kojong's father, the Taewŏn'gun ("grand prince"), had hoped to avoid the problem of a powerful consort clan. Queen Min proved to be an ambitious and resourceful politician, however, and the Min clan rose to prominence in the late 1860s. After Kojong attained majority in 1873, the Min clan became the most powerful political faction at court until the Queen's brutal assassination in October 1895.

As patron to her male relatives Queen Min insinuated family members into high bureaucratic posts during the regency of the Taewŏn'gun (1864–1873). The queen became a bitter enemy of her father-in-law. This enmity can be traced to the Taewŏn'gun's effort to name a concubine's son as crown prince after the death of the queen's first child in 1871. The Min clan were in power during the opening of Korea to foreign commerce in 1876, and they continued to dominate public policy thereafter.

The abortive 1882 army revolt challenged Min hegemony and attempted to restore the Taewŏn'gun to power. The queen's reputedly immoral deportment and the corruption of her relatives were the focus of widespread criticism in and out of government in the 1880s. During the Tonghak Rebellion (1894–1895) rebel memorials attacked the corruption of the queen and her family, and attempts were made to limit the queen's power institutionally during the subsequent Kabo Reforms (1895). [*See also* 1882 Uprising; Tonghak; *and* Kabo Reforms.]

In 1895 resident Japanese officials conspired to assassinate Queen Min in order to advance Japanese interests. On 8 October 1895 an armed group broke into the palace, murdered Queen Min, and burned her corpse. The plot backfired in a storm of diplomatic protest and disgust, but the assassination nevertheless marked the end of Min power in Yi politics.

[*See also* Kojong; Taewŏn'gun; *and* Yi Dynasty.]

MICHAEL ROBINSON

MINAMI KIKAN. Formally inaugurated on 1 February 1941, the Minami Kikan was a Japanese clandestine organization established to facilitate the cooperation of young Burmese nationalists with the Japanese military in its plans to occupy Southeast Asia. Its leader, Colonel Suzuki Keiji, or Bo Mogyo, as he was known to the Burmese, used Minami as a cover name while operating in Burma before the war. After the recruitment of the so-called Thirty Comrades, who formed the nucleus of the Burma Independence Army, Colonel Suzuki became commander of the group; when these forces, with the Japanese, entered Burma from Thailand in January 1942, Suzuki shared formal command with Aung San. Because of his advocacy of genuine Burmese independence in the face of contrary Japanese policy, Suzuki was later removed from control of the Minami Kikan.

[*See also* Burma Defense Army: Aung San; *and* World War II in Asia.]

ROBERT H. TAYLOR

MINAMOTO, surname granted to certain descendants (also called Genji) of the Japanese imperial family between 800 and 1050. As finances tightened in the early Heian era (794–1185), the imperial house found it could no longer support all its offspring. In addition, the northern branch of the Fujiwara family came to monopolize political offices in the capital, making political advancement for members of the imperial lineage all but impossible.

As a result, one of two surnames, either Minamoto or Taira, was bestowed on an emperor's child, ending his affiliation with the imperial line.

Altogether, nine emperors conferred the Minamoto name on their children: Saga, Junna, Nimmyō, Montoku, Seiwa, Murakami, Uda, Daigo, and Kazan. Of these offspring, the Murakami, Uda, Kazan, and the Seiwa Genji were the most significant. The Murakami line began in 1020, when Morofusa received the surname; Morofusa himself was appointed "minister of the right" and his second son succeeded in breaking the Fujiwara stranglehold on other high posts. Later, a member of the Murakami line known as Michichika became involved in intrigue against the Kamakura shogunate. After his demise the Murakami split into four branches. The Kazan Minamoto were the hereditary Shinto priests of the court; they were even allowed to use the title "prince." The Uda Genji rose only as high as the middle ranks of the aristocracy, but eventually became the founders of military houses such as the Kyōgoku and the Rokkaku.

By far the most illustrious of all the branches was the Seiwa Genji. Commencing with Minamoto no Tsunemoto in the mid-tenth century, the Seiwa house was famous as Japan's greatest military family. Tsunemoto began the tradition by helping to crush the revolts of Taira no Masakado in 940 and the pirate Fujiwara no Sumitomo in 941. His son Mitsunaka became the military enforcer for the Fujiwara as a result of his collaboration in the Anna Incident in 969. Mitsunaka's three sons founded new lines in the provinces of Settsu (Osaka), Yamato (Nara), and Kawachi (also Osaka); the Kawachi chief Yorinobu gained renown as the nemesis of Taira no Tadatsune, a rebel of eastern Japan. Yorinobu's descendants Yoriyoshi and Yoshiie campaigned in northeastern Japan in the Former Nine Years' War and the Latter Three Years' War in the second half of the eleventh century.

Yoshiie's heirs, however, were all unfit. The retired emperors, who had replaced the Fujiwara as heads of state, soon chose the Taira of Ise province to be their "teeth and claws." The two military houses clashed first in the Hōgen War in 1156 and later in the Heiji War of 1159; the Taira succeeded in vanquishing first Minamoto no Tameyoshi and then his son Yoshitomo. [See Hōgen and Heiji Wars.] The Minamoto remained in the shadow of the Taira until 1180, when Taira no Kiyomori's high-handed politics provoked another war. [See Taira no Kiyomori.] Under the adroit leadership of Minamoto no Yoritomo and the battlefield wizardry of his brother Yoshitsune, the Taira were destroyed, and Yoritomo established the first military government, the Kamakura shogunate. Yoritomo's line ended with the death of his son Sanetomo in 1219, but Minamoto influence lived on through numerous branch families such as the Takeda and the Ashikaga.

Jeffrey P. Mass, *Warrior Government in Early Medieval Japan* (1974). Helen McCullough, *Gikeiki* (1966) and "A Tale of Mutsu," *Harvard Journal of Asiatic Studies* 25 (1964): 178–211. Minoru Shinoda, *The Founding of the Kamakura Shogunate* (1960).   WAYNE FARRIS

MINANGKABAU. The Minangkabau, who make up approximately 90 percent of the inhabitants of the Indonesian province of West Sumatra (with a population of three million in 1975), are one of the largest matrilineal societies in the world and at the same time a devoutly Islamic people. Their original settlements were in the upland valleys of the region, particularly around the volcano of Mount Merapi in the three districts (*luhak*) of Agam, Tanah Datar, and Limapuluh Kota.

The first historical record of the Minangkabau appears in 1347 when inscriptions indicate that Adityavarman, a prince of mixed Javanese-Sumatran parentage, threw off allegiance to the East Java kingdom of Majapahit and ruled the gold-rich regions of Tanah Datar until at least 1375. Oral tradition traces the two systems of social organization that characterize the independent Minangkabau villages (*nagari*) from this period. Essentially federations of kinship groups governed by lineage headmen and with no effective supravillage authority, the *nagari* adopted either an autocratic or more democratic system of governance.

The Padri War (1803–1837) enabled the Dutch to gain control of the region, and much of their administration in the late nineteenth century was directed to controlling and monopolizing coffee production and export. When these controls were relaxed in the early twentieth century, Minangkabau traders and farmers became more active in a highly monetized economy based on coffee, rubber, and copra exports. Anticolonial feelings were strong among the Minangkabau, with sporadic uprisings against the Dutch (notably in 1908 and 1927) and with many Minangkabau assuming prominent leadership roles in the Indonesian nationalist movement. During the revolution (1945–1949), the Dutch eventually occupied most towns, but they never extended their control to the villages and rural areas, which remained loyal to the republican government. The Minangkabau region was the principal center of the regional rebellion against the Sukarno government in 1958. Suppression of that revolt accelerated traditional Minangkabau migration (*merantau*)—in 1930, according to the census, 11 percent of the Minangkabau lived outside their province—and in recent years there have been large-scale population movements to the large urban centers of Sumatra and Java, particularly to Jakarta.

[*See also* Indonesia, Republic of; Padri War; *and* Sukarno.]

Taufik Abdullah, *Schools and Politics: The Kaum Muda Movement in West Sumatra* (1971). Christine Dobbin, *Islamic Revivalism in a Changing Peasant Economy* (1983). E. Graves, *The Minangkabau Response to Dutch Colonial Rule* (1981). Joel Kahn, *Minangkabau Social Formations* (1980). Tsuyoshi Kato, *Matriliny and Migration* (1982).   AUDREY R. KAHIN

MINARET. The term *minaret* (Arabic, *manara*) refers to any Muslim tower. In modern usage it usually means a tower that is attached or adjacent to a mosque and used for calling the faithful to prayer.

Towers were employed before and after the advent of Islam as watchtowers and lighthouses and for other secular purposes. They may be traced back to the Indian *lats* erected in the third century BCE. They are found from West Africa to Indonesia and China and differ in both shape and construction according to location and available materials.

Characteristic shapes and materials vary from region to region in the Islamic world. For example, eastern minarets are often cylindrical in shape while western ones are often angular. The large, square-based minaret of North Africa bears a strong resemblance to a lighthouse, which it may once have been, and often has windows. Persian minarets, in contrast, are typically thin, tall spires, carefully decorated, with a primary function as religious art.

Herman Thiersch, *Pharos in Antike, Islam und Occident* (1909).   JAHAN SALEHI

MINDANAO, second largest of the islands of the Philippines, located to the extreme south of the archipelago. Its area encompasses 36,536 square miles; its population exceeds eight million. Historically it has been the island least well controlled by the Manila government, and often it has harbored antigovernment resistance.

During the Spanish colonial period, from the late sixteenth century to 1898, Mindanao was barely controlled by Manila, and its hispanized Christian population was small and confined to a few coastal cities. Parts of the island harbored large Muslim populations, and it served as a base for so-called Moro raids against the islands to the north, which were suppressed only gradually.

Mindanao was brought under control by the American authorities slowly, as late as 1913, long after most of the rest of the archipelago. Migration to Mindanao from the densely populated northern and central islands began in the 1920s and picked up after World War II, particularly when organized resettlement on the island was promoted among agrarian rebels who had joined the Hukbalahap movement and surrendered to government forces. Since the 1960s, antigovernment insurgency on Mindanao and in the Sulu Archipelago has increased, associated particularly but not exclusively with the large Muslim minority in the region.

[*See also* Moro; Moro Wars; *and* Huk.]

    DAVID K. WYATT

MINDON, king of Burma (r. 1853–1878). Among the kings of the Konbaung dynasty, Mindon alone is remembered as an enlightened monarch; his predecessors were famous for their martial qualities. Under Mindon, Burma enjoyed twenty-five years of relative peace and prosperity. His statesmanship and diplomacy enabled Burma to avoid conflict with the British, who were menacing the kingdom prior to its final annexation to British India in 1886.

Born to King Tharrawaddy and his fourth queen in 1814, Mindon served his half-brother King Pagan (1846–1852) as an officer of the Hluttaw, the supreme administrative council of the kingdom. Pagan's misrule and the Second Anglo-Burmese War (1852) gave Mindon and his younger brother, the Kanaung prince, a chance to revolt against Pagan and overthrow him. In 1853 Mindon was crowned king and Kanaung became the crown prince.

Territorially reduced and economically weakened by the war, Burma was now exposed to still further British encroachments. Mindon tried to uphold the independence of his kingdom by maintaining amicable relations with Britain. He brought the Second Anglo-Burmese War to an end, though he discreetly refrained from recognizing the British annexation of Lower Burma, and he cordially welcomed British diplomatic missions to his court. He signed commercial treaties with Britain to promote trade with

Lower Burma and amicably settled a dispute with the British over the district of Karenni. At the same time he preserved his dignity and prestige as an independent sovereign by refusing the demand of the British that they be allowed to enter his palace without removing their shoes, as was customary. To gain recognition from other European powers, he sent diplomatic missions to France, Italy, Spain, and Portugal. He explored every possible source to obtain arms and alliances in order to bolster defenses against the British threat but to no avail.

In 1857 Mindon built a new royal palace and founded a new capital at Mandalay and made it a center of culture, learning, and trade. To increase the prosperity of his landlocked kingdom he carried out tax reforms, introduced salaries in place of the traditional fief system, built factories, improved inland water transport, laid telegraph lines, and published a newspaper. Caught between modernity and tradition, he tried to steer his kingdom safely between them during this critical period.

Religion was one of the main pillars of Mindon's Burma and a tool for legitimizing his reign and consolidating his kingdom. The stability and prosperity of the kingdom were associated with the health of Buddhism, and Mindon carried out the purification of the Buddhist canon and the Burmese monkhood. He convened the Fifth Buddhist Council at his capital to revise the Buddhist texts and inscribe them on stone tablets. He founded the stricter sect called the Shwegyin with the hope of guaranteeing the survival of Buddhism.

Despite Mindon's good intentions and political wisdom, the basic political and economic problems of the kingdom remained unsolved. With many sons competing to take his place, a succession crisis loomed ominously after an abortive palace coup by two of his sons brought about the murder of the crown prince in 1866. Mindon's death in 1878 plunged the court into a power struggle that resulted in a bloodbath and the ascendancy of King Thibaw, the last king of Burma.

[*See also* Burma; Konbaung Dynasty; Anglo-Burmese Wars; Lower Burma; Mandalay; *and* Thibaw.]

Henry Yule, *A Narrative of the Mission to the Court of Ava in 1855* (1968).   MYO MYINT

MINES AND METALLURGY.

Along with stockbreeding, one of the principal foundations of the mixed agricultural and pastoral economy that evolved in the Eurasian steppe during the Andronovo phase of cultural development (lasting from about 1700 to 1000 BCE) was mining and forging of both farming implements and weaponry from iron. M. Gimbutas has presented evidence suggesting the very early development of metallurgical techniques in the Eurasian steppe and their diffusion to the Middle East and Europe by the Kurgan people during the course of their migrations to the Caucasus and into the Balkan lands as early as 2300 BCE. Forbes confirms the Central Asian provenance of metallurgical techniques and indicates that while the use of smelted iron was known very early in Mesopotamia (according to some, as early as 2500 BCE), it was only gradually introduced, at first for the manufacture of ceremonial weapons, between 1900 and 1400. Thus, while the techniques were certainly known, they were not generally familiar or widely used until the beginning of the "true" Iron Age, which began around 1200. Recent Soviet archaeological studies have uncovered evidence of an intensive exploitation of iron pits in the Altai Mountains and elsewhere in Central Asia dating from a significantly earlier period; these studies indicate the inauguration of a "true" Iron Age in these parts from at least 1400. The early exploitation of iron mines and the development of metallurgical techniques in the mountainous regions of the steppe may have had a direct bearing on the subsequent development of a specialized form of warfare that made use of iron-tipped arrows and lightweight armor for men and horses, against more primitively armed adversaries in the agricultural plain.

Other minerals besides iron, including precious metals such as gold and silver, are found in relative abundance in various sites in the Tian Shan, Kunlun Shan, and Altin Dagh ranges of northwest China. Because exploitation of such mines in later historical times tended to be a government monopoly under the control of minting and treasury departments of imperial states, the local economic impact felt from expansion or contraction of the mining industry was minimal.

[*See also* Metalwork.]

John P. Fletcher, "Ch'ing Inner Asia," in *Cambridge History of China*, vol. 10, *Late Ch'ing, 1800–1911, Part 1*, edited by John K. Fairbank (1978), pp. 35–106. R. Forbes, "Extracting, Smelting, and Alloying," in *A History of Technology*, edited by C. Singer, vol. 1 (1954), pp. 572–599. M. Gimbutas, *Bronze Age Cultures in Central and Eastern Europe* (1965).

RHOADS MURPHEY, JR.

MING DYNASTY.

The Ming dynasty ruled China from 1368 to 1644. While many of its literary, philosophical, and artistic developments were peculiar to the times, much of its social, institutional, and legal structure survived into the late Qing period.

The dynasty was founded by Zhu Yuanzhang (b. 1328, r. 1368–1398), a young man of peasant origin who joined an anti-Yuan rebel group in the Huai region in 1352, captured Nanjing in 1356, and from a base in the hinterlands of southeast China proceeded to dispose of his warlord neighbors one by one, finally expelling the Mongol court and taking Beijing in September 1368. Zhu Yuanzhang determinedly committed himself and his new regime to unity, agrarian reconstruction, and Confucian ethical regeneration.

Seventeen years of civil war left much of China ruined and depopulated, and the early Ming administrative apparatus was deliberately designed to create and sustain unity and foster recovery at the lowest possible cost. The Ming army, some two million strong, was originally made self-supporting, permitting land taxes to be pegged at very low rates. By compelling the people themselves to perform low-level judicial, police, and tax-collecting services without pay, the founder was able to trim the salaried civil bureaucracy to very small size. Decision-making authority and policy enforcement were made exclusive imperial prerogatives, especially after 1380, when the founder permanently removed all high-level coordinating offices from the bureaucracy. Savage penal regulations were formulated to destroy any sign of collusion, factionalism, and peculation among the officials. Confucian orthodoxy provided legitimation, a standard of official recruitment, and a means of general ideological control.

When the founder died in 1398 he had liquidated his top military command and placed the regional control of armies in the hands of his sons, enfeoffed as princes. His designated successor as emperor, however, was a young grandson, Zhu Yunwen (Jianwen; r. 1398–1402). The dynasty was, in effect, refounded after another bout of civil war, which ended in the seizure of the throne by one of the armed princes, the founder's fourth son, Zhu Di (Yongle; r. 1402–1424). It was he who moved the imperial capital from Nanjing to Beijing in 1421. [See also Zhu Yuanzhang and Zhu Di.]

Thus, by the early fifteenth century, the Ming state achieved its original goals, the unification of China and the rehabilitation of the traditional agrarian economy. Further demographic growth and regional economic development, however, soon stretched its capacities to the utmost. Constitutionally frozen in its original shape, too small and too underfinanced to manage the country effectively, the Ming state re-

TABLE 1. *Emperors of the Ming Dynasty*

REIGN TITLE	TEMPLE NAME	ERA YEARS*
Hongwu	Taizu	1368–1398
Jianwen	Huidi	1399–1402
Yongle	Chengzu	1403–1424
Hongxi	Renzong	1425
Xuande	Xuanzong	1426–1435
Zhengtong	Yingzong	1436–1449
Jingtai	Taizong	1450–1456
Tianshun	Yingzong	1457–1464
Chenghua	Xianzong	1465–1487
Hongzhi	Xiaozong	1488–1505
Zhengde	Wuzong	1506–1521
Jiajing	Shizong	1522–1566
Longqing	Muzong	1567–1572
Wanli	Shenzong	1573–1619
Taichang	Guangzong	1620
Tianqi	Xizong	1621–1627
Chongzhen	Zhuangliedi	1628–1644

*New reign titles took effect on the first new year's day following the accession of the emperor.

sisted fundamental reform, preferring to cope with changing conditions by passive, piecemeal, ad hoc, and occasionally illegal adjustments to hard realities.

Domestic Policy. As later emperors distanced themselves from active decision making, there emerged a kind of free-floating central authority that palace eunuchs, regular bureaucrats, and the constitutionally improvised grand secretaries continually vied to capture. Although partisan organization always remained an ill-defined statutory crime, there evolved among the regular bureaucrats a series of informal but wide-ranging networks inspired by ideas of moral rededication and Confucian renewal. These movements served to mobilize officialdom in the ongoing contest for authority. When the examination system became the chief mechanism for official recruitment in the early fifteenth century, the networks achieved a crucial capacity to influence education, examination criteria, and personnel placement.

The followers of Wang Yangming (Wang Shouren; 1472–1529), the premier Confucian theorist of Ming times, centered their drive for moral renewal on encouraging the building of academies outside the regular hierarchy of state Confucian schools. After a considerable history of success in placing adherents in officialdom, the movement was finally suppressed by Grand Secretary Zhang Juzheng in 1579. The next effort, founded in 1604 by Gu Xiancheng and others, had its operational base

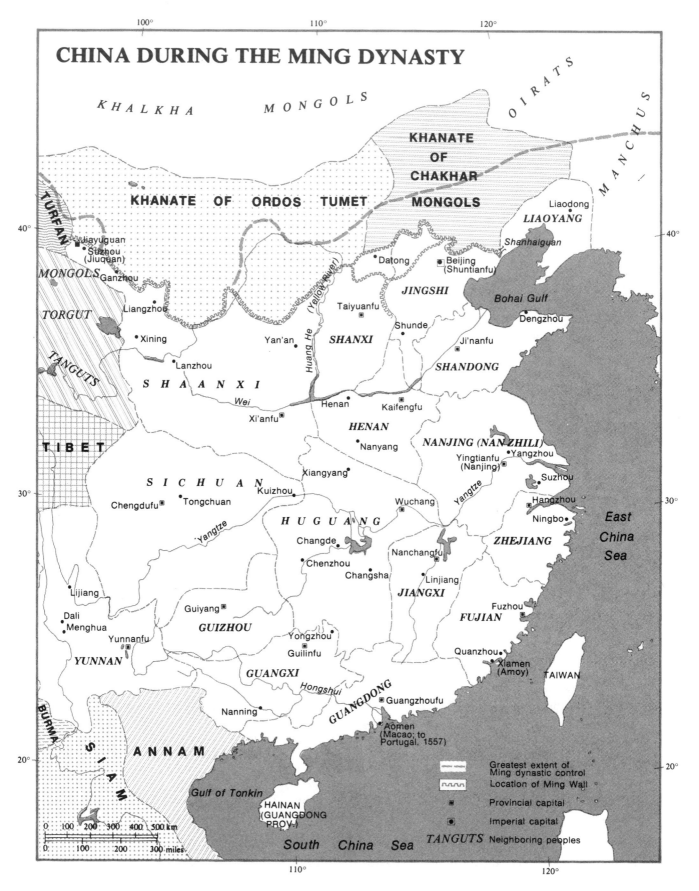

CHINA DURING THE MING DYNASTY

KHALKHA   *MONGOLS*   *OIRATS*

KHANATE OF ORDOS TUMET   **KHANATE OF CHAKHAR MONGOLS**

TURFAN   Jiayuguan
Suzhou (Jiuquan)
MONGOLS Ganzhou   Datong • Beijing (Shuntianfu)   Liaodong
LIAOYANG
Shanhaiguan
MANCHUS

TORGUT   Liangzhou   *JINGSHI*   *Bohai Gulf*

Xining   Taiyuanfu
TANGUTS   Yan'an *SHANXI* Shunde   Ji'nanfu   Dengzhou
Lanzhou   *Huang He (Yellow River)*

TIBET   *S H A A N X I*   *Wei*   *SHANDONG*
Henan Kaifengfu
Xi'anfu

HENAN
Nanyang   *NANJING (NAN ZHILI)*
Yingtianfu (Nanjing) • Yangzhou
S I C H U A N   Xiangyang   Suzhou
Chengdufu • Tongchuan Kuizhou   Wuchang *Yangtze* Hangzhou
Yangtze   *H U G U A N G*   Ningbo   *East China Sea*
Changde   *ZHEJIANG*
Chenzhou Nanchangfu
Changsha   Linjiang
Lijiang   *JIANGXI*
Dali   Guiyang   Yongzhou Fuzhou *FUJIAN*
Menghua   *GUIZHOU* Guilinfu
Yunnanfu   Quanzhou
YUNNAN   Xiamen (Amoy) *TAIWAN*
GUANGXI   Guangzhoufu
GUANGDONG
BURMA   Nanning *Hongshui*
Aomen (Macao; to Portugal, 1557)
S I A M   *A N N A M*

Gulf of Tonkin   HAINAN (GUANGDONG PROV.)

≈≈≈	Greatest extent of Ming dynastic control
⌐⌐⌐	Location of Ming Wall
▪	Provincial capital
⊡	Imperial capital
TANGUTS	Neighboring peoples

South China Sea

0 100 200 300 400 500 km
0   100   200   300 miles

in the Donglin Academy in Wuxi. The Donglin movement, while opposed to many of the ideas of Wang Yangming, was even more virulent in its pursuit of moral purity and more partisan in its outlook and organization. The palace eunuchs, led by the notorious Wei Zhongxian, crushed the Donglin in the sweeping and bloody purges of 1624 to 1627. At the time of the fall of the Ming in the 1640s, yet another Confucian renewal movement had been launched, this time in the form of a nearly nationwide coalition of local literary circles known as the Restoration Society (Fushe). It survived the Qing conquest and was dissolved only in 1661. [*See also* Wang Yangming; Zhang Juzheng; Donglin Academy; *and* Wei Zhongxian.]

Yet while Ming politics was preoccupied with the maintenance and purification of the existing system, China's society and economy were outgrowing the rational management capacities of that very system. It is likely that China's population more than tripled over the course of the dynasty. Several major regions took advantage of the availability of cheap water transport and sacrificed self-sufficiency for cash cropping and commercial exchange. The Yangtze River delta was a center of cotton and silk production and textile weaving. Coastal Fujian became known for tobacco and sugar cane. A strong commercial sector also developed on the northern frontier. Porcelain manufacture at Jingdezhen in Jiangxi achieved unprecedented outputs in the sixteenth and seventeenth centuries. A new proliferation of small market towns (rather than huge urban nodes) serves as an index to the colossal quantitative growth of the Ming commercial economy and also as testimony to its quasi-rural, decentralized, and heavily competitive structure. [*See* Jingdezhen.]

The Ming state could neither adequately tax this growth nor guide it through national fiscal policy. However, as more and more foreign silver entered the country through largely illicit trade channels during the sixteenth century, local officials made piecemeal adjustments to the new currency, and in this way the dynasty's fiscal base gradually shifted from personal services and taxes in kind to a lump-sum silver payment known as the "single whip" system (*yitiaobianfa*). Yet the state never coined this silver, nor was it ever able to control its supply. [*See also* Yitiaobianfa.]

Foreign Policy. Ming foreign policy mirrored the domestic in its ideological rigidity and high moralism coupled with curious exceptions and ad hoc adjustments. From the dynasty's inception, relations with organized states abroad were conducted within

FIGURE 1. *Ming-dynasty Figurine.* Depiction of the Daoist deity Xuandi. Porcelain, probably sixteenth century. Height 31.7 cm., width 16.2 cm.

the ideological and institutional framework of the so-called tribute system. Ming China considered itself not just the world's largest state, but also the moral center of the universe. It sought a moralized global supremacy but tried to confine actual contact with foreigners to limited and closely regulated channels. Early in the fifteenth century, Zhu Di aggressively advertised the might and virtue of the Ming in a series of embassies, including especially the imperial naval expeditions (the Zheng He voyages) to Southeast Asia, the Persian Gulf, Arabia, and East Africa. These gigantic flotillas conducted official trade and enrolled new and far-flung states into the Ming tributary system. [*See also* Zheng He *and* Tributary System.]

The Ming order of international relations did impose a latent peacekeeping obligation upon China. The ethically based interventionist implications of the tributary system became reality on several occasions. The most spectacular example was Zhu Di's involvement in Vietnam (1407–1427). Originally this was an act of military intervention in support of the legitimate but collapsing Tran dynasty, but the complexities of the situation rapidly led the Ming to an ill-advised attempt at outright annexation, which eventually had to be given up in the face of widespread armed resistance. The Ming dynasty's massive intervention in Korea (1592–1598), while undertaken in defense of a legitimate ruler against Japan's invasion of the peninsula, was also more clearly linked to China's own security needs than had been the case in Vietnam. The Ming court had never been able to establish a mutually satisfactory suzerain-vassal relationship with Japan, and further official links with it were cut in 1549.

Japan excepted, the official framework for the conduct of external relations seemed to work best with small and remote states. Along China's coastal and Great Wall frontiers, the maintenance of the framework required a thick infrastructure of border policing in order to discourage free trade and contact. Across the Great Wall frontier in Mongolia, the Ming court was faced with a dilemma. If it acquiesced in the rise of a unified Mongol power it then had reason to fear competition for the loyalty of the frontier population and perhaps another Mongol conquest of China. If Mongolia were to remain anarchic, however, then there was no way to reduce the threat of continual small-scale raiding into North China. The policy of the Ming founder, which Zhu Di continued, was to launch periodic campaigns out into the deep steppes in order to inhibit the rise of ominous Mongol coalitions, while at the same time thickening military defense installations on the Chinese side of the Great Wall line. The steppe campaigns ended after 1424, but the commitment to heavy garrisoning was sustained throughout the dynasty. Only in 1570 did the Ming court finally work out a satisfactory treaty relationship with a Mongol ruler, Altan Khan of the Tumet.

Defense was not a function of the Great Wall itself (which along most of its length was no more than a demarcation line), but of the colonies, garrisons, and fighting towers spotted along it. Yet the frontier zone was one of great social ambiguity, with many Chinese emigrants illegally settled in Mongol territory, large numbers of Mongols (many of them soldiers in Ming service) settled inside China, and Chinese garrison troops carrying on surreptitious trade and smuggling with the enemy. Here, Confucian theories of Sino-foreign relations had much less meaning than they appear to have had in Beijing. [See also Altan Khan and Great Wall.]

China's maritime frontier posed some analogous difficulties. Official interdicts on private trade ran up against the hard fact that there emerged during the course of the Ming an international East Asian maritime community, consisting of Japanese, Portuguese, Dutch, and especially Chinese sea venturers. With a network extending from the China coast to Japan, the Philippines, and Southeast Asia, Chinese maritime elites pursued profit and power of a sort perhaps acceptable in Venice but antithetical to the Confucian norms that the Ming state safeguarded. These sea venturers did not hesitate to turn to piracy and violence when official obstacles seriously hindered their activities. The China coast population was partly attracted inward to the continental Ming system and partly pulled outward in the direction of the traders and pirates, the offshore islands, and overseas emigration. Ming antipirate efforts finally achieved a measure of success in the mid-sixteenth century, largely because pirate suppression was accompanied by a partial relaxation of the maritime trade restrictions. Of this, the Portuguese establishment of an officially authorized trading base at Macao in 1557 is but the best-known example. [See also Piracy: Japanese Piracy in China and Macao.]

It was through both legal and illegal oceanic trade channels that Ming China came to be linked into an emerging global economy; while it benefited from it in boom times, it also proved very vulnerable to its depressions. China exported mainly silk and porcelain, and in return imported Japanese, Peruvian, and Mexican silver in ever-mounting quantities, beginning especially in the 1570s. The silver boom had a dramatic effect upon the continental economy and the dynasty's fiscal system. After around 1610, however, world silver flows suffered a series of downturns, and the impact of these slumps upon China was calamitous. The silver famine made its presence known in widespread tax defaults. These in turn occasioned a government payments crisis that put the northern defense system in serious straits, thus contributing to the fall of the Ming in 1644.

Rise of the Manchus. By the early seventeenth century the Ming court faced the problem of a hostile aggregation of tribes in Manchuria, a region where it had always sought to foster division and weakness. Led by Nurhaci (1559–1626), the Jurchen tribesmen (later renamed Manchus) inflicted a shocking defeat upon a much larger Ming army in Manchuria in 1619. That psychological blow, coupled with the dynasty's worsening fiscal crisis, prompted whole units of unsupplied and unpaid Ming frontier troops to turn to Mongol-style predatory outlawry inside China, especially after 1628. [See also Manchus and Nurhaci.]

The Ming dynasty did not expire easily, but by

the 1630s and 1640s the only question was whether it would be the Manchus or the Chinese military rebels now led by Li Zicheng who would fairly soon supplant it. The Manchus won, as it turned out, but less for military than for political reasons. Even by the time he captured Beijing in April 1644, Li Zicheng had not been able to control his outlaw followers or make a convincing case for his ability to found a new dynasty. Although non-Chinese, the Manchus had better political preparations and were able to arrange the defections of important Ming generals and their armies. Their occupation of Beijing in June 1644 proved final and irreversible.

There is more than a little irony in the fact that the last serious efforts at Ming resistance to the Manchu conquest of China should have been championed by Koxinga (Zheng Chenggong; 1624–1662), a half-Chinese, half-Japanese representative of the maritime trading community that the Ming court in its heyday had been so eager to suppress.

[See also Li Zicheng and Zheng Chenggong.]

Jerry Dennerline, *The Chia-ting Loyalists: Confucian Leadership and Social Change in 17th-Century China* (1981). Edward L. Farmer, *Early Ming Government: The Evolution of Dual Capitals* (1976). L. Carrington Goodrich and Chaoying Fang, eds., *Dictionary of Ming Biography, 1368–1644* (1976). Ray Huang, *1587, A Year of No Significance: The Ming Dynasty in Decline* (1981). Charles O. Hucker, ed., *Chinese Government in Ming Times: Seven Studies* (1969). Jonathan Spence and John E. Wills, Jr., eds., *From Ming to Ch'ing: Conquest, Region, and Continuity in 17th-Century China* (1979).

JOHN W. DARDESS

MINH MANG, second emperor of the Nguyen dynasty of Vietnam (r. 1820–1841). The future Minh Mang emperor was born 25 May 1791, the fourth son of the Nguyen lord Nguyen Phuc Anh (who later became the Gia Long emperor). His personal names were Dam and Hieu.

Prince Dam was educated in the Chinese classics and in 1816 was appointed heir to the throne. Dam was the eldest surviving son of the reigning emperor. Gia Long considered the other chief candidate, the son of the former heir Prince Canh, both too young and too heavily influenced by Catholicism.

As emperor, Minh Mang's major objective was to increase the power, and hence the freedom of action, of the monarchy. He hoped to improve upon the examples of the Ming and Qing emperors of China. To achieve this goal he engaged in a simultaneous process of bureaucratic centralization and gradual erosion of the prerogatives of the viceroys

of northern and southern Vietnam. This policy culminated in the establishment of a consolidated imperial secretariat (*noi cac*, 1829–1830) and the creation of a unified provincial administrative system (1831).

The difficulty of operating a Chinese-style administration in a Southeast Asian environment made Minh Mang throughout his reign unusually preoccupied with political, cultural, and educational orthodoxy, that is, conformity with Chinese precedent, which he saw as a universally applicable body of experience. One of his first acts as emperor was to prohibit the use of *chu nom* (Viet characters) in official documents. Other examples of this concern are the construction of an imperial academy (*quoc tu giam*) in Hue (1821), the renewal of the metropolitan and palace examinations (1822, 1829), the promulgation of ten moral maxims (1834), and a series of increasingly severe edicts against Christianity (1825–1836).

Christianity was particularly disturbing to Minh Mang, as it was the nexus of three distinct problems: heterodoxy, foreign (non-Sinitic) influence, and internal order. One Vietnamese scholar has counted 234 separate uprisings during the Minh Mang reign, the most serious of which were those of Phan Ba Vanh in the north (1821–1827) and of Le Van Khoi in the south (1833–1835). When it became evident that Christians were deeply implicated in the last rebellion, Minh Mang authorized the first executions of foreign missionaries (1833). The continuation of anti-Christian policies by Thieu Tri and Tu Duc, the son and grandson of Minh Mang, was the immediate cause of French intervention in Vietnam.

[See also Hue; Le Van Duyet; Le Van Khoi Rebellion; and Thieu Tri.]

M. Gaultier, *Minh Mang* (1935). Thomas Hodgkin, *Vietnam: The Revolutionary Path* (1981). A. B. Woodside, *Vietnam and the Chinese Model* (1971).

JAMES M. COYLE

MINTO, EARL OF. See Morley-Minto Reforms.

MIR, MUHAMMAD TAQI (1722–1810), along with Ghalib one of the two greatest poets of the classical Urdu style of poetry, the *ghazal*. Mir was born and grew up in Agra, but lived his adult life first in Delhi, then after 1782 in Lucknow, where he died. Moody, proud, quite conscious of his own preeminence, he was often on difficult terms with his relatives and patrons. But his brilliance as a poet was recognized even before his first *divan,* or group of poems, was collected around 1750; during his lifelong poetic career he produced a good deal of other Urdu and Persian poetry, together with an autobiography (in Persian) and an account of Urdu poets.

Mir's command of Persian, his fondness for pra-kritic vocabulary, and his wonderful capacity for wordplay give his language a piquancy that belies his reputation as a poet of unrelieved melancholy. More than any other poet Mir shaped the classical Urdu *ghazal* in its middle period; his popularity and influence remain very much alive.

[*See also* Ghalib, Mirza Asadullah Khan.]

R. Russell and K. Islam, *Three Mughal Poets: Mir, Sauda, Mir Hasan* (1968).   FRANCES W. PRITCHETT

MIR JA'FAR, the East India Company's first puppet nawab of Bengal (1757–1760), an adventurer who married the half-sister of Alivardi Khan, the nawab of Bengal, thus entering the new ruling group in Bengal. His best-known act as a general was to betray his master, Siraj ud-Daulah, at the Battle of Plassey. Ambition and personal loyalty to Robert Clive, rather than support for the company (whose trading abuses he protested) were his politics. Forced to abdicate in favor of his son-in-law Mir Qasim, he was reinstalled by the British when they declared war on his successor in 1763. Mir Ja'far died frustrated with British self-aggrandizement on 5 February 1765.

[*See also* Mir Qasim; East India Company; Clive, Sir Robert; Plassey, Battle of; *and* Siraj ud-Daulah.]

Abdul Majed Khan, *The Transition in Bengal 1756–1775: A Study of Saiyid Muhammad Reza Khan* (1969). Atul Chandra Roy, *The Career of Mir Jafar Khan 1757–1765* (1953).   FRITZ LEHMANN

MIR JUMLA (c. 1591–1663), popular name of Mir Muhammad Sa'id Ardistani, Persian merchant adventurer who entered the service of the Qutb Shahis of Golconda around 1630. From the rank of *havildar* of Masulipatam, he gradually rose to be the chief minister under Abdullah Qutb Shah—an appointment probably earned in appreciation for the military talent he displayed in the conquest of Udaygiri Fort in 1643. Master of a strong artillery in which even English gunners were employed, he carved out a dominion for himself by extensive conquests in eastern Karnataka.

Mir Jumla established an efficient financial and civil administration, organized messenger service between Hyderabad and Karnataka, and maintained a powerful army paid both in cash and *jagirs* (tracts of land). The geopolitics of the region brought him into conflict with the Bijapuris but his main thrust was concentrated against the Vijayanagar empire. When in April 1656 Mir Jumla transferred his allegiance to Shah Jahan, the title of Mu'azzam Khan was conferred on him; later he was appointed *diwan-i kul* (chief minister) of the Mughal empire. Under Aurangzeb he became governor of Khandesh and later viceroy of Bengal. He extended the Mughal frontiers to Cooch Behar and Assam. Mir Jumla's mining activities made him the owner of twenty-five maunds of diamonds. He lent money to the English and conducted trade with West Asia and the East Indies.

[*See also* Golconda; Aurangzeb; *and* Mughal Empire.]

J. N. Sarkar, *The Life of Mir Jumla—The General of Aurangzeb* (1951).   FARHAN AHMAD NIZAMI

MIR QASIM (d. 1777), nawab of Bengal (1760–1763), son-in-law of his predecessor, Mir Ja'far. Installed by the British, Mir Qasim refused to be a puppet. A more proficient administrator than Mir Ja'far, he doubled revenue collections and attempted to modernize the army. When the British refused to stop abusing their trade privileges, Mir Qasim boldly extended the same exemptions from tax to the Indian merchants. The outraged British declared war in June 1763 and brought back Mir Ja'far. Mir Qasim's alliance with Nawab Shuja ud-Daulah of Awadh and with the Mughal emperor culminated in his defeat at Baksar on 23 October 1764.

[*See also* Baksar, Battle of *and* Mir Ja'far.]

Nandalal Chatterji, *Mir Qasim, Nawab of Bengal, 1760–1763* (1935). Ram Gopal, *How the British Occupied Bengal* (1963).   FRITZ LEHMANN

MISHIMA YUKIO (1925–1970), Japanese novelist and playwright. Mishima is famous for his spectacular suicide at the headquarters of the Self-Defense Agency, a protest against what he saw as the spinelessness of modern Japanese youth and the loss of national identity. Of all modern Japanese novelists, however, he was the one most concerned to make an international name for himself, and much of his energy was spent in self-promotion. This may also be why his novels are carefully plotted and sometimes seem to be written to appeal to a foreign audience. His central theme was the inviolability of idealism and the justification of violence. Torn between spiritualism and materialism, Mishima glorified the self-sacrifice of the warrior and yet gave in to intense narcissism; these fused in the eroticism of death, illustrated most graphically in the short story "Patriotism" ("Yūkoku," 1960), in which ritual disembowelment is coupled with lovemaking.

Among Mishima's most important works are *Confessions of a Mask* (*Kamen no kokuhaku,* 1949), about a young man's discovery of his homosexuality, which in turn becomes a metaphor for general alienation; *The Temple of the Golden Pavilion* (*Kinkakuji,* 1956), in which an acolyte burns down a Buddhist temple when he finds that a beauty not his own can engender only hate; and *The Sea of Fertility* (*Hōjō no umi,* 1969–1970), which ends in a barren silence. His novels brought him great fame in Japan and abroad, but his unending succession of adolescent heroes acting out their fantasies may limit his future reputation. The idealism and willingness to sacrifice self stem not so much from a belief in what is right as from self-disgust and the horror of an empty center. Nevertheless, Mishima has a large readership both in Japan and abroad, and for many he embodies the more masculine traits of Japanese culture.

Donald Keene, *Landscapes and Portraits* (1971). Masao Miyoshi, *Accomplices of Silence* (1974). John Nathan, *Mishima: A Biography* (1974). Edward Seidensticker, "Mishima Yukio," *Hudson Review* 24.2 (1971): 272–282.   RICHARD BOWRING

MISSIONARIES. *See* Christianity *and* Jesuits.

MITHRA is an Iranian deity whose name is also a common noun meaning "an agreement between men." Most of his characteristics spring from his fundamental nature as the god of contracts. Because contracts were concluded in front of a fire, Mithra was associated with fire and in particular with its greatest representative, the sun. His roles as judge of dead souls and as a war god who destroys men who break their contracts are similarly derived.

The name *Mitra* (a form of the name *Mithra*) has been found in a treaty concluded about 1370 BCE between a Hittite king and an Indo-Iranian ruler of the kingdom of Mitanni in western Mesopotamia. Although not included in Zoroaster's revelation, Mithra occupies a prominent position in Zoroastrianism as it developed under the Achaemenids and

later. The hymn to him in the Avesta, the Zoroastrian scripture, was composed about the fifth century BCE, and Artaxerxes II (404–359) broke with tradition by invoking Mithra and Anahita along with Ahura Mazda.

The Mithraism that the Roman legions carried to the West, although it ultimately derives from the Iranian Mithra, had little to do with Iran.

[*See also* Ahura Mazda; Anahita; Artaxerxes II; *and* Zoroastrianism.]

Ilya Gershevitch, *The Avestan Hymn to Mithra* (1959). R. C. Zaehner, *The Dawn and Twilight of Zoroastrianism* (1961).   LUCIANNE C. BULLIET

MITRA, RAJENDRALAL (1822–1891), Bengali scholar, first Indian president of the Asiatic Society of Bengal (1875). A prodigious worker, he edited dozens of Sanskrit texts and inscriptions and supervised the collection of Sanskrit manuscripts. Mitra's work brought him many international honors, but his approach, which relied heavily on the authority of Sanskrit pandits, was gradually superseded by the emergence of "higher criticism" in Germany. Mitra was also the editor of two excellent general-interest Bengali newspapers. A leading member of the British Indian Association, he favored close cooperation between the respectable classes of Indians and British authorities, a view that found little favor among his younger contemporaries, who considered him a defender of landlord interests.

[*See also* Asiatic Society of Bengal.]

WARREN GUNDERSON

MITSUBISHI, postwar Japan's largest industrial group, founded in 1873 by Iwasaki Yatarō. Among prewar *zaibatsu* (financial conglomerates) it was second only to Mitsui. Three main financial factors explain its emergence: government subsidies to its shipping operation until 1885, its sale of NYK (Nippon Yūsen Kaisha) stock, and profits from mines. These factors enabled it to purchase more metal mines and vast real estate, including the Marunouchi area of Tokyo, and to strengthen its banking. Mitsubishi's move into heavy industry was made possible by state subsidies to shipping firms, for which Mitsubishi began building large vessels in the late 1890s. Shipbuilding then became the basis for further diversification into electrical engineering and ventures for acquiring raw materials such as iron ore and coking coal. These supplied the state-run Yawata Iron and Steel Works from which Mitsubishi purchased steel for its ships. During the ship-building slump that occurred after World War I, Mitsubishi's electrical and aircraft firms grew rapidly through the Mitsubishi Trading Company's import of foreign technology. Although this trading firm was temporarily dissolved by the Occupation, Mitsubishi quickly recovered in the 1950s thanks to its well-integrated base in heavy industry and the group loyalty of its salaried managers.

[*See also* Iwasaki Yatarō.]

Hidemasa Morikawa, "The Organizational Structure of the Mitsubishi and Mitsui Zaibatsu, 1868–1922: A Comparative Study," *Business History Review* 44.1 (Spring 1970): 62–83. William D. Wray, *Mitsubishi and the N.Y.K., 1870–1914: Business Strategy in the Japanese Shipping Industry* (1984).   WILLIAM D. WRAY

MITSUI, the largest of Japan's prewar *zaibatsu* (industrial conglomerates). The Mitsui family business became famous in the mid-seventeenth century for its Edo dry-goods store, which made major innovations in merchandising. It was also a powerful money-exchange agent for the *bakufu*. The precepts of the Mitsui House Code, which eschewed entrepreneurship and stressed survival of the house, served it well in the Meiji Restoration, when it became a banker for the Meiji government.

Despite its three strong enterprises in the early Meiji years—banking, trading, and mining—Mitsui's management and strategic direction remained unstable until its Family Council delegated more authority to salaried managers in the 1890s, first to Nakamigawa Hikojirō of the bank and then to Masuda Takashi of the trading firm. Under their direction Mitsui began industrial investments in textiles, electrical engineering, and shipbuilding that complemented its traditional dominance in commerce and banking. Through many sole agency contracts with producers outside the Mitsui *zaibatsu*, Mitsui's trading arm became an "organizer of the economy." In the interwar years its industrial investments, technological spin-offs from mining, and frequent takeovers gave Mitsui a strengthened position in heavy industry.

Takeovers of other firms made Mitsui more of a conglomerate than Mitsubishi. Because of this practice, however, the ties among firms within Mitsui were less cohesive than those within Mitsubishi. Failing to regroup as effectively as Mitsubishi after the Occupation, it fell to second among postwar industrial groups.

[*See also* Zaibatsu.]

Japan Business History Institute, ed., *The 100 Year History of Mitsui & Co., Ltd.* (1977). John G. Roberts, *Mitsui: Three Centuries of Japanese Business* (1973).

WILLIAM D. WRAY

MIZO, a Tibeto-Burmese-speaking hill people residing primarily in the Indian district of Mizoram (population 332,390); many live across the border in Burma and Bangladesh. Known to the British as Lushai after their chief clan, the Mizo claim to have migrated from the northeast, arriving in Mizoram in the fifteenth century.

Raiding the plains is part of the Mizo heritage, and the British fought intermittently with the hillmen from their first encounter in 1824. The Mizo peoples continued to assert their independence against India, forming a Mizo National Front in 1961 and fighting a bloody underground battle for autonomy. A peace accord in 1976 only partially mollified the tribesmen, and the Mizo region remains an extremely sensitive, as well as extremely strategic, area.

[*See also* Adivasis.]

T. Lewin, *A Fly on the Wheel* (1885). L. Thanga, *The Mizos* (1978).   CHARLES LINDHOLM

MIZUNO TADAKUNI (1794–1851), Japanese politician and reformer of the late Tokugawa period. Mizuno Tadakuni was born the son of the daimyo of Karatsu, becoming daimyo himself on his father's retirement in 1812. Within five years Tadakuni's domain had been transferred to Hamamatsu, and he was already launched on a political career in the Tokugawa *bakufu*. In 1834 he was promoted to the position of senior councillor (*rōjū*), but it was not until the death of the retired shogun Ienari in 1841 that Tadakuni was able to introduce what became known to posterity as the Tempō Reforms. Some of these were of a traditional kind, including the purge of almost a thousand officials identified with the old regime and the issuing of standard moralistic prohibitions against almost every kind of pleasurable activity. Naturally these had no more success than such doctrinaire paroxysms had had in the past. Other reform measures, however, were rather more innovative, and these seemed aimed at recouping some of the *bakufu*'s diminished authority in national affairs. Given Japanese fears of foreign invasion, this intention was perhaps no more than reasonable, but these initiatives aroused such resentment and suspicion among Tadakuni's peers that they forced his resignation in 1843 and hastily dismantled the entire reform program. Tadakuni was to be recalled briefly the following year to deal with a diplomatic emergency, but he soon resigned again, in the process losing part of his domain, the remainder of which was transferred to Yamagata. He was forced to retire in disgrace, and several of his colleagues were either executed or imprisoned.

[See also Tempō Reforms.]

HAROLD BOLITHO

MLECCHA ("barbarian"), an early Aryan concept applied to non-Aryan groups, both those indigenous to India (e.g., Dravidians, or tribals) and foreigners (e.g., Greek and Hun invaders). A derogatory term, mleccha implied ignorance of Sanskrit and nonobservance of caste ritual.   USHA SANYAL

MOELLENDORFF, PAUL GEORG VON (1847–1901), the first Westerner in the service of the Korean government. Born in the Prussian province of Brandenburg, he studied at the University of Halle and in 1869 was recruited by Robert Hart for the Chinese Maritime Customs Service. Disappointed, he resigned from Hart's services in June 1874 to become an interpreter in the German consulate. In the summer of 1882 he joined Li Hongzhang's staff. In mid-September 1882, when Korea requested an adviser on foreign affairs, Li recommended von Moellendorff, who arrived in Seoul on 13 December. His principal duties were connected with the Foreign Office and the Korean Maritime Customs Service. He enjoyed King Kojong's confidence and also held office in the traditional bureaucracy. He enthusiastically supported Korea's modernization program. As the head of the new mint he attempted to introduce a modern minting system. He also helped establish the government language school and invited several German experts (mining, sericulture, etc.) to Korea. Convinced that only Russia would be an effective counterbalance to Japanese aggression, he conducted unauthorized negotiations for hiring Russian army instructors. His secret diplomacy caused a storm of protests, and he was dismissed in the fall of 1885. He returned to the Chinese Maritime Customs, was appointed commissioner at Ningbo in 1897, and died mysteriously in 1901.

[See also Yi Dynasty.]

Martina Deuchler, Confucian Gentlemen and Barbarian Envoys: The Opening of Korea, 1875–1885 (1977).

MARTINA DEUCHLER

MOGULS. See Mughal Empire.

MOHAMED ALI (1878–1934), key figure in Indian politics during the first two decades of the twentieth century. He was editor of the Comrade and the Hamdard, two of northern India's most influential newspapers; the chief spokesman of Muslim interests; and the architect of the Khilafat campaign, which dominated Indian politics from 1919 to 1923.

Born in Rampur, Mohamed Ali was educated at Aligarh and Oxford. He returned to India in 1902 and found employment first in Rampur and later at Baroda. Toward the end of 1910 he decided on a career of journalism; the Comrade, launched on 14 January 1911, was his first venture. Soon afterward he aquired the Urdu-language Hamdard. These journalistic ventures received unprecedented popularity and provided a framework for the uneasiness and dissatisfaction of important Muslim groups, molding their attitudes toward government. Above all, the newspapers focused on the disturbing news from the Balkan front, which gave evidence of successive military reverses suffered by the Turkish armies and raised the specter of European forces advancing into the heartlands of the Islamic world.

For his views and involvement in the pan-Islamic upsurge, Mohamed Ali was sent to jail, first on 15 May 1915, later in November 1922. During his famous Karachi trial in October 1922, Mohamed Ali said, "The trial is not Mohamed Ali and six others versus the Crown, but God versus man."

During the Khilafat movement Mohamed Ali was a close ally of Gandhi and a staunch supporter of the Indian National Congress. But when Hindu-Muslim relations deteriorated in the aftermath of the Khilafat and noncooperation movements, Mohamed Ali became disillusioned with the Congress as well as with Gandhi.

The gulf that separated Gandhi and Mohamed Ali was confirmed by Mohamed Ali's open condemnation in April 1930 of the civil disobedience movement launched by the Mahatma. Mohamed Ali urged Muslims not to join it because its goal was the establishment of a Hindu raj.

[See also Ali Brothers; Gandhi, Mohandas Karamchand; and Khilafat Movement.]

Mushirul Hasan, Mohamed Ali: Ideology and Politics (1981). Mushirul Hasan, ed., Mohamed Ali in Indian Politics: Select Writings, 2 vols. (1982–1983).

MUSHIRUL HASAN

MOHENJO-DARO. *See* Indus Valley Civilization *and* India.

MOLUCCAS. *See* Maluku.

MOMOYAMA PERIOD. Narrowly defined, the term *Momoyama* as a period designation refers to those years when Toyotomi Hideyoshi was in power in Japan (1582–1598 CE); more broadly, it designates the era of revolutionary political and cultural change spanning the careers of the "three unifiers" who brought to a close more than a century of civil war in Japan and left to their successors a united, centrally administered state. This longer period (also known as the Azuchi-Momoyama period) covers the ascendancy, from 1568 to 1582, of Hideyoshi's predecessor Oda Nobunaga, the tenure of Hideyoshi himself, and the years between 1598 and 1615, when Tokugawa Ieyasu supplanted the Toyotomi heir, acquired the title of shogun, and laid the foundation for the long and peaceful rule of successive heads of his own family.

The designation *Azuchi-Momoyama* derives from the names of two spectacular castles that served as emblems of the glory and ambition of the leading warlords of the age. Azuchi was the site of Nobunaga's major enceinte, contructed between 1576 and 1579 on the southeast shore of Lake Biwa (Shiga Prefecture); it was destroyed during the struggle over succession that followed Nobunaga's death. Momoyama, literally "peach hill," was the site of Hideyoshi's final residence, a retirement "villa" constructed and reconstructed between 1592 and 1598 in the town of Fushimi, to the southeast of Kyoto. This castle also fell, during the succession wars provoked by Hideyoshi's death, although it was restored for a time as the western headquarters of Tokugawa Ieyasu. Eventually dismantled in the 1620s, the compound was replaced by a peach grove that gave the area its popular name.

In political terms, the Momoyama period covers the cataclysmic battles of military unification and the seminal changes in government that transformed the many hostile domains of the Sengoku ("warring states") period into a strong, orderly state. Consolidating their conquests with pacification policies of lasting import, the "three unifiers" fixed the boundaries of class and status, radically curtailed changes of occupation or residence, began the conversion of traditionally enfeoffed warriors into a stipended soldiery largely confined to towns, and disarmed farmers, tradespeople, and members of religious orders. Although they were architects of an authoritarian central administration whose jurisdiction ranged from the control of Christianity to the registration of land, the unifiers respected a degree of autonomy in more than two hundred newly federated domains that served as units of local government. Domain lords (or daimyo) continued to supervise local armies, taxation, and the administration of justice.

In cultural terms, the Momoyama period witnessed dramatic changes in style and taste affecting most forms of artistic expression—from architecture to gardening, from painting to ceramics, from music to dance. The Momoyama taste found its most powerful expression in the castles of the time and its most important patrons in the warlords who used artistic display to project authority. Surviving castles of this era (including Himeji Castle in Hyōgo Prefecture and Matsumoto Castle in Nagano Prefecture) indicate the hallmarks of the Momoyama style: theatricality, enormity of scale, and lavish ornamentation. Together with moats, labyrinthine walls, and donjons of up to nine stories, these compounds included opulent residences with reticulated ceilings, carved transoms, and lacquered and gilded columns. Golden finials and roof tiles, flamboyantly sculpted gates, and gardens rich in tropical plants also distinguished the castle complex.

Polychrome painting on walls and large folding screens are among the most important remains of the Momoyama period. Commissioned by monastic patrons and prominent merchants as well as by daimyo, these paintings often featured bold treatments of genre subjects, wild animals, and birds and flowers against a ground of gold leaf. Leading artists of the time included Kanō Eitoku, Kaihō Yūshō, and Hasegawa Tōhaku. The artistic explosion also affected the performing arts: prototypes of *kabuki* appeared in this era, the *samisen* (a three-stringed instrument introduced from the Ryūkyūs) became popular, and frenetic communal dances performed in large circles *(furyū)* flourished. A general tone of exuberance, even abandon, was intensified by an interest in the exotic—clothing inspired by European fashion, animals and birds imported from China and India, wines and foodstuffs introduced by Western traders.

Despite the dominance of the baroque style, practitioners of the widely popular tea ceremony set a second direction for Momoyama aesthetics. Celebrating the values of rusticity and restraint *(wabi)*, they favored rude vessels of clay and bamboo and simple tea huts of reeds, thatch, and plaster. The "tea taste," which continues to influence the Japanese arts, was largely developed by tea masters from mercantile circles.

Adding to the expansive character of the Momoyama period was a cosmopolitanism rare in premodern Japanese history. Following the arrival of the Portuguese in 1543, traders and missionaries from Portugal and Spain (and, eventually, traders from Britain and Holland) established bases in the ports of Kyushu. Missionary activity, constrained after 1587, provoked persecution by 1598 and mounting efforts to extirpate Christian belief throughout the first half of the seventeenth century. Yet European merchants, who introduced the Japanese to firearms and carried goods between Japan and China, received active support from major warlords throughout the Momoyama era. Japanese traders also engaged in foreign commercial ventures, sending ships to Indochina, the Philippines, and Taiwan.

Political innovation, artistic invention, and foreign contacts, while critical developments of the age, do not exhaust the richness of Momoyama experience. Increased urbanization, expanding domestic commerce, and heightened interest in Confucian philosophy contributed to the vitality and variety of one of the richest and most complex periods of Japanese history.

[See also Oda Nobunaga and Toyotomi Hideyoshi.]

C. R. Boxer, *The Christian Century in Japan, 1549–1650* (1951). Rand Castile, *The Way of Tea* (1971). Michael Cooper, ed., *They Came to Japan: An Anthology of European Reports on Japan, 1543–1640* (1965). Doi Tsugiyoshi, *Momoyama Decorative Painting,* translated by Edna B. Crawford (1977). George Elison, *Deus Destroyed: The Image of Christianity in Early Modern Japan* (1973). George Elison and Bardwell L. Smith, eds., *Warlords, Artists, and Commoners: Japan in the Sixteenth Century* (1981). The Metropolitan Museum of Art, eds. and comps., *Momoyama: Japanese Art in the Age of Grandeur* (1975). Yamane Yuzo, *Momoyama Genre Painting,* translated by John M. Shields (1973).

MARY ELIZABETH BERRY

MON, also known as Talaing, a people of great importance in the history of mainland Southeast Asia (Burma and Thailand) for their political and cultural innovations. Their numbers have shrunk to insignificance in modern times.

In the first millennium CE the Mon, who speak an Austroasiatic language, were spread over Lower Burma, the northern part of the Malay Peninsula,

and north, central, and northeastern Thailand. They are associated with the ancient kingdoms of Ramannadesa, Thaton, and Pegu in Burma and with Haripunjaya, Dvaravati, and Canasa in what is now Thailand. Mon-language inscriptions dating from the sixth to the sixteenth century are found in this area, extending from Irrawaddy Delta in the west to the Mekong River in the east. The Mon were among the region's earliest and most fervent Buddhists, particularly of the Theravada school, and are usually credited with transmitting Buddhism to the Burmese and Thai and perhaps also to the Cambodians. It was from Mon Thaton that King Anawrahta of Pagan is said to have obtained Buddhism, literature, and writing, for example.

With the rise of Burmese and Thai kingdoms from the eleventh century, however, the Mon increasingly were on the defensive. Their kingdom of Pegu, or Hanthawaddy, survived from the thirteenth to the sixteenth century, but an attempt to revive it in the eighteenth century brought a vicious Burmese counterattack; in the face of this, many Mon fled to exile in Siam, while those remaining in Burma were increasingly assimilated into Burmese society. Mon nationalism was last heard from in the years immediately following World War II, when a Mon National Liberation Front briefly operated in Burma and in Thailand. The Mon literary and cultural tradition barely survives, and through most of the area where Mons once lived it is virtually forgotten.

[See also Burma; Thailand; Ramannadesa; Thaton; Dvaravati; Anawrahta; Pagan; Pegu; and Austroasiatic Languages.]

G. Coedès, *The Indianized States of Southeast Asia,* translated by Susan B. Cowing (1963). G. Diffloth, *The Dvaravati Old Mon Language and Nyah Kur* (1984). R. Halliday, *The Talaings* (1917). G. E. Harvey, *A History of Burma from the Earliest Times* (1925; reprint, 1967).

DAVID K. WYATT

MONEY

MONEY IN EAST ASIA

China's first money was cowries imported from the South Seas. Strung in units of ten or twenty, these strings, called *peng,* were first used around the sixteenth century BCE. The earliest Chinese coinage was spades and knives cast uniformly in bronze around the mid-eighth century BCE. Frequently inscribed, they circulated mainly in northeastern China. Gold plates stamped in units of *yuan* together with bronze cowries were used in the Hubei-Jiangsu-

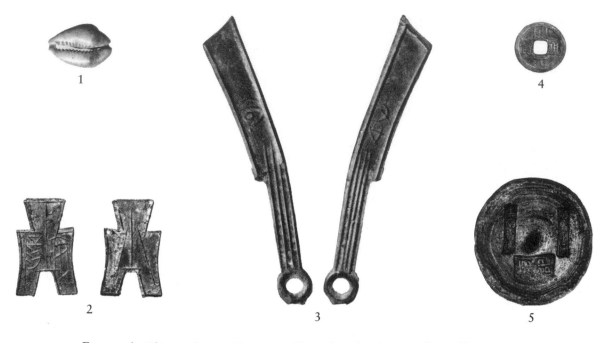

FIGURE 1. *Chinese Coins.* (1) cowry; (2) spade coin, Anyang, first millennium BCE (left, obverse; right, reverse); (3) knife coin, character on blade reading *Ming* (left, obverse; right, reverse); (4) *qian,* Tang dynasty (618–907); (5) silver ingot, Qing dynasty, Guangxu era (1875–1908).

Anhui area. By the third century BCE these early coins were replaced by round bronze ones with a hole in the center; these were of diverse sizes and weights and their circulation was localized (see figure 1).

As part of the standardization of weights and measures under the Qin dynasty, China's monetary system became unified in 221 BCE, when round bronze *banliang* (half-ounce) coins were made the sole official currency. Weighing initially 12 *zhu* each (24 *zhu* = 1 *liang,* or tael), they were reduced to 5 *zhu* each by 118 BCE. Gold was calculated in *yi* (20 *liang*) units. This system remained in effect until 620, when the *qian* became the standard. One *qian* was, in fact, one round copper coin with a square hole in the center and weighing one-tenth of a *liang.* The official exchange rate of silver and gold to coins was 1 *liang* to 1,000 and 10,000 copper *qian* respectively, although in reality, the rate fluctuated with the metals' market value. No basic change occurred until 1889, when cast coins were replaced by machine-struck ones in silver and copper, based on the tael unit. Since the establishment of the Chinese Republic in 1912, *yuan* and *jiao* ("dollar" and "cent") became the standard currency units. China

abolished the silver standard in 1935, and all Chinese coins—both in the People's Republic and in the Republic of China on Taiwan—are of base metals today.

Until 1912 China's monetary situation was complicated by concurrent but independent use of paper currencies, silver ingots, and foreign silver dollars. From 1024, when China issued the world's first real paper money, its economy had been plagued by overissues of paper notes that circulated independently of its coins. Gold and silver ingots, of between 10 and 50 taels each, were commonly used for commerce, especially during the Yuan (1279–1368) and Qing (1644–1911) dynasties, but they too formed a separate system of their own. Foreign silver dollars, valued for their silver content and chop-marked for authenticity by Chinese merchants, were important to China's economy from the time of their introduction in the sixteenth century even though they were outside the official monetary system.

Japan's first currency was modeled after China's *qian.* Between 708 and 958, twelve series of round bronze coins valued at one *mon* each were cast for circulation. Domestic minting ceased after 958, however, owing to internal political strife, and until

1587 Japanese currency was a miscellany of imported Chinese cash and what was left of the early coppers, the value of each being dependent on the fluctuating market. Powerful daimyo cast their own gold, silver, and lead coins for local use. Currency centralization was achieved under the Tokugawa shogunate (1600–1868). The Kinza and Ginza (gold and silver mints, respectively) supplied Japan with gold, silver, and copper coins, based on the system of 16 *shu* to 4 *bu* to 1 *ryo* for gold and silver coins, and the *mon* standard for copper ones, but there was no fixed exchange rate between the three metals (see figure 2). The Meiji Restoration (1868) brought Japan a Western-style coinage beginning in 1870, based on a system of 10 *rin* to 1 *sen,* and 100 *sen* to 1 *yen.* The new Osaka Imperial Mint became Japan's sole issuer of coins. Japan abandoned the silver standard in 1939 and modern coins are in copper-nickel, aluminum, or tin alloy. Paper money, privately issued since the 1620s, became nationalized in 1870. The Bank of Japan, the official agent, issues notes in *sen* and *yen* denominations.

Korea's earliest currency, iron coins cast in 996 and patterned after the Chinese cash, was unpopular because of its crudeness. It was quickly followed by copper cash coins that also failed to replace bartering completely. Korea's monetary situation

FIGURE 3. *Korean Coins.* (1) copper coin (1633–1891); (2) first struck silver coin (nineteenth century).

finally stabilized in 1633, when a greatly improved copper coinage of 1, 2, 5, 10, and 100 *mun* was established as the national currency. Silver coins of 1, 2, and 3 *chon* were cast in 1882 to facilitate trade, but these were short-lived because of hoarding and illegal exporting. In 1891 Korea began striking Western-style bronze and silver coins in *fun, yang,* and *whan* denominations (100 *fun* = 1 *yang,* 5 *yang* = 1 *whan*). Today, South Korea issues coins based on the *chon* and *won/hwan* system (100 *chon* = 1 *won/hwan*); since 1962, 1 new *won* has been equal to 10 old *won/hwan*. Paper money, in use since 1401, is issued in *sen* and *yen* (100 *sen* = 1 *yen*). North Korean currency, both in coins and bills, is also based on the *chon* and *won* (100 *chon* = 1 *won*) system (see figure 3).

Bank of Korea, eds. *The Money of Korea* (1960). Norman Jacobs and Cornelius C. Vermeule III, *Japanese Coinage* (1953). Edgar J. Mandel, *Cast Coinage of Korea* (1972). Yü-ch'üan Wang, *Early Chinese Coinage* (1951).

ROSE CHAN HOUSTON

MONEY IN PRE-ISLAMIC INDIA

Coins provide concrete evidence that a monetary economy existed in northern India as early as the sixth century BCE. Although money was to become increasingly important in Indian economies with the expansion of trade and industry and the rapid growth of urban life, barter and the use of cowrie shells and metallic dust also persisted as media of exchange for many centuries.

Despite lively and continuing debate, scholars have not proved that people in Rig Vedic times used minted money. The thousands of punch-marked coins (so named after their method of manufacture) found throughout India are the earliest known coins.

FIGURE 2. *Japanese Coins.* (1) *mon,* after 708; (2) *bu,* silver; (3) *ryō,* gold *koban.*

Most are made of silver, although copper punch-marked coins have also been found. They bear no inscriptions or portraits to aid in their dating. Their pictorial markings (animals, birds, etc.) have been studied to determine chronological sequence and to classify them by region. It is not certain, however, who issued the earliest punch-marked coins. It does appear that the indigenous Maurya empire (c. 320–c. 185 BCE) ran a well-organized mint to produce the later punch-marked coins.

Uninscribed copper coins (cast in molds) also circulated in northern and central India, perhaps as early as the Maurya period. Round and square shaped, they also bear pictorial markings. Following the invasion of India by Alexander the Great in 327/326 BCE, the conquered territories were ruled by the Indo-Bactrians, who brought lasting changes to the style and manufacture of Indian coins (c. 200 BCE–c. 20 CE). They popularized the technique of striking coins between two dies and introduced the use of royal portraits and inscriptions to identify the issuing authority.

Three empires emerged during the post-Maurya period (c. 200 BCE—c. 300 CE): the Kushan, Satavahana, and Saka. The temporal and geographical limits of the foreign Kushan empire in the northwest are still disputed, but the fact that it was the first to mint gold coins in India attests to its flourishing economy. Kushan coins were die-struck in gold and copper with royal portraits, identifying inscriptions, and a rich array of deities.

The native Satavahana dynasty (c. 100 BCE—225 CE) was the earliest to issue an extensive series of coins in the Andhra region. The majority are lead (round) and copper (round and square), die-struck with symbols commonly found in punch-marked coins. A smaller number of silver coins bearing portraits also exists.

The foreign Sakas ruled in western India from about 126 BCE to about 400 CE. They minted high-quality silver coins in great quantity and copper coins with types generally patterned after the Indo-Bactrian coins. Saka coins seem to have circulated alongside Kushan coins.

Scholars believe that while a monetary economy prevailed in northern India after the decline of Kushan power, the varied composition of coins minted thereafter and the types of minting authorities (kings, tribes, and cities) indicate that no one currency system prevailed. Although during this period punch-marking and casting techniques were still used to a limited degree in northern India, coins were generally die-struck and the style of Indo-Bactrian coins was followed.

Political decentralization prevailed throughout South India for more than three hundred years after the decline of Satavanaha power. Local variation in currency based on Satavahana models was the rule.

Indigenous rule witnessed a resurgence in the north as the Gupta empire rose to power (from about the fourth to the mid-sixth century CE). Gold, silver, and copper coins were issued, but it is the superbly designed and crafted gold coins that are most remarkable. Gupta currency is thought to have circulated throughout the empire.

After the Gupta empire declined, a great variety of coins was minted in northern and central India. Prior to the Ghaznavid invasion in the tenth century, the coins of those regions can generally be described as imitations or derivatives of the Gupta coin types. They show great divergence in weight, quality, and metallic value. Continuity in coin currency has proved difficult to establish for the medieval period in northern India.

Chalukya rule brought political integration to the south in the mid-sixth century. The power of the dynasty's eastern and western branches waxed and waned until the twelfth century, but evidence that the early Chalukyas issued any new coin series is scant. Knowledge of the currency systems in the south during this period is limited and highly tentative. Except for Pallava coins circulating in southernmost Tamil Nadu (c. third century CE), indigenous currency from the post-Satavahana period in the south is practically nonexistent until the mid-tenth century, when a regular currency was again issued in the Deccan.

G. L. Adhya, *Early Indian Economies* (1966). *Catalogue of Indian Coins in the British Museum*, 7 vols. (1884–1936). Brajadulal Chattopadhyaya, *Coins and Currency Systems in South India c. A.D. 225–1300* (1977). P. L. Gupta, *Coins* (1969).

BARBARA GOMBACH

MONEY IN SOUTHEAST ASIA

Although there are sizable deposits of gold, silver, and copper in Southeast Asia, by themselves they were not sufficiently large to sustain metal-based currency systems in the region during periods of substantial growth in internal trade. Consequently, from at least the beginning of the second millennium CE, the monetary systems of Southeast Asia have been founded primarily on inflows of coin and bar metal from other areas of Asia and beyond. Thus, in thirteenth- and fourteenth-century Vietnam the monetary system was based on the copper coins of China; from the fifteenth century onward, as the

Vietnamese economy began to experience coin shortages, there was an inflow of copper ore and coin from Japan. In the early seventeenth century lead coin imported from China circulated on Java, and probably in the ports to which Javanese traded, alongside Spanish and Portguese specie and Chinese trading bar silver.

Beginning in the late sixteenth century a large amount of silver was transported from the Americas into Southeast Asia, brought into the region either directly through the Spaniards in Manila or indirectly through trade with China, Japan, and India. By the eighteenth century the monetary systems of at least mainland Southeast Asia had become primarily silver based. The sustained inflow of silver had a marked expansionary impact on the economies of Southeast Asia and may have been an important consideration in the formation of strong indigenous states in the region from the middle of the sixteenth century onward.

As the economies of Southeast Asia directed themselves increasingly toward an expanding trade with the industrializing West in the later nineteenth century, the dominant coin in regional trade was the Mexican silver dollar. And in the case of Siam, for example, the large trade surpluses that emerged in this period led to a substantial net inflow of the Mexican silver dollar, which was in part melted down and reminted into the Siamese domestic coin, the *baht*. In this way the domestic money supply of the kingdom—and, to the extent that the economy was monetized, the level of domestic economic activity—was determined by the net inflow of silver coin required to balance trade and invisible payments. From the late nineteenth century onward, internal monetary payments in the states of the region were increasingly facilitated by the introduction of paper currencies, frequently by permitting the major Western banks in the East to act as banks of issue.

The declining value of silver in relation to gold during the last decades of the nineteenth century forced all the states of Southeast Asia to abandon their silver-based monetary systems and adopt the gold-exchange standard. This occurred in the Netherlands East Indies in 1877, in Burma in 1893, in Siam in 1902, in the Philippines in 1903, and in the Straits Settlements in 1904. French Indochina remained tied to silver until 1930. The disintegration of the world trading and payments structure during the late 1920s, however, forced each state in the region to abandon the gold-exchange standard, although all maintained a strict relationship with the currency of the metropolitan power. This relation-

ship continued, except during the years of Japanese occupation, until the end of the colonial period and, in some cases, beyond.

J. C. van Leur, *Indonesian Trade and Society: Essays in Asian Social and Economic History* (1955). Victor B. Lieberman, *Burmese Administrative Cycles: Anarchy and Conquest, c. 1580–1760* (1984). William F. Spalding, *Eastern Exchange, Currency and Finance* (1924).

IAN BROWN

MONEY IN THE ANCIENT NEAR EAST

The coinage-based monetary system in the ancient Near East was a direct outgrowth of the birth of coinage in the ancient Greek world sometime between 650 and 600 BCE. Datable archaeological evidence indicates that coins made their first appearance in the provinces of Lydia or Ionia on the western coast of present-day Turkey. From there the invention spread rapidly throughout the Greek world, and shortly thereafter to the Near East, where the use of coins was first adopted by the Achaemenid rulers of Persia after Cyrus subjugated Croesus and his Lydian kingdom in 546 BCE.

The Persian kings apparently continued to utilize the mint at Sardes, the Lydian capital, eventually replacing the gold and silver coins of Croesus with their own gold *darics* and silver *sigloi*, which served mainly as payment to western mercenaries. These are small bean-shaped pieces of about 8.35 grams in gold and 5.50 grams in silver on the Lydian standard; they share an obverse image depicting a royal archer, presumably the king. Two varieties of this type, introduced by Darius around 515 BCE, show the king at half length and the king drawing a bow. A third variety, which shows the king running with bow and spear, appeared in quantity probably during the reign of Xerxes after 486 BCE (see figure 1.1), and a fourth, the king with bow and dagger, continued to be struck in the fourth century. Only the second and third varieties are found on the *darics*. The reverses of all carry only an oblong incuse punch. These coins provided the major currency in the Near East until the arrival of Alexander the Great.

Alexander succeeded Philip II in 336 BCE and extended his father's empire from Macedonia to the Indus Valley. Mints immediately sprang up in the wake of conquest, striking gold and silver coins on the Attic standard (the *tetradrachm,* equal to 17.2 grams) that now bore only Alexander's chosen types: the head of Athena and winged victory on the obverse and reverse, respectively, of the gold *staters,* and on the silver *tetradrachms* and *drachms*

FIGURE 1. *Ancient Near Eastern Coins.* (1) gold *daric*, Persia (fifth century BCE); (2) silver *tetradrachm*, Antiochus I of Syria, Seleucia-on-the-Tigris (280–261 BCE); (3) silver *tetradrachm*, Phraates III of Parthia, Seleucia-on-the-Tigris (70–57 BCE); (4) silver *tetradrachm*, Demetrius of Bactria (c. 195–150 BCE). All shown left, obverse; right, reverse.

the head of Herakles in the scalp of a lion and Zeus seated on a throne. Alexander established mints as far east as Babylon and possibly Susa. After his death in 323 BCE, his vast empire was divided among his generals. Seleucus I, Alexander's successor in Syria, as well as later Seleucid rulers, included Susa, Ecbatana, and Bactra among their eastern mints. Their splendid series of royal portrait coins (see figure 1.2), which continued to be struck on the Attic standard, were to serve as direct models for the coinages of the Bactrian Indo-Greeks, the Parthians, and Persian vassal kingdoms such as Persis, Characene, and Elymais (formerly Susiana).

The Parthian coinage consists of silver and bronze pieces (see figure 1.3). While *tetradrachms* were struck only at Seleucia in Mesopotamia, several silver *drachm* mints operated in Iran proper. The Persian coin types in general dwindled gradually from the fine workmanship of the Greeks to a linear portrait style and garbled Greek legends that betray the hands of less skilled Near Eastern die engravers.

The Parthians, led by Arsaces, rose up against the Seleucids around 250 BCE but fell in turn to the Sasanids in 224. The coins of the Sasanids continue to bear the portrait busts of the kings, now resplendent in crowns that identify the individual rulers. Sasanid coinage, which consists for the most part of silver *drachms*, was finally terminated by the Islamic conquest in 651 CE. Some of the earliest Islamic coins, however, are imitations of Sasanid models.

The Indo-Greeks, under Diodotus I, rebelled against the Seleucids about the same time as the Parthians. Demetrius (r. circa 195–150 BCE) extended the Bactrian kingdom southeast into the Indus Valley, but in the process he lost Bactria and a portion of his possessions in Gandhara to Eucratides (r. circa 175–155 BCE). The *tetradrachms* of these two kings have provided some of the most handsome portraits in the history of Greek coinage (see figure 1.4).

Some of the distinctive features of the coins of the Bactrians are their use of nickel as a metal for coinage, along with silver and bronze; the use of bilingual legends in Greek and Bactrian; and production of square as well as round pieces. Many of the issues were imitated by the Indo-Scythians and Indo-Parthians.

[*See also* Achaemenid Dynasty; Alexander III; Bactria; Greeks; Metalwork; Mines and Metallurgy; Parthians; Sasanid Dynasty; *and* Seleucid Dynasty.]

Robert Gobl, *Sasanian Numismatics* (1971). Michael Mitchiner, *Indo-Greek and Indo-Scythian Coinage*, 9 vols. (1975–1976). David Sellwood, *An Introduction to the Coinage of Parthia* (2d ed., 1980).

NANCY M. WAGGONER

MONEY IN THE ISLAMIC WORLD

In manufacture and use, Islamic coins did not differ materially from those of the rest of the world (except East Asia). The distinguishing feature of Islamic coins is the absence of any image, in accordance with Islamic tradition; instead, they are covered with generally religious inscriptions in Arabic or other languages employing the Arabic script. This is not to say that all coins issued by Muslim rulers have had Islamic inscriptions. There are many Muslim issues that imitate or adapt the previous coinage of a newly conquered region, including the use of images, and there are instances of non-Muslim states issuing coins of Islamic type (with inscriptions only in Arabic) because of strong Muslim influence.

The first coins issued by Muslims were imitations of the coinage of the Byzantine and Sasanid empires. In Iran, for example, silver *drahms* displaying the portrait of the former Sasanid emperor and the Zoroastrian fire altar were issued by the Arabs at many mints from about 650 to 700. Islamic coinage was invented specifically to replace such imitations with coins more appropriate to the beliefs of the new

religious community. The first Islamic coins were gold *dinars* struck in Damascus in 697, followed two years later by silver *dirhams* issued at Damascus and at mints throughout the Islamic east from Basra to Balkh (see figure 1.1–2).

These first Islamic coins were anonymous, issued in the name of the community rather than an individual, but toward the end of the eighth century officials frequently began to put their names on gold and silver coins along with the standard religious inscriptions. In the ninth century this privilege was regularized and limited to the caliphs and their designated heirs, but the independent secular Muslim states that arose in the ninth and tenth centuries were granted, or simply asserted, the privilege of adding their names to that of the caliph. This became a standard feature of Islamic coinage, so that the inscription of a ruler's name on his coins was re-

FIGURE 1. *Islamic Coins.* (1) silver *dirham*, Bishapur mint, dated AH 47 (667/668 CE); (2) gold *dinar*, Damascus (c. 692–694 CE); (3) silver *dirham* with name of al-Mahdi, son of the caliph, Rayy mint, dated AH 145 (762/763 CE); (4) gold *dinar* with name of Caliph al-Mu'tadid, Madinat al-Salam (Baghdad) mint, dated AH 288 (900/901 CE); (5) silver *dirham* with name of Ilkhan Abu Sa'id, Tabriz mint, dated AH 723 (1323 CE); (6) gold *mohur* with name of Mughal emperor Jahangir, Agra mint, dated month Aban, seventh year of reign, AH 1021 (1612 CE). All shown left, obverse; right, reverse.

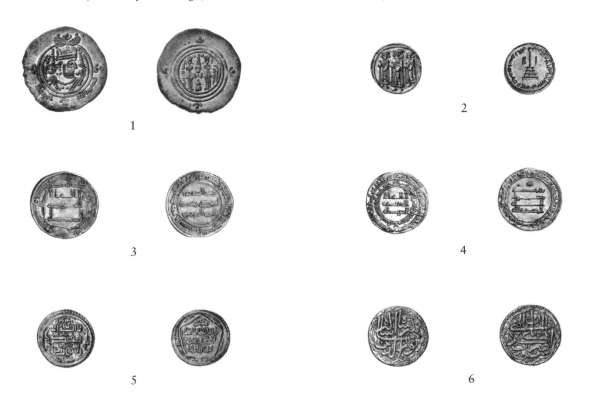

1

2

3

4

5

6

garded as one of the essential symbols of his sovereignty (see figure 1.3–4).

From the eighth to the thirteenth century, most coinage of Iran and its eastern neighbors conformed to a standard type, with several horizontal lines of inscription (including fundamental Muslim religious statements and the rulers' names) surrounded by one or two circular inscriptions. Those inscriptions included the place where the coin was struck and the date of its minting; thus, each Islamic coin is a miniature document of a specified time and place that indicates who ruled there and something of his religious beliefs.

The Mongol conquest resulted in major changes in Muslim coinage. Wide variety in arrangement and content of inscriptions became the norm among the Ilkhans and their successors, down to the nineteenth century and the introduction of machine technology (see figure 1.5). In India, Muslim coinage began about the time of the Mongol conquests in the early thirteenth century, and it took a rather different course of evolution from the western Muslim world, reflecting local conditions.

Muslims used all three of the common coinage metals, gold, silver, and copper. In the classical era, up to the thirteenth century, gold coins were called *dinars,* silver coins were called *dirhams,* and copper coins were called *fulus* (singular, *fals*). All three of these names came from Greek and Latin. Normally, gold and silver coins were as pure as possible. The standard weight of *dinars* was usually between 4.00 and 4.50 grams, and that of *dirhams* from 2.50 to just over 3.00 grams. The value relationship between gold, silver, and copper coins at any specified time and place depended on the precise weight standard and purity of each denomination, and also on supply and demand for each; with coins valued at nearly their worth in raw metal, it was impossible for governments to guarantee exchange rates in the face of market forces. In later centuries new denominations became common, such as the silver *rupi* (rupee) and gold *mohur* of India and Iran, both with a weight of about eleven grams, and the *ashrafi* of the Mediterranean and Iran, a gold coin of about 3.50 grams intended to compete with the ducat of Venice (see figure 1.6). The introduction of European mechanized coinage production in the nineteenth century brought with it the gradual replacement of Islamic coinage by the Western style coin with images, although a few Muslim states adhered to inscriptional designs or at least avoided the portrayal of humans.

[*See also* Dinar *and* Dirham.]

Michael L. Bates, *Islamic Coins* (1982). L. A. Mayer, *Bibliography of Moslem Numismatics, India Excepted* (2d ed., 1954). Michael B. Mitchiner, *Oriental Coins and Their Values: The World of Islam* (1977). C. R. Singhal, *Bibliography of Indian Coins, Part 2: Muhammadan and Later Series* (1952).   MICHAEL L. BATES

MONGKUT (1804–1868) was king of Siam as Rama IV from 1851 to 1868. Originally known as the Chao Fa prince (or high crown prince), Mongkut was the eldest surviving son of King Rama II by his chief queen. As a child he was educated in the palace, and for a short time he was a novice in a Buddhist monastery. Later, at age twenty, just before the death of his father, he again entered a monastery.

Mongkut was to live in the Buddhist *sangha* for the next twenty-seven years, and he did not leave the *sangha* until he was invited to become king in 1851. As a monk, Mongkut was free to follow his own intellectual and religious interests. He was an enthusiastic student of language, studying most of the languages of mainland Southeast Asia as well as Sanskrit and Pali, the classical languages of India. He made many pilgrimages to religious sites in Thailand. During one of his trips, in 1833, he discovered the inscription of King Ramkhamhaeng. Mongkut was responsive to new sources of knowledge; he studied Latin with Pallegoix, a French Catholic priest, and English with American Protestant missionaries Dr. Bradley and the Reverend Jesse Caswell. He sought out Western books and newspapers for information about foreign countries and modern science.

During the third reign Mongkut led a Buddhist reform movement that became the Thammayut sect of the *sangha*. Backed by many devout Buddhists who were concerned about the challenge of Christianity and the new scientific ideas, Mongkut sought a return to the Vinaya, the monastic discipline that at that time was most closely followed by the Mon *sangha,* and to the original teachings of the Buddha. This permitted a more rational approach to Buddhism, making a positive response to modern science possible. Mongkut's religious leadership was strengthened by his appointment as abbot of Wat Bowonniwet in 1837. He popularized his reform teachings through sermons in the Thai language and through the Buddhist tracts published by the Wat Bowonniwet's press.

Throughout his life, Mongkut's main concern was to assure the Thai of respect and status equal to that of any other nation. When he became king in 1851,

Mongkut devoted himself to the improvement of his country's international standing, carrying on an extensive correspondence with foreign heads of state, including Queen Victoria of Great Britain, Emperor Napoleon III of France, Pope Pius IX, and presidents Pierce, Buchanan, and Lincoln of the United States. Foreign missions were welcomed. Mongkut and his advisers followed a conciliatory policy toward the Western powers, accepting their demands for free trade, diplomatic relations, and other privileges. In 1855 the Thai met with Sir John Bowring and signed the Treaty of Friendship and Commerce with Great Britain. Several months later a similar treaty was signed with the United States. Treaties with France, Denmark, the Hanseatic Republic, and other European nations followed. The export of rice was legalized; it soon become the country's major export. Foreign advisers were hired and a large foreign community settled in Bangkok.

Mongkut was also concerned with the modernization of the Thai kingdom through legal means. He issued numerous edicts modifying or eliminating ancient customs that were now out of date. He reinstated the right of citizens to petition the king directly, and people were permitted to look at the king and to watch royal processions. His efforts to improve public health and welfare were many; he continued to encourage the medical work of the missionaries. Mongkut established a royal mint, which issued a standardized flat coinage, and began the publication of an official gazette.

Mongkut tended to leave administrative tasks to others. Krom Somdet Phra Dechadison, his elder half-brother, and Krommaluang Wongsathiratsanit, his younger half-brother, performed many administrative functions, as did Somdet Chaophraya Sisuriyawong (the Kalahom) and Chaophraya Nikonbodin (the Mahatthai). With the exception of two expeditions to the Shan States (1852–1854), no military campaigns were undertaken during Mongkut's reign.

Mongkut liked children, and by the end of his reign he was the father of eighty-two sons and daughters. His eldest surviving son was Chulalongkorn, who became Rama V. Mongkut often expressed concern about his family and took great interest in the education of his sons. The wives of the American missionaries were invited to the palace to teach English, and Anna Leonowens, whose career was later romanticized in the musical "The King and I," was employed as a tutor for his sons.

Mongkut's interest in science may have brought about his death: he died on 1 October 1868 from an illness contracted during a trip to the south to observe a solar eclipse. Mongkut had been a strong king, however, and his diplomatic skills helped preserve his kingdom's independence at a time when other Southeast Asian nations were losing theirs.

[*See also* Chulalongkorn.]

Abbot Low Moffat, *Mongkut, the King of Siam* (1961).

CONSTANCE M. WILSON

MONGMAO, oldest urban site yet to be uncovered in Burma, dates to about 200 BCE. Located in the eastern part of the Kyaukse Plain in the dry zone of Burma, Mongmao is linked, in cultural and probably economic and political ways, to the dozen or so other so-called Pyu sites. Mongmao has not been excavated as thoroughly as Peikthano, but findings suggest that the two sites might be contemporary or older, and Mongmao promises to be as significant a site as Peikthano. Mongmao is also significant in that it is the first site of its age to be found in the dry plains, the region that was long the cultural, political, and economic center of Burma. The site's brick structures, urn burial, coins, onyx beads, and its script are all virtually the same as those unearthed the other Pyu sites, suggesting that Mongmao had contact with places in India, Sri Lanka, and Thailand, which were in turn linked to the Rome-India-China trade.

[*See also* Peikthano.]

Michael Aung-Thwin, "Burma before Pagan: The Status of Archaeology Today," in *Asian Perspectives* (1987).

MICHAEL AUNG-THWIN

MONGOL EMPIRE. [*This entry consists of an overview, which details the rise and expansion of the Mongol empire and its successor states, and three discussions of the Mongol invasions of regions on the empire's periphery:* Mongol Invasions of Korea, Mongol Invasions of Japan, *and* Mongol Invasions of Southeast Asia. *These three focus on the effects of the invasions from the point of view of the countries involved. The ethnographic origins and social organization of the Mongols are treated in* Mongols.]

AN OVERVIEW

The Empire of the Great Mongols (*yeke mongghol ulus*) was the largest contiguous land empire in human history. In the mid-thirteenth century it included within its frontiers Korea, Manchuria, North and Southwest China, North Vietnam, Tibet, East and West Turkestan, Afghanistan, Kashmir, Iran, Mesopotamia, Asia Minor, the Caucasus, the Rus principalities, and southern Siberia. In constructing their state the Mongols visited great destruction upon the various centers of Eurasian civilization and inflicted endless misery upon the subject population. But these conquerors, by bringing under their dominion a multitude of peoples and cultures widely diverging in language, religion, and levels of social and economic development, also created conditions that facilitated the exchange of ideas and goods between West and East Asia.

Genghis Khan. The formation of the empire can be dated conveniently to 1206. In this year Temujin, the chieftain of the Mongol tribe, was proclaimed Genghis (more properly, Chinggis) Khan ("universal sovereign") after three decades of internecine conflict among the various nomadic tribes of the eastern steppe. *Mongol,* the name of the victorious tribe, came to be applied generically to the Naiman, Tatar, Kereit, and other subordinate tribes who had joined the emerging confederation through choice or compulsion.

Following the enthronement ceremonies, held along the lower course of the Kerulen River of eastern Mongolia, Genghis Khan systematically mobilized his new subjects. Utilizing a well-established nomadic tradition, he enrolled all adult males into *mingghan* (literally, "units of one thousand"). The 115 *mingghan* mustered at this time were in turn divided into smaller units of ten and one hundred. For large-scale operations ten *mingghan* were brigaded together to form a *tumen;* in command of each such formation Genghis Khan placed a trusted follower. As both soldiers and their families were made subject to the authority of a *mingghan* commander, these units served the new emperor as a means of administrative control as well as a mechanism for military mobilization.

Genghis Khan also recast and significantly expanded his personal bodyguard *(keshig)*. First established in 1204 with a complement of 1,150 troops, it was now enlarged to a body of ten thousand. In addition to providing for the security of the emperor, this body tended to his personal needs, took care of his possessions, and formed the nucleus around which the imperial government developed.

His military and administrative measures in place, the emperor ordered a series of military operations designed to expand the nascent empire's demographic and resource base. In 1207 the forest tribes of southern Siberia were subjugated, and an exploratory raid was launched against the Tangut kingdom of Xixia, located in the Ordos-Gansu region of China. Several years later a larger force was sent against the Xixia, and in 1211 the Tangut ruler, besieged in Zhongxing, his capital on the Yellow River, tendered his submission to Genghis Khan. In the wake of this military success several other sedentary states hastened to acknowledge Mongol overlordship. Chief among them were the Turkic-speaking Uighurs, an urbanized people of the Turfan Depression, from whom the Mongols acquired their alphabet and many of their fiscal and administrative institutions.

The Mongols' next objective was the Jurchen-ruled Jin dynasty of North China. On the heels of his victory over the Xixia, Genghis Khan initiated a series of annual campaigns against the Jin that culminated in the capture of Zhongdu (Beijing), the Jurchen capital, in early 1215.

Later that year, the emperor received an embassy from the Khwarazmshah, the ruler of West Turkestan and North Iran, that resulted in the establishment of friendly trade relations between the two powers. This amicable interlude came to a sudden end in 1218, when a Mongol trading caravan was slaughtered in the city of Utrar by one of the Khwarazmshah's local officials. Enraged, Genghis Khan invaded Khwarazm in 1219, and by 1223 the defending armies were crushed and most of the oasis cities of West Turkestan lay in ruins.

In 1224 Genghis Khan returned to Mongolia, intent upon settling with his erstwhile vassals, the Tanguts, who had failed to send auxiliary troops in support of the Khwarazm campaign. In the spring of 1226 he mobilized the Mongol armies. The Tanguts were soon on the defensive, and by early 1227 Zhongxing was under siege. Once his troops had surrounded the capital, Genghis Khan struck south toward the Wei River valley to pressure the Jin along their western frontier. In August 1227, somewhere south of the Liupan Mountains, the great warrior died from injuries received in a riding accident two years before. In accordance with his deathbed injunction, his demise was kept secret until the Tanguts were destroyed. In September Zhongxing capitulated and the Mongols halted operations. The Mongol princes and officials returned to the Kerulen to bury their fallen leader and to order the affairs of the realm. [*See also* Genghis Khan; Tanguts; *and* Jurchen Jin Dynasty.]

Ghenghis's Successors. In 1219 and again just prior to his death, Genghis Khan had designated his third son, Ogedei, as successor. To the heirs of his

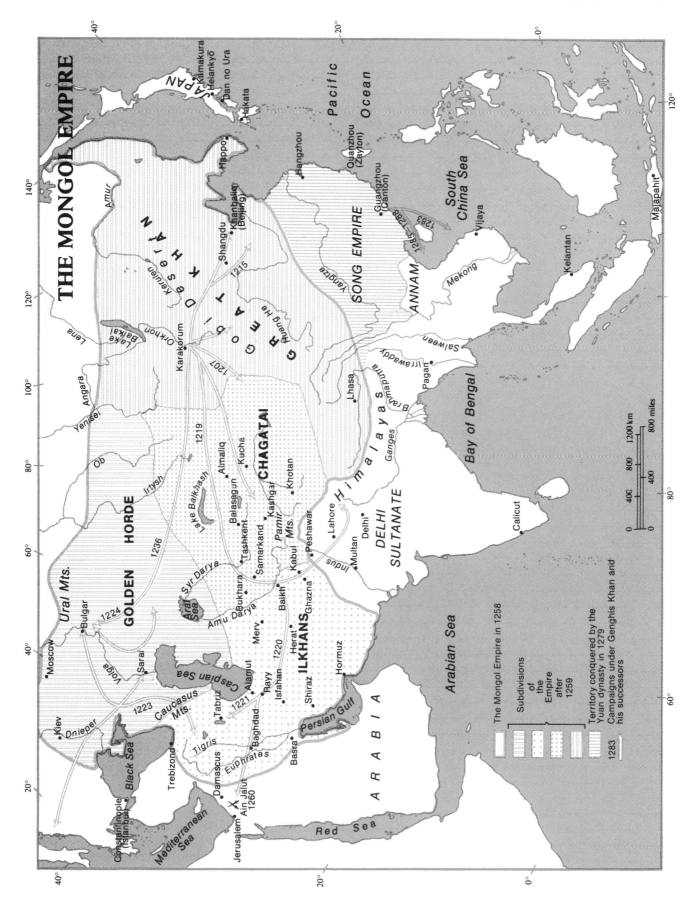

THE MONGOL EMPIRE

GREAT KHAN

GOLDEN HORDE

CHAGATAI

ILKHANS

Pacific Ocean

SONG EMPIRE

South China Sea

ANNAM

Bay of Bengal

Arabian Sea

DELHI SULTANATE

ARABIA

Red Sea

Mediterranean Sea

Black Sea

Caspian Sea

Aral Sea

Persian Gulf

GOBI Desert

Himalayas

JAPAN

Kamakura
Heiankyō
Dan no Ura
Hakata
Happo

Hangzhou
Quanzhou (Zayton)
Guangzhou (Canton)
Vijaya
Kelantan
Majapahit

Khanbaliq (Beijing)
Shangdu
Karakorum
Lake Baikal
Orkhon
Kerulen
Amur
Lena
Angara
Yenisei
Ob
Irtysh
Lake Balkhash

Almaliq
Kucha
Khotan
Kashgar
Balasagun
Tashkent
Samarkand
Bukhara
Amu Darya
Syr Darya
Pamir Mts.
Peshawar
Kabul
Balkh
Ghazna
Herat
Merv

Moscow
Bulgar
Saral
Kiev
Dnieper
Volga
Ural Mts.
Trebizond
Constantinople (Istanbul)

Lhasa
Ganges
Brahmaputra
Pagan
Irrawaddy
Salween
Mekong
Yangtze
Huang He

Lahore
Delhi
Multan
Jumna

Hormuz
Shiraz
Isfahan
Rayy
Tabriz
Alamut
Baghdad
Basra
Damascus
Tigris
Euphrates
Jerusalem
Caucasus Mts.

Ain Jalut 1260

Calicut

1215
1207
1219
1220
1221
1223
1224
1236
1285-1288
1283

The Mongol Empire in 1258

Subdivisions of the Empire after 1259

Territory conquered by the Yuan dynasty in 1279

Campaigns under Genghis Khan and his successors

400   800   1200 km
400   800 miles

eldest son, Jochi (who had died earlier in 1227), he granted the as-yet-unconquered western Eurasian steppe and the Rus principalities; to his second son, Chagatai, western Turkestan and parts of eastern Turkestan; and to the youngest, Tolui, the Mongolian homeland. While the latter three had their own territories and armies, each was to cooperate with and obey the new emperor (now titled *khaghan*) to further expand the empire's frontiers.

As soon as Ogedei was formally enthroned along the Kerulen in 1229, new campaigns of conquest were mounted. Between 1230 and 1233 the truncated Jin state was overwhelmed, and from 1236 to 1241 Batu, Jochi's second son and successor, brought the Kipchak steppe and the Rus principalities under Mongol control.

Because of the rapid expansion of the empire into areas of sedentary culture, the imperial guard, which performed the functions of a central government, could no longer adequately administer the realm by itself. Ogedei, upon his succession, established two regional secretariats to govern the empire's sedentary population. One, headed by Mahmud Yalavach, a Khwarazmian, had jurisdiction over east and west Turkestan; the other, led by Yelü Chucai, a sinicized Khitan, was responsible for North China. In each secretariat the Mongols employed numerous nonnative administrative specialists, often merchants, to work together with locally recruited officials. An extensive network of imperial agents *(darughachi)*, usually Mongols, monitored the work of regional and local officials on behalf of the *khaghan*.

Ogedei tried to regularize and rationalize the Mongols' rather ad hoc revenue system. Under the new scheme urged upon the ruler by Mahmud Yalavach and Yelü Chucai, official exactions were limited to an agricultural tax, a commercial tax, and *kubchir,* a tribute imposed on individual households in China and on all adult males in Turkestan. For each category of taxes, fixed schedules and rates of payment were established. Initially, these reforms brought a degree of relief from the endless extraordinary exactions the Mongols had traditionally imposed on conquered people, but toward the end of Ogedei's reign conditions again deteriorated. Given to hard drinking, Ogedei increasingly lost interest in the affairs of state; in 1239 he turned over the financial administration of North China to Central Asian merchants, an action that resulted in a dramatic rise in tax rates and huge profits for the merchants and their Mongol partners. The peasants, now unable to pay the exorbitant rates, had to turn to these same merchants for loans at usurious in-

terest rates to meet their obligations to the state. Ogedei soon came to realize the destructive character of this policy, but he was unable to improve the situation before his death in 1241. [*See also* Ogedei *and* Yelü Chucai.]

Following a lengthy interregnum in which Ogedei's widow, Toregene, served as regent, Guyug, the oldest son of the deceased *khaghan,* succeeded to the throne in 1246. Because of a long-standing personal difference with Guyug, Batu, leader of the line of Jochi, bitterly opposed his elevation; in the end Batu grudgingly recognized the new *khaghan* but refused to attend the enthronement ceremonies. During Guyug's brief and ineffectual reign (1246–1248) the authority of the central government further declined, in part because of the ruler's addiction to alcohol and in part because of Batu's intransigence.

After the death of Guyug, Batu, while conceding to Guyug's widow, Oghul Kaimish, the right to assume the regency, had no intention of allowing a descendant of Ogedei on the throne. With the active support of Sorghaghtani, the widow of Tolui, he convoked a *khuriltai* (diet of princes) south of Lake Balkash in 1250; there Mongke, eldest son of Tolui, was proclaimed *khaghan.* The lines of Ogedei and Chagatai refused to attend, claiming that such matters could only be transacted along the Kerulen. Mongke and his supporters bowed to tradition, and a second, "official" enthronement took place in Mongolia in 1251.

After suppressing opposition from the disgruntled and disorganized princes of the Ogedei and Chagatai lines, Mongke installed a new central government in Karakorum, the Mongol capital in the Orkhon River valley. An able and energetic ruler, Mongke quickly and forcibly reasserted the authority of the office of *khaghan*. Intent upon further conquest after the ten-year lull, he set about acquiring men and supplies to sustain his program of expansion. To this end he ordered a new census of the entire realm, reintroduced a regular scheme of taxation, and mobilized huge armies from the settled population.

Three major campaigns were set in motion by 1252. Hulegu, Mongke's brother, was commissioned to complete the conquest of western Asia and establish there a new regional khanate under direct control of the Tolui line. In 1256 Hulegu destroyed the order of Assassins (Isma'ilis) in their mountain castles of northwestern Iran and then pushed on to Baghdad. In early 1258 the Abbasid capital fell, and its hapless inhabitants were put to the sword. Mongol expansion continued westward until September of 1260, when the Egyptian Mamluks defeated Hulegu's armies in Syria at the Battle of Ain Jalut. [*See also* Hulegu.]

Simultaneously with the assault on western Asia Mongke reopened hostilities with Korea. The inhabitants of the peninsula, under Mongol pressure since 1218, tenaciously resisted the renewed onslaught, forcing the *khaghan* to commit reserves in 1258. By 1259, however, the tide of battle turned and the Korean king finally acknowledged Mongol overlordship.

The third of Mongke's campaigns was directed against the Song dynasty of China. As a first step, Kublai, another brother of Mongke's, led a force into Sichuan and Yunnan in 1252. In 1254 the Nanzhao kingdom, located along the southwestern frontier of the Song, capitulated, and Kublai returned to the north. Uriyangkadai, the responsible field commander, entered Annam in 1257 and in the spring of the next year forced the Annamese ruler to surrender. Soon thereafter Mongke entered Sichuan with a new army, preparing for a final descent upon the Song, but before telling damage could be inflicted, the *khaghan* died in August of 1259, and hostilities were halted.

For the Song, Mongke's death meant a twenty-year reprieve and for the Mongols a new and divisive succession crisis from which the empire never recovered. His failure to establish a clear line of succession precipitated a contest for the throne between his brother Kublai, whom he had placed in charge of North China, and Arigh Boke, whom he had left in command of Karakorum. Each of the two princes, eager for power, hurriedly convoked a *khuriltai* in his respective sphere of influence and proclaimed himself emperor. This split in the house of Tolui gave the other Chinggisid lines an opportunity to reassert themselves and to pursue their particularistic interests after nine years of effective central rule.

Initially, Arigh Boke received the support of the lines of Chagatai and Jochi; Kublai was supported by his brother Hulegu in Iran. In the civil war that followed, the Mongols of Iran (the Ilkhans) fended off Chagatai incursions into Khurasan and Jochi inroads into Transcaucasia. In the latter confrontation, Berke (r. 1257–1265), khan of the line of Jochi (known as the Golden Horde through later Russian usage), laid claim to the Ilkhanid province of Georgia and in 1262 sent to the south a large invasion force; after numerous battles the invaders withdrew from Ilkhanid territory in 1263. In preparing his drive toward Transcaucasia, Berke, a recent convert to Islam, enlisted the aid of the Egyptian

Mamluks, who had their own grievances against Hulegu. Although its immediate practical consequences were few, the Golden Horde–Mamluk partnership was an important step in the breakup of the Mongol empire, for it marked the first occasion in which a Mongol prince sought outside support in an internal political struggle. [*See also* Chagatai *and* Ilkhanid Dynasty.]

While these conflicts flared in the western half of the empire, Kublai and Arigh Boke were locked in bloody conflict for control of the imperial throne. Starting in 1260, the armies of the two pretenders fought a number of engagements in Mongolia, western China (Gansu), and eastern Turkestan. Kublai, relying on the abundant resources of China, gradually wore down his rival. In 1262 Arigh Boke's Chagatai allies abandoned him; two years later he was compelled to surrender to Kublai. The defeated prince, at first pardoned, was subsequently executed for his act of "rebellion."

The Empire of Kublai Khan. Kublai's restoration of empire in 1264 was at best tenuous and incomplete. The new *khaghan* controlled North China and Mongolia and enjoyed the recognition of the Ilkhans and the Chagatai, but Berke and his immediate successors, still disgruntled over territorial dispensations in Transcaucasia, continued their assaults on these provinces, refusing to acknowledge Kublai as sovereign. His transfer of the capital from Karakorum to Beijing in 1260 and his proclamation of a Chinese-style dynasty, the Yuan, in 1271 further undercut his legitimacy in the eyes of the more conservative Mongol princes who remained in the steppe.

At a *khuriltai* held along the Talas River in western Turkestan in 1269 Kaidu, a grandson of Ogedei, fashioned a coalition of princes in Central Asia dedicated to the ouster of Kublai and to the restoration of the line of Ogedei. This alliance, formed with the lines of Jochi and Chagatai, mounted attacks in Afghanistan, Mongolia, and eastern Turkestan throughout the 1270s and 1280s. The Ilkhans successfully held their ground in Khurasan, and the Yuan, despite heavy commitments of troops against the Southern Song (conquered in 1279), blunted the assaults on Mongolia. In eastern Turkestan, however, Kaidu made considerable headway, and in 1295, the year after Kublai's death, the Yuan abandoned this region and pulled back into Gansu.

While Kaidu's victory in eastern Turkestan was a substantial achievement, he was unable to capitalize upon it owing to dissidence among his allies. The princes of the Golden Horde, whose territories extended eastward to the Irtysh and thus abutted those of Kaidu in Dzungaria and Semirechie, grew increasingly wary of the growing power and ambition of the Ogedei line during the 1280s. Their unease resulted in 1294 in a major realignment of the princes in the Mongol civil war. The Golden Horde now joined the Yuan dynasty and the Ilkhans in a grand alliance again Kaidu and his principal collaborator, Du'a, the Chagatai khan. Following protracted negotiations, the Yuan and its partners launched a well-prepared offensive against Kaidu's coalition. In a decisive battle on the southern slopes of the Altai Mountains in September of 1301, the Yuan dynasty and the Golden Horde emerged victorious, and Kaidu was killed. Although greatly weakened by the defeat, Du'a and Chabar, Kaidu's son and successor, continued the struggle for several more years. Finally exhausted by the long conflict, Du'a and Chabar agreed to a truce. By the terms of a treaty signed in 1304 by the major Mongol princes, hostilities were to be terminated and trade routes reopened; practical results of this agreement were, however, minimal. Temur Oljaitu (r. 1294–1307), Kublai's successor on the Yuan throne, was duly acknowledged by the regional khans as emperor, but their recognition of his sovereignty was both nominal and fleeting. When Du'a and Chabar had a falling out in 1305–1306 the peace was soon shattered. The attempt to reunify the fragmented empire had failed; the leaders of the four independent and autonomous regional khanates—the Golden Horde, the Ilkhans, the Chagatai khanate, and the Yuan dynasty—made no further efforts in this direction.

Contacts and conflicts between the four polities gradually declined; the last generalized outbreak of hostilities occurred in the period from 1313 to 1319 when Uzbek, the khan of the Golden Horde (r. 1313–1341), unsuccessfully invaded Transcaucasia, and the Chagatai khan, Esen Bugha (r. 1310–1318), clashed with Yuan forces in Dzungaria and with the Ilkhans in Khurasan. Thereafter, the Yuan dynasty remained at peace with the other Mongol states. Although the Ilkhans still had to fend off further encroachments by the Golden Horde and the Chagatai, these conflicts now took on the character of local territorial disputes; the issue of succession to the imperial throne, which had engendered the civil wars of the preceding decades, had by this time lost much of its importance. [*See also* Kublai Khan *and* Yuan Dynasty.]

Trade. Strife among the Mongol princes, although frequent and destructive after 1259, did not prevent economic and cultural exchange between the regional khanates. The Mongol khans, like all previous nomadic rulers, were eager to profit from the lively trade that passed between eastern and western Eurasia. At least four major commercial arteries are known from the Mongol era: (1) a sea route from South China to the Persian Gulf; (2) the old Silk Road leading from West China into the Tarim Basin and West Turkestan, and thence into northern Iran; (3) a variant route that began in the lower Volga, followed the course of the Syr Darya, and then passed through Dzungaria to West China; and (4) a Siberian route, apparently pioneered by the Mongols, that started in the Volga-Kama region, traversed southern Siberia to Lake Baikal, and then struck south to Karakorum and Beijing. Although the civil war often hindered trade, at least one or two of the routes remained open at all times.

Along these lengthy commercial highways there passed a variety of luxury items. Valuable furs and gyrfalcons from Siberia reached the emporiums of China and the Middle East, and Chinese silk, porcelain, aromatic herbs, and mirrors traveled to Siberia, the lower Volga, and Iran. The merchants who transported these commodities were mainly Uighurs and Central Asian Muslims. Some were private, independent entrepreneurs, while others entered into partnerships with Mongol princes. The latter, known as *ortaq* in Turkish, operated with capital supplied by their princely sponsors. In the early empire *khaghans* such as Ogedei allowed *ortaq* merchants free use of the *jam*, the Mongols' system of postal relay stations, to transport themselves and their goods from market to market, a practice that substantially increased their profit margins. Another form of economic intercourse within the empire arose from the custom of granting to the prince of one Chinggisid line an appanage in the territory of another line. Thus, the Golden Horde, the Chagatai, and the Ilkhans all had their own properties in North China, while the Yuan emperors had appanages in western Turkestan and the northern Caucasus. From such properties the assignee derived both taxes and local products; Hulegu and his successors enjoyed, for example, the proceeds from 25,056 silk-producing households in Henan.

There were also exchanges of population among the khanates. Military contingents raised in one end of the empire were regularly sent great distances to meet manpower needs elsewhere in the Mongol domain. Uighur units were stationed in Yunnan (southwest China), Khurasan, and in the territory of the Golden Horde. Chinese sappers helped breach the walls of Baghdad in 1259, and Muslim catapult operators helped reduce Southern Song cities in the 1270s.

The "trade" in artists and craftsmen was also brisk. The Mongols took great pains to identify those of their subjects with useful skills and then put them to work on a variety of projects throughout the realm. The archaeological remains of Karakorum, for example, reveal the hand of Chinese, Tibetan, Uighur, Muslim, and Volga Bulghar artisans. Scientists and physicians, too, were transferred freely about the empire. Exchanges of this sort were particularly common between the Yuan dynasty and its longtime military ally, the Ilkhans of Iran; Bolad Chengxiang (d. 1313), a Mongol ambassador sent by Kublai to Iran in 1285, and Rashid al-Din (d. 1318), the Persian historian and high functionary at the Ilkhanid court, methodically exploited the unique cultural opportunities afforded by the Mongols' vast trans-Eurasian empire. Bound together by ties of friendship and shared intellectual interests, they commissioned Persian translations of Chinese works on medicine, agronomy, and governance and had an agricultural experiment station organized in Tabriz to test new seed strains from India and China. Rashid al-Din used his great personal wealth to support the work of Chinese physicians and astronomers brought to Iran; in return, the Ilkhans sent Muslim astronomers and physicians to China. Even food recipes were shared, for the Yuan dynasty's imperial dietary compendium contains a selection of Middle Eastern dishes, including directions for the preparation of sherbet.

The most enduring monument to their collaboration is undoubtedly Rashid al-Din's justly famous history, *The Collection of Chronicles*. This huge compendium, commissioned by the Ilkhan Ghazan (r. 1295–1304), provides a history of the Islamic dynasties, India, China, the Jews, the Franks, and the Mongol and Turkish tribes. Bolad supplied the Persian historian with data on the formative stages of the empire, from now-lost Mongol chronicles. He also furnished guidance for these sections of the history that touch on Kublai's reign in China; as a former high official in the Yuan government and as a member of Kublai's guard, Bolad was in a position to offer his colleague eyewitness testimony.

The Mongol Empire in Decline. The regional khanates that had emerged as de facto sovereign states from the civil wars of the latter half of the thirteenth century began to fall into decline in the middle decades of the fourteenth century. The first to succumb were the Ilkhans. During the reign of Abu Sa'id (1316–1335) struggles for power among Mongol and Turkish military commanders severely crippled the authority of the central government. After Abu Sa'id's death a series of ineffectual puppet rulers, placed on the throne by rival factions, followed one another in rapid succession until 1353, when the last Chinggisid sovereign of Iran met his death.

The Chagatai khanate experienced similar difficulties in the 1330s. Tensions within the Mongol and Turkish ruling elite between those who had embraced Islam and those still wedded to Mongol nomadic traditions led to destructive military confrontations and frequent changes in rulers. This state of affairs persisted down to the early 1380s, when the famous conqueror Timur (Tamerlane; 1336–1405), brought all of Turkestan under his control and reduced the last of the Chagatai khans to mere figureheads. [*See also* Timur.]

In the Yuan realm bitter rivalries among high Mongol officials at court during the 1350s and 1360s seriously impaired the Mongols' ability to maintain their authority over China. This, in combination with growing peasant unrest in South China provoked by decades of misrule, brought about the rapid collapse of the Yuan. In 1368 the last *khaghan* of the Mongol empire, Toghon Temur (r. 1332–1368), was ignominiously forced to flee Beijing under pressure of advancing Chinese rebel armies; he took refuge in Mongolia, where he died two years later. The large number of Mongols who remained in China when their emperor decamped subsequently found service with the new dynasty, the Ming (1368–1644).

After the collapse of the Yuan dynasty, the Mongols split into the Oirats, or western Mongols, who occupied the steppes north of the Tian Shan range, and the Northern Yuan, who moved north of China into eastern Mongolia. The Oirat confederation attacked and defeated the eastern Mongols in the early fifteenth century, but began to decline a generation later. The eastern Mongols then gained the ascendancy. Their leader Altan Khan, active in the mid-sixteenth century, was responsible for introducing Tibetan Buddhism to Mongol society. It is Altan Khan who first bestowed the title Dalai Lama on the leader of the Yellow Hat sect. [*See also* Oirats; Altan Khan; *and* Dalai Lama.]

From the mid-seventeenth to mid-eighteenth century, the Oirat Dzungar confederation rose to prominence in eastern Turkestan. They defeated the Chagatai and were a significant threat to Qing Chinese dominance of Tibet and Mongolia. Eventually the Qing dynasty controlled the entire region. [*See also* Dzungaria *and* Qing Dynasty.]

Farther west the Golden Horde, the longest lived of the Mongol khanates, began to weaken visibly in the 1370s and 1380s, by which time the ruling class was Turkish in speech and Islamic in religion. Disputes within the line of Jochi invited Timur's intervention in the affairs of the khanate after 1375; the resulting confusion gave Muscovite Russia an opportunity to challenge the military strength of their longtime Tatar masters at the Battle of Kulikovo Pole in 1380. The Russians won the day, but the Golden Horde overcame their difficulties, reasserted their military supremacy over the Russians two years later and, although still buffeted by domestic discord, managed to survive with some semblance of unity into the early decades of the fifteenth century. Thereafter, internal dissension and rivalry, aided by Muscovite diplomacy, intensified, and the Golden Horde disintegrated into a number of successor states. By the middle of the sixteenth century most of its major successors—the Great Horde and the khanates of Kazan and Astrakhan—had been incorporated into the expanding Muscovite state by force of arms, leaving the Crimean Tatars as the Russians' only serious rival in the steppe. The Crimean khanate, the last remnant of the once-mighty Mongol imperium, was subjected to Russian rule in 1771 and formally extinguished in 1783.

Thomas T. Allsen, "Mongol Census Taking in Rus, 1245–1275," *Harvard Ukrainian Studies* 5(1981): 32–53. J. A. Boyle, "Dynastic and Political History of the Īl-khāns," in *The Cambridge History of Iran*, vol. 5, *The Saljuq and Mongol Periods*, edited by J. A. Boyle (1968), pp. 303–421. John Dardess, "From Mongol Empire to Yüan Dynasty: Changing Forms of Imperial Rule in Mongolia and Central Asia," *Monumenta Serica* 30 (1972–1975): 117–165. Hsiao Ch'i-ch'ing, *The Military Establishment of the Yüan Dynasty* (1978). P. Jackson, "The Dissolution of the Mongol Empire," *Central Asiatic Journal* 22 (1978): 186–243. Rashīd al-Dīn, *The Successors of Genghis Khan*, translated by J. A. Boyle (1971). J. J. Saunders, *The History of the Mongol Conquests* (1971). Bertold Spuler, *The Muslim World*, part 2, *The Mongol Period* (1969). George Vernadsky, *The Mongols and Russia* (1953).   THOMAS T. ALLSEN

MONGOL INVASIONS OF KOREA

In the mid-thirteenth century the Mongols waged the campaigns that eventually placed most of Asia under their rule. In Korea, the Mongols met one of their most resolute foes; it took them more than forty years to subjugate the Korean people completely.

The Koryŏ kingdom (918–1392) first learned of the Mongols at the beginning of the thirteenth century, when Mongol forces tried to eradicate Khitan influence in the Yalu and Tumen river basins. In 1218 Koryŏ and Mongol soldiers joined forces to push the Khitan from the area. With the successful completion of this campaign, the Mongols immediately expected Koryŏ to submit to their demands. Initially Koryŏ, sensing danger, agreed to send tribute, but as Mongol requests increased and Mongol behavior grew more arrogant, Koryŏ prepared to resist.

In 1224 the murder of a Mongol envoy to Koryŏ caused a break in relations between the two. The Mongols, who were too heavily engaged in battle elsewhere to fight Koryŏ immediately, allowed seven years to elapse before their first invasion of Koryŏ in 1231. When that invasion failed to subjugate Koryŏ, the Mongols launched six more massive attacks, the last in 1254. None convinced the Koryŏ leadership to surrender. The immediate goal of the invasions was to avenge the murder of the Mongol official, but an invasion of the peninsular kingdom suited long-range Mongol strategy as well. In order to conquer China, the Mongols needed to secure their rear flanks by neutralizing Koryŏ. Furthermore, Koryŏ was a rich state with furs, horses, and armaments, all of which were useful supplies in the Mongols' campaigns.

Koryŏ's strength was revealed in its resistance. Troops were drilled and placed on alert, and when the invasion began Koryŏ soldiers resisted with uncommon valor. At the famous siege of Kuju (Kusŏng) in northern Korea, the Koryŏ troops' ability to withstand Mongol onslaughts astonished Mongol generals. When fortresses did fall, peasants and soldiers took to the hills and coastal islands, where they used guerrilla tactics to continue the fight. The entire society, including slaves and monks, participated in the resistance, slowing the Mongol attacks.

After the first Mongol invasion the court, then under the domination of the Ch'oe military house, evacuated the capital, Kaesŏng, and fled to Kanghwa, a nearby island. By taking advantage of the Mongols' dislike of naval warfare, the Koryŏ leadership was able to continue a splendid court life for some time, and they remained a symbol of Koryŏ's resistance to the invasion. Conscious of the suffering caused by the attacks, the court sent a royal relative to the Mongols but claimed that he was the crown prince (an indication of goodwill), in a ploy aimed at tricking the Mongols into a suspension of hostilities. Divine aid was also sought by sponsorship of a project to carve printing blocks for the entire Buddhist canon. The project, begun in 1236, reproduced the Tripitaka in some eighty-one thousand woodblocks that are still extant at Haeinsa, a monastery near Taegu. [See Koryŏ Tripitaka.]

Devastation followed in the wake of the invasions. As attack upon attack crisscrossed the kingdom, peasants lost their fields, homes, and lives. The *Koryŏsa*, the dynastic record, declares: "Those who died of starvation were multitudinous, the corpses of the old and weak clogged ravines, and in the end some even left babies tied in trees." Peasants bore the brunt of the invasions, but cultural loss also was great. To show their disdain for Koryŏ, the Mongols torched whatever seemed magnificent. Kaesŏng was sacked, temples destroyed, and pagodas that had stood for more than five hundred years were toppled and scattered. Libraries that housed many of Korea's literary treasures were burned, forever severing links with the past. Much of Korea's rich artistic and literary heritage was lost.

Confronted with the near obliteration of their culture, Koreans resisted anew. They looked to their past to praise it; some scholars discern the emergence of a rudimentary national consciousness at this time. Pride in the Korean past prompted the monk Iryŏn to write the *Samguk yusa (Memorabilia of the Three Kingdoms)* in the 1280s. It also caused Yi Kyu-bo, one of the great writers of the age, to declare that he wrote simply "to let the world know that our country always has been a land of hero-sages."

The Mongol invasions ended in 1259, when the court sent the real crown prince to the Mongols as a hostage; they returned to the capital on the mainland in 1270. This disengagement was complicated by strife within the leadership, as many military officials opposed the surrender. Civilians, on the other hand, weary of war and military domination, engineered a coup that restored some authority to the monarch and put a peace faction in power. The military officers of the *sambyŏlch'o* ("three elite patrols") revolted and retreated to the southwest coast and then to Cheju Island, where they were defeated in 1273 by a combined Koryŏ-Mongol force.

With the court in submission and resistance quelled, the Mongols took over Korea. They established numerous offices, extorted quantities of tribute, and impressed Koryŏ forces and wealth to extend the war into Japan. The Mongol invasions are a bitter memory in Korean history, made worse by the disastrous expeditions to Japan in 1274 and 1281. Mongol authority was not completely eliminated until the middle of the fourteenth century. The Korean people nevertheless emerged from these years with more confidence in themselves as the inheritors and transmitters of a rich, vibrant culture.

[*See also* Koryŏ.]

William E. Henthorn, *Korea: The Mongol Invasions* (1963).   EDWARD J. SHULTZ

MONGOL INVASIONS OF JAPAN

In the late thirteenth century Japan was subjected to two large-scale invasion attempts by the Mongols, who had previously conquered China and Korea. The invasions failed, but they represented the most serious foreign threat to Japan in the premodern era, posed severe problems of security for the warrior rulers of Japan, and galvanized an incipient consciousness of Japan as a divinely protected nation.

The Mongols, led by Kublai Khan, completed their protracted conquest of Song China in 1279. After the conquest of the Korean state of Koryŏ in 1268, Kublai, who had heard that Japan might be a source of gold and jewels, sent ambassadors to urge the Japanese to submit to Mongol authority. The demands of the Mongol envoys caused a flurry of dismay in the imperial court in Kyoto and angered the warriors who headed the military government, the *bakufu*, in Kamakura. Shrines and temples began to offer prayers for the safety of the country. It fell to the Hōjō regents, who dominated the *bakufu*, to organize the defense of the country. The Hōjō took a defiant line with Kublai. His demands were ignored or rejected and his envoys either executed or put in exile.

Kublai then resorted to direct action. In the late summer of 1274 he dispatched a large invasion fleet to Japan, manned by 8,000 Chinese and Koreans and bearing some 18,000 Mongol troops. After raiding the islands of Tsushima and Oki, the Mongols landed on the beaches of northern Kyushu. After sharp fighting they were driven back to their ships by Kyushu warriors from the Shōni, Otomo, Kikuchi, and other families. Before they could land again, their fleet was ravaged by a typhoon.

Warned by the scale of the first invasion, the *bakufu*, under Hōjō Tokimune (1251–1284), braced for another invasion. Tokimune ordered his Kyushu warrior vassals to be on constant alert and began the building of a defensive rampart on the coast of northern Kyushu. The second invasion fleet, which sailed into Japanese waters in the summer of 1281, was even larger than the first. It was divided into two fleets, bearing 40,000 and 100,000 men, respectively. Harassed at sea by Japanese warriors and struck by storms, the second invasion attempt also ended in disaster. In the belief that Kublai planned to launch a third invasion, Japan maintained its defenses. The threat, however, never materialized. Chinese resistance to the heavy levies imposed to build and equip another invasion fleet led to its cancellation.

The Hōjō regents and Kyushu warriors, who had borne the brunt of the defense of the country, and the temples and shrines that had prayed for its divine protection all gained some prestige from the rout of the Mongols. The storms that had wrecked the Mongol ships were referred to as "divine winds" (kamikaze), and the idea grew that Japan was a divinely protected land. In the long run, however, the burdens imposed on the warrior society may have outweighed the immediate glory. There were no spoils to be had in driving back a seaborne invasion. The costs of the defense of the country, which were borne by the bakufu and its Kyushu vassals, had been heavy. While the personal authority of the Hōjō may have been enhanced, many of their housemen (gokenin) were disgruntled and began to turn away from the Hōjō. Disaffection in the warrior society was compounded by growing samurai indebtedness and loss of land to moneylenders. The bakufu's resort to a debt moratorium, tokusei rei, in 1297 did little to restore alienated lands or to relieve the problem of samurai indebtedness. Because of the problems of samurai hardship and loss of control by the bakufu over its vassals after the invasions, some historians have seen the Mongol invasions as contributing to the weakening and ultimate collapse of the Kamkura bakufu.

Martin Collcutt

MONGOL INVASIONS OF SOUTHEAST ASIA

The Mongols, totally misunderstanding China's traditional tributary relationship with the people it considered the "southern barbarians," attempted to reestablish what they thought was the appropriate Chinese role in Southeast Asia by sending military expeditions into the south. Basing their view on misleading dynastic histories that emphasized the political rather than economic activities of past Chinese monarchs, the Mongols fully believed that Vietnam had in the past been part of China's political realm. Their efforts to "reestablish" China's political hegemony over the Vietnam region in the late thirteenth century were repulsed. In 1281 a Mongol army attempted to enter Vietnam but was defeated; Toghon, a son of the first Yuan emperor Kublai

Khan, returned in 1283 and captured the Vietnamese capital in 1285, but he was subsequently defeated by Tran Nhan Tong at Thanh Hoa, and his forces were driven north. The Mongol general Sogata, who had intended to attack the Vietnamese from Cham territory to the south, was captured by combined Vietnamese and Cham forces and was executed and decapitated.

Ignoring the normal Chinese diplomatic interaction with Southeast Asia, whereby Chinese forces were not sent into the south, the Mongols invaded Burma in the late thirteenth century. Unlike the Vietnam invasion attempts, the Mongol incursions into Burma were not undertaken for the purpose of territorial extension; instead they came about after the new Yuan dynasty warned the Burmese rulers that if they could not control political instabilities along the China-Burma border (especially the actions of those who had fled from Yuan rule and were using the mountain regions on the border as their base for rebellious activity against the Yuan) the Chinese would take matters into their own hands. Burma's Pagan-based dynasty ignored the repeated requests of Kublai Khan to send a delegation of princes and ministers to his Beijing court. After the ambassadors of the Yuan emperor to the Pagan court were either executed by the Burmese king Narathihapade or were murdered on their way back to China in 1273, and after Burmese forces plundered a Chinese tributary state on the China-Burma border in 1277, the Mongol emperor responded by sending invasion forces in 1277 and 1283, and Pagan was finally sacked in 1287. The Mongol invasions devastated Burma, precipitating a major transition in the Burmese dynastic system, but the Mongols themselves had no lasting impact on the resultant Burmese reorganization as the Chinese forces quickly withdrew.

Similarly, the Mongols appear to have dealt directly with the recurring piracy problem in the Southeast Asian maritime realm, launching naval expeditions against the pirate lairs of the southern Vietnam coast in the 1280s. The Yuan attempted to supplant Javanese control over the western Indonesian archipelago region. When Kertanagara, the ruler of Java, mistreated Kublai Khan's envoy, who had insisted that a member of the royal family travel to the Beijing court to present tribute, the emperor launched an ill-fated punitive expedition against the Javanese in 1292. Kertanagara died prior to the arrival of the Chinese fleet, and the mission had the unintended results of securing the throne for Kertanagara's legitimate heir and assisting his consolidation of a political base from which the powerful Majapahit state emerged.

[*See also* Kublai Khan; Pagan; Kertanagara; *and* Majapahit.]

G. Coedès, *The Indianized States of Southeast Asia,* translated by Susan B. Cowing (1968).

KENNETH R. HALL

MONGOLIAN. The Mongolian language family includes such dialects as Buriat, Kalmuk, Dagur, Ordos, and Chahar in areas to the north, west, and south of the present-day Mongolian People's Republic. The family forms a major branch of the Altaic language group and can be seen as a link with Turkic languages to the west and Manchu-Tunguz languages to the east. Speakers of all dialects number around three million.

The oldest written records are from the time of Genghis (correctly, Chinggis) Khan (thirteenth century) and employ the vertical Uighur script, which ultimately derives from Sogdian and Aramaic predecessors. The old script is still in use in the Inner Mongolia Autonomous Region of the People's Republic of China, but in the 1940s the Soviet-influenced Mongolian People's Republic began to use a modified Cyrillic system. In structure, Mongolian adds suffixes of fixed meaning in stipulated order to express the grammatical and syntactic functions of cases; it makes much use of verbal nouns and suspensory forms not marked for tense or person.

[*See also* Mongols *and* Turkic Languages.]

K. Gronbech and J. Krueger, *Introduction to Classical (Literary) Mongolian* (1976). N. Poppe, *Mongolian Language Handbook* (1970).

JOHN R. KRUEGER

MONGOLIAN PEOPLE'S REPUBLIC. The Mongolian People's Republic (MPR), formerly called Outer Mongolia, is the oldest people's republic in Asia, having taken that title in November 1924. The Mongols date their official independence from the time of their revolution in July 1921, when the Revolutionary Government of Mongolia was declared. Since that time, the MPR has followed a course of social, political, and economic development that closely parallels that of the USSR, its closest ally and greatest source of economic assistance.

Some aspects of Mongolia's development are unique among the nations of the socialist bloc because of the nature of its prerevolutionary pastoral nomadic society and the extensive influence of Mongolian Buddhism. Both of these elements have given way to socialism and to modernization on the Soviet model. More modern problems involve the small population, a serious lack of financial capital, a harsh climate, and the politics of the Sino-Soviet split.

The Land. The Mongolian People's Republic is the fifteenth-largest independent nation in the world by area, measuring 604,247 square miles (1,565,000 square kilometers). The country is landlocked between Siberia in the north and China in the south. It measures about twice as long (1,471 miles from east to west) as it is wide (782 miles from north to south), and averages about 5,100 feet above sea level.

Unlike the popular image of it as an arid desert, Mongolia is a land of great diversity and beauty, including alpine mountains, vast grasslands, rolling hills, and semideserts. Mountains are visible almost everywhere, although their appearance varies from forested to barren depending on location. The northern third of the MPR is geographically and climatically closer to Siberia, while the southern portion more nearly resembles Central Asia. The mountain ranges that give the country its definition and help form its climate include the Tannu-Ola in the northwest, the Mongolian Altai and the Gobi Altai to the west and southwest, the Khentei in the northeast, and the Khangai in the northwest central area. The highest peak in the MPR is listed as Mount Nairamdal in the Altai range, at 14,302 feet, while the lowest point is on the east Mongolian Plain, at 1,828 feet.

Because the southern half of the MPR tends to average less than 3 inches of annual precipitation, it is arid to semiarid and generally lacking in rivers of any size. The northern half averages above 10 inches of annual precipitation, which is augmented by run-off from the mountains. For these reasons, there are river valleys, such as the Onan and Kerulen in the north, and the Orkhan Selenga, and Tula in the northwest and northcentral mountain areas. About a quarter of the land is classified as *gobi* ("desert"), with little annual precipitation (from 0 to 3 inches) and terrain ranging from sand to gravel to salt marshes.

The People. Unlike most Asian nations, the MPR has a homogeneous population. In 1981 the total population was given as 1,685,400, or about 2.8 persons per square mile. Although the official census of the MPR now no longer lists the ethnic status of the population, the Khalkha Mongols were the dominant group in the 1969 census, making up almost

90 percent of the total. An additional 7 percent of the population was made up by other Mongol-speaking groups, such as the Oirats (50,000 in 1969), the Buriats (22,000), the Darigganga (16,000), and the Darkhat (7,000). Speakers of all these latter dialects are mutually intelligible to each other and to speakers of Khalkha. The largest non-Mongol group in Mongolia in 1969 was made up of Turkic-speaking Kazakhs (26,000), mostly resident in the western areas of the MPR. As late as 1970 there were about 10,000 Chinese living in various areas, but their present status has been unknown since the official expulsion order of 3 June 1983.

Cities and Towns. A major shift in the size of cities has occurred, primarily since 1945, as a result of the ongoing industrialization of the MPR. As a result, Ulan Bator, the capital, has a population of 435,400, the new steel-producing city of Darkhan (founded in 1962) has a population of 56,000, and the city of Erdenet (founded in 1975) already has reached 38,000 in size. Erdenet's central function is to serve as a copper and molybdenum processing center. Other cities of over 10,000 in population are now found in almost all the seventeen *aimags* (regions).

The rapid development of these cities and towns has transformed the MPR very rapidly from a traditional, rural country, in which only 21 percent of the population was urban in 1956, to one in which slightly more than half the population lives in urban areas. This number will probably continue to grow at a rapid rate as pastoral nomadism continues to decline as a base of the economy. Of the total population, 38 percent are now classed as rural by occupation.

Demographics. As might be expected, the rapid shift to an urban environment has brought changes as well to general population dynamics. There tend to be higher percentages of females than males in the more rural areas, while the reverse is true in the urban centers, owing to the urgent need for labor there. A further result of this movement of labor can be seen in the statistics for birthrates. The national birthrate in 1980 was 37.9 births per 1,000 population, while in Ulan Bator it was 32.3 and in Erdenet it was only 25.3. The figures for natural increase attest to the rising levels of health care and the successful struggle with certain endemic diseases. As recently as 1921, some observers believed that the native Mongol population was dying out, given the fact that the death rate exceeded the birth rate in most years. In 1980, the natural increase rate had

reached 27.5 per 1,000 population. The labor shortage is also reflected in the statistics for females in the work force. Women make up about 45 percent of all workers, and 54 percent of all women are employed.

Twentieth-Century History. The modern history and politics of Mongolia are tangled and confusing. As a result of the Treaty of Dolon Nor of 1691, Outer Mongolia became a province of the Chinese empire. This status continued until the fall of the Manchu Qing dynasty in 1911, at which time the Mongols declared themselves "autonomous." The government formed in 1911 was headed by a religious authority, the eighth Jebtsun Damba Khutukhtu, whose seat of rule was at the city of Urga. Czarist Russia and Japan recognized Outer Mongolia as part of the Russian sphere of influence in a series of secret treaties. The Tripartite Treaty of Kiakhta, signed by Russia, autonomous Mongolia, and China in 1915, accepted Mongolia's autonomous status but agreed that Mongolia was still under Chinese suzerainty. The formula was puzzling, but continued to define the legal status of Outer Mongolia until the plebiscite of October 1945, by which the MPR finally became independent. From 1911 until 1918, autonomous Mongolia was relatively free of direct foreign influence, although Chinese and Russian agents operated there for a variety of factions. In 1919 that situation changed.

In October 1919, an army of six thousand Chinese troops led by Xu Shuzeng arrived at Urga. The autonomous government was abolished and Chinese sovereignty was reestablished. All treaties were voided. This condition continued until the Russian civil war spilled into Mongolia in 1921. Baron von Ungern-Sternberg, a White Russian general with perhaps five thousand troops, invaded and occupied Urga in February 1921, ending the Chinese occupation but drawing Russian Red Army units into Mongolia in pursuit. In July 1921, the White forces were driven out of Urga and a Mongolian Revolutionary Government was established. The Baron was caught and executed.

The Russian Red Army units at Urga supported the establishment of a government composed of the followers of two revolutionary groups that had merged in 1920 to form the Mongolian People's Party. One group was led by Sukhe Bator; the other by Khorlogiyn Choibalsan. Their new government followed the example of the Soviet Union in its organization and ideology. Until 1924, however, the government continued to be nominally headed by the Jebtsun Damba Khutukhtu. At his death in

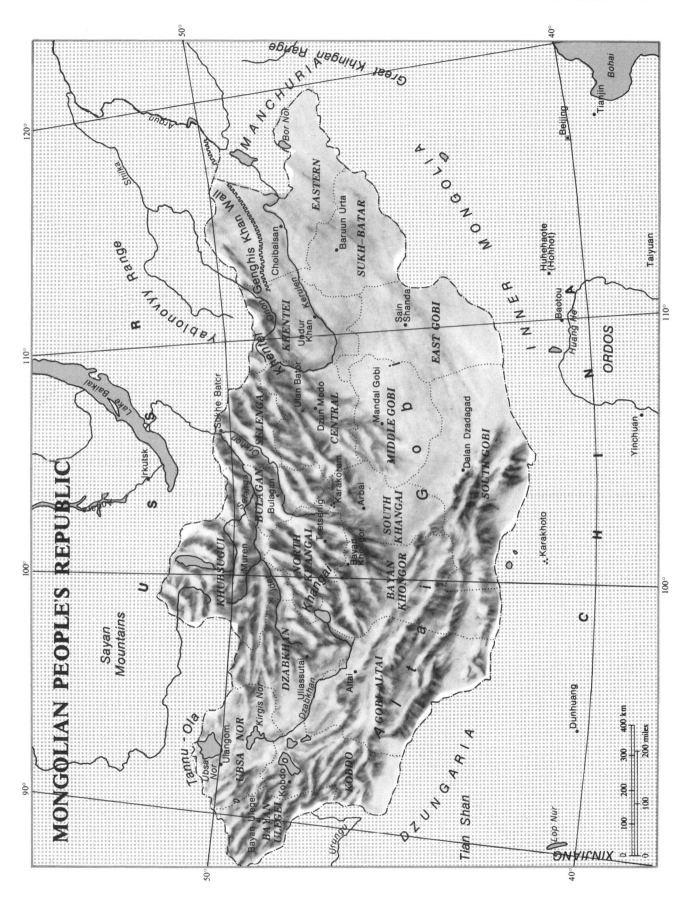

MONGOLIAN PEOPLE'S REPUBLIC

1924, the Mongolian People's Republic was declared. The Republic continued to accept the international status of autonomy, but was under Chinese suzerainty from 1924 until 1945. Since 1924 the MPR has been a firm ally of the USSR and has accepted its advice and direction in all aspects of development. International recognition of the MPR was heightened in October 1961 with its entry into the United Nations.

Economic Development. The MPR faced many serious problems at the start of its revolution in 1921. It was nonindustrial, feudal, and pastoral, with a variety of health problems, an illiterate population, and a huge territory without modern systems of communication. It did possess great reserves of natural resources, a homogeneous population unusually free of sectarian animosities, and a small populaton, which freed the social system from the pressures of explosive growth.

From the early years of the revolution, the economy has focused on centralized planning in the mode of three- and five-year plans. In the early years the plans sought to use the most readily available animal products to establish a capital-producing industry. Meat, milk, wool, and hides taken from an animal herd that has averaged about 25 million head of sheep, goats, camel, cattle, and horses fostered such industries as leather and carpet factories; meat, milk, and cheese processing plants; boot and shoe factories; and rendering plants. Although attempts were also made before World War II to establish heavy industry, these attempts were not successful until after 1950. As more investment capital became available in the form of loans and grants from the USSR and the PRC, greater attention has been paid to opening mines, steel mills, cement factories, and railroads. A gradual shift away from animal product industries to mineral resources related industries has resulted. This process has been aided by numerous technical advisors and laborers from the socialist countries. Increasingly, however, native Mongols are taking a greater role in modernization as Mongol technical institutes turn out larger graduating classes qualified to work in the new industries.

Politics and Government. The Mongol political system closely resembles that of the USSR. The Mongolian People's Revolutionary Party directs the affairs of the state, based on the definition of its role in the Mongolian constitution, derived from that of the Soviet Union. The constitution provides for a republic of seventeen *aimags* (regions) subdivided by *somons* (districts). The three largest cities, Ulan Bator, Darkhan, and Erdenet, are independent administrative units.

At the highest administrative level, the state functions through a parliament called the Great People's Khural, to which deputies are elected every three years. The Great Khural appoints a Council of Ministers and a Presidium of the Great Khural. Below the state level, local Khurals operate at the *aimag* and *somon* level. As in the Soviet Union, the first secretary of the Party is the highest political authority. To date, Mongolia has had only three first secretaries of note. Choibalson served from about 1932 until his death in 1952, Tsedenbal from 1952 until 1984, and Sambuu after 1984.

Charles R. Bawden, *The Modern History of Mongolia* (1968). William A. Brown and Urgunge Onon, trans., *History of the Mongolian People's Republic* (1976). Gerard M. Friters, *Outer Mongolia and Its International Position* (1949). George G. S. Murphy, *Soviet Mongolia* (1966). Robert A. Rupen, *Mongols of the Twentieth Century*, 2 vols. (1964).   LARRY W. MOSES

MONGOLS. The Mongols are a people of the Altaic language group inhabiting the steppe region north of China, from the Yellow River to Lake Baikal. They are best known for the great empire they founded in the thirteenth century under Genghis (Chinggis) Khan.

The term *Mongol* has had several different meanings. Originally, this was the name only of the small group of eastern Mongolian tribes that Genghis Khan was born into; after his conquests, however, the name of his tribe became associated with the whole of his tribal confederation. The same group of tribes was earlier known as Tatars, after the Tatar tribe that controlled them before Genghis Khan, and this name was applied to the Mongols in Russia and Europe after the great conquests. In recent times the term *Mongol* has acquired a specific ethnographic meaning, denoting peoples speaking the Mongolian language.

The early history of the Mongols remains obscure. The steppes to the north of China were inhabited by numerous nomadic tribes who depended for their livelihood on flocks of horses, sheep, goats and sometimes camels; to nourish their animals on the sparse vegetation of the steppe, they followed a regular migration among seasonal pastures. The basic unit of society was the tribe, whose leader controlled pasturages, but the tribes often banded together into confederations and attacked settled regions. Because nomadism lends itself well to military activity, such confederations were often able to conquer and rule northern China. [*See* Nomadism.]

The name of the Mongols first appears in Chinese

sources during the Tang period (618–907). In the twelfth century the Mongols formed a tribal confederation and soon became a worry to the Jurchen Jin dynasty of northern China, who in 1160 united with the Tatar tribe to destroy this first Mongol leadership. It was at about this time that Temujin—later Genghis Khan—was born. He was orphaned at an early age, but after a difficult youth became an important figure in the violent struggle for power among the tribes. In 1206 he convened a large gathering at which the tribal leaders who were allied with him raised him to the throne and bestowed upon him the title Genghis Khan, sometimes translated "universal sovereign."

Genghis soon began to extend his sway beyond the steppe, attacking the Islamic world and taking the major cities of Central Asia. When he died in 1227 during a campaign against the Tanguts, his empire was divided among his sons. It was during this next period that the Mongol empire expanded to its greatest extent.

Throughout the empire the supreme code of law was the *Jasagh*, a set of laws and precepts on military and social matters begun by Genghis Khan and continued under his successors. The office of khan was at once hereditary and electoral; the Mongols practiced both lateral and patrilineal inheritance and the choice among candidates was determined by agreement among prominent members of the dynasty. This system led to considerable delay in electing a new khan and later armed succession struggles became common, seriously weakening the cohesion of the Mongol empire.

The Mongols began to adapt themselves to the agrarian societies they ruled. Although most Mongols had followed their original religion, worshiping a universal sky god, Tengri, and a host of minor spirits, they had long been familiar with the major world religions, particularly Buddhism and Nestorian Christianity. Kublai, who established Mongol rule in China, adopted Buddhism in 1253 and when he became khan he installed the Buddhist church as a state institution. In 1295 the Ilkhans, the branch of the Mongol leadership that ruled Iran, restored Islam as the official religion of their realm and in the early fourteenth century the rulers of the Chagatai khanate and the Golden Horde, ruling Turkestan and the Volga region, respectively, followed suit. At this time also the Mongols in the western part of the empire began to speak Turkish, although they continued to use Mongolian for official correspondence. Thereafter, the culture of the western empire can best be characterized as Turco-Mongolian; this new combined tradition lasted long after the final breakup of the Mongol empire. Nonetheless, the empire retained a definite cultural unity, and different regions often developed along parallel lines. All of them continued to honor the Chinggisid *Jasagh* and to use many of the same Mongol offices and institutions.

The late eighteenth and nineteenth centuries were a period of political and economic decline for the Mongols and led in particular to the impoverishment of the lower classes, who were subject to exploitation not only from their secular and religious nobility but also from an increasing number of Chinese merchants and colonists. In the twentieth century the majority of the Mongolian population is divided between the Inner Mongolia Autonomous Region of the People's Republic of China and the Mongolian People's Republic (Outer Mongolia), which was established in 1921.

[*See also* Mongol Empire; Mongolian; Mongolian People's Republic; *and* Genghis Khan.]

C. R. Bawden, *The Modern History of Mongolia* (1968). Francis W. Cleaves, trans., *The Secret History of the Mongols* (1982). Christopher H. Dawson, *The Mongol Mission* (1955). René Grousset, *The Empire of the Steppes*, translated by N. Walford (1970). Henry H. Howorth, *History of the Mongols from the Ninth to the Nineteenth Century*, 4 vols. (1876–1927). S. Jagchid and Paul Hyer, *Mongolia's Culture and Society* (1979). Marco Polo, *The Description of the World*, edited and translated by A. C. Moule and Paul Pelliot (1938). John J. Saunders, *The History of the Mongol Conquests* (1971).

BEATRICE FORBES MANZ

MON-KHMER LANGUAGES. *See* Austroasiatic Languages.

MONTAGNARDS. *See* Vietnam.

MONTAGU-CHELMSFORD REFORMS. The Government of India Act (1919), based on the joint report of Edwin Montagu, the secretary of state, and Lord Chelmsford, the viceroy, introduced reforms known as dyarchy. In the provinces the governor was made responsible for such departments as finance and law and order and elected ministers were entrusted with the task of handling subjects pertaining to public welfare, such as education, public health, and public works. For the first time representatives of the people were given responsibility for a very limited sphere of administration. The British government officially laid down, as the goal of constitutional development, dominion status as well as responsible government. Franchise was extended and provision was made for an appointment of an Enquiry Commission, after a decade of working the constitution, to suggest whether to further extend responsibility or restrict it. Reforms fell short of Indian expectations.

[See also Government of India Acts.]

S. R. Mehrotra, *India and the Commonwealth, 1885–1929* (1965).   S. RAZI WASTI

MOORS. See Muslims in Sri Lanka.

MŌRI, a Japanese aristocratic lineage that ruled Chōshū *han* during the Tokugawa period. The Mōri claimed descent from Ōe Hiromoto. As of 1500 they resided on their own Yoshida manor in Aki. Mōri Motonari (1497–1571) followed Amako Haruhisa for a time and later joined the Ōuchi. The Ōuchi were overthrown by their steward Sue Harukata in 1551, but the Sue were displaced in turn by the Mōri in 1555. By enterprising generalship Motonari extended the Ōuchi's original holdings of Suō and Nagato to embrace eight other provinces as well.

Motonari's grandson Terumoto (1553–1625), ruling from his new seat at Hiroshima, succeeded in keeping Oda Nobunaga's armies out of his domain. Terumoto was active as a Toyotomi general at the Battle of Sekigahara (1600), however, so the Tokugawa victors reduced his lands to the original Suō and Nagato, known then as Chōshū.

The Mōri were a *tozama* house known for their sympathy toward the imperial line and for their tacit ambivalence toward Tokugawa authority. The Mōri gave their own samurai more leeway in managing *han* affairs than most lords, and their domain was unusually well run. Mōri Takachika (1819–1871) had reformist sympathies and accommodated the Restoration movement in Chōshū at the end of the Tokugawa period. He was persuaded by Chōshū reformers voluntarily to return *han* land registers to the emperor in 1869.

[See also Chōshū; Tozama Daimyo; *and* Kemmu Restoration.]

THOMAS M. HUBER

MORI ARINORI (1847–1889), bureaucrat, diplomat, essayist, and persistent introducer of Western thought and culture into Japan. Mori was born in Satsuma (Kagoshima). After the bombardment of Kagoshima by British naval forces in 1863, Satsuma *han* authorities sent him to England and America

for study (1865–1868). On his return, Mori became a bureaucrat in the new Meiji government and almost immediately caused an uproar by advocating the abolition of sword-bearing by samurai (1869). He then was sent to Washington as *chargé d'affaires* (1871–1873) and later posted as minister to the Court of Saint James (1880–1884).

Mori was among the few Meiji leaders able to associate with Westerners intimately and with perception. Among his associates were Thomas Lake Harris, Laurence Oliphant, and Herbert Spencer. He established Japan's first modern learned society, the Meirokusha (1874–1876), whose impact on Meiji intellectual and political life extended far beyond its short-lived existence. It was in the *Meiroku zasshi*, the society's journal, that he published his controversial feminist treatise (1874–1875). Mori wrote on subjects as disparate as physical fitness and constitutional government. He was not a professional pedagogue, but even before his eventful years as education minister (1885–1889), he was laying the foundation of modern Japan's educational system. This system, geared to serve state purposes, turned out a literate populace and a highly trained elite that enabled Japan to take major strides in modernization. Mori was stabbed by an assassin on 11 February 1889 and died the next day, putting an early end to an already notable career.

[See also Meiji Period.]

GEORGE K. AKITA

MORI ŌGAI (1862–1922), Japanese medical doctor, scholar, translator, writer, and army bureaucrat. Mori studied in Germany from 1886 to 1888 and returned to make a name for himself in both medical journalism and literary circles. He participated as chief medical officer in the Sino-Japanese and Russo-Japanese wars and in 1907 reached the rank of surgeon general. Mori was known during his lifetime as the introducer of many aspects of European culture and as a translator of German works, including three volumes of romantic poetry; more than eighty prose works, notably the novel *Improvisatoren* by Hans Andersen; and forty-six plays, such as *Faust* and works by Arthur Schnitzler, Henrik Ibsen, and August Strindberg. Mori is known today chiefly for his own literary products, however, in particular three early romantic novellas that deal with his years in Germany, *The Dancing Girl (Maihime)* being the most famous; a series of didactic and autobiographical stories produced in the period 1894 to 1912, including the well-known

"Vita Sexualis" and "The Wild Goose" ("Gan"); and, last, a number of historical novellas, such as *The Abe Family (Abe ichizoku)* and *Incident at Sakai (Sakai jiken)*, that investigate the samurai ethic of the preceding age. His last products were long historical biographies of a number of Tokugawa-era physician-scholars with whom he felt a certain affinity. Beginning in 1910 he became increasingly worried by the effects of government censorship. A tension between artistic expression and the bureaucratic mind was in many ways the source of his enormous energy. Mori and Natsume Sōseki were the two preeminent literary figures of the Meiji period.

[*See also* Meiji Period.]

Richard Bowring, *Mori Ōgai and the Modernization of Japanese Culture* (1979). David Dilworth and J. Thomas Rimer, trans., *The Historical Literature of Mori Ōgai*, 2 vols. (1977). Kazuji Ninomiya and Sanford Goldstein, trans., *Vita Sexualis* (1972). J. Thomas Rimer, *Mori Ōgai* (1975).   RICHARD BOWRING

MORLEY-MINTO REFORMS. The Morley-Minto Reforms instituted several administrative changes designed to increase native participation in the governing of British India. In 1907, John Morley, secretary of state for India (1905–1910), and later Lord Minto, viceroy of India (1905–1910), began to admit Indian advisers to the Council of the Secretary of State in London, to the Executive Council of the Governor-General, and to the councils of the regional governors.

More substantive reforms were instituted when the secretary and the viceroy collaborated to get the British Parliament to pass the Indian Councils Act of 1909, which opened the imperial and provincial legislatures to limited numbers of nonofficial, elected representatives. The act also gave the legislatures the right to discuss the budget and provided Muslims with separate, communal representation. Sometimes hailed as a fundamental constitutional change, the Morley-Minto Reforms gave very little real power to Indians and exacerbated the political divisions between Muslims and Hindus.

S. R. Wasti, *Lord Minto and the Indian Nationalist Movement, 1905–10* (1964). S. Wolpert, *Morley and India, 1906–10* (1967).   JAMES A. JAFFE

MORO. Spanish colonialism in the Philippines began with conquest of the coastal stretches of Luzon and the central Visayas in the second half of the sixteenth century. During that time, the Spaniards came into direct contact and conflict with various groups professing Islam in the southern part of the archipelago on Mindanao and in the Sulu chain of islands. The most important of these different people were the Taosug and Samal of the Sulu Archipelago, the Magindanao of Cotabato, and the Maranao of Lanao and Cotabato. The Spanish bureaucracy and friars called them Moros, a term that was originally used to describe the islamicized North Africans who, under Arab leadership, ruled the Iberian Peninsula from the eighth to the sixteenth century.

The term *Moro* provided an ideological prelude in the Philippines to the Spanish colonial state's drive (1565–1898) to colonize Mindanao and the Sulu Archipelago. The Spaniards created an image, a composite portrait, of the Muslim Filipino's "character," that became a major intellectual justification for Spanish retaliation and religious incursion against the Muslim south over the ensuing four centuries. Thus *Moro*, a foreign appellation imposed on the Muslim Filipinos, carried pejorative connotations. Until recently, it was synonymous with a specific social disposition and attitude associated with ignorance, depravity, and treachery, and the label *Moro*, in turning history into myth, connoted an Islamic people in the Sulu Archipelago and Mindanao who were considered to be savages, pirates, and slavers.

Since the 1970s a deepening Islamic consciousness and an increased unity among Muslim Filipinos in the face of the politics of national integration in the Philippines has led some to speak openly of themselves as Bangsa Moro ("the Muslim people"). In the context of the present conflict in the Mindanao Sulu area, the designation *Moro* is promoted by the Moro National Liberation Front as a way of giving Muslims a new sense of pride and self-awareness and of transcending the old ethnolinguistic categories of Taosug, Magindanao, Maranao, and Samal.

Peter Gordon Gowing, *Muslim Filipinos—Heritage and Horizon* (1979). Cesar A. Majul, *Muslims in the Philippines* (1973). James Francis Warren, *The Sulu Zone 1768–1898: The Dynamics of External Trade, Slavery, and Ethnicity in the Transformation of a Southeast Asian Maritime State* (1981).   JAMES FRANCIS WARREN

MORO NATIONAL LIBERATION FRONT, or MNLF, political organization founded in 1969 by young radical Muslim leaders in the Philippines. The Moro National Liberation Front had as its primary objective to "reacquire the Bangsa Moro people's political freedom and independence from the clutches of Filipino terror and enslavement." Its first leader was Nur Misuari, a Tausug Muslim and graduate of Asian studies at the University of the Philippines. The Bangsa Moro Army of the MNLF began fighting for secession after Philippine president Ferdinand E. Marcos declared martial law in September 1972. After several years of hostilities and thousands of fatalities, a cease-fire was arranged with diplomatic pressure from some Arab-league nations. With much of its leadership in exile, the MNLF is now dormant.

[See also Moro and Marcos, Ferdinand E.]

T. S. J. George, Revolt in Mindanao: The Rise of Islam in Philippine Politics (1980).   DAVID A. ROSENBERG

MORO WARS. Two perspectives have dominated the politico-religious history of the Moro Wars—slave raiding and piracy against the Spanish-ruled Christian parts of the Philippines and against the weaker, politically fragmented coastal societies of insular Southeast Asia. On the one hand, there is the persistent theme of the advent of Muslim piracy in the Malay world from the sixteenth century onward and the decline of the indigenous maritime power and trade. This is known as the decay theory, and its proponents have argued that the monopolistic trade practices of eighteenth-century Europe tore away the props that supported the economic base of many indigenous coastal and island states such as the Sulu sultanate. Severely weakened by the loss of revenue and commerce, these states (Johor, Aceh, Brunei, and Sulu) opportunistically turned to piracy and slave raiding.

A different approach to the history of the resistance of Muslim Filipinos to Spanish political and religious imperialism emphasizes the rivalry between Catholic Spaniards bent on expansion in the Philippines and the defiance of the Muslim population of Mindanao and the Sulu sultanate. In the pioneering histories of Sulu and Mindanao by Najeeb Saleeby and Cesar Majul, Moro piracy and slave raiding are interpreted, within the framework of the Moro Wars, as retaliation against Spanish colonialism and religious incursion. These authors provide some insight into the role of Muslim raiding and slavery from the sixteenth to the eighteenth century, but there is a clear historiographical problem in their writings. The term Moro Wars, like piracy, obscures the complexity of the phenomenon of maritime raiding. As other scholars have pointed out,

such raiding can have a political, economic, or even religious basis. Saleeby and Majul do not always clearly differentiate between Muslim ethnic groups engaged in these activities in different periods. While the Sulu (Taosug) did conduct raids in the earlier period, the printed chronicles of the sixteenth to eighteenth century point to the Magindanao as the principal slave raiders. More important, if this is so, there is a discontinuity between early and later slaving and raiding pursuits, their composition and organization, and the reasons for the accentuated tempo of these activities in the Philippines and insular Southeast Asia in the post-1768 period. In the earlier period, Magindanao raiders seem to have been primarily from Mindanao, and their marauding was then viewed as an extension of jihad (holy war), with religio-political and not simply economic motives. Between 1565 and 1780, the movement of captive peoples (including Tagalog and Visayan indios) in the context of the slave trade was to the stronger and wealthier European and Asian port cities, such as Melaka, Batavia, Makassar, and Penang.

Recent research demonstrates that this sort of slave trade was far less common, at least in the late eighteenth and nineteenth centuries, when increased trade with Europe and China led to an expansion of Sulu-based slave raiding. Most of the accounts of the Sulu sultanate written before 1780 indicate that the internal demand for slaves at Sulu was on a much smaller scale than it was destined to become in the nineteenth century. Driven by a desire for wealth and power, the Iranun and Balangingi Samal surged out of the Sulu Archipelago in search of slaves. Within three decades (1768–1798), their well-armed prahus scoured the coasts of the Indonesian world and sailed northward into the Philippines. They joined with other Iranun and Samal speakers living on the coasts of Borneo, Sulawesi, and Sumatra. The raiding system enabled the Sulu sultanate to incorporate vast numbers of people from the Philippines and eastern Indonesia into the Sulu population. Traffic in slaves reached its peak in Sulu in the period 1800–1848, founded on the trade with China and the West.

Meant primarily for European consumption, the classic Spanish accounts of the Moro Wars, as well as the writings of Sir Thomas Stamford Raffles and Sir James Brooke about the "nefarious activities" of the Iranun and Balangingi, relegated the Sulu sultanate to the status of a mere pirates' nest by the 1840s. This propaganda, portraying the Sulu Zone as the scourge of the seas from Singapore to Papua, became grist for antipiracy campaigns mounted to destroy these seafarers.

[*See also* Moro *and* Philippines.]

Reynaldo Ileto, *Magindanao, 1860–1888: The Case of Dato Uto of Buayan* (1971). Cesar A. Majul, *Muslims in the Philippines* (1973). Anthony Reid, ed., *Slavery, Bondage and Dependency in Southeast Asia* (1983). Najub M. Saleeby, *The History of Sulu* (1963). Nicholas Tarling, *Piracy and Politics in the Malay World* (1963). James Francis Warren, *The Sulu Zone 1768–1898: The Dynamics of External Trade, Slavery, and Ethnicity in the Transformation of a Southeast Asian Maritime State* (1981).

JAMES FRANCIS WARREN

MOSQUE, building used by Muslims for prayer and other religious and communal functions. The word derives from *masjid*, which means "place of prostration" in Arabic. A *jami* is a "congregational mosque" where the Friday noon prayer with its attendant sermon is held. Mosques have been the subject of some of Islam's most inspired architectural designs, and many regional styles have developed in different Asian and African nations.

RICHARD W. BULLIET

MOSSADEGH, MOHAMMED (1881–1967), an Iranian political leader best known for his role, during his tenure as prime minister, in the oil nationalization crisis of 1951–1953. Mossadegh led the National Front (Jebhe-ye Melli), a coalition of secular and religious political groups that was one of the most important forces opposing the Pahlavi monarchy.

Born into a wealthy, landed family, Mossadegh was educated at the École des Sciences Politiques in Paris and at Neuchatel University in Switzerland. He held various government positions from an early age, serving as a member of the Iranian Majles (parliament) from 1915 to 1917, again from 1925 to 1928, and finally from 1944 to 1953. Under the last of the Qajar monarchs, Mossadegh served as governor-general of the province of Fars (1920–1921), as minister of justice (1921), as governor-general of Azerbaijan (1922–1923), and as foreign minister (1924).

Mossadegh's support for constitutionalism and parliamentary democracy, coupled with his opposition to Reza Shah's increasing autocracy, led to his arrest in the late 1930s and temporary retirement from political life. He reentered the political arena in 1941 immediately following the forced abdication and exile of Reza Shah by the British.

It was in this period, from 1941 to 1943, that Mossadegh arose as the leader and spokesman for the secular nationalist faction of the Majles that was to become the National Front. Elected to the fourteenth Majles in 1943, Mossadegh spoke out strongly in opposition to continued foreign influence in Iran's government and economy, most specifically in the area of the already crucial oil industry.

Mossadegh made frequent, sometimes impassioned speeches in the Majles concerning the disadvantageous concessions Iran had often made to foreign interests. He proposed a bill, passed in December 1944, prohibiting any minister from negotiating oil concessions to a foreign party without the approval of the Majles. Three years later, he led the successful opposition to a proposed joint Soviet-Iranian venture to search for oil in northern Iran. Simultaneously, Mossadegh challenged the terms of the current agreement with the British in their oil concession in the south; this move quickly developed into a call for complete nationalization of Iran's oil industry.

From 1947 to 1949 Iran's government engaged in negotiations for new terms for the oil concession granted to the Anglo-Iranian Oil Company (AIOC); these ended in a highly unpopular compromise agreement that was accepted by the government but rejected by the Majles. Mossadegh and the National Front led the opposition to the oil agreement, and the Majles elections of 1950, in which the National Front candidates gained a large number of new seats, reflected the growing popular support for the anti-British, nationalist position long held by Mossadegh.

With his election as chairman of the oil commission of the Majles, Mossadegh immediately reiterated the call for nationalization of the oil industry. In 1951, after the assassination of Ali Razmara and a brief interim government led by Husain Ala, Mossadegh was elected prime minister. Under his premiership, Iran formally announced the nationalization of the oil industry.

The ensuing dispute between Iran and Great Britain led to a worldwide boycott of purchases of Iranian oil, with the United States initially supporting, then actively opposing, Iran's position. Great Britain interfered with Iran's foreign trade and banking and put diplomatic pressure on its allies to do the same. The United States, responding to repeated British requests, refused to lend Iran money until the oil dispute was resolved; at the same time the Americans made their own efforts to enforce the international oil boycott. Consequently, from 1951 to

1953 Iran experienced a severe economic decline, with only small sales of oil to Japan and Italy, which resisted pressure to join the boycott. The overwhelming importance of oil revenues to Iran's economy, together with the successful efforts of Great Britain and the United States to block foreign loans or new markets for Iran's oil, presented insurmountable stumbling blocks to Mossadegh's political and economic policies.

During his tenure, and in the midst of the oil crisis, Mossadegh attempted to reduce Iran's dependence on oil revenues, to reform the domestic tax and revenue structures, and to control government spending. He also sought a policy of nonalignment in foreign affairs, hoping to balance off the Soviet Union and the Western powers.

Within Iran, Mossadegh enjoyed widespread support throughout most of 1952; early in 1953, however, he was faced with a deepening economic crisis and the defection from the National Front of Husain Makki, Muzaffar Baghai, and the religious faction led by Ayatollah Kashani. Iran's major communist party, the Tudeh, initially supported then later attacked Mossadegh's leadership; Mossadegh, in turn, was cautious about accepting support from the Tudeh Party, in part because of its pro-Soviet stance. In addition, conflicts with the shah had led to a series of demonstrations in support of Mossadegh following arrests of various government officials on charges of treason and conspiracy.

Mossadegh's most serious internal opposition stemmed from growing disputes within the National Front. Once he had consolidated control of the government, after pressures that had held the National Front together were relaxed, some religious and leftist groups found themselves at odds with Mossadegh's policies. A number of social, economic, and political reforms that Mossadegh wished to implement alienated one group or another, and a growing sense of impatience and then alarm was expressed by some over Mossadegh's attempts at gaining control of the army, something he felt he had to have to ensure the stability of his government.

By the summer of 1953, the British and American governments had initiated plans for the covert overthrow of Mossadegh. British Intelligence and the United States Central Intelligence Agency had agreed to support the shah and opposition groups within Iran in carrying out a coup. The decision was made to replace Mossadegh with General Fazlollah Zahedi, one of those arrested in February on charges of plotting to overthrow the government. The shah and a group of military officers were informed of these plans, and they were put into effect in August.

On 19 August a group of tanks led by General Zahedi moved through Tehran and surrounded Mossadegh's residence. At the same time, hired strongmen from the bazaar commenced a noisy demonstration in support of the shah, while supporters of Ayatollah Kashani joined in to add to the confusion. Resistance to the coup was minimal, and in a matter of hours both Mossadegh and his top leaders were arrested and the shah was flying back to Iran. Several months later Mossadegh was put on trial for treason; he spent three years in jail and then was confined to his village, in political isolation, until his death in 1967.

Mossadegh remains a figure of tremendous stature in the history of modern Iran. As an individual, he had a reputation for honesty, integrity, and sincerity. He strongly opposed foreign, especially British and, later, American, influence in Iran at a time when most Iranians perceived many of their economic and political hardships as originating from such influence. He was an eloquent, impassioned orator, and his speeches are still widely read in Iran. [See also Pahlavi, Reza and Razmara, Ali.]

Richard W. Cottam, Nationalism in Iran: Updated through 1978 (2d ed., 1979). Sepehr Zabih, The Mossadegh Era: Roots of the Iranian Revolution (1982).

JAHAN SALEHI

MOTOORI NORINAGA (1730–1801), Japanese religious thinker, the most important figure in the Kokugaku ("national learning") school, a Shinto revivalist movement. Motoori Norinaga was the son of a cotton-goods merchant in the city of Matsuzaka. In 1752 he went to Kyoto to study medicine and Confucianism, but after reading the works of Keichū he became interested in Kokugaku. In 1757 he returned to Matsuzaka and conducted research on the Japanese classics while earning a living as a physician. In 1763 he became a student of Kamo no Mabuchi. As a leading scholar in the Kokugaku tradition, Norinaga devoted his life's work to demonstrating how rigorously empirical textual exegesis clarified the ancient "Way of the gods" (shintō) and why this indigenous Way made Japan superior to all other nations.

Norinaga's scholarship and thought may be seen as concerned with two areas, literature and the ancient Way. His ideas on literature were largely set before meeting Mabuchi in 1763 and changed little thereafter. In contrast, his studies on the ancient Way, through explication of the Chronicle of Ancient Matters, or Kojiki (compiled 712), were undertaken after meeting Mabuchi, and his monumental *Commentaries on the Kojiki* was finished in 1798, after thirty-four years of toil.

Norinaga turned first to Heian-era poetry and *monogatari* literature in search of an ethical counter ideal to what he considered the oppressively stern ways of Buddhism and Confucianism. These alien ways led men and women to hypocrisy, by claiming the ability to suppress genuine emotions such as love and affection. Norinaga's counter-ideal was *mono no aware*, or "the poignance of things," which keenly moved sensitive persons to be tolerant and forgiving, rather than abrasively faultfinding, when moral transgressions occurred. Such a nonnormative Way, he held, was particular to Japan and no less worthy than the Way of the Chinese Confucian sages.

But Norinaga went on to claim superiority for Japan's indigenous Way. He held that the Chinese sage kings were not holy personages: they were evil usurpers who had overthrown their rulers, and sought to keep from being overthrown in turn by their own followers. That is why they invented the moral norms—virtue, the mandate of Heaven, and the Way—that make up Confucianism. For Norinaga, Confucianism was no more than an ideology justifying political usurpation. The Chinese espoused its moral strictures, such as the "loyalty of subject for sovereign," but in truth they had in their history overthrown dynasty after dynasty. By contrast, Norinaga argued, the *Kojiki* recounted that Amaterasu, the sun goddess, ordered her descendants, the imperial house, to rule over Japan forever, and in fact the Japanese people submitted to this one dynasty throughout their history. Thus, he reasoned, the *Kojiki* shows that the Japanese always had obeyed and always would obey the gods' will by submitting unconditionally to their divine emperor—unlike the Chinese, who legitimized regicide and rebellion in the name of Confucian morality. Here, he asserted, was Japan's unique Way and the basis of her world preeminence.

Norinaga should not be dismissed as merely a prejudiced and irrational nationalist. True, he held that all *Kojiki* accounts, even those of a miraculous nature, must be accepted as revealed truth. But the philological erudition displayed in his *Commentaries on the Kojiki* commanded unlimited admiration from all quarters in an age when philology was the most prestigious of academic endeavors, and the work retains much scholarly value even today. Norinaga changed the Japanese intellectual climate decisively: he made it respectable, if not imperative, to claim Japan's uniqueness and moral excellence based on *Kojiki* myths that told of Japan's divine lineage of emperors descended from Amaterasu. Such a claim would have been rejected as absurd by Confucian rationalists at the beginning of the eighteenth century, but it was to find expression in the Meiji constitution at the end of the nineteenth.

[*See also* Kokugaku *and* Kamo no Mabuchi.]

Shigeru Matsumoto, *Motoori Norinaga* (1970).

BOB TADASHI WAKABAYASHI

MOUNTBATTEN, LOUIS

MOUNTBATTEN, LOUIS (1900–1979), first earl Mountbatten of Burma. Until 1917 he was known as Louis Francis Albert Victor Nicholas of Battenberg.

Born 25 June 1900, Lord Mountbatten was the great-grandson of Queen Victoria. Like his father, he was a naval officer. In 1921 he accompanied the Prince of Wales on a tour of India. Advancing rapidly in the service, he was appointed chief of combined operations against German-occupied Europe in 1942. The following year he became supreme allied commander, Southeast Asia, with responsibility for the recovery of Burma and Malaya from the Japanese conqueror. He directed the campaign in Burma, which culminated in the occupation of Rangoon on 3 May 1945, and was responsible for formulating British policy toward the Burmese nationalists who had cooperated with the Japanese. Against the prevailing policy he laid the dictum down that "no person shall suffer on account of political opinions honestly held." In August 1945 General MacArthur enlarged Mountbatten's responsibilities by adding the Netherlands Indies and French Indochina to his charge. He carried out the liberation of Malaya and introduced British Indian forces into Java and Saigon, continuing his policy of recognizing Southeast Asian nationalism despite protests from Britain's European allies. Mountbatten's appointment as "supremo" terminated on 31 May 1946.

In December 1946 he was asked by Prime Minister Clement Attlee to succeed Archibald Wavell as viceroy of India and was instructed to accelerate independence on the basis of a united India. Inducted as viceroy on 24 March 1947, he decided that this was impossible. The plan that he promulgated on 3 June 1947 provided for partition, and this came into effect on 15 August, when the two new nations, India and Pakistan, were born. Mountbatten hoped they would retain a common link by choosing him governor-general, but only India made the appointment. He continued as constitutional head of the new India until June 1948. Among important decisions he took was the acceptance of the accession of Kashmir to India, subject to a plebiscite. Subsequently, his service career was crowned by appointment as chairman of Britain's Defence Staff and Chiefs of Staff Committee. He was assassinated by the Irish Republican Army on 27 August 1979.

[*See also* Partition of India.]

Alan Campbell-Johnson, *Mission with Mountbatten* (1951). Philip Ziegler, *Mountbatten* (1985).

HUGH TINKER

MUDALIYAR, Tamil title. This surname is shared by certain members of the agricultural South Indian caste known as Vellalas. [See also Vellala.]

CAROL APPADURAI BRECKENRIDGE

MUGHAL EMPIRE, Indian empire founded by Babur (1526), which, with a short interregnum under the Surs (1540–1555), continued until the invasion of Nadir Shah (1739). The dynasty formally survived until 1857, when the last emperor, Bahadur Shah, was deposed by the British. Agra was the capital of the empire during most of its earlier period, but during the later years of Shah Jahan (r. 1628–1658), Delhi acquired this status. (Earlier on Fatehpur Sikri and Lahore served as capitals for short periods.)

Under Babur and Humayun (r. 1530–1556), the empire essentially functioned as a successor to the Lodi kingdom (1451–1526) and ruled an area largely confined within modern Afghanistan, the British North-West Frontier Province and Punjab, and the present Indian state of Uttar Pradesh. Extensive conquests by Akbar (r. 1556–1605) brought under subjugation the remaining parts of North India and a significant portion of the Deccan. The process of expansion in the Deccan continued under Jahangir (r. 1605–1627) and Shah Jahan, but it was under Aurangzeb (r. 1659–1707) that the maximum limits in the south were reached, the entire peninsula being annexed except for Kerala (see map 1).

Nonetheless during the same reign the rise of Maratha power under Shivaji (1627–1680) and his successors began to undermine Mughal authority. Nadir Shah's invasion (1739) exposed the empire's full weakness, and thereafter the Mughal emperor ceased to exercise actual control over much of the larger part of the empire. Many potentates in India (including the Marathas and the British East India Company) still thought it politic to bolster their authority by grants of offices from the emperor, but Shah Alam II (r. 1761–1806) became a mere pensioner of the English (1765–1771), of the Marathas (1771–1803), and, finally, of the English again, holding sway merely over the Red Fort. The 1857 rebellion gave the empire its last flicker. With the massacre of the princes by the English and exile to Burma of Bahadur Shah Zafar, the last emperor, its nominal existence too came to an end.

Administration. A centralized, heavily systematized administration was a notable feature of the Mughal empire. Its basic structure was established by Akbar. At the center, the emperor appointed ministers such as Wakilus Saltanat (after Bairam Khan, a largely titular office, usually unoccupied), the Diwan-i A'la (in charge of the financial administration), the Mir Bakhshi (in charge of grants of *mansabs*, upkeep of the army, and intelligence service), the Sadrus Sudur (in charge of appointments of the judicial officers and charity grants), and others. These ministers controlled fairly well-organized departments; their subordinates were posted in the provinces (*subas*). Akbar, too, had been responsible for dividing the whole empire into *subas*, appointing for each a governor (Sipahsalar, Nazim). The governor's powers were greatly restricted by his colleagues the Diwan, the Bakhshi, and the Sadr, who were responsible only to the corresponding ministers at the center. Each *suba* was divided into *sarkars*; commandants called *faujdars* were appointed to maintain law and order in the *sarkars*, though their actual jurisdictions did not always coincide with *sarkar* boundaries. Each district (*pargana*) had a Muslim judge (*qazi*) and two semihereditary officials (*qanungo* and *chaudhuri*) who were concerned with tax collection.

All higher offices (which until the eighteenth century never became hereditary and had, in actual practice, only short incumbencies) were filled by persons who belonged to the *mansab* cadre. Each of them held a "rank" (*mansab*) marked by double numbers, for example, 5,000 *zat*, 3,000 *sawar* (now conventionally represented as 5,000/3,000). The lowest *mansab* was 10/10. The first rank broadly indicated status and personal pay; the second determined the size of military contingent and the pay for it. Thus, every *mansab* holder was supposed to be a military officer as well; the higher *mansab* holders were called *umara*, or commanders. Apart from maintaining his contingent, the *mansab* holder could be appointed to any office or post, for which he did not receive any additional salary. The *mansab* was

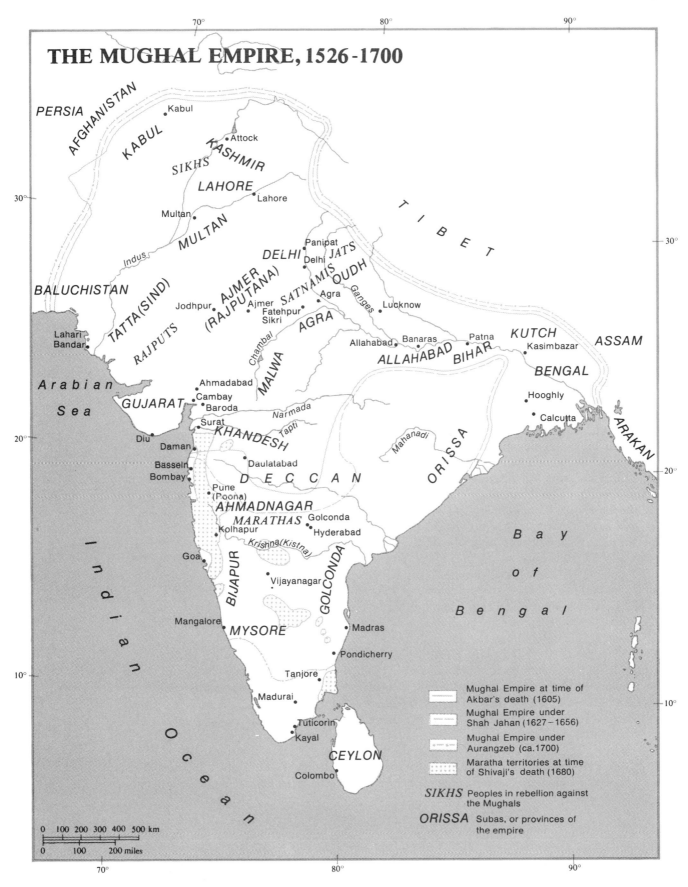

THE MUGHAL EMPIRE, 1526-1700

PERSIA

AFGHANISTAN

• Kabul

KABUL

• Attock

SIKHS KASHMIR

LAHORE

• Lahore

Multan •

MULTAN

BALUCHISTAN

Indus

TATTA (SIND)

AJMER
(RAJPUTANA)

DELHI

Panipat

Delhi • JATS

OUDH

Jodhpur •

Ajmer •

SATNAMIS

Fatehpur
Sikri

Agra •

Ganges

Lucknow •

RAJPUTS

Chambal

AGRA

Banaras •

Allahabad •

Patna •

KUTCH

Kasimbazar •

ASSAM

MALWA

ALLAHABAD

BIHAR

BENGAL

Arabian

Ahmadabad •

Cambay •

Baroda

Narmada

Hooghly •

Sea

GUJARAT

Calcutta •

Diu •

Surat •

Tapti

Mahanadi

ORISSA

ARAKAN

Daman •

KHANDESH

Basseln •

Bombay •

DECCAN

Indian

Pune
(Poona)

Daulatabad •

AHMADNAGAR

MARATHAS

Golconda •

Kolhapur •

Hyderabad •

B a y

Goa •

Krishna (Kistna)

BIJAPUR

GOLCONDA

o f

Vijayanagar •

Mangalore •

B e n g a l

MYSORE

Madras •

O c e a n

Pondicherry •

Tanjore •

Madurai •

Tuticorin •

Kayal •

CEYLON

Colombo •

	Mughal Empire at time of Akbar's death (1605)
	Mughal Empire under Shah Jahan (1627–1656)
	Mughal Empire under Aurangzeb (ca.1700)
	Maratha territories at time of Shivaji's death (1680)

SIKHS Peoples in rebellion against the Mughals

ORISSA Subas, or provinces of the empire

0 100 200 300 400 500 km

0   100   200 miles

regions

granted by the emperor alone, and a man rose as he received *mansab* enhancements. Imperial disapproval was usually shown by a reduction in *mansabs*.

The pay claims of *mansab* holders were met either in cash or by assignment of transferable *jagirs*, or revenue assignments. Each area with set limits was assigned a *jama* (or expected net revenue collection), and the *jama* of *jagirs* always had to equal the pay due to the *mansab* holder. The *jagirdar* arranged for tax collection through his own establishment of officials (*sarkar*); the principal revenue collector was called *amil*. Areas whose revenues were reserved for the Imperial Treasury were called *khalisa-i sharifa* and administered by imperial officials according to detailed rules. The *jagirs* were always transferable, and down to Aurangzeb's death (1707) the transfer system was maintained rigorously.

Land revenue was the empire's main source of income. The sovereign did not formally claim to be proprietor of the soil, as was alleged by contemporary European travelers (e.g., Bernier), but the land tax was heavy enough—often half the produce—to be practically equal to rent. Various methods of revenue assessment and collection were employed, such as simple crop sharing, crop sharing based on land measurement, cash-revenue rates imposed on different crops, lump sum demand on village, and so on. Cash nexus—an agglomerate of impersonal monetary factors specifically considered as the basis for human relations—prevailed over large areas. A share was always left for *zamindars*, or hereditary landed elements, and local officials such as village headmen.

High Culture. The Mughal court was the nucleus of a splendid flowering of art and culture, based on a blending of Indian and Perso-Islamic traditions. The most visible evidence of this high culture survives in the great buildings the Mughals have left behind, such as the palace-city of Fatehpur Sikri (built by Akbar), the forts at Agra and Delhi (built by Akbar and Shah Jahan), and, above all, the mausoleum of Shah Jahan's queen, Mumtaz Mahal, the celebrated Taj Mahal at Agra. [*See also* Fatehpur Sikri *and* Taj Mahal.]

Under the emperors' patronage, a distinct school of painting took shape. Descended from the Persian school, it liberally accepted both Indian and European influences. It produced such masters of miniature painting as Abu'l Hasan (who flourished under Akbar), Mansur (Jahangir), and Bichitr (Shah Jahan). Persian was the language of the Mughal court and administration, and Akbar's court brought together a notable assemblage of Persian writers. The poets Urfi and Faizi have permanent niches in the history of Persian lierature. Abu'l Fazl was not only a master of Persian prose (of the very ornate kind) but also a reflective writer, who compiled two distinctive works in Persian, a detailed history of Akbar's reign (*Akbarnama*) and a description, largely statistical, of Akbar's empire and administration (*A'in-i Akbari*). The Mughals did much to spread the use of Persian; ultimately, a literary language based on a blending of Hindi and Persian appeared in the eighteenth century in the form of Urdu, whose very name proclaimed its association with the court (*urdu* means "imperial camp"). Under Akbar, the Mughals patronized a liberal and scientific revival. [*See also* Abu'l Fazl.]

Called upon to govern a multireligious country, Akbar invoked pantheistic principles to justify a semidivine monarchy, not attached to any particular religion, but designed to secure "peace among all" (*sulh-i kul*). He had translations made of Hindu religious texts and held discussions with theologians of all faiths, including Jesuits. The tradition was continued by Prince Dara Shikoh (executed in 1659), who not only translated the *Upanishads* into Persian but also argued that Hinduism and Islam ultimately represented a single truth. Aurangzeb's orthodox religious policy partly thwarted this movement, but it was revived in the eighteenth century. Akbar displayed some interest in technology, and his minister Fathullah Shirazi invented mechanical devices, but this interest had no sequel. The patronage of astronomy proved more fruitful, leading to the establishment of the great observatories by Raja Jai Singh Sawai (d. 1743), which laid the basis for his great astronomical work, the *Zij-i Muhammad shahi*.

Society and Economy. W. H. Moreland estimated the population of India in 1600 at about 100 million; more recent estimates put it at about 140 to 150 million. It rose to about 200 million by 1800. The larger portion of the population lived in villages, the urban component being estimated at about 15 percent of the total population. Agriculture was mainly peasant based, but there was considerable production for the market. This combination has led to revisions of the nineteenth-century theories of the precolonial village community. It is true, however, that the sale of produce was largely induced by the imposition of the heavy land-revenue demand, which was mainly realized in money. Another feature of the agrarian scene was the presence of a class of hereditary intermediaries called *zamindars*, whose own fiscal and other rights are now much discussed by scholars. The main claimants to the land revenue were the *jagirdars*, who constituted the Mughal nobility. Since their *jagirs* were frequently transferred, the *jagirdars* tended to extort as much as possible from their temporary assignments, although the Mughal administration tried to impose a number of controls over them. Bernier (in India, 1658–1667) argued that the system tended to destroy the resources of the country and was a cause of the empire's decline; this, however, is debatable. On the basis of the large income of the *jagirdars* (as well as the emperor) there arose a flourishing urban economy, with a large craft sector. When direct trade began with Europe, through the Portuguese and then the Dutch (company established, 1602) and the English (1600), India exported large quantities of cotton cloth, silk, spices, indigo, and saltpeter, and it imported mainly silver and much smaller quantities of gold. The bullion imports were intended to raise prices in India and caused a moderate price revolution in the seventeenth century. Mughal India had a uniform currency system based on the silver rupee (178 grains) and a fairly developed indigenous system of commercial credit, bills of exchange, deposit banking, and transport and marine insurance.

[*See also* Babur; Aurangzeb; Humayun; Akbar; Shah Jahan; Jahangir; Nur Jahan; Zafar, Bahadur Shah; *and* Mansabdari System.]

M. Athar Ali, *Mughal Nobililty under Aurangzeb* (1966) and *Apparatus of Empire* (1985). Percy Browne, *Indian Architecture (Islamic Period),* 2 vols. (reprint, 1981), and *Indian Painting under the Mughals* (1924). H. M. Elliot and J. Dawson, *History of India* (1867; reprint, 1964). Irfan Habib, *Agrarian System of Mughal India* (1963) and *Atlas of the Mughal Empire* (1981). Ibn Hasan, *Central Structure of the Mughal Empire* (1936). W. Irvine and Jadunath Sarkar, *The Fall of the Mughal Empire,* 4 vols. (1932–1950). W. H. Moreland, *India at the Death of Akbar* (1920). A. A. Rizvi, *Muslim Revivalist Movements of the Fifteenth and Sixteenth Centuries* (1965). P. Saran, *Provincial Government of the Mughals* (1973). Jadunath Sarkar, *Short History of Aurangzeb* (1954). S. R. Sharma, *Religious Policy of the Mughal Emperors* (1962). R. P. Tripathi, *Rise and Fall of the Mughal Empire* (1956).   M. Athar Ali

MUHAMMAD, prophet of Islam and messenger through whom the Qur'an was revealed; founder of the *umma,* the Islamic community. While many of the details of Muhammad's life are verifiable by modern historical methods, the student should beware lest, by discarding the mythic elements as pious fiction, he or she overlook the true significance of the person of Muhammad in the religious life of Muslims.

Muhammad, son of Abd Allah, was born around the year 570 in the city of Mecca, a thriving commercial center in the Arabian Peninsula. His family was from the clan of Hashim of the prominent tribe of Quraish; at the time of Muhammad's birth, however, Hashim possessed only modest means. Muhammad's father died before he was born; his mother died while he was still a child.

Muhammad was raised by his uncle Abu Talib. Muslim tradition relates that he traveled with his uncle on commercial expeditions. On one of these trips the caravan halted by the hermitage of a Christian monk, Bahira, who recognized in the young Muhammad a future prophet. According to a second myth, Muhammad was seized by the angel Gabriel, who split open his chest and washed his heart with the sacred water of Zamzam, removing from it a black clot, the satanic element that infects the rest of mankind.

As a young adult Muhammad entered the employ of a wealthy widow, Khadija. They married when Muhammad was twenty-five and Khadija about forty. While she lived, Muhammad took no other wives. Khadija provided Muhammad with psychological support when, at about the age of forty (c. 610), he began to undergo experiences that both frightened and perplexed him.

Muhammad was accustomed to retiring to a cave called Hira outside of Mecca. It was here that he began receiving revelations. Muhammad feared for his sanity; it was Khadija who urged him to consult with her Christian cousin Waraqa Ibn Naufal, who helped assure Muhammad that the revelations were not the products of devils or *jinn* but were from God.

Muhammad's revelations, Muslim tradition relates, were mediated by the angel Gabriel. They were codified into book form (the Qur'an) some years after Muhammad's death. In addition to the Qur'an's overriding emphasis on the oneness of God and Muhammad's role as messenger of God, it stresses man's moral responsibility and the need for social justice. The text communicates as well a vivid awareness of hell and paradise. The Qur'an is not intended to abrogate the earlier revelations by God to the Jews and Christians. The process of revelation, begun with Adam and continued through hundreds of prophets and messengers, reached its culmination with Muhammad, the "Seal of the Prophets."

Khadija was the first to embrace Islam; among the earliest converts was Muhammad's cousin and future son-in-law Ali, Abu Talib's son. The reaction of the larger Meccan community to Muhammad's preaching was relatively benign until the leaders realized that any change in the religious status quo would seriously damage trade. Muhammad's insistence that Allah, the Lord of the Ka'ba, was the only god presumed the deposition of other deities. Thus, benign disregard by the Meccans soon turned into outright persecution. Around 615 a portion of Muhammad's followers emigrated to Abyssinia, seeking protection at the court of the Christian ruler. In 619 the death of Muhammad's beloved Khadija and his uncle Abu Talib added to the precariousness of his position at Mecca.

A city about two hundred miles to the northwest, Yathrib (now known as Medina), provided Muhammad with an opportunity to escape the hostile environment of Mecca and yet preserve his nascent community intact. Beginning in 620 negotiations took place between Muhammad and the feuding tribes of Medina that culminated in an invitation to him and his followers to emigrate. Muhammad would act as leader and arbiter among the warring factions. Muhammad's followers emigrated in small groups during the next two years. By 622 only Muhammad, Ali, and the trusted Abu Bakr remained at Mecca; they too soon slipped away. The emigration from Mecca to Medina (the Hijra) signals the establishment of Islam as a community, and it is from this crucial event that the Muslim dating system begins.

A relationship of brotherhood was established between the emigrants (*muhajirun*) and the Medinese, who were known as helpers (*ansar*). No longer was allegiance to be determined by tribal affiliation; from now on a Muslim was to find his or her identity with other Muslims in their common commitment to God and to Muhammad. The ideals of equality and close cooperation were institutionalized in a constitution prepared by Muhammad, which provided as well for the religious freedom of the Jewish tribes. Relations with the Jews, however, deteriorated quickly. Muhammad, it seems, was convinced that the Jews would accept his prophethood and the revelations of God. Muhammad's claims, however, were rejected and, according to Muslim tradition, ridiculed.

Because of the Jews' rejection of the revelation and their alleged complicity in plots to overthrow Muhammad, several military actions were taken against them. The tribe of Qainuqa was compelled to migrate in 624; a similar fate awaited the tribe of Nadir in 625. In 626–627 the Quraza were attacked and all of the men of the tribe put to death. In 630 the Jewish oasis of Khaibar was captured. On this occasion Muhammad established the norm for the treatment of Christian and Jewish minorities; the Jews remained on their lands but were obliged to pay a poll tax (*jizya*).

In 624 a Meccan army advanced against Muhammad. The armies met at Badr, reportedly three hundred Muslims against one thousand Meccans. Despite the odds, the Meccans were routed. The following year three thousand Meccans under Abu Sufyan engaged the Muslims outside of Medina at Uhud. Muhammad was wounded; rumors circulated that he had been killed. The Meccans, however, did not pursue their advantage.

In 626–627 the Meccans raised an army of ten thousand to lay siege to Medina. The Jews and certain bedouin tribes are said to have been accomplices in the Meccans' plot. The siege failed because Muhammad had a ditch dug around the exposed flanks of the town, thus halting the Meccans' advance. In 627 Muhammad proposed to the Meccans that he be allowed to visit the Ka'ba in Mecca. Although the Meccans refused, both parties concluded the Treaty of Hudaibiyya, which permitted Muhammad to visit the holy places the following year. Moreover, the treaty provided for a ten-year truce.

The visit to the holy places was accomplished in 629. At the end of that year Muhammad set out with an army for Mecca, insisting that the truce had been violated because his sympathizers in Mecca were suffering persecution. He entered the city without a struggle and destroyed the idols housed in the Ka'ba.

In March of 632 Muhammad made his last pilgrimage to Mecca. On the occasion of this farewell pilgrimage he is reported to have given a sermon that is still recited each year during the pilgrimage rites. In it he emphasized the human values at the heart of Islam and the need for social, political, and economic justice. Above all he stressed the solidarity of the Muslim community, whose members are to treat one another as brother and sister. A few months after the pilgrimage Muhammad fell ill, and on 8 June 632 he died unexpectedly. He was buried without ceremony under the floor of the home of his wife A'isha.

The greatness of Muhammad lies in his practical accomplishments and in his spiritual role as God's chosen instrument. No myth captures this more fully than the story of Muhammad's night journey and ascension. Muhammad was carried one night from the precincts of the Ka'ba at Mecca to the Aqsa Mosque at Jerusalem. On his fabled steed Buraq, he ascended through the seven heavens, where he was acclaimed by all the major prophets, especially Moses and Jesus. Eventually he reached the divine throne and the presence of God. The Dome of the Rock in Jerusalem commemorates the spot from which Muhammad is said to have ascended into heaven.

[*See also* Arabs; Islam; *and* Qur'an.]

Tor Andrae, *Mohammed: The Man and His Faith* (1936; reprint, 1977). A. J. Arberry, trans., *The Koran Interpreted* (1955; reprint, 1970). Arthur Guillaume, trans., *The Life of Muhammad: A Translation of Ibn Ishāq's Sīrat Rasūl Allāh* (1955; reprint, 1967). Maxime Rodinson, *Muhammad,* translated by Anne Carter (1980). Annemarie Schimmel, *And Muhammad Is His Messenger* (1985). William Montgomery Watt, *Muhammad at Mecca* (1953), *Muhammad at Medina* (1956), and *Muhammad: Prophet and Statesman* (1961).

PETER J. AWN

MUHAMMAD BIN QASIM, Arab general known for his conquest of Sind in 711 at the age of seventeen. Having consolidated his authority at Debul, he defeated Dahir and captured Brahmanabad, becoming master of Lower Sind. Aror (near modern-day Rohri), Multan, and the outskirts of Kashmir came under his control. A military leader par excellence, he was recalled at the zenith of his success and executed. It is untrue that he fell from grace for having molested slave girls meant for the caliph. Instead, the death of his father-in-law, Hajjaj, and the consequent political changes were responsible for his fall. His Brahmanabad Declaration assured religious and economic freedom to the Indians and won the cooperation of Indian officers like Moka, Sisakar, and Kaksa. The Sindhis constructed statues of him at Kiraj.

H. M. Elliot and J. Dawson, *History of India,* vol. 1 (1867; reprint, 1964). Mirza Kalichbeg Fredunbeg, *The Chach Namah, An Ancient History of Sind* (1900).

FARHAN AHMAD NIZAMI

MUHAMMADIYAH, a mission-minded social and educational organization for Muslims adhering to reformist teachings. Founded in Yogyakarta, Java, in 1912 by Kyai Haji Ahmad Dahlan (1868–

1923), Muhammadiyah grew rapidly in the politicized atmosphere of the late Dutch colonial period in Netherlands India. By 1983 it had achieved a membership of some 250,000. Muhammadiyah has been the dominating organizational force among modernist Muslims in Indonesia since the mid-1920s. It avoids overt political activity and concentrates instead upon its fundamentally social and religious mission, which it promotes through its nationwide branches and its network of schools, mosques, libraries, hospitals, clinics, and welfare institutions.

JAMES R. RUSH

MUHAMMAD SAID. *See* Mir Jumla.

MUJIBUR RAHMAN, SHEIKH (1921–1975), prime minister (1972–1975) and president (1975) of Bangladesh. Mujib began his political career as a student in Calcutta in 1940. He joined with Hussain Shahid Suhrawardy in forming the Awami League in 1949 and became organizer for East Bengal (later East Pakistan). He served jail terms under the Muslim League and Ayub Khan governments. He was minister of commerce in East Pakistan from 1956 to 1957 and assumed leadership of the East Pakistan Awami League after Suhrawardy's death in 1963. Mujib announced his six-point program for East Pakistani autonomy in 1966; the plan would have retained Pakistan as a confederal entity. He led the Awami League to overwhelming victory in the 1970 elections, winning all but two national assembly seats in East Pakistan and a majority in all of Pakistan. He was arrested by the Pakistan government as part of a military crackdown in March 1971 and held in jail in West Pakistan; he was released and returned to Bangladesh in January 1972.

Rahman led the new Bangladeshi parliament to adopt a parliamentary constitution and became prime minister. In the face of growing opposition he obtained parliamentary approval for a presidential system with himself as president in January 1975. This was followed by creation of a one-party state in June 1975 and increasing authoritarianism. He was assassinated on 15 August 1975 by disgruntled middle-grade military officers.

[*See also* Bangladesh; Pakistan; Awami League; *and* Suhrawardy, Hussain Shahid.]

Craig Baxter, *Bangladesh: A New Nation in an Old Setting* (1984), chaps. 4 and 5. Zillur Rahman Khan,

Leadership in the Least Developed Nation: Bangladesh (1983).

CRAIG BAXTER

MUJTAHID, Arabic, literally "one who exerts"; that is, a person who exerts the faculties of the mind to the utmost for the purpose of forming an opinion in a case of law. The case usually involves an ambiguous and unusual point of law in such a way that a new situation can be subsumed under a new solution as a result of the "exertion" of the *mujtahid*. This process of forming a new rule is known as *ijtihad*, and it is based on interpretation and application of the generalized principles derived from the two major sources of Islamic law, the Qur'an and the *sunna*. Although each individual Muslim can employ *ijtihad* and follow his own judgment, it is only those who are trained as *mujtahids* who have a right to formulate a new decision, and their decision must be followed by others, who are designated as *muqallids* (i.e., those who "follow" the *mujtahid*).

In the history of Islamic law, the founders of the four Sunni *madhhabs* (legal schools) are regarded as absolute *mujtahids* who have established the general principles of jurisprudence (*usul al-fiqh*) and have laid down authoritative texts containing a rule in support of their new legal ruling (*fatwa*). Subsequent jurists are considered *mujtahids* in a given school who issued their decisions on the basis of a relevant text or precedent in the past. In this sense, although each *mujtahid* was a *mufti* ("one who gives a *fatwa*"), not all *muftis* were capable of giving independent judgments without reference to a precedent within a given legal school.

In Shi'ite Islam, the *mujtahid* has always formulated a new rule based on *aql* (intellect), which is regarded as one of the major sources of law besides the Qur'an and the *sunna*. The use of the title *mujtahid* for the Twelver Shi'ite jurist occurs during the Qajar period, probably following the victory of the Usuli jurists over their Akhbari adversaries, who were against the use of *aql* in formulating a new decision. It is almost certain that by the time of the Qajars there was no dispute among the Twelver jurists regarding the position of a *mujtahid* during the concealment of the Hidden Imam, namely, that he was a deputy of the last imam. So construed, a well-qualified Shi'ite *mujtahid* was the functional imam during the absence of the actual authority of the imam proper. Accordingly, he was always absolute *mujtahid* and could not become a *muqallid*. It was in this position as the deputy of the twelfth

imam that the Shi'ite *mujtahid* could freely criticize and spearhead opposition to the actions of the shahs, who were regarded as the merely temporary preservers of order.

[*See also* Akhbari; Ayatollah; Mulla; Shari'a; Shi'a; Sunni; *and* Usuli.]

Fazlur Rahman, *Islamic Methodology in History* (1965).

ABDELAZIZ SACHEDINA

MUKDEN. *See* Shenyang.

MUKDEN INCIDENT, military clash on 18 September 1931 that started Japan's conquest of Manchuria (northeastern China) and set Japan on the path to war with China and involvement in World War II. Since 1906 Japan had garrisoned troops in Manchuria to guard the South Manchuria Railway. In 1931 radicals in the Japanese Kwantung Army were becoming fearful that the moderate civilian government in Tokyo would abandon Manchuria in the face of rising nationalism in China. Plotting without official authorization, the officers set a bomb on the night of 18 September that blew up a section of railroad tracks just north of Mukden (Shenyang). Alleging that Chinese were responsible for the bombing and claiming self-defense, the Japanese forces advanced outside the railway zone and by early 1932 completed the occupation of all Manchuria. In March of the same year, Japan established the puppet state of Manchukuo, ostensibly headed by Puyi, who had been deposed as emperor of China in 1912. The League of Nations condemned Japan in 1932 for its actions, but was not able to halt further Japanese aggression.

[*See also* Kwantung Army.]

LLOYD E. EASTMAN

MULLA, a title usually given to a male or female student of traditional Islamic sciences, including literature, and to a lesser member of the religious class in Twelver (Ithna Ashari) Shi'ism, who functions as a teacher and preacher. In its early usage, the title was given to any learned person who wore a turban, which indicated the high level of learning acquired through the process of *mulla raftan* ("to go to school, to learn"). In this sense, it served as a title for some leading Twelver scholars in the past. Later, when Shi'ism became institutionalized in the Safavid and post-Safavid era, the term *mulla* was applied to a person who was well grounded in the art of preaching and who was appointed to perform everyday religious functions, such as leading congregational prayer in the smaller mosques, teaching the Qur'an and literature, and preaching the Twelver faith, including the *ta'ziya*—the passion story of the sufferings of the Twelver imams Ali and Husain. The Persian word *akhun* or *akhund* is a virtual synonym of *mulla* in both the above senses.

[*See also* Education: Education in Iran and Central Asia.]

Roy P. Mottahedeh, *The Mantle of the Prophet* (1985).

ABDELAZIZ SACHEDINA

MÜLLER, FRIEDRICH MAX (1823–1900), German-born scholar who spent his career in England, primarily at Oxford. Although denied the Boden Professorship of Sanskrit in 1860, he became the most celebrated Indologist of the nineteenth century. To Müller we owe the first published edition of the *Rig Veda* with Sayana's commentary. This enterprise (1849–1873), commissioned by the East India Company, earned him the reverence of Indian scholars. Müller later turned his attention to comparative philology and comparative mythology. Many of his ideas were soon considered out of date; yet his personal charm and the lucidity of his English style made him a favorite of the European reading public. Müller conceived and edited the famous Sacred Books of the East series; begun in 1875, all but one volume and the index were published in his lifetime. Although he never visited India, he was in constant contact with Indians and displayed much interest in India's political and intellectual affairs.

The Life and Letters of the Right Honourable Friedrich Max Müller, Edited by His Wife, 2 vols. (1902). J. H. Voight, *Max Mueller: The Man and His Ideas* (1967).

LUDO ROCHER

MULRAJ, DIWAN, Hindu governor of Multan (1844–1848), precipitated the Second Anglo-Sikh War (1849) by leading a local anti-British insurrection in 1848. The Sikh kingdom was defeated.

[*See also* Sikhism.]

USHA SANYAL

MULTAN, today a district headquarters in lower Punjab, Pakistan, is reputedly the city from which Alexander the Great retreated after his decision not to invade India. It was a renowned center of sun worship; offerings to the main temple, which was destroyed in the seventeenth century, and to its deity provided revenue for Multan's Muslim governors. Originally appointed by the caliph, they controlled the city from the eighth century onward. By the tenth century Multan had become a stronghold for followers of a heretical Islamic sect, the Qarmatis, but Sunni Islam was restored by Mahmud of Ghazna in the early eleventh century. Upon the Ghorid conquest of North India, Multan was incorporated into the Delhi sultanate; this status lasted until 1438, when independent rulers assumed power. In 1528 the city became part of the Mughal empire. Subsequently Multan was under Afghan control, and in 1818, Ranjit Singh captured the city. By 1850 the British took Multan.

Famous for its tombs of early sultanate-period saints, the city is dominated by the enormous two-storied octagonal tomb of Rukn-i Alam Suhrawardi. It was reputedly constructed by the future sultan Ghiyas ud-Din Tughluq (d. 1325) as a tomb for himself, and he bestowed it upon his spiritual adviser, Rukn-i Alam. Constructed of brick and embellished with glazed blue tiles, it has recently been restored by Wali Ullah Khan.

J. Burton-Page, "Tomb of Rukn-i Alam," *Splendors of the East* (1965), pp. 72–81. "Directions in Diversity: The Winners of the 1983 Aga Khan Award for Architecture," *Mimar* 10 (1983): 16–48. Syed Muhammad Latif, *The Early History of Multan* (1963).   CATHERINE B. ASHER

MUNDA. About a million strong, the Munda have their homeland in the Ranchi district of Bihar, from which they have spread over adjoining areas of Orissa and West Bengal. Ethnologically they belong to the proto-Australoid stock. During the last two hundred years they have been influenced by Hinduism and Christianity and have also been a factor in the rise of the composite culture of Chotanagpur. They participated in the formation of the state by the Nagbanshi in the medieval period and bore the brunt of colonialism in the nineteenth century, during which time aliens dispossessed them of their land. They often rebelled; their best-known uprising, called the *ulgulan*, was led by Birsa Munda (1874–1901) and resulted in the enactment of the Chotanagpur Tenancy Act, which protected their land system. Primarily settled agriculturists, the Munda have also emigrated as laborers in tea gardens and elsewhere.

S. C. Roy, *The Mundas and Their Country* (1912).

K. S. SINGH

MUNRO, SIR THOMAS

MUNRO, SIR THOMAS (1761–1827), governor of Madras for the East India Company, responsible for introducing the *ryotwari* land settlement, in which renters were disposed of and a direct settlement with the *ryots* was entered into. Munro was Burkean in outlook, believing that indigenous systems should be preserved and strengthened. He opposed a free press in India, arguing that India was a conquered nation that could only slowly be brought to the advanced institutions of England.

[*See also* East India Company *and* Madras.]

T. H. Beaglehole, *Thomas Munro and the Development of Administrative Policy in Madras, 1792–1818* (1966).

LYNN ZASTOUPIL

MUONG. The Muong people primarily inhabit the area south and west of Vietnam's Red River, although groups of Muong did go to Laos and South Vietnam after the partition of Vietnam. The exact origin of the Muong has not been determined, but it seems probable that they have been in the region as long as the Vietnamese themselves, and the two peoples share many linguistic, religious, and social characteristics. During the nineteenth century the Muong instigated several anti-French uprisings, although the colonial government later worked to develop better relations with them, as did the Hanoi and Saigon governments after independence.

US Department of the Army, Ethnographic Study Series, *Minority Groups in North Vietnam* (1972).

BRUCE M. LOCKHART

MUQANNA, AL-, the epithet (meaning "the veiled one") of the leader of a religious-political revolt against Abbasid rule in Transoxiana in the eighth century CE. Al-Muqanna's insurrection received support from villagers in the Zeravshan and Kashkadarya valleys, the surrounding Turkish tribes, and even the Bukhar-Khuda Bunyat. It probably reflected resentment about Arab colonization, taxation, and efforts to bring this remote area under the control of the central administration.

Al-Muqanna allegedly taught heterodox doctrines (such as metempsychosis), permitted antinomian practices (including the common possession of women), and used deceptions, such as causing a false moon to rise from a well, to persuade people of his own divinity. The revolt was crushed, and al-Muqanna killed, in 779–780. A sect known as the White Raiments survived and awaited the messianic return of al-Muqanna to rule.

E. Daniel, *The Political and Social History of Khurasan under Abbasid Rule* (1979), pp. 137–147.

E. L. DANIEL

MURASAKI SHIKIBU (c. 973–?), author of the *Genji monogatari (The Tale of Genji)*, a masterwork of Japanese prose commonly cited as the world's first novel. The daughter of a middle-ranking Heian court official, Murasaki was chosen by Fujiwara no Michinaga to become tutor-cum-companion to Empress Shōshi, his daughter. She is thought to have entered court service in 1006, by which time some of her great prose work may have already been written. Besides the *Genji monogatari* there are a collection of poetry and some important memoirs known as the *Murasaki Shikibu Diary*. It is known from the latter that the *Genji* was read at court and that her talents were recognized, but little else is known of her life. The diary is a combination of semiofficial woman's court diary concerned with ceremonial and a series of personal reminiscences; the latter are at times extremely caustic, especially concerning contemporaries such as Sei Shōnagon. It also reveals the author's ambivalent attitude to court life: she was censorious of its frivolity but drawn to it as the only place she could practice her art. A similar tension between a strong awareness of impermanence and a delight in the physical manifestations of the cultured life lies behind the *Genji*, a vast and complex work that came to define her age for all later ages. The eponymous hero is an imperial prince made commoner, and a large part of the tale is devoted to his search for a lost mother figure through a series of subtly interrelated surrogates.

[*See also* Genji Monogatari *and* Fujiwara Period.]

Richard Bowring, *Murasaki Shikibu: Her Diary and Poetic Memoirs* (1982). Andrew J. Pekarik, ed., *Ukifune: Love in the Tale of Genji* (1982). Edward G. Seidensticker, trans., *The Tale of Genji* (1976). RICHARD BOWRING

MUROMACHI PERIOD, the 240-year period of Japanese history that takes its name from the Muromachi district of Kyoto, the seat of shogunal government during the period; it is also known as the Ashikaga period, after the Ashikaga warrior family, whose members held the office of shogun from 1338 to 1573. Most historians date the Muromachi period from 1336, when Ashikaga Takauji (1305–1338) ended the Kemmu Restoration (a short-lived attempt by the imperial court to reassert political power) by ousting emperor Go-Daigo from Kyoto; he then set up Kōmyō as a puppet emperor and laid the basis for a new military regime. [See Kemmu Restoration.] Others date the period from 1338, when Takauji assumed the title of shogun and formally established his shogunate, or *bakufu,* in Kyoto. The end of the Muromachi period is marked by the expulsion of the fifteenth Ashikaga shogun, Yoshiaki, from Kyoto by Oda Nobunaga in 1573. Some might argue, however, that for all practical purposes it had come to an end when Nobunaga marched into Kyoto in 1568.

Political History. Contrasted with its predecessor, the Kamakura *bakufu,* or with the later Edo *bakufu,* the Muromachi *bakufu* was a fundamentally unstable warrior government. The Muromachi regime has been described as a coalition of shogun and *shugo.* *Shugo* were powerful branch family members and vassals of the Ashikaga with military authority over one or more provinces. Some *shugo* enrolled local warriors as their vassals and expanded their control over neighboring provinces. The success of the central authority of the shoguns depended on their ability to dominate the coalition. Except during the reigns of the third through sixth shoguns (1370–1441), the Muromachi *bakufu* was weakened by factionalism and civil war, and there was difficulty in imposing shogunal authority over provincial agents, the *shugo.*

The Ashikaga were a warrior family from eastern Japan. In 1333 Ashikaga Takauji had helped emperor Go-Daigo topple the Kamakura *bakufu* and restore direct imperial rule. Dissatisfied with the meager political rewards granted to him by the restored imperial government, Takauji set up a puppet emperor, Kōmyō, and took the title of shogun after forcing Go-Daigo into exile; Go-Daigo set up a rival regime in Yoshino. This set in motion the sporadic but debilitating civil war between supporters of Go-Daigo and his Southern Court and those who supported the Ashikaga and the Northern Court. [See Nambokuchō.]

Thus, the inherent weaknesses of the Ashikaga *bakufu* were clearly exposed in its early decades. Unlike Minamoto Yoritomo in 1185 or Tokugawa Ieyasu in 1600, Takauji had not established his *bakufu* on the basis of a decisive military victory. Rather, he had shared power with Go-Daigo, and when he turned against Go-Daigo he was plagued by fratricidal strife and civil war. Because he had not won an overwhelming military victory, he had not acquired the military and political stature nec-

essary to impose his authority over his chief vassals, the *shugo.* Nor had he gained control over enough land to provide an adequate economic base from which to draw tax income and provide spoils. [See Ashikaga Takauji.]

Ashikaga Yoshimitsu (1358–1408), the third shogun, was more successful than Takauji in asserting his authority over the country. Politically adept and aided by loyal vassals in the office of shogunal advisor, *kanrei,* he imposed his will on the provincial *shugo.* Yoshimitsu isolated *shugo* who resisted his authority and mobilized rival *shugo* against them. He gained influence over the imperial court by healing the breach between the northern and southern lines and then used court titles to enhance his feudal authority. He enhanced his stature through lavish cultural patronage and the initiation of active trading and diplomatic relations with China. He took for himself the title "King of Japan." [See Ashikaga Yoshimitsu.] His successor, Yoshimochi, a less flamboyant shogun, was cool toward Yoshimitsu's policies, especially trade with China, but the shogunate again found an active, autocratic leader in Yoshinori, the sixth shogun. Yoshnori's assassination in 1441 by a disgruntled *shugo* was a serious blow to shogunal authority. The *bakufu*'s authority was further, and disastrously, weakened during the reign of Ashikaga Yoshimasa, the eighth shogun. Yoshimasa, a generous patron of the arts, was politically maladroit, and he allowed rivalries and succession disputes between powerful *shugo,* courtiers, and members of his family to break into open war in 1467. [See Ashikaga Yoshimasa.]

In the Ōnin War, 1467–1477, much of Kyoto was put to the torch. Monks and nobles fled to the provinces, and shogunal authority ebbed. After the warfare in the capital had subsided it continued as a desultory civil war in the provinces that ushered in what has been called the "age of warring provinces," *sengoku jidai,* or the time of "the lowly overturning the mighty," *gekokujō.* Although the shogunate survived, real power was held by those *shugo* who controlled the office of *kanrei.* Many of the former *shugo,* most of whose ties with their provinces had weakened through their residence in Kyoto, were overthrown by their deputies, or by local warrior families, *kokujin,* who established leaner, more tightly governed domains better suited for survival in an age of war. These were known as the *sengoku daimyō,* or "warring states barons." [See Ōnin War *and* Sengoku Period.]

By the mid-sixteenth century Japan was headed by an impotent shogunate and fragmented into some

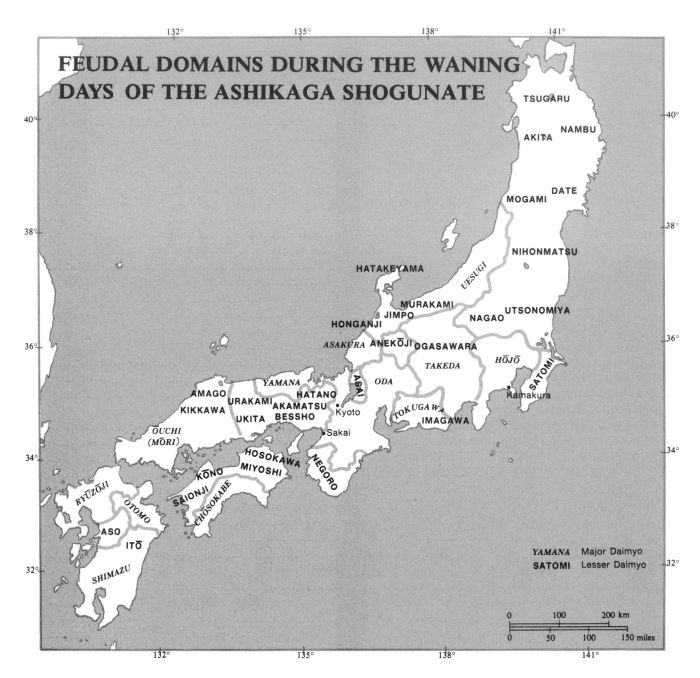

FEUDAL DOMAINS DURING THE WANING DAYS OF THE ASHIKAGA SHOGUNATE

YAMANA Major Daimyo
SATOMI Lesser Daimyo

250 domains whose leaders scoffed at the authority of the *bakufu* and did all in their power to strengthen their own military forces and exploit the resources of land and manpower under their control. At an extreme of decentralization, the country was ripe for reunification. Unification was set in motion by Oda Nobunaga, (1534–1582). Nobunaga, a restless and ruthless warrior, was a brilliant military tactician who used the new Western technology of the musket to offset his numerical weakness. He applied his energies to the conquest of rival daimyo and armed religious communities in central Japan.

Marching into Kyoto in 1568 to aid Yoshiaki, he soon fell out with the shogun and, in 1573, expelled him. Neither Nobunaga nor his brilliant successor Toyotomi Hideyoshi assumed the discredited title of shogun. They preferred to base their authority on their own force of arms and court titles. The shogunal title was assumed again by the third of the unifiers, Tokugawa Ieyasu, after his sweeping victory over supporters of Hideyoshi in 1600. Ieyasu looked back not to the Ashikaga shoguns but to Minamoto Yoritomo as his model. His *bakufu*, based upon a solid preponderance of military and economic power, was carefully structured to avoid the instabilities inherent in Ashikaga rule. [*See* Momoyama Period.*]

Economic Life. If the Muromachi period was one of political instability and warfare, it was at the same time a period of economic and commercial growth. Warfare and political fragmentation broke down old institutions and loosened social bonds, created new patrons, and stimulated new needs, all of which provided opportunities for growth and change in society. Two older institutions that felt the forces of change were the estate holdings, *shōen,* held by the nobility and the larger temples, and the older guilds, *za,* which the nobility and temples had also sponsored and drawn upon for service and income.

Shōen had been subjected to erosion and division in the Kamakura period as *jitō* and other local warriors sought to entrench and expand their influence in the provinces. The process of *shōen* erosion quickened during the civil warfare of the fourteenth and late fifteenth centuries. *Shugo* and *sengoku daimyō* cut into the absentee rights of Kyoto proprietors. *Sengoku daimyō,* in particular, resented any outside influence within their domains and simply rejected the claims of central proprietors to income from local estates. They adopted a similar attitude to the privileges and exemptions of the older *za,* seeking to replace their influence with that of new groups of local merchants who would be more beholden to the daimyo. Nobunaga's policy of freeing markets and guilds, *rakuichi rakuza,* marked the maturation of this attitude of hostility to the commercial privileges of the old central institutions. [*See* Shōen.]

The erosion of *shōen* and the decline of the older guilds were related to other economic changes. Farmers, freed from the closed economic worlds of the *shōen,* were able to divert more of their produce into markets. There is some evidence of an agricultural surplus during these centuries. Technological innovations, such as cropping, greater use of draft animals, and improved farming implements, may also have contributed to increased production. Markets became more widespread and regular. They stimulated the commercial activities of peddlers, merchants, and transport agents. By the late Muromachi period the produce of distant provinces was finding its way through commercial channels to wholesale markets in Kyoto and Kamakura. The military and building activities of the *sengoku daimyō* created a huge demand for building materials, arms and armor, and military supplies of all kinds.

Yoshimitsu's more active trading policies opened up commercial tally trade as well as diplomatic contact with Ming China. Goods from China, *karamono,* including art objects, silks, and medicines, were prized in Japan. This trade brought wealth to the merchants of Hakata, Sakai, and Kyoto. Unlike the Kamakura *bakufu,* the Muromachi *bakufu* did not have extensive lands under their control. To make up for this they seem to have resorted to a more active trading and commercial policy. In addition to their forays in foreign trade, the Ashikaga shoguns generated tax revenues by encouraging the commercial activities of the Kyoto guilds and sake brewers and wholesalers, *dosō.* From the 1540s, Portuguese and Spanish "black ships" brought merchants (as well as missionaries), and Japan found itself benefiting from, and drawn into, a commercial network that covered East Asia and had links with Western Europe.

One important spur to economic activity was the growing use of money. Copper coins, minted in Song China, were imported in the thirteenth century. In some areas annual taxes began to be paid in cash rather than rice. From the Muromachi period, Ming coins were a major import item and were widely used in markets and shops. The Ashikaga shoguns did not attempt to mint coins, and their dependence on coinage from China led to problems of supply and quality. Hoarding of good coins was only partially curtailed by "coin selection edicts" that forbade the damaging or hoarding of good coins. The growing availability of coinage and commercial wealth fostered moneylending by temples, merchants, and pawnbrokers. High rates of interest and problems of repayment created periodic demands for debt moratoria, *tokusei.* At times, as in 1428, 1441, and 1454, violent uprisings, *ikki,* were directed at pawnbrokers, or at the *bakufu* for its failure to redress financial hardhips. The *bakufu*'s passage of debt moratoria in response to the more threatening of these *ikki* offered only temporary relief to debtors and tended to add confusion to the marketplace by reducing the inducement for merchants to make loans.

Overall, the economic gains made during the Muromachi period probably outweighed the losses and dislocations. The disintegration of *shōen* created new opportunities for some merchants and farmers. Local merchants benefited from the relaxation of guild privileges and greater access to markets. A nascent merchant class emerged. Although coinage was not being minted in Japan, the use of money, bills of exchange, and pledges, were all accepted. Although the Muromachi *bakufu* did not develop a successful mercantile policy, it was more involved in trade and commerce than its predecessor had been. Japan was opened to foreign trade. When the Ashikaga shoguns lost active interest in the China trade in the late fifteenth century it was taken up by western daimyo like the Ōuchi and Hosokawa. Other *sengoku daimyō* recognized the important role played by commerce and provision merchants in the strengthening of their domains. Products from remote areas were feeding into central markets and maritime networks were being extended along the coasts of Japan. *Sengoku daimyō* fought for the new wealth being dug from gold and silver mines. Nobunaga and Hideyoshi were consolidating a richer and more powerful country than the Ashikaga shoguns had ever ruled.

Religion. Although the Muromachi period was doctrinally less creative than the preceding Kamakura era, it witnessed a vigorous diffusion and popularization of Buddhism. Shintō also experienced a revival, one that focused on the Ise Shrine and asserted the primacy of Shintō *kami* over the Buddhas. But there was also an interpenetration of Buddhism and Shintō at many temple complexes and shrines. By the end of the period, Christian missionaries from Portugal and Spain had established a presence in the country and had already converted many western daimyo and commoners. Until the proscription of the Christian missionary effort by Hideyoshi, it looked as if Christianity would come to rival Buddhism and Shintō for influence in Japan.

Within the Buddhist world the older monastic centers like Enryakuji, Kōyasan, Kōfukuji, and Negoro maintained their influence. They protected their religious, political, and land privileges through court connections and with powerful monastic armies. The power and influence of the older monasteries were not greatly reduced until Nobunaga attacked and burned Enryakuji in 1571 and Hideyoshi reduced the landholdings and military forces of Kōyasan and Negoro in the 1580s. Growth in Buddhism during this period came, however, not in the older schools, but in the diffusion of the so-called new schools of Buddhism that had been established by Hōnen, Shinran, Ippen, Nichiren, Eisai, and Dōgen in the late Heian and Kamakura periods. All the Pure Land lineages—the Pure Land, or Jōdo, teachings of Hōnen, the Timely, or Ji, school of Ippen, and the True Pure Land, or Jōdo Shin, tradition of Shinran—with their promise of universal salvation in Amida's Pure Land, flourished and found devotees and patrons at all levels of society. [*See* Pure Land *and* Amidism.]

The True Pure Land tradition established itself in this period as the most widely based school of Japanese Buddhism. Until the fifteenth century the many local groups, *montō*, of True Pure Land followers were divided by local rivalries and accusations of doctrinal unorthodoxy. They were united under the leadership of the powerful monastic center of Honganji by the priest Rennyo (1415–1499). [*See* Rennyo.] Because of their single-minded religious devotion and strong local bonds, these groups of

FIGURE 1. *Gilt Bronze Box.* This *kaitaibako* (a box for Buddhist ritual implements) of the fourteenth to fifteenth century is an example of the highly ornamented design applied to functional objects during the Muromachi period. 12.9 cm. × 35 cm.

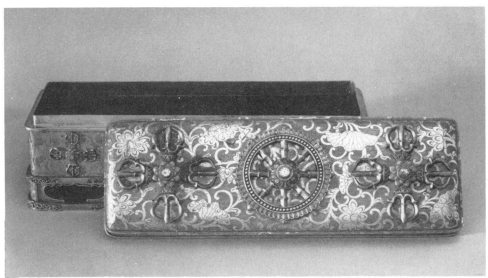

warriors and farmers were known as the *ikkōshū,* or "single-minded school." In many provinces the *montō* refused to acknowledge the authority of local *shugo,* and in Kaga in 1488 they actually took over the whole province in an *ikkō* uprising, or *ikkō ikki,* and controlled it for a century. These militant *ikkō* supporters were thorns in the flesh of daimyo struggling to win local territorial control. In order to gain control over central Japan, Nobunaga had to devote ten years of sporadic but bitter campaigning to the eradication of Jōdo Shin militancy.

Nichiren's teachings, based on the *Lotus Sutra,* also won a nationwide following during this period, especially among lesser samurai and farmers. One branch was particularly strong among townspeople in Kyoto. Like Jōdo Shin *montō,* Nichiren followers were militant in their determination to carry the teachings of the *Lotus Sutra* to nonbelievers. Nichiren's devotees were regarded with caution or suspicion by many daimyo. In Kyoto there was friction between Nichiren followers in the city and the monks of Enryakuji, who exercised influence on the economic and political life of the capital. In 1532, in Nichiren-school uprisings, known as *Hokke ikki,* followers seized control of parts of the city. In 1536 their temples were burned and they were expelled by soldier-monks from Enryakuji. This was not a permanent setback, however. They were permitted to return and continued to proselytize aggressively in Kyoto and the provinces. [*See* Enryakuji.]

Of the two principal branches of Zen, Rinzai attracted more adherents from the upper levels of warrior and court society. Under shogunal and daimyo patronage the *gozan* ("five mountains") system was extended by the building of Rinzai temples in every province. By 1600 there were several thousand provincial monasteries, large and small, in the *gozan* network. The non-*gozan* lineages of Daitokuji and Myōshinji found patrons among the merchants of Sakai and newly emerging *sengoku daimyō.* Dōgen's Sōtō Zen, made more accessible by the incorporation of popular prayer ceremonies, began to spread widely among farmers and local samurai families in northern and central Japan.

The period from 1540 to 1640 has been called the "Christian century" in Japan. Although Japan was still far from becoming a Christian country when the policy of persecution and eradication of Christianity was set in motion by Hideyoshi, the Jesuit mission effort had been impressive. Nobunaga used Christianity to offset the power of militant Buddhism. With his tacit acceptance, many daimyo, samurai, farmers, and townspeople accepted Christianity. Tens of thousands of converts were made. Churches, seminaries, and schools were built. A Japanese Christian priesthood was being trained, religious texts were printed and distributed, and Christian art was introduced. In the closing years of the Muromachi period, while Nobunaga was alive, the Christian mission effort looked promising. In 1573, when the fifteenth and last Ashikaga shogun was driven out of office, it must have seemed to many Japanese that Buddhism was on the defensive while Christianity was sweeping all before it.

Cultural Life. Muromachi culture is commonly divided into two major cultural epochs, Kitayama and Higashiyama. Kitayama ("northern mountains") refers to the early Muromachi cultural phase centering on Ashikaga Yoshmitsu and his Golden Pavilion in the northern hills of Kyoto. Higashiyama ("eastern mountains") refers to the eighth shogun Yoshimasa and his retreat, the Silver Pavilion, in the eastern hills. These terms are at once convenient and misleading. They are convenient because they point up the importance of shogunal patronage to Zen and the arts. They are misleading because they downplay the importance of the cultural contribution of other social groups as well as the continuum and diversity of Muromachi culture. And to these two major divisions we can add at least two more: Sengoku and Nanban culture. The warfare of the Sengoku period did not quench cultural activity. Rather it tempered it into new forms. And the "southern barbarians," *nanbanjin,* who came to Japan in the sixteenth century, brought with them cultural forms new and intriguing to the Japanese.

The contributions made to Japanese culture during the Muromachi period were rich and complex. The period witnessed the development of linked verse, *renga,* the maturation of the *nō* and *kyōgen* dramatic forms, and the elaboration of the tea ceremony, *cha no yu,* from a simple Zen monastic custom into a complex and refined aesthetic experience. Muromachi culture was also heavily influenced by Zen aesthetics in the arts of ink painting, which was brought to a high level of perfection by Sesshū Tōyō and the early masters of the Kanō school, and domestic architecture and garden design. In the later decades of the Muromachi period the monochromatic Zen-inspired artistic styles began to give way to a more grandiose, gilded style that derived its energy from the conquests of powerful daimyo and was displayed in their new castles.

Whereas the culture of the Nara and Heian periods had been largely shaped by emperors, courtiers, and monks, and that of the Kamakura period by the interaction between an old nobility and a new warrior elite, the culture of the Muromachi period drew on the intelligence, vision, experience, and patronage of all sectors of society. At the highest level, the decision to locate the Muromachi *bakufu* in Kyoto brought shoguns and *shugo*, many of whom were required to spend long periods of attendance in the capital, into close contact with the old court nobility. In a process that had already begun in the Kamakura period, warriors came to share courtly interests in the civilian arts, *bun*, including classical literature and the study of courtly etiquette. Courtiers and warriors alike consorted with Zen monks, especially the learned priests of the *gozan* monasteries, and from them acquired a deeper appreciation of all the Chinese cultural interests conveyed to Japan through Zen monastic channels: Buddhist and Confucian thought, Chinese poetry, ink painting, garden design, the preparation of tea, domestic architecture, and the arts of flower arranging and interior design.

Townspeople of Kyoto, Hakata and Sakai, some of them lowly actors, wandering jongleurs, and "riverbank dwellers," *kawaramono*, became active participants in urban cultural activities. Some men of modest social origins, many of them taking the Pure Land title *ami* as part of their names, rose to become cultural advisors, *dōbōshū*, to shoguns and daimyo. Among the most influential of these *dōbōshū* were Nōami, in painting and *renga*, Kan'ami and Zeami, for *nō*, and Zen'ami, for garden design. [*See* Zeami.] Wealthy townsmen of Kyoto and Sakai consorted with Zen monks like Ikkyū Sōjun and developed a passion for the cult of tea. Out of this milieu came the great tea masters of the age who were to set their mark on the tea ceremony, especially Murata Jukō, Takeno Jōō, and Sen no Rikyū, who brought to perfection the restrained beauty of tea in the *wabicha* style. [*See* Sen no Rikyū.] For the early part of the period cultural life tended to focus on Kyoto. Later, with the growth of Sakai, Hakata, Yamaguchi, and other "little Kyotos," helped by the dispersion of nobles and monks that accompanied the Ōnin war, cultural interaction reached across provincial and regional boundaries. The arrival of Christian missionaries and traders put Japan in direct contact with cultural influences from Southeast Asia and Western Europe.

Martin Collcutt, *Five Mountains: The Rinzai Zen Monastic Institution in Medieval Japan* (1981). Michael Cooper, ed., *They Came to Japan: An Anthology of European Reports from Japan, 1543–1640*. George Elison and Bardwell L. Smith, eds., *Warriors, Artists, and Commoners: Japan in the Sixteenth Century* (1981). John W. Hall and Toyoda Takeshi, eds., *Japan in the Muromachi Age* (1977). John W. Hall, Nagahara Keiji, and Kozo Yamamura, eds., *Japan Before Tokugawa: Political Consolidation and Economic Growth, 1500–1650* (1981). H. Paul Varley, *The Onin War* (1967) and *Imperial Restoration in Medieval Japan (1971)*.   MARTIN COLLCUTT

MURSHIDABAD, city on the Bhagirathi River in West Bengal. Murshidabad was a significant mercantile town when Murshid Quli Khan established the capital of Bengal there in 1704. Under him and the subsequent nawabs of Murshidabad, it became Bengal's preeminent cultural and political center until 1772. In 1757 the British under Robert Clive defeated Nawab Siraj ud-Daulah at the Battle of Plassey, effectively eclipsing the power of Murshidabad and paving the way for British control of Bengal and ultimately of India. Numerous monuments built by the nawabs and high-ranking nobles remain as a testimony to Murshidabad's former status.

[*See also* Murshid Quli Khan; Bengal; Clive, Sir Robert; Siraj ud-Daulah; *and* Plassey, Battle of.]

P. C. Mohsin, *Musnud of Murshidabad* (1905). Khan Mohammad Mohsin, *A Bengal District in Transition: Murshidabad, 1765–1793* (1973).

CATHERINE B. ASHER

MURSHID QULI KHAN (d. 1727), title of Muhammad Hadi, perhaps born a brahman, who was purchased and adopted by Haji Shafi Isfahani, a successful *diwan* (revenue administrator) in India from 1668 to 1690. The son began service under the *diwan* of Berar. The Mughal emperor Aurangzeb noticed his ability, leading to his appointment as *diwan* of Bengal in 1700; Orissa and Bihar were added to his domain in 1703 and 1704. Succession politics caused his transfer to the Deccan in 1708, but he returned home in 1710 and secured quasi-independent status in 1717; when he died, he bequeathed Bengal to his son-in-law, Shuja ud-Din Muhammad Khan. His exceptional administrative abilities made Bengal orderly and yielded high revenues, but English economic dominance beginning in his rule led to their political dominance as well.

[*See also* Diwani *and* Bengal.]

Abdul Karim, *Murshid Quli Khan and His Times* (1963). Jadunath Sarkar, *The History of Bengal: Muslim Period, 1200–1757* (reprint, 1973).   FRITZ LEHMANN

MUSIC

MUSIC IN CHINA

The earliest existing writings on Chinese music can be found in passages in the classics. Most of the standard histories contain an essay on music, and the musical pitches are discussed in some of the essays on the calendar. Such works usually present the official views on music and record the actual musical happenings at the imperial court. Other historical compilations and encyclopedias from various periods also have entries on music. Beginning in the Song period (960–1279), special treatises on music and discussions on music in individual literary works became more numerous. Archaeological finds of elaborate musical artifacts show the importance of music in rituals and state functions in even more ancient times.

Philosophy and History. Confucian orthodoxy recognizes the power of music and its importance in education. The music at the Confucian temple not only serves to accompany the ceremonies but also is supposed to demonstrate Confucian principles such as moderation. Other pre-Qin philosophical schools held different views on music; for example, the Daoists warned against anything that affected the senses; the Mohists considered musical activities wasteful. Occasionally there were also original thinkers such as Xi Kang (third century CE), who argued that music intrinsically has no emotional substance. During the Tang dynasty imported and entertainment music tended to displace Confucian music in the court, but the orthodox musical philosophy has nevertheless remained essentially Confucian throughout Chinese history.

There were many lively debates about how the proper Confucian ceremonial music was to be put into practice. Pitch measurement was a frequent topic because it was related to various cosmological considerations and also because it relates to the very practical matter of establishing standards of measurement in general.

Chinese musical historians usually draw a major dividing line at the end of the Tang dynasty (618–907). During the preceding millennium foreign influences were important, while music development following the Tang was relatively more independent. The introduction of Central Asian music into China along with Buddhism is well documented. There are references to new tunes, dances, instruments, foreign musicians, and systems of modes, all of which left a lasting impact upon Chinese music.

The second period was a time of consolidation of many of these foreign musical elements, which by the twelfth century had evolved into a coherent musical system, although the court music theorists claimed to be restoring Confucian musical ideals. Treatises from the Song period and following have offered more precise information on the musical systems, the instruments, and the forms of notation. Notable survivals include a few songs composed by the poet Jiang Kui (thirteenth century) and a set of Confucian ceremonial songs preserved in notation by the philosopher Zhu Xi (1130–1200), which became the model for ceremonial songs in later dynasties. Writings by the Song musical theorists became the guidelines for later theorists.

Ming and Qing dynasty theoretical treaties on music are abundant. Zhu Zaiyu of the late sixteenth century devised the mathematical method of creating a scale of twelve evenly divided tones within the octave, completing a search that had begun much earlier (by Jing Fang, first century BCE) for a symmetrical system that would be usable for cosmological purposes.

Instrumental Music. Iconographic evidence shows that in addition to Confucian ceremonial orchestras there were elaborate instrumental ensembles for court entertainments. In the Han dynasty there were military bands and indoor ensemble groups. In the Tang period the royal court kept orchestras of musicians of nine or ten different nationalities. Elaborate Yuan, Ming, and Qing court orchestras are described in detail. In all these orchestras the prominence of foreign instruments is notable.

In modern times ensemble groups are either private or are supported by various public institutions. The typical instruments contained in an ensemble differ from region to region. Basically there are two types: the gentler orchestra consisting mainly of stringed instruments and flutes (the Silk and Bamboo ensembles), and the more exciting orchestra containing the louder wind instruments such as the double-reed *suona* and various kinds of gongs, cymbals, woodblocks, and other percussion instruments (the Wind and Percussion ensemble). Under the influence of the Western orchestra, Chinese ensemble groups are undergoing many changes today.

Music notated for individual instruments such as the *pipa* (four-stringed lute) or the *zheng* (zither with movable bridges) is modest and for the most part relatively recent, although these instruments are of considerable antiquity. One isolated case is the set of twenty-five pieces for the *pipa* found in the Dunhuang caves, dated not later than the tenth century

FIGURE 1. *Moon Lutes.* Left: Siamese *sung*; length 73.7 cm., diameter (of face) 34.3 cm. Right: Chinese *yueqin* (no dimensions).

CE. They are written in a system of notation that is practically identical with that for the *biwa* in Japanese court music today.

The instrument that has commanded the most attention by Chinese writers is the seven-stringed zither, the *qin*. Its long history (with earliest mention in the *Book of Odes,* and earliest notated piece from the sixth century) and association with the literati have given it a special status in society. From a musical standpoint it is important because it has an enormous repertoire, containing works of great beauty and intricate structure. Up to the present day the playing of the *qin* has been transmitted through the oral tradition. Yet from the fifteenth century on a great number of *qin* pieces have been kept in notation. *Qin* notation is a tablature that provides detailed indication of the technique of finger movement rather than pitch. From these instruction books as well as from the actual performances one can see that the choreography of hand movements must have been an important factor in the creation of a piece.

Narrative and Dramatic Music. Evidence of musical narrative performances can be found among Han-dynasty tomb figures. The earliest surviving written document of the *shuochang* narrative form, that is, alternating song and speech, is in the *bianwen* texts of the tenth century. Chinese scholars believe them to be Buddhist adaptations of some kind of Chinese indigenous narrative forms, used to spread their own teachings. In the twelfth and thirteenth centuries the narrative art reached a sophisticated stage in the form of *zhu gong diao* (literally, a "medley of different modes"), in which the singing portions can make use of tunes from a variety of modes.

The principle of tune types involves the use of an existing stock of tunes again and again for different texts within a genre. Each tune can undergo various small changes when adjusted to words, while still maintaining its identity. Each narrative genre has its own repertory of tunes from which a selection is made to fit a specific story. The music of the narrative art is preserved only through oral tradition. With more than two hundred narrative genres from various regions, it is one of the richest areas in the Chinese music field today.

All traditional Chinese dramatic art is musical. The earliest surviving documents are texts written by literary men of the fourteenth century, preserved for their literary merits. No music was written down with these early texts, but the arias have tune titles with modal designations. Along with the development of the literary structure of the Yuan drama came a systematized convention of grouping tunes of the same mode together, and of using only tunes from one mode in each of the four standard acts of a play.

The earliest dramatic music existing in notation is the mid-eighteenth-century anthology of arias, *Jiugong dacheng,* from numerous operas, categorically arranged by modal types. It is written in pitch notation with fairly specific time indications. It is believed that some of the sources for this collection could date as far back as the Yuan dynasty. From the late eighteenth century on, anthologies of dramatic arias also appear, with whole acts intact. The richest collection of dramatic music surviving today is that for the *Kunqu,* a highly sophisticated form that flourished from the middle of the sixteenth century to the nineteenth century and is still performed today among small groups of connoisseurs. Musically all these dramatic forms are based upon the principle of the use of tune types. One of the very few individuals known for creating new tunes was Wei Liangfu (sixteenth century), who played a major role in developing the *Kunqu.*

During the latter part of the eighteenth century, the regional operas from Anhui and Hubei, which were popular in Beijing, gradually evolved into what is later known as the Beijing (Peking) Opera. Unlike its earlier contemporary *Kunqu,* which is characterized by its abundant lyrical arias, Beijing Opera uses tunes with sharp contrasts in rhythm and tempo, which, although far fewer in number, lend themselves more effectively to dramatization. The Beijing Opera also makes much use of percussion instruments, adding another dimension to the musical setting of drama with their hundreds of rhythm patterns. While the prestige of royal support greatly facilitated the development of Beijing Opera, its intrinsic qualities also made it a successful dramatic form. Thus, although the Beijing Opera originated from regional operas, it has become in turn a model for regional operas to emulate. Nevertheless some of the regional operas, besides having different sets of tune types, still have their own outstanding features; the Shantou (Swatow) operas are rich in the use of dances, and the Sichuan operas, in the use of backstage choral singing.

Music in the Modern Chinese Context. The most obvious example of social change influencing the state of music in China is the disappearance of work songs (sung by the boatmen, construction workers, pole carriers, vendors), which were once so prevalent. Today one comes across such music only very occasionally. Poetry chanting now and then can still be done by older scholars who have had a traditional education. Once in a while in a public park in the city of Kunming in southwestern China, or in a small town in Taiwan, one still finds old people sitting around at sundown, spontaneously singing traditional songs for their own entertainment. Professional narrative singers are now more often heard in theaters, or on radio and television, than in teahouses. In Hong Kong, Taiwan, Bangkok, and among Chinese communities in the US, besides regular commercial opera performances, one still can see performances offered in celebration of the birthday of certain deities. The forming of Beijing Opera and *Kunqu* clubs is still one of the most common amateur musical activities in Chinese communities all over the world. Confucian ceremonial music is annually performed in Taiwan. Buddhist music can still be heard in monasteries in Taiwan and in Hong Kong.

In the field of music theory, there are more objective historians than innovative theorists today. Yet on the issue of musical values, at least in official statements, the emphasis on the didactic function of music in present-day China does not seem to be very far from the Confucian ideas.

Significant amounts of Western music began to be introduced into China in the late nineteenth century through German-trained military bands, the churches, and the missionary schools. Western mu-

FIGURE 2. *Tibetan Trumpets.* Copper, inlaid with precious stones, eighteenth century.

sic also was imported through Japan, when modern-style schools modeled after Japanese examples were established. In the early decades of the twentieth century, the music first taught at schools was mostly the same kind of Western school music found in Japan. To this day, traditional Chinese music is rarely taught in schools as a part of general education.

Composing original works rather than re-creating from a stock of preexisting tunes is, of course, a very different process. Among the earlier generations of modern-style composers were Zhao Yuanren, Xiao Youmei, and Li Weining, who were all trained abroad and wrote essentially in the style of the Common Practice period. To these people, adopting the Western tonal system was an intellectual adventure as well as an artistic challenge. There were various experiments in adjusting Western harmony to Chinese melodies; works by Huang Zi and Liu Xuean are well-known early examples. Ma Sicong, who has written many instrumental pieces, has tried unconventional harmony for some folk songs with special modal characteristics. He Luding and Xian Xinghai are known for their melodies in Chinese folk song style. Among composers in recent times who have tried newer tonal experiments are Hsu Tsang-hui and Wen Long-shin in Taiwan, Doming Lam in Hong Kong, and Chou Wen-chung in the US.

Representing another trend in musical creation in modern China are works by Liu Tianhua, who had remained much closer to the traditional Chinese music style, although his compositions are completely original creations. His few works for the two-stringed fiddle (erhu) and the pipa have been influential enough to raise the social status of these instruments in Chinese society.

More recently there have been experiments in styles not obviously borrowed directly from the West, such as the sporadic two-part singing using open fifths, fourths, and octaves by a pair of young performers of the Beijing Drum Song, the responsorial chorus in a reformed Beijing Opera, or the use of an ostinato figure in the cello accompaniment for the dance narrative the Twirling Duet, which originated from the seasonal farmers' dances of northeastern China. The details could be inspired by contact with other regional Chinese or foreign arts, but the methods of using them are original.

K. J. DeWoskin, *A Song for One or Two: Music and the Concept of Art in Early China*, Michigan Papers no. 42 (1982). William Dolby, *A History of Chinese Drama* (1976). R. H. van Gulik, *The Lore of the Chinese Lute* (1940; reprint, 1969). Frederic Lieberman, *Chinese Music: An Annotated Bibliography* (1970). Colin Mackerras, *The Performing Arts in Contemporary China* (1981). Rulan C. Pian, *Song Dynasty Musical Sources and Their Interpretation* (1967). L. E. R. Picken, "The Music of Far Eastern Asia: China," in *The New Oxford History of Music*, vol. 1 (1957), pp. 83–134. A. C. Scott, *The Classical Theatre of China* (1957). Bell Yung, "Creative Process in Cantonese Opera," *Ethnomusicology* 27.1–3 (1983). See also articles on "China" in *Harvard Dictionary of Music* (1969) and *The New Grove Dictionary of Music and Musicians* (1980).   RULAN CHAO PIAN

MUSIC IN SOUTH ASIA

South Asians place high value on their long and culturally significant musical tradition. As an element of social life in South Asian history, music has usually been seen as associated with particular groups or with individuals whose group identity is fairly clear—from the gods who created it, to the priests who utilized it, the pandits who theorized about it, the musicians or communities who have made it, and the patrons who have fostered it. Furthermore, music in South Asia has always been one element in a cultural "performance" complex, whether part of a sacred ritual, a drama, a rite of passage, a gathering of musically educated elite patrons or musicians, a village festival, or some other type of activity. Also of primary importance has been the association of music with religious expression, whether as part of group worship or as expression of individual devotion. Probably as a result of this association, vocal music of various sorts has been predominant among types of music in South Asia.

The musical history of South Asia encompasses traditions of two primary groups: peoples of Dravidian culture and those of Indo-European culture. While sources for Dravidian musical history are primarily literary, the first major source for Indo-European music history is musical—Vedic chant, the oldest continually practiced body of ritual music to have been documented. Vedic chant is testimony to the fact that an oral tradition can be well preserved if practitioners intend to preserve it. [*See also* Vedas.] Beyond the Vedic period South Asian music history becomes distinguishable by more groups: first, socioreligious groups—primarily Buddhist, Hindu (and, in turn, various Hindu groups), and relatively late in South Asian history, Muslim. In addition, music history has been viewed as the traditions of sociocultural (and political) groups: folk, tribal, and elite. From the perspective of the musical traditions of cohesive groups and in accordance with the assumption of musical continuity, scholars have suggested links to the past in folk traditions—in the musical element of melodic contour, for example, linking melodies of repertoires of traditional folk song to the distinctive melodic contours of Vedic chant. A link with performance practice of more recent times is suggested, for example, in the use of a continuous melodic drone in the sacred chant tradition of a tribal group. Sometime in fairly recent history the primary South Asian performance ensemble of a melody instrument—often the voice—and a rhythm instrument was incremented by a drone instrument.

In sociopolitical terms the elite in South Asia has changed over time, but the valuing of music and the cultivation of musical knowledge have characterized the lifestyle of all elite groups. In strictly musical terms the elite in South Asian culture have been persons learned in *shastriya sangit*, that is, the extensively cultivated theory and practice of art music,

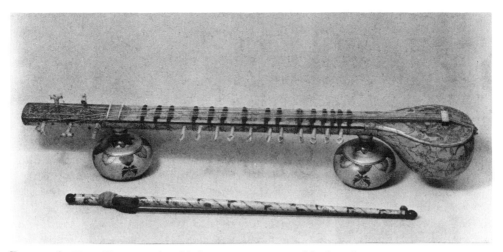

FIGURE 1. *Vina.* Two gourds added as resonates, movable threads.

whether in the South Indian (Karnatak) or the North Indian (Hindustani) tradition. To belong to this group a musician must demonstrate knowledge of the complex theoretical system of melodic modes *(raga)* and metric cycles *(tala)* of the art music traditions and, ideally, be familiar with treatises that expound the theory. Within the musical elite, relative status is also measured by the genre one performs—the highest status in the Karnatak tradition, for example, is given to singers of the demanding improvisational genre *ragam-tanam-pallavi;* in the Hindustani tradition it is given to singers of the equally demanding genre *alap-dhrupad,* which combines improvisation and traditional song.

Within each sociopolitical group musicians are likely to be organized into further groupings by some type of specialization. In folk music traditions, for example, specialists in drumming are particularly distinguished (often they belong to a particular caste), or a particular group enjoys hereditary status as entertainers in a traditional patronage situation, such as the Manganiyar in Rajasthan. In the elite music sphere groups such as the *sampradayas* of South India or the *gharanas* of North India cultivate not only certain genres of music, but particular repertoire and performance style as well. Such groups contribute to the continuity of tradition and rich diversity in the music of South Asia.

[*See also* Indo-Aryan Languages and Literatures *and* Dravidian Languages and Literatures.]

Alain Danielou, *Northern Indian Music,* 2 vols. (1949–1954). B. C. Deva, *Indian Music* (1974). Daniel Neuman, *The Life of Music in North India: The Organization of an Artistic Tradition* (1980). P. Sambamoorthy, *South Indian Music,* 6 vols. (1960–1969). Bonnie C. Wade, *Music In India: The Classical Traditions* (1979).

BONNIE C. WADE

MUSIC IN SOUTHEAST ASIA

Indigenous invention, local variation, elaboration of detail, borrowing from outside the region, and synthesis of unique forms are constant themes throughout the history of all major musical cultures in Southeast Asia. There is little evidence of the nature of the forms and functions of musical activities before the ninth century. Archaeological evidence of musical activities in the pre-, proto-, and early historical periods is scant, and that which exists can be interpreted effectively only in the light of ethnological, archaeological, and written evidence from the last thousand years.

Two kinds of prehistoric archaeological finds—Neolithic lithophones from Annam and bronze drums found principally in the highlands of the mainland and in southern Indonesia and dating from as early as the fifth century BCE—point to several strands of continuity from early times to the present. The lithophones are tuned in both five-tone anhemitonic and seven-tone tunings and demonstrate the early importance of percussion on instruments consisting of rows of keys or slabs. Bronze drums show the early significance of percussion on gong-chime instruments and present continuities of shape with the large gongs of Southeast Asian ensembles from the thirteenth to the twentieth century. Reliefs on a few bronze drums dating from the first centuries CE depict musicians playing rudimentary free-reed mouth organs, instruments still found today in various forms among inland peoples of the mainland. One form, the *kaen*, is regarded as a signal characteristic of Lao ethnic identity.

From the ninth century onward, there are more historical records and greater archaeological evidence of musical activities in some Southeast Asian societies. Over one hundred bas-reliefs on Borobudur (eighth–ninth century CE), for example, portray musicians singing and playing on more than forty different wind, string, and percussion instruments in royal, religious, and educational contexts. Drums are the most prevalent type of instrument, and no gongs or gamelan-like ensembles are depicted. Reliefs on Angkor buildings (eleventh–fourteenth century) feature gongs and gong-chime instruments several times, though the total number of different instruments depicted is considerably less than on Borobudur. Contexts for performances are mostly martial processions, battles, and royal audiences. By the fourteenth century, several new types of string and percussion instruments, including gongs and gong-chimes, appear in Javanese bas-reliefs, while many earlier types of strings, winds, and drums disappear or decline in frequency of depiction. In general, instruments that are more readily traceable to Indian models decline, while those with links to present-day instruments increase. Attempts, sometimes convincing, have been made to correlate musical components in Javanese bas-reliefs and literary references from ninth- to fourteenth-century sources. These attempts must deal with the changes in language and contexts for ensembles or instruments that occurred throughout the centuries, as well as with the multiple names used for instruments. From the fifteenth century onward, literary references increase and are more easily connected to recent musical references, while iconographic evidence declines.

Because Southeast Asian musical life during this period was so rich and varied, it is counterproductive to make generalizations about it. Furthermore, evidence from this period argues for a much richer and variegated musical life in earlier periods than the materials from those periods might allow. In pre-twentieth-century Southeast Asia, music permeated social and cultural functions, from the most mundane and simple (selling goods, soothing children, writing letters) to the most complex and special (installing kings, conducting funerals, evoking histories). Since the beginning of the twentieth century in most areas, pressures of expanding population, increasing interactions of cultures and societies, cultural and social dislocation and change caused by wars and migrations, and radical changes in communication, agriculture, and manufacturing have been paralleled by the growth of musical genres that show extensive influence from Western and westernized musical systems. For most modern nations of Southeast Asia, these are the most conspicuous types of music. Yet most of these types differ from nation to nation or, within one nation, from region to region.

M. Hood, "Southeast Asia," in *New Grove Dictionary of Music and Musicians* (1975). J. Kunst, *Hindu-Javanese Musical Instruments* (1968). O. W. Wolters, *History, Culture, and Region in Southeast Asian Perspectives* (1982).

MARTIN HATCH

FIGURE 1. *Bonang Barung Slendro*. Java, mid-twentieth century; wood, metal. One of the instruments that forms a gamelan ensemble.

MUSIC IN IRAN, AFGHANISTAN, AND CENTRAL ASIA

Iran, Afghanistan, and Central Asia span the distance, musically as well as geographically, from the Near East to India. Art music throughout the region has been modeled on Persian court traditions. From the middle of the nineteenth century, the music of the Afghan court was also strongly influenced (at least until 1978) by North India and Pakistan. Although the folk music of the various Iranian- and Turkic-speaking peoples has many features in common, each ethnic group has its own distinct style.

The practice of music is generally held in low regard in West and Central Asia. Professional musicians, especially members of hereditary families of entertainers, are often social outcasts. The disdain for music is generally attributed to Muslim teachings, but it probably stems more directly from the musicians' association with prostitution and other impure activities. At the same time, music is considered indispensable for certain social rites, such as weddings, and is greatly appreciated as entertainment in teahouses and on the radio.

Instruments. The human voice is the most favored vehicle for musical expression. Nevertheless, the region has produced a rich variety of musical instruments, many of which have spread westward to Europe and eastward to China and Japan. Long-necked, fretted lutes constitute the most impressive category; lutes appear in a bewildering variety of shapes and names, from the diminutive Persian *sehtar* to the Turkic *saz* and the Afghan *rabab*. Other stringed instruments include bowed fiddles *(kemanche, ghichak)* and a hammer dulcimer *(santur)*. The principal wind instruments are the end-blown reed flute *(nai, nar, nal)*, considered in most areas

to be suitable only for shepherds, and a shawm *(zurna, sorna)*, played exclusively by low-status professionals. The *zurna* is nearly always accompanied by a double-headed cylindrical drum *(tabl, dohol)*. Other drums include a large, round frame-drum *(doira, def)*, and a single-headed, goblet-shaped drum *(dombak, zarb, zirbaghali)*. The North Indian *tabla* pair is sometimes used in Afghanistan. Western instruments have been adopted in this century, particularly for use in military bands and commercial orchestras. The violin, more than any other Western instrument, has also found a place in traditional ensembles.

Mode and Melody. Folk performers generally rely on a small repertoire of melody types that can accommodate a variety of poetic texts. In art music, melodies are based on modal scales *(maqam, naghma)*, usually of five to seven tones, drawn from a background scale estimated by various theorists to include from seventeen to twenty-six tones. There is thus a greater variety of scales and more subtlety of intonation than in the Western system of twelve equal semitones. A *maqam* is more than a simple scale, however; it is a complex set of rules for composition and improvisation. The opening and final notes of a composition, as well as other prominent notes, are determined by the mode. The *maqam* also governs overall melodic flow, the choice of specific characteristic phrases, and modulation to other, related modes.

All members of an ensemble play the same basic melody, but each musician varies and ornaments it according to his own taste and the technical possibilities of his instrument. The main melody may be supported by a drone, but, in general, emphasis falls on the linear development of melody rather than on the simultaneous sounding of different pitches found in Western harmony. In rare instances, most notably the lute music of the Turkmens and the Kazakhs, a moving drone produces a polyphonic effect.

Rhythm. Fixed meters have regularly recurring patterns of strong and weak beats that may be varied or embellished slightly with each repetition of the cycle. Meters are frequently additive or asymmetrical, as in the Turkic *aksak* ("limping") rhythms. Unmeasured passages, where no regular metrical pattern can be perceived, appear as preludes or interludes between pieces, often as vehicles for vocal or instrumental improvisation.

Forms. In Iran and Central Asia, performances of art music have traditionally been organized in suite form. Successive pieces are set to a roughly predetermined sequence of different metrical structures,

FIGURE 1. *Naggara (Twin Drum)*. Pottery and leather, shown with wooden drumsticks.

which often alternate between free and fixed rhythm. The suite as a whole is unified by the use of a single melodic mode or a series of closely related modes.

Folk repertoires include a wide variety of forms, from work songs to epics, such as the tale of the Turkic hero Kuroghlu, to *ta'ziya*, Persian musical dramas reenacting the martyrdom of Shi'ite imams. Both lyric and narrative songs make frequent use of the quatrain form (*dubeiti, charbaiti, ruba'i*).

N. Chadwick and V. Zhirmunsky, *Oral Epics of Central Asia* (1969). Hiromi Lorraine Sakata, *Music in the Mind: The Concepts of Music and Musician in Afghanistan* (1983). Mark Slobin, *Music in the Culture of Northern Afghanistan* (1976). Owen Wright, *The Modal System of Arab and Persian Music: A.D. 1250–1400* (1978). Ella Zonis, *Classical Persian Music: An Introduction* (1973).

PHILIP D. SCHUYLER

MUSLIM LEAGUE. *See* All-India Muslim League.

MUSLIMS IN SRI LANKA. *Moor* is the name given to the Muslims of Sri Lanka who settled there prior to the British conquest of the island in 1795. As with the Muslims of the Philippines, known as Moros, the name is one that has been given to the Islamic population by Europeans; in both cases the people identify themselves as Muslims rather than Moors or Moros. They number slightly more than one million, and their historical background and social characteristics closely resemble those of the Muslims of peninsular India—the Mappilas of Kerala and the Labbais of Tamil Nadu. That is, Sri Lankan Muslims evolved from the commercial settlements of the Arab Muslim traders who first arrived in Sri Lanka in the late seventh or the early eighth century CE. Some of these Muslims probably came directly from Arabia while others arrived via Kerala, but the majority of the later settlers must have come from Tamil Nadu, as Tamil is the major language among them. The majority of Muslims in Sri Lanka still make their living as merchants, although there is a community of Muslim agriculturalists in eastern Sri Lanka.

[*See also* Mappilas *and* Moro.]

Mohamed Mauroof, "Aspects of Religion, Economy and Society Among the Muslims of Ceylon," *Contributions to Indian Sociology* 6 (1972): 66–83, and "Muslims in Sri Lanka: Historical, Demographic and Political Aspects," *Journal of the Institute of Muslim Minority Affairs* 1 (1980): 183–193.

STEPHEN FREDERIC DALE

MUSSO (1897–1948), Indonesian communist leader and an architect of the Indonesian Communist Party (PKI) uprisings of 1926–1927. Exiled to Moscow after the uprisings, he secretly visited Indonesia in 1935–1936 to establish the so-called Illegal PKI but returned to lead the Party only in August 1948, publicly announcing his intention to form a communist government. In his *New Road for the Indonesian Republic* (1948) he advocated a fusion of all working-class parties; a sharpening of class struggle, especially the elimination of feudalism; and closer alignment with the Soviet Union. He took part in the Madiun Uprising in late 1948 and was killed in battle.

[*See also* Madiun *and* Partai Komunis Indonesia.]

Ruth McVey, *The Soviet View of the Indonesian Revolution* (1957) and *The Rise of Indonesian Communism* (1965).

ROBERT B. CRIBB

MU'TAZILI, a theological school in Islam known primarily for the creation of a dogmatic system in which speculative reason played a crucial role. Although its roots can be traced back to the Umayyad period, it was not until the early ninth century that Mu'tazilis, under the influence of Hellenistic thought, came to form an organized school with a more or less coherent body of doctrine. In their intellectual endeavors, Mu'tazilis were motivated by a twofold concern: (1) the defense of Islam against a plethora of anti-Islamic tendencies current in the early Abbasid empire, and (2) the elaboration of the principal doctrines of Islam into a system of thought compatible with reason.

In its classical form as expounded by such leading Mu'tazilis as Abu al-Hudhail (d. about 850), Nazzam (d. about 845), and Bishr ibn al-Mu'tamir (d. 826), Mu'tazili thought came to be organized around five major theses. They are (1) that God is one and transcendent, (2) that his actions are compatible with the requirements of justice as established by reason, (3) that God will reward those who do good and punish those who do evil, (4) that Muslims who commit a grave sin are neither believers nor unbelievers but occupy an intermediate state, and (5) that it is incumbent on believers to encourage good and combat evil. Under the rubric of the first thesis, Mu'tazilis declared the Qur'an to be created in time, since to affirm otherwise would be tantamount to positing a quality in God distinct from his essence and thus to deny his unity.

Although Mu'tazili doctrine was adopted as the official dogma of the Abbasid empire by the caliph al-Ma'mun in 827, the traditionalists of Baghdad mounted a powerful opposition to it, and in 848 al-Mutawakkil was forced to withdraw state support for the school. With that Mu'tazili fortunes declined steadily during the century that followed. Under the Buyids (945–1055), the school did regain some of its lost influence, but its doctrine never again enjoyed the status of orthodoxy except in the Zaidi state of Yemen.

During the heyday of its influence, the Mu'tazili school established itself in many of the great centers of the Muslim world from Spain to Transoxiana. In general it found its greatest acceptance in those lands where Hanafi law prevailed.

William Montgomery Watt, *The Formative Period of Islamic Thought* (1973), pp. 209–250.

MERLIN SWARTZ

MUTINY, INDIAN.

MUTINY, INDIAN. The most serious challenge to British rule in India in the nineteenth century came in 1857, when mutinies among the Indian soldiers of the East India Company (which was still the nominal ruler, not the British government itself) were followed by uprisings among the civilian population in a number of important areas.

At the beginning of the year there were indications that the soldiers in the Bengal army, the most important of the three armies of the East India Company, were restless and dissatisfied. A rumor that the bullets being issued to the soldiers were greased with the fat of cows and pigs was one of the many signs of danger. But although there had been a number of cases of soldiers disobeying orders, the actual outbreak of violence came on 10 May, when the Indian soldiers of the regiments stationed at Meerut killed their British officers and marched to Delhi, thirty miles away. The insurgents captured the city without much difficulty and proclaimed the Mughal emperor, a helpless elderly man of eighty-two, as their leader. After a lull of three weeks there were new outbreaks among the civilian population in the Ganges Plain, especially in the former kingdom of Oudh (Awadh), and in central India. Here the leadership came from members of the old ruling classes, who had recently been dispossessed by the British. The battles evoked enormous interest in England, and there were many stories of savage attacks on British women and children, which inflamed opinion against the Indians.

Delhi was recaptured by the British in September after fierce fighting, and the two great cities of Lucknow and Kanpur in Uttar Pradesh were recovered six months later. The last remaining pockets of resistance in central India were overcome in July 1858, and by the end of the year British control had been completely restored, with the leaders of the uprising either killed in battle or put to death after summary trials. The fact that the areas that had been under British rule for nearly a century—Bengal, Bombay, and Madras—remained quiet suggests that the outbreaks were attempts by members of the old order to regain their power. Some historians have seen the uprisings as a reaction to the social changes introduced by the British, while others have argued that it was largely a Muslim-led revolt, but there is little evidence for either of these views.

The successful suppression of the uprisings probably convinced many Indians of the invincibility of the British, and there were few attempts in subsequent years to use violence to overthrow them. On the British side, there was undoubtedly an increase of racist feeling toward Indians. A favorite theme was to contrast the valor and heroism of the British with the barbarism of the Indians, with warnings to be on guard against trusting them. In the twentieth century, with the rise of nationalism, many Indians looked back at the events of 1857 as a war for Indian independence that was lost because of disunity among the people of India themselves.

[See also East India Company; Awadh; and Sepoy.]

Ainslie T. Embree, ed., *India in 1857* (1963). R. C. Majumdar, *The Sepoy Mutiny and the Revolt of 1857* (1957). S. N. Sen, *Eighteen Fifty-Seven* (1957). E. J. Thompson, *The Other Side of the Medal* (1925).

AINSLIE T. EMBREE

MUTSUHITO

MUTSUHITO (1852–1912), emperor of Japan from 1868 to 1912 under the era name *Meiji* ("enlightened rule"). It was during the Meiji period that Japan ended its policy of seclusion and embarked on a course of rapid modernization.

A strong-willed and able-bodied boy, Mutsuhito enjoyed Japanese wrestling and horseback riding. As a youth he is alleged to have been politically apathetic, but in the 1870s those close to the throne began a sterner education appropriate to his central position in a nation undergoing immense changes. Mutsuhito was particularly conscientious about military matters, attending military sessions day and night during the Sino-Japanese War of 1894 to 1895 and the Russo-Japanese War of 1904 to 1905. The work and anxiety during the latter aged him and damaged his health.

Although Mutsuhito was not fond of Western innovations, he apparently recognized some as inevitable, desirable, or both. He supported the imperial edict of 1875 promising constitutional government. He and the court adopted Western styles and diplomatic practices suitable to Japan's international aspirations. Breaking the centuries-old isolation of the emperor and imperial institution, he toured his country widely and met extensively with foreign and Japanese leaders and dignitaries.

Given the sanctity surrounding the throne, particularly in the latter half of his reign, Mutsuhito's personal influence in government is difficult to assess. Having been "restored" to direct imperial rule in 1868, his role as Japan's central political authority was dependent on those who had restored him. He was apparently distressed about going to war with China in 1894 and was most reluctant to engage tsarist Russia in 1904, pressing his ministers to negotiate with Russia until all hope was gone. On the eve of his death on 30 July 1912, the Tokyo correspondent of *The Times* of London wrote that "no problem of importance to the State might be decided without a conference in his Majesty's presence, and often on these occasions he surprised his ablest officials by a wonderful memory of all previous legislative and administrative details."

Mutsuhito's tall and robust appearance symbolized the newfound dignity that Japan had achieved at the time of his death. Venerated by most of his subjects to the point of worship, he had been the centripetal point for Japan's remarkable nation-building efforts. In 1912 Britain's Prime Minister Asquith told the House of Commons that "the death of the Emperor of Japan marks the close of the most memorable reign in modern history."

[See also Meiji Restoration *and* Meiji Period.]

John Whitney Hall, "A Monarch for Modern Japan," in *Political Development in Modern Japan,* edited by Robert E. Ward (1968). Marius B. Jansen, "Monarchy and Modernization in Japan," *Journal of Asian Studies* 36.4 (1977). Shumpei Okamoto, "Meiji, Emperor," in *Encyclopedia of Japan,* edited by Gen Itasaka (1983), vol. 5, pp. 153–154.   DAVID A. TITUS

MUTSU MUNEMITSU (1844–1897), Japanese government official of the Meiji period; foreign minister at the time of the Sino-Japanese War of 1894

to 1895. Mutsu was the son of a high-ranking samurai of Wakayama *han,* but, owing to his father's defeat in internal political strife, his family lived in hardship and poverty while he was still very young. At the age of fifteen he went to Edo and soon was engaged in the activities of those who wished to "revere the emperor and expel the foreigners." He was given special attention by Sakamoto Ryōma, who must have helped him find a position in the government immediately after the Meiji Restoration in 1868. His initial post was in the foreign service. From there his power increased rapidly.

Mutsu disliked the monopoly of power of Chōshū and Satsuma men, however, and he joined forces with those who conspired to topple the regime, taking part in the Satsuma Rebellion of 1877. He was arrested and imprisoned until 1883. On his release Mutsu sailed to Europe, where he deepened his understanding of European political theories, especially the utilitarian liberalism of Great Britain. Back in Japan, he served again in the government. He was made ambassador to the United States (1888), minister of agricultural and commercial affairs (1890), and foreign minister in the second cabinet of Itō Hirobumi (1892). In 1894 he succeeded in ending extraterritoriality by a new treaty with Great Britain, a breakthrough in Meiji Japan's efforts for treaty revision.

The climax of Mutsu's career came with the Sino-Japanese War, especially its conclusion. It appears that he integrated in the Treaty of Shimonoseki the cession of Liaodong Peninsula to Japan to placate public sentiment, even though he anticipated Russian opposition. When the Triple Intervention did indeed come, he secured public understanding by placing blame on the foreign pressure. His diplomatic memoir *Kenkenroku* (1895) gives a detailed account of how he handled difficult problems. Still at the height of his political career, he died of tuberculosis at the age of fifty-four.

[See also Meiji Period; Sino-Japanese War; *and* Shimonoseki, Treaty of.]

Marius B. Jansen, "Mutsu Munemitsu," in *Personality in Japanese History,* edited by A. M. Craig and D. H. Shively (1970). Mutsu Munemitsu, *Kenkenroku: A Diplomatic Record of the Sino-Japanese War, 1894–1895,* translated by Gordon M. Berger (1982).

KIMITADA MIWA

MUZAFFARID DYNASTY, fourteenth-century Iranian dynasty centered first in Yazd and then in Shiraz in western Iran. The dynasty's eponym, Sharaf ad-Din Muzaffar, was an official in the service of the Mongol Ilkhans. His son, Mubariz ad-Din, profited from growing disorder in the Ilkhan realm to seize control of Yazd. He defeated the Injuids in Shiraz and Isfahan in the 1350s. Mubariz ad-Din was a brutal ruler whose reign ended when his son Shah Shuja (r. 1358–1384) deposed and blinded him. Hafiz, one of the greatest of Persian poets, was one of the many artists who flourished under Shah Shuja's rule. Shortly after Shah Shuja's death, Timur defeated the Muzaffarids and ended their rule.

[*See also* Inju Dynasty *and* Hafiz.]

Lawrence Lockhart and Peter Jackson, eds., *Cambridge History of Iran*, vol. 6 (1986), pp. 11–16, 59–64, and 929–947.   RICHARD W. BULLIET

MYANMA HSOSHELIT LANZIN. *See* Burma Socialist Program Party.

MYOCH'ŎNG (d. 1136), Buddhist monk who led a major rebellion in 1135 that was decisively suppressed by the central aristocrats of the Korean kingdom of Koryŏ.

The reign of Injong (r. 1122–1146) was a period of intrigue. In 1126 the powerful aristocrat Yi Cha-gyŏm unsuccessfully tried to take control of the dynasty. Myoch'ŏng was a Buddhist monk who in the years after Yi Cha-gyŏm's uprising increasingly attended King Injong and advised him on Buddhist creed. He was evidently a charismatic individual, for within the capital, Kaesŏng, he attracted a considerable following in addition to the king.

Like Injong, Myoch'ŏng was concerned for the safety and prosperity of the dynasty and he formulated policies to rejuvenate it. A firm advocate of geomancy who said that the future of the dynasty was dependent on the location of its capital, Myoch'ŏng urged the king to move his capital north to P'yŏngyang, which enjoyed a more favorable topography. P'yŏngyang, known as Sŏgyŏng, or the western capital, was a secondary capital of Koryŏ. Myoch'ŏng believed that Yi Cha-gyŏm's rebellion, which resulted in the burning of the royal palace, had caused Kaesŏng to lose its luster and inhibited Koryŏ's rehabilitation. Furthermore, by transferring the capital north to P'yŏngyang, many of the entrenched Kaesŏng aristocrats who dominated the monarch would lose their base of power and be isolated, allowing for a newer group of officials to take charge. The move also had international ramifications. By moving north Koryŏ would be able to assert a more aggressive policy toward the Jurchen Jin dynasty that was displacing the Song in northern China. Myoch'ŏng was attempting through this ploy to declare Korea's independence of China and affirm its sovereignty. [*See also* Kaesŏng *and* P'yŏngyang.]

Myoch'ŏng's scheme encountered immediate opposition from the Koryŏ elite, who demanded that the dynasty be more realistic in its pursuit of policy. Myoch'ŏng's intention to challenge China, a strong continental power, seemed preposterous. Reconciliation and accommodation, not attack, were the fundamentals to a sound Koryŏ foreign policy. Furthermore, to the Kaesŏng elite, Myoch'ŏng's brand of geomancy was pure superstition, nothing but an attempt to hide his own designs on usurping royal authority. The king was less hostile, but confronting overwhelming oligarchic opposition in his capital, he remained neutral between the two groups. He followed Myoch'ŏng's suggestion and built a palace near P'yŏngyang in 1129; he also made several visits to the area, but did little else to implement Myoch'ŏng's designs.

Convinced that destiny rested with him, Myoch'ŏng raised an army in 1135, established P'yŏngyang as his capital, and founded his state called Taewi ("great accomplishment"). Within a year, however, government troops under the command of Kim Pu-sik toppled him.

The Myoch'ŏng rebellion has been interpreted by some as a watershed in Korean history. By one analysis Myoch'ŏng and his movement tapped the indigenous Korean tradition. A spokesman for "old" Buddhist ideas, as opposed to "new" Confucian ideology, Myoch'ŏng resisted foreign influence, spoke for a more aggressive stance against military threats from China, and wanted to reclaim Koryŏ's legacy in Manchuria. Kim Pu-sik and the Kaesŏng elite, on the other hand, represented a much more cosmopolitan, sinified worldview. Learned in Confucian ethics and well versed in politics, these men sought a cautious, realistic approach to Koryŏ's foreign affairs. With the victory of the Kim Pu-sik group, Koryŏ emerged tied to the Chinese cultural orbit. This interpretation, although simplistic, captures many of the major issues that troubled Injong's reign in twelfth-century Koryŏ. Although Myoch'ŏng failed to check the power of the central elite, a military revolt in 1170 broke the control of the literati over the kingdom.

[*See also* Koryŏ.]

EDWARD J. SHULTZ

MYSORE, the premier Hindu state of South India; its Wadiyar rulers traced their origins to 1399. There were two notable interruptions to their rule in Mysore. The first occurred in 1765 when Hydar Ali, their able Muslim general, usurped the throne. Tipu Sultan, his more erratic son and successor, presented a major obstacle to British expansion in South India until he was defeated by Arthur Wellesley, the future duke of Wellington, in 1799. The British restored the Wadiyar dynasty, whose rulers entered a subsidiary alliance with their patron. After a popular rebellion in 1831 the British assumed the administration of Mysore until 1881, when they once again returned control to the Wadiyar dynasty.

Mysore was known as a model princely state although it remained a benevolent autocracy. It had an efficient administration, a legislative assembly that was inaugurated in 1881, and significant industrial development, especially in gold mining and the generation of hydroelectric power. It also was unique among the princely states in having an active unit of the Indian National Congress. In 1931 Mysore had an area of 29,528 square miles and a population of 6,557,871. Although it was the fifth-largest state in size, it ranked second after Hyderabad in population and revenue. Acceding to India in 1947, Mysore has undergone various territorial adjustments and was renamed Karnataka in 1972.

[*See also* Karnataka *and* Wadiyar Dynasty.]

Bjørn Hettne, *The Political Economy of Indirect Rule: Mysore 1881–1947,* Scandinavian Institute of Asian Studies Monograph Series, no. 32 (1978). James Manor, *Political Change in an Indian State: Mysore 1917–1955,* Australian National University Monographs on South Asia, no. 2 (1977).   BARBARA N. RAMUSACK

N

NABOB, corruption of the Indo-Persian word *nawab* ("deputy"). Originally the term denoted the deputy of a Mughal emperor. In eighteenth-century India it came to designate an autonomous prince or ruler. In England at that time *nabob* became an epithet applied to *nouveau riche* Europeans who returned from the East with fortunes that they spent in an extravagant, ostentatious, and profligate manner. Robert Clive was undoubtedly the first and perhaps the archetypal nabob, even though many earlier servants of the East India Company made fortunes. Buying country estates and "rotten boroughs" (or even titles) that enabled them to get seats in Parliament, they peddled influence or became part of the India "interest" (i.e., lobby). Old and noble families scorned them for their lavish, loud, and boorish ways. The term was also applied to all Europeans who lived well in India.

[*See also* Raj *and* Clive, Sir Robert.]

H. E. Busteed, *Echoes of Old Calcutta* (4th ed., 1908). H. H. Dodwell, *The Nabobs of Madras* (1926). John Galt, *The Member* (1831; reprint, 1975). T. G. P. Spear, *The Nabobs* (1932; reprint, 1963).

ROBERT E. FRYKENBERG

NACIONALISTA PARTY, oldest political coalition in the Philippines. Although it was formed in 1907, the Partido Nacionalista had its origins in Manila opposition groups that were established by prominent *ilustrados* in 1901–1902 to counter the American-sponsored Federal Party and to gain recognition for themselves and for their differing views on the political future of the Philippines. In 1906 the opposition groups openly pursued their effort to form a wider coalition in preparation for the 1907 Assembly elections. Although the various Manila factions grudgingly coalesced around a platform calling for "immediate, complete, and absolute independence," the eventual formation of the party was due in large part to the remarkable political talents of two youthful provincial governors: Sergio Osmeña of Cebu and Manuel Quezon of Tayabas. After their impressive electoral victories, they took control of the Assembly and, with it as their base, transformed the Partido Nacionalista into a truly national political coalition. Thus established, the party remained the major political institution through which Osmeña (until 1922) and Quezon (1922–1941) maintained control over Philippine politics and Philippine-American relations.

No other party seriously challenged the Nacionalistas until after the Pacific War. In 1946 Manuel Roxas, a prewar Nacionalista, formed the Liberal Party and defeated Osmeña in the first presidential election of the Republic of the Philippines. The Liberals and Nacionalistas, functioning as a "one-party, two-faction" polity, traded politicians and power in local and national elections for the next two decades.

In 1972, when President Ferdinand Marcos declared martial law, the Nacionalista Party (of which he remained the nominal head) became inactive by Marcos's creation of a new political party, the KBL (New Society Movement). Former defense minister Juan Enrile, the acknowledged leader of the Nacionalista Party, ran his 1987 congressional campaign under this party. The Nacionalista Party has since become enfolded into a loose coalition of parties called the Grand Alliance for Democracy (GAD).

[*See also* Osmeña, Sergio; Quezon, Manuel Luis; *and* Marcos, Ferdinand E.]

Onofre D. Corpuz, "Filipino Political Parties and Politics," *Philippine Social Science and Humanities Review* 23 (1958): 141–157. Maximo M. Kalaw, *The Development of Philippine Politics (1872–1920)* (1927). Carl H.

Landé, *Leaders, Factions, and Parties: The Structure of Philippine Politics* (1965). Dapen Liang, *Philippine Parties and Politics* (1971).   MICHAEL CULLINANE

NADARS, a caste of India. In the early twentieth century various strategies enabled *shanars* of Tamil Nadu, who tapped palm trees to make toddy, to change their caste standing. They began to use the title *nadar;* they migrated north out of the semiarid agrarian regions of South India and into urban areas; they took up new occupations including merchandizing, particularly as middlemen; and they adopted standards of etiquette appropriate to middle-level castes.

[*See also* Caste.]

R. L. Hardgrave, *The Nadars of Tamil Nad: The Political Culture of a Community in Change* (1969).

CAROL APPADURAI BRECKENRIDGE

NADAUNGMYA, king of the Burmese kingdom of Pagan (r. 1210–1234). The son of King Narapatisithu, perhaps the most powerful of Pagan's monarchs, Nadaungmya inherited a vast kingdom with a bulging treasury, an effective military machine, a purified and well-controlled church, and a highly developed culture.

A myth about the king suggests that although he was probably last in line in succession, he attained the throne because of his military abilities. Indeed, he was called Htilominlo (meaning "as the umbrella [willed it, so] the king he became"), again suggesting that his military leadership insured his legitimacy. The name *Nadaungmya* means "[one with] many earrings" and reflected the king's extravagant lifestyle, which was supported by the massive treasury his father had amassed through conquests, the reform of the sangha, and other means. Nadaungmya used the treasury to patronize lavishly both lay supporters and the church and thus eliminate doubts about his questionable ascension. In one single donation, for example, he gave away in perpetuity 45,250 acres of choice irrigated land and a large number of people to support it. He built some of the largest and aesthetically most appealing temples found in Pagan: the Sulamani, Htilominlo, and Gawdawpalin. His reign, along with the reigns of his father and son, marked the height of Pagan's glory in terms of military power, cultural achievements, and standard of living.

[*See also* Pagan *and* Narapatisithu.]

Michael Aung-Thwin, *Pagan: The Origins of Modern Burma* (1985). G. E. Harvey, *A History of Burma from the Earliest Times* (1925; reprint, 1967). G. H. Luce, "Aspects of Pagan History—Later Period," in *In Memoriam Phya Anuman Rajadhon* (1970), pp. 139–146.

MICHAEL AUNG-THWIN

NADIR (1688–1747), more fully Nadir Shah Afshar, king of Iran from 1736 to 1747, ruler of an empire that stretched into India and Central Asia. He was born Nadr Quli Beg into a poor family of the Qirqlu clan of the Turkmen Afshar tribe during the annual migration to winter pastures near Mashhad.

Nadir acquired a reputation and a small army in the course of local intertribal warfare, and after the Afghan occupation of Isfahan in 1722 he was recruited by the Safavid claimant Tahmasp II. Renamed Tahmasp Quli Khan ("slave of Tahmasp"), Nadir had by 1726 supplanted Fath Ali Khan Qajar as Tahmasp's commander in chief, secured Mashhad, and subdued the surrounding Kurds and Turkmens. He then subjected the Abdali Afghans of Herat and, after battles near Shiraz, Damghan, and Isfahan, expelled the Ghilzai Afghans from Iran.

Tahmasp showered Nadir with honors, even giving him his sister in marriage. But when Tahmasp mounted a premature campaign against the Ottoman Turks, was defeated, and was forced to sign an unfavorable treaty, Nadir seized this pretext to depose him, charging incompetence. In 1732 he installed Tahmasp's young son on the throne as Abbas III. Denouncing the treaty, Nadir unsuccessfully besieged Baghdad, but by December 1733 he had forced the governor, Ahmad Pasha, to agree to evacuate the occupied Safavid provinces. Nadir next attacked the Ottomans in the Caucasus provinces, aided by a virtual alliance with Russia (which had agreed in 1732 to evacuate Iranian territory south of the Kura River); Ganja and Tiflis fell in 1735, and much of Daghestan was pacified. The Russians also relinquished Baku in 1735.

Nadir then called a grand national assembly (*quriltai*) of governors, notables, and Muslim clergy on the Mughan steppe at the confluence of the Aras and Kura rivers and, feigning a wish to retire, engineered his acclamation as shah. He accepted the office on the condition that the Iranians abandon the distinctively Shi'ite practices introduced under the Safavids, which he evidently saw as an obstacle to securing a firm treaty with the Turks. On 8 March

1736 Nadir Quli (as he was then known) was crowned Nadir Shah of Iran.

The following year Nadir reduced Kandahar, thus completing the subjugation of the Afghans. Leaving his son Riza Quli as regent of Iran, he embarked on a course of imperial expansion, lured by the wealth of India and the weakness of the Mughal emperor. After taking Peshawar and Lahore, he defeated the Mughal forces on 24 February 1739 at Karnal. At Delhi he was acknowledged as overlord by Muhammad Shah and took for himself the coveted royal treasures, including the Koh-i Nur diamond and the Peacock Throne. [See Koh-i Nur Diamond.] A rumor spread that Nadir had been poisoned, however, and some three thousand of his troops were killed in a popular uprising; in reprisal Nadir ordered a general massacre in which perhaps twenty thousand citizens were killed and large areas of the city looted and destroyed. Nadir secured the cession of all provinces north of the Indus, declared a three-year tax amnesty for Iran, and in 1740 advanced into Central Asia. The Bukharan khanate submitted peacefully, and Nadir took twenty thousand Uzbek and Turkmen reinforcements for his army; Khiva, the capital of the Khwarazm khanate, surrendered after some resistance.

After returning to Mashhad, Nadir mounted a second campaign in Daghestan to avenge the death there of his brother Ibrahim and perhaps to invade Russia's possessions in the Caucasus. Operations dragged on into the winter of early 1743; Nadir's forces were decimated by the mountaineers in the defiles of the Caucasus, and his reputation suffered correspondingly. At this time, too, an attempt was made on Nadir's life; it was attributed to his son Riza Quli, whom Nadir caused to be blinded.

The Ottoman sultan rejected Nadir's proposals for a peace treaty, and the shah advanced again into Iraq. He unsuccessfully besieged Mosul but established cordial relations with the pasha of Baghdad, made pilgrimages to both Shi'ite and Sunni shrines, and in December summoned an assembly of the clergy at Najaf in an attempt to work out a compromise on the religious question. Accounts of the discussions confirm that, on paper at least, the Iranians agreed to renounce Shi'ism, while the Sunni *ulama* (religious scholars) consented to recognize certain Iranian precepts embodied in the Ja'fari sect, based on the teachings of the Shi'ite imam Ja'far al-Sadiq, as a fifth school of orthodox Islamic law. [See Ja'fari.]

From early 1743 a spate of revolts in Iran, some on behalf of Safavid pretenders, claimed Nadir's full attention. In 1744 a new Ottoman campaign threatened Azerbaijan and Kurdistan, but a victory by Nadir at Murad Teppe in August 1745 put an end to the Ottoman threat. On 4 September 1746 a treaty was signed with Ottoman envoys at Kurdan that reestablished the frontiers of the two empires at those agreed to in the Treaty of Zuhab in 1639; it also stipulated free passage of pilgrims, the release of all prisoners of war, and an exchange of ambassadors every three years. Nadir, moreover, dropped his insistence on Ottoman recognition of the Ja'fari sect. A serious rebellion in Sistan, provoked by the exorbitant demands of Nadir's tax collectors, also threatened his metropolitan province of Khurasan when his nephew Ali Quli, sent to quell this, instead joined the rebels. Early in 1747 Nadir left Isfahan for Kerman and Mashhad, leaving at every halt a tower of the heads of those he had tortured and executed on suspicion of disloyalty. On his way to subdue a revolt by the Kurds of Khabushan (Quchan), near Mashhad, Nadir was assassinated in his tent on 20 June by the Afshar and Qajar chieftains who were in charge of his household guards. Ali Quli Khan soon arrived from Herat and was proclaimed ruler under the name of Adil Shah; Nadir's progeny were massacred, his army was dispersed, and his treasure was dissipated.

Nadir Shah's main achievement was the restoration of an Iranian state after the Safavid empire had collapsed and Iran had been partitioned by its neighbors. His imperial strategy was probably modeled consciously on that of Timur, and he has been compared with Frederick the Great and Napoleon. His peacetime administration was less astute: constant heavy taxation and requisitions were harmful to commerce and agriculture. This, together with his increasingly arbitrary and cruel punishments, his attempt to abolish the strongly rooted Shi'a, and his favoring of Afghan, Turkmen, and Uzbek troops and officers over Persians turned his subjects against him.

[See also Afsharid Dynasty and Safavid Dynasty.]

Jonas Hanway, *An Historical Account of the British Trade over the Caspian Sea*, 2 vols. (1754). Laurence Lockhart, *Nadir Shah: A Critical Study Based Mainly upon Contemporary Sources* (1938). Robert W. Olson, *The Siege of Mosul and Ottoman-Persian Relations 1718–1743* (1975).   JOHN R. PERRY

NAGA, the name of a tribe, which, although known from very early times, came to the fore in North India in the third century CE and contributed to the disintegration of the Kushan empire in the east. In the Puranas their strongholds of power were in Vidisha, Kantipuri, Mathura, and Padmavati. Seven kings at Mathura and nine at Padmavati (near Gwalior) had ruled before the Guptas came to power. Some Naga kings are named as exterminated by Samudragupta. Several of them minted coins. They were generally votaries of Brahmanical sects.

[*See also* Adivasis.]

K. A. Nilkanta Sastri, ed., *A Comprehensive History of India,* vol. 2 (1957). H. V. Trivedi, *Catalogue of the Coins of the Naga Kings of Padmavati* (1957).

A. K. NARAIN

NAGAI KAFŪ (1879–1959), Japanese author noted for his sketches, essays, novels, and diaries. Nagai is known as one of the first writers in modern Japan to react to modernization by actively turning his back on it. Sent by his father to the United States in 1903 in the hope that he might become a businessman, he traveled widely but showed no inclination for business and preferred to study French. He left for Paris in 1907 and there discovered that his real love was Tokugawa culture, or rather its remains.

On Nagai's return to Tokyo in 1908 he began a lifelong career as self-appointed poet of the rapidly disappearing city of Edo. His theme was the decay of beauty and the beauty of decay. He was not a novelist but rather a master of elegiac description, heightening the awareness of what was being irretrievably lost and rediscovering the city landscape as the repository of his cultural identity. Nagai supported himself by teaching French at Keio University from 1910 to 1916 and thereafter by his writing. Pieces such as *The River Sumida* (*Sumidagawa,* 1909), *Tidings from Ōkubo* (*Ōkubodayori,* 1913–1914), *Quiet Rain* (*Ame shōshō,* 1918), and *A Strange Tale from East of the River* (*Bokutō kidan,* 1936), all of which hover on the borders of fiction and discursive essay, are considered to be among the finest of modern Japanese prose. During the Pacific War he managed to avoid active support of the war effort and instead devoted himself to the writing of a remarkable diary.

Edward Seidensticker, *Kafū the Scribbler* (1965).

RICHARD BOWRING

NAGALAND. Lying on the hilly border between Assam and Burma, the Indian state of Nagaland has had a tumultuous history. Geographically, the region is made up of high ridges separated by swiftly flowing rivers, while the vegetation is secondary forest and scrub. The tribal people who inhabit Nagaland have historically been as fragmented as the rugged terrain they live on, with many different local groups engaged in continual warfare, both externally against lowland kingdoms and internally against one another.

The geography of the hills, combined with the mixed backgrounds of the peoples who have migrated there, has led to an efflorescence of cultural variation among the various tribes, despite the common designation *Naga,* which is applied to all of them. This term, however, has only recently been taken up by the hillmen themselves as a term of self-reference. Previously, they knew themselves by tribal names (Angami, Ao, Sema, Zemi, Rengma, Lhota, etc.) or by the names of local villages or clans. It is only in reaction to external encroachment, first by the British colonial power, then by the Indian government, that the Nagas gained a sense of common ethnic identity.

The diversity of the Nagas is evident at every level. The Thendu Konyak of the northeast, for instance, had hereditary absolute chiefs with the power of life and death; the Ao were loosely governed by age-graded councils of unmarried men; while among the Lhota "big man" entrepreneurs were influential. Traditionally, food production has also varied, with slash-and-burn cultivation of taro prevailing in the higher elevations, millet and rice cultivation in the lower hills, and extensive wet-rice terrace farming found among the Angami. Even such a "typical" Naga institution as the men's house (*morung*) has several forms: it is the chief's house among the Konyak, a men's dormitory among the Ao, and a mere model built in times of scarcity among the Sema; traditionally the Angami had no *morungs* at all.

Nonetheless, the Nagas do share a common repertoire of cultural traits from which each group takes its own unique combination. A sense of unity among the million or so Naga was fostered by British encouragement and by the spread of Christianity across tribal boundaries. The first intertribal group, the Naga club of government employees, was founded in 1918, and a number of similar organizations followed. The fight against the Japanese in World War II increased Naga solidarity and led to the formation of the Naga National Council in 1946.

Separatist sentiments among the Nagas were fanned by Indian Government policies that were considered assimilationist, and in 1954 a violent underground movement was begun by A. Z. Phizo, an Angami. More than twenty years of war followed, despite the Indian Government's naming Nagaland a separate state in 1963. Opposition between tribal groups broke the underground movement into rival factions, defusing its power. Conciliatory efforts were finally rewarded with a peace pact signed by all parties in 1975. Some groups soon repudiated this agreement, but the intensity of resistance did decrease considerably. Meanwhile, the center of the underground movement shifted to the less accultur-ated tribes along the Burmese border, who chal-lenged the leadership of the traditional lowland tribal elite, thus reasserting the continued impor-tance of local interests and loyalties in Naga politics.

[See also Adivasis.]

M. Aram, *Peace in Nagaland* (1974). V. Elwin, *Na-galand* (1961). C. von Fürer-Haimendorf, *The Konyak Nagas* (1969). J. Hutton, *The Angami Nagas* (1921). J. Mills, *The Ao Nagas* (1926). CHARLES LINDHOLM

NAGARAKERTAGAMA, Old Javanese poem from fourteenth-century Majapahit.

The panegyrical poem known as the *Nagaraker-tagama* and dedicated to King Hayam Wuruk was composed in 1365 by the Majapahit court poet Wi-nada-Prapanca, a young Buddhist courtier of high standing. The original work was entitled *Desha-warnana (Description of the Country)*, a title more accurately reflecting the text's contents than the present one, which was given by the writer of the first colophon and can be translated as *Book of Learning on the Good Order of the Realm*.

As a *lontar*, or palm-leaf manuscript, the *Nagara-kertagama* came into Dutch possession in 1894 when it was taken from the palace compound of the Balinese king Cakra Nagara during the course of the Lombok War. The poem's value to historical scholarship lies more in its content than its form; it relates the genealogy of the Singosari-Majapahit dy-nasty, describes the layout of the Majapahit capital in its heyday, and lists the kingdom's tributaries and neighbors. It also contains detailed descriptions of royal processions, hunts, ceremonies, and annual festivals, and it makes possible a relatively accurate reconstruction of the workings of fourteenth-cen-tury Majapahit administration. Most of the events in the poem were witnessed by the poet himself; information about earlier events was obtained from court records, annals, or private notes of his erudite contemporaries.

[See also Majapahit; Hayam Wuruk; Java; and Singosari.]

Thomas G. Th. Pigeaud, *Java in the Fourteenth Cen-tury. A Study in Cultural History. The Nagarakertagama by Rakawi Prapanca of Majapahit, 1353 A.D.* (1960–1963). M. C. HOADLEY

NAGARJUNA, important South Indian Buddhist philosopher of the second century CE. Founder of what was later called the Madhyamika school of Mahayana Buddhism, Nagarjuna reconciled the Prajnaparamita treatises with older textual tradi-tions in opposition to both the Nyaya—the school of Hindu logic—and to the Buddhist Abhidharma philosophers. Nagarjuna's logical dialectic seeks to expose all philosophical categories as dependent constructs and thus reduce them to emptiness *(shun-yata)*. Much of later Buddhist tradition builds on Nagarjuna's equating the ultimate reality of *nirvana* with *samsara*, the mundane world.

[See also Buddhism.]

T. R. V. Murti, *The Central Philosophy of Buddhism* (1955). Frederick J. Streng, *Emptiness: A Study in Reli-gious Meaning* (1967). TODD THORNTON LEWIS

NAGARJUNIKONDA, the largest Buddhist es-tablishment in South India, located in Andhra Pra-desh near the Krishna River. The center was actively supported by queens of the Iksvaku dynasty during the third and fourth centuries. Iksvaku kings—all Shaivites—are named in inscriptions at the site; these mention Shiva temples as well as the dedica-tions by the queens on behalf of several Buddhist sects. Numerous structures include self-contained groups focused on stupas, with one or two shrines housing Buddha images or small stupas, and central *mandapas* flanked by monastic residence cells. Brick stupas containing relic cases were lime-plastered and embellished with carved limestone slabs depicting stupas, Buddha images, and narrative scenes.

A. H. Longhurst, *The Buddhist Antiquities of Nāgār-junikonda, Madras Presidency*, Memoirs of the Archae-ological Survey of India, no. 54 (1938). H. Sarkar, *Studies in Early Buddhist Architecture in India* (1966).

GERI HOCKFIELD MALANDRA

NAGASAKI, city (population 447,091) in north-western Kyushu, Japan. Nagasaki has been a major port for Japan's foreign trade since the mid-sixteenth century, and from 1641 to 1855 it was the only Japanese port regularly and legally open to foreign ships.

A fishing village in the Ōmura domain, Nagasaki attracted Chinese traders as early as 1562. In 1569 Ōmura Sumitada, a Christian convert, invited the Jesuit missionary Gaspar Vilela to Nagasaki to preach. In 1570, Sumitada opened Nagasaki to Portuguese trading ships from Macao, hoping to make the village the major trading port in Kyushu, and in 1571 the first *galeota* entered the port. In 1580 Sumitada donated the town to the Society of Jesus, the first recorded alienation of Japanese territory to a foreign power, and for the next seven years Nagasaki was a center of Jesuit activity and the principal port for the Portuguese *galeota* from Macao. As there were no direct Sino-Japanese relations at the time, the Portuguese exploited their access to both countries at great profit, carrying Japanese silver to China and bringing Chinese gold and silks to Japan. [*See* Jesuits: An Overview.]

In 1587 Toyotomi Hideyoshi subjugated the various daimyo of Kyushu and, startled at the extent of Christian power in the island, ordered the expulsion of the Jesuits and the confiscation of Nagasaki. Hideyoshi was thus also able to exploit the Nagasaki trade for his own enrichment and to control relations with the Portuguese. As the principal port for Portuguese trade, Nagasaki was also the center for the importation of Iberian culture into Japan. [*See* Namban Bunka.] After 1603, the Tokugawa *bakufu* administered Nagasaki as one of the *chokkatsu toshi* (shogunal cities), which remained its status to the end of the Tokugawa period. As such, the town and the trade conducted there were administered by a shogunal deputy (*daikan*) or magistrate (*bugyō*) drawn from the ranks of the *hatamoto* (Tokugawa retainers). With the establishment of the *shuinsen* system of trade licensing in 1604, Nagasaki's position in Japan's overseas trade became more important still, although the city had to compete with the Chinese, the Dutch (after 1609), and the English (from 1613 to 1622) in Hirado to the north, as well as with other ports in Kyushu. The English, however, withdrew from Japan in 1622, while the Portuguese, because of their Catholic proselytizing, and the Spanish, for both their Catholicism and their suspected aggressive intentions, were increasingly restricted: in 1624, the Spanish were expelled, in 1634 the Portuguese were confined to the new man-made island of Deshima in Nagasaki harbor, and in 1635 Chinese traders were also limited to Nagasaki but were not confined

to a compound like the Portuguese. In 1639, as part of the increasingly stringent shogunal control of Christianity and foreign relations, generally referred to as the "seclusion" (*sakoku*) edicts, the Portuguese were expelled from Japan, and when in 1641 the Dutch were required to close their factory in Hirado and move to Deshima, Nagasaki became the sole port for foreign traders entering Japan, a status it retained until 1855. After 1688, as the *bakufu* attempted further to control foreign trade, Chinese traders in Nagasaki were also denied the freedom of the town and were confined to the Chinese compound (*tōjin yashiki*). [*See* Seclusion.]

Despite these hindrances Nagasaki remained the major entry point for foreign cultural, intellectual, and scientific influences in the Tokugawa period, especially after the eighth shogun Yoshimune eased import restrictions on foreign books. Most important were Western medical and scientific knowledge and the Dutch language, known collectively as "Dutch studies" (*rangaku*). [*See* Rangaku.] As Western pressure for Japan to open herself to unrestricted commerce mounted in the first half of the nineteenth century, Nagasaki was important in providing access to modern military science: the daimyo and the *bakufu* imported Western metallurgical technology (especially for artillery casting) and gunnery techniques. The *bakufu* established a shipyard in Nagasaki in 1855 and a steelmaking operation in 1861. In the last years of the shogunate, as the *bakufu* was no longer able to control access to Western scientific knowledge, nor even to Nagasaki, anti-*bakufu* activists gathered in the town to purchase Western arms, which would soon be used to overthrow the shogunate and establish the Meiji government.

After the Meiji Restoration Nagasaki continued as a port, though it was displaced in relative importance by ports, like Yokohama and Kobe, closer to the centers of Japanese populations; it remained a center of shipbuilding as well. The government shipyards were sold to the Mitsubishi combine in 1887 and are today the main shipyards of the Mitsubishi Shipbuilding Company. On 9 August 1945, three days after the atomic bombing of Hiroshima, a United States Army Air Corps bomber dropped an atomic bomb on Nagasaki, destroying most of the city and killing 122,000 people. The atomic bombings were a major factor in the Japanese government's decision to accept the terms of the Potsdam Declaration: the Japanese surrendered on 15 August 1945, thus ending World War II.

[*See also* Deshima.]

C. R. Boxer, *Jan Compagnie in Japan, 1600–1817* (2d rev. ed., 1950); *The Christian Century in Japan, 1549–1650* (1951); and *The Great Ship from Amaçon: Annals of Macao and the Old Japan Trade, 1555–1640* (1959). Engelbert Kaempfer, *The History of Japan Together with an Account of the Kingdom of Siam, 1690–1692*, 3 vols. (1906).   RONALD P. TOBY

NAGASHINO, BATTLE OF.

A turning point in Japanese warfare, the Battle of Nagashino was fought between the armies of Takeda Katsuyori and Oda Nobunaga at Nagashino in the province of Mikawa in 1575.

Takeda relied on traditional offensive tactics and organized waves of mounted warriors to charge into Nobunaga's defenses. Vastly outnumbered, Nobunaga entrusted his fortunes to a novel battlefield force—foot soldiers armed with muskets, a weapon that had been introduced into Japan only a generation earlier. Always an innovative general, Nobunaga stationed his three thousand men behind high wooden palisades; firing in rotation, they inflicted heavy losses on Takeda's mounted warriors while suffering only a relatively few casualties themselves.

This victory brought Nobunaga a step closer to domination of central Japan and opened an avenue of attack against the Ikkō sect adherents in Echizen and Kaga. Of broader significance, Nobunaga's victory had an immediate impact on battlefield tactics. Convinced of the superiority of muskets, all daimyo began to rely less on traditional mounted men armed with swords and spears, and instead started to organize large-scale battalions of foot soldiers *(ashigaru)*, some of whom were armed with muskets and some with lances and bows. [See Ashigaru.]

The use of muskets, and later cannon, also rendered obsolete the fortifications of the Sengoku daimyo, who had located their small castles in mountain areas that could be defended against the traditional bow and cavalry fighter. Daimyo now moved down onto the plains, where they could erect massive stone castles and protect them with concentric circles of battlements and moats. These new locations ultimately created the opportunity for daimyo to gain more direct control over transportation routes and the agricultural wealth of the plains villages. The importation of the musket thus hastened the reunification of Japan during the latter half of the sixteenth century.

[*See also* Tanegashima *and* Oda Nobunaga.]
                                JAMES L. MCCLAIN

NAGOYA,

the fourth largest city in Japan, located on the Nobi Plain in the Chūbu region of Honshu. Nagoya is the former castle town of the domain of the Owari clan, one of the "three houses" *(go-sanke)* of the Tokugawa period. It is the prefectural capital and largest city of Aichi Prefecture, with a population of 2.09 million (1982 est.). Conveniently located along the Tōkaidō railway line and a halfway point between Tokyo and the Kyoto-Osaka region to the south, the city serves as a regional economic and distribution center. It is also important as a center for heavy industry and chemical manufacture. Although adequate access to port facilities was not gained until 1907, when Nagoya absorbed the city of Atsuta, located on Ise Bay, it is today one of Japan's five major ports for foreign trade.

Nagoya's history dates to 1525, when Shiba Yoshimune, governor of the province of Owari, built a castle on the site for his son-in-law, Imagawa Ujitoyo. The castle was captured in 1532 by Oda Nobuhide, father of Nobunaga. It fell into a serious state of disrepair, however, when Nobunga abandoned it for his new residence at Kiyosu. Half a century later the site regained importance when Tokugawa Ieyasu commanded several western daimyo to undertake new construction of the castle, which was presented to Ieyasu's seventh son, Yoshinao, in 1609.   THOMAS R. SCHALOW

NAGPUR.

Named after the Nag streamlet, Nagpur is a city of 1.3 million people in the Indian state of Maharashtra. From indefinite beginnings it became capital, successively, of the tribal kingdom of Devgarh (1739), of the Bhonsla state of Nagpur (1743), of the British Central Provinces (1861), and of bilingual Madhya Pradesh (1947), losing this position when the state's Marathi-speaking areas joined Bombay State in 1956. Nagpur remains an administrative center but is increasingly important for commerce, industry, and mining. It has the largest orange market and cotton mills in India, and possesses a varied cultural life.

Maharashtra State Gazetteers, Nagpur District (rev. ed., 1966).   DAVID BAKER

NAHDATUL ULAMA,

Indonesian council of Islamic scholars and mullahs. It was founded in 1926 by traditional Islamic leaders from East Java who resisted the advance of modernist Islamic thought.

Although it was originally a nonpolitical organization, Nahdatul Ulama joined MIAI and its successor, Masjumi (then a political party uniting the Indonesian Islamic organization), during the Japanese occupation of Indonesia. In 1952 it left the Masjumi and became an independent political party, receiving 18.4 percent of the vote in the general elections of 1955. In 1973 it delegated its political role to the new Islamic party, the Partai Pesatuan Indonesia, and once again became a nonpolitical organization. East Java is still its main area of support.

[*See also* Masjumi.]

C. VAN DIJK

NAICKER, E. V. RAMASWAMI (1879–1973),
leader of the Dravidian movement in Madras, India, who worked for the cultural and political autonomy of the Tamil-speaking peoples of the region. Under the influence of the nationalist leader C. R. Rajagopalachari, Ramaswami joined the Indian National Congress and led the noncooperation movement in Madras in 1920. He became known as a champion of the Untouchables, but he resigned from the Congress because he believed it was dominated by brahmans. He became a bitter critic of Hinduism, arguing that religion had kept people enslaved to superstitions that prevented social and economic development.

In 1925 Naicker founded the Self-Respect Movement to promote the interests of backward groups, while at the same time he agitated against British rule. He was imprisoned in 1933 for inciting people to rebellion, and when he was in prison he was elected president of the Justice Party, an anti-Brahmanical nationalist group. He transformed this into the Dravida Kazhagam, or Dravidian Federation, which was accused of wanting to create a separate state for Tamils in South India. He opposed the attempt of the Government of India to make Hindi the national language and condemned the constitution of India as an instrument of Brahmanical oppression. To spread his message he made skillful use of dramas, street demonstrations, and pamphlets and newspapers written in Tamil.

A group of his followers later broke away and founded a new party, the Dravida Munnetra Kazhagam, which was less radical in its separatist demands, and they came to power in Madras (Tamil Nadu) in 1967. One of the last movements that he organized was the Superstition Eradication Conference, which demanded the end of discrimination based upon religion, language, and caste, and the right to criticize the beliefs and practices of all religions. While he was often depicted by his critics, especially in North India, as an enemy of united India and an anti-religious fanatic, he was very popular in the Tamil country and undoubtedly gave expression to views that were widely shared.

[*See also* Dravidian Languages and Literatures; Dravidian Movement; Indian National Congress; Rajagopalachari, Chakravarti; *and* Tamil Nadu.]

AINSLIE T. EMBREE

NAIDU, SAROJINI (1879–1949), Indian poet
and political leader. Her three volumes of poetry—*The Golden Threshold* (1905), *The Bird of Time* (1912), and *The Broken Wing* (1917)—were composed in English. The female images of grief and stasis that mark her poems stand in radical contrast to her public life as orator and politician. As early as 1903 she was active in the cause of national liberation. By 1906 this cause had become powerfully linked for her with the claim for women's rights. She met Mohandas Gandhi in 1914 and became one of his closest followers. In 1925 she became the first Indian woman to be elected president of the Indian National Congress.

Padmini Sengupta, *Sarojini Naidu: A Biography* (1966).

MEENA ALEXANDER

NAIRS (or Nayars), a caste of Kerala on India's
southwestern coast, once famed for its matrilineal customs. From the twelfth century until the second quarter of the twentieth century, Nair families traced their origin and descent through women. In the classic example (although there were regional variations), such families were matrilocal and did not include husbands and fathers. Children were the responsibility of the mother's house. The system, however, was not matriarchal: the manager of the family's property was the eldest male member. Although nominally *shudras*, Nairs were often soldiers and controllers of land.

Matrilineal customs began to collapse in the late nineteenth century. The practice was undermined by changes such as population increase, a rigid legal system, a cash economy, and new ideas of individualism, all vigorously exploited by Kerala's non-matrilineal groups. Beginning in 1925 legislation was passed in the various units of what is today Kerala to allow individuals to take their share of the corporate assets and separate from the matrilineal family. By the 1950s the matrilineal joint-family had almost vanished, although the legal loose ends were still being tied up in the 1970s. Today Nairs follow a patrilineal, patrilocal system similiar to Hindus elsewhere in India. The Nair Service Society, founded in 1915 by Mannath Padmanabhan (1878–1970), which aimed to reform Nair customs and create a cohesive community, is one of the wealthiest and most successful caste associations in India.

[*See also* Kerala *and* Shudra.]

C. J. Fuller, *The Nayars Today* (1976). Kathleen Gough, "Changing Kinship Usages in the Setting of Political and Economic Change among the Nayars of Malabar," *Journal of the Royal Anthropological Institute* 81 (1952): 71–88. Robin Jeffrey, *The Decline of Nayar Dominance: Society and Politics in Travancore, 1847–1908* (1976). Joan P. Mencher, "Changing Familial Roles among South Malabar Nayars," *Southwestern Journal of Anthropology* 18 (1972): 230–245.　Robin Jeffrey

NAKAE CHŌMIN (Tokusuke, 1847–1901), Japanese political theoretician and philosopher; popular rights activist of the Meiji period. A samurai from Tosa by birth, Nakae studied Dutch and French as a young man, and at the age of twenty-one he served as the interpreter for the French minister, Leon Roches. In 1871 he was sent to France as a government student, where he studied philosophy, history, and literature. On his return to Japan in 1874 he briefly served in the Genrō-in, but left the government in a dispute with Mutsu Munemitsu. Thereafter he devoted himself to teaching and writing.

In 1881, at the peak of the Popular Rights (Jiyū Minken) Movement, Nakae joined Saionji Kimmochi in publishing the *Tōyō jiyū shimbun* (*Oriental Free Press*), in which the two proposed to introduce liberal European political ideas. Nakae devoted himself mainly to French thought. In 1881 he brought out a superb translation of Jean-Jacques Rousseau's *Social Contract*. Three years earlier he incorporated many of Rousseau's ideas into the platform of the Liberal Party. Such efforts soon earned him the nickname the "Rousseau of the East." Nakae briefly flirted with active politics and in 1890 successfully ran for the Diet, but he soon resigned his seat, and his final years were devoted to writing. In addition to a large corpus of journal and newspaper articles, Nakae wrote many books, of which *Sansuijin keirin mondō* (*A Discourse of Three Drunks on Politics*), *Ichinen yūhan* (*A Year and a*

Half), and *Zoku ichinen yūhan* (*A Year and a Half Continued*) are best known. The latter two served as summaries of his political and philosophical ideas and were written shortly before his death in 1901.

[*See also* Meiji Period *and* Jiyū Minken.]

F. G. Notehelfer

NAKAMA AND TON'YA, leading Japanese business institutions of the Tokugawa period (1600–1868) that possessed monopolistic privileges, especially in distribution. *Ton'ya* traded in specialized commodities or services and in the early Tokugawa period promoted interregional trade. They eventually became organized in associations of merchant houses engaged in similar business. These associations were called *nakama,* or sometimes *kabunakama. Kabu* referred to the license or membership share required for entry to the *nakama.* The *kabu,* granted in exchange for tribute fees, could be inherited, purchased (subject to *nakama* approval), or obtained through an apprentice system.

Since the *nakama* regulated entry of outsiders, they were organizationally compatible with Tokugawa policy, which limited mobility between status groups. The *bakufu* came to recognize the *nakama* as its agents in directing the flow of commodities through the cities under its control. In the 1720s the *bakufu* gave special authorization to the *nakama* in exchange for license fees. By the 1770s the *nakama* began more regular payments (akin to taxes) in exchange for patents of monopoly that often extended beyond the jurisdiction of the cities. This program was intended to provide additional revenue for the *bakufu* and to protect the commercial sphere of the *nakama* against encroachment by rural merchants. By the late 1700s and early 1800s the emergence of an agricultural surplus in more developed regions and the growing of crops for cash led to diversification of the village economy into various cottage industries. Rural production and commercial facilities then began to challenge the marketing network of the urban-based *nakama.*

In the 1840s, the *bakufu* abolished the *nakama* monopoly rights in order to lower prices. This policy, which led to snags in distribution, was unsuccessful, and further *bakufu* efforts at reform were doomed by the coming of the West. By the late 1850s direct channels between rural areas and ports newly opened to foreign traders bypassed major cities and urban merchants. Many *nakama* thus collapsed, although some successor associations established after the 1840s continued business into the Meiji period (1868–1912).

William B. Hauser, *Economic Institutional Change in Tokugawa Japan: Ōsaka and the Kinai Cotton Trade* (1974). Charles D. Sheldon, *The Rise of the Merchant Class in Tokugawa Japan, 1600–1868: An Introductory Survey* (1958).   WILLIAM D. WRAY

NAKASONE YASUHIRO (b.1918), prime minister of Japan since 1982, the twelfth member of the ruling Liberal Democratic Party to hold that post since Japan's recovery of sovereignty in 1952. Born to a lumber merchant in Gumma Prefecture, sixty miles northwest of Tokyo, Nakasone attended the prestigious Tokyo Imperial University and entered the powerful Home Ministry in 1941. His bureaucratic career was interrupted by war service, and his ministry was abolished by the political reforms that followed the war.

Nakasone was elected to the Diet's House of Representatives in 1947 and won reelection in every contest thereafter. His aggressive personal style and publicly expressed doubts about Japan's postwar constitution kept him for some time from a central place in the Liberal Democratic Party, where Yoshida Shigeru's protégés long dominated. In 1967 Satō Eisaku appointed him minister of transport, however, and from then on Nakasone, leader of a growing faction in the lower house, held many cabinet posts, the most important of which were leadership of the Self-Defense Agency (1970) and the Ministry of International Trade and Industry (1972, under Tanaka Kakuei). By the time of Tanaka's fall from power Nakasone was a leading figure in the ruling party.

Nakasone has often been charged with ambition and opportunism by his critics, who have sometimes nicknamed him "Weathervane." On points of nationalism and national pride, however, he has been thoroughly consistent. He sponsored a private academy in his home community to inculcate national spirit, and he aligned himself with conservative members of the ruling party who were impatient with Japan's "low posture" approach to international affairs. He advocated revision of the constitution to make it a more Japanese document, and as prime minister he has worked for a stronger Japanese stance in world affairs through travel and greater participation in summit meetings. Despite a weak power base within his party, Nakasone has managed to provide effective and visible leadership.

MICHIO UMEGAKI

NAKHON SI THAMMARAT, ancient principality in southern Thailand. The geography of the

FIGURE 1. *Buddhist Temple.* Example of the typical Buddhist architectural style found in Nakhon Si Thammarat.

Malay Peninsula virtually dictated that an important center should be located in the region of Nakhon Si Thammarat. In ancient times it possessed a large harbor sheltered from the northeast monsoon; a transpeninsular land route led easily to Trang on the west coast; and it dominated the largest area suitable for rice cultivation in the middle section of the peninsula. From about the second century until the thirteenth it appears to have been the seat of the state of Tambralinga, which Chinese and South Indian texts record as being powerful and prosperous. At times Nakhon Si Thammarat fell under the influence—political or cultural—of Malay Srivijaya (based at Palembang in Sumatra), Java, Angkorian Cambodia, and Pagan Burma, and it was the subject of Chola maritime raids early in the eleventh century. In the mid-thirteenth century King Chandrabhanu twice sent military expeditions against Sri Lanka. Through much of the early period Nakhon Si Thammarat was an important center of Buddhism, and from there Buddhist monks carried Sinhalese Buddhism to Siam and Cambodia in the thirteenth century.

A major break in Nakhon's history occurs in the last third of the thirteenth century, between Chandrabhanu and King Ramkhamhaeng of the Thai Kingdom of Sukhothai, who in the 1290s claimed Nakhon Si Thammarat among the southernmost of the principalities dependent on him. It would appear that the growing Thai element in Nakhon's population (which also included Malays, Mon, and Khmer) had seized power from Chandrabhanu's line. These people allied themselves with Sukhothai, bringing with them Nakhon's traditional vassals, extending as far south as Pahang. This ruling house ultimately transferred its allegiance to Ayudhya in the last half of the fourteenth century but maintained some internal autonomy until the mid-sixteenth century, when Ayudhya, increasingly alert to the value of peninsula products in world trade, displaced the local rulers and began to station its own governors in Nakhon Si Thammarat and through them to control most of the Malay Peninsula. The governors of Nakhon occasionally sought independence from Siam, but they never succeeded for long, and Nakhon was fully integrated into Siam by the eighteenth century.

[See also Tambralinga; Srivijaya; Sukhothai; Chandrabhanu; and Ramkhamhaeng.]

The Crystal Sands: The Chronicles of Nagara Sri Dharrmaraja, translated by David K. Wyatt (1975).

DAVID K. WYATT

NALANDA, the most renowned Indian Buddhist monastery of ancient India. Founded during the Gupta period in Bihar, Nalanda became a huge educational complex supported by kings and revenues from more than one hundred villages. At Nalanda

FIGURE 1. *Remains of the Buddhist Monastic University at Nalanda.*

all the intellectual traditions of India—philosophy, grammar, and medicine—were taught, but Buddhism was preeminent. At its peak monks from throughout the Buddhist world as far as China and Southeast Asia came to Nalanda to study with the greatest masters. Muslim invasions of the twelfth century destroyed Nalanda; the ruins were unearthed in the nineteenth century.

[*See also* Buddhism: An Overview.]

Sukumar Dutt, *Buddhist Monks and Monasteries of India* (1962).   TODD THORNTON LEWIS

NAMAMUGI INCIDENT. *See* Richardson Incident.

NAMBAN BUNKA ("southern barbarian culture"), the language, customs, art, and cultural artifacts imported to Japan from southern Europe and the cultural artifacts produced in Japan, in both European and Japanese styles, in response to Japan's early contact with the *namban,* the Iberian and Italian missionaries, merchants, and mariners active in Japan between 1543 and 1639. The word *namban* derives from Chinese usage, in which non-Chinese peoples in each cardinal direction were designated by a specific name. Like other Europeans, the Iberians appeared to the Japanese from the south, yet they were distinguished from the northern European Dutch and English who arrived in the early seventeenth century and were called "red hairs" *(kōmō).*

Namban bunka included Iberian-style ships, firearms, food and clothing styles—which were immensely popular among the urban merchant and upper samurai classes—and art depicting the Europeans in Japan, or scenes of Europe that were either imagined from descriptions or copied from European models brought by the traders. Among the most popular Japanese-style works were pairs of painted folding screens *(byōbu),* often showing a Portuguese ship at anchor in Nagasaki harbor, with Portuguese merchants and Jesuit missionaries parading the deck or walking the streets of the town. Some sixty pairs of screens are extant, their vibrant excitement and rich visual detail a valuable source of information about the texture of life at the time and about Japanese perceptions of themselves and the foreigners.

Of signal importance in the development of Japanese painting in European style or on Christian themes was the arrival of the Italian Jesuit Giovanni

Niccolo, a gifted painter, in Nagasaki in 1583. He painted numerous devotional works as tools of evangelism, which were displayed in churches of the Jesuit mission in Japan, and taught painting and copperplate etching to students in the Jesuit schools of Kyushu, until he and all Jesuit missionaries were expelled from Japan in 1614. The *Martyrdom of the Three Saints,* a triptych in the Tokyo National Museum, is attributed to Niccolo. Besides paintings on Christian themes, the *namban* painters were active as cartographers as well, producing numerous maps of the world in Western style, as well as maps of Japan that combine sixteenth-century European cartographic style with the conventions of Japanese screen painting. *Namban* and Christian themes also entered the minor arts, as Japanese craftsmen produced lacquerware and inlay storage chests, letter boxes, and saddles with portrayals of *namban* on them, *tsuba* (sword guards) and water bowls with crucifix motifs, backgammon boards, chairs, clothing, and all manner of European-style gear.

Another major element of *namban bunka,* one with far-reaching effects, was the output of the Jesuit press, the first movable-type printing press in Japan, which was established by Alessandro Valignano in 1590. The press published twenty-nine books in its quarter-century of operation, including translations of religious tracts into romanized Japanese, transcriptions of Japanese literature in Latin script, and dictionaries and grammars of the Japanese language, which are valuable sources of information about the language of the day. The press was closed in 1614, when the mission was expelled from Japan.

Namban styles and customs were a powerful fad in late sixteenth- and early seventeenth-century Japan: a Jesuit missionary reported that Toyotomi Hideyoshi had "a great liking for Portuguese clothing, and members of his retinue, in emulation, are often attired in the Portuguese style." Another Jesuit, Joaõ Rodrigues, noted that Hideyoshi's taste for Portuguese styles had created such a fad that "the tailors of Nagasaki are all so busy that they have not a moment to spare," and that he had developed a taste for "hen's eggs and beef." The suppression of Christianity and the termination of Japanese overseas voyaging and the Portuguese trade by 1639 ended the *namban bunka* craze. Mere possession of an object judged to have a Christian theme might bring arrest and punishment. Thereafter the only *namban* form that remained active was the production of *fumie,* "trampling pictures," depicting the Madonna and child, which were used as a test of suspected Christians: believers would refuse to trample the sacred image, it was thought, and might thus be discovered. The *bakufu's* anti-Christian policies also brought about the destruction of much of the art on Christian themes, although remarkably much survives.

[*See also* Christianity: Christianity in Japan *and* Valignano, Alessandro.]

Michael Cooper, ed., *The Southern Barbarians* (1971). Yoshitomo Okamoto, *The Namban Art of Japan* (1972). Shin'ichi Tani and Tadashi Sugase, *Namban Art* (1973).

RONALD P. TOBY

NAMBOKUCHŌ. The name *Nambokuchō,* meaning "southern and northern courts," is used to refer to two courts of medieval Japan, headed by rival branches of the imperial family, that existed concurrently during the period 1336 to 1392. Their rivalry constituted the only major dynastic schism in Japanese history. The origins of the Northern and Southern courts lay in a succession dispute that arose in 1272 upon the death of the abdicated emperor Go-Saga (1220–1272). His sons, the former emperor Go-Fukakusa (1243–1304) and the reigning sovereign, Kameyama (1249–1305), both claimed that the imperial succession should be inherited by their descendants. Real power in the country at the time lay with Japan's first warrior (samurai) government, the Kamakura shogunate (1185–1333). But instead of decisively choosing either the senior (Go-Fukakusa) line or the junior (Kameyama) line, the shogunate wavered and finally allowed an arrangement whereby emperors were designated alternately from the two lines. This arrangement worked reasonably well until about the 1320s. By this time the Kamakura shogunate was in decline, and a loyalist movement to overthrow it formed behind the junior-line emperor Go-Daigo (1288–1339).

In 1331 officials of the shogunate seized Go-Daigo, sent him into exile, and replaced him as emperor with a member of the senior line. Still, the tide of opposition to the shogunate flowed strongly, with disaffected warriors joining the loyalist movement in ever-increasing numbers. In 1333 the shogunate was overthrown, and Go-Daigo returned from exile in triumph, proclaiming a restoration of direct rule by the emperor. But his restoration, called the Kemmu Restoration (1333–1336) after the Kemmu calendrical period (1334–1335), was an unmiti-

gated failure. A thorough reactionary, Go-Daigo wished to go back some five hundred years to a time when emperors still supposedly exercised power in deed as well as in name. But national power had decisively shifted in the late twelfth century from the emperor and courtiers of Kyoto to the provincial warrior class, and the overthrow of the Kamakura shogunate simply signaled the need for new warrior leadership in the land. Behind Go-Daigo's restoration lay a power struggle between chieftains heading two branches of the great Minamoto clan, Nitta Yoshisada (1301–1338) and Ashikaga Takauji (1305–1358). In 1336, Ashikaga, having defeated Nitta, forced Go-Daigo to abdicate and selected a member of the senior branch of the imperial family to be emperor. Soon after, Go-Daigo fled from Kyoto to Yoshino in the mountainous region to the south. There he reaffirmed his claim to the throne and founded the Yoshino, or Southern, Court. The court in Kyoto, where Ashikaga Takauji established the Ashikaga of Muromachi shogunate (1336–1573), became the Northern Court.

The Northern Court was a mere puppet regime of the Ashikaga, and the Southern Court became primarily a rallying point for warriors opposed to the shogunate. Although there was considerable fighting throughout the country for several decades between the armies backing the Northern and Southern Courts, and although the adherents of the Southern Court occupied Kyoto no less than four times in the period 1352 to 1361, the final outcome of the fighting was never truly in doubt. By at least the late 1360s the Southern Court had become little more than a fugitive government, moving from one place to another in the Yoshino region. In 1392 the Ashikaga shogun Yoshimitsu (1358–1408) persuaded the Southern emperor to return to Kyoto with the promise of a renewal of the alternate succession arrangement. But this promise was never honored, and the emperorship has been held from that time to the present by the senior, or Northern, branch of the imperial family.

Although the Southern Court failed to prevail, it was not forgotten. Thanks mainly to a famous war tale of the age, *Taiheiki,* the leading warriors who fought for the Southern cause, especially Kusunoki Masashige (d. 1336), became great folk heroes and were regarded as paragons of the military virtues and imperial loyalty. In 1911 the Japanese government actually decreed that the Southern Court be portrayed in primary school history texts as the legitimate seat of emperorship in the period 1336 to 1392.

[*See also* Go-Daigo; Kemmu Restoration; Ashikaga Takauji; *and* Yoshino Line.]

George B. Sansom, *A History of Japan: 1334–1615* (1961). H. Paul Varley, *Imperial Restoration in Medieval Japan* (1971) and *A Chronicle of Gods and Sovereigns* (1980).   PAUL VARLEY

NAMBOODRIPAD, E. M. S. (b. 1909), probably India's best known and most prolific communist theorist. Namboodripad was born into a wealthy, conservative brahman family of central Kerala. Involved as a youth in attempts to reform the repressive customs of Nambudiri brahmans, he left college in January 1932 to join the Gandhian civil disobedience campaign against the British. While in jail he studied Marxist writings, and he became a member of the Congress Socialist Party in 1934. A secret communist from about 1937, he was a leader of Kerala's Communist Party from its inception in 1940. After apparent hesitation he joined the Communist Party of India (Marxist) when the Communist Party of India split in 1964. He served as chief minister of Kerala from 1957 to 1959 and again from 1967 to 1969. He was elected to the Madras Legislative Assembly in 1939 and the Kerala Legislative Assembly in 1957, 1960, 1965, 1970, and 1977. He was general secretary of the undivided CPI in 1962 and 1963 and has served in the same position in the CPI(M) since 1977.

[*See also* Communism: Communist Parties in South Asia.]

E. M. S. Namboodripad, *How I Became a Communist,* translated by P. K. Nair (1976), and *Selected Writings,* vol. 1 (1982). T. J. Nossiter, *Communism in Kerala: A Study in Political Adaptation* (1982).   ROBIN JEFFREY

NAMCHE BAZAR, prominent Sherpa trading center and launching point for mountaineering expeditions to Nepal's Everest region, situated eighty-five miles northeast of Kathmandu at the foot of the Khumbu Valley. Namche lies along the trade route linking Nepal's fertile Dudh Kosi basin with the Tibetan province of Tingri. The Sherpas, who dominate the region's population, obtained exclusive trading rights in the region from the king of Nepal in 1828. Since that time, Namche has prospered as an entrepôt for such goods as Tibetan salt, yak tails, rice, and Chinese consumer goods and more recently as a tourist center.

Christoph von Fürer-Haimendorf, *Himalayan Traders* (1975).   RICHARD ENGLISH

NAMGYAL, PALDEN THONDUP (r. 1963–1982), the last of the hereditary rulers *(chogyals)* of Sikkim. When Palden Thondup succeeded to the Sikkimese throne, he was the twelfth ruler in a lineage that began in 1641. Begrudgingly he oversaw an era of political reform that resulted from pressures by the Nepalese majority of the Sikkimese population and by the Indian National Congress. His attempts to obstruct the passage of a new constitution by a popularly elected National Assembly in June 1974 led to widespread civil unrest and the eventual annexation of Sikkim by the government of India. Upon Palden Thondup's death in 1982, his son Wangchuk Namgyal was "illegally" proclaimed thirteenth *chogyal* by his Lepcha and Bhutia supporters. [*See also* Sikkim.]   RICHARD ENGLISH

NAM TIEN ("southward advance") refers to the gradual territorial expansion of the Vietnamese people from the Red River Delta. Beginning in the eleventh century, Vietnamese settlers colonized uncultivated Cham territory. These gains were consolidated by military conquest and marriage alliances with Champa, particularly under emperors Ly Thai Tong (1028–1054), Tran Anh Tong (1293–1314), Tran Thuan Tong (1388–1398), and Le Thanh Tong (1460–1497). The Nguyen lords completed the conquest of Champa in the late seventeenth century and went on to occupy parts of Cambodia. Expansion in the Mekong Delta continued until the final annexation of Ha Tien in 1780. [*See also* Champa.]   BRUCE M. LOCKHART

NAM VIET (Nanyue), a South China toponym closely associated with Vietnam. The original Nanyue, centered on Canton, was one of the Hundred Yue (Bach Viet) states of the fourth century BCE. It was attacked by Qin in 221 BCE but not entirely subdued. When Qin collapsed, power in the Canton region was assumed by Chinese officer Chao Tuo (Trieu Da), who proclaimed himself king of Nanyue in 207 BCE. Sometime after 179 BCE Nanyue obtained suzerainty over the Viet kingdom of Au Lac and was, in turn, absorbed by the Western Han in 111 BCE.

In 1804 the Nguyen dynasty sought recognition from China that they were the rulers of Nam Viet. The Qing, aware of the geographical implications of this name, changed it to Vietnam (Yuenan, "south of Yue," as opposed to "southern Yue").

[*See also* Bach Viet; Trieu Da; *and* Au Lac.]

Keith W. Taylor, *The Birth of Vietnam* (1983).

JAMES M. COYLE

NANAK (1469–1539), first of the ten Sikh gurus. He was born in the Punjab of Hindu parents. The traditional version of his life story derives from the hagiographic verses known as *janam-sakhis*. These narratives contain numerous anecdotes (many of them involving miracles) concerning his childhood, early adult employment, travels, and concluding years back in the Punjab. Particular attention has been focused on his travels, said to have carried him as far as Assam, Sri Lanka, Mecca, and Tibet. Some scholars in the West believe that the *janam-sakhis*, stripped of their miracles, can be regarded as essentially reliable. Others maintain that a more radical critique is needed and that little can be positively affirmed concerning the life of Nanak.

The teachings of Guru Nanak have also attracted some controversy in recent years. Whereas Sikh scholars emphasize his originality, others tend to locate him within the devotional *sant* tradition of northern India. External conventions such as temple or mosque attendance were firmly rejected by Nanak in favor of inward meditation. Akal Purakh, the Supreme Being, is everywhere manifest, his manifold presence constituting his *nam*, or "name." He who meditates on the *nam* will eventually achieve mystical bliss, thus breaking free from the bondage of transmigration.

[*See also* Sikhism.]

J. S. Grewal, *Guru Nanak in History* (1969). W. H. McLeod, *Gurū Nānak and the Sikh Religion* (2d ed., 1976).
W. H. MCLEOD

NANA SAHIB (b. 1824), born Dhundu Pant, the adopted son of the last Maratha *peshwa*, Baji Rao II. In the 1857 uprisings Nana Sahib declared himself *peshwa* and for a short period led the rebels in and around Kanpur. Although this role may have been forced upon him by his retainers, he did hold a grievance against the East India Company for the stopping of a family pension. He remained accused of responsibility for the murder of the defeated British defenders at Kanpur. Following defeat of his troops (16 July 1857) Nana Sahib fled, ultimately to Nepal and an unknown death.

[*See also* Marathas *and* Mutiny, Indian.]

P. C. Gupta, *Nana Sahib and the Rising at Cawnpore* (1963). R. C. Majumdar, *Sepoy Mutiny* (1963).

FRANK F. CONLON

NANBEI CHAO. *See* Southern and Northern Dynasties.

NANCHANG, Chinese city, capital of Jiangxi Province; population, 1,046,000 (1982 estimate). Traditionally a trade and administrative center on the main transport route from Beijing to Guangdong, since 1949 Nanchang has become an industrial city as well, concentrating on food processing, cotton textiles, and manufacturing. Nanchang was the site of a famous uprising in 1927, when a Communist army briefly defeated Nationalist troops. The anniversary of this event is now celebrated in China as the founding day of the People's Liberation Army.

JOHN A. RAPP

NANDABAYIN (r. 1581–1599) was the last king of the First Toungoo dynasty of Burma. Although possessed of determination and physical courage, he inherited an insupportable political legacy. As constituted under his father, Bayinnaung, the First Toungoo empire was a sprawling, incongruous entity, without geographic or economic coherence or effective administrative institutions. Outlying vassals were controlled through ceremonial and personal obligations and ultimately by their fear of invasion. Imperial control proved sufficiently difficult even in Bayinnaung's day, but after his death the dissolution of personal ties to the high king and the military rejuvenation of Siam (a key vassal) presented a challenge of unprecedented gravity. Limited manpower rendered Lower Burma, the only area under Nandabayin's direct control, particularly ill-suited to cope with the ensuing demands for military levies. Nor would Nandabayin consider saving the empire by reducing its scope.

Although he suppressed some major revolts, between 1584 and 1593 he sent no fewer than five unsuccessful expeditions against rebellious Siam.

With each reverse, nearer vassal principalities became less willing to supply auxiliary troops, while peasants in Lower Burma itself became more determined to escape military service. Nandabayin responded with a series of drastic measures of popular control—inquests to purge the Buddhist monkhood, tattooing of royal servicemen, exemplary executions—all to no avail. With some rice-growing districts practically deserted, famine gripped the Irrawaddy Delta. In late 1599 Nandabayin's cousin, the vassal king of Toungoo, finally sacked the capital, Pegu, and seized Nandabayin, who was later murdered together with his heir apparent. Although Toungoo sought to revive the southern-based empire, Lower Burma was too exhausted, and political authority eventually returned to the more populated north.

[See also Bayinnaung and Toungoo Dynasties.]

Maung Htin Aung, *A History of Burma* (1967). G. E. Harvey, *A History of Burma from the Earliest Times* (1925; reprint, 1967). Victor B. Lieberman, *Burmese Administrative Cycles: Anarchy and Conquest, c. 1580–1760* (1984). VICTOR B. LIEBERMAN

NANDA KUMAR. *See* Nuncomar.

NANJING ("southern capital"), Chinese city on the south bank of the Yangtze River approximately 300 kilometers from its mouth. Nanjing has been a major administrative and military center of South China ever since the fall of the Han in 220. Before then the town was of minor importance; the vicinity was ruled by Wu in the Spring and Autumn period and by Yue in the Warring States period until the conquest of the lower Yangtze area by Chu, which gave the town the name Jinling, changed by the Han to Moling.

During the civil wars at the end of the Han, Sun Quan (r. 222–252 as founding emperor of the Three Kingdoms state of Wu) and his advisers were impressed with the military advantages of the site of Nanjing. The Purple Mountain (Zijin Shan) or Bell Mountain (Zhong Shan) to the east and the Yangtze to the north and west shielded the city "like a coiling dragon and a crouching tiger," a phrase used until recent times to describe Nanjing's natural strength. Sun Quan made it his capital, calling it Jianye. The fall of Jianye in 280 temporarily reunified China under the Western Jin, ruling from Luoyang, but civil wars and barbarian invasions led to the collapse of the unified empire during the Yongjia period (307–313). The Eastern Jin regime survived until 420 in South China only and made its capital at Nanjing, renamed Jiankang. Jiankang remained the capital under the successive (Liu) Song, Southern Qi, Liang, and Chen dynasties. Along with the aforementioned Wu and Eastern Jin, Nanjing thus was the imperial capital under six dynasties, a term that has become a standard reference for South China between 222 and 589. [*See also* Six Dynasties.]

Owing to the fragmented nature of authority in this period, the survival of the successive imperial regimes often depended on the resources that could be mobilized in the immediate hinterland of Nanjing. Nanjing also became the center of imperially sponsored Buddhism, especially during the reign of the Liang emperor Wu (r. 502–549). During the destructive rebellion of Hou Jing (c. 548–552), Nanjing was sacked and occupied by the rebels. The weak Chen dynasty that followed was unable to maintain the independence of the South, which was extinguished in 589 when Nanjing fell to the Sui. Such of the great families as had survived the previous disorders were removed to Chang'an.

Nanjing (called Jiangning under the Sui and Tang, and Jiankang again under the Song) shared in the urban growth common to the lower Yangtze region in the following centuries. However, the construction of the Grand Canal under the Sui had the effect of transferring economic and political predominance to the cities along the canal, especially Yangzhou, Suzhou, and Hangzhou; Nanjing remained merely a middle-level city. After the Mongol conquest it was renamed Jiqing and given the administrative status of route (*lu*), one of thirty in the Yuan province of Jiangzhe, which was administered from the former Southern Song imperial capital at Hangzhou.

In 1355 the rebel leader Zhu Yuanzhang crossed the Yangtze. He captured Nanjing in 1356 and made it his base, giving it the suggestive name Yingtian ("responding to heaven"), which remained its middle-level administrative (*fu*) designation until 1912. In 1360 Zhu defeated his archrival Chen Youliang in a decisive battle fought in the immediate vicinity of Nanjing. In 1368 Zhu proclaimed himself emperor of the Ming dynasty, under the regnal designation Hongwu (1368–1398), and the city was called Nanjing for the first time. Hongwu kept Nanjing as his capital for his entire reign and settled his old soldiers there, thus both increasing the population and changing the local dialect to resemble that spoken north of the Yangtze. Extensive new city walls were constructed, running along the Qinhuai River in the south and west and the Xuanwu Lake in the north and reaching both the Purple Mountain and the Yangtze. The area thus enclosed has essentially defined the city down to the present. Hongwu's tomb, the Xiaoling, is located on the southern slope of the Purple Mountain. [*See also* Zhu Yuanzhang.]

In 1402 Hongwu's son Zhu Di (Yongle; r. 1402–1424) secured the throne by capturing Nanjing, and in 1421 he formally transferred the capital to Beijing, where it remains today. Nanjing continued to be a secondary capital, the political and military center of the region later divided into the provinces of Anhui and Jiangsu. The naval expeditions of Zheng He originated in Nanjing, and the great "treasure ships" were built in the Longjiang shipyard on the Qinhuai River. Culturally and economically, however, Suzhou and Hangzhou remained superior to Nanjing, and appointment to high office at Nanjing came to be regarded as a kind of quasi-exile for officials who had lost out at Beijing.

Briefly the center of late Ming resistance to the Manchus (from 1644 to 1645), Nanjing then was the seat of the Qing governor-generalship of Liangjiang, with jurisdiction over Jiangsu, Anhui, and Jiangxi. Its political predominance within the lower Yangtze thus continued under the new dynasty. The signing of the Treaty of Nanjing in 1842 inaugurated the period of the unequal treaties. Nanjing was more affected by internal developments, being captured by the Taiping rebels in 1853 and serving as the Taiping capital until 1864, when recapture by Qing forces devastated the city.

In the late nineteenth century Nanjing was garrisoned by Hunanese troops and ruled by a succession of Hunanese governors-general beginning with Zeng Guofan. Liu Kunyi, one of Zeng's successors, kept Nanjing and its dependent provinces neutral during the Boxer Rebellion of 1900. Nanjing grew into the acknowledged center of Christian missionary activity in China. While not comparable to Shanghai or Hankou as a commercial-industrial center, Nanjing's continuing economic importance was assured by the completion of trunk railway lines from both Shanghai and Tianjin.

During the 1911 revolution, Zhang Xun bravely defended Nanjing for the Qing. Nanjing was the seat of the assembly that successively elected Sun Yat-sen and Yuan Shikai to the presidency. Yuan returned the capital to Beijing, but Nanjing remained an important political-military center during the warlord period, especially as the capital of Sun Quanfang's Union of Five Provinces (Jiangsu, Anhui, Jiangxi, Fujian, and Zhejiang), which was destroyed by the Guomindang (Kuomintang, KMT, or Nationalist Party) Northern Expedition of 1926 to 1927. The victor, Chiang Kai-shek, was strongly

FIGURE 1. *Ming Tomb Guardians.* The tomb of the first Ming emperor serves as a reminder of Nanjing's history as a capital of Chinese dynasties.

impressed by the parallel to the Ming founding, in which Nanjing had served as the capital of a Chinese South triumphing over foreign rule emanating from Beijing. He made Nanjing his capital and buried Sun Yat-sen in an ornate tomb next to the Xiaoling on the southern slope of the Purple Mountain. The so-called "Nanjing Decade" of 1927 to 1937 represented the peak of KMT power.

Full-scale hostilities broke out between China and Japan in July 1937, and Nanjing fell in December. Extensive atrocities at Nanjing, shown vividly on the newsreels of the time, aroused American public opinion against Japan. However, Japan remained in occupation of a large part of China until its final defeat in 1945, and made Nanjing the seat of the collaborationist regime of Wang Jingwei. The KMT government came back to Nanjing after the war, and the KMT constitution was enacted there in 1947. This was only an epilogue; KMT rule in Nanjing came to an end with the Communist conquest of the region in 1950.

Under the People's Republic of China the political/economic dualism previously noted in the lower Yangtze has persisted. Shanghai remains the economic center of the region, but Nanjing, in addition to serving as the capital of Jiangsu Province, is also the headquarters of the Nanjing Military Region, with authority over Jiangsu, Anhui, and Zhejiang, as well as Shanghai Municipality. Nanjing and Wuhan are the sites of the only two road and railway bridges spanning the Yangtze. Nanjing thus retains the political and military centrality in the lower Yangtze that began in the Three Kingdoms.

Edward L. Farmer, *Early Ming Government: The Evolution of Dual Capitals* (1976).   EDWARD L. DREYER

NANJING, TREATY OF. See Treaty Ports.

NANNING, China's southernmost city; capital of the Guangxi Zhuang Autonomous Region, home to China's largest national minority, the Zhuang, as well as eleven other national minorities. Nanning was founded during the Yuan dynasty (1279–1368) as a market center on the trade routes that extended west to the Himalayan Plateau and south to China's tributary states in Southeast Asia. In the mid-nineteenth century Guangxi was the birth place of the Taiping movement. In the late nineteenth century Nanning was a treaty port where the French and British vied for influence. During World War II Nanning was captured by the Japanese, marking one of the farthest points of advance of the Japanese line. Today Nanning is an industrial center processing agricultural products and exploiting nearby mineral resources.

June T. Dreyer, *China's Forty Millions* (1976). Edward H. Schafer, *The Vermillion Bird: T'ang Images of the South* (1967).   SALLY HART

NAOROJI, DADABHAI (1825–1917), Indian nationalist, known as "the grand old man of India." A Parsi graduate (1845) of Elphinstone College, Bombay, professor of mathematics (1854–1855), and Young Bombay reformer, Naoroji helped set up the Students' Literary and Scientific Society, various girls' schools, a Parsi reform body, a newspaper, and the Bombay Association (1848–1855). To lobby Indian issues, he cofounded the East India Association (1866) in London and a branch in Bombay (1869). A founder of the Indian National Congress (1885) and one of its presidents (1886, 1893, 1906), he was also a member of the British Parliament (1892–1895) for the Liberal Party. Increasingly radical in later life, he wanted self-government for India, arguing in *Poverty and Un-British Rule in India* (1901) that India's poverty was the result of the drain of wealth by Britain.

[*See also* Indian National Congress.]

R. P. Masani, *Dadabhai Naoroji* (1960). R. P. Patwardhan, *Dadabhai Naoroji Correspondence*, vol. 2, part 1 (1977).   JIM MASSELOS

NAPIER, SIR CHARLES (1782–1853), British army officer who was responsible for the conquest and subjugation of Sind, in what is now Pakistan, by the British. An aggressive imperialist, he provoked war with the Amirs before annexing Sind in 1843. Napier borrowed from the model of the Irish constabulary to create a strong military administration in Sind. He was called back to India to meet the challenge posed by the Sikhs in 1847, and he reorganized the British army before resigning in a dispute with Lord Dalhousie.

[*See also* Sind.]

H. T. Lambrick, *Sir Charles Napier and Sind* (1952).
LYNN ZASTOUPIL

NAQSHBANDI, a Sufi order *(tariqa)* that began in Central Asia. Its legends identify Ahmad Ata Yaswi (d. 1116) as the order's founder, but the name derives from Bahauddin an-Naqshband (d. 1389). The order arrived in India at a fairly late date. Although the Mughal emperor Babar supposedly invited its adherents to India, Shaikh Baqi Bi'llah (d. 1603), who arrived in Delhi during Akbar's reign, was the first influential Naqshbandi to make his home there. During this period the spiritual program of the Naqshbandis was not yet solidly established. Baqi Bi'llah's own son was attracted to the pantheistic views of the Spanish mystic philosopher Ibn Arabi.

Baqi Bi'llah's favorite disciple, Ahmad Sirhindi (d. 1624), however, took a much more scripturalist approach, attacking Arabi's thought and bemoaning the influence of Shi'ites and Hindus in the royal court. Sirhindi's emphasis on the Qur'an, *shari'a*, and the personality of the Prophet as revealed in *hadith* literature helped to place Indian Naqshbandis at the center of the religious revival that took place in the Muslim world in the century after Sirhindi's death. Indian Naqshbandis living in the holy cities initiated many Indonesians and Central Asians into the order. The hospice of Mirzah Mazhar Jan-i Janan (d. 1780) was another notable Naqshbandi center. In contrast to the Chishtis, Naqshbandis favored private meditation (particularly intense concentration on the image of one's master) and rejected the use of music as a spiritual aid.

[*See also* Islam; Sufism; *and* Sirhindi, Ahmad.]

A. Ahmad, *An Intellectual History of Islam in India* (1969). F. Robinson, *Atlas of the Islamic World* (1982).

GREGORY C. KOZLOWSKI

NARAI, king of Ayudhya (r. 1656–1688), brought Siam into relations with Louis XIV of France. Born about 1631, Narai was the second son of King Prasat Thong (r. 1629–1656). On his father's death, Narai's elder brother Chai seized the throne. The next day, Narai deposed him and placed Prasat Thong's brother on the throne; ten weeks later (26 October 1656), with substantial aid from Ayudhya's foreign Asian community, Narai seized it for himself. The concerns of his early years were typical of Ayudhya monarchs: he surmounted the challenges of princely rivals and went to war with Lan Na and Burma. In the 1670s and 1680s he became increasingly alert to the possibilities of strengthening the kingdom through foreign diplomatic and commercial relations, and he made heavy use of Siam's resident Japanese, Malay, Makassarese, and Persian communities—as well as the Dutch East India Company and English private traders—to expand commerce. His "prime minister" (of the Mahattahai) until 1685 was of the Persian Bunnag family and was in turn replaced by the Greek adventurer Constantine Phaulkon, who worked assiduously to promote Narai's conversion to Christianity while promoting relations with France, Persia, and various Indian states. Narai sent two missions to Louis XIV's court at Versailles, and the French reciprocated with three, each more numerous and threatening than the previous; the 1687–1688 mission brought two hundred troops. Resentment of Phaulkon's promotion of France and of Christianity was fueled by his displacement of Chinese and Muslim trading interests and coalesced around Phra Phetracha, head of the Elephant Department and foster-brother to Narai. Siam's Glorious Revolution of 1688 brought the execution of Phaulkon in June and the elevation of Phetracha to the throne after Narai's death on 11 July.

[*See also* Ayudhya; Prasat Thong; Mahatthai; Bunnag Family; Phaulkon, Constantine; *and* Phetracha.]

Claude de Beze, *1688, Revolution in Siam,* translated by E. W. Hutchinson (1968). Simon de la Loubère, *A New Historical Relation of the Kingdom of Siam* (1693; reprint, 1969). John O'Kane, trans., *The Ship of Sulaiman* (1972). G. V. Smith, *The Dutch in Seventeenth-Century Thailand* (1977). David K. Wyatt, *Thailand: A Short History* (1984).

DAVID K. WYATT

NARAPATISITHU, king of the Burmese kingdom of Pagan (r. 1174–1211). He greatly expanded the influence of his kingdom, and his authority extended to Mergui and the Shan States. He exploited adjacent centers of power and increased the kingdom's revenues by settling people on virgin land that was made cultivable. He reorganized Pagan's military and made it highly effective, re-formed the administration into a centralized organization manned by crown officials, and patronized literature, the arts, and the *sangha* (the Buddhist monastic order). Under his reign Pagan became a center of learning and Buddhism. Its myriad temples, wrote one Sinhalese pilgrim, had peaks that "cry shame on Devendra's abode."

Narapatisithu left his successors with a large kingdom, a strong military, a full treasury, and what appears to be a sound administration. Sheltered from the rigors and problems of state building, and also locked into an ideological system that linked their legitimacy to largesse on the Buddhist church,

Narapatisithu's successors slowly depleted the resources of the kingdom. A century after Narapatisithu ascended the throne, the Pagan kingdom that he helped raise to such heights crumbled under the weight of its own structural and ideological problems and pressure from external enemies.

[*See also* Pagan.]

Michael Aung-Thwin, *The Origins of the Classical Burmese State: An Institutional History of the Kingdom of Pagan* (1985). G. H. Luce, "Aspects of Pagan History—Later Periods," in *In Memoriam Phya Anuman Rajadhon* (1970), pp. 139–146. Pe Maung Tin and G. H. Luce, trans., *The Glass Palace Chronicle* (1960).

MICHAEL AUNG-THWIN

NARA PERIOD (710–784), era of Japanese history named for the capital city of Nara (then called Heijō). The Nara period is distinguished by the pervasive influence of Chinese ideas and tastes. Although short, the period is well known, partly because in Nara (capital for all but five years of the period) one can still see such remarkable Nara-period sights as the great Buddhist temple of Tōdaiji, the famous fifty-three-foot statue of Vairocana Buddha housed in one of the world's largest wooden buildings, and the impressive Shōsō-in storehouse. Other well-known artifacts include artworks and manuscripts of notable quality, including an anthology of ancient poems (the *Man'yōshū*) and two of Japan's earliest extant court chronicles. Among historians this segment of Japanese history is also appreciated for the great advances that were made in the formation of a centralized bureaucracy, the completion and early deterioration of a system for bringing all land and people under state control, the rise of a statewide complex of Buddhist temples supported by the court, and spectacular developments in learning. All these changes and achievements came at a time when Japanese aristocratic leaders had become fascinated by the political power and cultural achievements of China during the Sui and early Tang dynasties.

The task of using Chinese bureaucratic forms to establish imperial control over all land and people was so closely linked with the enactment and enforcement of penal and administrative *(ritsuryō)* law that the resultant political order is frequently referred to as the *ritsuryō* state. The work of compiling a *ritsuryō* code was first undertaken during the reign of Tenchi Tennō (661–671), who adopted as well a number of other measures for strengthening and unifying imperial rule. These measures were initiated by men who were familiar with, and concerned about, the great power and achievements of seventh-century China. Thus, not simply penal and administrative law but the entire mechanism of political control was strongly influenced by Chinese principles and methods. Indeed, the 250-year period that begins with the great reforms in 645 and includes the ninth-century portion of the later Heian period were years in which Japanese politics and culture were affected in deep and lasting ways by Chinese models. Those two and a half centuries are therefore frequently described as a time of sinification, just as the last century of Japanese history is characterized as a time of westernization.

During the first decade of the Nara period, the *ritsuryō* network of administrative control was redefined in the Yōrō Penal and Administrative Code, which was completed in 718 but not promulgated until nearly forty years later. It was in the first decade that the city of Heijō became a grand capital built along the lines of Chang'an (the capital of Tang China), that coins were minted, roads constructed, and post stations built. Emperor Gemmei's edict of 713 ordered all provinces to submit information on their geography, traditions, and produce. The whole of the report *(fudoki)* submitted by the province of Izumo and portions of four others, have been preserved. Previous *tennō* (emperors) had also ordered the compilation of chronicles that would detail their genealogical descent from the sun goddess (Amaterasu) and record court events. The earliest such chronicles extant are from the first decade of the Nara period: the *Kojiki*, or *Record of Ancient Matters*, which is said to have been completed in 712, and the *Nihonshoki*, or *Chronicles of Japan*, which was submitted to the throne in 720. While the *fudoki* were expected to provide information needed for extending governmental control to outlying areas, the chronicles were meant to clarify and affirm—in the style of a Chinese dynastic history—a single line of imperial descent from the first *tennō*, preceded by a single line of *kami* (divinities, numinous forces) descended from the Sun Goddess (the ancestral *kami*).

The major political currents of the Nara period flowed from the shifts in the power of rulers to control and direct the affairs of the *ritsuryō* state. Throughout the period, the descendants of Temmu (who reigned from 673 to 686) occupied the throne, and for the most part they were, like Temmu, despotic rulers who tended to govern the state directly in the Chinese manner. But as early as the first decade of the Nara period, imperial power was shared with, if not diminished by, a strong leader of the Fujiwara *uji* (clan): Fujiwara no Fuhito (659–720). Fuhito became particularly influential after 707 when, following Mommu Tennō's death, a Mommu son by Fuhito's daughter was named crown prince. Plans were then made to move the capital to Heijō. Thus, the beginning of the Nara period is linked with the rise of Fujiwara no Fuhito to a position of great influence at the court.

The Fuhito years were also a time of ambitious imperial projects that, according to recent research, caused severe hardships among common people. A document of 711 states that many workers were deserting. Likewise, the tax burden on farmers had become so heavy that many fled to become *furōnin* (vagrants). The government was also finding it increasingly difficult to locate enough land suitable for rice cultivation to give each registered household member a plot of the prescribed size and productivity. Thus, while imperial control under the *ritsuryō* system probably reached its highest point during the first decade of the Nara period, political and economic pressures were already beginning to undermine the administrative structure.

When Fuhito died in 720 his position of influence at court was not taken over by another member of the Fujiwara *uji* but by a member of the imperial family: Prince Nagaya (684–729). Yet a son of Fuhito's daughter was placed on the throne as Shōmu Tennō in 723. Then in 729 Fujiwara leaders seem to have plotted the death of Prince Nagaya. Soon after the prince's death, a Fujiwara woman was designated empress *(kōgō)* and four Fuhito sons received prominent positions within the Council of State, temporarily ending the princely challenge to Fujiwara dominance. While the next eight years are known as the period of the "four Fujiwara brothers" regime, the rapid rise of Fujiwara fortunes came to an abrupt end in 737, when all four brothers died in a smallpox epidemic. From that year until the Fujiwara no Nakamaro rebellion of 764, the administration of state affairs was disrupted by continuous and often bitter rivalry among powerful *uji* and between Fujiwara leaders and female members of the imperial family.

The stormy middle four decades of the Nara period were notable for the emergence of a state system of Buddhist temples, with Tōdaiji (and its huge statue of Vairocana Buddha) located at the capital and provincial temples *(kokubunji)* in outlying regions. The support of Buddhism by members of the imperial family can be traced back to Prince Shōtoku (574–622), known as the founder of Japanese Buddhism. But the erection of a state temple system began with Temmu Tennō, who ordered Buddhist halls built, Buddhist statues made, Buddhist sutras deposited, and Buddhist rites held in each province of the land. He and his successors were undoubtedly influenced by reports of what was being done in Tang China to make Buddhism a state religion. But edicts issued by Shōmu Tennō in 739, when the country was suffering from a smallpox epidemic, were far more sweeping and specific than in China. At first Shōmu ordered one statue of Buddha, two statues of Kyōji Bosatsu, and one copy of the *Prajnaparamita Sutra (Daihannyagyō)* to be sent to each province as a prayer that Buddha would end the epidemic. The following year he ordered that each province have ten copies of the *Lotus Sutra* and a seven-story Buddhist pagoda. Finally, in 741 he handed down an edict proclaiming that every province maintain two temples (one for monks and another for nuns) and that monks and nuns perform rites assuring the elimination of catastrophe, good rice harvests, and the prosperity of the state.

In 743 Shōmu Tennō took another important step toward making Japan a Buddhist state by proclaiming, as a *tennō* possessed of all the people and land of the country, that the country's resources be used to erect a monumental statue of Vairocana Buddha at Tōdaiji. This was a costly and difficult undertaking that was not completed until 752. Shōmu eventually had to make a special plea for materials and labor, and even resorted to seeking the assistance of Gyōgi (668–749), a popular Buddhist priest whose earlier activities had caused the government to censure him. The casting of the fifty-three-foot statue seemed to receive the blessing of Vairocana himself when, in 749, officials from northern Japan suddenly reported the discovery of gold, just when it was badly needed for covering the entire statue with gold leaf. On this happy occasion Shōmu's daughter, who had succeeded Shōmu as *tennō* in 749 and who was also devoted to Buddhism, issued an edict in which she referred to herself as a "servant of the Three Buddhist Treasures," leaving the impression that Buddha now stood above Amaterasu. But a few days later she issued another edict in which she identified herself as "a *tennō* who is a manifest *kami*," indicating that she accepted the traditional view (clearly reflected in both the *Kojiki* and the *Nihonshoki*) that her legitimacy as a *tennō* was rooted in her descent, in an unbroken genealogical line, from Amaterasu.

Following the death of Shōmu Tennō in 756, his daughter Kōken arranged elaborate Buddhist services for him and had his treasured belongings collected and presented to Tōdaiji, the temple that, with the great statue of Vairocana Buddha, was now the centerpiece of Shōmu's statewide temple system. A check of the listings in the extant presentation document reveals that most of the items deposited in Tōdaiji's famous storehouse (the Shōsō-in) still exist, making the Shōsō-in and its contents impressive and comprehensive testimony to the cultural achievements of the Nara period. The collection contains, in addition to documents marked with the *tennō* seal, precious works of art, various implements and medicines, and even articles imported from countries as far west as Persia. [*See* Tōdaiji.]

While Shōmu Tennō had been on the throne the great Fujiwara *uji* continued to struggle against the Tachibana *uji* for dominance at court, and political tensions were constantly exacerbated by rivalry between two factions headed by female members of the royal family: Retired Emperor Genshō was aligned with the Tachibana, and Shōmu's consort (Retired Emperor Kōmyō) with the Fujiwara. And yet it seems that Shōmu had not been much restricted by the power of any one *uji* or female member of his family, although contemporary evidence suggests that the Fujiwara began to regain positions of influence after Fujiwara no Nakamaro (706–764) was appointed to a fairly high office in 743. In sum, Shōmu Tennō seems to have been a *ritsuryō*-state despot not unlike his great grandfather Temmu Tennō, although the high cost of building and maintaining Buddhist temples and unusually destructive natural disasters were arousing discontent among the common people and making it increasingly difficult for the government both to collect sufficient income and to find enough land suitable for distribution to registered members of households. Indeed, economic troubles were forcing the government to take steps toward encouraging the development of new lands for rice cultivation, since discontent over the shortage of land was beginning to undermine the *ritsuryō* order.

The twenty-year period between 749 and 770 was one in which Japan's political affairs were largely dominated by Shōmu's consort, Retired Emperor Kōmyō, and their daughter Kōken. The latter occupied the throne twice: first as Kōken Tennō between 749 and 758 and then as Shōtoku Tennō between 764 and 770, the year of her death. It appears that she was as despotically inclined as her father and became even more deeply devoted to the Buddhist cause than he was. But her life was constantly buffeted by conspiracy and civil war.

Like her mother, Kōken was closer to the Fujiwara than to the Tachibana, although during most of her first reign Tachibana no Moroe held highest office. Quite soon, however, Fujiwara no Nakamaro (706–764) received high-level appointments and began to act as if he were the most influential person at court, especially after Moroe's death in 756 and the appointment of a crown prince whose mother was a Fujiwara. The high point of Nakamaro's influence came in 757, when he arranged to have the Yōrō Code (largely the work of his grandfather Fuhito) promulgated, and in the following year, when he managed to have the crown prince placed on the throne as Junnin Tennō. Within a few months, he was granted three thousand households and one hundred *chō* of "merit land" in perpetuity and permitted to mint coins (even though private minting was normally considered an unpardonable crime), to make rice loans (*suiko*), and to use a seal that had as much authority as the seal of the Council of State. By 762 Nakamaro held the highest office and the highest rank that could be bestowed on a commoner.

After 762 Nakamaro's fortunes declined. Some feel that this began in 760 with the death of Shōmu's consort, Retired Emperor Kōmyō, who had supported Nakamaro and who may have exercised more influence over state affairs than her daughter Kōken or Junnin Tennō (who occupied the throne from 758 to 764). Retired Emperor Kōmyō had established a Chinese-style bureau (called the Kōgōgū-shiki) which, according to some scholars, had the standing of a ministry in the Council of State. After 755 this bureau (headed by Nakamaro) was reorganized and strengthened, until it seemed to stand above the Council of State itself. Other measures instituted at the time suggest that Nakamaro thought of Kōmyō as Japan's Empress Wu, the tyrannical ruler of Tang China between 691 and 705. But after Kōmyō's death in 760, Nakamaro was forced to obtain royal backing from Retired Emperor Kōken and Junnin Tennō. For two years he was moderately successful. Meanwhile, however, huge building projects (including forts on the northern frontier and a new detached palace at Hora no Miya), costly military ventures (centered on plans to invade Korea), a devaluation of Japanese coins, and successive years of famine were seriously weakening the economic base of his administration.

The year 762 was a time of crisis not only for Nakamaro but for the *ritsuryō* state. In the fifth month of that year, after they returned from the new palace at Hora no Miya, Retired Emperor Kōken and Junnin Tennō occupied different palaces at the capital; a split had occurred between them over Kōken's relations with a Buddhist priest, Dōkyō (d. 772), who had used esoteric methods to cure Kōken's illness and then had become intimate with her. As soon as the former and current emperors returned to the capital, it seems that Junnin Tennō (probably with the backing of Nakamaro) reproached Kōken over the Dōkyō affair. Kōken then called in high officials and issued an edict in which she proclaimed that henceforth she would be responsible for important matters of state and Junnin Tennō for unimportant ones. Nakamaro was suprised and upset, realizing that he had lost Kōken's support, which was apparently more important than that of the reigning Junnin Tennō.

After this edict had been issued, the influence of Buddhist priests and temples increased rapidly, and by 764 Nakamaro was plotting a military coup in a desperate effort to reestablish Fujiwara influence. But the plot was disclosed and Kōken mobilized troops for a showdown. Within a few days her forces emerged victorious. Nakamaro and many of his supporters were executed, Junnin Tennō was sent into exile, and Kōken herself reoccupied the throne as Shōtoku Tennō. It was Japan's most serious internal disturbance since the short succession war of 672.

Although Shōtoku Tennō had already become a Buddhist nun, as tennō she was the country's highest Shinto priestess in the worship of native kami, and thus she was impelled to issue an edict at the time of the great kami festival scheduled for the first month of 675. In it she attempted to explain why she, as a Buddhist nun, could still properly conduct rites as a high Shinto priestess. She admitted that it had been customary to avoid Buddhist associations when worshiping native kami but proclaimed that Buddhist scriptures had identified kami as divine beings that honor and protect Buddhism.

During the Shōtoku Tennō reign, Buddhist priests and institutions became especially powerful. High priority was assigned to building Buddhist pagodas, to the support of Buddhist priests and temples, to the completion of the provincial temple system, and to building a Saidaiji ("western temple") that would be the equal of the great Tōdaiji ("eastern temple"). Dōkyō himself was promoted to the high office of Priestly Ruler (hō-ō) in 766, and other priests received posts in the Council of State.

A priest from the great Usa Hachiman Shrine of northern Kyushu, one who was holding a position under Dōkyō's brother, suddenly appeared in the capital in the fifth month of 769 reporting that an oracular message had been received from the great kami Hachiman announcing that Dōkyō should be enthroned as the next tennō. Dōkyō was pleased to hear this but apparently Shōtoku Tennō was not. Hachiman appeared to her in a dream one night and advised her to have someone check the veracity of the oracle. For the assignment she picked Wake no Kiyomaro (733–799). When Dōkyō heard what was being done, he reportedly called in Kiyomaro and promised him a ministerial post if the original oracle message proved correct. But when Kiyomaro arrived at the Usa Hachiman Shrine and prayed to Hachiman, this revised version of the oracle was revealed to him: "A tennō must be a descendant of a tennō." After Kiyomaro returned to the capital and reported what Hachiman had really said, Dōkyō had Kiyomaro demoted and exiled. The incident did not therefore bring Dōkyō's administration to a close. That was brought about only by the death of Shōtoku Tenno in the eighth month of 770.

The rapid rise of Buddhist influence in state affairs placed additional strain on the economic foundations of the ritsuryō system. As early as 743 the government had been so hard-pressed for income-producing land that it had offered private ownership in perpetuity to persons or institutions that would convert virgin land to rice fields. These newly developed and privately owned fields could be sold or commended, and could not therefore be used by the state for allocations under the ritsuryō system. It was the Buddhist temples, such as the Tōdaiji at the capital, that were the major developers. By 749 the government had to set limits on the amount of land a temple could possess. But, in the face of heavy building costs, the Tōdaiji devised a plan of developing tax-free land holdings, called "early shōen," that soon appeared all over the country. As new Buddhist temples were built and old ones were expanded the temple system accumulated vast land holdings that lay outside of the state's tax system. At the time of Shōtoku Tennō's death in 770 the court was concerned not merely about the inordinate influence of Buddhist priests but also with the enormous wealth of Buddhist temples.

Since Shōtoku Tennō had not selected her successor, a complicated rivalry arose between the supporters of two princely candidates: a descendant of Temmu Tennō (whose descendants had occupied the throne since his death in 686); and a descendent of Tenchi Tennō (the Temmu brother who had preceded Temmu). The latter, supported by two powerful members of the Fujiwara uji, was finally enthroned as Kōnin Tennō. For the next several years the court was torn by rivalries between the supporters of the two lines, between the Fujiwara and other *uji*, as well as between different Fujiwara houses. But finally Kōnin's eldest son ascended the throne as Kammu Tennō in 781. Thereafter, Tenchi descendants ascended the throne as emperor.

The capital was moved to Nagaoka in 784 and then to Heian (now Kyoto) in 794, bringing to a close the brilliant Nara period. Within less than a century, a succession of despotic but colorful *tennō* of the Temmu line had been replaced by descendants of the Tenchi line; the Fujiwara *uji* had finally established itself in a position of dominance at court; the *ritsuryō* system, developed as a powerful support for *tennō* control, had begun to crumble; the danger that *tennō* rule would be replaced by Buddhist rule had been removed; and the tradition of great power being exercised by female members of the royal family (especially by consorts and daughters) had been broken. Not until several centuries later did another woman become *tennō*.

[*See also* Ritsuryō State; Tōdaiji; Fujiwara Lineage; Temmu; *and* Heian Period.]

George B. Sansom, *A History of Japan to 1334* (1958). J. B. Snellen, "Shoku Nihonji, Chronicles of Japan, for 697-791 A.D.," in *Transactions of the Asiatic Society of Japan,* series 2, vol. 2 (1934) and vol. 14 (1937).

DELMAR M. BROWN

NARATHIHAPADE, ruler of the Burmese kingdom of Pagan (r. 1255–1287 CE). He went down in Burmese history as the person responsible for the destruction of Burma's most glorious kingdom. He was said to have destroyed temples to build fortifications against external enemies, the gravest of errors in a Buddhist society. Contemporary inscriptions, however, tell a somewhat different story. According to them, Narathihapade, of plebeian origin, provided a calm respite of close to thirty years to a kingdom burdened with financial problems. He must have had the political skill and military ability to have attained the throne and to have kept it for so long. His great work of merit, the Mingalazedi, built in the style of Anawrahta's temples, survives; it was said to have enshrined in it miniature replicas of the royal family that ruled Pagan since the days of Anawrahta. Narathihapade's reign saw the end of the political apparatus that once had firm control over the plains of Burma, but the end had begun with King Nadaungmya and his largesse toward the *sangha* (the Buddhist monastic order); Narathihapade inherited a process over which he had little

effective control and one which was a fundamental characteristic of Burmese society.

[*See also* Pagan *and* Anawrahta.]

Michael Aung-Thwin, *The Origins of the Classical Burmese State: An Institutional History of the Kingdom of Pagan* (1985). Paul J. Bennett, *Conference under the Tamarind Tree: Three Essays in Burmese History* (1971). Pe Maung Tin and G. H. Luce, trans., *The Glass Palace Chronicle* (1960).   MICHAEL AUNG-THWIN

NARAYAN, JAYAPRAKASH (1902–1979), Indian political leader. Born in Bihar, "JP" was educated at the University of Wisconsin, where he joined the Communist Party; he later abandoned it in favor of Jawaharlal Nehru's nationalism, and finally deserted Nehru for an idealistic rural-based Gandhian socialism that eschewed political power. A prolific writer and widely regarded philosopher, Narayan worked closely with Vinoba Bhave in the Sarvodaya movement after Mohandas Gandhi's death in 1948. In the 1970s Narayan went into unreserved opposition to Indira Gandhi, whereas Bhave tried to remain outside of partisan debate.

Narayan was the unquestioned leader of the Janata coalition that defeated Indira Gandhi's Congress in the March 1977 elections. Hampered by a serious kidney ailment requiring dialysis in his later years, Narayan nevertheless insisted on residence in Bihar, where proper medical facilities were unavailable. His refusal to seek or accept political office for himself always assured him a large following among Gandhians and other Indians, who almost universally regarded him as a saintlike and well-meaning figure. Communists and radical socialists considered Narayan's organizations, including the Sarvodaya and the Janata Morcha, "mere camouflage for feudal, bourgeois, or landed interests." More moderate criticisms of Narayan revolve around his inability to build lasting institutions and his excessive reliance on his own charismatic appeal for support.

[*See also* Gandhi, Mohandas Karamchand; Bhave, Vinoba; Nehru, Jawaharlal; *and* Gandhi, Indira.]

Ajit Bhattacharjea, *Jayaprakash Narayan: A Political Biography* (1975). Jayaprakash Narayan, *Face to Face* (1971).   MARCUS FRANDA

NARESUAN, king of Ayudhya (r. 1590–1605), warrior king who regained Siam's independence from Burma. Born in 1555, Naresuan was the eldest son of King Mahathammaracha by his chief queen, who was the daughter of King Chakkraphat. He spent the years 1564 to 1571 in Burma as a hostage for his father's obedience to Burma. Although he was only sixteen on his return, he was named heir-presumptive *(uparat)* and sent to take charge of the Phitsanulok region. Throughout his father's reign he established himself as an able and daring general, though he was still a vassal of Burma. By the late 1580s, however, he had improved the kingdom's army and defenses and had broken with the Burmese. When his father died in June 1590, Naresuan succeeded to the throne, apparently naming his younger brother, Ekathotsarot, nominal coruler. The culmination of Ayudhya's half-century struggle with Burma came with the Battle of Nong Sarai on 18 January 1593, when Naresuan, astride an elephant, defeated the Burmese crown prince in single combat and the Burmese retreated. Throughout the rest of his reign Naresuan campaigned to extend Ayudhya's frontiers and strengthen its institutions. Following his death, which occurred on 25 April 1605 as he campaigned in the Shan States, Ekathotsarot succeeded him. Naresuan is one of a handful of Thai monarchs to have earned the epithet "the great."

[*See also* Ayudhya; Mahathammaracha; Chakkraphat; *and* Ekathotsarot.]

W. A. R. Wood, *A History of Siam* (1926). David K. Wyatt, *Thailand: A Short History* (1984).

DAVID K. WYATT

NASIR AL-DIN SHAH QAJAR. *See* Qajar, Nasir al-Din.

NASUTION, ABDUL HARIS. Born in 1918 in Kotanopan, North Sumatra, General Nasution has been one of the leading figures in the Indonesian army and its principal theoretician.

Trained in the Bandung Military Academy under the Dutch, he was a second lieutenant in the Dutch Indies Army at the time of the Japanese invasion of Indonesia. He joined the Republican army after independence and in May 1946 was appointed commander of its West Java division (later Siliwangi). He became deputy commander of the armed forces and chief of its operations staff in 1948 and was the prime mover in the republic's plans for rationalizing the armed forces. In December 1949 he was named chief of staff of the army but was suspended for his

role in the movement demanding dissolution of Parliament in October 1952.

Inactive from 1952 to 1955, Nasution was reappointed army chief of staff, a post he had until 1962, when he became chief of staff of the combined armed forces. He was minister of defense from 1959–1966. He led military actions against the regional rebellions of 1958 to 1961. Although often disagreeing with Sukarno, he actively supported the West Irian campaign and the Confrontation policies directed against Malaysia. [*See* Confrontation.]

He was a principal target of the attempted coup of 30 September 1965 but escaped with minor injuries, although his daughter was killed. He was elected chairman of Parliament in 1966 and held the post until 1972. He has been a prominent critic of the Suharto government.

In 1958 he formulated his middle-way concept of the army's political role, on which later theories of its "dual function" *(dwifungsi)* were based. His extensive writings include a three-volume history of the Indonesian army and a treatise on guerrilla warfare (translated as *Fundamentals of Guerrilla Warfare*).

Harold Crouch, *The Army and Politics in Indonesia* (1978). Herbert Feith, *The Decline of Constitutional Authority in Indonesia* (1962). David Jenkins, *Suharto and the Generals* (1984). Ulf Sundhaussen, *The Road to Power: Indonesian Military Politics 1945–1967* (1982).

AUDREY R. KAHIN

NATIONALIST PARTY. *See* Guomindang.

NATS. In Burma the word *nat* is used to mean a humanized spirit. *Nats* may be guardians of a particular phenomenon in nature, such as a tree or a mountain. They may be family, village, or territorial guardians of sorts. They may be Buddhist celestial forms, such as a Brahma or Mara. They may also be reputed to have been historical personages. The best-known grouping of these spirits is called the Thirty-Seven Nats.

According to custom, there are actually two sets of Thirty-Seven Nats. One grouping, the Inner Nats, is so called because images of them were allowed inside sacred buildings as Buddhist deities or adaptations of competing gods such as Shiva and Ganesha. Another somewhat variable list, the Outer Nats, originally kept outside temples, is primarily composed of legendary historical Burmese personages turned spirit whose "green" or violent end is poignantly recalled as often due to conflicts involving royal commands. The outer, more historical Thirty-Seven Nats have received the most attention in Burma, despite frequent attempts by some Buddhists to reduce their influence.

Propitiation of any number of the outer Thirty-Seven Nats has been an integral part of religious life for millennia, although Burmese and international scholars have long debated whether *nats* represent a separate animist religion or are a part of the Buddhist Burmese spectrum. Honoring the potential influence of *nats* by gifts and rituals is common in Burma, and certain individuals are known as susceptible to the state of *nat* spirit possession, particularly in complex dances peculiar to each *nat*. For centuries the stories of particular *nats* have been the subject of the traditional Burmese arts, such as sculpture, literature, dance, and music.

Maung Htin Aung, *Folk Elements in Burmese Buddhism* (1962). E. Michael Mendelson, "Observations on a Tour in the Region of Mount Popa, Central Burma," *France-Asie* 179 (1963): 786–807. Melford E. Spiro, *Burmese Supernaturalism* (1967). R. C. Temple, *The Thirty-Seven Nats: A Phase of Spirit-Worship Prevailing in Burma* (1906).   JOHN P. FERGUSON

NATSIR, MOHAMMAD (b. 1908), a Western-educated, Minangkabau, modernist Muslim intellectual and politician. Mohammad Natsir opposed secular Indonesian nationalism in the 1930s in favor of a more purely Islamic vision for any postcolonial Indonesian state. During the Indonesian revolution (1945–1949) he emerged as a cabinet minister representing Masjumi, an Islamic political party in which, for a time, modernists and those of more traditional leanings collaborated. He was Indonesia's first postrevolution premier (1950–1951) and in 1958 became vice-premier of an unsuccessful secessionist government known as Permesta. Released from five years of detention in 1966, he resumed his role as a leading figure among the modernists, chairing the Dewan Dakwah Islamiyah Indonesia (Indonesian Council for the Propagation of Islam) and serving as vice president of the World Muslim Congress.

[*See also* Indonesia, Republic of; Indonesian Revolution; Masjumi; *and* Pemerintah Revolusioner Republik Indonesia/Perdjuangan Semesta.]

Deliar Noer, *The Modernist Muslim Movement in Indonesia, 1900–1942* (1973).   JAMES R. RUSH

NATSUME SŌSEKI (1867–1916), Japanese novelist. Natsume graduated from Tokyo Imperial University in 1893 with a degree in English. He taught in Tokyo and then moved to the provinces, the first of many quixotic acts. In 1900 he accepted a government scholarship to study in London, where he spent a very uncomfortable two years and came close to mental breakdown. He returned to Japan in 1902 to replace Lafcadio Hearn as professor of English at Tokyo University. Natsume began writing fiction in 1904. His disillusion with academic life culminated in his resignation from the university in 1907, after which time he devoted himself to writing, producing two full-length novels each year.

Natsume's early successes include the satiric *I Am a Cat* (*Wagahai wa neko de aru,* 1905) and the bittersweet *Sanshirō* (1908), both of which retain a lightheartedness that was soon to fade. Later works such as *The Gate* (*Mon,* 1910) and *The Wayfarer* (*Kōjin,* 1913) became increasingly pessimistic about the possibilities of communication between individuals; his characters have been called "memorably unhappy." This negative outlook may have been one of the effects of the chronic ulcers that plagued him throughout his adult life and caused his death. His themes are the universal ones of alienation and identity in the modern world and the more parochial one of the nature of individualism in modern Japan. *Kokoro* (1914), perhaps his most powerful and certainly his best-known work, treats questions of betrayal and suicide largely in the style of the epistolary novel. For many Natsume is the novelist who best captures the sense of intellectual dislocation that has characterized Japan's entry into the modern world.

Howard Hibbett, "Natsume Sōseki and the Psychological Novel," in *Tradition and Modernization in Japanese Culture,* edited by Donald H. Shively (1971). Edwin McClellan, *Two Japanese Novelists: Sōseki and Tōson* (1969). Masao Miyoshi, *Accomplices of Silence* (1974). Natsume Sōseki, *Kokoro,* translated by Edwin McClellan (1957).   RICHARD BOWRING

NATYASHASTRA. Ascribed to the mythical sage Bharata, this treatise on dramaturgy is the main source of information on theater in ancient India. The *Natyashastra,* traditionally revered for its divine origin, enjoys the unique status of a prescriptive law book (*shastra*) expounding rules and regulations governing drama and theater and of an encyclopedia of theatrical practice, incorporating costumes and properties, acting styles and techniques, gestures, postures, and movements. It also contains the kernel of an aesthetic theory—the *rasa* theory—that underlies most critical and popular appreciation of art and literature in India.

The treatise is presented within the framework of a *purana* (mythology). Brahma, the Creator, in response to questions asked by Bharata, explains the nature of *natya*, that is, dance, drama, and music. Bharata expounds on this knowledge to his hundred sons, who become the first performers and stage a play for the gods.

The text is divided into thirty-six sections and was probably compiled and recast over several centuries: estimates range from the second to eighth centuries CE. The most complete extant text is preserved within the erudite commentary of Abhinavagupta (tenth to eleventh centuries), a monastic Shaivite from Kashmir.

The Nātyaśāstra Ascribed to Bharata Muni, 2 vols., trans. by M. M. Ghosh, 2d. rev. ed. (1967). Pramod Kale, *The Theatric Universe* (1974).   PRAMOD KALE

NAUNGDAWGYI (1734–1763), second ruler of the Konbaung dynasty (r. 1760–1763). Appointed crown prince in 1753 as the eldest son of Alaunghpaya (r. 1752–1760), Maung Hlauk took the throne on 7 June 1760 in the face of an unsuccessful challenge by his next-youngest brother, the future Hsinhpyushin. A weak, unpopular ruler, Naungdawgyi spent much of his short reign subduing the major rebellions mounted first by the able and popular general Mingaung Nawrahta and then by his uncle the viceroy of Toungoo. Naungdawgyi died suddenly on 28 November 1763, possibly poisoned by Hsinhpyushin, who succeeded to the throne legitimately, as Naungdawgyi's only son was a minor. [*See also* Konbaung Dynasty; Alaunghpaya; *and* Hsinhpyushin.]   WILLIAM J. KOENIG

NAW BAHAR, a toponym common to Bukhara, Samarkand, and Balkh signifying the site of a Buddhist temple complex. The complex discussed here is Balkh's, the best known of the three. At the beginning of the seventh century CE a Chinese traveler described the complex as containing a temple, north of which stood a 200-foot-high stupa. To the southwest of the first temple stood a second and much older one. The complex was destroyed after the Arabo-Muslim conquests of the late seventh century, but writers continued to describe the site for many centuries thereafter.

The Barmakids, an important family of viziers in late eighth-century Baghdad, traced their origins to this temple complex, which their ancestors had administered until the Muslim conquests. [*See also* Balkh.]

ROBERT MCCHESNEY

NAXALITES. The appellation *Naxalites* in India has come to mean groups of communists bent on achieving the immediate overthrow of existing society by violent acts particularly aimed against the rich, powerful, and landed. The movement grew out of the Communist Party of India (Marxist), or CPM, in the mid-1960s, when some members of this party left it, completely dissatisfied with its parliamentary methods. Led by Charu Mazumdar, a campaign of violence began in the Naxalbari area of northern West Bengal state in 1967. The outbreak was followed, as on every subsequent occasion, by ruthless state repression and reprisals. Spurred by the belief that they were following the correct Marxist line as enunciated by Mao Zedong, the Naxalites killed landlords and officials of the government, thinking that the moment of revolution had come. Other communists, in both the Communist Party of India (CPI) and the CPM, believed that Mazumdar was a left sectarian adventurer who would harm rather than help the cause of communism in India.

The outbreak in Naxalbari was followed by actions in Srikakulam (in Andhra Pradesh) and in the Debra-Gopiballabhpur area of Midnapore near the Bihar-Orissa border area. In April 1969 communists of the Naxalite persuasion formed the CPI (Marxist-Leninist), or CPI (M-L), with Charu Mazumdar as general secretary and Kanu Sanyal, Asim Chatterjee, and Sushital Ray Chaudhuri as leading members. There were soon splits in the movement in Bihar and in Andhra. The first party congress was held in Calcutta in May 1970 and was followed by an upsurge of violent actions by Naxalite youths in Calcutta. Government repression quickly followed and many members of the movement were murdered, some even within prisons.

After president's rule had been established in West Bengal in 1971, Mazumdar was captured in July 1972 and died shortly thereafter in captivity. Most of the active groups were crushed by this time, and many communists inside and outside the movement were critical of its emphasis on annihilation campaigns, on spontaneity, and on the even development of the revolutionary situation in India. Some argued that greater emphasis on mass mobilization and organization of the working class was necessary. Sporadic actions by individuals and small groups have continued into the present and diverse groups have operated under the label CPI (M-L).

[*See also* Communism: Communist Parties in South Asia.]

Sumanta Banerjee, *In the Wake of Naxalbari* (1980). Manoranjan Mohanty, *Revolutionary Violence: A Study of the Maoist Movement in India* (1977). Samar Sen, Debabrata Panda, and Ashish Lahiri, eds., *Naxalbari and After: A Frontier Anthology*, 2 vols. (1978).

LEONARD A. GORDON

NAYAKA. The Sanskrit term *nayaka* has had two different meanings in the political culture of South India. From the fourteenth to the sixteenth century it was used largely, although not exclusively, to designate a new supralocal military class whose membership included brahmans and nonbrahmans. From the late sixteenth to the eighteenth century it was associated with regional Hindu kings situated in select enduring core areas of South India, such as Ikkeri, Tanjore, Madurai, and Gingi. During this period Hindu kingship was critically and centrally tied to the worship of temple deities on the one hand, and on the other, to new forms of economic activity that included trade monopolies, revenue agents, and land-based political control.

[*See also* Tamil Nadu.]

R. Sathyanatha Aiyer, *History of the Nayaks of Madurai* (1924). K. D. Swaminathan, *The Nayaks of Ikkeri* (1957).   CAROL APPADURAI BRECKENRIDGE

NAYARS. *See* Nairs.

NEESIMA, JOSEPH HARDY. *See* Niijima Jō.

NEGRI SEMBILAN (Negeri Sembilan), one of the nine Malay states that, with the former British settlements of Melaka and Penang, make up the Federation of Malaysia. It is located on the west coast, fronting the Straits of Melaka, and is bordered by Selangor, Pahang, Johor, and Melaka.

The region of Negri Sembilan was first developed in the time of the sultanate of Melaka (1400–1511) but gained political coherence only in the eighteenth century with the addition of considerable Malay immigrants from the Indonesian archipelago, who were drawn there mainly by tin deposits. In 1773,

a time when old Johor was slipping into chaos, Dutch Melaka was dormant, and warfare seemed endemic on the west coast, nine chiefs of varying importance, each with authority in a single district and most of them of Minangkabau origin, joined together as the *negri sembilan* ("nine states"). These included Sungei Ujong, Naning, Rembau, Klang, Jelebu, Segamat, Ulu Pahang, Jelai, and Johol. Four of these chiefs installed Raja Melewar (or Raja Mahmud, r. 1773–1795) as the first *yang di-pertuan besar,* or "paramount chief."

Raja Melewar's successors had increasing difficulty maintaining their power and domains in the face of bitter struggles over the region's tin, disputed successions, and Bugis and Chinese intrusions. Like other Malay sultans, the *yam tuan* accepted British "protection" in 1874 and in 1895 joined the original Federated Malay States under the British.

From its beginnings, Negri Sembilan has enjoyed a unique constitution, with a ruler elected from among the four major chiefs, perhaps the pattern from which succession to the Malaysian throne was taken. Modern Negri Sembilan is highly developed, with an economy based on tin and plantation agriculture. Its population of about 600,000 is composed of 42 percent Malyas, 41 percent Chinese, and 15 percent Indians.

[*See also* Malaysia; Federated Malay States; Johor; Melaka; Minangkabau; *and* Pangkor Engagement.]

Barbara W. Andaya and Leonard Y. Andaya, *A History of Malaysia* (1982). Mubin Sheppard, *A Short History of Negri Sembilan* (1965). R. O. Winstedt, "Negri Sembilan: The History, Polity, and Beliefs of the Nine States," *Journal of the Malaysian Branch of the Royal Asiatic Society* 12.3 (1934), pp. 35–111.   DAVID K. WYATT

NEHRU, JAWAHARLAL (1889–1964), nationalist leader and the first prime minister of India (1947–1964), was born at Allahabad on 14 November 1889. The only son of Motilal Nehru, he was educated at Harrow and Cambridge and called to the bar in London. The seven years he spent in England were a formative period in which he acquired a rational and skeptical outlook and sampled Fabian socialism and Irish nationalism, which added to his own patriotic dedication. He returned to India in 1912. Legal work and a comfortable life failed to satisfy his restless spirit: it was not law but politics that called him. He joined the Home Rule movement in 1917, but his real initiation into militant politics came two years later when Mohandas Gandhi launched his campaign against the Rowlatt Bills. There was much about Gandhi that puzzled and baffled young Nehru, but he saw in Gandhi's *satyagraha* an effective alternative to armchair politics and sporadic terrorism, between which Indian politics was oscillating. At first Nehru's father did not like the idea of his twenty-nine-year-old son plunging into an unconstitutional agitation, but both father and son cast in their lot with Gandhi at the crucial session of the Indian National Congress held in Calcutta in September 1920. A year later they were jailed for six months. This was Jawaharlal's first prison term; in all he was to spend nine years in jail.

Despite intellectual and temperamental differences, Jawaharlal became a trusted lieutenant of Gandhi. He served as general secretary of the All India Congress Committee, whose office was located in the family house at Allahabad. While he was in Europe for the treatment of his ailing wife, Kamala, in 1926–1927, Nehru attended the Congress of Oppressed Nationalities Against Imperialism in Brussels and paid a brief visit to Moscow, which gave a radical edge to his politics. In December 1928, at the Calcutta session, he clashed with the Congress old guard on the issue of dominion status for India. A year later, he presided over the Lahore session, which declared complete independence and civil disobedience under Gandhi's leadership. Nehru was elected to the Congress presidency again in 1936, 1937, and 1946, and he came to occupy a position in the nationalist movement second only to that of Gandhi.

Passionately opposed to fascism, Nehru was eager for nationalist India to throw its full weight behind the Allied war effort. But he insisted that the British government recognize India's right to freedom. After the abortive Cripps Mission, he reluctantly fell in line with Gandhi's plans for the "Quit India" campaign and was imprisoned in August 1942. Released in 1945, he took a leading part in the negotiations that culminated in the emergence of the dominions of India and Pakistan in August 1947. [*See also* Cripps Mission.]

Nehru was fifty-seven when he assumed office as prime minister of India. Although his entire life had been spent in opposition, he made an effortless transition from a political agitator to a statesman. His government coped successfully with formidable challenges: the disorders and mass exodus of minorities across the new border with Pakistan, the integration of 500-odd princely states into the Indian Union, the framing of a new constitution, and the establishment of the political and administrative infrastructure for a parliamentary democracy.

Nehru's position in the Congress Party and the government was unchallenged throughout his seventeen years of power, except perhaps during the first three years of Sardar Vallabhbhai Patel's term as the deputy prime minister. [*See also* Patel, Sardar Vallabhbhai.] Nehru's aim, in his own words, was to convert India's economy into that of a modern state. He set up a Planning Commission, encouraged development of science and technology, and launched three successive five-year plans. His policies led to a sizable growth in agricultural and industrial production, but it was somewhat offset by an unprecedented increase in population.

Important as Nehru's influence was on domestic policy, it was decisive on foreign affairs. Long years of association with the nationalist movement under Gandhi's leadership had conditioned him against colonialism and militarism. He was also acutely conscious of the hazards of war in the thermonuclear age and refused to align India with either of the power blocs. Initially his independent stance put him out of court with both the United States and the Soviet Union. However, over time both countries increasingly appreciated his motives and aims. He played a constructive, mediatory role in bringing the Korean War to an end and in resolving other international crises, such as those over the Suez Canal and the Congo, offering India's services for conciliation and international policing. He contributed behind the scenes toward the solution of several other explosive issues, such as those of West Berlin, Austria, and Laos.

Nehru was unable to achieve a satisfactory equation with India's two major immediate neighbors, Pakistan and China. The Kashmir issue proved a stumbling block in reaching an accord with Pakistan, and the border dispute prevented a resolution with China. The Chinese invasion in 1962, which Nehru failed to anticipate, came as a great blow to him and probably hastened his death. [*See also* Kashmir; Aksai Chin; *and* McMahon Line.]

Nehru had the prescience to foresee the possibilities of liberalization in the post-Stalin Soviet Union and of the rift between the Soviet Union and China. He persevered, in the face of much skepticism and criticism, in his pleas for the admission of China to the United Nations, for détente between the United States and the Soviet Union, and for a more equitable economic relationship between the developing and the developed countries. He called for liquidation of colonialism in Asia and Africa and, with

Tito and Nasser, was one of the chief architects of the nonaligned movement.

Nehru was also a writer of distinction. His writings were a by-product of his intense involvement in the Indian nationalist movement, and his major works, *Glimpses of World History* (1934), his *Autobiography* (1936), and *The Discovery of India* (1946), were actually written in prison.

[*See also* Nehru, Motilal; Gandhi, Mohandas Karamchand; Indian National Congress; *and* Pakistan.]

M. Brecher, *Nehru, A Political Biography* (1959). S. Gopal, ed., *Selected Works of Jawaharlal Nehru*, 15 vols. (1972–1982). S. Gopal, *Jawaharlal Nehru: A Biography*, 3 vols. (1976–1984). R. K. Karanjia, *The Mind of Mr. Nehru* (1960). B. R. Nanda, *The Nehrus: Motilal and Jawaharlal* (1962). Jawaharlal Nehru, *An Autobiography* (1936) and *Speeches 1946–1964*, 5 vols. (1949–1969). B. N. Pandey, *Nehru* (1977). M. Chalapathi Rau, *Journalism and Politics* (1984).   B. R. NANDA

NEHRU, MOTILAL

NEHRU, MOTILAL (1861–1931), eminent Indian lawyer and nationalist leader. Motilal Nehru was born at Agra, where his father, Pandit Gangadhar (who had been a police officer in Delhi), had migrated after the revolt of 1857. Motilal was educated at Muir Central College at Allahabad. He qualified as a lawyer and built up an enormous legal practice. Robust, rational, and secular in his outlook, he defied the caste taboo on foreign travel; his home, Anand Bhawan in Allahabad, was one of the most westernized in North India.

In the early years Motilal took only a fitful interest in politics, and belonged to the moderate party both in the Congress and the provincial legislative council of the United Provinces. His politics took a radical turn under the influence of his son Jawaharlal. He presided over the Amritsar Congress in 1919 and plunged into the noncooperation movement led by Mohandas Gandhi in 1920, renounced his legal practice, and courted imprisonment. After the collapse of the noncooperation movement, he founded the Swaraj Party with C. R. Das for work in legislative councils. He proved an outstanding leader of the opposition in the Central Legislative Assembly (1924–1929). He chaired the All Parties Committee that prepared the Nehru Report and presided over the Calcutta Congress in December 1928. He was jailed in 1930, released on grounds of health, and died shortly afterward in February 1931.

Motilal became a legendary figure in Indian nationalist lore as the man who had sloughed off the luxuries of a lifetime at Gandhi's bidding. His son Jawaharlal and granddaughter Indira Gandhi became prime ministers, and his daughter Vijaya Lakshmi Pandit served in key diplomatic positions.

[*See also* Gandhi, Mohandas Karamchand; Nehru, Jawaharlal; Gandhi, Indira; *and* Pandit, Vijaya Lakshmi.]

Ravinder Kumar and D. N. Panigrahi, eds., *Selected Works of Motilal Nehru*, 3 vols. (1982–1984). B. R. Nanda, *The Nehrus: Motilal and Jawaharlal* (1962). Jawaharlal Nehru, *An Autobiography* (1936).   B. R. NANDA

NEIGE. *See* Grand Secretariat.

NEI MONGGOL AUTONOMOUS REGION.

NEI MONGGOL AUTONOMOUS REGION. *See* Inner Mongolia.

NEO-CONFUCIANISM

NEO-CONFUCIANISM. A reassertion and metaphysical transformation of Confucianism that developed in Song-dynasty (960–1279) China, orthodox Neo-Confucianism is represented by the teachings of Zhu Xi (1130–1200), who synthesized the formulations of Zhou Dunyi (1017–1073), Shao Yong (1017–1077), Zhang Zai (1021–1077), and the brothers Cheng Hao (1032–1085) and Cheng Yi (1033–1107). Zhu Xi's commentaries on the Confucian canon received government endorsement during the Yuan dynasty (1279–1368) and were accepted as the authoritative interpretations for the civil service examination from 1313 until 1905. Because every successful officeholder in China for nearly six centuries had at one time memorized Zhu Xi's commentaries, this tradition contributed to a remarkable educational homogeneity among China's elite.

Several features distinguished Neo-Confucianism from earlier Confucian teachings. It represented a complete metaphysical system that proved an attractive intellectual alternative to Mahayana Buddhist metaphysics. Orthodox Neo-Confucianism explained the world in terms of a combination of abstract principles *(li)*, which operate like a natural law, and material force *(qi)*, the dynamic physical matter of the universe. Principles are manifest in humans in one's original nature and incline one naturally toward goodness; one's feelings and emotions, however, can distract and disrupt one's mind, making good behavior difficult by obscuring the original nature.

One's quest for sagehood (perfect goodness) is

advanced by the quasi-scientific exploration of principles in the material world (the "investigation of things," *ge wu*) and by the inner cultivation of qualities of seriousness and reverence; in this way, one conforms to the Way of Heaven *(tian dao)*. Through maintenance of correct social relationships, one contributes directly to stability in the family, the realm, and the world as a whole. Neo-Confucianism also reorganized the Confucian canon by giving priority to the Four Books (the *Analects* of Confucius, or *Lunyu;* the *Mencius,* or *Mengzi;* the *Great Learning,* or *Daxue;* and the *Doctrine of the Mean,* or *Zhongyong*) over the Five Classics (*Book of History,* or *Shujing; Book of Odes,* or *Shijing; Book of Changes,* or *Yijing; Book of Rites,* or *Liji;* and *Spring and Autumn Annals,* or *Chunqiu*). These key works formed the heart of the Neo-Confucian curriculum throughout East Asia.

Government endorsement of orthodox Neo-Confucianism continued after the Yuan in both native Chinese (the Ming, 1368–1644) and nonnative (the Manchu Qing, 1644–1912) dynasties. Although Zhu Xi had notable rivals and challengers in his own day, such as Lu Xiangshan (Lu Jiuyuan; 1139–1193), the most popular alternative to Zhu's teachings during the Ming were those of Wang Yangming (Wang Shouren; 1472–1529), a famous general and respected scholar. Wang's activist and "heterodox" interpretation of Neo-Confucianism emphasized one's innate knowledge of and capacity for goodness, thus dispensing with much of the scholarly emphasis on learning and memorization that had accompanied the growth of orthodox Neo-Confucianism. Wang maintained that "knowledge is the beginning of action, and action is the completion of knowledge," that is, that one's innate knowledge of filial piety initiates the filial impulse, just as filiality completes that impulse. Wang's more radical interpreters inclined toward an extreme emphasis on spontaneity and "naturalness," resulting in a conservative response during the Qing, when Neo-Confucians generally emphasized more "concrete" subjects like textual studies.

In conjunction with Neo-Confucianism's central position in the civil service examination, and accompanying the formation of an early-modern popular culture, Neo-Confucian academies proliferated beginning in the seventeenth century; the most famous and prestigious of these was the Donglin Academy. The Donglin served a variety of functions, at times advising the government, at times criticizing it, but always functioning as an "old-boy" network for its "alumni." [*See also* Donglin Academy.]

From China, Neo-Confucianism spread to Vietnam, Korea, and Japan. As in China, in Korea's Yi dynasty (1392–1910) Neo-Confucianism was tied to the civil service examination, although permission to take the exam was restricted to members of the privileged *yangban* class. This contributed to an even greater degree of educational and social homogeneity in Korea's bureaucratic elite than that of China. Korean Neo-Confucianism generally adhered to orthodox interpretations, although Korea's greatest Neo-Confucian, Yi T'oegye (Yi Hwang; 1501–1570), showed originality in his interpretation of human emotions, which he described in easily understandable charts. Korean monarchs took Neo-Confucian principles more seriously than did their counterparts elsewhere in East Asia, an extreme example being the king Yi T'aejong, who in 1418 abdicated the throne when he became convinced that Heaven had withdrawn its mandate to him to govern. As in China, Neo-Confucianism in Korea contributed to the growth of scholarship, supported by printing; the Neo-Confucian interest in history inspired the completion in 1451 of the impressive *Koryŏ sa,* or *History of the Koryŏ [Dynasty]*. [*See also* Yi Hwang *and* Neo-Confucianism in Korea.]

Korea contributed greatly, although unintentionally, to the development of Neo-Confucianism in Japan. Prior to the Tokugawa period (1600–1868), Neo-Confucian teachings in Japan were for the most part institutionally housed in Zen monasteries, where they were regarded as useful adjuncts to Zen that might, if properly interpreted, point one toward the same truths. When Japan invaded Korea in the 1590s, Japanese troops plundered Korean libraries, sending back to Japan the writings of Yi T'oegye and others, thereby stimulating the Japanese appreciation of Neo-Confucianism as an independent doctrine with a more complex intellectual lineage than had been understood.

Neo-Confucianism in Tokugawa Japan benefited from a measure of interest from the Tokugawa government, or *bakufu,* but since the *bakufu* did not use an examination system in recruitment for its civil service, Neo-Confucian teachings did not enjoy the same degree of institutional suppport in Japan as elsewhere in East Asia. Throughout the Tokugawa period, Hayashi Razan (1583–1657) and his descendants served the *bakufu* as authorities on orthodox Neo-Confucianism. Arai Hakuseki (1657–1725) served as adviser to two Tokugawa shoguns, Ienobu (r. 1709–1712) and the infant Ietsugu (r. 1713–1716), influencing a broad range of legislation. Yamazaki Ansai (1618–1682) founded the most successful private school (the Kimon) in Japan for the study of Neo-Confucianism, which, in Ansai's interpretation, inclined toward a dour moralism and discouraged the study of such "frivolous" subjects as literature or history.

Neo-Confucian vocabulary and assumptions emerged in the popular culture of Tokugawa Japan, and since virtually all literate persons in Tokugawa Japan learned to read using a Neo-Confucian curriculum, the concepts enjoyed broad currency and acceptance. Perhaps because of its later development in Japan, the challenge to orthodox Neo-Confucianism was coeval with its growth. Wang Yangming's interpretation, known in Japan as Yōmeigaku, appeared in the mid-seventeenth century but reached its height of popularity during the last years of the Tokugawa, when its emphasis on combining thought with action inspired numerous political activists. The most forceful intellectual challenge to orthodox Neo-Confucianism in Japan, however, came from a school known as Ancient Learning (Kogaku), which insisted that the Four Books could be understood better through direct perusal than through the commentaries of Zhu Xi and others.

Although the national experiences of Neo-Confucianism have differed in the countries where its doctrines were taught, there are shared elements that constitute a Neo-Confucian legacy to the early-modern and modern societies of East Asia. Of these the two most prominent are humanism and rationalism. Neo-Confucianism placed the responsibility for societal stability and human development squarely on the shoulders of individuals, and, even though its emphasis on enduring principles and endorsement of social stratification represent powerful conservative elements within the tradition, Neo-Confucianism also embraced reformist and progressive themes. Further, its comprehensive metaphysics and emphasis on quasi-scientific enquiry encouraged a broad range of rationalist speculations that proceeded from the Neo-Confucian assumption that the world as a whole is ultimately comprehensible.

Further, Neo-Confucianism in general encouraged historical mindedness, since it argued that within the records of the past, one could find all lessons necessary for the improvement of life in the present. Thus, wherever Neo-Confucianism was studied, historical writings followed. In China this contributed to a degree of ethnocentrism, and elsewhere in East Asia one finds many examples of Neo-Confucian sinophiles, but the emphasis on the study of one's national past also encouraged the growth of broader nativist scholarship, particularly in Japan. This emphasis on scholarship and the growth of Neo-Confucian academies also contributed to high male literacy rates and an affirmative attitude toward learning throughout premodern East Asia.

In modern times Neo-Confucianism has generally been overshadowed in East Asia by the rise of competing ideologies, although Neo-Confucian assumptions continue to be evident in much modern East Asian thought. Nonetheless social scientists point to the Neo-Confucian legacy as one important component in the East Asian modernization process, and Neo-Confucian teachings and assumptions continue to contribute to the respect for learning and social stability that characterize East Asia today.

[See also Confucius; Confucianism; Lunyu; Mencius; Guwen; Jinwen; Kaozheng Xue; Song Dynasty; Cheng Brothers; Han Yu; Li Zhi; Lu Xiangshan; Wang Yangming; Zhang Zai; Zhou Dunyi; and Zhu Xi.]

Wing-tsit Chan, A Source Book in Chinese Philosophy (1963). Min-hong Choi, A Modern History of Korean Philosophy (1983). Wm. Theodore de Bary, Neo-Confucian Orthodoxy and the Learning of the Mind-and-Heart (1981). Masao Maruyama, Studies in the Intellectual History of Tokugawa Japan (1974). Thomas Metzger, Escape from Predicament (1977). David Nivison and Arthur Wright, eds., Confucianism in Action (1959). Peter Nosco, ed., Confucianism and Tokugawa Culture (1984). Tu Wei-ming, Neo-Confucian Thought in Action (1976).

PETER NOSCO

NEO-CONFUCIANISM IN KOREA.

Both Confucianism and Buddhism came to Korea from China during the fourth century, while the peninsula was still divided into the three rival kingdoms. Buddhist monks were frequently the carriers of Confucian as well as Buddhist learning, the former representing worldly learning, the latter, transcendent wisdom. Thus, the Confucianism from this period through the succeeding Silla (668–935) and Koryŏ (935–1392) dynasties remained largely a practical learning for government functionaries. It involved the ability to read and write literary Chinese and regard for several essential social virtues, such as loyalty and filial piety. In 682 a national Confucian Academy was established, and about a century later a civil service examination that tested ability in reading the Chinese classics was instituted. These essential Confucian institutions functioned only sporadically, however, and Confucianism did not have a major part in shaping the political or social institutions of the country.

This situation changed markedly with the advent of the Yi dynasty (1392–1910). The founders of the new dynasty explicitly adopted Confucianism as the official ideology of the country. In part this was designed to cut back the political and economic power of the Buddhist church, which had been swollen by centuries of government favor and private largess. It also reflected similar developments in China, where a major Confucian revival took place during the Song dynasty (960–1279). Traditional Confucian moral and social values had been completed with a new metaphysics, psychology, and ascetical system, and the powerful synthesis, known in the West as "Neo-Confucianism," became the major intellectual and spiritual tradition in China. Neo-Confucianism had been gradually gaining strength in Korean official circles for some decades, and young officials steeped in the new learning were the chief supporters and accomplices of Yi Sŏng-gye (1335–1408), the military leader who became the founder of the Yi dynasty. [See Yi Sŏng-gye.]

Although Confucianism had not been central in earlier Korean society, during the Yi dynasty Korea developed into what was undoubtedly the most Confucian (Neo-Confucian) society in East Asia. In part this might be the result of its being smaller, more tightly unified, and more homogeneous than the societies of China and Japan. In any event, from beginnings that were Buddho-Confucian at best, the Yi dynasty developed steadily toward Neo-Confucian orthodoxy. In the realm of practice it became famous for its adherence to strict Confucian norms of propriety and ritual. Intellectually Korea remained almost exclusively committed to the officially sanctioned Neo-Confucian school of Zhu Xi (1130–1200); it not only rejected the rival school of Wang Yangming (1472–1529) that enjoyed such popularity in China and Japan, but came to regard itself as the bastion of orthodoxy, the custodian of a truth from which its neighbors had faithlessly strayed.

These developments were not rapid. Throughout the fifteenth century the main focus was on the practical reform of institutions and mores to conform more closely with what Koreans discovered in Confucian classical texts such as the *Zhouli* and the *Liji*. Meanwhile, a parallel development of the rigorous moral self-cultivation aspects of Neo-Confucianism was taking place in the countryside. As men with this orientation began filtering into government they came into opposition with established and powerful interests, giving rise to a series of four bloody "literati purges" (1498, 1504, 1519, and 1545), complex political events stereotyped as acts of the corrupt and powerful that brought about the downfall of the pure and idealistic. [See Literati Purges.]

The Korean Neo-Confucian tradition came to complete intellectual maturity with the thought of Yi Hwang (Yi T'oegye; 1501–1570), the man commonly regarded as the premier thinker of the Yi dynasty. In him self-cultivation concerns were firmly incorporated into the full framework of Neo-Confucian metaphysics and psychological and ascetic theory. He is also responsible for a celebrated controversy regarding the metaphysical grounding of various kinds of feelings; metaphysical psychology is a central nerve in Neo-Confucian thought and this debate touched on issues of major importance, setting a distinctive intellectual agenda for Korean Neo-Confucian thinkers that was pursued for centuries afterward.

T'oegye was followed a generation later by Yi I (Yi Yulgok; 1536–1584), the second great thinker of the Yi dynasty. Yulgok picked up the opposing side of the above-mentioned debate, and the Korean tradition has ever since been divided between the partisans of these two thinkers. Neo-Confucian metaphysics is a dualism of "principle" (Chinese, *li*) and "material force" (Chinese, *qi*). T'oegye tended to emphasize the role of principle and Yulgok that of material force, themes further developed by their followers over the centuries. The full exploration of the implications of this dualism is the distinctive hallmark of the Korean Neo-Confucian intellectual tradition.

From Yulgok's generation onward endemic factionalism became a notable feature of the Korean Neo-Confucian world. Factions out of favor continued to exist through power bases in the countryside, especially the *sŏwŏn* (private academies), a Confucian institution that flourished to an unprecedented extent in Korea. Thus, factional conflict continued for centuries and left its mark on both political and intellectual life. [See Sŏwŏn.]

Modern Koreans often regard their Neo-Confucian tradition as a thing of the past, and blame it for the difficulties the country has experienced in the twentieth century. Nonetheless this heritage is still visible in the values surrounding the family, in the moral rhetoric common in public life, and in a distinctive sense of propriety or formality that marks the many small interactions of daily life.

[See also Yi Hwang *and* Yi I.]

Wm. Theodore de Bary and JaHyun Kim Haboush, eds., *The Rise of Neo-Confucianism in Korea* (1985). Martina Deuchler, "Neo-Confucianism: The Impulse for Social Action in Early Yi Korea," *Journal of Korean Studies* 2 (1980): 71–111. Woo-Keun Han, *The History of Korea*, translated by Kyong-shik Lee (1970). Ki-baik Lee, *A New History of Korea*, translated by Edward W. Wagner (1984). Edward W. Wagner, *The Literati Purges: Political Conflict in Early Yi Korea* (1974).

MICHAEL C. KALTON

NEPAL

HISTORY OF NEPAL

Nepal, the world's only Hindu kingdom, is a tiny, landlocked country with an area of 54,718 square miles, wedged in the central Himalayas. It is surrounded by India on three sides, and by Tibet in the north. Its history has been that of an independent political entity, buttressed by its abiding fame as a center of arts and crafts. The two main factors energizing its creativity were a steady trans-Himalayan trade and a long-surviving Buddhist tradition, which it transmitted to Tibet. Although Nepal's chronicles attribute to it a long history going back several millennia, much of this is probably mythical and not supported by any definitive prehistoric remains.

Modern Nepal's boundaries were formed in the nineteenth century in the wake of a series of territorial conquests started by Gorkha, a hill state about sixty miles west of the Kathmandu Valley, and given permanency by the 1816 Sagauli Treaty Nepal signed with the English government in India after the Anglo-Nepal War. The Nepal of earlier times was a far smaller physical entity restricted mainly to the Kathmandu Valley, where historical remains still abound and where its original inhabitants, the Newars, largely live.

Nepal's history is best understood in light of its physical and ethnic setting. Three factors in this regard seem to have helped to shape its historical course; first, its relative geographical isolation from the Indian plains; second, its intermediary location between India and Tibet; and, third, its multiethnic demography.

During the first millennium BCE the Himalayan foothills in the general area where Nepal is located were regarded by the writers of the Indian epics as a sort of frontier land of the Aryan expansion in India at the expense of the non-Aryan Kiratas. Later legendary accounts of Nepal's history (written between the fourteenth and nineteenth century CE) describe a long period of Kirata rule followed by a solar dynasty, probably the Licchavis, who were representatives of Aryan culture. [*See* Kirata.] Thus, Nepal became a meeting ground of the Hindus coming from the south with a host of local cultural and linguistic groups that produced a new cultural synthesis. As native groups were hinduized in this process, the Hindus themselves modified some of their rules regarding intermarriage with local women. Hindu predominance over Nepal dates from this time and has been maintained ever since.

Nepal's terrain is a transition zone between the Indian plains and the Tibetan Plateau. It can be considered a stepping stone for Indians going to Tibet across the Himalayas for cultural exchange or reasons of trade. This flow of travelers stopped only in 1904, when the English opened a new route through Sikkim. Despite Nepal's role as a trans-Himalayan axis, it remained isolated from all but the most adventurous outsiders. It was at least a twelve-day journey from the nearest city, Vaisali, near modern Muzaffarpur, across a malarial forest belt and rugged hills. Its physical isolation and enclosed space may have been responsible for Nepal's syncretic religion of Buddhism and Hinduism, and also its predilection for absorbing and perpetuating cultural and artistic traditions long lost in India.

Aside from references in Kautilya's *Arthashastra* (in which two types of woolen blankets "made in Nepal" and available in India are mentioned) and Samudragupta's Allahabad Pillar Inscription, both of the fourth century BCE, Nepal's early history relies on epigraphical and archaeological records, beginning with the Licchavi period in the fifth century CE. Licchavi rule lasted until about 733 and is marked by a high degree of indicization in Nepal, covering practically every aspect of the people's socioreligious, artistic, and cultural life. The Licchavis promulgated their edicts in Sanskrit and created a landed aristocracy under a Hindu monarchical system. [*See* Licchavi Dynasty.] Tibetan traditions speak of the marriage of a Nepali princess, Bhrikuti, to the Tibetan king Songzen Gampo (r. 620–649), and official Chinese annals of the Tang dynasty record exchange of embassies between Nepal and China during this period in the seventh century.

The period between the eighth century and the rise of Jayasthitimalla (r. 1382–1395) was a confusing period politically. There was a succession of insignificant kings and sometimes more than one king ruled simultaneously. Nepal continued to be a cultural crucible, however, assimilating the regular influx of people arriving from India. A team of art-

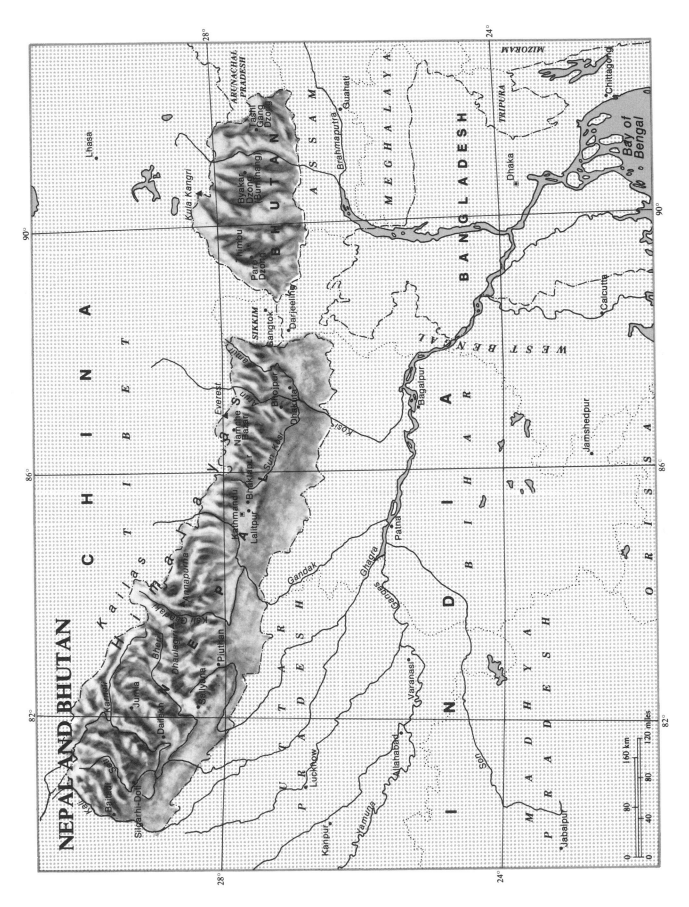

NEPAL AND BHUTAN

ists under A-ni-ko became quite famous in Tibet and China at the time of Kublai Khan in the mid-thirteenth century.

Jayasthitimalla's reign marks a period of political consolidation and social reorganization of Nepal along more definitive orthodox Hindu lines. The force of his social organization survives in the social life of the Newars today. [See Newar.]

In the time of Yaksamalla (1428–1480), Nepal split up again politically, which led to the emergence of the three kingdoms of Bhaktapur, Kathmandu, and Patan. All these were later incorporated by Gorkha in 1768 and 1769.

The absorption of Nepal by Gorkha marks a significant turning point in its history. Not only did a strong and enlarged political entity emerge out of it, but the reign passed to a Hindu line of a different ethnic background, that of the Nepali-speaking caste Hindus of the hills. The new state had a collectivity of ethnic groups, as its territories were far-flung. Historical Nepal's chief architects, the Newars, became an ethnic minority during this period. Their centuries-old plastic and architectural heritage broke its link with the past under the new political dispensation.

Outside the Kathmandu Valley the earliest historical beginnings in the hills of (modern) western Nepal are to be traced to the Khasa kingdom of Jumla in the twelfth century. It was a Hindu/Buddhist kingdom, whose rulers considered themselves *kshatriyas* and who ruled over their marginally hinduized Khasa subjects. It was a vast kingdom whose territories included Garhwal in India and portions of western Tibet. In the east, it raided the Nepal valley several times. Its enduring legacy to the later Nepal was its language, Nepali, whose early forms began there. Similarly, their hierarchy of castes and social milieu, which later became ubiquitous throughout Nepal's hills and was codified as law in the nineteenth century, first evolved there. The myriad states that sprang up throughout Nepal's hills in the sixteenth to eighteenth century, popularly called the Baisi and the Chaubisi clusters, were descendants of the fragmented Jumla kingdom of the fourteenth century. Their rulers were of different clans of the Thakuri, who claimed their descent from the Rajputs who fled to the Himalayas from the Muslim invasion of Rajasthan. Despite their political division, they were culturally and linguistically homogeneous groups, sometimes a single family establishing separate principalities under its breakaway collaterals and siblings. Their rapid proliferation in the hills resulted from their making inroads into the tribal areas of diverse Tibeto-Burman-speaking groups and establishing dominance over them.

Gorkha was one of the kingdoms of the Chaubisi cluster, established in the middle of the sixteenth century. Under its last ruler, Prithvinarayan Shah (1723–1775), Gorkha began territorial expansion, the crowning glory of which came in the conquest of the three kingdoms of Kathmandu, Patan, and Bhaktapur. [See Kathmandu; Patan; and Bhaktapur.] Its borders eventually reached Sikkim in the east. Prithvinarayan died early, but Gorkha's conquests in the west were continued by his successors, which by the early nineteenth century reached the Sutlej River in India. This expansion involved Nepal in wars with both China (1792) and the English in India (1814–1816). The latter confrontation had serious political consequences, one of which was the loss of a sizable portion of territory to the English. [See Prithvinarayan Shah.]

Prithvinarayan Shah's death set off a period of political instability marked by incessant intrigue and violence in the court at Kathmandu. The succeeding kings were minors and their appointed regents acted to further their own personal interests. This political situation prevailed throughout the early nineteenth century, and climaxed in a single night in 1846 with the Kot massacre of Nepal's high civil and military officials that brought Jung Bahadur Rana (r. 1846–1877) to power. [See Kot Massacre.] He established a century-long family autocracy of the Ranas in Nepal by taking over the king's powers and making the position of prime minister hereditary. In 1850 Jung visited England and France, the first native ruler from South Asia to do so. He led Nepal into a victorious war with Tibet in 1856, obliging it thereafter to pay Nepal a tribute of 10,000 rupees annually. He pursued a policy of friendship with the English and helped them suppress the Sepoy Mutiny of 1857. The Ranas later allowed the recruitment of Gurkha soldiers into the British army. This policy paid off in maintaining Nepal's political independence. [See Jung Bahadur Rana *and* Gurkhas.]

The Rana regime was overthrown by a popular uprising in 1951. King Tribhuvan briefly went into exile to India, lending his support to the anti-Rana movement. Finally, the Ranas yielded to India's pressure, and Tribhuvan returned to Nepal with full power restored to the monarchy. [See Tribhuvan, Bir Bikram *and* Rana.]

The year 1951 marks the beginning of Nepal's break with its feudalistic past and its movement into the modern era of popular rule and economic planning and development. Political modernization of a country steeped in tradition and centuries of isolation, however, was anything but a smooth task. Tribhuvan died early and was succeeded by his son, King Mahendra, in 1955. The latter had a different notion about Nepal's political destiny, with monarchy playing an active role. His first decisive action was to shelve permanently the idea of holding elections for a Constituent Assembly, which previously had been promised by Tribhuvan. Instead, an election was held for a parliament in 1959. In 1960, however, Mahendra dismissed the duly elected government of the Nepali Congress under B. P. Koirala. [See Koirala, Bishweshwor Prasad.] In 1962 he promulgated a partyless Panchayat system, in which various indirectly elected Panchayat bodies in several tiers from the village to the National Panchayat, its legislature, were formed. The king appointed all the ministers, who were responsible to him only. [See Panchayat.]

King Mahendra ruled with a strong hand as long as he lived. In 1972 he died and his son, King Birendra, succeeded him. [See Mahendra and Birendra.] Birendra began his reign with an emphasis on Nepal's economic development. Political opposition to the Panchayat system, however, had not ceased. The banned political parties were able to maintain constant pressure for political liberalization. A serious student agitation broke out that led the king to announce a referendum in 1980 to determine whether, in future, there would be a multiparty system of government or whether a reformed Panchayat system should be retained. The referendum's verdict was said to favor the Panchayat. In 1981 an election for the new legislature was held by universal suffrage and it elected Surya Bahadur Thapa as its prime minister. He and his cabinet were collectively made responsible to the legislature for the first time since 1960. He was voted out of power three years before his tenure expired, however, and was replaced by Lokendra Bahadur Chand in July 1983.

Francis Buchanan Hamilton, *An Account of the Kingdom of Nepal* (1819; reprint, 1971). Bhuwan Lal Joshi and Leo E. Rose, *Democratic Innovations in Nepal* (1966). Luciano Petech, *Mediaeval History of Nepal* (1958). D. R. Regmi, *Modern Nepal*, 2 vols. (1975). P. R. Sharma, *Preliminary Study of the Art and Architecture of the Karnali Basin, West Nepal* (1972). Rishikesh Shaha, *Essays in the Practice of Government in Nepal* (1982). Daniel Wright, ed., *History of Nepal* (1877; reprint, 1972).
PRAYAG RAJ SHARMA

NEPALESE ARCHAEOLOGY, ARCHITECTURE, AND ART

From the point of view of archaeology, architecture, and art, Nepal may be divided into three zones: the Tarai, which comprises the lowlands contiguous to the plains of India; the Pahad, or midmontane region, including the Kathmandu Valley, which contains much of the country's artistic heritage; and the Himalayan highland, or Bhota, the mountainous areas contiguous to Tibet. The last of these areas is the least studied and, although much of its cultural heritage is heavily influenced by Tibet, its history as well as the extent of local variation has yet to be investigated.

Archaeology. The prehistory of Nepal and the central Himalayas is still largely unknown. No Paleolithic or Neolithic sites have been definitely identified, but stone tools found on the surface throughout the country indicate the high probability of early human settlement. On the basis of some of these surface finds, it has been conjectured that the culture of the earliest settlers may be related to those of Southeast Asia as well as cultures to the west.

The most extensive excavations have been carried out in the Tarai. The largest of these was at Tilaurakot, where excavations were conducted by a team of Indian and Nepalese archaeologists in 1962. A primary objective was to establish the site firmly as that of Kapilavastu, the ancient city of Gautama Buddha. Although the high probability remains that Tilaurakot is indeed the site of Kapilavastu, the excavations have so far failed to establish the identification conclusively, and rival sites on the Indian side of the border have been proposed, none of which is any more certain. From a more general point of view, the site has yielded a rich find of terracotta ware, pottery, stone sculpture, coins, and brick structures, some of which may date back as early as the sixth century BCE. The most famous site in the Tarai is that of Lumbini, successfully identified as the birthplace of the Buddha through the Ashokan pillar discovered there in 1893. Here insufficient archaeological work has been done, and the integrity of the site is threatened by the planned establishment of a large tourist center for Buddhist pilgrims. [See Lumbini.]

In the Nepal Valley itself, excavations by Indian archaeologists in the 1960s near the Manesvara temple in the Hadigaon area of Kathmandu were conducted in the hope of identifying one of the royal palaces of the Licchavis (fifth to eighth century). Although the site yielded evidence of occupation during the Licchavi period, none of the structures appeared to be that of a royal palace.

In 1984 and 1985 excavations were carried out at Dumakhal, a village approximately ten kilometers northeast of Kathmandu. These excavations revealed stone and brick structures, many varieties of stamped pottery, terra-cotta figures, and stone artifacts that may date back to the Licchavi period, if not earlier. In the same year a team of Italian archaeologists began excavations near the Satyanarayana temple in Hadigaon. These excavations have uncovered extensive brick structures that also appear to date from the Licchavi period. [*See* Licchavi Dynasty.]

Architecture. Foundations at Tilaurakot, Lumbini, Kodan, and other sites in the Tarai demonstrate the existence of Buddhist stupas and Hindu temples, but little remains beyond foundations. The ruins indicate that the main medium of construction was brick, often beautifully decorated, with stone playing only a minor role. Most of these structures appear to derive from types developed in northern India.

In the Kathmandu Valley, which has escaped much of the destruction that visited North India, there are innumerable examples of the architecture that is often thought of as distinctively Nepalese. These include large Buddhist stupas, many small *caityas* that date from the Licchavi period, and the trabeate structures built by the Newars—mainly houses, royal palaces, temples, monasteries, and other public buildings. All of these are made of brick and are decorated with woodcarving and repoussé metalwork. The major stupas of the valley, despite changes in size and decoration through the centuries, may date from ancient times. The stupa of Svayambhunath may have been constructed by the Licchavi king Vrisadeva in the fifth century, according to inscriptional evidence. The great stupas of Patan, associated by the tradition with the emperor Ashoka, may date from an early period, but there is no hard evidence to associate them with the Maurya emperor.

Elements of the trabeate architecture of Nepal have been associated with the Kushans, but some scholars find the origins of this style in the domestic buildings of the Newars themselves. The latter argument, based on similarities in design and materials, is highly plausible, and it suggests that the royal palaces, temples, and monasteries are based on the same architectural concepts of tiered roofs and supporting struts. This form of Nepalese architecture therefore bears only passing resemblance

FIGURE 1. *Svayambhunath Stupa, Dome Detail.*

to architectural forms of Central and East Asia, with which it is easily confused. Despite early literary evidence for the existence of tiered buildings in Nepal (they are attested by Chinese pilgrims in the seventh century), no ancient examples survive. The oldest standing structures probably date from about the thirteenth century. The majority of extant historical buildings date from the Malla period (fourteenth to seventeenth century); these include the chief Hindu temples, Pasupatinath, Changu Narayan, and Kumbhesvara; the pavilion called the Kasthamandapa, from which the city of Kathmandu derives its name; Hanuman Dhoka, the royal palace of the Malla kings of Kathmandu; the palaces of Patan and Bhaktapur; the Nyatpola of Bhaktapur; and the overwhelming majority of Buddhist monasteries.

The Shah dynasty, which conquered the Kathmandu Valley in the eighteenth century, occupied the palaces of the Newar kings but introduced no new styles except for the mountain houses associated with the hills. Later, the Ranas, who ruled the country for more than one hundred years (1846–

FIGURE 2. *Rato Matsyendranath Temple, Ta Bahal, Patan.*

1951), were heavily influenced by European models. [*See* Rana.] Their residences, called *bhavan, darbar,* or *mahal,* are the first major forms of foreign architecture to be introduced into the valley in the modern period. The chief example of these dwellings is Singha Darbar, originally built as the residence of Prime Minister Chandra Samsher.

The extensive architecture of western Nepal, particularly that of the Karnali basin, is also significant. This area formed part of the medieval Khas empire with major settlements at Dullu, Jumla, and Guge. Neither the history nor the architecture of the area has been studied in detail. Extant temples appear to be heavily influenced by examples from Kumaon that date from the Katyauri period (eleventh to fourteenth century). They are of modest proportions and are in the plain *sikhara* style. The districts of Dailekh, Accham, and Jumla are rich in temples. Most of them are undated, but the earliest is one of a group of four temples at Vinayak I in Accham dated Saka 1202 (1280 CE).

In the northern highland regions, the architecture is almost entirely Buddhist, although there are important Hindu shrines at major places of pilgrimage. Despite its clear Tibetan cultural affinities, the area has considerable local variation. Buildings are generally constructed of wood and stone, with flat or sloping roofs, depending on climatic conditions, particularly rainfall, which tends to be far heavier in the east. The monastery facades are plain, even austere, and most decoration is reserved for the interiors, the walls of which are often covered with murals. Among the most important temples are Raling Gompa and the Kalashilto temple of Humla district in the northwest; the temples of Vishnu Lokesvara at Muktinath; the Dzong monastery in Mustang district; the Kutsapternga monastery, which contains some excellent painting; the temples of Chure Gyang, one of the oldest temples in the Helambu region; the temples of Karkegyang in the Sindhupalanchowk district; and, finally, the Thyangboche and Pangboche monasteries of the Solu-Khumbhu district. None appears to date prior to the seventeenth century.

Art. The art of the Tarai forms a continuity with that of North India, particularly with regard to terra-cotta and stone sculpture. There is little that is distinctively Nepalese about the art. Terra-cotta objects, both animal and human figurines, have been found that date from the Maurya, Kushan, and Gupta periods. Much of the stone sculpture is of the medieval period, although some pieces are datable to the time of the Kushans. Only a few examples of bronze sculpture have been found, and no painting.

The earliest pieces of bronze sculpture are of the Licchavi period, but the art of bronze casting reached its peak in the thirteenth and fourteenth centuries. At its best, the bronze sculpture of the Newar craftsman was unsurpassed in all of Asia, and their lost-wax techniques and metalworking skill became widely known in Tibet and China. The tures are the Vishnu images at Tilganga and Lazimpat (467 CE). Other sculptures known to date from the Licchavi period include the Jalasayana Vishnu at Budhanilkantha, the famous Vishvarupa Vishnu at the temple of Changu Narayan, and the image of Dhumbarahi in Vishal Nagar.

The earliest pieces of bronze sculpture are of the Licchavi period, but the art of bronze casting reached its peak in the thirteenth and fourteenth centuries. At its best, the bronze sculpture of the Newar craftsman was unsurpassed in all of Asia, and their lost-wax techniques and metalworking skill became widely known in Tibet and China. The

FIGURE 3. *Bodhisattva, Probably Avalokiteshvara*. Nepal, thirteenth century. Gilt copper with inlays of semiprecious stones. Height 47.5 cm.

tradition remained alive and buoyant well into the eighteenth century. The earliest extant examples of painting are on wooden book covers that date from the eleventh and twelfth centuries. Later, the painted cloth scroll made its first appearance, the earliest examples dating from the fourteenth century. Little remains of wall painting, although there are some excellent examples in the city of Bhaktapur. [*See* Bhaktapur.] It should be noted that the Newar craftsman excelled in the decorative arts, particularly in wood sculpture anad *repoussé* metalwork.

The stone sculpture of western Nepal is historically important but artistically inferior to the work done in other parts of the country. In the Himalayan highlands, the Buddhist *gompas* contain painting and bronze sculpture of importance. Much of it, as with the architecture, is of comparatively recent date, and none of it has been the subject of detailed study.

[*See also* Newar *and* Architecture: South Asian Architecture.]

Corneille Jest, *Monuments of Northern Nepal* (1981). Devala Mitre, *Excavations at Tilaura-Kot and Kodan and Explorations in the Nepalese Tarai* (1972). Pratapaditya Pal, *The Arts of Nepal*, part 1, *Sculpture* (1974). Prayag Raj Sharma, *Preliminary Study of the Art and Architecture of the Karnali Basin, West Nepal* (1972). Mary Shepard Slusser, *Nepal Mandala: A Cultural Study of the Kathmandu Valley*, 2 vols. (1982).   THEODORE RICCARDI, JR.

NESTORIANISM, a branch of Christianity named after Nestorius, a presbyter of Antioch who became patriarch of Constantinople in 428. In 431 his teachings concerning the relation between the human and divine natures of Christ were condemned at the Council of Ephesus, and Nestorius was deposed. But his teaching spread through much of the church in Syria and became popular in Persia. In 496 the Persian churches became independent of the churches in the Byzantine empire, and the Nestorian patriarchate eventually was established in Baghdad.

Although rooted in Persian soil, the Nestorian church employed Syriac for its scriptures and other writings. Nestorian missionaries spread throughout Central Asia, penetrating the Chinese Tang empire and settling in the capital Xi'an in 635. From there they moved into six other important cities of the empire. In 751 some of its members erected a handsome stele, inscribed in Syriac and Chinese, near Xi'an. It was later buried, possibly in the persecution of 845. Discovered in 1625, the stele became the subject of great interest to Roman Catholic missionaries, who translated the inscriptions.

The Nestorian church, banned in 845, returned to China under the Mongols. Its members established an archbishopric in Beijing (1275) and churches in three cities in the lower Yangtze River valley and elsewhere. In 1281 a pilgrim from the capital to Jerusalem was elected patriarch, and an envoy was sent to Rome and Paris. By the end of the Yuan, or Mongol, dynasty (1279–1368), however, the Nestorian church had disappeared from China.

[*See also* Christianity: An Overview.]

A. C. Moule, *Christians in China before the year 1550* (1930). P. Y. Saeki, *The Nestorian Documents and Relics in China* (2d ed., 1951).   L. CARRINGTON GOODRICH

NETHERLANDS EAST INDIA COMPANY. *See* Dutch East India Company.

NETHERLANDS EAST INDIES. Nederlandsch Indië, the official name for the "Asiatic possessions" of the Netherlands, was first used in the Regerings

Reglement (Government Regulatory Act or Fundamental Law) of 1815. The name remained the official designation of the Dutch holdings in the East Indian archipelago until 1942 in fact and until 1950 in law. By the mid-twentieth century the territory covered by this name stretched from Sabang (5° 53′ north latitude, 95° 17′east longitude) to Merauke (8° 30′ south latitude, 140° 22′ east longitude), a distance of some 3,000 miles. The major islands (or portions thereof) included in this colony were Borneo (Kalimantan, 208,285 square miles); Sumatra (182,859 square miles); West New Guinea (Irian Jaya, 162,927 square miles); Celebes (Sulawesi, 73,056 square miles); and Java and Madura (51,037 square miles). This colony is now the independent Republic of Indonesia. In the 1930 census the total population of the colony was about 61 million; close to 43 million, or about 70 percent, lived in Java and Madura. This ratio has remained the same into the present day.

The governance of the colony fell to the crown, which until 1848 meant the king and thereafter the king and Parliament. The governor-general was the highest official; he and a few other top officials were appointed by the crown. Batavia was the official seat of government, but since the governor-general resided much of the year in Buitenzorg (Bogor), much business was also transacted there. In the 1930s some departments were moved to Bandung. The Regerings Reglement (RR) was the crown's formulation of general principles of colonial rule that had to be put into practice by laws made in the colony. Before 1848 there were five RRs, but after that date there has been only one, dated 1854, which was modified in 1925. The decrees, ordinances, laws, and instructions signed by the governor-general were taken up in the Staatsblad van Nederlandsch Indië, or the official statute book. The Council of the East Indies, composed of senior Indies functionaries, was cogoverning with the governor-general from 1815 to 1836 and 1854 to 1925 and was advisory from 1836 to 1854 and after 1925, when its advice had to be sought on certain matters.

For most of the nineteenth century the area under the direct control of this government was limited to most of Java and Madura and a few other key places in the other islands. Its relationship with rest of the archipelago was regulated by treaties or contracts with local rulers that granted the government certain rights and privileges but left sovereignty with the local potentate. This was akin to relationships between states as regulated by international law. This situation changed only little during most of the nineteenth century when Java was the economic and administrative focus of the Dutch. In the last quarter of that century, however, economic development in the other islands and the colonial expansion of other powers led to the imposition of greater control over the outlying parts of the archipelago. Through force of arms and persuasion, the government extended its hegemony, either deposing local rulers or leaving them with only ceremonial rights. It fought the long and costly Aceh War (1873–1903) and successfully conquered Bali in 1906. By about the first decade of the twentieth century, the Netherlands East Indies was a centralized government controlling the territory described above.

Because of Java's centrality in Dutch plans and policies, the colony's organs of governance—administrative corps, judiciary, and military—were developed to meet conditions there. These organs were modified when they were introduced into the other islands at the end of the nineteenth century; by then, the central government had become more complex, with specialized bureaus and departments. Nonetheless many of the guidelines that had been established in Java remained central to Dutch administration. Insofar as their aims of economic exploitation and peace and orderliness allowed, the Dutch followed a policy of letting natives rule natives and of respecting native customs (adat) and religions. This meant that there was a great deal of indirection in the application of authority and a gulf between written European statutes and the way in which things got done. The efforts to reconcile and alter these basic principles, especially in the face of social modernization and economic growth, lie at the root of the historical changes that the Netherlands East Indies underwent during its existence.

[See also Dutch East India Company; Java; Madura; Aceh; Bali; and Adat.]

M. C. Ricklefs, *A History of Modern Indonesia* (1981). H. Sutherland, *The Making of a Bureaucratic Elite* (1979). A. Vandenbosch, *The Dutch East Indies* (1942).

ROBERT VAN NIEL

NEVA'I (1441–1501), pen name of Nizam al-Din Ali Shir, later called Mir Ali Shir, the most outstanding figure of Chagatai literature.

Neva'i was born in Herat (in present-day northwestern Afghanistan) into a family of Uighur scribes that had long been in the service of the clan of the Timurid dynasty that ruled Central Asia in the fifteenth century. Neva'i was in the service of his foster brother, the Timurid sultan Husain Baiqara, who ruled from his capital in Herat from 1469 to 1506. Although not a member of the hereditary military elite, Neva'i occupied a prominent position at the Timurid court as a private courtier and confidant of the sultan. Appointed to the rank of *amir* (or *beg*) in 1472, he also occupied such posts in the administration as keeper of the seal and governor of the province of Astarabad, but never that of *vazir*, a title often ascribed to him in the scholarly literature.

One of the wealthiest men of his time, Neva'i financed a wide range of cultural activities, including patronage of artists, calligraphers, musicians, and poets; and he donated nearly four hundred architectural monuments and complexes in and around the city of Herat. An extremely versatile literary author, he cultivated all forms of literature available to him in his day and was considered by his contemporaries to be the best poet in Chagatai, an eastern Turkic literary language that, on account of his contribution to its development, was sometimes called "the language of Neva'i."

Neva'i's most significant poetical work was the *Khamsa* (1483–1485), an imitation of and elaboration on five poems in rhyming couplets *(masnavi)* by the earlier Persian poets Nizami and Amir Khusrau, as well as by Neva'i's contemporary, the Persian poet Jami. Neva'i was also the author of four *divans* (collections of lyric poetry) in Chagatai and one in Persian in which he used the pen name Fani. Among his most noteworthy prose works are the *Majalis al-nafa'is,* the first Turkic biographical history of contemporary Persian and Chagatai poets; the *Muhakamat al-lughatain,* a linguistic comparison of the Chagatai and Persian languages; and the *Mizan al-awzan,* a treatise on prosody.

Neva'i's influence was considerable not only on later Chagatai authors, but on Azeri and Ottoman Turkish authors as well. He is now claimed by Soviet Uzbeks as belonging to the sphere of Uzbek literature.

[*See also* Baiqara, Husain; Chagatai Literature; *and* Jami.]

Wilhelm Barthold, *Four Studies on the History of Central Asia,* translated by V. and T. Minorsky (1956–1962), vol. 3. M. E. Subtelny, "Alī Shīr Navā'ī: *Bakhshī* and *Beg,*" *Harvard Ukrainian Studies* 3/4 (1979–1980), pt. 2, pp. 797–907.   MARIA E. SUBTELNY

NEWAR, an ethnic group whose culture shaped civilization in the Kathmandu Valley in Nepal from Licchavi times (464–850 CE) onward. The name *Newar* likely derives from *Nepal,* the original name for the valley proper. Newars share a common Tibeto-Burman language and Hindu-Buddhist heritage, but considerable diversity exists due to continuous mi-

gration and political divisions among the three principal cities of Nepal—Kathmandu, Bhaktapur, and Patan. Newars were known throughout Asia for their fine artistry, especially multi-roofed temple architecture, wood carving, fresco painting, manuscript illumination, and lost-wax metal-casting. Newar artisans were important in spreading Indian culture to Tibet and China.

Newars preserve many features of ancient Indian civilization that long ago disappeared on the subcontinent. Most notable is Mahayana-Vajrayana Buddhism, which still survives in a number of separate caste communities. The discovery of Newar manuscripts in the nineteenth century was a milestone in the study of Buddhism in the West.

[*See also* Kathmandu; Bhaktapur; Patan; *and* Nepal.]

Mary Slusser, *Nepal Mandala,* 2 vols. (1982).
                              TODD THORNTON LEWIS

NEW FOURTH ARMY INCIDENT, also known as the South Anhui Incident (5–15 January 1941), a merciless attack by Chinese Nationalist forces upon the headquarters detachment of the Communist New Fourth Army near Maolin, Anhui Province. Most of the detachment's nine thousand men were killed, captured, or dispersed. Commanding officer Ye Ding was captured; vice-commander and political officer Xiang Ying—in fact the army's real authority—was murdered as he fled, by a bodyguard who made off with the army's gold supply. Mao Zedong blamed Xiang Ying for this defeat, charging that, like Wang Ming, he had been too accommodating to the Nationalists, had not built a solid territorial base, and had not mobilized the masses.

[*See also* United Front; World War II in China; *and* Wang Ming.]

                              LYMAN P. VAN SLYKE

NE WIN (b. 1911), Burmese general. He led the Burmese army during the 2 March 1962 coup and from then until 1974 served as chairman of the Revolutionary Council, combining the roles of head of state, head of government, and chief lawmaking authority. Following the introduction of the 1974 constitution, Ne Win became president while remaining chairman of the ruling Burma Socialist Program Party. In 1981 he stood down from the presidency and was succeeded by a colleague, General San Yu, but remained chairman of the party and still the most powerful figure in Burma.

Ne Win began his political career in the 1930s while working in the Rangoon post office. As a member of the Thakin nationalist movement he was active in anti-British activities and in 1940, along with Aung San and twenty-eight other men, traveled to Hainan Island, where he received military training under the Japanese. These "thirty comrades" became the nucleus of the Burma Independence Army, which accompanied the Japanese on their 1942 invasion of British Burma. During the war years Ne Win became a leading officer of the Japanese-sponsored Burma army, but along with the rest of the officer corps, he rebelled against the Japanese in March 1945 and fought alongside the returning British until the war's end. [See Thirty Comrades.]

Following the Kandy Agreement between British commander Lord Mountbatten and Aung San, Ne Win was inducted into the British Burma Army and during 1946 and 1947 commanded troops in operations to clear dacoits and communists from central Burma. Soon after Burma's independence on 4 January 1948, Ne Win replaced the Karen commander of the army during the Karen and communist rebellions. For a brief period in 1949–1950 he served as minister for home affairs and for defense while continuing to command the army. With the return to more stable conditions in the early 1950s, Ne Win withdrew from politics, although many of his subordinate officers did not. In 1958 he was asked by Prime Minister Nu at the behest of other officers to form a caretaker government to restore domestic order and hold elections. This he did and then handed back power to Nu in 1960. However, when it appeared to him Nu's government was both denying the promise of the socialist revolution that many thought would accompany independence and also compromising the unity of the state by acceding to minority separatist demands, he carried out the 2 March 1962 coup. Subsequently Ne Win's policies were increasingly socialist and, in the Burmese context, politically radical. The 1974 one-party socialist constitution caps his revolutionary program.

[See also Burma Socialist Program Party; Mountbatten, Louis; Aung San; and Nu, U.]

Maung Maung, *Burma and General Ne Win* (1969).

ROBERT H. TAYLOR

NEW PEOPLE'S ARMY (NPA), the military arm of the Communist Party of the Philippines (CPP), which started with sixty people in 1969. Both the NPA and CPP are the major members of an umbrella organization called the National Democratic Front (NDF), whose main goal is to create a coalition of interests that historically "opposed martial law and imperialism." Under the regime of President Ferdinand E. Marcos, all three groups were outlawed by the Philippine government and had to operate underground. After President Aquino came to power, a first-ever, sixty-day cease-fire was negotiated. During the cease-fire, the NDF had access to the media so that it could publicize its cause.

A rural-based mass organization, the NPA advocates land redistribution and agrarian reform. Most of its members are young, and some have a college education. They are committed to Maoist ideals and armed struggle. Jose Sison, the founder of the CPP, who was released from prison by Aquino, has been touring abroad and is suspected of raising funds from friendly socialist countries.

The NPA's goals are long-range and do not pose an immediate threat to the government, but its influence has risen dramatically in recent years. It is known to operate more than forty guerrilla fronts. Its stronghold is Samar Island, where a reported one thousand cadres are working actively with the people, but it is also strong in northern Luzon, Bicol, and Mindanao. The CPP claims that there are sixteen thousand armed regulars all over the country; the government estimates NPA armed strength at a new high of twenty-four thousand. The Aquino administration's policy of reconciliation has not appreciably reduced the level of military action by the NPA and has been resisted and thwarted by the Philippine military.

The NPA's strength grew during the Marcos era. Military abuses, the government's neglect of rural areas, landlord excesses, usurious interest rates, and continuing poverty are some of the conditions the NPA is fighting against. In some cases it metes out "instant justice," especially against cattle rustlers, informers, and rapacious local officals.

The NPA is seen as the only thriving insurgency in Southeast Asia. Both the CPP and NPA were weakened politically by choosing to boycott the presidential elections that brought Cory Aquino to power in 1986, as well as by the overwhelmingly favorable vote (76 percent voted yes) for the Aquino constitution in February 1987. The CPP's current leadership is splintered; for example, the NPA of Northern Mindanao has independently negotiated a continued cease-fire with the government. Debate within the CPP currently centers on whether to settle for a peaceful parliamentary struggle. The NPA has a long way to go before it will be able to seize power, but is has become a major force in the political landscape of the Philippines.

[See also Philippines; Marcos, Ferdinand E.; Aquino, Corazon Cojuangco; and Communism: Communism in Southeast Asia.]

John Bresnan, Crisis in the Philippines: The Marcos Era and Beyond (1986). Ross Munro, "Dateline Manila: Moscow's Next Win?" Foreign Policy 56 (Fall 1984): 173–190.   BELINDA A. AQUINO

NEW RELIGIONS IN JAPAN.

The Japanese term *shinkō shūkyō*, or "new religions," refers to more than two thousand Japanese religious organizations, Buddhist, Shinto, Christian, and completely independent, large and small, urban and rural, that have arisen in Japan since the beginning of the nineteenth century. In that the rubric "new religions" is applied to groups with a history of nearly two centuries, it has become something of a misnomer, but it is nevertheless firmly embedded in scholarly literature.

Roughly one-third of the Japanese belong to one of the new religions, only a few of which can be thought of as marginal "cults." Most of the members of the new religions are traditional in their social behavior and conservative in politics. The larger groups, with longer histories, occupy a place among Japanese religions similar to the position of the Mormon or Christian Science church in American religious life.

New religions' "newness" may be sought in the contrast between them and shrine Shinto or temple Buddhism. In temples and shrines the priesthood holds a pre-eminent position, mediating for the laity to the deities, while the laity supports the priesthood. With a few exceptions, the priesthood is male, because pollution taboos prevent women from assuming a priestly role. The new religions are mainly lay groups, and their ministry is in principle open to all. It is possible for members to become leaders through training courses that do not require them to give up their jobs, renounce marriage, or undergo rigorous ascetic regimens. The distinction between leaders and followers is comparatively weak, and it is assumed that both have equal chances for salvation. The taboos barring women from full participation at temples and shrines, if not completely absent, are much less involved. Women participate enthusiastically and form the majority of most groups.

The new religions share a common worldview in which the self, the body, society, nature, and the universe are vitalized by a single principle; these various aspects of experience are ideally integrated in the manner of concentric circles emanating from a point, the animating principle. Religious practice consists of striving for continuous integration, harmony, and congruence of self with the body, society, nature, and the universe. Misfortune, illness, and strife result from a disruption of this integration, and the solution to these and all other problems is a return to the idealized harmony. When the self is fully in harmony, then nothing is impossible. This worldview is not an eccentric development, but rather an extension of pervasive and traditional cultural themes combined with a radical idealization of the power of the self to control circumstances.

In spite of their common approach to human problems, the doctrines of the new religions are extremely diverse. Most groups reserve a special place for ancestor worship, whatever their theological disposition. The supernaturals are, however, subject to the same fundamental principles that govern the human world. They do not stand outside these principles or manipulate the world in accord with an independent and unknowable will.

Each period of Japanese history that has seen the founding of new religions has also had an element of social disruption or crisis that has functioned as a catalyst to recruitment. However, the founders themselves have been motivated most immediately by mystical experience of possession by or revelation from a deity. As the meaning of their experience became clear to them, they constructed a method, or "Way," of religious practice and self-cultivation they believed would lead to the solution of the individual's problems and would bring society to harmony and the universe to peace.

History. The late Tokugawa period (1600–1868) gave rise to the first of Japan's modern new religions with the founding of Nyoraikyō (Buddhist; founded 1802), Kurozumikyō (Shinto; founded 1814), Tenrikyō (Shinto; founded 1838), Butsuryūkō (Buddhist; founded 1857), and Konkōkyō (Shinto; founded 1859). Whether Buddhist or Shinto, each of these groups differed from previous tradition in the centrality of the role of lay followers. These new religions were founded as the power of local elites over religious observances eroded, and all were powerfully influenced by contemporary enthusiasm for the Ise pilgrimage [See Ise Mairi.] They all clashed with preexisting religions over the practice of healing, challenging the previous monopoly of priestly healers, and they attracted most of their early following through their healing activities.

Tenrikyō exemplifies important trends found

NEW RELIGIONS IN JAPAN 115

widely among the new religions. Founded by Na-
kayama Miki (1798–1887), pious wife of a prosperous village landowner, Miki entered a state of
spirit possession *(kamigakari)* while in search of a
cure for her son, and in that condition she announced that a deity had come to reside within her.
She accumulated her first followers through healing
and through aiding women in childbirth, thus denying notions of pollution associated with childbirth. By 1865 there were followers throughout the
Kinki area, and Miki's writings, the *Mikagurauta*
(1867) and the *Ofudesaki* (1869), became the basis
of their creed. The deity ordered Miki and her family
to reduce themselves to proverty as the starting point
of the religious life. The idea of religious poverty
remains a pillar of the group's doctrine.

The deity possessing Miki revealed itself gradually
through a succession of names, such as Heavenly
Shogun, the Wheel-turning God (after the *chakra-
vartin* idea in Buddhism), and Parent Deity. None
of these names were known previously; thus Miki's
religion was in essence independent of both Buddhism and Shinto. In early Meiji, however, the group
was pressured to assume a Shinto identity in order
to escape persecution, and it participated in the
state-sponsored Great Proselytization Campaign
and otherwise cooperated with the state until 1945.
Nevertheless, the charismatic appeal of Tenrikyō
was taken as a threat by the state; Miki herself was
jailed eighteen times, and the group was subjected
to severe suppression in many areas. Today it has
some 2,600,000 members and a nationwide organization of churches.

Against a background of rural poverty, which
grew as the factory system, especially the textile industry, penetrated rural Japan, Ōmotokyō was
founded in 1892 by Deguchi Nao (1837–1918) and
her son-in-law Deguchi Ōnisaburō (1871–1948).
Ōmotokyō proclaimed the advent of the millennium
in Nao's *Ofudesaki.* These writings were considered
inflammatory in heralding the downfall of the rich
in favor of the weak. For this reason, Nao and her
followers were repeatedly suppressed, but after
Nao's death, Ōnisaburō attempted to bring the
group into the mainstream by formulating a nationalistic interpretation of Ōmoto doctrine. Nevertheless, the group's millenarian tendency was so
feared by the authorities that its headquarters were
destroyed. Ōmoto now has 168,000 members,
mainly in rural areas.

The early twentieth century saw the founding of
another wave of new religions, including Reiyūkai
(Buddhist; founded 1919–1925), Sōka Gakkai

(Buddhist; founded 1930), and Seichō no Ie (independent; founded 1930). Sōka Gakkai and Reiyūkai
derive from the Nichiren Buddhist tradition. [*See
Nichiren.*] In the prewar era Reiyūkai attracted a
large following of lower middle class self-employed
persons and owners of small or family-run busi-
nesses. It expounded a path to salvation and the
cure of all ills through a layman's worship of ancestors in a manner based on the Lotus Sutra and independent of the Buddhist clergy. Reiyūkai belief
and practice are continued, albeit with significant
modification, in the nearly twenty groups that have
originated from it through schism. Reiyūkai presently has roughly three million members, of whom
about 70 percent reside in urban areas.

The most phenomenal development among the
new religions since 1945 has been the rapid growth
of Sōka Gakkai, a gigantic organization claiming
sixteen million members and sponsoring publishing
houses, a national daily newspaper (circulation
4,540,000), a national network of meeting halls,
primary and secondary schools, a university (Sōka
University), and Japan's third-largest political party,
Kōmeitō.

Shortly after the end of the war, Sōka Gakkai
began to put up candidates for local elections, and
in 1964 it formed Kōmeitō. In 1967 Kōmeitō seated
twenty-five members in the Lower House. Kōmeitō's
original platform advocated clean government and
the expansion of welfare policies. It also promoted
a number of strictly religious issues, such as "Buddhist Democracy" and unification of the nation in
Sōka Gakkai worship. In the early days of Kōmeitō,
it and Sōka Gakkai were one and the same. Under
considerable public pressure, however, Sōka Gakkai
and Kōmeitō were formally separated in 1970, and
since that time Kōmeitō has begun to resemble more
and more other political parties that, like the German Christian Democratic Party, have no particular
religious slant. However, in that most Kōmeitō leaders are also executives in Sōka Gakkai, it would be
premature to say that Kōmeitō has thrown off all
religious associations.

Other new religions have also become involved
in politics, in part because politicians aggressively
court them in hopes of gaining the large blocks
of urban votes they represent. In 1951 the Union
of New Religious Organizations was founded; it
has eighty-four member groups. The political arm
of the Union now commands the machinery to
choose a common slate of candidates for all these
groups. How far the various new religions will in
fact cooperate politically remains to be seen, but

without a doubt they represent a political force of potentially immense influence.

The new religions represent the most vital sector of Japanese religion today. They thrive in contemporary society, while shrine Shinto and temple Buddhism are in decline. While infinitely diverse in doctrine, the members of the new religions share a common worldview in which cultural themes such as the solidarity of the family and respect for age and tradition are heightened and imbued with religious significance.

[*See also* Shinto *and* Christianity: Christianity in Japan.]

HELEN HARDACRE

NEW TEXT SCHOOL. *See* Jinwen.

NGAM MUANG, king of Phayao (1238–1318) in northern Thailand. The son of King Ming Muang, Ngam Muang is said to have studied at Lopburi in the 1250s and to have made the acquaintance there of the future King Ramkhamhaeng of Sukhothai. Returning home, he succeeded his father in 1258 and in 1276 concluded an alliance with King Mangrai of Lan Na. Mangrai subsequently mediated a dispute between Ramkhamhaeng and Ngam Muang in the 1280s, and the three kings joined together in 1296 to ceremonially inaugurate Mangrai's new capital at Chiang Mai. Ngam Muang died in 1318, outliving both of his more famous contemporaries. Only his son and grandson seem to have been styled kings, and within the next century Phayao was absorbed into the Lan Na kingdom.

[*See also* Phayao; Lopburi; Ramkhamhaeng; Mangrai; *and* Lan Na.]

David K. Wyatt, *Thailand: A Short History* (1984).

DAVID K. WYATT

NGHE-TINH UPRISING, peasant rebellion in the French protectorate of Annam in 1930 and 1931. High taxes, mandarin corruption, and the effects of the Great Depression had led to conditions of starvation and rising unrest in the central coastal provinces of Nghe An and Ha Tinh in the summer of 1930. Mobilized by Communist Party activists, peasants in several rural districts drove out the local imperial authorities and formed village self-help associations, called soviets, after the Chinese model.

The French struck back with force, and by the spring of 1931 the rebellion had been put down. In the process, the young Indochinese Communist Party was virtually destroyed. The origins of the rebellion have long been a source of dispute among scholars. Was it organized and directed by the Communists at the behest of Moscow, or was it a spontaneous uprising of desperate peasants? Current evidence suggests that both factors may have been in evidence.

[*See also* Indochinese Communist Party.]

Huynh Kim Khanh, *Vietnamese Communism, 1925–1945* (1982). James C. Scott, *The Moral Economy of the Peasant* (1976).   WILLIAM J. DUIKER

NGO DINH CAN (d. 1964), brother of Ngo Dinh Diem (1901–1963) and a hidden but powerful figure in South Vietnam under the Ngo regime. Involved in forcing Bao Dai to abdicate in June 1955, Can went on to develop a strong power base in Hue. He was concerned with restraining and suppressing the Viet Nam Quoc Dan Dang and Dai Viet parties and later used his forces to fight National Liberation Front (NLF) forces as well. Can's interests sometimes led him to oppose those of the Saigon government, particularly those of his brother Ngo Dinh Nhu (1910–1963). After Diem's fall, Can was executed publicly in 1964.

[*See also* Ngo Dinh Diem; Ngo Dinh Nhu; *and* Ngo Dinh Thuc.]

Dennis Duncanson, *Government and Revolution in Vietnam* (1968). Denis Warner, *The Last Confucian* (1964).   BRUCE M. LOCKHART

NGO DINH DIEM (1901–1963), first president of the Republic of Vietnam, usually referred to as South Vietnam. Born into an influential Catholic mandarin family in central Vietnam, Diem rose through the colonial administration and was appointed minister of the interior by Emperor Bao Dai in 1933. He soon resigned this position, however, on the grounds that the Vietnamese had no real power in the French protectorate.

Although he remained an active nationalist, both in Vietnam and abroad, for the next two decades, Diem did not take an official post again until June 1954. At this time he was made prime minister of Bao Dai's State of Vietnam, comprising the territory south of the seventeenth-parallel demarcation line, established as a "temporary" division by the July 1954 Geneva accords. Diem went on to obtain Bao

Dai's abdication and consolidate his own power, declaring the Republic of Vietnam in October 1956.

Allied with the United States, the Diem government blocked reunification of Vietnam and worked to establish a viable noncommunist state in the south. Despite Diem's relatively favorable nationalist credentials, however, his efforts were blocked by several major obstacles. While his Confucian upbringing and ideals tended to cut him off from the people under his leadership, his family's consistent promotion of Catholic interests further alienated the predominantly Buddhist Vietnamese. Although Diem and his brother Nhu (1910–1965) were initially able to suppress such movements as the Binh Xuyen, Cao Dai, and Hoa Hao, their repressive policies toward political opponents only isolated their regime. While Saigon's programs of rural development and pacification were backed by the United States, crackdowns on Buddhist protests in 1963 eroded American support. The November 1963 coup by a military junta headed by General Duong Van Minh received tacit American approval, if not covert backing. Diem and Nhu were assassinated on 2 November 1963.

[*See also* Ngo Dinh Can; Ngo Dinh Nhu; Ngo Dinh Thuc; *and* Vietnam, Republic of.]

Dennis Duncanson, *Government and Revolution in Vietnam* (1968). Bernard Fall, *The Two Viet-Nams* (1967). Stanley Karnow, *Vietnam: A History* (1983). Denis Warner, *The Last Confucian* (1964).

BRUCE M. LOCKHART

NGO DINH NHU (1910–1963), a younger brother of Ngo Dinh Diem (1901–1963). His closeness to Diem enabled Nhu to gain considerable power in his role of political adviser. He promoted the ideology known as Personalism, a conglomerate of ideas based on the thought of Emmanuel Mounier, but ultimately relied more on security forces and his Can Lao (Labor) and Republican Youth movements to suppress dissent in South Vietnam. Nhu's personal ruthlessness, together with the outspoken statements of his wife, Tran Le Xuan, eroded the Ngo regime's support among Vietnamese and Americans alike. He was assassinated with his brother during the November 1963 coup d'état.

[*See also* Can Lao; Ngo Dinh Can; Ngo Dinh Diem; *and* Ngo Dinh Thuc.]

Dennis Duncanson, *Government and Revolution in Vietnam* (1968). Jean Lacouture, *Vietnam: Between Two Truces* (1966).   BRUCE M. LOCKHART

NGO DINH THUC. Monsignor Pierre Martin Ngo Dinh Thuc, brother of Ngo Dinh Diem (1901–1963), exemplified the brand of politicized Catholicism characteristic of the Ngo regime in South Vietnam. Senior among Vietnamese bishops, Thuc had moved from his former diocese in the southern province of Vinh Long to join his younger brother Can (d. 1964) in Hue. The two men shared considerable power in central Vietnam. Thuc's efforts to promote his own interests and those of the church brought him into conflict with both his coreligionists and the Buddhists, and his actions played a major part in precipitating the 1963 Buddhist crisis. Thuc survived his family's regime, however, because he was away in Rome at the time of the coup.

[*See also* Ngo Dinh Diem; Ngo Dinh Can; *and* Ngo Dinh Nhu.]

Jean Lacouture, *Vietnam: Between Two Truces* (1966). Denis Warner, *The Last Confucian* (1964).

BRUCE M. LOCKHART

NGO DYNASTY (939–965), ruled over the kingdom of Dai Co Viet after Ngo Quyen (939–944) had obtained independence from Chinese rule. The Ngo capital was at Co Loa, royal city of An Duong Vuong in his kingdom of Au Lac in the third century BCE. After Ngo Quyen's death in 944, power was usurped by Duong Tam Kha. Ngo's son Xuong Van regained the throne in 951 and ruled until 963, reigning jointly with his brother Xuong Ngap between 951 and 954. His own death precipitated two years of chaos known as the Period of the Twelve Warlords, lasting until Dinh Bo Linh (965–979) proclaimed himself king in 965.

[*See also* Dai Co Viet; Ngo Quyen; Co Loa; An Duong Vuong; *and* Dinh Bo Linh.]

Keith W. Taylor, *The Birth of Vietnam* (1983).

BRUCE M. LOCKHART

NGO QUYEN (897–944), Vietnamese leader. Ngo was born at Duong Lam, west of present-day Hanoi, Vietnam, and served under Duong Dinh Nghe when Chinese soldiers were driven out of Vietnam in 931; he subsequently became Duong Dinh Nghe's son-in-law and was given command of Ai Province (Thanh Hoa). When Kieu Cong Tien killed Duong Dinh Nghe in 937, Ngo Quyen killed Kieu Cong Tien. In the Battle of Bach Dang River, fought during the 938/939 dry season, Ngo Quyen decisively defeated a Southern Han expedition responding to the internal Vietnamese disorders. He then proclaimed himself king and established a Chinese-style court at Co Loa, the ancient citadel of Vietnam's pre-Han kings. He died in 944.

[*See also* Co Loa.]

Keith W. Taylor, *The Birth of Vietnam* (1983).

KEITH W. TAYLOR

NGUYEN AI QUOC. *See* Ho Chi Minh.

NGUYEN DU (1765–1820), Vietnamese poet, began his career as a military mandarin under the Le dynasty. Strongly opposed to the Tay Son movement, he hoped for a Le restoration but was obliged to transfer his loyalty to the Nguyen. Under the new dynasty he served in the Ministry of Rites and also led a diplomatic mission to China. Nguyen Du is best known as a writer, however, and he composed prose and poetry in both classical Chinese and the Vietnamese *chu nom* script. The best known of his *nom* works is also the most famous piece of Vietnamese literature: the narrative poem *Doan-truong tan-thanh* (*New Cries from a Broken Heart*), often referred to as *Kim Van Kieu* (after the names of the three principal characters) or simply *Truyen Kieu* (The Tale of Kieu).

Written in the early Nguyen period, *Kim Van Kieu* is actually based on a Chinese novel from the Ming era. It is the story of a beautiful young woman named Kieu who is forced to sell herself into prostitution to prevent her father's execution. After years of wanderings and hardship, she is reunited with the man she loves. She considers herself no longer worthy to marry him, however, and they vow to love each other as brother and sister.

[*See also* Chu Nom.]

Huynh Sanh Thong, trans., *The Tale of Kieu* (1973) and *The Tale of Kieu: A Bilingual Edition of Truyen Kieu* (1983).   BRUCE M. LOCKHART

NGUYEN DYNASTY, ruling house of Vietnam (1802–1945), founded by Nguyen Phuc Anh, last of the Nguyen lords.

The conservative character of Nguyen rule was determined by the long struggle against the Tay Son. Experience had convinced the Gia Long emperor of the need to preserve internal security and imperial control of the administrative apparatus. The major policies of his reign—establishment of a centralized bureaucratic administration on the Chinese model, promulgation of a law code based on Chinese principles rather than Viet custom, maintenance of a large standing army, and the construction of roads, canals, dikes, and especially fortresses—were directed toward those ends.

While Gia Long had turned to Chinese doctrine in reaction to Tay Son practices, his son and successor, Minh Mang, firmly believed in the universal applicability of Confucian principles. During the reign of Minh Mang (1820–1841) the bureaucracy became more centralized and imperial rule more absolute than ever before. The emperor's concern for ideological orthodoxy caused him to regard Christianity, which may have been practiced by as many as 350,000 of his subjects, as a threat to the state. The practice of Christianity was discouraged in 1825 and missionaries confined to the capital, but it was not until Christians were deeply implicated in the Le Van Khoi Rebellion (1833–1835) that any missionaries were executed.

The campaign against Christianity, which was continued under both Thieu Tri (1841–1847) and Tu Duc (1847–1883), provided France with a cause for intervention in Vietnam. When threats and displays of force brought no concessions from the Vietnamese court, the French decided to intervene militarily. After an abortive attack on Da Nang (1858), Saigon and the surrounding areas were occupied (1859–1862). Tu Duc recognized the French conquests in the treaty of 5 June 1862.

Popular uprisings against the French began almost immediately but received no support from the court, which feared insurrection more than external aggression. The French used these attacks as a pretext for the occupation of the remaining provinces of southern Vietnam (Cochinchina) in 1867. When the potential commercial advantages of the Red River became apparent, France negotiated another treaty with Tu Duc (1874). Attempts by the French to enforce the provisions of this vaguely worded agreement led to the imposition of a French protectorate over the remainder of Vietnam in 1883–1884.

The French onslaught coincided with a crisis at the Vietnamese court. Tu Duc died childless in July 1883, leaving the government in the hands of a council of regency, which made and unmade three rulers (Duc Duc, Hiep Hoa, Kien Phuc) in rapid succession. The regents, dominated by the strongly anti-French Ton That Thuyet, then installed the

TABLE 1. *Nguyen Emperors*

EMPEROR	REIGN DATES
1. Gia Long (Nguyen Phuc Anh)	1802–1820
2. Minh Mang	1820–1841
3. Thieu Tri	1841–1847
4. Tu Duc	1847–1883
5. Duc Duc	1883*
6. Hiep Hoa (Prince Hong Dat)	1883*
7. Kien Phuc	1883–1884*
8. Ham Nghi	1884–1885*
9. Dong Khanh	1885–1889
10. Thanh Thai	1889–1907*
11. Duy Tan	1907–1916*
12. Khai Dinh	1916–1925
13. Bao Dai	1926–1945*

*Deposed or resigned.

twelve-year-old Ham Nghi as emperor. In July 1885 Thuyet instigated an unsuccessful attack on the French garrison in Hue, then fled with the emperor to Quang Tri Province. The French used this opportunity to declare Ham Nghi deposed and place his older brother Dong Khanh (1885–1889) on the throne. Ham Nghi was captured and exiled in 1888.

Under French rule the Nguyen continued to reign as shadow emperors, but sovereigns who expressed the slightest dissatisfaction with their status were promptly deposed, as were Thanh Thai (1889–1907) and Duy Tan (1907–1916). The last of the Nguyen emperors, Bao Dai, abdicated in favor of the Democratic Republic of Vietnam on 25 August 1945.

[*Some of the Nguyen monarchs are the subject of independent entries. See also* Nguyen Lords; Tay Son Rebellion; Le Van Khoi Rebellion; *and* Vietnam, Democratic Republic of.]

John Cady, *The Roots of Imperialism in Eastern Asia* (1954). Thomas Hodgkin, *Vietnam: The Revolutionary Path* (1981). Nguyen The Anh, *The Withering Days of the Nguyen Dynasty* (1978). Alexander B. Woodside, *Vietnam and the Chinese Model* (1971).

JAMES M. COYLE

NGUYEN HOANG

NGUYEN HOANG (1525–1613), Nguyen lord (1558–1613) and son of Nguyen Kim (d. 1545). Despite the ambitions of his brother-in-law Trinh Kiem, Nguyen Hoang was able to obtain the governorship of Thuan Hoa in 1558. Supported by loyal family followers, he consolidated his military and administrative control over the Thuan Hoa-Quang Nam region. He was conscious of growing Trinh power in the north and strenthened his own position while vowing fidelity to the Le. After repelling an invasion from Champa, he was able to annex Cham territory as far as Phu Yen in 1611. Nguyen Hoang was succeeded by his son Phuoc Nguyen (Sai Vuong, 1613–1635). [*See also* Nguyen Lords; Nguyen Kim; *and* Trinh Kiem.]

BRUCE M. LOCKHART

NGUYEN KIM

NGUYEN KIM (c. 1467–1545), resistance leader against the Mac usurpers in Dai Viet. Having fled to a Lao kingdom with supporters of the Le dynasty, Nguyen Kim led a movement loyal to the emperor Le Trang Ton, whom he had enthroned in 1533. In 1535 he sent a mission to China to plead the Le cause. Nguyen's forces grew increasingly powerful and expanded the territory under their control. After his death, the struggle was carried on by his son-in-law Trinh Kiem, whose rivalry with Nguyen Kim's son Nguyen Hoang foreshadowed the long Trinh-Nguyen conflict. [*See also* Mac Dynasty; Mac Dang Dung; Nguyen Hoang; Trinh Kiem; *and* Trinh-Nguyen Wars.]

BRUCE M. LOCKHART

NGUYEN LORDS

NGUYEN LORDS (Vietnamese, Chua Nguyen), autonomous governors of southern Dai Viet, or Dang Trong (1558–1777), and predecessors of the Nguyen dynasty.

The Nguyen, one of the oldest Vietnamese clans, were originally from Thanh Hoa Province. Active supporters of Le Loi, they rose to modest prominence during the reign of Le Thanh Tong when the future emperor Hien Tong was born to a Nguyen empress.

Nguyen Kim (1468–1545), a retired official, fled to Lan Sang at the usurpation of Mac Dang Dung (1527) with the intention of restoring the fallen Le dynasty. By the time of his death, the restoration movement had wrested from the Mac control of Dai Viet from Thanh Hoa southward.

In 1558 Trinh Kiem, son-in-law of Nguyen Kim and leader of the restoration forces, allowed Kim's second son, Nguyen Hoang, to become governor of the inhospitable province of Thuan Hoa, in the far south. Nguyen Hoang used this opportunity to form an autonomous territory but continued to cooperate with the Trinh until his death in 1613. His successors, however, claiming that the Trinh lords had

TABLE 1. *Nguyen Lords*

LORD	REIGN DATES
1. Nguyen Kim	1533–1545
2. Nguyen Hoang (Chua Tien)	1545–1613
3. Nguyen Phuc Nguyen (Chua Sai)	1613–1635
4. Nguycn Phuc Lan (Chua Thuong)	1635–1648
5. Nguyen Phuc Tan (Chua Hien)	1648–1687
6. Nguyen Phuc Tran (Chua Nghia)	1687–1691
7. Nguyen Phuc Chu (Chua Quoc)	1691–1725
8. Nguyen Phuc Tru (Ninh Vuong)	1725–1738
9. Nguyen Phuc Khoat (Vo Vuong)	1738–1765
10. Nguyen Phuc Thuan (Dinh Vuong)	1765–1777*
11. Nguyen Phuc Anh	1778–1802

*Deposed.

usurped the power of the Le emperors, refused to pay tribute to the northern court. This brought on a period of bloody and inconclusive warfare between the two regions, which ended in mutual exhaustion and de facto recognition of the partition of Dai Viet, although both Trinh and Nguyen lords continued to recognize the theoretical authority of the Le dynasty.

During this period and in the succeeding century, the Nguyen lords opened new areas for cultivation, established a formal administration, conducted their own examinations, promoted commerce, and extended the area under their control as far as the Mekong Delta, at the expense of Cambodia and the remnants of the Cham kingdom. They also encouraged successive waves of Chinese refugees to settle in the delta and in the regions of Ha Tien and the Ca Mau Peninsula.

The death of Chua Vo Vuong in 1765 ushered in a period of turmoil. The succession struggle that ensued ended in the enthronement of the late lord's sixteenth son, a boy of twelve. Power was exercised by a regent, Truong Phuc Loan, whose self-aggrandizing fiscal policies helped trigger a massive peasant uprising, the Tay Son Rebellion, in 1771.

The rebellion gave the Trinh an opportunity to profit from the confusion in the south. Breaking the century-old truce, a Trinh army invaded Nguyen territory and captured the capital, Phu Xuan (Hue), in March 1775. The Nguyen family fled to the Mekong Delta where, aided by the local Chinese, they put up an increasingly feeble resistance to the Tay Son. In October 1777 the *chua,* his designated heir, and most of the Nguyen clan were killed by Tay Son forces. A grandson of Vo Vuong, Nguyen Phuc Anh, escaped the slaughter and founded the Nguyen dynasty twenty-five years later.

[*Several Nguyen lords are the subject of independent entries. See also* Nguyen Dynasty; Mac Dang Dung; Le Dynasties; Mac Dynasty; Trinh Kiem; *and* Trinh-Nguyen Wars.]

Thomas Hodgkin, *Vietnam: The Revolutionary Path* (1981).   JAMES M. COYLE

NGUYEN PHUC ANH. *See* Gia Long.

NGUYEN THAI HOC (1902–1930), first chairman of the Viet Nam Quoc Dan Dang (Vietnam Nationalist Party, or VNQDD). As a student, he petitioned the French authorities for colonial reforms in Indochina. Receiving no answer, however, he began to advocate more violent methods and helped found the VNQDD in 1927. When the Party was implicated in the assassination of a French official in 1929, the government arrested many of its leaders, but Nguyen was able to escape. After several months as a fugitive, he became involved in the abortive Yen Bay Uprising of February 1930. This time he did not escape arrest and was beheaded.

[*See also* Vietnam Nationalist Party *and* Yen Bay Uprising.]

William J. Duiker, *The Rise of Nationalism in Vietnam, 1900–1941* (1976). Nguyen Phut Tan, *Modern History of Vietnam 1802–1954* (1964).   BRUCE M. LOCKHART

NGUYEN THAT THANH. *See* Ho Chi Minh.

NGUYEN TRAI (1380–1442), scholar, poet, and counselor to Le Loi (later Emperor Le Thai-To, r. 1428–1433). During Le Loi's rebellion against the Ming occupation, Nguyen Trai helped plan strategy and drafted letters urging the Chinese generals to surrender. He formulated an ideology of strong royal authority based on the principles of *nhan* (Chinese, *ren,* "humanity") and *nghia* (Chinese, *yi,* "justice"). He came into conflict with the military elite in the Le court, however, was falsely accused of regicide, and was executed in 1443. His most famous literary work is the *Binh Ngo dai cao* (*Great Proclamation of the Pacification of the Chinese*).

[*See also* Le Loi *and* Lam Son Uprising.]

Thomas Hodgkin, *Vietnam: The Revolutionary Path* (1981).   BRUCE M. LOCKHART

NIAN REBELLION. Etymologically meaning "to twist and bundle together," *Nian* originally referred to a conglomeration of feuding and autonomous gangs in the Huaibei area of China in the early nineteenth century. Composed of the human debris of the White Lotus Rebellion (1796–1805)—uprooted peasants, remnant sectarians, and disbanded soldiers—these early Nian groups were predatory gangs involved in banditry and smuggling. They forged strong links with local communities along kinship lines, and their leaders were powerful lineage heads who turned entire villages into militarized bases populated by seasonal outlaws.

By the early 1850s the hardship and dislocation created by the shifting course of the Yellow River, together with the confusion caused by the arrival of the Taiping army in Huaibei, changed the character of the Nians. A sense of unity and signs of shared political consciousness emerged. Rallying under the leadership of Zhang Luoxing, an affluent salt smuggler of Zhiheji (Woyang County, Anhui Province), the erstwhile diverse gangs now assumed the word *Nian* as a proper noun for their movement.

The Nian Rebellion had two distinct phases. The first comprised the decade up to early 1863, when Zhang Luoxing was captured and executed; the second lasted from 1864 to 1868, when Zhang's nephew Zongyu waged a wide-ranging cavalry war with the government all across the North China Plain. During the first phase the Nians were entrenched in their earth-wall communities and the few large cities they took, launching regular raids on adjoining provinces and inspiring separate local rebellions along the way. During the second phase, however, they were forced to abandon their nest areas and to engage in a mobile guerrilla warfare with the government. The Nian Rebellion finally ended with the defeat and suicide of Zhang Zongyu in August 1868, but the government also lost one of its most decorated commanders, the Mongol prince Senggerinchin.

[*See also* Qing Dynasty; Rebellions in China; *and* Senggerinchin.]

Siang-tseh Chiang, *The Nien Rebellion* (1954). K. C. Liu, "The Ch'ing Restoration," in *The Cambridge History of China*, vol. 10, edited by John K. Fairbank (1978), pp. 456–477. Elizabeth J. Perry, *Rebels and Revolutionaries in North China 1845–1945* (1980).   RICHARD SHEK

NICHIREN (1222–1282), Japanese religious reformer and founder of the Nichiren, or Hokke ("lotus"), school of Japanese Buddhism. Nichiren was born in the province of Awa (modern Chiba Prefecture) and always took pride in his claim to have been born the son of a humble fisherman. At the age of eleven he entered the religious life as a novice in a local Tendai monastery. After visiting monasteries in Nara and on Mount Kōya for further study, he spent ten years in Enryakuji, the great Tendai center on Mount Hiei established by Saichō. [*See* Enryakuji.] It was there that he attained his first deep spiritual insight and took the name Nichiren. The character *nichi* means "sun" or "light" and also connotes the nation and land of Japan. *Ren* means "lotus" and thus expressed his lifelong devotion to the *Lotus Sutra*. At that time Tendai Buddhism was heavily influenced by esoteric Shingon and Pure Land practices. Nichiren regarded these as evils distorting the true Tendai doctrine advocated by Saichō, the practice of which he was convinced lay in exclusive devotion to the *Lotus Sutra*.

Quitting Enryakuji in 1253, Nichiren began to preach his message of the absolute efficacy of the *Lotus Sutra*. He believed that the *Lotus* contained within it the power of all the Buddhas, past and future. It was, therefore, the perfect scripture for opening people's eyes to the truth and offering access to salvation in an age of degeneration of Buddhism, *mappō*. The saving power of the *Lotus,* moreover, could be called upon by the simple invocation of the phrase "Namu myōhō renge kyō" ("praise to the *Lotus of the Wonderful Dharma*"). This invocation, known as the *daimoku*, became the basis of religious practice for Nichiren and his followers.

Salvation, he taught, was not remote but rather easily within reach in this life for those who trusted the *Lotus* and lived diligently. Without the *Lotus,* however, men and women would inevitably be led astray by false teachings in a degenerate age. Just as Nichiren advocated his *Lotus* teaching aggressively, so he virulently attacked all other teachings as heretical. He regarded himself as a reincarnation of the bodhisattva Jōgyō, who had originally been entrusted with the protection and promotion of the *Lotus Sutra*.

Nichiren saw his role, therefore, as an unflinching advocate of the true teaching and as a savior of individuals, of society, and of the country. This role involved rooting out heresy. He was particularly hostile to Pure Land and Zen Buddhism. In his *Rissho ankoku ron* (*Treatise on Establishing Right and Pacifying the Country*, 1260), written a little more than a decade before the first invasion attempt by the Mongols, he argued that if the *bakufu* did not promote the *Lotus* and eradicate all other heretical teachings, the country would suffer invasion. This intolerant stance was unusual in Japanese Buddhism and set Nichiren at odds not only with other Buddhists but with the political authorities. He was so outspoken in his condemnation of other schools of Buddhism, and of political authorities for harboring them, that he was sent into exile in 1261 to Izu and later sentenced to death, pardoned, and then exiled again, to the island of Sado (1271–1274).

Punishment and exile merely strengthened his resolve. He used the periods of exile to write and make new converts among farmers and local warriors. While he was on Sado he wrote the *Kaimokushō, (Eye Opener),* in which he made a threefold vow to be the bearer and defender of religious truth as the pillar of Japan, the eyes of Japan, and the great vessel of Japan. Nichiren was pardoned in 1274 and allowed to return to Minobu, near Mount Fuji, where he spent the remainder of his life. His disciples and successors shared his robust, intransigent sincerity. Although frequently divided by issues of orthodoxy of transmission and teaching, they carried Nichiren's devotion to the *Lotus* throughout Japan and laid the foundations for the vigorous Nichiren school of Buddhism. Of the six disciples that Nichiren designated before his death, Nikkō, Nichiren's oldest disciple, established a temple near Mount Fuji; Nichirō and Nisshō were active in Kamakura and eastern Japan; and Nichiji became a missionary to the Ainu in Hokkaidō. In later generations, Nisshin (1407–1488) was a vigorous evangelist in Kyushu and Kyoto, while Nichiō (1565–1630) led an uncompromising group known as Fuju-fuse ("accept nothing, give nothing," referring to their refusal to have any dealings with nonbelievers).

The seven branches of the Nichiren school active today have some two million adherents. With these, however, should be considered those new religious movements that derive at least in part from Nichiren Buddhism and have particular devotion to the *Lotus Sutra.* Among these are Reiyūkai, claiming three and one-half million members; Risshō Kōseikai with two million followers, and Sōka Gakkai with ten million.

[*See also* Tendai *and* New Religions in Japan.]

Masaharu Anesaki, *Nichiren the Buddhist Prophet.* (1916). Joseph M. Kitagawa, *Religion in Japanese History* (1966). MARTIN COLLCUTT

NICHOLSON, JOHN

NICHOLSON, JOHN (1821–1857), British military hero. Nicholson joined the Bengal infantry in 1839 and fought in the First Afghan War (1839–1842). Involved in the Sikh wars from 1845 to 1849, he later helped "settle" the frontier Pathans (Pakhtuns) from 1851 to 1856. Nicholson forcefully

quelled rebellion in the Punjab in the 1857 Mutiny. He was killed while leading an attack on Delhi. [*See also* Mutiny, Indian.] USHA SANYAL

NIHONBASHI

NIHONBASHI, an area of southeastern Tokyo, Japan, lying between the city's financial center in the Marunouchi-Ōtemachi district and the Sumida River. Nihonbashi is a part of Tokyo's Chūō ward, one of the twenty-three wards of which the city is composed, and is the home of Japan's stock market, the Bank of Japan, and such well-known department stores as Takashimaya and Mitsukoshi.

The area derives its name from the main bridge in this section of the city, one of hundreds of bridges constructed in Tokyo (then called Edo) during the Tokugawa period. The bridge, traversing the Nihonbashi River, was first built in 1603 and has been rebuilt nineteen times since. The present structure dates from 1911 and measures 48.6 meters in length and 27 meters in width.

Nihonbashi is perhaps most famous as the starting point for the five main roads, the Tōkaidō, Nakasendō, Ōshūkaidō, Kōshūkaidō, and Nikkōkaidō, that linked Edo to all points within Japan during the Tokugawa period. All distances to Edo were measured as starting from this bridge.

[*See also* Tokyo.]

Edward Seidensticker, *Low City, High City: Tokyo from Edo to the Earthquake* (1983).

THOMAS R. SCHALOW

NIHON SHOKI

NIHON SHOKI *(Chronicle of Japan),* Japan's first court history, an official document written in Chinese. Commissioned in 681 by Emperor Temmu, the chronicle was completed by a committee of high-ranking nobles under Imperial Prince Toneri in 720. The history is based on aristocrats' diaries, official documents, foreign chronicles, and imperial records *(teiki, kuji);* it describes Japan from its creation to the reign of Empress Jitō (r. 686–697).

The authors' major purposes in writing the *Nihon shoki* were to glorify the imperial line and legitimize Japan's supremacy over the Korean kingdom of Silla. Thus Japan's mythical first emperor, Jimmu, was given divine parents and his reign pushed back into the dim past (660 BCE). A mythical Japanese "invasion" of Korea was chronicled in the reign of Empress Jingū.

The account of the mid-seventh century also served the ideological purposes of Japan's ruling house; only the chronicles of the reigns of Temmu and Jitō approach historical objectivity. However, Tsuda Sōkichi, a scholar of the 1920s, proved that critical study of the *Nihon shoki*, in combination with study of the *Kojiki (Records of Ancient Matters*, 712) and archaeological data, can provide numerous insights into the Japanese past.

[*See also* Kojiki.]

W. G. Aston, trans., *Nihongi* (1896).

WAYNE FARRIS

NIIJIMA JŌ (Joseph Hardy Neesima; 1843–1890), Japanese educator and Christian leader. Niijima was born in Edo, the son of a samurai from Annaka. Educated in Chinese and Dutch learning, he developed a growing curiosity about the outside world and a desire to learn more about Christianity, which he had read of in Chinese and Dutch books. In 1864 he managed to make his way to Hakodate, where he taught Japanese to Nikolai, the Russian priest who introduced the Russian Orthodox Church to Japan. [*See* Nikolai.] Later the same year he secretly left Japan for Shanghai, and in 1865 he arrived in Boston aboard the clipper ship *Wild Rover*. Alpheus Hardy, the ship's owner, hearing of Niijima's plight and desire for an education, sent him to Phillips Academy, Amherst College, and Andover Theological Seminary. In 1874, after graduating from Andover and being ordained as an "evangelist," he returned to Japan as a member of the American Board of Commissioners for Foreign Missions.

In the years that followed Niijima devoted himself to what he regarded his life mission—the founding of a Christian college in Japan. With the help of Alpheus Hardy and the American Board he turned the American Board's Kyoto Training School into Dōshisha College and later Dōshisha University. In this effort he was assisted by missionaries such as Jerome D. Davis and in 1876 by the arrival in Kyoto of the Kumanoto Band, the brilliant group of students who had been converted to Christianity by Captain L. L. Janes at the Kumamoto School for Western Learning. Niijima died in 1890, leaving behind a reputation as the leading Christian educator of his generation.

[*See also* Christianity: Christianity in Japan.]

F. G. NOTEHELFER

NIJŌ CASTLE, the official residence of the Tokugawa shogun in the Japanese imperial capital of Kyoto. Nijō castle was built and steadily expanded

FIGURE 1. *Nijō Castle.*

between 1602 and 1626. Although rarely used by the shogun themselves, who governed from the city of Edo (present-day Tokyo) and failed even to visit Nijō between 1634 and 1863, the castle remained both a symbol of military power in Kyoto and the headquarters of Tokugawa deputies (*shoshidai*), who made it the seat of urban administration until 1868. Surrounded by a moat, stone walls, and the residences of great lords (daimyo) who served the Tokugawa house, the Nijō complex occupied approximately sixty-five acres within the grid of Kyoto's streets. At its heart was the shogunal mansion, a magnificent wooden building with a cypress-bark roof and several wings that epitomized the tastes of the period. The walls were covered with polychrome paintings on gold leaf and the transoms carved into flamboyant shapes. A donjon, which was moved from Fushimi castle in 1623, occupied an area of raised ground to the west of the mansion until its destruction by fire in 1791. Also included within the complex were spacious gardens, several minor residences and reception halls, various towers (*yagura*), barracks, storehouses, and service facilities. Much of the original rampart, a number of gates and towers, the principal garden, and the shogunal mansion remain today, now under the care of the Kyoto city government. (Nijō castle should not be confused with Nijō *gosho*, a residence constructed during 1569 in a different location by Oda Nobunaga for the last Ashikaga shogun and later used by the imperial family; this residence was destroyed in 1582.)

[*See also* Kyoto *and* Tokugawa Period.]

Hirai Kiyoshi, *Feudal Architecture of Japan*, translated by Hiroaki Sato and Jeannine Ciliotta (1973). John B. Kirby, *From Castle to Teahouse: Japanese Architecture of the Momoyama Period* (1962). R. A. B. Ponsonby-Fane, *Kyoto: The Old Capital of Japan* (reprint, 1956).

MARY ELIZABETH BERRY

NIKITIN, AFANASI (d.1475). A Russian merchant who resided in India from 1469 to 1472, Nikitin left an account of his travels that is one of the earliest extant European descriptions of the South Asian subcontinent. A native of the important commercial city of Tver (subject to Moscow), Nikitin visited India only as an attempt to recoup the losses that he had suffered when he was plundered by the subjects of Shirvan Shah in the southern Caucasus. His memoir, which focuses principally on the Bahmani sultanate, is brief and of limited value, and had no evident effect on Russian trade with India, which Nikitin himself actively discouraged.

R. H. Major, ed., *India in the Fifteenth Century* (1857).

STEPHEN FREDERIC DALE

NIKOLAI (born Ivan Kasatkin; 1836–1911), Russian priest and founder of the Orthodox church in Japan. First attracted to Japan by reading Golovnin's account of his captivity, Nikolai was sent from Saint Petersburg to serve as consular chaplain in Hokkaido. Arriving in Hakodate in 1861, he studied Japanese (for a time with the American-educated Japanese Christian Niijima Jō) and began his missionary work. In 1872, after returning briefly to Russia and being officially appointed a missionary to Japan, he left his work in Hakodate for Tokyo, where he established a church and school at Surugadai in Kanda. A gifted linguist and scholar, he made an intensive study of the Japanese language, the history of Buddhism and Confucianism, and Japanese society. Working largely by himself he attracted large numbers of Japanese to the Orthodox faith. A man of dignity, he was held in great esteem by his followers, and even during the Russo-Japanese War (1904–1905) he maintained his rapport with the broader Japanese public. Preacher, teacher, translator, and student of Japanese culture, Nikolai was among the group of outstanding early Meiji-period missionaries who introduced modern Christianity to Japan.

[*See also* Christianity: Christianity in Japan.]

F. G. NOTEHELFER

NILGIRI HILLS, a mountain range (*nilgiri* means "blue hills") in South India that straddles the state boundaries of Kerala, Karnataka, and Tamil Nadu.

Known as a summer resort for Madras-based British officials in the nineteenth century, the Nilgiris contain the hill stations of Ootacamund and Coonoor, as well as the industrial city of Coimbatore. Tea and coffee are grown in the Nilgiris; the highest point is Dodabetta (8,760 feet).

Mollie Panter-Downes, *Ooty Preserved* (1967).

ROBIN JARED LEWIS

1911 REVOLUTION. *See* Xinhai Revolution.

NINGXIA, Chinese province, first separated from Gansu Province in 1928. In 1954 it again became part of Gansu, although in 1958 it regained provincial-level status as an autonomous region for Hui (Chinese Muslim) peoples. With a population of 3,895,706 (1982 census), Ningxia occupies an area of 77,000 square kilometers and is located west of Inner Mongolia and south of the Mongolian People's Republic. In the central area of the Ningxia plain, irrigation allows the naturally arid land to produce nonglutinous rice, spring wheat, millet, gaoliang (Chinese sorghum), soy beans, cotton, tobacco, and hemp. After the arrival of the railway in the late 1950s some mining and industry developed, particularly the coal-mining center of Shicuishan at the north end of the plain. Animal husbandry, especially sheep and horses, is more prominent in the south and the desert northwest. Yinchuan, the provincial capital, is an important highway center and contains some industry, including textiles. Chinese Muslims constitute about one-third of Ningxia's population, which also includes Mongols in the sparsely populated west and northwest.

JOHN A. RAPP

NINOMIYA SONTOKU (1787–1856), Japanese expert on agricultural administration during the late Edo (Tokugawa) period. Ninomiya Sontoku was born to a wealthy peasant family that suffered economic ruin during his boyhood. Through ceaseless toil and thrift, he, as an orphan, regained the family's former landholdings and revived its prosperity. His talents gained recognition from several daimyo in the area centering on Edo, and he helped restore some six hundred villages to varying degrees of economic health. In 1842, Mizuno Tadakuni, head of the *bakufu*, appointed him to minor posts in charge of Tone River water-control projects and the economic resuscitation of the *bakufu*'s Nikkō domain.

Sontoku accepted the Tokugawa sociopolitical

order as a given and sought economic reform by working within it. He taught that the peasants' economic improvement depended on their prior moral improvement. He attacked their prevalent fatalistic ideas of poverty being due to "Heaven" or destiny. Such a passive resignation, he believed, resulted in moral sloth. He preached that men must perceive themselves as both responsible for their economic plight and capable of improving it, through unflagging effort, thrift, village cooperation, and the honest management of rationally planned finances.

BOB TADASHI WAKABAYASHI

NIRVANA, a term common to several ancient Indian traditions indicating spiritual emancipation. Consistent with its etymology, *nirvana* means "blowing out" the implied "flame" of personal attachments. For most Indian religions, the realization of *nirvana* signifies cutting off the cycle of rebirth and death. To the devotee, the term suggests human perfection, unshakeable beatitude, and the attainment of extranormal powers.

Nirvana is especially associated with Buddhism, where it is seen as the salvation resulting from perfecting ethical conduct *(shila),* mind training *(samadhi),* and phenomenological insight *(prajna).* For the Hinayana schools, *nirvana* is the highest human ideal, the attainment of the *arahat;* for the Mahayana schools, their exemplars, the bodhisattvas, must develop six or ten perfections *(paramitas)* and keep a vow to lead all other beings to *nirvana* before they attain salvation.

[*See also* Buddhism: An Overview; Hinduism; *and* Jainism.]

Theodore Stcherbatsky, *The Concept of Buddhist Nirvana* (1927; reprint, 1977). E. J. Thomas, *The History of Buddhist Thought* (1933).   TODD THORNTON LEWIS

NISHAPUR, paramount city of eastern Iran from the ninth through the thirteenth century. Located near the end of the eastward extension of the Elburz mountains on a narrow arable plain separating the mountains from the central Iranian desert, Nishapur was the main entrepôt for caravans entering Iran from Central Asia, China, Afghanistan, and India.

The Sasanid city, called Abarshahr, was a military strongpoint with only a few thousand inhabitants. Nishapur grew rapidly after the Arab conquest, largely as a center for the growing Islamic society. By 1000 it had attained a peak population of 100,000–150,000. The Tahirid, Samanid, Saffarid, Ghaznavid, and Seljuk dynasties used it, at times,

FIGURE 1. *Ceramic Bowl.* Nishapur, late tenth century. Glazed pottery with white slip over red body and calligraphic design. Height 10.8 cm., diameter 35.8 cm.

as a primary or secondary capital. As a center of Islamic religious learning it rivaled Baghdad. Its economy rested on transit trade, cloth manufacture, and grain cultivation.

Religious factionalism and the general economic decline of Iran afflicted Nishapur in the late eleventh century. In 1161–1162 the feuding of religious factions and nomadic depredations caused the abandonment of the bulk of the city. A smaller city built in the suburb of Shadyakh flourished until the Mongols destroyed it in 1221. Also beset by several earthquakes, Nishapur sank permanently to a secondary rank, and Mashhad took its place as principal eastern Iranian city.

Richard W. Bulliet, *The Patricians of Nishapur* (1972) and "Medieval Nishapur: A Topographic and Demographic Reconstruction," *Studia Iranica* 5 (1976): 67–89.

RICHARD W. BULLIET

NITOBE INAZŌ (1862–1933), Japanese educator, essayist, and cultural interpreter. It is in this last role that Nitobe is best remembered. He introduced many greats of the Western literary tradition to Japan and addressed the Western world in fluent English.

Nitobe was born a samurai in northern Japan. His father and grandfather had just completed an ambitious irrigation development that changed arid upland into paddy. Inazō graduated with a degree in agronomy from a college established by the Meiji government in Hokkaido. He then studied in the United States and Germany; he returned when he was twenty-eight years old with two further degrees. He also brought back an American bride. Mary and Inazō subsequently worked in close cooperation.

Nitobe then helped form two schools, taught agronomy (1891–1897), restructured the economy of colonial Taiwan (1901–1903), administered Japan's most prestigious preparatory school (1906–1913), taught colonial policy (1913–1920), served as first president of Tokyo Women's Christian College (1918–1920), and helped strengthen the agricultural cooperative movement (1931–1933). While so engaged, he was also able to publish numerous books and essays.

Most famous among Nitobe's works was *Bushido, the Soul of Japan* (1900), which he dictated in English while recuperating from a nervous breakdown. Its appearance in more than ten languages brought him world renown. *Bushido* became the standard against which other evaluations of Japanese culture were measured. Because of it, Nitobe became the first Japanese exchange professor to the United States. He also served as the first non-European undersecretary of the League of Nations (1920–1927) and subsequently became head of the Japan branch of the Institute of Pacific Relations (1929–1933). After attending a conference in that capacity, he died in Victoria, British Columbia, Canada.

The Pacific War made it appear that Nitobe's lifelong ambition to bridge the Pacific had failed. Subsequently, he has been recognized as Japan's greatest internationalist.

Sukeo Kitagawa, *The Life of Dr. Nitobe* (1952). Inazō Nitobe, *Bushido, the Soul of Japan* (1900; reprint, 1969).

JOHN F. HOWES

NIZAM AL-MULK

NIZAM AL-MULK (lit., "order of the realm"; 1017/1019–1092), honorific title of Abu Ali Hasan ibn Ali Tusi, vizier to the Seljuk sultans Alp Arslan and Malikshah.

Nizam al-Mulk is generally regarded as the principal architect of the Seljuk state. He began his administrative career under the Ghaznavids, from whom he would draw inspiration for both theory and practice throughout his life. Then, following the victories of the Seljuks, he entered their service in Khurasan, becoming Alp Arslan's vizier and succeeding with him to imperial power.

Nizam al-Mulk combined his administrative skills with the military ventures of his sovereign to consolidate Seljuk authority from the Mediterranean to beyond the Oxus River. Although he was able to dominate the young Malikshah, Alp Arslan's son and successor, the vizier and the sultan later fell out, probably because of Nizam al-Mulk's arrogance as well as resistance at the court, due in part to his extensive use of nepotism.

Nizam al-Mulk's greatness lies in his championing of traditional Perso-Islamic practices of government and his attempt to adapt them to the new context of the Islamic Middle Ages. His goal was to return substantial power to a civilian Persian bureaucracy; here he was unable to reverse the trend toward Turkish military dominance. Ironically, he contributed to the growing autonomy of local military leaders: by introducing reforms in the land grant (iqta) system, he institutionalized it to the point that it would serve as a basis for their expanded power, influence, and independence. He was able, however, to contribute to the spread of a common educational and intellectual standard throughout Islam by supporting his own schools for Islamic scholars, the Nizamiyya *madrasas*.

Nizam al-Mulk's practice was complemented by his theories, which were articulated in the *Siyasatnama (Book of Government),* a collection of advice, quotations, traditions, sayings, anecdotes, longer stories, contemporary events, and historical narratives, written in the last five years of his life. The *Siyasatnama* takes a well-deserved place in both the development of Persian literature and the refinement of Islamic political theory.

The first part of the book contains chapters about the king's public function ("Concerning assignees of land and inquiry into their treatment of the peasantry," "On obtaining information about the conduct of tax-collectors, judges . . .") as well as his more personal life ("Concerning boon companions and intimates . . . ," "Concerning the rules and arrangements for drinking parties . . ."). The second part is foreboding, dealing almost exclusively with heresy and various revolts, in particular with the contemporary activities of the Isma'ilis.

Nizam al-Mulk's pessimism was warranted; he was assassinated in 1092 by an Isma'ili, possibly with the complicity of the enemies he had gathered at court over three decades. Malikshah died shortly thereafter. These dual voids would not be filled; thus the decline of the Seljuk empire in favor of smaller regional and local states was ensured.

[*See also* Seljuk Dynasty; Education: Education in Iran and Central Asia; *and* Madrasa.]

C. E. Bosworth, "The Political and Dynastic History of the Iranian World (A.D. 1000–1217), " in the *Cambridge History of Iran,* vol. 5, *The Saljuq and Mongol Periods,* edited by J. A. Boyle (1968). Marshall G. S. Hodgson, *The Venture of Islam,* vol. 2 (1974). Ann K. S. Lambton, "The Internal Structure of the Saljuq Empire," in *The Saljuq and Mongol Periods,* already cited. Nizām al-Mulk, *The Book of Government or Rules for Kings,* translated by Hubert Darke (2d ed., 1978).

RUSSELL G. KEMPINERS, JR.

NIZAMI (1141–1203), more fully, Ilyas ibn Yusuf Nizami, born in Ganja; the greatest Persian poet of the southern Caucasus. His epic work consists of five separate poems compiled by later generations into a collection called the *Khamsa (Quintet).* Each poem is composed in a different meter and evokes a different tradition. *Makhzan al-asrar (Treasury of Secrets)* is an ethical-philosophical poem rich in parable and allegory; *Khusrau u Shirin,* said to be inspired by Nizami's grief over the death of his first wife, is an interpretation of a tragic, semihistorical Middle Iranian love story; *Laila u Majnun,* also a romantic tragedy, is based on Arabic folklore; *Haft paykar (Seven Portraits)* gives an account of the education and reign of an ideal king, here Bahram Gur. The fifth epic, which consists of two parts, *Sharafnama (Book of Honor)* and *Iqbalnama (Book of Happiness),* is a portrait of Alexander the Great as warrior, philosopher, and king.

Of the presumed twenty thousand lyrical verses of Nizami, two thousand have survived to attest to his mastery of the genres of *ghazal* (love poetry) and *qasida* (panegyric). A large number of imitators in Iran and in areas under the influence of Persian culture, such as Turkey, Central Asia, and India, composed Khamsas of their own; thus, the formal conventions and mythology of the original were widely circulated.

[*See also* Persian Literature.]

Nizami, *Mirror of the Invisible World: Tales from the Khamseh of Nizami,* translated by Peter J. Chelkowski (1975). J. Rypka, *History of Iranian Literature* (1968).

MARIAM PIRNAZAR

NIZAM UD-DIN AULIYA (d. 1324), one of the most celebrated Sufi saints of India. Disciple of Shaikh Farid Ganj-i Shakar of Ajodhan (d. 1265), he worked in Delhi for the moral and spiritual culture of people for more than half a century. According to the historian Barani all sorts of people from the cities as well as from the rural areas visited him. Nizam ud-Din kept an open kitchen and entertained his visitors irrespective of their caste or creed. He sent his disciples to distant parts of the country and through their efforts the Chishti order attained a pan-Indian status. Eminent figures from all walks of life—princes, nobles, scholars, administrators, poets, businessmen, and others—joined his discipline. The shaikh identified religion with the service of humanity and considered helping the needy to be more important than prayers or penitence. He believed in instructing people through example rather than spinning fine ideas. He kept away from the rulers and the politics of the day and if a *khalifa* (higher disciple) accepted government service, he expelled him from the discipline. The *Fawa'id-Fu'ad* is a collection of is conversations. During the centuries his tomb has remained an important place of pilgrimage.

[*See also* Chishti Tariqa *and* Sufism.]

Wahid Mirza, *The Life and Works of Amir Khusrau* (1935), pp. 112–119. K. A. Nizami, *Some Aspects of Religion and Politics in India during the Thirteenth Century* (1961).

KHALIQ AHMAD NIZAMI

NŌ, a classical Japanese theater form. Emerging from peasant origins in the fourteenth century, *nō* had reached a high degree of refinement by the mid-fifteenth century under the patronage of Ashikaga Yoshimitsu. Yoshimitsu's patronage was largely owing to his attraction to the eleven-year-old boy actor Zeami (1363–1443), who became *nō*'s most famous actor-playwright. Tradition has it that half the surviving canon of 230 plays are Zeami's, but by modern scholarship only 25 are usually recognized to be his work. He is, however, the theater's foremost theoretican, placing great emphasis on the ability to control an audience through the art of suggestion. After Zeami's death *nō* continued to flourish; during the long period of civil strife, and particularly as reflected in the work of Zenchiku (1405–1468), the aesthetics of *nō* came strongly under the influence of Zen. In the late sixteenth century the possibility of a permanent shift to more realistic drama emerged when Hideyoshi patronized *nō* for his own pleasure and amusement, but this was reversed during the Tokugawa period, when *nō* became institutionalized as part of official shogunate ritual. Although today it might seem to be fossilized, it is in fact as alive as opera is in the West. The form has in many respects returned to the aesthetically severe style that is thought to have been Zeami's and Zenchiku's ideal.

Nō is difficult to classify as drama because there is no necessary conflict involved and there is no plot; it is a combination of highly wrought verse, musical accompaniment, and dance. The text of each play is usually only a few pages long, but an average performance now takes from one to two hours, not only because of slow, deliberate delivery but also because of interludes of dance and long periods of silence. The stage is usually bare except for a few symbolic props, the intention being to give an impression of sacred space, an atemporal dream world into which the spectator has a privileged glance. Both acting and text are remarkable for their abstract qualities. There are no characters, only roles whose function it is to give voice to powerful emotions. The roles are "main actor" *(shite)*, "second actor" *(tsure)*, and "side actor" *(waki)*. In addition, there is a chorus that does not comment on the action but merely provides yet further vocal counterpoint; the effect of these various roles is to share the poetry so that it is never allowed to become the prerogative of one specific figure. Masks are used frequently by both *shite* and *tsure* to enhance the other-worldliness of the play; the *waki*, as representative of this world introducing us into the dream, never wears a mask.

Nō plays have traditionally been classified into five types: god, warrior, woman, mad or realistic, and demon plays. Originally the pace must have been faster than today, for we know that performances often included one play from each type arranged in ascending order of emotional impact. Today, most audiences can sit through only one performance at a time, so demanding is the combination of slow pace and lack of plot.

[*See also* Zeami.]

Donald Keene, *Nō: The Classical Theater of Japan* (1966), and *Twenty Plays of the No Theater* (1970). J. Thomas Rimer and Masakazu Yamazaki, eds., *On the Art of the No Drama* (1984).   RICHARD BOWRING

NOGI MARESUKE (1849–1912), Japanese general and war hero. Commissioned in the newly formed Japanese army in 1871 and given a regimental command, Nogi took part in quelling the Satsuma Rebellion in western Japan in 1877, although his regiment lost its flag in combat, a disgrace that haunted him for the rest of his life. During study in Germany in the mid-1880s Nogi developed a strong military idealism based on traditional samurai values. He commanded an infantry brigade in the Sino-Japanese War of 1894 to 1895, served as governor-general of Taiwan from 1896 to 1898, and commanded the Third Army in its bloody, futile attacks on Port Arthur during the Russo-Japanese War of 1904 to 1905. Despite his rather ineffective leadership in the final campaigns in Manchuria

FIGURE 1. *Scene from a Nō Play.*

against Russian forces, Nogi's stoic acceptance of the loss of his two sons in combat brought him immediate adulation from the Japanese public, which welcomed him back as a war hero. Given the title of count in 1907, Nogi was appointed head of the prestigious Peers School. Nogi committed ritual suicide with his wife on the evening of the funeral of the Meiji emperor in 1912, an act that shocked the nation because it supposedly was an act of protest against the luxury and profligacy of contemporary Japan. It may also have been, however, an act of personal atonement.

[See also Sino-Japanese War and Russo-Japanese War.]

MARK R. PEATTIE

NŌHONSHUGI, a brand of agrarian nationalism that flourished in some parts of Japan in the first half of the twentieth century and was connected with the terrorist outbursts of the early 1930s.

The rapid industrialization of Japan provoked a romantic reaction that stressed the priority of agriculture and the superiority of an autonomous rural life, which had presumably existed in premodern times. In the 1920s Nōhonshugi turned into a protest movement against big government, big industry, and big cities. It encompassed landlords, small farmers, and peasants who felt threatened by the capitalist economy and by "decadent" Western culture.

The main spokesmen of the movement were Gondō Seikyō and Tachibana Kōzaburō. Gondō advocated a loose federation of autonomous rural communities under the titular leadership of the emperor. Tachibana organized a rural cooperative movement in Ibaraki Prefecture. Both were extreme nationalists, calling for an expanded Japanese empire. This combination of virulent nationalism and anticapitalism attracted village youths and young military officers.

The rural distress that struck Japan in the early 1930s radicalized the movement. In February and March 1932 two village youths who had been organized by Inoue Nisshō assassinated former Finance Minister Inoue Junnosuke and Mitsui's director, Dan Takuma. In May members of the movement, together with young naval officers and army cadets, made an abortive attempt at a coup d'état in which Prime Minister Inukai Tsuyoshi was assassinated.

Following these incidents the Nōhonshugi movement was suppressed and its leaders were arrested. Gondō was soon released, but Tachibana and Inoue were sentenced to life imprisonment. They were released in the 1940 general amnesty. Japan's growing dependence on heavy industry and bureaucratic management, increased by the outbreak of the war with China in 1937, eliminated much of the ideological attraction of the movement.

[See also Shōwa Period.]

Thomas R. H. Havens, *Farm and Nation in Modern Japan* (1974). Masao Maruyama, *Thought and Behavior in Modern Japanese Politics* (1963).

BEN-AMI SHILLONY

NOM. *See* Chu Nom.

NOMADISM, general term for a wandering way of life. The term is now usually limited to "pastoral nomadism," a regular pattern of migration within a specific area in which all of the population participates, based on year-round herding in the open. In Asia, nomads are found in the polar deserts and tundra zone (where they herd reindeer); in the steppes and deserts that stretch from the Danube River to North China in the temperate zone; as well as in Afghanistan and the Middle East. In recent times peoples that were formerly nomadic have increasingly settled down. In the past, however, nomads have often played a critical role in Asian history, one out of all proportion to their actual numbers.

As raiders, conquerors, and empire-builders in the steppe, Central Asia, and China, nomads have decisively affected the development of Asian civilization. Among the more important nomadic empires have been those of the Xiongnu (c. third century BCE–fourth century CE); the Turks (sixth to eighth century); the Uighurs (eighth to ninth century); and the Mongols (twelfth to fifteenth century), the last creating a world empire whose influences are still felt from China to Eastern Europe. Modern China, Russia, and the Middle East would undoubtedly have taken quite different shapes without repeated infusions of nomadic rulers, populations, institutions, and ideas. Yet nomads themselves have left few records or monuments, while histories written by settled peoples have stereotypically portrayed them as greedy, cruel, and uncivilized, and have provided little information about their actual life. Reconstruction of their histories is thus difficult, and has depended to a large extent on insights derived from the anthropological study of nomadic communities in the modern world, as well as on historical sources. This process is further complicated by the difficulty of fitting nomadic life into general theories, a problem that has given rise to an extensive literature on such questions as the existence of nomadic feudalism.

Formerly believed to be a survival of a general primitive way of life that antedated agriculture, nomadism is now more commonly believed to have evolved in a marginal areas out of settled agriculture, at a time after the domestication of animals. A highly specialized way of life, it permits exploitation to the limit of the scarce resources of the narrow ecological niche provided by the steppes, deserts, and other areas too dry for agriculture, but where herding is possible. The narrow specificity of nomadic adaptation to the environment renders such societies inherently unstable and vulnerable. Nomads lack reserves of fodder that would enable them to survive setbacks; they have few economic skills other than herding, and thus little possibility of shifting livelihood; furthermore, their culture is so closely attuned to the needs of their life as to render difficult the adoption of another way. Grazing disasters, the *jud* so feared by the Mongols, can devastate a population, with the effects still reflected (e.g., in the age structure of herds) a decade or more later. In nomadic societies balance and stability in the short run are difficult to attain, a fundamental fact that determines much about their relationship with the settled world.

Insofar as nomads are not autarkic, requiring products of sedentary cultures such as grains and metals, and since demands are not always reciprocal (settled peoples generally need few nomadic products, although horses for warfare have been an exception), economic tensions between the two realms have frequently arisen. Because the instability of the nomadic life has made the establishment of regular trade relations difficult, and because sedentary polities have often been unwilling to deal with nomads on equal terms, or at all, this tension has often as not led to warfare. To extract what they need, nomads have turned to raiding and to conquest.

That societies as rudimentary as nomadic ones should transform themselves into organizations capable of successfully waging coordinated warfare on settled areas may appear paradoxical. Nomadic society usually lacks much organization above small herding units, loosely linked to one another, and certainly lacks a fixed state structure. Divorced from settled life, nomadic societies furthermore appear relatively static: their economies do not evolve, nor does their population become socially differentiated.

In other words, the sorts of dynamic internal processes usually credited with state formation in other societies appear to be lacking, yet nomadic states nevertheless appear.

Historical reconstruction suggests this happens for purely political and military reasons: state formation seems to occur primarily for the purpose of extracting wealth from neighboring sedentary states. Modern anthropological fieldwork has not documented this process, however, probably because the nomadic groups studied are no longer warriors; they have been conquered and incorporated into a larger polity, although they still retain many specific nomadic traits. Historians have argued convincingly that the Huns of Europe, far from being of exclusively Inner Asian composition, in fact contained many local people, assimilated by fictive kinship ties, and survived to a considerable extent on subsidies extorted from the Romans that supplemented the pastoral economy. Analysis of the Xiongnu empire likewise shows a pattern of nomadic state formation for the purpose of entering into economic relations with China; similar linkage may be traced between Mongol polities and the Ming dynasty.

At times, nomads took an even more active role within settled areas, as contenders for power or as conquerors. Such a role was evident in North China during the period between the fall of the Han (220 CE) and the emergence of the Tang (618), a dynasty that manifested many nomadic traits; and in the Yuan (1279–1368), which saw direct Mongol rule extended over China proper. While one should not underestimate the degree to which nomads ruled through existing sedentary institutions and were themselves assimilated (the Mongol Yuan even faced difficulties with dissident nomadic Mongols in the north), neither should one neglect to note that many settled states have nomadic origins and take basic organizational features from the nomadic world. The governmental institutions of late imperial China well illustrate the synthesis of nomadic elements into an enduring sedentary civilization.

[*See also* Central Asia; Mongol Empire: An Overview; Oirats; Tribes; *and* Xiongnu.]

Thomas J. Barfield, *The Central Asian Arabs of Afghanistan: Pastoral Nomadism in Transition* (1981). Frederik Barth, *Nomads of South Persia: The Basseri Tribe of the Khamseh Confederacy* (1961). Wolfram Eberhard, *Conquerors and Rulers: Social Forces in Medieval China* (2d rev. ed., 1970). Sechin Jagchid, "Patterns of Trade and Conflict between China and the Nomads of Mongolia," *Zentralasiatische Studien* 11 (1977): 177–

204. A. M. Khazanov, *Nomads and the Outside World* (1983). Luc Kwanten, *Imperial Nomads: A History of Central Asia, 500–1500* (1979). Rudi Paul Lindner, *Nomads and Ottomans in Medieval Anatolia* (1983). *Pastoral Production and Society: Proceedings of the International Meeting on Nomadic Pastoralism* (1979).

ARTHUR N. WALDRON

NOMONHAN, BATTLE OF.

Nomonhan, the site of a cairn and a frontier outpost in desolate western Manchuria, lent its name to undeclared hostilities between Japan and the USSR in 1939. The battle is known to the Russians as Khalkhin Gol or Halha River. Pursuing guidelines from the Kwantung Army and goaded by the Outer Mongolians' penetration of the disputed Halha line in mid-May, a local Japanese commander dispatched a punitive expedition. In late May Russian units, not the Mongolians the Japanese had scorned, annihilated a large Japanese unit. The troubles escalated to include Soviet bombings inside Manchukuo (the Japanese puppet state of Manchuria) and Japanese air strikes into Mongolia (27 June) that were not authorized by Tokyo. Japanese troops crossed the Halha into Mongolia on 2 July and were stopped, as were Japanese tanks pressing from the east. Reinforced by artillery, the Japanese tried new attacks on 23 July and were checked again. Incomparably stronger Soviet forces under G. K. Zhukov then unleashed an irresistible surprise offensive on 20 August that overran the Japanese in ten days and reached objectives thirty kilometers beyond Halha. When the often-insubordinate Kwantung Army threatened revenge, the Tokyo High Command seized its reins in early September, ousting General Ueda Kenkichi and senior officers in Manchuria and Japan. When World War II began in Europe, Soviet and Japanese diplomats arranged a cease-fire that became effective on 16 September.

Nomonhan presaged the blitzkrieg to come and cost Japan 20,000 casualties; the Russians admitted losing 9,284. The antagonists expended hundreds of aircraft. Japan handled the crisis fitfully; outgeneraled, the Japanese army learned little. The Russians orchestrated matters deftly and enabled Stalin to look westward, while the discomfited Japanese turned their attention to the less imposing battleground of Southeast Asia.

[*See also* Kwantung Army *and* World War II in Asia.]

Alvin D. Coox, *Nomonhan: Japan Against Russia, 1939* (1985).   ALVIN D. COOX

NOMURA KICHISABURŌ

(1877–1964), Japanese admiral and diplomat. Nomura gained a reputation within the navy as a moderate who favored continued cooperation with the Anglo-American naval powers in limiting naval armaments. He was naval attaché in Washington during World War I and on the Naval General Staff in the 1920s. After his retirement in the early 1930s, he served briefly as foreign minister (late 1939). Because of his close ties with influential officers in the US Navy, Nomura was selected to be ambassador to the United States and was thus responsible for the conduct of the ill-fated negotiations with American Secretary of State Cordell Hull of April to December 1941. Despite his integrity and good intentions, Nomura was professionally ill prepared to handle this demanding diplomatic assignment and ill served by an aggressive government that by the fall of 1941 had concluded that war with the United States was inevitable, yet kept him ignorant of its specific plans to open hostilities. [*See also* Pearl Harbor.]

MARK R. PEATTIE

NORGAY, TENZING

(1914–1986), Sherpa mountaineer. Born in the mountain village of Thami in eastern Nepal, Tenzing Norgay Sherpa migrated to Darjeeling at the age of eighteen and joined the 1935 British assault on Mount Everest via the North Col. Tenzing participated in five subsequent Everest attempts and was a member of teams that scaled Nanda Devi and Nanga Parbat in the Indian Himalayas and Tirich Mir in the Karakorams. As *sirdar* (guide) for the Hunt expedition to Everest in 1953, Tenzing won international acclaim after reaching the 29,028-foot summit with Sir Edmund Hillary. In 1954 Tenzing joined the newly formed Himalayan Mountaineering Institute in Darjeeling, where he directed the training of an entire generation of Sherpa mountaineers.

[*See also* Everest.]

Tenzing Norgay, *Tiger of the Snows* (1955) and *After Everest* (1977).   RICHARD ENGLISH

NORODOM

(1838–1904), king of Cambodia (r. 1860–1904), succeeding his father, Ang Duang (r. 1848–1860). Norodom spent much of his childhood in Bangkok, as a protégé of the Thai court; he returned to Cambodia halfway through his father's reign. For this reason, and because of his rather intransigent personality, he had little personal following, and when his father died, Cambodia plunged immediately into a civil war, forcing Norodom to flee to Bangkok. Soon after he returned in 1863, French naval officers, fresh from colonizing southern Vietnam, offered him vaguely worded protection in exchange for commercial privileges. Hoping to loosen the Thai grip on his court, Norodom willingly accepted without perceiving that France's long-term plans were to turn Cambodia into a colony, along the lines of the different segments of Vietnam.

Until the 1880s, Norodom retained considerable freedom of action, but after the French suppressed a royally sponsored uprising in 1886, they reduced Norodom's powers and secretly promised the throne to his pro-French younger brother, Prince Sisowath. Norodom's declining years were marked by his increasingly feeble struggles against French control and by outbursts of authoritarianism at the court. During these years, the French trained a pliable bureaucratic elite, drawn primarily from hangers-on at the court, to administer Cambodia on their behalf and placed French *résidents* throughout the kingdom. In economic terms, Cambodia remained a backwater, partly because of King Norodom's reluctance to play a completely subordinate role. Although he had welcomed the French in 1863, Norodom became embittered about them in the 1880s and 1890s. For this reason, he has been treated as a nationalistic hero by many Cambodian historians.

[*See also* Ang Duang *and* Sisowath.]

M. E. Osborne, *The French Presence in Cochinchina and Cambodia* (1969).   DAVID P. CHANDLER

NORODOM SIHANOUK (b. 1922), Cambodian political leader and royal prince, was born in Phnom Penh. His mother's father, Sisowath Monivong, reigned as king from 1927 to 1941. His father, Norodom Suramarit, was a grandson of King Norodom (r. 1860–1904). Sihanouk, the only child of this unhappy marriage, was educated privately and at a French high school in Saigon, from which he was summoned, before his graduation, to be king. For the rest of World War II, he was closely supervised by French advisers, except for the period from March to October 1945, when the Japanese imprisoned French authorities throughout Indochina and encouraged Sihanouk to declare Cambodia's independence.

When the French returned at the end of 1945, Sihanouk, although attracted to the idea of eventual independence, decided to welcome them. During the years 1946–1953, he quarreled frequently with the nationalist members of Cambodia's elite, who wanted independence on their terms, rather than on terms acceptable to the French. In 1953, to outflank this group (and to counter Communist-led guerrilla opposition to the French) Sihanouk dramatically embarked on a "Crusade for Independence," threatening to abdicate if the French persisted in political and economic control. The French caved in and granted Cambodia's independence at the end of 1953. This decision was ratified in 1954 at the Geneva Conference.

In 1955, King Sihanouk abandoned the throne, had his father named as king, and set out on a full-time political career. His main objective was to smash Cambodia's political parties, and he did so by founding his own political movement, the Sangkum Reastr Niyum, which remained the dominant political force in Cambodia for the next fifteen years. Indeed, the years 1955–1970 can justifiably be called the Sihanouk years. The prince, under various titles, including prime minister and chief of state, dominated Cambodian political life and the conduct of foreign affairs. In 1956, for example, he opted for a neutralist foreign policy, which enabled him to obtain economic aid from the communist bloc as well as from Western powers. The United States' disapproval of his policies and US involvement in anti-Sihanouk plots led the prince to sever diplomatic relations with the United States in 1965. For the next five years, as fighting intensified in Vietnam and Laos, he attempted to maintain a neutral course, but opposition to his rule increased on both left and right.

A full-scale civil war directed against communist-led Cambodian guerrillas (the so-called Khmer Rouge) broke out in 1968. By this time, Sihanouk's own behavior had become increasingly erratic. He spent much of his time directing and starring in popular films that dramatized Cambodia's past. His support among government workers in the capital and among younger members of the Cambodian elite began to diminish.

In March 1970 he was overthrown by his own government while he was traveling abroad. The new regime, led by Lon Nol, named itself the Khmer Republic and plunged into an alliance with the United States and warfare against communist forces inside the country. Sihanouk himself, taking refuge in Beijing, where he had long enjoyed the patronage of Zhou Enlai, almost immediately became the titular head of a government in exile. Real power was in the hands of the clandestine Communist Party of Kampuchea (CPK), directed by Saloth Sar, soon to be known as Pol Pot—the people who had been trying to overthrow Sihanouk since 1968 and probably before.

In April 1975, CPK forces triumphed over those of the Khmer Republic. With victory, the CPK set in motion a series of economic and political measures that were, by the end of 1978, to tear Cambodia apart. In early 1976, Sihanouk was brought back to Phnom Penh, forced to resign as chief of state, and placed under house arrest. The regime in power named itself Democratic Kampuchea. When Vietnamese forces invaded Cambodia at the end of 1978 (following two years of warfare), Sihanouk was flown to Beijing and the United Nations to plead Democratic Kampuchea's case. Before very long, once Democratic Kampuchea had been deposed, Sihanouk was expressing anticommunist ideas and setting himself up as an acceptable alternative to the pro-Vietnamese Communist government now ensconced in Phnom Penh. In 1981, he agreed to form a coalition government in exile alongside the leaders of Democratic Kampuchea and a Cambodian elder statesman, Son Sann, who had served as his prime minister in the 1960s. Sihanouk was able to gain credibility among governments unfriendly to Vietnam. The coalition succeeded in holding Democratic Kampuchea's seat at the United Nations.

By the mid-1980s several factors tended to reduce Sihanouk's popularity among Cambodians. Some opposition came from older people, who recalled his erratic performance as chief of state in the closing years of his regime. Still more stemmed from his marriage of convenience with the CPK and from his failure to dissociate himself from the surviving leaders of Democratic Kampuchea. Moreover, Sihanouk's contempt for political associates, his impatience with other people's ideas, and his belief that he embodied the aspirations of all the people of Cambodia combined to narrow his political base, except perhaps among older peasants who associated his rule with a golden age. Although he is undoubtedly a sincere and hardworking patriot, Sihanouk's frequent changes of direction have bewildered his associates and convinced his opponents that he seeks political power at any price.

An eloquent orator, Sihanouk is also a fluent writer. He has defended his record in several volumes of memoirs.

[See also Cambodia; Sangkum Reastr Niyum; Khmer Rouge; Khmer Republic; Lon Nol; Pol Pot;

Kampuchea, Democratic; and Kampuchea, People's Republic of.]

David P. Chandler, A History of Cambodia (1983).

DAVID P. CHANDLER

NORODOM SURAMARIT (1896–1960), king of Cambodia (r. 1955–1960), succeeding his son, Norodom Sihanouk, who left the throne to take up a full-time political career. Suramarit's wife, Princess Kossamak, was the daughter of King Sisowath Monivong (r. 1927–1941). During the French protectorate, Suramarit served without fanfare in various advisory posts. Following his death, his widow was named queen of Cambodia. Although Suramarit's mild, fun-loving personality enhanced his popularity while he was king, and indeed throughout his life, he neither sought nor obtained significant political power. [See also Norodom Sihanouk.]

DAVID P. CHANDLER

NORTH, FREDERICK (1766–1827), first governor of the British-controlled Maritime Provinces of Sri Lanka (1798–1805). The Oxford-educated third son of the second Earl of Guilford, North brought to his office powerful political connections but failed to impose a strong personal authority over the administration he headed. His governorship was marred by protracted conflicts among the senior colonial officials and by the abject failure in 1803 of the invasion of the Kandyan kingdom he initiated. North's major accomplishment was setting the tone and tenor of the new administration as one that was distinctively English, in sharp contrast to the previous rule of the Dutch East India Company.

[See also Sri Lanka and Dutch East India Company.]

Dictionary of National Biography (1885–1900), vol. 14, pp. 609–610.   VIJAYA SAMARAWEERA

NORTH EAST FRONTIER AGENCY. Now known as Arunachal Pradesh, the North East Frontier Agency (NEFA) comprised the largest and most sparsely populated of the "seven sister" states of India's northeast. It was also perhaps the wildest and least explored, and it was certainly the most diverse internally, encompassing twenty major tribes and between ninety and one hundred lesser groups, all speaking Tibeto-Burman languages with the exception of the Kachin-speaking Tai. Most of the tribes share certain traits, such as a patrilineal ideology, a village-centered polity, government by elders, men's dormitories, and age grading.

The area was first administered by the British after battles with the tribal people in 1911, but the difficulty of the terrain kept British intervention at a minimum, and groups in the foothills were relatively untouched until the 1950s. Christian missionaries, although prohibited from the interior, had great success in the NEFA, but efforts to revitalize local culture and to limit conversions have been made by the local government with Indian approval. Because of its location on the Tibetan border, the NEFA area is crucial to India's defense, and a massive program has been inaugurated to modernize the region while still maintaining tribal integrity. The program has been remarkably successful, and the people of the NEFA have suffered little of the dislocation and oppression found in other tribal areas.

[See also Arunachal Pradesh.]

U. Bower, *The Hidden Land* (1953). C. von Furer-Haimendorf, *A Himalayan Tribe: From Cattle to Cash* (1980). B. Shukla, *The Daflas of the Subansiri Region* (1959). CHARLES LINDHOLM

NORTHERN EXPEDITION, the military phase of Sun Yat-sen's plans for a national revolution in China. Since 1917 Sun had advocated a military expedition to sweep away warlord factionalism and China's disunity. Striking northward from his base in Guangzhou (Canton), such a force, he envisioned, would unite progressive elements against entrenched militarism and foreign imperialism. The Northern Expedition thus became the single most important project of the Guomindang (Kuomintang, or Nationalist Party) during the 1920s. Most of Sun's own actions before his death in 1925, and those of his successors until 1930, were devoted to working out its problems.

In July 1926 the National Revolutionary Army (NRA), with eight army corps totaling 150,000 men, started northward. Chiang Kai-shek was its commander; the Soviet Union its chief foreign supporter. NRA forces comprised an amalgam of loyal officers trained at the Nationalist Party's Whampoa Military Academy, plus older units with warlord characteristics. The small Chinese Communist Party actively participated in the first stage of the Northern Expedition.

Once underway, the Northern Expedition split into three fronts. The first important action occurred on the Hunan front. NRA armies there were accompanied by the chief Soviet adviser, Michael Borodin, and many left-wing Chinese Nationalists. They struck toward the inland city of Wuhan. The main central column, under Chiang Kai-shek's command, marched into Jiangxi Province and made for Nanchang and then Nanjing. Finally, a coastal column under He Yingqin, a general loyal to Chiang Kai-shek, followed through Fujian and Zhejiang.

The Nationalists intended to enlist progressive warlords along the way. The Guangxi clique's troops, led by Bai Chongxi and Li Zongren, were an important element in the Northern Expedition from the beginning. It was hoped that Feng Yuxiang and Yan Xishan, two progressive northern powerholders, would join once the expedition was underway.

The opposition boasted 500,000 troops, assembled into an unstable coalition of warlords. Wu Peifu and Sun Chuanfang between them divided control over the central and lower Yangtze River valley, along with parts of the North China Plain. Zhang Zuolin, the dominant warlord in the Northeast (Manchuria), controlled Beijing and influenced Zhang Zongchang in Shandong. Foreign states, aside from the Soviet Union, varied in their disapproval of the Northern Expedition, but all were worried about the safety of their nationals and anxious to preserve their special privileges.

The Northern Expedition had three stages: a successful military campaign from July 1926 until March 1927, in which the NRA won control over the central and lower Yangtze Valley; a year-long second stage of internal division and realignment from March 1927 to March 1928; and a swift offensive from March to June 1928, in which the reorganized NRA routed the opposition from Beijing. The NRA armies in Hunan won handily against Wu Peifu and his allies in the initial stage, partly through defections to the Nationalist cause. The central front in Jiangxi saw greater resistance from Sun Chuanfang, but NRA forces won major battles in November 1926.

In the second stage the split between left and right in the Nationalist movement became a reality. Differences between the two had widened since the Zhongshan gunboat incident of March 1926. Open conflict became inevitable when the left established its own interim national government at Wuhan on 1 January 1927. In April the central forces under Chiang Kai-shek linked up with He Yingqin's columns and then massacred the Communists in Shanghai. Then Chiang created his own interim government at Nanjing. The ensuing maneuverings among the left and right within the Nationalist movement along with those of the Chinese Communists and Soviet policymakers have become a major fascination for historians.

In brief, the Chinese Communists were expelled by the Wuhan government, the Soviet advisers departed for home, and finally the left's government itself collapsed. Its demise was hastened by General Feng Yuxiang. In May 1927 he had intervened on their behalf in a stalemated offensive into Henan undertaken by the Wuhan government against the northern warlords. Feng's army saved the day, but he declined further cooperation with the left. Instead, on 21 June Feng sealed an alliance with Chiang Kai-shek, and with it the fate of the Wuhan government. Under Moscow's direction the Chinese Communists then undertook to organize revolts behind the NRA front against the new Nationalist order. These Autumn Harvest Uprisings of August 1927 failed.

This second stage also saw a reshaping of Chiang Kai-shek's wing of the Nationalist movement. He managed to acquire financial support in Shanghai and also to calm rural landlord fears of a radical social revolution. His new alliance with Feng Yuxiang was shaky but promising. Chiang even convinced the Western governments, although not Japan, that despite xenophobic outbreaks at several inland treaty ports during the expedition's first stage, the Nationalists were not rabidly antiforeign.

Against these successes, Chiang also suffered two setbacks. First, in the fall of 1927 he insisted on pushing the NRA into a northern campaign that stalled and brought open rebellion from Chiang's own generals. Chiang temporarily resigned as commander. His second failure came during a visit to Japan, where he could not convince the cabinet of Tanaka Giichi to drop its opposition to the Northern Expedition.

In January 1928 Chiang Kai-shek resumed command of the NRA. His reorganized forces had more than 600,000 troops composed of a First Army Group under Chiang's own command, a Second Army Group under Feng Yuxiang, and a Third Army Group under Yan Xishan. These armies won a series of swift victories against warlord armies beginning in March. In Shandong the NRA clashed with Japanese units in the Ji'nan Incident in early May, but pushed quickly on to Beijing. [See also Ji'nan Incident.] Zhang Zuolin withdrew from the old capital without a fight, but was assassinated by Japanese officers who dynamited his train on 4 June as he returned homeward.

The military phase of the National Revolution was thus finished, but Chiang Kai-shek faced the problem of how to provide for the 2.2 million troops gathered under the Nationalist banner since the Northern Expedition had left Guangdong. Most of these remained loyal to their warlord commanders, and the difficulties of disbanding these forces became a major problem for the government of the new Republic of China.

Events of the Northern Expedition decisively shaped Chinese politics for the next twenty years as a result of the new political alignments that it produced. These include Chiang Kai-shek's own leadership, which was closely connected to the great emphasis on the Northern Expedition as the Nationalist movement's primary goal. Others include the fateful split between the Nationalists and Communists, the ability of warlord allies to limit the authority of the Nanjing central government, Japan's adoption of a policy of armed intervention in China, and the reconciliation between the Nationalists and the Western powers.

[See also Chiang Kai-shek; China, Republic Period; Warlord Cliques; and Guomindang.]

C. Martin Wilbur, "The Nationalist Revolution: From Canton to Nanking, 1923–1928," in *The Cambridge History of China*, vol. 12, *Republican China, 1912–1949, Part 1*, edited by John K. Fairbank (1983), pp. 527–720.

David D. Buck

NORTHERN LIANG KINGDOM (397–439),

a Xiongnu state in Gansu; one of the Sixteen Kingdoms formed in North China between the collapse of the Western Jin dynasty and the consolidation of the Northern Wei.

[See also Six Dynasties and Sixteen Kingdoms.]

Edward L. Farmer

NORTHERN QI DYNASTY (550–577), one of

the small successor states generated after the breakup of the Northern Wei dynasty into the Eastern and Western Wei dynasties.

The early medieval conquest states of North China tended to disintegrate as a result of the divergent evolution of their civil and military elites. The military power supporting the state was vested in tribal structures adapted to mobile combat in steppe Asia, while the civil administration was both confronted with the problem of governing a large, sedentary, Chinese population and tempted by the urban civilization that the agricultural surpluses of such a population could support. Unsure of their place in a state run on Chinese lines, the military leaders were likely to rebel in the name of traditional tribal values.

In the year 534 one of these disaffected commanders, Gao Huan, of Xianbei tribal extraction, set up a puppet emperor as ruler of the Eastern Wei at Ye, in northeast China. In 550 a cousin named Gao Yang declared himself the first emperor of the Northern Qi dynasty. The brief and violent history of the Northern Qi is dominated by the endless fighting that went on with its fellow successor state to the west, the Northern Zhou dynasty, and with the Chen dynasty in the South. Weakened by losses of territory to the Chen, the Northern Qi was finally overwhelmed by the Northern Zhou, which thus managed a feeble reunification of North China. The defeat of the Northern Qi by the Northern Zhou is another demonstration of the strategic dominance of the northwest over the northeast, a major feature of Chinese history from the earliest times until the transfer of the socioeconomic center of gravity to the southeast during the latter half of the Tang dynasty (618–907).

[See also Northern Wei Dynasty and Southern and Northern Dynasties.]

DENNIS GRAFFLIN

NORTHERN WEI DYNASTY (386–534), most powerful and significant of the conquest regimes in early medieval North China. The Northern Wei was the precursor to the reunification and expansion of the Chinese empire that took place under the Sui and Tang dynasties.

During the early fourth century, China north of the Yangtze River was a chaotic mixture of the indigenous Chinese population with numerous non-Chinese groups (the origins and ethnic backgrounds of which are poorly understood), which had taken advantage of the weakness of the central government to move into Chinese territory. The kaleidoscopic interaction of peoples and institutions resulted in the creation of a multitude of short-lived states. [See also Sixteen Kingdoms.]

Rising slowly out of this situation to a position of political importance was the Tuoba, a loose confederation of tribal units containing both Turkic and Mongol elements. From 338 to 376 they formed a semi-sinicized state known as Dai on the north-central frontier of China, submitting briefly to the Tibetan state of Former Qin when it carried out its reunification of North China in the late fourth century. The defeat of the Former Qin in 383 at the Battle of the Fei River, as it attempted to invade South China, caused its northern empire to disintegrate, and in 386 the Tuoba reasserted their independence as the Northern Wei. [See also Fei River, Battle of.]

Like all the conquest states, the Wei was confronted with the incompatibility of the social institutions of its ruling elite with the administrative necessities of governing a large agricultural population. Either the traditional tribal structures could be preserved, at the cost of failing to exploit the potential of the Chinese majority of the population, or the rulers could learn to govern in the style of Chinese emperors, at the cost of breaking down the old structure of their own society. The need to maximize agricultural production and manpower resources in an era of endemic conflict drove ambitious rulers into the arms of surviving Chinese elite families, which possessed the training and experience to handle the land and tax policies of an agrarian state.

Learning from the mistakes of earlier Sino-foreign hybrid regimes, the Northern Wei had managed to reunify North China by 439. The combined effects of intermarriage with the Chinese and a conscious policy of sinicization finally came to a head during the reign of Emperor Xiaowen (r. 471–499). Traditional historiography credited the initiatives of his reign to his personal leadership, but W. F. J. Jenner has argued that the real stimulus came from his stepgrandmother, Empress Dowager Feng (441–490). Her influence on the court had increased after the death of her husband in 465 and became paramount after the death of his successor in 476 (following abdication in 471). The empress dowager was both Chinese and ardently Buddhist, an additional foreign factor in the equation. Buddhism had come into North China along the Central Asian trade routes, just as had the alien invaders. Hostile to the political culture of the native Chinese, foreign rulers were quick to seize upon Buddhism as an alternative source of ideological reinforcement. This made the North China regimes particularly careful to ensure that the Buddhist church, as an institution with lands, wealth, and a sizable proportion of the literate manpower of the society, stayed firmly under government regulation.

In 460 the Northern Wei appointed Tanyao, a powerful churchman, to a watchdog position in the government. Along with his surveillance function, which was passed on to later Chinese regimes as one of a number of Northern Wei legacies, he also acted as a conduit for imperial patronage, under the auspices of powerful believers such as Empress Dowager Feng. From roughly 460 to 500 tremendous effort was put into carving Buddha images and temples into the living rock at Yungang, near the Northern Wei capital of Pingcheng (modern Datong, in northern Shanxi Province). The intimacy of the link between Buddhism and the state is shown by the fact that the faces of the Buddha images are supposed to be idealized representations of the Northern Wei emperors, claiming for secular rulers the status of living Buddhas (see figure 1).

The logic of progressive sinicization in the Northern Wei argued strongly for a different capital city. Pingcheng, while appropriate for a steppe kingdom, was poorly located to be the capital of a regime that derived its sustenance increasingly from the peasant cultivators of the North China Plain. Standing at the end of a long and difficult supply line, it also left the emperors hostage to the most unreconstructed elements in Tuoba society. Ease of administration, waterborne grain transport, and the desire for legitimation in Chinese terms all led to a decision to transfer the throne to Luoyang, the ancient Chinese capital site on the Yellow River, in 493–494. At about the same time, sweeping efforts were made to encourage the spread of Chinese language, dress, surnames, customs, and spouses among the Tuoba elite. Almost immediately after the transfer, thought was given to creating a new rock temple complex, resulting in massive labor between 500 and 540 at Longmen, a short distance away from Luoyang (see figure 2). The two complexes, at Yungang and Longmen, remain the most striking physical evidence of the way in which Buddhism and tribal military power were welded into a new form of absolutism in the Sino-foreign hybrid states. [*See also* Longmen *and* Buddhism: Buddhism in China.]

Inevitably, there were many in Tuoba society who could not or would not make the adjustment to the new sinicized pattern. Preeminent among them were the tribal military commanders, who saw their influence directly threatened by the growing power of Chinese civil officials. The first of a series of military rebellions that would ultimately bring down the Northern Wei broke out in 524. In a situation of rapidly worsening social and political disorganization, two powerful families attempted to save from the wreckage what they could by forming local states in the region of their greatest strength. The Gao family propped up a Tuoba puppet emperor in the eastern part of the country in 534, forming the Eastern Wei dynasty. The maneuver was matched by the Yuwen family to the west, forming the Western Wei dynasty in 535. Gao impatience led to an explicit usurpation of the throne in 550, creating the Northern Qi dynasty; a similar evolution in the west resulted in the establishment of the Northern Zhou dynasty in 557.

FIGURE 1. *Yungang Caves, Datong.* Constructed during the second half of the fifth century.

FIGURE 2. *Longmen Caves, Luoyang.* Although construction of the Longmen site began when the Northern Wei moved its capital to Luoyang in 494, work continued for the next two hundred years, into the Tang dynasty, when these figures were carved.

The facts of early medieval demography meant that the eastern zone was the rallying point for the Chinese elite and for aliens sympathetic to the process of sinicization. Conversely, the western zone benefited from the services of the still tribalized components of Northern Wei society. It is characteristic of this entire period that it was the tribal west that triumphed over the sinicized east, reuniting North China in 577. From that victory, through the usurpation in 581 by Yang Jian, who founded the Sui dynasty (581–618) and went on to reunify all of China, can be traced the thread of a new structure of imperial power that made possible the achievements of the later dynasties.

Institutional historians point to two innovations in particular that had major consequences for the late medieval Chinese empire. The first of these was the "equal field" (*juntian*) land system. In essence, it attempted to match the dispossessed of war-torn North China with the abandoned fields left in the

wakes of the restless armies. To the extent that it was successful it solved several serious problems simultaneously, eliminating the refugee problem, bringing land back into cultivation, checking the rate of growth of powerful landowning families, and increasing the government's tax base. As originally conceived, the system contemplated retrieving most of the land from people as age or disability reduced their ability to work it effectively, and redistributing it to young people coming to maturity. This assumed both regular, exhaustive census-taking and zero population growth, neither of which was likely to occur in reality; there is serious doubt that the redistributive aspect of the system ever operated. In areas in which the central government was powerful, however, various forms of the *juntian* system seem to have operated for centuries thereafter to provide willing cultivators with land when possible.

The second development of note is more properly credited to the Western Wei/Northern Zhou successor regimes. This is the militia (*fubing*) system. Each of the Sino-foreign hybrid states found that as it adopted a Chinese style of organization, its military forces tended to deteriorate, based as they were on the social order of a pastoral steppe society. There was thus a desperate need for some way to generate effective military power, at least for defensive purposes, out of a peasant population. Under the militia system, peasants were organized on a local basis, given military training, and then required to serve in pseudo-tribal military formations. This substitution of village organization for tribalism worked well enough to provide for defense needs well into the Tang dynasty.

[*See also* Fubing System; Sui Dynasty; *and* Tang Dynasty.]

W. J. F. Jenner, *Memories of Loyang: Yang Hsüan-chih and the Lost Capital (493–534)* (1981), see in particular part 1.   DENNIS GRAFFLIN

NORTH-WEST FRONTIER PROVINCE.

Formally created in 1901 by Lord Curzon as a separate administrative unit, the North-West Frontier Province (NWFP) of Pakistan is divided between indirectly administered "tribal areas" and directly administered "settled areas." Under British rule the tribal area extended along the entire Afghan border, but the princely states of the North—Dir, Swat, and Chitral—have since been annexed into the settled area by the government of Pakistan. Indirect rule continues to prevail, however, in the arid hills around the Khyber Pass that are the homeland of the Karlanri Pathan (Pakhtun) people: the Afridi, Waziri, and others who have lived in this harsh environment as long as history records. The settled area of the northern mountains and the Indus plains is inhabited by other Pathan groups: the Yusufzai in Swat, Dir, and Mardan; Mohmand, Khalil, Daudzai, Khatak, and Muhammadzais in the Peshawar plain; and assorted settled Ghalji groups—Marwats, Lohanis, Niazis, and so forth—to the south.

Pathans are not the only people of the NWFP: Chitral is populated by Koh speakers, Hazara by Hindko speakers, and Dera Ismail Khan by mixed nationalities. Peshawar city is home for an array of specialized groups. In the North, Gujri-speaking nomads and Dardic-speaking "mountain men" (Kohistanis) fill their separate ecological niches among the Pathans of Swat.

Pathan culture is nonetheless dominant in the region. It is a culture that has traditionally made government in the NWFP a difficult affair. Pathan social organization strongly resembles that of other Muslim tribal peoples of the Middle East, such as the Berbers or Kurds. It is structured on alliances and oppositions between patrilineal kinsmen, a system that permits unity in struggles against external invasion, but that tends to fragment into warring factions in the absence of an outside threat. Leadership is ephemeral and task-oriented, usually devolving on a religious practitioner. Only Dir (probably because of its relationship with the ancient kingdom in Chitral) ever developed a long-lived Pathan state in the NWFP. Primary values are equality, bravery, and independence, and the cardinal virtues are hospitality, sanctuary, and revenge. Traditionally a warrior people, Pathans have augmented their sparse incomes by raiding and levying fees on caravans passing through their territories. They have always resisted rule from any quarter, and have defeated the armies of the Mughals, the Afghans, and the British.

On this volatile frontier of rough terrain and warlike tribes the British played out the "Great Game" against Russia. Oscillating between a costly "Forward Policy" of invasion and a "Closed Border Policy" of sanctions and fines, British control in the region was always tenuous, despite the great efforts and resources expended. Outbreaks occurred throughout British rule; the largest, in 1897, inflamed the entire tribal area, and a serious revolt shook Waziristan throughout the 1930s. Nor were the plains totally pacified, as Abdul Ghaffar Khan led his anticolonial Red Shirt movement for an independent "Pukhtunistan." [See also Khan, Abdul Ghaffar.]

After achieving independence Pakistan withdrew troops from the tribal areas, trying instead to integrate the border peoples through economic aid. This effort has been partially successful, although the NWFP remains relatively impoverished and underdeveloped. The Soviet invasion of Afghanistan and the migration of huge numbers of refugees into the NWFP has increased pressure on the economy, as well as increasing the number of Pakistani troops on patrol in the hills. Balancing these disruptive elements is a greater sense of solidarity with Pakistan and a decrease in separatist sentiments.

[See also Pakhtun; Swat; and Khyber Pass.]

A. Ahmed, *Pukhtun Economy and Society* (1980). O. Caroe, *The Pathans* (1958). M. Elphinstone, *An Account of the Kingdom of Caubul* (1815). A. Embree, ed., *Pakistan's Western Borderlands* (1977). E. Howell, *Mizh* (1931).   CHARLES LINDHOLM

NOSAKA SANZŌ (b. 1892), member of the Japan Communist Party (JCP) since its organization in 1922 and chairman of the party's central committee from 1958 to 1982 and again in 1985. Nosaka has held seats in both Japan's House of Councillors (upper house) and its House of Representatives (lower house) during the postwar period.

Nosaka became involved in Japan's socialist movement while still a university student. His work with the labor organization known as the Yūaikai provided him with an opportunity to visit England in 1919 to witness the activities of the labor movement in that country. After returning to Japan he joined the JCP and continued his activities with the labor movement. He was interned briefly in 1923 as a result of the government's first attempt to suppress the Communist Party and once again in 1928 in response to the March Fifteenth Incident, during which leftists were arrested for their alleged violation of the 1925 Peace Preservation Law. His election to the central committee of the JCP came in 1931, the same year he became the Japanese representative to the Comintern. In 1940 Nosaka traveled to China to oppose Japanese aggression in that country and did not return to Japan until after World War II. In both the prewar and postwar periods he has been criticized for his willingness to subordinate the JCP to the will of Moscow, but in his later career he directed the JCP into policies that stressed the creation of a welfare state.

[See also Communism: Communism in Japan.]

George M. Beckmann and Okubo Genji, *The Japanese Communist Party, 1922–1945* (1969). Robert A. Scalapino, *The Japanese Communist Movement, 1920–1966* (1967).
THOMAS R. SCHALOW

NOW RUZ, "new day," the beginning of the Iranian year. It was the holiest festival of the ancient Iranians; the Achaemenids celebrated it in the spring, probably in imitation of the Babylonians. Under the Sasanids Now Ruz was celebrated at the autumnal equinox in a calendar reform. Later, the vernal equinox (21 March) became the New Year's Day of Iranians as well as other peoples in the Near East.
RICHARD N. FRYE

NU, U (Thakin; b. 1907), prime minister of Burma from 1947 until 1956 and again in 1957–1958 and 1960–1962. Nu was a leading member of the prewar Burmese nationalist movement as well as an important writer and religious thinker. Born in 1907 to a prosperous landowning family in the Irrawaddy Delta, he studied at Rangoon University in the early 1930s. Returning to study law, he became active in student politics and strikes and, with Aung San and others more radical than he, entered the Thakin nationalist movement. After the Japanese invasion in 1942, he bacame minister of foreign affairs and of information in the government of Ba Maw as well as leader of the Dobama-Hsinyeitha Party. At the end of the war and with the temporary return of British rule, Nu attempted to withdraw from politics to write, but in mid-1946 he was elected vice president of the Anti-Fascist People's Freedom League and chairman of the constitutional assembly.

Upon the assassination of Aung San and other members of the Governor's Executive Council in July 1947, the British governor called upon Nu to form a new government, and from then until the military coup of 2 March 1962 he was the leading politician of Burma. While he was never a socialist, he justified his government's policies as a blend of Burmese Theravada Buddhist thought and socialist ideology. In foreign affairs Nu's government followed a policy of strict nonalignment. One of the founders of the nonaligned movement, Nu made efforts to bridge the gulf between the West and Communist China and Russia during the height of the Cold War in the 1950s.

When his government coalition collapsed in 1958, Nu was induced to invite General Ne Win to form a military caretaker government, which returned power to Nu following elections in 1960. Ne Win ousted Nu in a coup in 1962, and he was placed under arrest for five years. When he was permitted to leave Burma for medical treatment, he quickly set about organizing a movement, based in Thailand, to return himself to power in the name of parliamentary democracy. This effort failed, however, and in the early 1970s Nu settled near a Buddhist monastery in India. In 1980 he returned to Burma at the invitation of Ne Win, accepted a state pension and honors, and began a project to translate Burmese Buddhist texts into English. This final activity in such a full political career highlights his very deep religious concerns. His plays and other works of fiction are highly didactic.

[See also Ne Win.]

Richard Butwell, *U Nu of Burma* (1969). Nu, *U Nu—Saturday's Son* (1975).
ROBERT H. TAYLOR

NUNCOMAR (Nanda Kumar Ray; 1721–1775), *naib subahdar* (deputy governor) of Bengal (c. 1765). Originally from the Murshidabad region, he had been *amin* of the Hijli and Moisadal before Robert Clive took him to Patna as his agent (*vakil*). As officer in charge of Hughli, he joined Nawab Mir Jafar in struggle against Mir Qasim. In 1764 and 1765 Emperor Shah Alam gave him titles, the East India Company made him Collector of Burdwan, Nadia, and Hughli in place of Warren Hastings, and he became *naib subahdar*, only to be displaced quickly by Muhammad Reza Khan.

In 1772 Nuncomar made the charges that enabled Hastings to depose Reza Khan, to abolish the system of "double government" (providing a pension for the infant nawab in Murshidabad), and to concentrate all power in Calcutta, having his son, Raja Gurudas, put in charge of the nawab's household. But in 1775, when he brought charges against Hastings before the Bengal Council, he soon found himself before justices of the Supreme Court, sitting as king's magistrates on a charge of forgery. Found guilty, Nuncomar was sentenced to death and hanged. Chief Justice Elijah Impey had a large role in this event.

[See also Hastings, Warren; Impey, Elijah; Bengal; Mir Ja'far; *and* Mir Qasim.]

J. M. Derrett, "Nandakumar's Forgery," *English Historical Review* 75 (1960). N. K. Sinha, "The Trial of Maharaja Nandakumar," *Bengal Past and Present* 78 (1959).
ROBERT E. FRYKENBERG

NUNG, a Tai ethnic group originating in the Chinese province of Guangxi and inhabiting both sides of the China-Vietnam border. In Vietnam the Nung are concentrated in the provinces of Cao Bang and Lang Son, with settlements in the coastal area north of Haiphong as well. There were Nung in the region before Vietnam's independence in the tenth century, but large-scale migration did not begin until the sixteenth century. Although the Nung have often resisted Vietnamese control, in recent years Viet Minh and Democratic Republic of Vietnam policies gained considerable support among them, and Nung participation in political and economic activities increased considerably.

Department of the Army Ethnographic Study Series, *Minority Groups in North Vietnam* (1972).

BRUCE M. LOCKHART

NURHACI (1559–1626), unifier of the Jurchen tribes and founder of the Manchu dynasty. Nurhaci was a member of the Tong clan, which was later renamed Aisin Gioro. Since 1412 his ancestors had commanded the left branch of the Jianzhou Guards in Manchuria, created by the Ming dynasty of China to pacify the Jurchen tribes. Late in 1582 his father and grandfather, Taksi and Giocangga, were killed in action when they helped the Ming garrison attack the right branch of the Jianzhou Guards. With their deaths as a pretext Nurhaci started his state-building work in 1583.

Nurhaci subjugated Jurchen tribes by warfare and diplomacy. Through the same method he dealt with the Ming court, the Korean government, and many Mongol chieftains. In 1595 the Ming conferred upon him the high title "General of the Dragon and Tiger" (Longhu Jiangjun); in 1606 the Mongols gave him the title Kundulun Khan (Divinely Martial Ruler). When he felt powerful enough, he proclaimed himself ruler of the kingdom of Jin in 1616 and thereafter frequently defeated the Ming army. In 1626, however, he experienced his first major military setback in Ningyuan, a Ming stronghold. A short time later he died of a back ulcer.

Nurhaci founded two institutions of lasting effect. The Manchu writing system he created in 1599 bonded the Jurchen people together politically and culturally. In addition, between 1601 and 1615 he organized the Manchu Eight Banners, a military institution indispensable to the Manchu Qing dynasty (1644–1911). [*See also* Banners.]

Ruthless and iron-handed, Nurhaci punished any disobedient individuals, including Cuyen, his crown prince. Although he had most likely designated Daisan, his second son, to succeed Cuyen as crown prince, he deposed Daisan because of a conduct problem in 1620. In his last years, Nurhaci's stated preference was that after his death the eight princes in charge of the eight Manchu banners would rule. Finally, Huang Taiji emerged as his successor.

[*See also* Huang Taiji; Manchus; *and* Qing Dynasty.]

Arthur W. Hummel, ed., *Eminent Chinese of the Ch'ing Period (1644–1912)*, vol. 1 (1943), pp. 594–599. Sei Wada, "Some Problems Concerning the Rise of T'ai-tsu, the Founder of the Manchu Dynasty," *Memoirs of the Research Department of the Tōyō Bunko* 16 (1957): 35–73.

PEI HUANG

NURI, FAZL ALLAH (1842–1909), Iranian religious scholar chiefly known for his promotion of *mashruta-yi mashru'a* (constitutional government in accordance with Islamic law) during the Constitutional Revolution. An early supporter of constitutionalism, Nuri began to express reservations in early 1907, when a supplementary fundamental law passed the Majles with the inclusion of provisions he regarded as incompatible with Islam. He organized a protest meeting at the shrine of Shah Abd al-Azim to the south of Tehran, published broadsheets attacking the allegedly secularist turn taken by the constitutional movement, and effectively became an ally of the court in the suppression of the constitution. When the constitutionalists triumphed in the spring of 1909, Nuri was arrested. He was executed on 31 July 1909. Long execrated in Iran, Nuri was rehabilitated after the triumph of the Islamic Revolution of 1978–1979.

[*See also* Constitutional Revolution.]

Abdul-Hadi Hairi, "Shaykh Fazl Allah's Refutation of the Idea of Constitutionalism," *Middle Eastern Studies* 13 (1977): 327–339.

HAMID ALGAR

NUR JAHAN (1577–1645), title of Mehrunnisa, daughter of I'timad ud-Daulah, who had moved from Persia to India to enter into the service of the Mughal court. Mehrunnisa was married to Ali Quli Khan, who served Prince Salim (later Jahangir) in military campaigns and was given the title Sher Afghan. They had a daughter. Following his coronation Jahangir raised I'timad ud-Daulah and his son, Asaf Khan, to high positions. In his sixth regnal year Jahangir married Mehrunnisa, who had been a widow for four years, and gave her the title Nur Jahan ("light of the world"). Nur Jahan was cultured, courageous, and ambitious; she saw to it that her daughter married a prince and sought to promote him at Shah Jahan's expense. She inherited all privileges of her father's office on his death and generally dominated the court in the last decade of Jahangir's life. On Jahangir's death in 1627 she withdrew herself from the court until her own death.

[*See also* I'timad ud-Daulah; Jahangir; *and* Shah Jahan.]

Beni Prasad, *History of Jahangir* (1962).

HARBANS MUKHIA

O

OCCUPATION OF JAPAN. Resulting from defeat in World War II, the Occupation of Japan began on 2 September 1945 with the signing of the surrender documents on the deck of the USS Missouri in Tokyo Bay and ended on 28 April 1952, when the San Francisco Peace Treaty went into effect.

On 26 July 1945 the United States, China, and Great Britain (later joined by the Soviet Union) issued the Potsdam Declaration to Japan. It warned Japan to surrender or face "complete destruction" of its armed forces and "utter devastation" of its homeland, and listed the terms of surrender, which included a military occupation. It was not until 15 August that Japan finally surrendered.

Japan surrendered formally to the victorious Allies, but the Occupation was in fact an almost completely American operation. Only American land, sea, and air forces were in a position to move rapidly into Japan to initiate the Occupation. Consequently, General Douglas MacArthur, with the approval of America's allies, was placed in command of the Occupation, with the title Supreme Commander for the Allied Powers (SCAP).

The role of other Allied powers in the Occupation was limited and ineffectual. Some months after the surrender an Allied Council for Japan was created to act as an advisory body to MacArthur in Tokyo, but it was almost completely powerless because of his refusal to tolerate any interference. The Far Eastern Commission was also established as an Allied organ sitting in Washington to deal with policy for the Occupation, but it was rendered largely ineffective by the comprehensiveness of American Occupation policy (which it endorsed) and its isolation from Japan. The US government decided that the Japanese government would be allowed to continue to administer the country's internal affairs during the Occupation, although the Supreme Commander was given complete authority over the emperor and the Japanese government. The reason for this decision was simple: neither the United States nor its allies had sufficient personnel with the knowledge of Japanese language and society that would make possible the creation of a military government that could rule Japan directly, as was being done in Germany.

The nerve center of the Occupation was General Headquarters, Supreme Commander for the Allied Powers (GHQ, SCAP, usually abbreviated SCAP). This was the command organization that served General MacArthur until he was relieved by President Truman in April 1951. General Matthew Ridgway then succeeded to the position until the end of the Occupation.

GHQ, SCAP consisted of a number of staff sections that were responsible for dealing with the Japanese government in the execution of Occupation policy and for evaluating progress toward policy goals. Their responsibilities covered virtually every aspect of Japanese life. The relations between SCAP and the Japanese government were remarkably smooth. They were characterized by discussion and negotiation, but it was always understood that ultimate authority lay with SCAP. On occasion the Japanese succeeded in getting SCAP to accept modification of its original position on an issue, but never in cases where SCAP believed basic Occupation policy might be adversely affected. Once agreement was reached the Japanese government acted either by issuing a cabinet or ministerial order or by enacting appropriate legislation.

Outside Tokyo the Occupation was monitored by tactical army units centered around civil affairs teams located in prefectural capitals. Their primary responsibilities were to observe how the Japanese local authorities acted to carry out central government instructions designed to achieve Occupation objectives and to report to SCAP on progress.

The work of SCAP was governed by a carefully developed policy worked out by the US government from mid-1942 to the end of the war in 1945. The policy was set forth in a document entitled "U.S. Initial Postsurrender Policy for Japan." It was formally approved by President Truman on 29 August 1945 and immediately sent to General MacArthur for his guidance.

The policy's two basic objectives were to ensure that Japan would not again become a menace to the United States or to the peace and security of the world and to bring about "the eventual establishment of a peaceful and responsible government" based on principles of "democratic self-government." The four means to achieve the objectives were to limit Japan's territory to what it was in the nineteenth century; to disarm and demilitarize Japan completely; to encourage the Japanese people to desire individual human liberties and to respect fundamental human rights; and to permit the development of a peacetime economy. The policy also listed in some detail the steps that should be taken to bring the means into operation and thus to achieve the ultimate goals.

The work of the Occupation fell into two broad phases, the first and shorter being punitive or destructive and the second, constructive. The destructive phase involved the elimination of the old militaristic and authoritarian order. It included disarmament (a process well started by the war itself), the elimination of ultranationalistic propaganda from the media and from education, the purge of militarists and their civilian supporters from public office, the dissolution of militaristic and ultranationalistic organizations and the breakup of *zaibatsu* firms, the abrogation of all laws restricting fundamental human rights, and the ending of the repressive powers of the police. It took less than a year for the Occupation to complete this phase of its work.

The constructive phase took longer because it involved a successful attempt to create the conditions for the development of a democratic order by the Japanese. This phase included such matters as the establishment of fundamental human rights, the encouragement of democratic political parties and labor unions, a land reform that enabled farmers to become owners of their land, a reform of the educational system, and the granting of political and legal rights to women. This phase was completed in roughly the first three years. The remaining three years of the Occupation witnessed the consolidation by the Japanese—under the observation of SCAP—of the earlier constructive reforms.

A vital step taken by the Occupation was constitutional reform. Within weeks after the start of the Occupation General MacArthur and his advisers decided that in order to eliminate the old authoritarian order and to create a lasting new democratic system it was necessary for Japan to have a new constitution. Under orders, the Japanese government produced a draft of a revised constitution that was deemed unacceptable. SCAP then drafted its own version, which the Japanese government was ordered to issue as its own in early March 1946. After some months of discussion, debate, and negotiation resulting in modification of the SCAP draft, the new constitution was approved by the Imperial Diet and became effective on 3 May 1947.

The three basic principles of the constitution were popular sovereignty, respect for fundamental human rights, and the renunciation of war; these embodied the goals of Occupation policy. Its links with the Occupation made the constitution controversial, but it became the foundation of Japan's democratic order and has remained unamended.

The Occupation achieved the objectives of American (and Allied) policy and initiated changes that proved to conform with Japanese desires and trends. It ranks as one of the most successful military occupations in history.

[*See also* MacArthur, Douglas A.]

John Curtis Perry, *Beneath the Eagle's Wings: Americans in Occupied Japan* (1980). Kazuo Kawai, *Japan's American Interlude* (1960).   JOHN M. MAKI

OC EO. Located in the western part of Vietnam's Mekong Delta, the site known as Oc Eo is believed to have been an early trading port, probably flourishing between the second and fifth century. Archaeological excavations have unearthed numerous inscriptions in various languages, as well as objects from several different cultures. Of particular interest are Roman medals from the mid-second century. Oc Eo is associated with a hinduized culture known as Funan, long believed to have been a powerful kingdom but now viewed as more probably a group of smaller polities. [*See also* Funan.]

BRUCE M. LOCKHART

OCHTERLONEY, SIR DAVID (1758–1825), an officer of the East India Company's army who figured largely in the transfer of power in North India from the Mughal emperor to the British. He took part in the unsuccessful campaign against the Jats in 1803, and then in the war against Nepal in

1814–1815 and against the Marathas in 1817–1818. As resident, or representative, of the East India Company in Delhi, he defended the maintenance of the dignity of the Mughal emperor against those who saw him as a useless expense. As resident in Rajputana he supported the claims of the young raja of Bharatpur and was dismissed by the governor-general. The great column in Calcutta, now designated as a monument to Bengal nationalists, but erected in Ochterloney's memory, is a reminder of the great fame he enjoyed among his British contemporaries in India.　Ainslie T. Embree

ODA NOBUNAGA (1534–1582), Japanese warlord and political administrator. Son of a minor military lord in Owari Province (Aichi Prefecture), Oda Nobunaga rose from modest origins to control nearly one third of Japan by the time of his death. He was the first conqueror of the Sengoku ("warring states") period, an age of bitter civil war that commenced in 1467, to approach the goal of national unification under a single hegemon. His career centered upon widespread and protracted military campaigns that led his armies across much of Honshu and involved confrontations not only with competing warlords but also with religious communities, leagues of peasants and townspeople, and the leaders of the old regime. Nobunaga's strategies of pacification, his centrist style of administration, and his conception of political legitimacy are also significant.

Nobunaga broke upon the national scene in 1560 when his then small army ambushed and defeated the huge complement of Imagawa Yoshimoto, a regional warlord who was attempting to penetrate Owari en route to an intended seizure of the capital, Kyoto. Following a string of victories and treaties in the provinces east of the capital, Nobunaga himself entered Kyoto in 1568. He was bolstered by overtures from the imperial court, a debilitated but still symbolically important authority in the nation, and by entreaties from a claimant to headship of the shogunate, a long-eviscerated military government struggling to recover the power it had exercised in the fourteenth and fifteenth centuries. Nobunaga used his influence in Kyoto and an expanding army recruited from conquered domains to wage war against distinguished martial households (including the Asai, Asakura, and Takeda), to attack the religious establishments of Mount Hiei and Ishiyama Honganji, and to take command of the city of Sakai. By 1573 he was sufficiently strong to defeat the defenders of the Ashikaga shogunate, to send the last shogun into permanent exile, and to install his own deputy as governor of Kyoto.

During the last nine years of his life, between 1573 and 1582, Nobunaga directed campaigns stretching from the Kantō to Bizen (Okayama Prefecture), and from the Sea of Japan to the Pacific Ocean. Aided by a superior arsenal, control of major mines and centers of arms production, and powerful mercantile connections, Nobunaga found his principal strength in brilliant subordinates capable of leading far-flung initiatives as the small and localized contests of an earlier day gave way to cataclysmic battles for national hegemony. Nobunaga's men obliterated their opposition and engaged in slaughter on a large scale. They were the vanguards in a reign of terror that threatened to annihilate all forms of provincial dissent and independence, making way for an absolutist regime based on the rule of force.

Nobunaga's policies of pacification included the widespread destruction of castles and fortresses once held by opponents and the disarmament of peasants who fought for the Honganji establishment in Kaga Province (Ishikawa Prefecture). He encouraged systematic efforts to register land, thus enhancing methods of investiture, taxation, and conscription. He eliminated market fees and guild protection in several commercial centers, hence increasing trade in his own domain and drawing merchants away from competitors.

The centrist qualities of Nobunaga's regime—apparent in his control of religious bodies, takeover of major cities, and rigorous cadastral surveys—were clearest in the administration of his expanding domain. As Nobunaga's conquests spread, defeated lords were replaced by a small body of longtime Oda deputies who exercised the rights of local government but remained fully accountable to Nobunaga. Submitted to regular rotation, harsh discipline, and frequent calls to battle, they also ruled their domains as Nobunaga's agents, subordinate to him in matters of taxation, justice, and most administrative decisions. Such treatment was instrumental in provoking one Oda deputy, Akechi Mitsuhide, to violence. Nobunaga died in the Kyoto temple of Honnōji while under attack from this assassin. [See Akechi Mitsuhide.]

Nobunaga's claim to political legitimacy, founded originally upon alliance with the Ashikaga shogunate and honorary titles awarded by the imperial court, derived finally from his power of force. Renouncing courtly honors in 1578, Nobunaga rooted his authority in successful conquest, the obeisance of the ruled, and the identification of his personal interest with the good of the realm. He increasingly projected authority through grand display, including the construction of a magnificent castle at Azuchi (Shiga Prefecture), military processions, and lavish entertainments. The era of unification consequently came to be associated with an age of grandeur.

[See also Sengoku Period and Momoyama Period.]

Mary Elizabeth Berry, *Hideyoshi* (1982). George Elison and Bardwell L. Smith, eds., *Warlords, Artists, and Commoners: Japan in the Sixteenth Century* (1981). John W. Hall, *Government and Local Power in Japan, 500 to 1700* (1966). John W. Hall, Nagahara Keiji, and Kozo Yamamura, eds., *Japan before Tokugawa: Political Consolidation and Economic Growth, 1500 to 1650* (1981).

MARY ELIZABETH BERRY

ODORIC OF PORDENONE (1265?–1331), Christian traveler and missionary to Asia. A member of the Franciscan order, Odoric went to China by way of India and Southeast Asia about 1321 and returned by the overland route through Central Asia about 1328 to 1330, arriving back in Italy in 1330. Before his death he dictated his narrative to a Franciscan brother. While not the first Franciscan in China, his written record is the most complete of any left by the medieval friars.

Odoric's work describes his voyage from Europe to western India and northern China, and includes accounts of the Western religious missions to the Mongols, Uighurs, and Chagatai. His depictions of the Franciscan cathedral and houses at Zayton (Quanzhou), the port near Amoy (Xiamen), and the Nestorian churches at Yangzhou are particularly noteworthy.

Of the early Western descriptions of East Asia available in the Renaissance, Odoric's narrative was second in popularity only to Marco Polo's. Scores of manuscript copies of the work are still extant, and the first printed version was made in 1513. The book of travels of John Mandeville, so highly regarded in Renaissance Europe but later proved to be a hoax, was largely appropriated from the work of Odoric.

Henry Yule, ed. and trans., *Cathay and the Way Thither*, vol. 2, newly edited by Henri Cordier in *Works Issued by the Hakluyt Society*, ser. 2, vol. 33 (1914).

THEODORE NICHOLAS FOSS

OGATA KŌAN (1810–1863), scholar, physician, and headmaster of a well-known Dutch studies (*rangaku*) academy in Tokugawa Japan. Ogata was the son of a low-ranked samurai from Bitchū Province (part of present-day Okayama Prefecture). At the age of sixteen, after informal Confucian training, he began the study of Dutch, first in Osaka, then in Edo (Tokyo) and Nagasaki. In 1838 he returned to Osaka, where he opened a medical practice and a school; he spent the next twenty-four years as a Dutch scholar, town doctor, and educator. In 1862, at the peak of his fame, he was brought to Edo as director of the *bakufu's* medical center. He died there, ten months after his arrival, at the age of fifty-three.

As a scholar, Ogata wrote the first general text on pathology and internal medicine in Japan. He also was the first translator of a book describing the anatomy of the chest and the treatment of pulmonary tuberculosis. As a physician, his most important accomplishment was the establishment in 1849 of a vaccination clinic that in 1858 became the first to receive official recognition. Ogata Kōan is best known, however, as the headmaster of the leading Dutch studies school of his time, a private academy called Teki Juku.

Ogata's school allowed students great personal freedom, but it also encouraged competition and rewarded intellectual achievement, unlike many of the official schools of the time. As a result of their advanced training in Dutch language many Teki Juku students became experts in areas relating to the technology and culture of the West. Some, most notably Fukuzawa Yukichi, emerged as important leaders during the Meiji period (1868–1912).

Ogata Kōan's Teki Juku is one of the few Dutch studies academies that can be visited with profit today. In the early 1980s an authentic reconstruction of the building was completed in Osaka. The interior, also authentic, is used to display manuscripts and paraphernalia from Teki Juku and from nineteenth-century medical practice in Japan.

[See also Rangaku and Fukuzawa Yukichi.]

Eiichi Kiyooka, *The Autobiography of Yukichi Fukuzawa* (1968). Richard Rubinger, *Private Academies of Tokugawa Japan* (1982).   RICHARD RUBINGER

OGEDEI (1186–1241), third son and successor of Genghis Khan as leader of the Mongol domains. Elected by an assemblage of the Mongol nobility in 1229, Ogedei was the first to adopt the title *khaghan*, or "khan of khans." He continued his father's expansionist policies, crushing the Jurchen Jin dynasty and seizing North China in 1234, and pacifying Korea in 1235. To the west, he initiated the spectacular campaigns that led to the conquest of Russia, Georgia, and Armenia and that reached as far as Hungary and Poland. Yet territorial expansion was not the only achievement of Ogedei's reign. With the help of the sinicized official Yelü Chucai, he established a civilian administration, recruited Confucian scholars as bureaucrats, and devised an equitable tax system for his Chinese domains. He also ordered the construction of Karakorum, the first Mongol capital, which was located along the banks of the Orkhon River in the present-day Mongolian People's Republic. Ogedei's policies paved the way for the Mongols' efforts to govern, rather than simply to plunder, the territories they had conquered.

[*See also* Genghis Khan; Kublai Khan; Yelü Chucai; *and* Mongol Empire: An Overview.]

John Andrew Boyle, trans., *The Successors of Genghis Khan* (1971).   MORRIS ROSSABI

OGHUZ. *See* Ghuzz.

OGYŪ SORAI (1666–1728), Japanese Confucian whose Kogaku ("ancient learning") school dominated Japanese intellectual circles from the early to middle eighteenth century. The son of a physician, Ogyū Sorai was born near Edo. He served Yanagisawa Yoshiyasu, an influential political adviser to the shogun Tokugawa Tsunayoshi, from 1696 to 1709. Thereafter he devoted himself to research, teaching, and literary pursuits.

Sorai shared with Itō Jinsai an attitude characteristic of the Kogaku: all mistaken interpretations and commentaries of the Chinese thinker Zhu Xi (1130–1200) and other latter-day Confucians must be rejected for a strict, philologically empirical method of arriving at the "original meaning" revealed in China's ancient classics. This "original meaning" constituted the Way (Chinese, *dao*; Japanese, *dō*), which, they believed, was replete with validity and worth for all men in all ages. But in contrast to the ethical concerns dominating Jinsai's philology and interpretation of the Way, Sorai interpreted the classics and defined the Way for a baldly political reason: to convince skeptical warrior-rulers in Edo that Confucianism really was indispensable to successful administration and to the longevity of their regime.

Zhu Xi scholars claimed the Way to be a product of *yin* and *yang* cosmic forces and thus reduced it to a metaphysical "principle," *li*. They defined rituals, music, laws, and administration as mere "teachings," or the curriculum men needed for personal moral cultivation. Sorai, however, argued that the ancient sages created rituals, music, laws, and administration as "techniques" for government, and that these techniques constituted the Way. In other words, the Way was a sagely contrivance to effect political control.

This claim rested on his conviction that the sages were infallible and that by implementing their Way the *bakufu* would solve its political and fiscal ills. The impoverishment of warriors and peasants and the enrichment of townsmen, he held, stemmed from policies created by fallible men—policies such as the separation of warrior and peasant classes and the alternate attendance system that forced daimyo to squander wealth unproductively. By returning warriors to the soil and restoring a rice-based economy of self-sufficient farming villages, Sorai believed, the *bakufu* would bring its administration back in line with the Way.

[*See also* Itō Jinsai.]

Olof G. Lidin, *Life of Ogyū Sorai* (1973). J. R. MacEwan, *The Political Writings of Ogyū Sorai* (1962). Maruyama Masao, *Studies in the Intellectual History of Tokugawa Japan* (1974).   BOB TADASHI WAKABAYASHI

ŌHIRA MASAYOSHI (1910–1980), prime minister of Japan from 1978 to 1980; inheritor of Ikeda Hayato's "income doubling" plan of the 1960s, hailed as savior of the Liberal Democratic Party for his success in arresting the conservative electoral decline in 1980.

Ōhira was born in Kagawa Prefecture on the island of Shikoku in 1910. After graduation from Tokyo University of Commerce he entered the Finance Ministry (1936). Steady progress in his bureaucratic career brought him to the attention of Ikeda Hayato, the prime minister who later engineered the "income doubling" plan that lowered political tempers stirred by the security pact demonstrations. Ōhira left the bureaucracy to enter politics and was elected to the House of Representatives in 1952, and there he became a loyal protégé of Ikeda. His financial expertise and skill in the management of the conservative party's factional politics, bolstered by a reputation for integrity, made it possible for him to emerge as a major-faction leader in 1970, when he inherited the original Ikeda faction. He served as foreign minister and minister of finance under prime ministers Tanaka Kakuei and Miki Takeo.

Ōhira began to assert himself as candidate for general party leadership in the 1970s, and when new methods of selection of party president were introduced under Fukuda Takeo, Ōhira was the beneficiary. As prime minister he hosted a summit meeting of leaders of industrial nations. A Diet setback forced him to call elections in 1980; shortly after he died of exhaustion during the campaign an astonishing resurgence of votes and seats proved a startling reversal of conservative electoral decline. Much had been expected of Ōhira's quiet, thoughtful leadership, and the electoral results were seen as an expression of popular approval of his style.

MICHIO UMEGAKI

ŌI KENTARŌ (1843–1922), popular rights activist and leader of the left wing of the Liberal Party in Meiji Japan. Born in Buzen, modern Ōita Prefecture, Ōi went to Nagasaki in 1862 to study Dutch and Western science, after which he was employed by the shogunate. In 1869 he began to study French with Mitsukuri Rinshō and developed an interest in French liberal thought. In 1874, in the wake of the petition to establish a parliament, Ōi came to national prominence by debating with Katō Hiroyuki over the issue of popular rights and the need for a national assembly. Thereafter he established himself as a leader of the radical wing of the Popular Rights (Jiyū Minken) Movement.

By the mid 1880s, as the confrontation between the government and popular opposition intensified, Ōi became a leading spokesman for the extremist branch of the Liberal Party that called for "direct action" against the government. A leader in the Chichibu Shakintō, a group that led a major unsuccessful rebellion in 1884, Ōi joined other of his former Liberal Party radicals in 1885 in a plan to assist the Progressive Party in Korea to produce a "liberal revolution" there. Having failed in such a revolution at home, it was hoped that Korea might be used as a base for future agitation in Japan. The so-called Osaka Incident occurred when Ōi and thirty of his accomplices, including several women, were about to sail for Korea with arms and ammunition. In total more than 130 members of the plot were arrested and sentenced to prison terms. After a brief period of political activity in the 1890s, Ōi's final years were spent in organizing labor and tenant groups.

[See also Meiji Period and Jiyū Minken.]

F. G. NOTEHELFER

OIRATS. A general designation for speakers of the dialects of the Western Mongolian group, the name *Oirat* is perhaps derived from *Dorben Oirat* ("four confederates"), the name used by several of the group in the thirteenth century; some are also called Kalmuks. The ancestors of the Oirats were among the unrelated tribes that eventually joined the Mongol nation created by Genghis (Chinggis) Khan. After the defeat of the Mongol Yuan dynasty in 1368, hegemony in the steppe was contested between the Oirats and the Chinggisid leaders of the Eastern Mongols. Brief success by Esen in the first half of the fifteenth century was followed by defeat; the Oirats took refuge in the north, fought and were defeated by Altan Khan, and emerged again in the eighteenth century as the Dzungar state in northern Xinjiang. Oirats today live in the USSR, the Mongolian People's Republic, and the Inner Mongolian autonomous region of the People's Republic of China.

[See also Central Asia; Dzungaria; Kalmuks; Mongol Empire: An Overview; and Nomadism.]

C. R. Bawden, *The Modern History of Mongolia* (1968).

ARTHUR N. WALDRON

OKADA KEISUKE (1868–1952), naval officer and prime minister of Japan (1934–1936). Born in Fukui Prefecture, Okada graduated from the Naval Academy in 1889 and from the Naval Staff College in 1901. In 1923 Okada was vice-minister of the navy; one year later he was appointed commander of the combined fleet and promoted to the rank of full admiral. He served twice as navy minister, from 1927 to 1929 in the cabinet of Tanaka Giichi and from 1932 to 1933 in the cabinet of Saitō Makoto. In 1933 Okada retired from active service, and in 1934 he was appointed prime minister, a post that he held until after the February Twenty-sixth Incident of 1936.

Okada belonged to the moderate faction of the Japanese navy, but as prime minister he often bowed to the demands of the extremists. Thus, when the Minobe controversy (centered around Minobe Tatsukichi's view that the emperor was subject to the law, not above it) flared up in 1935, he first tried to defend Minobe, but later changed his position and forced Minobe to resign.

When the February Twenty-sixth Incident broke out, Okada was one of the main targets of attack. The rebels stormed his official residence, but mistakenly killed his brother-in-law, Colonel Matsuo Denzō. Okada, presumed dead, was spirited out of his occupied house on the following day, disguised as one of the mourners who had come to attend his memorial service. When the rebellion was suppressed, Okada tendered his resignation. In 1944, in his capacity as a *jūshin* (senior statesman), he was instrumental in toppling the cabinet of General Tojo Hideki.

[*See also* February Twenty-sixth Incident.]

Thomas F. Mayer-Oakes, ed., *Fragile Victory* (1968). Ben-Ami Shillony, *Revolt in Japan* (1973) and *Politics and Culture in Wartime Japan* (1981).   BEN-AMI SHILLONY

OKAKURA TENSHIN (1862–1913), Japanese art historian, critic, and art administrator. Okakura Tenshin was a prominent intellectual of the Meiji period (1868–1912), especially as an ideologue for Japan's attempts to conserve, protect, and develop traditional arts and crafts at a time of extensive westernization in national life. At the same time, his unique versatility in the English language and his secure knowledge of classical Chinese scholarship enabled him to promote broad understanding of Eastern arts and aesthetics in the English-speaking world, particularly America.

Okakura Kakuzō (Tenshin was his artistic name) was born in Yokohama; his father was a minor samurai-retainer who had become a merchant. Okakura began studying English at the age of seven and classical Chinese two years later. When he was eleven years old his family moved to Tokyo to start an inn, and Okakura entered the Tokyo School of Foreign Languages. In 1875, still only thirteen years old, he entered Tokyo Kaisei School, which soon became Tokyo University; there he studied under Ernest Fenollosa. His associations with Fenollosa continued until 1901, first as an interpreter and later as Fenollosa's colleague in the preservation of traditional Japanese art.

Although Okakura majored in government and political economy at Tokyo University, his graduation thesis was on aesthetics. After graduation in 1880 Okakura was employed by the Music Research Section of the Mombushō (Ministry of Education) and later by the Curriculum Section and served, along with Fenollosa, as a member of the Committee for Training and Research of Paintings within the ministry. In 1885 the ministry established the Committee for Research and Registration of Paintings, with Okakura and Fenollosa as two of its members. The members of this committee later became the founding faculty of the Tōkyō Bijutsu Gakkō (To-

kyo Art Academy; later Tokyo University of Arts and Music), which officially opened in 1887. The ministry sent Okakura to Europe and America to observe art educational institutions and museums and appointed him the academy's director in 1890. Ideological controversies both inside and outside the academy brought about his resignation in 1898.

From 1889 Okakura was also curator of fine arts of the Imperial Household Museum (now Tokyo National Museum). Under these auspices he went to China in 1893 for six months to investigate Chinese art. In 1901 Okakura was sent to India for one year. In 1904 he was invited by the Boston Museum of Fine Arts to catalog more than thirty-six hundred Japanese paintings in its collection, and he was appointed curator of Chinese and Japanese art there in 1910.

The last several years of his life were spent between Boston and his home in Izura, Ibaraki Prefecture. He also returned to China in 1906 and 1907 and to India in 1912, specifically to acquire art objects for the Boston Museum. In early 1913 Okakura fell ill and took a leave from the Boston Museum to return to Izura. In September of that year he died of a kidney infection and heart disease.

Okakura's activities and thoughts as historian and critic of Eastern art are well chronicled in numerous publications, both in Japanese and English. In 1889 Okakura founded Japan's earliest monthly art journal, *Kokka (National Culture)*. In 1903, two years after his trip to India, he published his first book in English, *The Ideals of the East*. His second English book, *The Awakening of Japan*, was published in 1904, and the third and most well-known book, *The Book of Tea*, in 1906. In 1911 Okakura was awarded an honorary master of arts degree by Harvard University.

Okakura's thoughts are lucidly articulated in his books in English, which were widely read abroad. He saw Asian art as a cultural manifestation distinct from that of the West. He held that India, China, and Japan shared the broad philosophical strains of Buddhism, Daoism, and Confucianism. As a historian Okakura was a diffusionist: he was instrumental in shaping the West's perception of the East through his slogan "Asia is one." The foundations of his ideas are to be found in his early polemical essays published in Japanese in 1882 that defended Eastern calligraphy as an art form. The salient points he made about calligraphy and its unique aesthetics remained the basis of his subsequent thoughts on Eastern art and culture.   YOSHIAKI SHIMIZU

OKINAWA, Japan's southermost prefecture, embraces the islands between Kagoshima and Taiwan. Historically, *Ryūkyū* (Chinese, *Liuqiu*), the name of the archipelago, has also been used to refer to the governments there. The island inhabitants of two thousand years ago were linguistically and culturally linked to the Japanese in Kyushu, but over the centuries a distinct culture and language evolved.

The first royal dynasty was established in 1187 by King Shunten. Buddhism was officially sponsored and students were sent to Japan for study in the period of the Eiso dynasty (1260–1349), but in the Satto dynastic period (1349–1395) the Chinese influence predominated. Tribute missions (the first in 1372), accompanied by students, were sent to the Chinese capital, and merchants remained at Fuzhou to trade while the Ming emperor dispatched technicians and scholars to assist the Ryūkyū government. With initial encouragement from King Satto (1321–1401) overseas commerce flourished, and Ryūkyū merchant vessels became important carriers of commercial goods between the ports of Southeast and East Asian countries. The resultant wealth contributed to the flowering of Ryūkyū culture, the construction of magnificent buildings, and the development of roads and bridges.

The fifteenth century was a time of relative domestic tranquillity. Under the First Shō dynasty (1406–1469) the island of Okinawa was unified (1422), and during the Second Shō dynasty (1470–1879) local rulers were disarmed and made to reside at the royal capital. The *nuru,* influential priestesses of the indigenous shamanist religion, became royal appointees.

External circumstances in the early sixteenth century adversely affected the Ryūkyū kingdom. The arrival of the Spaniards and Portuguese in Southeast Asia, growing disorder on the Chinese mainland, and piracy on the high seas curtailed its overseas trade. The cessation of civil strife in Japan enabled the Satsuma army to invade Ryūkyū (1609) and take the king hostage; he signed a treaty (1611) that relegated his kingdom to dependency on the Satsuma. However, this relationship was concealed, as the Satsuma hoped to benefit from the Ryūkyū kingdom's contacts with China. The Ryūkyū-China trade was made an official monopoly shared by the king and the lord of Satsuma. An imperial Chinese investiture mission continued to install each new Ryūkyū king officially, but the royal succession depended upon the approval of the Satsuma.

Despite the initial shock of defeat in 1609, the seventeenth and eighteenth centuries were times of social, economic, and cultural progress in Okinawa. Population expanded as agricultural productivity rose; land under cultivation increased as private ownership was allowed for reclaimed plots. The introduction of the sweet potato and improved techniques for extracting sugar from sugar cane were significant economic factors. Scholars compiled genealogies, wrote multivolume histories, and composed poems and other literary works, while artists and artisans made notable contributions in music, drama, and arts and crafts, bringing Ryūkyū to a cultural peak.

International rivalries enmeshed the kingdom in the nineteenth century. French and British warships visited Ryūkyū from 1844 to 1846 and exerted pressure for trade and diplomatic relations, and in 1853 Commodore Matthew C. Perry forcibly established an American coaling base at Naha harbor preparatory to his trip to Edo Bay, Japan. In 1874 the Meiji government responded militarily to the killing of Ryūkyū natives by aborigines in Taiwan, thus establishing Japan's claim to Ryūkyū, over China's protests. In 1879 the kingdom was abolished and Okinawa was established as a prefecture of Japan. A governor was sent from Tokyo to administer the islands, but islanders did not share fully in the obligations and privileges of Japanese citizenship. Compulsory education began in 1880 but universal military conscription for men was not enforced until after the Sino-Japanese War of 1894–1895; and it was not until 1919 that Okinawans were able to participate directly in national parliamentary government.

The Pacific War (1941–1945) was a particularly devastating experience for Okinawans, who were subjected to the full onslaught of the last major battle of the war. After the war Okinawa became the major base for American military forces in East Asia. The San Francisco Peace Treaty, ratified in 1952, left Okinawa under American military administration, with Japan given "residual sovereignty" over the islands. Okinawans found themselves without a government to which they could appeal their grievances concerning compensation for land expropriated for military purposes, the inhibition of democratic political processes, and the denial of the Okinawan wish to revert to Japanese sovereignty. These economic and political conditions were gradually ameliorated between 1945 and 1972, as it became clearer that the deep frustrations of the Okinawans impaired the security and effectiveness of the American military base. On 15 May 1972 Okinawa was reunited with Japan, and American military bases were placed under the same restrictions as elsewhere in Japan. The Japanese government, in its desire to build support and promote development, made Okinawa the site of the International Ocean Exposition in 1975.

Ta-taun Ch'en, "Investiture of Liu-Ch'iu Kings in the Ch'ing Period," in *The Chinese World Order*, edited by John K. Fairbank (1968). George H. Kerr, *Okinawa: The History of an Island People* (1958). Robert K. Sakai, "The Ryukyu (Liu Ch'iu) Islands as a Fief of Satsuma," in *The Chinese World Order*, edited by John K. Fairbank (1968). Mitsugu Sakihara, "History of Okinawa," in *Uchinanchu: A History of Okinawans in Hawaii*, edited by the United Okinawan Association of Hawaii (1981). Frederick L. Shields, *America, Okinawa, and Japan: Case Studies for Foreign Policy Theory* (1980).

ROBERT K. SAKAI

ŌKUBO TOSHIMICHI (1830–1878), with Itō Hirobumi and Yamagata Aritomo, one of the three principal statesmen-architects of the Meiji state in Japan.

Ōkubo was born in Satsuma (Kagoshima) to a samurai family whose respectable status disguised its modest means. He followed his father into the *han* bureaucracy while still in his teens (1846), became embroiled in *han* politics, was twice discharged and twice returned. By 1861 he was among the leading policy makers in the *han*, which was now active in national politics. He played an important role in the formation of the four-*han* coalition of Satsuma, Chōshū, Tosa, and Hizen and forged ties with Iwakura Tomomi, the ablest of the nobles who would later serve the Meiji state. Before the Meiji Restoration in 1868, Ōkubo was thus experienced in three spheres that would serve him well: administration, politics, and diplomacy.

Ōkubo had no part in the military campaigns against the *bakufu* and concentrated immediately on strengthening the new government. He tried early on to put his stamp on Meiji fiscal policy, in order to make it moderate and noninflationary. He was a follower rather than leader on the *hanseki hōkan* policy of 1869, in which the territories of daimyo would be returned to the emperor, but he may be credited with a major role in implementing the *haihan chiken* policy of 1871, in which the *han* were dissolved and prefectures under the control of the central government established in their place. His importance and influence in the Meiji government can be charted in the succession of positions he held. He was a *san'yō* (junior councillor) in 1868 and a

sangi (state councillor) the following year. He was appointed state minister *(kyō)* to the two most powerful ministries, the Finance Ministry (1871–1873) and the Home Ministry (1873–1874). By this time, holding these positions in tandem with his position as *sangi,* he was de facto prime minister, with a hand in fiscal-economic policies and a powerful voice in the "heart and center of the domestic bureaucracy."

Ōkubo, described as forceful, tough, and of "steely implacable will," was single-mindedly devoted to the creation of the Meiji state, but he was of two minds about the West. On the one hand, he saw the advanced Western nations as a source of learning, and it is in this spirit that he led the Iwakura Mission to the United States and Europe (1871–1873). [*See* Iwakura Mission.] On the other hand, the Western powers were seen as real threats to Japan's independence. They were to be given no pretext to establish a military presence in Japan. He therefore led the decision against military action in Korea (1873), declaring that the "most mature consideration and forethought is essential in order to . . . protect the land and its people." This principle guided every major foreign policy decision of the Meiji state.

One of Ōkubo's last acts was the crushing of the Satsuma Rebellion (1877), which pitted him against his erstwhile comrade Saigō Takamori. He followed Saigō in death by less than nine months, when he was killed by ex-samurai from Kanazawa.

[*See also* Meiji Restoration *and* Meiji Period.]

GEORGE K. AKITA

ŌKUMA SHIGENOBU (1838–1922), Japanese government leader of the Meiji period. Ōkuma was born to a samurai family in Hizen (Saga). He was a lifelong learner and was reputed to be, along with such other national figures as Itō Hirobumi, Yamagata Aritomo, and Fukuzawa Yukichi, a voracious reader. He played no prominent part in the Meiji Restoration in 1868 but came to the attention of Inoue Kaoru, who recommended his appointment as *san'yō* (junior councillor) in Tokyo. He won acclaim by standing up to Sir Harry Parkes, the British minister to Japan, over an issue involving Japanese Christians. He rose quickly in the most important ministries: the Foreign Ministry, the Finance Ministry, and the Home Ministry. By 1880 he was one of the most influential men in the government, with talented protégés scattered throughout the central administration. These protégés, however, did not constitute a power base and Itō Hirobumi easily outmaneuvered him and ousted him and his protégés from the government in 1881.

After 1881 Ōkuma divided his considerable energies and gifts between three areas. He established major political parties, the Rikken Kaishintō (1882), the Shimpotō (1896), and, with Itagaki Taisuke, the Kenseitō (1898). This coalition lasted briefly and Ōkuma became president of the Kenseihontō (1898). He served in the government as foreign minister (1888–1889; 1896–1897; 1898), prime minister (1898; 1914–1916), agriculture and commerce minister (1897), and privy councillor (1889–1891). He became an educator, founding the Tokyo Semmon Gakkō (1882), which later became Waseda University, serving as its president in 1907.

Ōkuma was living proof that having been purged by the Meiji government was not an insurmountable political handicap. In fact, he presented the Japanese political system with important alternatives—political parties and English constitutional concepts. He was also a cosmopolite, but he never traveled to the West and spoke English with difficulty. Still, he was, with Itō, the Japanese public figure most foreigners eagerly sought out.

[*See also* Meiji Period.]

GEORGE K. AKITA

ŌKURA KIHACHIRŌ (1837–1928), Japanese trader who utilized close political and military contacts to establish a *zaibatsu*, or large conglomerate. In 1865 he set up a firm to buy guns from Western merchants and sold them to both the Tokugawa *bakufu* and the domains. In the Meiji period (1868–1912) Ōkura became the official purveyor to the army, and his imports of weapons stigmatized him as "the merchant of death." Among trading companies he pioneered the opening of overseas offices, setting up a branch in London in 1874. From contacts there and his base in the arms trade, he diversified into imports of machinery, locomotives, generators, and other technical equipment.

The Ōkura *zaibatsu's* core companies were in trading, construction, and mining, but its most distinctive feature was its early overseas investments. Ōkura established enterprises successively in Korea in the early Meiji period, in Japan's newly acquired colony of Taiwan after the Sino-Japanese War (1894–1895), and in China following the Russo-Japanese War (1904–1905). Most of his mining operations were in southern Manchuria, where he set up a successful coking coal, iron ore, and steel complex, which he tried to secure with politically ten-

dered loans to Chinese military cliques. Ōkura was also a leading figure in the domestic business world, cooperating with Shibusawa Eiichi in founding the Tokyo Chamber of Commerce. As a *zaibatsu* leader, however, he was slow to move into heavy industry or chemical manufacture or to develop an effective administrative structure. His Chinese investments presented problems after World War I, and following Ōkura's death his firm declined relative to other *zaibatsu*.

[*See also* Zaibatsu.]

Johannes Hirschmeier and Tsunehiko Yui, *The Development of Japanese Business* (2d ed., 1981). Yoshihara Kunio, *Sogo Shosha: The Vanguard of the Japanese Economy* (1982).

WILLIAM D. WRAY

OLD PERSIAN, the written language of the Achaemenid court as preserved in cuneiform inscriptions, all of which are royal. The syllabic alphabet was probably ordered by Darius I, or at least it was first used extensively by him. The language is archaic and similar to Avestan. Artaxerxes III (359–338 BCE) is the last ruler to have used Old Persian in inscriptions at Persepolis, although an Old Persian inscription written in the Aramaic alphabet also exists at Naqsh-i Rustam.

[*See also* Avestan *and* Cuneiform.]

R. G. Kent, *Old Persian* (1953), p. 6.

RICHARD N. FRYE

ŌNIN WAR (1467–1477), civil war of medieval Japan, fought mainly in Kyoto and named after the reign era, Ōnin (1467–1469), in which it began; the war plunged the country into a century of disunion and strife.

After the overthrow of Japan's first warrior (samurai) government—the Kamakura shogunate (1185–1333)—a new military government, the Ashikaga, or Muromachi, shogunate (1336–1573), was established in Kyoto. Weaker than its Kamakura predecessor, the Ashikaga shogunate was plagued by regionalism. Provincial chieftains, appointed *shugo* (constables) by the shogunate, rose to control large territories (often two or more provinces) and to arrogate regional governing powers. The Ashikaga shogunate at its height (about the year 1400) was a balance of power between the shogun and his leading *shugo*. Most of the *shugo* houses, economically weak and often challenged by unruly vassals, however, steadily declined during the fifteenth century. A common manifestation of such decline was the succession dispute (to the office of *shugo*); and in the mid-1460s a dispute over succession to the position of shogun broke out in the Ashikaga family.

This dispute was the proximate cause of the Ōnin War: various *shugo* and even feuding *shugo* contenders formed great camps behind the two Ashikaga candidates for shogun; in 1467 these camps commenced warring. Although there was related fighting in the provinces, the Ōnin War was waged largely in Kyoto and its environs. The shogun, long deprived of real power, was a feeble bystander. As the *shugo* and *shugo* contenders exhausted themselves in seemingly futile conflict in Kyoto, their vassals took control of parts or all of their domains. When the war ended in 1477 Kyoto was almost completely devastated; the Ashikaga shogunate was a government in name only; and most *shugo* houses were either in ruins or about to be ruined. The century known as the "age of the country at war" (*sengoku jidai*) had begun.

[*See also* Muromachi Period *and* Sengoku Period.]

H. Paul Varley, *The Ōnin War* (1967).

Paul Varley

ONN BIN JA'AFAR, DATO (1895–1961), Malay statesman and political leader, recognized as the father of the United Malays National Organization (UMNO), the first political party to represent purely Malay interests. The son of a politically prominent Johor family, he had become the chief minister of Johor by the 1940s. Following World War II, he organized opposition to the Malayan Union plan. With others, he formed the UMNO in 1946 and was named its first president. In 1951, after his attempt to broaden the party's base by admitting non-Malays was opposed, Dato Onn resigned from the UMNO and formed the Independence of Malaya Party (IMP) with a multiracial membership. While it gained some initial support, the IMP lost most of the offices in the first municipal elections to the communal parties. Thereafter he remained on the fringes of Malay political life. His son, Hussein bin Onn, was prime minister of the Federation of Malaysia between 1976 and 1981.

[*See also* United Malays National Organization; Johor; Malayan Union; *and* Independence of Malaya Party.]

Ishak bin Tadin, "Dato' Onn, 1946–1951," *Journal of Southeast Asian History* 1.1 (March 1960): 62–69.

Carl A. Trocki

OPIUM, narcotic made from the processed sap of the opium poppy (*Papaver somniferum*). Although it was cultivated and used as a drug since Neolithic times, it was not until the sixteenth century that the inhabitants of South Asia and Persia began using opium as a "recreational" drug. It was usually eaten or drunk in a variety of preparations. In the seventeenth century the Chinese devised a method for smoking opium, a practice apparently initially related to the use of tobacco. The great expansion of the opium trade came in the mid-eighteenth century as a result of the British East India Company's (EIC) conquest of Bengal in 1750, which gave the British control over one of the major opium-producing areas of the subcontinent. In subsequent years the export to China was encouraged as a means of helping to balance the company's deficit caused by tea purchases.

System of Production in British India. After 1780, opium was produced under a monopoly of the company, whose agents (one at Patna in Bihar, and one at Ghazipur, near Varanasi) advanced money to Indian peasants through a hierarchy of local agents and collectors. Opium, a pasty black-brown sap, was obtained by cutting the green seed pod of the opium poppy. This was collected in factories of the East India Company, where it was purified, shaped into balls of approximately 3 pounds, wrapped in poppy petals, and packed in wooden boxes, or "chests" (forty balls to a chest), weighing about 140 pounds. Opium was then taken to Calcutta, where it was auctioned to private British traders who carried it to Southeast Asia and China.

Initially much of the opium was sold in Southeast Asian ports for reshipment to China, but increasingly country traders delivered the opium to smugglers off the South China coast. Country traders paid off their bills of exchange at the EIC godowns in Canton, and the company used the silver to finance tea purchases. By about 1800, opium sales had balanced the company's tea deficit, and production of opium under EIC monopoly in India was averaging about four thousand chests (280 tons) annually.

Growth of the Trade. Over the next half century, the opium trade was important to the British imperial advance both in the subcontinent and to the east, in Southeast Asia and China. In India, the East India Company had come to rely on opium as the second largest source of revenue (after the land tax). Attempts to restrict the production of opium in the Indian states on the Malwa plateau was a major factor in British relations with them. Finally it became possible to funnel all this production through Bombay, where a very heavy tax was laid on it.

British concern for the security of the trade led to territorial expansion in the Malay world and the founding of British settlements, first at Penang in 1786 and then at Singapore in 1819. The same concerns led to the Opium War (1840–1843) and the negotiation of a series of treaties that "opened" China to European economic and political domination. The number of Chinese smokers continued to increase unabated for the next fifty years. Indian production, both from British territories and the so-called Malwa states, approached an annual total of one hundred thousand chests, and at least an equal amount was being produced by China itself by 1880.

Suppression of the Trade. Initially, the opposition to the opium trade came almost exclusively from Europeans, especially Protestant missionaries and physicians, who ultimately formed the Society for the Suppression of the Opium Trade. The society was successful in calling international and humanitarian attention to problems of widespread addiction and raised a call for reform. Although some restrictions were introduced, the trade, together with taxed, regulated, and legalized usage, continued throughout nearly the whole of Asia into the twentieth century, despite the emergence of both national and international bodies, commissions, conferences—religious, governmental, and otherwise—in opposition to the traffic.

The British, who continued to be the major force in the opium trade, refused to move toward any kind of regulation until 1905, when a newly elected Liberal government acceded to the reformers. As a result of a number of international conferences and conventions (1909, 1915, 1930, etc.), most of the major powers, and later other countries, undertook the responsibility to restrict and ultimately prohibit international traffic in opium and opium derivatives (morphine, codeine, heroin).

While the legitimate trade and manufacture had slowed to a trickle by the 1930s, the production of opium was continued illegally in many places. In Southeast Asia, colonial governments continued to draw revenues from opium monopolies (at much higher prices) until 1942, when opium usage was finally suppressed by Japanese occupation forces.

Following the victory of the Communists in 1950, effective steps were taken to eradicate opium usage and production throughout China. By 1960 opium production in Southeast Asia had been confined to a few isolated areas in upper Burma, Laos, and Thailand. During the Vietnam War, however, production by the various tribal peoples in these areas was encouraged by a number of irregular armed groups, including the remnants of Chinese Guomindang (Kuomintang) forces that had settled in the region after 1950, anti-Burmese rebels, and the so-called secret army of the Hmong, which was controlled by the General Vang Pao and supported by the American Central Intelligence Agency. These efforts combined to make the Golden Triangle one of the major centers of illegal opium production at the present time.

[*See also* China Trade; Country Trade; East India Company; *and* Malwa.]

House of Commons, *First Report of the Royal Commission on Opium With Minutes of Evidence and Appendices,* 7 vols. (1894–1895). Bruce D. Johnson, "Righteousness before Revenue: The Forgotten Moral Crusade Against the Indo-Chinese Opium Trade," *Journal of Drug Issues* (Fall 1975): 304–326. John C. Kramer, M.D., "Speculations on the Nature and Pattern of Opium Smoking," *Journal of Drug Issues* (Spring 1979): 247–256. Alfred McCoy, *The Politics of Heroin in Southeast Asia* (1972). D. E. Owen, *British Opium Policy in China and India* (1934). Joshua Rowntree, *The Imperial Drug Trade: A Restatement of the Opium Question in the Light of Recent Evidence and New Developments in the East* (2d ed., 1906).
                                                    CARL A. TROCKI

OPIUM WAR. *See* China Trade *and* Lin Zexu.

ORANG ASLI. The Orang Asli ("original people") are the aboriginal inhabitants of the Malay Peninsula. Two-thirds of the over 60,000 Orang Asli are speakers of Austroasiatic, Mon-Khmer languages subdivided into three groups of Aslian stock. These are the Northern Aslian (Kensiu, Kentaq Bong, Jehai, Mendriq, Batek dialects, Mintil, Chewong, with an additional 300 Tonga and Mos speakers found in southern Thailand), Central Aslian (Semnam, Sabum, Lanoh Jengjeng, Lanoh Yir, Temiar, Semai dialects, Jah Hut), and Southern Aslian (Semaq Beri, Semelai, Temoq, and Mah Meri or Besisi). The remaining 20,000 are Austronesian speakers of Malay dialects collectively termed Aboriginal Malay, including Temuan, Orang Hulu (Jakun), Orang Kanaq, and Orang Selitar.

This linguistic classification differs from the three categories, based on ethnic and cultural critera, commonly used to describe the Orang Asli: Semang, or Negrito; Senoi; and Aboriginal Malay. The 2,700 Semang comprise all Northern Aslian speakers except the Chewong, as well as the Lanoh, Semnam, and Sabum. Sometimes called Negritos, the Semang were traditionally nomadic hunter-gatherers living in small bands in the lowland tropical rain forests of the foothills in northern Malaysia. Semang camps contain five to fifteen elementary families consisting of parents and their children. Food obtained by the elementary family was usually distributed throughout the camp; however, individual families retained political autonomy and constantly changed their residence from band to band. Political authority also remained within the elementary family, although elders of either sex might emerge as nominal leaders in certain camps. Semang shamans communicate with superhuman beings *(hala asal* or *cenoi)* during dreams and while journeying in trance as leaders of singing sessions. Some Semang groups have recently been prompted by the Department of Orang Asli Affairs to adopt settled agriculture.

The Senoi, basically Mongoloid peoples, include the Chewong, who are linguistically North Aslian. The Senoi division includes 18,000 Semai, the largest Orang Asli group, living from highland and lowland jungles to the city's edge in Perak, Pahang, and Selangor. The Temiar (who have a population of 11,500) dwell in Kelantan, Perak, and Pahang in the tropical rain forests on either side of the mountainous divide running down the center of the Malay Peninsula. Dispersed in small settlements of 30 to 150 along the rivers and their tributaries, the semisedentary Senoi traditionally move their settlements within a limited hereditary area every few years to locate new swidden (slash-and-burn) agricultural plots, where they grow tapioca, hill rice, and other crops. They also hunt, fish, and gather forest products for their own use and for exchange. Senoi villages consist of extended families linked by kinship or marriage to a core sibling group. Village leaders are usually elder males of this core group, some of whom received additional sanction as headmen from traditional Malay authorities, a process continued today by the Department of Orang Asli Affairs. However, their mode of leadership through coordination rather than coercion remains essentially egalitarian. During trance-state dance and singing sessions held for entertainment, healing, or to end a period of mourning, Senoi spirit mediums act as conduits for spirit guides, who reveal songs through dreams that are later performed in ceremonies. The Temiar and Semai have become known in the West as the models for Senoi dream therapy, a psychotherapeutic technique based on an embellished interpretation of Senoi dream practices.

Except for the Mah Meri and some Semaq Beri who exhibit Senoi physical characteristics, the South Aslian and Austronesian-speaking Orang Asli groups are ethnically and culturally placed in the third descriptive category: Aboriginal Malays or Proto-Malays. The Jah Hut, while linguistically and physically Senoi, are culturally linked with the groups living to the south. The term *Jakun,* sometimes used to refer to this descriptive category as a whole, has also been used to label the largest tribal group of Aboriginal Malays (with a population of 9,800), currently called Orang Hulu (people of the interior), who live in Pahang and Johore. The Aboriginal Malays are Mongoloid peoples found from the rivers of the interior to the coast in the southern portion of Malaysia. They subsist on swidden and wet-rice farming, fishing, and trading. The Jah Hut and Mah Meri have gained fame for their woodcarvings, which adapt traditional themes to the requirements of the recent tourist trade. Except for the Orang Seletar who live on boats, the Aboriginal Malays are more permanently settled than the Semang or Senoi. Political authority was traditionally invested in a system of ranked offices that linked several villages into a regional policy under the jurisdiction of a territorial chief.

Currently administered by the Malaysian government's Department of Orang Asli Affairs, the Orang Asli have recently formed an indigenous pantribal political organization, the Persatuan Orang Asli Semenanjung Malaysia, or POASM (Orang Asli Association of Peninsular Malaysia).

[*See also* Malaysia; Senoi; *and* Malays.]

I. Carey, *Orang Asli: The Aboriginal Tribes of Peninsular Malaysia* (1976). R. K. Dentan, *The Semai: A Non-Violent People of Malaya* (1973). S. Howell, *Society and Cosmos: Chewong of Peninsular Malaysia* (1984). Alun Jones, "The Orang Asli: An Outline of Their Progress in Modern Malaya," *Journal of Southeast Asian History* 9.2 (1968): 286–305. W. C. Solhein, "Searching for the Origins of the Orang Asli," *Federation Museums Journal* 25: 61–75. S. A. Wurm and S. Hattori, eds., *Language Atlas of the Pacific Area,* part 2, map 37 (1983).

MARINA ROSEMAN

ORANG LAUT ("men of the sea") were a people who lived by harvesting the products of the sea and coastal jungles of the Malay Archipelago. Known to early European travelers as Cellates, Saletters, or Zalatters (from Orang Selat, "men of the [Melaka] Straits"), they were feared for their unrivaled knowledge of the narrow waters and navigational hazards of the area, which gave them a decided advantage when they turned to piracy. They played a leading role in the power structure of the Melaka/Johor empire, providing war fleets and keeping the sealanes open until displaced by Bugis in the eighteenth century.

[See also Johor.]

Leonard Y. Andaya, *The Kingdom of Johor, 1641–1728* (1975). David E. Sopher, *The Sea Nomads* (1965).

DIANNE LEWIS

ORD, SIR HARRY (1819–1885). After serving as a soldier and administrator principally in West Africa and the West Indies, Major-General Ord was appointed the first Colonial Office governor of the Straights Settlements (1867–1873). He reorganized the straits on Crown Colony lines, but his brusque manner alienated subordinates and the local mercantile community. Lacking instructions, Ord attempted to increase British influence in the Malay States until the Colonial Office prohibited intervention (1868). When London decided on action (1873), it entrusted the task to Sir Andrew Clarke, in whom it had more confidence. Ord was governor of Western Australia from 1877 to 1879.

[*See also* Straits Settlements.]

C. D. Cowan, *Nineteenth-Century Malaya* (1961).

A. J. STOCKWELL.

ORDOS REGION, broadly speaking, the area of the great loop of the Yellow River—more properly, only the desert it encloses—in Inner Mongolia. Although north of the line where rainfall is sufficient to support agriculture, the waters of the Yellow River make farming possible in parts of the Ordos, and through history this has given the area unusual strategic significance. In Chinese hands the Ordos served as a base for controlling or fighting nomads, while in nomadic hands it posed a grave threat to China. The struggle for control of the area is one of the grand themes of Asian history, beginning even before the unification of the Chinese state.

G. B. Cressey, "The Ordos Desert of Inner Mongolia," *Denison University Bulletin* 28.8 (1933): 155–248. Owen Lattimore, *Inner Asian Frontiers of China* (1940).

ARTHUR N. WALDRON

ORIENTALISM has traditionally been the name of the academic discipline that undertakes the study of non-Western cultures by Europeans and, more recently, by Americans. Currently, Orientalism also designates the underlying attitudes and motivations of the men and women who have pursued this avenue of research and the consequences these attitudes and motivations have had on the discipline itself and on society in general.

Interest in non-Western cultures by Europeans dates back to the Renaissance. The primary focus was philological, with special attention paid to Hebrew and the Hebrew scriptures. The study of language, however, was not the sole prerogative of academics. By the nineteenth century Christian missionary movements had expanded to many parts of the non-Western world. The study of language was essential if the scriptures were to be translated and the central dogmas of the Christian faith communicated to the indigenous populations.

It is important to bear in mind that Christianity, like the other religious traditions of the West, Judaism and Islam, sees itself as the sole possessor of the fullness of revealed truth. Salvation is considered extremely difficult, if not impossible, without initiation into the Christian community through baptism. The missionary enterprise, therefore, was predicated on two presuppositions: Christianity is superior to all other religions, and the missionary is the only physician capable of curing the disease of spiritual ignorance. Both of these presuppositions easily contribute to attitudes of cultural and racial superiority, for religion is not a collection of abstract dogmas, but a worldview incarnated in a sociocultural milieu. Consequently the cultural matrix in which the only true religion flourished was frequently presumed to be the only true culture.

Religious mission was not the only catalyst for involvement in Asian cultures. Trade and empire building both encouraged the acquisition of linguistic skills and any other practical tools needed to ensure the establishment of stable markets and secure colonial borders. These movements, like the Christian missions, were not principally concerned with understanding the intricacies of other cultures, except insofar as understanding translated into concrete gain.

During the eighteenth and nineteenth centuries, at the same time that important inroads into "the Orient" were being made in the name of religion, trade, and empire, the growth of interest in non-Western cultures increased in academic circles. France, England, and Germany were at the forefront; many other European countries made substantial contributions. The accomplishments of these scholars in many areas—language, literature, history, religion, philosophy, and so forth—were prodigious; their work remains influential today. It is often presumed, however, that the academic study of other cultures is less biased and utilitarian than that initiated for more pragmatic reasons. Intellectual inquiry, it is hoped, is predicated on a quest for objective knowledge, not material gain or power. There is little doubt that such an idealized view of the intellectual life is overly romantic.

This does not mean that scholars are dishonest or that they deliberately distort their findings. The point to be made is that scholars are men and women who usually share the prejudices as well as the strengths of their own culture and generation. Some may see farther and more clearly than their contemporaries; others, on the contrary, may be chronically myopic. It is to be hoped, nevertheless, that Orientalists will remain open to criticism and that they will take special pains to avoid reinforcing the popular caricatures of non-Western cultures prevalent at a particular point in time.

The challenge to men and women who study non-Western cultures is to communicate as honestly and thoroughly as possible the complex web of human realities that comprise changing societies. Some in the past and present have succeeded, others have not. The failures, however, are as profoundly significant as the successes. To fail in this endeavor is to contribute to the body of fictitious myths about non-Western peoples that are passed from scholar to scholar, to student, to government, to business, and so forth. The myths become self-perpetuating paradigms for dealing with foreign cultures. For example, the Arab is depicted as untrustworthy, primitive, and degenerate; the Indian is passive, duplicitous, and a religious primitive. Peoples are massed together and dealt with in broad, general terms. If such myths remain uncriticized, they become institutions and the bases for the economic and political policies of the West toward "the Orient."

The study of Asian cultures should no longer be considered the private preserve of a small group of specialists; it is an endeavor that has implications for all men and women and should, therefore, be of concern to all. The fact that Orientalism (a term that is often being replaced by the less ethnocentric *Asian Studies*) as a scholarly discipline is undergoing scrutiny and reevaluation from both within and without the academic community does not imply its imminent demise. The ability to integrate intelligent criticism and grow from it is a sign of health, not morbidity.

The present critique of Orientalism should act as a reminder that all scholarship, be it concerned with other cultures or with another area of study, needs to be continually evaluated. No writer is free of prejudice; pure objectivity is an illusion. The struggle to communicate one's ideas honestly and carefully is nevertheless no vain enterprise. Moreover, it is the excitement engendered by the process that makes the pursuit of Orientalist scholarship rewarding and unquestionably relevant to the modern world.

Ainslie T. Embree, "The Tradition of Mission—Asian Studies in the United States, 1783 and 1983," *Journal of Asian Studies* 43 (1983): 11–19. Bernard Lewis, "The Question of Orientalism," *The New York Review* (24 June 1982), pp. 49–56. K. M. Panikkar, *Asia and Western Dominance* (1959). Edward Said, *Orientalism* (1978). R. W. Southern, *Western Views of Islam in the Middle Ages* (1962).   PETER J. AWN

ORISSA, Indian state wedged between West Bengal and Andhra Pradesh and bordered in the east and south by the Bay of Bengal. Different physical environments, from lush jungle and mountainous terrain to rolling river valleys and coastal plains, make it a land of sharp contrasts. Dense forest, fearful during the monsoon rains, mellow at other times, is felt by many of its inhabitants to endow the land with primitive power. Of a population of 26,272,054 (1981 census), 25 percent make up the scheduled tribes who inhabit the hilly forested interior; they have their own languages, which are different from Oriya, the regional, sanskritic language. Another 15 percent represent the scheduled castes. Together they make up the economically and educationally backward communities in the state. [*See* Adivasis *and* Untouchability.]

Like most other regions of India, Orissa's history dates from Vedic times (c. 1500–500 BCE). It is believed that the original inhabitants were primitive tribes akin to the Saoro and Juang who today constitute important groups living in the remote hinterland. There is no doubt that the proportion of tribal peoples to the general population in earlier centuries must have been much greater than what it is today, the inaccessible terrain shaping them into an independent unit with their distinctive customs and rituals.

Today Orissa remains only a fraction of the vast empire of Kalinga that was so powerful around the beginning of the common era. [*See* Kalinga.] A landmark in Orissan history is its conquest by the Maurya emperor Ashoka, when he massacred thousands in the Kalinga war of 261 BCE. Later, Ashoka embraced Buddhism, carving his famous rock edicts on Dhauli Hill. [*See* Ashoka.] The first and second centuries BCE witnessed the reign of Kharavela, whose far-reaching conquests were instrumental in embodying those cultural influences that in the course of time led to the development of the superb temple architecture of Orissa. Around this time too, the people of Kalinga became the pioneers of Indian colonization in the Indian archipelago. For the next few centuries they maintained a maritime trade with Indonesia, Malaysia, and other eastern lands.

The eighth to the thirteenth century CE was a fervent period of temple building that culminated in the elaborate Konarak Temple; it was a period representing the Oriya craftsman's search for the beatific vision in the realm of art and aesthetics. The temple city of Bhubaneswar contains some of the finest examples of Hindu art. [*See* Bhubaneswar.]

In 1568 Orissa ceased to exist as an independent Hindu kingdom. Conquered by the Afghans, the Mughals, and the Marathas successively, Orissa was finally occupied by the British in 1803. Unhappy with the British administration, Orissa burst forth into rebellion with the *paika* (the landed militia of the princes) uprising in 1817, which was eventually crushed. Annexed to Bengal at first, and then to Bihar and Orissa Province, Orissa was at last granted separate and political identity in 1936.

Mainly agricultural, the Oriyas continue to live amid temples and shrines, with their own festivals, feasts, and fasts. Their religious belief is centered around Jagannath, a deity of tribal origin who has been assimilated into Hinduism.

[*See also* Architecture: South Asian Architecture; Santal; *and* Bihar.]

JAYANTA MAHAPATRA

ORKHON INSCRIPTIONS

ORKHON INSCRIPTIONS, the name given to a group of funerary monuments *(balbal)* erected by Turkic rulers and princes. They were discovered by the Russian archaeologist N. M. Yadrintsev in 1889 in present-day Outer Mongolia near the old course of the Orkon River, and in successive expeditions to the Yenisei and Orkhon regions organized by the Finns (A. O. Heikel), Poles (W. Kowicz), and others. The significance of these finds is that they represent the earliest surviving record of written Turkish from a time (mid-eighth century CE) when the old national alphabet (called variously Runic, Gok Turkic, and Aramaic/Iranian) was still in use and the language retained a form as yet little diluted by foreign influences.

The best-preserved monuments, dating from 732 and 735, are four-sided limestone slabs measuring about twelve feet in height on which are carved bilingual versions of texts in the Orkhon Turkic and Chinese languages. Apart from general eulogizing of the battle prowess and bravery of the Turkic commanders and warriors, the content of the two principal inscriptions erected by Kul Tegin and Bilge, two sons of the ruler Ilterish Kagan (d. 692), includes some sermonizing and advice to the people, chiefly warnings concerning the threat posed to their national identity and autonomy by sinicizing influences. The words of the Kul Tegin inscription instruct the people to maintain their martial self-discipline and ignore the "sweet words and soft materials" (Tekin translation, p. 261) of the Chinese.

G. Clauson, "The Origin of the Turkish 'Runic' Alphabet," *Acta Orientalia* 23 (1970): 51–76. T. Tekin, *A Grammar of Orkhon Turkic* (1968).

RHOADS MURPHEY, JR.

OSADAMEGAKI HYAKKAJŌ

OSADAMEGAKI HYAKKAJŌ, basic code of civil and criminal procedure in Tokugawa Japan, compiled by the order of the eighth shogun Tokugawa Yoshimune in 1742. Yoshimune had strong interests in administrative procedure, and his assistants utilized codes of the Ming dynasty in China in addition to other precedents. While earlier Tokugawa legislation had been based upon the regulations for court nobles and military houses, the code of Yoshimune reflected the growing importance of structuring procedures for commoners in the growing commercialization and urbanization of Japanese life.

More correctly known as *Kujikata osademagaki*, Yoshimune's codes mark a watershed in the development of Japanese law. Initially "100 articles" *(hyakkajō)*, they became 103 and were issued in two volumes, one of instructions and one of precedent and justification. The code was revised and amended in 1790 by Matsudaira Sadanobu.

The code was not published or addressed to the people subject to its provisions, but kept secret from them lest it encourage litigious behavior. It was meant specifically to guide the magistrates of finance, temples and shrines, and cities in their work. Its provisions were echoed in the legislation of other Tokugawa-period domains, notably those of Fukui, Morioka, and Kameyama. Taken as a whole, these developments may be said to mark the turn from the rather capricious, individual administrative practices of early Tokugawa years to the more structured and orderly procedures of the later Tokugawa period.

[*See also* Tokugawa Yoshimune.]

John Carey Hall, *Japanese Feudal Laws: The Tokugawa Legislation, Part IV: The Edict in 100 Sections* (1906; reprint, 1979). Dan Fenno Henderson, *Conciliation and Japanese Law: Tokugawa and Modern*, vol. 1 (1965), and "The Evolution of Tokugawa Law," in *Studies in the Institutional History of Early Modern Japan*, edited by John Whitney Hall and Marius B. Jansen (1969).

MARIUS B. JANSEN

OSAKA, Japan's third largest city (after Tokyo and Yokahama), with a population of 2,648,180 (1980). The Osaka-Kobe industrial and financial zone along the Inland Sea has a concentration of economic strength comparable to the Tokyo-Yokohama area three hundred miles to the east. Osaka City is the capital of Osaka Prefecture (Osaka-fu), Japan's second largest prefecture in population (8,473,446), although the smallest in area.

The many archaeological remains found in the Osaka coastal plain from the Jōmon (c. 10,000 to 300 BCE) and Yayoi (300 BCE to 300 CE) periods indicate that it was already in prehistorical times one of Japan's more populous areas. The two largest burial mounds *(kofun)*, those of the emperors Nintoku and Ōjin of the early fifth century, are near the city. One of the first major Buddhist temples, the Shitennōji, was built there by Shōtoku Taishi in 593. Then known as Naniwa, the city was the site of the imperial court for brief periods from the fifth to eighth centuries and the port for missions to China and trade with the continent. In medieval times, Sakai, a short distance to the south, and other nearby ports were more active, but Osaka regained importance with the establishment there of the Ishiyama Honganji monastery in 1496. Three years after the fall of Ishiyama Honganji in 1850, Toyotomi Hideyoshi (1536–1598) built Osaka Castle on its site by the Yodo River and made this his primary military and political headquarters in his drive to reunify Japan. After his death in 1598, the castle was the residence of his heir until it was besieged and captured in 1615 by Tokugawa Ieyasu.

The castle and the surrounding city were rebuilt by the Tokugawa, who placed the city under their direct administration. Daimyo of most of the country established warehouses on the canals and rivers of Osaka in order to more effectively market rice and other products of their domains. Before the end of the seventeenth century Osaka replaced Kyoto as the central marketplace of Japan, earning it a reputation as the country's "kitchen." Its population had reached 330,000, the equal of Kyoto's, which was exceeded only by that of Edo, the shogun's capital. The prosperity of this largely commercial

FIGURE 1. *Osaka Castle.*

city nurtured the development of the popular culture of the urban commoners *(chōnin)* in the Kyoto-Osaka area. Among the innovators in the arts active in Osaka at the end of the seventeenth century (Genroku period) were the *haiku* poet Nishiyama Sōin (1605–1682), the story writer Ihara Saikaku (1642–1693), the playwright Chikamatsu Monzaemon (1653–1725), the *kabuki* actor Sakata Tōjūrō (1647–1709), and the reciter of puppet play texts *(jōruri)* Takemoto Gidayū (1651–1714). [*See* Genroku Culture.]

In the middle of the eighteenth century the population of Osaka reached 400,000, but it declined steadily thereafter, until it stood at less than 300,000 at the time of the Meiji Restoration (1868). When the modern municipal administration was established in 1889, Osaka had 472,247 people. It grew rapidly, to 3,252,340 by 1940, but during World War II one-third of the city was devastated, and the population had fallen to 1,102,959 by 1945.

From the beginning of industrialization in the late nineteenth century Osaka was a leader in textiles. More recently the leading industries have been machinery, steel, chemical products, metals, and electrical equipment. The city has one of Japan's major concentrations of universities, libraries, and museums. As in Tokugawa times, Osaka continues to be the home of the puppet theater, now called *bunraku*. The Tenjin Festival of the Shinto shrine Temmangu is known as one of the three major festivals of Japan. The main keep of the castle burned in 1868, but it was rebuilt in ferroconcrete in 1931 and continues to be a major tourist attraction. The massive masonry of the moats and several surviving gates and turrets attest to the grand scale of the original castle complex.

William B. Hauser, *Economic Institutional Change in Tokugawa Japan: Osaka and the Kinai Cotton Trade* (1974).   DONALD H. SHIVELY

OSAKA CAMPAIGNS. The Osaka campaigns of 1614 and 1615 extinguished the Toyotomi cause and completed the national unification by Tokugawa Ieyasu, ending the warfare that had wracked Japan for a century or more. At the decisive battle of Sekigahara in 1600 a coalition of central and eastern lords under Tokugawa leadership had crushed southwestern claimants to power, but Toyotomi Hideyoshi's young heir Hideyori had not taken formal part; the major contestants continued to profess their association with the Hideyoshi legacy. In the years that followed, Tokugawa Ieyasu's drastic rearrangement of domains to reward his vassals and weaken possible opponents, and his elevation to the office of shogun in 1603 (transferred to his son Hidetada in 1605) signaled early assumption of full hegemony for the Tokugawa.

The presence of Hideyoshi's heir Hideyori, with his mother Yodogimi, in the virtually impregnable castle of Osaka made for a possibly dangerous secondary power center. Hideyori held lands rated at 650,000 *koku* and had court rank second only to Ieyasu's, and the numerous lords and temples indebted to his father could be expected to favor his cause. In 1614 Ieyasu manufactured an alleged insult on which he challenged the Osaka leaders. Yodogimi called on major daimyo for help, but none responded. Displaced lords and their vassals recently victimized by the post-Sekigahara settlement did rally to the Osaka cause, however, and in the "winter campaign" several hundred thousand men were involved. After inconclusive fighting a truce was arranged whereby the Osaka defenders agreed to remove their outer defences. Ieyasu's vassals charged with filling in the outer moats went on to deal with the secondary defenses also, and when Hideyori refused Ieyasu's demand that he accept a new domain elsewhere and give up the Osaka castle, fighting resumed in the "summer campaign." This ended with the death of Hideyori and his mother Yodogimi in the flames of Osaka castle.

Although the Shimabara revolt of 1637 extended local Tokugawa vassals several decades later, the Osaka victory secured the Tokugawa hegemony for the centuries that followed. The massive redistribution of lands carried out by the early Tokugawa shoguns, however, continued to produce discontented warriors and contributed to volatile conditions that required careful monitoring by Edo authorities for some time.

[*See also* Sekigahara, Battle of; Tokugawa Ieyasu; *and* Tokugawa Period.]

A. L. Sadler, *The Maker of Modern Japan: The Life of Tokugawa Ieyasu* (1937).   MARIUS B. JANSEN

OSMEÑA, SERGIO (1878–1961), leading political leader of the Philippines before the Pacific War. An illegitimate child from the disinherited side of one of the wealthiest and most prominent Chinese *mestizo* (mixed Chinese-Filipino) families of Cebu City, Osmeña's early rise to political prominence was based on his intelligence and educational attainments. Through considerable nonfamily sponsorship, he completed his secondary education at the local Seminario-Colegio de San Carlos (1892) and proceeded to the University of Santo Tomas in Manila to study law. Because of interruptions caused by the political upheavals in 1896 and 1898, he was unable to complete his law degree until 1902. Nevertheless, he returned to Cebu in 1898 as one of a small number of Manila-educated Cebuanos, earning him the status of *ilustrado*.

An ambitious youth, he achieved early recognition as an aide to one of the last Spanish governors (1897) and acquired economic security through his first marriage (1901) to the daughter of one of Cebu's wealthiest Chinese businessmen, Estefania Ch. Veloso. He avoided involvement in the 1896 rebellion, which had little impact in Cebu, and was only peripherally involved in the Filipino resistance to the Americans.

In early 1900, he emerged as the editor of Cebu's first daily newspaper, *El Nuevo Dia* (1900–1902). Propagating a moderate nationalist viewpoint, *El Nuevo Dia* gained for Osmeña the respect of the American community and a national reputation as an effective spokesman of nonmilitant *ilustrado* aspirations; his rational approach to the quest of elite nationalist and reformist objectives met with wide approval. With the establishment of peace in Cebu by early 1902, Osmeña withdrew from journalism, completed his law degree, passed the bar exam (1903), and set up a law practice in Cebu, becoming one of twelve qualified attorneys in the city at the time. By the end of 1903, Osmeña was the leading protégé of the incumbent governor of Cebu, was an active leader in several political groups among the city's educated young men, and had been elected to the municipal council with the highest vote.

His political rise was accelerated in 1904 by two fortuitous developments. He was named acting governor for three months, while the incumbent toured the United States; immediately thereafter, he was appointed provincial attorney *(fiscal)* to fill a recent vacancy in this prestigious post. These positions gave him considerable responsibility and exposure (at the age of twenty-six) and led to his being widely acknowledged as Cebu's most promising young leader. Although he was initially unsure of how to pursue his ambitions, either through bureaucratic advancement or politics, in 1906 he chose politics. He resigned his post to run for governor of Cebu, winning by a very large majority.

As governor he established ties with several of the leading American authorities of the day (especially with William Cameron Forbes) and reestablished his relationship with his former classmate, Manuel Quezon, then the governor of Tayabas. Osmeña was one of the first Filipinos to realize the importance of the Philippine Assembly in the political developments of his time, and he began early to prepare for his role in this legislative body. During the next year and a half (1906–1907), he consolidated his political base in Cebu, participated actively in the formation of the Nacionalista Party in Manila, and strengthened his personal and political ties with Filipino colleagues and American colonial authorities. He easily won his seat in the Assembly from Cebu's second district, including Cebu City. After three months of additional campaigning, he and Quezon captured the leadership in the Assembly; Osmeña was chosen speaker by a unanimous vote, making him the highest-ranking Filipino official.

Using the Assembly as their institutional base, the two young politicians succeeded in bringing the factionalized Nacionalista Party into existence, transforming it from a Manila-based opposition group to a truly national coalition. For the next fifteen years, Osmeña ran both the Assembly, as speaker, and the Nacionalista Party, as president. He was reelected as the assemblyman or representative from Cebu's second district four times (1909, 1912, 1916, and 1919), the last three times unopposed. During this period, Osmeña maintained a firm grip on Cebu politics, carefully selecting his local political representatives.

In 1918 his first wife died, leaving him ten children. In 1920, he remarried, this time to the daughter of a wealthy and prominent Chinese Filipino family of Manila, Esperanza Limjap, with whom he had four more children. It was also during this time that Osmeña expanded his economic holdings in Cebu, acquiring, among other things, a large portion of the Osmeña family landholdings in the city and province. In 1916, with the establishment of the Philippine Senate, the competition between Osmeña and Quezon for political leadership intensified. Quezon entered the Senate and controlled it as president. In 1921–1922, Quezon challenged Osmeña's leadership of the party. In an effort to meet Quezon head on and to avoid a major political challenge to his leadership in Cebu's second district, Osmeña decided to run for the Senate. He easily won his seat but lost his struggle with Quezon; Osmeña became president pro tempore under Quezon, who also took over the leadership of the party.

Although his control over Cebu politics was less pervasive in the 1920s and 1930s, Osmeña had no difficulty winning reelections to the Senate (in 1928 and 1934). In 1931 he was sent to the United States at the head of a mission with Manuel Roxas, speaker of the House, and others to negotiate an independence bill with the US Congress. In 1933, operating under politically favorable conditions, they succeeded in obtaining the passage of the Hare-Hawes-Cutting Act. Quezon, for various reasons (mostly political), opposed the act, had the Philippine legislature reject it, and once again split the Nacionalista Party in a show of force against the perceived political challenge of Osmeña. Returning to the United States, Quezon was able to obtain the Tydings-McDuffie Act, only slightly different than the previous act. In the 1934 election, Quezon once again triumphed, setting the stage for his election as president of the Philippine Commonwealth (1935–1946).

In the 1935 commonwealth elections, Osmeña chose not to contest Quezon and ran and easily won the vice-presidency. Both were reelected in 1941, on the eve of the Japanese invasion of the Philippines. As a last-minute decision, Osmeña was evacuated together with Quezon and General Douglas MacArthur in early 1942; Osmeña was forced to leave behind his wife and family. After Quezon's death in August 1944, Osmeña was inaugurated as commonwealth president in Washington, D.C. In October 1944 President Osmeña waded ashore with General MacArthur at Leyte, as the beginning of the major offensive to drive the Japanese forces from the islands.

For the next year and a half, the aging prewar politician attempted to regroup his political coalition and family, run the government in the midst of war, chaos, and destruction, and prepare for Philippine independence, to be granted on 4 July 1946. Saddened by personal tragedies (the death of two sons, accusations of collaboration against two others, and the destruction of his home and personal files) and uncomfortable about the political role he was forced to play, he was unwilling to campaign for the presidency of the nascent republic. His opponent, Manuel Roxas, established the Liberal Party and campaigned vigorously around the country. In April 1946 Osmeña lost an election for the first time in his long career. Afterward, he congratulated his opponent, called for unity among all political parties and factions, attended the independence ceremony, and then retired permanently to private life in Cebu City. He died quietly in a Manila hospital on 19 October 1961, while his son, Sergio Osmeña, Jr., then a congressman from Cebu, was campaigning as an independent candidate for the vice presidency.

[See also Philippines; Ilustrado; Cebu; Forbes, William Cameron; Quezon, Manuel Luis; Nacionalista Party; Roxas, Manuel; Tydings-McDuffie Act; and Philippines, Commonwealth of.]

Vincente Albano Pacis, *President Sergio Osmena: A Fully-Documented Biography*, 2 vols. (1971). Theodore Friend, *Between Two Empires: The Ordeal of the Philippines, 1929–1946* (1965). Carlos Quirino, *Quezon: Paladin of Philippine Freedom* (1971).

MICHAEL CULLINANE

OSSO, a form of popular protest, usually against economic conditions, misrule, or excessive fiscal burden, in Tokugawa Japan. *Osso* were complaints directed to levels of government (including the shogunate) beyond those directly above the people involved owing to popular perceptions of nonresponsiveness of immediately superior officials—hence the name, meaning "bypass" petition. Given the strict adherence to hierarchical process and status in Tokugawa Japan, such petitions were a direct affront to the system and (although the substantive plea was often responded to) were therefore punished severely, with execution common. Petitioners were most often village representatives although in the later Edo era petitions by common peasants themselves increased. *Osso* had several variants, including *kagoso* (submitting a petition to an official in his palanquin), *hariso* (a posted petition), *suteso* (an appeal scattered about the streets), and *kadoso* (demonstration before a high official's gate).

[See also Ikki.]

JAMES W. WHITE

ŌSUGI SAKAE (1885–1923), Japanese anarchist. The son of a low ranking army officer, Ōsugi was born in Marugame on the island of Shikoku but shortly afterward moved to Shibata in Niigata Prefecture. In 1899 he entered the Nagoya Cadet School, from which he was expelled in 1901. Turning his back on a military career, he studied French at the Tokyo School for Foreign Languages and graduated in 1905. During this period he became involved with the Heiminsha and became a socialist. In the years after 1906 he was involved in numerous left-wing confrontations with the police, was arrested on five occasions, and spent more than three years in jail. Introduced to anarchism by Kōtoku Shūsui, his years of study and incarceration confirmed these beliefs, and in the decade following

Kōtoku's death he remained among a small minority of left-wing activists and labor organizers who, despite government repression, persisted in pursuing the anarchist-syndicalist vision of reform. A prolific writer, polemicist, and organizer, he played a central role in the debates between anarchists and Bolsheviks that flared after the Russian Revolution. In 1920 he traveled to Shanghai and Paris. In 1923, in the wake of the Kantō earthquake, he was murdered by a military policeman while in custody. [See also Kōtoku Shūsui.]   F. G. NOTEHELFER

ŌTSUKI GENTAKU (1757–1827), Japanese scholar, physician, and educator who expanded the field of Dutch (European) studies *(rangaku)* in late eighteenth-century Japan by his manifold activities. The son of a physician from Ichinoseki *han* (now part of Iwate Prefecture), Ōtsuki Gentaku began his Dutch studies in Edo in 1778 with the pioneers of Western medical research in Japan, Sugita Gempaku (1733–1817) and Maeno Ryōtaku (1723–1803). Following a year of language study in Nagasaki, he returned to Edo in 1786 as a physician in the service of Sendai *han*.

Gentaku wrote and translated on a variety of subjects, from language studies to Western culture and natural science, thus considerably widening the scope of *rangaku* beyond its initial concern with Western medicine. His most popular book, *Rangaku kaitei* (published in 1788), explained Japanese scholarship on the Dutch language in terms nonspecialists could understand. In all of his work he argued forcefully for the importance of Western learning and protested against the intellectual domination of Confucianism. Gentaku's enthusiasm for Western ways extended to promoting New Year's Eve parties complete with European-style tables, chairs, knives, forks, and Dutch costumes.

However, Gentaku may have made his most significant contributions as an educator. In 1789 he opened the first *rangaku* academy in Japan, Shirandō, and provided students from throughout the country with access to the best *rangaku* scholarship, presented in a more systematic fashion than previously. Although the number of students was small, many returned home to pioneer *rangaku* in their local areas. In addition, Gentaku's language skills and broad interests led students into new areas of research, such as electricity, internal medicine, and pharmacology.

In 1811, in what subsequently became a pattern of official recognition for leading *rangaku* scholars,

Ōtsuki was made director of the *bakufu*'s newly established office for translation of Western books. [*See also* Rangaku.]

Donald Keene, *The Japanese Discovery of Europe, 1720–1830* (1969). Richard Rubinger, *Private Academies of Tokugawa Japan* (1982).   RICHARD RUBINGER

OTTAMA (d. 1939), Burmese Buddhist monk and nationalist leader. U Ottama returned to Burma in 1918 after traveling to India, Egypt, France, and Japan and then joined in the activities of the Young Men's Buddhist Association and the General Council of Burmese Associations (GCBA). Initially spurned by most established monks for his argument that until Burma was free of British rule Buddhists would be unable to attain their religious goals, he was nonetheless important in mobilizing younger monks to participate in the nationalist movement. U Ottama was also connected with the Indian National Congress. For his advocacy of GCBA boycott campaigns and for allegedly proposing the use of violence, he was repeatedly arrested by the British government.

[*See also* Young Men's Buddhist Association; General Council of Burmese Associations; *and* Indian National Congress.]

Donald Eugene Smith, *Religion and Politics in Burma* (1965).   ROBERT H. TAYLOR

OUDH. *See* Awadh.

OUDONG, capital of Cambodia from 1602, following the abandonment of Lovek, until 1811, and again between 1848 and 1866. Frequently abandoned in the turmoil of the eighteenth century, Oudong was restored by King Ang Eng (r. 1794–1797). When the Vietnamese came to control the Cambodian court in 1811, the capital shifted to Phnom Penh, returning to Oudong under Ang Duang (r. 1848–1860), a protégé of the Thai. Duang's son, Norodom (r. 1860–1904), moved the capital to Phnom Penh again, at the request of French authorities. In the 1970s, the temples and monuments of Oudong were heavily damaged in fighting between Cambodian Communist and republican troops.   DAVID P. CHANDLER

OUYANG XIU (1007–1072), leading Northern Song literatus. Ouyang's early career was closely tied to that of the reformer Fan Zhongyan (989–1052).

He was demoted between 1035 and 1038 for his defense of Fan, brought to court with Fan in 1043, and demoted once again in 1045 after Fan's fall. He returned to the capital in 1054 to hold a series of influential positions, including that of assistant chief minister, until being forced out in 1067.

Ouyang was the most influential scholar and literary stylist of his time. He coedited the *New Tang History* and privately wrote an account of the Five Dynasties that was officially adopted as the *New History of the Five Dynasties*. He was largely responsible for establishing the preeminence of the "ancient style" in literature through his own writings and service as director of the 1057 examinations. He promoted the trend of dispensing with the study of traditional commentaries on the classics in favor of seeking larger meanings and universal principles. Ouyang's prose and poetry helped create a new and typically literati style of literature, one in which the individual, creative expression of meanings and attitudes was valued above literary complexity. His claim that Song literati could gain a new and better understanding of the enduring values of the cultural tradition than their predecessors and his belief that literati were responsible for defining the common interest profoundly influenced the further development of literati thought and culture.

[*See also* Fan Zhongyan; Neo-Confucianism; *and* Song Dynasty.]

Ronald C. Eagan, *The Literary Works of Ou-yang Hsiu (1007–1072)* (1984). James T. C. Liu, *Ou-yang Hsiu, an Eleventh Century Neo-Confucianist* (1967).

PETER K. BOL

OVERSEAS CHINESE. Counting all persons of Chinese background, there were more than 20,000,000 "Overseas Chinese," or "Chinese" people living outside of China, in 1984. This figure excludes Chinese in Hong Kong and Macao, who have a different relationship to China. More than half reside in Southeast Asia; the remainder are found in the United States, Canada, Latin America (chiefly Peru and Brazil), Australia, New Zealand, Japan, South Africa, and Western Europe (especially England, France, and the Netherlands). Singapore and Malaysia are exceptional: 75 percent and 35 percent of their respective populations are Chinese. Elsewhere, ethnic Chinese make up no more than 10 percent of the population of any other Southeast Asian country; outside of Southeast Asia, they are usually less than 1 percent of any country's population. For example, at most 1.5 percent of the Ca-

nadian population is of Chinese origin; perhaps .5 percent of the American population; and perhaps one of every five thousand persons in the Japanese population.

Periods of Migration. Overseas Chinese is an appropriate term in the sense that most of this migration has been over bodies of water, although there has always been some overland migration to mainland Southeast Asia from the Chinese provinces of Guangxi and Yunnan. Continuous overseas migration and settlement in significant numbers began in the sixteenth century. The important periods are: (1) 1550–1850; (2) 1850–1900; (3) 1900–1950; and (4) since 1950. In the first period, migration was closely associated with maritime trade, and hence went to Japan, Vietnam, Cambodia, Thailand, Malaya-Singapore, Indonesia, and the Philippines. The earliest Chinese migrants were speakers of the Hokkien dialect from the counties around the Fujian trading ports of Quanzhou and Zhangzhou. Some were big merchants engaged in long-distance trade; others were laborers or clerks. Changes in trade patterns and in the relative importance of local merchant groups in China encouraged changes in migration. Teochiu-speakers from the Chaozhou region of Guangdong and Cantonese from a dozen counties near Canton also began to settle in Southeast Asia. Although the earlier arrivals, the Hokkiens, maintained their monopoly over major forms of Chinese long-distance commerce in many parts of Southeast Asia, the Teochius, in particular, were able to achieve similar positions in places like Cholon (in southern Vietnam) and Bangkok, where they dominated the rice trade. Like the Hokkiens and Teochius, the Cantonese engaged in a wide variety of commercial and light industrial occupations. By the eighteenth century Hakkas from Guangdong had joined the others, farming in West Borneo and mining in various parts of Southeast Asia. In Japan, the Nagasaki trade attracted merchant settlers from the lower Yangtze region as well as Fujian and Guangdong. Meanwhile, small numbers of Chinese found their way to Mexico and Peru via the Manila Galleon.

The second Chinese diaspora (1850–1900) included new forms of migration, new destinations, and an additional set of migrants. Rapid steamship service developed, encouraging the use of "credit ticket" systems of financing and "chain migration." The volume of migration expanded greatly and the "chain migration" of fathers, sons, and nephews produced portions of families overseas. The infamous "coolie trade" transported Chinese laborers under horrible conditions to where they were in demand—principally Cuba, Peru, and parts of Southeast Asia. Gold discoveries and railroad building led to migration—especially by Cantonese and Hakkas—to the United States, Canada, Australia, New Zealand, Mexico, and Peru. The opening of new international trading ports in Japan brought more Chinese settlers there. Hainanese, the last major Overseas Chinese subethnic group, now joined the others in Southeast Asia. Like the Hakkas, they found a place in occupations left open by the earlier arrivals.

In the third period (1900–1950) most Western Hemisphere countries and Australia and New Zealand cut off or restricted Chinese immigration. Migration now increased to those Southeast Asian countries still open and extended to South Africa and Europe. Taiwanese from Japan's new colony became the major component of Japan's Chinese population. The fourth period (since 1950) has been marked particularly by new types of migrants. Besides merchants and laborers, there are now also highly educated, cosmopolitan professionals with language skills and wealth. There is also much more movement from one overseas site to another and hence many more "second country" Overseas Chinese. Family migration also characterizes this period—a further development of the practice of wives joining husbands overseas that began in the 1900 to 1950 era.

Motivations. Historically, the motives for migration have been both those of "pull" and "push." Economic opportunity abroad has been the major "pull"; since 1900 educational opportunity has also been important. "Push" factors have included population pressure on resources in China, which has consistently been important, and political refuge, which has occasionally been of great importance. Especially before 1950, Chinese were often sojourners abroad, partially supporting family in China with remittances and intending to return there in retirement. Often, however, they were pioneers, intending to have their families with them when possible. Given the opportunity, they would commit themselves completely to their country of overseas residence.

Occupations. Although Overseas Chinese have engaged in mining, farming, artisanry, domestic service, and various kinds of labor, they have gravitated toward commerce when able to do so. They have thus tended to concentrate in the cities, in anything from small shops to large commercial operations and, eventually, in manufacturing and industrial enterprises and professional work. But a characteristic "frontier" form of Chinese enterprise overseas has been the small-town general store, whether in Southeast Asia or in parts of North America, supplying commercial, banking, and other services to a local clientele, while frequently buying up and forwarding local products as well.

Reception Overseas. Hostility toward Overseas Chinese has appeared in many countries. The reasons have been economic, cultural, and political. Resentment of Chinese success and fear of Chinese competition are two economic reasons. Cultural remoteness, and sometimes cultural aversion, have complicated the issue. Politicians have found a politically weak and culturally unpopular Chinese minority useful as a scapegoat. Like other vulnerable minorities, Overseas Chinese are most in peril during times of economic depression, when economic competition, cultural aversion, and political opportunism interact most strongly against them. This has been most pronounced in Southeast Asia, where Chinese have been preeminent in certain economic fields. Anti-Chinese episodes have ranged from the massacres in the Spanish Philippines and Dutch Indonesia during the seventeenth and eighteenth centuries, to isolated anti-Chinese incidents. Between these extremes there has been systematic exclusion of Chinese immigration and expulsion of large numbers of already resident Chinese. Long-term forms of discrimination have been a feature of many host societies. Nor are such measures all in the distant past. Major anti-Chinese policies have been a characteristic of several Southeast Asian societies since 1950. Expulsions and bloody incidents marked Indonesian Chinese history in the 1960s and Vietnamese Chinese history in the late 1970s. In Malaysia, ethnic confrontations involving the Chinese reached a peak in 1969.

Adaptation. Chinese adaptation to their host societies has varied with the situation there and the claims of China in each case. At one extreme were the Chinese *mestizos* of the Philippines and the Chinese Thai of pre-twentieth-century Thailand. Descendants of early Chinese immigrant fathers and indigenous mothers, individuals in this group were readily assimilated into Philippine and Thai societies. A second group of similar parentage, the *peranakans* of Java and the *babas* of Malaya, created unique forms of Sino-Malay culture that lasted for several generations. At the other extreme were Chinese who arrived abroad after large Chinese communities had been built up. Particularly after 1900, Chinese nationalism claimed their attention at the same time as local nationalisms and nativisms were rejecting Chinese efforts to be part of local societies. Since 1950 it has become difficult for Overseas Chinese to be deeply involved in China's affairs and more families have been reunited overseas; in fact, the majority of Overseas Chinese in recent years have been born outside of China.

Since 1950 Overseas Chinese and others have debated the appropriateness of assimilation (in which Chinese attributes would disappear), or integration (in which some kind of "Chineseness" would remain) as possibilities of adaptation to host environments. The larger cultural questions raised by such debates are made more complex than before by changing and contradictory definitions of Chinese culture emanating from the People's Republic of China (PRC), Taiwan, and the Overseas Chinese societies themselves. From the perspective of host society governments, the issues of Overseas Chinese assimilation and integration have centered on economic and cultural nationalization and citizenship policies. Since the 1950s Indonesia, the Philippines, and various Vietnamese governments have tried to remove the Chinese from retail trade. In many host countries Chinese schools have been forced either to accept nationalizing-content restrictions or to close. Overseas Chinese citizenship, as a problem, goes back to 1909, when China's citizenship law claimed all persons born of Chinese fathers overseas as Chinese, whatever other citizenship they might claim. Since 1950 the PRC has signed treaties of citizenship clarification with some Southeast Asian states and since 1957 has stated its intention that Overseas Chinese unambiguously become, when free to do so and if they so desire, citizens of their host countries. Subsequent ambiguities in policies emanating from Beijing and Taiwan's continued adherence to the principles of 1909 have maintained the complexity of the problem.

Organizations. Chinese communities abroad have sustained themselves in large part through organizations that have drawn consistently on models in China and have been adapted to local situations. The following are the most important types of Overseas Chinese organizations.

1. The joint-stock mining or farming community. These groups, called *gongsi*, were most often found in certain parts of Malaysia.
2. The single community headman, or *kapitan*. Found in Japan, the Philippines, Java, and Malaya from the seventeenth to the early twentieth century, the headman was often the leader of a group

of officers, chosen by the Chinese themselves, by officials of the host society, or by both. He frequently enjoyed certain monopoly tax and local economic development rights as well.
3. Secret societies. Offshoots of the Hong Men in southeast China, these societies were often organized by subethnic group (Hokkiens, Teochius, Hakkas, etc.) and usually competed for control of economic resources. They were most prominent in nineteenth-century Southeast Asia and in the United States in the nineteenth and early twentieth centuries.
4. District associations. The district associations united Chinese of the same county or other small district in China into *huiguan*, which provided mutual benefits and sought control over economic resources. These were found almost everywhere.
5. Clan associations. Linking persons of a common surname, the clan association's functions were comparable to those of the district associations and were especially prevalent in Malaya, Singapore, the Philippines, and North America.
6. "Umbrella organizations." Of federative type, these groups, such as Chinese benevolent associations and chambers of commerce, attempted to speak for the community as a whole while mediating its internal disputes. They were found almost everywhere.
7. Fraternal-political organizations. The political groups possessed a widely recruited membership, and were not only concerned with politics in China until 1950, but also served as focal points of local Chinatown politics. Prime examples are the political parties derived from the Guomindang (Kuomintang) and Hong Men, such as the Zhigongtang.

There have also been organizations of local reference, ranging from the *peranakan* political parties of 1950s Indonesia to various trade and athletic associations and Chinese versions of such North American organizations as the Lions Club. [*See also* Gongsi; Kapitan China; *and* Secret Societies.]

Relations with China. Private economic relations between Overseas Chinese and China have been continuous since the sixteenth century. Political relationships, on the other hand, have gone from almost nonexistence (before 1850), to growing affiliation (1850–1900), to intense interaction (1900–1950), to a distant and ambiguous contact (post-1950). Before 1850 Chinese central governments had little to do with Overseas Chinese. They did not protect their lives or properties, regarded them as politically suspect for leaving China, and sometimes prohibited overseas trade and migration. Policy changed after 1850. Overseas Chinese remittances to relatives in Guangdong and Fujian came to be seen as valuable to the economies of those provinces, and Overseas Chinese investments of money and skills as helpful to the modest modernization program China was then attempting. Chinese embassies and consulates were established overseas, in part to protect Overseas Chinese lives and properties, and Chinese diplomacy negotiated the end of the shocking coolie trade.

In the 1900 to 1950 period China's politics came to the Chinatowns of the world. Chinese abroad were caught up in China's new nationalism and radical attempts at modernization. Reformers, revolutionaries, and conservatives wooed the Overseas Chinese with offers of titles and government positions, and China claimed them as its citizens. Chambers of commerce were formed in overseas cities, as in China, in part to link the government in China with Overseas Chinese leadership. Overseas Chinese supplied Sun Yat-sen and others with much of the funding that made the 1911 Revolution possible. Not all Overseas Chinese supported that movement, however, and China's politics continued to divide Chinatowns around the world. The very term "Overseas Chinese," with its strong implication of ties to China, came into being in this period as a verbal claim of Chinese governments to the loyalty and support of persons of Chinese descent outside of China. Their support, when given, was not necessarily political. Many contributed primarily in support of modernization in their home districts (funds for railroads or modern schools) or invested in the development of overseas "home base" area cities like Amoy (Xiamen), Swatow (Shantou), and Canton (Guangzhou). Japanese encroachments on China's sovereignty and, ultimately, the Pacific War of 1937 to 1945 brought strong financial support from overseas for China's resistance. Southeast Asian Chinese support was outstanding until Japanese conquests after 1941 made it almost impossible to continue. Thereafter, North American Chinese carried the greatest burden.

1950 marks a cutoff date in the political and other relations of Overseas Chinese with China. The land reform in the PRC affected many Overseas Chinese families and clearly changed expectations for all. Subsequent special programs for Overseas Chinese and, especially, their dependents in China were suspended during the Cultural Revolution and only restored in 1978. Meanwhile, Taiwan, although it had

its economic and political supporters, was not an easy substitute as a home district. The reopening of investment, technical aid, and other oppporunities for Overseas Chinese in the PRC after 1978 raised both new opportunities and old problems.

[See also Coolie Trade and Emigration: Chinese Emigration.]

Maurice Freedman, The Study of Chinese Society: Essays by Maurice Freedman, edited by G. William Skinner (1979). Stephen Fitzgerald, China and the Overseas Chinese (1972). Mary F. Somers Heidhues, Southeast Asia's Chinese Minorities (1974). Victor Purcell, The Chinese in Southeast Asia (2d ed., 1965). G. William Skinner, Chinese Society in Thailand: An Analytical History (1957). Wang Gungwu, Community and Nation: Essays on Southeast Asia and the Chinese (1981). E. Wickberg, H. Con, R. Con, G. Johnson, and W. E. Willmott, From China to Canada: A History of the Chinese Communities in Canada (1982). Yen Ching-hwang, The Overseas Chinese and the 1911 Revolution (1972).

EDGAR WICKBERG

OXUS RIVER. Oxus is the ancient Greek name for the Amu Darya, the largest river of Soviet Central Asia. Originating in the Hindu Kush and Pamir mountain ranges, the river extends 1,578 miles to the Aral Sea. Two-thirds of the flow is concentrated in the period from May to August, the result of melting from the glaciers and perennial snow fields of the high mountains. The Oxus forms part of the boundary between Afghanistan and the USSR and divides the deserts of the Kara Kum and Kizil Kum in the Turan Lowland.   MICHAEL BONINE

ŌYAMA IWAO (1842–1916), Japanese field marshal, prince, and genrō (elder statesman) of the Meiji period (1868–1912). Born to a samurai family in Satsuma (now Kagoshima Prefecture), Ōyama gained military distinction during the Meiji Restoration (1868). He studied military science in France, served several times as army chief of staff, and was army minister in four different cabinets between 1880 and 1892. He gained fame as a field commander during the Sino-Japanese War (1894–1895) and as field marshal and commander in chief of the victorious Japanese forces in Manchuria during the Russo-Japanese War (1904–1905). He retired from active service in 1907, when he was rewarded with the title of prince, but he continued his respected advisory service to the emperor as an elder statesman. In 1914 he became lord keeper of the privy seal, a court office close to the throne, and died in that post in 1916.   ROGER F. HACKETT

OZAKI YUKIO (1859–1954), modern Japanese politician. Elected to Japan's first parliament in 1890, Ozaki subsequently served twenty-four consecutive terms, until his retirement from political office in 1953. He has been justly labeled the "political conscience of modern Japan" and "protector of constitutional government."

Ozaki's political career began in 1882, when he joined the Progressive Party, organized by Ōkuma Shigenobu. In 1887 he was banished from Tokyo for three years for speaking out against the Meiji government. He took this opportunity to visit Europe, where he fell under the spell of the British liberal spirit. After returning to Japan he made a successful bid to serve as representative for Mie Prefecture in Japan's first elected parliament. While serving as education minister in the coalition cabinet of Ōkuma Shigenobu and Itagaki Taisuke, Japan's first party cabinet, he made a speech that contained an allusion to republicanism. This brought such con-

demnation for his supposed disrespect for the position of the emperor that the cabinet was forced to resign. A similar incident in 1942, during which he brought his criticism against the cabinet of Tōjō Hideki for its disregard of constitutional procedures, brought him a criminal conviction for lese majesty, although this conviction was later overturned by a higher court.

Throughout his lifetime, Ozaki spoke as a voice for the democratic spirit in Japan. He was often critical of the Japanese people for their failure to understand that spirit, but his faith in constitutional government never wavered. He was not a particularly "successful" politician, with little more to his credit than the mayorship of Tokyo from 1903 to 1912 and a limited number of cabinet posts, but there have been few men who have exerted such influence on the political conscience of Japan for such a long period of time. It was during Ozaki's tenure as mayor of Tokyo that the cherry trees were presented to Washington, D.C.

Douglas H. Mendel, "Ozaki Yukio: Political Conscience of Modern Japan," *Far Eastern Quarterly* 15 (May 1956): 343–356.   THOMAS R. SCHALOW

P

PADAHLIN. Burma's equivalent of the Lascaux caves, Padahlin, a Neolithic site of two caves, is located one thousand feet above sea level on a spur of the Nwalabo Range, just west of the Shan Plateau in the Taunggyi District. It seems to be part of the Hoabinhian, the broad Southeast Asian prehistoric culture. Excavations of one of the caves revealed more than sixteen hundred stone tools, most of them unfinished, suggesting the presence of a toolmaking workshop. Among the tools are probable hammerstones, anvils, hand axes, adzes, ring stones, and whetstones, specimens of which reveal a transitional technique between flaking-chipping and grinding-polishing. The cave's most significant find appears to be red-ocher drawings of palm prints, the sun, a bison, a boar and perhaps an elephant, cattle, and a fish skeleton. Results of faunal identification and soil analysis are still pending, but radiocarbon tests of charcoal suggest a terminal date of about 6,500 before the present, while bone-collagen tests show 11,250 and 13,400 years before the present. Both Burma's Paleolithic and Neolithic cultures derive their influence from the east (China, Thailand, and the rest of Southeast Asia) rather than the west (India and the Middle East).

U Aung Thaw, "The 'Neolithic' Culture of the Padahlin Caves," *Asian Perspectives* 14 (1971): 123–133.

MICHAEL AUNG-THWIN

PADANG, capital of the province of West Sumatra, Indonesia. Padang (population approximately 240,000) was a fishing and salt-making village until the Acehnese came to dominate it in the early seventeenth century as one of their west-coast pepper entrepôts. It was taken over by the Dutch East India Company (VOC) in 1664, and the Dutch made it the center for exporting gold and pepper from the region. The British captured the town in 1793 and garrisoned it, returning it to the Dutch in 1819. Padang prospered in the late nineteenth century as an export center for coffee from the highlands. A new railway line connected it with the interior, and a new port (Emmahaven, now Teluk Bayur) was constructed six miles south of the town to ship coal from the Umbilin coalfields. Padang is the main exit port for cement from Indarung and for West Sumatra's other major exports of rubber, copra, cloves, coffee, cinnamon, and rattan.

AUDREY R. KAHIN

PADRI WAR. Starting in the highlands of West Sumatra in the early nineteenth century, the Padri (Paderi) War was initially an Islamic revivalist movement, inspired and led by followers of the Arab Wahhabis, that developed into a civil war encompassing much of the upland interior of Sumatra. Padri attempts to impose their ideas by force throughout the region provided the Dutch with a pretext for intervening in Sumatra beyond their footholds on the coast; they responded to requests from local aristocracy for help in combating the religious armies of the Padri. War raged between Dutch and Padri forces from 1819 to 1825 and again from 1831 to 1837, when the Dutch succeeded in capturing and exiling the last great Padri leader, Tunku Imam Bondjol, and were then able to impose their own administration throughout central Sumatra.

[*See also* Imam Bondjol.]

Christine Dobbin, *Islamic Revivalism in a Changing Peasant Economy* (1983). Muhamad Radjab, *Perang Paderi* (1954).

AUDREY R. KAHIN

PAEKCHE, kingdom in southwestern Korea that, with Koguryŏ and Silla, was one of the Three Kingdoms of Korean history. According to Sino-Korean chronicles of the twelfth and thirteenth centuries, Paekche was founded in 18 BCE. However, no early Chinese source mentions the existence of the state at this time. As late as the third century the Chinese history *Sanguozhi* shows, in the course of an exceptionally detailed account of Korea, that the whole of the southern third of the peninsula was at that time divided up among the Korean Han tribes. These tribes, agriculturalists who had inhabited the area for several centuries, comprised three major divisions that were, however, geographical rather than political: Mahan in the southwest, Chinhan in the southeast, and Pyŏnhan or Pyŏnchin between them. It is clear that there was no overall state structure within any of these divisions; because of the mountainous terrain the farming communities of the valleys enjoyed a natural self-sufficiency and mutual independence. Mahan itself contained more than fifty of these autonomous units, and although one of these was indeed called Poqi, the Chinese equivalent of Paekche, the *Sanguozhi* does not distinguish it from the rest in any way. Clearly at this time there was nothing that could be termed a kingdom of Paekche.

By the end of the third century the situation was beginning to change, and Chinese historians of that period refer to a "lord of Mahan." Modern scholars have conjectured that this "lord" may simply have been one of the Han chieftains who was used by the Chinese administrators of the Lelang and Daifang commanderies as an intermediary in their dealings with the tribes. Since the authority of such a figure must have depended very largely on his relations with the suzerain power, when Chinese rule in Korea (and in North China) collapsed early in the fourth century, the position of the lord of Mahan must have been threatened.

At this point a new element entered the picture. All sources treating the kingdom of Paekche agree that its ruling house was derived from the Manchurian kingdom of Puyŏ. Puyŏ itself is known from contemporary Chinese records to have been devastated by an invasion in 285, whereupon certain members of the royal family fled to northeastern Korea and there gained control over the Okchŏ tribes, establishing a state called Eastern Puyŏ. In their account of the founding of Paekche, the Sino-Korean chronicles of the twelfth and thirteenth centuries describe how certain Puyŏ princes arrived in southern Korea, where they were given lands by the king of Mahan. Eventually the realm founded by the Puyŏ princes Piryu and Onjo is said to have grown strong enough to annex the rest of Mahan;

this was the beginning of the state of Paekche. This story makes little sense in the context of the first century BCE, in which, as already seen, it is placed by the chronicles. It is, however, much more plausible as a recollection of events in the early fourth century CE, when the lord of Mahan may well have welcomed Puyŏ princes moving south from eastern Puyŏ in an attempt to bolster up his fading authority. [*See also* Puyŏ *and* Three Hans.]

After its establishment Paekche rapidly absorbed not only the other Mahan communities but also the settlements of the old Chinese commandery of Daifang, now isolated from China proper. The fact that Paekche later emerged as the most sinicized of all the Korean states suggests that the new kingdom may have inherited many of the former Chinese ruling elite of Daifang. Indeed, the pace of sinicization in Paekche is indicated by the fact that already by the middle of the fourth century the Paekche court was keeping records, presumably in Chinese, and by the beginning of the succeeding century Paekche scholars were introducing the Chinese classics into Japan.

The rise of Paekche coincided with the southward advance of the kingdom of Koguryŏ into the former Chinese commandery of Lelang. Paekche and Koguryŏ thus entered into competition to absorb the remains of the old Chinese colonies, and around 371 King Soe of Koguryŏ fell defending P'yŏngyang, the former headquarters of Lelang, against a Paekche attack. After this, however, Paekche, which was much the smaller of the two states, rapidly lost ground to Koguryŏ. Searching for allies, the rulers of Paekche renewed contacts with the Chinese court, now in exile south of the Yangtze River; more practical help was afforded by an alliance with the Japanese Yamato kingdom. As is recorded in the stele inscription at the tomb of King Kwanggaet'o of Koguryŏ (r. 391–413), Yamato despatched troops into Korea to fight against Koguryŏ late in the fourth century.

The Paekche connection with Yamato was to have considerable importance in the cultural history of East Asia. It was from Paekche, called Kudara by the Japanese, that, as already seen, Chinese writing and the Chinese classics were introduced into Japan at the beginning of the fifth century; it was also from Paekche that the Buddhist religion was introduced into Japan in 552. Buddhism had reached Koguryŏ from North China in 372, but was separately introduced into Paekche in 384 by a group of monks from southern China, one of whom, Malananda, is said to have come from Central Asia. Buddhism rapidly became more influential in Paekche than in Koguryŏ: it was enthusiastically supported by the royal house, one ephemeral king at the end of the sixth century even going so far as to order the release of all hunting falcons and the destruction of all hunting and fishing gear. Several Buddhist statues ascribed to Paekche craftsman still survive, the most famous being the so-called Kudara Kannon (i.e., the Avalokiteshvara from Paekche), which is kept at the Hōryūji in Nara. The stylized elongation of this standing figure creates a sense of otherworldliness, characteristic of Paekche art, a style copied in Silla and Japan. [*See also* Buddhism: Buddhism in Korea.]

Another cultural export from Paekche to Japan may well have been the beginnings of Japanese historical writing. When the first Japanese histories, the *Kojiki* and the *Nihongi*, were written early in the eighth century, they were modeled not on the elaborate composite histories then in vogue in China, but on a simpler annalistic form. This form seems to have been developed in Paekche during the fourth, fifth, and sixth centuries, to judge from the few fragments of Paekche chronicles that survive in the form of quotations embedded in the *Nihongi*.

In spite of this high level of cultural activity, the political history of Paekche was dismal. Beginning in the fifth century it retreated in the face of pressure by Koguryŏ, moving its capital south from Hansŏng to Ungjin in 474, and from Ungjin to Sabi (the modern Puyŏ) in 538. Meanwhile, in a further effort to stave off the southward advance of Koguryŏ, Paekche allied itself with the rival state of Silla in southeastern Korea. This alliance came to an end in 552, when Silla seized the Hansŏng area that the two allies had just won back from Koguryŏ. When King Sŏng of Paekche (r. 523–554) attempted to recover the stolen territory, he was killed in battle; thereafter Paekche had to face enemies on two fronts.

The reunification of China by the Sui in 589 posed a threat to all the Korean states, since the Sui were determined to recover the lost Han empire. During the ensuing Sui wars with Koguryŏ, Paekche—still on hostile terms with both Koguryŏ and Silla—remained effectively neutral, although in theory supporting China. Soon afterward, however, the danger from Silla brought Paekche and Koguryŏ together, a combination that produced repeated appeals from Silla for Chinese assistance. Eventually these appeals led the emperors of the new Tang dynasty (618–907) to threaten Paekche that, unless peace was maintained with Silla, China would be forced to intervene. Since it was always Koguryŏ that had

borne the brunt of Chinese aggression in the past, these warnings were ignored in Paekche; in the summer of 660, however, a massive Chinese army under general Su Dingfang landed on the coast of Paekche, while Silla launched an invasion across Paekche's eastern frontier. So little preparation had been made to defend the capital against an attack from the sea that on 24 August Sabi surrendered; King Ŭija (r. 641–660) and his family were deported to China, along with all his leading officers and several thousand inhabitants of Sabi.

It was the Tang court's intention to use Paekche as a base from which to attack Koguryŏ, and at the same time to restore the long lost Chinese colonies in Korea. The territory of Paekche was divided into five governorships and some ten thousand Chinese troops were stationed there. Resistance in the provinces of Paekche, however, was far from being crushed. A relative of King Ŭija, Prince Poksin, raised a rebellion against the Chinese in company with the Buddhist priest Toch'im; he also made contact with the Yamato court and secured the intervention of a Japanese fleet. The Japanese installed as king a son of King Ŭija who was living in Yamato as a hostage, and for a time the rebels enjoyed considerable success. Eventually there was a falling out within the royal family; Prince Poksin murdered Toch'im and was himself put to death by Prince P'ung, the new ruler of Paekche. Finally the Chinese defeated the Japanese in a naval battle fought off the mouth of the Kŭm River on 4 October 663, a conflict that constitutes the first known direct clash between the two countries. The Japanese lost more than four hundred ships and withdrew from the war, the Paekche resistance movement collapsed, and Prince P'ung sought refuge in Koguryŏ.

For a few years the Tang attempted to rule Paekche through another son of King Ŭija, Prince Yung, who was made to swear a covenant of peace with the king of Silla. After the fall of Koguryŏ in 668, however, Chinese forces were required on other frontiers and the Tang government found that it could no longer afford the continuing drain on its resources entailed by the Korean campaigns. Within a few years Silla resumed its encroachment on Paekche territory. Prince Yung fled back to China, and in spite of a few halfhearted attempts at punitive action by the Chinese, by 673 virtually all the former lands of Paekche had been taken over by Silla.

Even after the Silla conquest, much of southwestern Korea tended to retain a distinctive culture. It was in this area that the warlord Chang Po-go flourished in the ninth century, while in 900 a certain

Kyŏn Hwŏn established the state of Later Paekche, which endured for thirty-six years. [*See also* Chang Po-go.] The cultural tradition of Paekche was also kept alive for a while by numerous craftsmen who migrated to Japan and there enriched the art of the Asuka period.

[*See also* Koguryŏ *and* Silla.]

Jonathan W. Best, "Diplomatic and Cultural Contacts between Paekche and China," *Harvard Journal of Asiatic Studies* 42.2 (1982): 443–501. K. H. J. Gardiner, "Some Problems Concerning the Founding of Paekche," *Archiv Orientalni* 37 (1969). W. E. Henthorn, *A History of Korea* (1971).
                                KENNETH H. J. GARDINER

PAGAN. Located in the dry plains of central Burma where the Irrawaddy River makes a sharp turn to the west, Pagan was the capital city of the first Burman state. The state rose to prominence in the mid-ninth century and continued as the center of a flourishing civilization for approximately 350 years, until it declined as a political force in the late thirteenth century. Even after the kingdom's political demise, the example set by Pagan inspired subsequent Burmese dynasties in their efforts to unify the country. Today, Pagan is the museum of Burma's classical culture, testifying not only to its political and cultural heritage but also to its religious devotion, the ultimate measure by which Burmans still define themselves.

The history of Pagan began when the power of the Pyu people, after a millennium of domination, was destroyed by the Nanzhao kingdom, located in western Yunnan. Its troops descended into the plains of the Irrawaddy River in the middle of the ninth century and sacked at least two of the Pyu political and economic centers of power, Halin and possibly Old Prome. The Burmans, thought to have been related to the Lolo-speaking peoples of Nanzhao and apparently on the scene, seized this opportunity and established their authority in the central plains. A brick fortress was built near the turn in the Irrawaddy, a strategic location that controlled central Burma's vital irrigated rice lands lying to the southwest, north, and east of the fortress. By the tenth century, a ruling family had begun to dominate the political and economic apparatus, and a royal dynasty had been formed. Its power was largely military, by which it extended its control over the entire plains area carved out by the Irrawaddy River. By the mid-eleventh century, an able monarch, King Anawrahta, mobilized his forces and began marching in all directions, first securing the strategic areas in the north along the length of the Irrawaddy River, building over forty forts along its banks as defensive outposts against traditional northern enemies; then sweeping southwest to secure that frontier; and finally moving farther south down the Irrawaddy to assert his hegemony over the port cities on the Gulf of Martaban and the Isthmus of Kra.

This last effort provided the inland, agrarian Burman civilization a window to the rest of the Asian and international world, which it needed to become more than a simple military power. With this contact, Burma, under the eleventh-century king Kyanzittha, reestablished its Theravada Buddhist foundations by restoring the Sarvastivadin (Hinayana) traditions of the Pyu while adding to them the new orthodoxy of Sri Lanka, with which the kingdom had come in contact in Lower Burma. Pagan's forces took these influences back to the dry hinterland, and with one brief exception, the intensively irrigated plains of central Burma remained the economic, as well as the political, cultural, and spiritual center of the country until it was colonized by the British in 1886.

The civilization of Pagan featured an agrarian economy based largely on wet-rice cultivation; a pyramidal social and political system of royalty, officialdom, and commoners in which principles of hereditary kingship and ideologies of legitimation steeped in Buddhist assumptions of man and the cosmos prevailed; a religious community of monks, nuns, and their retainers that made up a large portion of Burmese society, the beneficiaries of a tremendous program of temple and monastery construction (over two thousand temples still stand today in the twenty-six square miles that was Pagan); an administration based on a system of "fiefs" granted at "the royal compassion" temporarily as well as in perpetuity; a justice system based on a written civil and criminal code and a hierarchical organization of courts to enforce it; and a belief system based on Theravada Buddhism, though intermingled in various ways and to different intensities with other great and little traditions.

Several institutional reasons and immediate events brought this magnificent civilization to a political end in the late thirteenth century. The belief in merit as a means to eventual salvation and an ideology of legitimation based on patronage of the religion and church stimulated an attitude of continual and generous giving to the Buddhist church. These gifts were in the form of the best irrigated rice lands, as well as skilled labor, endowments that were both tax-exempt and held in perpetuity. With the supply of labor continually low in precolonial Southeast Asia, with hereditary occupation hindering mobility, and with population growth limited to a stable rate relative to resources, infant mortality, and other such factors, a point was reached when the human and material resources no longer produced what the state needed in order to sustain its power and lifestyle. But the belief in salvation by merit, as well as certain ideologies of legitimation concerning leadership and the state, compelled the system to continue, for significant change of the system implied destruction of the society's reason for being. With the state thus weakened, the various factions at court were provided with the necessary milieu and justification for rebellion, while tributary states capitalized on the situation to declare their independence. Finally, in the last decade of the thirteenth century, a series of events destroyed the kingdom of Pagan as a viable political entity. A Mongol invasion, followed by Shan attacks, left the central plains a decentralized political arena until it was once more unified briefly in the mid-fourteenth century by a king who founded the next dynasty (Ava), who legitimized his rule by adopting the same ideas, myths, and historical figures important to the Pagan monarchs.

The significance of the Pagan kingdom lies in its establishing the essential principles of a classical Burmese tradition. Burma owes its heritage to this initial classical form, which continued to influence the structural and ideological direction its successors were to take. Because the kingdom of Pagan became the exemplary model for future generations, subsequent Burmese institutional history witnessed far more continuity than change.

[Several monarchs mentioned above are the subject of independent entries. See also Pyu; Prome; *and* Shan.]

Michael Aung-Thwin, "The Role of *Sasana* Reform in Burmese History: Economic Dimensions of a Religious Purification," *Journal of Asian Studies* 38 (1979): 671–688, and "Jambudipa: Classical Burma's Camelot," *Contributions to Asian Studies* 16 (1981): 38–61. G. E. Harvey, *A History of Burma from the Earliest Times* (1925; reprint, 1967). G. H. Luce, *Old Burma—Early Pagan* (1969). Than Tun, "History of Burma: A. D. 1300–1400," *Journal of the Burma Research Society* 42 (1959): 119–134.
MICHAEL AUNG-THWIN

PAGAN MIN (1811–1880), ninth ruler of the Konbaung dynasty (1846–1853) in Burma. Eldest son of Tharrawaddy (r. 1837–1846), Pagan took the throne through a palace coup in November 1846 and placed his mentally disturbed father under house arrest. He had almost no control over the officials, and maladministration and disorder were even more a feature of his reign than his father's. Although strongly anti-British, he was drawn into a war with Britain, largely not of his making, in 1852. With defeat and the British annexation of Lower Burma, he was deposed by a younger brother, the Mindon prince, in February 1853 and lived in the palace until his death in 1880.

[*See also* Konbaung Dynasty *and* Anglo-Burmese Wars.]

D. G. E. Hall, *A History of Southeast Asia* (4th ed., 1981).
WILLIAM J. KOENIG

PAHANG, largest state in peninsular Malaysia. Based on the long Pahang River and its tributaries, Pahang has always been sparsely populated. Although the royal capital, Pekan, is situated on the east coast, the majority of the people have tended to live in the interior region. Pahang was mentioned in an Arab source of the tenth century and described in the twelfth century as a tributary of Srivijaya, the Sumatra-based empire. In the fifteenth century Pahang was brought under the sway of Melaka.

During the next two centuries Minangkabau migrated from Sumatra to the interior of the state, where they mined gold and established wet-rice cultivation. These migrants maintained a close association with the Minangkabau of Negri Sembilan. Pahang formed a part of Johor (the successor state

TABLE 1. *Kings of Pagan*

KING	REIGN DATES
Sawrahan	956–1001
Kyaungphyu	1001–1021
—	?
Anawrahta	1044–1077
Sawlu	1077–1084
Kyanzittha	1084–1113
Alaungsithu	1113–1169/70
Kalakya	1169/70–1170
Naratheinkha	1170–1174
Narapatisithu	1174–1211
Nadaungmya	1211–1230
Kyaswa	1235–1249
Uzana	1249–1255
Narathihapade	1255/56–1287
Kyawswa	1288–1297

of Melaka) from the seventeenth century onward and became the special province of the *bendahara* ("chief minister") of that empire during the 1800s. Eventually Pahang achieved independence from its suzerain, and in 1882 Bendahara Ahmad assumed the title sultan and established his own court on the old Johor model.

After protracted negotiations, the British forced the sultan to accept a resident in 1888. A broad-based revolt occurred and was not suppressed until 1895. During the next decade the British provided Pahang with an economic infrastructure. Although developing slowly in comparison with Perak and Selangor, Pahang attracted tin- and gold-mining enterprises as well as rubber planting. The Chinese and other immigrants were more involved than the local Malays in these activities, but British intervention also promoted an expansion of wet-rice agriculture and cash cropping among the peasantry.

In the postindependence period widespread agricultural development and timber felling have taken place in Pahang, and by the 1980s the population had become ten times the sixty thousand estimated a century earlier. Pahang remains a relatively backward and isolated state.

[*See also* Malaysia.]

Hayi Buyong Adil, *Sejarah Pahang* (1972). R. G. Cant, *An Historical Geography of Pahang* (1972). W. Linehan, "A History of Pahang," *Journal of the Malaysian Branch of the Royal Asiatic Society* 14 (1936): 1–256.

A. C. MILNER

PAHANG WAR (1857–1863), civil war in which several neighboring states became embroiled. It originated in the rivalry between two sons of Bendahara ("chief minister") Ali: Ahmad and Mutahir. Ahmad fought in the name of Sultan Muhmud (the deposed sultan of Lingga and claimant to the sultanship of Johor-Pahang) and received support from the Sultan of Trengganu. The Temenggong of Johor and the British in Singapore assisted Mutahir. The British even bombarded Trengganu (1862) in an attempt to prevent Sultan Mahmud and the Siamese from interfering in Pahang affairs. Ahmad won the war but then ceased to pay allegiance to the Johor-Pahang empire.

[*See also* Pahang; Johor; *and* Trengganu.]

W. Linehan, "A History of Pahang," *Journal of the Malaysian Branch of the Royal Asiatic Society* 14 (1936): 1–256. A. C. Milner, *Kerajaan: Malay Political Culture on the Eve of Colonial Rule* (1982). A. C. MILNER

PAHLAVI. The word *pahlavi* is an adjective that, in its Middle Iranian form *pahlavig*, designated the Parthians, the politically most prominent ethnic group in Iran during the Arsacid period (c. 250 BCE–226 CE), and stood in contrast to Middle Iranian *parsig* (modern *farsi*), which designated the Persians, an ethnic group predominant in southwestern Iran that became the most prominent group during the succeeding Sasanid period (226–651). During the early Islamic period (seventh to eleventh century) this contradistinction between *pahlavi* and *farsi* retained its chronological implication as the designation for the older literary Persian of the Sasanids and the new literary Persian written in Arabic script, respectively.

Pahlavi, the official Sasanid literary language, represented a variety of Middle Iranian speech of the ethnic Persians in southwestern Iran (Persis) and was distinguished by its heterographic writing system, which was a direct paleographical development of the Achaemenid style of written Aramaic as it persisted and developed in this Persian-speaking area of Iran during the centuries following the end of Achaemenid administration (330 BCE). It was used not only in official circles by the imperial chancellery for royal inscriptions, coins, and other government documents, but also by private individuals for a variety of purposes (e.g., inscriptions and letters). At least two prominent Sasanid religious communities, the Zoroastrians and the Nestorian Christians, used it extensively for religious writings and inscriptions. During the early Islamic period, Pahlavi continued to be used for Zoroastrian writings (ninth century) as well as on the inscriptions and coins of some local Iranian dynasts (seventh to eleventh centuries).

[*See also* Farsi; Parthians; *and* Zoroastrianism.]

Mary Boyce, "Middle Persian Literature," in *Handbuch der Orientalistik*, edited by Bertold Spuler, part 1, vol. 4, *Iranistik: Literatur* (1968), pp. 31–66. E. W. West, "Pahlavi Literature," in *Grundriss der iranischen Philologie*, vol. 2, *Literatur, Geschichte und Kultur* (1896–1904), pp. 75–129.

DAVID A. UTZ

PAHLAVI, ASHRAF (b. 1919), twin sister of the late shah of Iran, Mohammad Reza Pahlavi, active in Iranian political and social welfare activities. She founded the Imperial Organization for Social Services in the 1940s and represented the Iranian government in an official trip to the USSR in 1946 to discuss the critical issue of the communist-backed Autonomous Republic of Azerbaijan that was established in Iran in 1945. In the 1950s she formed the Women's Organization of Iran; the organization was largely responsible for the passage of the Family Protection Act in 1975. She was sent into exile twice, first in 1951 by the prime minister Mohammed Mossadegh, ostensibly because of corruption and her opposition to the oil nationalization bill. She returned to Iran in 1953 after the fall of Mossadegh and resumed her political and social activities. She again followed her brother into exile in 1979.

[See also Mossadegh, Mohammed; and Pahlavi, Mohammed Reza.]

W. Forbis, *Fall of the Peacock Throne* (1980). G. Lenczowski, *Iran under the Pahlavis* (1978).

NEGUIN YAVARI

PAHLAVI, MOHAMMED REZA (1919–1980), shah of Iran from 1941 to 1979 and last monarch before the establishment of the Islamic Republic. Mohammed Reza Shah was the son of Reza Shah, the founder of the Pahlavi dynasty. He and his twin sister, Ashraf, were born in Tehran while their father was still an officer with the Cossack Brigade. Mohammed Reza was named crown prince at the coronation of Reza Shah in 1926. His father made a conscious effort to educate him to be a future shah. From 1931 to 1936 Mohammad Reza attended private schools in Switzerland. When he returned to Iran, he studied military science for two years at the Military College in Tehran, then served as inspector of the army for three years.

Mohammed Reza was named shah in September 1941, following the abdication of his father under pressure from Great Britain and the Soviet Union, whose forces had jointly invaded Iran. The foreign troops continued to occupy parts of Iran until May 1946. Thus, Mohammed Reza Shah began his reign under the national humiliation of foreign intervention. He and his fellow citizens would continue to be concerned about the role of foreign governmental interference in Iran's internal affairs throughout his entire rule.

The forced abdication of Reza Shah and the presence of foreign troops in Iran for more than four years helped to stimulate the revival of political parties opposed to the concentration of power in the hands of the monarch. Consequently, the first twelve years of Mohammed Reza Shah's reign were characterized by intense rivalry between the shah and his supporters and the elected members of the Majles who preferred a strictly constitutional king. By 1951 the Majles was able to nominate its own choice for

prime minister, and Mohammed Reza Shah was obliged to acquiesce. In 1953 the Majles nationalized the petroleum industry, then owned by the British government, precipitating an international crisis; the shah was forced to flee the country, but a proroyalist, military coup d'état against the government of Prime Minister Mohammed Mossadegh enabled Mohammed Reza to return to reclaim the throne.

After 1953 Mohammed Reza Shah asserted himself more forcefully. Independent political parties were banned, press censorship was imposed, elections to the Majles were controlled, and political leaders who insisted upon expressing opposition in public were jailed. The repressive measures provoked periodic political disturbances, most notably the riots of June 1963, which spread to several cities and resulted in hundreds of casualties. Nevertheless, until 1977 most of the period after 1953 was characterized by relative political calm despite the general resentment of the shah's authoritarian rule.

Mohammed Reza Shah was interested, as had been his father, in promoting what he believed was the modernization of his country. Thus, he initiated projects to expand industrial capacity. These included direct government investment in petroleum refineries, steel works, and various heavy industries, as well as easy term loans and subsidies for private investors. The revenues from the sale of oil were used to finance multiyear development plans and major projects such as dam construction, extensions of the Trans-Iranian Railway, and new highways.

Mohammed Reza Shah also was interested in agricultural development. He supported the implementation of a major land reform program that led to the redistribution of approximately one-half of the cultivated land to peasant sharecroppers. Low interest loans to large landowners encouraged the increased production of industrial and export crops. The government also invested in and subsidized the development of agribusinesses, agricultural machinery manufacture, and irrigation networks.

Mohammed Reza Shah also promoted social changes by expanding the state-supported school system, especially at the secondary and college levels, and by supporting legislation to improve the legal status of women. Some of the social changes that occurred as a result of these policies, as well as social changes that resulted from economic development policies, were resented by various classes of people who felt threatened by the rapidity of social change. By 1977 those who opposed social changes have begun to ally with groups who were disaffected on account of political and/or economic grievances.

Consequently, a popular movement against the shah developed in the latter part of 1977 and throughout 1978. In January 1979 Mohammed Reza Shah decided to leave Iran voluntarily in order to stem the tide of discontent. His departure failed to dampen the antimonarchy sentiments, and in a referendum in April an overwhelming majority of the population voted to abolish the institution of shah and replace it with a republic.

Mohammed Reza Shah did not return to Iran. He lived in exile in various countries and died of cancer in Egypt in 1980.

[See also Mossadegh, Mohammed; Pahlavi, Reza; and Pahlavi, Ashraf.]

Ervand Abrahamian, Iran between Two Revolutions (1982), pp. 169–529. Robert Graham, Iran: The Illusion of Power (1979). Fred Halliday, Iran: Dictatorship and Development (1979). Eric Hooglund, Land and Revolution in Iran, 1960–1980 (1982). Nikki Keddie, Roots of Revolution: An Interpretive History of Modern Iran (1981), pp. 113–182. Muhammad Reza Pahlavi, Answer to History (1980).   ERIC HOOGLUND

PAHLAVI, REZA (1878–1944), shah of Iran from 1925 to 1941; founder of the Pahlavi dynasty. Reza Shah was born in an Elburz mountain village near the Caspian Sea in Iran's Mazandaran Province. His father, a small landowner and an officer in a locally recruited regiment of Nasir al-Din Shah's army, died when Reza was still an infant. Subsequently, his mother took him to Tehran, where Reza was raised in the household of a maternal uncle. While he was an adolescent his uncle had him enrolled in the Russian-officered Cossack Brigade in about 1893. The future shah was to spend almost thirty years with the cossacks, rising from the ranks to become one of the brigade's most influential Iranian officers and, eventually, commander of the entire army.

Reza Shah's interest in politics developed as early as World War I. After the Iranian government dismissed all remaining Russian officers of the Cossack Brigade in 1920, Reza, then a general, was made commander of the regiment based in Qazvin. This position enabled him to exercise a degree of political power, and he was soon in contact with civilian leaders who were plotting to install a new government in Tehran. In February 1921 he collaborated with a prominent journalist in the coup d'état that would lead to his emergence as the single most powerful leader in Iran.

Following the coup d'état, Reza served initially as chief of the army, then as minister of war, and in October 1923 was appointed prime minister. After he became prime minister, he entertained the idea of establishing a republic in Iran. Opposition to a republic, led by prominent clergymen who feared that a republican government would institute secular programs like the 1924 reforms in Turkey, persuaded Reza that a monarchical form of government should be retained. Consequently, in December 1925 he encouraged his supporters in the Majles to abolish the Qajar dynasty and establish a new royal family, the Pahlavi, with himself as Reza Shah.

During his reign Reza Shah instituted various economic and social reforms that were collectively called modernization. The focus of his economic policies was the industrialization of Iran. The state invested in manufacturing enterprises and encouraged private capital to set up factories for producing consumer goods. An infrastructure of roads, railways, and renovated harbors was built to promote the industrial development.

Reza Shah's social policies were equally significant. Legal reforms secularized the judicial system; a state-run, public school system was established for the entire country; universal male conscription was introduced and a national army created; and public dress codes were enforced for men and women. Some of his social policies were controversial, but Reza Shah did not tolerate public opposition after 1925. Consequently, the programs instituted during his reign, while often resented by different classes of the population, effected a major transformation of Iranian urban society.

Reza Shah viewed the social and economic policies he undertook as necessary measures to make Iran a strong country that could resist pressures from the European powers. He regarded the foreign intervention in Iranian affairs, especially in the years 1911–1921, as a matter of national dishonor and was determined that such interference not recur. He sought to minimize the influence of Great Britain and Russia—the two countries that historically had been most deeply involved in Iran—by cultivating diplomatic relations with rival countries such as Germany, France, and the United States.

Reza Shah's efforts to prevent foreign intervention proved to be futile. In August 1941, soon after Great Britain and the Soviet Union became allies in war against Germany, they used the fact of Iran's diplomatic relations with Germany as an excuse to invade and occupy Iran. Great Britain insisted upon Reza Shah's abdication and exile from Iran. He died in Johannesburg, South Africa, in 1944.

[See also Persian Cossack Brigade; Qavam, Ahmad; Trans-Iranian Railway; *and* Tripartite Treaty of Alliance.]

Ervand Abrahamian, *Iran between Two Revolutions* (1982), pp. 102–165. Amin Banani, *The Modernization of Iran, 1921–1941.* Wilfrid Knapp, "1921–1941: The Period of Riza Shah," in *Twentieth Century Iran,* edited by H. Amirsadeghi (1977), pp. 23–51. Donald Wilbur, *Riza Shah Pahlavi: The Resurrection and Reconstruction of Iran, 1878–1944* (1975).   ERIC HOOGLUND

PAINTING

CHINESE PAINTING

The Chinese have regarded great architectural monuments as well as sculpture, bronze vessels, ceramics, and lacquerware as the work of artisans, not artists as the term is defined today. For this reason, the names of the makers of such objects are rarely recorded in historical sources, while those of hundreds of painters are known. Painting, considered the pursuit of a proper Confucian gentleman, possesses a certain prestige and value well established in Chinese culture.

One of the reasons why painting has been so highly regarded throughout Chinese history is that it is one of the best expressions of the Chinese mind. Subject matter is often drawn from the stories and figures of history and literature most memorable to the Chinese people, as well as from natural scenes and objects. As it developed, painting became increasingly humanistic in approach, expressing the pure and noble spirit of Chinese intellectuals, and their desire to lead the simple and free life of the scholar-hermit. In later periods painting represented a means for the pursuit of pure aesthetic goals.

Chinese painting has been produced, for the most part, on three types of ground: wall surfaces, silk, and paper. The basic tools are the Chinese brush, made of animal hair (such as that of rabbit, goat, horse, or wolf), usually formed into a round bundle with a pointed tip; ink, manufactured from charcoal into an inkstick, which, when ground on an inkstone, produces the ink; and colors, mostly mineral and vegetable. In the early periods, up to the end of the Tang dynasty (618–907), wall paintings were quite common, especially in palaces and Buddhist temples. After the Tang, when Buddhism declined, paintings on silk and paper became popular. During the later periods (Yuan, Ming, and Qing) artists found paper most appropriate to their expressive intent.

In paintings on both silk and paper, three formats are most common. Although in earlier periods paintings on silk or paper were often mounted on screens, none exists today, except as recorded in pictures of early life. It is generally believed that wall painting and screen painting were replaced by the hanging scroll, which is easy to roll up and store. The handscroll and the album are other important formats. The handscroll is probably the oldest form among the three, for it was based on the form of a piece of silk, usually about one foot wide, with a length of any measurement, ranging from a few to dozens of feet. The album presumably first appeared in the form of a round fan painting. A number of fans, removed from their ribs, can be mounted as leaves in an album form. In later periods, the album assumed many different forms, usually rectangular. The number of leaves ranged from as few as four to as many as twenty-four or thirty-six or more, but the standard count was eight or twelve.

Paintings on silk and paper are usually mounted on a paper backing and framed on the four sides by pieces of silk. A dowel is attached to the end of the scroll for the purpose of rolling it up when in storage or to hold it straight when hung or unrolled. Chinese paintings, unlike their Western counterparts (usually oil on canvas), are rather fragile, but convenient for displaying, storing, and shipping. Because of this fragility, few paintings older than one thousand years have survived. On the other hand, because of the convenience of handling, many paintings have survived the abundance of wars and disasters in Chinese history.

Early Chinese writers trace the origin of Chinese painting to the beginning of the writing system in legendary history. Reflecting the belief that painting and writing share a common origin, early Chinese records attribute their beginning to Cangjie, an official under the Yellow Emperor, who invented the pictographic writing system based on his observations of natural phenomena. At present, the earliest types of painting in China can be found in decorations on painted pottery, the earliest of which appeared about 5000 BCE. Writing, on the other hand, had its earliest appearance on the oracle bones and bronze vessels of the late Shang period in Anyang, as early as the fourteenth century BCE. However, the origins of writing must have been somewhat earlier, as the examples found at Anyang already represent a rather high degree of sophistication.

Definite references to painting already occurred in writings dating to the early Zhou dynasty (1122?–256 BCE). Because none of the early palaces still stands, however, the existence at such an early date

FIGURE 1. *Boat with Eight Men (The Golden Image of Chang Gansi)*. Dunhuang wall painting, Tang dynasty. 50.8 cm. × 94 cm.

of paintings of legendary figures, emperors, and kings cannot be proven. Our first examples of paintings all come from tombs, the earliest of which dates to the period of the Warring States, or about the fourth century BCE. These paintings were funerary in nature, and reflected the mythological world in which the people of that time believed. Usually the deceased is depicted as traveling to the heavenly world, surrounded by mythical creatures such as dragons, serpents, fantastic fish, and winged figures.

The best extant examples of this depiction of the mythological world occur in the tomb paintings of the Western Han period, during the first and second centuries BCE, including those excavated from the tombs of the family of the marquis of Dai at Mawangdui, Hunan Province, datable to the second century BCE. An expanded version of heaven, earth, and the underworld is depicted as filled with mythical creatures, above and below. Such figures as the King Father of the East and Queen Mother of the West; the original ancestors, Fu Xi and Nu Wa; and many winged figures and animals are part of the major images in Western Han paintings, found in either tombs or shrines. One of the most constant themes of these Han paintings was the desire for immortality, sought by emperors and commoners alike. The object of their interest was the Isles of the Immortals, a mythical paradise that was the subject of many Han works of art.

With the development of social stability and prosperity in the Eastern Han period, the Chinese turned their attention away from the world of the immortals to the everyday world, dominated by Confucian ethics. In many tomb paintings and wall reliefs, from Shandong and Jiangsu in the east to Shaanxi and Sichuan in the west, the most common subjects spanned the standard Confucian themes of virtuous kings and emperors, paragons of filial piety, and lessons from history to scenes of contemporary life, such as family feasts and entertainment, hunting, farming, and marketing. They remain the best documents recording the daily life of the Han people.

The flourishing of Buddhism during the period of the Northern and Southern Dynasties (third to sixth century CE) introduced to China religious images combining elements of Western and Indian origins, both subject and style. The Chinese began to depict not only images of the Buddha (and his manifestations), attendants, and followers, but also episodes from his life, the Jataka tales (his previous incarnations), and related stories. The colorful, dramatic, and effective narrative style represented a new contribution to the development of Chinese painting. During the Tang period, the popularity of the Pure

Land sect of Buddhism led to the widespread depiction of the Western Paradise, the eternal resting place for the saved souls of Buddhists. Most of these Buddhist paintings, usually decorating the walls of temples during the period from the third to the ninth century, have disappeared with the crumbling of buildings and cities. A considerable number of wall paintings, however, are still well preserved in the several hundred caves of Dunhuang, an oasis in the northwestern part of Gansu Province, and some of the caves at Kizil and several other locations in Xinjiang Province. [*See also* Dunhuang.]

While from Han to Tang the major subjects of pictorial depiction were either mythological figures or Buddhist images, the world of man and his activities was also the subject of painting, especially in court circles. Tang artists are noted for their ability to depict not only Buddhist and Daoist images in realistic expressions and movements, but also emperors, ministers, scholars, and court ladies. Yan Liben (c. 600–674) is noted for his depiction of tribute-bearers from various countries under the Tang sphere of influence. Wu Daozi (fl. 710–760) is famous for his realistic scenes of suffering in hell. Zhang Xuan (fl. early eighth century) and Zhou Fang (fl. late eighth century) were both masters of portraying court ladies in daily life. The same realism was also applied to the depiction of animals, particularly horses and water buffaloes, such as those by Han Gan (mid-eighth century) and Dai Song (eighth century). In their ability to capture the true expressions of humans and animals, Tang painters set the standard for later periods.

By the late Tang era, Chinese art criticism had developed to the point that Zhang Yanyuan, in *Painters of the Various Dynasties* (dated 845), could state, "Painting promotes culture and strengthens human relationships. It penetrates all the mysteries of the universe. It serves thus the same purpose as the Six Classics, and like the rotation of the four seasons, originated from nature and not from human tradition." This statement established painting as an important cultural activity that contained strong Confucian overtones and philosophical implications.

The development of landscape painting represents the high point in Chinese painting. During the earlier periods, the landscape (although rare) had served mainly as a background for human action. Although records indicate that the landscape was considered an important subject in Tang painting, very few actual examples have survived to testify to this claim. However, landscape painting probably emerged as the major expression of Chinese painters during the periods of the Five Dynasties and Northern Song (960–1127). Landscapes became the focus of artistic vision, reflecting a new synthesis in the evolution of the art that resulted from a refinement of techniques,

FIGURE 2. *Ladies in the Palace.* Copy of an original by Zhou Wenzhu, c. 1140. Song-dynasty handscroll, ink on silk; 25.7 cm. × 177 cm.

the perfection of realistic depiction, and a deepening of philosophical meaning.

This development was achieved by a series of painters. In the North, along the Yellow River, Jing Hao and Guan Tong (both early tenth century) were pioneers in choosing landscapes, rather than figures, as their major means of expression. By the late tenth century, Li Cheng (919–967) achieved mastery of seasonal effects by portraying wintry trees with crabbed branches. He also achieved control of deep spatial recession by the depiction of distant mountains that seemed to stretch for a thousand miles. Fan Kuan at the beginning of the eleventh century perfected the depiction of realistic mountains and rocks. Yan Wengui (late tenth century) and Xu Daoning (mid-eleventh century) both captured the grandeur of mountain ranges and deep valleys. Guo Xi (late eleventh century) revealed the mysterious changes in nature, described in his famous *Essay on Landscape* and best represented in his painting *Early Spring* (1072), now in the Palace Museum, Taipei. Further changes in the evocation of atmospheric effects occurred in the cloudy mountains of Mi Fei (early twelfth century) and his son Mi Youren (mid-twelfth century), depicted in broad brushwork and ink washes.

In the South, along the Yangtze River, Dong Yuan (fl. mid-tenth century) and Ju Ran (fl. 970) developed landscape depicted in free brushwork, evoking the moist atmosphere, luxuriant vegetation, and secluded hills and rivers of the Yangtze delta, from which this type of scenic view took its name, the "Jiangnan landscape." During the Southern Song period (1127–1279), landscape painting shows a further exploration of the mysteries of nature by an increasing use of mist and clouds. Li Tang (early twelfth century) was the transitional figure who explored this new possibility, and the paintings of Ma Yuan and Xia Gui (both active in the early thirteenth century), dominated by an intangible void sur-

FIGURE 3. *Bare Willows and Distant Mountains*. By Ma Yuan (fl. 1190–1224), Southern Song dynasty. Round album leaf; ink and colors on silk. 23.8 cm. × 21.2 cm.

FIGURE 4. *Bamboo (Section 3)*. Attributed to the Song-dynasty literatus Su Dongpo (Su Shi; 1036–1101) but probably from the Yuan or early Ming dynasty. Handscroll, ink on paper; 28.3 cm. × 29.5 cm.

rounded by vaguely seen objects, represent the culmination of this development.

All these innovations took place during the period of rapid development in Neo-Confucianism, which was an effort to synthesize traditional Chinese Confucian ethical ideas with Indian Buddhist speculative thought into a new philosophical system. In the same way, Chinese landscape painters attempted to combine direct depiction of the outward forms of nature with an expression of the moral and philosophical overtones that pervade the universe. Thus, in their landscapes, they tried to attain spiritual communion between man and nature, which is best reflected in the theory and practice of Song painting.

During the Yuan period (1279–1368), when Mongol rule led to a great cultural crisis in China, literati painting became the dominant force, which continued into the early twentieth century. The ideas regarding literati painting were first developed by a group of scholar-officials during the late eleventh century, including Su Dongpo (Su Shi; 1036–1101), Wen Tong (1019–1079), Mi Fei (1051–1107), and Li Konglin (d. 1106). Separating themselves from the painters of the imperial academy, they emphasized the scholar-artist approach to painting as distinguished from that of the artisans. In particular, they viewed painting as a personal expression for scholars as amateurs, not as professionals. As such it must reflect their individual worth, their background, their education, and their knowledge of the past. It should also combine all of the three highest art forms: poetry, calligraphy, and painting. Although these ideas were already developed during the Northern Song period, they became prominent during the Yuan, when Chinese artists, reacting against Mongol domination, endeavored to find a new way of expression.

Guided by these ideas of literati painting, artists of the early Yuan period, especially Qian Xuan (fl. 1235–1301) and Zhao Mengfu (1254–1322), were pioneers in a long period of revivals of the manners of the Northern and Southern Dynasties, Tang, and Northern Song. Paintings of figures, horses, birds and flowers, buildings and palaces, and landscapes from those early periods were copied and imitated as a means to search for the antique spirit in art. From these explorations came the realization that landscape and the three friends of winter (bamboo, plum blossoms, and pine) were the best vehicles for the expression of the literati's feelings and ideals. Four landscape painters of the late Yuan were considered by later critics to be the best exponents of literati painting. The art of Huang Gongwang (1269–1354) was known for its spontaneity and freedom, derived from Dong Yuan's works. Wu Zhen (1280–1354) drew some ideas from Ju Ran to form his own dark and flowing manner. Ni Zan (1301–1374) personalized his landscape into the most austere and purest form. In contrast, Wang Meng (1308–1385), inspired by works of the Five Dynasties, developed a complex and nervous energy in his paintings. These individual styles became quite influential to the evolution of later periods of Chinese painting.

During the Ming period (1368–1644), styles generally conformed to the theory of literati painting—the pursuit of the idea of *xieyi* (expression) combined with the use of earlier models—in particular, that of the Wu school painters in Suzhou (the region known as Wu). Drawing upon elements in the style of Wang Meng, Huang Kongwang, Wu Zhen, and Ni Zan, Ming painters such as Shen Zhou (1427–1509), Wen Zhengming (1470–1559), Lu Zhi (1496–1576), and Chen Shun (1483–1544) all formed their own personal manner. Pure representation of nature was replaced by complex allusions to the past, combined with an emphasis on brushwork for its own sake. These elements are typical of Ming literati painting.

Another group of painters, known as the Zhe school because they were natives of the Hangzhou area (in Zhejiang Province) or related to the Hangzhou artists in style, developed their ideas from the Southern Song manner of Ma Yuan and Xia Gui, in contrast to the Wu school artists. Although their works were varied, they tended to be more decorative and imitative, and served the interests of the court in Beijing well. The painter most representative of the school was Dai Jin (fl. mid-fifteenth century). Another group of painters in Suzhou, who also painted in a decorative manner, included Shou

Chen and Qiu Ying (both early sixteenth century), and an artist who combined the characteristics of this group and the literati, Tang Yin (1470–1523). They were considered to be professionals, in contrast to the literati painters.

The most important literati painter in late Ming times was Dong Qichang (1555–1636), poet, painter, calligrapher, and art theorist. Summarizing all the major ideas of literati painting, he strongly criticized the professional and academic tradition. He established the direct development of literati painting: the poetic, free, personal expression of certain artists from the Tang through the Ming period. Dong emphasized the importance of the independence of painting from nature, the primacy of brushwork as the chief means of expression, and the close relationship between poetry, calligraphy, and painting. Through the influence of Dong's theories, the supremacy of literati painting was assured.

The late Ming and early Qing periods revealed a great vitality in Chinese painting. The great number of different directions and trends reflects a great upsurge in creative energy among painters. This wide range of styles includes: archaism in the works of Chen Hongshou (1599–1652) and Cui Zichong (d. 1644); the fantasy of Wu Bin (c. 1568–1621) and Ding Yunpeng (c. 1584–1638); the realism of Zhang Hong (1580–c. 1660) and Yuan Shangtong (1570–1661?); the transformation of the Ni Zan

FIGURE 5. *Marsh Scene with Birds (Section 5).* Attributed to Shen Zhou (1427–1509), Ming dynasty. Handscroll, ink on paper; 29.2 cm. × 454 cm.

FIGURE 6. *Landscape.* By Wu Bin (c. 1568–1621), dated 1603. Fan mount.

tradition by Cha Shibiao (1615–1698) and Hongren (1610–1663); the brooding, melancholy landscapes of Gong Xian (d. 1689); the strange creatures of Zhu Da (1625–c. 1705); the innovative brushwork of the Mount Huang painters, such as Mei Qing (1623–1697) and Daoji (1641–c. 1720); and the traditionalism of the Four Wangs—Wang Shimin (1592–1680), Wang Jian (1598–1677), Wang Hui (1632–1717), and Wang Yuanqi (1642–1715).

After the Manchu conquest of China in the middle of the seventeenth century, Chinese painting narrowed from the great variety of directions of the earlier periods to the popularity of the official line under the patronage of the new regime. Receiving the blessing of the court, the art of Wang Hui and Wang Yuanqi attracted hundreds of followers. Essentially based on Dong Qichang's emphasis on an intensive study of the Song and Yuan masters and imitation of their styles using more refined brushwork, their art became the standard for the next three hundred years. The other diverse schools, however, owing to their loyalty to the Ming, began to lose their following. Consequently, the manner of the Four Wangs became the orthodoxy for much of Qing painting.

During the eighteenth century, the insatiable desire of the emperors (from Kangxi to Yongzheng to Qianlong) brought most of the important paintings of the past into the imperial collection. The influence of the Four Wangs, therefore, became even more prominent. In the prosperous city of Yangzhou, however, a number of painters (some natives of the area and some attracted to it from other parts of China) developed a simple, free, spontaneous style in subjects mostly of bamboo, orchid, plum blossoms and other flowers, and figures. These "Eight Eccentrics of Yangzhou" are best represented by Jin Nong (1687–c. 1764), Zheng Xie (1693–1765), and Huang Shen (1687–1766), whose works show great ingenuity, vitality, and originality, in contrast to the imitative landscapes of the Wang tradition.

During the twentieth century, Chinese painting developed in the tradition of the Four Wangs, while a parallel trend consisted in reverting for inspiration to some late Ming painters, especially Daoji. Some artists continued in the literati tradition, but further expanded these ideas. Huang Binhong (1864–1955), Qi Baishi (1863–1959), Fu Baoshi (1904–1965), and Pan Tianshou (1889–1971) represent the most interesting new development along traditional lines. Another group, influenced by the West, began to experiment with various new ways to combine Chinese and Western elements to form a new art. The most interesting artists are Xu Beihong (1895–1953) and Lin Fengmian (b. 1900), in addition to some younger artists working both on the mainland and in Taiwan.

Susan Bush, *The Chinese Literati on Painting: Su Shih (1037–1101) to Tung Ch'i-ch'ang (1555–1636)* (1971). James Cahill, *Chinese Painting* (1960), *Hills beyond a River: Chinese Painting of the Yuan Dynasty, 1279–1368* (1976), *Parting at the Shore: Chinese Painting of the Early and Middle Ming Dynasty, 1368–1580* (1978), and *The Distant Mountains: Chinese Painting of the Late Ming*

Dynasty, 1570–1644 (1982). Shen Fu and Marilyn Fu, *Studies in Connoisseurship: Chinese Paintings from the Arthur M. Sackler Collection* (1973). John Hay, *Ancient China* (1973). Laurence Sickman and Alexander Soper, *Art and Architecture of China* (1956; 3d ed., 1968). Osvald Sirén, *Chinese Painting: Leading Masters and Principles,* 7 vols. (1956–1958) and *The Chinese on the Art of Painting* (1936).   CHU-TSING LI

SOUTH ASIAN PAINTING

The most characteristic paintings of South Asia are page-sized miniatures, executed from the fifteenth century onward for the purpose of illustrating manuscripts. Significant survivals of earlier paintings of the fifth century include the murals in the Buddhist monastic caves at Ajanta in India and the paintings on the rock fortress at Sigiriya in Sri Lanka. The Ajanta artists covered walls and ceilings with illustrations from Buddhist legend. They painted scenes bustling with activity: the female figures in these scenes, dressed in translucent garments and placed in eye-catching poses, are well known. At Sigiriya, extraordinarily free line-drawings pre-

FIGURE 1. *Ajanta Wall Painting.*

sent an exquisite group of celestial maidens, half-emerging from the clouds. [*See* Ajanta *and* Sigiriya.]

In the twelfth century paintings on long, narrow palm leaves began to appear on a large scale, both in Bengal, where Buddhist texts were copied, and in western India, where Jain manuscripts were illustrated. Jain artists painted in hues of rich blue and deep red, and they used gold lavishly; faces are in three-quarter profile with one eye shown projecting beyond the face. The Muslim invaders brought with them the technique of paper-making, and Jain painters abandoned the palm leaf but retained its long, narrow format. It is with Mughal artists that the page assumed the upright format that is the norm today.

Mughal painting owes its inspiration to the emperor Humayun's visit to the Safavid court of Persia, where he persuaded two Persian artists to return with him to India. These Persian masters were placed in charge of Emperor Akbar's atelier and given the task of training the more than one hundred painters recruited mainly through Akbar's conquests of Hindu kingdoms. Mughal painting is in many ways eclectic, with the Persian masters overseeing and adapting the conventions of the Hindu artists. The department of painters was closely attached to the Royal Library, since most of their work consisted of illustrating manuscripts. Artists developed specialized skills and frequently three or four would work on a single painting, and their names are found inscribed on the margins. Akbar himself supervised work, making comments, giving out rewards, and adjusting salaries; Mughal painting was closely controlled by the wishes of the monarchs, and the painters frequently produced illustrated biographies of their patrons. [*See* Akbar *and* Mughal Empire.]

Rajput miniatures transport us into a different and enchanted realm in which love is the leitmotiv. Women are beautiful, demure, yet passionate; valiant men are out fighting wars; and nature is in tune with human emotions. Love is the recurrent theme of all Rajput painting and even the months of the year and the musical modes are interpreted in terms of human love. The main religious motif, the love of the god Krishna for his beloved Radha, further emphasizes the significance and supremacy of love. Rajput painting, both of the Punjab hill states and of the Rajasthan plains, shows clear knowledge of the Mughal tradition. In some cases, as at Kangra, the connection is direct. When Nadir Shah of Iran sacked Delhi in 1738, families of artists aban-

FIGURE 2. *Illuminated Page from the Bhagavata Purana.* Rajput school, southern Rajasthan, probably Mewar, about 1550. Manuscript page, ink and color on paper. 17.8 cm. × 22.8 cm.

doned the dying Mughal empire and migrated to the hills, where they found enthusiastic patrons. The much admired Kangra miniatures are characterized by an ethereal delicacy; frequently the sole themes of the paintings are the beautiful Kangra women with their finely chiseled features and large gentle eyes, wearing high-waisted dresses that accentuate their slim grace and elegance. [*See* Rajput *and* Kangra.]

The adjoining state of Basohli, where painting began in the seventeenth century, presents us with a striking contrast in style. The impact of Basohli derives from its primitive directness, its sense of movement, and its hot, disturbing colors. The feminine face is unusual with large, sloping foreheads, wide, expressive eyes, and large, rounded chins. These miniatures are clearly the products of a sophisticated and mannered court. Similar strong contrasts in style

exist among contiguous states in the plains, between the majestic elegance of Kishangarh, for instance, and the direct strength of Bundi. [*See* Bundi.] Rajput painting, like that of the Mughals, was a courtly art that flourished in an atmosphere of royal patronage. It is only in the present century, with the dispersal of numerous royal collections, that South Asian miniatures have come to be widely viewed and appreciated.

Contemporary Indian painting has not sought to go back to ancient roots but has turned to the West for inspiration. For the first time artists are using oils, and paintings are being produced for display on walls. Several painters, among them M. F. Husain, have achieved a certain international recognition; it still remains to be seen if a distinctive South Asian style of modern painting will emerge.

[*See also* Architecture: South Asian Architecture.]

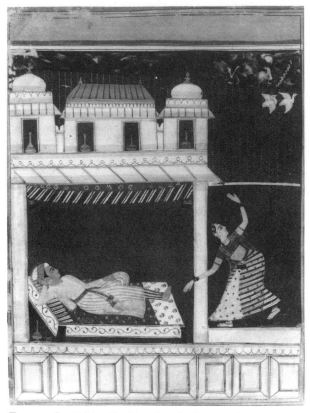

FIGURE 3. *Abhisarika Nayaka (A Heroine Comes to Her Lover through the Rain)*. Malwa school, c. 1630. Manuscript page, ink and color on paper. 22.8 cm. × 16.8 cm.

W. G. Archer, *Indian Minatures* (1960). Douglas Barrett and Basil Gray, *Indian Painting* (1978). P. Pal, *Court Painting of India* (1983). C. Sivaramamurti, *South Indian Painting* (1968). S. C. Welch, *The Art of Mughal India* (1963).   VIDYA DEHEJIA

JAPANESE PAINTING

The history of Japanese painting proper begins with the introduction of themes and techniques from the Asian mainland in about the sixth century of the common era. Thereafter, Japanese painting developed under the combined influences of both continental and indigenous aesthetic canons.

Materials and Techniques. Whatever its format, Japanese painting is done either on paper made of hand-molded bark fibers (principally from *kōzo*, or paper mulberry) or silk (protein in substance, consisting of the fibrous strands of the silkworm cocoon). Other materials are used for support, such as wood for panel paintings and the white clay ground of dry fresco for wall painting, but these are far outnumbered by the more fragile paper and silk.

The silk, when stretched on a stretcher, is usually sized by a thin wash of *dōsa* (a solution of horse bone or hide glue [*nikawa*] and alum). When sized, the cloth stretches as tightly as the face of a drum. The sizing is done in order to prevent paint or ink from quick absorption and running. Paper, too, is often sized in order to ensure an enduring adhesion of the medium, whose binder is also *nikawa*.

Whether done on paper or on silk, painting for a hanging scroll *(kakejiku)* is first back-papered and then attached to the mounting material, often a silk brocade with or without gold embroidery. On top and bottom the painting is bordered by the stripes of different silk brocade known as *ichimonji*. Made of the same material as the *ichimonji,* a pair of vertical strips called *fūtai* (literally, "wind sash") hang symmetrically from the upper end of the scroll. The upper and lower edges of the entire hanging scroll is attached to sticks, the lower one being heavier and larger and serving as a roller. The two ends of each stick may be capped by short cylinders of gold, silver (often with open-work design), ivory, or sandalwood (frequently with intricate carvings). When not on view, a hanging scroll is rolled up and placed in an oblong box (often of paulownia wood) for storage. When on view, a hanging scroll quietly occupies the wall of the *tokonoma,* an alcove especially reserved for that purpose. Handscrolls (*makimono*), either of silk or paper, were also frequently used to unfold a continuous landscape or a narrative. Paintings were also done on fans (*senmen*).

For a large screen (*byōbu*) or sliding door panels (*fusuma*) the ground may be premounted ready for painting. On the inside are layers of paper glued and stretched over a grilled wooden framework. A screen, usually paired, may serve as a partition to screen off an area to be concealed. Larger screens may decorate the interior for special occasions. The sliding door panels in actual use are mounted on double wooden rails, the two end panels being on one rail and the two inside panels on the other. Screen panels (usually six) are connected in sequence joined by an intricate system of interlocking paper hinges. Most screens are conceived in that form from the time of their creation but occasionally paintings designed as sliding door panels are later remounted as screens. In the same way a group of independent hanging scrolls may be remounted as a set, or an album leaf can be independently mounted as a hanging scroll.

Dry pigments of both vegetable and mineral kinds are employed along with Chinese ink, or *sumi,* for Japanese painting. They are applied with the binder *nikawa* and water. The even application of such mineral pigments as green malachite, when applied thickly, produces the sandy texture revealing the pigment particles. When thinly applied, it produces an effect similar to that in Western watercolor painting. While Japanese painters use both opaque and transparent pigments in much the same way as Western artists do, one unusual technique should be noted, especially as applied to painting done on silk: the *ura-zaishiki*, a method of applying pigments (or in some instances, gold) from the back to obtain luminosity and solidity. It is a technique transmitted from China and found most frequently in the Middle Ages (Heian through Muromachi periods), most notably in Buddhist paintings.

A distinct type of painting apart from the polychrome is *suibokuga*, or ink painting, which became a major artistic medium in the early Muromachi period (fourteenth century). Done in various tones of Chinese ink applied with a flexible brush, an ink painting can be as finished and expressive as a painting in polychrome. When applied with a less conventional implement such as a straw brush, or even one's fingernails, the black ink is capable of rendering explosive forms and motion. An unusual combination of media, such as polychrome and ink or ink and gold, may be seen in some Japanese paintings; it produces an extraordinary artistic effect (see figure 1).

The ground for Japanese painting may be prepared entirely in gold. Monumental screens or sliding door panels made after the late Muromachi and Momoyama periods (from the late fifteenth century on) are prepared by gold grounds *(kinji)*, which may be in gold leaf *(kinpaku)* or gold powder suspended in water *(kindei)*, rendering a soft atmospheric effect. The use of areas of cut pieces of gold or silver leaf *(kiri-haku)* is frequent and masses of still smaller flakes of gold and silver *(sunago)* are also common. These artistic techniques are shared with traditional crafts, such as lacquer art, indicating that there is a close relationship between painting and other crafts in Japanese artistic history.

A Japanese painting may or may not bear the artist's signature. When signed, usually in the lower corner of a composition, it may show only the artist's studio name in a seal form (square, oblong, or circular; in relief or intaglio); his pseudonym and the family name combined; or a long inscription in which his title, family name, sobriquet, studio name, and pseudonym are all included. The combination of signatures and seals identifying authorships did not begin to appear until the fourteenth century.

Historical Development. The history of Japanese painting can be divided into three main epochs in terms of dominant patronage, mode of production, genre, and artistic style. First is the epoch under Buddhism of the Asuka and Nara periods and that of the courtly culture of the Heian period—from the seventh century to the end of the twelfth century.

FIGURE 1. *Uji Bridge.* Artist unknown, Kanō school, six-panel folding screen; Japan, second half of the seventeenth century.

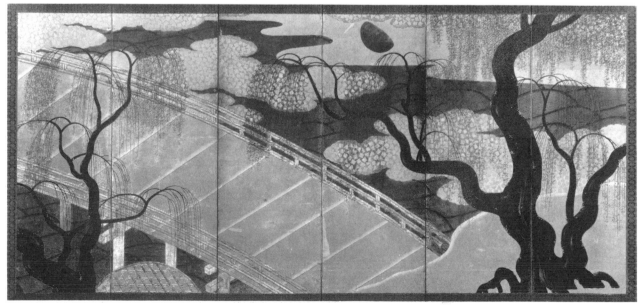

Second is the epoch in which art was appropriated by the warrior families who ruled the nation from Kamakura and, later, Kyoto, from the end of the twelfth century to the end of the sixteenth century. Third is the epoch under the Tokugawa shogunate, which ruled the nation from Edo (modern Tokyo) from the early seventeenth century through the mid-nineteenth century.

Buddhism of the Asuka and Nara periods gave rise to religious painting in a variety of forms under monastic patronage. As with other artistic media such as sculpture, calligraphy, and metalwork, Buddhist paintings of this period were inspired by Chinese examples known to the Japanese via Korea and particularly through works brought by returning envoys and Buddhist pilgrims. Significant numbers of recorded painters of this period were descendants of earlier Chinese and Korean émigrés, who had brought their skills to Japan. These artists, working for the Buddhist establishment of Nara, were effectively organized into a unit of production called *edakumi no tsukasa,* or the Office of Painters, attached to a monastery. The Office of Painters operated as a craft studio with its own head, who was in charge of the administrative aspects of the office, and painters and assistants who were in charge of production.

After the move of the capital to Heiankyō (modern Kyoto) at the end of the eighth century, two new centers of patronage came into being: one was the Imperial Palace at the capital; and the other, the new religious establishment of Tendai and Shingon Buddhism. These developments meant, on the one hand, an appropriation of artistic patronage by an aristocracy that demanded an art of its own, and, on the other hand, a proliferation of new types of Buddhist icons required by the increasingly complex Buddhist liturgy that characterized the Buddhism of this period. At the Kyoto court in the tenth century a Bureau of Painting *(edokoro)* was established within the governmental bureaucracy. The *edokoro* was headed by an artistic director *(edokoro azukari),* under whom the assistants performed specialized chores, such as mixing colors and preparing paper. By the early twelfth century the artistic director's position had become hereditary and was successively assumed by the talented members of the aristocracy. Developing further the structure of the earlier Office of Painters of the Nara monasteries, and emulating the workshop organization at court as a model, similar units were organized at Buddhist and Shinto shrines across the land; in the thirteenth century, the term *edokoro* became synonymous with "painter's studio" in general.

Under the aristocratic patronage of the Heian court a new genre of secular painting emerged. Called *Yamato-e* ("pictures of Yamato," i.e., Japan), it represented subject matters inspired by native literature, particularly poetry *(waka),* and by annual and monthly events observed at court. *Yamato-e* developed narrative picture scrolls *(emakimono)* and paintings mounted on screens *(byōbu-e).* Stylistically and thematically, *Yamato-e* was contrasted with *Kara-e* ("pictures of Kara," i.e., China), in which the subject matter was Chinese. *Yamato-e* appealed to the native sensibility; highly abstract forms, conceptual lines, and subtle colorism characterize works done in this tradition, and in time these aesthetic properties began to appear in Buddhist paintings as well.

By the thirteenth century aristocratic patronage at court had weakened, and the *edokoro*'s activities declined. By the mid-fourteenth century, the artistic director's position had become virtually nominal, and it was assumed for some generations by members of the Tosa family. Tendai and Shingon Buddhist paintings of this period also lost much of the earlier aesthetic finesse and spiritual intensity, reflecting a general loss of vitality in patronage of the arts at various centers. Locally, however, a handful of Buddhist as well as Shinto establishments continued to produce works that were to form a new genre of painting, notably that of temple histories and hagiographical narratives that were executed in the style of *Yamato-e.* Produced at temples and shrines, these works indicate that the painters, including the Tosa artists who were trained in the aristocratic mode of *Yamato-e* at court, found a new demand for their trade. The *Yamato-e* developed, from this period on, a wider appeal for the commoner population, moving well beyond the aristocracy from which it had originally sprung.

With the arrival of Zen Buddhism and the spread of its monasteries under the patronage of the warrior families—the Hōjō in Kamakura in the thirteenth century and the Ashikaga in Kyoto in the fourteenth and fifteenth centuries—ink painting *(suibokuga)* developed as part of the broad sinophile activities espoused by the Zen clerics. Inspired by the imported Chinese monochrome paintings that were in temple and private collections, ink paintings of this period show a broad range of subject matter, including figures, birds and flowers, and landscapes using a variety of formats (hanging scrolls, handscrolls, album leafs, and screens) and executed in an equally broad range of pictorial styles.

Beginning in the late fifteenth century, as the political power of the Ashikaga shogunate weakened in the capital, the patronage of the Zen monastic system and of the arts collapsed. Zen monk-painters in Kyoto (Sesshū Tōyō, for example) left Kyoto and sought the patronage of local provincial lords. [*See* Sesshū Tōyō.*] Kyoto was without active patronage of arts until, during the second half of the sixteenth century, the warlord unifiers Oda Nobunaga, Toyotomi Hideyoshi, and Tokugawa Ieyasu in turn took over political power and provided active patronage for artists. Painters who responded to the new patrons were professionals of the Kanō family, who were themselves descendants of a provincial warrior. The Kanō, who were earlier patronized by the Ashikaga shogunate at the end of the fifteenth century, adopted a workshop tradition, which had several centuries of history, by forming a guildlike organization. Their family members established satellite studios with increasing tendency to compete for and monopolize commissions coming from various patrons. Their specialty was painting executed primarily in ink and representing Chinese subjects, hence the name *Kanga* ("painting of Han," i.e., China), but they also adopted the *Yamato-e* tradition of the Tosa school (see figure 2). The adoption was at once artistic and familial, as a daughter of Tosa Mitsumochi became the wife of Kanō Motonobu, the second head of the family. The two main pictorial traditions merged in the Kanō works, subtly differentiating each style in terms of subject matter and format, especially in the monumental screens and sliding door panels of the patrons' residences and military castles. [*See* Kanō School.*]

As the Tokugawa government moved from Kyoto to Edo in the early seventeenth century, artistic patronage also shifted. The Kanō family studios also moved to Edo. By the end of the century, there were five branch studios in Edo and one in Kyoto. In Edo, the head of each studio was given the official title of *oku-eshi* (painter in service of the inner quarters of Edo Castle). The *oku-eshi* were given annual stipends and ranked equal to the *hatamoto* (banner bearers) of the warrior class. Kanō painters enjoyed a virtual monopoly of official commissions throughout the rest of the premodern period. Works by the Kanō painters of this period were characterized by recurrent themes such as didactic historical accounts of Chinese origin and executed in the predictable style perpetuated within the family. By the end of the eighteenth century the Kanō painters' activities had extended into the provinces where local lords created a demand for their services. Before the collapse of the Tokugawa shogunate and the feudal system in the nineteenth century, Kanō painting had

FIGURE 2. *Landscape.* By Bunsei (active mid-fifteenth century), Muromachi period; ink and slight color on paper. 73.2 cm. × 33 cm.

established itself as the orthodox school of Japanese painting. While the Kanō school was consolidating its firm foothold in the artistic arena around the new patronage, there emerged during the early decades of the seventeenth century artists outside the Tokugawa shogunate's sphere of influence who pro-

FIGURE 3. *Poem Scroll with Bamboo.* Calligraphy by Hon'ami Kōetsu (1558–1637), painting by Tawaraya Sōtatsu (active early seventeenth century); Edo period, dated to 1626. Handscroll, ink and gold on silk. 32 cm. × 524.5 cm.

vided paintings that appealed to affluent townsmen. Their art, free from the constraints of official themes and style, soon began to create their own patrons. Of the several schools of painting that can be identified among these artists, four are most notable. One, centered in Kyoto, is the school of Hon'ami Kōetsu and Tawaraya Sōtatsu (early seventeenth century) and their follower Ogata Kōrin (d. 1716). Known as Rimpa, this school specialized in a lyrical and decorative style of painting inspired by the indigenous tradition of *Yamato-e* (see figure 3). In their output the best forms of traditional crafts and pictorial style can be said to have merged. Emerging earlier in Kyoto and developing later in Edo, was the school of *ukiyo-e* ("pictures of the floating world"), which, like the popular woodblock prints with which it shared themes of urban pleasure quarters and familiar native landscapes, blossomed in the eighteenth century and continued into the nineteenth century. Yet another was a school of Realists or "Sketchers" of Kyoto, who were to no small degree influenced by Western pictorial conventions introduced through European copper-plate prints that were brought to Japan by Chinese and Dutch traders. Finally, there was also the school of Nanga or Bunjinga ("literati painting"), which specialized in works that emulated the Chinese scholar-painters' movement of the Ming and Qing dynasties. The Nanga movement was a widespread national phenomenon, and continued to survive well into the early twentieth century.

[*See also* Ukiyo-e *and* Woodblock Prints, Japanese.]

Terukazu Akiyama, *Japanese Painting* (1977). Robert Treat Paine and Alexander Soper, *The Art and Architecture of Japan* (1955).   YOSHIAKI SHIMIZU

PAINTING IN SOUTHEAST ASIA

Premodern Southeast Asian painting is predominantly of a didactic nature, informed by Buddhism, Hinduism, or Islam. It includes paintings on the walls of temples and portable works on wood, cloth, bark, and other materials. Very few of these fragile works have survived the tropical elements; those that remain are concentrated in Burma and Thailand. Other Southeast Asian countries had flourishing painting traditions as well, but we have an imperfect knowledge of their development. Media closely related to painting include Burmese and Thai lacquer, Indonesian textiles, tattoo motifs, drawings on bamboo, leather shadow-play figures, and decorated metalwork.

The earliest wall paintings to have survived relatively intact are dry frescoes from temples at Pagan in Burma. The compositions, dating to the eleventh and twelfth centuries, depict the Jatakas (tales of previous lives of the Buddha) and the life of the Buddha and were meant as pious reminders to the faithful. The paintings are predominantly Theravada Buddhist, although examples of a Tantric or Mahayana character are known. The classic Pagan style had a major impact on the mural paintings of later Burma, such as those of the Konbaung dynasty period (1752–1885).

In Thailand, the creators of Ban Chiang pottery (first millennium BCE) used fanciful painted and incised designs on their funerary wares. The first vestiges of painting from the eighth century are painted bricks from U Thong and Nakhon Pathom. During the Sukhothai period a series of engravings on stone from Wat Si Chum (mid-fourteenth century) depict the Jatakas in a linear style that is also preserved in fragmentary paintings from Si Sacchanalai. The earliest relatively complete examples of painting are from Wat Rajapurana (1424 CE) in Ayudhya, discovered in 1957. They continue the Sukhothai tradition; some were possibly executed by a Chinese artisan. From this point, examples of Thai painting become more numerous. In addition to the Bangkok school in the south, a northern school, designated as Lan Na, produced significant works, particularly on the theme of the Prince of the Golden Conch.

The themes of Thai painting, as well as those of neighboring Burma and Cambodia, include the Jatakas, scenes from *The Three World,* the Buddhas of the past, and the life of the Buddha. Wall paintings predominate, although examples in a palm-leaf format and illuminated *khoi*-paper accordion-folded manuscripts are well known. Painted cotton banners and hangings are equally common.

After prehistoric cave paintings, the first significant examples of painting from the islands of Southeast Asia (Malaysia, Indonesia, and the Philippines) are eighteenth- and nineteenth-century hangings and illuminated manuscripts, including calendars, executed on bark cloth, cotton, and imported European paper. They attest to a long-lived Hindu-Buddhist painting tradition heavily influenced by the shadow play *(wayang),* with a significant impact by Islam in later centuries. Influence of the shadow play, where figures are shown in strict profile with exaggerated poses, can be found in Java's *wayang beber* and Bali's *ider-ider,* in which stories are recounted using bark-cloth painted scrolls. Other ritual and narrative hangings show varying degrees of *wayang* influence. Some indication of their historical roots are to be found in the low-relief carvings of Indonesia's temples and religious shrines, such as can be found at Borobudur, Prambanan, and Panataran.

[*See also* Pagan; Ban Chiang; Sukhothai; Lan Na; Borobudur; Prambanan; *and* Panataran.]

Tibor Bodrogi, *Art of Indonesia* (1972). Jean Boisselier, *Thai Painting* (1976). Alexander B. Griswold et al., *The Art of Burma, Korea, and Tibet* (1964). Claire Holt, *Art in Indonesia: Continuities and Change* (1967).

ROBERT S. WICKS

IRANIAN AND CENTRAL ASIAN PAINTING

Both Central Asia and Iran have long traditions of painting on pottery, wood, cloth, and lacquer. The discussion here, however, will be limited to wall painting and book illustration, the two most significant types of Iranian and Central Asian painting.

Wall Painting. The few surviving examples of wall paintings, supplemented by textual descriptions, suggest a continuous tradition of figural wall painting that dates back to the Buddhist civilization that flourished along the Silk Route in Central Asia in the first millennium CE. The caves at Kizil (c. 500) show scenes of the life of the Buddha with sensitively modeled round figures in bright colors. The Uighurs took over the Turfan oasis in the ninth century, and frescoes from the temple complex near Kocho depict local rulers and rich merchants, supporters of the monasteries, dressed in splendid red robes. The Sogdians, meanwhile, controlled western Central Asia; their palace at Panjikent was embellished with frescoes depicting epic scenes and heroes like Siyavush.

The Islamic world adopted this Central Asian tradition of palatine wall painting. Among the paintings found at the Abbasid palaces at Samarra (ninth century) were scenes of servants and dancing girls. The tradition was in turn borrowed by the Ghaznavids (twelfth century); French excavations of the capital at Bust in Afghanistan revealed frescoes on the walls of the throne room depicting the imperial guard. Texts describe paintings of battle scenes on Ilkhanid palaces, and the seventeenth-century Safavid palaces at Isfahan (Chihil Sutun and Hasht Bihisht) preserve large frescoes of battles and receptions and individual vignettes illustrating court figures or scenes from lyric poetry. Not only do these palace wall paintings illustrate courtly pleasures and pursuits such as feasting, hunting, and battle, they also glorify the ruler by association with epic heroes.

Manuscript Painting. The origins of Persian manuscript painting are obscure and controversial. A few fragments of eighth- and ninth-century Manichaean manuscripts were found in the Turfan oasis; they depict religious ceremonies in rich colors. Surviving contemporary manuscripts from the western Iranian world, like other Arabic manuscripts, are decorated with illumination or with astronomical figures. However, the earliest surviving Persian manuscripts with illustrations date only from the end of the thirteenth century. From that point, a continuous development of imperial or metropolitan painting from the Ilkhanid through the Safavid periods (fourteenth to seventeenth century) can be established.

The *Shahnama,* the Persian national epic, was by far the most popular subject for illustration, but, although later rulers maintained the tradition of commissioning a personal copy of the *Shahnama,* lyric poems—especially Nizami's *Khamsa (Quintet)*—became increasingly popular. Prose works such as histories, cosmologies, and even the occasional religious text were also illustrated.

Three imperial manuscripts of the *Shahnama* illustrate the development of manuscript painting

FIGURE 1. *Leaf from Nizami's Khamsa.* Dated 1525.

from the Ilkhanid through the Safavid periods. The first was probably commissioned around 1335 in Tabriz by the last Ilkhanid ruler, Abu Sa'id; it has been cut up and is now dispersed in European and American collections. A second was ordered by the Timurid prince Baysonghor at Herat in 1439–1440 and is now in the Gulistan Library in Tehran. A third was done for the Safavid shah Tahmasp at Tabriz, probably between 1522 and 1535, and is now in New York's Metropolitan Museum of Art and other collections.

All three are large-format manuscripts, measuring at least ten inches by fifteen inches, but the Ilkhanid and Safavid ones have a much higher rate of illustration. The former is estimated to have contained 250 miniatures; the latter has 258. By contrast, the Timurid manuscript has only twenty illustrations, in addition to a double-page frontispiece. While this lower rate of illustration might reflect the lower status of the patron as prince rather than king, more probably it is due to the court's discriminating taste for quality over quantity, for many Timurid manuscripts contain a small number of extremely fine miniatures.

The relationship of text to image also changed. Most of the miniatures in the Ilkhanid manuscript are rectangular blocks inserted into the text; a few are stepped to increase the drama and impact of the action. During the fourteenth and fifteenth centuries, miniatures continued to expand and spill into the margin, so that by the Safavid period the miniature envelops the text.

The Ilkhanid illustrations are experimental. Individual miniatures differ dramatically in color, from monochromatic washes to cool greens and browns to vivid blues and golds. A variety of devices such as triangular compositions, gaze, repoussé figures, and overlapping planes are used to depict spatial depth. The large figures seem ready to burst from the picture frame and readily evoke an emotional response from the viewer.

In complete contrast, the Timurid illustrations epitomize the classical moment in Persian painting. Pristine, jewel-like colors are meticulously balanced throughout the miniature. Small, neat figures drawn with a clear line are uniformly set against a high horizon. Space thus becomes a vertical plane, with the objects at the bottom meant to be read as nearer and those higher up as farther back. Such technical perfection and rational conception meant the loss of the earlier emotional tone. Instead, birds twitter and figures stand in a frozen, timeless space; gory battles are reduced to ballets.

By the Safavid period this classical norm had yielded to fantasy and detail. The modulated colors became lusher, with a heavier use of violet. Line is more exuberant. Humor and caricature enter the picture: cushions spin, demons cavort as their tails are tweaked, monsters and dragons swirl out of anthropomorphic rocks. The viewer's eye is lost in the riot of color, pattern, and detail.

This evolution in physical layout and style may reflect a change in the way manuscripts were produced. Very little is known about the organization of ateliers, or *kitabkhanas;* based on textual references and analogy with illuminated manuscripts, it seems that at first the calligrapher was the painter, but with the development of miniature production, specialization increased. The first signed miniatures date from the late fourteenth century, and the most celebrated Persian miniature painter, Bihzad, flourished in the late fifteenth and early sixteenth centuries. He began at the Timurid court of Sultan Husain Baiqara at Herat, and the Safavids recruited him to Tabriz, where he was appointed head of the royal library, in charge of all librarians, calligraphers, painters, gilders, marginal draftsmen, gold mixers, gold beaters, and lapis lazuli washers. Only in sixteenth-century works can individual hands and schools be distinguished.

Such manuscripts were obviously luxury items, produced in court workshops at metropolitan centers. Cities like Shiraz and Yazd also maintained a standard of book production for anonymous patrons, presumably rich merchants or bourgeois. Another group of manuscripts with stocky figures, stock motifs, and broad drawing has been attributed to Turkmen circles. Other miniatures of weird beasts and distorted humans, mostly preserved in albums in Istanbul, probably reflect the taste of another sector of society.

Manuscript illustration began to wane in the second half of the sixteenth century. Shah Tahmasp turned against painting, so that the royal ateliers were disbanded and staggering numbers of artists emigrated to India. A new class of non royal patrons emerged who preferred individual drawings or album pages. These were often done with voluptuous curves and sensitive modeling, into which a master like Reza Abbasi injected a note of satire and caricature. In the seventeenth century European prints circulated in Iran; thus, Muhammad Zaman based his miniatures on Western models. Finally, under the Qajars miniature painting was almost completely supplanted by tinted drawings, watercolors, and oil portraits on canvas.

[See also Baiqara, Husain; Bihzad; Herat; Nizami; Panjikent; and Shahnama.]

Laurence Binyon, J. V. S. Wilkinson, and Basil Gray, *Persian Miniature Painting* (1933; reprint, 1971). Oleg Grabar and Sheila Blair, *Epic Images and Contemporary History: The Illustrations of the Great Mongol Shahnama* (1980). Basil Gray, *Persian Painting* (1961). Herbert Hartel and Marianne Yaldiz, *Along the Ancient Silk Routes: Central Asian Art from the West Berlin State Museums,* edited by M. E. D. Laing (1982). Tehran Imperial Palace Library, *An Album of Miniatures from the Baysonghuri Manuscript of the Shahnameh* (1971). Stuart Cary Welch, *A King's Book of Kings: The Shah-nameh of Shah Tahmasp* (1972).   SHEILA S. BLAIR

PAJAJARAN, Sundanese kingdom of West Java (fourteenth to sixteenth century). According to the Old Sundanese commemorative inscription of Batu Tulis, the royal palace of Pajajaran, called Pakuan and located near present-day Bogor, was founded in the year 1333. One of the few pieces of historical evidence attesting to Pajajaran's importance in a quasi-international context comes from the Majapahit history work the *Pararaton.* There it is related that the Majapahit king, Hayam Wuruk, decided upon a marriage with a Sundanese princess of Pajajaran. Yet when she and her entourage arrived at the Majapahit port of Bubat in 1351, they were met by chief minister Gajah Mada's demand that the bride be handed over as a token of submission rather than as a symbol of alliance between Java's most powerful kingdoms. This was unacceptable to the Sundanese delegation, which was led by its king, and although they defended themselves as best as they could they perished in the bloodbath that followed. While the short reference to the event in the *Pararaton* is given poetic embroidery in the much later *Kidung Sunda,* neither it nor the Pajajaran kingdom are mentioned by the *Nagarakertagama,* written at the Majapahit court a decade afterward. That more peaceful contacts existed at this time between the island's eastern and western halves is attested to by the wanderings of a Sundanese Buddhist monk, Bujangga Manik. According to an Old Sundanese manuscript written by Bujangga Manik, his travels from Pakuan in West Java through Central and East Java, as well as to Bali and home again, must have taken place at the end of the fourteenth or beginning of the fifteenth century.

As late as 1522 Pajajaran still controlled the harbor of Sunda Kalapa (present-day Jakarta). Within a few years, however, this passed under the control of its aggressively Islamic neighbor, the kingdom of Banten. According to the *Sejarah Banten (The History of Banten),* the coup de grâce for the Pajajaran heartland came in the 1570s with the capture of the royal palace, the slaughter of its royal family, and the forced conversion of its subjects to Islam at the hands of Banten's Panembahan Yusup. Even so the reputation of the kingdom's last ruler, Prabhu Siliwangi, lived on as a symbol of the glories of the precolonial period of Indonesia's history.

Another, younger branch of the kingdom, Galuh, was located around Ci Amis to the south of Cirebon in the Eastern Priangan highlands. Toward the end of the sixteenth century Galuh fell under Mataram control, ultimately passing into Dutch hands in 1705, when the territory was formally ceded to the Dutch East India Company by the hard-pressed Sultan Mangkurat II of Mataram.

[See also Majapahit; Hayam Wuruk; Gajah Mada; Nagarakertagama; Banten; and Mataram.]

M. C. HOADLEY

PAK CHŎNG-HŬI. See Park Chung Hee.

PAKHTUN and *Pashtun* are the terms by which the speakers of Pakhtu/Pashtu inhabiting the present territory of Afghanistan and the North-West Frontier Province of Pakistan have preferred to be known. Outsiders, however, have more frequently referred to them as Pathans or Afghans.

The Pakhtu language seems to be derived from Saka, a language spoken by Central Asian nomads who conquered the present habitat of the Pakhtuns in the second millennium BCE. But there is little historical evidence or agreement on the ethnogenesis of the Pakhtuns. Stressing their monotheism, the Pakhtuns, in their folklore, equate their origin with the origin of Islam: Qais, their putative ancestor, is said to have led his followers from Ghur, in central Afghanistan, to Muhammad, the prophet of Islam, in Medina; there he was converted by the prophet in person and renamed Abd al-Rashid.

The Pakhtuns represent their social relations in an organizational chart of hierarchical patrilineal segments, starting with Qais and his three or four sons and reaching those living in the present. In this principle, every Pakhtun should know every chain of segmentation; in practice, however, a male Pakhtun has to know the name of his seven male ascendants and how their living descendants are linked to him. Beyond this minimal unit, he is required to know only the major segments, rather than the precise line of individuals through which his minimal unit is linked to the higher-named segments.

There are no words in Pakhtu that refer exclusively to a "lineage," in which descent is demonstrated, or a "clan," in which descent is merely assumed; the suffixes *zai* and *khel,* added to names of males to imply descent from them, can mean either "lineage" or "clan." The ambiguity, however, is very useful in practice. Instead of allowing their genealogy to dictate their behavior, the Pakhtuns can manipulate their tables of organization in such a way as to change the significance of levels of segmentation to the extent of incorporating totally alien groups within their genealogical fold.

Durrani, Ghilzai, and Karlanri have been for the last two centuries the names of the major groups of Pakhtun clans. The major clans in the Durrani group are the Achakzai, Alikozai, Alizai, Barakzai, Ishaqzai, Nurzai, and Popalzai; in the Ghilzai group are the Andar, Hotak, Kharoti, Nasir, Sahak, Sulimankhel, Taraki, and Tokhi; and in the Karlanri group are the Afridi, Bangash, Khatak, Khugiani, Mahsudi, Mangal, Orakzai, Utmankhel, and Wazir.

Symbolically, the unity of the Pakhtuns is expressed through their adherence to *pakhtunwali,* the ideal code of behavior stressing honor, hospitality, and revenge. *Pakhtunwali* is also a customary system of mediation that includes provisions for settling disputes ranging from theft to homicide. The social agencies through which *pakhtunwali* has been practiced are the *jirga* (assembly) and the *khan* (chief). In its juridical sense, *jirga* refers to a gathering of experts on *pakhtunwali* who are chosen by parties to a case to mediate between the disputants. In its political sense, *jirga* refers to a gathering of all members of a clan, heads of households or lineages, or the representatives of clans, who serve as intermediaries between a Pakhtun group and outside powers. The *jirga* is, thus, always considered representative, but the *khan* may or may not be.

In the sixteenth century the title *khan* was bestowed by Mughal and Safavid emperors on Pakhtun notables appointed to safeguard the long-distance trade between India and Iran. The consolidation of the office of khan soon led to the emergence of *khankhels* (chiefly, lineages) that laid exclusive claim to the office. Khans, however, were often polygamous, and as the Pakhtun have had no preferential rules of succession to high office, the intense rivalry among aspirants to the office of khan often resulted in internal factionalism and unfavorable external alliances. The odds against unified Pakhtun action were thus great, and the few leaders who have succeeded at the task are fondly remembered by all Pakhtuns. The best known of these Pakhtun heroes are Khushal Khattak (1613–1689), the poet-warrior who led the Pakhtun resistance against the Mughals; Mir Wais Hotak (d. 1715), who freed Kandahar from the Safavid yoke and founded the Hotak state; and Ahmadshah (r. 1747–1773), who founded the Durrani empire. Unfortunately, the Soviet invasion of Afghanistan in December 1979, which has subsequently driven most Pakhtuns out of the country, has neither produced unified action nor given rise to leaders with a vision of the future.

[*See also* Afghanistan; Durranis; *and* Ghilzais.]

Olaf Caroe, *The Pathans 550 B.C.–A.D. 1957* (1958). David Dichter, *The Northwest Frontier of Pakistan* (1967). Louis Dupree, *Afghanistan* (1980). Ainslie Embree, ed., *Pakistan's Western Borderlands* (1977). Charles Lindholm, *Generosity and Jealousy: The Swat Pukhtun of Northern Pakistan* (1982).   ASHRAF GHANI

PAKISTAN. On 14 August 1947 Pakistan emerged as the single largest Muslim state in the world. A fascinating (and by far the bloodiest) instance in the history of postwar decolonization, the creation of Pakistan was accompanied by the largest demographic movements in recorded history. Nearly seventeen million people—Hindus, Muslims, and Sikhs—are reported to have moved in both directions between India and the two wings of Pakistan. Of the ninety-five million Muslims in the Indian subcontinent at the time of partition, some sixty million became citizens of Pakistan. Paradoxically, the establishment of a predominantly Muslim state in the northwest and the northeast of the subcontinent left thirty-five million Muslims inside India—the largest Muslim minority in a non-Muslim state.

Scarred from birth, Pakistan's quest for survival has been as compelling as it has been uncertain. Despite the shared religion of its overwhelmingly Muslim population, Pakistan has been engaged in a precarious struggle to define a national identity and evolve a political system based on the consensus of its linguistically diverse constituent units. Chronic regional tensions, successive failures in constitution-making, three full-scale wars with India, a strategically exposed northwestern frontier, a series of economic crises, and the continued difficulties of allocating scarce financial resources in an equitable manner underpin the dilemma Pakistan has faced in reconciling the goal of national integration with the imperatives of national security.

The breakaway of its eastern wing and the establishment of Bangladesh in 1971 following a military defeat at the hands of India was the most dramatic manifestation of this dilemma. Political developments in Pakistan continue to be marred by provincial jealousies and, in particular, by the deep resentments in the smaller provinces of Sind, Baluchistan, and the North-West Frontier Province against what is seen to be a monopoly by the Punjabi majority of the benefits of power, profit, and patronage. Pakistan's political instability has been matched by a fierce ideological debate about the form of government it should adopt, Islamic or secular. In the absence of any nationally based political party, Pakistan has long had to rely on the civil service and the army to maintain the continuities of government. Pakistan has been under military rule for twenty-two of its thirty-eight years of existence. The Punjabi dominance of the civil bureaucracy and army has served to accentuate regional grievances, especially since constitutional government, which might have provided a better balance between the provinces, has been in abeyance for extended periods of time.

The roots of Pakistan's multifaceted problems can be traced to the period immediately preceding its creation. It was in March 1940, a mere seven and one-half years before partition, that the All-India Muslim League formally orchestrated the demand for a Pakistan consisting of Muslim-majority provinces in the northwest and the northeast of India. By asserting that the Indian Muslims were a nation, not a minority, the Muslim League and its leader, Mohammad Ali Jinnah, had hoped to negotiate a constitutional arrangement that could provide for an equitable share of power between Hindus and Muslims once the British quit India. The demand for a "Pakistan" was Jinnah's and the League's bid to register their claim to be the spokesmen of all Indian Muslims, both in provinces where they were in a majority as well as in provinces where they were in a minority. Jinnah and the League's main bases of support, however, were in the Muslim-minority provinces; in the 1937 general elections, the league had met a serious rebuff from the Muslim voters in the majority provinces.

There was an obvious contradiction in a demand for a separate Muslim state and the claim to be speaking for all Indian Muslims. During the remaining years of the British Raj in India neither Jinnah nor the Muslim League explained how Muslims in the minority provinces could benefit from a Pakistan based on an undivided Punjab, Sind, North-West Frontier Province, and Baluchistan in the northwest, and an undivided Bengal and Assam in the northeast. Yet the lack of clarity on the part of Jinnah and the League was more seeming than real. Jinnah at least had tried to get around the inconsistencies by arguing that since there were two nations in India—Hindu and Muslim—any transfer of power from British to Indian hands would necessarily entail a dissolution of the unitary center created by the imperial rulers. Any reconstitution of the Indian union would have to be based on either confederal or treaty arrangements between Pakistan (representing the Muslim-majority provinces) and Hindustan (representing the Hindu-majority provinces). Jinnah also maintained that Pakistan would have to include an undivided Punjab and Bengal. The substantial non-Muslim minorities in both these provinces were the best guarantee that the Indian National Congress would see sense in negotiating reciprocal arrangements with the Muslim League to safeguard the interests of Muslim minorities in Hindustan.

Despite Jinnah's large claims, the Muslim League failed to build up an effective party machinery in the Muslim-majority provinces. Consequently the

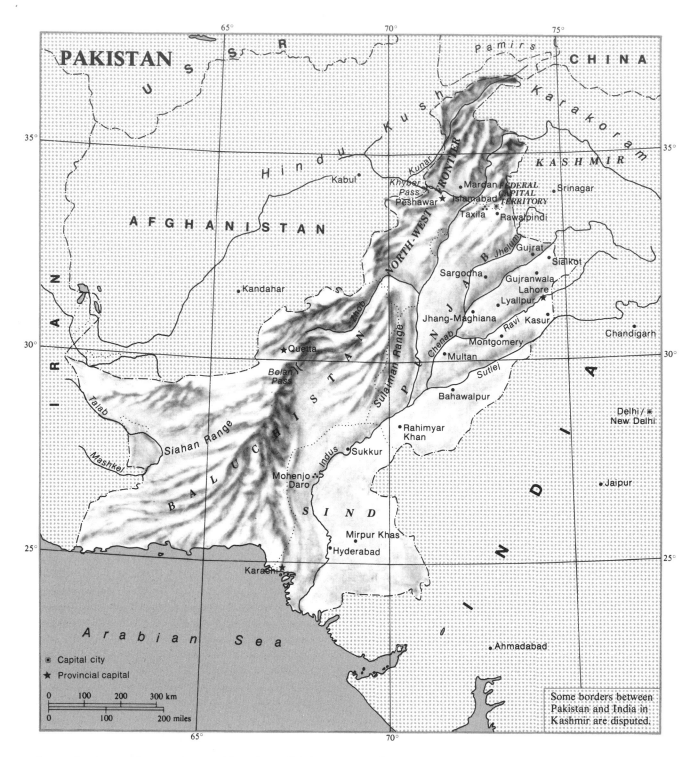

league had no real control over either the politicians with whom it came to hurried accommodations or the populace at the base who were mobilized in the name of Islam. The uncertain commitment of the Muslim-majority province politicians to the Muslim League's purposes and the expectations aroused by the demand for Pakistan, critically narrowed Jin-

nah's options during the final negotiations with the British and the Congress. The outbreak of communal troubles constrained Jinnah further still. In the end he had little choice but to settle for a Pakistan stripped of the non-Muslim majority districts of the Punjab and Bengal and to abandon his hopes of a settlement that might have secured the interests of all Muslims. But the worst cut of all was Congress's refusal to interpret partition as a division of India between Pakistan and Hindustan. According to the Congress, partition simply meant that certain areas with Muslim majorities were 'splitting off' from the "Indian union." The implication was that if Pakistan failed to survive, the Muslim areas would have to return to the Indian union severally; there would be no assistance to recreate it on the basis of two sovereign states.

Indeed, nothing stood in the way of the reincorporation of the Muslim areas into the Indian union except the notion of a central authority that had yet to be firmly established. To establish a central authority over provinces that for so long had been governed from New Delhi was all the more difficult, given the separation of Pakistan's eastern and western wings by one thousand miles of Indian territory. If Islamic sentiments were the best hope of keeping the Pakistani provinces pulling in the same direction, their particularistic traditions and linguistic affiliations were formidable stumbling blocks. Islam had certainly been a useful rallying cry, but it had not been effectively translated into the solid support Jinnah and the League had needed from the Muslim provinces in order to negotiate an arrangement on behalf of all Indian Muslims. [See Jinnah, Mohammad Ali.]

The particularisms of Pakistan's provinces, therefore, were a potential threat to central authority. While the provincial arenas continued to be the main centers of political activity, those who set about creating the new center in Karachi were either politicians with no real bases of support or civil servants trained in the old traditions of British Indian administration. The inherent weaknesses of the Muslim League's party machinery, together with the absence of a central administrative apparatus that could coordinate the affairs of the state, proved to be a crippling disadvantage. The socioeconomic dislocations in the provinces and the presence of millions of refugees called for urgent remedial action by a central government that had neither adequate resources nor capacities. The commercial groups had yet to be cajoled into investing in some desperately needed industrial units. And the need to extract revenues from the agrarian sector called for state interventions that sooner rather than later pitched the administrative apparatus against the landed elite who dominated the Muslim League.

To complicate matters, the security of Pakistan's newly demarcated frontiers required substantial outlays for defense. With 17.5 percent of the assets of undivided India and one-third of the armed forces, Pakistan was responsible for the defense of the strategically vulnerable northwestern frontier. Afghanistan's claims on parts of the North-West Frontier Province hinted at the potential problems on that front. There was also the need to defend Pakistan's far-flung eastern wing. The initiation of hostilities with India, especially over the Muslim-majority princely state of Kashmir, so soon after the establishment of the state entailed a diversion of very scarce financial resources—inevitably extracted from the provinces—into a defense procurement effort that might best have been postponed until after political processes in Pakistan had become more clearly defined.

While a less than representative seventy-nine-member Constituent Assembly debated the future constitution, and the military dispute with India drained the state of its financial resources, solutions to Pakistan's manifold problems became increasingly intractable. It was not long before the regional and the internal factors combined with the imperatives of the postwar international political system to shift the institutional balance of power away from the political center in Karachi and toward the military headquarters in Rawalpindi. Political leaders, notably Prime Minister Liaqat Ali Khan (assassinated in October 1951), were reluctant to join British and American sponsored defense organizations without a firm territorial guarantee for Pakistan. The perspective of the defense establishment was different. Anxious to secure modern armaments, its top echelons were ready to commit Pakistan to Western security arrangements. By 1955 Pakistan had formally joined both the Southeast Asia Treaty Organization (SEATO) and the Central Treaty Organization (CENTO) and had become a major recipient of American military and economic aid.

Since neither the military nor the civil bureaucracy had entirely escaped the dislocations wrought by partition, it took a continuing cycle of political and economic crises to witness the eclipse of politicians as the symbolic bearers of authority in the evolving structure of the Pakistani state. Raging controversies over the issue of the national language, the role of Islam, provincial representation, and the distribution of power between the center and the provinces delayed constitution-making and postponed general elections. In October 1956 a consensus was cobbled together and Pakistan's first constitution promulgated. The experiment in democratic government was short but not sweet. Ministries were made and broken in quick succession and in October 1958, with national elections scheduled for the following year, General Mohammad Ayub Khan carried out a military coup with confounding ease.

Between 1958 and 1971 Pakistan experienced a process of centralization without the inconvenience of unstable ministerial coalitions that had characterized its first decade after independence. The alliance of a predominantly Punjabi army and civil bureaucracy with the small but influential industrial class as well as segments of the landed elite was all the more important because parliamentary government was replaced in 1959 by a system of "basic democracies." The 1962 constitution formalized the system. It aimed at depriving parties and politicians with provincial bases of any role in the political system by extending the scope of bureaucratic patronage, both economic and political, to the localities. This was to be achieved by establishing direct links between the center and the local councillors through the local officers of what by now was a highly centralized civil service. The local councillors (initially eighty thousand divided equally between the two wings and later increased by another forty thousand) served as the electorate for a presidential form of government.

By giving the civil bureaucracy a firm hand in electoral politics, Ayub had hoped to bolster central authority, a necessary accompaniment to his ambitious, and largely American-directed, program for Pakistan's economic development. But these policies exacerbated existing disparities between the provinces as well as within them, giving the grievances of the eastern wing a potency that threatened the very centralized control Ayub was trying to establish. In West Pakistan, notable successes in increasing productivity were more than offset by growing inequalities in the agrarian sector, an agonizing process of urbanization, and the concentration of wealth in a few industrial houses. In the aftermath of the 1965 war with India, mounting regional discontent in East Pakistan and urban unrest in West Pakistan helped undermine Ayub's authority, forcing him to relinquish power in March 1969. [See Ayub Khan, Mohammad.]

The period of Pakistan's second military regime under General Agha Muhammad Yahya Khan underlined the extent to which the process of centralization under bureaucratic and military tutelage had fragmented Pakistani society and politics. The general elections of 1970 on the basis of adult franchise revealed for the first time ever in Pakistan's history how regionalism and social conflict had come to dominate politics despite the efforts at controlled development. The Awami League, led by Mujibur Rahman, campaigned on a six-point program of provincial autonomy, capturing all but one seat in East Pakistan and securing an absolute majority in the national assembly. In West Pakistan the Pakistan People's Party, led by Zulfiqar Ali Bhutto, had a populist platform that stole the thunder from the Islamic parties and emerged as the largest single bloc. The prospect of an Awami League government was anathema to politicians in West Pakistan who in collusion with the military leadership prevented Mujib from taking the reins of power. [See Awami League.] The political stalemate leading to armed rebellion in East Pakistan and a military intervention to crush it resulted in a third war with India, thus clearing the way for the establishment of Bangladesh in 1971. [See Mujibur Rahman, Sheikh and Bhutto, Zulfiqar Ali.]

The dismemberment of Pakistan discredited both the civil bureaucracy and the army, and saw the formation of a representative government under the Pakistan People's Party (PPP), led by Bhutto. Bhutto's electoral strength, however, was confined to the Punjab and Sind, and even there it had not been based on solid political party organization. This, together with the PPP's lack of following in the North-West Frontier Province and Baluchistan, meant that Bhutto could not work the central apparatus without at least the tacit support of the civil bureaucracy and the military high command. The 1973 constitution made large concessions to the non-Punjabi provinces and provided the blueprint for a political system based on the semblance of a national consensus. But Bhutto failed to implement the federal provisions of the constitution. This was dramatically highlighted by his unceremonious dismissal of the non-PPP governors of the North-West Frontier Province and Baluchistan on charges of fomenting secessionist demands and, above all, by his use of the army and air force to squash an armed insurrection of Baluchi tribesmen. By relying on the coercive arm of the state to snuff out political opposition and by neglecting to build the PPP as a truly popular national party, Bhutto missed the opportunity afforded to him by the military debacle in East Pakistan. The gap between his popular rhetoric and the marginal successes of his somewhat haphazard economic reforms prevented Bhutto from consolidating his social base of support. Thus, despite a temporary loss of face in 1971 the civil bureaucracy and the army remained the most important pillars of the state structure. Although Bhutto's

PPP won the 1977 elections, the Pakistan National Alliance—a nine-party coalition representing five years of accumulated disaffections—charged him with rigging the vote. Violent urban unrest gave the army under General Zia-ul Haq the pretext to make a powerful comeback to the political arena, and on 5 July 1977 Pakistan was placed under military rule yet again.

Upon assuming power General Zia banned all political parties and expressed his determination to recast the Pakistani state and society into an Islamic mold. In April 1979 Bhutto was executed on murder charges and the PPP's remaining leadership was jailed or exiled. By holding nonparty elections and initiating a series of islamization policies, Zia sought to create a popular base of support in the hope of legitimizing the role of the military in Pakistani politics. The Soviet invasion of Afghanistan in December 1979 gave Zia's regime the international support it had courted with limited success during its first two years in office. Although Pakistan has now formally disentangled itself from both SEATO and CENTO and joined the nonaligned movement, it is regarded by the West as an important front-line state and is a major recipient of American military and financial aid. Despite a string of statistics advertising the health of the economy, murmurs of discontent, though muffled, continued to be heard. On 30 December 1985, after confirming his own position in a controversial "Islamic" referendum, completing a fresh round of nonparty elections to the provincial and national assemblies, and introducing a series of amendments to the 1973 constitution, Zia finally lifted martial law and announced the dawn of a new democratic era in Pakistan. Whether Zia's political system can withstand the inherent imbalance between military and civil institutions in Pakistan remains to be seen.

With a population of more than ninety million divided unequally among four linguistic provinces—the Punjab (56 percent), Sind (23 percent), the North-West Frontier Province (13 percent), and Baluchistan (8 percent)—Pakistan faces the unenviable task of setting government priorities in accordance with the needs of its diverse and unevenly developed constituent units. Irrespective of the form of government—civilian or military, Islamic or secular—solutions to the problem of mass illiteracy and economic inequities on the one hand, and the imperatives of national integration and national security on the other, will eventually determine the degree of political stability, or instability, that Pakistan faces in the decades ahead.

[See also Partition of India; Zia-ul Haq, Mohammad; Liaqat Ali Khan; Bangladesh; Bengal; Bhutto, Zulfiqar Ali; Punjab; Sind; North-West Frontier Province; Baluchistan; and All-India Muslim League.]

Rashid Amjad, *Industrial Concentration and Economic Power in Pakistan* (1974). G. W. Choudhury, *Constitutional Development in Pakistan* (2d ed., 1969). Hassan Gardezi and Jamil Rashid, eds., *Pakistan: The Roots of Dictatorship* (1983). Ayesha Jalal, *The Sole Spokesman: Jinnah, The Muslim League and the Demand for Pakistan* (1985). K. B. Sayeed, *The Political System of Pakistan* (1967). Anwar Syed, *Pakistan: Islam, Politics and National Solidarity* (1982). Lawrence Ziring, *Pakistan: The Enigma of Political Development* (1980).

AYESHA JALAL

PAKNAM INCIDENT (1893), climactic event in Siam's war with France that led to the establishment of French control over Laos. Following their takeover of central and northern Vietnam in 1885, the French claimed to succeed to alleged Vietnamese "suzerainty" over Laos, and in pressing these claims they encountered Siamese military resistance, notably at Khammouane early in 1893, when a French officer was killed. France thereupon sent two gunboats that forced the Siamese defenses at the mouth of the Chaophraya River and steamed upriver to Bangkok. With French guns literally leveled on the Royal Palace, Siam had to accede to French demands for a huge indemnity and the cession to France of all Laos east of the Mekong River.

[See also Laos.]

Chandran Jeshurun, *The Contest for Siam, 1889–1902* (1977). Hugh Toye, *Laos: Buffer State or Battleground* (1968). DAVID K. WYATT

PAKUALAMAN, the minor court established in Yogyakarta on 22 June 1812 when Sir Thomas Stamford Raffles (in office as lieutenant-governor of Java, 1811–1816) recognized Pangeran Natakusuma, a son of Sultan Hamengkubuwana I (r. 1749–1792), as Pangeran Aria Pakualam I (r. 1812–1829). A highly intelligent man and a shrewd politician, Pakualam I succeeded in ingratiating himself with the British (especially Raffles and John Crawfurd) through a shared interest in Javenese literature. By a contract of 17 March 1813, he was accorded an independent apanage of 4,000 households (*cacah*) and a monthly stipend to maintain a corps of one hundred horses as government auxiliaries. The corps, however, never achieved the importance of the Mangkunagaran Legion in Surakarta, and after Pakualam I's death in December 1829, the court began to move into a closer relationship with the sultanate.

In the early twentieth century, members of the Pakualaman played a prominent role in the early stages of the Budi Utomo cultural organization, and during the Indonesian national revolution against the Dutch (1945–1949), Pakualam VIII (r. 1937 to present) cooperated closely with Sultan Hameng-kubuwana IX (r. 1939 to present). This association has been maintained to the present day for purposes of the local administration of the Yogyakarta Special Region (Daerah Istimewa Yogyakarta).

[See also Yogyakarta; Raffles, Sir Thomas Stamford; Crawfurd, John; Mangkunagaran; Budi Utomo; and Indonesia, Republic of.]

Peter Carey, ed., *The British in Java, 1811–16: A Javanese Account* (1985).
PETER CAREY

PAKUBUWANA. The name *Pakubuwana* has been borne by twelve *susuhunans* ("kings") of Kartasura and Surakarta in Central Java since Pakubuwana I (r. 1704–1719). Pakubuwana II (r. 1726–1749) was one of the least able and most unfortunate monarchs of the Mataram dynasty. Pakubuwana IV (r. 1788–1820) was a mercurial man who tried to overturn existing political arrangements in Central Java and only narrowly escaped deposition by the Europeans on three occasions (in 1790, 1812, and 1815). Pakubuwana VI (r. 1823–1830) was exiled by the Dutch for fear that he would rebel. Pakubuwana XII (r. 1944 to present) was kidnapped by Indonesian revolutionaries, and his prerogatives were abolished in 1946.

[See also Kartasura; Surakarta; and Mataram.]

M. C. Ricklefs, *A History of Modern Indonesia, c. 1300 to the Present* (1981).
M. C. RICKLEFS

PAK YŎNG-HYO (Prince Kŭmnŭng; 1861–1939), the son-in-law of Korean King Chŏlchong (1831–1863; r. 1849–1863) and a prominant civil servant, reformist thinker, and political activist during the twilight years of the Yi dynasty (1392–1910).

Early in Pak's youth he came under the influence of progressive thinkers belonging to the *sirhak* ("practical learning") tradition of Korean Confucianism. During a short visit to Japan in 1882 as an official Korean envoy, Pak became very interested in Japanese modernization endeavors and returned to Seoul as an advocate of reform. During 1883, while serving as a local magistrate in Kwangju and as mayor of Seoul, Pak instituted many reforms, including helping Yu Kil-chun and Yun Ch'i-ho start Korea's first but short-lived newspaper, the *Han-sŏng sunbo,* published every ten days. He also became an active member of the progressive circle known as the Independence Party.

After the suppression of the Independence Party's 1884 coup, he fled to Japan. Except for a short visit to the United States in 1885, Pak remained there until 1894, learning English at Meiji Gakuin, a Protestant school, and studying Christianity and Western civilization. While there he expressed his support for the idea of converting Koreans to Christianity as a way of making their country "enlightened and prosperous." Pak is also known to have had many contacts with the Japanese publicist and reformer Fukuzawa Yukichi. Perhaps inspired by Fukuzawa's school, Keiō Gijuku, Pak also set up a school in Tokyo called Ch'inrin Ŭisuk (Japanese, Shinrin Gijuku; "good neighborliness school"). [See also Fukuzawa Yukichi.]

Pak is best know for writing a "reform memorial" to King Kojong in 1888 from his Japanese exile. In this 13,000-character document he discussed 114 specific proposals for reform, covering all major aspects of Korean life. Practically all the ideas the Independence Party and Independence Club championed are covered to a greater or lesser degree in the memorial.

With the backing of Japan, Pak returned to Seoul in 1894 and served as home minister in the new reform government. In July 1895, however, he once again had to flee to Japan when he was implicated in an antithrone plot. His association with Japan continued to plague his reputation, although Pak never became a Japanese puppet but remained a strong nationalist. In 1907, with the control of Japan over Korea becoming firmer than ever, Pak once again returned to Seoul to serve as palace affairs minister. After the Japanese annexation of Korea in 1910, Pak was appointed to the new Privy Council as an adviser; he later became a member of the Japanese peerage.

Pak was one of those progressive Koreans who, while remaining wedded to Korean nationalism and modernization, could not help aligning himself with Japan under the belief that such help was indispensable to the successful achievement of his hopes for his country. He unwittingly helped the Japanese in their expansionist designs on Korea.

[See also Independence Party and Club; 1884 Coup d'État; Yu Kil-chun; Yun Ch'i-ho; Kojong; and Korea, Japanese Government-General of.]

Hilary Conroy, The Japanese Seizure of Korea, 1868–1910 (1960). Harold F. Cook, Korea's 1884 Incident (1972). Young-Ick Lew (Yu Young-ik), "The Reform Efforts and Ideas of Pak Yŏng-hyo," Korean Studies 1 (1977): 21–61.   VIPAN CHANDRA

PALA DYNASTY. Following a period of political instability in eastern India, the Pala Dynasty rose to power about 750 CE and continued to rule much of Bihar and Bengal until the middle of the twelfth century. The Palas were Buddhists and established several important monasteries, Vikramasila and Paharpur among them, both founded by the second Pala king, Dharmapala (c. 783–818). A subsequent

FIGURE 1. *Pala-period Stele with Khasarpana-Lokeshvara.* Bengal, late tenth to early eleventh century. Black chlorite. Height 139 cm.

king, Mahipala (c. 991–1040), who restored the dynasty's authority after a period of decline and briefly extended its realm as far west as Varanasi, provided patronage for many Buddhist sites from Sarnath to Bengal.

[See also Buddhism: An Overview and Bengal.]

A. M. Chowdhury, Dynastic History of Bengal (c. 750–1200 A.D.) (1967). B. A. Sinha, The Decline of the Kingdom of Magadha (cir. 455–1000 A.D.) (1954).

FREDERICK M. ASHER

PALEMBANG. From the late seventh to the early eleventh century Palembang was the head of the loosely knit Srivijaya empire of trading ports. Palembang was strategically located between the Strait of Melaka and the Sunda Strait, and from this upriver Musi River port in southeastern Sumatra, Srivijaya's rulers were able to control the international trade routes that passed through their realm. Reports of Palembang's fabulous wealth circulated widely among early Asian traders. In 1025 the South Indian Cholas plundered Palembang, and the Srivijaya capital subsequently shifted to Jambi. Early fourteenth-century Chinese records indicate that by that time Palembang had to force ships to use its harbor. A Chinese pirate chief controlled Palembang in 1407, when he was arrested by the Ming eunuch admiral Zheng He. By the sixteenth century an independent sultanate had assumed control over Palembang and based its existence on the marketing of local pepper.

In the early seventeenth century the English and Dutch traded at Palembang, but when the Palembang sultan murdered the Dutch factors and the crews of two Dutch ships in 1658, the Dutch responded by forcing the sultan to allow them to construct a fortress and to sell local pepper to them exclusively. The British briefly assumed authority over the Dutch fortress during the Napoleonic era, but in 1825 Palembang was brought completely under Dutch rule. By the end of the nineteenth century Palembang had become a center of the Dutch rubber industry.

[See also Srivijaya; Jambi; and Zheng He.]

O. W. Wolters, The Fall of Srivijaya in Malay History (1970).   Kenneth R. Hall

PALLAVA DYNASTY. It is believed that the rulers of this South Indian dynasty emerged as early as the second century CE, and that they were brahmans who came from North India. By the late third or early fourth century the Pallava Sivaskandavarman

FIGURE 1. *Pallava-period Sculpture (Seated Queen?)*. South India, Pandya area, eighth to ninth century. Buff granite. Height 170.2 cm., width 88.3 cm.

controlled many parts of the Tamil country and probably sizeable areas of present-day Karnataka and Andhra Pradesh. The latter half of the sixth century was the period of the great Pallavas, who ruled from their capital at Kanchipuram. Pallava territory expanded under Simhavishnu (ruled c. 556–589), who fought against the Cholas, Kalabhras, Gangas, and Chalukyas in the north, and the Pandyas and the kings of Kerala in the extreme south. His successor was the well-known Mahendravarman (ruled c. 590–629), author of the Sanskrit play *Mattavilasa prahasana*. Some of the temples of Mahabalipuram were hewn out of rock during his time. Under Narasimhavarman (ruled c. 630–668), war against the Chalukyas culminated in the sack of the Chalukyan capital, Vatapi. Narasimhavarman also invaded Sri Lanka on behalf of a

Sinhala prince. Both the port and the temple complex at Mahabalipuram were expanded in his reign. Mahendravarman II and Paramesvaravarman succeeded him. The latter fought against the Chalukyas, Gangas, and Pandyas. In the reign of Narasimhavarman II (r. 690–729), the famous Kailasanatha temple at Kanchipuram was built and Sanskrit literature flourished. Narasimhavarman developed contacts with China. His successors Paramesvaravarman II and Nandivarman II faced crushing attacks by the Chalukyas. In the early ninth century the Rashtrakutas, who superseded the Chalukyas, captured Kanchipuram and held it for some years. Under Nandivarman III, who ruled briefly in the mid-ninth century, overseas trade increased, Tamil traders went as far as Takuapa in Thailand, and Mahabalipuram grew. The last effective Pallava ruler, Nripatunga (r. 869–900), in alliance with the Pandyas, was involved in a war against Sri Lanka.

[*See also* Mahabalipuram; Tamil Nadu; *and* Sri Lanka.]

R. Gopalan, *History of the Pallavas of Kanchi* (1928). G. Jouveau-Dubreuil, *The Pallavas* (1917). C. Minakshi, *Administration and Social Life under the Pallavas* (1938). K. A. Nilakanta Sastri, *A History of South India from Prehistoric Times to the Fall of Vijayanagar* (1955).

MEERA ABRAHAM

PALLEGOIX, DENIS-JEAN-BAPTISTE (1805–1862). A French Roman Catholic priest, Pallegoix spent much of his life in Thailand. He arrived in Bangkok in 1830 and eight years later was appointed bishop of Mallos, vicar-apostolic of Siam. An active student of language, history, and culture, Pallegoix published a Thai-Latin grammar, a dictionary of the Thai language, and an account of the country's history, religion, products, and geography. He became close friends with the future king, Mongkut. The two met frequently; Mongkut taught Pallegoix Pali, while Pallegoix taught Mongkut Latin. Later, Pallegoix served as translator and assistant to French visitors to the Thai court.

[*See also* Mongkut.]

CONSTANCE M. WILSON

PAMIRS, the high-altitude mountains of Central Asia located mostly in the Tajik republic of the USSR and Xinjiang, China. The range constitutes a mountain knot from which other major ranges extend: the Hindu Kush to the west, the Karakoram to the east, and the Tian Shan to the north. Containing numerous glaciers and peaks above 20,000 feet, the Pamirs include the 24,590-foot Communism Peak in the USSR and the 25,325-foot Gongger in China. [*See also* Hindu Kush *and* Tian Shan Range.]

MICHAEL BONINE

PANATARAN, fourteenth-century temple complex in the East Java kingdom of Majapahit. It is the largest and most important monument of the eastern Javanese period. Lying in the upper reaches of the Brantas River valley, the complex dates to 1369, although work on it must have commenced earlier and certainly continued until the early fifteenth century. Panataran provides a fine example of *candi* architecture, characteristic of East Java during the thirteenth and fourteenth centuries and imitated on Bali until modern times. Candi Panataran, along with Jago, Kedaten, and Surawan, represents the culmination of the *wayang* style of reliefs, which were carved on walls, balustrades, and bases. Figures and their surroundings are presented in a flat, almost two-dimensional and highly stylized pattern, closely resembling the flat leather-carved shadowplay puppets from Bali, which are less elongated than their Javanese counterparts. [*See also* Majapahit.]

C. Holt, *Art in Indonesia: Continuities and Change* (1967).

M. C. HOADLEY

PANCASILA (from Sanskrit, *panchashila,* "five principles"), the Indonesian state ideology to which all organizations in the country must adhere. It was enunciated by Sukarno in June 1945 and incorporated into the preamble to the 1945 constitution. The ideology calls for (1) belief in one supreme deity, (2) a just and civilized society, (3) national unity, (4) people's rule guided wisely through consultation and representation, and (5) social justice for all Indonesian people.

Despite changes of regime, the five principles have remained almost universally acceptable, although their intepretation has varied. The first principle, conceived as an alternative to an Islamic state, was invoked against atheistic communism in 1965. In the 1980s, government-sponsored Pancasila indoctrination courses helped limit the scope of permissible political debate. [*See also* Indonesia, Republic of *and* Sukarno.]

CHARLES A. COPPEL

PANCHAYAT ("council of five"), a group of recognized Indian leaders who convene to adjudicate disputes or render decisions affecting the group they represent.

Various kinds of *panchayats* have long existed in India. Traditionally, local and regional caste groups and villages have had councils that meet irregularly in response to specific problems. Elders or respected persons—almost exclusively male—gather to ponder pertinent issues and reach decisions by consensus. Meetings range from impromptu gatherings of a few local leaders to planned convocations of representatives from many villages. Enforcement of judgments depends upon united public opinion and action.

After Indian independence, formally elected village and multivillage *panchayats* were established by statute as local democratic governmental bodies to encourage economic and social change. Elected members are often young, and in some cases are female. Decisions are reached by voting and may be enforced with the assistance of government officers.

Oscar Lewis, *Village Life in Northern India* (1958). David G. Mandelbaum, *Society in India* (1970).

DORANNE JACOBSON

PANCHEN LAMA, the second most important religious hierarch in postreformation Tibet, believed to be a member of a line of incarnations like the Dalai Lama. Losang Chokyi Gyantsen (1570–1662) was formally installed as the first Panchen, abbot of Tashilhunpo Monastery in southern Tibet, although the incarnation line was traced back to Khaydrub Jay (a foremost disciple of Tsong Khapa, founder of the Gelugpa order). The dates of the second through the seventh Panchen Lamas are as follows:

Panchen Losang Yeshi (1663–1737)
Panchen Penden Yeshi (1738–1780)
Panchen Tenpai Nyima (1782–1853)
Panchen Tenpai Wangchuk (1855–1882)
Panchen Thupten Chokyi Nyima (1883–1937)
Panchen Tinlay Lhundup (b. 1938)

The present Panchen Lama was imprisoned by the Chinese from 1965 until 1979 for refusing to denounce the Dalai Lama and serve as puppet head of the Chinese regional administration of Tibet. He is now a layman, living in Beijing and serving on the Minorities Commission, trying to begin the process of rebuilding the shattered culture of Tibet. [*See also* Dalai Lama.]

ROBERT A. F. THURMAN

PANDIT, VIJAYA LAKSHMI (b. 1900), daughter of Motilal Nehru and sister of Jawaharlal Nehru. She was educated at home, and married Ranjit S. Pandit in 1921. She participated in the nationalist struggles led by Mohandas Gandhi and was imprisoned three times. Pandit was minister of health and local self-government in the Congress ministry in the United Provinces from 1937 to 1939. She headed the Indian delegation to the United Nations in 1946 and served as India's ambassador to the USSR (1947–1949) and to the United States (1949–1951). Her longest diplomatic assignment was as high commissioner for India in London from 1954 to 1961. She was a member of the Indian Parliament (1952–1954 and 1964–1969), and the governor of Maharashtra (1962–1964). She was president of the United Nations General Assembly in 1953–1954. In *The Scope of Happiness, A Personal Memoir* (1979), she gives her reminiscences of the nationalist movement and of the eminent personages she met during her varied diplomatic career. [*See also* Nehru, Jawaharlal.]

B. R. NANDA

PANDYA DYNASTY. The traditional territory of the Pandyas was the Tamil-speaking country of South India. Madurai was their capital. The Pandyas are first mentioned in the Sangam age, after which they reemerge in history toward the end of the sixth century CE. Pandya expansionism led to clashes with the Pallavas, Chalukyas, and Kongu and Kerala chiefs. In the early tenth century the Pandyas were defeated decisively by the Cholas. As Chola power declined in the thirteenth century the Pandyas again became important. In the second half of the thirteenth century Pandya territory included Kongu and may have extended north to Nellore. Pandya overseas trade was important. Their effective rule ended with the raid of Malik Kafur, followed by the establishment of the Muslim sultanate at Madurai in 1329–1330.

[*See also* Tamil Nadu *and* Madurai.]

K. A. Nilakanta Sastri, *The Pandyan Kingdom: From the Earliest Times to the Sixteenth Century* (1929) and *A History of South India from Prehistoric Times to the Fall of Vijayanagar* (1955).   MEERA ABRAHAM

PANGKOR ENGAGEMENT, a treaty between the British government and the chiefs of the Malay state of Perak, signed on 20 January 1874 at Pangkor Island off the coast of Perak, that placed the state under British protection and subsequently was the model used by the British to extend their control over the states of Malay Peninsula.

By introducing a permanent British presence, the Pangkor Treaty brought a truce both to factional warfare between competing groups of Chinese miners in Perak and to conflict between the Malay chiefs of the state over succession to the sultanate. The key clauses of the treaty were Clause 6, "that the Sultan (of Perak) receive and provide a suitable residence for a British Officer, to be called Resident, who shall be accredited to his Court, and whose advice must be asked and acted upon in all questions other than those touching Malay religion and custom," and Clause 10, "that the collection and control of all revenues and the general administration of the Country be regulated under the advice of these Residents." This so-called residential system was extended to all the rest of the Malay states of the peninsula over the next several decades, early to Negri Sembilan, Selangor, Pahang, and Johor; later to Trengganu, Kelantan, Kedah, and Perlis.

The Pangkor Treaty was a two-edged sword. On the one hand, it provided an opening through which Britain could turn "advice" into control, which in many cases proved absolute, and brought the forced reform and modernization of the administration of the states concerned. On the other hand, by reserving powers over "Malay religion and custom" to the Malay rulers, it unintentionally enhanced traditional authority and institutions, thereby providing, in the long run, a basis upon which Malay identity and nationalism could be developed.

[*See also* Birch, James W. W.; Ord, Sir Harry; Perak; Federated Malay States; *and* Unfederated Malay States.]

Barbara W. Andaya and Leonard Y. Andaya, *A History of Malaysia* (1982). C. D. Cowan, *Nineteenth-Century Malaya* (1961). R. O. Winstedt, *A History of Malaya* (1935). R. O. Winstedt and R. J. Wilkinson, *A History of Perak* (1934; reprint, 1974).   DAVID K. WYATT

PANINI (fourth century BCE), author of the *Ashtadhyayi*, the earliest surviving Sanskrit grammar. The culmination of a long tradition, it is composed of more than four thousand brief mnemonic sutras in a highly technical language. Because of Panini's thoroughness and scholarly excellence, it not only totally eclipsed earlier work, but is the source of almost all South and Southeast Asian indigenous linguistic literature since. It has also been an important influence in the development of modern Western linguistics.

George Cardona, *Pāṇini: A Survey of Research* (1976).
RANDOLPH M. THORNTON

PANIPAT, BATTLES OF.

The region of Panipat, a town and district in the state of Haryana in India, about fifty miles north of Delhi, was the scene of a number of important battles. Situated in an open plain on the Yamuna (Jumna) river, it controlled access to the Delhi area. It was here that Timur defeated the armies of the Delhi sultan in 1398, leading to the massacre of 100,000 Indian soldiers and the sack of Delhi. In 1526 it was site of the decisive battle in which Babur, invading India from his base in Afghanistan, defeated Ibrahim Lodi, the Delhi sultan, making possible the establishment of the Mughal empire. Then in 1556, Akbar, Babur's grandson, defeated a combination of his enemies and restored Mughal power. Another decisive battle was fought at Panipat in 1761 when Ahmad Shah Durrani, the Afghan invader, defeated the Marathas, who had already beaten the Mughal armies at Delhi. The Marathas, who had seemed likely to become the inheritors of the Mughals, were greatly weakened by their losses at Panipat. The Sikhs, who were becoming an important military power in the Punjab, fought a number of battles with the Mughal armies at Panipat in the 1770s, but they failed to mount a drive toward Delhi. The Panipat district passed into the control of the British in 1803.

[*See also* Delhi Sultanate; Lodi Dynasty; *and* Akbar.]

AINSLIE T. EMBREE

PANJIKENT,

a Sogdian city in present-day Tajikistan about sixty kilometers east of Samarkand. Soviet archaeologists have brought to light there a series of wall paintings that, though dating mainly from the eighth century CE, are of great documentary value for understanding Sogdian culture, religions, and history from the fifth to the eighth centuries. One set focuses on the mourning of a group of brown-haired, light-skinned men and gods for a young prince widely identified as Siyavush. Another set illustrates the exploits of Rustam in his famous seven stages. The site gained fame as the capital of Prince Devasti, whose archive from Mount Mugh has produced documents in Sogdian containing valuable data on the economic and cultural history of Central Asia.

[*See also* Painting: Iranian *and* Central Asian Painting *and* Sogdiana.]

Guitty Azarpay, *Sogdian Paintings* (1981). G. Frumkin, *Archaeology in Soviet Central Asia* (1970).
A. SHAHPUR SHAHBAZI

PAN-MALAYAN ISLAMIC PARTY,

or Partai Islam Se-Malaysia (PAS), Malaysian political party. Formed by a number of Islamic groups in 1951, the PAS has been the chief rival of the United Malays Nationalist Organization, drawing strength from its firm attachment to Islamic and nationalist principles, whatever its difficulties in explaining the practical implications. It formed a coalition with the Alliance Party in 1973 and joined the National Front in 1974 but returned to opposition in 1977. Its main strength has been in Kelantan (where it participated in the state government from 1959 to 1978), Terengganu, Kedah, and Perlis. The party split in 1983. [*See* Malaysia *and* United Malays National Organization.]
R. S. MILNE

P'ANMUNJŎM PEACE TALKS.

From July 1951 to July 1953, five representatives from each of the two sides in the Korean War conferred in agreed neutral territory between the opposing lines—briefly in Kaesŏng, then at P'anmunjŏm—to negotiate an armistice agreement to halt military hostilities. Talks began following Soviet United Nations Representative Jakov Malik's suggestion in June 1951 that the Communist side was willing to negotiate. The senior United Nations Command delegate until May 1952 was Admiral C. Turner Joy of the United States Navy; Joy was then replaced by Major General William K. Harrison, Jr., of the United States Army. Major General Paik Sun Yup represented the Republic of Korea Army. The representatives of the (North) Korean Peoples' Army and Chinese People's Volunteers included General Nam Il as senior delegate, and Lieutenant General Tong Hua.

By 26 July 1951 initial procedural details and an agenda had been worked out in meetings at Kaesŏng. The agenda included four substantive topics: fixing the military demarcation line between forces; arrangements for entering and enforcing the ceasefire and armistice; disposition of prisoners of war; and recommendations to governments on nonmilitary matters. Eight months later the demarcation line and most aspects of implementation were agreed upon, as was the recommendation for a political conference. The principal obstacle to final agreement was Communist resistance to the UN Command's support of the principle of voluntary repatriation of prisoners of war, which the Communists resisted because so many of their captured soldiers (nearly thirty thousand) preferred not to go home. Lesser obstacles were rehabilitation and construction of airfields, which the UN side wanted to prohibit (but eventually accepted), and the composition of the Neutral Nations Supervisory Commission. In April 1952 the United Nations side presented a package proposal that the Communists refused. An impasse resulted, and meetings were recessed indefinitely at UN initiative from October 1952 until March 1953.

During the recess the United Nations adopted an Indian resolution supporting the voluntary repatriation principle and proposing dispatch to a neutral country for prisoners of war not desiring to return to their own side. Sick and wounded prisoners were exchanged in April 1953; plenary sessions then resumed, and a variant of the Indian proposal was adopted.

Final agreement was put in jeopardy at the last moment by South Korean President Syngman Rhee's unilateral release of twenty-seven thousand prisoners of war on 18 June, but was nonetheless reached in a signing ceremony on 27 July 1953. The two principal delegates signed in the P'anmunjŏm conference room; the supreme commanders signed the documents in their respective headquarters at Kaesŏng and Munsan.

Procedural as well as substantive difficulties impeded negotiations. The Communist side apparently viewed the proceedings as a political extension of the basic conflict, and exploited them in every possible way for strategic and propaganda advantage—including germ-warfare charges. The UN side, prepared to accept the status quo, wanted speedy and businesslike negotiation of a practical truce. The differences in approach and psychology resulted in acrimonious tirades during plenary sessions, extensive delays, and frequent recesses—in two cases, for several months. Subcommittees of one representative from each side sometimes provided a means of resolving problems with fewer procedural complications.

[See also Korean War.]

C. Turner Joy, *How Communists Negotiate* (1970). *Panmunjom*, compiled by the Democratic People's Republic of Korea Foreign Languages Publishing House (1969). *Special Report of the Unified Command on the Korean Armistice Agreement* (1953). William H. Vatcher, Jr., *Panmunjom: The Story of the Korean Military Armistice Negotiations* (1958).   DONALD S. MACDONALD

P'ANSORI, Korean narrative verse form and popular performing art that flourished in the eighteenth and nineteenth centuries. It is performed by a single professional singer (*kwangdae*), who both narrates and assumes the role of the characters, accompanied by a single drummer. In addition to his superior voice and memory, the singer was expected to master narrative and dramatic techniques in order to recreate the mood of a given story and the protagonist's state of mind. Holding a fan or a handkerchief in his hand, he thus sings, narrates (*aniri*), and acts (*pallim*). Around a core story comprising one or more folktale motifs, the plot of a *p'ansori* gradually accumulated episodes during its transmission from one generation to the next. These were created or reworked by the singer during performance and include elements of folklore, romance, and high literature.

The *p'ansori* stories were transmitted orally and grew in size through frequent performance until they were written down in the nineteenth century (the earliest extant text dates from 1754). The repertoire consists of twelve titles, the most popular of which is the *Song of a Faithful Wife, Spring Fragrance*. There are six tempos according to the mood of a story, and three schools of singing. Some popular stories, known as *p'ansori* tales, are outgrowths of the *p'ansori*.

Originally the singer had to eke out a meager living by performing at a wealthy patron's home, but his social position improved in the late nineteenth century, when the literati began to appreciate the art. Since the 1950s people of all classes have learned to sing *p'ansori;* annual contests and concerts play to large audiences. Famous singers have been designated as intangible national treasures.

Peter H. Lee, *Anthology of Korean Literature: From Early Times to the Nineteenth Century* (1981).

PETER H. LEE

PAPER has been in use in China from perhaps as early as 100 BCE. Produced from the process of pounding and stirring rags in water, paper was made from a variety of materials, the best including hemp, jute, flax, ramie, rattan, mulberry bark, grasses such as bamboo, reeds, and stalks of wheat. It was used for such varied purposes as wrapping, sanitary purposes, shoe linings, and fans. By the first century paper came to displace bamboo and silk for writing. An office was instituted in the imperial palace for the Secretariat during these decades. The dynastic history for the year 105 CE reports that an official of the Board of Works informed the court of improvements in the art of paper manufacture.

Within a century paper made its appearance in Korea, where further improvements were made. Before the seventh century it had already made its way to Japan, Indochina, and India. A Chinese traveler in the next century noted that certain Chinese prisoners of war had started the manufacture of paper in Samarkand, and by 794 another paper mill was begun in Baghdad. From there it spread to Damascus in Syria, and thence to Africa by the ninth century, replacing papyrus. Spain and Italy were the next to adopt it. The earliest use of paper for printing came after 700; the earliest extant example is a *dharani* (a short magical or sacred formula) dated 704–751, printed in Chinese.

Hans Bielenstein, *The Bureaucracy of Han Times* (1980), pp. 55–56. T. F. Carter and L. Carrington Goodrich, *The Invention of Printing in China and its Spread Westward* (2d ed., 1955), pp. 4–5. L. Carrington Goodrich, "Printing: A Preliminary Report on a New Discovery," *Technology and Culture* 8.3 (1967): 376–378.

L. CARRINGTON GOODRICH

PARACEL ISLANDS (Chinese, Xisha Jundao), group of small islands about 200 miles west of the central coast of Vietnam in the South China Sea. Occupied periodically by the Chinese empire during the premodern period, they were claimed and seized by the French in 1931, who cited alleged prior ownership by the Vietnamese empire. In 1951 several of the islands were seized by the new Communist government on mainland China. Later, some of the remaining islands were occupied by troops of the government of South Vietnam. They were driven out by Chinese forces in 1974. Today both China and the Socialist Republic of Vietnam claim ownership over the islands, and the naval units of the two countries have clashed periodically in the area.

Harold Hinton, *The China Sea: The American Stake in Its Future* (1980). Lim Joo-Jack, *Geo-Strategy and the South China Sea Basin: Regional Balance, Maritime Issues, Future Patterns* (1979).   WILLIAM J. DUIKER

PARAKRAMABAHU I (1153–1186), Sri Lankan king who unified the country after a long period of civil war; reformed the Buddhist monastic community (*sangha*); helped heal the longstanding schism between the Mahavihara and the Abhayagiri monasteries; built a remarkable series of irrigation works, including the massive Parakrama Samudra

("the sea of Parakrama"), the largest irrigation tank of ancient Sri Lanka; and commissioned public and religious monuments. His reign marks the last major phase in the development of irrigation technology in ancient and medieval Sri Lanka. He conducted an active foreign policy, sending his navy on a punitive expedition against Burma in a dispute over a trade agreement, and his army to South India in support of a Pandyan claimant to the throne. While this latter expedition failed after initial success, the Burmese mission fared better.

The reign of Parakramabahu, with all its achievements and its revival of ancient grandeur, proved to be the last flowering of Sinhalese greatness. Indeed his vigorous rule, in particular his ambitious foreign policy, may have contributed to the suddenness and completeness of the collapse that followed so soon after his death.

[*See also* Sri Lanka.]

K. M. de Silva, *A History of Sri Lanka* (1981), pp. 59–78.   K. M. DE SILVA

PARAKRAMABAHU II (1236–1270), Sri Lankan king. His long reign at Dambadeniya, a rock fortress in northwest Sri Lanka, was a patch of stability during a lengthy period of political decline, unstable conditions, and loss of vitality. His power extended over the central hills, throughout Rohana, and to the border regions between the Sinhalese kingdom and the newly established Tamil kingdom in the north. He annexed Polonnaruva and held his coronation there but could not establish that city as his capital nor could he control the Tamil kingdom. A scholar in his own right, his rule is associated with a revival of Buddhism and a revitalization of literature and the arts.

[*See also* Dambadeniya *and* Polonnaruva.]

K. M. de Silva, *A History of Sri Lanka* (1981), pp. 81–96. A. Liyanagamage, *The Decline of Polonnaruva and the Rise of Dambadeniya* (1968).   K. M. DE SILVA

PARAMARA DYNASTY. Among the several kin dynasties ruling in western and central India, only the Paramara dynasty of Dhara and Ujjayini (Ujjain) in Avanti, or Malwa, attained sovereignty and political ascendancy, this under Harsha Siyaka II (r. 950–973), who engineered a spectacular victory over the last Rashtrakuta emperor and plundered his capital, Manykheta, in 972. Succeeding monarchs, Vakpati II Munjaraja (r. 973–996) and Bhoja the Great (1010–1055), ruled over most of modern Madhya Pradesh and parts of the adjoining states, while compaigning as far afield as Orissa in the east and Haryana in the north. Their patronage of the arts and sciences earned them more enduring fame than their short-lived political paramountcy. Subsequent Paramara rulers maintained a precarious existence amid plundering raids of surrounding powers until the Khalji sultanate extinguished their rule in 1305.

P. Bhatia, *The Paramāras, c. 800–1305 A.D.* (1970). D. C. Gamguly, *The History of the Paramāra Dynasty* (1933).   SHIVA BAJPAI

PARARATON (*Book of Kings*), Javanese chronicle, composed in the late fifteenth century. Its central figure is Ken Angrok (Rajasa), a man of low origin who usurped the Javanese throne and established a new court at Singosari. A brief history of Singosari's kings up to the foundation of Majapahit is presented, and then the chronicle records the affairs of the Majapahit dynasty during the fourteenth century. The *Pararaton* is used by historians to balance the *Nagarakertagama*, the chronicle of the mid-fourteenth-century Majapahit court. The *Pararaton* seems to look backward in an attempt to glorify the Majapahit age, but it also reaches an understanding of why the Majapahit state fell from power. It is a syncretic Hindu text but reflects a different concern than the magico-religious focus of most earlier Javanese literature. While earlier works project the image of a sanctified court, the *Pararaton* recognized the importance of the nonreligious political and economic affairs of the Majapahit state.

[*See also* Ken Angrok; Singosari; Majapahit; *and* Nagarakertagama.]

C. C. Berg, "The Javanese Picture of the Past," in Sodejatmoko et al., *An Introduction to Indonesian Historiography* (1965), pp. 87–118.   KENNETH R. HALL

PARCHAM. *See* Percham.

PARHAE (Chinese, Bohai), state located in northern Korea and southern Manchuria that was a major force in northeast Asian politics from its founding in 698 to its collapse in 926. When the Korean kingdom of Koguryŏ fell to the combined forces of Silla and Tang China, much of southern Koguryŏ was incorporated into the Silla domain, but former Koguryŏ aristocrats gradually took control over Koguryŏ's northern extremities. A Koguryŏ general, Tae Cho-yŏng (King Ko; r. 698–720), taking advantage of a revolt in southern Manchuria and aided

by a group of rebels, established the kingdom in 698, first calling it Chin and in 713 taking the name Parhae. That same year he sent a son as hostage to the Tang court and was invested as king. People of Koguryŏ descent became the Parhae ruling elite and dominated the Malgal nomadic tribes that had been living in the area from Koguryŏ times.

The international position of Parhae at its founding was precarious, for it soon asserted its independence from Tang authority and sought to expand. It took over the area between the Amur River in the north, the Liao River in the west, and the Taedong River on the Korean peninsula. Parhae even carried out a naval expedition against the Tang in 732, resulting in an alliance between Silla and the Tang empire against it. Parhae responded to this challenge by fostering ties with Japan and other northeast Asian people. In the reign of Tae Hum-mu (King Won; r. 738–794) relations between Parhae and China were normalized, and Parhae scholars and monks traveled to study in China. Relations with Silla, however, remained tense.

Although Tang political influence was curtailed, Tang cultural influence remained strong. The formal governmental structure that administered the kingdom through three chancelleries and six ministries was based on the Tang model. The Parhae capital, Sanggyŏng ("high capital") near modern Dongjingcheng, Heilongjiang Province, China, was constructed according to the grid used in the Tang capital at Chang'an. Parhae possessed a good system of roads with five major routes connecting the various parts of the kingdom. It quickly achieved a level of cultural sophistication; Confucian principles played an important role in governing, and education was the mark of an official.

Earlier Koguryŏ traditions also influenced the kingdom. The *ondol* system of heating through hot-air flues in the floor has been found at Parhae sites. Tombs built by Parhae aristocrats with horizontal entrance shafts, Buddhist statuary, and temple roof tiles all reveal Koguryŏ culture. In addition to its major capital at Sanggyŏng, Parhae had four secondary capitals, a tradition quite probably inherited from the Koguryŏ administration system of five *pu*. Furthermore, many of the ruling class had the Koguryŏ royal surname Ko. Parhae leaders, referring to Parhae as the "state of Ko[gu]ryŏ," saw themselves as the successors to Koguryŏ.

During the reigns of King Mun and King Son (r. 819–831), Parhae was culturally and politically at its peak. Its borders extended far across much of Manchuria into the Korean peninsula and a strong central authority rules over a prosperous state whose population exceeded 500,000 people. Chinese histories described it as "the flourishing land in the east."

Late in the ninth century, when China collapsed into anarchy following the Huang Chao Rebellion, trade contacts between Parhae and the Tang came to an end. At the same time Parhae came under increased pressure from Khitan tribes, now unified under Abauji, the founder of the Liao dynasty. When this was combined with increased opposition from the Malgal people, the Parhae leadership forfeited its last capital (in 926) and fled south. The kingdom was incorporated into the Liao state. Parhae refugees, including members of the ruling house, fled south and were incorporated into the ruling elite of the Koryŏ state, which established itself as successor to Silla. In this way the traditions of Koguryŏ and Puyŏ, which Parhae had revived, were transmitted to Koryŏ. Within two centuries the Malgal would expel the Khitan and found their own state, the Jurchen Jin (1115–1234). The fall of Parhae marked an end to Korean influence in Manchuria.

[*See also* Koguryŏ; Silla; Liao Dynasty; *and* Jurchen Jin Dynasty.]

William E. Henthorn, "Some Notes on Parhae (P'ohai)," *Transactions of the Korea Branch of the Royal Asiatic Society* 38 (April 1961): 63–81.

EDWARD J. SHULTZ

PARIAN (derived from an old Tagalog word for "marketplace"), Chinese residential districts within Philippine urban areas during Spanish rule. Early Spanish authorities, particularly in Manila, maintained a persistent fear of ethnic uprisings and isolated the Chinese into segregated quarters to facilitate control over them. The Parian of Manila was established in 1581 near the Intramuros, and similar *parianes* grew up in other urban areas. Manila's Parian was the center of commercial life until its destruction in 1790, at which time Chinese residence shifted across the Pasig River. As the numbers of resident Chinese decreased in the late eighteenth century, the second largest Parian, of Cebu, was transformed into a wealthy Christian Filipino-Chinese (*mestizo*) community. [*See also* Intramuros.]

MICHAEL CULLINANE

PARIS PEACE CONFERENCE. Negotiations to settle the Vietnam (Indochina) War began in Paris in 1968. The real negotiations occurred in private, unofficial meetings between Henry Kissinger of the United States and Le Duc Tho of North Vietnam; the formal sessions of the peace conference also included representatives of South Vietnam and of the Provisional Revolutionary Government (made up of South Vietnamese Communists).

After a prolonged diplomatic stalemate, Kissinger and Tho reached an agreement in October 1972. President Thieu of South Vietnam found it totally unacceptable and persuaded Kissinger to ask for major alterations in it. Tho responded by asking for alterations of his own, and the negotiations soon approached collapse.

From 18 to 30 December 1972, the United States launched the "Christmas bombing"—massive attacks by B-52 bombers against Hanoi, Haiphong, and other targets in North Vietnam. In January 1973, serious negotiations resumed and quickly produced an agreement very similar to the one tentatively reached the previous October. It called for the withdrawal of US military forces from South Vietnam but not for the withdrawal of North Vietnamese forces. All prisoners of war were to be released. There was to be a cease-fire in place (exact procedures not adequately explained), and the future of South Vietnam was to be settled by peaceful political processes (likewise vaguely defined).

It is doubtful that either Thieu or the Communists ever intended to abide fully by this agreement or that either expected the other to do so. It did not actually end the shooting for even one day. Its most important result was to remove the United States from the fighting.

[*See also* Indochina War; Le Duc Tho; Vietnam, Provisional Revolutionary Government of; *and* Vietnam.]

Arnold R. Isaacs, *Without Honor: Defeat in Vietnam and Cambodia* (1983).

EDWIN E. MOISE

PARK CHUNG HEE (Pak Chŏng-hŭi; 1917–1979), Korean general and president of the Republic of Korea (1963–1979).

Park was born in a small, poor village near Kumi, North Kyŏngsang Province, to an impoverished tenant farmer's family with leftist connnections; one older brother was shot as a Communist in 1946. Park graduated from a normal school in nearby Taegu and then taught in Mun'gyŏng for two years. In 1940 Park entered the Manchukuo Military Academy, finishing as a top student in the Tokyo Military Academy in 1944. He served a year as a second lieutenant in the Japanese army in Manchukuo (Manchuria), reportedly in a special internal control intelligence unit.

After the war Park joined the South Korean Constabulary, rising to the rank of major with its expansion. In 1947 he was recruited by a communist friend of his brother's to indoctrinate officer trainees in a conspiracy that surfaced in the October 1948 Yŏsu-Sunch'ŏn rebellion. Subsequent investigations revealed his role; he was condemned to death and saved himself by cooperating with Korean Counter-Intelligence Corps search parties in ferreting out other cryptocommunists, many of whom met their deaths through him. Cashiered from the constabulary, Park was a civilian adviser to G-2 (the military intelligence section of the army) when the Korean War erupted; he was quickly reinstated by his former academy classmates, rose rapidly, performed well in many commands until 1961, and never gave further grounds for suspicion. Reserved and antisocial, he was a compartively obscure major-general when he took power.

Already before President Syngman Rhee's overthrow in 1960, General Park and his communist brother's son-in-law, Lieutenant General Kim Jong Pil (Kim Chong-p'il), were leading a group of dissident officers in planning a coup. The army, then coming to institutional hegemony in South Korea, viewed with mounting outrage the vagaries and corruption of the civilian government. Park and his group sought a "surgical operation" to remove Korea's faults, reduce economic and social inequities, and establish a guided "administrative democracy." The April 1960 student overthrow of Rhee forestalled these plans but when the democratic regime was perceived as unavailing against social chaos, Park and some 250 officers and 1,600 troops struck on 16 May 1961, quickly toppling the unprepared government of Chang Myŏn, ending freedoms, purging thousands, and establishing a military Supreme Council for National Reconstruction whose legislation superseded the constitution. Within weeks Park was the council's chairman; as acting president (1962–1963) and then president, Park ruled South Korea for eighteen years. [See April Nineteenth Student Revolution; Rhee, Syngman; and Chang Myŏn.]

Park's lasting achievements were economic, derived from three well-planned and well-executed development plans that from 1963 to 1976 brought 10 percent average annual real growth of the gross national product and an export increase of thirty-six times the 1963 figure. Park took a leading role in the industrialization, urbanization, and coordinated development of the economy and infrastructure, altering South Korea irreversibly.

Park's political legacy was unhappy in contrast. He abhorred politics and distrusted politicians. Although junta rule was weaned to a constitutional, semicivilian rule with two reasonably fair elections in 1963 and 1967, restraints on a third term were removed in 1969 and promises that it would be his last were conveniently forgotten. Park instituted a coup against his own system in October 1972 with the new authoritarian constitution expanded by draconian decrees forbidding almost all criticism. Political parties remained undeveloped, the media was controlled, and politics and its institutions, including labor unions, were suppressed. Park's Central Intelligence Agency director, convinced that such a system was untenable in the face of rising resentment, assassinated the increasingly isolated and morose Park, who had already been widowed by assassination, on 26 October 1979. His rule was replaced by that of Chun Doo Hwan (Chŏn Tuhwan), who became president of the newly established Fifth Republic of Korea in 1980.

Park's overall achievements are marred by his repression and vindictiveness. His economic legacy, however, continues to be an essential factor in modern Korea's history.

[See also May Sixteenth Coup d'État; Korea, Republic of; and Chun Doo Hwan.]

Gregory Henderson, *Korea: The Politics of the Vortex* (1968). Kim Chong-shin, *Seven Years with Korea's Park Chung-hee* (1967). Se-jin Kim, *The Politics of Military Revolution* (1971).   GREGORY HENDERSON

PARLIAMENT OF INDIA. The Parliament of India consists of the president of the republic, the Lok Sabha ("house of the people"), and the Rajya Sabha ("council of states"). The president is considered an integral part of Parliament, but is neither a member nor dependent on legislative votes of confidence. He summons, prorogues, and may dissolve Parliament. He may address Parliament or send messages and must sign all bills before they become law.

The Lok Sabha, the lower house of Parliament, has 544 members. Of these, 542 are directly elected by adult franchise and 2 may be appointed by the president to represent the Anglo-Indian community. In order to ensure representation of disadvantaged communities, a portion of the elected seats are reserved for scheduled castes and tribes. Seats are allocated among the states and union territories on the basis of population, and constituencies are roughly equal in the number of voters. Under a constitutional amendment passed in 1976, the size of the Lok Sabha, based on the 1971 census, was frozen until the year 2001 in an effort to ensure that states would not be disadvantaged for pursuing rigorous family planning programs.

The Lok Sabha is modeled after the British House of Commons and follows many of its practices, procedures, and traditions. It is elected for five years, may pass motions of confidence, and may be dissolved by the president at any time upon the advice of the government. The life of Parliament may be extended for up to one year during periods of national emergency, but it may not continue beyond six months following the end of emergency rule. [*See* Emergency in India, The.]

Constitutionally, the House must meet at least twice a year, but in practice it averages three sessions per year. The Lok Sabha has twelve committees to assist in its business and is presided over by a speaker, who is elected from among the members, serves as an impartial presiding officer, and enjoys considerable power in the conduct of parliamentary business.

The position of the Lok Sabha in the Indian political system is limited. Although India's first prime minister, Jawaharlal Nehru (1947–1964), treated Parliament with deference, subsequent prime ministers have reduced its importance. Members have also contributed to the decline of Parliament. Desultory debates, lack of interest, and poor attendance have limited the importance of parliamentary proceedings; legislative business has dropped sharply; and the ability of the House to ventilate grievances and ensure accountability has declined. The government therefore resorts to the frequent use of ordinances.

The Rajya Sabha is presided over by the vice president of India and is composed of 250 members, of whom twelve are nominated by the president. Seats are allocated among the states based on population, and one-third of the members are elected by state legislative assemblies every two years for six-year terms. The Rajya Sabha has failed to evolve a distinctive role for itself and tends simply to duplicate the composition and work of the Lower House.

[*See also* Nehru, Jawaharlal.]

R. B. Jain, *The Indian Parliament* (1976). A. B. Lal, ed., *The Indian Parliament* (1956). W. H. Morris-Jones, *Parliament in India* (1957). S. Srivastava, *Constitution and Functioning in the Rajya Sabha* (1979).

STANLEY A. KOCHANEK

PARSIS, Indian Zoroastrians of Iranian descent who migrated to India in the tenth century to escape Muslim persecution. Under the Samanids (874–999 CE), Zoroastrians in Khurasan (in northeastern Iran), seeking to escape persecution and forced conversion to Islam, dwelt in the mountains of Kuhistan for one hundred years before proceeding to the Persian Gulf port of Hormuz. They stayed there for fifteen years and thereafter sailed to the island of Diu near Kathiawar, Gujarat, where they spent nineteen years and learned Gujarati before finally reaching the coast of Gujarat in western India. Their date of arrival is assigned by Parsi tradition to Vikram Samvat 992, that is, 936 CE. Through confusion between the local script and *devanagari* numbers this date came to be read as Vikram Samvat 772, or 716 CE, and this latter, incorrect date is still widely reproduced.

The local raja, Vajjardevrai of the Silhara dynasty, granted them asylum, but decreed that they uniformly adopt the Gujarati language, perform marriages only at night, and ensure that the women wear saris. The immigrants founded the settlement of Sanjan, and came to be termed Parsis, meaning "Persians." Sometime later the Parsis consecrated an *atash bahram* ("victorious fire") named Iran Shah ("the king of Iran"), which remained their only sacred fire for more than eight hundred years. Most religious rituals were performed using hearth fires. During the following three hundred years Parsis dispersed to towns along the coast, such as Navsari (1142), Surat, Anklesar, Cambay, and Broach, as farmers, toddy planters, carpenters, weavers, and merchants. Each priest ministered to a few families, called his *panthak*, with this association becoming hereditary. Around 1290 the priests divided Gujarat into five *panths* (ecclesiastic groups): the Sanjanas at Sanjan, the Bhagarias serving Navsari, the Godavras at Anklesar, the Bharuchas at Broach, and the Khambattas of Cambay.

By the thirteenth century extensive contact between Parsis and Iranian Zoroastrians had commenced, with several religious texts being transferred to India. The *jizya* ("poll-tax") was imposed upon all non-Muslims in 1297, when the Delhi Muslim sultanate conquered Gujarat. This caused hardship for the Parsis and served as an instrument for conversion to Islam. [*See* Jizya.] Yet, in 1350, the Dominican friar Jordanus encountered active Parsi communities who exposed corpses in *dakhmas* ("funerary towers"), a Zoroastrian practice. Sanjan was sacked by the Muzzafarid sultan Mahmud Begada, probably in 1465. Parsi priests rescued the *atash bahram* and guarded it in a cave for fourteen years before transporting it to the town of Bansda. Two years later the fire was enthroned at Navsari. The main source for this early history of the Parsis is the *Qissa-e Sanjan,* a narrative poem in Persian based upon oral tradition, composed in 1600 by Bahman Kekobad Sanjana, a Parsi priest.

Pressure from Hindus compelled Parsis to make religious and social changes. Ritual sacrifice of bulls and cows was abandoned owing to Hindu reverence for these animals; the Parsis then established the custom of keeping sacred bulls for procuring *gomez* (consecrated urine) and tail-hair sieves used in Zoroastrian rituals. *Khwedodah* (kin-marriage) was gradually forsaken. The Parsis came to be regarded as a caste within Hindu society; thus the religion became hereditary, with no converts being accepted.

The Mughal emperor Akbar conquered Gujarat in 1572. [*See* Akbar.] In 1578 a Bhagaria priest, Meherji Rana, was summoned to the Mughal court for a religious conference and greatly impressed the emperor. Shortly thereafter Akbar abolished the *jizya.* Contact between the Parsis and Europeans increased with the establishing of trading factories in the seventeenth century. According to Europeans the Parsis adhered strictly to their own customs, with violators being excommunicated or even executed. As trade increased so did the wealth and size of the Parsi community. In the seventeenth and eighteenth centuries the port of Surat had the largest Zoroastrian population in the world, with more than a hundred thousand Parsis.

Owing to a dispute with the Bhagarias in 1741 the Sanjana *panth* transferred the Iran Shah *atash bahram* from Navsari to Udwada, where it burns to the present day. The Bhagarias consecrated their own *atash bahram* in 1765. In 1746 a disagreement relating to the calendar caused division of the community into Kadmis, who accept the *qadimi* ("ancient") Iranian calendar, and Shenshais, or Rasimis ("traditionalists"), who maintain the original Parsi calendar. Since 1906 another group, the Fasalis, who calculate the calendar by the *fasl* ("season"), has broken off.

In 1661 Bombay came under the administration of the British East India Company. Here Parsis such as the *wadia* ("shipbuilder") Lowji Nassarwanji (1702–1744) and Sir Jamsetji Jijibhai (1785–1859) built the community's success on shipbuilding and the cotton and opium trade with China. Parsis also established themselves in textile manufacture and banking. The community became the mercantile arm of the British and controlled India's foreign

trade for more than two centuries. The Parsis promoted education and philanthropy, founding schools, hospitals and trusts, and developed into an urbanized middle class. The Parsi Panchayat, initially a council of elders, was established in 1728 to regulate community affairs. In 1854 the Parsis sent Manekji Limji Hataria to the Qajar court in Iran to intercede on behalf of Iranian Zoroastrians. Hataria succeeded in having the *jizya* abolished by the Qajars in 1882. During the eighteenth and nineteenth centuries European scholars concluded that Zarathushtra (Zoroaster) had preached a monotheistic faith that was debased by his followers. This viewpoint gained the acceptance of many Parsis who sought to reform their religion. The introduction of theosophy and other doctrines further attenuated doctrinal unity among the Parsis, but lack of doctrinal unity and a decline in theological learning continue to the present day.

In the late nineteenth century Parsis entered politics, with Dadabhai Naoroji (1825–1917), the architect of Indian nationalism, becoming in 1892 the first Indian member of the British parliament. [*See* Naoroji, Dadabhai.] Other Parsis closely associated with the Indian nationalist movement were Sir Pherozeshah Mehta (1845–1915) and Sir Dinshaw Wacha (1844–1936). The community helped found the industrial base of modern India. Pioneers include J. N. Tata (1839–1904), who established the iron and steel industries, hydroelectricity, and the Indian Institute of Science, and Homi J. Bhabha (1909–1966), who developed atomic energy research. [*See* Tata Family *and* Bhabha, Homi Jehangir.] International dispersion of Parsis occurred between the 1950s and 1980s. The community now numbers about 82,000 in India; 5,000 in Pakistan; and approximately 10,000 in Great Britain, Canada, the United States, and Australia. Small groups are also present in Hong Kong, Singapore, and Sri Lanka. Low birthrate and intermarriage have contributed to their decline in numbers.

M. Boyce, *Zoroastrians* (1979). S. H. Hodivala, *Studies in Parsi History* (1920). D. F. Karaka, *History of the Parsis,* 2 vols. (1884). P. Nanavutty, *The Parsis* (1977).

JAMSHEED K. CHOKSY

PARTAI KOMUNIS INDONESIA (PKI), or the Indonesian Communist Party. The PKI was founded in May 1920 to succeed the Indies Social Democratic Association (ISDV). Its leaders, Semaun and Darsono, argued that capitalist imperialism had proletarianized Indonesian society and that the national and proletarian struggles thus coincided. They pioneered the "bloc within" strategy as members of the nationalist party the Sarekat Islam (SI). Expelled from SI in 1921, the PKI won wide support in Java and Sumatra, attracting the attention of the Dutch police. To maintain its élan and forestall repression, the party launched uprisings in Banten (1926) and West Sumatra (1927). Supported by Musso and Alimin but opposed by Tan Malaka, these uprisings were abortive and led the Dutch to suppress the party and exile many cadres to West New Guinea.

In 1935 Musso established the Illegal PKI, which followed an antifascist line and remained underground until 1948. An aboveground party was established in 1945 and briefly led by Muhammad Jusuf, later by Alimin and Sardjono. It was subordinate to the underground party, and party members were active in several parties within the ruling Sayap Kiri ("left wing"). The PKI supported negotiations with the Dutch to ensure the Indonesian Republic's survival, but after the fall of Amir Sjarifuddin's cabinet in January 1948 it increasingly favored armed struggle by workers and peasants. In August 1948 the PKI emerged openly as leader of the Front Demokrasi Rakyat (People's Democratic Front) under Musso and Sjarifuddin but was suppressed militarily for its involvement in the Madiun Affair (September 1948).

After Madiun, the PKI, under Tan Ling Djie, resumed the strategy of working through front parties. This policy, however, was discarded in 1951 by the new-generation leadership—D. N. Aidit, M. H. Lukman, Nyoto, and Sudisman—who rehabilitated the party politically by stressing its nationalist commitment and renouncing armed revolution. The party survived repression by the Sukiman government and expanded its membership by broadening its base to include the peasantry, especially through one of its affiliates, the Barisan Tani Indonesia (Indonesian Peasants' Front). It won 16.4 percent of the vote in the 1955 elections and later claimed three million members.

Although it obtained political protection from Sukarno by backing his program of Guided Democracy and emphasized that its primary enemy was Dutch and American capital, the PKI drew the hostility of many intellectuals for its insistence on ideological correctness. The PKI also angered civilian and military officials as a result of its attacks on corruption and privilege and alienated the rural elite (often associated with Muslim parties) because of its support of peasant interests, especially its unilateral actions

(*aksi sepihak*) in 1964 to carry out an as yet unimplemented land reform law in Central and East Java.

After the 1965 Gestapu Affair, army units and Muslim youth conducted a pogrom in which perhaps 400,000 PKI members and supporters died and 100,000 were jailed. The party was banned in March 1966 but briefly conducted guerrilla operations near Blitar, East Java, and in West Kalimantan. PKI exiles in Beijing, led by Jusuf Ajitoropo, later publicized a self-criticism (*otokritik*) condemning the Aidit leadership for alleged revisionism and announcing a new Maoist program advocating armed revolution.

[*See also* Sarekat Islam; Musso; Alimin, Prawirodirdjo; Tan Malaka; Gestapu; Amir Sjarifuddin; Madiun; *and* Indonesia, Republic of.]

Donald Hindley, *The Communist Party of Indonesia 1951–1963* (1964). George McTurnan Kahin, *Nationalism and Revolution in Indonesia* (1952). Ruth T. McVey, *The Rise of Indonesian Communism* (1965). Rex Mortimer, *Indonesian Communism under Sukarno* (1974).   ROBERT B. CRIBB

PARTAI MURBA, or Proletarian Party, Indonesian left-wing nationalist party founded in October 1948 by Ibrahim Datuk Tan Malaka and led after his death by Sukarno. It gathered together leftists who were unhappy with the Indonesian Communist Party's (PKI's) alleged accommodation with the West during the revolution and its emphasis on class struggle within Indonesia thereafter. Murba was ideologically close to Sukarno, arguing for an all-encompassing national front or state party, but it was unable to deliver significant popular support for him. Under PKI pressure, it was declared inactive in January 1965 and was formally banned in September. Restored to legality for the 1971 elections, it polled poorly and in 1973 was incorporated into the Partai Demokrasi Indonesia (PDI).

[*See also* Tan Malaka; Partai Komunis Indonesia; *and* Sukarno.]

ROBERT B. CRIBB

PARTAI NASIONAL INDONESIA (PNI), or the Indonesian Nationalist Party, was formed in 1927 by Sukarno and other nationalist leaders, some of them recently returned from study in the Netherlands. It quickly became the main voice of Indonesian nationalism. Under Sukarno's chairmanship the party aimed at a mass membership, sought the union of all nationalist organizations in the pursuit of independence, and practiced noncooperation with the colonial regime. Within two years it claimed a membership of approximately ten thousand.

After Sukarno's arrest, trial, and conviction in 1930, the PNI dissolved itself and formed the Partindo (Indonesian Party), also to be deprived of its leaders and effectively immobilized two years later.

The PNI was reformed after the Proclamation of Independence in 1945. Although in theory it was a new party, its leadership and its ideas came primarily from the original PNI. After 1950 it became one of the main elements in the domestic political balance. It saw itself as the party of radical nationalism, seeking indonesianization of the economy and an independent foreign policy. The PNI participated in the Masjumi-led Sukiman government (1951–1952) and was the main partner in the Wilopo government (1952–1953) and the Ali Sastroamidjojo governments (1953–1955 and 1955–1956). The 1955 elections confirmed it as one of the big four parties (the others were Masjumi, Nahdatul Ulama, and the Indonesian Communist Party, or PKI). In 1957 the PNI supported Sukarno's Guided Democracy plans, although their effect, in the end, was to undermine party activity. It continued to support Sukarno after 1959.

The 1971 elections under President Suharto saw all remaining parties overwhelmed by Golkar, the government-sponsored organization. In 1973 an enforced rationalization of parties led to the amalgamation of the PNI and other non-Muslim parties into the Indonesian Democratic Party (Partai Demokrasi Indonesia).

[See also Sukarno; Indonesia, Republic of; Masjumi; Sukiman, Wirjosandjojo; Wilopo; Nahdatul Ulama; and Partai Komunis Indonesia.]

Herbert Feith, *The Decline of Constitutional Democracy in Indonesia* (1962). George McT. Kahin, *Nationalism and Revolution in Indonesia* (1952). J. E. Rocamora, *Nationalism in Search of an Ideology: The Indonesian Nationalist Party, 1946–1965* (1975).   JOHN D. LEGGE

PARTAI SOSIALIS INDONESIA (PSI), Indonesian Socialist Party. The PSI was formed in February 1948 by Sutan Sjahrir's followers. It was the ideological descendant of the Pendidikan Nasional Indonesia, formed by Hatta and Sjahrir in 1931 to train a socialist leadership for the Indonesian nationalist movement. After Indonesia became independent, the PSI was influential in Parliament and the civil service. It was seen as the party of the in-

tellectuals and was noted for a pragmatic and rational approach to political issues. It lacked electoral support, however, and was virtually eliminated in the 1955 elections. Some of its members were implicated in the 1958 rebellion, and in 1960 Sukarno banned the party. [*See also* Indonesia, Republic of; Sjahrir, Sutan; Hatta, Mohammad; *and* Sukarno.]

JOHN D. LEGGE

PARTHIANS, an ancient Iranian people. The northeastern Iranian region of Parthia (Old Persian, Parthava; Greek, Parthyene) had been a province of the Achaemenids. After Alexander's campaigns, Parthia became a satrapy of the Macedonian Seleucids. The satrap, Andragoras, had revolted against Antiochus II, but was himself deposed by the invading nomadic Iranian Parni tribe.

Arshak (Greek, Arsaces), the Parni leader, was crowned in 247 BCE as the first king of the Arsacid dynasty, which was to be the longest-lived of the three great pre-Islamic Iranian empires. He was succeeded by his brother Tirdat (Greek, Tiridates), who preserved Arsacid Parthia despite Seleucid advances. Ardavan I (Greek, Artabanus) succeeded him around 211 and increased Parthian domains; Mihrdat I (Greek, Mithridates; r. c. 171–138) reconquered the remainder of Iran from the Greeks and issued coins at Seleucia-on-the-Tigris.

The administrative center of the Arsacids then shifted from the old city of Nisa in Parthia (now

near Ashkhabad, Turkmen SSR) to the city of Ctesiphon, founded opposite Seleucia. From 130 to about 124, invasions of the nomadic Sakas in the east weakened Arsacid authority generally, but Mihrdat II (r. c. 124–87) restored order and, apparently regarding his deeds of pacification and empire building as worthy of Darius I, had a bas-relief carved at Behistun, beneath that of the Achaemenid monarch. Mihrdat also called himself King of Kings on his coins, using for the first time in the dynasty the old Achaemenid title.

Parthian Military Power. From the first century BCE until the end of the dynasty in the third century CE, the Arsacids faced Rome as their principal rival, along the boundary of the two empires at the Euphrates. In 54 BCE the Roman Crassus boasted that he would conquer Parthian Mesopotamia; the Parthian ambassador held out his palm and warned, "Hair will grow here before you see Seleucia." Plutarch has preserved a dramatic account of the famous Roman debacle at Carrhae (Harran) in 53. The slow-moving Roman legions were decimated by the swift Parthian mounted archers, the *clibanarii*, glittering with armor that protected horse and rider. The light Parthian cavalry attacked, then retreated with the backward-fired "Parthian shot." The din of kettledrums and the unearthly sight of the long, coiling "dragon" banners of the Iranians reduced the Romans to terror. The victorious Parthian general Suren had the head of Crassus delivered to the Armenian capital, Artashat (Greek, Artaxata), where the Armenian and Parthian kings were celebrating a royal wedding with a performance of scenes from *The Bacchae* of Euripides. According to Plutarch, the Greek actor Jason lifted the severed head of Crassus and recited Agave's victorious ode over the dead Pentheus.

Armenia, which was subject alternately to Roman and Parthian influence, retained close cultural and religious ties to Iran; in 65 CE the Roman emperor Nero affirmed the balance of power by placing the Armenian crown on the head of Tirdat, brother of the Parthian king Valakhsh I (Greek, Vologases). The Armenian branch of the Arsacid (Armenian, Arshakuni) dynasty was to survive the Iranian by some two hundred years, to be abolished by the Sasanids in 428.

Arsacid Decline. The first two centuries of the common era saw the steady deterioration of centralized rule in Parthian Iran: in the east, the powerful Kushan dynasty was on the rise; in the west, the province of Pars (Greek, Persis) enjoyed virtual independence. By about 18 BCE, silver was no longer

minted—an indication of a faltering control of commerce. At the beginning of the third century, the house of Sasan wrested power from the satrapal kings of Fars, and in about 224 Ardashir I, taking advantage of the internecine fighting that incessantly plagued the Arsacid house in the latter half of its ascendancy, overthrew the last king, Ardavan V.

The Parthian Cultural Legacy. Most information on the Parthians comes from Greek and Latin sources. Although there is a wealth of Zoroastrian Parthian proper names inscribed in heterographic Aramaic script on the ostraca from Nisa, these documents are brief, repetitive, and uninformative vineyard records. There are few inscriptions in rock from the Arsacid period, although Parthian was used in the inscriptions of the early Sasanids, so there was probably some earlier tradition of historical writing. The flowery opening of an official letter in Parthian has been found on a fragment of parchment from Dura-Europos. Most of Parthian literature was oral verse on epic and romantic themes, sung to the accompaniment of musical instruments by skilled *gosans* ("minstrels") who are remembered in later Iranian literature. One Parthian work or fragment of a work, identifiable by the large proportion of Parthian words and by a possible reference to the *gosan* tradition, is preserved in the Zoroastrian Pahlavi literature: the *Ayadgar-i Zareran (Memorial of Zarer),* on the struggle of Vishtaspa (Greek, Hystaspes), of the semilegendary Kayanian line of heroes, to protect the newly received Zoroastrian faith. Much of the heroic legendry of the *Shahnama* must have been transmitted by the Parthians, and Parthian noblemen and kings themselves appear in Firdausi's epic.

The Pahlavi *Denkard* attributes to one of the Arsacid kings named Valakhsh the first redaction of the Zoroastrian sacred texts of the Avesta. Isidore of Charax, whose itinerary *Stathmoi Parthikoi (Parthian Stations)* covers the trade route from Syria through the Parthian empire toward China, records the maintenance of an ever-burning fire at Asaak in Parthia—apparently a Zoroastrian fire temple—and one of the three great sacred fires of the Sasanids, Adur Burzen Mihr, was in Parthia; its name is Parthian. Statues apparently belonging to the Zoroastrian cult of the spirits of royal ancestors have been found by Soviet archaeologists at Nisa. Much of the information we possess about Parthian Zoroastrianism is corroborated and amplified by the practices of the Armenians, who had a similar ancestor cult, as well as fire temples devoted to the divinities of Zoroastrianism.

The Parthians under Sasanid Rule. The Parthian nobility continued to occupy a prominent place in the hierarchy of the Sasanids, and Parthian language and literature survived in the east of Iran, where the religion of Mani, himself a Parthian of noble parentage, flourished down to the end of the first millennium CE. Parthian was the sacred language of the eastern Manichaean church, and hymns and prose works were composed in it. Buddhism appears to have spread among the Parthians as far west as Margiana (Merv), and Chinese sources record the activity of two Parthian Buddhist missionaries in China in the latter half of the second century BCE. Parthian art seems also to have influenced the style of the Han dynasty. In central and western Iran, however, the Parthian language was overwhelmed by Middle Persian by the mid-Sasanid period.

The Sasanids appear to have preserved many Parthian institutions and cultural traditions, while exercising much more centralized control over their domains. Although the Parthians have been deprecated as slavish imitators of Hellenism, notably for the use of Greek, including the epithet *Philhellenos,* on their coins, the fact is that the use of Greek seems to have been mainly an expedient concession to the Greek-speaking commercial element, and legends on coins minted in the Iranian hinterland had had Parthian legends from the start. Parthian architecture preserved and developed traditional Iranian features such as the *iwan* and the squinch-supported dome; it also provided the prototype of the Sasanid fire temple with its square inner cells and perambulatory passage.

The Parthians had a distinctive style of dress, with bashlik helmet, trousers (Greek, *anaxyrides*), soft leather boots, and the Iranian short sword (Greek, *akinakes*). They wore abundant jewelry, particularly pearls, and dressed their long hair. There was a distinct tradition of Parthian painting very different from that of the Greeks, which is amply reflected in the frescoes of the Dura-Europos synagogue. Although mainly orthodox Zoroastrians themselves, the Parthians were tolerant of other faiths. After the destruction of the Temple at Jerusalem by the Romans in 70 CE, centers of Jewish life and learning flourished in Parthian and later Sasanid Mesopotamia, and many Jews linked their messianic hopes to Iranian power. Christians, too, found in the Parthian empire a refuge from Roman persecution, and the New Testament legend of the Magi refers to Parthian Zoroastrian priests (Middle Iranian, *magu;* Greek, *magos;* Latin, *magus;* pl., *magi,* from which is derived the word *magician,* for the Iranian priests were said to possess miraculous powers).

[*See also* Achaemenid Dynasty; Manichaeism; Pahlavi; *and* Seleucid Dynasty.]

M. Colledge, *Parthian Art* (1977). N. C. Debevoise, *A Political History of Parthia* (1938). D. Sellwood, *An Introduction to the Coinage of Parthia* (2d ed., 1980). Ehsan Yarshater, ed., *The Seleucid, Parthian and Sasanian Periods* (1983), vol. 3 of the *Cambridge History of Iran.*

JAMES R. RUSSELL

PARTITION OF INDIA. The partition of the Indian subcontinent and the establishment of Pakistan was first envisaged in a vague and shadowy form under the terms of the resolution adopted by the Muslim League at Lahore in March 1940. This demanded independent states in northwest and northeast India. The Indian National Congress insisted that India was a territorial unity and all its peoples were one nation—kept apart only by Britain's "divide and rule" policies. The British response was to recognize Indian nationhood as a political goal but to insist that until the various groups could agree upon a constitution there must be safeguards for the minorities.

Mohammad Ali Jinnah was a late convert to the "two nations" theory and even in 1941 was talking only of an awakening Muslim national consciousness. [*See* Jinnah, Mohammad Ali.] Muslim intellectuals were devising various schemes for subnational groupings of provinces and princely states, but these played no real part in serious political discussion. The first possibility that a future Indian union might not include the whole of India was provided in the Cripps proposals of March 1942, conceding that certain provinces might choose to stay out of his scheme and eventually become separate entities. However, the Congress decision to challenge British rule in August 1942, leading to the incarceration of the Congress leaders, effectively froze Indian politics until after World War II. [*See* Cripps Mission.]

The advent of the postwar Labour government in Britain signaled an acceleration in the pace of the withdrawal from empire. Lord Wavell as viceroy attempted to induce the Indian National Congress and the Muslim League to enter an "interim government" on a basis of parity. This effort failed. As an alternative, elections were called throughout India for both provincial and central legislatures. The Congress made an almost clean sweep of the "general" constituencies, but the league captured the great majority of the separate Muslim seats. Only in the North-West Frontier Province (NWFP) did the pro-Congress Red Shirts defeat the candidates of the Muslim League.

The NWFP was a vital element in the demand now clearly enunciated for a separate Pakistan, composed of two eastern provinces, Bengal and Assam, and four in the northwest: Punjab, Sind, Baluchistan, and NWFP. The British still persisted in regarding the Pakistan demand as a cover for obtaining maximum concessions in a federated Indian union. Wavell prepared a secret plan under which the Indian National Congress and the Muslim League would be invited to cooperate in an interim government leading to independence. If Jinnah refused, he would be told he could have a Pakistan composed only of those areas in which the Muslim population was in the majority. This would entail dividing Bengal and the Punjab and conceding only one Muslim-majority district of Assam. The belief was that this reduced offer would call Jinnah's bluff. The contingency plan that Wavell presented to the Labour government proved to be identical with the solution eventually adopted. The Cabinet would have nothing of it, however, and instead dispatched a Cabinet Mission to India to negotiate with the Indian leaders. [See Cabinet Mission.]

Fortified by the solid evidence of Muslim electoral support for Pakistan, Jinnah pressed for the full six provinces. Congress would accept only a constitution agreed upon by an Indian Constituent Assembly—in which Congress had an unassailable majority. Cripps produced an ingenious formula designed to reconcile the irreconcilable. His "three tier plan" distributed the powers of the state at three levels: that of the province, the center (for defense, foreign affairs, etc.), and at the level of "groups" formed by the provinces: Group A, the major portion of the subcontinent; Group B, the Punjab, NWFP, Baluchistan, Sind; and Group C, Bengal and Assam. Although Congress whittled away parts of the Cripps formula, Jinnah and the Muslim League accepted this plan because (so they argued) it could eventually yield a six-province Pakistan. Congress belatedly announced its acceptance, but subsequently dismissed the grouping feature as irrelevant.

The Labour government went on attempting to induce Congress to accept the grouping formula from June to December 1946. When Jawaharlal Nehru disavowed grouping, however, Jinnah angrily decreed a "day of action," 16 August 1946, and on this day violence erupted in Calcutta that was not suppressed until after four thousand people had been killed. The Great Calcutta Killing convinced Wavell that the British grip on India was no longer effective: he pressed Prime Minister Clement Attlee to announce a terminal date when the British would withdraw. Attlee professed to find Wavell "defeatist"; nevertheless, he had no alternative, and on 20 February 1947 he announced that British rule would end before June 1948. He also announced that Lord Mountbatten would take over as viceroy.

Attlee's announcement offered no solution to the Indian problem. Recognizing the absence of agreement he admitted that the British might hand over "in some areas to the existing provincial governments." In other words, India would be fragmented. Within Congress the realists, led by Sardar Patel, admitted that Pakistan was a better alternative to fragmentation. [See Patel, Sardar Vallabhbhai.] They concentrated on giving Jinnah as little as they could. Mountbatten rapidly decided that there was no hope of a united India, and directed his staff to draw up plans for a partition that would "place the responsibility of dividing India conspicuously on the Indians themselves." In accordance with Attlee's announcement the decision would be taken by votes in the provincial legislatures: voting whether to be incorporated in an Indian union or to join a new assemblage (Pakistan was not mentioned by name). In Punjab and Bengal the legislators would vote separately as Muslims and non-Muslims: if either faction called for the division of the province, this would prevail.

Both Nehru and Jinnah reacted in predictable fashion to the proposals, but on 3 June 1947 Mountbatten was able to inform the peoples of India that their leaders had accepted his plan. [See Nehru, Jawaharlal.] In addition to the votes taken in the legislatures, there were plebiscites to decide for or against Pakistan in Sylhet District of Assam and in the NWFP. Baluchistan made its choice by a process of consultation. In every case the Muslim-majority areas opted for Pakistan.

The actual line of division in both Bengal and Punjab was determined by a Boundary Commission composed equally of Muslims and non-Muslims with a British chairman, Cyril Radcliffe. The most critical area was central Punjab, where any boundary drawn to separate Muslims and Hindus necessarily had to carve through the land inhabited by the Sikhs. Forming only 15 percent of the total population of the Punjab, the Sikhs were nevertheless strongly conscious of their individual identity and strongly represented in the armed forces. [See Sikhism.]

Radcliffe was compelled to make the partition award on his own, since his colleagues were in total disagreement. The award contained certain surprises. The new East Bengal, or East Pakistan, incorporated the Chittagong Hills District, lacking any Muslim inhabitants, but did not include Murshidabad District with its Muslim majority. [See Murshidabad.] The greatest controversy, however, surrounded Radcliffe's allotment of Gurdaspur District in the Punjab, with its Muslim majority and its strategic position as the gateway to Kashmir, to India.

The actual line of partition was made known to the leaders of the two new countries in a meeting presided over by Mountbatten on 16 August 1947. Both sides were disconcerted and disgusted by aspects of the award. Already by that date a vast exodus was taking place in Punjab, with Muslims pouring into Pakistan and Hindus and Sikhs into India. About four million moved east, and another four million moved west. In the process about two hundred thousand died. In Bengal, the exchange of population and the slaughter were on a lesser scale and took place over a longer period. The elimination of the Hindu population in East Bengal continued into the months before the birth of Bangladesh (1972) and the crossborder migration continues in the 1980s.

[See also All-India Muslim League; Indian National Congress; Mountbatten, Louis; Pakistan; Punjab; Sind; North-West Frontier Province; Baluchistan; Bengal; Assam; Kashmir; and Bangladesh.]

Nicholas Mansergh, ed., *The Transfer of Power, 1942-1947*, vols. 7–12 (1977–1983). V. P. Menon, *The Transfer of Power in India* (1957). Penderel Moon, *Divide and Quit* (1961). R. J. Moore, *Escape from Empire: The Attlee Government and the Indian Problem* (1983). Hugh Tinker, *Experiment with Freedom: India and Pakistan 1947* (1967) and "Pressure, Persuasion, Decision: Factors in the Partition of the Punjab August 1947," *Journal of Asian Studies* 36.4 (1977).   HUGH TINKER

PASAI, the first important Muslim state in Southeast Asia, was situated on the best natural harbor of northern Sumatra, near modern Lhokseumawe. Its earlier and alternative name, Samudra, was extended by Arab and European sailors to the whole island of Sumatra. Adopting Islam in the 1290s, Pasai was for the following century and a half the major port of the Melaka (Malacca) Straits area, despite a conquest by Majapahit (Java) about the 1360s. It had diplomatic contacts with China, Siam, and India, and was visited by Marco Polo (1292) and Ibn Battuta (1355). It lost its commercial preeminence to Melaka in the late fifteenth century, suffering from constant internal turmoil that was accentuated by Portuguese intervention in 1512–1520. Muslim and mercantile forces were therefore ready to support Aceh, the new Muslim power of Sumatra, in its conquest of the state in 1524.

[See also Majapahit; Melaka; and Aceh.]

ANTHONY REID

PASARGADAE, capital of Cyrus II ("the Great"; r. 559–530 BCE) and coronation place of his successors, 140 kilometers northeast of Shiraz, Iran. The town had no wall, but many royal structures, built by Cyrus and completed by Darius and Xerxes, were scattered within a large park. They included a fort on a mound artificially extended with rusticated slabs; a tower tomb; a shrine with two altars; a residential palace; a gate house, the door jambs of which were ornamented with the figure of a man with four wings and an Egyptian crown; an audience palace; and the tomb of Cyrus himself, a gabled-roof stone chamber set on a six-tiered base. Artisans of various lands were involved in contructing and ornamenting these monuments, which consequently ranked as fine creations of Near Eastern art. Alexander seized the treasury of Pasargadae, and Cyrus's tomb, guarded by priests as a shrine until Alexander's conquest, was robbed by a Macedonian notable, although its sanctity was preserved locally by claims that it was the tomb of Solomon's mother.

[See also Achaemenid Dynasty and Cyrus II.]

Sylvia A. Matheson, *Persia: An Archaeological Guide* (2d ed., 1976), pp. 214–220. C. Nylander, *Ionians in Pasargadae* (1970). D. Stronach, *Pasargadae* (1978).

A. SHAHPUR SHAHBAZI

PASISIR, Javanese word for "coast," usually used to refer to the north coast of Java, an area that fell under Dutch political control between 1619 (the date of the foundation of Batavia) and the end of the eighteenth century. At the Central Javanese courts of Surakarta and Yogyakarta the term *pasisir* later came to mean any area (whether coastal or otherwise) outside the boundaries of the princely states. Throughout modern Javanese history, from the Majapahit period (1294–c. 1527) up to the final establishment of Dutch rule in the eighteenth century, the *pasisir* areas existed in a dynamic and often tense relationship with the Javanese court centers in the interior. From the fifteenth century onward, the establishment of islamized port cities on the north coast gradually undermined the authority of the Hindu-Buddhist Majapahit empire in Java, and in the seventeenth century, the successor state of Mataram proved itself unable to control the *pasisir* regents (Javanese, *bupati*), who looked on the Dutch East India Company (VOC) as a political ally against the Javanese court. During this last period the north-coast areas became ever more important for the Dutch as sources of rice and other agricultural products for their trade with the spice-producing islands of eastern Indonesia. The large numbers of Chinese immigrants who settled in the *pasisir* from the late seventeenth century onward also gave the area a special character. The Dutch scholar Th. G. Th. Pigeaud has identified a special *pasisir* culture that was much more heavily influenced by Islam and the presence of foreign traders (especially Malays, Chinese, Arabs, and Europeans) than that of the Central Javanese courts. Contacts between the coast and the interior, however, were always maintained through commerce and intermarriage among the Javanese elite.

[*See also* Surakarta; Yogyakarta; *and* Mataram.]

Th. G. Th. Pigeaud, *Literature of Java*, 4 vols. (1967–1980). D. E. Willmott, *The Chinese of Semarang* (1960).

PETER CAREY

FIGURE 1. *Krishna Mandir, Durbar Square, Patan.*

PATALIPUTRA, ancient name of modern Patna, situated on the confluence of the Ganges and Son rivers. Founded in the fifth century BCE, it became the capital of Magadha and of the Maurya and Gupta empires. As a metropolitan city of political and cultural importance it attracted people from various reaches of these empires. The Seleucid kings kept the Greek residents Megasthenes and Deimachos in Pataliputra at the court of Chandragupta and Bindusara in the fourth and third centuries BCE. Megasthenes gave a vivid description of the city's fortification, a stockade, and a moat as well as its municipal administration and royal splendor. Archaeology has confirmed the essential details and character of the city.

[*See also* Megasthenes; Patna; Maurya Empire; Gupta Empire; *and* Magadha.]

R. C. Majumdar, ed., *The Age of Imperial Unity* (1968).

A. K. NARAIN

PATAN. The town of Patan (Newari, Yala) lies southeast of Kathmandu, Nepal, separated from it by the Bagmati River. It is the historical legacy of an independent Newar kingdom of Patan, which the raja of Gorkha conquered in 1768. Patan is a compactly built town with winding cobbled lanes and open public squares and tanks, an old palace, and numerous temples. Until the early eighteenth century it was complete with a surrounding wall and gateways. Its history of first settlement dates perhaps from Magadha's king Ashoka (reigned c. 273–236 BCE), who, according to tradition, built five stupas, which are still extant. Patan was probably the site of the Licchavi seat of Managriha, known as Yupagrama. It was Nepal's political capital also in the medieval period. The town is of Buddhist orientation, with a total of 143 *viharas* (monastic compounds). It is a famous craft center for the Newars.

[*See also* Newar; Nepal: History of Nepal; *and* Kathmandu.]

John K. Locke, *Karunamaya: The Cult of Avalokitesvara-Matsyendranath in the Valley of Nepal* (1980). Mary Slusser, *Nepal Mandala: A Cultural Study of the Kathmandu Valley* (1982).

PRAYAG RAJ SHARMA

PATANI (also Pattani), city and ancient kingdom of the Malay Peninsula, now in southern Thailand. Early Patani owed its importance to its position at the mouth of the river draining an extensive rice plain and as the eastern terminus of an overland trading route across the peninsula. Under the name Langkasuka it entered into trade relations with China by the sixth century CE and was an early center of Buddhism and Indian religion. As a trading port it was among the objects of the naval expeditions of Rajendracola (1017–1025). In the thirteenth century it was brought under the sway of the rising Thai Buddhist state centered on Nakhon Si Thammarat.

Patani's Malay population was converted to Islam probably in the fifteenth century, and to this day it remains a major center of Islamic teaching and scholarship. The state's independence and trade grew in the wake of the Portuguese capture of Melaka in 1511, and Patani became a leading South China Sea port for Asian and European trade with Japan and China. As the Thai kingdom of Ayudhya attempted to control this trade in the seventeenth century, Patani was drawn into conflict with the Thai and succumbed to Thai control in 1785. After rebelling against Bangkok, Ayudhya's successor, in 1817, Patani was subdivided into seven small provinces and thereafter was too weak to successfully challenge the growing power of Siam. Further rebellions against the imposition of Bangkok's authority in 1901–1902 and 1946–1948 were ineffective, but Muslim Malay resentment of Thai control in Patani remains strong.

[See also Ayudhya; Bangkok; Langkasuka; Melaka; and Nakhon Si Thammarat.]

A. Teeuw and David K. Wyatt, *Hikayat Patani: The Story of Patani* (1970).   DAVID K. WYATT

PATEL, SARDAR VALLABHBHAI (1875–1950), a leader of the Indian National Congress and deputy prime minister of India from 1947 to 1950. A barrister practicing in Ahmadabad, Gujarat, Patel was drawn into an active role in the Congress during the Bardoli *satyagraha* movement in 1922. He rose in the party to become Congress president in 1931. Outside of India he was the least known of the three major leaders (the others were Mohandas Gandhi and Jawaharlal Nehru), but in the party he was recognized as the strong man in the organization. His pragmatic acceptance of partition in 1947 was crucial to Lord Mountbatten's plan. He entered the Interim Cabinet in 1946 as home minister and re-

tained that post as well as the deputy premiership after independence until his death. Among his major achievements was the successful integration of the princely states. He was generally more conservative than Nehru as well as more pragmatic than Gandhi. His death removed a possible conservative challenge to Nehru.

[See also Indian National Congress; Princely States; Gandhi, Mohandas Karamchand; and Nehru, Jawaharlal.]

Durga Das, ed., *Sardar Patel's Correspondence, 1945–50*, 10 vols. (1971–1974). K. L. Punjabi, *The Indomitable Sardar* (1962).   CRAIG BAXTER

PATENOTRE TREATY (1884). Signed on 6 June 1884 and ratified in May 1885, the treaty established the French protectorate over Vietnam, Tonkin coming under more direct supervision while the court at Hue theoretically had more control over Annam. In large part because of the conflict with China over French policy toward her vassal, the final version of the treaty somewhat softened the original Harmand Agreement of 1883, particularly where Hue's sovereignty over certain provinces was concerned. Other clauses of the treaty dealt with the status and rights of the French in the protectorate, as well as various aspects of internal administration. [See also Harmand, François-Jules.]

BRUCE M. LOCKHART

PATERNO, PEDRO (1858–1911). Born to a wealthy Manila family of mixed Tagalog, Chinese, and Spanish origin, Paterno was among the most prominent *ilustrados* of his time. Highly educated (B. A., Ateneo, 1871; LL.D., Madrid, 1880), he was a prolific writer whose large body of works reflects his participation in the reform movement and expresses his views on Filipino national heritage. In 1897 he negotiated the Pact of Biaknabato, the agreement ending the first phase of the Philippine Revolution against Spain. Although at first reluctant, Paterno supported the 1898 republic, serving as a personal aide of Emilio Aguinaldo until his capture by the Americans in late 1899. Subsequently, Paterno was unable to achieve the recognition and position he so desperately sought, finding himself displaced by a younger generation of political leaders. [See also Ilustrado; Philippine Revolution; and Aguinaldo, Emilio.]   MICHAEL CULLINANE

PATHAN. See Pakhtun.

PATHET LAO. The term *Pathet Lao* (PL), meaning "land of the Lao," was first used in 1950 by Lao forces that followed the Viet Minh's lead and refused to accept the accommodation with the French to which other Lao nationalists had acceded the previous year. The term gained international currency when it was used at the Geneva Conference of 1954, even though representatives of the PL forces were not seated at the conference and it was a Viet Minh general who signed the cease-fire with the French on their behalf. The name remained in common use as a generic term for the Lao Communists despite the fact that a legal political party, the Neo Lao Hak Sat (NLHS, or Lao Patriotic Front), was formed in early 1956. Therefore, although Pathet Lao was properly the name only of the armed forces of the Lao Communists between 1950 and 1965, it was used colloquially to include all components of the Lao Communist movement. Among them were the People's Party of Laos (Phak Pasason Lao), the semisecret Communist party whose name was changed in 1972 to the Lao People's Revolutionary Party (Phak Pasason Pativat Lao); the Lao Patriotic Front (Neo Lao Hak Sat); the Lao People's Liberation Army (Kongthap Potpoi Pasason Lao); and the administration in the Communist zone of Laos. Since the seizure of full power by the Communist movement and the proclamation of the Lao People's Democratic Republic in December 1975, the term *Pathet Lao* is no longer used. [*See also* Viet Minh; Geneva Conference of 1954; *and* Laos.]

JOSEPH J. ZASLOFF

PATIALA, one of the former princely states of India, located in the Punjab, south of the Sutlej River. The largest of the semiautonomous states in the region, it had further importance since the ruler was a Sikh and therefore had preeminence in his community. It was known as one of the three Phulkian states (the other two were Jind and Nabha), from *Phul,* the name of a remote ancestor of the rulers. The family belonged to the great Jat caste or clan, but they also claimed Rajput ancestry. At the end of the seventeenth century ancestors of the Patiala ruler, along with many other Jat families in the area, became followers of the Sikh leader Guru Gobind Singh. In 1762 the Afghan invader Ahmad Shah Durrani gave the chief of Patiala the title of raja in return for assistance against the Mughal emperor, but in the following year the raja made himself independent. By the beginning of the eighteenth century the state was threatened by Ranjit Singh, the

powerful Sikh chieftain who had made himself supreme in the rest of Punjab. In 1809 the raja of Patiala made an alliance with the British, who by this time were establishing their authority in the Delhi region, in return for protection from Ranjit Singh. During the Mutiny of 1857 the ruler supported the British, thus ensuring them from being attacked by the other Sikh chieftains of the Punjab. The capital, also known as Patiala, was founded in 1763 and at the end of the nineteenth century it became an important road and rail center. After Indian independence in 1947, the state was merged into a union with other states in eastern Punjab; in 1956 this union was integrated into the state of the Punjab. [*See also* Princely States; Singh, Ranjit; *and* Sikhism.]

AINSLIE T. EMBREE

PATNA, capital of Bihar state, India. In ancient times it was known as Pataliputra. After the Guptas, the city declined under medieval feudalism until the sultanate revival of trade and urban life. Sultan Ala ud-Din Husain Shah of Bengal built a cathedral mosque in 1510–1511, a sign of substantial Muslim settlement. Sher Shah built a fort in 1541, and the emperor Akbar conquered the city for the Mughals in 1574. The English and Dutch East India companies established factories in 1640 and 1666. The English crowned Shah Alam in their factory on 12 March 1761; began governing Patna in 1766; and made it a municipality in 1864 and provincial capital in 1912. With the first newspaper (in Urdu) in 1855, the railway in 1862, and Patna College in 1863, Patna was launched into modern life. Population estimates of 200,000 in 1641 and 312,000 in 1811 seem inflated. The 1901 census counted 134,785, with increases to 196,415 in 1941 and 475,300 in 1971.

[*See also* Pataliputra *and* Bihar.]

Surendra Gopal, *Patna in the 19th Century* (1982). Hameeda Khatoon Naqvi, *Urban Centres and Industries in Upper India 1556–1803* (1968). FRITZ LEHMANN

PATTANI. *See* Patani.

PAVIE MISSIONS, a series of explorations of French Indochina and adjoining territories, carried out between 1879 and 1895 under the guidance of the French explorer and engineer Auguste Pavie (1847–1925). The series was broken into four parts and each of these was further subdivided into several component expeditions.

The earliest missions (1879–1885) involved surveys for telegraph lines running through Cambodia into Thailand (then Siam). The second series of missions, from 1886 to 1889, mapped much of the terra incognita now known as Laos, as well as adjoining areas of what is now northern Vietnam, in sixteen separate expeditions. These continued between 1889 and 1891, with missions fanning out into southwestern China and unmapped portions of Cambodia as well. The final group of missions, between 1892 and 1895, accompanied the imposition of French control over much of the areas previously mapped, which had been tributary to Bangkok or had enjoyed ambiguously independent relations with China. Pavie himself, an indefatigable traveler with considerable diplomatic skills, has been credited almost single-handedly with removing those parts of Siam now known as Laos from Thai control. The bravery and skills of his companions, and the accuracy of their cartographic and ethnographic work, are reflected in the eight-volume description of the explorations, which appeared in 1898–1904. Pavie has been ranked with Francis Garnier as one of the most inspired and heroic actors in the drama of French colonialism in Southeast Asia.

[See also Garnier, Francis.]

DAVID P. CHANDLER

PEACE PRESERVATION LAW,

the symbol of repressive legislation in interwar Japan. Overwhelmingly approved by the Diet in 1925, the measure outlawed the acts of organizing or joining an association that aimed at "altering the national polity [kokutai] or denying the system of private property." The crimes carried maximum prison sentences of ten years. Critics charged Katō Takaaki's cabinet, which had sponsored the legislation, with attempting to stifle the potential of the cabinet-sponsored institution of universal manhood suffrage to bolster the liberal left. Government spokesmen insisted, however, that the Peace Preservation Law was specifically aimed at the Communist Party—not scholarly research or social democratic parties and unions. On 15 March 1928 the cabinet of Tanaka Giichi, in cooperation with conservative officials of the Ministry of Justice, used the law to arrest 1,600 suspected communists. Tanaka next revised the original law so that organizing an association to alter the national polity would carry a sentence of death. The government also established new "thought prosecutors" and extended the "thought police" (Special Higher Police) so as to be able to police the entire nation.

During the 1930s officials steadily broadened the scope of the Peace Preservation Law so that it could be applied to liberals, religious organizations, allegedly communist-infiltrated cultural groups, and even subversive rightists. A complete revision in 1941 reinforced these tendencies. From 1928 to 1944 the government invoked the law within Japan to arrest some 68,500 people, prosecuting 6,227. By order of the American Occupation the law was repealed on 15 October 1945.

[See also Katō Takaaki and Tanaka Giichi.]

Richard H. Mitchell, *Thought Control in Prewar Japan* (1976).
SHELDON M. GARON

PEARL HARBOR,

Hawaiian Islands site of a surprise aerial assault by a Japanese carrier task force on American naval, military, and air facilities on 7 December 1941, thus opening the Pacific War. Contingency planning for the assault was begun early in 1941, as the Japanese government pondered the alternatives of war and negotiation as means for retaining a free hand in China, for breaking the American embargo of oil supplies to Japan, and for obtaining control of the vital resources of Southeast Asia.

Strategically, the plans were based on the assumption that superior American industrial capacity made it unlikely that Japan could win a protracted war with the United States and that, therefore, Japan would have to strike such a devastating blow at the outset that the American government would be forced to agree to a negotiated settlement on Japanese terms. The coordinated and complex strategy called for the early destruction of the United States Pacific Fleet so that it could not threaten the Japanese Navy's support of rapid military offensives that were to conquer the territories and resources of Southeast Asia. Tactically, the plans were grounded on the conviction that if carried out by surprise, a massed torpedo and plane attack against warships at anchor in harbor would bring about a decisive victory, since the surface ships would be unable to take evasive action. As the US Pacific Fleet was frequently at anchor at Pearl Harbor, it made an ideal target for such an attack.

Admiral Yamamoto Isoroku (1884–1943), commander of the Japanese combined fleet, who had consistently opposed a war with the United States as unwise, now energetically undertook overall responsibility for planning the operation. Early in 1941 Yamamoto ordered feasibility studies of torpedo attacks at short range in shallow waters, and in September of that year selected Japanese pilots began secret training in such tactics in Kagoshima Bay, Kyushu, while personnel attached to the Japanese consulate in Honolulu began close surveillance of the US Pacific Fleet at Pearl Harbor. In early November 1941 the Japanese cabinet and general staffs decided that Hawaii would be attacked if the nation's statesmen and diplomats could not reach a satisfactory settlement with the United States.

On 22 November the task force of six aircraft carriers, two battleships, and twenty-seven other warships and support ships assembled in the Kurile Islands north of Hokkaido under its commander, Admiral Nagumo Chūichi (1887–1944). It departed on 26 November for Hawaii, taking a course through the North Pacific well clear of normal navigational routes. If not recalled the task force was to launch its aircraft so as to strike Hawaii at 8:30 A.M. on 7 December, which would be thirty minutes after the Japanese ambassador in Washington had delivered the note telling that Japan, having concluded that progress through cooperation had "finally been lost," had decided to break off negotiations. As it turned out, because the task force launched its planes thirty minutes ahead of schedule and because the Japanese embassy staff in Washington was inefficient, the declaration was delayed until well after 8:30 A.M. Hawaii time, with disastrous consequences to the American view of Japanese intentions.

The attacking aircraft arrived over Hawaii a little before 8:00 A.M., having achieved complete surprise. Japanese pilots were disappointed to find that no American aircraft carriers were in Pearl Harbor, but torpedo and dive-bombing attacks were launched with devastating effect on the capital ships that were at anchor and on nearby army and air bases; these attacks were followed by a second strike at 9:15. Despite the destruction of these ships and facilities, the attackers neglected to damage less tempting yet more important strategic targets: the machine shops and oil storage facilities that were critical to Pearl Harbor's effectiveness as a base. What had been achieved by the time the planes departed was dramatic enough: four battleships and two other vessels sunk, twelve ships severely damaged, 188 aircraft destroyed, and some 3,700 American servicemen killed and wounded. Japanese losses were only twenty-nine aircraft and a few midget submarines. Although some of his staff argued heat-

edly for a third strike, Admiral Nagumo, fearing a counterattack from American carriers, whose whereabouts were unknown, ordered a withdrawal to the west at high speed.

The Pearl Harbor attack was one of the most dramatic tactical victories in the history of modern warfare, achieved by brilliant planning and incredible luck. It was also a disastrous strategic mistake for Japan, for by the destruction of a number of overage American battleships, Japan, owing to the apparently infamous circumstances of the assault, had at one stroke united the deeply divided American people in an outraged determination to wreak vengeance on the aggressors and to wring from them unconditional surrender.

[See also World War II in Asia.]

A. J. Barker, *Pearl Harbor* (1969). Herbert Feis, *The Road to Pearl Harbor* (1965). Gunther Prange, *At Dawn We Slept* (1982).   MARK R. PEATTIE

PECHENEGS, a Turkic tribal confederation that figured prominently in Byzantine, Khazar, Rus, and Danubian affairs from the ninth to the eleventh century. The earliest reference to them, found in an eighth-century Tibetan translation of a Uighur report on the "peoples of the north," places them in the Syr Darya basin. They were evicted thence by the Oghuz in the late eighth to early ninth century and forced into the area between the Volga and Ural rivers. Steady Oghuz pressure drove them into Khazar territory in the ninth century. One of the consequences of this migration was the displacement of the Hungarian tribal union at the end of the ninth century and its settlement in present-day Hungary.

After 920, the Pechenegs periodically raided or allied themselves (especially after 980) with various Rus factions. In 972, having replaced the Khazars as the leading power in the Pontic steppes, they killed the Kievan prince Sviatoslav. Vladimir I (r. 980–1015) and Iaroslav I (r. 1036–1054) mounted major campaigns against the Pechenegs that, together with Oghuz pressure, drove them toward Byzantium's Danubian-Balkan borders. A Byzantine-Cuman alliance against them culminated in their massacre at Levunion in 1091. A last Pecheneg effort against Byzantium in 1122 ended unsuccessfully. Thereafter, Pechenegs were found in the Balkans, Hungary, and Rus, often functioning as border guards.

The Pechenegs appear to have spoken a form of Kipchak Turkic and may have used a type of runic script. Their loosely knit union of eight tribes did not have a strong monarchic tradition. The religion of the Pechenegs was in the main shamanistic.

PETER B. GOLDEN

PEDIR (Acehnese, Pidie) is the most intensively cultivated district of Aceh, centered on the town of Sigli on the northern coast of Sumatra. It flourished briefly as an independent Islamic kingdom in the fifteenth century, when it produced large quantities of pepper and silk for export. Its predecessor was probably the Nakur visited by the Aheng He expedition (1412–1415) and the cannibalistic Dagroian of Marco Polo (1292). After a brief flirtation with the Portuguese, Pedir was conquered by Aceh in 1524. Although remaining the most populous and productive dependency of that sultanate, it was progressively divided into numerous rival fiefdoms. [*See also* Aceh *and* Zheng He.]

ANTHONY REID

PEGU. A major political and symbolic center in Lower Burma, Pegu, located north of Rangoon, is usually associated with the Mon, one of the important ethnic groups in Burmese history. Legend attributes its founding in the ninth century to two brothers. However, the first mention of Pegu in contemporary sources (Old Burmese inscriptions) comes only in the twelfth century. It was not until the fifteenth century, when a Mon dynasty was founded there by Byinnya-U, that any evidence emerges of Pegu's efflorescence, and only subsequently did it receive its classical name, Hamsavati (Hanthawaddy).

Pegu attained its greatest prominence in the mid-sixteenth century when it became the capital of Tabinshweihti of the Toungoo dynasty. Its political and economic grandeur lasted for two centuries until King Thalun moved his capital back to central Burma in 1635 and reestablished Ava as the seat of central government in Burma. Finally in 1757 King Alaunghpaya of the last (Konbaung) dynasty once more placed Pegu under inland hegemony after a last effort by Lower Burma to become the dominant political force in the country failed. In 1852, after the Second Anglo-Burmese War, with the rest of Lower Burma, Pegu was annexed by the British.

Pegu is significant in Burmese history for several reasons. Its proximity to (if not on) the coasts of Lower Burma made it a valuable commercial center (hence, a lucrative revenue source for the hinterland powers) during most of its early existence. But the continued buildup of silt from the Pegu River finally prevented ships from docking there after the sixteenth century, and thereafter it began to lose its commercial importance. Yet central Burma's control of Pegu not only served as a guarantee against attack from the rear—the north was the primary concern of most Burman governments—but also kept open the central region's access to Lower Burma and thus to the rest of the Asian commercial and religious world. It further provided a buffer for the center of Burmese culture, located farther north, against attacks from the southeast during the centuries when the Thai reasserted their power in the region. When the British annexed Pegu to the Indian empire in 1852, their major reason for doing so was once again economic: teak, for which Pegu and its environs were known, had become important as an export commodity. Not until the late nineteenth century were Pegu's swamps drained and turned into the vast plains of cultivated rice with which we are familiar, and perhaps only then did its role as supplier of the national staple surpass that of central Burma. Pegu was important also in religious and cultural terms. It was regarded as a center of pure Buddhism for many centuries, largely because under the fifteenth-century Mon king Dhammaceti (Dhammazedi), one of the major purifications of the *sangha* (the Buddhist monastic order)—one that continued to be a model for subsequent reforms—occurred in Pegu. The Shwemawdaw Pagoda of Pegu, whose towering stupa of 375 feet is actually higher than the more reknowned Shwedagon of Rangoon, is still one of the premier holy places in Burma. And for many centuries Pegu remained the symbol of Mon and regional political-cultural independence and a rallying point for resistance to inland, agrarian Burman rule.

[*See also* Burma; Mon; Tabinshweihti; Toungoo Dynasties; Alaunghpaya; Konbaung Dynasty; Anglo-Burmese Wars; Lower Burma; Shwedagon Pagoda; *and the map accompanying* Ayudhya.]

Michael Aung-Thwin, *Historical Sites in Burma* (1972). Gasparo Balbi, "Gasparo Balbi, His Voyage to Pegu, and Observations There, Gathered Out of His Owne Italian Relation," in *Hakluytus Posthumus or Purchas His Pilgrimes*, edited by Samuel Purchas, vol. 10 (1625; reprint, 1905–1907), pp. 143–164. R. Halliday, *The Talaings* (1917). R. Halliday, trans. and ed., "Slapat Rajawan Datow Smin Ron—A History of Kings," *Journal of the Burma Research Society* 13 (1923): 5–67. G. E. Harvey, *A History of Burma from the Earliest Times* (1925; reprint, 1967). Arthur P. Phayre, *History of Burma* (1883).

MICHAEL AUNG-THWIN

PEIKTHANO, or Beikthano Myo, one of the earliest urban sites found in Burma (dating from between the first century BCE and second century CE) and the best excavated. It is located between Sri Ksetra and Pagan, east of the Irrawaddy River but in its valley. According to Burmese legend, Peikthano is not the first city, but it is one of the oldest, and it is thought to have been built by the Pyu. Excavations have revealed information that links Peikthano with contemporary and near-contemporary urban sites in Burma that are also attributed to the Pyu. These sites have been found from the central dry plains to the coasts of Lower Burma.

Peikthano represents the archetypical center in terms of city plan, architecture, cultural artifacts, and recognizable ideology. Its temple and monastic remains are virtually identical in style to those of the other urban sites, and it seems that it also shared certain practices, such as urn burial, coinage, and building materials, with these sites. With the exception of Mongmao, which has not been fully excavated, Peikthano is the oldest urban site yet discovered in Burma, and evidence implies that it is linked with other similar sites in Burma as well as with contemporary ones in Sri Lanka, India, and Thailand.

Peikthano has more than chronological significance, however; it suggests the presence of a common culture in the Irrawaddy Valley almost a millennium prior to the rise of Pagan in the mid-ninth century CE.

[See also Pyu; Mongmao; and Pagan.]

U Aung Thaw, ed., *Excavations at Beikthano* (1968) and *Historical Sites in Burma* (1972). Michael Aung-Thwin, "Burma Before Pagan: The Status of Archaeology Today," in *Asian Perspectives* (1987).

MICHAEL AUNG-THWIN

PEKING. See Beijing.

PEMERINTAH REVOLUSIONER REPUBLIK INDONESIA/PERDJUANGAN SEMESTA, known as the PRRI/Permesta, two interrelated rebellions against the Indonesian republic. They took place on Sumatra and Sulawesi.

A revolutionary government, headed by Sjafruddin Prawiranegara, was proclaimed in Padang on 15 February 1958, after the Indonesian central government had turned down an ultimatum from the Dewan Banteng of Central Sumatra (chaired by Lieutenant-Colonel Achmad Husein) to change the government. The Piagam Perdjuangan Semesta had been read on 2 March 1957 by the military commander of East Indonesia, Lieutenant-Colonel Ventje Sumual. It called for a better division of foreign income over the regions. The PRRI/Permesta, inspired by a combination of political and economic grievances, regional sentiments, and dissatisfaction over the personnel policy of any army command, was soon repressed. Within a year its major force had been defeated. Some rebels did fight on, joining forces with the Darul Islam and founding the Republik Persatuan Indonesia. [See also Sjafruddin Prawiranegara.]

C. VAN DIJK

PENANG (also known as Pinang), an island off the west coast of the Malay Peninsula, opposite Kedah; site of early British settlement; now a constituent state within Malaysia.

In the 1780s, the sultan of Kedah was under intense pressure from Siam because he had offered less than full resistance to Burmese armies during the Burma-Siam warfare of the previous two decades. The British East Indian Company (EIC) was seeking a naval base and trading station on the east shore of the Bay of Bengal to secure its growing trade with China. Francis Light secured the cession of Penang from Kedah to the EIC in return for a promise to defend Kedah and an annual payment of $30,000. The EIC took possession of Penang in July 1786, naming it Prince of Wales Island, and subsequently failed to carry out fully the terms Light had negotiated, cutting the annual payment to $6,000. To assure the island's security and agricultural base, the EIC negotiated the cession of adjacent territory on the mainland, "Province Wellesley," in 1800, with an increase in the annual payment to $9,000.

Over the next century Penang's principal port, George Town, became a major focus for the economic development of the west coast of the peninsula. It handled the region's overseas trade and became a center of Chinese entrepreneurial activity. Penang economic interests pressed strongly for the extension of British control on the mainland in the 1870s, and it became a center for tin smelting and rubber processing. On Malayan independence in 1957, Penang and Province Wellesley together became a sultanless state in the federation, with an elected government headed by a governor.

[See also Kedah; Light, Francis; East India Company; Malaysia; Province Wellesley; Straits Settlements.]

Barbara W. Andaya and Leonard V. Andaya, *A History of Malaysia* (1982). R. Bonney, *Kedah 1771–1821*

(1971). C. D. Cowan, *Nineteenth-Century Malaya* (1961). R. O. Winstedt, *A History of Malaya* (1935).

DAVID K. WYATT

PENG DEHUAI (1899–1974), one of the most important Chinese Communist military leaders from 1928 until his purge by Mao Zedong in 1959. Born in the same county of Hunan Province as Mao, and like Mao the son of a rich peasant family, Peng left home at an early age to work at various menial jobs. In 1915 he returned to his native area and within a year led a peasant attack on a rich merchant. Soon after, as a member of the Hunan provincial army, he participated in abortive plots against the governor of Hunan, for which he was eventually imprisoned.

After Peng was released he rejoined the army, from which he was admitted to the Hunan Military Academy in 1922. He graduated in 1924 and was made a battalion commander. Peng joined the Guomindang (Kuomintang, KMT, or Nationalist Party) on the Northern Expedition in 1926 as a regimental commander in the Fifth Independent Division of Tang Shengzhi. By 1928, when he joined the Chinese Communist Party (CCP), Peng had risen to brigade commander first in Tang's army and later in the KMT 35th Army. In July he helped to start the Pingjiang Uprising in Hunan as the commander of the newly organized Fifth Red Army. After establishing the Hunan Soviet Government, Peng led part of his army to Mao's headquarters at Jinggang Shan, where he merged his forces into the Fourth Red Army of Mao Zedong and Zhu De and became its deputy commander. From that time on he played a leading role in the rise to power of the CCP.

From 1929 to 1930 Peng's forces were primarily involved in defending the Jinggang Shan base area, with northward excursions into Hunan and Hubei. In the middle of 1930, when Li Lisan's policy of urban insurrection was the dominant line of the CCP, Peng's army led two assaults on Changsha, the capital of Hunan, from which they retreated to Jiangxi with the Zhu-Mao forces. In the Fudian Incident of late 1930 Peng refused the entreaties of rebels among his own forces and declared his unequivocal support for Mao.

In the period of the Jiangxi Soviet, Peng played an important role in the CCP defense against the first four of Chiang Kai-shek's Extermination Campaigns. He was a member of the Central Executive Committee of the first and second Chinese soviets and was elected to the CCP Central Committee in 1934. As commander of the Third Army Corps of the First Front Army, he played a crucial role in the famous Long March of 1934 to 1935. At the key Zunyi and Maoerkai conferences of the CCP in January and July 1935, Peng threw his weight behind Mao's successful effort to take complete control of the CCP. As commander of the First Front Army and later as deputy commander in chief of the Eighth Route Army, Peng led the fight against the Japanese, most notably in the Battle of One Hundred Regiments of August to December 1940. From 1941 to 1942 he also served as secretary of the CCP North China Bureau.

Peng was elected to the Seventh Central Committee and named an alternate member of the Politburo in June 1945, concurrently serving as head of the CCP Military Commission and deputy commander in chief of the Peoples' Liberation Army (PLA). In the civil war with the KMT he led PLA forces in the conquest of the northwest, recapturing Yan'an in 1948 and taking Xi'an, Lanzhou, Xining, and Yinchuan from May to September 1949.

From the founding of the People's Republic in 1949 until the end of 1954 Peng served on the Central People's Government Council, the People's Revolutionary Military Council, and the Sino-Soviet Friendship Association. From October 1950 to September 1954 he commanded the Chinese People's Volunteers (CPV) in Korea, signing the armistice in Kaesŏng in July 1953 and returning to a hero's welcome. After 1954 Peng achieved his greatest influence, as Politburo member, vice-premier of the State Council, vice-chairman of the National Defense Council, and most importantly, minister of national defense, posts he continued to hold until 1959. In 1955 he was named one of the ten marshals of the PLA, the highest military rank, and received the three top army decorations. In the period of close alliance between the People's Republic of China (PRC) and the Soviet bloc, he also led many delegations to the Soviet Union and Eastern Europe.

Peng's abrupt fall came in July 1959, at the Lushan Plenum of the CCP Central Committee, where he gave talks and circulated a letter to Mao in which he criticized the excesses and failures of the Great Leap Forward. At Mao's insistence, he was purged in August as the leader of an "anti-Party clique." Since Peng, unlike earlier CCP purge victims, had not conspired secretly but had openly expressed his criticisms within Party councils, his fall represented, according to some scholars, the first real break with inner Party norms after the founding of the PRC. Some military analysts have speculated that Peng's purge was related to a split in the PLA between a purely military line and a line stressing the primacy of ideology, in which the military professionals may have sought closer ties with Moscow in order to strengthen China's defenses. Indeed, after the purge of Peng and several top associates, Mao learned that Peng had expressed his criticism of the Great Leap to Khrushchev while in the Soviet Union, criticism that Khrushchev later echoed while the Lushan meetings were under way.

Nevertheless, scholars such as Frederick Teiwes find neither collusion with the Soviets nor differences in military policy to be at the core of Peng's purge, since other leaders including Mao had criticized domestic Chinese policies to their Soviet "elder brothers" in the 1950s, and since even Lin Biao, the top representative of the supposed "political" line in the PLA, nevertheless intensified military training and decreased the allocation of army manpower to civilian tasks after replacing Peng as defense minister in 1959. Instead, many scholars believe that the key factor in Peng's fall was Mao's personal identification with the Great Leap policies.

Within the top Party and state leadership, much resentment over Mao's actions remained, as evidenced by Peng's continued Party and Politburo membership after 1959, and by top-level support for his repeated attempts in the early 1960s to obtain a "reversal of verdicts." He remained in a number of minor posts, mostly in the southwest, until the mid-1960s, and reportedly even had a conciliatory meeting with Mao sometime in that period.

The outbreak of the Cultural Revolution, however, thwarted Peng's attempted comeback. Indeed, an attack on *Hai Rui's Dismissal,* a historical play widely viewed as an allegorical defense of Peng, was the opening salvo of the Cultural Revolution. Peng received rough treatment at the hands of the Red Guards, beginning in December 1966/January 1967, when he was arrested and paraded through the streets as a "capitalist roader."

With the rise of Deng Xiaoping to top leadership in late 1978 and the reversal of verdicts on the Cultural Revolution, Peng was at last officially rehabilitated, although it was revealed at the same time that he had died in November 1974 after a long period of solitary confinement. Since early 1979, when favorable accounts of his career first appeared in the Chinese press, Peng Dehuai has become one of the chief symbols of the oppression and injustice of the final twenty years of the rule of Mao Zedong.

[*See also* China, People's Republic of; Communism: Chinese Communist Party; Chinese People's Liberation Army; Great Leap Forward; Great Proletarian Cultural Revolution; *and* Mao Zedong.]

Ellis Joffe, *Party and Army: Professionalism and Political Control in the Chinese Officer Corps, 1949–1964* (1965). Donald W. Klein and Anne B. Clark, *Biographical Dictionary of Chinese Communism, 1921–1965* (1971). Roderick MacFarquhar, *The Origins of the Cultural Revolution,* vol. 2, *The Great Leap Forward, 1958–1962* (1983). Frederick C. Teiwes, "The Dismissal of P'eng Tehuai," in *Politics and Purges in China: Rectification and the Decline of Party Norms, 1950–1965* (1979). Union Research Institute, eds., *The Case of Peng Teh-huai* (1968). *Who's Who in Communist China* (1966).

JOHN A. RAPP

PENGHU ISLANDS. *See* Pescadores.

PENG ZHEN (b. 1902), former member of the Politburo of the People's Republic of China; chairman of the Standing Committee of the National People's Congress.

Born in Shanxi to a poor peasant family, Peng Zhen found an opportunity to attend middle school only when he was twenty-one years old. He joined the Chinese Youth League in 1921 and then the Chinese Communist Party two years later. For his underground Party work he was twice imprisoned in the 1930s. During the anti-Japanese war he worked as an important organizer and political commissar in North China, eventually emerging as a leading figure in the region. He was promoted to be a member of the Seventh Central Committee in 1945, and in 1952 was elected to the Politburo as well as being named first party secretary of Beijing, positions he kept until his purge in 1966.

Peng was the first high-ranking Party leader to be purged in the Cultural Revolution for his protection of Wu Han against Mao Zedong's wishes. After Mao's death, he made his first public appearance in 1979. Peng served as chairman of the Legal Commission of the National People's Congress and then assumed the chairmanship of the Standing Committee of the National People's Congress.

[*See also* Great Proletarian Cultural Revolution.]

HONG YUNG LEE

PEOPLE'S ACTION PARTY of Singapore (PAP) was founded in November 1954 in response to British promises of elections and self-government. Its early membership included democratic socialists and procommunists; its platform included repeal of the internal security laws and independence as part of Malaya. Initially the PAP pursued leftist policies and fomented much labor unrest. Soon, however, a bitter internecine struggle was waged between the moderates under Lee Kuan Yew and the procommunists. In 1957 the procommunists actually won control over the Central Executive Committee (CEC); they were soon displaced by the moderates, chiefly because colonial officials placed most procommunists under detention.

The left wing finally broke away in July 1961 and formed the Barisan Sosialis. Badly shaken by this proximity to disaster, the party leadership ever since has exercised tight discipline to screen out radicals. Never again has the PAP permitted rivals to share power; it keeps the identity of party cadres secret, and the CEC now exerts total oversight of all party and government activities. Electorally, the PAP has been victorious in every contest since it first formed an elected government in 1959.

In its twenty-five years in office it has been remarkably successful. The PAP relentlessly pursues a policy of economic development based on foreign investment and state capitalism; it has constructed vast public housing estates; it provides abundant goods and services; its leadership and structures are efficient and incorruptible; and it continues to permit electoral democracy, albeit under its own terms. The PAP's genius lies in its ability to detect potential problems before they occur and then to take effective preventive measures. The party's task today is to ensure that the second generation of leadership is equipped to both manage political conflict and adopt policies to meet the challenges of a changing international economic system.

[See also Lee Kuan Yew; Barisan Sosialis; and Singapore.]

Chan Heng Chee, The Dynamics of One-Party Dominance: The PAP at the Grass Roots (1976). Pang Cheng Lian, Singapore People's Action Party: Its History, Organization, and Leadership (1971).

STANLEY BEDLINGTON

PEOPLE'S COMMUNES, the basic unit of government in the Chinese countryside. They were established in 1958, during the Great Leap Forward. Since 1980 the Chinese Communist Party has moved gradually to separate the economic and political functions of these institutions.

The organizational history of the communes can be divided into three stages. The period from 1958 to 1962 marks the stage of origin and evolution. Communes combined industry, agriculture, trade, education, and military affairs, and integrated government administration and rural economic management. They arose out of the functional need for a larger unit of rural organization in the countryside to manage water conservancy projects and to extend Party control. Previously, the countryside had been organized into collective farms of approximately 200 households each. In 1958 more than 23,000 communes were hurriedly established, with an average of 5,443 households in each. Communes were vigorously promoted by Mao Zedong, who saw them as a vehicle by which the Chinese countryside could approach a communistic society.

Mao's utopian views did not last long, however, as problems with the new organizations quickly emerged. They were too large, incentives for peasants to produce were lacking, and cadres blindly ordered people around. One attempt to solve these problems resulted in the establishment of two subdivisions within the commune, the brigade and the team. By 1962 the team, of twenty to thirty households, was the basic unit of organization and management within the commune.

The second period, from 1962 to 1978, marks the stage of the mature commune system. During this period the three-level ownership system (the commune, the brigade, and the team) was institutionalized. There were 52,000 communes, 690,000 brigades, and about 5 million teams in 1978. Teams were responsible for agricultural production. Brigades coordinated team activity and ran some rural industry. Communes controlled larger rural industries, supervised the teams and brigades, managed education and health activities, and were the lowest level of government administration in rural areas.

Since 1980 the Communist Party has experimented with dividing the communes into separate economic and administrative entities. Leaders felt that the previous unified structure of communes facilitated the abuse of power by commune, brigade, and team officials. Progress has been slow in implementing the new system however. This third period marks the stage of dissolution.

Urban communes were also briefly established during the Great Leap Forward. However, these disappeared in the early 1960s and have never been revived.

[See also Agriculture, Collectivization of; China, People's Republic of; Great Leap Forward; Mao Zedong; and Responsibility System.]

Anita Chan, Richard Madsen, and Jonathan Unger, *Chen Village* (1984). Frederick W. Crook, "The Commune System in the People's Republic of China, 1963–1974," in *China: A Reassessment of the Economy*, compiled by the Joint Economic Committee of the Congress of the United States (1975), pp. 366–410. William L. Parish and Martin King Whyte, *Village and Family in Contemporary China* (1978). Vivienne Shue, "The Fate of the Commune," *Modern China* 10.3 (July 1984): 259–284.   DAVID BACHMAN

PEOPLE'S LIBERATION ARMY. *See* Chinese People's Liberation Army.

PEOPLE'S PARTY OF BURMA,
political party formed in 1925 by merging the Twenty-One, or National, Party led by U Ba Pe, the Swaraj Party led by U Paw Tun, and the Home Rule Party led by Tharrawaddy U Pu. Its candidates pledged not to accept office under the dyarchy constitution introduced by the British in 1923. In the 1928 elections the People's Party won 40 of the 59 legislative seats it contested. In the 1932 elections the party favored separation from India and lost seats to the Anti-Separation League. The party collapsed before the 1936 elections because its leaders disagreed on whether they should accept office under the new 1935 constitution. The majority faction followed U Ba Pe in forming the Ngabwinsaing ("five flowers") alliance, winning 46 seats out of 132.

[*See also* Anti-Separation League; Ba Pe; *and* General Council of Burmese Associations.]

John F. Cady, *A History of Modern Burma* (1958).
                                    ROBERT H. TAYLOR

PEOPLE'S PARTY OF THAILAND.
On 24 June 1932, a group of middle-level military and civilian officials who called themselves the People's Party staged a coup d'état overthrowing absolute monarchy in Thailand. The party's leaders, who had first met when they were students in Paris, were concerned with the rigidity of absolutism, particularly when their professional advancement could be frustrated by ascriptive criteria.

The leaders of the 1932 coup, known as promoters, could be divided into two groups: those who met in Paris (Pridi, Phibun, Khuang), and senior officers led by Phraya Phahon and Phraya Song Suradet. After the coup, the promoters chose an outsider, Phraya Manopakorn, a civilian judge, to head the cabinet. Mano was soon replaced by Phahon. By 1938, the young promoters came of age when Phibun succeeded Phahon as prime minister. The leadership of the People's Party remained relatively intact until Phibun and Pridi disagreed over policy toward Japan in 1941. Pridi subsequently organized the Seri Thai in opposition to the Japanese presence in Thailand.

[*See also* Pridi Phanomyong; Phibunsongkhram, Luang; Khuang Aphaiwong; Manopakorn Nitithada; Phahon Phonpayuhasena; *and* Free Thai.]

Kenneth P. Landon, *Siam in Transition* (1939). David Wilson, *Politics of Thailand* (1962).

                                    THAK CHALOEMTIARANA

PEPPER
is the fruit of *Piper nigrum*, a shrub indigenous to the Malabar coast of southwest India. Perfect for the luxury trade, light and small in volume, and slow to spoil, pepper became a staple of Indian trade to Europe in Roman times and was increasingly popular in China from the seventh century onward. It was being cultivated in the Malay Archipelago by the twelfth century, for though it had been unimportant in the export trade of Srivijaya, the "pepper ports" of North Sumatra, Pidie, and Sumadra-Pase were enjoying an expanding trade by the fourteenth century. Increasing control of the pepper-growing regions stimulated Melaka's growing trade in the fifteenth century.

At the end of that century the Portuguese came to Asia to compete for the rich trade in pepper and other spices. They captured several strategic ports, including Melaka, hoping thereby to control the traffic in pepper and spices. The Asian traders, however, transferred to new ports—most importantly Aceh in North Sumatra and Bantam in West Java—and continued as before.

The early seventeenth century brought a new wave of merchants from north Europe. The strongly organized Dutch obtained monopolistic contracts with pepper-producing areas, but they were no more successful than the Portuguese in excluding other buyers. In the eighteenth century the European pepper trade declined, but the China trade became increasingly important, and growing numbers of English private, or country, traders came seeking pepper to take to China.

Consequently, in the nineteenth century production of pepper increased, especially in the rich alluvial soils of northeast Sumatra. Immigrant Chinese added greatly to the number of pepper growers, and

European and American vessels went directly to the local ports. In the name of suppression of piracy, European governments prevented the sultans from enforcing their traditional rights. Penang and Singapore became the great centers of the pepper trade, which, reduced temporarily by the Aceh War, was increasingly conducted by Europeans.

[See also Srivijaya; Sumatra; Melaka; Aceh; Penang; and Singapore.]

J. S. Bastin, *The Changing Balance of the Southeast Asian Pepper Trade* (1960). M. A. P. Meiliknk-Roelofsz, *Asian Trade and European Influence in the Indonesian Archipelago between about 1500 and 1630* (1962). Anthony Reid, *The Contest for North Sumatra* (1969). John Wills, *Pepper, Guns, and Parleys* (1974).

DIANNE LEWIS

PERADENIYA, a suburb of Kandy, Sri Lanka. The earliest reference to Peradeniya was as the site of a royal residence in the mid-fourteenth century. Its importance in modern times began with the establishment of the Royal Botanical Gardens there in 1821, and its development into one of the great tropical botanical gardens of the British empire. Peradeniya had been the location of a royal garden under the Kandyan king Rajadhi Rajasinha (1780–1798). It is the site of the University of Peradeniya, formerly the University of Ceylon. [See also Kandy.]

K. M. DE SILVA

PERAK. Although the basin of the Perak River, on the west of the Malay Peninsula, has neither rich flats suitable for agriculture nor deep-water ports on its coast, it does have a major asset: tin. Readily available quantities of this metal attracted settlers by the sixteenth century, when the area is first mentioned as a dependency of the Melaka empire. Possessing great potential wealth but no capacity to sustain a large population, Perak was bound to be a perpetual pawn. On the fall of Melaka, Perak gained its other notable asset—a sultan descended from the old Melaka line—when the elder brother of the sultan of Melaka/Johor, disappointed in his hopes of ruling the larger empire, established his court in Perak.

But the small tin-rich state was soon swallowed by the growing North Sumatran power of Aceh. After they captured Melaka in 1641, the Dutch tried to monopolize Perak's tin output, and ties with Aceh were broken. The people of Perak, however, resented and evaded this heavy-handed monopoly,

and the Dutch withdrew by the end of the seventeenth century. Perak enjoyed a brief and uneasy independence, and its inability to stand alone forced reconciliation with the Dutch in 1746. This strategic alliance, which preserved Perak's independence during the eighteenth-century expansion of Bugis power, lasted until the fall of the Dutch East India Company in 1795.

In the nineteenth century Britain became the dominant power in the region. Tin production expanded rapidly to meet a growing market, drawing large numbers of Chinese miners backed by Penang merchants. The new wealth created problems for the traditional Malay political structure. When, in the second half of the century, lawlessness—engendered by these problems and compounded by the growing rivalry among different groups of Chinese immigrant miners—rose to a height dangerous to their investments, Penang merchants agitated for British intervention. A disputed succession in 1874 supplied the opportunity, and the Pangkor Engagement installed in Perak a British officer (an "adviser") with sufficient powers to bring order to Perak in the interests of the expanding tin industry (and its Penang backers). Ostensibly this action was undertaken to help the Perak Malays, but in reality the resident and his English bureaucracy ruled and the Malays advised. The first resident failed to heed this advice and was murdered. Swift British retribution quelled further attempts to evade the new overlord, and Perak remained under British "protection" till the Japanese invasion.

The short period of British rule saw great changes in Perak's economic and demographic structure, as plantations of rubber and other cash crops supplemented the ever-expanding tin mining. Chinese (and to a lesser extent Indian) immigration continued on a large scale. British policy was to use these immigrants to fuel the expanding economy, leaving the Malay population to go its traditional way. At the same time Perak was linked economically, bureaucratically, and physically with its neighbors Pahang, Selangor, and Negri Sembilan; in 1895 it became a member of the Federated Malay States, a confederacy joining these British-ruled Malay states. The events of World War II and the Communist Emergency (1948–1960) strengthened these ties, as did new nationalist awakenings in a multiracial environment. In 1957 Perak became a member of the newly independent Federation of Malaya (expanded in 1965 to include the former British-ruled Borneo territories of Sabah and Sarawak as the Federation of Malaysia).

[*See also* Melaka; Aceh; Pangkor Engagement; *and* Federated Malay States.]

Barbara W. Andaya, *Perak, The Abode of Grace* (1979). Barbara W. Andaya and Leonard Y. Andaya, *A History of Malaysia* (1982). J. M. Gullick, *Indigenous Political Systems of Western Malaya* (1956). C. Mary Turnbull, *A Short History of Malaysia, Singapore and Brunei* (1980).   DIANNE LEWIS

PERCHAM (lit., "banner"), the second major faction that split from the People's Democratic Party of Afghanistan (PDPA) in 1967. Babrak Karmal, the Afghan president following the Soviet invasion in December 1979, belonged to this faction. The Perchamis favored more moderate domestic economic reforms and were closer to the Soviets than was the PDPA; they also had more support among the Tajiks, a Persian-speaking ethnic group, and among the urban Pakhtuns. The faction published a weekly newspaper called *Percham*.

In 1977 Percham united with the other major communist faction, Khalq, to overthrow the government of Daud Beureu'eh. After the coup the Perchamis were quickly eliminated from positions of power. Some were arrested; others remained abroad, mostly in Eastern Europe. Khalqis accused Perchamis of plotting a coup against them. With the Soviet invasion, the balance of power was shifted in favor of Percham. The Perchamis came to dominate the government. They sought to expand the base of power of the regime and win the war against the partisans known as the Mujahedin. They established a communist-dominated National Fatherland Front, expanding the Communist Party, moderating some of the Khalqi reforms, and establishing several security organizations.

[*See also* Karmal, Babrak; Daud Beureu'eh, Mohammed; *and* Khalq.]

ZALMAY KHALILZAD

PERERA, NANAYAKKARAPATHIRAGE MARTIN (1905–1979), leader of the Lanka Sama Samaja Party (LSSP) in Sri Lanka from 1935 to 1979. Perera's leadership of the party was characterized by a deep commitment to parliamentary democracy and by a pragmatism that rejected doctrinaire Trotskyite approaches. Perera served in the national legislature from 1936 to 1977 and twice held cabinet portfolios, from 1964 to 1965 and 1970 to 1975. [*See also* Lanka Sama Samaja Party.]

VIJAYA SAMARAWEERA

PERLIS, Malay sultanate, now a state of Malaysia, on the northern border with Thailand.

In the eighteenth century Perlis was a district of the sultanate of Kedah, and by the 1770s it became the power base for ones lower in the succession to the throne of Kedah. The long conflict between Kedah and Siam, culminating in the revolt of 1838–1839, resulted in the restoration of the sultan of Kedah to his throne and in the division of Kedah. As a result, Perlis became an independent sultanate and both Kedah and Perlis remained vassals of the Siamese king. According to the agreement outlined in the Anglo-Siamese Treaty of 1909, Perlis (along with Kedah, Kelantan, and Trengganu) was ceded to Britain. Perlis was incorporated into the Unfederated Malay States without formal agreement with Britain until 1930, when the position of a British adviser there was regularized. After World War II, Perlis became part of the Federation of Malaya, and since 1957 it has been a constituent state of Malaysia.

[*See also* Malaysia *and* Kedah.]

Barbara W. Andaya and Leonard Y. Andaya, *A History of Malaysia* (1982). R. Bonney, *Kedah 1771–1821* (1971). W. F. Vella, *Siam Under Rama III* (1957).
DAVID K. WYATT

PERMESTA REBELLIONS. *See* Pemerintah Revolusioner Republik Indonesia/Perdjuangan Semesta.

PERRY, MATTHEW C. (1794–1858), American naval commander whose expedition to Japan marked the opening of that country to the West.

Following the Opium War in China in 1842, it was widely expected that there would be a large increase in the volume of China's foreign trade. Japan was important to the United States in this context as a potential staging-point on shipping routes being planned across the Pacific. In May 1851 Washington decided to send a naval squadron to seek an agreement opening Japanese ports, which were still closed to all foreign vessels except those of the Netherlands and China. Commodore Matthew C. Perry was given command of the expedition in March 1852.

Perry's squadron, famous in Japan as the "black ships," reached Uraga at the entrance to Edo Bay in July 1853 via the Atlantic and Indian oceans. His approach to negotiations, which emphasized the needs of shipping more than trade, reflected his belief that previous Western approaches to Japan had failed because of a lack of evident determination. Thus, he pursued a policy of "gunboat diplomacy."

On 14 July 1853 Perry handed Japanese officials a letter from President Millard Fillmore, requesting a treaty of friendship and commerce, together with one of his own urging "the necessity of averting unfriendly collision between the two nations." He would, he stated, return next year with a larger squadron to receive the Japanese reply. This he did; in February 1854 he came back with eight ships, rather than four, negotiating this time at Kanagawa (Yokohama). There he concluded a treaty on 31 March, opening Shimoda and Hakodate as ports of call for American ships. This treaty marked the end of Perry's active career. He returned to the United States soon after and spent much of the next two years preparing a detailed account of the expedition, published in 1856.

[See also Kanagawa Treaty.]

Samuel Eliot Morison, "Old Bruin": Commodore Matthew C. Perry, 1794–1858 (1968). Roger Pineau, ed., The Japan Expedition, 1852–1854: The Personal Journal of Commodore Matthew C. Perry (1968).

W. G. BEASLEY

PERSEPOLIS, dynastic center built by Darius I (522–486 CE), Xerxes, and Artaxerxes, 60 kilometers northeast of present-day Shiraz, Iran. Persepolis became "the richest city under the sun," according to Diodorus Siculus. It was sacked by Alexander in 330 BCE. Only the acropolis (locally known as Takht-i Jamshed) represents the city now. Standing on a platform that measures 450 by 300 meters, it is ascended by a staircase with double reversed flights, each with 111 steps. Darius planned and built a treasury, a private palace (the Tachara), and a 32-columned hall with 12-columned porticoes on three sides (the Apadana). Xerxes finished the Apadana; constructed a great hall with 100 columns, a gate house, a central palace, and a private residence (the Hadish); and enlarged the treasury. Artaxerxes finished these and built a new palace on the southeast corner. Only minor additions were made after 450 BCE. The monuments had stone foundations and thick mud-brick walls faced partially with glazed tiles ornamented with inscriptions and figures of plants, animals, and soldiers. Door jambs and stairway facades bore sculptured figures of kings attended by officials as well as of servants carrying provisions (in private palaces), soldiers (in guard rooms and official buildings), processions of guards (on foot), nobles, and gift-bearers (in audience palaces). Doorway frames and larger columns were carved from local marble; smaller columns were made of wood encased in colored plaster, and the rafters were made of Lebanese cedar.

Persepolis was a crucible in which Near Eastern

FIGURE 1. *Tachara Palace Relief, Persepolis.* Frieze on the western staircase.

skills and artistic traditions were blended to produce a truly majestic creation. Artists, artisans, and laborers from Ionia, Anatolia, Egypt, Mesopotamia, Media, eastern Iran, and Central Asia were hired—many cuneiform tablets recording their payments have survived—to build an architectural complex that embodied all aspects of Near Eastern art and yet was distinct in nature and design. Persepolis still retains a certain religious significance locally and is admired universally, especially after the systematic excavations by E. Herzfeld, E. F. Schmidt, and Ali Sami and the restorations by G. Tilia revealed its glory more clearly.

[See also Darius I and Xerxes.]

Sylvia A. Matheson, *Persia: An Archaeological Guide* (2d ed., 1976), pp. 225–234. Edith Porada, *The Art of Ancient Iran* (1965), pp. 144 ff. E. F. Schmidt, *Persepolis* (1953–1969).   A. SHAHPUR SHAHBAZI

PERSIA. *See* Iran.

PERSIAN COSSACK BRIGADE, Iranian military force in existence from 1882 to 1921. The Cossack Brigade was formed at the instigation of Nasir al-Din Shah (1848–1896) to serve as an imperial guard. It had Russian officers who, until 1917, were also on active duty with the Russian army. The Cossack Brigade gradually expanded to become an army of more than ten thousand men, and it played a significant political role in the Constitutional Revolution of 1905 to 1911, the turmoil of World War I, and the 1921 coup d'état that led to the eventual deposition of the Qajar monarchy. Reza Shah spent more than twenty-five years as a member of the Cossack Brigade. After he became minister of war in 1921 he merged the brigade with smaller military forces to form Iran's national army.

[See also Constitutional Revolution; Qajar, Nasir al-Din; and Pahlavi, Reza.]

Firuz Kazemzadeh, "The Origins and Early Development of the Persian Cossack Brigade," *The American Slavic and East European Review* 15 (1956): 342–363.
ERIC HOOGLUND

PERSIAN LITERATURE. The term *Persian literature* refers to the body of poetry and generally nonutilitarian prose written in the New Persian language from the ninth century to the present day. While a good deal of literary writing in this language appears outside of Iran proper (as in India, Afghanistan, Pakistan, and Turkey) the following discussion is limited to the literature of the Iranian tradition.

Pre-Islamic Period. The only surviving ancient Iranian texts valuable for literary investigation are the Avestan *Gathas* and *Yashts*, which contain prosodic and thematic elements to which later literary developments can be traced. Very few Middle Iranian texts (third century BCE to eighth century CE) have survived; on the basis of text fragments and orally preserved literary traditions, however, three genres of poetry can be distinguished: *surud* (panegyric), *chikama* (narrative), and *tarana* (lyric). In all three genres, the meter is quantitative and based on stress; rhyme is used only occasionally. Among the surviving Pahlavi (southwestern Middle Iranian) texts, *Ayadkar-i Zareran* (a short epic), *Karnamag-i Ardashir-i Papakan* (a mythic/historical account of the founder of the Sasanid dynasty), *Bundahishn* (a compilation of Zoroastrian myths and traditions), and *Artak-Viraz-namak* (a Zoroastrian priest's wanderings through heaven, hell, and purgatory) are noteworthy. Two fifth-century Pahlavi texts, now lost, that are significant in the evolution of Iranian literary tradition are the *Khwatainamak* (*Book of Lords,* the Pahlavi version of the national epic recreated by Firdausi in the tenth century), and *Hizar afsana* (*A Thousand Tales,* which contains stories from *A Thousand and One Nights* as well as the frame tale of Shahrzad).

Post-Islamic Period. The emergence of New Persian (Farsi) coincides with the islamization of Iran at the beginning of the seventh century and is marked by the influences of a transitional period. While there is little evidence of original literary activity during this time, it is a mistake to consider this period a disruption in the evolution of Persian literature. The role of the oral tradition in preservation of the literary tradition notwithstanding, as the result of the political and ideological domination of the Arabic language, most Iranian men of letters who sought protection and opportunity in the courts of the caliphate engaged in translations of original Pahlavi texts or of translations into Pahlavi of Greek and Sanskrit texts; they also produced works of scholarship and of original literary composition in Arabic. The work of such prose writers as Ibn al-Muqaffa, Sibawaihi, and al-Jurjani and such poets as Bashshar ibn Burd and Abu Nuwas established a dialogue between the Persian and Arabic traditions that proved significant for the development of both literatures.

In literary scholarship the "science" of *aruz* (prosody) and the "techniques" of *balagha* (rhetoric and poetics) that emerged during this period are part of a formative stage in the history of Persian literature. "Classical" poetry (also called *shi'r-i aruzi*) adopted some of the quantitative meters of Arabic as well as the use of genre-specific rhyme patterns (e.g., *aa ba ca . . .* in *ghazal* and *qasida; aa bb cc . . .* in *mathnavi;* and *aa ba* in *ruba'i*). The importance of the use of *balagha* techniques can be observed in the rivalry between the Khurasani and Iraqi styles of poetry. The Iraqi style, with its use of complex tropes and figures, is directly influenced by Arabic poetry, while the Khurasani style is less ornamental in language and centered upon more purely Persian themes. The same stylistic devices are used in prose; the epitome of "arabization" was the "artificial prose" *(nathr-i masnu)* of the thirteenth century. In the formation, as opposed to formalization, of genre, Iranian literature continued along the line of its indigenous tradition.

With the establishment of independent dynasties in Iran in the ninth century, literary activities in New Persian flourished, manifesting the conventions that would later result in sharp distinctions among styles and genres. The poetry of Rudaki (the "father" of Persian poetry) and Farrukhi is the epitome of the Khurasani style, while the beginnings of the Iraqi style are detectable in the work of Unsuri, Asjudī, and Manuchihri. Firdausi, whose epic masterpiece, the *Shahnama*, revitalized the linguistic, historical, and cultural integrity of Iran, must be singled out among the poets of the Khurasani period (ninth to eleventh century). In prose, the histories of Bal'ami and Baihaqi and the introduction to the *Shahnama* of Abu Mansur are of particular literary value.

With Anvari, who incorporated his knowledge of philosophy and sciences into his poetry, and with Sana'i and Attar, who introduced Sufi themes into poetry, a new symbolism with its own technical, arabized language developed during the Seljuk period (eleventh to mid-twelfth century). Khaqani's poetry exemplifies the complex signification of the poetic conventions of the era. Nasir Khusrau, the epic poet Nizami, and Omar Khayyam, whose quatrains are well known, are among the major poets of this time. Among the important prose works of this period are the *Siyasatnama, Qabusnama, Marzbannama, Chahar maqala,* and especially *Kalila-u-Dimna*.

Three of the most powerful figures in the literary history of Iran belong to the Iraqi period (late twelfth to fourteenth century): Rumi, whose *Mathnavi* and *Ghazaliyyat* are the most complete and brilliant literary expositions of Sufism; Sa'di, in whose *Gulistan, Bustan,* and *Ghazaliyyat* the excellence of the Iraqi style is attained; and Hafiz, whose *ghazals* reach the perfection of the genre and the exquisite formalized ambiguity associated with it. In effect, the literature of this period reflects the maturity of classical poetry in the form of a perfect balance of the lucidity of the Khurasani school with the complexity of the Iraqi, and with Jami the classical era comes to a close. The histories of Juvaini, Rashid al-Din, and Nasir al-Din Tusi and the works of Aufi and Shams Qais-i Razi are among the most important prose works of this time.

It is generally agreed that no literature comparable in greatness to that of the classical era appeared during the so-called period of decline (fifteenth to nineteenth century). The predominant Hindi style, with its overly intricate allusions and metaphors, as in the poetry of Sa'ib, Urfi, and Kalim-i Kashani, is often overlooked. The development of prose fiction is the most important literary contribution of this period. While some textural versions of stories in the oral tradition appeared prior to this time (e.g., *Bakhtiyarnama, Abu-Muslim-nama, Samak-i ayyar*), a large number of such texts date from this period (*Tutinama, Razmnama, Shirinnama,* etc.).

Reaction in the nineteenth century against the artificial language and stagnant forms of the previous era led to a return to the less rigid conventions of the Khurasani and Iraqi styles. While not entirely devoid of innovation, the poetry of Saba, Visal, Mushtaq, Qa'ani, and Mahmud Khan-i Malik al-Shu'ara is modeled to a great extent on the classics. Translations introduced the European genre of the novel, and the Persian version of James Morier's *Haji Baba of Isphahan* brought the form close to home.

The greater part of literary production in the early twentieth century was circulated via the new phenomena of newspapers and magazines; it was largely political in content. The essays of Mirza Agha Khan-i Kermani, Shaikh Ahmad-i Ruhi, Talibuf, Dihkhuda, Kasravi, and others did much to change the attitude of the public toward literature, and with *Siyahatnama-yi Ibrahim Beg* the novel emerged as a new and promising genre. Iraj, Arif, Bahar, Adib-i Pishavari, Parvin I'tisami, and other poets of the period brought about no structural changes in poetry; many of them, however, displayed the rebellious spirit that later led to fundamental changes in the form and nature of Persian poetry.

Contemporary Literature. In spite of an intensifying atmosphere of political repression a new tradition of Persian literature began to emerge in the middle of the twentieth century and continues to develop, creating a wealth of works in new genres and styles, in theory and criticism, and a new literary aesthetic on the whole. In poetry, Nima Yushij freed poetry and the idea of poetry from traditional structural binds; his work was followed by a new generation of poets (e.g., Shamlu, Kasra'i, Farrukhzad, Nadirpur, and Akhavan Sales) whose break with tradition is based on a deep knowledge and appreciation of it. In the novel, the novella, and the short story, the works of Jamalzada, Hejazi, Afghani, Chubak, Al-Ahmad, Mirsadiqi, and Danishvar stand out, while the novellas of Sadiq Hidayat enjoy the highest critical esteem. In drama, plays by Sa'idi, Baiza'i, Mufid, and Sultanpur, based to a greater or lesser degree on traditional forms, have been successfully performed. A further contemporary development has been the appearance of women on the literary scene. While the poetry of Rabi'a (tenth century), Mahasti (twelfth century), and Parvin I'tisami (early twentieth century) has traditionally received literary recognition, it is with Furugh Farrukhzad and Simin Danishvar that women have acquired a permanent voice outside the oral literary tradition.

[*See also* Avestan; Old Persian; Pahlavi; Dari; Farsi; Shahnama; Firdausi; Hafiz; Jami, Kasravi, Ahmad; Khayyam, Omar; Nizami; Rudaki; *and* Sa'di.]

A. J. Arberry, ed., *The Legacy of Persia* (1953). A. J. Arberry, *Classical Persian Literature* (1958). E. G. Browne, *A Literary History of Persia*, 4 vols. (1928). R. Levy, *An Introduction to Persian Literature* (1923). Ibn al-Nadim, *The Fihrist of al-Nadim*, translated by B. Dodge (1970). T. Ricks, ed., *Critical Perspectives on Modern Persian Literature* (1984). J. Rypka, *History of Iranian Literature* (1968). C. A. Storey, *Persian Literature: A Bio-Bibliographical Survey* (1927–1958).

MARIAM PIRNAZAR

PESCADORES (Chinese, Penghu), a group of islands along the Tropic of Cancer in the Formosa Straits west of Taiwan. First known as a base for Chinese pirates at the end of the Yuan dynasty (1279–1368), the Pescadores (Spanish for "fishermen") were used historically as a staging point for conquerors of Taiwan, including the Dutch, Koxinga (Zheng Chenggong) and his Ming loyalists, the Manchus, and the Japanese. Since 1949 the islands have been controlled by the Nationalist regime on Taiwan, which maintains strong military bases there. The Pescadores are inhabited by fewer than 150,000 people, almost half of whom live in Magong, the county seat. The main products of the islands are sweet potatoes, peanuts, and gaoliang (Chinese sorghum), along with coral, shells, and seafood.

JOHN A. RAPP

PESHAWAR (original Sanskrit name, Purushapura), situated near the foot of the Khyber Pass, is the capital of the North-West Frontier Province. It is also the name of the district and valley in which the city is located.

The valley was ruled by Hindu and Buddhist kingdoms until it was conquered by Mahmud of Ghazna in the early eleventh century. Peshawar city was a center of Buddhism from the time of the Kushans and is thought to have been the capital of the emperor Kanishka in the first or second century CE.

The Pakhtuns (or Pathans), the dominant ethnic group in the valley today, are believed to have moved into it in the fifteenth century. Peshawar city served as a strategic garrison town under the Mughals, Durranis, and Sikhs, but none of them entirely pacified the surrounding valley.

Peshawar Valley was annexed by the British in 1849 and was governed as part of the Punjab Province until the North-West Frontier Province was created in 1901, with the city as its capital. The valley has become the center of nationalist activity in the frontier since the beginning of the twentieth century and became part of Pakistan in 1947. It was integrated into the province of West Pakistan in 1954 and was recreated as a separate province in 1969.

[*See also* North-West Frontier Province *and* Pakhtun.]

A. H. Dani, *Peshawar: Historic City of the Frontier* (1969). S. M. Jaffar, *Peshawar Past and Present* (1946).

STEPHEN RITTENBERG

PESHWA. The office of *peshwa* (a Persian term meaning "foremost") was introduced in the Deccan, India, by Muslim rulers. After his coronation as Maratha ruler (*chhatrapati*) in 1674, Shivaji appointed Moropant Pingle as *peshwa* (or prime minister) but did not make the office hereditary, although Moropant's two sons, Nilakantha and Bahiropant, enjoyed it until 1713. Balaji Vishwanath Bhat (1713–1720), a Chitpavan brahman from Shrivardhan, appointed as *peshwa* in 1713, by Shahu Chhatrapati and his son and successor Bajirao I (1720–1740), virtually made the peshwaship hereditary in the Bhat family. After the death of Shahu, during the peshwaship of Balaji Bajirao (1740–1761), for want of an able *chhatrapati*, the *peshwa* became the de facto head of the Maratha state and the leader of the confederacy. This transfer of power was silently and gradually accomplished by the Bhat family. Madhavrao I (1761–1772), the fourth *peshwa* in this line, restored the Maratha prestige obliterated by the Third Battle of Panipat (1761). [*See* Panipat, Battles of.] His brother Narayanrao (1772–1773), the fifth *peshwa*, was murdered. His uncle, Raghunathrao, then claimed the peshwaship in vain. Madhavrao II (1774–1795), son of Narayanrao, was the sixth *peshwa*. The last *peshwa*, Bajirao II (1795–1818), son of Raghunathrao, surrendered the Maratha power to the British in 1818.

[*See also* Marathas *and* Shivaji.]

N. K. Wagle and A. R. Kulkarni, eds., *Vallabha's Parasrama Caritra* (1976).   A. R. KULKARNI

PETA, the Pembela Tanah Air ("defenders of the homeland"), also known as Giyugun, volunteer army units formed in October 1943 by Japanese authorities on Java and Sumatra. While ostensibly formed to defend the islands against expected Allied invasions, the PETA was also a concession to Indonesian nationalist demands for military training and aided the inculcation of Japanese values in Indonesian youth. Its officers, up to battalion level, were Indonesians, but there was no hierarchial link between battalions independent of the Japanese army. In February 1945 PETA troops at Blitar (East Java) revolted unsuccessfully against the Japanese. PETA officers formed much of the officer corps of the Indonesian army.

[*See also* Indonesia, Republic of.]

Nugroho Notosusanto, *The PETA Army During the Japanese Occupation of Indonesia* (1979).

ROBERT B. CRIBB

PHADKE, VASUDEO BALWANT (1845–1885), Indian revolutionary and bandit. A Chitpavan brahman, he went to school in Pune and in 1864 became a clerk in the commissariat department. Disturbed by agrarian and famine distress, he wanted to overthrow the British and reestablish Hindu rule by rural rebellion. To fund his activities, he led a band of mainly poor peasants and tribals in raids

on Indian moneylenders in villages around Pune in 1879 but was captured, sentenced to be transported (banished), and died in Aden.

V. S. Joshi, *Vasudeo Balwant Phadke: First Indian Rebel against British Rule* (1959).   JIM MASSELOS

PHAGS-PA (1235–1280), nephew of the pandit of the Sakyapa sect of Tibetan Buddhism. In 1253 he was invited for a visit by the then Prince Kublai when the latter was conquering Yunnan. He became a confidential adviser to Kublai and a "chaplain" to the Mongol royal house. An energetic thinker, he provided the Mongols with a pseudohistorical legitimating theory, which incorporated them into the line of succession of Buddhist universal emperors, the *chakravartins*. He also invented an alphabet for writing preclassical Mongolian, still known as Phags-pa script. When he died, the Mongol court conferred great honors upon him.

Herbert Franke, "Tibetans in Yuan China," in *China under Mongol Rule*, edited by John Langlois (1981).

JOHN PHILIP NESS

PHAHON PHONPHAYUHASENA (1887–1947), Thai political leader. Born Phot Phahonyothin in Bangkok, Phahon was the son of Colonel Phraya Phahon Phonphayuhasena, whose father had held the same title. At twelve, Phahon entered the military academy, and four years later he won a scholarship to continue his studies in Germany. After graduation, Phahon served in the German army and was sent to Denmark for further education in 1912. He returned to Thailand in 1913 and joined Luang Phibunsongkhram and Pridi Phanomyong to help plan the coup d'état in 1932 that ended absolute monarchy in Thailand.

Phahon was the acknowledged leader of the People's Party senior faction, which included Colonel Phraya Songsuradet and Phraya Ritthiakhane. These senior officers resented the fact that the top echelon of the army was still the reserve of members of the royal family. Following the 1932 coup, Phahon became the minister of defense in the Manopakorn Nitithada cabinet.

In 1933 Phraya Mano, reacting to Pridi's proposed Economic Development Plan, which many thought to be communistic, suspended Parliament and proceeded to rule by decree. Mano passed an anticommunism law shortly afterward, and Pridi voluntarily returned to France for a brief exile. But within three weeks of the closing of Parliament, the army, led by Phraya Phahon, staged a coup against the Mano government. With Mano exiled in Penang, Phahon was appointed prime minister.

The new Phahon government faced a rebellion mounted by provincial army units led by Prince Boworadet, a grandson of King Chulalongkorn and a former minister of defense. The rebels accused the government of encouraging disrespect toward the monarchy and promoting communism, and they demanded that the government resign. Government forces led by Phibunsongkhram, however, soon defeated the rebels.

The rebellion, added to the controversy of Pridi's economic plan, strained relations between the government and Rama VII, and in 1935, two years after the Boworadet Rebellion, the king left for England, eventually abdicating. Phahon remained prime minister until 1938, when he was succeeded by his protégé Phibun. On 14 February 1947, Phahon died of a stroke.

[See also Thailand; Phibunsongkhram, Luang; Pridi Phanomyong; People's Party of Thailand; Manopakorn Nitithada; and Prajadhipok.]

David K. Wyatt, Thailand: A Short History (1984).

THAK CHALOEMTIARANA

PHALKE, DHUNDIYAJ GOVIND (1870–1944), regarded as the father of Indian cinema. The son of a Sanskrit scholar, Phalke was born near Nasik, Maharashtra. He studied painting at art schools in Bombay and Baroda, where he developed a special aptitude for photography. He launched and successfully ran a block-making and engraving works.

Forced out by business feuds, Phalke turned his energies and innovative talents to making swadeshi motion pictures. A brief visit to London provided him with the basic know-how and essential equipment. Surmounting innumerable difficulties, he made the first Indian motion picture to be released commercially: it had its debut at the Coronation Cinema, Bombay, on 3 May 1913, and it became a great hit.

As a moviemaker Phalke exploited the magical elements of Hindu mythology. Although he made some ninety movies, he never could master the intricacies of the movie business. He died in Nasik, spending his last years in obscurity and near-poverty.

Eric Barnouw and S. Krishnaswamy, Indian Film (1963).

PRAMOD KALE

PHAM HONG THAI (1896–1924), Vietnamese anti-French revolutionary. Born Pham Thanh Tich, son of a local Can Vuong leader, he was educated in Hanoi but later worked as a manual laborer. In 1918 he departed with other young revolutionaries for Canton, where they contacted Phan Boi Chau's organization. Dissatisfied with the group's efforts, however, Pham and his companions established the more activist Tam Tam Xa (Association of Like Minds). On 18 June 1924 Pham threw a bomb at visiting Governor-General Merlin of Indochina. Merlin was not killed, and Pham drowned trying to flee across the Pearl River. His eulogy was written by Phan Boi Chau.

[See also Can Vuong and Phan Boi Chau.]

William J. Duiker, The Rise of Nationalism in Vietnam, 1900–1941 (1976). David Marr, Vietnamese Anticolonialism, 1885–1925 (1971).   BRUCE M. LOCKHART

PHAM QUYNH, an influential journalist and conservative politician during the colonial period in Vietnam. Born in 1892 in Hai Duong Province, he attended interpreters' school in Hanoi and later studied at the École Française d'Extrême Orient. In 1917, with official support, he founded the cultural journal Nam Phong, through whose pages he promoted the development of a distinctive Vietnamese literature and the adoption of quoc ngu, a romanized form of the Vietnamese written language. Conservative in his political views, he favored a continued French presence in Vietnam and served in Emperor Bao Dai's cabinet in the 1930s. In 1945 he was assassinated by the Viet Minh.

[See also Quoc Ngu and Bao Dai.]

William J. Duiker, The Rise of Nationalism in Vietnam, 1900–1941 (1976).   WILLIAM J. DUIKER

PHAM VAN DONG (b. 1906), veteran Communist Party leader and former prime minister of the Socialist Republic of Vietnam. Born of a mandarin family in Quang Ngai Province, he was educated at the National Academy in Hue. Joining the Communist movement in 1926, Pham Van Dong was arrested in 1931 and spent six years on Poulo Condore. During World War II he became a trusted associate of Ho Chi Minh and rose to the Party Politburo in 1951. He was named minister of finance in the new Democratic Republic of Vietnam in 1946 and headed the Ministry of Foreign Affairs three years later. He was named prime minister in 1955.

His resignation was announced December 1986 during the sixth national Vietnamese Communist Party Congress.

[*See also* Vietnam, Democratic Republic of.]

Thomas Hodgkin, *Vietnam: The Revolutionary Path* (1981). Huynh Kim Khanh, *Vietnamese Communism, 1925–1945* (1982).   WILLIAM J. DUIKER

PHAN BOI CHAU (1876–1940), leading patriotic and revolutionary figure in colonial Vietnam. Born in Nghe An Province, he received a Confucian education and earned a regional degree in 1900. But Phan was resentful of growing French domination over his country and refused an official career in the imperial bureaucracy. In 1904 he formed the Vietnam Modernization Association, the objective of which was to overthrow French rule and set up a constitutional monarchy under Prince Coung De, a member of the ruling Nguyen dynasty. In 1905 Phan set up his headquarters in Japan, from which he hoped to receive assistance in evicting the French and restoring Vietnamese independence. For the next three years he became the chief publicist of the movement, writing essays and books on Vietnamese history and current conditions and attempting to attract Vietnamese patriots to serve in his organization. Several attempts at revolt failed, however, and when his party was evicted from Japan he turned to China, seeking help from Sun Yat-sen and forming a new party, the Vietnam Restoration League, on the Chinese republican model.

The new organization had no more success than the previous one had, however, and in 1914 Phan was arrested and imprisoned in South China. Released in 1917, he remained in China and attempted to resume his revolutionary activities but was increasingly viewed by young radicals as an anachronistic figure from the past, admired but not followed. In 1925 he was betrayed by a colleague and seized by French agents in Shanghai. Brought back to Hanoi, he was sentenced to death. Eventually the sentence was commuted to house arrest in Hue, where he died in 1940. Today he is one of the most admired Vietnamese patriots.

[*See also* Cuong De; Vietnam Modernization Association; *and* Vietnam Restoration League.]

William J. Duiker, *The Rise of Nationalism in Vietnam, 1900–1941* (1976). Thomas Hodgkin, *Vietnam: The Revolutionary Path* (1981). David G. Marr, *Vietnamese Anticolonialism, 1855–1925* (1971). David G. Marr, ed., *Reflections from Captivity* (1978).   WILLIAM J. DUIKER

PHAN CHU TRINH (1872–1926), Vietnamese nationalist. In 1908 Phan was arrested for his alleged complicity in inciting peasant riots in central Vietnam. At first condemned to death, he was later transferred to Poulo Condore. In 1911 he was permitted to live in exile in France, where he spoke out occasionally on colonial policy. In 1925 he returned to Vietnam and presented two major addresses calling for reform and a synthesis of the best values of East and West. He died of illness in March 1926, and his funeral occasioned a great outpouring of nationalist feeling. While many Vietnamese did not agree with his rejection of violence in seeking independence, the sincerity of his patriotic views earned wide respect.

William J. Duiker, *The Rise of Nationalism in Vietnam, 1900–1941* (1976). David G. Marr, *Vietnamese Anticolonialism, 1855–1925* (1971).   WILLIAM J. DUIKER

PHAN DINH PHUNG (1847–1895), high-ranking mandarin scholar and later prominent leader in the Can Vuong movement. In 1885 he organized anti-French actions in his native Ha Tinh, together with his trusted lieutenant Cao Thang. Initially coordinating sporadic attacks by *nghia-quan* ("righteous troops"), he later concentrated on developing a strong network of guerrilla bases. Although by 1894 his forces had been shattered, Phan Dinh Phung refused to surrender, responding to a written appeal from the collaborator-scholar Hoang Cao Khai with a letter famous for its affirmation of loyalty to his monarch and his country.

[*See also* Can Vuong *and* Ham Nghi.]

David G. Marr, *Vietnamese Anticolonialism, 1885–1925* (1971). Nguyen Phut Tan, *Modern History of Vietnam 1802–1954* (1964).   BRUCE M. LOCKHART

PHAN THANH GIAN (1796–1862), important Vietnamese mandarin under Tu Duc. After the four years of fighting following the French attack on Tourane in 1858, Phan was appointed to negotiate a treaty. The result was the 1862 Treaty of Saigon, according to which Vietnam ceded three provinces, including Saigon, to France. An unsuccessful trip to France in 1863 to renegotiate the treaty stimulated him to propose certain reforms for Vietnam, but no results were forthcoming. Caught between the demands of the militarily powerful French and pressures from the court, Phan was unable to avoid the cession of three more provinces in June 1867. Claiming responsibility for the loss, he committed suicide, urging his sons to refrain from collaboration.

[*See also* Vietnam *and* Saigon, Treaty of.]

Nguyen Phut Tan, *Modern History of Vietnam 1802–1954* (1964). BRUCE M. LOCKHART

PHAULKON, CONSTANTINE (1647–1688),

Greek "prime minister" of Siam during part of the reign of King Narai (1656–1688). After a youth spent in the fleet of the British East India Company, Phaulkon came to Ayudhya in 1678, entered the service of the Phrakhlang (civilian) ministry as interpreter and accountant, and became the king's leading minister. He schemed to convert the king to Christianity and promoted an alliance between Siam and France, then ruled by Louis XIV. His policies antagonized both the English and the Siamese bureaucracy and sparked a plot that resulted in his death, in June 1688, and the end of the French alliance.

[*See also* Ayudhya; Narai; *and* Phetracha.]

Claude de Beze, *1688, Revolution in Siam,* translated by E. W. Hutchinson (1968). E. W. Hutchinson, *Adventurers in Siam in the Seventeenth Century* (1940). David K. Wyatt, *Thailand: A Short History* (1984).

DAVID K. WYATT

PHAYAO, ancient principality in northern Thai-

land. Founded perhaps in the eleventh century by members of the same ruling family that founded Lan Na, Phayao came briefly to prominence during the reign of King Ngam Muang (r. 1258–1318), when it was briefly the equal of Lan Na and Sukhothai. Within the next century it was absorbed by Lan Na.

[*See also* Lan Na; Ngam Muang; *and the map accompanying* Sukhothai.] DAVID K. WYATT

PHAYRE, SIR ARTHUR P. (1812–1885). Born

in England, Phayre went to Burma in 1834 and was appointed commissioner of Burma in 1852 by Lord Dalhousie, the governor-general of India. Unlike most English officials in Burma, Phayre was sensitive to Burma's predicament as a twice defeated and truncated sovereign state. As commissioner and later chief commissioner he redesigned the city of Rangoon and maintained diplomatic relations with the Burmese court at Amarapura and Mandalay. He wrote voluminously to Governor-General Dalhousie and in 1883 published his still valuable *History of*

Burma. Little is known of his private life, and he seems to have been satisfied to avoid publicity so long as he could maintain control of local policy.

D. G. E. Hall, *The Dalhousie-Phayre Correspondence, 1852–1856* (1932). Hugh Tinker, "Arthur Phayre and Henry Yule: Two Soldier Administrator Historians," in *Historians of South-East Asia* (1961). Oliver B. Pollak, *Empires in Collision: Anglo-Burmese Relations in the Mid-Nineteenth Century* (1979). OLIVER B. POLLAK

PHETRACHA, king of Ayudhya (r. 1688–1703),

leader of Siam's Glorious Revolution of 1688. Of rural origins, Phra Phetracha was raised as a virtual foster brother to King Narai (r. 1656–1688) and during the latter's reign established himself as a general and head of the Elephant Corps. As leader of the opposition to the king's Greek prime minister, Constantine Phaulkon, Phetracha and his son Luang Sorasak led the coup that eliminated Phaulkon and his French allies and managed Phetracha's accession to the throne. His reign was challenged by rebellions, but he succeeded in establishing a dynasty that was to last until the kingdom's end in 1767.

[*See also* Ayudhya; Narai; *and* Phaulkon, Constantine.]

Claude de Beze, *1688, Revolution in Siam,* translated by E. W. Hutchinson (1968). E. W. Hutchinson, *Adventurers in Siam in the Seventeenth Century* (1940). David K. Wyatt, *Thailand: A Short History* (1984).

DAVID K. WYATT

PHETSARATH (1890–1959), Laotian prince. He

was the son of Prince Boun Khong, viceroy, or second king, of the protected kingdom of Luang Prabang in the French colony of Laos. Educated in Paris (1905–1913), he joined the French chief resident's staff in Vientiane in 1914 and from 1917 onward traveled widely with him. In this way the prince added recognition and influence throughout the country to his immense inherited prestige. In 1919 he became director of the Laotian Civil Service, which he transformed; in 1923 he was inspector of Laotian Political and Military Affairs and a member of the Government Council for Indochina. He rapidly attained the highest positions open to him, becoming by far the most important personality of the Laotian elite. The constitutional changes made by France after the forced cession of royal territory to Thailand in 1941 left Phetsarath viceroy and prime minister of all of northern Laos. In March 1945, after Japan evicted the French, the prince reached the height of his power. A proud, aristocratic authoritarian who brooked no opposition, he was liked by few, least of all perhaps by the increasingly influential Crown Prince Savangvatthana.

Japan capitulated in August 1945, and it seemed for a few confused weeks that the French might not return to Laos. The danger for Laos was that the Vietnamese, long openly covetous of Laotian territory and actually outnumbering the Laotian population in Vientiane, would replace the French. Pressed by the rebel group Lao Issara, Phetsarath tried to temporize, reaffirming the independence granted by the Japanese and preventing the liberated French from resuming control. He advised the king in Luang Prabang to declare the union of Laos, including southern Laos, not hitherto part of his domains, and ignore the French. But the king already had announced the resumption of the French protectorate and had welcomed a French mission, as had Prince Boun Oum, the dominant personality in southern Laos.

Circumstances prevented a resolution of the impasse. The French were in Luang Prabang and the south. Phetsarath, between them in Vientiane, was not anti-French, but a Vietnamese force under his half-brother Prince Souphanouvong, who was stridently so, would soon arrive; furthermore, Chinese forces, with anti-French ambitions of their own, were entering Laos by Allied arrangement. Under these pressures Phetsarath himself proclaimed the union of Laos on 15 September. For this, for his actions against the French, and for his subsequent encouragement of the Lao Issara, he was never forgiven. King Sisavangvong dismissed him on 10 October, and when the French returned in strength six months later, Phetsarath fled with the Lao Issara to Thailand.

While rapid political progress was made in Laos, the movement slowly crumbled in Thailand. In 1949 Souphanouvong joined the Vietnamese, and the remaining Lao Issara leaders returned under an amnesty to a united and independent Laos. But Phetsarath, cousin-german and brother-in-law of the king, had been excluded from the new constitution. He remained bitter in Thailand until circumstances allowed his return in March 1957. He was given the honorary title of viceroy of Luang Prabang—a kingdom that had vanished—and died in retirement on 15 October 1959.

[See also Laos; Luang Prabang; Savangvatthana; Lao Issara; Boun Oum; Souphanouvong; and Sisavangvong.]

3349 (pseudonym, largely Phetsarath), *Iron Man of Laos*, translated by John B. Murdoch (1978). A. J. Dommen, *Conflict in Laos* (1984). J. M. Halpern, *Government, Politics, and Social Structure in Laos* (1964).

HUGH TOYE

PHIBUNSONGKHRAM, LUANG (1897–1964), Thai political leader. The son of a durian farmer, Phibunsongkhram, whose real name was Plaek Khitasangkha, was born in Nonthaburi Province near Bangkok. He received his early education at temple schools near his home and in Bangkok and entered the royal Thai Military Academy at the age of twelve, graduating in 1915. Among his classmates at the academy were General Luang Adun Adundetcharat, General Mangkorn Phromyothi, and Field Marshal Phin Chunhawan.

Phibun's first assignment was in Phitsanulok, where he met and married a fifteen-year-old schoolteacher. As the 1924 valedictorian of the Army General Staff College, Phibun received a scholarship to study artillery science in France. While in France, he met frequently with other politically aware students—Pridi Phanomyong, Prayun Phamonmontri, Khuang Aphaiwong, and others—to talk about the future of Thailand. After his return to Bangkok in 1927, Phibun wrote numerous articles on modern artillery warfare. As the first Thai graduate of the French Artillery School, Phibun was highly respected by his fellow officers.

Together with Pridi, Phibun helped plan the coup of 24 June 1932, which overthrew absolute monarchy in Thailand. Because of their youth and relative inexperience, Pridi and Phibun left the leadership of the People's Party to the senior clique led by Phibun's immediate superior, Colonel Phraya Phahon Phonphayuhasena. Following the takeover of power, the promoters (as members of the People's Party were known) convinced the respected jurist Phraya Manopakorn Nitithada to lead Thailand's first parliamentary government. Following his summary closing of Parliament in 1933, Mano's cabinet was ousted by a Phahon-led coup d'état. Phibun played an important role in this coup and shortly thereafter led the government troops that suppressed the Boworadet Rebellion.

As a young and promising promoter in the People's Party, Phibun became a member of Thailand's first cabinet, approved by Parliament on 28 June 1932. Two years later, he assumed the powerful position of minister of defense in the Phahon government. It became clear that Phahon was grooming Phibun for the premiership.

Between 1935 to 1938, Phibun survived two shootings and one arsenic poisoning. His narrow escapes from these three assassination attempts convinced the public that he had special qualities and merit. In 1938, Phibun succeeded Phahon as prime minister. With the help of his friend and former classmate Police Chief Luang Adun Adundetcharat, Phibun had scores of people arrested for treason; eighteen were eventually executed. The most prominent person arrested was Phibun's political rival Colonel Phraya Song Suradet, a fellow promoter and contemporary of Phraya Phahon. Phraya Song was forced into exile abroad.

Phibun's tenure as prime minister can be divided into two periods: the first lasted from 1938 to 1944, the second from 1947 to 1957. Prior to World War II, Phibun's regime promoted militarism, irredentism, and social development through cultural enrichment. His government's nationalistic policy resulted in campaigns against the local Chinese. His irredentist aspirations led to a brief war with France in 1941 that forced France to return former Thai territories in Laos and Cambodia to Thailand. Through the Ministry of Culture, Phibun promoted the emulation of Western practices and etiquette, such as the wearing of dresses, hats, and gloves. Thais were asked to follow Phibun, the leader, so that the nation would survive external threats during World War II.

Phibun's decision to allow Japanese troops to pass through Thailand to fight in Burma and Malaya (1941) created a rift within the leadership of the People's Party. Phibun's policy was opposed by both Pridi and Luang Adundetcharat, who formed and led the anti-Japanese resistance organization Seri Thai (Free Thai). When it became clear that Japan would lose the war to the Allies, Phibun's government fell by a parliamentary vote of no confidence. Phibun resigned on 26 July 1944.

From 1944 to 1947 Thailand had six civilian governments. Pridi himself became prime minister for five months in 1946. Following the mysterious death of King Ananda, a coup d'état against the Pridi-backed Luang Thamrong government was carried out by the army, which was led by General Phin Chunhawan and other officers who had been demobilized at the end of World War II. After the brief Khuang Aphaiwong interim government, Phibun was again asked to form a new government.

The postwar Phibun regime gave lip service to the benefits of democratic processes and institutions. Pro-Americanism and anticommunism became its prominent policies. Through the initiative of the United States, Thailand became an active leader of the Southeast Asia Treaty Organization, a mutual defense agreement designed to thwart the spread of communism into the region.

By the mid-1950s, Phibun's leadership was challenged by army strongman Sarit Thanarat and by Police Chief Phao Siyanon. Sarit used the public uproar over the "dirty" elections of February 1957 as a pretext for a coup d'état against the Phibun government.

Sarit's 16 September 1957 coup ended Phibun's long political career. Although the new regime made no public threats toward him, Phibun chose exile and lived in Japan until his death.

[*See also* Pridi Phanomyong; Khuang Aphaiwong; People's Party of Thailand; Phahon Phonphayuhasena; Manopakorn Nitithada; Free Thai; Franco-Siamese War; Southeast Asia Treaty Organization; *and* Sarit Thanarat.]

David Wilson, *Politics in Thailand* (1962). David K. Wyatt, *Thailand: A Short History* (1984).

THAK CHALOEMTIARANA

PHILIPPINE-AMERICAN WAR (1899–1902),

a forty-one-month struggle between the United States and Philippine revolutionary forces that saw the fall of the first Philippine Republic and victory for the US claim to sovereignty over the Philippine archipelago.

Following the negotiation of the Spanish-American Treaty of December 1898, relations quickly worsened between US Army troops under General Elwell Otis and Filipino soldiers, led by Emilio Aguinaldo, surrounding the American trench lines on the outskirts of Manila. Military conflict was virtually inevitable. The Americans demanded Filipino acquiescence to US sovereignty; the Malolos Republic insisted on the right of the Philippine people to an independent national existence. On the night of 4 February 1899, two American sentries fired on Filipino pickets in the Santa Mesa sector, and a general engagement followed. Otis brushed aside a proposal for a military truce, and Aguinaldo issued a formal declaration of war against "the American army of occupation." The war that followed was labeled in Washington as an insurrection; for the Filipinos, it was the second chapter of what they call the War for Philippine Independence.

The war may be divided into three stages. The first covered the months of February to November 1899. Following the outbreak of hostilities, US troops mounted an attack on a succession of towns along the railroad north of Manila. The Filipinos fought from fixed entrenchments and suffered heavy casualties. On 30 March Aguinaldo was forced to evacuate his capital at Malolos, and by June US troops had penetrated San Fernando. Aguinaldo's soldiers successfully harassed their enemy in a series of skirmishes during the rainy season of June–September, but in October, General Otis mounted a three-pronged offensive designed to entrap Aguinaldo and his "insurgents" as they were driven north along the central plain of Luzon. As a result of the procrastination of General Lloyd Wheaton, the trap was not closed in time. Aguinaldo and a portion of his army scaled the mountains of Benguet and eventually gained the haven of Isabela province.

Some weeks before his escape, Aguinaldo had issued a proclamation at Bayambang, disbanding the regular Philippine army and proclaiming that henceforth the patriot forces would fight a guerrilla war. This proclamation initiated the second stage of the Philippine-American War, beginning in November 1899 and ending with Aguinaldo's capture in March 1901. This period saw the Filipino forces at their most effective and the American soldiers periodically beleaguered and frustrated. Aguinaldo of necessity had relinquished the idea of a military victory; his strategy was to increase the human and financial costs of American occupation in the hope that the American public would become discouraged and demand an end to colonial adventure.

The US strategy sought to combine military subjugation and political pacification. General Arthur MacArthur succeeded Otis as military governor in May 1900, and in June and December of that year he issued two decrees that embodied the US political-military strategy of persuasion and coercion. The first decree promised amnesty to any guerrilla who would surrender his rifle and acknowledge the sovereignty of the United States. This was coupled with a renewed effort to gain the support of the propertied and professional classes and create an Americanista Party among those Filipino leaders prepared to desert Aguinaldo and the cause of Philippine independence. In December MacArthur proclaimed that neutrality was no longer an option available to the Filipinos. The American army would combine search-and-destroy missions with permanent garrisoning of towns suspected of aiding the guerrillas. The following months would see increased acts of terrorism by the guerrillas against suspected collaborators and the use of the water torture by US troops determined to extract information from suspected guerrilla sympathizers.

The daring and duplicitous capture of Aguinaldo by General Frederick Funston in March 1901 marked the beginning of the third and last stage of the War for Philippine Independence. Aguinaldo was brought back to Manila and on 1 April took the oath of allegiance. In the next months, generals Mascardo, Alejandrino, Lucon, and Cailles surrendered, and by the summer of 1901 the only sizable guerrilla units in the field were those of General Lukban in Samar and General Malvar in Batangas. Both would figure prominently in the anticlimactic and bloody conclusion of the Philippine-American War. By the end of April 1902, Lukban and Malvar had capitulated, and on 4 July 1902 President Theodore Roosevelt proclaimed a general grant of clemency for the defeated Filipinos.

For both countries the war was a costly tragedy. The US Army suffered battle losses of over 4,200 men killed and over 2,800 wounded. The Filipinos suffered battle losses of over 16,000 killed and as many as 200,000 civilian casualties, victims of war-related disease and famine. The damage to Philippine national pride and identity defies statistical enumeration.

[See also Philippines; Aguinaldo, Emilio; Philippine Revolution; and Malolos Republic.]

Leandro H. Fernandez, The Philippine Republic (1926). Teodoro M. Kalaw, The Philippine Revolution (1969). Stuart C. Miller, "Benevolent Assimilation": The American Conquest of the Philippines, 1899–1903 (1982). William T. Sexton, Soldiers in the Sun (1939). Leon Wolff, Little Brown Brother (1961). Gregorio F. Zaide, The Philippine Revolution (1954).

RICHARD E. WELCH, JR.

PHILIPPINE COMMISSIONS. To avoid political corruption, late nineteenth-century Americans often turned to expert commissions to study public issues and administer government efficiently. After deciding to retain the Philippines, President William McKinley appointed two such commissions.

The first, the Schurman Commission (after its head, Jacob Gould Schurman, 1854–1942), appointed in 1899, gathered information about the Philippines and recommended policies. Although impeded in its work by fighting between American and Philippine forces, the commission succeeded in identifying reforms and developmental programs that could entice elite Filipinos into collaboration with the United States. Calling Filipinos "wholly unprepared for independence," its final report (January 1900) urged the United States to replace military with civilian government, assure individual liberties, and promote local self-government where possible.

The second Philippine commission exercised both legislative and executive power in the colony from 1900 until 1916. Until the election of the first Philippine Assembly in 1907, the commission was the unicameral legislature of the civil government. Between then and 1916, it functioned as the upper house of a bicameral legislature. Originally composed of five appointed Americans who divided among themselves the executive portfolios of the government, the commission grew to eight in 1901 to allow the appointment of Filipinos, without portfolio. A ninth seat was created in 1908 when the first Filipino cabinet secretary was appointed. Following the election of President Woodrow Wilson in 1913, Filipinos replaced Americans in the majority, paving the way for the Jones Act's elimination of the commission in favor of an elected senate in 1916.

Given the standards of the time, the Philippine commission administered the colony progressively and professionally. Under the leadership of William Howard Taft, civil governor from 1901 to 1903, the commission quickly gave Filipinos local self-government and devoted itself to such tasks as modernizing legal codes, providing reliable currency, and improving roads, ports, education, and public health. Although unable to neutralize the Filipino desire for independence, these policies did assure peace and relative prosperity.

Although the commission form of government ended with the Jones Act, the patterns established by the Philippine commissions continued throughout the colonial era: collaboration with politically conservative but modernizing elites, rapid devolution of authority to local units and to elected Filipino officials, heavy emphasis upon modernization and improvement of public services, and peaceful progress toward independence.

[See also Philippines and Jones Act.]

Kenneth Hendrickson, Jr., "Reluctant Expansionist—Jacob Gould Schurman and the Philippine Question," *Pacific Historical Review* 36 (1967): 405–421. James A. LeRoy, *The Americans in the Philippines* (1914). Peter W. Stanley, *A Nation in the Making: The Philippines and the United States, 1899–1921* (1974).

PETER W. STANLEY

PHILIPPINE INDEPENDENT CHURCH.

The Philippine Independent Church (PIC), or Iglesia Filipina Independiente, is headed by a supreme bishop *(obispo máximo)* elected by a general assembly of lay and clerical delegates and claims a membership of 3.5 million with five hundred priests and sixty four bishops. It uses a vernacular liturgy in Catholic tradition as reformed by the modern liturgical movement and trains most of its priests in Saint Andrew's Theological Seminary, a Philippine Episcopal Church institution jointly staffed by both churches. A member of the World Council of Churches, the PIC has concordats with the Old Catholics in Europe and most of the national churches of the Anglican Communion.

The PIC was proclaimed in August 1902 by journalist Isabelo de los Reyes as a break with Rome over the issue of a native hierarchy, and nationalist appeal soon swelled its membership to one-fifth the total population. It was headed for almost forty years by Gregorio Aglipay y Labayan, a patriot-priest excommunicated while vicar-general of the Revolutionary Army, and is sometimes called the Aglipayan Church. Reyes was a modernist free-thinker who wrote a late nineteenth-century rationalism into the church's doctrinal literature, but after Aglipay's death the hierarchy affirmed an orthodox trinitarian position and received apostolic orders through the American Episcopal Church.

[See also Aglipay y Labayan, Gregorio.]

Pedro S. de Achútegui and Miguel A. Bernad, *Religious Revolution in the Philippines*, 4 vols. (2d ed., 1961–1972). Mary Dorita Clifford, "Iglesia Filipina Independiente: The Revolutionary Church," in *Studies in Philippine Church History*, edited by Gerald H. Anderson (1969), pp. 223–255. John N. Schumacher, *Revolutionary Clergy: The Filipino Clergy and the Nationalist Movement, 1850–1903* (1981).   WILLIAM HENRY SCOTT

PHILIPPINE LANGUAGES.

The Philippine languages are a subgroup of the Austronesian language family, which extends through insular Southeast Asia and eastward from Madagascar on the west to Easter Island and Hawaii on the east and from Formosa (Taiwan) on the north to Australia on the south. The Philippine languages include all of the Austronesian languages spoken in the Philippines. In addition, some of the languages of Sarawak and Sabah and the northern arm of Sulawesi are considered to be in the subgroup of the Philippine languages.

The total number of languages in this group is unknown because the language names that are commonly given usually refer to the areas in which they are spoken, and in many cases no systematic language surveys have been conducted. For example, the designation *Visayan* refers to the central portion of the Philippines, and at least twelve different languages are commonly referred to as Visayan. In the Philippines alone, there are somewhere in the neighborhood of a hundred languages, most, if not all, of which belong to the Philippine subgroup. A non-Austronesian language, Chabacano, is also spoken in the Philippines, in Zamboanga, Mindanao, and in a few villages of Cavite province in Luzon. This language is a hispanization of a Portuguese creole that was brought to the Philippines from Ternate in the Moluccas (Maluku) in the seventeenth century.

Although the Austronesian languages of the Philippines are numerous, they resemble each other closely in grammatical structure and vocabulary. They are characterized by a rich and elaborate system of morphology and a simple phonology and uncomplicated way of adding affixes to a root. The similarity in structure among all these languages is probably the result of centuries of interethnic contact, in which languages in contact tended to become like each other. They either borrowed from one another or, in cases where languages spread to a new population, the new population spoke the language they took on with retentions from their original language. Thus Masbateño, which is spoken on Masbate where Bikol, Samar-Leyte, Hiligaynon, and Cebuano all meet, consists of elements taken from all four languages and probably came to be that way by repeated language shifts and multilingualism over the generations. Similarly, Abaknon of Capul Island off Samar, a Samalic language brought north from the Sulu Archipelago in the seventeenth century, has been strongly influenced by the Cebuano of Capul and has come to resemble Cebuano in many important ways. The Abaknon and Masbateño situations have been repeated many times over throughout the Philippines, giving the Philippine languages a closeness in grammatical structure.

This closeness in structure and layers of mutual influence make it impossible to subgroup the Philippine languages on other than large-scale terms. The languages of northern Luzon (including Ilocano), of the Cordillera, and of the Cagayan Valley are clearly in one subgroup. Tagalog and Bikol, the languages of the Visayas, and most of the languages of the eastern third of Mindanao are in another subgroup, called Tagalic. Interestingly, Tawsug (Jolohano) from Sulu is also in this group and must have been brought west to the Sulu Archipelago from Agusan in the eastern third of Mindanao. However, most of the languages from Luzon, including Pangasinan, Pamango, and Sambal, fall in a category between the northern Luzon languages and differ from the major languages in this area. The languages of central Mindanao, including Maranao, Magindanao, and the various Manobo languages, are in another subgroup.

Most Philippine languages are spoken by small populations and are used only as home languages in their native areas. The vast majority of the population of the Philippines, on the other hand, speaks one of the major languages. The most important of these is Tagalog (also called Pilipino), which is the national language and is spoken as a language of wider communication in urban areas outside of its homeland. Tagalog is the language of the metropolitan Manila region and surrounding provinces and counts some ten to twelve million native speakers. The next most important language, Cebuano, comes from the central Visayas and northern Mindanao and has more native speakers than Tagalog; it is known as a language of wider communication through much of Mindanao. Equally important is Ilocano, spoken throughout most of the lowlands of northern Luzon into the Cagayan Valley. Other languages in the Philippines with speakers numbering in the hundreds of thousands are Pangasinan, Pampango, Ibanag, Sambal, and Bikol on Luzon; Samar-Leyte, spoken on Samar and Western Leyte; Aklan, Kinaray-a, and Hiligaynon, on Negros and Panay; and finally the non-Austronesian Chabacano from Zamboanga.

Most of the major Philippine languages are known from grammars, religious texts, and dictionaries that date to the seventeenth century. (In fact, for Tagalog they date to the end of the sixteenth century.) There is little, however, by way of older literature. Most of the literature is folkloric in nature and is lost or dying out. For Tagalog there is a fairly large body of literature dating from the last century. For Cebuano and Ilocano there is literature only from this century, and for the other major languages very little has been published at all. A large number of the minor languages have become known in recent years through the work of the Summer Institute of Linguistics, which has published schoolbooks and translations as well as grammatical studies and word lists. Nonetheless, many of the minor languages, especially those spoken by lowland Christian groups, remain unrecorded.

The lowland languages spoken by populations under strong Spanish influence show heavy borrowing from Spanish in the lexicon. Many of the Spanish forms have moved on into the languages spoken by populations that were not under Spanish control, but for the most part these languages do not show as heavy a Spanish overlay. The languages of the Muslims, especially Tawsug and Samal, reveal heavy borrowing from Malay. Tagalog also shows a strong Malay influence that dates from pre-Hispanic times. At present Malay and Spanish have little role in the Philippines, and the source of outside influences for all of the languages of the Philippines is English and Tagalog.

Many groups of the Philippines had an indigenous writing system, with syllabaries indirectly of Indic origin. Among the christianized groups, knowledge of the native alphabets had disappeared by the eighteenth century, and practically no manuscripts and little else by way of evidence have survived. A few groups on Mindoro and Palawan have maintained local writing systems, but no manuscripts of length are extant. Despite the lack of native documents, however, the Philippine languages are an important source of information on the history of the Philippines. A study of loanwords and language influence sheds light on contacts that existed in prehistoric times. Language comparisons yield evidence for origins and movements of populations, and other types of studies of the lexicon can provide information on Philippine life and culture in bygone times.

[See also Austronesian Languages and Tagalog.]

Andrew Gonzalez, *Language and Nationalism: The Philippine Experience Thus Far* (1978). Teodoro A. Llamzon, *Handbook of Philippine Language Groups* (1978). JOHN U. WOLFF

PHILIPPINE REVOLUTION. The seeds of the Philippine Revolution were sown in the nineteenth century with the breakdown of Spain's enforced isolation of the Philippines. As parts of the archipelago became tied to European markets, a new class of prosperous, mostly hispanicized mestizos, the *ilustrados,* emerged to challenge their colonizers. Their sons attended European universities, where they were influenced by the liberal ideas sweeping Europe. In 1868 a liberal government in Madrid instituted colonial reforms, but these were rescinded in 1872 when a revolution in Cuba helped return Spain's conservatives to power. This loss of reforms triggered a workers' rebellion in Cavite, south of Manila, that was brutally suppressed.

Over the next thirty-five years, *ilustrado* intellectuals pressed for restoration of the reforms. The unofficial leader of these efforts, which came to be known as the Propaganda Movement, was Jose Rizal, a celebrated surgeon, poet, artist, and linguist. Rizal's novel, *Noli Me Tangere,* had a galvanizing

effect on Filipino nationalism, although the propagandists never demanded independence.

Millenarian and messianic cults also fomented peasant uprisings. Somewhat closer to this tradition was a radical secret society, the Katipunan, which was founded by Andres Bonifacio in 1892, on the very day that Rizal was banished from Manila. Betrayed in the confessional, Bonifacio was forced to begin the revolution prematurely on 26 August 1896; as a result of the betrayal, many followers were rounded up in a wave of hysteria that soon led to Rizal's execution. Rizal became a martyr for a revolution he had rejected.

The rebels' only success took place in Cavite and was led by a young *katipunero,* General Emilio Aguinaldo, who also outflanked Bonifacio by displacing the Katipunan with a revolutionary government. When he objected, Bonifacio was executed for treason after a farcical trial. Aguinaldo was forced to retreat to Biaknabato, a mountain redoubt near Manila, from which he directed guerrilla warfare until Spain negotiated peace at the end of 1897. Both sides quickly violated the pact. In exile, Aguinaldo and a band of leaders plotted a second round, while some rebels rejected the peace and others secreted weapons rather than surrender them. Spain ignored the amnesty and never paid more than a third of the stipulated indemnities.

When the war over Cuba between the United States and Spain was imminent, Aguinaldo's junta conferred with American diplomats and naval officers in Hong Kong and Singapore. Once war was declared in April 1898, the US Navy transported the junta back to Luzon to take charge of a renewed rebellion. Admiral Dewey turned over captured Spanish arms to them, while the American consul in Hong Kong purchased more with money Aguinaldo had given him. Thus, a de facto alliance clearly existed.

Aguinaldo laid siege to Manila and successfully attacked Spanish garrisons elsewhere on Luzon. A declaration of independence, almost a paraphrase of the earlier American one, was signed on 12 June and bore the signature of an American colonel among the witnesses. On 1 August, the *presidentes* of towns throughout Luzon gathered at Bacoor to ratify independence.

Meanwhile, American troops continued to arrive at Cavite. With no written agreement, Aguinaldo relied on America's anticolonial tradition to respect his revolutionary government. He even made room on his line of siege for Americans, who then stormed Manila on 13 August after a prearranged sham battle designed to keep the Filipinos out. A shocked Aguinaldo resumed the line of siege, explaining that Manila could revert to Spain in the peace negotiations then under way in Paris, from which he was also excluded. This action enraged the American command, which began a diplomatic offensive designed to humiliate the Filipinos by forcing them to retreat from the suburbs they occupied.

Since the armistice ignored his government, Aguinaldo expanded his campaign against the Spaniards to other islands. Moving his capital to Malolos, twenty-five miles northwest of Manila, he inaugurated a Philippine Congress that ratified a constitution after much debate. Nevertheless, the functioning Philippine Republic that controlled most of the archipelago was ignored in the Treaty of Paris, signed on 10 December, and the islands were ceded to the United States. Ironically, the Filipino government was dominated by conservative *ilustrados* eager for American protection in exchange for internal autonomy and willing to cede bases, had Washington bothered to recognize and negotiate seriously with it.

Tensions continued to mount outside Manila, when, on the evening of 4 February 1899, two Nebraska sentries shot three unarmed Filipino soldiers who had refused to halt at a hotly disputed outpost. Although not the first such incident, heavy firing erupted, mostly from American volunteers, already famous for their lack of discipline with a rifle. In spite of few casualties and a cease-fire at 2:00 AM, the Americans executed a prearranged plan, bombarding Filipino positions at dawn before charging them. Aguinaldo's appeals for a truce were dismissed, and over the next eleven months he was steadily pushed back to a mountain refuge near Luzon's northeast coast.

The guerrilla phase began in 1900 and lasted, officially, another thirty months, with many atrocities committed by both sides. Over 4,000 Americans, up to 20,000 Filipino combatants, and possibly 200,000 civilians perished in the war. The *ilustrados* had largely abandoned the cause early, often serving the Americans in civilian capacities. The Macabebes, traditional enemies of the Tagalogs, who dominated the revolution, fought for Americans as Philippine Scouts and were instrumental in the capture of Aguinaldo in March 1901. He quickly pledged allegiance to the United States and urged his followers to surrender. Many of them did over the following year, but the struggle limped along years longer, suppressed largely by the Philippine Constabulary and often by former revolutionary leaders who had been elected as governors of provinces as the Filipinos were granted greater self-rule. A Katipunan revival, various fanatical religious sects, and finally the Huks continually renewed the struggle against the conservative *ilustrado* government that evolved under American tutelage until the Philippines were granted full independence in 1946. The Moros never fully bowed to Manila any more than they did to Washington.

[*See also* Philippines; Ilustrado; Cavite Mutiny; Rizal, Jose Mercado; Katipunan; Bonifacio, Andres; Aguinaldo, Emilio; Malolos Republic; *and* Moro.]

Teodoro Agoncillo, *The Revolt of the Masses: The Story of Bonifacio and the Katipunan* (1956). Reynaldo C. Ileto, *Pasyon and Revolution: Popular Movements in the Philippines, 1840–1910* (1979). Benedict J. Kirkvliet, *The Huc Rebellion: A Study of Peasant Revolt in the Philippines* (1977). Stuart Creighton Miller, *"Benevolent Assimilation," The American Conquest of the Philippines, 1899–1903* (1982). John M. Schumacher, *The Propaganda Movement, 1880–1885* (1973). Peter W. Stanley, *A Nation in the Making: The Philippines and the United States, 1899–1921* (1974). David R. Sturtevant, *Popular Uprisings in the Philippines, 1840–1940* (1976). Richard E. Welch, Jr., *Response to Imperialism: The United States and the Philippine-American War, 1899–1902* (1979). Gregorio F. Zaide, *The Philippine Revolution* (1954).

STUART CREIGHTON MILLER

PHILIPPINES, Southeast Asian island nation with a predominantly rural and Catholic population of fifty million.

Prehistory. Over five thousand years ago, successive waves of Malays from the Asian mainland settled in small, widely dispersed villages along the coastlines and rivers of the Philippines and lived by fishing, hunting, and shifting cultivation. The most common unit of settlement was the *barangay*, headed by a *datu* (local chieftain) and consisting of freehold farmers, warriors, and indentured servants. [*See* Barangay.] The absence of any precolonial central government or elite culture has endowed the country with a strong tradition of localism.

Spanish Period. In 1521 Ferdinand Magellan arrived in search of spices and converts for Prince Philip, later King Philip II, whose name was bestowed on the islands. Lapulapu, a native chieftain of Cebu, resisted Magellan's claim of Spanish sovereignty with a mortally wounding spear thrust. In 1565 Miguel Lopez de Legazpi established the first permanent Spanish settlement in Cebu. [*See* Legazpi, Miguel Lopez de.] By the end of the century, most of the country was under Spanish control except for

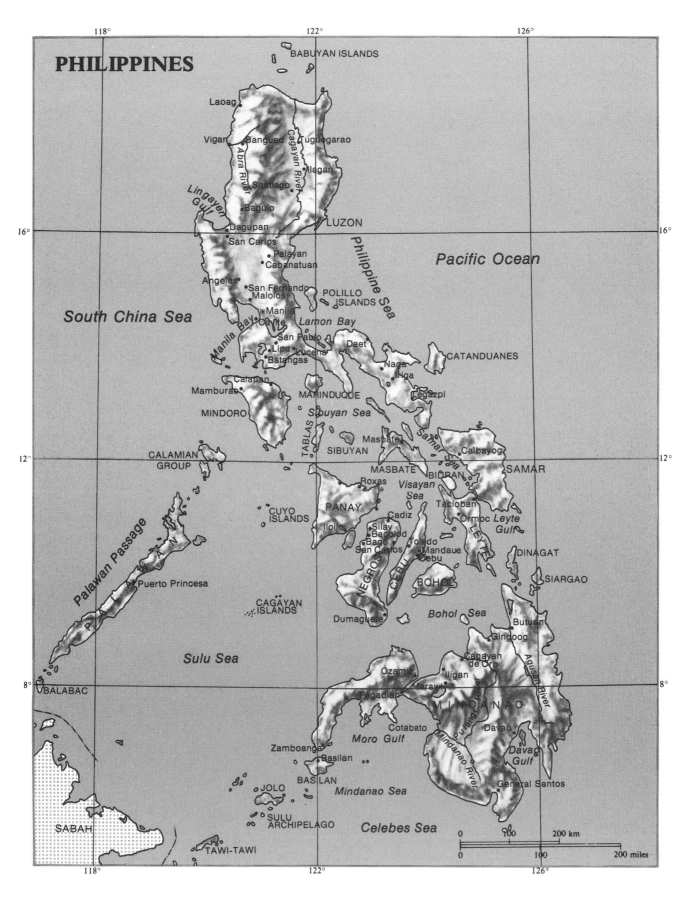

PHILIPPINES

BABUYAN ISLANDS

Laoag

Vigan Bangued Tuguegarao

Abra River Cagayan River Ilagan

Lingayen Gulf Santiago

Baguio

Dagupan LUZON

San Carlos

Palayan Pacific Ocean

Cabanatuan

Angeles San Fernando POLILLO

Malolos ISLANDS

South China Sea Manila

Cavite Lamon Bay

San Pablo

Manila Bay Lipa Daet

Lucena Naga

Batangas Iliga CATANDUANES

Calapan Legazpi

Mamburao MARINDUQUE

Philippine Sea

MINDORO Sibuyan Sea

Maspate Samar

TABLAS SIBUYAN Calbayog

CALAMIAN MASBATE BILIRAN SAMAR

GROUP Roxas

Visayan Tacloban

CUYO Sea

ISLANDS PANAY Cadiz Ormoc Leyte

Iloilo Silay Gulf

Palawan Passage Bacolod

Bago Toledo LEYTE

San Carlos Mandaue DINAGAT

Puerto Princesa Cebu

NEGROS CEBU SIARGAO

CAGAYAN BOHOL

ISLANDS Dumaguete Bohol Sea

Butuan

Gingoog

Sulu Sea Cagayan de Oro

Ozamis Iligan Agusan River

BALABAC Marawi

Pagadian MINDANAO

Cotabato Davao

Zamboanga Moro Gulf Davao

Basilan Gulf

BASILAN General Santos

JOLO Mindanao River

SABAH Mindanao Sea

SULU

ARCHIPELAGO Celebes Sea

TAWI-TAWI

0   100   200 km

0   100   200 miles

the southern islands, where Muslim Filipinos remain a highly autonomous cultural minority. Although there were seldom more than a few hundred priests in the country, the Roman Catholic church did not encourage the development of a Filipino clergy or the teaching of Spanish to Filipinos. Only the Spanish village priests could speak both Spanish and the local languages; hence they exercised considerable power as indispensable intermediaries between colonial and church authorities and the rest of the indigenous population. [See Friars *and* Catholicism in the Philippines.]

Colonization was encouraged through the *encomienda* system, which rewarded Spaniards for their services to the crown with the exclusive right to control public affairs, including tax collection, in a certain locality. The system was gradually abandoned during the seventeenth century after widespread criticism of extortion and other abuses. The *datu* was made official head of the *barangay* and given the power to collect taxes. Private ownership of land was introduced by the Spaniards, and many *datus* strengthened their position by taking over *barangay* lands that had been previously held in common. The new property laws and the concentration of church, government, and market activities in towns gave rise to the *principalia*, a local aristocracy, and *caciques*, other local leaders, who formed an indigenous elite class. [See Principalia *and* Cacique.] At the top of the political hierarchy was the governor-general, who ruled with almost unlimited powers because of his control over the courts and military and the great distance between Manila and Madrid. He was also permitted to engage in commerce for private profit. Both public and private revenues were increased during the sixteenth and seventeenth centuries, when Manila was an important entrepôt for the galleon trade between Mexico and China. [See Manila *and* Manila Galleon.] This trade attracted a large Chinese community, which has continued to play a vital role in Philippine commerce. After the galleon trade monopoly ended in the early nineteenth century, foreign merchants expanded commercial export agriculture in tobacco, indigo, sugar, hemp, and coffee.

Few Filipinos were able to read, write, or speak Spanish. Demands for reforms and public disturbances were frequent and sometimes violent, as in the Cavite Mutiny of 1872. [See Cavite Mutiny.] The very few Filipinos from wealthy or prominent families who were able to study abroad began a campaign, known as the Propaganda Movement, to appeal to Spanish authorities in Madrid for more lenient policies in the Philippine colony. [See Propaganda Movement.] Jose Rizal, physician and author, returned home from Spain in 1892 and organized the Liga Filipina to press for reforms; however, Spanish authorities in Manila responded with only token concessions. Rizal was arrested, exiled, and finally executed in 1896 as a subversive. This precipitated the Philippine Revolution, led by the Katipunan, a secret revolutionary society founded by Andres Bonifacio in 1892. The Spanish retaliated and forced the rebels to retreat. Emilio Aguinaldo, military commander of the rebel forces, seized the leadership of the Katipunan, and in December 1897, after receiving promises of reforms, he signed a cease-fire with the Spaniards, who paid him a large sum to withdraw with other rebel leaders to Hong Kong. [See Rizal, Jose Mercado; Liga Filipina; Philippine Revolution; Katipunan; Bonifacio, Andres; *and* Aguinaldo, Emilio.]

In the meantime, the Spanish-American War broke out off the shores of Cuba. On 1 May 1898, Commodore George Dewey sailed into Manila Bay and sank the Spanish fleet. [See Manila Bay, Battle of.] He then called on Aguinaldo to help defeat the Spanish land forces in exchange for US support. Aguinaldo and his forces routed Spanish forces around Manila, and on 12 June 1898 he declared the independence of the first Philippine Republic. A constitutional convention was convened in Malolos, and in January 1899 Aguinaldo became president of the new government. [See Malolos Republic.]

American Period. President William McKinley decided to annex the Philippines, a decision formalized in the Spanish-American Treaty of Paris signed on 10 December 1898 and ratified in the US Senate by a narrow one-vote margin over the required two-thirds majority. The United States paid Spain $20 million for the colony, but Filipino forces rejected American claims of sovereignty, and hostilities soon broke out. Thousands of lives were lost in the Philippine-American War (1898–1901) until Aguinaldo was captured. [See Philippine-American War.] Warfare then subsided, and civil government replaced military occupation. Two Philippine commissions sent by President McKinley advised preparation for self-government and eventual independence for the new colony. In 1901, William Howard Taft, a federal judge and later US president, became the first governor of the colony. [See Philippine Commissions *and* Taft, William Howard.] In 1907 an elective legislative assembly was established, the first in Southeast Asia. Under the Jones Act of 1916, the commission was abolished and replaced by an elected senate; the act also promised independence "as soon as a stable government can be established." [See Jones Act and Harrison, Francis Burton.]

Under US rule, major improvements in public health and education were achieved; progress in agricultural and industrial development, however, was limited. The Payne-Aldrich Tariff Act of 1909 provided free trade between the Philippines and the United States, severely retarding industrial growth in the islands. Sugar plantation and mill owners profited greatly from their access to the protected US market, thus reinforcing the economic base of the landed aristocracy. Tenancy increased steadily, and peasant rebellions, such as the Sakdals, broke out, especially in central Luzon in the 1930s. [See Sakdal.]

The elections of 1907 established the predominance of the proindependence Nacionalista Party, whose two political leaders, Sergio Osmeña and Manuel Quezon, competed with each other to get the best possible terms and the earliest possible date for independence. [See Nacionalista Party; Osmeña, Sergio; and Quezon, Manuel Luis.] The Tydings-McDuffie Act of 1934 scheduled independence after an interim ten-year commonwealth government and set US quotas and tariffs on Philippine goods. A constitution was quickly drafted, and the commonwealth was inaugurated on 15 November 1935 with Quezon elected as president and Osmeña as vice-president. [See Tydings-McDuffie Act and Philippines, Commonwealth of.]

Japanese forces invaded in December 1941 and forced Philippine-American troops to retreat and surrender on Corregidor and Bataan. The Japanese occupation (1942–1945) met widespread Filipino resistance, especially in central Luzon, where the Huk were a strong guerrilla force. [See Huk.] The Huk, under communist leadership, also redistributed lands from landlords who had gone to the Japanese-occupied cities to the many tenant farmers among their followers. Allied forces under General Douglas MacArthur returned in 1944, but severe fighting continued until the Japanese surrender in August 1945. Manuel Roxas, a leading collaborator supported by MacArthur, formed the Liberal Party and campaigned successfully to become president of the second independent Republic of the Philippines on 4 July 1946. [See Roxas, Manuel.]

Independence. Although wartime destruction was enormous, US reconstruction aid was limited. Aid was tied to Filipino acceptance of onerous conditions in the Bell Trade Act, which provided free trade between the United States and the Philippines, tied the peso to the dollar, and gave US citizens parity, or equal access, to Philippine natural resources. The United States also acquired a ninety-nine-year lease on many military bases throughout the country. [See Bell Trade Act.]

Another source of contention was the differential treatment accorded collaborators, many of whom were given amnesty, and Allied guerrilla fighters, many of whom were not recognized or remunerated for their efforts. Wartime agrarian reforms by the Huk were reversed, and Huk supporters elected to the first Congress were denied their seats. These events, along with widespread fraud in the 1949 election of President Elpidio Quirino, precipitated the Huk rebellion of 1949–1953. This communist-led uprising was finally halted by a comprehensive counterinsurgency campaign led by the secretary of national defense, Ramon Magsaysay, with considerable US aid. [See Magsaysay, Ramon.] The popular and charismatic Magsaysay went on to win the presidential elections of 1953. When he died in a plane crash in 1957, he was succeeded by his vice-president, Carlos P. Garcia. [See Garcia, Carlos P.] But neither Garcia nor his successor, Diosdado Macapagal (1961–1965), was able to reduce economic inequalities or implement basic social reforms underlying the insurgency. [See Macapagal, Diosdado P.]

Campaigning against graft and corruption in government and calling for new efforts in economic development, Ferdinand E. Marcos defeated Macapagal in the presidential election of 1965. As a result of his domestic policy initiatives and massive campaign expenditures, Marcos was reelected to the presidency in 1969, becoming the first president to serve a second term. [See Marcos, Ferdinand E.] Foreign relations were broadened with Japan and the nations of the Association of Southeast Asian Nations (ASEAN); diplomatic relations with the Soviet Union, China, and other communist nations were established. A constitutional convention was convened to chart basic reforms and to curb the strong US influence in the country. Domestic policies, however, foundered on a sagging economy. At the start of 1970, student demonstrations led to major antigovernment protests. Violence broke out again with the still-unexplained bombing of the opposition Liberal Party's rally in Manila in 21 August 1971. Several opposition leaders were killed, and President Marcos suspended the constitutional writ of habeas corpus to try to quell the growing public disorder. As he came to the end of the two-term limit in office, Marcos called on the constitutional convention to adopt a parliamentary system of government.

Martial Law. After disastrous flooding in central Luzon and a series of mysterious bombings around Manila, Marcos proclaimed martial law throughout the country on 23 September 1972. He dissolved Congress, suspended the Constitutional Convention, curtailed civil liberties, and arrested many prominent Filipinos. Recently enacted limitations on foreign enterprise were voided. Strikes were banned, and a major land reform program was launched. In January 1973, Marcos announced the ratification of a new "constitutional authoritarian" form of parliamentary government with a unicameral legislative assembly, the Batasang Pambansa. His stated objective was to achieve a "New Society" through his extensive emergency decree powers.

Armed opposition to martial law, led by the secessionist Moro National Liberation Front with some foreign assistance from Arab League nations, began in the Muslim areas of the south. [*See* Moro *and* Moro National Liberation Front.] After several years of intermittent warfare and thousands of fatalities, the civil war subsided and a cease-fire took hold. A resurgent Communist Party of the Philippines, with its New People's Army (NPA) and a political coalition, the National Democratic Front, spread throughout the country and was able to carry out military strikes against government forces, especially in Mindanao. [*See* New People's Army.]

Martial law was formally lifted in January 1981. The new constitution was amended to provide for a strong executive presidency, and in June 1981 Marcos won a six-year term in elections marked by voting abuses and a widespread boycott. The finance minister, Cesar Virata, was appointed prime minister. As economic performance deteriorated and violence increased, Marcos relied increasingly on the military, the constabulary, and his decree powers to govern.

In August 1983, former senator Benigno Aquino, Jr., a political rival who had been imprisoned by Marcos for seven and one-half years, returned from exile. He was assassinated seconds after arriving at Manila International Airport, prompting a storm of protest and massive anti-Marcos demonstrations. A commission appointed to investigate the assassination found that several of Marcos's close allies in the military were responsible, but all the defendants were acquitted when a trial—controlled by Marcos—was held. Under President Corazon Aquino a new trial is being held.

After the assassination, moderate opposition leaders, who had formed the United Nationalist Democratic Organization, joined the Catholic church and many business leaders in charging the Marcos government with widespread violations of human rights and of property rights. Marcos responded to this crisis of confidence in his administration by calling for snap presidential elections, to be held in early 1986, although his term as president extended until 1987. Met with pleas that only she could successfully unite the opposition and beat Marcos at the polls, Corazon Aquino, the widow of Benigno Aquino, ran against the president. Amid widespread charges that Marcos won by electoral fraud, Aquino claimed victory in February 1986 and called on Marcos to concede defeat. [*See* Aquino, Corazon Cojuangco.] When Marcos ordered the arrest of Juan Enrile, his defense minister, and of General Fidel Ramos on the basis of an alleged plot to assassinate him, he triggered a four-day "people power" revolution, which began when Cardinal Sin called Filipinos to the streets. By forming a human barricade at Camp Aguinaldo in Manila, the people prevented Marcos forces from reaching Enrile and Ramos. Marcos's twenty-one-year rule of the Philippines ended on the night of 25 February 1986, when he was evacuated from the country by the US military.

Shortly after coming to power, President Aquino disbanded the Batasang Pambansa, proclaimed a provisional government under an interim "freedom constitution," and appointed a commission to draft a new constitution. The first-ever cease-fire, lasting sixty days, was negotiated with the NPA, and in the meantime the newly drafted constitution was overwhelmingly approved in a plebiscite that gave Aquino a six-year term as president and paved the way for congressional and local elections.

With a restored constitutional democracy, the Philippines still struggles for an economic recovery, which many believe will require drastic social reforms, especially the breaking-up of traditional family landholdings. Numerous political uncertainties continue to beset the country in this time of perilous transition.

John Bresnan, *Crisis in the Philippines: The Marcos Era and Beyond* (1986). Frederica M. Bunge, ed., *The Philippines: A Country Study* (1984). Theodore Friend, *Between Two Empires: The Ordeal of the Philippines, 1929–1946* (1965). Carl H. Landé, *Leaders, Factions and Parties: The Structure of Philippine Politics* (1965). John Leddy Phelan, *The Hispanization of the Philippines: Spanish Aims and Filipino Responses, 1565–1700* (1959). David A Rosenberg, ed., *Marcos and Martial Law in the*

Philippines (1979). Peter W. Stanley, *A Nation in the Making: The Philippines and the United States; 1899–1921* (1974). David Joel Steinberg, *The Philippines: A Singular and a Plural Place* (1982).

DAVID A. ROSENBERG

PHILIPPINES, BRITISH OCCUPATION OF.

During the Seven Years War, a combined British naval and land force attacked and occupied Manila (1762). The British forces were under the commands of William Draper and Samuel Cornish. The Spaniards were unaware that war had been declared between England and Spain, so surprise played a major role in the conquest. In a direct frontal attack, the British landed unopposed about a mile from the city walls, but in spite of overwhelming numerical superiority the Spaniards could not overrun the enemy position. A ransom of over a million pesos was offered the British to prevent them from pillaging the entire city.

The original scheme of the British was to disrupt Spanish shipping in the East and possibly establish a permanent British settlement in the Philippines. Neither goal was accomplished. The war ended in 1762, and notice of the cessation of hostilities was received in the Philippines the next year. The British force withdrew in 1763.

[*See also* Philippines *and* Manila.]

Nicholas Cushner, *Documents Illustrating the British Conquest of Manila, 1762–1763* (1971).

NICHOLAS P. CUSHNER

PHILIPPINES, COMMONWEALTH OF,

the government of the Philippines from 1935 to 1946. According to the Tydings-McDuffie Act of 1934, the Commonwealth of the Philippines was the form of political self-rule prescribed for the ten-year transition period to Philippine independence. Following the will of the American Congress, a constitution was written by the Filipinos and approved by the American president, national elections were held, and Manuel L. Quezon (1878–1944) was inaugurated as first president of the Commonwealth of the Philippines on 15 November 1935.

Thus, the very first instance of decolonization began with both Filipinos and Americans uncertain about their respective powers and privileges. The Tydings-McDuffie Act had provided that during the ten-year transition period the United States would reserve control of foreign affairs, defense, finance, and immigration and that a high commissioner would reside in Manila as the representative of the American president and would oversee and advise the commonwealth government. After 1935 it became increasingly evident that these stipulations often tended to generate a disputatious atmosphere.

According to Theodore Friend (1965), "The major problems of the Philippine Commonwealth were three: maldistribution of political power, slow and uneven economic development, and military insecurity." Quezon's style and persona, exacerbated by his resentment of his semipresidency, combined with tradition and circumstances to augment his authoritarian executive dominance of the commonwealth. In addition, after 1935 both Americans and Filipinos recognized that some changes in the economic conditions of separation were necessary if the Philippines was ultimately to survive as an independent entity. Accordingly, in 1939 the US Congress, though by then uninterested in and disenchanted by the Philippines, enacted ameliorative legislation. Full of his customary self-confidence, General Douglas MacArthur, who had been hired by Quezon as his military adviser, assured the commonwealth president that he could inexpensively build an indigenous military force fully capable of defending the islands.

Moreover, the commonwealth's "dilemma of semisovereignty" was directly affected by the expanding power of the Japanese, which came at the same time as the anticipated American withdrawal from the region. As a result Quezon and his administration developed a modus vivendi with Japan, significantly strengthening Philippine-Japanese relations. Thus Philippine diplomacy, although theoretically nonexistent, was honed at a time of complex international tensions.

When war between Japan and the United States began in December 1941, and when, despite MacArthurian grandiloquence, the Philippines was overrun by the Japanese, Quezon and the commonwealth government, responding to American pressure, fled to the United States. In exile, Quezon insisted that his presidency continue beyond its prescribed constitutional limits. In 1944, however, he died in Saranac Lake, New York, and Sergio Osmeña (1878–1961), who had been vice president since the inception of the commonwealth, became president.

Osmeña returned to the Philippines in November 1944 with the reconquering American troops and reestablished commonwealth authority on Philippine soil. Although he ran for another term as president of the soon-to-be-independent republic, Os-meña lost to Manuel Roxas (1892–1948). On 4 July 1946, in accordance with the provisions of the Tyd-ings-McDuffie Act, the commonwealth ended, and the Republic of the Philippines was launched.

[See also Philippines; Tydings-McDuffie Act; Quezon, Manuel Luis.; Osmeña, Sergio; and Roxas, Manuel.]

Theodore Friend, Between Two Empires (1965). Grant K. Goodman, Four Aspects of Philippine-Japanese Relations, 1930–1940 (1967). Joseph R. Hayden, The Philippines: A Study in National Development (1942).

GRANT K. GOODMAN

PHILLIPINES INDEPENDENCE LAW. See Tydings-McDuffie Act.

PHNOM PENH, capital of Cambodia since 1866. It is the country's most important city and has a population of about four hundred thousand. Founded in the fifteenth century, following the abandonment of Angkor, Phnom Penh rapidly became a commercial center, acting as an entrepôt for goods coming south along the Mekong, southeast along the Tonle Sap, and northward from the Mekong Delta. In 1811, when the Vietnamese established hegemony over Cambodia, Phnom Penh was made the capital at the expense of Oudong, which became the capital again in 1848.

The major expansion of the city occurred during the French protectorate (1863–1954), when swamps were drained, the royal palace built, and tree-lined avenues, modeled on those of provincial France, were laid out. The city's population rose gradually in the colonial era, swelled by considerable numbers of immigrants from China and Vietnam. Cambodia's first high school was founded there in 1935. During the early years of independence, Phnom Penh's population continued to grow, reaching approximately five hundred thousand in 1970. During the Cambodian civil war of 1970–1975, approximately 2 million Cambodian refugees sought asylum in the city. The entire population was evacuated to the countryside and brutally mistreated by the victorious regime of Democratic Kampuchea (1975–1979). When this regime was overthrown, thousands of former residents flocked back into the city to find public services nonexistent and much of the city's infrastructure in ruins. Since 1980, services have been gradually restored, and the city has resumed its commercial importance and continues to

house government offices, embassies, and industrial enterprises. Phnom Penh also continues to serve as an important freshwater port. Its name ("Penh mountain") derives from a small hill at the northern edge of the city.

[See also Cambodia.]

DAVID P. CHANDLER

PHOT SARASIN (b. 1906), Thai political leader. Born in Bangkok, he is the son of Phraya Sarasin Saphamiphak, an expert on parasites and the first Thai to graduate from New York University Medical School. Phot was educated in both the United States and England and joined a law firm in Bangkok after graduation. He became good friends with Luang Phibunsongkhram, then prime minister, and was appointed senator in 1947. He became deputy minister of foreign affairs in Phibun's 1948 cabinet, and four years later he became Thailand's ambassador to the United States and the United Nations. Upon his return to Thailand, Phot assumed the position of secretary general of the Southeast Asia Treaty Organization (SEATO). Following the Sarit Thanarat coup of 1957, Phot was asked to form an interim government to supervise elections to be held within three months. From 1963–1972 Phot served as minister of development under Thanom Kittikachorn. [See also Phibunsongkhram, Luang; Sarit Thanarat; and Thanom Kittikachorn.]

THAK CHALOEMTIARANA

PHOUI SANANIKONE (1903–1983), Laotian politician. Born in Vientiane, Phoui Sananikone served as prime minister of Laos from 1950 to 1951 and from 1958 to 1959; he was foreign minister and held other ministerial portfolios during the 1950s and 1960s. He also served as president of the Chamber of Deputies from 1948 to 1950 and from 1960 to 1974 and was president of a conservative political group, Rassemblement du Peuple Lao, from 1962 to 1974.

When the Communists seized power in May 1975, Phoui fled to Thailand and subsequently emigrated to France. In September 1975, he was sentenced to death in absentia by the new government. In France, Phoui provided leadership for the formation of a Lao government in exile, announced in Perpignon on 14 October 1978, and he was its prime minister. Phoui died in Paris on 4 December 1983.

[See also Laos.]

JOSEPH J. ZASLOFF

PHOUMI NOSAVAN (b. 1920), Laotian politician. Phoumi was a leader of the Vichy French youth movement in Laos during World War II. At the end of the war he joined the Lao Issara and was a member of a guerrilla unit under the command of Prince Souphanouvong in central Laos, later switching to the French forces commanded by Prince Boun Oum. Phoumi advanced to become chief of staff of the Royal Armed Forces in 1955. He attended the French War College in Paris, from which he graduated with honors.

In 1958 Phoumi joined with other conservative military officers and politicians to form, with the support of the US Central Intelligence Agency, the Committee for the Defense of the National Interests (CDIN). In December 1959, General Phoumi and members of the CDIN seized power in Vientiane through a coup de'état. Following a neutralist-oriented coup led by Captain Kong Le in August 1960, Phoumi served as a deputy prime minsiter in a coalition government formed by Prime Minister Souvannaphouma. Several months after the formation of this government, Phoumi withdrew to Savannakhet where, with Prince Boun Oum, he formed a revolutionary committee that acquired US and Thai support and retook Vientiane, forcing Souvannaphouma into exile.

Following the Geneva Conference of 1962, which brought an accommodation to the factional conflict in Laos, Phoumi represented the rightist forces in the newly established tripartite government, serving as a deputy prime minister, with Prime Minister Souvannaphouma representing the neutralists and Deputy Prime Minister Souphanouvong representing the left. After this tripartite government effectively collapsed in 1964, Phoumi attempted another coup, in 1965, against the government of Souvannaphouma, who retained the support of the United States. With the coup's failure, Phoumi fled to Thailand.

Phoumi has lived in Thailand since 1965 and has been active in exile politics in opposition to the communist government of Laos since its seizure of power in 1975.

[See also Laos; Lao Issara; Souphanouvong; Boun Oum; Kong Le; and Souvannaphouma.]

JOSEPH J. ZASLOFF

PHRAKHLANG (or Barcalon), a ministry of civil government in premodern Thailand. The functions of the Phrakhlang were outlined in the laws of King Borommatrailokanat of Ayudhya in the mid-fif-

teenth century. The Phrakhlang served as the king's treasury, and because it also ran royal trading monopolies it was responsible for the kingdom's foreign relations.

The minister heading the Phrakhlang was also generally known by the title, and it was he with whom most foreign emissaries dealt until a separate Ministry of Foreign Affairs was created in 1885. King Chulalongkorn's government reorganization of 1888–1892 created a new Ministry of Finance.

[See also Ayudhya; Borommatrailokanat; and Chulalongkorn.]

H. G. Quaritch Wales, *Ancient Siamese Government and Adminsitration* (1934; reprint, 1965).

DAVID K. WYATT

PHRAKHLANG DIT BUNNAG (1788–1855), eldest son of Chaophraya Yommarat of Siam, appointed *phrakhlang*, in charge of trade and foreign affairs, in 1822. In 1830, he was also given the post of *kalahom*. These positions made him a highly powerful official, close to the king. As a military leader, he conducted campaigns against rebellious southern states in 1832 and against the Vietnamese in 1833–1834. As an active diplomat, present at all negotiations with foreign representatives between 1824 and 1855, he favored increasing contacts with the West and in the 1850s was the leader of the faction backing open relations with the West.

Walter F. Vella, *Siam under Rama III* (1957). David K. Wyatt, *Thailand: A Short History* (1984).

CONSTANCE M. WILSON

PHRA NANG KLAO, or Rama III (1776–1851), king of Siam (r. 1824–1851). The third monarch of the Chakri dynasty, Phra Nang Klao was the eldest son of King Rama II by a nonroyal wife. Under the title of Prince Chetsadabodin, he had gained considerable experience in state affairs. In a number of ways, his reign was a traditional one. An active supporter of Buddhism, he made many donations to the Buddhist monastic order and contributed to the construction and repair of Buddhist temples. He encouraged painting, sculpture, and the decorative arts but tended to neglect literature and the theater.

Interested in the expansion of Thai territory, he oversaw a large number of military campaigns. The rebellion of Chao Anu of Vientiane was put down in 1827–1828 and a number of Lao townships brought under Thai administration. In 1831–1832 and 1838–1839, two rebellions in the Malay south were crushed and Thai authority reasserted. Three campaigns directed against Vietnamese activities in Cambodia in 1833–1834, 1841–1842, and 1845–1847 restored partial Thai control over the region.

His reign was innovative in two ways. He promoted Chinese immigration, employing the Chinese as tax farmers and as paid labor. Trade with China became more important to the economy. Phra Nang Klao also accepted an increase in contacts with the Western world. The Catholic mission was revived in 1830, and permanent Protestant missions functioned after 1833. Diplomatic missions were received from Great Britain in 1825 and in 1850 and from the United States in 1833 and in 1850. A treaty with the British East India Company was signed in 1826 and a second with the United States in 1833. Despite an anti-Western reaction at the end of the reign, these early relations with the West helped to prepare the way for the establishment of full diplomatic and commercial relations during the fourth reign.

[See also Thailand and Chakri Dynasty.]

Walter F. Vella, *Siam under Rama III, 1824–1851* (1957).
                                        CONSTANCE M. WILSON

PHRA PATHOM CHEDI, major Buddhist monument and shrine at Nakhon Pathom, Thailand. The region to the west of Bangkok, near the mouth of the Khwae River, was the scene of commerce and Buddhism as early as the first centuries CE, as attested by finds of Roman and Mediterranean objects in the vicinity of Nakhon Pathom. Various towering reliquaries, reputed to enshrine relics of the Buddha, were constructed there, the most recent of which, the Phra Pathom Chedi, was reconstructed on the base of earlier ruins by Mongkut in the 1860s.

[See also Dvaravati and Thiphakorawong Kham Bunnag.]

Prince Dhani Nivat, *The Excursion to Nakhon Pathom* (1957). Piriya Krairiksh, *Buddhist Folk Tales Depicted at Chula Pathon Cedi* (1974).
                                        DAVID K. WYATT

PHRA PHUTTHALOETLA NAPHALAI, or Rama II (1768–1824), king of Siam (r. 1809–1824).

The eldest son of King Rama I, he received the title Prince Isarasunthon in 1785, becoming king in 1809. During his reign he continued to share his father's concerns with law and with religion, issuing new edicts and adding to the buildings in the temple compounds at Phra Phutthabat, Wat Arun, and Wat Suthat.

Rama II maintained diplomatic relations with China, Vietnam, Cambodia, and Burma, and he also accepted missions from Portugal and from John Crawfurd of the British East India Company. He was, in addition, a noted poet, author of *Inao,* and a contributor to the classical theater.

[See also Thailand and Crawfurd, John.]

B. J. Terwiel, *A History of Modern Thailand* (1983). David K. Wyatt, *Thailand: A Short History* (1984).
                                        CONSTANCE M. WILSON

PHRA PHUTTHAYOTFA CHULALOK, or Rama I (1737–1809), king of Siam (r. 1782–1809), the first king of the Chakri dynasty of Bangkok. Born to a well-connected Ayudhyan noble family, Thong Duang was recruited by his younger brother to the cause of Taksin during the anarchy following Ayudhya's destruction by the Burmese in 1767. Thong Duang and his brother served Taksin well, winning brilliant victories against the Burmese in northern Thailand and against the Lao states along the Mekong. By 1775 Thong Duang had become the *chakri,* chief minister and general over all the Siamese forces—hence the title by which his dynasty is known. When Taksin's behavior grew so aberrant that he alienated his support among the kingdom's elite, General Chakri—because of his outstanding leadership and because he held the goodwill of most of that elite (as well as having kin ties with a surprising number of important families)—was the obvious choice to succeed Taksin when the latter's removal was deemed imperative.

Rama I's reign is commonly seen as a period of reconstruction and restoration. One of Rama I's first acts as king was to begin building a new capital, Bangkok, across the Chaophraya River from Thonburi, Taksin's uncompleted capital. This signaled that the reign was to be a new start and not a continuation of Taksin's false start at reconstructing the Siamese kingdom after Ayudhya's fall. Rama I also hastened to reestablish the *sangha,* the Buddhist monastic order, badly demoralized by Taksin's demands, and he cultivated a good working relationship with the kingdom's elite, restoring their confidence in royal justice. Aware of his own origins in the class on whose support he depended, he never adopted a remote and inaccessible royal style, and, although he clearly ruled as well as reigned, he apparently allowed a good deal of open discussion at his court, his decisions tending to reflect a previously agreed upon consensus. He emphasized that all his decisions were taken with abstract Buddhist principles of justice in mind, implying in turn that all his acts were to be measured against such principles. His reign thus took on a self-consciously Buddhist cast in contract to the late Ayudhya period, when the kingdom's identification with Buddhism had the air of owing as much to ancient custom as to reasoned commitment.

During Rama I's reign the Burmese threat to Siam was broken, the last serious invasion being repelled in 1785; thereafter Rama I's generals went on the offensive. By the end of the reign Siam's empire included all of present-day Laos and Cambodia as well as territories that are now part of Burma, China, Vietnam, and Malaysia.

Trade, interrupted during the wars with Burma, revived with royal encouragement, especially the trade with China. The reign also saw an artistic and literary flowering, since an entire cultural heritage was lost in the sack of Ayudhya and needed to be replaced. Literary classics, histories, even Ayudhya's ancient law code were recomposed, not merely re-copied, so that they, like the murals on the walls of Bangkok's temples, became living reflections of the new kingdom they adorned. Rama I died in 1809 and was succeeded peacefully by his eldest son.

[See also Bangkok; Chakri Dynasty; and Taksin.]

Klaus Wente, *The Restoration of Thailand under Rama I* (1968). David K. Wyatt, "The 'Subtle Revolution' of Rama I," in *Moral Order and the Question of Change*, edited by A. B. Woodside and David K. Wyatt (1982), and *Thailand: A Short History* (1984).

LORRAINE M. GESICK

PHRA PIN KLAO, second king of Siam (1808–1866). The full brother of King Mongkut, Phra Pin Klao was known as Prince Chuthamani before he was crowned, at Mongkut's request, as second king in 1851. Phra Pin Klao was noted for his interest in martial affairs, science, and sports. As a prince he studied English with the American missionaries and from them acquired a knowledge of modern science and mechanics. Reputedly the most westernized of the Thai elite, he had close relations with the foreign community in Bangkok. As second king he participated in diplomatic affairs and served as head of the European-trained artillery and naval forces.

[See also Mongkut.]

William L. Cowan, "The Role of Prince Chuthamani in the Modernization of Siam," *Journal of the Siam Society* 55. 1 (January 1967): 41–59.

CONSTANCE M. WILSON

PHRA WIHAN. *See* Preah Vihear.

PHULE, JOTIRAO GOVINDRAO (1827–1890), Indian social revolutionary. From a Mali (gardener caste) family, Phule studied at the Poona (Pune) Scottish Mission School until 1847. He taught there part-time from 1854 and became a government contractor in 1868.

A theist influenced by Paine's *Rights of Man*, he attacked caste inequality and brahman supremacy, asserted women's rights, and urged free, compulsory primary education. In Pune, despite orthodox opposition, he started the first schools and library for low-caste women and men (1848–1852) and opened a night school for adults (1855) and a shelter for orphans and widows (1860). He founded the Satyashodak Samaj ("truth-seeking society") to promote lower caste and Untouchable rights (1873). A member of the Poona Municipality (1876–1882), he gave evidence to the Education Commission (1882), and in late life worked among Bombay mill-hands. An 1888 public meeting awarded him the title Mahatma. His Marathi books included *Slavery, Priestcraft Exposed*, and *Life of Shivaji*.

[See also Untouchability.]

D. Keer, *Mahatma Jotirao Phooley* (1964). G. Omvedt, *Cultural Revolt in a Colonial Society* (1976).

JIM MASSELOS

PHU XUAN. *See* Hue.

PIGNEAU DE BÉHAINE, PIERRE (1741–1799), bishop of Adran, French missionary, and adviser to Prince Nguyen Anh. Responsible for Christian communities in the Ha Tien area of Vietnam, the bishop came in contact with Nguyen Anh after the outbreak of the Tay Son rebellion. In 1784 he was entrusted with the royal seal and the young Prince Canh. After months of unsuccessful attempts to obtain French support for the Nguyen cause, he returned to France and negotiated the 1787 Treaty of Versailles. When France failed to carry out the agreement, however, he returned to Vietnam with arms and a small contigent of troops. He served as Nguyen Anh's adviser until his death in 1799.

[*See also* Gia Long *and* Versailles Treaty of 1787.]

Nguyen Phut Tan, *Modern History of Vietnam (1802–1954)* (1964).   BRUCE M. LOCKHART

PILAR, MARCELO H. DEL (1850–1896), shares with Jose Rizal the role of preparing the ground for the Philippine Revolution against Spain. While del Pilar was still a law student, his brother Toribio, a priest, was exiled to Guam for his participation in the Cavite Mutiny. As a lawyer del Pilar held minor bureaucratic posts and made contacts with anticlerical Spanish bureaucrats, who helped him in his efforts to end the influence of friars in Filipino affairs, secular or religious. Dedicated to the same end on a national level, del Pilar left for Spain in 1888. Here he was commissioned to organize a newspaper representing Filipino interests and to negotiate with liberal Spanish politicians to legislate reforms in the Philippines that would destroy the theocracy.

Del Pilar arrived in Barcelona just as the Filipino expatriates were about to found a newspaper, *La Solidaridad,* of which he gradually obtained actual control, as he did of Revolución, the Filipino colony's Masonic lodge. In October 1889 he transferred the newspaper to Madrid, converted the city's defunct Masonic lodge Solidaridad into a Filipino lodge, and founded the Asociación Hispano-Filipina as a joint Spanish-Filipino lobby for reforms. The *asociación* was able to use Spanish masonry to gain thousands of signatures and to summon Spanish politicians as advocates for reforms in the Philippines, in particular for Filipino representation in the Cortes, the first step in del Pilar's plan. At the same time, del Pilar stirred activity in the Philippines through antifriar pamphlets and *La Solidaridad,* which was smuggled into the country. The influential Filipino leader Jose Rizal, however, believed that Spanish politicians could not be depended on and that the struggle had to be carried out in the Philippines. With the break between the two leaders in 1891, del Pilar's organization weakened, and by 1895 it had collapsed because of a lack of funds. In 1896, while awaiting money for his return to the Philippines, del Pilar died of tuberculosis, just weeks before the revolution was begun by the separatist secret society the Katipunan.

[*See also* Philippine Revolution; Propaganda Movement; Friars; *and* Rizal, Jose Mercado.]

Marcelo H. del Pilar, *Monastic Supremacy in the Philippines,* translated by Encarnacion Alzona (1958). John N. Schumacher, *The Propaganda Movement* (1973).

JOHN N. SCHUMACHER, S.J.

PILGRIMAGE. Pilgrimage can be defined as a religious journey, long or short in duration, to a particular site, or set of sites, that is invested with sanctity by a particular religious tradition. Pilgrimage has been a major historical force in the integration of Asia's complex religious civilizations. In recent years, there has been a resurgence of interest in this phenomenon in both the human and social sciences. This has resulted in novel translations and interpretations of pilgrimage texts informed by current trends in semiotics and the study of comparative symbolism. Social scientists have concentrated on the integrative consequences of pilgrimage. These integrative effects are of three types: individual or psychological; cultural, in the sense that pilgrimages relate basic cosmological assumptions to culturally defined notions of social and historical identity; and sociological, in that spatial patterns of pilgrimage bear historical relation to the organization of economic and political regions. Viewed from the perspective of religious experience, Victor Turner notes that pilgrimage creates for participants a sense of "communitas," a feeling of community and fellowship brought about by an awareness of a temporary release from the structured ties of normal social order. Turner also likens pilgrimage to a form of "exteriorized mysticism" paralleling metaphorically the mystic's interior pilgrimage. Stein (1978) and others, more interested in the cultural and sociological effects of pilgrimage, have tried to develop a conceptual framework for elucidating the connection between pilgrimage as a cultural performance and pilgrimage as a pattern of human interaction with important economic and political effects. In this view, pilgrimage contributed greatly to indigenous conceptions of the "cultural region" as it developed in different parts of Asia.

Muslim Pilgrimage. For Muslims of the Sunni and Shi'a sects pilgrimage takes two forms: (1) the *hajj,* the pilgrimage to Mecca in Saudi Arabia, and (2) *ziyarah,* visitation to holy places, including those, such as Medina, associated with the Prophet Muhammad or his family and companions, as well as the tombs of imams, *pirs,* and other personages worshiped throughout the Muslim world. As one of the "five pillars of Islam" set out in the Qur'an, the *hajj* is central in the set of codified rituals that mark initiation and identification in the Islamic faith. *Hajj* is prescribed for all adult Muslims who are healthy in body and financially capable of making the journey at least once in a lifetime. Believed to have been established in Ibrahim's time, *hajj* is an important expression of social and religious unity in Islamic culture. A history of pilgrims' efforts to reach Mecca would make an interesting chapter in the history of travel and transportation. For instance, the opening of sea travel in the nineteenth century broke down the isolation of Indonesian Muslims from the sources of their tradition in the Middle East. Pilgrims who returned to Java and established Qur'anic schools there are credited with strengthening orthodox Islam in that country.

The pilgrimage takes place on three days beginning on the eighth day of Dhu al-Hijjah, the twelfth month of the Muslim lunar year. *Hajj* proper consists of visiting the following sites in sequence: a preliminary circumambulation of the Ka'bah stone in the Great Mosque at Mecca, known as the *'umrah,* or the "lesser pilgrimage"; standing at Mount Arafat; "hurrying" to Muzdalifah; and performing several rituals at Mina, such as throwing seven stones at the pillar of Aqaba and sacrificing a lamb or goat and eating it afterwards in the feast known as Id al-Adha. Before starting the pilgrimage, adepts enter a state of purity known as *ihram,* wherein they wear special clothes, shave, and refrain from defiling behavior. After the sacrifice and feast at Mina, pilgrims enter a phase of deconsecration that is complete after they make a final circumambulation of the Ka'bah.

Seen against the uniformity of the *hajj,* the varying nature of visits to the tombs of saints underscores the diversity of Islam's many cultural settings and the history of schisms within the faith. After Mecca, many pilgrims visit the Prophet's tomb in Medina. For Shi'ism, the state religion of Iran since Safavid times, pilgrimage to Ali's tomb in Karbala and to Imam Rida's tomb in Mashhad in western Iran rivals the *hajj* in importance. This is attributable to the veneration given the imam as a figure of spiritual authority in the Shi'a tradition. Shi'ites trace Muhammad's succession from Ali, his cousin and son-in-law, who, in their reckoning, was the legitimate caliph and the first imam.

Within the larger Sunni sect, the practice of worship at the tomb of *pirs,* or saints, was widely dispersed by the various Sufi orders that radiated out of Central Asia beginning in the twelfth century. In the Sufi view, saints have the power to answer pilgrims' needs because they share in Allah's miraculous gifts and grace. *Pirs* are not conceived of as dying; rather, their souls are believed to linger on at a shrine, protecting all who seek their help and answering their wishes. Worship practices at saint's tombs *(dargah)* are fairly uniform throughout this region. Pilgrims flock to the tomb on the anniversary of the saint's death *(urs).* They consult attendants at the shrine and purchase amulets from them. They leave memories of their requests to the saint in the form of bits of cloth tied to the tomb, or small clay replicas of objects desired, such as cattle or a child's bed, left as honor offerings in the tomb. In any one area, the relative importance of tombs rests more on the efficacy of the saint's magic than on his importance in his own lifetime. When vows are granted, pilgrims return to the shrine to reward the saint's descendants with cash and other gifts. The best known tombs in Afghanistan are those of the Timurid saint Khwaja Abdullah Ansari Herawi, near Herat, and Hazrat Ali's tomb at Mazar-i-Sharif; in Swat, Pakhtun tribesman visit tombs of Pir Baba and Saidu Baba, among others.

The *pir* tradition is very strong in North India, where Sufi orders set up a network of hospices in the twelfth century. Of particular importance today are two tombs: that at Ajmer of the Chishti saint Muin ud-Din, the founder during Ghurid times of the Chishtiyya order in India, and that of his successor Nizam ud-Din Auliya in south Delhi. Chishti tombs are also found in Punjab and Sindh in North India and in Karnataka state in the South. [*See also* Chishti Tariqa *and* Nizam ud-Din Auliya.]

As a form of pilgrimage, saint worship was more adaptable to syncretic religious practices than was the more doctrinal *hajj.* Saint worship in India coincided with the development of other devotional forms of religion, such as those associated with Kabir and Guru Nanak, saints whose followers were drawn from diverse religious backgrounds.

Buddhist Pilgrimage in South and Southeast Asia. Visits to places associated with events in the Buddha's life and to shrines housing his relics are meritorious acts and an important step to the realization of the Buddha nature within oneself. In the Pali text that describes the Buddha's *parinibbana* ("final cessation"), the Buddha himself recommends pilgrimage to four places in India: the place where he was born, where he gained Enlightenment, where he preached his first sermon, and where he drew his final breath. From epigraphal evidence, Emperor Ashoka (270–232 BCE) is known to have made pilgrimage to Bodh Gaya, the second of the four sites mentioned above. Ashoka is credited in ancient

Buddhist legend with dividing the Buddha's relics after his death and distributing them throughout South and Southeast Asia. The original ten stupas (reliquary mounds) were opened in Ashoka's time and the relics divided in eighty-four thousand parts. These relics became the focus of pilgrimage throughout the Buddhist world.

Relics are of three types: bodily relics; objects that the Buddha used in his lifetime, such as his alms bowl or the Bo tree; and traces of his shadow or footprints, as well as representations of him in votive images, stupas, and other Buddhist monuments. The most complete records of early Buddhist pilgrimage are those of Faxian and Xuanzang, Chinese pilgrims who visited this region during Gupta times, in the fifth and seventh centuries, respectively. These provide vivid descriptions of social and cultural aspects of India, Sri Lanka, and Java during this period. [*See also* Faxian *and* Xuanzang.]

Cultic representations of the Buddha also became powerful symbols of legitimation for Buddhist kings. Buddhists make a distinction between the Buddha's "*dharma* body," which was traditionally linked to the scriptures and the community (*sangha*) of monks who recited and preserved the scriptures, and the Buddha's relics, or "*rupa* body," which have political importance because of their association with kings who have constructed architectural representations of the Buddha's body and venerated them. The Pali text *Mahavamsa* mentions sixteen places said to have been visited by the Buddha in Sri Lanka; more than half of these can be linked to the ancient kingdom of Anuradhapura. The increased importance of pilgrimage to the Temple of the Tooth (Dalada Maligava), not one of the original sixteen, is linked to the rise of the Kandyan kingdom in the fifteenth century. In Thai and Laotian kingship, the Holy Emerald Jewel, an image of the Buddha, has played a similar role. [*See also* Emerald Buddha.] The spatial layout of pilgrimage sites, such as with those associated with the twelve-year cycle in northern Thailand, could serve to reconcile the realities of a fragmented political topography with successively larger religious communities, in this case uniting the individual pilgrim with other Buddhists in northern Thailand, with Burmese and Lao Buddhists, and even, symbolically, with the Buddha heaven itself. The symbolism of large stupa complexes such as Borobudur or Angkor Wat serves a similar purpose of linking political and moral communities in the world to Buddhist cosmological principles. [*See also* Borobudur *and* Angkor Wat.]

For centuries, Buddhist pilgrimage was confined to lands outside of India, but with the advent of international travel and the Buddhist revival movement in the nineteenth century Buddhist pilgrims returned to the Indian sites. Buddhists from all over the world can be seen today at Bodh Gaya, Sarnath, or Sanchi.

Buddhist Pilgrimage in East Asia and Tibet. The best known pilgrimage sites on mainland China are the "five peaks," thought to be significant for the protection of the entire country. The "five peaks" are Mount Tai, a Daoist site, and four Buddhist sites, each associated with a particular bodhisattva who is thought to appear to pilgrims in human form. The latter four are Emei in Sichuan Province, presided over by the bodhisattva Samantabhadra; Wutai in Shanxi, presided over by Manjusri; Putuo in Zhejiang, presided over by Avalokiteshvara; and Jiuhua in Anhui, presided over by Ksitigarbha. A visit to Mount Tai was incumbent on all newly invested emperors in ancient China; in Buddhist times, the mountain became associated with the world of the dead and with a cult of the goddess of childbirth. Tibetan Buddhism was introduced at Mount Wutai by Mongol rulers during the Yuan dynasty (1272–1368). This site remained popular with Mongolian pilgrims throughout later Chinese history. These mountain sites were located in remote regions of China and attracted monks and lay pilgrims alike. Wandering monks hoped to visit all four mountains and to engage in meditation and to study Buddhist scripture under authorities resident at each site. Lay pilgrimage, referred to as "journeying to a mountain and offering incense," attracted bands of banner-waving pilgrims who made these arduous journeys on the feast days of the mountains' presiding deities. They returned home with vows fulfilled, wishes granted, and their pilgrims' satchels stamped with insignia of the various places visited.

Pilgrimage places with the broadest appeal to all classes of Japanese society have been the Shinto shrines at Ise and Kumano, and the larger Buddhist circuits of the thirty-three stations of Saikoku, dedicated to Kannon (Avalokiteshvara), and the eighty-eight stations on Shikoku. As early as the Heian period (794–1185), members of the imperial family, other aristocrats, and Buddhist monks made pilgrimages to mountain shrines, such as Kumano in the southern part of Wakayama Prefecture. Popular or mass pilgrimage, as we know it today, reached its height in the Tokugawa period (1610–1868) with the Saikoku and Shikoku pilgrimages. In these pilgrimages, temples and shrines were visited in fixed order, the sites often spread out over wide distances.

Origin myths associated with these pilgrimage circuits trace them to the early visits of monks and emperors. [*See also* Ise Mairi.]

Pilgrimage guidebooks produced in large numbers during the Tokugawa and later periods are a valuable source on Japanese pilgrimage. Guidebooks are divided into two parts, a fixed itinerary and, as an addendum, a list of places to visit while on pilgrimage, bits of local history and folklore, and even mention of the diverse entertainments to be had at places along the way of the amusement-seeking pilgrim. The itineraries give the prescribed order of pilgrimage—sites to be visited, legends describing their religious importance, song texts, directions for erecting placards, and details of other performances appropriate to the site. Foard (1982) notes that while itineraries remain fairly fixed over time, the addenda change in a way that reflects changing perceptions of what it meant to be Japanese.

Tibetan pilgrimage traditionally involves visits to major temples in Lhasa and to outlying monasteries famous as the original seats of lamas who founded sects within Tibetan Buddhism. Tibetans also visit natural sites, such as Mount Kailasa, which is surrounded by three concentric routes. In accordance with the meditative focus of this tradition, Tibetans espouse belief in millenarian pilgrimages to "hidden countries" concealed by Padmasambhava, places of refuge and meditation. Yogis and others adept in meditation are believed capable of reaching the mythical paradise of Shambhala.

Hindu Pilgrimage. *Tirtha-yatra* (literally, "journey to the sacred ford"), the Sanskrit term for pilgrimage, implies that pilgrimage involves a sacralized intersection of some sort. The term *tirtha* is also applied to holy persons, giving it a wide semantic range that rests on the metaphor of passing over to the sacred in some way through various ritual and meditational means. The earliest toponymy of sacred places appears in the *Mahabharata* epic (c. 300 BCE). The later Puranas, composed between 300 and 1200, give detailed descriptions of pilgrimage places, the deities enshrined at each, the praises due them, and the fruits *(phala)* that accrue to those who visit a site. Classical texts are still invoked by ritual specialists at these places, and, in many senses, these texts can be seen as validating charters for current pilgrimage practices.

There have been numerous attempts to classify Hindu pilgrimage places. A common distinction is made between water-associated sites and temple sites; the former are marked by bathing rituals and propitiation of ancestors, the latter by temple rites, such as dressing the temple image and offering it food and other items. Perhaps the most useful classification is that between North and South Indian pilgrimage, wherein the North is characterized by defining sacred space in horizontal terms and imbuing natural objects and places with sacredness, the South by a more temple-focused tradition of pilgrimage. Pilgrimage in the North more frequently involves traversing a sacred circuit, or *kshetra*. The largest of these *kshetra* are the six-hundred-mile concourse in the Himalayas above Rishikesh and the circuit that covers the entire length of the Ganges. South Indian pilgrimage is generally oriented to a single temple, as at Tirupati, or to a cluster of temples, such as the five *bhutalingas* sacred to Shiva, the six centers of Murukan, or the six centers of Ayyapan.

A major focus of research has been the organization of Hindu sites into a hierarchy of nested catchment areas. Seen in these terms, Hindu pilgrimage is a massive circulation system that can be viewed from several hierarchical levels. At the highest level are found places of civilization-wide importance. Termed "transsectarian," these sites attract pilgrims from all over the subcontinent and are instrumental in affirming pan-Indian values in the face of the country's overwhelming linguistic and cultural diversity. Sites at this level include the sacred rivers, the "four abodes of Vishnu" *(chardhama)* located at the four quarters of India, and the "seven holy cities" *(saptamahatirtha)*. Prayag, Nasik, and Hardwar, associated with the massive Kumbh Mela, the bathing festival held every twelve years, also fall into this group.

Beneath this comes sites of regional and sectarian importance. Into this group fall Somnath, Kedarnath, and Amarnath, of interest to worshipers of Shiva; Tirupati, Srirangam, and Udipi in the South, Pandharpur in Maharashtra, and Vrindavana and Ayodhya in Uttar Pradesh, all of which follow the *pancharatra* system of ritual favored by Vaishnavas; and many of the Devi shrines, known as *shaktapithas*. Goddesses asssume great importance at the regional and local levels. The best known goddess shrines (there are 106 of them mentioned in Tantric textual sources) are those of Kali in Calcutta, Kamakhya in Assam, Minakshi in Tamil Nadu, and Jvalamukhi in Himachal Pradesh.

Local sites, most expressive of the diversity in Hindu belief systems and ritual practice, come lowest in the hierarchy of sites. Pilgrims' relations to deities at this level are highly personal and their goals take the form of particularistic appeals to deities for help with personal or material problems. Bhardwaj (1973) relates local pilgrimage in Himachal Pradesh to other, more inclusive nodes in the Hindu pilgrmage system in this region. He concludes that nodes at various levels of the circulation system enable us to grasp both common and diverse features of Hinduism.

A point that emerges in many recent studies of Hindu pilgrimage (Morinis, 1984) is that the diversity of regional practices is limited by structural paradigms of meaning and action that are common throughout India. Seen in relation to these structural paradigms, regional traditions can be seen as structural microcosms of the pan-Indian system. In this bipolar view, structural paradigms, much like Dumont's purity/pollution dichotomy, enable regional pilgrimage traditions to differ from one another to some extent while, at the same time, preserving features of the greater Hindu system.

Samuel Beal, trans., *Si Yu Ki: The Buddhist Records of the Western World* (1884; reprint 1969). Surinder Mohan Bhardwaj, *Hindu Places of Pilgrimage in India* (1973). James Foard, "The Boundaries of Compassion: Buddhism and National Tradition in Japanese Pilgrimage," *Journal of Asian Studies* 41 (1982): 231–251. G. von Grunebaum, *Muhammadan Festivals* (1976). E. Alan Morinis, *Pilgrimage in the Hindu Tradition* (1984). Bardwell Smith, ed., *Religion and the Legitimation of Power in Thailand, Laos, and Burma* (1973). Burton Stein, ed., *South Indian Temples: An Analytical Reconstruction* (1978).
PAUL M. TOOMEY

PILIMA TALAUVE (d. 1811), first *mahadigar*, or chief minister, of Kandy. Leader of the Sinhalese aristocratic faction in the court and a master politician, Talauve was a major factor in the politics of the Kandyan kingdom in its last phase. His greatest success was the placement of his protégé on the Kandyan throne in 1798. The independence of the new king led Talauve to plot the downfall of Sri Vikrama Rajasimha and the replacement of the Nayakkars, who originated from South India, with a Sinhalese dynasty. His intrigues, including those with the British, eventually moved the king to strip him of his offices in 1810. Talauve unsuccessfully rebelled and was executed.

[*See also* Kandy *and* Sri Lanka.]

VIJAYA SAMARAWEERA

PILLAI, ANANDA RANGA, an eighteenth-century agent of the French governor of Pondicherry, who kept a personal diary that has been trans-

lated from Tamil into English and French. Its multifaceted commentary provides information on everything from everyday life to social, commercial, political, and historical matters during the critical period of transition (1736–1761) to British rule in South India.

[*See also* French East India Company.]

J. F. Price and K. Rangachari, eds. and trans., *The Private Diary of Anadaranga Pillai* (1904–1908).
CAROL APPADURAI BRECKENRIDGE

PINANG. *See* Penang.

PINDARIS (lit., "plunderers"), independent bands of freebooters who traveled throughout Central India in groups of several thousand mounted warriors. At the time of the breakup of the Mughal empire it appeared as if the Marathas might be the likely successors to their power. Constant competitive raiding drained much of the wealth of the Marathas, however, and as the Maratha chiefs failed to pay their troops, their armies began to dissolve. Pindaris came from all regional, ethnic, and religious groups. Constantly in motion, they were able to attack, disperse if challenged, and regroup. The British made several attempts to disperse them, but did not finally succeed until 1818.

[*See also* Marathas.]

Vincent A. Smith, et al., *The Oxford History of India* (1919; 4th ed., 1981).
GREGORY C. KOZLOWSKI

PINYIN, or *Hanyu pinyin* (lit., "Chinese spelling"), is the sole official system of romanization presently employed in the People's Republic of China. It was formally endorsed by the State Council on 1 November 1957 and subsequently approved for official use by the National People's Congress on 11 February 1958. In China it is used in schools for the teaching of correct pronunciation and in the promotion of the standard language, *putonghua*. In 1979 *pinyin* was made official in China's dealings with foreign countries; in that year all foreign-language publications originating in China, including dispatches from the New China News Agency, began to use *pinyin*. In recent years *pinyin* has also increasingly come to replace the Wade-Giles system in scholarly publications concerned with China in the English-speaking world.

[*See also* Wade-Giles Romanization.]

JERRY NORMAN

PIRACY

JAPANESE PIRACY IN KOREA

Although marauders from Japan (Japanese, *wakō;* Korean, *waegu;* Chinese, *wokou*) had plagued the Korean coastline from early times, they became particularly burdensome in the fourteenth and early fifteenth centuries. Their effect was felt throughout the country and especially along the southeastern coastal areas closest to Japan. Pirate raids became so serious in the late fourteenth century that peasants withdrew inland, causing much fertile land to lie fallow. The raids also threatened Korean coastal shipping and particularly shipments of grain tax revenues to the capital, endangering the kingdom's economy. An attack against Kanghwa Island, fewer than twenty miles from Koryŏ's capital, Kaesŏng, threw the court into panic. Pirate raids from Japan also bothered China, especially along the coast north of the Yangtze River.

The pirates traveled in groups, sometime numbering only one or two vessels. On other occasions there were raids by as many as five hundred ships in varying sizes. Not all marauders were Japanese. The *Koryŏsa*, a Korean dynastic record, indicates that impoverished Korean peasants would disguise themselves as bandits from Japan to plunder at will. Chinese thieves undoubtedly tried the same tactic. Nevertheless, the bulk of the raiders came from Japan.

The causes of the incursions were many. The first record of the marauders in the Koryŏ period occurred in King Kojong's reign (1213–1259), in the middle of the Mongol invasions. The Mongol invasions weakened Koryŏ's coastal defenses, enabling bandits to run unchecked. Pirates, taking advantage of Koryŏ's administrative and military collapse, attacked the coast with ease. When the Mongols took their war to Japan, they spread disaster further, and even though their invasions of Japan failed, they weakened Japan's central authority, enabling banditry to grow in outlying districts. [*See* Mongol Empire.] With the Mongol attacks over, Koryŏ power waned, and in the final years of the dynasty, and especially in King U's reign (1374–1388), piracy peaked with 378 incidents in a fourteen-year period. Koryŏ's collapse was one cause of the piracy, and the problem was not resolved until Korea's new Yi (Chosŏn) dynasty established its authority.

Conditions in Japan also contributed to the piracy. In addition to problems resulting from the Mongol invasions, Japan in the fourteenth century experienced a number of wars; as Ashikaga replaced Kamakura, central control declined. Offshore islands and areas along the southwestern coast were notoriously disorderly. Tsushima in particular became a center of piracy. As in Europe, trade and piracy were related. When blocked in their peaceful pursuit of trade, some Japanese, desperate for Korean goods, turned to plunder.

The Koreans responded to the piracy through a variety of techniques. At first they sent written protests to the Japanese leaders, demanding a halt to the raids. They also fortified their defenses; several Korean generals gained renown for their attacks against these marauders. Yi Sŏng-gye, who in 1392 established the Yi dynasty, was one such general. Koreans also attempted to refine their technology to produce better weapons modeled on those used by the Chinese. Establishing the Superintendency for Gunpowder Weapons, they perfected the use of cannons. They also built improved ships. In 1419 King Sejong (r. 1418–1450) equipped and sent an expedition to Tsushima that successfully eradicated the pirates there. The Korean leadership also tried to enlist support from the Ashikaga shoguns and powerful regional families such as the Ouchi to help check piracy by agreeing to allow more formal trade between Korea and Japan. As the central Korean authority became stronger and other avenues for commerce increased, piracy slackened.

M. S. Seoh, "A Brief Documentary Survey of Japanese Pirate Activities in Korea in the 13th–15th Centuries," *Journal of Korean Studies* 1 (1969): 23–39.

EDWARD J. SHULTZ

JAPANESE PIRACY IN CHINA

Piracy by various East and Southeast Asian peoples seems to have existed to some degree in East Asian waters throughout history, but it was not until the latter half of the fourteenth century that plundering by fierce Japanese seafaring adventurers became a major problem along the coasts of China and Korea. The Chinese called these pirates *wokou;* the element *wo* has the perjorative connotation "dwarf" and had been used since Han times to refer to the people inhabiting the Japanese islands. The *wokou* were no doubt encouraged by the decline of Mongol domination on the continent and the political turbulence preceding the creation of new dynasties in both countries. This initial phase of *wokou* disturbances was soon largely quelled by new Chinese measures implemented by the Ming dynasty founder: a strong coastal defense system, a policy of strict controls limiting maritime trade and foreign contact, and diplomatic initiatives designed to prod the Japanese ruler (shogun) into halting his countrymen's marauding. The establishment of a regular tributary relationship with Japan by the third Ming emperor in the early fifteenth century also proved effective in channeling Japanese desires for commerce (one of the root causes of piracy) into a more peaceful mode.

In the early sixteenth century Japanese demands for more trade than the restrictive tributary system allowed led to the flourishing of coastal smuggling involving the collusion of Chinese from all levels of society. This clandestine trade led to outbreaks of violence and a renewal of piracy. A vigorous effort by Ming authorities to suppress Chinese participation in smuggling in the 1540s was thwarted by local opposition and only drove more Chinese into the ranks of the pirates. Furthermore, the abandonment of the suppression campaign coincided with the collapse of Japanese tributary relations and the decline of central power in Japan. With the ranks of the pirates now inflated, a renewed phase of violent *wokou* invasions began in the 1550s, lasting more than a decade and proving nearly unstoppable. This time, however, the so-called *wokou* were mainly Chinese and Chinese-led, although they often acted in league with Japanese and used Japanese islands as bases.

During these years the Chinese coast from Jiangsu to Guangdong suffered repeated invasions and plundering. The resulting devastation and loss of life were factors contributing to Ming decline. Indecisive and ill-managed military campaigns indicated deterioration of central leadership; defense expenditures depleted financial resources; and the devastation of the coast destabilized the region's society and economy and eroded public confidence in the regime.

[*See also* Ming Dynasty.]

Charles O. Hucker, "Hu Tsung-hsien's Campaign Against Hsü Hai, 1556," in *Chinese Ways in Warfare*, edited by Frank A. Kierman, Jr., and John K. Fairbank (1974). Y. S. Kuno, *Japanese Expansion on the Asiatic Continent*, 2 vols. (1940–1967). Kwan-wai So, *Japanese Piracy in Ming China during the 16th Century* (1975).

ROLAND L. HIGGINS

PIRACY IN THE MALAY WORLD

The term *piracy* is essentially a European one and appears in the Malay literature only in the second half of the eighteenth century. The term had the effect of criminalizing activities that the indigenous populations had hitherto considered political or commercial in nature. The indigenous maritime po-

litical systems of the Malay world were largely financed by commercial monopolies and by large cosmopolitan entrepôts that drew foreign traders. Raiding, or *merompak,* was a major feature of Malay political activity. It was a principal mechanism of commercial competition, political warfare, and tax collection. It was also the means by which young chiefs proved themselves.

If a warrior chief could unify a large group of sea peoples and set up an entrepôt at some strategic location in a major strait (e.g., Melaka, Johor, Riau, Sulu, etc.), then neighboring states would be subdued and international commerce would be channeled into the entrepôt. Exchange, while usually secure, was conducted under the supervision of the ruler. Slave raiding also formed an important part of the system.

After 1800, as English and Dutch colonial empires began to expand in the Malay world, indigenous political and commercial practices were seen to conflict both with liberal principles such as free trade and antislavery as well as with imperial aspirations. The foundation of an English base at Singapore in 1819 as a free port effectively destroyed the old Johor sultanate, cutting off the Johor chiefs and their followers from a share in the revenues of the increased trade. The decay of the Malay political system, together with the increased trade, may have actually increased the level of raiding and other maritime violence.

By 1837, the Singapore government began conducting its own raids against Malay villages with "piratical" reputations. Within a few years steamships arrived, and English naval vessels such as the *Dido* under Sir Henry Keppel and independent adventurers such as James Brooke began sweeping the Riau Archipelago and the Borneo coast in a campaign that eliminated many of the sea peoples and native traders. The increasing dominance of square-rigged trading vessels owned by Europeans and Chinese also contributed to the elimination of the maritime way of life.

[*See also* Johor; Singapore; Lingga; Riau; *and* Orang Laut.]

Nicholas Tarling, *Piracy and Politics in the Malay World: A Study of British Imperialism in Nineteenth Century Southeast Asia* (1963). Carl A. Trocki, *Prince of Pirates: The Temenggongs and the Development of Johor and Singapore 1784–1885* (1979).   CARL A. TROCKI

PIRES, TOMÉ (1468–c. 1539) was a Lisbon apothecary who resided in Melaka (Malacca) from 1512–1515, immediately after its conquest by the

Portuguese in 1511. His book *Suma Oriental,* which was rediscovered in 1937, is perhaps the most complete account of Southeast Asia produced during the first half of the sixteenth century. Pires personally visited India and Java and may have traveled to Vietnam, Siam, and Cambodia. While he was working for the Portuguese government at Melaka, he avidly collected disparate information from traders concerning the entire Southeast Asian realm. The *Suma Oriental* is not accurate in every detail, but most of what Pires wrote is consistent with other fragments of evidence from this period and facilitates the historian's use of these other sources. After the *Suma* was completed, and in recognition of his accomplishments as a factor, writer, and drug merchant, Pires was appointed the first Portuguese ambassador to China in 1516.

Armando Cortesão, trans. and ed., *The Suma Oriental of Tomé Pires* (1944).   KENNETH R. HALL

PITT, THOMAS,

PITT, THOMAS, governor of Madras (Fort Saint George) from 1698 to 1709. An outstanding merchant governor of the East India Company, Pitt's dual purpose was to advance mercantile trade and to accumulate a private fortune. Under his tenure cotton fabrics from the Coromandel—calico, chintz, muslin, dungaree, and so forth—came into common use in Europe. Following his purchase of the Golconda diamond, which weighed 410 carats (136 after cutting), the hitherto-derided "Pirate Pitt" (designating "a desperate fellow . . . [who would] not stick at doing any mischief") became better known as "Diamond" Pitt. Until he managed to sell it to the regent of France for 135,000 pounds, he feared for his very life. His fortune enabled the rise of the earls of Chatham: William Pitt, "The Great Commoner," and the "Younger" William Pitt, who faced Napoleon, were among his descendants.

C. Lawson, *Memories of Madras* (1905). J. Talboys Wheeler, *Madras in Olden Time* (1861), vol. 1, pp. 335–406; vol. 2, pp. 1–107.   ROBERT E. FRYKENBERG

PLASSEY, BATTLE OF,

PLASSEY, BATTLE OF, fought in Bengal between the army of Nawab Siraj ud-Daulah and the forces of the (British) East India Company on 23 June 1757. The battle was the climax of a carefully manipulated conspiracy to oust Siraj in favor of a nawab more amenable to British interests and more acceptable to some of the courtiers and merchants of Bengal. In the battlefield the nawab's army made an impressive and colorful appearance in the late Mughal procession style of warfare. It numbered nearly fifty thousand men with fifty-three pieces of artillery, mainly of heavy caliber. Robert Clive's army consisted of three thousand men—mostly sepoys—with eight cannons; eighteen were killed and fifty six wounded. Five hundred on the nawab's side perished. Siraj was later hacked to death by the son of his leading commander, Mir Ja'far. Mir Ja'far was proclaimed nawab as the protégé of the East India Company, which became the virtual master of Bengal.

[*See also* Mir Ja'far *and* Sepoy.]

Holden Furber and Kristof Glamann, "Plassey: A New Account from the Danish Archives," *Journal of Asian Studies* (1960). S. C. Hill, *Bengal in 1756–57* (1905).

PRADIP SINHA

PO CHÜ-I. *See* Bai Juyi.

POLIGAR. In the seventeenth century *poligars* (Tamil, *palaiyakkarar*) were small-scale kings situated largely in the semiarid central spine of South India. Often migrants from language regions other than the one in which they became kings, and almost always rooted in social systems that were based more on clan than on caste, these leaders were the staunchest exemplars of a ritual-based Hindu kingship in late pre-British South India. In military encounters with British-led eighteenth-century militias, one entire generation of *poligar* leadership was liquidated before those who remained were transformed (from the British point of view) into landholding *zamindars.*

[*See also* Land Tenure and Reform: Land Tenure, Revenue, and Reform in South Asia.]

K. Rajayyan, *The Rise and Fall of the Polygars of Tamil Nadu.* (1974).   CAROL APPADURAI BRECKENRIDGE

POLO, MARCO (1254?–1324?), medieval European traveler to East Asia. His travels throughout Asia from Baghdad to the China Sea during the years 1271 to 1295 are known through his book, *Description of the World.* After his return to Europe, Polo joined his native Venetian forces, who were fighting Genoa. He was captured in 1296, and while in prison for two years he dictated an account of his travels, known through dozens of manuscripts and first printed in a German edition of 1477. During the Renaissance it was one of the main Western sources of information on the East, especially on Cathay and Mongol-controlled Central Asia.

The unification of continental Asia under the Mongol dynasty of Genghis Khan in the thirteenth century led to the *pax Mongolica* and made possible Polo's travels throughout the East. Polo's may be said to be the most renowned record of an exploration from one end of the Eurasian continent to the other. In recounting his voyage and the customs of the inhabitants, Polo told of not only "all the great wonders" he had seen but also those he had "heard of as true"; thus, not all of his work is based on his own eyewitness experience. Sometimes he chose to include exaggerated or somewhat fabulous accounts, yet European audiences took much of what Polo recorded from personal experience as fabulous as well. As his book was filled with a vast number of wonders, Polo's work was dubbed as "Il Milione."

Marco's father, Niccolo Polo, and uncle Maffeo Polo had earlier made a trading expedition from Venice to Constantinople (1253–1260). As they were prevented by war from returning to Italy, they journeyed eastward to Cathay, reaching Kublai Khan's eastern capital of Khanbaliq (Beijing) in 1266. Appointed by the khan as emissaries to the pope in Rome, they returned to Europe in 1269. They were to request that the Vatican send one hundred learned men to the khan's court to engage in a scholarly and religious debate. After a delay caused by the election of a new pope, Gregory X, the Polos were appointed apostolic delegates to the khan's court. They set out for Cathay with Niccolo's son, Marco, and two Dominican friars deputed to represent Western learning to the court at Khanbaliq. The missionaries soon abandoned the party, which reached Kublai Khan at his summer palace in 1275, and the Polos joined the many other foreigners in the Mongol imperial administration. During the Yuan dynasty (1279–1368), the Mongol conquerors successfully diluted Chinese control of the government by employing non-Han people in positions of authority. In his account Marco Polo maintains that he was employed by the khan for some seventeen years to carry out various official duties in areas throughout the Chinese empire. In 1292 Niccolo, Maffeo, and Marco were deputed to escort a royal bride to her betrothed, the khan of Persia. The Polos arrived back in Venice in 1295.

The prologue of *Description of the World* tells of Polo's life, while the body of the book relates the customs and nature of the various lands of the Eurasian landmass that Marco had visited or heard of. Polo describes his route through the Middle East to Cathay. In great detail he tells of the government and exploits of Kublai Khan; he is particularly vivid in recounting his personal experiences within the political realms of Mongol China. While Polo describes much that was unknown to Europe of the time—coal, asbestos, and paper currency, for example—he fails to mention tea cultivation, the fishing cormorant, footbinding, and book printing. Indeed, he himself told his amanuensis that he was telling "only half of what he knew."

While Polo was very much interested in the size and nature of the cities—their economies, architecture, canals, rivers, ports, and industries were far more advanced than those in Europe of the time—his merchant background may account for the particular attention he pays to the natural resources, flora, and fauna of each region. Marco was little interested in Chinese high culture, and he made little mention of literary or religious pursuits. He often identifies adherents of the religious practices of a particular land with the single word *idolaters*. The only religion that seems to have attracted his attention was Buddhism, largely because of what he perceived as its dark, parodic likeness to aspects and practices of Christianity.

Polo was the first to describe Japan ("Zipangu") to European audiences, although his was only a hearsay account. He told of Japan's riches and of the unsuccessful attempt of Kublai Khan to invade and conquer the islands.

While Polo had traveled to China by the land route, he returned to Europe by sea via Sumatra, Ceylon, the Malabar coast, and the Persian Gulf. In his account he describes these places as well as lands and cities that he did not visit but had heard about during his homeward journey: Java, the interior of India, and the coast of East Africa as far south as Zanzibar.

Description of the World was an extraordinary work. Its vivid descriptions of the East strained the credulity of its readers; many considered it a colorful romance, and it was not until the rediscovery of East Asia in the sixteenth century that Polo's work was seen to be largely factual. Indeed, until the nineteenth century the portions that deal with Central Asia continued to be a unique document of the society of the time.

L. F. Benedetto, *Il Milione* (1928). A. C. Moule and Paul Pelliot, eds., *Marco Polo: The Description of the World* (1938); corrigenda for this edition are found in A. C. Moule, *Quinsai with Other Notes on Marco Polo* (1957). Leonardo Olschki, *Marco Polo's Asia: An Introduction to His "Description of the World"* (1960). Paul Pelliot, *Notes on Marco Polo*, 3 vols. (1959–1973). Henry

Yule and Henri Cordier, eds., *The Book of Ser Marco Polo*. 2 vols. (3d ed., 1903; reprint, 1921); a third volume, *Notes and Addenda*, by Henri Cordier (1920), is still useful for its commentary.   THEODORE NICHOLAS FOSS

POLONNARUVA, Sinhalese city. When and by whom it was founded are not known, but we do know that the region around Polonnaruva had been developed long before the capital was shifted there in the eleventh century.

Its transformation into a gracious cosmopolitan capital city was the work of three kings, Vijayabahu I, Parakramabahu I, and Nissanka Malla. During Nissanka Malla's reign (1187–1196) it reached the peak of its development as a capital city, with architectural features rivaling those of Anuradhapura: water tanks, stupas, palaces, and gardens. Perhaps its most notable religious monument was the Gal Vihara, a rock-cut temple fashioned at the command of Parakramabahu out of an enormous granite outcrop from which were carved four great statues of the Buddha. Its landscape, like that of Anuradha-

FIGURE 1. *Large Seated Buddha, Polonnaruva.*

pura, was dominated by massive stupas and tanks; the most conspicuous tank was the enormous Parakrama Samudra.

Polonnaruva's importance as a capital did not last beyond the mid-thirteenth century. Efforts made in the thirteenth and fourteenth centuries to revive its glories met with only temporary success. Like Anuradhapura it was soon covered by the jungle tide, and rehabilitation was later thwarted by malaria. Rehabilitation only came in the twentieth century, when the town became the center of a massive colonization effort based on the great tanks of the past, Minneriya and the Parakrama Samudra, restored to their ancient levels of peak efficiency. Polonnaruva is now one of the main rice-producing areas of the island.

[*See also* Parakramabahu I; Vijayabahu I; Anuradhapura; *and* Sri Lanka.]

K. M. de Silva, *A History of Sri Lanka* (1981). W. Geiger, *Culture of Ceylon in Medieval Times*, edited by H. Bechert (1960).   K. M. DE SILVA

POL POT (b. 1928), pseudonym of Saloth Sar, Cambodian communist politician and prime minister of Democratic Kampuchea (DK) from 1976 to 1979. Pol Pot was born into a prosperous peasant family that enjoyed the patronage of the Cambodian court. Several relatives worked in the palace in Phnom Penh; one of Pol Pot's sisters was a minor wife of King Sisowath Monivong (r. 1927–1941). Pol Pot was educated in Phnom Penh and Kompong Cham. In 1949, perhaps because of his palace connections, he was awarded a scholarship to study electrical technology in Paris. After repeatedly failing his examinations, and probably joining the French Communist Party, Pol Pot returned to Cambodia in 1953 and served briefly in anti-French guerrilla forces controlled by the Vietnamese.

In 1960, he was named to the central committee of the Communist Party of Kampuchea (CPK); two years later, after being named secretary, he went into hiding in the northeastern area of the country. He visited China, Vietnam, and North Korea in the mid-1960s. After Norodom Sihanouk's government had been overthrown in 1970, Pol Pot assumed command of guerrilla forces seeking to overthrow the Khmer Republic. His forces won the civil war in 1975, although his own role, and that of the CPK, was kept a secret until 1977. In the meantime, the regime of Democratic Kampuchea, secretly controlled by the CPK, embarked on a radical transformation of Cambodian society, during which perhaps a million people were assassinated or died of malnutrition or overwork. Pol Pot revealed that he was prime minister of the regime in 1976. In 1977–1978, he instigated purges of the CPK and began to encourage a cult of personality in his honor. Overthrown by a Vietnamese invasion in 1979, Pol Pot took command of guerrilla forces along the Thai border, while publicly renouncing political office.

[*See also* Cambodia; Kampuchea, Democratic; Norodom Sihanouk; Khmer Republic; *and* Communism: Communism in Southeast Asia.]

Ben Kiernan and Chanthou Boua, *Peasants and Politics in Kampuchea* (1983). Michael Vickery, *Cambodia 1975–1982* (1984). DAVID P. CHANDLER

PONDICHERRY. *See* French East India Company.

POONA SARVAJANIK SABHA, one of the most articulate and powerful of the associations that preceded the Indian National Congress. Established in 1870, the "Public Association of Poona [Pune]" was unique in its early concern for agrarian problems and its requirement that each member be the acknowledged representative of at least fifty others. Mahadev Govind Ranade became the mentor of the *sabha* in 1871, while G. V. Joshi as secretary encouraged *swadeshi* (homegrown) products. The *sabha* voiced concerns over governmental policy regarding recurrent famine, excise tax, Legislative Council reform, civil service recruitment, and representation in Parliament. The *sabha* would have been host to the first session of the Indian National Congress in 1885 but for a cholera outbreak that forced a move from Pune to Bombay.

[*See also* Ranade, Mahadev Govind.]

Gordon Johnson, *Provincial Politics and Indian Nationalism: Bombay and the Indian National Congress 1880–1915* (1973). S. R. Mehrotra, "The Poona Sarvajanik Sabha: The Early Phase (1870–1880)," *Indian Economic and Social History Review* 6.3 (1969): 294–321.
ELEANOR ZELLIOT

POONCH, a district in Jammu and Kashmir state now divided by the ceasefire line between India and Pakistan. It occupies an area of 1,689 square miles and has a population of 170,598. The administrative center in the town of Poonch lies on the ceasefire line between India and Pakistan. The district is bounded on the north by the Jhelum River and on the east by the Pir Panjal range. [*See also* Kashmir.] WILLIAM F. FISHER

POOR MAN'S PARTY. *See* Sinyetha Party.

POPULAR RIGHTS MOVEMENT. *See* Jiyū Minken.

POPULATION

AN OVERVIEW

[*The statistics cited in this article reflect a definition of Asia that includes the Arabian Peninsula, the Levant, and Turkey. For the more limited definition of Asia observed elsewhere in the encyclopedia, see the discussion in the preface.*]

Asia comprises 27 percent of the earth's land surface and, in 1983, included 58 percent of the total world population of 4.7 billion. Asia's proportion of the total population has been roughly the same at least since 1650, when the estimated population of Asia was 330 million and of the world 550 million. The growth rate of the population was so slow (less than 1 percent per year) that Asia's population did not exceed the 1 billion mark until 1920. Net additions have grown progressively larger ever since. By 1970 the population reached 2 billion and was estimated as 2.7 billion in 1983. The United Nations medium-level projection for Asia's population in the year 2000 is 3.5 billion, equivalent to the world's total in 1968.

The countries of Asia present greater variation in demographic characteristics than those of any other continent. Moreover, reliable demographic data are available only for recent decades. Hence, generalizations about all of Asia are often of dubious value. Comparative analysis of countries and regions is more meaningful. The two demographic giants—China and India, with their respective populations of 1.04 billion and 732 million in 1983—contain almost two-fifths of humanity. The latest estimates of selected demographic and socioeconomic measures for these two nations and for five other Asian countries with a population exceeding 50 million are presented in table 1. These seven countries account for 84 percent of Asia's population. With population growth in recent decades as a point of departure, the following discussion will center around mortality, fertility, determinants of fertility decline, and urbanization.

Population Growth. The average annual growth rate of Asia's population during the period 1970 to 1980 was 2.1 percent—slightly higher than the world average of 1.9. Among the seven major Asian countries, the rate ranged from 1.1 percent in Japan

TABLE 1. *Recent Estimates for Seven Asian Countries with a Population Exceeding 50 Million in 1983*

COUNTRY	POPULATION SIZE IN MILLIONS (1983)	POPULATION GROWTH RATE (1970–80)	CRUDE BIRTH RATE (1980–85)	CRUDE DEATH RATE (1980–85)	INFANT MORTALITY RATE (1980–85)	LIFE EXPECTANCY AT BIRTH IN YEARS (1980–85)	PER CAPITA GNP IN U.S. DOLLARS (1982)	NUMBER OF GIRLS ENROLLED IN PRIMARY SCHOOL AS A PERCENTAGE OF AGE GROUP[1]
China	1,040	1.9	18.5	6.8	38	67	310	106
India	732	2.2	33.2	13.3	118	53	260	64
Indonesia	159	2.3	30.7	13.0	87	53	580	94
Japan	119	1.1	12.4	6.7	8	77	10,080	100
Bangladesh	96	2.8	44.8	17.5	133	48	140	47
Pakistan	96	2.8	42.6	15.2	120	50	380	31
Philippines	52	2.5	32.3	6.9	50	65	820	108
Total Asia	2,731	2.1	27.4	10.2	87	58	—	—
Total World	4,685	1.9	27.3	10.6	81	59	—	—

1. For countries with universal primary education, the gross enrollment ratios may exceed 100 percent because some pupils are below or above the official primary-school age.

SOURCES: For columns 1 to 6, United Nations (1984); for columns 7 and 8, World Bank (1984).

to 2.8 percent in Bangladesh and Pakistan. The average growth rate for Asia was slightly lower in this period than in the decade 1960 to 1970 (2.2 percent). The decline was higher in East Asian countries than in other Asian regions. China's natural growth rate (birth rate minus death rate) is reported to have declined precipitously in the latter half of the 1970s, from 2.6 percent in 1970 to 1.2 in 1979.

The rapid population growth during recent decades in all Asian countries except Japan, which is considered a developed country, is a matter of increasing concern to development planners and policymakers. Although the growth rate in Asia reached its peak in the period 1965 to 1970, the annual increase in population for most countries continues to be too high for their level of economic and social development. Under conditions existing in these countries, rapid population growth slows, sometimes drastically, the absorption of vast numbers of the population into the modern, high-productivity economy. In the dynamic economies of a few relatively small countries of East Asia, with national incomes increasing by 8 to 10 percent annually, population growth of about 2.0 percent is a comparatively minor issue, but most countries of Asia can take no such comfort.

Popular discussions in the 1960s of population "pressure"—often colored by the terms "explosion" and "bomb"—predicted catastrophic effects of worsening population-natural resource ratios. To the surprise of many doomsayers of that decade, the rate of foodgrain production during the past two decades in most Asian countries, particularly China

and India, was higher, on average, than the population growth rate. The central policy question, however, is not, "Can a country cope with such a high or low population growth?"; rather, it should be, "Is it better for the country's development to lower or raise the population growth rate, and how is this to be achieved?" For most countries of Asia, a significant decline in the growth rate would be desirable. The prevalence of this viewpoint is exemplified by the fact that 94 percent of the population in Asia (excluding Japan) lives in countries that have adopted an official policy to reduce population growth and have given official support to family planning activities.

The rate of population growth depends on rates of fertility, mortality, and migration. Since international migration from and to any major Asian country accounts for a small proportion of its total population, a reduction in the growth rate can occur only if the mortality rate increases and/or the fertility rate decreases.

Mortality. Table 1 presents estimates of current (1980–1985) mortality levels in seven major Asian countries as measured by the crude death rate (number of deaths per 1,000 population in a year), infant mortality rate (number of babies that die in a year per 1,000 born), and expectation of life at birth. Not surprisingly, Japan has reached a mortality level—as measured by all three indexes—equivalent to that of Western countries. The remaining six countries vary considerably in each of the three indexes of mortality. The range of variation is highest for the infant mortality rate. However, a reasonable consistency exists among the three indexes: for example, China has the lowest and Bangladesh the highest mortality level, as measured by each index.

Although a modest gain in life expectancy or decline in mortality started during the 1920s in a few less-developed countries, such as India, significant annual gains in life expectancy in all Asian countries began soon after World War II. These gains were achieved directly through large-scale government public health programs aimed at the control of selected infectious diseases, such as malaria, smallpox, yellow fever, cholera, tuberculosis, and measles. Improvement in living standards also contributed to the gains.

Recent evidence suggests, however, that since the mid-1960s the earlier promising tempo of mortality decline in Asia has declined. In Asia the average annual increase in life expectancy at birth was 0.70 years from 1950 to 1955 and 1955 to 1960, and 0.52 years from 1965 to 1970 and 1970 to 1975. One main reason for the deceleration in life expectancy gains is the incapacity of public health and medical care programs to deal with the major causes of death that have replaced the previous ones. For example, diarrhea, pneumonia, and malnutrition, which singly or synergistically cause the majority of infant and child deaths, pose a serious challenge to current medical and health programs. There are also suggestions, notably those of Davidson R. Gwatkin, of slowdowns with respect to a number of social and economic programs considered directly relevant to mortality decline.

The acceleration of the population growth rate in most Asian countries since World War II was mainly due to reductions in levels of mortality. The rise in fertility levels owing to the declining practice of breastfeeding, erosion of traditional practices of sexual abstinence, and improvement in the health of women might also have contributed toward this acceleration in some regions or sectors of the population. The more recent modest decline in the population growth rate in many countries, beginning around 1970, can be attributed to the reduction in levels of fertility.

Fertility. Table 1 shows that the pattern of variation in current estimates of crude birth rates among the seven major Asian countries is similar to that of the mortality indexes—countries with lower mortality levels have generally lower fertility levels. Japan's birth rate is the lowest (12.4 per 1,000); among the remaining six countries, China currently has the lowest rate (18.5) and Bangladesh the highest (44.8). Within large countries, there are wide regional or statewide variations. For example, in India, Kerala state had a birth rate of 26 in 1981, compared to 40 in Uttar Pradesh. All countries exhibit large rural-urban and educational differentials in fertility.

Except in Japan and Hong Kong, the crude birth rate around 1950 in all Asian countries was 40 per 1,000 population or higher. Since then the rate has declined in all countries, but the most spectacular drop has occurred in China, particularly in the decade from the late 1960s to the late 1970s. During this period China lowered its crude birth rate from 32.4 to 21.3—a decline of 34 percent. During the same period, the rate in Indonesia, India, and the Philippines declined by 22, 16, and 11 percent respectively, while in Pakistan and Bangladesh it declined by 8 and 6 percent, respectively. Among the countries not listed in table 1, the following experienced significant declines in fertility: Hong Kong, Malaysia, Singapore, South Korea, Sri Lanka, Taiwan, Thailand, and Turkey.

The two important mechanisms through which a decline in fertility level occurs are the rising age at marriage and increased use of contraception. The countries recording a sharp decline in fertility have experienced both phenomena, but their relative importance varies between countries and by different stages in the transition to lower fertility. Available evidence suggests that the fertility decline in Malaysia and Sri Lanka occurred largely through an increase in age at marriage, while the decline in several other Asian countries (e.g., Thailand and Taiwan) occurred largely through increased use of contraception.

One indicator of the aggregate use of contraception in a country is the percentage of married women of reproductive age (MWRA) using contraceptive methods at some defined point in time. Recent estimates of this indicator for the countries listed in table 1 suggest a high contraceptive prevalence rate in China (70 percent in 1982) and Japan (61 percent in 1975), medium prevalence in the Philippines (48 percent in 1981), Indonesia (36 percent in 1981), and India (24 percent in 1982), and low prevalence in Bangladesh (12 percent in 1980) and Pakistan (6 percent in 1980). In 1981 and 1982 more than 87 percent of all Indian couples practicing contraception were protected by sterilization of either husband or wife. In other Asian countries, contraceptive methods used by couples are more evenly distributed, the popularity of specific methods in different countries varying widely.

India was the pioneer in establishing a government family planning program (in 1952); a few other Asian countries quickly followed. By 1982 all Asian countries except the following two groups had family planning programs with reduction of the birth rate as an objective: (1) Afghanistan, Iraq, and North Korea—countries in which the government supports family planning programs for nondemographic reasons, mainly in the interests of health and human rights; and (2) Burma, Kampuchea, Saudi Arabia, Syria, and Yemen—countries that range from neutral or laissez-faire with respect to population growth to those with an avowed pronatalist position.

It appears that the acceptance of contraception by married couples in Asian countries takes place in two stages. The first stage is characterized by acceptance primarily by older couples seeking to terminate their childbearing. This is followed by the stage in which younger couples, wishing to space their childbirths, also adopt contraception. The establishment of family planning programs initially serves well the latent demand for contraception among those older couples who have already attained their desired family size and preferred sex composition (which in most Asian countries is biased in favor of sons). The second stage of more widespread use of contraception accompanies a change in attitude toward family size and in sex preference. Family planning programs can do very little to initiate such a change; it depends mostly on the pace of economic and social development, including institutional changes that reduce the demand for children or the net value of children to their parents.

Determinants of Fertility Decline. The two principal factors affecting fertility—age at marriage and contraceptive use—are known to be associated with socioeconomic development and institutional change, but there is as yet no generalized theory of fertility that can explain fertility transition in terms of specific aspects of such development and institutional change. Table 1 provides recent estimates of three developmental indexes that are often found to be associated with fertility—per capita gross national product (GNP), infant mortality rate, and the number of girls enrolled in primary school as a percentage of the total number of girls of primary-school age.

Japan, with a per capita GNP far above other Asian countries, has the lowest fertility level among the seven countries, but the association between income and fertility is apparently weak when the other six countries are compared. All three continental

South Asian countries have relatively low income and high fertility, but China, with a per capita income (US $310) lower than that of Pakistan ($380), has a much lower crude birth rate (18.5) than the latter (42.6). A comparison between Sri Lanka and Saudi Arabia shows more dramatically that a high level of income is neither necessary nor sufficient for fertility decline. The crude birth rate in Sri Lanka is 27 per 1,000 population, compared to 43 in Saudi Arabia; Sri Lanka's per capita GNP is $320 compared to $16,000 in Saudi Arabia.

In less developed countries the infant mortality rate and the literacy rate (particularly female)—two indexes reflecting social development—seem to be more closely correlated with fertility level than any index reflecting economic development. Since comparable data on female literacy for Asian countries are not available, the proportion enrolled in primary school is used as its proxy in table 1. China, with the lowest fertility level among the six less developed countries of Asia, has the lowest infant mortality rate and full enrollment of girls in primary school. As a contrast, Bangladesh, Pakistan, and India, countries with high fertility levels, have high infant mortality rates and low levels of primary school enrollment of girls.

Among Asian countries, Japan was the first to experience the demographic transition. Its current economic and social development indexes are comparable to those of Western countries. The birth rate in Japan started declining in the 1920s and, after a temporary rise between 1940 and 1947, has declined steadily over the last three decades. The postwar fertility decline in Japan can be attributed mainly to the country's dramatic pace in economic and social development, spurred by unparalleled progress in industrialization. As in many Western countries, Japan's current demographic concern is not with its high population growth rate but with a shortage of labor and with the social security of its growing number of elderly people.

After Japan, significant fertility decline started in the so-called Asian Gang of Four—Hong Kong, Singapore, South Korea, and Taiwan. Following World War II, these countries experienced a consistently high economic growth rate, accompanied by rapid social changes. In South Korea and Taiwan the extraordinary growth of manufactured exports, achieved in a favorable international economic environment, occurred in combination with steady improvement in agricultural productivity, stimulated by an effective program of land reform. A simultaneous expansion of education, health, and family planning programs under stringent government administrative and political control contributed to fertility decline.

The factors responsible for the rapid decline in fertility level in China are somewhat unique. The country's campaign for the one-child family has been in effect since 1980, but a significant decline in fertility started in the late 1960s. A crucial factor in the success of the Chinese family planning program is the direct pressure on individual families by the program cadres and other officials who are themselves under pressure to achieve quick results. Equally important is the fact that the radical reforms of the 1950s, including the establishment of collectivized agriculture, gave the rural territorial units ("teams" and "brigades") much more economic autonomy than exists in villages of other Asian countries. Because the teams and brigades were obligated to fund most of their social services, they were interested in controlling population growth within their territorial units and tended to establish local family planning targets that in a large measure conformed to the national policy. More direct government pressures, through antinatalist and delayed-marriage campaigns, pushed in the same direction.

Sri Lanka and Kerala (one of the poorest states of India) are the best known instances of low rates of fertility and mortality being reached without any apparent stimulus from a dynamic economy and without a strong politico-adminstrative system. In certain respects, particularly in the wide availability of equitable (in terms of male-female and rural-urban) education and health services, both places are substantially more advanced than their aggregate production performance would suggest. A different source of possible explanation is found in the nature of their evolving labor markets—the extensive pattern of labor commuting from rural to urban areas in Sri Lanka, the organization of agricultural trade unions in Kerala, and, in both, the relative lack of employment opportunities for children.

Urbanization. The problem of rapid growth of urban areas, particularly large cities, is often viewed as different from that of rapid population growth at the national or regional level. Of the thirty less developed countries in Asia and the Pacific region that responded to a United Nations query about their concern with population issues, only two declared the spatial distribution of their populations "acceptable." Twelve replied that it was "unacceptable to some degree," and sixteen declared it to be "largely unacceptable." Part of the concern reflects a belief that the increasing migration from rural to urban areas is a consequence of unjustifiable urban bias in development planning. Government concerns include administrative and financial difficulties in providing urban services in the face of unplanned changes and an implied threat to the existing social order.

Contrary to the popular view, neither the level nor the rate of urbanization in Asia (by past or present standards) is spectacular. In 1980, 27 percent of Asia's population lived in urban areas, compared to 65 percent in Latin America and 29 percent in Africa. Excluding the city-states of Hong Kong and Singapore, Japan and Israel are two Asian countries that have exceptionally high levels of urbanization. The rate of change in Asian urban percentage between 1950 and 1975 (from 15 percent to 26 percent) was about the same as the rate in the United States between 1850 and 1875 (from 15 to 27 percent).

Although the rate of urbanization (change in the proportion of the population living in urban areas) has not been unprecedented in Asia, the growth rate of the urban population has been. The explanation lies not in rapid growth of the urban population produced by rural-urban migration, but in the high rates of natural increase (excess of births over deaths) in both rural and urban areas. For example, the proportion of urban growth between 1961 and 1971 attributable to natural increase was 67.7 percent in India and 64.3 percent in Indonesia. The rate of natural increase in urban areas of Asia, as in rural areas, can only be reduced through policies and programs to reduce the fertility level.

To mitigate the problems posed by rapid growth of urban populations, particularly in metropolitan cities, many Asian countries have adopted policies and programs specifically designed to alter the existing pattern of population distribution. These efforts fall into four categories: (1) reversing population flows by encouraging or compelling urban residents to relocate in rural areas (China, Kampuchea), (2) stopping or discouraging rural migrants from leaving their communities or from entering large cities (Indonesia in relation to Jakarta and the Philippines in relation to Manila), (3) resettling migrants in frontier areas (Indonesia, Malaysia), and (4) redirecting rural migrants from metropolitan centers to new industrial "growth poles" located in nonmetropolitan cities (almost all Asian countries). The outcome of these policies and programs has ranged from almost total failure to moderate success. Their overall impact on the rapid growth of Asia's urban population seems modest at best.

[See also Economic Development.]

China Financial and Economic Publishing House, *New China's Population* (1987). Kingsley Davis, "Asia's Cities: Problems and Options," *Population and Development Review* 1.1 (1975): 71–86. Davidson R. Gwatkin, "Indications of Change in Developing Country Mortality Trends: The End of an Era?" *Population and Development Review* 6.4 (1980): 615–644. W. Parker Mauldin, "The Determinants of Fertility Decline in LDC's: An Overview of the Available Empirical Evidence," in *Selected Papers of the International Population Conference, Manila, 1981*, edited by the International Union for the Scientific Study of Population (1981), vol. 1, pp. 5–24. Geoffrey McNicoll and Moni Nag, "Population Growth: Current Issues and Strategies," *Population and Development Review* 8.1 (1982): 121–140. Moni Nag, "Modernization and its Impact on Fertility: The Indian Scene," *India International Centre Quarterly* 8.3–4 (1981): 235–247. Dorothy L. Nortman and Joanne Fisher, *Population and Family Planning Programs: A Compendium of Data through 1981* (11th ed., 1982). Samuel H. Preston, "Urban growth in Developing Countries: A Demographic Reappraisal," *Population and Development Review* 5.2 (1979): 195–216. K. Srinivasan, "Fertility Trends in Asian Countries," in *Conference of the Asian Forum of Parliamentarians on Population and Development, 17–20 February 1984*, edited by Sat Paul Mittal (1984), pp. 16–22. United Nations, *The Determinants and Consequences of Population Trends*, vol. 1 (1973), and *World Population Prospects as Assessed in 1982* (1984). World Bank, *World Development Report, 1984* (1984).   MONI NAG

POPULATION IN CHINA

For many centuries the people of Asia have constituted more than one-half and, at times, close to two-thirds of the world's population. While North and Central Asia remained sparsely settled, South and East Asia have been densely populated. Two countries, China and India, have been the most populous in the world. China alone approached one-third of the world total in the first half of the nineteenth century and in the second half of the twentieth century has only gradually dropped below one-quarter of the expanding world total.

China's population buildup occurred intermittently over several millennia. With the advent of agriculture and the organization of urban government, the population of North China grew in the final two millennia BCE. During the Han dynasty (206 BCE–220 CE), the census of 2 CE recorded 60 million people, roughly the same total as found in the Roman empire. Despite declines in population in times of endemic war and political instability, the total rose to more than 100 million in the Song dynasty (960–1279). Settlement of South China by Han Chinese was steadily shifting the balance of population below the Yangtze River. In the next few centuries the occupation of North China by non-Han conquerors and the spread of new strains of rice that permitted multiple cropping favored population growth in the South.

Recovering from the devastation of the Mongol conquest, China's population in the Ming dynasty (1368–1644) doubled to more than 150 million, then doubled again in the Qing dynasty (1644–1911) to more than 400 million in 1850. Such a large increase was made possible by the intensive cultivation of rice, supported by carefully maintained irrigation systems. New areas were brought into cultivation through upland terracing and the introduction of New World crops such as the sweet potato. Some migration to southwest China occurred, but the vast stretches of outer lands in an arc from Tibet to Manchuria were off limits or insecure for Han settlers almost until the twentieth century. Harsh conditions led to female infanticide in some regions of China, sometimes resulting in a recorded sex ratio for a prefecture or province as high as six males to five females. Nevertheless, population growth continued, leading already crowded villages to stringent conservation measures in order to sustain additional hundreds of residents.

More than any other country, China has attracted attention in recent years for its stringent population controls. Unstable conditions had kept death rates high through the first half of the twentieth century, but China's population began to skyrocket from a level of 550 million after the Communist victory in 1949. At first leaders opposed population controls, based on the assumption that a larger population was a source of national strength. In stages, they came to realize a need for late marriage, family planning techniques, and finally the one-child policy that went into effect in 1979. Convinced that further growth of a population already numbering one billion would impair efforts to modernize their country, China's leaders permitted families to have only one child each. While by 1984 some exceptions were being made (e.g., where the married couple themselves had no siblings), the Chinese succeeded in bringing birth rates down sharply. They envisaged stopping the growth of China's population at 1.2 billion before the end of the century.

GILBERT ROZMAN

POPULATION IN JAPAN

For many hundreds of years Japan has ranked among the densely settled East Asian countries in which rice cultivation has produced the staple food for most people. In the Kamakura, Muromachi, and Sengoku periods (twelfth to sixteenth century) it was one of a handful of countries throughout the world with a population close to or in excess of ten million. Rapid population growth in the seventeenth century brought the population total to roughly 30 million—a figure unsurpassed in Europe until the end of the eighteenth century. In the late twentieth century, with a population of 120 million, Japan remains among the seven most populous countries.

The Tokugawa-era (1600–1868) population increase from 1600 until about 1720 was caused by an era of uninterrupted peace and expanding agriculture. Previously marginal lands were opened to rice cultivation and fertilizer was applied in growing amounts to raise yields. As conditions grew more crowded, households and communities took measures that led to a reduction in fertility. They delayed the age of marriage and made it difficult for non-inheriting sons to establish new households in the community. Some evidence has been presented to the effect that abortion and infanticide were also used to plan the spacing of births. After 1720 the population grew slowly. In eastern Japan, areas that sent many migrants to large cities lost population, and mortality crises in the 1780s and 1830s had some lingering impact. In contrast western Japan continued to experience population growth through the 1840s.

In the mid-nineteenth century the population growth rate increased. By the 1920s the population had doubled to sixty million. By that time birth rates were steadily declining. The sharpest declines came from 1947 to 1955; legalization of contraception and abortion were important factors. Large numbers of abortions continued to take place in the 1980s as Japanese remained reluctant to adopt modern forms of contraception such as the pill. By world standards, Japanese birth rates fell very rapidly and they eventually stabilized at a low level, even for an industrialized country.

In recent years Japanese reproductive behavior has been remarkably homogeneous. Women marry between the age of twenty-two and twenty-five and have two children by the age of thirty, after which they stop having children. The result is a population that is likely to remain in the 120 to 130 million range for many years to come.   GILBERT ROZMAN

PORBANDAR, town in western Gujarat state, India, situated on the Arabian Sea. It was the capital of the princely state of Porbandar (680 square miles) under British paramountcy and was the chief city of the Jethwa clan of Rajputs. It is perhaps best known as the birthplace of Mohandas Gandhi; his father, uncle, and grandfather all served here as *diwans,* or prime ministers. Before the growth of Bombay, Porbandar was a minor port trading with Arabian Sea ports, East Africa, and the west coast of India.

[*See also* Gandhi, Mohandas Karamchand *and* Princely States.]

P. C. Govinden, ed., *The Kathiawar Directory,* 3 vols. (1921–1923). J. W. Watson, *Statistical Account of Porbandar* (1979).   HOWARD SPODEK

POROS, the Greek name of Parvataka, was the ruler of the country between the Jhelum and Chenab rivers in the Punjab. He fought a heroic battle with Alexander, who found it one of the toughest of his campaigns. Although defeated, this brave and powerful king of imposing personality impressed Alexander so much that he made friends with him and not only reinstated his kingdom but added more territories to his care.

[*See also* Alexander III.]

R. C. Majumdar, ed., *The Age of Imperial Unity* (1968).   A. K. NARAIN

PORT ARTHUR (Chinese, Lüshun; Japanese, Ryojun), deep-water, ice-free harbor at the southern tip of the Liaodong Peninsula, China, dominating the entrance to Bohai Gulf (Zhili); briefly occupied by Japanese troops (1894–1895); leased from China by the Russians (1898), who fortified it "impregnably." In February 1904, Japanese destroyers surprised and crippled the Russian flotilla anchored in the roadstead. General Nogi Maresuke's Third Army invested Port Arthur from the landward side. By August he concentrated 80,000 men and 474 artillery pieces against General Anatoli Stoessel's 40,000 troops and 506 guns positioned on high ground. Massed Japanese infantry attacked endlessly but suffered great losses while making progress. Vital to the defenses was Hill 203, commanding the harbor below. Fierce Japanese assaults from 27 November to 5 December cost Nogi 11,000 lives before his siege guns crushed the last 2,200 Russians atop the hill. On 2 January 1905 Stoessel surrendered Port Arthur and 10,000 combatants. Nogi's losses numbered 59,000 killed, wounded, or missing; in addition, there were 34,000 who were sick. Having secured Liaodong, the Third Army veterans marched north. The Portsmouth Treaty of 1905 awarded Japan the Port Arthur leasehold.

[*See also* Russo-Japanese War.]

Denis Warner and Peggy Warner, *The Tide at Sunrise: A History of the Russo-Japanese War, 1904–1905* (1974).

ALVIN D. COOX

PORTSMOUTH, TREATY OF. Signed in Portsmouth, New Hampshire on 5 September 1905, the Treaty of Portsmouth brought an end to the Russo-Japanese War of 1904 to 1905.

By the summer of 1905 the war was placing such a severe strain on both countries that they were willing to accept President Theodore Roosevelt's offer of mediation. Russia was suffering from internal difficulties and the disadvantage of fighting a war at the end of a long and undependable supply line. Even though it had been victorous on both land and sea, Japan was under severe economic strain produced by the cost of the war.

The principal terms of the treaty, apart from the restoration of peace, involved Russian recognition of Japan's paramount position in the Korean peninsula; both parties' evacuation of Manchuria (except for the Liaodong Peninsula) and the restoration of Chinese rule there. In addition, Russia assigned all its rights in the Liaodong Peninsula to Japan, it turned over the South Manchuria Railway, and it ceded the southern half of Sakhalin Island to Japan. Japan did not gain an indemnity from Russia to help pay the cost of the war and also failed to obtain all of Sakhalin. As a result, popular demonstrations broke out in Japan against the treaty. [*See* Hibiya Incident.]

The effects of the treaty were to eliminate Russia as an important factor on the Asian continent and to establish a firm foothold for Japan in Manchuria and Korea. The elimination of Russia from Korea was to lead to Japan's annexation of Korea in 1910, and the Japanese takeover of the Russian position in Manchuria was to result in the eventual occupation of that area by Japan.

[*See also* Russo-Japanese War.]

Raymond A. Esthus, *Theodore Roosevelt and Japan* (1966). John Albert White, *The Diplomacy of the Russo-Japanese War* (1964).

JOHN M. MAKI

PORTUGUESE

PORTUGUESE IN INDIA

The Portuguese established the first European presence in India and were the last to leave their colonies there. Vasco da Gama arrived in Calicut in 1498, the first European to reach India via the Cape of Good Hope. Although older literature refers to the Portuguese search for "Christians and spices," recent research stresses economic motives, not religious ones. During the sixteenth century the Portuguese empire in India consisted of a string of forts on the west coast, similar to others all over seaborne Asia. In South Asia their main fortified areas were Goa (their center as of 1510), Daman, Diu, Colombo, Cochin, and Bassein.

These forts were bases to facilitate the main Portuguese ambition in India and Asia, which was to monopolize the trade in spices to Europe and to control and tax other trade. The Portuguese hoped to dispossess the Muslim spice traders who controlled the trade to the Mediterranean by way of the Red Sea, and so achieve a monopoly over the supply of spices to Europe through the Cape of Good Hope route. But this ambition was never realized: by the middle of the sixteenth century as many spices were reaching Europe through the Red Sea as through the Cape in Portuguese ships, as Asian traders learned how to evade the Portuguese patrols in the vast Indian Ocean. The Portuguese failure to establish a base to block the Red Sea entrance at Aden made evasion even easier.

The second economic aim of this maritime empire was to force Asian traders to take Portuguese passes and pay customs duties at Portuguese forts. Because of their possession of Daman and Diu they were able to enforce this system of extortion fairly effectively over the large sea trade of Gujarat. In other areas of western India the Portuguese had less success, and in the entire Bay of Bengal the Portuguese official presence was minimal. Instead they were best known for their roles as traders, missionaries, pirates, and mercenaries. Indeed, nearly all Portuguese in India, from the governor on down, traded actively as individuals.

Much effort and money went into the attempt to convert Indians to Roman Catholicism, but little was achieved beyond areas ruled by Portugal, where coercion was sometimes used. In 1600 the number of converts in South Asia was about 175,000, out of a total population of about 150 million.

Portuguese power in India declined rapidly in the seventeenth century under Dutch attack. By 1658 Sri Lanka was conquered, and all Portuguese forts in Malabar had fallen by 1663. After losses to Indian powers during the eighteenth century, only Goa, Daman, and Diu remained. Yet despite this political decline, vestiges of Portuguese culture—language and, especially, religion—remained influential in some coastal areas of India into the nineteenth century. Portugal's three remaining areas were forcibly "liberated" by India in 1961 after the Portuguese dictator Antonio de Oliveira Salazar had refused to negotiate with independent India. Portuguese influence in Goa continues to decline, apart from the continuing role of the now indianized Catholic church.

[*See also* Gama, Vasco da *and* Goa.]

C. R. Boxer, *Portuguese India in the Mid-Seventeenth Century* (1980). J. Correia-Affonso, ed., *Indo-Portuguese History: Sources and Problems* (1981). A. R. Disney, *Twilight of the Pepper Empire* (1978). K. S. Mathew, *Portuguese Trade with India in the Sixteenth Century* (1983). M. N. Pearson, *Merchants and Rulers in Gujarat: The Response to the Portuguese in the Sixteenth Century* (1976).   MICHAEL N. PEARSON

PORTUGUESE IN SOUTHEAST ASIA

When they reached India in 1497, the Portuguese soon discovered that they could not sell their inferior trade products in the sophisticated Asian marketplace. They therefore used their naval superiority in the Indian Ocean to create a system of institutionalized piracy, to sell letters of passage, and to establish customs houses at strategic positions like Hormuz and Socatra in the west and Goa on India's western coast. When word of Melaka's (Malacca's) great wealth, which had been received from Asian traders in India, reached him, the Portuguese king Dom Manuel (r. 1495–1521) dispatched Diogo de Sequeira to find Melaka, to secure a treaty with its ruler, and to stay there as Portugal's commercial representative east of India. Sequeira was initially well received by Sultan Mahmud Syah (r. 1488–1528) upon the former's arrival in 1509, but when Sequeira began to build a fortified factory, Melaka's international trading community convinced Sultan Mahmud that the Portuguese were a threat to his sovereignty. Melaka's troops drove the Portuguese out, capturing several of Sequeira's men, killing others, and forcing Sequeira's four ships to return to India. In April 1511 Affonso de Albuquerque (c. 1459–1515) led a force of 1,200 men and seventeen or eighteen ships from Goa to Melaka, which finally fell to the Portuguese and their superior firepower in August.

Although they controlled Melaka, the Portuguese soon found that this did not give them their desired control over the flow of pepper and spices from Southeast Asia. To avoid the Portuguese, Asian traders shifted their base of operation to rival ports in Java, Johor, and Aceh, where they were subject to lesser duties and where prices were lower. The Portuguese were almost powerless to maintain their monopoly. Melaka was dependent on Asian suppliers

for its food and trade goods. The Portuguese administration was inefficient, confused, and corrupt; Portuguese governors even traded for their own personal gain at Malay ports in violation of the monopoly that they were supposed to maintain. The Portuguese's technological superiority was quickly diffused to their Southeast Asian competitors, who employed Portuguese military personnel to teach them how to mount cannons on more sturdy ships and how to fight more effectively using guns and European infantry formations. Johor and Aceh soon became Melaka's naval and military equals, and by the second half of the sixteenth century Portuguese Melaka was one of various ports in the western Indonesian archipelago that competed for Asian trade.

While the Portuguese never established a monopoly over Southeast Asian trade, they did disrupt the organization of this trade. In the sixteenth century many members of the Asian trading community left Melaka and settled in some of the other ports that were bitterly competing among themselves to become the new dominant center of Southeast Asian trade.

The Portuguese also had a cultural impact on the eastern Indonesian archipelago's Spice Islands. Immediately after the conquest of Melaka, the Portuguese took advantage of the temporary decline of Javanese and Malay sailings to the east, caused by the destruction of the Javanese fleet at Melaka in 1511. In 1512 Francisco Serraro established commercial relations with Ambon, Ternate, and Tidore in the Moluccas (Maluku). Between 1522 and 1575 the Portuguese had a fortified trade base at Ternate. When the Ternate population drove them out, they established a new fortress at Tidore, but Ambon became their main center of commercial operations until it finally fell to the Dutch in 1605. Francis Xavier (1506–1552), a cofounder of the Jesuit order with Ignatius Loyola, worked among the Ambon, Ternate, and Morotai (Moro) populations in 1546–1547; by the 1590s there were some 50,000 Catholic converts in the Maluku region. Over the centuries the Ambonese have continued to maintain their syncretic Portuguese-Indonesian heritage.

[*See also* Goa; Melaka; Albuquerque, Affonso de; Johor; Aceh; *and* Maluku.]

C. R. Boxer, *The Portuguese Seaborne Empire, 1415–1825* (1969). M. A. P. Meilink-Roelofsz, *Asian Trade and European Influence in the Indonesian Archipelago between 1500 and about 1630* (1962).

KENNETH R. HALL

PORTUGUESE IN SRI LANKA

The island of Sri Lanka, long known in European fable as a source of precious stones and curiosities, was first visited by the Portuguese in 1506. A fortress-factory was established in Colombo in 1518. Over the next 140 years the Portuguese were actively involved in Sri Lanka in both political and religious affairs. In the early sixteenth century Sri Lanka was divided into three small kingdoms. The Portuguese were able to turn the king of Kotte, in the south and southwest, into their protégé: indeed, in 1557 they converted the king, who became Dom João Dharmapala, and who, on his death in 1597, bequeathed his kingdom to the king of Portugal. Both before and after this time the Portuguese were embroiled in warfare in Sri Lanka, especially with Buddhist kings and their supporters who opposed foreign Portuguese rule. In the seventeenth century their main opponent was the ruler of Kandy, who from 1638 was helped by the Dutch. These allies slowly drove out the Portuguese: Colombo fell in 1656, and two years later Portuguese forces in the northern Tamil area capitulated. In the first half of the seventeenth century Sri Lanka represented the largest territory ruled by the Portuguese in Asia: nowhere else were they driven to such extensive and expensive warfare.

Religion and commerce fostered this involvement. Cinnamon was increasingly in demand in Europe, and at times the Portuguese made large profits from their control of areas growing this spice. Sri Lanka was also a major conversion field. Followers of Francis Xavier made many converts in the Jaffna area, and later, after the conversion of the king of Kotte, in the south. In all perhaps 100,000 Sri Lankans had converted by 1600, and more followed later. As in other areas of Asia, Portuguese language and religion survived both military defeat and Dutch persecution. Even today a form of Portuguese is spoken by some coastal communities, and Roman Catholics remain an important minority in the the population.

[See also Sri Lanka and Dharmapala, Dom João.]

T. Abeyasinghe, *Portuguese Rule in Ceylon, 1594–1612* (1966). C. R. de Silva, *The Portuguese in Ceylon, 1617–38* (1972). P. E. Pieris, *Ceylon and the Portuguese, 1505–1658* (1920). G. D. Winius, *The Fatal History of Portuguese Ceylon: Transition to Dutch Rule* (1971).

MICHAEL N. PEARSON

PRACTICAL LEARNING, SCHOOL OF. See Sirhak.

PRAJADHIPOK (Rama VII), last absolute monarch of the kingdom of Siam (r. 1925–1935).

Prajadhipok was born on 8 November 1893, the last son and seventy-sixth child of King Chulalongkorn, his ninth by Queen Saowapha. He was trained in England (at Eton and Woolwich Military Academy) and in France for a military career, and returned to Siam only in 1924. The royal succession law provided that the sons of Chulalongkorn by Queen Saowapha stood first in line for the throne, failing a son from the then-reigning monarch, King Vajiravudh (r. 1910–1925). All Prajadhipok's elder brothers predeceased him, and he became king on 26 November 1925, having never expected to be king. He admitted he was unprepared for his duties, and facing serious financial difficulties and a general loss of confidence in the monarchy, he brought back to public life the senior princes of the royal family whom Vajiravudh had ignored.

He had moderate success in restoring economic stability before the world depression intervened. On several occasions during his brief reign, the last in March of 1932, he seriously explored making major political changes in the direction of increasing public political participation; but on each occasion he was dissuaded by his senior advisers (notably Prince Damrong Rajanubhab). Perhaps his major failing was his lack of self-confidence, his unwillingness to go against the advice of his senior uncles. The combination of economic crisis and political paralysis precipitated the Thai revolution of 24 June 1932. Prajadhipok unhesitatingly accepted the political change, agreeing to serve as a constitutional monarch, but relations between the king and the ruling military junta rapidly deteriorated to the point where, on 2 March 1935, he abdicated, stating "I am willing to surrender the powers I formerly exercised to the people as a whole, but I am not willing to turn them over to any individual or any group to use in an autocratic manner without heeding the voice of the people." Prajadhipok died in England on 30 May 1941.

[See also Thailand; Chakri Dynasty; Damrong Rajanubhab; Manopakorn Nitithada; People's Party of Thailand; Phahon Phonphayuhasena; Phibunsongkhram, Luang; and Pridi Phanomyong.]

B. A. Batson, *Siam's Political Future: Documents from the End of the Absolute Monarchy* (1977) and *The End of the Absolute Monarchy in Siam* (1984). David K. Wyatt, *Thailand: A Short History* (1984).

DAVID K. WYATT

PRAMBANAN. The ancestor temple complex at Prambanan in Central Java is normally identified by the name of the Lara Jonggrang temple that is dedicated to Shiva's consort Durga. It is believed to have been constructed during the reign of King Pikatan about 856 to validate the transition from the previous Sailendra monarchs to the new dynastic line of kings who traced their lineage to Sanjaya.

The central Shiva temple is flanked by smaller temples to Brahma (south) and Vishnu (north). Facing them are four smaller sanctuaries that house their mounts, and at the northern and southern gates of the central complex are smaller shrines that once contained gold, jewels, and other treasures. There were originally three descending tiers of 156 shrines surrounding the central temples, and beyond these were living quarters for priests, monks, ascetics, and pilgrims. The Shiva temple has three sequences of reliefs, one of the Guardians of the Cardinal Points, one of celestial dancers and musicians, and one that illustrates the *Ramayana* epic up to the crossing of the monkey army from India to Sri Lanka. This story is concluded on the Brahma temple, and the Vishnu temple's reliefs show scenes from the life of Krishna. Art historians note that the tone of Prambanan's art is more dramatic than that of the earlier Borobudur.

[*See also* Java; Sailendra; Sanjaya; Borobudur; *and* Architecture: Southeast Asian Architecture.]

Claire Holt, *Art in Indonesia: Continuity and Change* (1965).   KENNETH R. HALL

PRAPHAS CHARUSATHIAN (b. 1912), Thai political leader. Born in Udorn Province, Praphas was educated at the Royal Thai Military Academy and briefly at Thammasat University. A junior member of the 1947 Coup Group (which overthrew the government of Prime Minister Pridi Phanomyong), Praphas rose to national prominence in February 1949 when he and Thanom Kittikachorn stormed the Royal Palace to quell an attempt by the Free Thai to overthrow Luang Phibunsongkhram and restore Pridi to power. The operation was led by Sarit Thanarat.

After Sarit Thanarat staged his coup against Phibun in 1957, Praphas was appointed deputy prime minister and minister of interior in the Thanom cabinet. Following Sarit's death, Praphas emerged as one of the heirs to Sarit's political and economic fortunes. Until he was forced out by the student uprisings of 14 October 1973, Praphas held the position of deputy prime minister, minister of interior, deputy supreme commander of the armed forces, commander-in-chief of the army, and acting director of the police department. After the 6 October 1976 coup d'état Praphas returned to Thailand from a brief exile.

[*See also* Pridi Phanomyong; Thanom Kittikachorn; Free Thai; Phibunsongkhram, Luang; *and* Sarit Thanarat.]

John Girling, *Thailand* (1981).

THAK CHALOEMTIARANA

PRARTHANA SAMAJ ("prayer society"), a theistic Hindu reform movement launched in Bombay in 1867. Although apparently influenced by the Brahmo Samaj, the society put emphasis upon personal devotion to a single, aniconic deity. Although many of its prominent members were active social reformers, the Prarthana Samaj remained firmly within the Hindu society of Maharashtra.

[*See also* Brahmo Samaj.]

C. H. Heimsath, *Indian Nationalism and Hindu Social Reform* (1964).   FRANK F. CONLON

PRASAD, RAJENDRA (1888–1963), president of India (1950–1962). Influenced by Mohandas Gandhi, Prasad abandoned a legal practice in 1920, committed himself to noncooperation and Indian nationalism, and became a leader in the Congress party. After independence he was elected India's first president. A staunch Gandhian and somewhat conservative thinker, Prasad was at times uneasy with post-independence policies that promoted modernization. He was an accomplished writer in English and Hindi, and his publications provide a rare insight into the man and his period.

[*See also* Gandhi, Mohandas Karamchand.]

R. L. Handa, *Rajendra Prasad: Twelve Years of Triumph and Despair* (1978). R. Prasad, *Portrait of a President: Letters of Dr. Rajendra Prasad*, 2 vols. (1974, 1976). S. M. Wasi, *President Prasad* (1962).

FRANKLIN A. PRESLER

PRASAT THONG, king of Ayudhya (r. 1629–1656), first Siamese king to have extensive dealings with the West. A cousin of King Song Tham, he controlled the Kalahom ministry as Phraya Siworawong. On Song Tham's death in 1628 he enthroned and killed several young princes and then took the throne for himself. As Prasat Thong, "king of the golden palace," he skillfully balanced the

Dutch East India Company against Asian trading interests to bolster his kingdom's economic strength and worked to expand its power on the Malay Peninsula.

[*See also* Ayudhya *and* Song Tham.]

George Vinal Smith, *The Dutch in Seventeenth-Century Thailand* (1977). David K. Wyatt, *Thailand: A Short History* (1984).   DAVID K. WYATT

PRATIHARAS (c. 730–1050), also known as the imperial Gurajara Pratiharas or Priharas of Avanti/Malwa and later of Kanyakubja (Kanauj); they were the last great empire builders of northern India and the chief bulwark of defense against the Muslim Arab expansion beyond Sind. Actively pursuing the goal of a pan-Indian hegemony, the Pratiharas conquered the Ganges Plain, transferring their capital to imperial Kanyakubja in about 815, and built a vast empire extending from the eastern to the western sea and from the Himalayas to the Vindhyas under their kings Mihira Bhoja (836–885) and Mahendrapala (885–914). They were unable, however, to end the Arab rule in Sind and achieve a pan-India paramountcy, on account of the intermittent Rashtrakuta invasions from the South. They succumbed to the Ghaznavid invasions in 1018 and 1022.

[*See also* Kanyakubja.]

R. C. Majumdar, *Readings in Political History of India* (1976). B. N. Puri, *The History of the Gurjara-Pratīhāras* (1975).   SHIVA BAJPAI

PRAYAG. *See* Allahabad.

PREAH VIHEAR, temple that in the 1950s and 1960s was the focus of a border dispute between Thailand and Cambodia.

After Cambodia's independence in 1954, Prince Sihanouk pursued a neutral and independent foreign policy that alarmed the Thai government. Distrust between Thailand and Cambodia had been simmering, especially since Thailand had given sanctuary to Son Ngoc Thanh, Sihanouk's political rival. The conflicts between the two countries were symbolized by their dispute of sovereignty over Preah Vihear.

In response to Cambodia's accusation that the 1902 Franco-Siamese Treaty placing the temple in French Indochina was signed under duress, the Thai government claimed in 1958 that its reoccupation of the area following the Franco-Siamese War of 1941 was legitimate. The infant regime of Thai prime minister Sarit Thanarat (in power from 1959 to 1963) used this issue to rally public support for his leadership. Ultimately both governments agreed to have the case settled by the International Court of Justice, and in 1962 the court ruled in favor of Cambodia by a vote of nine to three. The Sarit government permitted a brief demonstration of public outrage but did not pursue the matter further.

[*See also* Norodom Sihanouk; Son Ngoc Thanh; Franco-Siamese War; *and* Sarit Thanarat.]

Michael Leifer, *Cambodia* (1967). Roger Smith, *Cambodia's Foreign Policy* (1965).

THAK CHALOEMTIARANA

PREMCHAND, pseudonym of Dhanpat Rai (1880–1936), novelist, short story writer, and journalist who pioneered the development of Indian realistic fiction, first in Urdu, later in Hindi. His twelve novels and almost three hundred short stories, at first devoted to patriotic themes, partly under the influence of Mohandas Gandhi and Maxim Gorki, became increasingly preoccupied with social injustice and poverty and championed the cause of women. His last completed novel, *Godan* (1939), his masterpiece, has been translated into English twice. Other important novels include the Gandhian *Premashram* (1918), and *Nirmula* (1925), which attacks traditionally arranged marriages.

Premchand, *The Gift of a Cow*, translated by Gordon Roadarmel (1968). Robert O. Swan, *Munshi Premchand of Lamhi Village* (1969).   DAVID RUBIN

PRIANGAN, the mountainous inland territories of West Java. The Priangan region embraces the eastern three-quarters of West Java, from the mouth of the Cipamalis River on the east to that of the Ciluwung (Jakarta) on the west. It is a predominantly Sundanese-speaking area that over the centuries has been subjected to Javanese colonization. During the early seventeenth century the region was acquired by the Dutch East India Company, which imposed a form of indirect rule on the local rulers, who were subsequently termed regents. The Priangan's rugged physical relief and low population density provided not only optimal conditions for the cultivation of pepper, coffee, and tea but also a place of refuge for rebels, social malcontents, and religious leaders. [*See also* Java *and* Dutch East India Company.]

M. C. HOADLEY

PRIDI PHANOMYONG (1900–1983), Thai political leader; prime minister for five months in 1946.

Born in Ayudhya Province, Pridi, the son of farmers, showed promise as a scholar when he graduated from high school at the age of fifteen. Too young to start postsecondary education, he worked on the family farm for two years before enrolling in the Ministry of Justice's Law School. By nineteen he had passed his law examinations, and in 1920 he went to France to study law. On his way to a doctorate, Pridi organized, and later led, the Thai Students' Association. He frequently met with students (such as the future leaders Luang Phibunsongkhram and Khuang Aphaiwong, among others) and junior-level government officials studying in Europe to discuss politics and explore avenues for change. Before returning to Thailand, he helped form the People's Party.

On 26 June 1932 the People's Party staged a coup d'état that overthrew absolute monarchy in Thailand. A constitutional government led by Phraya Manopakorn Nitithada, a prominent jurist who was not a member of the People's Party, was inaugurated. Pridi was appointed minister in the Mano cabinet and assigned one of the major tasks of the new government—to present Parliament with a National Economic Development Plan. Pridi's proposal, however, proved too radical for many, both in and out of Parliament. Calling for income redistribution and state supervision of key economic enterprises, the plan was criticized as communistic, and Phraya Mano used the controversy it stirred as an excuse to suspend Parliament. Because of the uproar over his proposal, Pridi left for a brief exile in Paris but returned after Phahon Phonphayuhasena, a leader of the People's Party, ousted the Mano government by a military coup d'état on 20 June 1933. Phahon became prime minister, and in late October Parliament gave Pridi a vote of confidence on his appointment to the Phahon cabinet. Pridi promised that he would "never act in a communistic fashion" at the Parliament session.

From 1933 until the Japanese landed in Thailand in 1941, Pridi was a key figure in the governments of Phahon and Phibun, who became prime minister in 1938. Pridi was the acknowledged leader of the civilian faction of the People's Party and was given important portfolios—Interior, Finance, and Justice. In 1933–1934, Pridi founded Thammasat University. He remained rector until 1952.

After the Japanese landing—and Phibun's decision to allow free passage of Japanese troops through Thailand—the rift between Pridi and Phibun widened. Because of Pridi's opposition to a policy of cooperation with the Japanese, he was removed by Phibun from the cabinet and given the prestigious, but powerless, position of regent. This position gave Pridi ample time to organize the Seri Thai (Free Thai) movement, an underground resistance group that undermined Japan's position in Thailand and helped prepare for Japan's eventual defeat. Although it did not see much combat, the Free Thai played a vital role in assisting the Allies in intelligence-gathering operations. More important, because of its anti-Japanese activities, its leaders, Pridi and Seni Pramote, were able to negotiate a lenient peace settlement with the Allies at the end of World War II.

Phibun and the army were discredited for backing the wrong power, and in March 1946, Pridi became prime minister. His tenure, however, was cut short by the mysterious death of the young King Ananda. Although he was not directly implicated in the death, Pridi had to shoulder most of the blame for it. In 1947, the army, under the leadership of General Phin Chunhawan, staged a coup d'état, overthrowing the Pridi-backed government of Admiral Luang Thamrong Nawasawat. Pridi fled the country. The schism between the army and civilian leaders continued, however, and it came to a head on 26 February 1949, when Pridi supported a coup against the government of Phibun, who had become prime minister again in 1948. Pridi's followers included factions from the navy and members of the Free Thai. This attempted coup, known as the Palace Rebellion, was routed by troops led by Sarit Thanarat, Thanom Kittikachorn, and Praphas Charusathian. Pridi went into exile in the People's Republic of China.

He remained in China until 1970. From 1970 until his death on 2 May 1983, Pridi and his wife lived in Paris. Throughout his long exile, Pridi remained a controversial but respected leader.

[See also Thailand; Phibunsongkhram, Luang; Khuang Aphaiwong; People's Party of Thailand; Prajadhipok; Manopakorn Nitithada; Phahon Phonphayuhasena; Free Thai; Ananda Mahidol; Sarit Thanarat; Thanom Kittikachorn; and Praphas Charusathian.]

David K. Wyatt, *Thailand: A Short History* (1984).

THAK CHALOEMTIARANA

PRINCELY STATES. The princely states of India and their rulers are usually portrayed as decadent remnants of traditional Indian culture or as artificial creations of British imperialists. In either case they are seen as hopelessly diverse and perplexingly numerous. These states and their rulers, however, embodied the interests of local magnates, military adventurers, caste groups, and large landholders who pursued various options to maintain their positions of dominance whenever threatened by a centralizing political force. When the British began to expand as a political power in India from the mid-eighteenth century, they were only the most recent example of a contender for empire in India who utilized local political leaders as allies and eventually as clients. The Mughal empire (1526–1858) had provided an excellent example of the successful use of client states in its relations with the Rajputs, and of an ineffective use in its relations with the Marathas.

There were three basic patterns for the evolution of princely states during the eighteenth century. First, there were the states that predated the Mughals and survived as their formal or informal allies, primarily those in Rajputana. Then there were those formed by Mughal provincial governors acting autonomously during the Mughal decline, namely Hyderabad, Awadh, and Bengal. Finally, there were the political entities or little kingdoms created by regional chiefs and military men who extended their authority as Mughal control weakened. This category included the Maratha pentarchy in western and central India that was initiated by Shivaji and expanded by later generals based at Baroda, Gwalior, Indore, and Nagpur; Mysore in the South; Sikh-ruled states in the Punjab; and those on the Mughal periphery such as Travancore and Cochin on the western coast of India. Some states in this group, especially those in South India, were territorially compact but most were geographically dispersed. This jigsaw puzzle arrangement reflected the political disorder of the late 1700s and the British intervention, which arrested the usual process of territorial consolidation. This classification also included many of those petty landholders, largely in western India around Kathiawar, who lacked most attributes of political autonomy but were lumped together with the princes for the sake of expediency. They constituted about 280 of the usually cited figure of 600 princely states.

After the British East India Company began to acquire revenue rights in Bengal and then around Madras and Bombay, they discovered that direct political control in India involved high costs in personnel and money. Since India was never viewed as a colony for settlement as were British claims in North America or Australia, the British sought col-laborators within Indian society. The Indian princes and their states were integrated as clients into the British imperial system through the use of subsidiary alliances beginning in the 1760s. Greatly expanded by Lord Wellesley, governor-general from 1799 to 1805, and consolidated by Lord Hastings, governor-general from 1813 to 1822, this treaty system provided for a delicate balance of interests. Although the company was the dominant patron, the princes received protection from internal revolts and external attacks in exchange for their loyalty and military and financial subsidies. The princes remained autonomous within their states but had to surrender control over their foreign policy, defense, and communications to their imperial overlord. The British thus acquired indirect control over vast areas but did not have to bear the burden of direct administration.

Throughout the first half of the nineteenth century the British continued to annex and rule directly some areas while allowing others to remain under princely rule. The policy of annexation was accelerated by Lord Dalhousie, governor-general from 1848 to 1856, as the British sought to rationalize their imperial administration, to extend "civilization" throughout India, to contain the threat of an expansionist Russia, and to increase their own resource base. These annexations, especially that of Awadh in 1856, were one factor that triggered the revolt of 1857.

Although a few rulers, such as Rani Lakshmi Bai of Jhansi, joined with the rebels, most princes either were too passive to challenge British authority openly or perceived the ultimate futility of contesting the British military strength. Their loyalty or indifference earned for the quiescent princes Queen Victoria's public renunciation of further annexations. Thus in 1858 the political map of India was frozen into British Indian provinces and princely states. The British directly administered three-fifths of the territory and two-thirds of the population of the Indian subcontinent while they controlled the remainder indirectly through the princes who were supposedly autonomous within their states.

Princely states were generally scattered on the periphery of British India and included economically unproductive areas or those whose geography made physical access and political control difficult. The major concentrations of princely states were in Rajputana around the Thar Desert; in the mountainous tracts of central India; in the remote districts of western India; in the Himalayas; in jungly Orissa; and in South India. The five largest states in territory were Jammu and Kashmir (85,885 square miles), Hyderabad (82,698 square miles), Kalat (73,278 square miles), Jodhpur (35,066 square miles), Mysore (29,475 square miles), and Gwalior (26,382 square miles). The five most populous states were Hyderabad, Mysore, Travancore, Jammu and Kashmir, and Gwalior. At the opposite extreme were twenty-four states in western India with less than one square mile of territory and fewer than one hundred people.

During the second half of the nineteenth century the British increasingly intervened in the internal affairs of the princely states, especially in succession disputes. They argued that as the paramount power in India they had the right and duty to ensure that good government would prevail. The Government of India exerted its influence through the advice of British political officers who handled relations with the states, the use of British officers or indigenous collaborators as administrators within the states, the threat of commissions of enquiry into alleged princely misdeeds or maladministration, the rewards of viceregal visits and new titles, and the proposed or actual deposition of a ruler.

As the challenges to their imperial authority shifted from military attacks to political agitations by Indian nationalists, the British evolved new functions for their princely clients. The princes were eulogized as natural leaders of voiceless peasants and were encouraged as both political and military allies. Schemes for an advisory council of princes to serve as a counterweight to legislative councils in British India were proposed in the 1870s and culminated in 1921 with the inauguration of the Chamber of Princes. The princes also aided less overtly in containing political disruption and acquired some influence in religious or communal politics. Nizam Usman Ali Khan of Hyderabad and Begum Sultan Jahan of Bhopal emerged as Muslim spokespersons, Maharaja Jai Singh of Alwar and Maharaja Madho Singh of Jaipur as Hindu protectors, Maharaja Madho Rao of Gwalior as a champion of Marathas, and maharajas Bhupinder Singh and Yadavindra Singh of Patiala as intermediaries with the Sikhs.

During the first half of the twentieth century the princes had an ambivalent relationship with their British patron. A new type of Indian prince was becoming prominent. Maharaja Ganga Singh of Bikaner was a prime example. Educated by British tutors privately or in a chiefs' college, accustomed to travel abroad, and possessing financial resources, some of the personally ambitious princes were seeking broader political arenas than those provided by their usually middle-sized states. They were, therefore, ready to move into new political roles. At the same time, many of these princes were concerned about the extent of British intervention in the internal affairs of their states. They sought to limit the exercise of paramountcy through resolutions in the Chamber of Princes, through testimony before the Indian States Committee of 1928, and finally through federation with the provinces of British India.

The federation that was provided for in the Government of India Act of 1935 was never achieved. One key reason was the debate over who should control the selection of representatives from the states to the federal assembly. This controversy reflected the shifting balance of power within princely states. In general, Indian princes were autocrats whose political authority was checked only by a feudal nobility (which included lineage members or military allies who helped in the creation of the states) and by the local British political officer. Princes were assisted by a *diwan,* or chief minister, and administrators who headed departments such as finance, revenue, household affairs, and public works. Frequently the *diwan* was a "foreigner," that is, either a Briton or an Indian from outside the state, such as the Tamil brahman *diwans* in Travancore or the Punjabi Muslims in Patiala. Middle-level administrative personnel could also be "foreign," such as the Kayasths in Hyderabad, who came from other regions of India but in time became natives, or they might be clan fellows of the prince. The administrator closest to the peasant subjects were the headmen and accountants selected by the village community.

There was a bureaucratization of the princely state administrations around 1900 but it proceeded unevenly. It was more extensive in states with greater resources and produced the much praised administrations of Mysore, Travancore, Cochin, and Baroda. These states acquired a progressive reputation because of the expansion of social services and public works, and the introduction of legislative assemblies. By the 1920s, however, most states experienced increasing demands from both their subjects and the British for more efficient administrations and more responsive governments. The main requests were for a defined privy purse, an independent judiciary, and fewer restrictions on the press and public meetings.

Political activity within the states was initially dominated by a small elite dependent on the prince or possessing large landholdings. They had a style

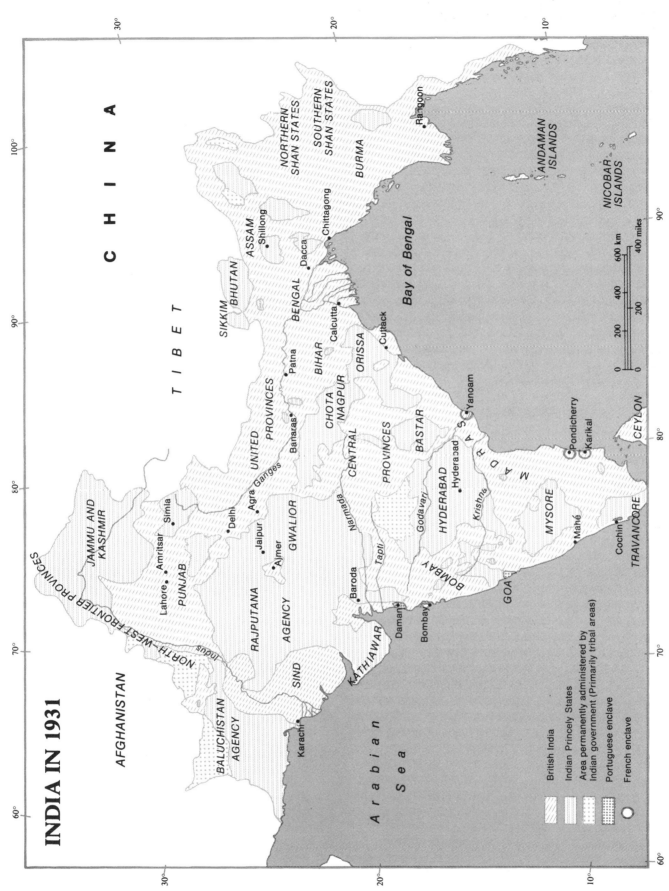

INDIA IN 1931

British India

Indian Princely States

Area permanently administered by
Indian government (Primarily tribal areas)

Portuguese enclave

French enclave

AFGHANISTAN

NORTH-WEST FRONTIER PROVINCES

CHINA

TIBET

Indus

BALUCHISTAN
AGENCY

SIND

JAMMU AND
KASHMIR

PUNJAB

Lahore

Amritsar

Simla

Delhi

Jaipur

Ajmer

RAJPUTANA
AGENCY

GWALIOR

KATHIAWAR

Karachi

Arabian
Sea

Baroda

Damani

Bombay

GOA

BOMBAY

Narmada

Tapti

UNITED
PROVINCES

Agra

Ganges

Banaras

Patna

BIHAR

CHOTA
NAGPUR

CENTRAL
PROVINCES

BASTAR

HYDERABAD

Hyderabad

Krishna

Goda Vari

MADRAS

MYSORE

Mahé

Cochin

TRAVANCORE

CEYLON

Pondicherry

Karikal

Yanoam

Cuttack

ORISSA

Calcutta

BENGAL

Dacca

Chittagong

Shillong

ASSAM

SIKKIM

BHUTAN

NORTHERN
SHAN STATES

SOUTHERN
SHAN STATES

BURMA

Rangoon

Bay of Bengal

ANDAMAN
ISLANDS

NICOBAR
ISLANDS

600 km

400 miles

400

200

200

0

30°

20°

10°

30°

20°

10°

60°

70°

80°

90°

100°

60°

70°

80°

90°

100°

marked by personal relationships, private negotiations, intrigue, and consensus. By the 1920s more popularly based political leaders started to form states' people's associations. These groups sought the ouster of "foreign" *diwans,* the establishment or expansion of legislative assemblies, and the election of state representatives to a federal assembly as opposed to their appointment by the princes. Sometimes based in British India because of princely opposition, the states' people's groups formed regional and national networks, which culminated in the All India States' People's Conference. Although the Congress Socialist Party, formed in 1934, was outspoken in its support for states' people's groups, the Indian National Congress, and more particularly, Mohandas Gandhi, pursued ambivalent policies toward states' people's groups. The Congress wanted to avoid an overextension of its resources and to maintain some leverage in future negotiations with the princes; therefore as an organization it formally abstained from involvement in the states. However, its Haripura resolution of 1938 allowed individual Congress members to participate in states' people's agitations.

The end of the British empire in 1947 resulted in the integration of the princely states into the two newly independent states of India and Pakistan. Physical integration had been fostered by an expanding network of common services, such as rail, postal, and telegraph and telephone systems, and the porous nature of territorial boundaries between British India and the princely states. The failure of most princes to institute democratic reforms had undercut their political viability once their imperial patron and protector was removed from the scene. Sardar Vallabhbhai Patel and V. P. Menon negotiated the actual accession of the states to the Indian Union and Mohammad Ali Jinnah and Liaqat Ali Khan had ultimate responsibility for the process in Pakistan. Most princes acceded quickly in return for a guaranteed privy purse and other personal privileges. Junagadh and Hyderabad joined India only after police actions; Jammu and Kashmir still remains divided between India and Pakistan. The largest princely states, such as Hyderabad and Mysore, joined India as distinct units, as did Bahawalpur and Khairpur in Pakistan. Many middle-sized states were grouped together, such as Patiala and East Punjab States Union (PEPSU); Rajasthan state and the smallest states were amalgamated with the neighboring British Indian province.

The consolidation of West Pakistan into one unit in 1954 and the States Reorganization Act of 1956 in India have erased most princely states as distinct territorial units. Only Mysore has survived as the core of Karnataka and Travancore and Cochin are the center of Kerala. The princely states had outlived their political usefulness with the advent of democratic central governments, but the local political and economic interests they secured now utilize other instruments more appropriate to electoral politics.

[*Most of the individuals, caste groups, and princely states mentioned in this article are the subject of independent entries; see also* East India Company.]

S. R. Ashton, *British Policy toward the Indian States, 1905–1939* (1982). Maharaja of Baroda, *The Palaces of India* (1980). Mohandas K. Gandhi, *The Indian States' Problem* (1941). Robin Jeffrey, ed., *People, Princes and Paramount Power: Society and Politics in the Indian Princely States* (1978). V. P. Menon, *The Story of the Integration of the Indian States* (1956). Urmila Phadnis, *Towards the Integration of the Indian States, 1919–1947* (1968). Barbara N. Ramusack, *The Princes of India in the Twilight of Empire: Dissolution of a Patron-Client System, 1914–1939* (1978).   BARBARA N. RAMUSACK

PRINCIPALIA, the body of indigenous officials who administered municipal (*pueblo*) governments under Spanish rule in the Philippines. The *principalia* was composed of former and incumbent *cabezas de barangay* (responsible for tribute collection, labor service obligations, and maintenance of order within their *barangay*), the *gobernadorcillo* (later *capitán municipal,* the equivalent of a municipal mayor and justice of the peace), and several municipal lieutenants. The office of *cabeza de barangay,* initially hereditary, was later filled mostly by appointment. The *gobernadorcillo* and his lieutenants were elected indirectly each year by an electoral board made up of thirteen members of the *principalia* selected by lots. The members of the *principalia,* the *principales,* were exempt from tribute and labor services. Most historical writing on the Philippines has depicted the *principalia* as an indigenous, elite upper class or aristocracy that not only controlled access to local bureaucratic positions but also dominated the local society and economy. Although this may have been so, relatively little is known about the evolution of the *principalia* during the first two centuries of Spanish rule. Nevertheless, a large number of *principales* emerged as a rural gentry—a municipal elite—having profited from the economic changes that began to occur in the late eighteenth century.

In the nineteenth century most observers described Philippine rural society as two-tiered, consisting of the *principalia* and peasant farmers. Recent studies have suggested a greater social and economic complexity, both above and below the *principalia,* in most municipalities during the late nineteenth century. *Principales* everywhere played leading roles in the major events, especially at the turn of the century and in particular in the Philippine Revolution (1896) and the Philippine-American War (1899–1902).

[*See also* Philippines; Barangay; Philippine Revolution; *and* Philippine-American War.]

Onofre D. Corpuz, *Bureaucracy in the Philippines* (1957). Norman G. Owen, "The Principalia in Philippine History: Kabikolan, 1790–1898," *Philippine Studies* 22 (1974): 297–324.   MICHAEL CULLINANE

PRINSEP, JAMES (1799–1840), an East India Company servant famed for his Orientalist research. Prinsep served under H. H. Wilson and followed Wilson as secretary of the Asiatic Society of Bengal. Prinsep is known for deciphering the Pali script on the Ashokan pillars and for his research into Indian coinage. [*See also* Asiatic Society of Bengal.]

LYNN ZASTOUPIL

PRITHVINARAYAN SHAH (1723–1775), known as the founder of modern Nepal. His career of conquest started in 1743 when he became king of Gorkha, a hill state sixty miles west of Kathmandu. Its peak was reached in the subjugation of the three Newar kingdoms of the Kathmandu Valley in 1768–1769. He wanted his hard-earned state to endure and so made a testament at his death, gathered in a book called the *Divya upadesha*. Here Prithvinarayan warns his successors about the dangers of an indolent and luxurious life, and the intentions of the English on Nepal.

[*See also* Nepal: History of Nepal.]

D. R. Regmi, *Modern Nepal,* 2 vols. (1975). L. F. Stiller, *Prithvinarayan Shah in the Light of Dibya Upadesh* (1968).   PRAYAG RAJ SHARMA

PRITHVIRAJ CHAUHAN (b. 1166; r. 1178–1192), foremost ruler of the Chauhan dynasty of India. He ascended the throne at Ajaymeru (Ajmer) and consolidated his rule in 1180 by suppressing revolts and fortifying his northwestern frontier against the Muslims. In pursuit of a North Indian paramountcy, he triumphed against the traditional enemies of his dynasty, notably the Chalukyas of Gujarat and the Chandellas of Jejakbhukti, and defeated Muhammad Ghuri in a spectacular victory in the battle of Tarain in 1191. But a reckless campaign against the Gahadavala king Jayachandra of Kanauj in 1191 enabled the strengthened Muhammad Ghuri to defeat the now weakened Prithviraj in 1192 on the very same battlefield. Prithviraj lost the war as well as his life, and Muslim rule was established in North India.

[*See also* Chauhan Dynasty.]

D. Sharma, *Early Chauhan Dynasties* (2d ed., 1975).

SHIVA BAJPAI

PRIYAYI, the traditional governing upper class of Java. *Priyayi* might be aristocrats, officials holding a high position in the court, or local chiefs. The ideal of the *priyayi,* defined by the court of Mataram (Central Java) and its successors, influenced other parts of Java and other ethnic groups (Sundanese, Madurese) as well as Javanese. Ideally a *priyayi* was well born and versed in the aristocratic culture of the courts (classical literature, music and drama, shadow-puppet plays, philosophy, and mysticism). He was expected to display integrity and honor, having a duty to both ruler and people.

Although in theory all *priyayi* derived their authority from the ruler, in practice local chiefs in outlying regions had considerable autonomy. As the Dutch extended their sway over Java, they detached the provincial *priyayi* elite from the Javanese courts and worked through it. Under the Dutch East India Company (VOC) this did not require radical change in the position of the *priyayi,* but economic expansion in the nineteenth and twentieth centuries demanded a more efficient and rational bureaucracy. This led to increasing westernization of the *priyayi* and, in consequence, to their identification with the Dutch and alienation from the people. Agrarian protest movements in Java were as often directed against the *priyayi* as against their Dutch masters.

The *priyayi* themselves were never allowed to become more than junior partners of the Dutch, and the Javanese members of the Western-educated intelligentsia that created the Indonesian nationalist movement originated in the *priyayi* class. Despite the extensive changes that have occurred since Indonesian independence, the *priyayi* ethos is still invoked in the Indonesian civil and military bureaucracies.

Clifford Geertz's division of Javanese religion into three variants has been influential among English-speaking students of Indonesia, but it has been criticized by Indonesian scholars for confusing social class (*priyayi*) with religio-cultural variants (Islamic *santri*, syncretic *abangan*).

[*See also* Java; Mataram; Dutch East India Company; Santri; *and* Abangan.]

Clifford Geertz, *The Religion of Java* (1960). Soemarsaid Moertono, *State and Statecraft in Old Java: A Study of the Later Mataram Period, Sixteenth to Nineteenth Century* (1968). H. Sutherland, "The Priyayi," *Indonesia* 19 (April 1975): 57–77.   CHARLES A. COPPEL

PROHIBITION IN INDIA. Large numbers of experiments with prohibition have taken place at state and national levels in modern India. Much of the impetus for this is derived from Mohandas Gandhi's strong emphasis on prohibition as a measure for improving the plight of India's poor. The most ambitious policy was undertaken by Prime Minister Morarji Desai (1977–1979), who excluded from his cabinet anyone known to drink alcohol and who surrounded himself with teetotalers from the upper-echelon bureaucracy. [*See* Desai, Morarji.] When Desai failed to get national laws banning liquor, he pushed through piecemeal administrative orders to bottleneck sales, including limits on the size of liquor retail outlets so that one had to stoop to enter and could barely move once inside them. The remants of such bottlenecks, plus continued bans on sales in some states, has sustained continued controversy, provided a source of revenue for organized crime, and resulted in a number of tragic cases of death from bootleg liquor.

Mohan Ram, "India's Liquor Trade," *Far Eastern Economic Review* 105 (1979).   MARCUS FRANDA

PROME. Old Prome, or Sriksetra, was one of the urbanized sites of the Pyu peoples of Burma. Located on the Irrawaddy River between Pagan and the Lower Burma coasts, it was about 180 miles north of present-day Rangoon. It has been dated as early as the middle centuries of the first millennium CE, and it reached its apogee between the sixth and ninth century, when a royal dynasty, known in the epigraphs as the Vikramas, was in power.

Although the walled capital city appears to have been circular, all its distinctive features are similar to those found in the more familiar rectangular and square cities of Burma. Evidence of monastic establishments, sizable brick stupas, numerous silver coins used as specie (and symbolically), a variety of bronze and stone sculptures (some secular, some with Hindu-Buddhist themes), and stone burial urns typical of other first-millennium sites in Burma suggest that Sriksetra was a major political, economic, and cultural center of the Pyu. It is thought that by the first quarter of the ninth century Sriksetra declined when the forces of Nanzhao upset the balance of power in the Irrawaddy River valley, allowing the Burmans to establish their dominance over Burma for the next millennium. The capital of the Pyu for most of their paramountcy, Old Prome was thereafter an important provincial center during this formative age in Burma's history.

[*See also* Pyu.]

Aung Thaw, *Historical Sites in Burma* (1972).

MICHAEL AUNG-THWIN

PROPAGANDA MOVEMENT, movement in the Philippines to acquire greater rights from Spain. Historians have given different dates for the Propaganda Movement depending on their understanding of it; as understood in this article it took place from 1880 to 1895. In the strictest sense it takes its name from the Comité de Propaganda, a small group of men in Manila who delegated Marcelo H. del Pilar to carry on the work of obtaining reforms for the Philippines in Spain and who agreed to support the work. Del Pilar arrived in Barcelona in 1889, finding the Filipino colony there already proposing the foundation of a newspaper called *La Solidaridad,* with Graciano Lopez Jaena, a longtime expatriate with radical connections among Spanish republicans, as editor. In fact, however, del Pilar was the main organizer and source of finances from Manila. In October 1889 del Pilar became editor and moved the fortnightly newspaper to Madrid, where it remained until it closed down for lack of funds in 1895.

La Solidaridad's goals were assimilationist, that is, it asked for such reforms as freedom of press, speech, and association, such as existed in Spain, and for representation in the Spanish Cortes. The basis of its campaign was that the Philippines was an integral part of Spain, and hence should be ruled by the same laws. In addition it called for the expulsion of the friars from the Philippines and their substitution by secular priests. Del Pilar also wrote a number of anonymous antifriar parodies in Tagalog for Philippine consumption, as well as serious works intended for Spanish politicians, such as his *La soberanía monacal en Filipinas (Monastic Supremacy in the Philippines).*

In a wider sense the Propaganda Movement has been taken to include the years 1880–1895, the period in which the Filipinos in Spain, through various newspapers and negotiations with Spanish politicians, attempted to make the Philippines and its needs known in Spain. This has been called the reform movement because its ostensible purpose was reform. But many of those involved, such as Jose Rizal and del Pilar, used reform merely as a facade; they were committed to the eventual separation of the Philippines from Spain.

[*See also* Philippines; Philippine Revolution; Pilar, Marcelo H. del; Friars; *and* Rizal, Jose Mercado.]

Leon Ma. Guerrero, *The First Filipino* (1963). Cesar A. Majul, *The Political and Constitutional Ideas of the Philippine Revolution* (1957). Marcelo H. del Pilar, *Monastic Supremacy in the Philippines,* translated by Encarnacion Alzona (1958). John N. Schumacher, *The Propaganda Movement.*   JOHN N. SCHUMACHER, S.J.

PROVINCE WELLESLEY, small territory on the mainland of the Malay Peninsula opposite Penang Island, administratively connected to Penang since 1800.

Relations between the British East India Company (EIC) and the sultans of Kedah were strained following the British occupation of Penang in 1786: the sultan was not getting the protection against Siam he thought he had been promised, and the British were nervous about insecurity on the mainland opposite the island. The EIC was all the more alarmed when Sultan Abdullah (r. 1778–1798) of Kedah began to develop a port at Kuala Perai, opposite George Town. Both to quash competition and to secure Penang's safety and food supply, the EIC negotiated with Sultan Diya ud-Din Mukarram Shah (r. 1798–1803) the lease of 285 square miles of land on the mainland, between the Krian and Muda rivers, in return for an annual rent and further vague promises to assist in the defense of Kedah against Siam. Today, Province Wellesley is part of Penang State, a constituent part of Malaysia.

[*See also* Penang; Kedah; *and* Malaysia.]

R. Bonney, *Kedah 1771–1821* (1971). Barbara W. Andaya and Leonard W. Andaya, *A History of Malaysia* (1982).   DAVID K. WYATT

PULGUK TEMPLE (Korean, Pulguksa), one of the oldest monasteries of the Korean Buddhist tradition, located in modern North Kyŏngsang Province, near the old Silla capital of Kyŏngju. According to the *Pulguksa kogŭm ch'angki* (*Record of the Past and*

FIGURE 1. *Pulguk Temple, Kyŏngju.*

Present Construction of Pulguksa), the monastery was founded in 528, one year after the official acceptance of Buddhism in Silla, and was reconstructed in 574. The *Samguk yusa* (*Memorabilia and Mirabilia of the Three Kingdoms*) relates that a major expansion of the temple took place in 751 under the direction of the prime minister, Kim Taesŏng (700–774). During the Silla period the monastery was an important site for state ritual observances, such as national protection rites. Sŏkkuram, a stone grotto enshrining the most famous Buddha-image in Korea, is located in the mountains behind the monastery. Several other Korean national treasures are preserved on the temple grounds, including the Tabo-t'ap (Stupa of Abundant Jewels), and a massive stone pagoda 10.4 meters tall, built in a style unique in Korea.

Robert E. Fisher, "Stone Pagodas of Korea," *Korean Culture* 2.1 (February 1981): 8–15.

ROBERT E. BUSWELL, JR.

PULO CONDORE. *See* Con Son Islands.

PUNE (Poona), city in Maharashtra, India. It is first mentioned in the copper plates of the Rashtrakuta king Krishna I (dated 758 and 768) as Punya Vishaya or Punya Vishayak; *vishaya* was an administrative unit. As it is on the confluence of Mula and Mutha rivers, it was also called Punnak and Punyapur. After the Yadavas, Pune came under Muslim rulers (1340–1595), who fortified it with a mud wall. In the fifteenth century it was a great center of learning. The *nizamshah* granted it to Maloji Bhonsale, grandfather of the Maratha hero Shivaji, and it remained with the Marathas until 1818. Morar Jagdeo, the Adil Shahi noble, destroyed the city in 1631. Under Shahaji, Dadoji Kondadev, the monitor of his son Shivaji, rehabilitated it and built the Lal Mahal, a palace where Shivaji, along with his mother Jijabai, spent his childhood. For his capital, however, Shivaji preferred hill forts like Rajgad and Raigad, rather than Pune, an open place.

The Mughals captured Pune in 1685 and it remained with them for a short period. Aurangzeb renamed it Mohiyabad in 1703. Pune came to prominence under the Peshwas. Bajirao I received it from Shahu in 1725 and constructed the Shanwar Palace (1730–1732). His son Balaji developed and beautified it by building temples on Parvati Hill. Pune became political center of the Maratha country after Shahu's death in 1749, and because of brahman dominance, it developed as a cultural center. Pillaged and ransacked by the *nizam* (1763), Daulatrao Shinde (1797), and Yeshwantrao Holkar (1802), Pune was finally occupied by the British in 1817–1818. It declined for some time after the fall of the Peshwas but again came to prominence when the British declared it their second capital. Next to Bombay in size, it is developing as an industrial city with an urban agglomerate population of 1,685,300 (1981 census).

[*See also* Maharashtra *and* Shivaji.]

D. B. Parasnis, *Poona in Bygone Days* (1921). S. B. Sawant, *The City of Poona* (1978).   A. R. KULKARNI

PUNJAB. The word *Punjab* or *Panjab* is derived from two Persian terms, *panch* ("five") and *ab* ("waters"), and refers to the land through which flow five rivers: the Jhelum, Chenab, Ravi, Beas, and Sutlej. The exact borders of this area are not fixed and have often included all land between the Indus River, further west of the Chenab, and the Sutlej on its eastern edge. Under the British, Punjab had as its eastern border the Jumna (Yamuna) River rather than the Sutlej. To the north, the Punjab includes the Siwalik Hills, the lowest range of the Himalayan barrier, and to the south it roughly terminates at the confluence of the Indus and Panjnad rivers. Between the rivers lie the doabs, elevated strips of land separated by two river basins. The Punjab plains are dry and subject to undependable rainfall. Consequently, agriculture developed along the rivers, as did most of the cities and towns, while the doabs were used primarily for grazing until irrigation systems could open them to farming. The Punjab, with its location west of the Ganges Plain and east of the Iranian Plateau, has been crisscrossed by several major trade routes since antiquity.

The Punjab was a major site of the Indus Valley Civilization (c. 2700 BCE–c. 1700 BCE), an agricultural society that encompassed the entire Indus River basin. [*See* Indus Valley Civilization.] A nomadic people, the Aryans, entered the Punjab from the northwest about 1700–1500 BCE and conquered and replaced the Indus civilization with their own village society. By 1000 BCE towns reappeared on the eastern edge of the Punjab and, as civilization extended into the Ganges basin, the Punjab became a border area sometimes dominated by empires to the east and at other times by states to the west. In the sixth century BCE, Darius I, ruler of the Achaemenid empire, annexed the Punjab. The Persians held it until Alexander of Macedon destroyed their empire. Alexander penetrated the Punjab in 327–325 BCE, fought against the local rulers, and then departed. [*See* Alexander III.] In the fourth century the Punjab came under control first of the Nanda dynasty and then under the Maurya empire, whose base was in Bihar. [*See* Maurya Empire.] The Punjab remained part of an extensive Indian state from the fourth to the second century BCE. When the Maurya empire disintegrated after 182 BCE, the Punjab again became a path of immigration from Central Asia through Afghanistan and the passes on the eastern edge of the Iranian Plateau. Following the steps of the Aryans and Persians came Indo-Greeks in the second century BCE, Sakas in the first century BCE, Kushans in the first century CE, and Hunas in the sixth century. Although these dates are still being debated, it is clear that the population of the Punjab underwent considerable modification as new groups of invaders were added to the original inhabitants. It was a center of both physical and cultural intermixing, particularly the Gandhara region on the northwestern edge of the Punjab.

At the end of the tenth century the Punjab underwent the beginnings of a fundamental change in its culture. Under the leadership of the sultan of Ghazna, an empire centered in eastern Afghanistan, Muslims began raids into the Punjab and further east. Raiding continued through the eleventh century and by the end of the twelfth century it shifted to the process of annexation. The Afghan kingdom of Ghur replaced Ghazna and sections of the Punjab were absorbed by this state. Between 1192 and 1206 the army of Muhammad Ghuri conquered northern India as far east as Bengal, founding the Delhi sultanate, which lasted from 1206 to 1526. [*See* Delhi Sultanate.] Once again the Punjab became a border province of an empire, this time based in Delhi and ruled by a Muslim military elite. The Mongols raided Punjab during the fourteenth century, but the Delhi sultanate succeeded in holding them at bay. In 1398 the Persian ruler Timur fought his way through the Punjab to Delhi and sacked the city before returning once more through the Punjab. A new empire was created by Babur, founder of the Mughal empire. The Punjab remained under control of the Mughal empire from the mid-sixteenth century until its decline in the first half of the eighteenth century. The loss of power by the Mughals led to another period of incursions from the northwest and the south, as Afghans, Mughals, Marathas, and a new historic force, the Sikhs, struggled to control the Punjab.

The long history of Muslim dominance has created a sizable community of Punjabi Muslims in this region both through immigration and conversion. It had also seen the destruction of Jain and Buddhist communities. Guru Nanak (1469–1539) began the creation of a new religious community. He founded a quietist sect that stressed a strict morality and monotheism while rejecting caste, idolatry, and the role of brahman priests. Nanak drew on the rich Sant tradition of Hinduism and on Islamic mysticism. The Sikh disciples grew and under the leadership of ten gurus a religion developed with its own scriptures, rituals, and customs. In 1606 Guru Arjun, the fifth in the line of succession, was executed by the Mughal emperor Jahangir. Afterward an intense animosity developed between the Sikhs and the Mughal government. [See Mughal Empire.] Following the execution of Guru Tegh Bahadur by Emperor Aurangzeb in 1675 antagonism became warfare. Under the leadership of Guru Gobind Singh (1675–1708) the Sikh religion was reshaped and fused with military values, ending a transition from the original teachings of Nanak to an aggressive religious community engaged in a lengthy military struggle. In 1799 the Sikhs established their own kingdom under the leadership of Maharaja Ranjit Singh, who ruled the Punjab until his death in 1839. [See Singh, Ranjit.] In 1846 the first Anglo-Sikh War resulted in the British annexation of the Jullundur Doab and in 1849, after the Second Anglo-Sikh War, the British-Indian government seized the entire Punjab.

Under British administration the Punjab was given a set of English laws, new concepts of land ownership, a system of roads and railways, and the introduction of schools teaching literacy in both English and the vernaculars. The British also introduced an extensive system of canal irrigation that produced a significant rise in agricultural productivity. They were accompanied by aggressive Christian missionaries who heightened existing religious competition. In 1891 the Punjab was divided into three major religious communities: Muslims (50 percent), Hindus (38 percent), and Sikhs (12 percent). Punjabis were drawn into competing socio-religious movements: the Arya Samaj, Dev Samaj, and Sanatana Dharm Sabha among Hindus; the Ahmadiyya, Ahl-i Hadis, and Ahl-i-Qur'an among Muslims; and the Namdharis, Nirankaris and Singh Sabhas among the Sikhs. By the close of the nineteenth century religious competition intensified as each community became associated with a particular language and script: Muslims with Urdu written in the Arabic script, Hindus with Hindi in the Devanagari script, Sikhs with Punjabi in the Gurmukhi script, and Christians with English in the Roman script. [See Arya Samaj; Ahmadiyya; and Ahl-i Hadis.]

During the first half of the twentieth century the Punjab was subject to religious and political conflict. Sikh and Hindu revolutionaries of the Ghadr Party turned to open rebellion in the years 1913 to 1915 and on 13 April 1919, the city of Amritsar was the scene of the Jallianwala Bagh massacre in which 379 protestors were killed and more than 1,200 wounded. [See Ghadr and Jallianwala Bagh Massacre.] In the years 1920 to 1925 militant Sikhs launched the Gurdwara reform campaign, a struggle that employed both nonviolent and violent tactics. It also led to the creation of the Shiromani Gurdwara Prabandhak Committee and the Akali Dal, two organizations that still dominate Sikh politics. [See Akali Dal.] Through the 1920s and 1930s the rural-based Unionist Party dominated Punjab politics, but by the mid-1940s it lost power to communal organizations as the Punjab was divided by rival forms of nationalism. [See Unionist Party.] The Punjab was formally bifurcated in 1947 with the creation of two new nation states, India and Pakistan. The new international border ran north and south between the cities of Lahore and Amritsar. Refugees fled the Punjab: Muslims moved west, while Hindus and Sikhs fled east. The Punjab became a border area for two nations and was the scene of fighting in the Indo-Pakistani wars of 1965 and 1971. [See Partition of India.]

Pakistani Punjab was initially a separate province within the new country, but in October 1955 West Pakistan became a single administrative and political unit. [See Pakistan.] A separate Punjab province ceased to exist until it was reinstated in October 1970 when Punjab became one of four states in the divided Pakistan. After independence, Indian Punjab consisted of the British-administered territories. In 1957 these districts were fused with several princely states to create a state of Punjab. At the same time the Punjab hill states were joined together to form a new political division, Himachal Pradesh. [*See* Himachal Pradesh.] In 1966 Indian Punjab was divided into a Punjab state made up of the northern Punjabi-speaking area and Haryana, composed of the southern Hindi-speaking districts. [*See* Haryana.] At the same time hill tracts formerly part of the Punjab were added to Himachal Pradesh. Indian Punjab remains torn by religious conflict, this time between Hindus and Sikhs, while Pakistani Punjab is the scene of competing linguistic and cultural groups. Culturally the Punjab has become increasingly divided. The Urdu language in Pakistani Punjab is steadily evolving toward close links with Arabic and with Middle Eastern culture, while Hindi and Punjabi have lost much of the Perso-Arabic influence built over centuries of Islamic domination.

[*See also* Amritsar; Lahore; Sikhism; *and* Nanak.]

Bridget Allchin and Raymond Allchin, *The Birth of Indian Civilization: India and Pakistan before 500 B. C.* (1968). G. S. Chhabra, *The Advanced History of the Punjab,* 2 vols. (1962).   KENNETH W. JONES

PURANAS. The Puranas are a class of ancient Sanskrit texts, dating from about the fourth century BCE to the fourteenth century CE, whose subjects are the traditional history and genealogies of gods, *rishis,* heros, and kings, as well as many other subjects.

The Puranas, literally meaning "old, ancient," are texts reworked by brahman redactors based on earlier *kshatriya* traditions that had been handed down orally by the nonbrahman bards *(suta).* According to tradition, Krishna Dvaipayana Vyasa, who arranged the Veda, also compiled the original Purana from various stories, and it seems that there was a core text going back to *suta* traditions from the time of the Mauryas, based on traditions dating from the Vedic period. The older Purana texts were well known by the Gupta period.

Although in a broad sense Purana can include history *(itihasa),* in its narrow sense it refers to a group of eighteen major texts. These are called Mahapuranas and included the *Brahma, Padma, Vishnu, Vayu, Bhagavata, Brihannaradiya, Markandeya, Agni, Bhavishya, Brahmavaivarta, Linga, Varaha, Skanda, Vamana, Kurma, Matsya, Garuda,*

and *Brahmanda* Puranas. There are similar related texts called Upapuranas ("sub-Puranas"). There are discrepancies in some of the lists—some Upapuranas being considered Mahapuranas and vice-versa. Their manuscript traditions offer a wide variety of interpretations.

The Puranas claim for themselves five topics of interest: creation of the world; its dissolution and recreation; lineages *(vamsha)* of gods, sages, and kings; the deeds of the royal dynasties; and the cosmic ages of the world *(manvanatara).* Much else is included, however, ranging from sacred geography to Dharmashastra. Most of the major Puranas also display some sectarian bias, either Vaishnavite or Shaivite. The *Bhagavata Purana,* for instance, is one of the most important source texts for the Krishna tradition.

[*See also* Hinduism.]

R. C. Hazra, *"Puranas,"* in *The Cultural Heritage of India,* vol. 2 (2d ed., 1962). F. E. Pargiter, *Ancient Indian Traditions: A Historical Account of Vedic and Puranic Traditions* (1922; reprint, 1979). J. L. Shastri, ed., *Ancient Indian Tradition and Mythology Series. Puranas in Translation* (1968–).   RANDOLPH M. THORNTON

PURE CONVERSATION. *See* Qingtan.

PURE LAND. The Pure Land (Japanese, Jōdo) is a concept central to a popular strain of Buddhism that took root particularly in Japan. The term refers to the Western Paradise of the Buddha called in Sanskrit Amitabha (Chinese, Amituofo; Japanese, Amida). Pure Land Buddhism, therefore, is the current of Buddhist devotionalism focused on Amitabha and entry to his paradise. The emphasis in Pure Land Buddhism is less on the attainment of salvation or enlightenment by one's own efforts (Japanese, *jiriki*), than on salvation through the saving power of another *(tariki),* in this case Amitabha.

The Pure Land has been vividly described in sutras, commentaries, and artistic representations by Chinese and Japanese monks. Early descriptions of the Pure Land and means of access to it are provided in the three principal Pure Land sutras: the *Larger Sukhavativyuha Sutra,* the *Smaller Sukhavativyuha Sutra,* and the *Amitayurdhyana Sutra (Guan wuliangshou jing). Sukhavati* means "pure and happy land," and the sutras describe the infinite pleasures of the paradise presided over by Amitabha. This early vision of the Pure Land was added to by Chinese and Japanese commentators, including the

Chinese Pure Land master Shandao (613–681) and the Japanese Tendai monk Genshin (942–1017). Paintings of Amida welcoming the deceased into his Pure Land and Pure Land halls, in which statues of Amida were enshrined, rank among the finest expressions of East Asian art and architecture.

In early Pure Land belief, as outlined in the longer version of the *Sukhavativyuha*, access to the Pure Land was to be attained by sincere devotion to Amida expressed in the accumulation of karmic merit by prayer and good works. In the shorter version of the sutra less emphasis was placed on merit accumulation and more on faith. For centuries the Pure Land was believed to be accessible only to monks and nuns or to very devoted laypeople who could give themselves fully to prayer and contemplation of the virtues of Amitabha. Surges of popular Pure Land devotion took place in China from the sixth and seventh centuries and in Japan from the twelfth and thirteenth centuries, when entry to the Pure Land was promised to all men and women and made readily attainable by the faithful invocation of Amida's name. This practice, known in Japan as *nembutsu* (Chinese, *nianfo*) was believed to trigger the compassionate vows of Amitabha to save all beings. Those monks who popularized the Pure Land in China included Huiyuan (334–417), Daochuo (562–645), and Shandao. The principal Pure Land pioneers in Japan were Kōya (903–972), Genshin, Hōnen (1133–1212), Shinran (1173–1262), Ippen (1239–1289), and Rennyo (1415–1499).

[*See also* Amidism.]

Wm. Theodore de Bary, ed., *The Buddhist Tradition in India, China, and Japan* (1969). John M. Rosenfield and Elizabeth ten Grotenhuis, eds., *Journey of the Three Jewels* (1979), pp. 115–163.   MARTIN COLLCUTT

PUSHYABHUTI DYNASTY.

The Pushyabhuti (or Pushpabhuti) dynasty ruled from Thaneshwar (present-day Haryana) during the early sixth century CE and is best known for its final and by far most famous king, Harsha (606–647). He assumed the throne at Kanauj, dominating much of Uttar Pradesh, Bihar, and Bengal at the peak of his reign. Although a Shaivite, Harsha provided such generous patronage for Buddhists, at Nalanda for example, that he is often assumed to have been a Buddhist. Harsha's history is known from the *Harshacharita* by Bana, the celebrated poet under his patronage, as well as from epigraphic sources and the account of the Chinese pilgrim Xuanzang.

[*See also* Harsha; Kanyakubja; *and* Nalanda.]

Brijnath Sharma, *Harṣa and His Times* (1970). R. S. Tripathi, *History of Kanauj to the Moslem Conquest* (1964).   FREDERICK M. ASHER

PU SONGLING (1640–1715), Chinese author, best known for *Liaozhai zhiyi*, a collection of 431 literary-language short stories. In content like the supernatural tales of the Tang and Song dynasties, the stories are distinguished by a sense of local color, a graceful style and diction, and by literary allusions. Circulated in manuscript form in Pu's lifetime (published 1766), the collection was the chief work in the genre of literary narrative that was widely appreciated by literati.

Jaroslav Prušek, "P'u Sung-ling and His Work," in *Chinese History and Literature: Collection of Studies* (1970), pp. 109–138. Pu Songling, *Strange Stories from a Chinese Studio*, translated by Herbert A. Giles (reprint, 1969).   SHAN CHOU

PUYI. *See* Xuantong Emperor.

PUYŎ (Chinese, Fuyu), a people of central Manchuria who migrated to the Korean peninsula. The Puyŏ were already settled on the upper Sungari River when the Chinese first made contact with them late in the third century BCE. The Puyŏ were agriculturalist tribesmen, and in later centuries traded some of their nonagricultural products—horses, sable fur, and precious stones—for silk and embroidered cloth from Han China. The ruling group in Puyŏ consisted of a relatively small elite controlling a subject population of semiservile status. When members of the elite died, their dependents were buried with them, often in considerable numbers, as had been the practice in China itself during the Shang dynasty. Other Puyŏ customs, such as the practice of levirate, were more similar to those of the surrounding nomadic peoples.

At some time in the remote past, a group of five tribes broke away from the main Puyŏ confederacy and moved south toward the headwaters of the Yalu River, being compelled by their new environment to take up a way of life that was heavily dependent on hunting and fishing. From at least as early as the first century BCE this group became the clients of the Chinese commandery of Xuantu; they were to form the nucleus of the later kingdom of Koguryŏ, throwing off all Chinese control after 12 CE. Until this time, Puyŏ itself had remained very much on the fringes of the Chinese world, but as Koguryŏ raids threatened both Puyŏ and the Chinese frontier, China and Puyŏ were drawn into an alliance. In 121 the Puyŏ king Wigut'ae led a force of twenty thousand men to relieve the Chinese garrison of Xuantu, which was being besieged by the ruler of Koguryŏ. At this time Puyŏ was at the height of its power, and the kingdom had extended its control over various less sophisticated groups, particularly those inhabiting the area between the Sungari basin and the coast of what is now the Soviet Maritime Province.

Toward the end of the second century CE the warlord Gongsun Du came to power in Liaodong and continued the traditional Chinese policy of friendship with Puyŏ by giving a girl of his own clan in marriage to the Puyŏ king, whose name is again given as Wigut'ae. When, in 238, the Gongsun lordship of Liaodong fell before the armies of the Wei dynasty, a series of Puyŏ "tribute missions"—in reality trading ventures—visited the Wei court at Luoyang. By this time Puyŏ was growing steadily weaker, and the tribes east of the Sungari had succeeded in throwing off Puyŏ control. Communications between Puyŏ and China were also threatened by the settlement of the Murong branch of the Xianbei nomads north of the Chinese commandery of Liaoxi. At this period of crisis Puyŏ's king was the child Ŭiryŏ, who had succeeded to the throne at the age of five or six. In 285 Puyŏ was sacked by Murong Hui, an exceptionally able prince who had just become ruler of his tribe. The attack was completely successful; Ŭiryŏ committed suicide in despair, and several of his relatives fled southeastward to take refuge among the Okchŏ tribes of northeastern Korea, where they eventually set up the kingdom of Eastern Puyŏ.

This Murong victory alarmed the Chinese court, which saw it as an undesirable change in the balance of power along the northern frontier. The Chinese intervened to restore a son of Ŭiryŏ to the Puyŏ throne, and this new kingdom managed to survive until 345, although constantly plundered and harassed by the Murong Xianbei. In 345 it was conquered by Murong Hui's son Murong Huang, but after the collapse of the Murong state in 370 some of the Puyŏ tribes managed to regain a measure of independence until they were finally annexed by Koguryŏ in the fifth century. By this time Koguryŏ had also conquered Eastern Puyŏ, but not before a branch of the Puyŏ ruling house there had moved further south into the Korean peninsula to set up the important state of Paekche, for centuries the bitter rival of Koguryŏ.

Puyŏ played a vital role in transmitting a sinicized version of northern nomad culture to the peoples of Korea and the littoral of northern East Asia. Moreover, Puyŏ culture was also kept alive by the ruling group of the state of Parhae, which emerged in the eighth century as the successor to Koguryŏ.

[See also Koguryŏ and Paekche.]

KENNETH H. J. GARDINER

P'YŎNGYANG, one of the oldest cities in Korea, now the capital of the Democratic People's Republic of Korea. Destroyed during the Korean War (1950–1953), P'yŏngyang has been rebuilt with broad streets, government buildings, and apartment blocks designed for institutional efficiency. Little of its past heritage remains. Plazas, museums, statues, and billboards garishly extol Kim Il Sung (Kim Il-sŏng) and his heir apparent, Kim Jong Il (Kim Chong-il).

Human settlement has long been established on the P'yŏngyang plain; archaeological evidence indicates the close relations this region had with China. The mythical founder of P'yŏngyang, Kija (Chinese, Jizi), a Chinese sage, settled his followers between the Taedong River and its tributary, the P'otung, in the shelter of some low hills in 1122 BCE. Lelang, a Chinese colony or tributary state, was located near P'yŏngyang during the Chinese Han dynasty (206 BCE–220 CE). A Korean kingdom extending into Manchuria, Koguryŏ (37 BCE?–668 CE), had its capital at P'yŏngyang. After Korea was unified by the Silla dynasty (668–918), P'yŏngyang became a frontier headquarters and subcapital, a status maintained during the Koryŏ dynasty (918–1392). P'yŏngyang was the capital of P'yŏngan Province, bordered on the north by the Yalu River, during the Yi Dynasty (1382–1910).

At the opening of Korea to the Western world in the late nineteenth century, P'yŏngyang was the second largest city in Korea. It was modernized under Japanese colonial control (1910–1945) with straight streets, office buildings, and wooden homes. American missionary efforts resulted in many churches, schools, and hospitals; a large missionary compound was west of the Korean city. A modern arsenal and factories were built south of the city and across the Taedong river.

The old city of P'yŏngyang and its modern appendages were destroyed in the Korean War (1950–1953), and Japanese and Christian influences were erased. Symbols of "Kim Il Sung Thought" emerged, including an immense museum and the twenty-two-story tower of Kim Il Sung University. New bridges were built across the Taedong and urban expansion moved eastward. Broad streets and a deep subway tie the city together. P'yŏngyang, including its industrial and apartment suburbs, had a population of 1.5 million people in 1985.   SHANNON MCCUNE

PYU. The earliest urban civilization in Burma, which existed from 200 BCE to the mid-ninth century, has been attributed to the Tibeto-Burman-speaking people called the Pyu. Although the evidence for the Pyu civilization is clear, the etymology of the word *Pyu* is still conjectural. It is suspected that the Pyu predate both the Burmans and the Mon and were not the so-called advance guard of the Burmans when they allegedly swooped down into the plains of central Burma in the ninth century; the civilization attributed to the Pyu had already been present and paramount in Burma for at least a millennium.

Their origins may be unclear, but it is fairly certain that the Pyu were part of the general cultural milieu of Southeast Asia and that several features of their culture laid the foundations of the later kingdom of Pagan. The Pyu buried their dead in urns, recalling similar practices in mainland Southeast Asia; they were part of the Rome-India-China trade network of the early first millennium CE; and they were Buddhists, apparently of the Sarvastivadin branch of the Hinayana school, many of whose doctrines the Burmans of Pagan adopted. The techniques and styles of their religious buildings continued to be used in the Pagan period, and their political and military influence was almost as extensive as that of the Pagan dynasty, stretching from the dry plains of central Burma to the Isthmus of Kra, whose provincial centers served as the nuclei for later seats of political and military power. Only in the mid-ninth century was their last capital, Halin, sacked by Nanzhao, allowing the Burmans to establish the kingdom of Pagan, which dominated Burma for the next four centuries.

[*See also* Pagan.]

Aung Thaw, *Report on the Excavations at Beikthano* (1968) and *Historical Sites in Burma* (1972). Michael Aung-Thwin, "Burma Before Pagan," in *Asian Perspectives,* edited by Jae Kyu Park (1987). G. H. Luce, "The Ancient Pyu," in *Journal of the Burma Research Society, Fiftieth Anniversary Publications* 2 (1960).

MICHAEL AUNG-THWIN

Q

QADI, Islamic judge. In theory, the judiciary in Islam was independent and the competence of the *qadi* extended to all fields of Islamic law, but in practice this varied, and the tribunals of the *qadi* were usually superseded in criminal and fiscal law by other institutions for the administration of justice. Only Muslims came under his jurisdiction; non-Muslim communities retained their own courts. The *qadi* sat in a single-judge tribunal and based his judgments on the authoritative texts of the school of law to which he belonged. He could impose discretionary punishments, and his decisions were final. An important and influential official, the *qadi* also had wide powers outside his court in functions that involved the public welfare in general.

Joseph Schacht, *Introduction to Islamic Law* (1964).
JEANETTE A. WAKIN

QAJAR, AHMAD, shah of Iran from 1909 to 1925. Ahmad Shah, also known as Sultan Ahmad, was the last ruler of the Qajar dynasty. He was elected shah by the First Majles (national assembly) after his father, Muhammad Ali, had been deposed and sent into exile. He was crowned in 1914 following a regency of five years.

Ahmad Shah did not succeed in asserting his authority over the government and was unable to prevent the anarchic decentralization of power in Iran during and immediately after World War I. He had to acquiesce in the 1921 coup d'état that brought Reza Khan, the future Reza Shah, to power as minister of war. As Reza Khan consolidated power, the status of Ahmad Shah was reduced to that of a mere symbol. In 1923, just after appointing Reza Khan as prime minister, Ahmad Shah departed Iran for France. He never returned to his country; in October 1925 the Majles deposed him as shah, abolished the Qajar family as the royal dynasty, and established the Pahlavis as the new royal family.

[*See also* Pahlavi, Reza *and* Qajar Dynasty.]

George Lenczowski, "Foreign Powers' Intervention in Iran during World War I," in *Qajar Iran: Political, Social and Cultural Change 1800–1925*, edited by E. Bosworth and C. Hillenbrand (1983), pp. 76–92. Malcolm Yapp, "The Last Years of the Qajar Dynasty," in *Twentieth Century Iran*, edited by H. Amirsadeghi (1977), pp. 1–22.
ERIC HOOGLUND

QAJAR, MUHAMMAD ALI, shah of Iran from 1907 to 1909. Muhammad Ali Shah's brief reign was marked by constant conflict between the court and the constitutionalists over the respective roles of the monarch and the newly established Majles (parliament). Muhammad Ali Shah was suspected of complicity in the assassination of the prime minister, Amin al-Sultan, in 1907, and in 1908 he ordered the Cossack Brigade to bombard the Majles building. This led to a year-long civil war during which the shah's forces were defeated by the constitutionalists and Muhammad Ali was deposed. In 1911 Muhammad Ali made an unsuccessful attempt to regain the crown with the tacit support of Russia.

[*See also* Constitutional Revolution *and* Persian Cossack Brigade.]

Ervand Abrahamian, *Iran between Two Revolutions* (1982), pp. 89–101. Nikki Keddie, "The Assassination of the Amin as-Sultan (Atabak-i A'zam)," in *Iran and Islam*, edited by C. E. Bosworth (1971), pp. 315–329.
ERIC HOOGLUND

QAJAR, NASIR AL-DIN (1831–1896), monarch (shah) of the Qajar dynasty in Iran from 1848 to 1896. Nasir al-Din acceded to the throne upon the death of his father, Muhammad Shah. For the first three years of Nasir al-Din's reign, real power was wielded by his prime minister, Mirza Taqi Khan Amir Kabir, who founded Iran's first institution for higher education, the Dar al-Fonun (Polytechnic Institute), and initiated a wide range of economic and political reforms inspired mainly by European models of centralization and modernization. Nasir al-Din perceived many of these attempted reforms as a threat to his own power, and in 1851 dismissed Amir Kabir; the following year he ordered Kabir's assassination. [See also Amir Kabir and Dar al-Fonun.]

From 1852 until 1890 Nasir al-Din's reign was a period of relative domestic stability marked by an increasing foreign involvement, chiefly British and Russian, in Iran's economy and politics. An unsuccessful attempt to regain Herat from the British between 1856 and 1857 was the only military conflict of note in the half-century of his rule. Iran in this period had virtually no standing army, with the most important armed force being the Persian Cossack Brigade led by Russian officers, which Nasir al-Din created in 1873 following the first of three trips to Europe. [See also Persian Cossack Brigade.]

Owing to gradually worsening economic conditions in the latter half of the century, Nasir al-Din Shah initiated a practice, carried on by his successor, of raising money for the crown by selling economic concessions to foreign subjects or governments. The concessions were eagerly sought after and competed for, especially by Great Britain and Russia. In 1872 the largest of these concessions was granted to a British subject, Baron Julius de Reuter, awarding exclusive rights for the development of Iran's minerals, railroads, irrigation, and a host of other industrial and agricultural resources. In addition, de Reuter was conceded the right to found what was later to become the Imperial Bank of Persia, Iran's major banking institution into the twentieth century.

Although the Reuter Concession was annulled in 1873 under pressure from both Russian and domestic opposition, significant portions of the concession were renegotiated and continued in effect. Among other concessions granted by Nasir al-Din Shah were telegraph construction rights to the British, fishing rights in the Caspian to the Russians, and tobacco sales and export to a British subject. It was this last that triggered the famous Tobacco Protest of 1891, an event that marked the first concerted effort by Iranian merchants, Muslim clergy, and secular opponents of the shah's economic policies to unite in protest and resistance. An effective national boycott of all tobacco products coupled with mass demonstrations forced Nasir al-Din Shah to cancel the concession less than a year later and expressed the increasing domestic hostility to both British and Russian influence in Iran's internal affairs and economy. [See also Reuter Concession and Tobacco Rebellion.]

Nasir ad-Din and his prime ministers, several of whom attempted secular reforms along Western lines, increasingly became the target of antiforeign sentiment inside Iran, most notably in the pages of a pan-Islamic, anti-British newspaper published in Paris by Jamal al-Din al-Afghani. At a time when internal Iranian dissatisfaction and unrest were steadily increasing, it was a follower of al-Afghani who assassinated Nasir al-Din Shah on 1 May 1896 at a shrine near Tehran. Subsequent Qajar monarchs were unable to resolve the problems of external political and economic pressure and internal resistance that plagued the final years of Nasir al-Din Shah.

[See also Qajar Dynasty and Afghani, Jamal al-Din al-.]

JAHAN SALEHI

QAJAR DYNASTY. *Qajar* designates both a dynasty that ruled Iran and a Turkic-speaking tribal confederation of pastoral nomads. Aqa Muhammad Qajar, the founder of the dynasty, was crowned in 1796; the last Qajar, Ahmad Shah, left Iran to be replaced by Reza Shah Pahlavi in 1925 (crowned 1926).

The earliest extant historical references to the Qajar tribes date from the late fifteenth century and place them in Anatolia and subsequently in Azerbaijan. At the very beginning of the sixteenth century the Qajars were one of the Kizilbash tribes that supported the rise to power of Shah Isma'il and the Safavid dynasty. Individual Qajars held important administrative positions throughout the Safavid era (1501–1722), and by its end the Qajar tribes were centered to the east of the Caspian Sea. From this base in northeastern Iran, the Qajars were involved in both internecine struggles and battles for supremacy over greater Iran with the various eighteenth-century contenders. With the death of Karim Khan Zand in 1779 and the imminent collapse of Zand sovereignty over central and southern Iran, Aqa Muhammad established Qajar hegemony. Significantly, Qajar tribal power waned as the dynasty established itself, for its founder had to deal not only with consolidation of his power, but with Russian challenges in the Caucasian provinces as well. In 1797 Aqa Muhammad was assassinated by two slaves; having died childless (he had been castrated as a youth), he was succeeded by his nephew, Fath Ali Shah (1797–1834).

Fath Ali withstood challenges for the throne, but fraternal rivalry meant uncertainty for all the Qajar rulers of the nineteenth century, especially at the times of their accessions—Muhammad in 1834 (the heir apparent, Abbas Mirza, had predeceased his father in 1833) and Nasir al-Din in 1848—despite Russian and British support for the designated successor. In the 1880s Nasir al-Din had to contend with one son, Zill al-Sultan, whose mother was not a Qajar and who had been passed over in favor of a younger brother, who ruled as Muzaffar al-Din (1896–1907). Muhammad Ali Shah ruled only from 1907 to 1909 before being deposed by the new Majles (parliament); he was succeeded by Ahmad Shah (r. 1909–1925), the last Qajar ruler.

The Qajar era constituted a period of significant change in Iran. In the first century of their reign the Qajars acted as traditional autocrats over a decentralized realm, according considerable autonomy to whole regions, cities, and tribes, or to locally based officials and institutions, as well as to the bureaucracy, the *ulama,* the military, and the landowners. (The royal family and officials, military and tribal leaders, and landowners were not wholly distinct classes.) The Qajars' failure to develop a centralized bureaucracy and a standing army meant that they could retain power only through Russian and British support and divide-and-rule policies. Consequently, regional centers of power emerged around prince-governors in Tabriz, Isfahan, and Shiraz or around magnates, leaders of the *ulama,* and tribal leaders, some of whom revitalized the Bakhtiyari and Qashqja'i confederations. Qajar attempts at reform were short-lived; such attempts included military reforms under Abbas Mirza and administrative ones under Amir Kabir, who pushed for the establishment of Dar al-Fonun (1851), a technical institute. Shortcomings in the Qajar monarchy, vested interests, and the absence of an effective bureaucracy are to blame for these failures; the military, religious, and local opposition to centralization, together with Russian and British policies, were contributing factors as well.

Qajar ineffectiveness in the face of foreign domination (indeed Qajar acquiescence to it) and the increasing Russian and British interest in Iran, situated as it was between Russia and British India, constitute another major theme of this era. Such interest was first expressed diplomatically, militarily, and politically, later economically and culturally. Two wars with Russia in the first third of the nineteenth century ended with the irrevocable loss of the Caucasian provinces, and in the 1850s conflict with Britain resulted in the cession of western Afghanistan. Territorial losses, foreign political manipulation, and increasing economic domination resulted in xenophobia; by the end of the nineteenth century nationalism had become a significant political force.

The Western impact forced change and brought the new ideas accompanying it. Earlier religious disputes and dissent laid the basis for the challenges to the state inherent in Shi'ism; greater authority was vested in *mujtahids,* the highest-ranking religious leaders. The emergence of secularism and ideas of equality and progress began to challenge Muslim society. New religious and political ideas, along with internal and external pressure for change within the *ulama* and society as a whole, called for new roles for the *ulama.* The Babi challenge to religious and political authority was crushed by the middle of the century, but opposition toward the Qajars would grow into a major crisis in 1890–1891 with widespread protest against the tobacco concession granted to a British firm. For many Iranians the concession was a symbol of the sale of Iran to Europeans, and in the end it had to be canceled. Here the *ulama* played an important leadership role, as it had earlier in demonstrations against Russia. With the sweeping 1871 Reuter Concession, later withdrawn, for all minerals, a state bank, and railways and communications, and with subsequent concessions, Iranian dissatisfaction had already been increasing.

Qajar ineptness, extravagance, and corruption, combined with continued European exploitation and escalating demonstrations, brought together a coalition of *ulama,* merchants, traditional leaders, and new nationalists, who now demanded a constitution and a representative assembly. Muzaffar al-Din Shah granted a constitution in 1906 that allowed for the election of representatives to the Majles. His death in January 1907, however, brought his anticonstitutionalist and pro-Russian son Muhammad Ali Shah to the throne. Muhammad Ali's reactionary policies were defeated by Tabriz and Rasht nationalists and the Bakhtiyari confederation, and the shah abdicated in favor of his young son, Ahmad Shah. Divisions within the Majles, *ulama* opposition to political and legal reforms (especially secular ones), and Russian intervention in 1911 (with British acquiescence) ended the hopes brought about by the Constitutional Revolution. Meanwhile, in this same critical period, Britain and Russia had divided Iran into spheres of influence with the Anglo-Russian Convention of 1907, and the newly discovered oil in Khuzistan reinforced Iran's strategic importance and increased Iranian nationalist sentiment for national sovereignty.

Iran declared its neutrality during World War I; it was nevertheless the scene of major fighting during and after the war. The weakness of the central government notwithstanding, the Majles rejected the Anglo-Persian Agreement of 1920 that would have made Iran a British colonial dependency. Britain, however, continued to play a critical, if indirect, role through its diplomatic mission and through the Anglo-Persian Oil Company. The Russian Revolution of 1917 had essentially removed the other major power as an important factor in Iran's politics until World War II. Nevertheless, Iran appeared doomed to fragmentation by separatist movements such as the one in Gilan, initially supported by the Soviets, combined with an increasingly incapacitated government. With these conditions as background, Sayyid Ziya al-Din Tabataba'i, a nationalist journalist, and Reza Khan, commander of some 2,500 soldiers of the Iranian Cossack Brigade, successfully staged a coup d'état in 1921. Within three months Sayyid Ziya al-Din was ousted as prime minister; Reza Khan, the new minister of war, set out to reform the military in order to reestablish the authority of the central government. In 1923 Reza Khan became prime minister; by 1925 he had convinced the Majles to depose Ahmad Shah and to elect him shah. At his coronation as Reza Shah Pahlavi in 1926 the Qajar era was brought to an end.

As a consequence of nineteenth- and twentieth-century Qajar misrule and domination by the European powers, the Iranian people faced extraordinary economic changes. Iran's integration into the world market system, while hindered by a number of geographical and political factors—drought, earthquakes, a hostile climate, the ruggedness and isolation of the Iranian terrain, internal and ethnic divisions, the localization of the economy, the land tenure system, and the lack of an infrastructure for trade and communication—tended to exacerbate the weaknesses inherent in the Iranian social and political sphere. For Iran, as for many other parts of the non-European world, the dominance of world markets by European financiers, merchants, and consumer tastes created a situation of economic dependency in which the Iranians had decreasing control of their economy. Thus, by the end of the nineteenth century Iran had been transformed from a subsistence-level agricultural, industrial, and commercial economy to a rather inflexible system largely dependent on imports. Despite a currency outflow, cash shortages, and rising credit demands, Iranian merchants were able to affect the number of imports and to play key roles in the face of European and Indian inroads on the economy. Increased production of cash crops such as silk, opium, tobacco, cotton, and rice did help to offset imports, but with the end result that Iran became a net importer of cereals. The revived carpet industry gained importance in the national economy, and the oil industry, a new factor, was to become significant in the Pahlavi era, although it symbolized continued British domination. The overwhelmingly negative consequences of the change from subsistence to dependency—inefficient, unjust administration and inflation—compounded national and political frustrations, underlining a general sense of Qajar failure.

Iran's transformation from a traditional Islamic society to a modern nation-state took place in the Qajar period. The emergence of the new ideas and programs of nationalism, liberalism, secularism, and constitutionalism was accompanied by significant social changes, one of the most important of which was the formation of an intelligentsia, exemplified by such figures as Jamal al-Din al-Afghani (d. 1897) and Malkom Khan (d. 1908). Ironically, the *ulama* was revitalized in its opposition to such changes, but the implications of this revitalization were not to be fully realized for perhaps two generations. The subsequent centralized Pahlavi governments were to play new active, modern roles unlike those of their traditional Qajar forerunners. What is often overlooked, however, in the generally negative assessments of the 129 years of Qajar rule, is that the new social, economic, and cultural relationships of the Pahlavi period, as well as the accompanying developments in literature, journalism, art, architecture, and education, have their roots in the Qajar era.

[*See also* Qajar, Nasir al-Din; Qajar, Muhammad Ali; Qajar, Ahmad; Pahlavi, Reza; Constitutional Revolution; Zand Dynasty; Abbas Mirza; Dar al-Fonun; Babi; Tobacco Rebellion; Reuter Concession; Persian Cossack Brigade; Malkom Khan; Amir Kabir; and Afghani, Jamal al-Din al-]

Ervand Abrahamian, *Iran between Two Revolutions* (1982). Shaul Bakhash, *Iran: Monarchy, Bureaucracy and*

Reform under the Qajars, 1858–1896 (1978). Mangol Bayat, *Mysticism and Dissent: Socioreligious Thought in Qajar Iran* (1982). Edmund Bosworth and Carole Hillenbrand, eds., *Qajar Iran: Political, Social and Cultural Change, 1800–1925* (1983). George N. Curzon, *Persia and the Persian Question* (1892). Charles Issawi, *The Economic History of Iran, 1800–1914* (1971). Nikki R. Keddie, *Sayyid Jamal al-Din "al-Afghani": A Political Biography* (1972). Ann K. S. Lambton, "Persia: The Breakdown of Society," in the *Cambridge History of Islam,* edited by P. M. Holt et al. (1970), vol. 1, pp. 430–446; and "Persian Society under the Qajars," *Journal of the Royal Central Asian Society* 48 (1961): 123–139.

GENE R. GARTHWAITE

QARAQOYUNLU. *See* Karakoyunlu.

QAVAM, AHMAD (1873–1955), controversial Iranian politician and several-time prime minister of Iran. From 1919 to 1921 he was the governor of Khurasan and, with the support of Reza Khan, successfully defeated the nationalist uprising of Colonel Mohammad Taqi Khan Pesyan. In 1922 Reza Khan appointed him prime minister. During that period the British-supported virtually autonomous shaikh of Khuzistan was defeated; thus, Qavam acquired an anti-British reputation, which at that period of Iranian history implied that he was pro-Russian. In 1922 Qavam, who opposed Reza Khan's quest for kingship, joined Sayyid Hasan Moddares and others in a coup against him.

After the Soviet Union refused to withdraw its troops from Iran and actively supported the autonomy-seeking Azerbaijan Republic, established in 1945, Qavam was brought back to the political scene in 1946, when Mohammed Reza Pahlavi, in an effort to exploit Qavam's pro-Soviet reputation, asked his help in negotiating with the Soviets. Qavam was made prime minister again. Although the role of Qavam in these negotiations is still uncertain, he succeeded in striking a deal, and the Soviets agreed to withdraw (albeit faced also with US threats of intervention) in exchange for a northern Iranian oil concession. Upon completion of the withdrawal, however, Mohammed Reza Shah refused to comply with the treaty and ousted Qavam from his post. He was made prime minister again for an extremely short period in 1952, as part of the shah's unsuccessful effort to prevent Mohammed Mossadegh's premiership. Qavam was again asked to resign in July 1952.

[*See also* Mossadegh, Mohammed; Pahlavi, Mohammed Reza; *and* Pahlavi, Reza.]

Ervand Abrahamian, *Iran between Two Revolutions* (1982). R. Cottam, *Nationalism in Iran* (1979). H. Katouzian, *The Political Economy of Modern Iran, 1926–1979* (1981). G. Lenczowski, *Russia and the West in Iran* (1949) and *Iran under the Pahlavis* (1978).

NEGUIN YAVARI

QI, one of the Warring States of ancient China. Qi expanded its territory on the eastern edge of the North China Plain by absorbing non-Han peoples until it controlled the Shandong Peninsula. The name *Qi* is still applied to the modern province of Shandong. Qi emerged as one of the powers in the seventh and sixth centuries BCE as the fortunes of the Zhou dynasty (1122?–256 BCE) declined. Qi's most famous ruler was Duke Huan (684–642 BCE), who became the first person to hold the title hegemon (*ba*) when a group of states formed an alliance against Chu in the south. Equally famous was Duke Huan's minister, Guan Zhong, who helped him devise effective methods for organizing the population into groups that enabled the state to directly raise military forces without depending on the hereditary nobility. A philosophical text known as the *Guanzi* is attributed to Guan Zhong. Qi came to an end in 221 BCE when the state of Qin completed its unification of China.

Kung-chuan Hsiao, *A History of Chinese Political Thought,* vol. 1, translated by F. W. Mote (1979).

EDWARD L. FARMER

QIANLONG EMPEROR. Hongli (temple name Gaozong; 1711–1799), fourth son of Yongzheng, ruled Qing-dynasty China from 1736 to 1796 as the Qianlong emperor. From his abdication as emperor until his death in 1799, in the third year of what is officially known as the Jiaqing reign, Qianlong continued as de facto ruler of China. On ascending the throne he had expressed a desire to emulate his grandfather, the Kangxi emperor (r. 1661–1722), but he considered that to exceed the length of Kangxi's reign, which had encompassed a complete Chinese cycle of sixty years, would be to display a lack of filial piety.

The Qianlong period represents, at its best, the height of Qing dynastic splendor. By the end of the eighteenth century, however, increasing corruption in government, in particular under Heshen, and the consequences of a population explosion combined to set in motion an irreversible decline. Further, after

1757 foreign traders had been allowed to reside and trade in Macao and Canton (Guangzhou); they increasingly resisted Chinese authority. Thus, the seeds of the domestic weakness that in the nineteenth century was to hamper China so severely in its dealings with Western powers were sown during this period.

Qianlong's military successes resulted in a dramatic expansion of the Chinese empire to twice its former size. In 1757 General Zhaohui (1708–1764) brought Ili (Dzungaria) under Chinese suzerainty, overcoming persistent rebellious activity on the part of the Khoit leader Amursana, who as a Qing assistant commander had been instrumental in the early stages of the Chinese conquest of Ili. In 1759, with the aid of Fude (d. 1776) and Agui (1717–1797), Zhaohui completed the conquest of what came to be known as Xinjiang, or the New Province, by defeating Muslim insurgents in Turkestan. [See also Dzungaria.]

Muslim rebellions occurred again in 1781 and 1784 in Gansu but were put down by Agui and Fukang'an (d. 1796), respectively. In Sichuan the Qing twice (in 1747–1749 and 1771–1776) pacified, after difficult campaigns, Jinquan aboriginal rebels. In 1774 followers of Wang Lun's popular millenarian uprising in Shandong, relying on magical formulas as well as on weapons, occupied the strategic Grand Canal city of Linqing and killed many officials before their defeat by government troops. At the end of the Qianlong reign China was again in turmoil as a result of the White Lotus Rebellion (1786–1805), the adherents of which claimed that corrupt officialdom had driven them to rebel. This claim was supported by such statesmen as Hong Liangji (1746–1789), who was exiled for a time because of his criticisms. [See also White Lotus Society.]

In 1787 and 1788 Fukang'an put down a rebellion in Taiwan, and from 1788 Burma and Annam became tributary states. They were joined by Nepal four years later, after Qing troops defeated the Gurkhas deep in Nepalese territory.

The enormous cost of these various campaigns added to the expense incurred between 1751 and 1784 by six imperial tours of southern China. The expansion of arable land and doubling of the population generated increased revenue. Demographic pressure eventually outpaced economic growth, however, leading concurrently to great ecological changes; deforestation resulted in erosion, which in turn caused the silting of rivers. On several occasions, famine-stricken regions had to be excused from tax payment. Yongzheng's reforms had placed national finances on a firm footing and for most of Qianlong's reign the treasury showed a surplus. Toward the end of the period, however, with the increasing corruption of an enlarged bureaucracy, the depletion of reserves began to contribute to China's problems.

Local and interregional markets expanded during this period, and the European demand for Chinese silk, tea, and ceramics helped stimulate considerable commercialization of the domestic economy. Agriculture intensified and mineral extraction flourished. Some historians view these developments as evidence of the spontaneous sprouting of capitalism in China independent of Western influence.

In the early part of his reign Qianlong's chief advisers were Ortai (1680–1745) and Zhang Tingyu, both experienced administrators. The emperor's brother-in-law Fuheng was ranking grand councillor from 1749 until 1770, when he died of an illness contracted on a Burmese campaign. His incumbency was the longest of the reign and the ten senior posts he is listed as holding concurrently (in 1752) suggest that Qianlong had exceptional confidence in him, even though it is unlikely that Fuheng could actively have fulfilled all the duties of those offices.

Qianlong's last minister, Heshen, began his career as an imperial bodyguard in 1772. Heshen's rise was meteoric. Within three years he became a grand councillor, a minister of the imperial household, general commandant of the Beijing forces, and superintendent of customs at one of the gates of Beijing, a lucrative post he held for eight years rather than the customary one year. Later he was appointed to many other senior administrative and honorific offices.

Many dark stories have circulated in an attempt to explain Heshen's sway over Qianlong, whose complete confidence he enjoyed. Some Qing writers suggested he attracted the emperor's attention because of his resemblance to a concubine of Yongzheng's to whom Qianlong had been greatly attracted but with whom any liaison was excluded under Chinese incest laws. It is unlikely that the truth will ever be known, owing to the probable suppression by the Jiaqing emperor (Yongyan, r. 1796–1820), Qianlong's fifth son and successor, of any record incriminating to the memory of his father. Heshen's power was unrivaled and his corruption was notorious. The government was filled with men of his faction and bribery became the norm. Those who dared to protest were cashiered and often killed. Heshen's wealth was proverbial; many tales have been told of his extravagance. Five days after Qianlong died Heshen was summarily stripped of his ranks and imprisoned by Jiaqing; within a month he was "permitted" to hang himself in his cell. [See also Heshen.]

Heshen's supremacy has been attributed in part to senility on the part of the aging Qianlong. However, members of the British mission under Lord Macartney in 1793 described the emperor as erect and vigorous. This mission sought to establish, among other things, extended trading rights and diplomatic relations with China. Qianlong politely rejected these proposals, saying, "We possess all things. I set no value on objects strange or ingenious, and have no use for your country's manufactures." Shortly thereafter he warned the governor-general in Canton to beware of England's naval and mercantile superiority.

During Qianlong's reign Christian missionaries continued to work in China despite periodic prohibitions and persecutions. One difficulty they encountered was that the Chinese sometimes confused Christianity with Islam, whose adherents rebelled several times during this period. At court the Jesuits Castiglione and Attiret were employed as official painters and helped design a new Summer Palace of great splendor. (It was to be destroyed by the British in 1860.) Jesuits assisted in surveys of newly conquered areas and established a workshop within the Inner City of Beijing where they trained Chinese people in various Western skills. After the abolition of their order in 1773 the Jesuit mission to China was taken over by the Lazarists in 1784. [See also Jesuits: Jesuits in China.]

The major literary achievement of Qianlong's reign was the compilation under his auspices of the Imperial Manuscript Library (siku quanshu) between 1772 and 1784. In 1773 Ji Yun (1724–1805) and Lu Xixiong (1734–1792) were appointed chief editors. The project involved an exhaustive search for rare works. The editors undertook a critical review of every work available to them and selected the works to be included, which then had to be transcribed, collated, and bound. Some 3,450 works were selected out of more than 10,000 reviewed. The Imperial Catalog (Siku quanshu zongmu tiyao), which included comments on the works in the collection, was presented to the throne in 1781 but subsequently underwent revisions; it remains a major reference work of Chinese bibliography.

The systematic search for works to be considered for inclusion in the Imperial Library facilitated a wide-ranging literary inquisition. Anything that was found to be antidynastic was destroyed. Included in this category were works disparaging earlier non-Chinese dynasties, rebellious writings, works violating such taboos as using Qing emperors' personal names, biased discussions of the early seventeenth-century conflict between the Chinese and Manchus, works on such topics as naval defense and frontier topography deemed potentially prejudicial to national security, works unfavorable to Confucius, and works by certain proscribed authors. The literature lost as a result of this censorship was enormous, although some banned works survived in private libraries and in Japan.

One of those who worked on the project was Dai Zhen (1724–1777), who is associated with the kaozheng xue ("school of empirical research"), which developed out of seventeenth-century scholarship and which accepted nothing without conclusive evidence. Textual criticism formed a fundamental part of Dai Zhen's work, prompting him to reject the scholarship of those scholars who regarded Han works as necessarily authentic because of their proximity to antiquity. Further, Dai Zhen's attacks on Neo-Confucian theory completed the erosion of the latter's intellectual domination, although the philosophy continued to form the basis of the examination system until the end of the dynasty in 1911. [See also Dai Zhen and Kaozheng Xue.]

One of those who disagreed with Dai Zhen's school was Zhang Xuecheng (1738–1801), an important figure in Chinese historiography. He regarded all records of the past as materials for the study of history and sought their methodical preservation. Zhang favored a general type of history, with annotations of important individual events, over the traditional chronological and biographical treatment, and devoted particular attention to local histories. [See also Zhang Xuecheng.]

During the Qianlong period different intellectual schools flourished, especially in the lower Yangtze region. Many academies were established for the education of aspiring scholars and officials.

[See also Grand Council; Kangxi Emperor; Yongzheng Emperor; and Qing Dynasty.]

Derk Bodde and Clarence Morris, Law in Imperial China, Exemplified by 190 Ch'ing Dynasty Cases (translated from the Hsing-an hui-lan), with Historical, Social and Juridical Commentaries (1967). T'ung-tsu Ch'u, Local Government in China under the Ch'ing (1962). J. L. Cranmer-Byng, ed., An Embassy to China; being the Journal Kept by Lord Macartney during his Embassy to the Emperor Ch'ien-lung, 1793-1794 (1963). Benjamin Elman, From Philosophy to Philology: Intellectual and So-

cial Aspects of Change in Late Imperial China (1984). L. Carrington Goodrich, *The Literary Inquisition of Ch'ien-lung* (1935). Harold L. Kahn, *Monarchy in the Emperor's Eyes: Image and Reality in the Ch'ien-lung Reign* (1971). Susan Naquin, *Shantung Rebellion: The Wang Lun Uprising of 1774* (1981). David S. Nivison, "Ho-shen and his Accusers: Ideology and Political Behavior in the Eighteenth Century," in *Confucianism in Action,* edited by David S. Nivison and Arthur F. Wright (1959).

JOANNA WALEY-COHEN

QI BAISHI (1863–1957), one of contemporary China's most original artists. Using the traditional medium of brush and ink, he was best known for bold lines and vividly colored paintings depicting insects, birds, small animals, and flowers and fruit. Qi drew inspiration from traditional nature themes and Chinese folk art to create an unpretentious individualistic style of painting that has made him popular both in China and abroad.

After the establishment of the People's Republic of China in 1949, Qi Baishi, then eighty-six years old, was honored by the government. He also was selected as a delegate from his native province of Hunan to the First National People's Congress in 1950. He died in 1957 at the age of ninety-five, and willed all of his paintings, seals and impressions, and writings to the Chinese government.

Howard L. Boorman, *Biographical Dictionary of Republican China* (1967), pp. 302–304. Arnold Chang, *Painting in the People's Republic of China: The Politics of Style* (1980). T. C. Lai, comp., *Ch'i Pai-shih* (1973).

ANITA M. ANDREW

QIN DYNASTY. Originally a kingdom of China's Warring States period, Qin emerged through military superiority to unify China as its first empire. Although the dynasty was short-lived (221–207 BCE), barely outlasting the death of its founder, the administrative and bureaucratic systems established during the Qin became the standard means of ruling the Chinese empire for the next two thousand years.

The State of Qin. The ancestors of the Qin royal house were members of a combat force brought from eastern China to the western border of the Zhou royal domain in the early Zhou dynasty (1122–256 BCE). They were assigned to raise horses for the royal stable and to defend the Zhou territory against the "barbarian" foreigners who encroached upon Chinese farmland. They had frequent contact with the local pastoralists, eventually intermarrying

with them. The fall of Western Zhou in 772 BCE left the former royal domain with a power vacuum, one gradually filled by the Qin warriors through control of the entire Wei River valley, the ancient seat of Chinese civilization.

During the Spring and Autumn period (722–481 BCE), the state of Qin moved steadily from caretakers of the former royal domain to a full-fledged dukedom and finally to the status of indisputable hegemony of the western lands through the annexation of territories of other small states in Chinese as well as "barbarian" regions. From the reign of Duke Mu (659–621 BCE), Qin became one of the four major powers in the Chinese multistate system, although it generally exercised regional influence only.

At the beginning of the Warring States period (403–221 BCE), Qin's power and influence decreased in relation to the other Chinese states. This was in part the result of chaos related to the succession to the throne, as well as the rapid economic advancement in the eastern Chinese states, especially the state of Jin. Qin was inefficient in the production and mobilization of resources. As a peripheral state, the Qin also faced great shortages in locally produced talent. The Qin government, for example, often had to recruit advisers, strategists, and diplomats from the eastern states, where higher cultural and educational opportunities provided the opportunity to develop useful talents. Qin entered into a period of most profound change during the reign of Duke Xizuo (361–338 BCE), who entrusted an easterner, Shang Yang, to launch a series of political reforms.

Shang Yang's Reforms. Following the general trend in all the major states of the time, Shang Yang upgraded the power of the ruler into that of an absolute monarch. Aristocratic ranks and generous rewards were granted to those who achieved merit on the battleground, while the old hereditary peers lost their titles. Good farmers were honored; those who produced more grain or clothes than was average were given tax exemptions. Households that had more than one adult male were compelled to divide. In Qin the farming units were made of nuclear families working on small farmsteads, a way to encourage production. Meanwhile, households were organized into groups of five and ten, the members of which were held responsible to watch for the security of the neighborhood.

Shang Yang also reorganized the Qin administrative system. Old boundaries of feudal domains were broken into plots for private landholdings that were then taxed by kinds of grain. Scattered settlements were incorporated into counties that served as the local administrative unit. Originally there were thirty counties, but the number continued to increase throughout the period. County magistrates were appointed rather than hereditary overseers. The authority of codified law was emphasized, and no one, even the heir apparent of the Qin throne, could enjoy privilege beyond the law. Punishments and rewards were made in accordance with behavior judged by law. Bronze weights and capacity units recovered from archaeological sites bear testimony to the Qin standardization of measurements. A new capital was built at a location much closer to the eastern end of the Wei Valley, symbolizing the determination of the Qin court to expand eastward.

Within twenty years Shang Yang completed one of the most thorough reformations in ancient China. The impact was profound in reshaping the Qin economy, society, and state power structure. Because of these reforms, the Qin were the most law-abiding people in the Warring States period. Production increased; direct taxation gave the state more revenues than the tributary feudal system could have delivered. Qin was regarded not only as the best governed state by its contemporaries, but it was also regarded as the most efficiently organized of the states that were competing for power. The systems established by Duke Xiao and Shang Yang allowed Qin's unification of China.

The Wars of Unification. In 340 BCE Qin tried its strength in a war against Wei, the strongest power and also the immediate neighbor of Qin. Qin won the war decisively. From then on, Qin was constantly involved in the attempt to subjugate the eastern states for the purpose of unifying the entire Chinese cultural sphere. The Qin strategy was to consistently divide its enemies by befriending distant states and attacking neighboring ones. A universal military service system drafted able-bodied male adults between fifteen and fifty-six years old to rotate in active service. These law-abiding commoners were organized into armies of well-disciplined soldiers who carried out the plan of conquest. Their counterparts in other states were often mercenaries who were probably professionally competent, yet not as abundant as the universal draft could supply.

During the reign of King Huiwen (337–311 BCE), Qin annexed territories along the great arch of the Yellow River, as well as the fertile basin in Sichuan and the upper reaches of the Han River. With newly secured resources and strategic positions, Qin actively engaged in the effort to make further con-

quests. The six eastern states, facing a common threat of a formidable Qin, began to organize alliances against Qin, the so-called "vertical union." The Qin took advantage of discordance between states, causing a break of alliances and the establishment of temporary friendships with a few select states that were geographically distant from Qin, a strategy called "horizontal alliance." Again and again the eastern states united, yet Qin always broke the union by means of diplomatic manipulation.

The accumulated effect during the period 319 to 247 BCE was repeated Qin victories. The joint resistance of the eastern powers gradually dissolved, the casualties of individual battles having amounted to several million. By the time the thirteen-year-old Prince Zheng succeeded to the throne in 245 BCE, the final unification under Qin was inevitable. In fact, the campaigns in the early years of King Zheng were not much more than cleanup operations. In 256 and 249 BCE, the figurehead rulers of the Zhou royal house had already yielded their tiny domain to Qin. From 230 BCE on, one after another of the capitals of the major eastern states fell to the Qin troops until the last, Qi, was overcome in 221 BCE. The whole of China was then ruled by King Zheng, who adopted the new title *shihuangdi,* or "first emperor." Thus, a unified empire was established in China.

Rise and Fall of the Unified Empire. Qin Shihuangdi, aided by a group of capable advisers, established a bureaucracy to govern China. There were no more hereditary aristocrats in the court. Government officials, from the chancellor to sheriffs, from generals to captains, all were appointed and subject to periodic reviews of their performance. China was divided into thirty-six provinces; later, more provinces were added as new territories along the frontiers were incorporated. Each province was ruled by a governor who reported to the king. The Qin territory reached the Korean peninsula in the east, the Sichuan basin in the west, the edge of the Gobi Desert in the north, and the South China Sea in the south. The Qin thus established what were to be the borders of China proper in later Chinese dynasties.

Militarily, the Qin empire maintained a large army consisting of recruited draftees. Whole troops of life-size models of Qin soldiers have been excavated from the tomb of the First Emperor. They appear to have been well armed, and their battle formations show that the Qin had developed an advanced war machine. A well-built highway network linked provinces to the capital, Xianyang in the Wei Valley. In order to defend Chinese farmland from the newly rising nomadic Xiongnu empire on the Eurasian steppe, the First Emperor sent hundreds of thousands of soldiers and conscripted laborers to build a wall along the northern border. Essentially, this "Great Wall" defense system consisted of a series of fortresses, pikes, ditches, and long sections of walls made out of packed earth and stone blocks, some of which had been constructed by various states even before the unification. [*See also* Great Wall.] Canal systems were constructed to facilitate transportation. One such canal linked the Yangtze River system and the Pearl River system. Garrisoned troops were constantly stationed along the northern borders as well as on the southern frontiers.

By means of strong edicts, Qin Shihuangdi banned criticism by the intellectuals. Education was provided only by government officials to teach literacy to those who intended to serve in the government. Books whose subject matter was anything other than pragmatic knowledge were forbidden to circulate, leading to the infamous "burning of the books" in 213 BCE. [*See also* Burning of the Books.] Local elite and wealthy people were forced to move to the capital so that there would be no local leaders in the provinces to organize rebellions. The First Emperor himself, an energetic person, worked from dawn to midnight to exercise his dictatorship. He also repeatedly toured the empire to assure that his rule would not be challenged. He died on one such trip in 210 BCE. His reign was an era of authoritarian governance. The government controlled every subject and guided every aspect of life. Recently discovered Qin legal codes and administrative regulations are evidence that administrative rules were explicitly spelled out to the most minute detail for the local magistrates to follow.

Qin Shihuangdi was succeeded by the Second Emperor, a prince too young and too incapable to step into the shoes of the father. China had been heavily burdened by corvée labor and military services that constantly kept no less than one-third of the able-bodied male adults at state service, a hardship that was difficult for the population to bear any longer. The strong dictatorship that the First Emperor had established could hardly continue effectively in the hands of his successor. In 209 BCE the peasants who were drafted to serve in the frontier missed the assigned date of arrival because of a delay on the road in the rainy season. They chose to lead a few hundred fellow conscripts to rebel rather than be executed. Without weapons, the rebellious peasants fought the imperial army with plain implements. Similar uprisings sprang up elsewhere.

The Qin government hastily organized an army of conscript laborers who were gathered to construct the imperial mausoleum of the First Emperor. The rebels formed several armies. Some of these were led by the elite and nobles of the six former states. Others were led by peasant generals whose followers were often conscripts on their way to a designated site of public construction or a garrison station. Qin instantly lost all of the east.

In 206 BCE, the vanguard of an allied force of the rebels reached Xianyang. The Second Emperor was killed by his own trusted eunuch chancellor, who tried to reach a truce with the rebels. An infant was put on the throne, but the rebels swarmed into Xianyang. The Qin dynasty had ended.

The Qin Legacy. Although the Qin dynasty lasted a brief time, the Qin put into place an imperial system that the Han was to inherit. After Qin, hereditary feudalism ceased to exist. The Qin society was one with an open structure in which, other than the imperial house, everyone, theoretically, could move from one social position to another, either upward or downward. Personal merits, notably military abilities during the Qin period and those of government service during the Han period, could bring a person of obscure social origin to high social status, because even the aristocracy was disposable under a strong imperial despotism.

Another important legacy was a vast bureaucratic machinery consisting of a hierarchy of commanding channels from the chancellor down to local sheriffs. A significant feature of the Chinese bureaucracy was the institution of examinations in which supervisory inspectors judged the performance of officials. The Qin, of course, gave to the world the term *China*, derived from the dynastic name, by which foreigners continuously identified the nation and the state of the Middle Kingdom.

[*See also* Warring States Period; Qin Shihuangdi; Legalism; Li Si; Lü Buwei; *and* Junxian System.]

Derk Bodde, *China's First Unifier: A Study of the Ch'in Dynasty as Seen in the Life of Li Ssu* (1938). J. J. L. Duyvendak, trans., *The Book of Lord Shang* (1938). Cho-yun Hsu, *Ancient China in Transition* (1965) and *Bibliographic Notes on Studies of Ancient China* (1982). Yu-ning Li, *The First Emperor of China* (1975).

CHO-YUN HSU

QINGDAO, Chinese port city located on the southeast side of the Shandong Peninsula in Jiaozhou Bay; its population in 1983 was 1,210,000. Qingdao had begun to be developed by the Qing dynasty in the 1880s for the North Sea

(Beiyang) Fleet when it was invaded by the Germans in 1897. Germany developed Qingdao as a port and a modern city, the headquarters for their Jiaozhou leasehold and other rights in Shandong. These included a railroad to the provincial capital at Ji'nan and exploitation of coal and iron mines in Shandong's interior.

Japan invaded Qingdao in 1915 and took over administration of all German holdings in Shandong Province. Confirmed in this position by the Treaty of Versailles, Japan came under pressure from China and the United States to settle the Shandong question by turning Qingdao and other German rights back to China. Japan did so in 1923, but retained considerable control by virtue of Chinese government inability to pay for Japanese improvements to the German leasehold. Japan again occupied Qingdao from 1927 to 1929 during the Northern Expedition, but the Republic of China's government at Nanjing assumed direct administrative control of Qingdao in May 1929. From 1915 to 1945 Qingdao grew as a center for food processing, textile manufacture, and transportation, with Japanese capital the dominant force both before and after 1923.

In 1937 the Japanese quickly reoccupied Qingdao. The United States Navy took over from the Japanese in September 1945 and the city became a major base for the Republic of China's forces in Shandong until 1949. Since 1950 Qingdao has continued to grow as a major North China port and an industrial center. It remains famous as a summer beach resort.

Leon Wilson Godshall, *Tsingtao under Three Flags* (1929).
DAVID D. BUCK

QING DYNASTY. Founded by Manchu conquerors in 1644, the Qing was the last dynasty to rule China. It was overthrown by the 1911 Revolution, which marked the establishment of the Republic of China.

The Rise of the Manchus. The Manchus were a hunting, fishing, and farming people of central Manchuria, the region northwest of China proper. Although descended from the Tunguz Jurchen tribes that had founded the Jin dynasty (1115–1234) in North China, they were politically divided and under loose Chinese suzerainty by the middle of the Ming period (1368–1644). [*See also* Jurchen.]

Late in the sixteenth century the Jurchen chief Nurhaci (1559–1626) unified the tribes over a span of thirty years. He consolidated his power by establishing a walled fortress, employing armorers and blacksmiths, recruiting Chinese advisers, and reorganizing the Jurchen tribes. Nurhaci's most important innovation was the banner system. The entire population was enrolled in quasi-military units, each identified by a colored banner. The banner organization became the basic administrative unit of the Manchu state. Because banners crossed tribal lines and were commanded by appointed officers rather than hereditary chiefs, they marked a shift from tribal to bureaucratic organization. Four banners initially were established; four more were added later. Eventually the system added eight Mongol and eight Chinese banners to incorporate the Manchus' non-Manchu allies. [*See also* Banners.]

Nurhaci also sponsored the invention of a Manchu writing system, based on the Mongolian alphabet. It facilitated the keeping of records (hitherto kept in Mongolian); moreover, translations of the Ming law code and Chinese classical works enabled the Manchus to adopt Chinese administrative practices and Confucian ideology.

In 1616 Nurhaci renounced fealty to the Ming. Two years later he invaded Ming territory in southern Manchuria. In 1625 he moved his capital to the recently captured city of Shenyang (Mukden). Nurhaci died in 1626 and was succeeded by his eighth son, Huang Taiji (Abahai; 1592–1643). As he eliminated rivals among his brothers and subjugated other Manchu princes, Huang Taiji began the transformation of Manchu rule from collective government by princes to autocratic rule. He depended increasingly on Chinese models and collaborators. In Shenyang he organized a central government based on Chinese institutions.

Huang Taiji also expanded the Manchu state, incorporating Inner Mongolia and the Amur River valley. He also forced Korea to accept Manchu suzerainty. Manchu forces raided China as far south as Shandong. In 1636 Huang Taiji proclaimed the establishment of the Qing ("pure") dynasty, implicitly claiming succession to the Ming. He died in 1643. His ninth son, Fulin (1638–1661), came to the throne as the Shunzhi emperor on the eve of the Manchu invasion of China. [*See also* Manchus; Nurhaci; *and* Huang Taiji.]

The Qing Conquest of China. The Manchu invasion was facilitated by the collapse of Ming authority in North China, where popular uprisings had brought much of the country into turmoil. Li Zicheng (1605?–1645) had emerged as the most powerful contender for power. In the spring of 1644 Li marched eastward and occupied Beijing. A Ming general, Wu Sangui (1612–1678), thereupon joined forces with the Manchus against Li. With the help of Wu and other Chinese generals, the Manchus overran North China and easily defeated the divided resistance. Initially meeting with little opposition, the Manchus won the allegiance of government officials and local gentry, many of whom welcomed the Qing as deliverance from banditry and rebellion. In October 1644 the Qing capital was transferred to Beijing.

The conquest of South China was much more prolonged. The Ming government there had not been destroyed by rebellion. Several Ming loyalist regimes vied for succession, and one controlled parts of southwest China for fifteen years. Zheng Chenggong (1624–1662), also known as Koxinga, led a sustained Ming loyalist movement on the southeast coast and Taiwan. In 1673 Wu Sangui and two other Chinese generals, Shang Kexi and Geng Jimao, rebelled and set up separatist regimes in the south. This rebellion was quelled in 1681. Two years later the Qing conquered Taiwan and defeated the last Ming resistance. [*See also* Li Zicheng; Zheng Chenggong; Wu Sangui; Shang Kexi; *and* Three Feudatories Rebellion.]

Qing Government. The Qing dynasty became more sinicized under the Shunzhi emperor (r. 1644–1661). The first Manchu monarch to master the Chinese language, he revived the Hanlin Academy, a stronghold of Confucian scholarship and orthodoxy, and relied greatly on Chinese officials and eunuchs. The pendulum swung back toward Manchu control upon his death. His seven-year-old son was chosen to rule as the Kangxi emperor (r. 1661–1722), aided by a regency of four Manchu princes. After Kangxi assumed personal power in 1669, he institutionalized the privileged position of Manchus by reserving for them top positions in the bureaucracy. Each of the Six Boards had one Chinese and one Manchu minister: only half of the grand secretaries were Chinese. Although Chinese were often appointed provincial governors and filled almost all lower positions, they were generally supervised by Manchu, Mongol, or Chinese bannermen serving as governors-general. [*See also* Kangxi Emperor.]

Qing government followed Ming administrative practices, with some minor modifications. Each of the eighteen provinces was administered by a governor. He was supervised by a governor-general, who usually oversaw two provinces. Below the provincial administration was a hierarchy of circuits, prefectures, and districts. The district magistrate, representing the lowest level of formal government, was aided in his duties by local gentry, mostly degree holders and their families.

TABLE 1. *Emperors of the Qing Dynasty*

REIGN TITLE	TEMPLE NAME	ERA YEARS
Shunzhi	Shizu	1644–1661
Kangxi	Shengzu	1661–1722
Yongzheng	Shizong	1723–1735
Qianlong	Gaozong	1736–1795
Jiaqing	Renzong	1796–1820
Daoguang	Xuanzong	1821–1850
Xianfeng	Wenzong	1851–1861
Tongzhi	Muzong	1862–1874
Guangxu	Dezong	1875–1908
Xuantong		1908–1911

Under the Yongzheng emperor (r. 1723–1735), the monarchy became more autocratic, and state administration further centralized. Yongzheng established a small and informal group of advisers, the Grand Council, to aid him in governing; he developed a secret memorial system to allow confidential communication between the emperor and his most trusted officials; and he took direct control over all banners, some of which had been commanded by Manchu princes.

The tax system was reformed under Kangxi and Yongzheng. In 1713 the head-tax quota was frozen. Yongzheng reformed tax collection by legitimizing and limiting certain surcharges and by supplementing officials' salaries with "integrity-nourishing" allowances in order to bring corruption under control. [*See also* Yongzheng Emperor *and* Grand Council.]

Qing Expansion into Inner Asia. The Qing began to expand into Inner Asia not long after consolidating its control over China proper. These Qing conquests were motivated at least in part by strategic concerns: nomadic cavalry could threaten sedentary civilizations, and the Mongols had been a constant threat to the Ming. The Manchus began to deal with the Mongols as early as the 1630s, when they conquered the Eastern Mongols. The Western Mongols remained independent, however. Moreover, the Manchu relationship with the Mongols was complicated by the religious ties between the Mongols and Tibetans, both predominantly Lamaist.

In the 1670s a Western Mongol prince of the Dzungar tribe, Galdan (1644?–1697), conquered the Islamic cities of eastern Turkestan, creating a Dzungar empire in what is now Xinjiang. Eventually Galdan invaded Outer Mongolia and threatened Beijing before being turned back. In 1696, however, Qing armies expelled the Dzungars from Outer Mongolia, which was incorporated into the Qing

CHINA DURING THE QING DYNASTY

RUSSIAN EMPIRE

AMUR

DZUNGARIA

OUTER MONGOLIA

MANCHURIA

Lake Balkhash

Lake Baikal

Yining
(Kuldja)

Urumqi

Kucha

Kashgar *Tarim*

Yarkand

Khotan

Hami

XINJIANG
(CHINESE TURKESTAN)

Anxi

ALASHAN

INNER MONGOLIA

Mukden
(Shenyang)

Niuzhuang

ZHILI Jehol

Beijing
(Shuntianfu)

Tianjin

Baoding

Chefu
(Yantai)

Port Arthur
(Luda)

Weihaiwei

KOREA

Sea
of
Japan

QINGHAI

GANSU

Xining

Ningxia

Lanzhou

Taiyuan

SHANXI

Huang He
(Yellow River)

Ji'nan

Qingdao

SHANDONG

Xi'an

SHAANXI

Kaifeng

HENAN

Nanjing

Suzhou

JIANGSU

TIBET

Lhasa

NEPAL

BHUTAN

INDIA
(BRITISH
EMPIRE)

Chindwin

SICHUAN

Chengdu

Chongqing

Yangtze

Yichang

Hankou

Wuchang

Jiujiang

ANHUI

Anqing

Yangzhou

Shanghai

Hangzhou

Ningbo

ZHEJIANG

Wenzhou

Changsha

Nanchang

HUNAN

JIANGXI

FUJIAN

Fuzhou

Taibei

GUIZHOU

Guiyang

Yunnan

YUNNAN

Guilin

GUANGXI

BURMA

Irrawaddy

Nanning

GUANGDONG

Guangzhou
(Canton)

Xiamen
(Amoy)

TAIWAN

Tainan

Shantou
(Swatow)

Macao
(Port.)

Hong Kong
(Brit.)

TONKIN

FRENCH
INDOCHINA

SIAM

Gulf
of
Tonkin

Mekong

East China Sea

States and regions formerly
under Chinese dominance:

Amur, 1689; to Russia, 1858
Dzungaria, 1757; to Russia, 1847
Korea 1627; to Japan, 1895
Taiwan, 1683; to Japan, 1895
Nepal, 1792; fully independent, 1908
Burma, 1769; to Britain, 1886
Tonkin; to France, 1884

0 200 500 800 km

0 200 500 miles

◼ Imperial capital

★ Provincial capital

ZHILI Province

MANCHURIA Regions

Boundaries of Qing
Empire ca.1900

Boundaries of China proper

Provincial boundaries

empire. [*See also* Dzungaria; Xinjiang; *and* Galdan.]

Both the Dzungars and the Qing became involved in Tibetan succession disputes. When the Dzungars occupied Tibet in 1717, the Qing responded with an invasion of Tibet. The Qing army took Lhasa in 1720 and established a protectorate. Qing control over Tibet was enforced by a permanent Manchu garrison.

In the years that followed, internecine strife weakened the Dzungars. In the 1750s the Qing defeated the Dzungars in a series of campaigns and subjugated the Turkic populations of eastern Turkestan. By 1760 the Qing reached its greatest extent of territorial control.

Qing Society and Economy. China enjoyed a long period of domestic peace and prosperity from the 1680s to the 1790s. New lands were opened to settlement, especially in the southwest. Newly introduced American food crops such as maize, sweet potatoes, and peanuts were grown on land unsuit-

FIGURE 1. *Qing-dynasty Porcelain Dish.* Jingdezhen blue-and-white ware, eighteenth century. Large dish with decoration of finches on a flowering branch in Xuande manner; porcelain with underglaze decoration in cobalt blue. Height 8.9 cm., diameter 50.1 cm.

able for other crops, bringing marginal land in every region into cultivation. Cash crops such as tea and cotton furthered the commercialization of agriculture, especially in the lower Yangtze region. Economic development increased the concentration of land ownership, particularly south of the Yangtze.

The proliferation of guilds, credit institutions, and market towns indicate a growing volume of trade in the eighteenth century. There was large-scale textile production in factories, particularly in Suzhou and Hangzhou. Copper mining became highly developed in Yunnan. European trade brought in an influx of silver, increasing the amount of money in circulation. Some historians have regarded this period as one of incipient capitalism.

Probably as a result of the expansion of agriculture and mid-Qing prosperity, China's population grew from roughly 150 million in 1700 to twice that a century later. Agricultural development barely kept pace with demographic growth. Migration to frontier areas alleviated population pressure, but promised no long-term solution to the problem.

This population explosion also produced political repercussions. The government did not grow to keep pace with demographic growth. In addition, examination quotas were not raised; competition for degrees and official positions thus intensified. The formal mechanisms for social mobility lagged behind population growth.

Qing Thought and Literature. The trauma of the Manchu conquest led Chinese scholars to concern themselves with the causes of Ming collapse. Huang Zongxi (1610–1695) advocated checks on the power of monarchs and delegation of authority; Gu Yanwu (1612–1682) criticized Neo-Confucian scholasticism and called for the pursuit of practical knowledge. Scholars continued to regard the classics as the basis of all learning. Gradually a "school of empirical research" (*kaozheng xue*) emerged, based on close examination of classical texts and use of the inductive method. This led to advances in philology and etymology, and also to reassessment of orthodox interpretations of the classics—particularly by Dai Zhen (1724–1777). [*See also* Huang Zongxi; Gu Yanwu; Dai Zhen; *and* Kaozheng Xue.]

The state sponsored and controlled most academic activity. The Qianlong emperor (r. 1736–1795) ordered the compilation of the 36,000-volume "Complete Library of the Four Treasuries." At the same time, he ordered a literary inquisition to destroy books regarded as seditious.

Fiction flourished during the Qing period. Novels reached their acme with *Honglou meng* (*The Dream of the Red Chamber,* also entitled *The Story of the Stone*) by Cao Xueqin (1715?–1763). Another well-known novel of the period is Wu Jingzi's *Rulin waishi* (*The Scholars*). [*See also* Chinese Literature; Cao Xueqin; Wu Jingzi; *and* Rulin Waishi.]

Dynastic Decline. By the end of the eighteenth century many of the classic signs of dynastic decline had appeared. Administrative deterioration was exemplified by the career of Heshen (1750–1799), a Manchu courtier who became a favorite of the Qianlong emperor and rose rapidly from bodyguard to grand councillor. Heshen's high status symbolized official corruption and demoralization. [*See also* Heshen *and* Qianlong Emperor.]

The White Lotus Rebellion, sparked by a millenarian religious sect, broke out in 1796. The sect had won adherents among the volatile and unsettled population of west central China, and was motivated in part by opposition to official oppression. Armed groups such as bandits and smugglers joined the uprising, which the regular Qing banner forces proved unable to subdue. Eventually the uprising was put down by a locally organized militia, and by 1805 the White Lotus rebels had been annihilated. [*See also* White Lotus Society.]

The rebellion was both a symptom and a cause of dynastic decline. It resulted from social pressures and administrative deterioration, and it hastened the fiscal and military decline of the dynasty. As a result, the Qing was already weakened when challenged by the Western powers.

Relations with the West. Until the nineteenth century, Sino-Western contact posed little threat to the Qing. As it expanded into Inner Asia, the Qing met Russian continental expansion; after some minor conflicts, however, the two empires signed the treaties of Nerchinsk (1689) and Kiakhta (1727) to regulate trade and define their borders.

Western maritime trade with China began early in the sixteenth century with the arrival of Portuguese and Dutch ships on the southeast coast. By 1760 the Qing government had restricted Western maritime trade to Canton (Guangzhou). European merchants were permitted only seasonal residence in Canton and allowed to trade only with the Cohong, a government-chartered merchant guild. [See Cohong.]

Great Britain emerged as China's major Western trading partner. The tea trade, monopolized by the East India Company, became an important source of British revenue. In order to improve Britain's unfavorable balance of payments, the East India Company began to grow opium in India and sell it to private traders who smuggled it into China. British opium trade with China doubled in the 1830s. The opium trade was illegal—China outlawed opium, a severely addictive and debilitating drug, in 1729. Moreover, the opium trade reversed the trade balance, disrupting the Chinese economy. The Qing government in 1838 dispatched Commissioner Lin Zexu to Canton to suppress the opium trade. British resistance sparked the Opium War (1839–1842). [See Lin Zexu *and* China Trade.]

The Treaty System. After three years of warfare, China sued for peace and was forced to sign the Treaty of Nanjing in 1842. The treaty opened five ports to British trade and gave British subjects extraterritorial privileges in China. In addition, China was required to pay an indemnity and cede the island of Hong Kong (Xianggang) to Britain.

Other Western countries soon signed similar treaties with China. Each successive treaty expanded foreign privileges. Eventually the treaty system opened inland waterways, allowed missionaries into China's interior, and deprived China of tariff autonomy. After Britain and France defeated China in the Second Opium War (also known as the Arrow War; 1856–1860), China permitted foreign legations to be established in Beijing for the first time. [See Hong Kong; Arrow War; *and* Treaty Ports.]

Nineteenth-century Rebellions. The Opium War and the shift of trade to treaty ports north of Canton disrupted the economy of Guangdong Province. Economic dislocation increased popular unrest and provided the backdrop to the Taiping Rebellion (1851–1864).

The Taiping movement was led by Hong Xiuquan (1813–1864), who had been exposed to Christianity in Canton. Convinced that he was the younger brother of Jesus, Hong founded a sect and in 1851 proclaimed the inauguration of the "Heavenly Kingdom of Great Peace" *(taiping tianguo)*. His army marched north and by 1853 took Nanjing, which became the Taiping capital.

Taiping ideology combined elements of Christianity with Chinese utopian thought. It envisioned equal distribution of land, sexual equality, and communal property. Taiping social policies prohibited use of opium, slavery, polygamy, and the binding of women's feet. However, the Taiping movement suffered from internecine warfare; moreover, its religious intolerance and hostility to much of traditional culture lost it popular support. Qing loyalists eventually rallied behind provincial armies organized by Zeng Guofan (1811–1872) and others. The Taipings were suppressed by 1864. [See also Taiping Rebellion *and* Hong Xiuquan.]

The Taiping Rebellion coincided with the Nian Rebellion in North China (1853–1868) and three separate Muslim rebellions: in Yunnan (1856–1872), in Shaanxi and Gansu (1862–1877), and in eastern Turkestan (1864–1878). The Qing suppressed the rebellions at the expense of the central government's authority as provincial officials led military operations and won fiscal autonomy. At the same time, Han Chinese officials increased their influence and the Manchus became less powerful. [See also Nian Rebellion.]

Self-Strengthening and Imperialism. After 1860 the Qing adopted a conciliatory policy toward the West. Under the leadership of Prince Gong (Gong Yixin; 1833–1898) and Empress Dowager Cixi (1835–1908), the government established the Zongli Yamen (a foreign affairs office) and a foreign language school. Zeng Guofan and his protégé Li Hongzhang (1823–1901), leaders of the suppression of the Taipings, sought to increase China's power by introducing Western military technology. This effort, known as the Self-Strengthening Movement, resulted in establishment of the Jiangnan Arsenal (1854) and the Fuzhou Shipyard. Eventually, the movement also promoted industrial development. Several enterprises were established under government supervision and with private capital. [See also Gong Yixin; Empress Dowager; Zongli Yamen; Zeng Guofan; and Li Hongzhang.]

The Self-Strengthening Movement failed to increase China's military strength significantly, however. In 1884 French ambitions in Vietnam, a Chinese protectorate, sparked the Sino-French War (1884–1885). Poor coordination and leadership resulted in China's defeat. Ten years later a clash with Japan over Korea resulted in the Sino-Japanese War (1894–1895), which Japan won easily. [See also Sino-Japanese War.]

After China's defeat, a "scramble for concessions" ensued. Germany, Russia, France, and Britain all forced China to lease ports and recognize foreign spheres of influence over Chinese territory. Nominal Chinese sovereignty was preserved in the foreign areas, mainly because the competing powers checked each others' ambitions. Nonetheless, imperialist pressure threatened to destroy China's unity and independence. [See also Imperialism.]

Late Qing Reform. This crisis brought a group of reformers to the attention of the Guangxu emperor (r. 1875–1908). Their leader, Kang Youwei (1858–1927), reinterpreted Confucianism to sanction radical innovation. In the summer of 1898 the emperor issued a series of decrees calling for wide-ranging institutional reforms and economic development, but official resistance blocked implementation of the reforms. In September 1898, conservatives led by Empress Dowager Cixi staged a coup d'état. The emperor was placed under house arrest; the reformers fled into exile or were arrested.

The new conservative government soon threw its support behind the Boxers (more properly, Yihetuan, "righteous and harmonious society"), a popular movement dedicated to driving Westerners out of China. The Boxers occupied Beijing in the summer of 1900 and besieged the foreign legations with the connivance of the Qing government, which declared war on the foreign powers. Regional officials in central and southern China, however, ignored the declaration of war and maintained friendly relations with the powers. An international force occupied Beijing in August 1900. In 1901 China was forced to sign the Boxer Protocol, which provided for a foreign military presence in North China, punishment for Chinese officials implicated in the Boxer movement, and an indemnity. [See also Yihetuan.]

The chastened Qing government thereupon undertook an extensive reform program, similar in many ways to the one aborted in 1898. A new public education system was inaugurated, and in 1905 the civil service examination system, based on the Confucian classics, was abolished. The traditional Six Boards were replaced with new ministries. Modern military academies trained a new officer corps and Yuan Shikai (1859–1916) established the Beiyang Army, a modern military force.

Japan's defeat of Russia in 1905 appeared to prove the superiority of constitutionalism over autocracy. The Qing government slowly began to establish representative assemblies. Provincial assemblies, with advisory functions but not legislative powers, were established in 1909. A consultative National Assembly met the following year. Nevertheless, the Manchu princes controlling the government moved cautiously and continued to monopolize the highest positions, thereby increasing Chinese frustrations and resentment.

The Revolution of 1911. In the decade following the Boxer Rebellion, expatriate reformers and revolutionaries vied for support. Kang Youwei, in exile in Japan, remained loyal to the Qing and opposed attempts to overthrow the dynasty. His disciple Liang Qichao (1873–1929) became familiar with Western political ideas and spread them in the journals he published in Tokyo. [See also Kang Youwei and Liang Qichao.]

Their most important rival was another Chinese exile, Sun Yat-sen (1866–1925). Sun was a Western-educated Cantonese with ties to overseas Chinese communities. In 1905 Sun established a revolutionary organization based in Tokyo, the Tongmenghui (Revolutionary Alliance). He promoted republicanism and his "Three Principles of the People"—nationalism, people's rights, and people's livelihood.

On 10 October 1911 revolutionary soldiers in the Qing army garrison in Wuchang mutinied. The authority of the Qing government rapidly collapsed; provincial assemblies in southern and central China declared their independence from the Manchus, and a provisional government was established in Nanjing. Sun Yat-sen returned from a sixteen-year exile to be inaugurated as the first president of the Republic of China.

The Qing court called upon the retired general Yuan Shikai to deal with the revolutionaries. Sun offered to resign the presidency in favor of Yuan if Yuan were to support the republic. Yuan engineered the abdication of the five-year-old Xuantong emperor in February 1912, and accepted the presidency, ending China's two millennia of imperial rule.

[See also Xinhai Revolution; Xuantong Emperor; Sun Yat-sen; Yuan Shikai; and China, Republic Period.]

Hao Chang, *Liang Ch'i-ch'ao and Cultural Transition in China* (1971). Joseph Esherick, *Reform and Revolution in China: The 1911 Revolution in Hunan and Hubei* (1976). John K. Fairbank, *Trade and Diplomacy on the China Coast: The Opening of the Treaty Ports, 1842–1854* (1953). Ping-ti Ho, *Studies on the Population of China, 1368–1953* (1959). Immanuel C. Y. Hsu, *The Rise of Modern China* (2d ed., 1975). Arthur W. Hummel, ed., *Eminent Chinese of the Ch'ing Period, 1644–1912*, 2 vols. (1943–1944). Daniel L. Overmyer, *Folk Buddhist Religion: Dissenting Sects in Late Traditional China* (1976). Dwight H. Perkins, *Agricultural Development in China, 1368–1968* (1969). Denis Twitchett and John K. Fairbank, eds., *The Cambridge History of China* (1978–). Mary Clabaugh Wright, ed., *China in Revolution: The First Phase* (1968).   ROBERT ENTENMANN

QING EMPIRICISM. *See* Kaozheng Xue.

QINGTAN, "pure conversation," refers to a tradition of philosophical speculation and a style of literary discourse associated with the revival of philosophical Daoism in the Wei–Jin period (220–420) in China. Étienne Balazs divides *qingtan* into three generations. Philosophers of the first generation, who were closely associated with the rise to power of Cao Cao (155–220) and his followers, reinterpreted Daoism as allowing participation in government service. They did so by equating *dao* with *wu*, or nonbeing, a move that, Richard Mather argues, allowed them to justify Cao Cao's rise to power "out of nowhere" instead of through family or aristocratic connections.

The second generation is exemplified by the so-called Seven Sages of the Bamboo Grove, an informal group of scholars and poets who refused office after the Sima family's coup against Cao Cao's descendants in 249. In their metaphysical discussions emphasis was placed on *ziran*, the spontaneous or natural, as a way of life opposed to Confucian tradition and as a justification for refusal to serve in the new regime. This generation therefore most epitomizes *qingtan*, which includes not only witticisms but also anecdotes of nonconformist behavior, including wine drinking, nudity, and other free-spirited and unconventional acts. After the execution of the host of the Seven Sages, Xi Kang (223–262), and the consolidation of Sima rule under the Jin dynasty (265–420), the libertarian tendencies of the second generation degenerated into libertine behavior for its own sake on the part of the children of the aristocracy. In this final generation of *qingtan*, Daoism was again reinterpreted to allow partici-pation in government, if only for individual gain and survival in the chaotic late-Jin epoch.

Many examples of *qingtan* were collected around 430 in the *Shishuo xinyu (A New Account of the Tales of the World)* of Liu Yiqing. The most important works of those associated with *qingtan* include the commentaries on the *Laozi* and the *Yijing* by Wang Bi (225–249), the Xiang Xiu–Guo Xiang commentary on the *Zhuangzi*, the third-century Daoist work *Liezi*, and the poetry of Ruan Ji (210–263), one of the Seven Sages. In fact, the *ziran* of his generation became most influential in the "southern" style in art and poetry, as opposed to the meticulous and painstaking "northern," or court, style, and is perhaps the most important way in which the *qingtan* movement helped convey Daoism to later generations.

[*See also* Seven Sages of the Bamboo Grove *and* Daoism.]

Étienne Balazs, "Nihilistic Revolt or Mystical Escapism: Currents of Thought in China during the Third Century A.D.," in *Chinese Civilization and Bureaucracy: Variations on a Theme*, edited by Arthur F. Wright and translated by H. M. Wright (1964), pp. 226–254. Liu I-ch'ing (Liu Yiqing), *A New Account of Tales of the World*, translated by Richard B. Mather (1976). Richard B. Mather, "The Controversy over Conformity and Naturalness during the Six Dynasties," *History of Religions* 9.2–3 (1969–1970): 160–180. Holmes Welch, *Taoism: The Parting of the Way* (1965).   JOHN A. RAPP

QIN SHIHUANGDI (r. 221–210 BCE), known to history as the king of the state of Qin who conquered all rivals for power at the end of the Warring States period (403–221 BCE) and emerged as the creator of the Qin dynasty (221–206 BCE), China's first universal empire.

The term *shihuangdi*, "first emperor," was adopted in 221 BCE by King Zheng of Qin to institutionalize his position as the absolute authority of the empire. The lords of the independent kingdoms of the period prior to unification had used the designation "king" *(wang)*. The victorious Qin sovereign combined the title of *huang* ("august sovereign") and *di* ("lord") to place himself in a category of ruler superior even to the legendary sage kings. By calling himself First Emperor he anticipated the continuation of a dynastic line that would last for ten thousand generations.

It has been suggested by a number of modern scholars that the highly centralized government established by the Qin dynasty was largely influenced by Li Si, Qin Shihuangdi's grand councillor. The measures introduced by Li Si followed the dictates of Legalism, a system of government that advocated promotion of agriculture and warfare to strengthen the imperial state. Under Li's stewardship, all Qin territory was centrally controlled, the population was held in check by a system of strict rewards and punishments, and there was a standardization of weights, measures, coinage, script, and axle-lengths for carts.

The state system established by Qin Shihuangdi and Li Si was quite harsh by any standard. The conscription labor demanded of the people to complete massive projects intended as symbols of Qin Shihuangdi's power caused great suffering. These projects included the formation of the Great Wall by joining the walls that earlier states had built along the empire's northern frontier, the construction of a system of roads connecting the empire at the capital (near the present-day city of Xi'an in Shaanxi Province), and the emperor's massive subterranean tomb. These undertakings took their toll in great loss of life and heavy taxation burdens. In addition, the Qin showed no mercy in meting out punishment and in eliminating intellectual opposition to its policies. (A "burning of the books" in 213 BCE served to suppress ideologies hostile to Qin Shihuangdi's rule.)

The harsh Qin regime had been held in place by the powerful personality of the First Emperor. However, the dynastic system that supposedly would last for ten thousand generations survived only three years after his death in 210 BCE.

[See also Burning of the Books; Legalism; Li Si; and Qin Dynasty.]

Derk Bodde, *China's First Unifier: A Study of the Ch'in Dynasty as Seen in the Life of Li Ssu 280?–208 B.C.* (1967). Hsiao Kung-chuan, *A History of Chinese Political Thought,* vol. 1, translated by F. W. Mote (1979). Burton Watson, trans., *Records of the Grand Historian,* 2 vols. (1961).   ANITA M. ANDREW

QIPCHAKS. *See* Kipchaks.

QIQIHAR, leading city in the Nanjiang River plain of Heilongjiang Province, China. A Manchu post first settled by Chinese in the eighteenth century, its development into an industrial city began with the arrival of the Chinese Eastern Railway in 1903 and became more extensive under the Japanese occupation (1932–1945). Since 1949 Qiqihar has grown to a population of 1,222,000 (1982 estimate). Its industry includes railway locomotive and rolling stock factories, as well as sugar refining, paper milling, and food processing.   JOHN A. RAPP

QIU JIN (1875–1907), early Chinese feminist and revolutionary martyr. Born to a lower gentry family, Qiu received a good education as a child. Unhappy with her marriage to a conservative son of a merchant family and increasingly concerned about foreign powers scrambling for territorial and economic concessions in China, she left her husband and departed for Japan to study in 1904. Qiu was quickly drawn into radical Chinese student circles in Tokyo. Now thoroughly convinced that China was plunging toward destruction unless the Manchu regime was overthrown, Qiu became a revolutionary.

A woman with an unusually compelling personality and romantic vision, Qiu enjoyed horseback riding and marksmanship. She was perennially fascinated by the stories of Chinese female knights-errant and warriors (such as Hua Mulan) and of Russian tragic-heroic anarchists (such as Sophia Perovskaya). Her adoption of the name Jianhu Nüxia ("female knight-errant of Jian Lake"), after the lake near her hometown, vividly revealed her fervent aspirations for a romantic-revolutionary role. She joined the revolutionary Guangfuhui (Restoration Society) in the spring of 1905, and the newly formed Tongmenghui (Revolutionary Alliance) a few months later, becoming an active member in both organizations.

Qiu returned to Shanghai in early 1906. For a while she devoted herself both to gradual feminist reforms and violent revolutionary changes. Extremely sensitive to the plight of Chinese women, she founded and wrote for *Zhongguo nübao (Chinese Women's Journal)* in Shanghai in 1907; in this journal she condemned such practices as arranged marriages and footbinding, and called for equal rights and modern education for women. Her ultimate aim, however, was revolution. In 1907 Qiu was made head of the Datong School, which had been established by Xu Xilin, Qiu's cousin and a leader of the Guangfuhui, as a front for the headquarters of revolutionaries. When Xu's attempted uprising in Anhui failed, Qiu was implicated. She was arrested and executed in July 1907.

Mary B. Rankin, *Early Chinese Revolutionaries: Radical Intellectuals in Shanghai and Chekiang, 1902–1911* (1971). Jonathan D. Spence, *Gate of Heavenly Peace: The Chinese and Their Revolution, 1895–1980* (2d ed., 1982).

CHANG-TAI HUNG

QIZIL BASH. *See* Kizilbash.

QOM, to the south of Tehran, Iran's second major shrine town. In medieval times the city was a winter capital and later a royal and noble mausoleum town; in this century Qom is Iran's premier center for training religious leaders. Hazrat-i Fatima, the sister of the eighth imam (Ali al-Rida), is buried here; her shrine is the second most important shrine (after that of the eighth imam in Mashhad) in Iran. Qom has a population of some 200,000 people, is known for producing fine carpets, has little industry, and is still a relatively traditional town based on farming, weaving, selling to pilgrims, and providing services to the sizable *madrasa* population. Since the establishment of the Islamic Republic of Iran in 1979 it has become a livelier place as the seat of various cliques and organizations with government connections.

After the Islamic conquest of Iran, Qom remained Zoroastrian for a time; the Sasanid ritual fire in the nearby village of Mazdijan was extinguished only at the end of the ninth century by the governor of Qom. During the ninth century Qom developed a reputation for resisting Sunni governors and their tax demands: at least five times the city had to be militarily reduced before taxes could be collected. At this time there were 266 Shi'ite and 14 Sunni *ulamas* (religious scholars) in the town.

By the fifteenth century Qom had become a winter hunting capital. The Safavid shahs Isma'il and Tahmasp continued using Qom as a winter capital and built the city into something much grander. The tombs of Shah Abbas II, Shah Safi, Shah Sulaiman, and Shah Sultan Husain were placed by the shrine. An administrator for the shrine was brought from Lebanon by Shah Tahmasp, and his descendants remained in the job until 1965, when Shah Mohammed Reza Pahlavi ousted them. By the time of the Safavids at least, the shrine became an important place of sanctuary *(bast-nishin),* where one could take refuge from the law until a judgment thought to be unfair could be sorted out.

In 1920 Shaikh Abd al-Karim Ha'eri-Yazdi came to Qom and reestablished the *hauza-i ilmi* (center of learning), this time not with royal or aristocratic patronage, but as part of the exodus back to Iran by Shi'ite leaders who were concerned that the transition between Ottoman and British rule in Iraq might jeopardize their position in the *atabat* (shrine towns of Iraq).

Qom soon became an arena of struggle between the modernization efforts of the Pahlavi monarchy and the conservative vision of the *ulamas* and their students. In January 1978 the city became the site of the first major violence of the revolutionary process that ousted the Pahlavi monarchy. Ayatollah Khomeini, who came to prominence in the 1963 revolt but was exiled the following year, returned to Iran in 1979 as the leader of the revolution; he went first to Qom and established a headquarters in the Madrasa Faiziyya. His heir apparent, Ayatollah Hossein Ali Montazeri, remains seated in Qom.

[*See also* Ayatollah *and* Mashhad.]

Michael M. J. Fischer, *Iran: From Religious Dispute to Revolution* (1980). Roy P. Mottahedeh, *The Mantle of the Prophet* (1985).   MICHAEL FISCHER

QUANZHOU. *See* Zayton.

QUEMOY. *See* Jinmen.

QUETTA, the capital of Baluchistan Province in Pakistan, is located near the eastern entrance of the Bolan and Khojak passes. In early historical references, the city was called Shal or Shalkot. It changed hands several times in the seventeenth century between the Mughals and Safavids, and under the British it served as the administrative and military headquarters of Baluchistan from 1876 until the creation of Pakistan in 1947. [*See also* Baluchistan.]

STEPHEN RITTENBERG

QUEYROZ, FERNAO DE (1617–1688), Portuguese Catholic clergyman of the order of the Society of Jesus who spent fifty-three years in the service of the society in India and rose steadily in its hierarchy, finally becoming provincial of the order (1677–1680). He served in Cochin, Goa, Diu, Tana, Bassein, and Salsette. A reputable scholar, he wrote a number of works, but most have been lost. Two major works survive in manuscript form—his biography of Pedro de Basto, a Jesuit lay brother in India, and *Conquista temporal e spiritual do Ceylao (Temporal and Spiritual Conquest of Ceylon).* The latter is an important source for the history of Sri Lanka, describing the Portuguese conquest, administration, and loss of the island; the work was completed in 1686 but was not published until 1916.

[*See also* Jesuits: Jesuits in India; Portuguese: Portuguese in India; *and* Sri Lanka.]

Fernao de Queroz, *The Temporal and Spiritual Conquest of Ceylon*, 3 vols., translated by S. G. Perere (1930).

S. ARASARATNAM

QUEZON, MANUEL LUIS (1878–1944), first president of the Commonwealth of the Philippines, was the dominant Filipino political leader of the American colonial era. Born in the remote town of Baler in Tayabas (now Quezon) province, Quezon received his early schooling from his Spanish *mestizo* parents and local clergy and his secondary education at the Colegio de San Juan de Letran in Manila. A law student at the University of Santo Tomas when the revolution against Spain began in 1896, Quezon returned home and sat out the fighting with his loyalist parents. He did, however, serve in the Philippine army during the Philippine-American War, which began in February 1899, and eventually achieved the rank of major. Surrendering in April 1901, he spent an embittering period in prison before resuming his legal studies and, in 1903, becoming a licensed attorney.

Returning to Tayabas, Quezon quickly won the political backing of regional American officials looking for progressive-minded Filipinos to fill positions in local and provincial government. With the active support of American constabulary officers, he was elected governor of Tayabas in 1906. The next year Quezon was elected to the first Philippine Assembly, where he became floor leader of the majority Nacionalista Party, whose platform called for early independence from the United States. From 1909 until 1916 he represented the Assembly as resident commissioner to the United States, becoming the chief lobbyist for Philippine independence in Washington. Quezon was instrumental in President Woodrow Wilson's choice of Francis Burton Harrison, a patrician anti-imperialist, to be governor-general of the Philippines, and he helped to both draft and lobby for passage of the Jones Act in 1916. On the strength of these successes, he became first president of the new Philippine Senate.

The ambivalence at the heart of Quezon's public career was thus evident from the beginning. Intellectually acute, personally charismatic, and driven by ambitions for both himself and the Philippines, Quezon played the game of colonial politics with virtuosity. His nationalism was tempered, however, by loyalty and indebtedness to many Americans and by the conviction he shared with them that modernization, development, and political stability ought to precede independence. Privately, he recommended that the United States grant the Philippines increased autonomy and guarantee the Filipinos' right to independence; caught in a cross-fire between American retentionists and Filipino advocates of independence, however, he aligned himself with the latter and became their leader.

Quezon used the period of conservative retrenchment under Republicans in the 1920s to consolidate his political leadership, defeating his lifetime rival Sergio Osmeña for control of the Philippine legislature and the Nacionalista Party and then engineering a dramatic confrontation with the colonial administration. When Osmeña and Assembly Speaker Manuel Roxas subsequently negotiated congressional passage of the Hare-Hawes-Cutting Act, which provided for Philippine independence in ten years, Quezon deposed his rivals from office and persuaded Congress to recast its independence legislation as the Tydings-McDuffie Act (1934).

Elected president of the transitional Commonwealth of the Philippines in 1935, Quezon struggled with mixed success to achieve military preparedness, economic stability, and social justice. Although presented as steps toward a new "distributive state," his social and economic programs failed to arrest the rise of agrarian and labor discontent. At his insistence, the National Assembly gave Quezon emergency economic powers and amended the constitution to allow him a second presidential term. He was reelected in 1941 by a margin of seven to one. Briefly tempted by thoughts of resistance or collaboration, Quezon fled the Japanese at the outbreak of World War II and established a war cabinet in Washington. He died of tuberculosis in 1944 and was succeeded by Vice President Osmeña, who had accompanied him into exile.

Quezon's political virtuosity eased the Philippines' progress toward independence but diluted the substance of his country's political life. Ambivalent himself, Quezon nevertheless invoked "the discipline of the independence movement" to stifle the emergence of other issues and defeat his rivals. A formative figure in modern Philippine political culture, he shaped the practice of electoral politics, guided the evolution of his country's multilayered relationship with the United States, and perhaps unwittingly provided precedents for the centralization of power in the hands of a strong leader.

[*See also* Philippines; Philippines, Commonwealth of; Philippines-American War; Nacionalista Party;

Harrison, Francis Burton; Jones Act; Osmeña, Sergio; Roxas, Manuel; *and* Tydings-McDuffie Act.]

Michael Cullinane, "The Politics of Collaboration in Tayabas Province: The Early Political Career of Manuel Quezon, 1903–1906," in *Reappraising an Empire: New Perspectives on Philippine-American History,* edited by Peter W. Stanley (1984). Theodore Friend, *Between Two Empires: The Ordeal of the Philippines, 1929–1946* (1965). Manuel Luis Quezon, *The Good Fight* (1946). Carlos Quirino, *Quezon, Paladin of Philippine Freedom* (1971). Peter W. Stanley, *A Nation in the Making: The Philippines and the United States, 1899–1921* (1974).

PETER W. STANLEY

QUM. *See* Qom.

QUOC NGU ("national language"), a romanized Vietnamese script originating in the efforts of various seventeenth-century European missionaries, particularly Alexandre de Rhodes (1591–1660). Although long confined to Catholic communities, *quoc ngu* became more widespread during the French colonial period. The French advocated its use both to aid in religious conversion and to oppose the traditional Confucian system represented by Chinese characters. Promoted by scholars such as Truong Vinh Ky, Huynh Tinh Cua, and Pham Quynh, *quoc ngu* was also popularized in newspapers, such as *Gia Dinh Bao, Dong Duong Tap Chi,* and *Nam Phong.* Since 1945 it has been the standard script for writing Vietnamese.

[*See also* Chu Nom; Rhodes, Alexandre de; *and* Truong Vinh Ky.]

John DeFrancis, *Colonialism and Language Policy in Viet Nam* (1977). Milton Osborne, *The French Presence in Cochinchina and Cambodia* (1969).

BRUCE M. LOCKHART

QU QIUBAI (1899–1935), leader of the Chinese Communist Party (1927–1928). Qu was born in Jiangsu Province to an impoverished gentry family. As a youth he studied English, French, and Russian, becoming particularly proficient in the latter. While still a young man he became known for his translations of Tolstoy, Gorky, and other Russian writers.

In 1921 Qu went to Moscow as a news correspondent. There he served for two years as a lecturer and interpreter for Chinese students at the Communist University of Toilers of the East. In February 1922 he joined the Communist Party. Upon returning to China, Qu was elected to the Party Central Committee. He was the editor of several Communist publications and a prolific writer, his works appearing under about fifty pseudonyms. In August 1927 he replaced Chen Duxiu as leader of the Chinese Communist Party when Chen was blamed by the Comintern for the 1927 massacre of Communists by the Guomindang (Kuomintang, or Nationalist Party) in Shanghai.

Qu's tenure as Party leader was brief. Condemned for his disastrous policy of aggressive urban and rural insurrection, Qu was called to Moscow for reeducation. In the USSR he established a reputation under the name Strakhov for his work in the Comintern. Back in China in 1931, Qu became active in the League of Left-wing Writers and was a close friend of Lu Xun. In 1934 he assumed the post of Education Commissioner for the Central Soviet government in Ruijin. Sick with the tuberculosis from which he had suffered for over a decade, Qu was too ill to go on the Long March when the Communists abandoned Ruijin. He was captured by National Government troops and executed on 18 June 1935.

[*See also* Communism: Chinese Communist Party *and* Comintern.]

Donald W. Klein and Anne B. Clark, *Biographic Dictionary of Chinese Communism, 1921–1965* (1971). Paul Pickowicz, *Marxist Literary Thought in China: The Influence of Ch'u Ch'iu-pai* (1981).   PETER J. SEYBOLT

QUR'AN, the sacred scripture of Islam, containing the revelations received from God by Muhammad over twenty-odd years (c. 610–632). For Muslims, the Qur'an is the actual word of God, and thus doctrine has come to hold that it is uncreated and coexistent with God, sharing a place on a heavenly tablet with former revelations. It follows that the Qur'an must always be recited in Arabic, although it may be read accompanied by a translation.

The Qur'an's 114 *suras,* or chapters, traditionally divided into those received at Mecca or at Medina, are of unequal length and were arranged, shortly after the death of Muhammad, not in the order in which they were revealed but in order of length. The doctrine of the inimitability of the Qur'an arises as much from its striking poetic qualities as from its content. Some of the prominent themes are the unity and transcendence of God, his goodness and mercy,

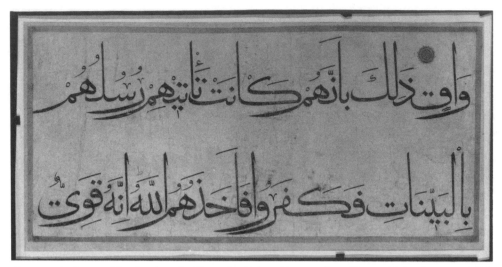

FIGURE 1. *Page of the Qur'an.* Attributed to Prince Baysonghur, Herat, Afghanistan, c. 1430. Two lines of the Qur'an, last word of chapter 40, verse 21 to near end of verse 22. Ink, gold, and colors on paper. 97.2 cm. × 44 cm.

the last judgment, and ethical teachings for the new society. Muslims everywhere show unbounded reverence for the Qur'an, often memorizing the book as children.

[*See also* Islam *and* Muhammad.]

A. J. Arberry, trans., *The Koran Interpreted* (1955). Fazlur Rahman, *Major Themes of the Qur'ān* (1980). W. Montgomery Watt, *Bell's Introduction to the Qur'ān* (1970).   JEANETTE A. WAKIN

QUTB UD-DIN AIBAK (d. 1210), a Turkish slave officer of Shihab ud-Din Ghuri, who established the Delhi sultanate. Unsettled conditions in Turkish lands pushed him into slavery; Shihab ud-Din admitted him to his slave household and assigned him important duties. He played an important role in the Battle of Tarain (1192), which facilitated the establishment of Turkish power in India. As Shihab ud-Din's viceroy he conquered major towns of northern India. On Shihab ud-Din's assassination, Aibak informally ascended the throne on 25 June 1206; formal recognition of authority, including probably the letter of manumission, was received from Ghazna in 1208. He died in Lahore while playing polo.

[*See also* Delhi Sultanate.]

M. Aziz Ahmad, *Political History and Institutions of the Early Turkish Empire of Delhi* (1949). M. Habib and K. A. Nizami, *Comprehensive History of India, vol. 5* (1970).   KHALIQ AHMAD NIZAMI

QU YUAN, Chinese official and poet of the late Warring States period (403–221 BCE). According to Sima Qian's account *(Shiji),* he served two kings of the southern state of Chu in the central valley of the Yangtze River at the end of the Warring States period. Qu Yuan was of aristocratic background and enjoyed an early success as royal adviser. Through court intrigue, however, he fell out of favor and was exiled. While in exile he wrote poems that formed the anthology *Chu Elegies (Chuci).* As the state of Chu lost successive battles against Qin, the dismayed Qu Yuan drowned himself in the Milo River. Every year on the fifth day of the fifth lunar month his death is commemorated by the celebration of the dragon boat festival.

This ostensibly straightforward tale hides a multitude of anthropological and literary puzzles. The collection itself, the *Chu Elegies,* is extremely diverse. The long epic poem "Encountering Sorrow" tells of a fantastic journey into the heavens. The enigmatic "Heavenly Questions" is a collection of riddles and questions elliptically outlining pre-Han cosmological and mythological beliefs. The eleven short poems known as the "Nine Songs" as well as the long poem "Summoning the Soul" are thought to be librettas based partially on shamanistic ritual. The character of Qu Yuan is also more complex than Sima Qian's account would indicate. The dragon boat festival, one of the most important holidays in the sacred calendar in China, in fact predates Qu Yuan. It is associated with the worship of river gods and goddesses who require sacrifice on the fifth day of the fifth month of the lunar calendar.

The chief intermediary in these ceremonies was the shaman. Thus, the festival and the literary material of the *Chu Elegies,* while associated with Qu Yuan, in fact predate him by as much as a century and probably derive from shamanistic practices characteristic of Chu religion. The myth of Qu Yuan grew; from the Han dynasty on he became a cult figure and was regarded as China's first major poet.

[*See also* Warring States Period.]

David Hawkes, *The Songs of the South, An Ancient Chinese Anthology* (1962) and "The Quest of the Goddess," *Asia Major* 13 (1967): 71–94. Arthur Waley, *The Nine Songs* (reprint, 1973).   VICTORIA B. CASS

R

RADHAKRISHNAN, SARVEPALLI (1888–1975), Indian philosopher and statesman. He devoted his life to finding a cultural synthesis between East and West that would pave the way to a new world civilization and to world peace. His "Neo-Vedantic" and "idealist" philosophy of religion, or religious philosophy, rooted in both Vedantic and Western rationalist thought, was essentially optimistic in outlook. Coming to politics late in life, Radhakrishnan held high public office as India's first ambassador to the USSR (1948–1952), vice president of India (1952–1962), and president (1962–1967). In 1964 he played a crucial role in ensuring a smooth political succession following Prime Minister Nehru's death.

[See also Vedanta.]

Sarvepalli Radhakrishnan, *Eastern Religion and Western Thought* (1939). Paul Arthur Schilpp, ed., *The Philosophy of Sarvepalli Radhakrishnan* (1952).

USHA SANYAL

RADHASOAMI SATSANG, a new religious tradition in India based on the teachings of the medieval poet-saints of northern India, the Sants, whose numbers include Nanak and Kabir. Today there are some thirty lineages of Radhasoami masters who trace their spiritual ancestry to the founding teacher, Swami Shiv Dayal Singh (1818–1878), a Punjabi from a Khatri caste of moneylenders, who in 1861 established a religious fellowship *(satsang)* in Agra. The word *Radhasoami* is a type of mantra, but in the movement's cosmology it is also the name of the highest region of spiritual consciousness. Members of the tradition do not accept the notion of priests or an anthropomorphic form of God. [See also Nanak *and* Kabir.]

The largest branches of the tradition are at Dayalbagh, near Agra, where a complex of educational institutions, dairies, and factories were developed in the 1920s and 1930s in the interest of creating a spiritual social utopia, and at Beas, in the Punjab, where the headquarters serves as a retirement home for several thousand members and as a temporary city for over a hundred thousand on festival days. The various branches of the movement claim over a million followers worldwide. Groups that trace their origins to the Radhasoami tradition, or have based their ideas on it, include such popular movements in the West (in the 1970s) as Ruhani Satsang, Eckankar, and the Divine Light Mission led by the "boy guru," Maharaj-ji.

[See also Bhakti.]

Mark Juergensmeyer, *Radhasoami Reality· The Logic of a Modern Faith* (1986). A. P. Mathur, *Radhasoami Faith: A Historical Study* (1974).

MARK JUERGENSMEYER

RAFFLES, SIR THOMAS STAMFORD (1781–1826), was the most famous of those Englishmen who, in the early nineteenth century, worked to establish a permanent British presence in the heart of the Malay Archipelago. Raffles started as a clerk in the British East India Company's London office in 1796. Promoted in 1805 to assistant secretary to the first governor of Penang, Raffles rapidly learned the language of the Malays and became interested in their culture. He came to believe Malay institutions were decayed and corrupt and that the Malays would benefit from "enlightened Western rule." He also deeply distrusted the Dutch, who had for decades tried to exclude other Europeans from the archipelago.

Raffles was appointed lieutentant-governor of Java in 1811, and, though his superiors plainly intended to return Java to the Dutch at the end of the Napoleonic wars, proceeded to introduce reforms dictated by his liberal beliefs and his desire to create favorable conditions for British trade. He instituted a land-rent system, designed to increase the cash flow among the population of Java and weaken the hold of the Javanese regents, and he abolished slavery. In 1816 Java was returned to the Dutch. Appointed lieutenant-governor of Benkulen in 1817, Raffles continued to implement such administrative reforms as he felt necessary and possible (among them the emancipation of company slaves and the establishment of schools for the local population), and to pursue schemes to extend British control over the independent Malay states, provoking bitter Dutch hostility. His efforts culminated in the foundation of Singapore on 29 January 1819.

Politically, his aims were realized with the retention of Singapore by the Anglo-Dutch Treaty of 1824. Administratively, his important contribution to the development of British and Dutch colonial policy was that he based his administration upon humanitarian principals. Raffles made notable contributions to the study of the archipelago and encouraged similar work whenever possible; his *History of Java* was published in 1817.

[*See also* Java; Singapore; *and* Anglo-Dutch Treaty.]

J. S. Bastin, *The Native Policies of Sir Stamford Raffles in Java and Sumatra* (1957). M. Collis, *Raffles* (1966). Syed Hussein Alatas, *Thomas Stamford Raffles, Schemer or Reformer?* (1971). C. E. Wurtzburg, *Raffles of the Eastern Isles* (1954).   DIANNE LEWIS

RAHMAN, ZIAUR (1936–1981), effective leader of Bangladesh from 1975 to 1981. He was commissioned in the Pakistan Army in 1953, and served in regular posts. In March 1971 Zia led his unit in Chittagong against Pakistanis and proclaimed Bangladeshi independence on March 27. He led the "Z Force" during the civil war, from which he emerged a hero. He held Bangladesh Army appointments and became chief of staff in August 1975, following the assassination of Mujibur Rahman. [*See* Mujibur Rahman, Sheikh.] Zia became deputy chief martial law administrator in November 1975, and chief martial law administrator in 1976. He was president of Bangladesh from 1977 to 1981, having been elected to that post by popular vote in 1978, when he resigned from the army. He was assassinated on 30 May 1981.

Zia is widely regarded as a capable, pragmatic, and charismatic leader whose efforts were directed toward rural development, food self-sufficiency, and family planning at home, and toward the creation of the South Asia Regional Cooperation organization in the wider area.

[*See also* Bangladesh.]

Craig Baxter, *Bangladesh: A New Nation in a New Setting* (1984). Talukder Maniruzzaman, *The Bangladesh Revolution and its Aftermath* (1980).   CRAIG BAXTER

RAHMAT ALI, CHAUDHURI (1897–1951). Rahmat Ali's only significant political act was the publication of a pamphlet in 1933 entitled *Now or Never* that was signed by himself and three other Cambridge students. Although a number of leaders in the 1930s, most notably Muhammad Iqbal, called for the establishment of an independent Muslim political entity in northwestern India, they did not have a name for it. Rahmat Ali is best known for having supplied that. Taking the initial letters from the various "homelands" of Muslims: *P* for Punjab, *A* for Afghania (North-West Frontier Province), *K* for Kashmir, *S* for Sindh, *Tan* for Baluchistan (also Tukharistan and Afghanistan), he came up with *Pak-i-stan*, meaning "land of the pure." Bengal was not included in the scheme until 1937; significantly, it never received its own letter. When working politicians like Mohammad Ali Jinnah took over the name, they dismissed Rahmat Ali as a grandiose dreamer.

[*See also* Pakistan *and* Partition of India.]

P. Hardy, *Muslims of British India* (1972).

GREGORY C. KOZLOWSKI

RAI, a Tibeto-Burman-speaking Mongoloid people inhabiting the eastern hills of Nepal. Rais observe the customs and beliefs of the country's Hindu majority but for the most part attend to a complex of ancestor rituals that link them with the tribal populations of northeastern India. Since the Hindu conquest in the 1790s, Rais have combined subsistence agriculture with service in the Gurkha regiments of the British and Indian armies. Large numbers are settled in the Darjeeling hills—they are the descendants of Rais who migrated to work on British tea plantations in the late nineteenth century.

[*See also* Darjeeling.]

C. McDougal, *The Kulunge Rai* (1979).

RICHARD ENGLISH

RAI SAN'YŌ (1780–1832), late Edo-period Japanese historian, poet, and scholar of Chinese learning. Rai San'yō was the son of a Hiroshima merchant, Rai Shunsui, who became a Confucian scholar. One year after San'yō's birth, Shunsui obtained a teaching post in Hiroshima domain, where San'yō grew up. At the age of twenty-one San'yō attempted to leave for Kyoto without domain consent *(dappan)*, a serious crime that, in Hiroshima domain, warranted summary execution. However, San'yō was pardoned and allowed to continue his studies under three-year house arrest. Later, he studied for one year under the renowned Hiroshima scholar Kan Sazan, and from 1808 to his death in 1832 he lived and wrote in Kyoto.

San'yō was and continues to be most famous as a historian of Japan. He completed his masterpiece, *An Unofficial History of Japan,* in 1826. This work, written in crisp, classical Chinese, relates the rise and fall of Japan's military houses from the Heike and Genji down to the Tokugawa. San'yō argued that each house flourished to the extent that it was loyal to the emperor and then fell when it became disloyal. His purpose was to show conclusively that Tokugawa supremacy was historically inevitable, owing to the devotion to the imperial court of its founder, Ieyasu.   BOB TADASHI WAKABAYASHI

RAIYATWARI SETTLEMENTS. *See* Land Tenure and Reform: Land Tenure, Revenue, and Reform in South Asia.

RAJ, derived from the Sanskrit *raja* (king), by extension denotes the realm, kingdom, or sovereignty of a ruler. The term *raj* often is used to mark out a particular era, as in *Congress Raj.* By itself in colloquial usage *the Raj* refers to the period of British rule in India. [*See also* India *and* East India Company.]   THOMAS R. METCALF

RAJA, a Sanskrit term used throughout South and Southeast Asia to denote a ruler. It is not accurate, however, to translate it as "king," since it was often applied to petty chieftains who owed allegiance to a more powerful ruler, usually called a *maharaja.* In India it was sometimes used as an honorific for a poet or musician to denote his mastery of his art. The term *raja* was most commonly applied, however, to the hundreds of chieftains and warlords recognized by the British government in India in the nineteenth century as rulers of what were known as native, or princely, states. It was used almost wholly

for Hindu rulers; the Muslim equivalent was a *nawab.* In Southeast Asia the term had broader political implications; the use by the Malays of the term *kerajaan* ("the state of having a raja") to communicate their concept of a political unit illustrates the central and essential role of the raja in traditional Malay polities.

DIANNE LEWIS and AINSLIE T. EMBREE

RAJAGOPALACHARI, CHAKRAVARTI (1870–1972), governor-general of India from 1948 to 1950 and prominent nationalist leader before Indian independence in 1947. From an orthodox South Indian brahman family, he was educated wholly in India. From 1919, when he met Mohandas Gandhi, until his death, he was actively involved in politics. He became chief minister of Madras in 1937 but resigned in 1939 in protest when, without consulting its ministries, the central government of India declared the country at war with Germany. Rajagopalachari expressed his support, however, for the Allies over against the Axis powers. He differed from Gandhi and Nehru during the negotiations for the transfer of power, arguing, in what was known as the "C. R. Formula," that the Muslims should be given the choice of having Muslim-majority provinces in a federal system. He was governor of West Bengal in 1947 before he was appointed to succeed Mountbatten as governor-general. He served again (1952–1954) as chief minister of Madras, but becoming increasingly concerned that Nehru's foreign and domestic policies were socialist oriented, he helped found the Swatantra party, which supported free enterprise and closer ties with the West.

[*See also* Swatantra Party.]

AINSLIE T. EMBREE

RAJA MUDA, the traditional title of the heir apparent in a Malay state. It normally was not an executive post, but in the early eighteenth-century Raja Muda Tun Mahmud of Johor displaced the four chief ministers and took control of affairs in an attempt to strengthen the hold of his family on the throne. His effort failed, and the Bugis who restored his nephew to the throne demanded the post of *raja muda* in perpetuity. Throughout the eighteenth and early nineteenth centuries the Malays struggled constantly to regain their old power, but the Bugis stood their ground, and the Malay nobles finally withdrew to the outer territories.

[*See also* Johor; Tun Mahmud; Bendahara; Bugis Raja; *and* Malays.]

Ali Haji ibn Ahmad, *The Precious Gift (Tuhfat al Nafis)*, trans. by Victoria Matheson and Barbara Watson Andaya (1982). D. G. E. Hall, *A History of South East Asia* (1970). DIANNE LEWIS

RAJASINHA I (1543?–1593), Sri Lankan ruler. In 1521 the kingdom of Kotte in Sri Lanka was partitioned among three brothers, one of whom, Mayadunne, ruled over his portion from the capital city of Sitawaka. An able and ambitious ruler, he coveted the share of his brothers and waged continuous war on them with the assistance of his son Rajasinha. When Mayadunne died in 1581 he bequeathed to his son the largest Sinhalese kingdom and a hatred of the Portuguese, who were protectors and allies of his chief rival, the ruler of Kotte.

Under Rajasinha the kingdom of Sitawaka expanded westward toward the coast and eastward into the highlands. In 1582 he succeeded in annexing the kingdom of Kandy and expelling its ruler, who took refuge with the Portuguese. Thereafter, Rajasinha concentrated his hostilities on the Portuguese and annexed almost the entire territories of the kingdom of Kotte, isolating the Portuguese in their coastal stronghold of Colombo. He besieged Colombo from land a number of times but was unable, in the absence of sea power, to conquer it.

To divert his attention from Colombo and the west coast, the Portuguese adopted a strategy of opening a second front. They sent an expedition to Kandy to establish on the throne a descendant of the king whom Rajasinha had deposed. The strategy succeeded, although not in the way the Portuguese had planned, for on the death of their candidate, Kandy came into the possession of Vimal Dharma, who was equally hostile to the Portuguese and to Rajasinha. It did have the effect of diverting Rajasinha's attention, and in an expedition to subdue Kandy he died.

A lengthy career of military activity and some significant successes against the Portuguese made Rajasinha a legend in Sinhalese history. His struggle against Portuguese domination and against the king of Kotte after this king had embraced Christianity took on a nationalist and cultural aspect, although his own beliefs extended beyond Buddhism and he patronized and supported Shaivism and Shaivite practices as well.

[*See also* Sri Lanka; Portuguese: Portuguese in Sri Lanka; Kotte; *and* Kandy.]

T. B. H. Abeyasinghe, *Portuguese Rule in Ceylon 1594–1612* (1966). C. R. de Silva, *The Portuguese in Ceylon 1617–1638* (1972). S. ARASARATNAM

RAJASINHA II (1600?–1687), Sri Lankan ruler. The youngest son of Senarat, king of Kandy in Sri Lanka from 1604 to 1635, Prince Maha Asthana, as he was then known, ascended the throne on his father's death with the regnal name Rajasinha II. Senarat's eldest son had died earlier and the second son, Prince Vijayapala, became ruler of the principality of Matale under the jurisdiction of Kandy. Vijayapala had his own ambitions and intrigued with the Portuguese against Rajasinha. He was defeated by his brother in 1641 and defected to the Portuguese, after which Rajasinha ruled over the entire territories of the kingdom of Kandy.

Rajasinha inherited from his predecessors a bitter hatred of the Portuguese and an ambition to expel them from the island. He continued the wars against the Portuguese in the western lowlands but was conscious of the need for seapower to achieve ultimate victory. With this intention he negotiated a treaty in 1638 with the Dutch admiral Adam Westerwolt. Under the terms of the treaty he promised the Dutch the monopoly of the cinnamon trade and some ports for settlement along the coast in return for Dutch military and naval assistance in his war against the Portuguese.

The allies cooperated successfully for some time against the Portuguese and a few Portuguese ports were taken. It soon became clear to Rajasinha that the Dutch were anxious to entrench themselves in some of the more important ports taken from the Portuguese. As the allies became suspicious of each other's aims Rajasinha continued to cooperate with the Dutch, as he felt them to be the lesser of two evils. In 1656, when Colombo was taken by the Dutch and not handed over to him, the worst of his suspicions were confirmed and he retreated to the interior and maintained a constant harassment of the Dutch along the coast.

Rajasinha had difficulty controlling the nobility in his territories and had to face a serious rebellion in 1664. Robert Knox, an English sea captain who spent seventeen years as a shipwrecked prisoner in the Kandyan kingdom, has left a fascinating account of the kingdom and of the administration of Rajasinha.

[*See also* Kandy; Portuguese: Portuguese in Sri Lanka; Dutch East India Company; Colombo; *and* Knox, Robert.]

S. Arasaratnam, *Dutch Power in Ceylon 1658–1687* (1958). K. W. Goonewardene, *The Foundation of Dutch Power in Ceylon* (1958). Robert Knox, *An Historical Relation of the Island Ceylon in the East Indies* (1681).

S. ARASARATNAM

RAJASTHAN, state in modern India. Covering approximately 132,000 square miles, Rajasthan is the second largest of the states in terms of land area but with an estimated 37 million people (in 1986) it is ninth in terms of population, giving it the second lowest density in the country, after Jammu and Kashmir. It has strategic importance, since it is a border state, with a boundary on the west and northwest for 660 miles with Pakistan, but much of the line runs through very inhospitable deserts. The capital is Jaipur, famous for its handsome red sandstone and stucco buildings laid out in the early eighteenth century in a geometric grid pattern.

The whole of Rajasthan constitutes what geographers have identified as one of the perennial nuclear regions of the Indian subcontinent, that is, a region that has maintained relatively permanent political and cultural boundaries throughout recorded history. The area was known in its own traditions as Rajwarra, and then in the British period as Rajputana, with these names indicating its salient historical position as the home of rajas, or kings and chieftains, who belonged to a number of clans that constituted a ruling class of warriors, not just in Rajasthan itself, but in much of North and central India. The legends and traditions of these warriors, known as Rajputs, have been preserved in bardic poems that celebrate the chivalric code of honor, centered on loyalty to one's chief and the martial virtues. The most familiar repository of these heroic legends is, however, the remarkable collection made in the 1820s by an English official, Colonel James Tod, called *The Annals and Antiquities of Rajasthan*. Tod's interpretation of Rajput history is influenced by European romanticism, particularly Walter Scott's novels of feudal life, and so it is difficult to say how accurately Tod was reflecting the Rajputs' own understanding of their history, but since it is the source that made the legends accessible to both modern Indians and Westerners, it has helped shape the image and self-identity of Rajasthan.

Rajasthan is divided into two natural divisions by the Aravallis, one of the oldest mountain ranges in the world, which stretch in a southwesterly direction from Delhi to Gujarat, with the highest point being Mount Abu, at the southwestern end. The division to the northwest of the Aravallis is dry and arid, but it had two trade routes that gave it great importance in Indian history. One led from Agra through Marwar (modern Jodhpur) to the port of Surat in Bombay. Another led across the Thar Desert to the magnificent fortress of Jaisalmer, and then on to the Indus River. Southeast of the Aravallis, in the second of the divisions of Rajasthan, the soil is somewhat more fertile. Mewar (modern Udaipur), the oldest of the Rajput states, was in this area. The combination of deserts and mountains made it possible for chieftains to construct numerous forts that could guard their own possessions while serving as refuges from their enemies and as strongholds from which to launch attacks. These strategically located forts play a large part in Rajasthan's long history of battles and heroic deeds.

There are no natural lakes in Rajasthan, but there are a number of large artificial reservoirs that preserve the scanty rainfall; there is only one important perennial river, the Chambal, in the southeastern region. The annual rainfall, while low everywhere, is quite variable, with the southeastern division getting about twenty-six inches and the desert area in the northwest receiving only six inches. Despite this arid climate, Rajasthan has been the center of a rich culture and of a dramatic history.

The Rajput rulers made their appearance in North Indian history in the ninth century, and historians have speculated that they were descendants of the Huns who had invaded India in the fifth and sixth centuries. Not much is known of how they established their power in Rajasthan, but by the eleventh century numerous chieftains had carved out principalities for themselves. The most important of these was Mewar, whose ruler fought tenaciously against the Turks after they had conquered Delhi at the end of the twelfth century and began the great expansion of the Delhi sultanate throughout India. [*See* Delhi Sultanate.] Many of the Rajput chieftains were forced to become vassals of the new Islamic power, but two of them, Mewar and Marwar, managed to preserve their independence. As the Delhi sultanate weakened in the fifteenth century, more of the chieftains asserted their independence, and when the new Turko-Afghan dynasty of the Mughals was established in the sixteenth century the Rajput chieftains were a major threat to them.

The subjugation of the Rajasthan area was largely the work of the emperor Akbar (r. 1556–1605). [*See* Akbar.] His first great victory came in 1562 when he defeated the ruler of Amber (modern Jaipur) and made him his vassal. Akbar's treatment of the Amber ruler became the Mughal pattern for dealing with the Rajasthan chieftains: if they acknowledged the Mughal emperor as suzerain, gave a daughter to the royal harem, sent the chief's heir to serve as an officer in the Mughal army, and agreed to pay tribute, then in return the Rajput chieftains were allowed to keep their territories so long as they remained loyal. In this way the Rajput chiefs were of great importance for the maintenance of imperial power. Many of them became leaders of the Mughal armies, notably Jai Singh of Amber (1617–1667), one of the greatest of Mughal commanders. [See Jai Singh.]

The Rajput chieftains borrowed many architectural, artistic, and administrative elements from the Mughals, but they did not accept Islam, nor is there much evidence that attempts were made to convert them. Many of them were patrons of Hindu religion and learning, and their courts kept alive many aspects of the Hindu tradition.

In the eighteenth century the Mughal emperor lost control of the empire, and throughout India regional powers struggled for mastery. The great Rajput chieftains, such as those of Mewar, Marwar, Jaipur, Bikaner, and Jaisalmer, all consolidated their kingdoms, often fighting with each other or with lesser chiefs, many of whom became vassals of one or other of the major rulers. The rulers were also attacked from outside by the Marathas, who were extending their power over North India. It was during this time, however, despite all the seeming turmoil, that many of the Rajput states became centers of art, and even small ones like Bundi, Pratapgarh, and Kotah had schools of painting that were remarkable for their beauty and vitality. The Rajput courts also preserved much of the elegance and ceremony of the Mughal court.

The establishment of British power in India by the East India Company brought in a new period in Rajasthan history, as the rulers, in much the same way as they had with the Mughals, accepted British suzerainty between 1817 and 1823 in return for a large measure of internal control within their states. Rajasthan, or Rajputana, became the center of what was known as "Princely India," that is, the two-fifths of the subcontinent that was left in the hands of Indian rulers, in contrast to British India, which was under direct British rule. In the nineteenth century Rajasthan became an intellectual and cultural backwater, isolated from the forces of westernization and nationalism that were transforming the rest of India. With their rule guaranteed by the British, the princes had little incentive to bring about social change, and many of them spent the revenues of their states on palaces and personal pleasure.

The coming of independence to India brought about great changes in Rajasthan. In common with other Indian princes, the Rajasthan rulers acceded to the new government of India in return for payments known as privy purses, and the complex array of rulers and their feudatories were brought into a single administrative framework. The area lacked the uniform system of administration, law, and education of the rest of India, and had no experience of the workings of representative government. Considerable opposition to the new order came from the Rajputs, who had been both rulers and landowners, but they gradually came to terms with it. The area is now fully integrated into the economic and political mainstream of Indian life, and there has been a great increase in agricultural and industrial productivity. The state government and many of the individual princes have used the area's romantic and colorful past to attract tourism, which has become a major source of income.

[See also Rajputs; Princely States; Bikaner; Chitor; Jaipur; Jaisalmer; Mewar; Marwar; Udaipur; Mughal Empire; Marathas; and Painting: South Asian Painting.]

V. N. Desai, ed., *Life at Court: Art for India's Rulers* (1985). R. Jeffrey, ed., *People, Princes, and Paramount Power: Society and Politics in the Indian Princely States* (1978). P. Pal, *Court Paintings in India* (1983). K. R. Qanungo, *Studies in Rajput History* (reprint, 1960). James Tod, *Annals and Antiquities of Rajasthan*, 3 vols. (1920; reprint, 1971).   AINSLIE T. EMBREE

RAJPUT. The word *Rajput* is derived from the Sanskrit term *rajaputra* ("son of a king") and refers both to a caste of northern and central India and to male members of this caste (female members are called Rajputnis or Rajputanis). In modern India Rajputs have many occupations and professions, but the traditional occupation of the Rajput caste is warfare, and it is in this sense that the Rajput is regarded in premodern historical literature.

Current historical opinion on the origin of the Rajput caste is divided. One school of historians believes that the existence of this caste is long standing and can be proved from texts as old as the Vedas (c. 1200 BCE). A second asserts that the Rajput caste developed fully only with the coming of the Mughals to India (post-1500 CE). A third maintains that the

Rajputs were of Central Asian or Afghan origin and came to India after the fall of the Gupta empire (c. 500). None of these theories, however, appears to be wholly adequate. It seems evident from literary and epigraphic sources in Sanskrit and Prakrit that the Rajput caste developed during the period from 800 to 1200 and included both indigenous and exogenous elements.

According to the Kashmiri chronicle entitled *Rajatarangini* (compiled c. 1150), the Rajputs were divided into thirty-six great families. Later sources indicate that these families belonged to three great clans: the Suryavamsa, or Solar Clan; the Somavamsa, or Lunar Clan; and the Agnivamsa, or Fire Clan. Lists of these families vary considerably according to when and where they were written, indicating both flexibility in the composition of the caste over time and a variety of regional claims to supralocal status. In the period 800 to 1200, the Chahamanas (Chauhans) of Ajmer and Delhi, Chalukyas of Gujarat, Paramaras of Malwa, and Pratiharas of Kanauj were the most influential Rajput families, but in the late medieval period (1300–1700) the most famous of the Rajputs were from Rajasthan: the Sisodiyas of Mewar, Rathors of Marwar, and Kachchhwahas of Amber (near Jaipur). It was these Rajputs who allied themselves with the Mughals and provided the emperors with wives and a steady stream of loyal soldiers throughout much of the sixteenth and seventeenth centuries.

Besides sharing myths of descent, the Rajput warriors adhered to a common code of conduct termed *kshatriya-dharma*, roughly translated as "the way of the warrior." This code enjoined the Rajput male to die the good death on the field of battle and to maintain his personal honor and masculine integrity in all situations. The Rajput woman had her own code, the most exacting demand of which was to join her dead husband on the funeral pyre and become a *sati* ("virtuous woman") by perishing in the flames. [*See* Sati.] In sieges, Rajput women sometimes would commit their bodies to the fire before their husbands rushed out for a final, fatal onslaught against the foe. Such ritual mass suicide was called *jauhar* and became a dismal commonplace of medieval Indian life under the intense pressure of the Muslim sultanates against the Rajput kingdoms trying to maintain their independence. Infamous *jauhars* occurred in 1303, 1535, and 1568 at Chitor in Mewar and in 1315 at Jaisalmer.

[*See also* Rajasthan; Kshatriya; Chitor; Mewar; Jaisalmer; Sisodiya Dynasty; Rathors; Chauhan Dynasty; Paramara Dynasty; *and* Pratiharas.]

G. Morris Carstairs, *The Twice-born: A Study of a Community of High-caste Hindus* (1957). Alexander Kinloch Forbes, *Rās Mālā; or Hindoo Annals of the Province of Goozerat in Western India,* 2 vols. (1924). James Tod, *Annals and Antiquities of Rajasthan,* 3 vols. (1920; reprint, 1971).
                                        RICHARD DAVIS SARAN

RAKUGO, literally "drop word," that is, "punch line," a genre of Japanese comic monologue in which a kneeling person relates a tale in dramatic fashion, representing each of the individual characters through voice inflection, facial expression, gesture and dialect. The tone of *rakugo* is that of poking fun at human foibles. The ancestors of modern *rakugo* performers were professional entertainers who traveled with warlords on military campaigns, providing entertainment by telling valorous tales or humorous anecdotes. Anthologies of these stories were kept, and at the beginning of the Tokugawa period new anthologies, containing more diverse topics, began to appear. In the mid-seventeenth century the performers first began to make distinctions between characters through the use of dialect and gesture, and then to concentrate on humorous tales, two characteristics of *rakugo* that have remained to the present. In the latter half of the eighteenth century *rakugo* became popular among the townsmen of Edo, with dilettantes trying their hand at writing and performing their own stories. These became known as *otoshibanashi* ("dropping tales"), because they most often ended in a strong punch line. Theaters for the performance of *rakugo* began to spring up at the end of the eighteenth century, and by 1842 there were over one hundred twenty theaters in Edo alone. The Tempō Reforms of 1841–1843 reduced this number to fifteen, but afterward the numbers again increased, along with the popularity of *rakugo*. This popularity continued into the Meiji period, not only because of the availability and modest cost of *rakugo* performance (one-third the price of Kabuki performance) but also because it addressed an expanding range of topics that appealed to the ever-growing population of Tokyo. *Rakugo* popularity suffered with the advent of opera and cinema in the 1920s and 1930s, and during World War II it fell into disfavor with the government because of its failure to adjust its themes to fit wartime ideology. In postwar Japan, *rakugo*'s adaptability to radio and television has assured its survival, and it remains a popular form of entertainment.
                                        J. SCOTT MILLER

RAM, JAGJIVAN (b. 1908–1986), a major spokesman for the Untouchables in India. Ram was the only person included in every cabinet formed in India between 1947 and 1979. The eighth and last child of a Chamar agricultural laborer from Bihar, Ram attended Banaras Hindu University on a scholarship from the Birla family and entered politics through his association with Mohandas Gandhi. Holding successively almost every major portfolio, Ram's ministries seemed blessed by luck. His defection from Indira Gandhi's Congress Party at the end of the Emergency in 1977 was instrumental in bringing down the Indira government and installing the Janata party in power.

[See also Untouchability *and* Emergency in India, The.]

Nau Nihal Singh, *Jagjivan Ram: Symbol of Social Change* (1977).   MARCUS FRANDA

RAMA. *For the Thai kings who have ruled under the name* Rama, *see* Ananda Mahidol *(Rama VIII),* Bhumibol Adulyadej *(Rama IX),* Chulalongkorn *(Rama V),* Mongkut *(Rama IV),* Phra Nang Klao *(Rama III),* Phra Phutthaloetla Naphalai *(Rama II),* Phra Phutthayotfa Chulalok *(Rama I),* Prajadhipok *(Rama VII), and* Vajiravudh *(Rama VI).*

RAMADAN, the ninth month of the Muslim lunar calendar, held sacred as the month when the first revelation of the Qur'an occurred. Ramadan is thus a period of atonement, forgiveness, and good works, a month when Muslims fast from dawn to nightfall, abstaining from food, drink, and sexual intercourse. The obligation to fast is considered the most important religious duty in nearly every Muslim country. Economic life often comes to a halt during part of the day, but the nights are livened in breaking the fast, intense social activity, and public entertainment.

[See also Id Fitr *and* Id Qorban.]

C. Snouck Hurgronje, *Mekka in the Latter Part of the Nineteenth Century,* translated by J. H. Monahan (1931). G. E. Von Grunebaum, *Muhammadan Festivals* (1951; reprint, 1976).   JEANETTE A. WAKIN

RAMAKIAN (or *Ramakien*), the Siamese (Thai) version of the Indian epic of Rama, the *Ramayana* of Valmiki. Evidence of the *Ramakien's* currency in Siam runs through the Ayudhya period, but it was not until the reign of King Rama I that a complete Thai version of the epic was produced, by the king and his courtiers in 1797. Although Valmiki's story is intact, the setting and the characters and their values are clearly those of the Thai of Bangkok. Similar transformations are present in most of the countries of Southeast Asia.

[See also Phra Phutthayotfa Chulalok.]

S. Singaravelu, "A Comparative Study of the Sanskrit, Tamil, Thai and Malay Versions of the Story of Rama," *Journal of the Siam Society* 56:2 (1968).

DAVID K. WYATT

RAMAKRISHNA (1836–1886), or Sri Ramakrishna as he is more commonly known, was an Indian religious teacher of great magnetism. Though a temple priest at Dakshineswar north of Calcutta and devoted to the goddess Kali, he experimented with other religions and proved to his satisfaction that there were several equally viable paths to God. Using earthy wisdom and parables, Ramakrishna persuaded westernized Bengalis that there was much of value in their own traditions. He did not engage in social reform work, but encouraged his disciples to undertake God's work in the world through social service. After his death they founded the Ramakrishna Order and the Ramakrishna Mission.

[See also Vivekananda.]

The Gospel of Sri Ramakrishna, edited by M. [Mahendra Nath Gupta], translated by Swami Nikhilananda (4th ed., 1964). Christopher Isherwood, *Ramakrishna and His Disciples* (1965).   LEONARD A. GORDON

RAMANATHAN, SIR PONNAMBALAM (1851–1930), the foremost Sinhalese nationalist from the time he entered the Legislative Council in 1879 until the spread of Sinhala-Tamil communalism in the 1920s. A Tamil Vellala, he was elected to the sole "Educated Ceylonese" seat in 1912 with the support of the Sinhalese Goyigama caste voters, who preferred him to a Sinhalese of the Karava caste.

[See also Sri Lanka *and* Vellala.]

M. Vythilingam, *Ramanathan of Ceylon: The Life of Sir Ponnambalam Ramanathan,* 2 vols. (1971).

PATRICK PEEBLES

RAMANNADESA. The early Arab geographers refer to Lower Burma as Ramannadesa. An urban culture had emerged by the sixth century around the cities of Thaton and Pegu, but the archaeological and epigraphic remains of this civilization prior to the ninth or tenth century are extremely limited. Almost all the history of this society is derived from later Burmese chronicles that provide lists of kings and a mythical account of early Mon civilization. These accounts, however, are problematic. For instance, the later chronicles depict the early Mon as patrons of Theravada Buddhism, but archaeological remains are largely Hindu. In 825 the Ramannadesa civilization was said to have culminated when the legendary twin brothers Samala and Vimala from Thaton founded the city of Pegu.

[*See also* Mon.]

Paul Wheatley, *Nagara and Commandery: Origins of the Southeast Asian Urban Traditions* (1983), pp. 199–230.   KENNETH R. HALL

RAMANUJA

RAMANUJA (1056–1137?), medieval Indian philosopher, founder of the school of Vedanta known as Vishishtadvaita, or "qualified nondualism." Active in South India in the second half of the eleventh century, Ramanuja's important contribution was the development of a philosophical framework for the resurgent Vaishnava *bhakti* (devotionalism) of the period. In contrast to Shankara, Ramanuja holds that individual souls and the material world have a qualified reality since they are contained within God, the highest reality. They are in fact the body of God, distinct pluralities within the unity of the whole.

His principle works are the *Vedantadipa*, the *Vedantasara*, the *Vedarthasamgraha*, and two important commentaries: the *Shribhashya* on the *Brahmasutra*, and the *Gitabhashya* on the *Bhagavad Gita*.

[*See also* Vedanta; Shankara; *and* Bhakti.]

M. A. Ayyangar, *The Philosophy of Ramanuja* (1958). J. A. B. van Buitenen, *Ramanuja on the Bhagavadgītā* (1968).   RANDOLPH M. THORNTON

RAMATHIBODI I

RAMATHIBODI I, king of Ayudhya (r. 1351–1369), founder of the kingdom of Ayudhya (Siam).

In the early fourteenth century, as the power of the kingdoms of Sukhothai and Angkor waned, the Chaophraya River basin was fragmented into small principalities. In one of these, Phetburi, Prince U Thong ("golden cradle") was born in 1314, perhaps to a powerful Chinese merchant family. He may subsequently have been connected by marriage to the ruling houses of Lopburi and Suphanburi. Legends claim that he was chosen king in the wake of an epidemic and led large numbers of people to a site at which the Pasak River empties into the Chaophraya. There he founded a new capital and kingdom on 4 March 1351. This strategic riverine junction facilitated both communications with the interior and international trade, and from the beginning Ayudhya's power was based in part on commerce.

To use its natural advantages, U Thong—who became King Ramathibodi—worked to blend the bureaucratic skills of the old Khmer kingdom of Lopburi with the Thai manpower resources of Suphanburi and the western provinces. He began the creation of a centralized bureaucracy, while sending his relatives to govern key provinces—his wife's brother, Pha-ngua, to Suphanburi, and his son, Ramesuan, to Lopburi. In international affairs, he was concerned to define his eastern frontier with Angkorian Cambodia and to gain diplomatic recognition from China as an independent kingdom. Some chronicles claim that he captured Angkor, but the evidence is insufficient to prove the point. On his death in 1369 he was succeeded by his son, Ramesuan.

[*See also* Ayudhya; Sukhothai; Lopburi; Ramesuan; *and* Borommaracha I.]

Charnvit Kasetsiri, *The Rise of Ayudhya* (1976). David K. Wyatt, *Thailand: A Short History* (1984).

DAVID K. WYATT

RAMAYANA

RAMAYANA, a sacred scripture of ancient India; the fuller title *Valmiki-Ramayana* is used to distinguish the ancient Sanskrit epic poem, traditionally attributed to the authorship of Valmiki, from later versions in other Indian languages. The *Ramayana*, consisting of about twenty-four thousand verses in seven books, is much shorter than the *Mahabharata* and is more homogeneous in style and structure; its nucleus probably dates from between 500 and 300 BCE. The epic hero Rama is associated with the line of Iksvaku kings that ruled the Gangetic kingdom of Kosala from their capital in Ayodhya in the sixth and fifth centuries BCE.

Legends surrounding the royal house and the adventures of Rama form the core of the epic, books two to six. The narrative of book two centers on events at the court of Rama's father, Dasaratha, in Ayodhya. Dasaratha has four sons, Rama, Bharata, Shatrughna, and Lakshmana, by his three wives. Rama is married to Sita, daughter of the king of Videha, and is appointed heir apparent, but the intrigues of Queen Kaiheyi to place her son Bharata on the throne result in Rama's exile. In books three to six characters and events are representative of mythic types traceable to older Vedic and non-Vedic sources. The forest wanderings of Rama with Sita and Lakshmana, the abduction of Sita by the demon king Ravana, and Rama's campaign to recapture her with the aid of his monkey allies, culminating in the attack on Ravana's fabulous island kingdom of Lanka, provide the main narrative frame. As a prince, Rama is the embodiment of order and duty *(dharma),* in contrast to Ravana, who represents the chaos of evil. The addition of the first and last books transformed the narrative into sacred text glorifying Rama as an incarnation of the god Vishnu.

The popularity of the epic throughout South and Southeast Asia is attested in many ways. Its story provides the inspiration of numerous literary works, including independent Indian vernacular versions, such as the Tamil of Kamban, the Hindi of Tulsidas, and the Bengali of Krittibas. Local versions are also important as national epics in Java, Malaya, Vietnam, Cambodia, Laos, and Thailand.

[*See also* Mahabharata.]

Robert P. Goldman, trans., *Balakanda,* volume 1 of *The Ramayana of Valmiki* (1985). H. Jacobi, trans., *Das Ramayana* (1893; English trans., 1960). H. P. Sastri, trans., *The Ramayana of Valmiki,* 3 vols. (1952–1959).

BARBARA STOLER MILLER

RAMESUAN, king of Ayudhya (r. 1369–1370, 1388–1395), worked to establish the new kingdom of Siam as a power on the Southeast Asian mainland. The son of Ramathibodi I, his first brief reign was ended by his uncle Borommaracha, against whom he retaliated by deposing that king's son eighteen years later. Ramesuan may have had kinsmen with courtly Cambodian traditions in Lopburi, where he spent Borommaracha's reign. As king, Ramesuan strengthened the central administration and exerted Thai military power against Cambodian Angkor while maintaining amicable relations with Thai Sukhothai. He was succeeded by his son Ramaracha.

[*See also* Ayudhya; Ramathibodi I; Borommaracha I; Lopburi; Angkor; Sukhothai; *and* Mahathammaracha II.]

Charnvit Kasetsiri, *The Rise of Ayudhya* (1976). David K. Wyatt, *Thailand: A Short History* (1984).

DAVID K. WYATT

RAMKHAMHAENG, king of Sukhothai, a small kingdom in what is now central Thailand; the first Thai to rule over a substantial lowland state.

Born perhaps in the 1240s, Ramkhamhaeng was the second son of the chief of the minor principality of Muang Bang Yang (near Sukhothai) who joined with a neighboring chief to end Cambodian overlordship in the region and establish Sukhothai's independence, following which he took the title of Sri Indraditya. Ramkhamhaeng earned his name, which means "Rama the brave," in battle under his father.

Ramkhamhaeng succeeded his elder brother as king about 1279 and dramatically expanded the kingdom in all directions, accepting as his vassals rulers from Luang Prabang in the north to Nakhon Si Thammarat in the south and from Vientiane to Martaban. He worked to contrast his state's administration to that of Cambodian Angkor by relaxing restrictions on trade and making justice accessible. In 1283 he is said to have invented an alphabet for writing Thai, and he used that alphabet in his celebrated inscription of 1292. In it, writing mainly in the first person, he described his city and his administration, beginning, "In the time of King Ramkhamhaeng this land of Sukhothai is thriving. There are fish in the water and rice in the fields." He did much to introduce orthodox Theravada Buddhism of the Sinhalese school to the region. He was careful to cooperate with the other major Thai states of his time, notably Lan Na (at Chiang Mai) and Phayao, with which he concluded an alliance in 1287, thus mobilizing a united Thai front against old Angkor. He cultivated good relations with the Mongols in China, but the legend that he personally visited Beijing is untrue. He died in 1298 and was succeeded by his son Lo Thai.

[*See also* Sukhothai; Lo Thai; Angkor; Lan Na; Phayao; Mangrai; Nakhon Si Thammarat; Ngam Muang; *and* Sri Indraditya.]

A. B. Griswold and Prasert na Nagara, "The Inscription of King Rama Gamhen of Sukhodaya (1292 A.D.)," *Journal of the Siam Society* (1971). David K. Wyatt, *Thailand: A Short History* (1984).   DAVID K. WYATT

RAMPUR, a princely state of India, incorporated into Uttar Pradesh in 1949. Rampur came into existence in the wake of the rise of the Rohilla power. During the eighteenth century an Afghan adventurer, Daud Khan, distinguished himself in the Maratha wars and received a grant of land near Badaon from the Mughal emperor. His adopted son Ali Muhammad Khan received the title of nawab, the rank of *panj-hazari,* and a large land grant in Rohilkhand in recognition of his success against the Barha Saiyyids. Despite initial setbacks Ali Muhammad managed to establish himself in Rohilkhand, and in 1747 Ahmad Shah confirmed his title to the region. He was succeeded by his son Faizullah Khan (d. 1793) who was granted Shikohabad by Ahmad Shah for his role in the Battle of Panipat (1761). Faizullah initially sided with Rahmatullah Khan but later entered into an alliance with the British and had his possessions secured under the Treaty of Laldhang in 1774. Faizullah founded the city of Rampur, initially called Mustafabad, in 1775. After the Revolt of 1857, as a reward for the services rendered by the then nawab of Rampur, Yusuf Ali Khan, to the British, some villages in Bareilly and Moradabad were granted to him. The last ruler of Rampur was Raza Ali Khan.

The Rampur state was surrounded by Naini Tal in the north, Bareilly in the east, Badaon in the south and Moradabad in the west. The two main rivers of this fertile region are the Kosi and Nahal. As testament to its history, the region has some exceptional mosques, palaces, and mausoleums.

[*See also* Rohillas.]

Gazetteer of the Rampur State (1911). *Statistical, Descriptive and Historical Account of the North-Western Provinces of India,* vol. 9, part 3, *Rampur* (1883).

FARHAN AHMAD NIZAMI

RAMSAY, JAMES ANDREW BROUN (marquis of Dalhousie; 1812–1860), governor-general of India from 1848 to 1856. His administration was marked by conquest, consolidation, and development; this earned him the epithet "the great proconsul." His early rise in public life was marked by brilliance and recognition (Privy Council, 1843; Board of Trade president and cabinet member, 1845). As governor-general, Dalhousie was noted for annexing the Punjab in 1849; for establishing the so-called Punjab school of administration under Henry and John Lawrence (eventually favoring John); for laying down plans for canals, railways, an imperial post, a telegraph system, and departments of education and public works; for conquering central Burma; and for reformulating the "Doctrine of Lapse." Under this doctrine, on failure of natural heirs, many princely states such as Satara, Nagpur, Tanjore (Thanjavur), Jhansi, and Awadh (Oudh) were annexed when their rulers failed to produce natural heirs. Annexation of Awadh for flagrant misgovernment had been ordered by London and urged by Dalhousie's council. Blamed for the Revolt, or Mutiny, of 1857 and exhausted and broken from overwork, Lord Dalhousie died (in Malta) without trying to defend his policies.

[*See also* Governor-General of India; Lawrence, Sir Henry Montgomery; Lawrence, John Laird Mair; Awadh; *and* Mutiny, Indian.]

J. G. A. Baird, *Private Letters to Dalhousie* (1910). W. W. Hunter, *Dalhousie* (1895). W. Lee-Warner, *The Life of the Marquis of Dalhousie* (1904; reprint, 1972).

ROBERT E. FRYKENBERG

RANA, the lineage of prime ministers that was the de facto ruling family of Nepal for more than a century. In 1846, Jung Bahadur Rana wrested political power from Nepal's Shah dynasty in a bloody coup which won him the office of prime minister and key positions in the country's administration for his immediate family. Rana authority was subsequently confirmed by order of the figurehead Shah ruler Surendra who, in 1856, granted the Ranas and their descendants absolute political authority. The Ranas ruled Nepal in the manner of feudal lords, erecting a rigidly centralized system of administration to insure the uninterrupted extraction of agricultural revenues for their personal indulgence. On the initiative of Jung Bahadur, subsequent Rana rulers maintained amicable relations with the British in India. This policy won the Ranas important allies against rival factions in Kathmandu and ultimately secured British acknowledgement of Nepal's internal sovereignty. The Rana oligarchy was not long able to resist the triumph of India's nationalist movement. Five years after the British relinquished their rule in India, Nepali advocates of democratic reform, with the support of India's Congress Party leadership, spearheaded a revolt that overthrew the Rana regime and restored the Shah dynasty.

[*See also* Jung Bahadur Rana.]

B. L. Joshi and L. Rose, *Democratic Innovations in Nepal* (1966).   RICHARD ENGLISH

RANADE, MAHADEV GOVIND (1842–1901), Indian intellectual and nationalist. Ranade was a Chitpavan brahman who studied at Elphinstone College, graduating with both a master of arts and a bachelor of laws degree from Bombay University in 1864.

After teaching at Elphinstone College and writing for local papers he joined the Bombay judiciary (1871), rising to judge in the Small Causes Court in Pune (1884), and the Bombay High Court (1893). Ranade was appointed to the Bombay Legislative

Council in 1885 and to the Finance Commission in the following year.

Precluded by his judicial role from political activism, he directed Pune's political association, the Sarvajanik Sabha, and helped to found the Indian National Congress. Working toward national regeneration on all fronts, Ranade pushed for religious reform through the Prarthana Samaj, for economic reform in his writings, and for social reform as president of the National Social Conference. He wrote *The Rise of the Maratha Power; Essays on Indian Economics; Religious and Social Reform;* and *Miscellaneous Writings.*

[*See also* Indian National Congress *and* Prarthana Samaj.]

P. J. Jagirdar, *Studies in the Social Thought of M. G. Ranade* (1963). R. P. Tucker, *Ranade and the Roots of Indian Nationalism* (1977).   JIM MASSELOS

RANGAKU ("Dutch studies"), a term used by the Japanese during the Tokugawa period (1600–1868) to refer not only to Dutch studies per se (the Dutch came to be the only sanctioned European residents in Japan) but to Western science in general, which the Japanese studied through the medium of the Dutch language. By the end of the Tokugawa period, Japanese interest in the West broadened to include other Western languages and cultures, and the term *yōgaku* ("Western studies") was used.

In 1639 a series of seclusion edicts culminated in the expulsion from Japan of all Europeans except the Dutch, who until 1854 were the only Westerners permitted to reside in Japan. The Dutch were favored because they had convinced the Tokugawa *bakufu* (shogunate) that their interests were commercial rather than religious. In 1641, the Dutch were confined to their trading station (or factory, as it is often called) on the man-made isle of Deshima in Nagasaki harbor and their intercourse with Japanese was greatly restricted.

As a consequence of the seclusion laws, access to information from the West during the seventeenth century was strictly limited. The importation of Western books (even in Chinese translation) was severely restricted. Japanese contacts with Dutch residents were confined to a small group of official interpreters attached to the Nagasaki magistrate's office. A coterie of Japanese doctors also managed to exchange scientific information with the resident physician on Deshima when he accompanied the Dutch on official visits to the shogun's court in Edo (Tokyo). Generally, the Dutch in Japan were far more interested in commerce than in cultural exchange, but when the doctor on Deshima was a serious scholar with an interest in Japan, as were Engelbert Kaempfer, Carl Peter Thunberg, and Philipp Franz von Siebold (none of whom was Dutch), the encounters were mutually beneficial.

By the eighteenth century Dutch studies had moved from the sporadic efforts of Japanese doctors to improve their medical skills to the efforts of translators to provide wider access to European science and culture. By the nineteenth century scholars were reading Dutch texts in the original language. The process may have begun as early as 1720, when Yoshimune Tokugawa, convinced that certain aspects of Western knowledge could be useful in governing, eased the restrictions on importation of foreign books, except for those dealing directly with Christianity. He commissioned the compilation of a Dutch dictionary and encouraged study in areas that had practical applications, such as astronomy (useful in constructing accurate calendars) and military tactics. These developments inspired a group of Edo doctors to produce the first scholarly translations of Dutch medical texts. The best known of these works was *Kaitai shinsho*, translated from a Dutch work on anatomy by Sugita Gempaku (1733–1817), Maeno Ryōtaku (1723–1803), and Nakagawa Jun'an (1739–1786) in 1774.

The significance of *Kaitai shinsho* went beyond the improvements it made possible in medical practice. It ushered in a wealth of translations of Dutch texts in the late eighteenth century that introduced Japanese scholars to Western works in fields as diverse as geography, botany, military strategy, and the arts and inspired Japanese experimentation in these areas.

The intellectual climate of late eighteenth-century Japan was greatly affected by the work of the translators. When Sugita Gempaku and others discovered that the Western works on medicine they were translating were far more accurate than the Chinese texts they had been relying on, they began to raise doubts about the intellectual supremacy of Chinese learning. This shift in attitude had profound implications, for it suggested that no longer could traditional learning, and by extension traditional authority, be accepted uncritically.

The *bakufu* maintained an ambivalent attitude toward Dutch studies in the late eighteenth and early nineteenth centuries. It patronized individual scholars in fields like language, medicine, and military strategy and set up an official translation office for Western books in 1811; but it also established restrictive policies and punished scholars for transgressing its rules. In 1789 the Ban on Heterodoxy forbade all but orthodox Zhu Xi Confucianism in the *bakufu* college, Shōheikō, and placed new restrictions on contacts with Westerners and the acquisition of foreign books. In 1828, the so-called Siebold Incident led to the expulsion from Japan of a leading European physician for the possession of forbidden information. In 1839, several prominent Dutch-studies scholars, including Takano Chōei (1804–1850) and Watanabe Kazan (1793–1841), were arrested for political insubordination. As late as 1849, the entrenched power of the Confucians led the *bakufu* to prohibit all Dutch medicine in official facilities, with the exception of surgery and treatment of the eye. It was not until the final decades of the Tokugawa period, when the need for experts in science and military technology became a matter of national survival, that the *bakufu* made a strong commitment to building facilities for what was now called Western studies: a Western medical center was created in 1861, a Western-style military school was established in 1854, and the *bakufu's* translation office was expanded in 1856 and made into a leading center for Western studies by 1863.

During the first half of the nineteenth century, the most important advances in Dutch studies came not from official encouragement or patronage but from the research and teaching of individual scholars in their private Dutch studies academies in cities like Edo, Osaka, Kyoto, and Nagasaki. Schools run by scholar-physicians like Ōtsuki Gentaku, Philipp Franz von Siebold, and Ogata Kōan, provided systematic access to the best Dutch scholarship. By the 1840s, a limited availability of reference works on Dutch grammar, such as *Grammatica* (1842) and *Syntaxis* (1848), along with the Doeff Dutch-Japanese dictionary (1817), enabled advanced students and scholars to read Dutch texts in both the sciences and humanities in the original. In the 1850s, faced with a national crisis, the *bakufu* and the *han* recruited these students for their expertise in areas related to the culture and technology of the West. Many emerged from these positions as important national leaders following the Meiji Restoration of 1868.

By the late 1850s and early 1860s, following the treaties of friendship and trade with America and the European powers, Japanese studies of the West broadened considerably, and English, French, and German began to supplant Dutch as the medium for importation of Western knowledge. But during the long period of Japan's isolation from the world, it was only through their Dutch studies that a few dedicated scholars maintained intellectual contact with European civilization. Their work contributed to the diversity of thought in Tokugawa Japan and helped develop new and independent lines of inquiry, some of which would eventually challenge official orthodoxy. The remarkable skills of the early Meiji leadership group in adapting Western ideas, methods, and institutions to Japanese conditions is explained, in part, by their training in Dutch studies in the late Tokugawa period.

[*See also* Seclusion; Deshima; Kaempfer, Engelbert; Thunberg, Carl Peter; Siebold, Philipp Franz von; Ōtsuki Gentaku; Ogata Kōan; *and* Watanabe Kazan and Takano Chōei.]

John Z. Bowers, *Western Medical Pioneers in Feudal Japan* (1970). C. R. Boxer, *Jan Compagnie in Japan* (1936). Marius B. Jansen, *Japan and its World* (1980). Donald Keene, *The Japanese Discovery of Europe, 1720–1830* (1969). Richard Rubinger, *Private Academies of Tokugawa Japan* (1982). George B. Sansom, *The Western World and Japan* (1973).   RICHARD RUBINGER

RANGOON, Burma's largest city and capital. Like many ancient Asian urban centers, the origins of Rangoon are obscured by the myth-laden character of the sources in which they are mentioned. The area of present-day Rangoon, which developed in the last half of the nineteenth century, first appears in history as the site of the Shwedagon, a Buddhist pagoda that was said to house strands of the Gautama Buddha's hair. Although Dagon, as the small settlement near the shrine was called from ancient times, was widely known for its annual market by the fifteenth century, its population remained small and its buildings, excepting the pagoda, were unimpressive. During the last decades of the sixteenth century, shifts in the course of the tributaries of the Irrawaddy River, which formed the alluvial delta where Dagon was located, led to the rise of the port city of Syriam, east of Dagon on the Pegu River. It is in this period that Dagon first appears in the accounts of European travelers, some of whom describe it in extravagant terms.

During the wars between the Burmans and Mon in the mid-eighteenth century, the armies of Alaunghpaya, the founder of the Konbaung dynasty, sacked Syriam. Burma's new ruler made Dagon the chief center of administration and commerce in Lower Burma and renamed it Rangoon ("end of strife"). Under Konbaung rule, Rangoon remained a small town of thatched houses, surrounded by a wooden stockade. The town's population of several thousand was made up mainly of Burman soldiers and administrators, Burman and Mon monks, and small groups of indigenous and foreign merchants.

After the first Anglo-Burmese War (1823–1826), in which Rangoon was captured by British forces, a new city was laid out away from the Rangoon River and called Ukkalapa, after the kingdom that was said to have ruled the area in ancient times. At the end of the second Anglo-Burmese War in 1852, the British annexed the Irrawaddy Delta region to their Indian empire, and Rangoon became the capital, main commercial and processing center, and chief port of the province of Burma. On the basis of extensive planning, a new town, built on an elaborate grid system, grew up at the juncture of the Rangoon and Hlaing Rivers.

Between 1852 and the end of British rule, brought about abruptly as a result of the Japanese invasion in 1941, Rangoon's population increased from several thousand to more than four hundred thousand, the majority of whom were immigrant Indian laborers and merchants. During this period Rangoon also became Burma's major center of higher education and home of a growing Western-educated elite, while remaining a major focal point of Burmese Buddhism. The convergence of Burmese nationalism, Buddhist revivalism, and economic dislocations linked to reverses in the world market made Rangoon a major arena of nationalist agitation and communal conflict during the 1920s and 1930s. With independence and Burma's self-imposed isolation, Rangoon's population declined, then stagnated, and the city's grand buildings, constructed during the colonial era, fell into disrepair. The well-gilded and tended Shwedagon, however, endures as one of Burma's most revered shrines.

[*See also* Burma; Shwedagon Pagoda; *and* Anglo-Burmese Wars.]

B. R. Pearn, *A History of Rangoon* (1939). O. H. K. Spate and L. W. Trueblood, "Rangoon: A Study in Urban Geography," *Geographical Review* (1942).

MICHAEL ADAS

RANI OF JHANSI. *See* Lakshmi Bai.

RANN OF KUTCH, large bipartite, seasonally inundated salt wasteland lying mainly in the Indian state of Gujarat. The Great Rann of Kutch extends 220 miles eastward from the Arabian Sea and between 25 and 50 miles north–south between the Gujarati district of Kutch and the Pakistani province of Sind. The Little Rann of Kutch, south and east of the district of Kutch, extends 65 miles eastward from the Gulf of Kutch and up to 35 miles from north to south, being joined to the Great Rann during the high-water period of the monsoon season when Kutch becomes an island. Located in a area of frequent seismic disturbances, the level of the Rann has fluctuated markedly in historic times. At times the area has been navigable, at times traversable by land in all seasons. Pakistan's claims to much of the Great Rann led to serious armed clashes with India in 1965. An international boundary tribunal awarded Pakistan roughly 300 square miles in 1968.

[*See also* Gujarat.]

Hari Ram Gupta, *The Kutch Affair* (1969). Indian Society of International Law, *The Kutch-Sind Border Question: A Collection of Documents* (1965). Joseph E. Schwartzberg, ed., *A Historical Atlas of South Asia* (1978).

JOSEPH E. SCHWARTZBERG

RASHTRAKUTA DYNASTY. The Rashtrakutas, rulers of the Deccan, India, from 752 to 972, moved north in the early seventh century from Lattalura, Maharashtra. Dantidurga (r. 733–758), first a feudatory of the Chalukyas, defeated his overlords in about 752. His uncle Krishnaraja I took the throne in 758 and sponsored excavation of the Kailasa temple at Ellora, the first Rashtrakuta capital. (A permanent capital was later established at Manyakheta or Malkhed.) Succeeding kings Dhruva (r. 780–793), Govinda III (r. 794–814), and Indra III (r. 914–922) carried out successful military campaigns into northern India; the dynasty extended its control over the Pratiharas, Palas, Eastern Chalukyas, and Cholas. The end of the dynasty came with the capture of Manyakheta by the Paramara king Siyaka in 972.

[*See also* Deccan.]

A. S. Altekar, *Rāshṭrakūtas and Their Times* (1934).

GERI HOCKFIELD MALANDRA

RASHTRIYA SWAYAMSEVAK SANGH (National Servants' Society). Founded in 1925, the RSS has been stereotyped as a rigidly doctrinaire, closed, and secret organization attempting to promote Hindu cultural revival through militant ideological and political activities. In its early years its exclusive emphasis was a fascist-like psychological and physical training of youth, but with increasing participation in electoral politics the RSS has now become heavily involved in cultural organizations, voluntary work, and development activities. A 1978 article in *The Organiser,* the weekly journal of both the RSS and the Bharatiya Jana Sangh (the political party supported by the RSS), pointed out that "Swayamsevaks have been engaged in uplift [development] activities at some sixty centres throughout the country for several years now." According to its leaders, what the RSS offers is a complete revitalization of Indian civilization by stressing "discipline and *esprit de corps"* along with "modern progress" and "basic virtues" like truth, physical exercise, honesty, and religious values.

Since the mid-1970s two major RSS factional positions have become evident. One supports cooperative meetings with non-Hindus, including Muslim attendance at RSS educational institutions and joint Hindu-Muslim celebration of Hindu festivals (such as Holi). The second supports militant, often violent, RSS activities directed at non-Hindus in local neighborhoods.

[*See also* Jana Sangh.]

Craig Baxter, *The Jana Sangh: A Biography of an Indian Political Party* (1971). Robert G. Wirsing, *Socialist Society and Free Enterprise Politics: A Study of Voluntary Associations in Urban India* (1977).   MARCUS FRANDA

RATHORS. The Rathor Rajputs ruled Marwar, India, west of the Aravalli hills in Rajasthan's Thar desert, from the fourteenth century. Rao Jodha (d. 1487) founded Jodhpur, the capital, in 1459. Brought under Mughal rule by the emperor Akbar, the Rathors suffered Maratha depredations in the eighteenth century, and came under British "protection" in 1818. [*See also* Rajput; Jodhpur; *and* Marwar.]   USHA SANYAL

RATU ADIL, the Javanese "just king" who, it was believed, would appear after a time of turbulence and depravity to institute a new age of justice and plenty. The belief was linked with the popular Jayabaya prophecies that had foretold the circumstances under which the *ratu adil* would arise and was later (especially in West Java) associated with the coming of an Islamic *mahdi* figure. In modern Javanese history, several princely rebels and popular leaders have styled themselves as the *ratu adil,* among them Dipanagara.

[*See also* Jayabaya *and* Dipanagara.]

Soewito Santoso, "Hérucakra," *Review of Indonesian and Malaysian Affairs* 10 (1976): 82–90.   PETER CAREY

RAZADARIT, also known as Rajadhiraja (r. 1385–1423), third and greatest of the Mon kings of Pegu in Burma. Born Binnyanwe, the eldest son of King Binnya U (r. 1353–1385), Razadarit seized the throne on his father's death and for the first time brought some order to the struggling kingdom. He had to contend with adventurous Shan and Burmese rulers to the north, as well as with highly developed localism along the coast. Having secured his state within the first decade of his reign, he was content to manage and sustain it through the rest of his reign. He was succeeded by his sons, Binnyadammayaza (r. 1423–1426) and Binnyaran (r. 1426–1446).

[*See also* Burma; Mon; *and* Pegu.]

G. E. Harvey, *A History of Burma from the Earliest Times* (1925; reprint, 1967). Arthur P. Phayre, *History of Burma* (1883; reprint, 1969).   DAVID K. WYATT

RAZIYYA (d. 1240), daughter of the Mamluk sultan Iltutmish (r. 1210–1235) and the ruler of India from 1236 to 1240. With the support of the people of Delhi, she overthrew her brother and ascended the throne. She curbed the power of the Turkish officers and encouraged non-Turkish elements as a counterpoise. When Turkish nobles conspired against her, she married Altuniah, but finally she was defeated (12 October 1240) and executed. A Carmathian revolt took place during her time. She declined alliance with the Khwarazmian governor of Ghazna, Hasan Qarlugh, against the Mongols.

[*See also* Delhi Sultanate *and* Iltutmish.]

Aziz Ahmad, *Political History and Institutions of the Early Turkish Empire of Delhi* (1949). Mohammad Habib and Khaliq Ahmad Nizami, *Comprehensive History of India,* vol. 5 (1970), pp. 237–244.

KHALIQ AHMAD NIZAMI

RAZMARA, ALI (d. 1951), prominent member of the Iranian elite from a wealthy landowning family and prime minister of Iran from 1950 to 1951, during the critical years of the oil nationalization process. Razmara was allegedly opposed to the oil nationalization bill and as prime minister had completed a new oil concession with the British in 1951. Owing to his pro-British and antinationalization tendencies, he was murdered in 1951 by a member of the Fida'iyan-i Islam, an extremist, nationalist religious group founded by Ayatollah Abu al-Qasim Kashani in Qom in 1945.

Ervand Abrahamian, *Iran between Two Revolutions* (1982). R. Cottam, *Nationalism in Iran* (1979).

NEGUIN YAVARI

READING, MARQUIS OF. *See* Isaacs, Rufus.

REBELLIONS IN CHINA. China's long history since the founding of the imperial system in the third century BCE has been punctuated by a series of massive rebellions that either resulted in the changing of dynasties or at least brought irreparable damage to the existing ones. The frequency, size, and intensity of these rebellions had so conditioned the outlook of the Chinese that they accepted, perhaps even expected, such outbreak of violence. Illustrative of this sentiment is the opening line of the popular novel *Romance of the Three Kingdoms,* "After a long duration of unity, the realm is bound to be torn asunder by rebellions."

What made rebellions such a permanent feature of Chinese history is a complex conglomerate of factors: official malfeasance, socioeconomic exploitation, natural or man-made disasters, and so forth. From the religio-philosophic point of view, however, two concepts are particularly relevant to the explanation of the frequent outbreak of rebellion in China. The first is that of the mandate of Heaven *(tianming).* First formulated during the Zhou dynasty in the first millennium BCE, this notion interpreted political authority and legitimacy as a commission or mandate from Tian—the ultimate source of being. Furthermore, it postulated the conferral of this mandate as a result of the ruler's moral fitness to rule. In other words, the ruler's power was tied directly to his morality, which at the same time implied that his loss of moral rectitude would result in the revocation of this mandate and its transference to someone else. Consequently this allowed, on the theoretical level at least, any aspirant to the throne to claim the right to rebel by arguing that the reigning monarch was no longer morally fit to rule. Rebellion was thus religiously and ethically justified.

Complementing this notion was the belief in the "mutual correspondence between human [secular] and cosmic [religious] events" *(tianren ganying).* Any disturbance or unusual occurrence in nature and society was interpreted as reflective of the tension and displeasure felt in the cosmic realm—potential signs for the withdrawal and transference of the mandate. In this manner cosmic change and the fate of the mundane monarch were inexorably linked, and the line between secular and sacred became blurred.

While rebellion was philosophically and religiously justifiable, indeed its recurrence expected, it was for obvious reasons seldom glorified or positively assessed by the guardians of culture and the political elites. They viewed all rebels with fear and contempt, and vilified all rebellious sentiments. Instead they preached the merits of social harmony and loyalty, dismissing popular uprisings as the result of a temporary lapse in good government or the machination of incorrigible elements in society.

With the triumph of the Communist revolution in 1949, however, mainland Chinese historians undertook a new appraisal of the historical rebellions. Inspired by Mao Zedong's 1939 assertion that "the class struggles of the peasants—the peasant uprisings and peasant wars—alone formed the real motive force of development in China's feudal society," they were nearly unanimous in their euphoric glorification of the revolutionary nature of the peasants and their rebellions. Between the 1950s and the mid-1970s they produced numerous symposia and published hundreds of articles on the "antifeudal class struggles" of the Chinese peasantry. In their assessment, the Chinese peasants possessed and often displayed a revolutionary consciousness that paralleled, and at times even surpassed, that of the European proletariat, thereby putting China in the forefront of the world struggle for liberation, despite its lack of a bourgeois revolution and a modern labor movement.

About a dozen "great peasant rebellions" have been identified for detailed study. They include:

1. The anti-Qin revolt (209 BCE)
2. The revolts of the Red Eyebrows and the Green Forests (18–27 CE)
3. The Yellow Turban Rebellion in the Latter Han (184)
4. Revolts of the Six Dynasties period, notable among which was the one led by Sun En and Lu Xun in the lower Yangtze area (398–417)
5. The anti-Sui revolts (610–624)
6. Late Tang revolts such as that headed by Wang Xianzhi and Huang Chao (874–884)
7. The revolts of the Song period, led by Wang Xiaobo and Li Shun in Sichuan (993–995), Fang La in Fujian and Zhejiang (1120–1122), and Zhong Xiang and Yang Yao in Hunan-Hubei (1130–1135)
8. The late Yuan White Lotus movement (1351–1368)

9. Mid-Ming revolts (fifteenth and sixteenth centuries)
10. Late Ming revolts of Li Zicheng and Zhang Xianzhong (1627–1645)
11. The White Lotus Rebellion in mid-Qing (1796–1805)
12. The Taiping Rebellion (1850–1864)
13. The Nian and Boxer rebellions (mid- and late nineteenth century)

Under the terms of this analysis, while each of these rebellions opposed exploitation, they also progressively evolved toward higher forms of struggle, becoming truly antifeudal after the Tang era and antiimperialist as well after the nineteenth century.

Since 1978, however, a swing of the pendulum toward the opposite has become noticeable in Chinese historiography on peasant rebellions. Perhaps partly as a reaction to the excesses of the Cultural Revolution, the current view is to downplay the revolutionary nature of the peasant uprisings and even of the peasants themselves. Their fatalistic, monarchistic, and hierarchical views have been presented as limited and "backward." Even the overall contribution of peasant rebellions to China's historical development has been cast in doubt.

Among Japanese and Western scholars, one interesting angle in the study of Chinese rebellions has been the role played by religion. At issue is the fundamental perception of the nature of such rebellions themselves. Were they staged by downtrodden peasants merely to redress socioeconomic exploitation, or were they motivated by "mindful peasants" bent on changing the world in their pursuit of the millennium? Studies have shown that many such uprisings were informed by an amalgam of Buddhist salvationism, Daoist messianism, and Manichaean chiliasm. Whether their religious vision was directly responsible for their rebellious activities remains open to question; but some rebels did embrace antinomian values and maintained organizational networks that made rebellion a distinct possibility.

[See also Fang La; Han Liner; Huang Chao; Hong Xiuquan; Li Zicheng; Nian Rebellion; Red Eyebrows; Red Turbans; Secret Societies; Taiping Rebellion; White Lotus Society; Yellow Turbans; Yihetuan; Zhang Xianzhong; and Zhu Yuanzhang.]

James P. Harrison, *The Communists and Chinese Peasant Rebellions: A Study in the Rewriting of Chinese History* (1969). Kwang-ching Liu, "World View and Peasant Rebellion: Reflections on Post-Mao Historiography," *Journal of Asian Studies* 40.2 (February 1981): 295–326. Susan Naquin, *Millenarian Rebellion in China: The Eight Trigrams Uprising of 1813* (1976). Daniel L. Overmyer, *Folk Buddhist Religion: Dissenting Sects in Late Traditional China* (1976). Frederic Wakeman, Jr., "Rebellion and Revolution: The Study of Popular Movements in Chinese History," *Journal of Asian Studies* 36.2 (February 1977): 201–237.   RICHARD SHEK

REDDY, N. SANJIVA (b. 1913), president of India from 1977 until 1982. Sanjiva Reddy is a landholder who rose within the ranks of the Congress Party to become chief minister of Andhra Pradesh and a leading member of "The Syndicate," the group of a half-dozen party bosses who ran the Congress Party in the 1960s. Nominated for the presidency of India in 1969, Reddy was defeated when Indira Gandhi chose to support his opponent, V. V. Giri, and split the Congress Party in the process. Reddy was elected president with the backing of the Janata government after the Janata had defeated Mrs. Gandhi in the 1977 elections.

[See also Gandhi, Indira *and* Giri, Varahagiri Venkata.]

Current Biography (1981), pp. 331–334. *India Today* (August 1–15, 1977).   MARCUS FRANDA

RED EYEBROWS, one of the rebel bands instrumental in toppling the Wang Mang regime (8–23 CE). Painting their eyebrows red to symbolize their loyalty to the Han and to distinguish themselves from Wang Mang's soldiers while fighting, they rebelled in 18 CE under the leadership of Fan Chong. Although successful in their campaigns against government forces and another rival rebel army, the Green Forests, they failed to earn the full support of the populace owing to their lack of administrative expertise and a viable political program. They were finally defeated by Liu Xiu, founder of the Eastern (Latter) Han, in 27 CE.

[See also Rebellions in China; Wang Mang; *and* Han Dynasty.]

Hans Bielenstein, "The Restoration of the Han Dynasty," *Bulletin of the Museum of Far Eastern Antiquities* 26 (1954): 1–210; 31 (1959): 1–288; 39 (1967): 1–198.   RICHARD SHEK

RED FORT, or Lal Qila, a name derived from the red Sikri sandstone used for their outer walls, is popularly applied to the Mughal forts of Agra and Delhi; the contemporary fort at Allahabad, also of the same medium, does not bear this name. Agra's Red Fort was built by Akbar between 1565 and

FIGURE 1. *Red Fort, Delhi.* View shows sandstone wall and west (Lahore) gate.

1573; construction was supervised by Qasim Khan Mir-i Bahr. Included were some five hundred buildings in the styles of Bengal and Gujarat, but few remain, for Shah Jahan replaced them with white marble structures. The Delhi fort is the imperial citadel adjoining Shah Jahan's newly created capital, Shahjahanabad, constructed between 1639 and 1648 by imperial architects Hamid and Ahmad. While Shah Jahan's public and private audience halls are still intact, many structures were replaced by British barracks.

Abu al-Fazl, *Akbar Nama,* 3 vols. (reprint, 1972–1973). Archaeological Survey of India, *List of Muhammadan and Hindu Monuments: Delhi Province,* vol. 1, *Shahjahanabad* (1916).   CATHERINE B. ASHER

RED GUARDS, Chinese student activists of the period of the Cultural Revolution. In August 1966, when the Chinese Communist Party adopted the "Sixteen Articles" initiating the Cultural Revolution, some college and high school students organized themselves as Red Guards to lead the student movement. As Mao Zedong gave his blessing to the organizations by, for instance, making public appearances with a Red Guard arm band and offering free transportation to Beijing, the Red Guard movement swept every part of China. Mao reviewed almost ten million Red Guards in six gigantic mass rallies during the latter part of 1966. Meanwhile, the Red Guards engaged in what they considered revolutionary activities: changing the names of streets and shops into more revolutionary ones, struggling against anyone whom they considered to be opposed to Mao, raiding private houses, and destroying temples and other cultural relics.

Initially the membership of the Red Guards was limited to the children from good class backgrounds, but this restriction was soon removed, allowing any student to form a Red Guard organization or join the existing ones. As a result, the Red Guard organizations multiplied with a wide variety of names, forming alliances and quarreling among themselves. To make matters worse, the various political factions at the top level also manipulated the Red Guard movement to protect themselves and to gain power. Thus, the Red Guard movement soon degenerated into bloody armed struggles, completely disrupting the basic fabric of Chinese society. Even though Mao initially viewed the Red Guards as an effective instrument for fighting against what he regarded as the revisionist trend among the top Party leaders, he changed his mind and used the military to end the Red Guard movement. The twist and turns of the Cultural Revolution and ensuing vicious power struggles among the elite groups eventually led the Red Guards—even those who participated in the movement out of their sincere faith in Mao and his version of socialism—to feel that they were no more than pawns used by the political elites in the power struggle. Consequently, the Red Guard generation became so severely alienated from the political process that they are often referred to as "the wounded generation" in present-day China.

[*See also* Great Proletarian Cultural Revolution.]
                                        HONG YUNG LEE

RED SPEARS were local Chinese self-defense groups organized and led by rural elites to fight against roving bandits, unruly soldiers, and rapacious warlords. Popular and powerful in the Huaibei area in the 1920s, they were the direct descendants of the Boxers. Red Spears followers claimed physical invulnerability to swords and bullets through magical incantations and the drinking of charm water. Although their name derives from their custom of decorating their spears with a red tassel, there were offshoots that used other colors, such as white, yellow, and black. The Red Spears were also active in the anti-Japanese guerrilla wars of the late 1930s.
[See also Yihetuan.]

Elizabeth J. Perry, *Rebels and Revolutionaries in North China, 1845–1945* (1980). Roman Slawinski, "The Red Spears in the Late 1920's," in *Popular Movements and Secret Societies in China, 1840–1950,* edited by Jean Chesneaux (1972).   RICHARD SHEK

RED TURBANS, large millenarian rebel bands that appeared throughout the Chinese empire toward the end of the Yuan dynasty (1279–1368). Donning red sashes—turbans may be a misnomer—these rebels subscribed to the chiliastic belief of White Lotus-Maitreyanism. There were two major camps of Red Turbans, one headed by Han Shantong and Liu Futong, the other centered around Peng Yingyu and Xu Shouhui.

Han Shantong's family had been devout worshipers of Maitreya for generations. Taking advantage of the widespread disaffection toward Mongol rule, Shantong predicted that "the empire will be in great turmoil and the Maitreya Buddha will incarnate [to save it]." This inspired his disciple Liu Futong to make preparations for rebellion, which broke out in early 1351 in Yingzhou (Anhui). Shantong, however, was immediately captured and executed, but his widow and son Liner escaped arrest and rejoined Liu Futong four years later. Liner was enthroned as the Small King of Light, and took Song as his dynastic name. Numerous military leaders fought under his nominal command, and Zhu Yuanzhang, future founder of the Ming dynasty, was among them.

Peng Yingyu, religious leader of the other camp of Red Turbans, had been the planner of an earlier abortive revolt. In 1351 he and his disciples made Xu Shouhui, a traveling merchant, their emperor and rebelled in Macheng (Hubei). These Red Turbans also believed in the imminent incarnation of Maitreya. Military leaders in this camp included Chen Youliang, who replaced Xu as emperor in 1360, and Ming Yuzhen, who occupied Sichuan and styled himself emperor of Xia.

While sharing similar beliefs and equally intense anti-Mongol sentiments, leaders of the two camps of Red Turbans also fought one another for supremacy. In the end, it was Zhu Yuanzhang who emerged triumphant in 1368, having disposed of all his rivals through ingenuity and treachery.

[See also Han Liner; Ming Dynasty; White Lotus Society; Yuan Dynasty; and Zhu Yuanzhang.]

John Dardess, "The Transformation of Messianic Revolt and the Founding of the Ming Dynasty," *Journal of Asian Studies* 29 (May 1970): 539–558.

RICHARD SHEK

REFUGEES. Asia has been a continent of mass migrations and refugees in the post–World War II era. The region has experienced some of the largest single population transfers in the world, and cumulatively more population movement across borders than any other region. These mass migrations reflect most of the major economic, social, and political upheavals of postcolonial Asia and the persisting tensions of north-south relations.

The United Nations has framed the legal terms of refugee movement and rights. The 1948 Universal Declarations of Human Rights guarantee all persons the right to leave and return to any country, including their own. Refugees were defined in the United Nations 1951 Convention and 1967 Protocol Relating to the Status of Refugees as persons who flee their countries with "a well-founded fear of persecution." Certainly, Asia's refugees have often moved with well-founded fears. The experience of individual persecution, however, has often been secondary to that of internal wars, external interventions, boundary problems, political dissension, and nationality disputes. Refugees in Asia have more often moved because of their group membership than because of personalized persecution, and generally, therefore, have moved with large groups rather than alone. These two characteristics, similar to population movements in postcolonial Africa, have transformed the nature of international responses to refugee problems and the understanding of political turmoil in the Third World.

Causes of Movement. Refugees can be identified by both the causes of their movement and the political environment in which they move. The causes of flight often resemble population movement outside the continent as well: civil wars and wars of intervention, religious and ideological conflicts, and political and economic differences among governments and their citizens. These categories alone encompass most of the region's refugees in the last four decades, including:

1. *War:* the Korean conflict and the partition of Korea; the Indochinese conflicts and the partition of Vietnam, with refugees from Cambodia, Laos, Thailand and Vietnam; civil war in Pakistan and the Indian intervention in East Pakistan; civil war and Soviet intervention in Afghanistan.
2. *Ideological conflict:* the flight of Nationalist Chinese to Formosa to form the Republic of China (Taiwan); the flight of Tibetans to India after religious conflicts with the government of the People's Republic of China.
3. *Political persecution:* the flight and exile of opponents of new and changing regimes, particularly after the imposition of military rule or martial law, in the Philippines, Indonesia, Pakistan, Cambodia, and Bangladesh; the flight of opponents of governmental economic policy and ideology, from the People's Republic of China, Vietnam, Cambodia, and Laos.

The enormous movement of populations after the 1947 partition of the Indian subcontinent falls into a category all its own. The largest organized transfer of population, accomplished mostly in the period immediately after Indian and Pakistani independence, it reflected the uncertain expectations of Muslims, Hindus, and Sikhs about political independence, and set the tone for postcolonial subcontinental politics.

Regional Environment. The political environment in Asia that has generated and received refugees more accurately reflects large-scale changes in the continent than specific causes of movement. While the international community often recognized refugees who left the Third World for the north (such as Koreans and Vietnamese who moved to Europe and the United States), postwar refugee phenomena more often concern those who remain in the region after leaving their homes. On occasion, stranded populations have taken on the characteristics of refugee groups: Urdu-speaking Biharis were left in Bangladesh after the 1971 war even though they were legally Pakistani citizens, and Karen ethnic-group members lived for many years in limbo on the Burma-Bangladesh border.

Political conflict in Asia often involves large populations that move across close borders with the intention of returning home again. Their existence as large, often homogenous and geographically identifiable populations have become in themselves facts of political and sometimes strategic life in the region. Refugees from Cambodia have lived on the Thai-Cambodian border for years, just as refugees from Afghanistan have lived along the Iranian and Pakistani borders. Both groups not only provide havens for refugees from war, but act as supply centers and training grounds for conflicts at home. Thus, while these refugees conform to traditional definitions of their status as populations in danger, they also help determine the future of the geopolitical conflicts that initially created their refugee status. The fact that these groups live in historically contentious and strategically vital areas is part of a continuing struggle to establish viable, enduring states in Asia.

International Action. International humanitarian agencies have traditionally helped resettle or repatriate refugees since World War II. The massive population transfers after the partition of India and Pakistan were accomplished largely by the two new countries themselves. Since them, refugee aid in Asia has developed unique patterns of responsibility, cooperation, and assistance. The appearance of Vietnamese "boat people" in the mid-1970s initiated new efforts not only to raise funds, but to establish intermediate safe haven (first asylum) in neighboring countries of the Association of Southeast Asian Nations (ASEAN). Thus, international organizations and northern countries alike were forced to recognize that absorbing large refugee groups might breed new instabilities for receiving countries. Relief efforts among Cambodian refugees in transit camps in Thailand gave United Nations agencies unusual primacy and importance. At the same time, while refugee assistance funds for Afghans in Pakistan were raised primarily in Islamic countries and the West, the Pakistan government assumed the predominant role in directing assistance efforts.

Continuing political instability in Asia will generate and maintain refugee populations. Some assume the characteristics of semipermanent residents of host countries; others ultimately repatriate or resettle in other countries. In the postwar, postcolonial period, there has been no time when Asia has not had to contend with the forced movement of millions of people. The next decades will therefore test not only its humanitarianism, but also its political and economic resilience.

Guy S. Goodwin-Gill, *The Refugee in International Law* (1984). Kathleen Newland, *Refugees: the New International Politics of Displacement* (1981). United Nations, *39th Session Supplement: Report of the United Nations High Commissioner for Refugees, no. 12* (1984).

PAULA R. NEWBERG

REGENTS, name given by the Dutch to the local chiefs and provincial heads in Indonesia (especially Java) who ruled in areas that had passed under the authority of the Dutch East India Company (VOC) from the early seventeenth century onward. The word was the same as the Dutch term used for the patrician oligarchs in Holland.

In Java, the regents (Javanese, *bupati*) were central to the Dutch exploitation of local agricultural and labor resources through the VOC system of contingents and forced deliveries. Attempts by early nineteenth-century reformers such as Herman Daendels and Thomas Stamford Raffles to bypass them in the interests of more efficient government failed, and after 1830 the regents came into their own once more as junior partners to the Dutch residents in the administration of the cultivation systems. From the 1870s onward, a series of reforms stripped the regents of many of their personal and fiscal privileges and turned them into salaried officials of the colonial state. At the same time, higher educational requirements forced the younger generation of regents to study at Dutch high schools and colleges of administration. By the early years of the twentieth century, those who had proved themselves sufficiently capable formed part of a new bureaucratic élite that was totally dependent on the Dutch and remained loyal to them until the end of the colonial period in 1942.

[*See also* Dutch East India Company; Java; Daendels, Herman Willem; *and* Raffles, Sir Thomas Stamford.]

Heather Sutherland, *The Making of a Bureaucratic Elite: The Colonial Transformation of the Javanese Priyayi.* (1979). PETER CAREY

REIYŪKAI. *See* New Religions in Japan.

RENNYO (1415–1499), eighth patriarch of the True Pure Land school (Jōdo Shinshū) of Japanese Buddhism. Rennyo was the son of Zonnyo the abbot (*zasu*) of Honganji, and he became *zasu* himself in 1457. Rennyo is revered as the second founder of Jōdo Shinshū. He revived the original teachings of the founder Shinran (1173–1262) and suppressed heretical interpretations that had sprung up among True Pure Land followers by issuing "pastoral letters" *(ofumi)* expressing his own and Shinran's teachings on Amida Buddha and the *nembutsu* in simple terms.

Following Shinran, Rennyo stressed faith in, and submission to, Amida. Faith *(shinjin)* itself, he argued, derived from Amida. Thus the very act of faithfully invoking Amida's sacred name through the *nembutsu* was an act of gratitude as much as it was an appeal for salvation. Rennyo was also successful in unifying the various, and often feuding, groups of Jōdo Shinshū believers *(monto)* under the leadership of the Honganji, which he made into the arbiter of Shinshū orthodoxy.

Many of the Jōdo Shinshū groups were tightly organized and militant. For this they had earned themselves the name "single minded school" *(ikkō-shū)*. Rennyo was critical of the militant role that *monto* played in the armed uprisings after 1473 known as *ikkō ikki*. He issued *ofumi* encouraging *monto* to restrain their attacks on rival religious groups and the legitimate political authorities but was unable to halt the uprisings that won the *ikkō* followers some territorial conquests. These uprisings ultimately set the *monto* in self-destructive opposition to powerful warriors like Oda Nobunaga, who were seeking to reestablish unchallenged political control over the country.

[*See also* Pure Land; Amidism; Shinran; *and* Ikki.]

Stanley Weinstein, "Rennyo and the Shinshū Revival," in *Japan in the Muromachi Age*, edited by John W. Hall and Toyoda Takeshi (1977). MARTIN COLLCUTT

RENVILLE AGREEMENT. *See* Indonesian Revolution.

REPUBLICAN PARTY OF INDIA. Established in 1956 by Dr. B. R. Ambedkar (1892–1956), the Republican Party was an attempt to broaden the base of his previous parties, the Independent Labour Party (1936) and the Scheduled Castes Federation (1942.) Its platform stresses social and economic equality. The party commands votes in Maharashtra and areas of Uttar Pradesh, Punjab, Karnataka, and Gujarat, but holds a neglible number of seats.

[*See also* Ambedkar, Bhimrao Ramji.]

Dhananjay Keer, *Dr. Ambedkar: Life and Mission* (3d ed., 1971). Eleanor Zelliot, "Buddhism and Politics in Maharashtra," in *South Asian Politics and Religion*, edited by Donald Eugene Smith (1966).

ELEANOR ZELLIOT

RESCRIPT ON EDUCATION. *See* Imperial Rescript on Education.

RESCRIPT TO SOLDIERS. *See* Imperial Rescript to Soldiers.

RESPONSIBILITY SYSTEM, a general term for a number of strategies whereby households or groups of farmers in China agreed to perform agricultural tasks or to work specified fields on a contract basis. The effect of these arrangements was to stimulate production by giving peasants an incentive by allowing them to sell for profit crops exceeding the contracted output target. These reforms were first pioneered in Sichuan Province and, since 1978, extended to the rest of China under the leadership of Deng Xiaoping. The responsibility system marks a trend away from collectivization of agriculture and back toward a rural market economy, although land remains collectively owned.

[*See also* Agriculture, Collectivization of; Deng Xiaoping; *and* Zhao Ziyang.]

EDWARD L. FARMER

REUTER CONCESSION. The 1872 Reuter Concession was the most extensive economic concession ever granted by Iran. It was sold cheaply by Nasir al-Din to a British subject, Baron Julius de Reuter, of news agency fame, and granted exclusive rights to build railroads, streetcars, irrigation works, a national bank, and many mineral, industrial, and agricultural rights. Britain, however, did not support the concession, and it was opposed by Russia and by several important Iranians. In 1873 the shah found a pretext to cancel the concession by not letting Reuter begin railroad construction on time. The shah kept the £40,000 that Reuter had put up as caution money; the British then backed Reuter's claims against Russian railroad schemes. In 1889 Reuter's claims were settled by a concession for a national bank with attached mineral rights.

[*See also* Qajar, Nasir al-Din.]

Nikki Keddie, *Religion and Rebellion in Iran: The Tobacco Protest of 1891–1892* (1966). NIKKI KEDDIE

REVOLUTIONARY COMMITTEES. The Revolutionary Committee (Chinese, *geming weiyuanhui*) made its appearance in January 1967 as a "provisional organ of government," symbolizing the new and allegedly progressive form of authority born in China's Great Proletarian Cultural Revolution. It was authority nonetheless: in the convulsive atmosphere of the time, the ruling Communist Party and many government bureaucracies had ceased to function, brought to their knees by rampaging mass factions of student Red Guards and worker "revolutionary rebels." Some mass factions, encouraged by Chairman Mao Zedong, grew anarchic, espousing the slogan "doubt everything, overthrow everything." Revolutionary Committees subsequently were approved by Mao to check the unwelcome anarchic current.

The early province-level committees, beginning with the one organized on 31 January 1967 in Heilongjiang, were dominated by former Party officials. Later committees, finally the one organized on 5 September 1968 in Xinjiang, were dominated by military representatives and reflected the growing influence of the army in bringing the Cultural Revolution to a close.

For a few years after the Cultural Revolution, Revolutionary Committees replaced the earlier provincial People's Congresses, or equivalent bodies at other levels, as the nearly universal administrative governing body for local governments, ministries, and communes. By 1978, however, when the Cultural Revolution period and all its trappings had come under severe attack as a dangerous "extreme left" deviation, all Revolutionary Committees were abolished.

[*See also* China, People's Republic of; Communism: Chinese Communist Party; Great Proletarian Cultural Revolution; *and* Mao Zedong.]

Richard Baum, ed., *China in Ferment: Perspectives on the Cultural Revolution* (1971). GORDON BENNETT

REYES Y FLORENTINO, ISABELO DE LOS (1864–1938), Filipino journalist, businessman, politician, and amateur theologian. Born in Vigan, Ilocos Sur, he graduated from the University of Santo Tomas and published two volumes of Philippine folklore and the first vernacular newspaper in the colony, *El Ilocano.* Exiled to Spain during the Philippine Revolution, he translated the New Testament into Ilocano and published the anti-American *Filipinas ante Europa.* He returned in 1901, founded the Philippine Independent Church (PIC) and the Democratic Labor Union, was jailed for labor agitation, and became the archtypical *intransigente* (irreconcilable). Straightforward criticism of American imperialism elected him to the Manila City Council and the Senate, and colorful exposure of collusion and the introduction of social legislation won him a reputation as father of Philippine socialism. He was a successful businessman, thrice widowed, and the father of twenty-seven children, one of whom—Isabelo, Jr.—was supreme bishop of the PIC for twenty five years.

[*See also* Philippine Independent Church.]

WILLIAM HENRY SCOTT

REZANOV, NIKOLAI PETROVICH (1764–1807)

a Russian nobleman and high official who attempted to establish trade relations with Japan and to strengthen Russian influence in Alaska and the west coast of North America. In 1795 Rezanov became the majority stockholder and chairman of the Russian-American Company, which had been founded to develop trade with Japan and North America and possibly to establish a Russian colony in North America.

In 1793 the Russian lieutenant Adam Laxman had been told by Japanese officials in the north that requests for trade would be honored at Nagasaki. In 1802 Tsar Alexander I named Rezanov envoy to Japan, giving him instructions to return four Japanese castaways and to demand trade on the basis of the promise given Laxman.

His two ships left Russia for Japan by way of the Cape of Good Hope in August 1803 and arrived at Nagasaki in October 1804. After months of waiting and negotiation he was told that he could not trade and was ordered to leave Japan immediately. After his departure he devised a scheme to open Japan by force by attacking Japanese settlements in Hokkaido and Sakhalin. A small force was sent to attack the settlements, but it did not succeed in opening the country. Thus Rezanov's second and indirect attempt to open trade with Japan also failed.

After his experiences in Japan Rezanov traveled to Alaska and as far south as San Francisco in search of trade. He died after a long illness on 13 March 1807 while en route to Saint Petersburg.

[*See also* Seclusion.]

Gertrude Atherton, "Nikolai Petrovich Rezanov," *North American Review* 189 (1909). George Alexander Lensen, *The Russian Push toward Japan* (1959).

JOHN M. MAKI

RHEE, SYNGMAN (Yi Sŭng-man; 1875–1965),

the Republic of Korea's first president (1948–1960) and stubborn lifelong fighter for Korea's cause. Syngman Rhee was born in Hwanghae Province of central Korea and died in Honolulu, Hawaii.

A distant relative of the Korean royal family, Rhee studied the Confucian classics, but then entered the American missionary Paejae High School in 1894. His activity in the reformist Independence Club led to imprisonment in 1897. Tortured at first, he later could write a somewhat prosaic political testament, "The Spirit of Independence," which was subsequently published in the United States. He was converted to Christianity while in prison.

Released in 1904, Rhee went to the United States to plead unsuccessfully for American support against Japanese hegemony. With missionary support, he studied successively at George Washington, Harvard, and Princeton universities, earning his doctoral degree. In 1911 Rhee returned to Korea—now a Japanese colony—as a YMCA teacher-evangelist, but Japanese suspicions soon drove him back to the United States. From 1913 to 1940 he based his activities in Hawaii, where he was principal of a Korean school and leader of a Korean expatriate faction called Tongjihoe (Comrades' Society). He continued his vigorous campaigning for Korean independence. His work was plagued then and subsequently, however, by dissension with Korean political and church leaders.

Rhee's stature as a fighter and spokesman for Korea's cause was such that after the Korean national independence uprising of 1 March 1919, he was named president of the Korean Provisional Government in Exile at Shanghai. His relations with the leaders at Shanghai, however, were strained. In 1925 the Provisional Government impeached him and replaced him as president with Kim Ku, but Rhee refused to recognize the action. [*See also* March First Independence Movement *and* Kim Ku.]

In his youth, Rhee had a traditional arranged marriage; his wife gave birth to one son, who died. In 1933, while trying to present the Korean case to the League of Nations in Geneva, he met and later married Francesca Donner, an Austrian, who became Korea's first lady.

In 1940 Rhee moved to Washington, published a book called *Japan Inside Out,* and sought recognition for Korea in the coming conflict. Following the Japanese attack on Pearl Harbor, he sought American recognition for the Korean Provisional Government, but the Department of State, weary of importunities from rival Korean factions and leery of expatriates, largely ignored his overtures. By 1943 Rhee was suggesting that the Soviet Union was responsible for failure to recognize the Provisional Government. His adamant anti-Soviet and anticommunist stand won him many American admirers.

Rhee returned to Korea on 16 October 1945 with the encouragement of his own group of conservative American supporters and of the American military occupation authorities, whose commander, General John Hodge, personally introduced him to a press conference at the capital. Rhee assumed a supra-partisan stand over the many competing political factions, organized his own National Society for the Rapid Realization of Korean Independence, and sought a national coalition. For many reasons, including Rhee's own uncompromising personality and doctrinaire anticommunism, the effort failed.

In December 1946, in defiance of the American authorities, Rhee campaigned in the United States for the establishment of a separate state in South Korea, continuing to work for it upon his return. In the end, he had his way. US-Soviet negotiations for unification of the two occupation zones failed, and Rhee was elected president of the Republic of Korea following UN-observed elections in the South in May 1948. Thereafter, he never ceased to call for a "march north" to unify the country by force.

Rhee was reelected president in 1952, 1956, and 1960. His control involved a skillful blend of political strategy and coercion. The Korean public respected his age, status, and nationalist credentials. They also admired his manipulation of Americans, such as his unauthorized release of twenty-eight thousand prisoners of war in June 1953 to frustrate negotiations for an armistice in the Korean War, and his successful bargaining for massive American economic and military support as his price for acquiescence in the truce.

Rhee's inability to work with others and his lack of concern or understanding for economics, however, retarded the progress that the people expected; opposition grew and public support diminished. Rhee's supporters resorted increasingly to coercion and fraud to keep him in power, thus losing for him much of his deserved place in history. In April 1960 blatant election fraud, popular demonstrations, and police violence led to his resignation. Rhee, by now verging on senility, went into exile in Honolulu, where he died five years later.

[*See also* Korea, Japanese Government-General of; Korean War; Korea, Republic of; *and* April Nineteenth Student Revolution.]

Richard C. Allen, *Korea's Syngman Rhee: An Unauthorized Portrait* (1960). Chong-sik Lee, *The Politics of Korean Nationalism* (1963). Robert T. Oliver, *Syngman Rhee: The Man behind the Myth* (1960).

DONALD S. MACDONALD

RHODES, ALEXANDRE DE (1591–1660), Jesuit missionary in Vietnam. A native of Avignon, de Rhodes first came to Cochinchina in late 1624. He spent eleven of the next twenty-one years there until expelled for good in 1645. His greatest accomplishment was the *quoc ngu* script, which he "codified, regularized, and popularized" based on earlier missionaries' romanization systems. Using this script, de Rhodes published a bilingual Vietnamese catechism and a trilingual dictionary in 1651. After his return to Rome, he wrote descriptions of his travels in the Far East and worked to help establish the Society for Foreign Missions, founded in 1664 after his death.

[*See also* Quoc Ngu.]

Solange Hertz, trans., *Rhodes of Vietnam* (1966).

BRUCE M. LOCKHART

RIAU (Riouw, Rhio), on the island of Bentan in the Riau-Lingga Archipelago, just south of Singapore, was for a century the main entrepôt of the Malay world, the heir of Srivijaya and Melaka.

Riau's prosperity blossomed in the late seventeenth century after the Dutch had captured Melaka and the North Sumatran state of Aceh had declined, loosening its control of the tin- and pepper-rich areas of East Sumatra and the west of the Malay Peninsula. In the eighteenth century the intervention of the Bugis in Johor politics coincided with the growth of European trade to China, and by 1760, with the Bugis Raja Muda Daeng Kemboja firmly in control, Riau was a major trade center. Tin, pepper, spices, rice, and other foodstuffs; cloth and opium from India; and china goods were all freely available. The Dutch jealously watched this smuggling trade from Melaka and Batavia, but they did not interfere till the English Company, needing a safe port in the straits for its China fleets, looked to Riau. In 1784 Batavia took action, capturing and occupying the Johor port. The English adopted alternative ports at Penang and Singapore, drawing off Riau's trade.

Riau remained a center for gambier production, which had been established on Bentan by the Bugis. In the nineteenth century the word *Riau* came to designate the whole province ruled by the *raja muda* of Riau, including Bentan, Batam, and the Karimon Islands.

[*See also* Melaka; Bugis; *and* Johor.]

Barbara W. Andaya and Leonard Y. Andaya, *A History of Malaysia* (1982). Dianne Lewis, "The Growth of the

Country Trade to the Straits of Malacca 1760–1777," *Journal of the Malaysian Branch of the Royal Asiatic Society* 43.2 (1970): 114–130. DIANNE LEWIS

RIBEIRO, JOÃO (1622–1693), a soldier in the Portuguese army from 1640 to 1660 who served in Ceylon during the years that the Portuguese were fighting a desperate war to save their maritime possessions in the island from the Dutch and the Sinhalese. On retiring to Lisbon, Ribeiro wrote an account of his experiences in Ceylon entitled *Fatalidade historica da Ilha do Ceilao (Historical Tragedy of the Island of Ceylon),* which, however, was not published until 1836. This work is valued as an outstanding source for the political and social history of the period, especially because of Ribeiro's eyewitness accounts of the Portuguese wars.

[*See also* Portuguese: Portuguese in Sri Lanka.]

Joao Ribeiro, *The Historical Tragedy of Ceilan,* translated by P. E. Pieris (1925). S. ARASARATNAM

RICCI, MATTEO (known to the Chinese as Li Madou; 1552–1610), the primary formulator of Jesuit accommodation in China and the outstanding Christian missionary to serve there. Ricci was born in Macerata in the Ancone Mark (now part of Italy), the son of Giovanni Battista Ricci, a pharmacist, and of Giovanna Angiolelli, who belonged to the noble family of the marquisate of Castelvecchio.

Jesuit influence upon Ricci started at an early age, beginning with his tutor, who later became a Jesuit, and then with the newly opened Jesuit school in Macerata. He was sent to Rome in 1568 with the initial purpose of studying law and greatly agitated his father by entering the Society of Jesus in 1571 without first obtaining approval. But fatherly assent was eventually forthcoming and Ricci continued his studies at the Collegium Romanum as a Jesuit novice. He initially expressed the wish to serve in the mission in India and departed from Rome in 1577. Because of the Portuguese *padroado* (Portuguese monopoly on Asian missionary activities), it was necessary at this time to obtain exit visas from Lisbon. After doing so, Ricci departed from Lisbon on board the *S. Luis* in March 1578 and arrived in Goa in September of the same year. He concluded his theological training in Asia and was ordained at Cochin in 1580, although, as was typical of Jesuits of that time, he did not take his final vows until nearly sixteen years later in 1596.

During this time it was decided by the Jesuit visitor, Alessandro Valignano, that Ricci should serve in the China Mission, and he consequently arrived at Macao in August 1582. After one year's intensive study of Chinese, Ricci was ordered to accompany Pompilio (Michele) Ruggieri to establish a mission at Zhaoqing, just west of Canton (Guangzhou). The experience at Zhaoqing was marked by antagonism and hostility on the part of the Chinese and frustration and failure on the part of the Jesuits. Much was learned at Zhaoqing, however, and it is here that Ricci first began to understand how to communicate with the Chinese literati. An early mistake was the adoption, at the insistence of the local prefect, of Buddhist dress, which by this time in Chinese history the literati had come to despise. Rather, Ricci discovered that the way to impress the Chinese scholar-officials was through his erudition; he had been doubly blessed, first, with a brilliant mind and, second, with an education provided by some of the most eminent European scholars of the day. In addition, Ricci was a charming conversationalist and he found that his mnemonic skills impressed the Chinese, whose educational curriculum laid great emphasis on memorizing large parts of the classics. With his knowledge of mathematics and geography, Ricci composed a map of the world that not only fascinated the Chinese but also flattered their cultural sensibilities by placing China at the center of the world, where the Chinese had traditionally held China to be located. Although it satisfied traditional Chinese belief, this placement did not violate the arbitrary nature of where one fixed the prime meridian in longitudinal reckoning.

In 1589 Ricci and his confreres abandoned Zhaoqing for the somewhat more northerly town of Zhaozhou. Here they showed how much they had learned from the disaster at Zhaoqing, and their lives, as well as their church architecture, became more sinicized. Zhaozhou proved fertile, and they began to make their first conversions of the literati, beginning with Qu Taisu. Soon thereafter they discarded the clothing of the Buddhist monks for that of the literati. Establishing a mission in the Chinese capital of Beijing had long been Ricci's aim, and now he was in an improved position to work toward this goal. Leaving the successful mission at Zhaozhou in the hands of other Jesuits, Ricci moved north to establish missions in Nanchang and Nanjing.

Ricci's first arrival in Beijing in 1599 was inauspicious because war with Japan had aroused Chinese distrust and suspicion of all foreigners. After a successful retreat to Nanjing, however, Ricci returned to Beijing in January 1601. This time the reception was more positive. After successfully outmaneuvering the eunuch Ma Tang, who sought to appropriate for himself Ricci's carefully selected assortment of gifts, Ricci was able to have his gifts presented to the Wanli emperor (r. 1572–1620). Although the emperor was reclusive and had no direct contact with the Jesuits, his fascination with the mechanical clock that Ricci had presented and the need to have the clock maintained was eventually transformed into an invitation to take up residence in Beijing. Ricci had learned his lessons well. His calculated but sincere request of being allowed to live and to die in China was granted and he proceeded to pursue the Jesuit dream of establishing a mission in the Chinese capital. By the time of his death in 1610, this dream had been realized.

Ricci's remarkable abilities in mastering the Chinese language combined with his penetrating and flexible intellect made him the leading formulator of a policy of accommodation that was both a daring mission strategy and a profound formula for the meeting of Chinese and European cultures. Ricci's policy of accommodation was grounded upon an intensive study of Chinese literature and culture and upon integration into Chinese literati society. The Jesuits in China were not missionaries on short-term service who viewed China as a place that they would eventually leave. Rather, they were to follow the model of Ricci in declaring their intention of spending the remainder of their lives in China. Such an attitude was not merely Jesuit missionary policy, but reflected the only terms on which the Chinese would admit foreigners as residents in China. Permanent residence in China had the effect of changing the missionaries. This was eminently true of Ricci, who entered China when he was thirty years old and who never left during the remaining twenty-seven years of his life. Ricci's model for sinicizing the Jesuits in China made them different from their confreres in Europe and created fundamental differences in understanding that would contribute greatly to the so-called Rites Controversy.

At the heart of Ricci's program of accommodation was the Confucian-Christian synthesis. This embodied both a perception of the nature of the Confucian tradition and a tactical approach for introducing Christianity into China. Ricci perceived the Confucian tradition as a recurring source of orthodoxy in Chinese history that was traceable not merely to Confucius, but to the most ancient sages of China. In making this interpretation, Ricci understood Confucian tradition well enough to know

that such a perception was reinforced by Confucius himself, who claimed to have been a transmitter of the teaching of the ancient sages rather than an originator of a new and novel teaching. Down through the ages, Chinese had accepted this continuity of orthodoxy without necessarily agreeing to the same interpretation of it. In fact, nearly every exponent of Confucianism would claim to be rejecting other interpretations on the grounds that his interpretation recaptured the original and true meaning of the sages of antiquity. Ricci applied this traditional approach to claim that the Confucian-Christian synthesis represented such a return and he thereby rejected competing interpretations, such as Neo-Confucianism, as a distortion of this original and true meaning.

Ricci's tactical approach for establishing the Confucian-Christian synthesis was aimed at displacing the role of Buddhism with Christianity on the grounds that the teaching of Christianity more truly complemented and completed the teaching of Confucius than did Buddhism. This approach had been developed with the assistance of Christian literati such as Xu Guangqi. [See also Xu Guangqi.] To this end, Ricci stressed the superstitious element of Buddhism and contrasted this with the rationalistic emphasis of Christian theology. One must add here that Ricci's plan for a Confucian-Christian synthesis was more appropriate during his age than in other times because the cultural atmosphere of the late Ming dynasty was syncretic and stressed syncretic formulations, such as the claim that the Three Teachings (Confucianism, Buddhism, and Daoism) were essentially the same. When this cultural climate changed after 1644 with the Manchu conquest of China, Ricci's proposal of accommodation was in need of modification to suit the altered cultural atmosphere. It may be debated whether Jesuits after Ricci gave his accommodation program the type of modifications that were necessary for its implementation and success in China or whether Ricci's approach, as brilliant and insightful as it was, was (because of inherent weaknesses or Chinese indispositions) doomed from the start to failure in China.

[See also Jesuits: Jesuits in China and Ming Dynasty.]

Pasquale M. d'Elia, ed., *Fonti Ricciani*, 3 vols. (1942–1949). George L. Harris, "The Mission of Matteo Ricci, S. J.: A Case Study of an Effort at Guided Culture Change in China in the Sixteenth Century," *Monumenta Serica* 25 (1966): 1–168. Matthew Ricci (Matteo Ricci), *China in the Sixteenth Century: The Journals of Matthew Ricci, 1583–1610*, translated by Louis J. Gallagher (1953). Jonathan D. Spence, *The Memory Palace of Matteo Ricci* (1984).   DAVID E. MUNGELLO

RICE. *See* Agriculture *and* Sawah.

RICE RIOTS, popular disturbances in Japan occurring from late July to mid-September 1918 in response to sharp increases in the price of rice. Fed by new urban demand and speculation, rice prices doubled between early 1917 and June 1918, increasing another 50 percent in the first ten days of August. The riots were unprecedented in their nationwide scope and in their critique of the political-economic order.

The first disturbances broke out in a Toyama fishing village when women protested the shipment of scarce rice to Osaka. By mid-August, similar incidents had erupted in most large cities, as crowds looted rice warehouses, attacked the homes of rice merchants, and clashed with police. Demanding wage increases, more than 34,000 factory workers and miners mounted strikes during August and September. Small farmers, who often bought rice themselves, denounced landlords and rice merchants for buying low and selling high. The rice riots involved between one and two million people and occurred in all but four prefectures. The government used police and 92,000 armed troops to arrest thousands and restore order. Officials also sought to reduce the sources of unrest, however, by delivering cheaper rice and by encouraging the importation of less expensive rice from colonial Korea and Taiwan. While lacking coordination, the rice riots represent the first instance of mass political expression in the post-1918 era of so-called Taishō Democracy. The protests discredited the oligarchic Terauchi Masatake cabinet, ushering in the first party cabinet, led by Hara Takashi.   SHELDON M. GARON

RICHARDSON INCIDENT, also known as the Namamugi Incident, the first major clash between Britain and Japan. Following the treaties concluded with Japan by America and others in 1858, samurai opposition to the opening of Japanese ports was often manifested in attacks on foreigners. The British legation in Edo was attacked in 1861 and 1862. On 14 September 1862 a party of British merchants riding at Namamugi, near Yokohama, was attacked by Satsuma samurai. One of them, named Richardson, was killed. The British government decided to take punitive action. It demanded from the *bakufu* an apology and an indemnity of £100,000; from Satsuma it demanded punishment of the guilty samurai and compensation of £25,000. Failing this, the British naval commander was empowered to take steps of reprisal or blockade.

After long negotiations the *bakufu* agreed to pay an indemnity (June 1863), but Satsuma made no move. A squadron of seven British warships was sent to Satsuma in August to enforce the demands. Fruitless talks led to general fighting, in which both the city of Kagoshima and the British squadron suffered much damage. At Yokohama the following November Satsuma negotiators agreed to pay the £25,000, although the samurai concerned were never punished.

[*See also* Kagoshima Bombardment.]

W. G. Beasley, ed., *Select Documents on Japanese Foreign Policy, 1853–1868* (1955). Grace Fox, *Britain and Japan, 1858–1883* (1969).   W. G. BEASLEY

RIPON, EARL OF. *See* Robinson, George Frederick.

RISHI, anglicized form of the Sanskrit *ṛṣi*, term used to refer to a sage or inspired seer, usually an ascetic, in ancient India. The word refers both to famous human sages, who may have been historical, such as the authors of the "family books" of the *Rig Veda*, and also to mythological figures, especially to the seven rishis born of Brahma, the creator god, who were the progenitors of the human race in each cycle of ages *(manvantara)* and from whom brahman families claim descent.

John E. Michiner, *Traditions of the Seven Ṛṣis* (1982).   RANDOLPH M. THORNTON

RISSHISHA (1874–1883), A Meiji-period political association central to the Popular Rights (Jiyū Minken) Movement in Japan. Organized by Itagaki Taisuke in Kōchi in 1874 as a "self help" society for displaced samurai, the Risshisha functioned predominantly as a political association designed to unite popular opposition to the Meiji government.

Active in assisting other local organizations concerned with the development of a political infrastructure in the early Meiji period, the Risshisha is sometimes regarded as Japan's first modern political party. Its political position was clearly outlined in its opening declaration, which stated that the society stood for self-government, local autonomy, natural rights, the equality of all classes, and the establishment of a legislative assembly. In 1877 it published a nationwide memorial calling for an extension of the rights of the people as opposed to those of the state. From 1877 to 1880 the Risshisha served as a leading voice demanding the establishment of a constitution. In 1880 it spearheaded a petition movement that garnered 250,000 signatures requesting a national assembly. Among the Risshisha's leaders were Itagaki Taisuke, Kataoka Kenkichi, and Ueki Emori, all liberals who used the association as a springboard to found other political societies, such as the Aikokusha and the Liberal Party (1881). By the mid 1880s, with the promise of a constitution, the Risshisha declined in influence and was absorbed by the Tosa branch of the Liberal Party.

[*See also* Jiyū Minken; Itagaki Taisuke; *and* Ueki Emori.]

F. G. NOTEHELFER

RITES CONTROVERSY. *See* Jesuits: Jesuits in China.

RITSURYŌ STATE, a designation used for the political structure of Japan during the late seventh through twelfth centuries CE, a structure resulting from the enactment and enforcement of penal and administrative laws *(ritsuryō)* based on Chinese models.

The work of compiling a *ritsuryō* code was first undertaken during the reign of Tenchi Tennō (661 to 671), who adopted a number of other measures in order to strengthen and unify imperial rule. Neither this first code (the Omi Administrative Code) nor the next one (the Asuka Kiyomihara Administrative Code, compiled during the reign of Temmu) has been preserved. The third one (the Taihō Penal and Administrative Code, promulgated in 702) has also been lost, but contemporary chronicles tell us a good deal about its compilation and contents. It is the extant Yōrō Penal and Administrative Code, completed in 718 and promulgated in 757, that gives us the clearest and most detailed picture of the *ritsuryō* system. In all of the laws issued and compiled during this period, one sees so many Chinese influences that one is tempted to consider the entire system a transplant from China. But a closer look reveals significant adjustments to the special situation in Japan.

The administration supporting the imperial court was divided into a Council of State (Dajōkan) and a Department of Shrines (Jingikan). The former included eight ministries (with their own departments and bureaus), a Board of Censors, and five military-police units. Almost every part of the Council had its counterpart in the administrative structure of Tang China. But laws pertaining to the Department of Shrines, although replete with titles and words introduced from China, outlined functions focused on the worship of deities *(kami)* that were uniquely Japanese, a worship that legitimized the position of the *tennō* (emperor) as a direct descendant of the sun goddess (the *tennō*'s ancestral *kami*) and as Japan's leading priest or priestess. Thus, while Chinese techniques and forms were utilized in the Council of State for strengthening the *tennō*'s administrative control, Japanese beliefs were used in the Department of Shrines for enhancing his or her divine authority.

In order to establish control over the country's people and land, two interlocking arrangements were outlined in *ritsuryō* law. The first gravitated about the requirement that everyone be listed on a household register *(koseki)* according to age, sex, and occupation; and that the *koseki* show how much land had been allotted to every registered individual. The second arrangement was centered on allotting an area of rice land *(handen)* to each registered person, the size of which varied according to sex, age, and class of the person registered (an adult male received the most and a slave child the least) and according to the productivity of the land allotted. Both the *koseki* and *handen* systems were first developed in China, but in Japan there was a tendency to hold the household, rather than the individual farmer, responsible for the payment of taxes.

The *ritsuryō* system also included (1) a local government organization made up of sixty provinces, each having several counties *(kori)* that contained numerous villages with fifty households each; (2) a system of court ranks for members of the ruling elite (whether at the capital or in the provinces) that reserved the highest ranks for the highest officials, who enjoyed appropriate stipends and perquisites; and (3) a military organization of conscripted soldiers with a unit in each province.

The imperial despotism and the cultural achievements of the Nara period have been associated with, if not attributed to, these *ritsuryō* arrangements, but other developments were crucially important: (1) the creation of a network of *kami* shrines (with Ise Shrine serving as the central shrine, where the *tennō* served as chief priest or priestess) by which organized *kami* worship was used to reinforce imperial authority; (2) the building of a statewide system of Buddhist temples that undergirded imperial authority in intellectual and cultural (as well as spiritual) ways; and (3) the formation of an educational system that not only trained individuals for service in *ritsuryō* offices but also gave aristocrats the ability to record the chronicles, commentaries, poems, and stories that are prominent cultural achievements of the period.

By the middle of the Nara period economic and political pressures were already weakening the integrity of the *ritsuryō* system, accounting for much of the decentralization of power and political conflict that preceded the emergence, during the twelfth century, of Japan's military regime (the *bakufu*). Imperial power, especially after the Shōkyū War of 1221, became largely symbolic; military shoguns and daimyo, not *tennō,* controlled most of Japan's land and people.

[*See also* Nara Period.]

John W. Hall, *Government and Local Power in Japan, 500-1700. (1966).* Ishii Ryosuke, *A History of Political Institutions in Japan.* (1980).   DELMAR M. BROWN

RIZAL, JOSE MERCADO (1861–1896), Filipino writer and patriot who became the national hero of the Philippines. He is the major figure of the nationalist movement not because of his political leadership of the Propagandists (where he had to yield to Marcelo del Pilar) but because he articulated the ideas that inspired the Philippine Revolution (1896–1898), primarily in his political novels *Noli me tangere* (1886) and *El Filibusterismo* (1891). He forms the principal link between the incipient national awareness found in the thinking of Friar Jose Burgos (1837–1872) and the revolutionary radicalism of the Katipunan, the secret separatist society founded by Andres Bonifacio in 1892.

In recent years, more for ideological than historical reasons, an effort has been made to contrast Rizal, the bourgeois who denounced the revolution he had prepared, to Bonifacio, the proletarian revolutionary. As a prisoner on trial for his life (1896), Rizal did condemn the revolution, but as the Spanish prosecutor observed, it was its inopportuneness rather than its justice that Rizal condemned. In his letters and, more obliquely, in his novels it is clear that he had aimed for separation from Spain even in the late 1880s. He preferred peaceful means but increasingly became ready to accept revolution if it proved necessary.

Rizal was born of a well-to-do family that leased almost five hundred hectares of the Dominican hacienda of Calamba. His brother Paciano had been living with Burgos in 1872 and was forced to leave school; to avoid association with them Jose adopted the surname Rizal. Burgos's desire to demonstrate the equality of Filipino and Spaniard remained central to Rizal's thought, as did Burgos's belief that the Filipinos could prove themselves by education. This particular belief became an obsession with Rizal and a source of friction with many companions in Spain, whom he berated for their sloth and lack of dedication.

A brilliant and devout pupil of the Ateneo Municipal, Rizal retained his affection for the Jesuits even after he had discarded most of his belief in Catholicism. Arriving in Spain in 1882, he quickly became the catalyst of the Filipino colony in Madrid, and he himself became increasingly radicalized. While a medical student there, he began to write his novel *Noli me tangere,* which he completed in Germany. Here he not only laid bare the racism and abuses inflicted on Filipinos by the Spaniards but also castigated Filipinos for their subservience to, and their acquiescence in, the hypocritical religion preached by the friars. While Rizal is careful not to opt for revolution, the book warns that it is inevitable if reforms are not forthcoming. *Noli me tangere* became the charter of the Propaganda Movement.

Although Rizal returned to Manila in 1887, Spanish denunciations soon forced him to return to Europe, where he spent a year working in the British Museum, preparing his edition of the seventeenth-century *Sucesos de las Islas Filipinas* by Antonio de Morga. In his copious annotations Rizal reconstructs pre-Hispanic Filipino culture, concluding that Spain had destroyed a flourishing civilization. Although it proved to be written too much from a scientific point of view, the book had a strong nationalist impact on Bonifacio and other future revolutionaries. Rizal had now portrayed the Filipino present and the past; his next book would point to the future.

Having come to Madrid to pursue a family lawsuit challenging Dominican ownership of the Calamba hacienda, which was intended to show that Filipinos could successfully challenge friars, Rizal clashed with del Pilar over leadership of the expatriate Filipinos. He rejected del Pilar's political activism in Spain as inefficacious and left for Brussels to finish his *El Filibusterismo* in 1891. This novel expresses Rizal's conviction that separation from Spain is inevitable but eschews both immediate violence and continued political intrigue in Spain. The essential prerequisite of separation, he argues, is the education of the people to national unity and awareness of their dignity; this will be accomplished not in Spain but in the Philippines.

Rizal left Europe for Hong Kong, where he found that the resisting tenants of Calamba had been evicted or imprisoned by the Spanish governor. After vacillating between a plan to found in Sabah a Filipino refuge under British protection and returning to the Philippines to seek his family's freedom from the new governor, he went to Manila in 1892. He obtained the pardon of his family, then secretly founded the Liga Filipina as a concretization of his desire to stimulate Filipino national awareness and unity. A few days later, he was arrested and exiled to Dapitan, a Jesuit mission town in Mindanao, in the hope that his Jesuit friends might win him back to Catholicism and Spain.

Removed from political activity, Rizal devoted himself to science and medicine, but in 1896 he volunteered to serve as an army surgeon in Cuba to get free. Since by this time Bonifacio had begun the revolution despite Rizal's dissuasion, Rizal was brought back from Spain to face trial for complicity. He was executed on 30 December 1896, after having signed a retraction of Freemasonry (though these were not his political beliefs) and returned to Catholicism under the influence of his Jesuit professors. Although its authenthicity and significance have been controverted, the retraction is now believed to be genuine; its sincerity, however, remains a matter of unverifiable and differing judgments.

[See also Philippines; Propaganda Movement; Pilar, Marcelo H. del; Philippine Revolution; Burgos, Jose; Friars; Katipunan; Bonifacio, Andres; and Liga Filipina.]

Austin Coates, *Rizal: Philippine Nationalist and Martyr* (1968). H. de la Costa, trans. and ed., *The Trial of Rizal* (1961). Leon Ma. Guerrero, trans., *Noli me tangere* (1961) and *El Filibusterismo* (1962). Leon Ma. Guerrero, *The First Filipino* (1963). John N. Schumacher, *The Propaganda Movement, 1880–1895* (1973).

JOHN N. SCHUMACHER, S.J.

RIZA SHAH PAHLAVI. See Pahlavi, Reza.

ROBE-WRAPPING CONTROVERSY, monastic dispute in Burma during the reign of King Sane (1698–1748). This bitter disagreement emerged between two rival factions of the (Buddhist) Parakama

tradition, both of which traced their strict orthodoxy through a succession of teachers to the fount of purity in Sri Lanka. It dealt with how the monastic outer robe should be worn when monks walked into villages and towns and stood while the laity earned merit by filling the monks' food bowls. One monastic group, the Ayon Gaing, covered both shoulders at such times; the other group, the Atin Gaing, covered only one shoulder. Monastic Vinaya courts (courts convened to rule on matters of Vinaya, or Buddhist monastic law) debated the issue for decades until 1784, when royally appointed monks, under the guidance of King Bodawhpaya, ruled in favor of covering both shoulders. This is still the custom in modern times.

E. M. Mendelson, *Sangha and State in Burma: A Study of Monastic Sectarianism and Leadership,* edited by John P. Ferguson (1975). JOHN P. FERGUSON

ROBINSON, GEORGE FREDERICK (Lord Ripon; 1827–1909), viceroy of India from 1880 to 1884. He was British prime minister W. E. Gladstone's third choice for the viceroyalty; despite this inauspicious beginning, Ripon's administration symbolized the attempt to implement Gladstonian liberalism in India. With peace, retrenchment, and reform as his prime minister's motto, Ripon first sought to consolidate British territorial acquisitions and to withdraw from newly conquered territories in Afghanistan. In so doing, however, he invited Russian intervention and the British government eventually was forced publicly to guarantee Afghanistan's borders.

Ripon introduced India's first factory legislation, removed restrictions on freedom of the press, and sought to transfer the control of some public service expenditures to the localities. His judicial reforms, promulgated in the Ilbert Bill (1883), were designed to allow Indians to serve as magistrates with jurisdiction over Europeans. But the outcry against the bill, the so-called White Mutiny, mobilized conservative opposition and dealt both the viceroy and the reform movement a significant moral and political defeat.

[See also Ilbert Bill *and* Government of India.]

S. Gopal, *The Viceroyalty of Lord Ripon, 1880–1884* (1957) and *British Policy in India, 1858–1905* (1965). JAMES A. JAFFE

ROE, SIR THOMAS (1581?–1644), ambassador under James I to the Mughal emperor Jahangir's

court from 1614 to 1618. Building upon the achievements of William Hawkins, Roe obtained various trading privileges for the British factory at Surat and laid the foundations for the future greatness of Bombay. His *Journal* provides a valuable account of life at the Indian court.

[*See also* Hawkins, William; East India Company; *and* Jahangir.]

The Embassy of Sir Thomas Roe to India, 1615–19, as Narrated in his Journal and Correspondence, edited by W. Foster´ (1899; rev. ed., 1926). USHA SANYAL

ROHANA, one of the three main territorial divisions of ancient Sri Lanka. Extending across the southeastern plain of the island, Rohana was widely dependent upon irrigation. The area was symbolic of the particularism that was a perennial problem in ancient Sri Lanka. It was the home of lost and viable causes, the refuge of Sinhalese kings overthrown by foreign invaders, and a bridgehead for the liberation of Anuradhapura from foreign rule. Its rulers conducted their affairs as if independent potentates, and Rohana's status varied from time to time from that of a mere administrative division of the Anuradhapura kingdom to a principality and a semi-independent kingdom.

[*See also* Anuradhapura.]

K. M. de Silva, *A History of Sri Lanka* (1981).

K. M. DE SILVA

ROHILLAS. The Rohillas, originally from the region of Roh in Afghanistan, ruled Rohilkhand in India (territory now including Moradabad, Bijnor, and Bareilly, in western Uttar Pradesh) from approximately 1740 to 1785. The founder, Ali Muhammad Khan (d. 1749), a soldier whom the Mughal emperor recognized as nawab of Rohilkhand, rose to power amid the unsettled conditions of invasions by Nadir Shah and Ahmad Shah Abdali. The Rohillas had an uneasy relationship with neighboring Awadh (Oudh), but became allies under the Maratha threat. Their possessions were repeatedly overrun by the Marathas between about 1750 and 1770, and they were decisively defeated in 1774 by the combined forces of Awadh and the British. In 1801 Rohilkhand became British territory.

[*See also* Awadh.]

Syed Altaf Ali Brelvi, *Life of Hafiz Rahmat Khan,* translated by Mohammad Hamiuddin Khan (1966). John Strachey, *Hastings and the Rohilla War* (1892).

USHA SANYAL

RŌJŪ ("senior councillor"), principal shogunal advisers and government officials of the Tokugawa period (1600–1868) in Japan. Usually four or five in number, the *rōjū* were selected from the ranks of loyal, castle-holding *fudai* (inner) daimyo with incomes in excess of 25,000 *koku*. In time, it became customary for one of the group to serve as chief senior councillor (*rōjū shuseki*). The *rōjū* took monthly turns as "duty officer," but important national issues were decided collectively. Most *rōjū* had prior administrative experience within the shogunal bureaucracy, as well as a large network of friends throughout the *bakufu*; these two qualities greatly enhanced their value as shogunal advisers and government officials by making them much better informed about the world beyond the castle than the shogun, who spent much of his life in the castle proper. The *rōjū* also enjoyed the privilege of affixing the shogunal seal to official documents.

Each of the *rōjū* had individual offices within the confines of the shogunal castle in Edo, but joint deliberations were conducted in the council rooms (*yōbeya*). From these offices the *rōjū* also supervised a plethora of important governmental offices, including Edo City commissioner (*Edo-machi bugyō*), finance commissioner (*kanjō bugyō*), inspectors-general (*ō-metsuke*), and chamberlains (*sobashū*). Among famous *rōjū* of the Tokugawa period were Tanuma Okitsugu (1772–1786), Matsudaira Sadanobu (1787–1793), and Mizuno Tadakuni (1844–1845), each of whom was associated with a major reform effort designed to rectify structural and functional flaws within the Tokugawa system.

[*See also* Tanuma Okitsugu; Matsudaira Sadanobu; *and* Mizuno Tadakuni.]

Harold Bolitho, *Treasures among Men: The Fudai Daimyo in Tokugawa Japan* (1974). Conrad Totman, *Politics in the Tokugawa Bakufu, 1600–1843* (1967).

RONALD J. DICENZO

ROKUMEIKAN, a social club built near the site of the Tokyo Imperial Hotel in 1883 by the Meiji government of Japan. Designed by the English architect Josiah Condor, the club was designed to show and to further the westernization of Japanese society and customs. Its name, "Deer Cry Pavilion," was taken from the Chinese *Book of Songs,* in which a banquet poem reads, "Here is a man that loves me / And will teach me the ways of Zhou." Western guests who attended banquets and balls to "teach the ways of Zhou" remarked on the sudden fad of Western dress and fashion that engaged the Japanese leaders. At court Western clothes prevailed, and the emperor himself appeared only in Western military uniform. The campaign was expected to help in reform of Japan's "unequal treaties" with the West, but when projected changes proved disappointing a wave of disillusion and anger extended to disapproval of uncritical adoption of Western forms. In 1890 the Rokumeikan became a Peers' Club; it was razed in 1941, but survives as a symbol of the "crash westernization" programs of the 1880s.

Donald H. Shively, "The Japanization of the Middle Meiji," in *Tradition and Modernization in Japanese Culture* (1971).   MARIUS B. JANSEN

ROLIN-JAEQUEMYNS, GUSTAVE (1835–1901), Belgian adviser to King Chulalongkorn of Siam. The son of a cabinet minister, Rolin-Jaequemyns was trained as a lawyer, entered politics as a Liberal, and was minister of interior in Belgium from 1884 to 1886. While Rolin-Jaequemyns was in Egypt for legal work, he was recruited by Prince Damrong Rajanubhab in 1891 to serve King Chulalongkorn as general adviser at a time of major governmental reform. Advising on administrative changes and foreign affairs from the perspective of a neutral at a time when Siam was under French and British pressure, Rolin-Jaequemyns was highly valued, and he achieved rare distinction as a *chaophraya*, the highest civil rank, in 1896. He left Siam for health reasons in 1899 and died in 1901.

[*See also* Chulalongkorn; Damrong Rajanubhab; *and* Paknam Incident.]

C. de Saint-Hubert, "Rolin-Jaequemyns (Chao Phya Aphay Raja) and the Belgian Legal Advisors in Siam at the Turn of the Century," *Journal of the Siam Society* 43.2 (1965): 181–190.   DAVID K. WYATT

ROMAN EMPIRE. Romans did not venture politically or militarily in Asia except in western parts, where they succeeded the Hellenistic Greeks. With major areas of Asia, particularly with India and China, their relations were indirect and based primarily on trade. Cicero's remark that "the credit of the Roman money market is intimately bound up with the prosperity of Asia" and Pliny's oft-quoted statement about Roman drainage of gold for spices and silk from the east and his lament that "so dearly we pay for our luxury and our women" cannot be ignored in any study of Roman relations with Asia. Sources such as Ptolemy's geography and the *Periplus of the Erythraean Sea* as well as Indian traditions, particularly from South India, and Chinese annals are supported by archaeological, epigraphic, and numismatic discoveries made particularly in India and Central Asia.

The heyday of Rome's dialogue with Asia took place in the first two or three centuries of the common era. Both land and sea routes were used, the former through the Central Asian steppes, now popularly known as the Silk Route, and the latter, taking advantage of the discovery by Hippalus with the help of Arab and Indian sailors of the monsoon winds, across the Arabian sea to the western and southern coasts of India and thence across the Bay of Bengal through the Isthmus of Kra to the China Sea. While the land routes were controlled by the Parthians and the Kushans, the passage through sea, although not free from pirates and natural hazards, was more independent.

Roman trade with China was so controlled by middlemen that while the Romans received considerable quantities of silk from China, the Roman items in China consist only of sporadic finds of coins and possibly glass and amber. On the other hand, *Periplus* gives a long list of commodities Rome imported from India, which included a variety of spices, precious stones, ivory, diamonds and sapphires, tortoise shell, cotton, muslin of all kinds, mallow cloth, and yarn, among other things. In return, Rome sent primarily large quantities of gold and silver coins, glass, deluxe pottery, copper, tin and lead, wine, singing boys, and beautiful maidens. Tamil poems of South India refer to the Yavanas, now a generic name for all Westerners, as coming laden with gold in their ships and returning with spices, and to Indian princes being exhorted to drink the cool and fragrant wines brought by them. *Silappadikaram* describes the warehouses and abodes of the Yavanas in the port of Kaveripattinam. Indian kings employed bodyguards of Western mercenaries and artisans.

The archaeological discoveries at Begram, Charsadda, Taxila, and Arikamedu and the large number of hoards of Roman coins found in India, and the discovery of an ivory statuette in Pompei and references of Indian embassies to Rome confirm the story of Indo-Roman trade relations. From all accounts it is clear that the balance of trade was in favor of India. Discovery of Roman objects of art and motifs on coins and seals in South Asia have lent suggestions about influences on art traditions and numismatic devices of South Asia in early centuries of the common era.

[*See also* Silk Route.]

Owen Lattimore and Eleanor Lattimore, *Silks, Spices and Empire* (1968). W. H. Schoff, *The Periplus of the Erythraean Sea* (1974). E. H. Warmington, *The Commerce between the Roman Empire and India* (2d ed., 1974). R. E. M. Wheeler, *Rome beyond the Imperial Frontiers* (1954).   A. K. NARAIN

ROMULO, CARLOS P.

ROMULO, CARLOS P. (1899–1986), distinguished Filipino writer in English, educator, and diplomat. Born in Manila, he received his B.A. from the University of the Philippines in 1918 and M.A. from Columbia University in 1921. One of his country's most successful public figures, Romulo served every Filipino president since Manuel L. Quezon.

In the 1930s Romulo engaged in press and radio work, and before the war in 1941 he won the Pulitzer Prize for a series of articles written on a trip through Asia. As General MacArthur's aide-de-camp in Bataan, Corregidor, and Australia, Romulo was at the invasion of Leyte and the liberation of Manila. After independence in 1946, he was a major factor in the evolution of Philippine foreign policy, especially with regard to the country's relations with the United States. He served successively as resident commissioner to the United States (1944–1946), ambassador to the United States (January 1952–May 1953; February 1954–September 1955 as personal envoy of President Magsaysay; September 1955–February 1962), and chief of the Philippine mission to the United Nations (1945–1954). He was also president of the fourth UN General Assembly (1949–1950) and president of the UN Security Council for two consecutive terms (1957). He was foreign affairs secretary under President Quirino (1950–1952). His final term as foreign minister began in 1969 and ended with his retirement in 1984.

Romulo was also an educator, at one time an associate professor of English at the University of the Philippines and a member of the university's Board of Regents (1931–1941). In 1962 he became the university's ninth president (until 1968) while also serving as the country's secretary of education. He has been credited with making the University of the Philippines the "best university for the Filipino" and a center of learning in Southeast Asia.

The one honor that was denied Romulo was the presidency of his country. He declined the vice presidency twice. On 21 June 1955, he cofounded the Democratic Party, which had seceded from the Liberal Party, and ran as its presidential candidate, only to withdraw in favor of Ramon Magsaysay. Romulo realized that he lacked political experience and was hardly known by the people; his prominence in public life had been achieved while he was abroad. He had to live down his image as a hopelessly pro-American Filipino before his country could take him seriously. In January 1984 he retired from public service at age eighty-five.

[*See also* Philippines *and* Magsaysay, Ramon.]

Adele Louise De Lieuw, *Carlos P. Romulo, The Barefoot Boy of Diplomacy* (1976). Carlos P. Romulo, *I Saw the Fall of the Philippines* (1942), *I Saw the Philippines Rise* (1946), and *I Walked With Heroes* (1961).

BERNARDITA REYES CHURCHILL

RONG HONG

RONG HONG (1828–1912), better known by the Cantonese rendering of his name as Yung Wing; the first Chinese graduate of an American university and one of China's earliest advocates of Western-style modernization. He was the primary force behind the Chinese Educational Mission of 1872 to 1881.

Born to a humble family in coastal Guangdong Province, Rong Hong received his early education from the pioneer Protestant missionaries in the nearby Portuguese enclave of Macao and later, after the "opening" of China in 1842, in British Hong Kong. In 1847, he was given the opportunity of continuing his Western studies in the United States, where he first attended Monson Academy in Massachusetts and then Yale University. He graduated from Yale in 1854.

On his return to China, Rong's ambition was, as he put it in his autobiography, "that the rising generation of China should enjoy the same educational advantages that I had enjoyed; that through Western education China might be regenerated, become enlightened and powerful" (1909, p. 41). At the same time, however, his thoroughly Western education had put him well out of the mainstream of Chinese official life. No one in authority in the 1850s showed any interest in him or his ideas.

In 1863, at the beginning of the Self-Strengthening Movement following the Second Opium War (1856–1860), Rong Hong finally came to the attention of the powerful official Zeng Guofan. As Zeng's expert in foreign matters, one of his first tasks was to buy machine-building equipment for the new Jiangnan arsenal near Shanghai. He later convinced Zeng that the arsenal should establish a technical school to train its own machinists rather than having to depend on foreign employees. It was not until 1870, however, that he was able to persuade Zeng Guofan and Zeng's junior colleague Li Hongzhang to set up the Chinese Educational Mission.

The aim of the mission, which was first implemented in 1872, was to send a group of 120 Chinese boys between twelve and fifteen years old to attend American schools for fifteen years, after which they would return to China and lead the country's modernization efforts. Rong Hong was appointed as one of the two joint heads of the mission, with its headquarters in Hartford, Connecticut. Unfortunately, the mission did not quite work out as he had hoped. Because of anxieties among conservative officials that the Chinese youths were becoming too westernized, Li Hongzhang in 1881 consented to the early termination of the project. All the boys, as well as Rong, who by then had also been appointed associate minister to the United States, were recalled to China.

Frustrated in his career as an official, Rong returned to Hartford in 1883 to be with his ailing American wife and, following her death, to raise their two sons. In 1895, after the shock of China's military defeat by Japan, he was summoned back to his homeland, but despite a more receptive intellectual climate than before, he was unable to gain official support for any of his reform proposals. He left China permanently in 1902 and retired to Hartford, where he died ten years later.

[See also Zeng Guofan; Li Hongzhang; and Qing Dynasty.]

Arthur W. Hummel, ed., *Eminent Chinese of the Ch'ing Period, 1644–1912*, 2 vols. (1943–1944), pp. 402–405. Thomas E. LaFargue, *China's First Hundred* (1942). Edmund H. Worthy, Jr., "Yung Wing in America," *Pacific Historical Review* 34 (1965): 265–287. Yung Wing (Rong Hong), *My Life in China and America* (1909).

EDWARD J. M. RHOADS

ROOT-TAKAHIRA AGREEMENT.

ROOT-TAKAHIRA AGREEMENT. Designed to relieve tensions in US-Japanese relations, the Root-Takahira Agreement was embodied in an exchange of diplomatic notes between the Japanese ambassador, Takahira Kogorō, and the US secretary of state, Elihu Root, on 30 November 1908.

Rivalry between the two nations was growing because both were then emerging as major actors in world affairs, and increasing friction was developing over their policies regarding China. In 1899 the US had enunciated its famous Open Door policy, which was designed to blunt domination of China by other powers, including Japan, and to safeguard American rights and privileges. Growing Japanese naval power, demonstrated in the destruction of the Russian fleet, also posed problems for American defense of the Philippine Islands.

By 1908 Japan had won wars against both China and Russia, gaining as a result a firm foothold in Korea (which it was to annex in 1910) and in Manchuria, still recognized as Chinese territory. The Japanese foothold on the continent threatened both China and the American rights and interests there. In the Root-Takahira Agreement the two powers agreed to encourage the free and peaceful development of their trade in the Pacific Ocean area, to maintain the status quo in the area and defend the principle of equal opportunity for trade and commerce in China (the "open door"), to respect each other's territorial possessions in the region, and to support the independence and integrity of China.

Raymond A. Esthus, *Theodore Roosevelt and Japan* (1966). A. Whitney Griswold, *The Far Eastern Policy of the United States* (1938). JOHN M. MAKI

ROXAS, MANUEL

ROXAS, MANUEL (1892–1948), first president of the Republic of the Philippines.

Manuel Roxas y Acuña was born in Capiz (now Roxas City) in the province of Panay and studied law at the University of the Philippines. He began his career in local politics, serving as governor of Capiz from 1919 to 1921, then was elected to the House of Representatives, where he served until 1933, for a time as Speaker of the House. Roxas served in the Philippine Constitutional Convention in 1934 and as a member of the National Assembly from 1935 to 1937. He became secretary of finance in the commonwealth government in 1938 and was elected to the Senate in 1941. Captured by the Japanese in 1942, Roxas was forced to support the Japanese-sponsored regime but covertly assisted the underground resistance. As president of the Senate at the end of the war, he was elected president of the Philippine Commonwealth and became the first president of the new republic on its independence, 4 July 1946. Roxas died while delivering a speech at the Clark Field US military base on 15 April 1948.

[See also Quezon, Manuel Luis and Osmeña, Sergio.]

Theodore Friend, *Between Two Empires: The Ordeal of the Philippines, 1929–1946* (1965). George E. Taylor, *The Philippines and the United States* (1964).

DAVID K. WYATT

ROY, MANABENDRA NATH

ROY, MANABENDRA NATH (1887–1954), a leading spokesman on India in the Third Communist International until he was purged by Stalin in the late 1920s; he then returned to India and became an important figure in the political and intellectual activity of the country until his death.

Born Narendra Nath Bhattacharya in a village in West Bengal, he joined the revolutionary movement while young. He was sent to meet German officials in Batavia in 1915; they promised to supply arms for an Indian revolution. When these plots fell through, he traveled through East Asia to the United States. Here he took the name M. N. Roy and, while on bail, fled to Mexico, where he met Michael Borodin, who helped convert him to communism and invited him to Moscow. He reached the Soviet Union in 1919 and worked with the Comintern to try to organize communists in India, although he remained abroad. He wrote one of the first Marxist analyses of India, *India in Transition* (1922); this work, along with his other writings, was smuggled into India.

After an unsuccessful trip to China in 1927 Roy was purged and fled to Western Europe. In 1930 he secretly returned to India, but was caught and imprisoned for six years. Upon his release, he joined the Congress, but broke with it on the issue of the war and formed the Radical Democratic Party. This party fared badly in the 1946 elections and he disbanded it and led the Radical Humanist movement until his death. He was a prolific and influential writer.

[*See also* Communism: Communist Parties in South Asia.]

G. Adhikari, ed., *Documents of the History of the Communist Party of India,* 2 vols. (1971–1974). John Patrick Haithcox, *Communism and Nationalism in India: M. N. Roy and Comintern Policy, 1920–1939* (1971). M. N. Roy, *M. N. Roy's Memoirs* (1964).

LEONARD A. GORDON

ROY, RAMMOHAN

ROY, RAMMOHAN (1772–1833), Indian social and religious reformer. Rammohan Roy is revered in the historiography of the Bengal or Indian Renaissance as the father of modern India. According to the standard accounts, Roy, while still a youth and without formal education, mastered Arabic, Persian, Sanskrit, and Hebrew in order to read the major sacred texts in their original languages. He then traveled extensively through South Asia in quest of spiritual truth. He learned English at age twenty-two while employed by the East India Company, and he finally settled in Calcutta in 1815.

In 1815 Roy openly declared his intention of leading a reformation of Hindu society and religion. He began to publish new versions of ancient texts, such as the Vedanta, intending to challenge the errors and misconceptions of Brahmanical orthodoxy. He also sought to historicize the pre-Muslim past, building on the scholarship of British orientalism. In the process, he rediscovered a Hindu golden age (1500–600 BCE), when there was no burning of widows, no Kulin polygamy, no child marriage, no caste rigidity, no purdah, and no restrictions on eating meat. In 1815, he institutionalized his initiatives with the founding of the Atmiya Sabha, or "society of friends," which in 1823 became the Calcutta Unitarian Committee and in 1828 the Brahmo Sabha, or "society for the worship of the one true god." It was from the latter society that Debendranath Tagore drew his inspiration for establishing in 1843 the famed Hindu reform community and movement known as the Brahmo Samaj.

Perhaps no other Indian has come so close to meaning all things to all men as has Roy. Until he converted the Baptist William Adam ("the second fallen Adam") to Unitarianism, Roy was a favorite of missionaries, who were convinced he would become the Luther of India. Roy, considered a Benthamite by some, died in the home of an English Unitarian in 1833, just before his intended trip to the United States to meet William Ellery Channing, the American Unitarian. Muslims and Hindu Saktos have prepared convincing arguments to prove that Roy's original inspiration for Hindu reform came from their traditions. A case has been made that Roy authored the *Mahanirvana Tantra* and that his compassion for women, the cornerstone of his social reform program, was derived from Tantrism. Even Naxalites, who have repudiated most of the Bengal Renaissance heroes as tools of British imperialism, have found in Roy's writings the seeds of their own revolutionary struggle against the tyranny of the Indian bourgeoisie.

Although recent disclosures have shown a certain disparity between word and deed, Roy's charisma has diminished very little. His continued popularity may be explained by the readiness with which his vision of a regenerated India became a model for subsequent generations of Hindu modernizers. He neither defended the defects of quotidian Hinduism nor accepted westernization as a viable alternative for India's future. He advocated a syncretism between new techniques and ideas from the West and revitalized Hindu institutions and practices.

[*See also* Brahmo Samaj.]

Brajendra Nath Bandyopadhyay, *Rammohun Roy* (1942). S. C. Chakrabarti, ed., *Father of Modern India Commemoration Volume, 1933* (1935). V. C. Joshi, ed.,

Rammohun Roy and the Process of Modernization in India (1975). Rammohun Roy, *The Man and His Work*, edited by A. Home (1933).   DAVID KOPF

RUAN YUAN (1764–1849), Chinese scholar and official. A native of Yizheng in Yangzhou Prefecture, Jiangsu Province, Ruan was born into a family of modest means with both a military and merchant background. He received broad training from distinguished local scholars and advanced rapidly through the civil service examinations to appointment in the Hanlin Academy in 1789. A decade later, Ruan began a life-long career as a leading provincial official serving in the southern provinces, where he directed primary attention to problems of internal security and control. As a reform-minded official, Ruan circumspectly proposed modifications within the existing institutional framework. An avowed eclectic, he advanced the latest trends in *kaozheng* scholarship.

[*See also* Kaozheng Xue; Neo-Confucianism; *and* Qing Dynasty.]

Wei Peh T'i, "Internal Security and Coastal Control: Juan Yuan and Pirate Suppression in Chekiang, 1799–1809," in *Ch'ing-shih wen-t'i* 4.2 (December 1979): 83–112.   JUDITH A. WHITBECK

RUDAKI (d. 940/941), Abu Abd Allah Ja'far ibn Muhammad, Persian musician, singer, and above all poet, considered the father of Persian poetry. Next to nothing is known of his early life. Born in Rudak near Samarkand, he presumably received the customary education of the time, reportedly having memorized the Qur'an by the age of eight. His music and poetry eventually led him to the cultured court of the Samanid *amir* Nasr ibn Ahmad and brought him the kind of fame and fortune that became proverbial among later poets. The vizier Bal'ami considered him peerless among both Arabs and Persians. A well-known story recorded by Nizami Arudi illustrates the profound effect of his poetry and music on the *amir,* who showered him with gifts, as did his nobles. Rudaki was blind, but it is not known whether he had been born as such; it is improbable that he had been blinded after having fallen from favor, as has been suggested. His alleged Isma'ili sympathy is also a matter of speculation.

A tremendous output of poetry is credited to Rudaki, although only two complete *qasidas* (panegyrics) and a few fragments and lines, totaling fewer than one thousand lines, are extant. His versified

Kalila wa Dimna is also lost. In one report Rudaki is credited with the invention of the *ruba'i* (quatrain) form.

[*See also* Persian Literature.]

E. G. Browne, *A Literary History of Persia* (1928), vol. 1, pp. 355–356, 455–458. "Rudaki," in *The Encyclopaedia of Islam* (old ed., 1913–1938). J. Rypka, *History of Iranian Literature* (1968), pp. 144–145.

MANOUCHEHR KASHEFF

RUIJIN, Chinese city, the county seat of Ruijin County, southeastern Jiangxi Province. It is notable historically as the capital of the Chinese Communists' Central Soviet Government from 7 November 1931, when the First National Congress of the Chinese Soviet Republic was convened there, until 10 November 1934, when it was taken by National Government troops. Prior to its fall most Communist administrative personnel and troops had abandoned the town and embarked on the famous Long March.

James P. Harrison, *The Long March to Power: A History of the Chinese Communist Party, 1921–1972* (1972). John Rue, *Mao Tse-tung in Opposition, 1927–1935* (1966).   PETER J. SEYBOLT

RULIN WAISHI, Chinese novel in fifty-five chapters by Wu Jingzi (1701–1754), completed 1750. In the work, commonly translated as *The Scholars,* members of the literati class are depicted in their pursuit of wealth, fame, and position. Spanning a hundred years in the Ming dynasty (with an introductory Yuan-dynasty episode), the plot episodes are brief, tenuously linked, and mostly satiric. The longest plot segment concerns a group of good scholars at Nanjing who build and dedicate a temple. Partially autobiographical and containing some sharp portraits of contemporaries, *Rulin waishi* has been much admired for its stylish prose.

[*See also* Chinese Literature.]

H. C. Chang, *Chinese Literature: Popular Fiction and Drama* (1973), pp. 329–381. Wu Jingzi, *The Scholars,* translated by Yang Hsien-yi and Gladys Yang (1957).

SHAN CHOU

RUPEE (from Sanskrit, *rupya,* "wrought silver"), the basic monetary unit of India, Pakistan, Nepal, Sri Lanka, Bhutan, Mauritius, and the Seychelles. The rupee was formally introduced as standard currency by Sher Shah in 1542 on the basis of silver coinage that dated to at least the thirteenth century. In the 1830s the British restandardized the weight to 180 grains and the silver content to 165 grains. Fluctuations in the ratio of the rupee to the British pound occasioned frequent nationalist protest in India.

B. R. Ambedkar, *History of Indian Currency and Banking* (1947). *Hobson-Jobson: A Glossary of Colloquial Anglo-Indian Words and Phrases,* edited by Henry Yule and A. C. Burnell (1903; reprint, 1968).

HOWARD SPODECK

RUSSO-JAPANESE WAR. Vexed by Russia's expansion into the Liaodong Peninsula after the humiliating Triple Intervention of 1895, challenged by Russian troops in Manchuria even after suppression of the Boxers in China, and denied recognition of its claim to exclusive rights in Korea, Japan spent a decade on countermeasures: application of its Chinese war indemnity to ground and naval build-up, consummation of a defensive alliance with England, and direct negotiations with Russia. When diplomacy foundered in early 1904 Japanese hard-liners prevailed and Tokyo opted for hostilities. Control of the sea lanes to the continent was prerequisite. Japan broke off its diplomatic relations with Russia on 6 February and then struck by surprise on 8 February, when Japanese destroyers mauled the Russian squadron at Port Arthur (Chinese, Lüshun; Japanese, Ryojun). Both parties declared war on 10 February.

The Imperial General Headquarters was established at the Imperial Palace in Tokyo. General Kuroki Tamemoto's First Army landed in Korea, easily pressed north, brilliantly defeated the Russians at the Yalu River (30 April–1 May), at a cost of 1,000 men (as opposed to 2,700 Russians), and crossed the river into Manchuria. To encircle and eliminate Russian naval and military power in Liaodong, Nozu Michitsura's Fourth Army debarked west of the Yalu in May; Oku Yasukata's Second Army was placed northeast of Port Arthur. After fierce fighting Oku took Nanshan Hill in late May, allowing entry into the fine Liaodong commercial port of Dalian (Japanese, Dairen; Russian, Dalny). Nogi Maresuke could now bring in his Third Army to besiege the formidable defensive complex at Port Arthur, just south of Dalian. Blockaded by sea and stormed by land, the fortress finally capitulated on 2 January 1905.

Meanwhile, Marshal Ōyama Iwao, commander in chief of the Manchuria Army, ably seconded by General Kodama Gentarō, deployed three field armies, numbering 125,000 men, in positions enveloping Liaoyang (200 miles north of Port Arthur), which was defended by 158,000 Russians under General Alexei Kuropatkin. After ten days of stiff fighting, the Russians abandoned Liaoyang, although they lost fewer men than the Japanese (18,000 Russians to 23,600 Japanese). Enfeebled by casualties and low on ammunition, Ōyama could not exploit the Russian retreat, capably conducted by Kuropatkin. Both sides having received reinforcements, a second major battle was fought at the Sha He (5–17 October), pitting between 131,000 and 170,000 Japanese against between 200,000 and 232,000 Russians. At a cost of 21,000 men, the Japanese inflicted twice as many casualties. Both sides then entered winter quarters. Kuropatkin, however, wanted to defeat Ōyama before Nogi could arrive. In late January 1905, 300,000 Russian troops attacked Ōyama's 220,000 men in confused fighting in the snow at Heikoutai-Sandepu. Failing to achieve their objectives, the Russian recoiled toward Mukden (Shenyang).

Now Ōyama wanted success before massive Russian reinforcements from Europe arrived. Incorporating Nogi's Third Army and Kawamura Kageaki's Army of the Yalu, Ōyama launched a preemptive offensive in late February along a broad front at Mukden, generating the largest military engagement in history to that date: 207,000 Japanese (with 992 artillery pieces) versus 291,000 Russians (with 1,219 artillery pieces). In hard-fought combat, 75,000 Japanese fell, while the Russians lost 69,000 dead and wounded, 22,000 prisoners, and mountains of ordnance. On 10 March Kuropatkin fell back toward Harbin; he soon was replaced by N. P. Linievitch. The Japanese were too spent to inflict a mortal blow. Although no major ground combat followed, on 27 and 28 May Admiral Tōgō Heihachirō shattered Z. P. Rozhdestvenski's motley flotilla, sent around the world from the Baltic, in the senseless battle of Tsushima Straits.

Both countries were now ready to talk, the Russians being nudged by Japanese seizure of Sakhalin Island in July and by revolutionary disturbances. Renewal and strengthening of the invaluable English alliance bolstered Japan's hand. President Theodore Roosevelt mediated the consequent Portsmouth Treaty (5 September 1905), under the terms of which Russia recognized Japan's paramountcy in Korea, transferred Liaodong's lease (including Da-

FIGURE 1. *Rock Garden at Ryōanji.* The Zen garden at Ryōanji, dating from the late Muromachi period, is one of the best known in Japan.

lian and Port Arthur) and the South Manchurian Railway and other economic interests, ceded southern Sakhalin (Karafuto), and yielded fishing rights. These terms mirrored the impressive Japanese victory but, poisoning Japanese relations with the honest broker, the United States, provision emerged for indemnity by Russia—a source of frustration for a country whose coffers were bare after expending 1.5 billion yen. At the human cost of 90,000 dead (from mobilized forces exceeding one million men), Japan was catapulted into the prestigious club of imperialistic powers. As a result of their generally unexpected triumph over a major European country, the Japanese exerted enormous influence on colonial peoples, although they ruthlessly quelled nationalism burgeoning among Asians within their own orbit. Tapping wellsprings of patriotism and fealty, the victorious Japanese army and navy laid groundwork for aggression abroad and ascendancy at home for the next four decades.

[*See also* Tsushima Straits, Battle of; Port Arthur; Anglo-Japanese Alliance; *and* Portsmouth, Treaty of. *For the extent of Japan's acquisitions resulting from this war, see the map accompanying* Meiji Period.]

Shumpei Okamoto, *The Japanese Oligarchy and the Russo-Japanese War* (1970). Denis Warner and Peggy Warner, *The Tide at Sunrise: A History of the Russo-Japanese War, 1904–1905* (1974).   ALVIN D. COOX

RYŌANJI, Zen temple in Kyoto, Japan, belonging to the Myōshinji branch of Rinzai Zen Buddhism, built in 1450. Ryōanji attracted the patronage of the Hosakawa family, who founded it, and Toyotomi Hideyoshi and Tokugawa Ieyasu. In modern times it is renowned chiefly for its rock and sand garden, consisting of fifteen rocks of varying sizes, arranged in a bed of white sand that is raked daily. The garden is credited to the artist Sōami (d. 1525), and interpretations of its meaning are varied.

[*See also* Kyoto.]

Stanley Weinstein, "Ryōanji," in *Encyclopedia of Japan* (1983), vol. 6, p. 347.   MARIUS B. JANSEN

S

SAADABAD PACT. The Saadabad Pact, signed on 8 July 1937 in Tehran between Iran, Turkey, Iraq, and Afghanistan, was a treaty of nonaggression that included provisions for regular meetings of the powers involved, nonintervention in internal affairs, respect for the inviolability of their common frontiers, and consultation. The treaty falls within the broader foreign policy framework of Reza Shah Pahlavi of Iran aimed at securing friendly regional alliances to be manipulated in case of domestic or foreign turmoil. Clause VII, which provided for the banning of subversive organizations in any of the states that could pose a threat to the government either of that state or of any of the other signatories, was generally regarded as a mutual promise to hinder communist activity in the signatory states.

[*See also* Pahlavi, Reza.]

G. Lenczowski, ed., *Iran under the Pahlavis* (1978). R. Ramazani, *The Foreign Policy of Iran, 1500–1941* (1966).   NEGUIN YAVARI

SABAH, Malaysian state situated in the northeastern corner of Borneo. With an area of 29,000 square miles, Sabah has wide coastal plains that gradually rise into forested hills and interior mountain ranges dominated by Southeast Asia's highest peak, Mount Kinabalu (13,455 feet). Several major rivers, most notably the Kinabatangan, drain the watershed. Sabah's 1970 population of 633,000 included Kadazans (28 percent), Chinese (21 percent), Bajaus (12 percent), Muruts (5 percent), and others (32 percent); over a third of its inhabitants profess Islam.

Sabah's history must be viewed in the wider framework of archipelago history. Neolithic boat builders along the east coast were already involved in extensive interregional trade by the Iron Age (sixth-seventh century CE). Islam apparently first reached Sabah from the south in the 1400 or 1500s, followed by the imposition of Malayo-Muslim political control under Brunei auspices. Many coastal peoples embraced Islam, but the interior peoples largely retained their traditional religion until recent times. In the early 1700s Brunei transferred its claims over much of Sabah to the sultan of Sulu, but actual Sulu power remained chiefly limited to taxation except in the northeast. Occasional resistance to Brunei or Sulu influence, as well as extensive coastal raiding and confusion over suzerainty, invited Western interest in the area beginning in the eighteenth century. Despite short-lived American activity, British power proved most decisive. Britain had already acquired the offshore island of Labuan in 1846; in the 1860s it gained a toehold in Sabah proper when a British merchant founded an east-coast settlement at Sandakan on lease from Sulu. Sandakan soon became Sabah's leading town and the base for further British activity. By 1881 the British had obtained rights to much of Sabah and launched the North Borneo Chartered Company, which ruled Sabah as a British protectorate from 1881 to 1941. The company operated the state in the interest of its British shareholders but never really prospered because of its poor management and high overhead; its sixty years of rule, however, established the administrative, legal, political, and economic framework of modern Sabah.

The company employed many British officers with colonial experience and devoted scarce resources to establishing and maintaining control of the state, including co-opting indigenous elites and mounting bloody "pacification" campaigns against recalcitrant subjects. Company policies generated considerable sociocultural change, including the establishment of Christian missions. Immigrant Chinese and Indonesians provided a plantation work force; later, Chinese merchants came to dominate the middle sectors of the economy. By 1939 Sabah's population had reached 277,000. Many non-Muslims responded to change by joining millenarian or neo-traditional religious movements, while others turned to occasional violent resistance. The company concentrated on developing Sabah's economy for the benefit of its shareholders; hence British North Borneo came to possess a basically extractive economy rooted in Western-owned tobacco and rubber estates and forest exploitation. The company did create a single state out of many local societies, and some Sabahans living in or near towns were able to gain modern education. But it also employed divide-and-rule policies to keep the Chinese separate. Officials tolerated little political activity.

The Japanese occupation (1941–1945) brought an end to company dominance and proved a difficult experience; in 1943 the Japanese brutally crushed a Chinese-led rebellion. The liberation of Sabah by the Allies also proved costly, as bombs leveled the major towns. In 1946 Sabah became the crown colony of British North Borneo, with its capital moved from Sandakan to Jesselton (now Kota Kinabalu). The seventeen years of colonial rule succeeded in rebuilding and eventually expanding the economy. Rubber and timber provided the basis for postwar economic growth, which occurred under the control of a few powerful British, and later Chinese, companies. Health and education facilities only slowly permeated the areas outside the towns. But political consciousness began to spread, especially among the Kadazan, with the development of radio and newspapers. Political activity accelerated with the mooting of the Malaysia proposal by Malayan and British officials in 1961. Several communally based political parties appeared to represent the interests of the Kadazan, Muslim, and Chinese communities. The first popular elections were held in 1962 and 1963, with all major parties accepting the idea of independence through merger with Malaysia, a sentiment that increased after the Philippines claimed Sabah based on former Sulu suzerainty.

Between 1963 and 1967 the Kadazan-led government suffered from chronic tensions between coastal Muslim and interior non-Muslim interests. In the 1967 elections Tun Mustapha became chief minister at the head of a Muslim-Chinese coalition and proceeded to rule the state with an iron hand, co-opting or repressing opponents, promoting Islam, and establishing powerful, often corrupt, quasi-official institutions. Since then Sabah has developed at a furious pace, with the state using timber and mineral profits to fund development projects. In 1975, however, an increasingly unpopular and independent government was defeated in elections by a multi-ethnic, multireligious coalition, known as Berjaya, that was allied with the federal government. Berjaya continues to preside over a high rate of economic growth, purchased by the rapid exploitation of Sabah's bountiful natural resources. Although peninsular sociopolitical patterns increasingly influence the state, Sabah remains the child of a unique historical development.

Ian Black, *A Gambling Style of Government: The Establishment of Chartered Company Rule in Sabah, 1878–1915* (1983). Kay Kim Khoo, ed., *Sabah: History and Society* (1981). Edwin Lee, *The Towkays of Sabah* (1976). Margaret Roff, *The Politics of Belonging: Political Change in Sabah and Sarawak* (1974). K. G. Tregonning, *A History of Modern Sabah: North Borneo, 1881–1963* (1965).   CRAIG A. LOCKARD

SABUKTIGIN. *See* Sebuktigin, Abu Mansur.

SADHU, Sanskrit term meaning "straight, unerring," used in the *Mahabharata* to mean "well-born," or "righteous." The term now denotes a Hindu holy man or wandering ascetic.

USHA SANYAL

SA'DI (1209/1210–1291), pen name of Abu Muhammad Musharrif al-Din Muslih ibn Abd Allah Shirazi, one of the great poets of the world and truly the best and most multifaceted author in Persian literature. He is often referred to by his countrymen as Afsah al-Mutakallimin ("most eloquent of speakers"). He was born in Shiraz to a family of religious scholars and received his earliest education from his father. His father died while Sa'di was still very young, and he continued his education under the direction of his maternal grandfather. Sa'di might have continued his education in Shiraz, then a major center of learning, had not political turmoil in 1224, when the province of Fars was ravaged by the forces of the Khwarazmshah, forced him to leave his home town for further study at the Nizamiyya college of Baghdad. Sa'di's teachers at the Nizamiyya included Jamal al-Din Abu al-Faraj ibn Yahya al-Jauzi, a lecturer at the Mustansariyya college in Baghdad, to whom Sa'di refers in his *Gulistan*. During the years that Sa'di was studying in Baghdad, Iran was being severely ravaged by the Mongol hordes, who destroyed cities and massacred their populations. In about 1227, rather than going back

FIGURE 1. *Leaf from the Bustan of Sa'di.* Artist unknown; Buhera, Iran, c. 1525–1535. Illustration from the chapter "Yusuf and Zulaykha." 18.4 cm. × 11.7 cm.

The enormous respect and reputation that Sa'di enjoyed during his lifetime only increased after his death and is unmatched by any other poet in the Persian language. His own remark that his poetry was eagerly sought after like gold leaves is hardly an exaggeration. His contemporary, Amir Khusrau, a great poet in his own right, felt embarrassed that he dared to write poetry in Sa'di's age. His poetry was put to music in China only half a century after his death. His impact on later poetry has been tremendous, and his prose marked a turning point in Persian literary style. For centuries his *Bustan* and *Gulistan* have been the standard textbooks for serious students of Persian.

Sa'di's works (known as the *Kulliyyat*) include the *Sa'dinama,* or *Bustan (Orchard),* completed in 1257, in ten versified chapters; *Gulistan (Rose Garden),* an entertaining book on practical wisdom in rhymed prose (in the form of anecdotes) interspersed with short poems (it was called the "Bible of the Persians" by Emerson); *ghazals* (lyrics); *qasidas* (odes, a few in Arabic); satires; and a few short pieces in prose.

[See also Persian Literature *and* Shiraz.]

A. J. Arberry, *Shiraz, the Persian City of Saints and Poets* (1960), pp. 112–138. E. G. Browne, *A Literary History of Persia* (1928), vol. 2, pp. 525–543. J. Rypka, *History of Iranian Literature* (1968), pp. 250–255. G. M. Wickens, trans., *Morals Pointed and Tales Adorned: The Bustān of Sa'dī* (1974). John D. Yohannan, *Persian Poetry in England and America: A Two Hundred Year History* (1977).   MANOUCHEHR KASHEFF

to Shiraz, Sa'di embarked on a traveling adventure in the Middle East, visiting scholars, theologians, Sufi shaikhs, and other distinguished figures of the time. He made several pilgrimages to Mecca (fourteen by one account) and, if a story in his *Gulistan* is to be taken as true, was taken captive by the Crusaders in Tripoli. The stories of his visits to India and Central Asia are most probably fictitious. In 1257 he was back in Shiraz, which, under the wise administration of the Salghurid *atabegs,* had managed to escape unscathed the destruction brought by the Mongols to the other parts of Iran. He became attached to the court of Atabeg Abu Bakr ibn Sa'd and his son Sa'd; except for another pilgrimage to Mecca Sa'di spent the remaining years of his life in peace in Shiraz, enjoying the great honor and esteem that he deservedly received as a sage and great poet from kings, noblemen, and commoners alike. He died in Shiraz and was buried to the east of the modern town, where his mausoleum, the Sa'diyya, now stands.

SAFAVI, the name given by Shaikh Safi al-Din Ishaq to a Sufi order *(tariqa)* located in the province of Gilan in northern Persia. The order was known as the Zahidiyya up to the year 1301, when Shaikh Safi became its head. Shaikh Safi transformed what had been a Sufi order of purely local significance into a religious movement whose influence was felt throughout Persia, Syria, and Asia Minor.

The Persia of Shaikh Safi's time was under the rule of the Mongol Ilkhans. Under Shaikh Safi's son and successor, Sadr al-Din (d. 1391/1392), the Safavid *da'wa,* or religious propaganda, was said to have made converts among the Mongol military commanders. Sadr al-Din selected the town of Ardabil in eastern Azerbaijan as the new headquarters of the order, and from this center lieutenants of the shaikh, known as *khalifas,* carried out proselytizing missions in eastern Anatolia, northern Syria and Iraq, the Armenian highlands, and in Persia itself.

This network of adherents to the order was controlled by an official known as *khalifat al-khulafa;* his office has been called by Vladimir Minorsky the "special secretariat for Sufi affairs."

The early shaikhs of the order were Sunni Muslims, but at some point, probably when Khwaja Ali was its head (1391/1392–1427), Ithna Ashari (Twelver) Shi'ite tendencies became apparent, and, under Junaid (1447–1460), the order became an openly militant movement aiming at temporal power. This aspiration brought the order into conflict with the political rulers of the day, and three successive leaders of the order were killed in battle (Junaid in 1460, Haidar in 1488, and Ali in 1494). Yet the order survived. Three factors enabled it to do so: (1) its tightly knit organization, compared by Minorsky to the single-party organization of a modern totalitarian state; (2) the military prowess of the disciples of the order, drawn largely from the Turkish tribes living in areas affected by Safavid propaganda; and (3) the fanatical devotion of these disciples to their leader (commented on with astonishment by contemporary Italian merchants visiting Persia). This devotion stemmed from the belief that their leader possessed quasi-divine powers or was even a manifestation of God incarnate. In 1501 the Safavi order achieved its goal of political power when its leader, Isma'il, became shah of Persia and established the new Safavid dynasty.

[*See also* Isma'il I *and* Safavid Dynasty.]

Vladimir Minorsky, *Tadhkirat al-mulūk* (1943). Roger M. Savory, *Iran under the Safavids* (1980).

ROGER M. SAVORY

SAFAVID DYNASTY,

SAFAVID DYNASTY, rulers of Iran (Persia) effectively from 1501 to 1722 and, through two *rois fainéants,* to 1736. The first king of this dynasty, Shah Isma'il I, came to power in 1501. His accession marked the culmination of two hundred years of preparation, initially by means of quiet propaganda on behalf of the Safavid family, ultimately through revolutionary activity. After the establishment of the Safavid state, its rulers deliberately tampered with historical evidence that showed that the early Safavid leaders were Sunnis, and consequently the origins of the family remain obscure.

It seems certain that Isma'il's ancestors were of native Iranian stock and probably hailed from Kurdistan, although some scholars have claimed that he was a Turk. It is true that Isma'il, and most if not all of his successors, spoke Azeri, the dialect of Turkish used in Azerbaijan, but this was necessitated by the fact that the vast majority of their supporters, both during the revolutionary phase of the Safavi movement and during the formative period of the Safavid state, were Turkmen tribesmen from eastern Anatolia, the Armenian highlands, and northern Syria and Iraq, who became known as Kizilbash ("red heads") because of their distinctive headgear commemorating the twelve Ithna Ashari Shi'ite imams.

Theocratic State under Isma'il I (1501–1524). At the time of his accession, Isma'il was master only of the province of Azerbaijan in northwestern Persia. During the first decade of his reign, Safavid power was consolidated throughout the rest of Persia. This process culminated with the withdrawal of the Uzbeks from the important northeastern frontier province of Khurasan following their defeat in a great battle outside Merv on 22 November 1510. Isma'il also extended Safavid sovereignty over two regions outside Persia proper: the province of Diyar Bakr (corresponding today to northern Iraq), and the principality of Shirvan in the southern Caucasus, an area in which both his grandfather and great-grandfather had met their end in battle.

Isma'il attempted to find solutions to a number of urgent problems that faced him at his accession. Both he and his successors devised short-term solutions, but their failure to solve them permanently played its part in the eventual decline and fall of the dynasty. In 1501 Isma'il I promulgated the Ithna Ashari form of Islam, which had been espoused by supporters of the Safavids during the fifteenth century, as the official religion of the newly established Safavid state. This decision, taken primarily for political reasons, was designed to create a sense of national identity among his subjects and to differentiate his realm from that of the Sunni Ottoman empire. Many Persians had adopted the Ithna Ashari form of Islam in early Islamic times as a form of protest against political and social domination by their Arab conquerors. In 1258 the caliphate, the symbol of the unity of the Islamic world and of the dominance of that world by the Sunni form of Islam, was destroyed by the Mongols as they swept through the region. Thereafter, Shi'ism steadily increased its influence and power in Persia and elsewhere, often using Sufi orders (*tariqas*) as a vehicle for its propaganda.

Unfortunately, Isma'il's decision institutionalized another problem that has remained unsolved to this day, namely, the problem of government in such a state. According to Ithna Ashari political theory, the

SAFAVID IRAN, 1501-1722

only legitimate ruler of an Ithna Ashari Shi'ite state is the twelfth imam, known as the Hidden Imam or the Mahdi. Since 940, when Ithna Ashari Shi'ites ceased to hope for the imminent return to earth of the Mahdi, and the period of the "Greater Occultation" began, they have accepted the claim of the *mujtahids* (leading scholars in religious jurisprudence and theology) to act as the representatives on earth of the Mahdi. Isma'il's decision thus made inevitable a struggle for power between the *mujtahids,* endowed with the aura of infallibility of the imams and aspiring to establish theocratic government, and the shahs, representing secular government.

The Safavid shahs attempted to defuse this potentially explosive situation by claiming that they, and not the *mujtahids,* were the legitimate representatives on earth of the Mahdi. This claim, based on a spurious genealogy linking the Safavid family with the seventh imam, was largely accepted by the common people but not, of course, by the religious classes. In effect, Isma'il preempted the role claimed by the *mujtahids* by himself establishing a theocratic state. He attempted to secure political control over the religious classes by appointing as their head an official termed the *sadr,* who was answerable to himself for their good behavior. Isma'il's aura of infallibility and invincibility was shattered by the crushing defeat inflicted on him by the Ottomans at the battle of Chaldiran on 23 August 1514. Henceforth, the shahs were able to stave off the challenge to their authority from the *mujtahids* only if they were strong and effective rulers.

A second problem that faced Isma'il was how to incorporate the revolutionary organization of the Safavi *tariqa* into the fabric of the state. Isma'il tried to solve the problem by creating the office of *vakil-i nafs-i nafis-i humayun*. This officer was to act as the shah's vicegerent in both temporal and spiritual matters, and his office was intended to constitute an umbrella under which the *khalifat al-khulafa*, the head of the Sufi order, could find shelter. The latter, however, resented the diminution of his authority implicit in the creation of the office of *vakil*, and he and his successors remained a thorn in the flesh of the shahs at least until the time of Abbas I. Isma'il also hoped that the *vakil* would act as a bridge between the two rival ethnic groups in the early Safavid state: the Turkish military elite and the Persian bureaucratic and religious classes. This idea also failed. If a Kizilbash chief was *vakil*, he became too powerful; if the office was held by a Persian, the jealousy of the Kizilbash was such that on several occasions they assassinated a Persian *vakil*.

Domestic Dissensions and External Threats (1524–1588).

Tahmasp was only ten and a half years of age when he succeeded his father Isma'il as shah. This gave the Kizilbash chiefs, no longer constrained by their mystical loyalty to a semidivine leader, the opportunity to challenge the shah's authority in a turbulent manner reminiscent of the behavior of the barons of medieval England. For the first ten years of Tahmasp's reign, power was taken away from him by successive groups of Kizilbash chiefs. In 1533 a group of seditious Kizilbash had the temerity to pursue their private quarrel into the shah's apartments, and an arrow shot by one of them struck the shah's hat. Tahmasp managed to quell the mutiny and assert his authority as ruler. Between 1533 and 1574, when the serious illness of Tahmasp prompted a recrudescence of factionalism, the shah walked a precarious tightrope between the various internal factions. Despite Kizilbash disloyalty, and the treachery of two of his own brothers, he succeeded in holding the state together but was not able to keep inviolate its boundaries. Between 1524 and 1538 the Uzbeks launched five major attacks on Khurasan. Between 1533 and 1553 Sulaiman the Magnificent, the greatest of the Ottoman sultans, made four large-scale invasions of Persia. Baghdad was recaptured by the Ottomans. Tabriz, the Safavid capital, was occupied on several occa-

sions, and Tahmasp transferred his capital to Qazvin, a city farther from the Ottoman frontier. Tahmasp has not been given sufficient credit for the way in which, with numerically far inferior forces, he kept these powerful enemies at bay. In 1555 he negotiated with the Ottomans the Treaty of Amasya, which was not totally unfavorable to Persia, and gave it a much-needed respite from war for more than thirty years.

Between 1540 and 1553 Tahmasp waged four campaigns in the southern Caucasus against the "infidel" Georgian, Circassian, and Armenian populations of that region. From the last of these campaigns, thirty thousand prisoners were brought back to Persia, but it is not clear whether Tahmasp intended to use these new ethnic elements to offset the power of the Kizilbash in the formal, institutionalized manner later devised by Abbas I.

When the illness of Tahmasp in 1574 led to a further struggle for power, the new "third force" in the state, the Georgians, Circassians, and Armenians, made its presence felt for the first time. Those Georgian and Circassian women in the royal harem who were mothers of princes engaged in constant intrigue, assisted by ambitious bureaucrats and members of the royal household, in order to secure the throne for their favorite son. The Kizilbash awoke rather belatedly to the realization that their hitherto dominant position in the state was threatened. Their problem was that only two of Tahmasp's nine sons were the offspring of Turkmen mothers, and one of these, Muhammad Khudabanda, was purblind and was initially considered ineligible for kingship.

Following the death of Tahmasp in 1576, the Kizilbash, in order to block the accession of a Caucasian candidate, were thus obliged to place on the throne as Shah Isma'il II the only remaining Turkmen candidate. It soon became clear that Isma'il II's mind had been impaired by nearly twenty years of incarceration in the fortress-prison of Qahqaha, and his brief and bloody reign was terminated by his assassination by the Kizilbash in November 1577. The Kizilbash now had no alternative but to put on the throne Isma'il's elder brother Muhammad Khudabanda. Subject to the physical disability already mentioned, and of a mild and scholarly disposition, Sultan Muhammad Shah, as he was styled, was a puppet in the hands of two ambitious and ruthless women: his own wife, Mahd-i Ulya, and his sister Pari Khan Khanum, who had assisted the assassins in murdering his younger brother Isma'il II. Mahd-i Ulya had her rival, Pari Khan Khanum, strangled; she then directed the affairs of state for eighteen months until she, too, was murdered by the Kizilbash because she had, in their view, acted contrary to the considered opinions of the Kizilbash elders, and had constantly attempted to humiliate them by giving appointments to Persians. A turbulent period followed the assassination of Mahd-i Ulya, and the Ottomans seized the opportunity to occupy Tabriz in 1585. In 1588, a Kizilbash coup d'état deposed Sultan Muhammad Shah and placed his son, Abbas, on the throne.

The Safavid Empire under Shah Abbas I (1588–1629). Abbas I did not come to the throne at an auspicious moment in the history of the Safavid state. Rent by Kizilbash factionalism, it appeared to be powerless before the attacks of its traditional enemies, the Ottomans and the Uzbeks. However, Abbas approached his task with strength and determination. In order to free his hands to deal with pressing internal problems of restoring law and order and the machinery of government, Abbas signed with the Ottomans in 1589–1590 a peace treaty that ceded to them large areas of Ottoman-occupied Persian territory. Among Abbas's achievements were the creation of a standing army, of which regiments drawn from "third force" elements formed a conspicuous part, and the sequestration to the crown of a number of provinces formerly under the jurisdiction of Kizilbash military governors. The provinces thus sequestered were placed under the administration of royal intendants, and their revenues were remitted to the royal treasury to pay for the new standing army. Abbas also opened the highest offices of the state to "third force" elements by means of a training system designed especially for them, and he reorganized the administrative system in ways designed to effect a greater degree of centralization; he was responsible for the development of diplomatic and commercial relations with the West and the fostering of a climate of religious tolerance that encouraged Armenian and Jewish merchants to trade freely, a policy that in turn increased the economic prosperity of the country. During his reign arts and crafts were patronized on a large scale, and a new capital at Isfahan remarkable for its beauty and imaginative planning was created; roads and bridges were constructed and improved, and caravansaries were built along the main highways for the benefit of the wayfarer. The considered opinion of the shrewd Huguenot jeweler Chardin, who spent much time in Persia in the seventeenth century, was that, "When this great prince ceased to live, Persia ceased to prosper!"

The Decline and Fall of the Safavid Dynasty. The decline of Safavid fortunes indeed begins with the reign of Abbas's successor, his grandson Shah Safi. This decline, checked by Abbas II (1642–1666), began again and accelerated during the second half of the seventeenth century. Forty years ago, Vladimir Minorsky listed the basic causes of the decline of the Safavid dynasty: (1) the disappearance of the "basic theocratic nucleus" of the state and the failure to substitute for it "some other dynamic ideology"; (2) the antipathy between Turkish and Persian officers in the military command structure; (3) the practice of converting "state" into "crown" provinces, which solved the immediate problem of finding funds with which to pay the newly created standing army, but in the long term reduced the fighting efficiency of the army; (4) "the irresponsible character of the 'shadow government' represented by the harem, the Queen Mother and the eunuchs"; (5) "the degeneration of the dynasty whose scions were brought up in the atmosphere of the harem, in complete ignorance of the outside world." This analysis is still valid, but to it should be added (6) the breakdown of the concordat between the ruler and the religious leaders. As noted earlier, the latter regarded any form of secular government as illegitimate, but, since they had benefited from the promulgation of Ithna Ashari Shi'ism as the official religion of the Safavid state, they had tolerated, though grudgingly, the rule of strong Safavid kings. Weak kings, however, gave them the opportunity to increase their power, and an important feature of the last half-century of Safavid rule is the greatly enhanced authority of the religious classes, as they freed themselves progressively from political control. Ithna Ashari Shi'ism was formulated in ever more dogmatic terms by powerful theologians, whose religious bigotry eroded the multicultural society developed by Abbas I.

The military weakness of the state was dramatically demonstrated in 1699 and again in 1709, when marauding bands of Baluchi and Afghan tribesmen, respectively, penetrated deep into southeastern Persia. The Afghans were not the only neighbors of Persia to sense that the collapse of the Safavid state was near. In 1715 a Russian ambassador reported to Tsar Peter the Great that the Persian army was so demoralized and inefficient that the country could easily be conquered by a small Russian army. In 1721 the Afghan chief Mahmud invaded Persia, reaching Isfahan, the Safavid capital. After defeating a Persian army outside Isfahan on 8 March 1722, he laid siege to the city and starved it into surrender on 12 October; at least eighty thousand people are said to have perished from starvation and disease. Mahmud assumed the throne of Persia, and he and his cousin and successor Ashraf controlled central and southern Persia until 1729. The last substantive Safavid shah, Sultan Husain, was put to death by Ashraf in 1726. One of the shah's sons, Tahmasp, who was as weak and ineffectual as his father, escaped to Qazvin, the former Safavid capital, where he proclaimed himself Shah Tahmasp II.

Effective resistance to the Afghans, however, was organized by a Kizilbash chief, Nadir Khan Afshar, who offered his services to Tahmasp II. Together they drove the Afghans out of Isfahan in November 1729, and shortly afterwards from Persian territory. Nadir Khan placed Tahmasp II on the throne but was himself the de facto ruler. In 1732, in order to increase his power still further, he deposed Tahmasp II in favor of the latter's infant son, who was crowned as Abbas III. Finally, on 8 March 1736, Nadir Khan abandoned the fiction of Safavid rule and installed himself on the throne as Nadir Shah, the first ruler of the new Afsharid dynasty. Although the Safavid state no longer existed as a political reality, the mystique that had surrounded its shahs and its institutions was so strong that Safavid pretenders continued to appear until 1773.

[See also Abbas I; Afsharid Dynasty; Isfahan; Isma'il I; Ithna Ashari; Kizilbash; Mujtahid; Nadir; Safavi; and Shi'a.]

Marshall G. S. Hodgson, *The Venture of Islam*, 3 vols. (1974), vol. 3, pp. 16–58. Laurence Lockhart, *The Fall of the Safavi Dynasty and the Afghan Occupation of Persia* (1958). Vladimir Minorsky, *Tadhkirat al-Mulūk* (1943). Roger Savory, *Iran under the Safavids* (1980).

ROGER M. SAVORY

SAFDAR JANG (1708–1754), second nawab, or ruler, of the North Indian state of Awadh (Oudh) from 1739 until his death. Nephew, son-in-law, and successor to Sa'adat Khan, and like him an immigrant from Nishapur, he expanded his territory in the Ganges River valley while retaining as much power as possible within the declining Mughal empire. He fought a civil war in and around Delhi in 1753 over the control of imperial offices, which by then were virtually powerless but invested with residual authority throughout India. Although his reign marks the emergence of Awadh as an autonomous successor state, his tomb, a splendid example of late Mughal architecture, stands in what is now New Delhi.

[See also Delhi; Awadh; and Mughal Empire.]

Z. U. Malik, *The Reign of Muhammad Shah, 1719–1748* (1977). A. L. Srivastava, *The First Two Nawabs of Awadh* (2d ed., 1954).   RICHARD B. BARNETT

SAFFARID DYNASTY. The Saffarids were a significant power in the Islamic world for only half a century (867–911), but they existed as a minor dynasty in the province of Sistan (essentially the Helmand River valley in Iran and Afghanistan) until the fifteenth century. The dynasty was founded by a military adventurer named Ya'qub ibn Laith. Ya'qub was of common origin, by profession a *saffar,* or coppersmith, from which term the name of the dynasty was derived. He began his career as a member of a band of *ayyar* operating near the town of Bust. The *ayyar* were at best a kind of popular militia that enforced some semblance of order during times of political weakness and protected local interests against outside powers; at worst, they were little more than brigands. In any event, Ya'qub managed to become the leader of the *ayyar* in Sistan and by 861 was the de facto ruler of the province.

Once in power, Ya'qub launched a series of military operations, each of which served quite different purposes. His first efforts were aimed primarily at breaking the strength of the Kharijite groups in Sistan. The Kharijites, who were mostly Arab tribesmen, had endorsed an unconventional variety of Islam that held, among other things, that legitimate political power should be held by the most pious person in the community. According to their view, Muslims who had committed a "grave sin" forfeited their status as believers and could be killed or dispossessed by the true, Kharijite, Muslims. Some of the Kharijites had fled to remote Sistan to evade the authority of the caliphs and the hostility of the Sunni Muslims; they thus came to play a major, if turbulent, role in the politics of that province. Ya'qub seems to have attacked them primarily in order to tame them rather than out of dislike for their religious views; once he defeated them, he incorporated them into his own forces.

Ya'qub initiated a second series of campaigns directed against the remaining pagan areas of Afghanistan and the Indian frontier. He was able to crush the Zunbil of Zamindavar and to capture and plunder Kabul. His seizure of many gold and silver idols from the pagan temples (along with the silver mines of central Afghanistan) contributed to the financial success of the early Saffarids and temporarily helped them capture the imagination and respect of the Muslim world, particularly since Ya'qub sent a portion of the spoils to the caliph, a deed required by Islamic law. Thus, some sources refer to Ya'qub and his forces as "volunteer fighters for the faith," and in this capacity they might be compared to the *ghazis* of later times. However, the Saffarid reputation as champions of the faith suffered considerably when Ya'qub began a third series of wars, this time against the Muslim areas to the north and west of Sistan. In the course of these campaigns, Ya'qub wrested control of the important province of Khurasan from the Tahirids and in 876 attempted unsuccessfully to occupy Baghdad. Although the Abbasid caliphs were thus compelled to recognize the rule of the early Saffarids over southern Iran, they were always distrustful of Saffarid intentions, attempting to stir up popular resistance to them and withdrawing the certificates of investiture they had granted whenever possible.

Upon the death of Ya'qub in 879, leadership of the dynasty was assumed by his brother Amr. Amr attempted to expand Saffarid territories at the expense of another favored client of the Abbasids, the Samanids of Transoxiana. He first appointed his own governor of Khwarazm and then, in 898, invaded Samanid territory directly. However, his army was decisively defeated, and Amr himself was taken prisoner (to be sent to the caliph and executed in 902). Amr's death marked the final collapse of the Saffarids as a regional power. The Samanids took Khurasan, representatives of the caliph gradually reclaimed Fars and Kerman, and Sistan itself was occupied twice by the Samanid forces. Yet the dynasty itself survived all these calamities, in addition to later invasions by the Ghaznavids (1003) and the Mongols (1221), until it finally disappeared around 1480.

The essentially popular and local character of the Saffarid dynasty is attested in the copious anecdotal material about Ya'qub and Amr as well as by what little we know of the society and culture they represented. Although one important source gives the Saffarids a glorious genealogy tracing their descent from ancient Iranian kings, the family does not appear to have made a concerted effort to disguise their humble origins. The Saffarids certainly made some attempt to copy the traditions, institutions, and etiquette of Islamic courts, but they are just as often depicted on campaign, sharing the simple diet and rough life of their military comrades. They were often praised for their zeal in protecting the poor and weak in matters of taxation and water supply as well as for championing local interests against outside exploitation. Saffarid culture was essentially unpretentious; Ya'qub is famous for having been unimpressed by praise of his accomplishments in Arabic verse and instead promoted the use of the Persian vernacular for his "court" poetry.

In short, the Saffarids are something of an anomaly in Islamic history: they broke virtually all of the rules of conventional political behavior in their dealings with the caliphs and their subjects, and yet their dynasty survived for more than six hundred years—one of the longest dynastic successions in all of Islamic and Iranian history. This longevity is extremely difficult to explain on the basis of anything other than their genuine popularity and their ability to represent, as C. E. Bosworth put it, "the national interests and aspirations of the people of Sistan, from whose ranks they themselves had sprung."

[See also Samanid Dynasty; Sistan; Tahirid Dynasty; and Zunbil.]

C. E. Bosworth, *Sistan under the Arabs* (1968), pp. 109–123. Milton Gold, trans., *Tārīkh-e Sīstān* (1976). Theodore Nöldeke, "Yakūb the Coppersmith and His Dynasty," in *Sketches from Eastern History,* translated by J. S. Black (1892). S. M. Stern, "Ya'qūb the Coppersmith and Persian National Sentiment," in *Iran and Islam,* edited by C. E. Bosworth (1971), pp. 535–555.

E. L. DANIEL

SAGA REBELLION, samurai rebellion in Kyushu, Japan, in 1874. During the 1870s, following the Meiji Restoration of 1868, Japan was undergoing a tremendous transformation. In quick succession, the fall of the Tokugawa shogunate was followed by the creation of an imperial government bent on modernizing Japan and, in 1871, by the liquidation of the feudal domains. The reform policies destroyed privileges enjoyed by the ruling samurai class for many centuries. As a result, the new imperial government began to be criticized for its disruptive policies of modernization, not only by former samurai but also by government officials sympathetic to them.

Etō Shimpei, a former samurai activist for the imperial restoration from Saga, was one such government official. Etō aligned himself with Saigō Takamori, who was extremely popular among former samurai, to support the sending of a "punitive" military mission to Korea, which had the purpose of diverting the discontent of disgruntled former samurai. When the proposal failed to gain government support, Etō, along with other dissenting government officials, resigned. He immediately began to seek ways to make the government accountable not only to his own policy preferences but also to the samurai discontent in general. In January 1874 Etō returned to Saga, where he and some three thousand followers, most of whom were former samurai, took up arms against the imperial government. Etō's rebellion marked the beginning of a series of samurai rebellions that eventually culminated in the Satsuma Rebellion of 1877, led by Saigō Takamori. Etō's

Saga Rebellion was not supported by samurai from other domains, and he was captured and executed.

[*See also* Etō Shimpei; Saigō Takamori; *and* Meiji Period.]

MICHIO UMEGAKI

SAICHŌ (767–822), posthumously known as Dengyō Daishi, one of great religious leaders of Japan and the founder of the Japanese school of Tendai Buddhism. Born into a local aristocratic family of Chinese ancestry in Omi Province not far from what was later to become the Heian capital, Saichō was ordained in 785 at Tōdaiji and began his training for the monastic life in the great Nara monasteries, where he began to study the Chinese Tiantai (Japanese, Tendai) doctrines made known in Japan by Ganjin and other Chinese immigrant monks.

Dissatisfied with monastic practice in Nara, Saichō built himself a small retreat on Mount Hiei in 788. In 804 he was sent to China by Emperor Kammu to study the latest trends in Chinese Buddhism, especially those most suitable for adoption at the new capital of Heian. During a year in China he studied with Tiantai, Zen, and Tantric masters and became convinced that the Tiantai teachings articulated by Zhiyi and based on the *Lotus Sutra* were the supreme expression of the Buddha's teaching, opening the path to salvation for all beings and offering protection to the state that sponsored them.

He returned to Japan and his former monastery, renamed Enryakuji, loaded with Buddhist texts. With imperial backing he established a new Tendai school of Buddhism and a thriving monastic community where Zen, the Vinaya, Shingon, and Pure Land teachings were introduced alongside Tendai. Although honored and successful as a monk, Saichō's latter years were clouded by two disappointments: his estrangement from the Shingon master Kūkai and his inability to secure permission to build an ordination platform on Mount Hiei and thus secure the full independence of Tendai from Nara Buddhism. The autonomy of Tendai was achieved shortly after Saichō's death when Enryakuji, by imperial decree, was permitted to conduct its own ordinations.

[*See also* Enryakuji; Tendai; *and* Kūkai.]

Wm. Theodore de Bary, Ryusaku Tsunoda, and Donald Keene, eds., *Sources of the Japanese Tradition* (1958). Paul Groner, *Saichō and the Establishment of the Japanese Tendai School* (1984). Joseph M. Kitagawa, *Religion in Japanese History* (1966).   MARTIN COLLCUTT

SAIGON. *See* Ho Chi Minh City.

SAIGON, TREATY OF. Signed on 5 June 1862, the Treaty of Saigon was the first of several agreements establishing French rule in Indochina. Faced with military pressure from Franco-Spanish forces under admirals Charner and Bonnard, as well as the loss of southern rice and a rebellion in Tonkin, Tu Duc had consented to negotiate through Phan Thanh Gian. The treaty ceded three provinces, including Saigon itself; allowed the free practice of Christianity; opened three ports, including Tourane, to European trade; and imposed a heavy indemnity upon Vietnam. Although numerous popular insurrections followed, the Hue court was forced to ratify the treaty in April 1863.

[*See also* Tu Duc *and* Phan Thanh Gian.]

Joseph Buttinger, *The Smaller Dragon: A Political History of Vietnam* (1958).   BRUCE M. LOCKHART

SAIGŌ TAKAMORI (1827–1877), one of the most powerful leaders of the transition between the Tokugawa and Meiji periods in Japan. Although of low samurai status, Saigō first achieved prominence as confidant and agent of the brilliant Shimazu Nariakira, lord of Satsuma. After Nariakira's death in 1858, Ii Naosuke's purge of his critics forced Saigō and the loyalist priest Gesshō to seek refuge in Kagoshima, but the new ruler Shimazu Hisamitsu refused to shelter him. After an unsuccessful suicide attempt, Saigō was sent into his first of two exiles (1858–1862; 1862–1864). He was released in the spring of 1864 and placed in charge of Satsuma troops at Kyoto, where he ousted Chōshū radicals from the capital. In the punitive *bakufu* expedition against Chōshū (fall 1864) Saigō personally negotiated moderate terms of punishment for the Chōshū leaders. The generous act paved the way for an anti-Tokugawa Satsuma-Chōshū alliance that helped bring about the humiliation of the *bakufu* in its second effort to chastise Chōshū (1866).

During 1866 and 1867 Saigō and Ōkubo Toshimichi were busy countering *bakufu* influence at the imperial court and forging a coalition of influential *han* against the Tokugawa. Their tactics finally brought about a military showdown on the outskirts of Kyoto, where Chōshū and Satsuma troops routed the shogun's forces. As chief of staff, Saigō led imperial forces toward Edo, but at Hakone he negotiated with Katsu Awa of the *bakufu* for the peaceful transfer of power from the Tokugawa shogun to the Meiji emperor.

After establishment of the Meiji government in 1868, Saigō was torn between loyalty to the emperor and unhappiness with the new regime's social and economic reforms, which stripped his followers of samurai status and slashed their stipends. Nevertheless, in 1869 he contributed to the smooth transfer of authority from local domains to prefectural governments. During the Iwakura Mission (December 1871–summer 1873) the government approved Saigō's plan to demand an apology from Korea for a diplomatic affront, but with the return of the mission the decision was reversed. [See Iwakura Mission.] Saigō angrily resigned from office and retired to Kagoshima, where he established private academies to employ his men and provide military and administrative training.

The Satsuma Rebellion (February–September 1877) erupted when academy members obstructed efforts of the central government to remove weapons from the Satsuma arsenal. Although he disapproved the rash action of his followers, Saigō agreed to lead them in a protest march to Tokyo. Blocked and defeated at Kumamoto by government forces, the Satsuma rebels slowly retreated to Kagoshima, where Saigō met his death in a suicidal charge against forces led by his former friends and colleagues.

[See also Meiji Restoration.]

W. G. Beasley, *The Meiji Restoration* (1972). Ivan Morris, *The Nobility of Failure* (1976).   ROBERT K. SAKAI

SAIGYŌ (1118–1190), a medieval Japanese poet and monk who wrote in the thirty-one-syllable *waka* form. Saigyō's highly personal, forthright poetic style sets him apart from such other famous poets of his time as Fujiwara Shunzei (1114–1204), Shunzei's son Teika (1162–1241), and the monk Jakuren (d. 1202). Reclusive by nature, Saigyō became known to the aristocratic poetry circles of the capital, Kyoto, only through his longstanding friendship with the influential critic Shunzei. Saigyō's lack of exposure to the latest fashions in *waka* enabled him to write poetry that was essentially a direct expression of his own feelings, stated in simple language. This style, which differed significantly from the more complex, polished approach then favored, struck the Kyoto poets as refreshing. Toward the end of Saigyō's life, his poetry was highly esteemed: Teika, as editor of the famous *waka* anthology *Shinkokinshū*

(c. 1205), included ninety-four of Saigyō's poems, larger than any other poet's contribution.

Saigyō's lay name was Satō Norikiyo. He was born in 1118 to a prominent military family and served as a guardsman to the former emperor Toba (1103–1156) in Kyoto. He became a Buddhist monk, for unknown reasons, at age twenty-two, taking the name En'i; *Saigyō* is a pen name. He lived on Mount Kōya, the headquarters of the Shingon sect, from about age thirty through age sixty, later retiring near Futami Bay in Ise. Saigyō made many pilgrimages during his life, and his experiences while traveling provided him with material for his poetry. During a journey north to raise funds for rebuilding the Great Buddha Hall of Tōdaiji in Nara, Saigyō was granted an audience with the shogun Minamoto Yoritomo (1147–1199) in Kamakura and answered the great man's questions on poetry. Saigyō died near present-day Osaka in 1190.

[See also Fujiwara Period.]

Robert H. Brower and Earl Miner, *Japanese Court Poetry* (1961). William R. LaFleur, trans., *Mirror for the Moon: A Selection of Poems by Saigyō (1118–1190)* (1978). Hiroaki Sato and Burton Watson, eds., *From the Country of Eight Islands: An Anthology of Japanese Poetry* (1981).   AILEEN GATTEN

SAILENDRA. An inscription from Nakhon Si Thammarat in the Malay Peninsula dating from 775 makes reference to the Srivijaya empire of Sumatra; on the reverse of the same stone is an undated inscription that speaks of the Sailendra family, which is known to have ruled Java in the same eighth-century era. Using the Nakhon Si Thammarat inscription as evidence that Srivijaya was the dominant political entity in the Southeast Asian archipelago during that age, some historians have proposed a "Sumatra period" in Javanese history. They see the ruler of Srivijaya as dominating central Java's politics and culture in the eighth and ninth centuries, a period characterized by Srivijaya's Mahayana Buddhist influence and Java's most impressive temple architecture. But an 860 inscription from Nalanda, the Mahayana Buddhist monastery in the Bihar region of northeastern India, honors a Southeast Asian *maharaja* ("great king") who sponsored a religious foundation and notes that this *maharaja* was descended from the Sailendra family of Java and ruled Srivijaya. The Nalanda inscription suggests an interpretation quite different from that of the Nakhon Si Thammarat inscription: that Java-based rulers of the Sailendra family held authority over the Srivijaya realm and that during the eighth and ninth centuries it was Java, not southeastern Sumatra, that dominated the Southeast Asian archipelago.

The Sailendras came to power around the mid-eighth century. They introduced the Indic title *maharaja*—a foreign-sounding title to awe their subjects and to distinguish themselves from other regional chiefs—and established their base in Central Java. Sacred rituals, and especially the encouragement of temple construction by Sailendra monarchs, were intended to maintain and enhance Sailendra prestige. During the height of their power in Central Java, the Sailendras, patrons of Buddhism, constructed impressive monuments and temple complexes, the best known of which is the Borobudur on the Kedu Plain. Their court attracted Buddhist scholars from afar and was acclaimed internationally as a center of Buddhist learning. They were the precursors of a new concept of statecraft in Java—the concentration of political power in a single authority—which was clearly being realized by the tenth century.

The most widely accepted reconstruction of Sailendra history was done by J. G. de Casparis, who stressed the intermarriage between the Java-based Sailendra and the Sumatra-based Srivijaya royal houses, as well as the consequent assumption of rule over Srivijaya by Sailendra-related monarchs after rival Javanese elite had superseded the authority of Sailendra monarchs in Java. At this time, Sailendra kings lost their seat in Java and ended up ruling Sumatra in the late ninth century.

[*See also* Java *and* Srivijaya.]

Kenneth R. Hall, *Maritime Trade and State Development in Early Southeast Asia* (1985). F. H. van Naerssen and R. C. de Iongh, *The Economic and Administrative History of Early Indonesia* (1977).   KENNETH R. HALL

SAIONJI KIMMOCHI (1849–1940), Japanese noble who was a major government leader during the Meiji period (1868–1912). Saionji was the second son of Tokudaiji Kinzumi and was adopted into the Saionji family when he was two years old. He served the emperor Kōmei (r. 1847–1866), who preceded the Meiji emperor. Iwakura Tomomi (1825–1883), one of the Meiji government's most influential statesmen, recognized his potential and appointed him *san'yō* (junior councillor) in the Meiji government when he was nineteen. He was the nominal commander of the new government forces that fought in northeastern Japan. The important Meiji statesman Yamagata Aritomo, more than ten years his senior, was his "subordinate."

Saionji then spent ten years in France (1871–1880), where he was influenced by Emile Acollas' social-democratic ideas. Upon his return, he founded and became editor of the newspaper *Tōyō jiyū shimbun* (1881). Nakae Chōmin, a fiery advocate of popular rights, and Matsuda Masahisa, later a stalwart in the political party Seiyūkai, were his cohorts. The Meiji leaders looked askance at this venture and had the emperor command him to return to the fold. In 1882 he went to Europe with Itō Hirobumi to study constitutional systems; this period of study together was the beginning of their close ties. He spent six years in Europe as minister to Austria-Hungary (1885–1887) and to Germany and Belgium (1887–1891).

During the next decade Saionji plunged deeply into politics. He was vice president of the House of Peers (1893) and education minister in the second (1894–1896) and third (1898) cabinets of Itō Hirobumi. He played an important role in the formation of the Seiyūkai in 1900 and, when Itō retired, succeeded him as president of the party in 1903. In the meantime, he served as president of the Privy Council (1900–1903). He was twice prime minister (1906–1908 and 1911–1912). Japan achieved some foreign policy successes under his ministries, but he had a more difficult time in domestic politics and was forced to resign over the army's proposal for two new divisions. In 1914 he handed over the Seiyūkai's reins to Hara Takashi. Except for a brief appearance as chief delegate to the Paris Peace Conference (1919), Saionji henceforth remained behind the scenes, and after Matsukata Masayoshi's death in 1924, he was the last *genrō* (elder statesman).

Saionji loved to discuss politics and political issues, but he lacked the energy and consuming desire to gain and exercise power. Yamagata Aritomo once said, "No one should lose his grip on power, so I for one, exert myself to maintain it." That Saionji recalled with distaste this remark seven years later suggests their different perceptions about the uses of political power. In the 1930s, although he had the final say on the decision to appoint the prime minister, his reclusiveness gave greater voice on this matter to the emperor's immediate advisers, such as the lord keeper of the privy seal. He finally refused to participate in Prince Konoe Fumimaro's nomination to the prime ministership in 1940.

[*See also* Meiji Period *and* Seiyūkai.]

GEORGE K. AKITA

SAIPAN, second largest of the Mariana Islands of Micronesia. A Spanish possession until 1898, then briefly owned by Germany, Saipan was occupied by Japanese naval forces in 1914 and became a district headquarters of the Japanese administration of Micronesia under a League of Nations mandate from 1922 to 1944. With the development of a sugar industry on Saipan in the 1930s considerable numbers of Japanese migrated to the island, and toward the end of that decade it was developed by Japan as a military base.

During the latter half of the Pacific War Saipan became the pivotal bastion of the Marianas defense perimeter, which was hurriedly strengthened early in 1944 to block the further advance toward Japan of American amphibious forces. Despite the inability of the Japanese to prepare adequate defenses on the island by the time that a large American task force approached Saipan in June 1944, the Japanese were able to dispatch nearly thirty thousand troops who were well entrenched and determined to shatter the American offensive or perish in the attempt. The Japanese navy took the occasion to sally forth and engage American naval forces in that part of the Pacific, but the annihilation of its naval aircraft by the American task force obliterated all hope of any Japanese air support reaching Saipan, which was now assaulted by three American divisions. The Japanese defenders on the ground resisted from caves and pillbox fortifications with frenzy and futility. Tragically, great numbers of the considerable Japanese civilian population chose to perish with them, leaping to their deaths off the rocky cliffs at the northern end of the island. On the orders of the senior military commander, General Saitō Yoshitsugu, the Japanese launched one final counterattack, the collapse of which marked the end of effective resistance on Saipan. The island was secured by American forces by early July. Because the Japanese government under Tōjō Hideki had staked so much on the outcome of the battle, the loss of Saipan was a major turning point in the Pacific War. Tōjō himself was forced from office by more moderate elements with the government, who began to seek ways to end the war.   MARK R. PEATTIE

SAKA DYNASTIES. The Sakas were the easternmost of the Indo-European-speaking Scythian tribes of Central Asia. While their earlier movements related to Indo-Iranian protohistory cannot be defined, those who stayed behind in the upper Ili region were destabilized in the middle of the second century

BCE because of Yuezhi pressure. Some of them moved south and founded several new states in the Tarim Basin, in the Pamirs, and in adjoining regions. Their languages and culture flourished (in Khotan, for example, until the arrival of the Turks).

By about 100 BCE the Sakas had entered the Indian subcontinent via the northern Karakoram passes. Their king Maues conquered Taxila and the Swat Valley from the Indo-Greeks, who had ruled there since the time of Alexander the Great. Maues reigned from about 95 to 75 through a satrapal system of government; under his reign coins similar to those of the Indo-Greeks were issued. The successors of Maues were driven out by the Pahlavas, who came from Sistan. The Sakas then established themselves at Mathura, where the best known of their rulers were Rajula and Sodasha. The Sakas were pushed out by the Kushans, and they resettled in Malwa, Gujarat, Maharashtra, and Rajasthan, in most parts of which they ruled for more than three hundred years.

These Sakas are known as the "Western Kshatrapas" because they used the designations *Kshatrapa* and *Mahakshatrapa* in coin legends and inscriptions. In Gujarat, Castana was one of their early kings, and the beginning of the Saka era in 78 CE perhaps marks his accession to the throne. The leader Rudradaman, who ruled in the middle of the second century, was the most powerful of this group. The Junagadh inscription of 150 CE, noted for the purity of its Sanskrit in contrast to the local Prakrit of their brahman Satavahana rivals, records Rudradaman's exploits and his repair of Sudarsana lake, an irrigation dam built by Chandragupta Maurya.

More than two dozen successors ruled in western India until the end of the fourth century, when they were vanquished by the Guptas. They issued a series of silver coins, each of which was stamped with its year of issue as well as the name and title of the ruler and his father. Saka political power and security in Gujarat depended to a large extent upon successful control of the seaports of western India and the resultant commercial benefits from trade relations with the Western world.

[See also Taxila; Mathura; Greeks; Alexander III; Kushan Dynasty; and Gupta Empire.]

H. W. Bailey, *The Culture of the Sakas in Ancient Iranian Khotan* (1982). S. Chattopadhyaya, *Sakas in India* (1967). G. K. Jenkins and A. K. Narain, *The Coin-types of the Saka-Pahlava kings of India* (1957). J. E. van Lohuizen-de Leeuw, *The "Scythian" Period* (1949). A. K. Narain, *The Indo-Greeks* (1980).   A. K. NARAIN

SAKAI. Now an industrial municipality in Osaka Prefecture, Japan, Sakai was one of Japan's largest and most affluent port cities in the Muromachi era (1338–1573), and has enjoyed a reputation as a "free city." The name *Sakai*, which means "boundary," first appeared in the Heian period (794–1185) referring to the area on the Settsu-Izumi provincial border.

The city was not an official administrative unit but grew naturally out of two *shōen* (manor, estate), Sakai Izumi no Shō (Kita no Shō) and Sakai Settsu no Shō (Minami no Shō). The first reference to a town on the site is in the chronicle *Ōei ki*, which describes the Battle of Sakai (1399), in which a *bakufu* coalition destroyed "a myriad houses" and killed the daimyo Ōuchi Yoshihiro, who had fortified the city. The residents' primary economic activity was as *toimaru*, those who forwarded estate rents, in this case especially to Kōyasan and the temples of Nara.

The Ōnin War (1467–1477) greatly spurred Sakai's growth, as it became in 1469 the port that handled the *bakufu*'s tally trade with Ming China, replacing Hyōgo, which had fallen to the shogun's enemies. In the ensuing prosperity Sakai experienced a cultural flowering that included such figures as the teaman Takeno Jōō and the *renga* poet Botange. Administratively, the Egōshū, a city council of leading merchants, managed municipal affairs autonomously; the Hosokawa gained proprietary rights in 1490. In 1504 the Miyoshi, principal Hosokawa retainers, fortified the city and defended it, establishing in 1521 a Sakai *mandokoro* (administrative office) for its control.

With reunification Sakai fell under direct central authority. Oda Nobunaga, after entering Kyoto in 1568, demanded the shogun give him the right to place his deputy in the Sakai *mandokoro*. Initially the townsmen resisted, but with teamen such as Imai Sōkyū mediating, the city capitulated. Toyotomi Hideyoshi and the Tokugawa shoguns also held Sakai directly. The *mandokoro* became, as the shogun's representative, the Sakai *bugyō* (magistrate). In the Azuchi-Momoyama period (1568–1600), especially, Sakai was a cultural center, with Imai Sōkyū, Tsuda Sōgyū, and Sen no Rikyū serving as *sadō*, tea masters, for both Nobunaga and Hideyoshi.

Hideyoshi's location of his castle in Osaka, immediately to the north of Sakai, substantially overshadowed the port, but it continued to function as an active trading center for *shuin* merchants and members of the Ito Wappu guild, which managed the silk trade. Sakai reached a peak population of about 70,000 in 1665. After flood control work on the nearby Yamato River caused Sakai's port to silt up from the eighteenth century on, the city lost much of its economic activity, and population fell until the nineteenth century.

Following the Meiji Restoration in 1868 Sakai became a prefecture and underwent several administrative reforms before it was incorporated into Osaka Prefecture in 1881 and became a municipality *(shi)* in 1889.

[*See also* Muromachi Period *and* Tea Ceremony.]

V. Dixon Morris, "Sakai: From Shōen to Port City," in *Japan in the Muromachi Age*, edited by John W. Hall and Toyodo Takeshi (1977). V. Dixon Morris, "The City of Sakai and Urban Autonomy," in *Warlords, Artists, and Commoners*, edited by George Elison and Bardwell Smith (1981), pp. 23–54. Toyota Takeshi, *Sakai* (1957).

V. DIXON MORRIS

SAKAI INCIDENT. On 8 March 1868 Japanese samurai from the Shikoku domain of Tosa who were guarding the port city of Sakai fired on a party of French sailors from the warship *Dupleix* who failed to understand or ignored the Tosa commanders' signals to return to their launch. Sakai was not an open port, and the Tosa samurai, without interpreters and full of the antiforeign enthusiasm of late Meiji Restoration days, were quick to carry out expulsion *(jōi)* of the "barbarians."

The Meiji government, in its first weeks of existence and eager for foreign recognition, quickly accepted the drastic demands presented by French minister Leon Roches: capital punishment for the Tosa commanders and men responsible and payment of an indemnity of 150,000 Mexican silver dollars. On the French side, a petty officer and eleven others had been killed and five wounded. Twenty Tosa samurai, including the two commanders, were sentenced to commit *seppuku* in the presence of foreign witnesses. Sentence was carried out at the Sakai Myōkokuji on 16 March; the commander of the *Dupleix* declared himself satisfied after eleven Tosa men had immolated themselves. The Meiji writer Mori Ōgai made the incident famous in a historical tale that focused on the shift in morality surrounding the ritual suicide.

[*See also* Mori Ōgai.]

D. Dilworth and J. T. Rimer, eds., *The Incident at Sakai and Other Stories*, vol.1 of *Historical Literature of Mori Ogai* (1977). MARIUS B. JANSEN

SAKAMOTO RYŌMA (1836–1867), activist in Japan's Meiji Restoration of 1868, the mediator of the Satsuma-Chōshū alliance, and author of the plan under which the last shogun agreed to resign his political powers, before he was finally outmaneuvered by the leaders of the future Meiji government.

Sakamoto was born in the Shikoku province of Tosa to a low-ranking (gōshi, "rural") samurai family with merchant antecedents. He had only a modest education in formal terms and in ordinary times could have expected little participation in local affairs and none at all in national politics.

Sakamoto began as a young swordsman in the following of Takechi Zuizan (Hanpeita), a charismatic leader who organized a loyalist party of young followers after the Edo bakufu forced the Tosa lord, Yamauchi Yōdō (Toyoshige), into retirement for his involvement in efforts to influence the Tokugawa succession. The loyalist manifesto he signed expressed indignation that the emperor's will had been ignored in the matter of the treaty negotiated with Townsend Harris. Tosa loyalists went on to assassinate the domain's first minister, Yoshida Tōyō, and led the new domain administration into efforts to increase the court's power at the expense of the bakufu (kōbu gattai), but by then Sakamoto had already fled Tosa jurisdiction to take up the life of a masterless samurai, or rōnin.

Sakamoto next entered the employ of a forward-looking bakufu official, Katsu Kaishū, but, when Katsu was forced out of his position (as organizer of a naval training school), Sakamoto found protection in the southwestern domain of Satsuma. Satsuma leaders helped him form a small shipping company, the Kaientai, and with these resources he was able to help supply the domain of Chōshū during its stand-off with the Tokugawa. As the pace of events accelerated, with Chōshū victories over the second Tokugawa expedition in 1866, Sakamoto and his Tosa associate Nakaoka Shintarō were instrumental in mediating the alliance between Satsuma and Chōshū. Next, he was restored to the registers and good graces of his Tosa superiors, and through them he introduced the suggestion that the shogun resign his powers, under an arrangement that would presumably leave him politically influential and his territories intact. This was not to be, however, as Satsuma, Chōshū, and court leaders precipitated the short civil war that brought down the shogunate. Almost immediately after the last shogun, Tokugawa Keiki (Yoshinobu) offered to resign his powers, however, Sakamoto and Nakaoka were murdered by members of a rōnin vigilante organization in the shogunate's employ. Sakamoto's buoyant enthusiasm, quick intelligence, and early death combined to make him a hero for documentary and fictional representations of the Meiji Restoration in Japan after World War II.

[See also Meiji Restoration.]

Marius B. Jansen, Sakamoto Ryōma and the Meiji Restoration (1961).   MARIUS B. JANSEN

SAKANOUE NO TAMURAMARO (758–811), Japanese general renowned for his victories against the warlike peoples of northeastern Japan (the emishi). The Sakanoue were skilled hunters and horsemen of Chinese stock. During the mid-eighth century, Tamuramaro's father, Karitamaro, was so useful to the court that his family was elevated to a more prestigious title (kabane).

The court had attempted the conquest of northeastern Japan since the 760s, but the fierce inhabitants of the Tōhoku proved more than a match for the court's expeditionary forces. In 794 Tamuramaro served in a series of bitterly fought battles in the frontier region. Two years later he was named general of Fort Taga. In 801 he headed forty thousand troops as the "barbarian-subduing general" (sei-i tai shōgun), dealing his enemy a serious defeat. His victory led to the construction of Fort Izawa and the end to emishi resistance in the area.

Tamuramaro played a crucial role in crushing the revolt of Fujiwara no Kusuko in 810. He was eventually promoted to the third court rank and given permission to participate in policy debates. His obituary describes him as having a "red face and yellow hair" and "retainers beyond number." It became customary for military leaders to visit Tamuramaro's grave in Uji to pray for success in battle.

George Sansom, A History of Japan to 1334 (1958).

WAYNE FARRIS

SAKDAL, the Tagalog word for "protest," was the name of a vitriolic weekly newspaper founded in 1931 by the charismatic Filipino radical Benigno Ramos (1893–1945). In 1933 Ramos established the Sakdalista Party, which was at first a vehicle for traditional political action. The Sakdalistas advocated immediate and complete independence for the Philippines as well as total opposition to the "tyranny" of American and local capitalism, of the Quezon "dictatorship," and of the Catholic church. On 2–3 May 1935 Ramos's personal demagoguery, the fantastic belief by his followers that Japan would come to their assistance militarily, and the profound economic frustration of the poverty-stricken central Luzon tenant farmers combined to produce a quixotic but bloody uprising. Although the rigorous suppression of this outbreak put an end to the potential power of the Sakdalista Party, grievances from which its following developed were to give rise subsequently to another, better organized and more radical political movement—the Hukbalahap.

[*See also* Quezon, Manuel Luis; Catholicism in the Philippines; *and* Huk.]

Grant K. Goodman, *Four Aspects of Philippine-Japanese Relations, 1930–1940* (1967). Joseph R. Hayden, *The Philippines: A Study in National Development* (1942).
GRANT K. GOODMAN

SAKDI NA, measure of hierarchical rank in premodern Thailand. By the fifteenth-century laws of King Borommatrailokanat, all in the kingdom were assigned numerical ranks that indicated their status. Both male and female commoners, for example, had a *sakdi na* of 15 *rai;* a watchman, 25; a scribe, 50; government officers ("nobles") from 400 to 10,000; and princes from 6,000 to 100,000 *rai*. Scholars have long argued about the meaning of these terms. *Sakdi na* might literally be translated as "rice-field power," while *rai* were measures of land equal to 0.4 acre; thus it would appear that all were measured in terms of land. However, since even obviously landless people were assigned *na* ranks, and since those higher in the order controlled land only by their control over those lower in the order, it is reasonable to regard the *sakdi na* system as measuring abstract relationships rather than physical units of land. Misleadingly, modern Thai authors have used *sakdi na* as a synonym for *feudalism*.

[*See also* Borommatrailokanat.]

H. G. Quaritch Wales, *Ancient Siamese Government and Administration* (1934; reprint, 1965). B. J. Terwiel, *A History of Modern Thailand 1767–1942* (1983).
DAVID K. WYATT

SAKOKU. *See* Seclusion.

SAKUMA SHŌZAN (1811–1864), Japanese Confucian scholar and political reformer of the late Tokugawa period. Sakuma Shōzan was born to a low-ranking samurai family in Matsushiro domain, now Nagano Prefecture. After studying in Edo in the mid-1830s his position in the domain rose, and in 1841, when his daimyo became a leader in efforts to reform the *bakufu*, Shōzan was ordered to draft proposals on how to strengthen coastal defense. Shocked by reports of British victory in the Opium War, he began to study Western gunnery techniques and the Dutch language so that he might assimilate Western technological knowledge. He opened in Edo an academy of Dutch (European) studies, or *rangaku,* and taught prominent men such as Katsu Kaishū, Sakamoto Ryōma, and Yoshida Shōin. In 1854, when Yoshida was captured in an abortive attempt to steal away to study conditions in America, Sakuma was implicated and imprisoned. Later he was released, but was assassinated in 1864 by an antiforeign extremist.

Sakuma was a strict scholar of the Chinese Neo-Confucian tradition inaugurated by Zhu Xi (1130–1200), but believed that Western technology was compatible with Confucian moralism and that a combination of the two would suffice to repel Western encroachment. He advocated opening the country to foreign trade and diplomacy under *bakufu* initiative.

[*See also* Rangaku.]

Harry Harootunian, *Toward Restoration* (1970).
BOB TADASHI WAKABAYASHI

SALA, Javanese royal city founded on the left bank of the Sala River (Bengawan Sala) by Sunan Pakubuwana II (r. 1726–1749) on 17 February 1745 after the occupation of his previous *kraton* (Kartasura) by rebels during the *prang Cina* (Chinese troubles) of 1742–1743. The new Surakarta *kraton* was first occupied early in 1746 and has remained a royal seat until the present.

After the Treaty of Giyanti, signed on 13 February 1755, Surakarta politics were dominated by the rivalry with the newly established court at Yogyakarta, which controlled half the princely territories in Central and East Java. The recognition of the Mangkunagaran by the Dutch in mid-March 1757 added another potential rival and led to a further division of the Surakarta polity, with one-fifth of the city on the south bank of the Kali Pepe being allocated to the new court.

Despite the difficulties occasioned by periodic floods, Surakarta proved to be a much more prosperous city than Yogyakarta since it was able to carry out a flourishing trade with East Java by the Bengawan Sala and was situated in the midst of well-irrigated rice lands. The Laweyan area of the city was renowned for its rich *santri* traders and batik manufacturers, and it later (1911) became the home of the important Sarekat Dagang Islam organization. The Surakarta court developed an especially refined artistic style that was much softer and less martial than that of Yogyakarta. Several of the Surakarta rulers, particularly Sunan Pakubuwana IV (r. 1788–1820) and Sunan Pakubuwana VII (r. 1830–1850), proved themselves discerning patrons of the arts.

From the late eighteenth century onward, the court remained on good terms with the Dutch, and like the Mangkunagaran (but unlike Yogyakarta) it was open to European influence in matters of dress, education, and social style. During the Indonesian Revolution against the Dutch (1945–1949), however, it acted equivocally toward the nationalist leadership, and the court was stripped of its remaining privileges.

[*See also* Giyanti, Treaty of; Yogyakarta; Mangkunagaran; Santri; *and* Sarekat Islam.]

M. C. Ricklefs, *Jogjakarta under Sultan Mangkubumi 1749–1792: A History of the Division of Java* (1974). Soewito Santoso, *The Kraton of Surakarta Hadiningrat* (1974). Soejatno, "Revolution and Social Tensions in Surakarta 1945–50," translated by Benedict Anderson, *Indonesia* 17 (April 1974): 99–112. PETER CAREY

SALAR JANG I (1829–1883), young nobleman who succeeded his uncle as *diwan* of Hyderabad State in the Deccan in 1853. He established himself with the support of indigenous bankers and the British East India Company, and he remained diwan of the subcontinent's largest princely state for the next thirty years. British officials initially viewed him as a modernizer; he supported them in the Mutiny of 1857. Traditionally educated, he carried out limited administrative reforms while trying to preserve the Mughal nobility and bureaucracy. He strove to maintain Hyderabad's autonomy and had to contend with three successive *nizams,* eleven British residents, and powerful Hyderabad nobles, bankers, and military men to do so. His pride, strength of character, and aggressive efforts to regain the Berar districts, ceded to the Company in early 1853, later provoked British hostility. Following Salar Jang's sudden death in 1883, British Indian policies and administrators increasingly dominated Hyderabad affairs. [*See also* Hyderabad *and* East India Company.] KAREN LEONARD

SALAT, obligatory ritual prayer in Islam, in contrast to voluntary individual prayer. *Salat* is observed at five specific times during the day, usually, although not necessarily, in a mosque. It is preceded by a public call to prayer and ablutions by the worshiper. The ritual itself consists of a sequence of bodily attitudes with recitations of formulas, some from the Qur'an, as the worshiper faces the direction of Mecca. An imam, who can be any member of the congregation, leads the group. Special *salats* are held on certain occasions, the most important being the Friday midday prayer, during which a sermon is delivered. The emphasis of *salat* on humility and acknowledgement of the omnipotence of God is reflected in the calm and sober demeanor of the participants. JEANETTE A. WAKIN

SAMANID DYNASTY. The Samanids were a prominent family of Iranian aristocrats who ruled much of central Asia from 864 to 999. They were much admired by Muslim historians; Ibn Khallikan considered the Samanids to have been "one of the best dynasties that ever ruled."

Several different genealogies purporting to trace the ancestry of the Samanids are preserved in the available sources. Most depict the Samanids as an offshoot of the Mihran, one of the great feudal families of pre-Islamic Iran with ties to the Arsacid dynasty, and as descendants of Bahram Chubin, a general who distinguished himself in guarding Iran's eastern borders and who attempted to usurp the throne in late Sasanid times. While of dubious authenticity, this genealogy was clearly intended to emphasize the image the Samanids wished to project of themselves: members of an aristocratic military elite, champions of eastern Iran and its culture, and defenders of the Central Asian frontier against the nomadic threat.

The first member of this family mentioned in Muslim historical sources was known as Saman Khudah, a name that implies that he was the petty ruler (probably the *dihqan*) of the town of Saman (variously located near Samarkand or, more likely, Balkh), which he had founded. Narshakhi, author of a history of Bukhara, noted that this Saman Khudah had fled from Balkh to Merv, where he was assisted by the Umayyad governor of Khurasan, Asad ibn Abd Allah al-Qasri (d. 738), in defeating his foes and returning to Balkh. In gratitude, Saman Khudah supposedly converted to Islam and named his own son Asad in honor of his benefactor. Narshakhi does not name the enemies of Saman Khudah, but it may

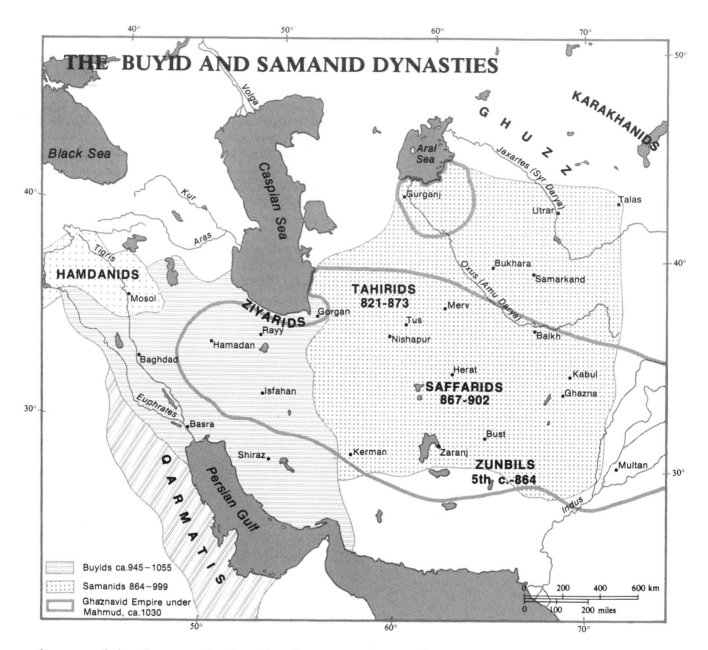

be assumed that they were the Turgesh tribesmen who, with encouragement from the Chinese, were harassing the borders of Khurasan. This is quite credible since it is well known that Asad advocated a policy of cooperation between the Arabs and the noble Iranian families (i.e., the military aristocracy) in order to deal with their common enemies and that he led several campaigns against the Turgesh in the environs of Balkh.

Saman Khudah's grandchildren further distinguished the family by coming to the assistance of the Abbasids against the rebel Rafi ibn Laith, who had seized control of most of Transoxiana during the caliphate of Harun al-Rashid (786–809). Some sources allege that the four sons of Asad ibn Saman Khudah interceded with Rafi and negotiated a settlement of this rebellion at the request of Ma'mun (Harun's son who was serving as governor of Khurasan). When Ma'mun became caliph, he rewarded each of the four brothers with the governorship of a district: Ilyas in Herat, Yahya in Shash (modern Tashkent), Ahmad in Ferghana, and Nuh, the oldest, in Samarkand. Ilyas played a prominent role in the Tahirid army, served for a while as governor of Egypt, and returned to Herat, where he died in 856. His son, Ibrahim, apparently lost Herat to the Saffarids after a battle near Pushang in 867, and so the line of Ilyas is of little importance. The fortunes of the family fared much better in Transoxiana, which was gradually united under the rule of Ahmad ibn Asad. For reasons that are not clear, one of Ahmad's sons, Nasr, took over Samarkand upon the death of Nuh (842), and another, Ya'qub, assumed power in Shash when Yahya died in 855.

Nasr ibn Ahmad became the head of the family when his father died in 864; he continued to govern from Samarkand. Following the destruction of the Tahirid dynasty by the Saffarids in 873, the Abbasid caliph al-Mu'tamid recognized Nasr as the legitimate ruler of all Transoxiana in hopes of blunting further expansion by the Saffarids. In 875, Nasr sent his brother, Isma'il, to govern Bukhara in response to an appeal from citizens of Bukhara alarmed by the collapse of law and order after the fall of the Tahirids. The two brothers, however, soon began to quarrel, and war between them broke out in 885. Isma'il defeated Nasr in 888 but allowed him to return to Samarkand, where he remained as nominal head of the family until his death in 892.

Under Isma'il ibn Ahmad (r. 892–907), the Samanids became the preeminent power in Central Asia and eastern Iran. Not only did he succeed in uniting Transoxiana under his rule, but he also compelled a number of local rulers in adjacent areas (such as Khwarazm and Khuttal) to recognize Samanid sovereignty. He conquered Talas (Taraz), Ushrusana, Gorgan, and part of Tabaristan; he drove back the Turkish nomads on the northern and eastern frontiers; and, most importantly, he defeated Amr ibn Laith and expelled the Saffarid forces from Khurasan. His son, Ahmad (r. 907–914), completed the conquest of Sistan. Nasr ibn Ahmad (r. 914–943) suppressed various revolts in the outlying areas and maintained the integrity of the Samanid principality. His reign marked the political and especially the cultural zenith of the dynasty. Subsequently, the Samanids became embroiled in a number of dynastic struggles, internal problems, and external conflicts that resulted in the precipitous decline of the dynasty.

The accomplishments of the early Samanids were manifold. The sophisticated and elaborate bureaucracy of their court and chancellery was praised by Narshakhi and Nizam al-Mulk and served as a model for later rulers. Isma'il himself was regarded as the ideal type of ruler: just, pious, magnanimous, and concerned with the welfare of his subjects. Samanid patronage of the arts and sciences made Bukhara and Samarkand two of the leading intellectual centers of the Islamic world. A host of famous religious scholars, scientists, poets (both Arabic and Persian), men of letters, and talented officials surrounded the Samanid court. The Samanids also pursued a vigorous religious policy as champions of Sunni "orthodoxy" (although Nasr flirted with Isma'ili Islam). In particular, they promoted and popularized the Hanafi school of Islamic law, professed loyalty (but not subservience) to the Abbasid caliphate, and encouraged missionary activities to spread Islam among the Turks in and on the borders of their territory. Because of their conquests and maintenance of law and order, the Samanids were also able to stimulate trade between their cities and China, Iraq, and eastern Europe. A key element in Samanid commercial success was their virtual monopoly of the trade in Turkish slaves. The recruiting, training, and indoctrination of these Turks (described at length by Nizam al-Mulk) were of tremendous importance in both the islamicization of the Turks and the turkicization of Central Asia.

A number of factors contributed to the decline of Samanid power. Most fundamentally, an emphasis on trade seems to have led to a neglect of the agricultural base of the economy of Khurasan and Transoxiana as well as a movement of population from the rural areas to the major cities. (Bukhara, despite its newfound political and cultural glory as the Samanid capital, was notoriously filthy, overcrowded, and prone to urban violence owing to sectarian strife.) At the same time, the Samanids, although probably of *dihqan* origins themselves, contributed to the downfall of the *dihqan* class, which had been the backbone of eastern Iranian society. This was partly the result of the neglect of rural interests and partly that of the Samanid preference for basing their military power on Turkish "slave troops." It was increasingly difficult for the Samanids to control the Turks in their service: some became involved in politics and dynastic succession squabbles; others were able to break away and form their own states. In addition, Turkish tribes in areas outside Samanid control gradually infiltrated Samanid territory. Samanid slave-raiding and missionary activities probably stimulated them to do so, and the decline of the *dihqans* and the depopulation of the countryside must have helped to make that infiltration possible. In any case, the newly islamized Karakhanid Turks seized Bukhara from the Samanids in 999. Without support from the non-Turkish rural and urban population, the dynasty collapsed completely by 1005.

[See also Abbasid Dynasty; Bukhara; Karakhanid Dynasty; *and* Saffarid Dynasty.]

Wilhelm Barthold, *Turkestan down to the Mongol Invasion* (2d ed., 1958). R. N. Frye, *Bukhara, the Medieval Achievement* (1965). Narshakhī, *The History of Bukhara,* translated by R. N. Frye (1954). Nizām al-Mulk, *The Book of Government,* translated by Hubert Darke (1960).

E. L. DANIEL

SAMAR, third largest island in the Philippines, was the first beachhead of the Spanish conquest of the Philippines. The Spaniards landed on 16 March 1521 in Homonhon, an islet off the coast of eastern Samar. In 1649 the island was the center of one of the biggest rebellions in the Philippines. The Samareños protested the massive conscription of laborers for the building of ships used in the Manila galleon trade. Although Samar was not involved during the Philippine Revolution of 1896, the Samareños fiercely resisted American occupation of the island in 1898. The Americans established civil rule in 1902.

[*See also* Manila Galleon.]

Horacio De la Costa, S.J., *The Jesuits in the Philippines, 1581–1768* (1967). Joseph L. Schott, *The Ordeal of Samar* (1964).   MILAGROS C. GUERRERO

SAMARKAND, ancient capital of Sogdiana and later of Timur, conquered by the Russians in 1868. The city, then called Maracanda, was destroyed by Alexander in 329 BCE, but little is known of its earlier history. It lies in the fertile loess valley of the Zeravshan, a tributary of the Oxus (Amu Darya), about half-way downstream from the source in the Pamirs where it first debouches onto the high plains. It appears as Samarkand in the historical record at the time of the Arab conquest.

Under the Samanids Samarkand enjoyed great prosperity and cultural splendor and probably exceeded 100,000 inhabitants at the time of its siege by Genghis Khan in 1220. Much of its well-being resulted from its location on the major east-west caravan route across Central Asia to China, although Samarkand also exported local products including cottons, fruits, and silks, as well as servicing the caravans. The city was walled and supplied with water by an underground aqueduct from the hills to the south. Samarkand surrendered to the Mongols in 1220 after a brief siege but was nevertheless ruthlessly pillaged; much of the city was destroyed, and many of its citizens were deported. It did not recover substantially until the time of Timur, who chose it as his capital in 1369 and carried out extensive building on a grand scale. During his reign, Samarkand is said to have had 150,000 inhabitants, and nearly all of the pre-nineteenth-century structures surviving today date from that period, including three religious colleges *(madrasas),* Timur's summer palace, and his tomb. Timur's grandson Ulug Beg (d. 1449) further embellished the city with his palace and a famous astrological observatory. By the eighteenth century Samarkand had greatly declined, owing in part to the diversion of the trade routes that had fed it. Since 1871 a new Russian city has grown beside the old city and has become a rail and industrial center.

[*See also* Shahrukh; Sogdiana; Timur; *and* Ulug Beg.]

Wilhelm Barthold, *Turkestan down to the Mongol Invasion* (2d ed., 1958).   RHOADS MURPHEY, JR.

SAM FANG KAEN (r. 1401–1441), one of the two fifteenth-century builders of the kingdom of Lan Na at Chiang Mai in Thailand. Born in 1389 in what is now Chinese Yunnan, where his father, King Saen Muang Ma, was campaigning, Sam Fang Kaen succeeded to the throne in 1401 at the age of eleven and soon afterward had to withstand both internal rebellion and a Chinese invasion (1404–1405). Throughout his reign Sam Fang Kaen worked to strengthen his control over outlying provinces, building the resources that his son, Tilokaracha, would use to make Lan Na a major power on his succession to the throne in 1441.

[*See also* Lan Na *and* Tilokaracha.]

N. A. Jayawickrama, trans., *The Sheaf of Garlands of the Epochs of the Conqueror* (1968). David K. Wyatt, *Thailand: A Short History* (1984).   DAVID K. WYATT

SAMIL MOVEMENT. *See* March First Independence Movement.

SAMKHYA, meaning *enumeration,* is one of the six systems of classical Indian philosophy. Although formalized at a relatively late date by Ishvarakrishna (second–fourth century?) in his *Samkhyakarika,* early Samkhya thought, with its nontheistic, dualist notions of the evolution of plural souls *(purusha)* in a material world *(prakriti),* and their liberation from suffering through knowledge alone, was very influential in the formation of early Indian thought, especially as expressed in the Upanishads, the *Bhagavad Gita*, and the system of classical yoga. [*See also* Yoga *and* Hinduism.]

Gerald J. Larson, *Classical Sāṁkhya: An Interpretation of its History and Meaning* (2d ed., 1979).

RANDOLPH M. THORNTON

SAMSKARA, often translated as "sacrament," is the term in Hinduism for a set of important rituals and their karmic effect on the personality. Classically sixteen in number, the *samskaras* mark crucial points in the life cycle from conception to funeral. Included is the Upanayana ceremony, which is the assumption of the sacred thread, or the "second-birth" for upper castes. [*See also* Hinduism.]

R. B. Pandey, "The Hindu Sacraments (Saṁskāras)," in *The Cultural Heritage of India*, vol. 2 (2d ed., 1962).

RANDOLPH M. THORNTON

SAMURAI, warrior class of Japan that emerged in the provinces in the early Heian period (794–1185). The samurai ("those who serve"), also known as *bushi* ("military gentry"), became the rulers of the country upon the founding of the Kamakura shogunate in 1185, and held power until the Meiji Restoration of 1868, when Japan entered the modern age. The samurai class was dissolved in the 1870s as part of the creation of a modern social structure.

In the Taika Reform of 645, the Japanese government, centered on the emperor's court, nationalized all the rice-producing land in the country and instituted a system of allotting equal-sized plots of land to members of the peasantry. Various taxes were attached to the allotted lands, including a corvée labor assessment that was used mainly to recruit manpower for a national army. With the decline of the allotment system and the establishment of private estates (*shōen*) in the eighth century, however, military conscription through corvée became increasingly unfeasible. Finally, in 792 the government abandoned conscription and directed district officials (the country was divided into some 66 provinces and 593 districts) to maintain local militia to keep the peace.

Two years later the court government, which had been in Nara from 710 until 784, was established in the newly constructed capital of Heian (modern Kyoto). Although the court organized mercenary armies to subdue recalcitrant tribesmen in the north during the first decade of the Heian period, it thereafter ceased to be directly involved in military affairs. When disturbances occurred in the provinces, the court commissioned provincial leaders to deal with them. Increasingly, the court neglected not only the police function but other aspects of provincial administration as well. A brilliant cultural and social life evolved in Kyoto, and the courtiers immersed themselves in it, leaving management of the provinces largely to the provinces themselves. Thus were created the conditions that gave rise in provincial society to the samurai class and to the institutions of feudalism: the growth of private estates; the weakening of central control of provincial government; and the taking up of arms to maintain local order.

The first significant glimpse we get of samurai society in the provinces is in the war tale *The Chronicle of Masakado*, which recounts the unsuccessful rebellion of Taira no Masakado (d. 940) in the Kantō, or eastern region, in the late 930s. The Kantō was frontier land in that age, and became the birthplace of the samurai.

In addition to describing the methods of fighting of eastern warriors in the mid-tenth century *The Chronicle of Masakado* informs us that these warriors were organized into bands called *bushidan*. During Masakado's time the *bushidan* was made up mostly of men related to the band's chieftain by blood. Later, however, the *bushidan* came to include nonrelated warriors as vassals of the chieftain. A distinctive feature of the lord-vassal relationship—one of the key elements of feudalism—as it evolved in samurai society was the use of fictive kinship terms, such as *ke'nin* ("houseman") and *ie no ko* ("child of the house"), to identify the vassal as a "child" or "son" of the lord, his "father." (The fictive parent-child relationship—*oyabun-kobun* in modern Japanese—is also found in many other social groupings: e.g., in factions within modern political parties and among members of the underworld.)

Leadership of the samurai class, as it evolved in the provinces in the middle and late Heian period, was assumed by members of court society, indeed by descendants of the imperial family itself. Emperors were polygamous and had many offspring; and it became the practice to exclude surplus princes from the imperial family, bestowing upon them surnames (the imperial family has no surname) such as Taira (or Heike) and Minamoto (or Genji). Some of these former princes stayed in Kyoto and founded courtier lines; others accepted posts in the provinces, often remaining in their regions after their terms of office expired. During the tenth century two great clans—the Kammu Taira (Taira descended from Emperor Kammu, 737–806) and the Seiwa Minamoto (Minamoto descended from Emperor Seiwa, 850–880)—arose as leaders of samurai society. So impressive and admired did the names Taira and Minamoto become that many warriors assumed them even though they were not consanguineously related. As a result Taira and Minamoto branch families sprang up rapidly in many parts of the country. Taira branches, for example, became numerous in the Kantō in the tenth century, and indeed the rebellion of Masakado was caused by infighting among the Taira in that region.

An important stage in the development of the samurai class was the series of campaigns fought by the Minamoto over a thirty-year period in the late eleventh century against independent-minded families ensconced in satrapies in northern Honshu. Confronted with rugged terrain and often inhospitable climatic conditions, the Minamoto established a great fighting tradition at this time, a tradition stirringly recorded in a brief war tale entitled *A Tale of Mutsu*. Perhaps the most important legacy of these northern campaigns, as they are described in *A Tale of Mutsu*, was the elevation of one of the Minamoto chieftains, Yoshiie (1039–1106), to the status of a "god of war." Ever after, the Minamoto looked back to Yoshiie as the spiritual forebear of their clan. Of more immediate importance, people began, in the wake of the Minamoto victories in the north, to commend lands directly to Yoshiie for protection, thus presenting the Kyoto court with the ominous possibility of the creation of a separatist warrior adminstration in the east and north.

The rise of the samurai in the Heian period was, in institutional terms, a process whereby arms-bearing men in the provinces, forming a warrior elite and organizing themselves into bands (*bushidan*), became the de facto managers of both estates and district- and province-level governments. In many provinces, for example, the governors were absentee courtiers or princes, and affairs were handled by local samurai serving as vice-governors.

By the mid-twelfth century court government in Kyoto was rent by conflict, with courtiers opposing one another and members of the imperial family (an emperor and a former emperor) vying for advantage. Samurai chieftains of both the Taira and Minamoto were drawn into this conflict, which polarized into opposing factions, and in 1156 and 1159 there were two clashes of arms in the capital. As a result, the leadership of the Minamoto, descended from Yoshiie, was decimated, and a branch of the Taira (the Ise Taira or Taira from the province of Ise) became a dominant force in court government. Following the practice of courtier families before them, the Taira sought to consolidate their power by marrying into the imperial family. In 1180 the Taira leader, Kiyomori (1118–1181), who had already acquired high court rank and office for himself, became the grandfather of a child emperor. In this same year, however, Minamoto clansmen rose in the provinces and precipitated a five-year war from 1180 to 1185, that led to the total destruction of the Ise Taira and the establishment by the Minamoto chieftain Yoritomo (1147–1199) of the Kamakura shogunate (1185–1333).

The flourishing of the Taira and the Taira-Minamoto war are the subjects of the *Tale of the Heike*, the greatest of the war tales. More literature than history, the *Tale of the Heike* pictures the Taira, having achieved great heights but also having become haughty, as fated to fall. In addition, the Taira are depicted, especially as they suffer the agonies of defeat in war with the Minamoto, as surrogates for the courtiers, who were being displaced historically at this time by the samurai as the ruling elite of the country. Indeed, in later literature and theater the Taira are frequently portrayed as the possessors more of courtly than samurai qualities. The Minamoto, on the other hand, are shown in the *Tale of the Heike* as hard-fighting, intrepid warriors who symbolized the qualities and virtues esteemed of the samurai of the coming medieval age. [*See* Minamoto *and* Taira no Kiyomori.]

The founding of the shogunate at Kamakura in the Kantō, long the seat of the Seiwa Minamoto, ushered in the medieval age. Minamoto Yoritomo received from the emperor the title of *sei-i tai shōgun* ("barbarian-subduing generalissimo," often abbreviated to *shōgun*); and although he retained this title only briefly, it later became the standard designation for a warrior hegemon who headed a government called *bakufu* (translated into English as "shogunate"). The selection of Kamakura as the capital of the shogunate reflected the fact that, at base, this new warrior regime was a Kantō hegemony. Although Yoritomo was authorized by Kyoto to appoint his officials—stewards (*jitō*) to estates and constables (*shugo*) to provinces—throughout the country, the shogunate always retained its eastern character.

A great challenge was presented to the Kamakura shogunate in the late thirteenth century when China,

FIGURE 1. *Samurai Armor*. A suit of *ō yoroi* ("great armor"), fourteenth century.

then under Mongol rule, twice (in 1274 and 1281) invaded Japan. The invasions, made in the Hakata region of northern Kyushu, were brief, and both ended in failure when typhoons—which the Japanese believed were *kamikaze*, or "divine winds"— forced the Mongols to return to their ships and, having suffered great losses, to put back to sea. One particularly interesting feature of the Mongol invasions was the contrast in fighting styles of the Mongols, organized largely into units of foot soldiers, and the Japanese samurai, who fought individually on horseback. The Mongol invasions placed great strain on the Kamakura shogunate, because the medieval samurai fought in anticipation of rewards in land; in this case there were no lands

to confiscate from a defeated enemy to distribute to the "victors." [*See* Mongol Empire: Mongol Invasions of Japan.]

The Kamakura shogunate was overthrown in 1333 by a coalition of forces supporting the loyalist movement of Emperor Go-Daigo (1288–1339). After a short, abortive attempt to restore rule by the emperor the Ashikaga, or Muromachi, shogunate (1336–1573) was founded in Kyoto in 1336. [*See* Go-Daigo *and* Kemmu Restoration.] From the outset, the government of the Ashikaga shoguns was beset with problems of regionalism. Institutionally, the history of the Muromachi period is in large part a record of several stages in the development of the domains of regional samurai rulers known as daimyos. The shogunate reached its peak about 1400, when the Ashikaga shogun presided over a hegemony comprising daimyo domains located mainly in the central and western parts of the country. But the hegemony declined steadily in the fifteenth century, and was totally destroyed in the Ōnin War (1467–1477) and its aftermath. [*See* Ōnin War.]

The period of nearly a century following the Ōnin War, 1478–1568, is called the "age of the country at war" (*sengoku jidai*). Gradually, a new breed of daimyo emerged and carved out independent and more solidly controlled domains, which in the late sixteenth century became the territorial building blocks for unification.

The Sengoku period was an exciting, although bloody, era in Japanese history. It was preeminently the age of the samurai, who engaged lustily in their profession of fighting. No great war tales were written to romanticize the samurai of Sengoku times. Hence we can observe their behavior rather more realistically than in earlier centuries. Perhaps the strongest impression we receive is how unromantic and fundamentally brutal the samurai life was. Whereas the war tales of former times had extolled such virtues as spotless honor and undying loyalty, we find countless examples in the Sengoku period of devious scheming and outright treachery. Indeed, we are apt to conclude that scheming and treachery were the true hallmarks of the samurai way. Although, as we shall see, a warrior code called *bushidō* (the way of the *bushi*, or samurai) was formulated after warfare ceased and the Tokugawa *bakfu* was established in 1600, no such code existed in the Sengoku period. The Sengoku samurai were little inclined to philosophize about themselves; rather, they behaved according to a roughly conceived "way of men" (*otoko no michi*). Honor to them seems, for example, to have been based more on a crude sense of personal "face" than on any devotion to higher principles. [See Sengoku Period.]

The age of unification, which began when Oda Nobunaga (1534–1582) entered Kyoto in 1568 and established himself as an emergent hegemon, was a heroic and dynamic period in Japanese history. The symbol of the age was the castle, which samurai warlords built as much for display as for military security and defense. Adding color to the times was the arrival of Europeans in Japan. The Portuguese came first in 1542, bringing with them trade, guns, and Christianity. The introduction of guns (muskets) could well have undermined and eventually destroyed the samurai class, since firearms can be adequately handled by almost anyone and do not require the skills of an elite military class. Guns were difficult to acquire during the age of unification, however, and when they did become widely available, about 1600, the country was unified and, with the founding of the Tokugawa shogunate (1600–1868), peace was made lasting.

Toyotomi Hideyoshi (1536–1598), who succeeded to the position of Nobunaga after the latter's assassination in 1582, completed unification in 1590. As fundamental to the process of unification as military conquest were the social policies implemented by Hideyoshi. Until his time, there had been no clear division between samurai and peasants. But Hideyoshi ordered all samurai who had not already done so to leave the countryside and take up residence in the towns and cities. At the same time, by means of a "sword hunt," Hideyoshi disarmed the peasantry and decreed that only samurai could possess weapons.

When Hideyoshi died in 1598, Tokugawa Ieyasu (1542–1616) emerged as the leading warlord of the land and, after a great victory of the Battle of Sekigahara in 1600, founded the Tokugawa shogunate. The new shogunate, which had its seat at Edo (modern Tokyo) in the Kantō and directly controlled about one-fourth of the rice-producing land in the country, constituted a hegemony over some 250 daimyo domains. In the 1630s the shogunate, fearful that Christianity was undermining Japanese society and that the European countries, trading in Kyushu ports, might join militarily with certain western daimyos to oppose it, instituted a national seclusion policy, which limited contact with the outside world to trade with a small number of Chinese and Dutch at the single port of Nagasaki. [See Seclusion.]

The great majority of samurai during the Tokugawa period were idle stipendiaries, separated from the land and obliged to live on fixed incomes based on the revenues of their former landed fiefs. They possessed the symbols, including swords, of a warrior class, but had no battles to fight. In addition, they suffered the indignity of a steady erosion of their purchasing power as peace brought an increase in commerce, which in turn caused inflation and benefited not the samurai, the ruling elite, but the merchants, who were officially regarded as the lowest class in society.

Bushidō, the "way of the warrior," evolved essentially in the attempt to justify the existence of the samurai class during the Tokugawa period. It was in part a glorification of the samurai fighting tradition of the past. More importantly, however, it stressed high ideals of service, honor, and loyalty, and spurred the samurai to develop their intellectual faculties through education as well as their physical prowess through military preparedness. Whereas the disorder of the Sengoku period, as noted, provided ample opportunity for samurai to ignore the warrior ideals and pursue their own interests, the fixed structuring of Tokugawa society—everyone had his place and was expected to remain in it—forced the samurai to accept the positions of feudal service into which they were born. Such forced feudal service, as it happens, instilled a strong sense of loyalty. The typical Tokugawa period samurai was fiercely loyal to his daimyo, even though the daimyo himself may have been incompetent (e.g., an infant) or personally unworthy. Tokugawa society, in short, produced a powerful loyalty ethic, an ethic that not only governed the behavior of the samurai but of the other classes as well.

The arrival in Edo (Tokyo) Bay of a flotilla headed by Commodore Matthew Perry of the United States in 1853 brought an end to Japan's seclusion policy. It also set in motion a series of events that led in 1867 to the dissolution of the Tokugawa shogunate and commencement of the Meiji Restoration, which brought Japan into the modern world. The Meiji Restoration was the work of a loyalist movement, headed by the samurai of certain key domains (e.g., Satsuma and Chōshū), who asserted that the shogun's government was no longer worthy and called for a restoration of power to the emperor. Imperial power, however, was "restored" in name only. The rulers of the new Meiji government (Meiji oligarchs) were for the most part former samurai, especially from Satsuma and Chōshū domains.

The Meiji Restoration was not a social revolution in its early stages, inasmuch as it was carried out primarily by the samurai, the ruling class of Tokugawa society. The great majority of samurai who helped bring about the Restoration no doubt expected that they would thenceforth serve the emperor directly as his "vassals." But the new Meiji period rulers, although themselves samurai, realized that it would be necessary to do away with the samurai class and its special privileges in order to construct a modern social order. Thus, samurai status was abolished during the period 1873 to 1876, and the samurai were given bonds as terminal payment for the stipends they had received during Tokugawa times and in the early Meiji years.

Although the samurai class was officially abolished, former samurai provided leadership in many areas of pursuit for a modernizing Japan, including government and the political parties that emerged in the 1870s to challenge the entrenched power position of the Meiji oligarchs. Moreover, the "samurai spirit" remained a highly valued guide to personal behavior for the Japanese until at least the end of World War II.

[See also Shogun; Bakufu; and Bushidō.]

John W. Hall, *Japan, From Prehistory to Modern Times* (1970). George Sansom, *A History of Japan*, 3 vols. (1958–1963). G. R. Storry, *The Way of the Samurai* (1978). S. R. Turnbull, *The Samurai: A Military History* (1977). H. Paul Varley, *The Samurai* (1970).

PAUL VARLEY

SANCHI, Buddhist site of the third century BCE to the twelfth century CE in Madhya Pradesh, India, near ancient Vidisha. A brick stupa and polished

FIGURE 1. *Gate at the Great Stupa, Sanchi.* Shunga and early Andhra periods (third century BCE to early first century CE). The gates are elaborately carved with scenes from the life of the Buddha.

stone pillar were erected during Ashoka's reign (third century BCE). The stupa was enlarged and two others were erected between the second to first century BCE; two of the stupas were embellished with stone railings and gateways, on which were carved Jataka and other narrative scenes. Additional stupas were erected in the Gupta period, as were many monasteries and temples, such as a flat-roofed structure with a four-pillared portico of the early fifth century and a pillared, apsidal hall housing a stupa of the seventh century.

J. Marshall, A. Foucher, and N. G. Majumdar, *The Monuments of Sānchī*, 3 vols. (1940).

GERI HOCKFIELD MALANDRA

SANFAN REBELLION. *See* Three Feudatories Rebellion.

SAN FRANCISCO TREATY. Signed on 8 September 1951, the San Francisco Treaty brought an end to the war between Japan and the forty-eight nations that signed it.

The signatories other than Japan were nations that had declared war on Japan in World War II or new nations that had been created since that war in areas that had been occupied by Japan. The Soviet Union, while it attended the San Francisco conference, did not sign the treaty because it claimed that the United States, the author of the treaty, had acted in contravention of international agreements regarding the occupation of Japan. The Republic of China (Taiwan) and the People's Republic of China were not invited to the conference because of the ambiguous diplomatic status of those two governments since the civil war that had ended two years earlier.

On 19 October 1956 the Japanese and Soviet governments signed a declaration in Moscow ending the state of war between them and establishing normal diplomatic relations, but no treaty of peace was negotiated because of the Soviet occupation of Japan's northern islands. The Republic of China and Japan signed a separate treaty of peace on 28 April 1952. It was not until 12 August 1978 that the People's Republic of China and Japan signed a treaty of peace and friendship.

Under the provisions of the San Francisco Treaty, in addition to an end of the state of war, Japan renounced all territories acquired or occupied between 1895 and 1945 and agreed to honor the security provisions of the United Nations charter; the

Allied powers recognized Japan's "inherent right of individual or collective self-defense" under the United Nations charter and its right to enter into collective security arrangements. The Occupation of Japan came to an end, economic relations between Japan and the other signatories were restored, and, in addition, Japan agreed to pay reparations in the form of goods and services.

At the same time as they signed the peace treaty, the United States and Japan signed a security treaty under the terms of which the United States would defend Japan against armed attack from without, in return for Japanese provision of bases for US forces. The security treaty was regarded as necessary by the two governments because American bases in Japan were vital to the war then being waged in Korea and because at that time Japan possessed only minor paramilitary defense forces.

[*See also* World War II in Asia.]

Frederick S. Dunn, *Peace-Making and the Settlement with Japan* (1963).   JOHN M. MAKI

SANGHA, Sanskrit term for a religious community in ancient India. It was used predominantly by Buddhists to designate their monastic community as one of the "three jewels" (*triratna*), along with the Buddha and the Dharma (his teachings). The early *sangha* was composed of initiated monks (*bhikshus*) and nuns (*bhikshunis*) and was governed by the Vinaya, one of the "three baskets" of early texts. Throughout Asian history the chief duty of the Buddhist laity has been to support the *sangha*.

[*See also* Buddhism: An Overview.]

Sukumar Dutt, *Buddhist Monks and Monasteries of India* (1962).   TODD THORNTON LEWIS

SANGKUM REASTR NIYUM ("People's Socialist Community"), a nationally oriented Cambodian political movement founded by Prince Norodom Sihanouk in 1955, shortly after his abdication as king. A condition of membership in the Sangkum was nonmembership in any other political party. Sihanouk founded the movement to mobilize support for himself and to dismantle Cambodia's multiparty political system, which had grown up since 1946. In the parliamentary elections of 1955, the Sangkum won 80 percent of the votes and all the seats in the National Assembly. It remained the dominant political organization in Cambodia until Sihanouk was overthrown in 1970.

[*See also* Norodom Sihanouk.]

DAVID P. CHANDLER

SANGUO PERIOD. *See* Three Kingdoms.

SANJAYA. The reign of Sanjaya (732–c. 760), king of Mataram, the southern part of Central Java, is considered to have been critical to the development of the themes of ritualized sovereignty practiced by subsequent Javanese states; most Javanese monarchs have expressed their legitimacy by tracing their ancestry to Sanjaya. Sanjaya's Cangal inscription of 732 provides information about the royal Shiva cult that Sanjaya instituted, at the beginning of his reign, in north-central Java's Dieng Plateau, on a sacred "mountain of the gods" that had been a center for the worship of indigenous deities but by the sixth century became the locus of a Javanese Shiva cult. According to the inscription, Sanjaya erected a *lingam* that he associated with a mountain, praising Shiva, Brahma, and Vishnu and invoking the immortals residing in the cosmic universe. Sanjaya thereby claimed to be the current and intimate representative of the ancestors as well as the patron of the Indian gods. The inscription further notes that from the time that Sanjaya subdued neighboring kings there was peace and prosperity and an end to fear.

[*See also* Mataram.]

Kenneth R. Hall, *Maritime Trade and State Development in Early Southeast Asia* (1985). F. H. van Naerssen and R. C. de Iongh, *The Economic and Administrative History of Early Indonesia* (1977).   KENNETH R. HALL

SANKIN KŌTAI ("alternate attendance"), system institutionalized in Japan by the Tokugawa shogunate (1600–1868) to maintain effective control over its vassal daimyo and certain liege vassals (*hatamoto*) by requiring them to spend alternative years in Edo in attendance upon the shogun. The *sankin kōtai* system had pre-Tokugawa precedents stemming from the nature of the relationship between feudal lord and vassal.

Initially, attendance was voluntary on the part of daimyo who wished to demonstrate their loyalty to Tokugawa Ieyasu (1542–1616) by journeying to Edo to swear allegiance. The first step in the direction of making it compulsory occurred in 1609, when all daimyo were ordered to attend the Tokugawa shogun at New Year's; in 1635, under the third Tokugawa shogun, it was institutionalized in the form that would continue until well into the nineteenth century. Each daimyo was required to spend alternate twelve-month periods in Edo. Strict regulations governed the time of the trip to and from

Edo; the route to be followed (in 1821 the Tōkaidō was the most heavily traveled, followed by the Ōshū Kaidō, the Nakasendō, and the Mito Kaidō); the size and composition of each daimyo's retinue; the number and size of Edo residences (*yashiki*), as well as their military and bureaucratic staffs (in 1721 daimyo with incomes in excess of 200,000 *koku* were entitled to have in Edo 15–20 cavalry, 120–130 infantry, and 250–300 attendants); the seating assigned to each daimyo in Chiyoda Castle when attending the shogun; and the nature and quantity of gifts (silver, silk, horses, falcons, swords) that were exchanged to symbolize the feudal relationship between the Tokugawa shogun and his vassal daimyo. Also strictly enforced was the provision that each daimyo's wife and legal heir were to be permanent residents in Edo as guarantees of his loyalty.

As a control mechanism designed to prevent insurrection, the *sankin kōtai* system was an integral part of a series of restraints imposed upon the Tokugawa daimyo, including constraints on castle repairs and new castle construction, the banning of intermarriage among daimyo houses without express shogunal approval, the dispatching of inspectors (*metsuke*) on surprise tours to daimyo domains, and the prevention of unauthorized meetings between daimyo of different domains. The *sankin kōtai* system was an immense success as a control mechanism; it accomplished its goal of preventing daimyo insurrection for several reasons: (1) it placed the daimyo under the close supervision of the shogunate for extended periods of time; (2) status and rank considerations kept the daimyo in constant competition with one another; and (3) it effectively impoverished the daimyo who, it has been estimated, spent as much as 70 to 80 percent of their annual incomes on *sankin kōtai*–related expenses (especially the upkeep of their Edo *yashiki*), and as a result were deprived of the financial means necessary to launch a successful anti-Tokugawa insurrection.

Critics of the system did emerge, with two of the most famous being Kumazawa Banzan (1619–1691) and Ogyū Sorai (1666–1728), both of whom were Confucian scholars who condemned the *sankin kōtai* system as doing more harm than good since the impoverishment of the daimyo had significant repercussions for the rest of society. Despite such critics, however, the system continued without significant change (the exception being the 1722–1730 emergency suspension) until 1862 when the shogunate, in a last desperate attempt to retain daimyo support, began to dismantle the system. The impact of the *sankin kōtai* system transcended the objectives of its creators, for, in addition to effectively controlling the daimyo, it also fostered the development of Osaka and Edo, the stimulation of a national commercial economy, and the growth of a merchant class.

Toshio Tsukahira, *Feudal Control in Tokugawa Japan: The Sankin Kōtai System* (1966). RONALD J. DiCENZO

SANSKRIT. *See* Indo-Aryan Languages and Literatures.

SANSKRIT IN SOUTHEAST ASIA. The Sanskrit language was the means by which such Indian literary expression as the mythology of the *Ramayana*, *Mahabharata*, and the *Puranas* (the sacred laws of Hinduism) and the texts of Mahayana Buddhism were communicated to Southeast Asia. These texts were the sources on which the court culture in Southeast Asia's earliest states was based. Sanskrit was the language of sacred court ceremony, record keeping, and scholarship in these states. It was used to sanctify kings and other ruling elite. The oldest surviving Southeast Asian written records, fourth-century rock inscriptions from the Malay Peninsula, southern Vietnam, Java, and Borneo, were written in Sanskrit. Scholars disagree whether North or South India was the source of the alphabet used in this earliest Sanskrit writing. By the seventh century Southeast Asians began to express themselves in their own vernacular, but they still frequently employed Sanskrit as the language of sacred ceremony while using their own languages and alphabets to express the affairs of this world. This joint usage largely ended by the fourteenth century after the Southeast Asian island realm began converting to Islam and the states of the mainland adopted Theravada Buddhism, which used Pali as its sacred language.

[*See also* Indianization.]

G. Coedès, *The Indianized States of Southeast Asia*, translated by Susan B. Cowing (1968).

KENNETH R. HALL

SANTAL, the largest tribe of indigenous peoples in India, numbering 3.6 million in 1971. They are classified ethnologically as proto-Australoid, and their language, Santali, has been classified with the Munda group as belonging to the Austroasiatic subfamily. It has no script of its own, but in the twentieth century a script called *ol chiki* was fashioned by Raghunath Murmu, a Santal master.

Originally inhabitants of southern Bihar, the Santals moved into Bengal and then into eastern Bihar, where they founded their reserve, the Demin-i-Koh. With a legendary reputation as reclaimers of land, they are now engaged in cultivation as landowners, sharecroppers, and agricultural laborers. The Santals have also been long exposed to influences of Hinduism and Christianity, although most of them still adhere to their ancient religion.

[*See also* Adivasis.]

P. C. Biswas, *The Santals* (1956).   K. S. SINGH

SANTRI, Javanese term for a student of religion, especially one who studies at a religious school *(pesantren)* where instruction is given in Islam and Qur'anic exegesis. Scholars of modern Java often apply the term to those who adhere more or less strictly to Islamic principles, as opposed to the so-called *abangan* ("red ones"), who take their religion less seriously. But such a hard and fast distinction cannot always be maintained in practice. Historically, all members of the Javanese-Islamic religious communities were referred to as *santri* and were distinguished by their style of dress, social origins, and areas of settlement from the Javanese nobility and officials *(priyayi)*. But there were many social contacts between the two groups (e.g., *priyayi* families would usually send their male children to be educated at *pesantren*).

[*See also* Abangan *and* Priyayi.]

Clifford Geertz, *The Religion of Java* (1960) and *Islam Observed: Religious Development in Morocco and Indonesia* (1968). M. C. Ricklefs, "Six Centuries of Islamization in Java," in *Conversion to Islam*, edited by Nehemia Levitzion (1979).   PETER CAREY

SANYAN, or "three words," refers to the volumes of Chinese short stories compiled and edited by Feng Menglong (1574–1646). The collection was published in three installments: *Instructive Words to Enlighten the World* (1620?), *Popular Words to Admonish the World* (1624), and *Lasting Words to Awaken the World* (1627). These works are known as the *Sanyan* collection from the repetition of the graph for "word" *(yan)* in each title.

The *Sanyan* collection is an important example of vernacular fiction linking the Chinese oral and written traditions. The themes of crime and adventure, love, and the supernatural reflect the manners and mores of the urban middle-class culture of China in the seventeenth century.

[*See also* Chinese Literature.]

Cyril Birch, *Stories from a Ming Collection: The Art of the Chinese Story-teller* (1958). Liu Wu-chi, *An Introduction to Chinese Literature* (1966). Jaroslav Prušek, *Chinese History and Literature* (1970).

ANITA M. ANDREW

SAPRU, TEJ BAHADUR (1875–1949), Indian politician who made a very important contribution to Indian independence as the leading figure in the group known as the Liberal Party. He was a member of the Legislative Council of the United Provinces (1913–1916), then of the Imperial Legislative Council (1915–1920). When the new constitution (the Montagu-Chelmsford Reforms) came into force in 1921, he was appointed law minister by the governor-general. He opposed Mohandas Gandhi's non-cooperation movement, arguing that the best hope for India's freedom was to work within the constitutional framework that had been created in 1921, even though it fell far short of the nationalist demands. He was knighted for his services to the government, and in 1934 was appointed a member of the Privy Council in London. While a staunch supporter of Indian independence, he criticized the Indian National Congress for its opposition to the new constitution of 1935 and for its "Quit India" movement in 1942. Outside his political activities, Sapru supported measures for reform of Hindu law and he favored land reform that would give the peasants a better return for their labor. Sapru's career is a reminder that there were many Indians of great distinction who worked for independence outside the Indian National Congress.

[*See also* Gandhi, Mohandas Karamchand; Indian National Congress; *and* Montagu-Chelmsford Reforms.]

USHA SANYAL

SARABHAI, a leading family of Ahmedabad, Gujarat, India, eminent in industry, science, social reform, and the arts. Ambalal Sarabhai (1889–1969) founded an industrial textile empire. His contribution in 1915 rescued Mohandas Gandhi's ashram from financial ruin after Gandhi had admitted Untouchables. His sister Anasyuaben founded the Gandhian Ahmedabad Textile Labour Association. His daughter Gira created the Calico Museum of Textiles. Another daughter, Bharatiya, was a dramatist, writing mostly in England. A third daughter, Mridula, was the founder of the Gandhian women's welfare association, the Jyoti Sangh, and was active in national politics. His three sons were educated at

Oxford: Suhrud died at age twenty-nine; Gautam, with multinational cooperation, extended the family business into chemicals and pharmaceuticals; Vikram was chairman of India's Atomic Energy Commission and pioneer in atomic energy research. Vikram's wife Mrinalini was founder-director of the Darpana Academy of Dance.

Erik H. Erikson, *Gandhi's Truth* (1969). Howard Spodek, "The 'Manchesterization' of Ahmedabad," *Economic Weekly* 17.11 (March 13, 1965): 483–90. *Times of India, Directory and Yearbook, Including Who's Who, 1914–* (annual).   HOWARD SPODEK

SARAWAK, largest state in Malaysia, located on the northwestern coast of Borneo and adjoining Sabah, with which it constitutes East Malaysia. In 1970 its recorded population was 976,000, including several major ethnic groups, among them Iban (31 percent), Chinese (30 percent), Malays (19 percent), Melanaus (5 percent), and other Dayak (5 percent). Sarawak has three distinct geographical regions: an often swampy coastal plain; an intermediate, forested hill zone, suitable for shifting cultivation; and rugged interior highlands. Several important rivers traditionally provided the major routes into the interior. Settlement patterns mostly correspond to the geographical setting, with Malays, Melanaus, and Chinese living along the coast; Dayak in the hills; and a few hunters and gatherers roaming the mountains.

Sarawak's history can best be understood in the context of the wider realm of Borneo. Bone and artifact discoveries at Niah Cave confirm human occupation of the region perhaps as early as 40,000 BCE. Sarawak entered the Iron Age by 600 CE as coastal towns traded with both China and India as well as the interior. Islam arrived in the fifteenth century, and over several centuries many coastal dwellers adopted Islam and the Malay language, in the process styling themselves Malays. The coastal districts soon came under the loose suzerainty of the Malay-dominated Brunei sultanate. Malay attempts to control the Dayak interior often failed, especially after the aggressive headhunting Iban people commenced their migrations into Sarawak.

Sarawak's history entered a new stage when English adventurer Sir James Brooke intervened in a revolt against Brunei control and was appointed raja (governor) of the Sarawak River basin by the sultan of Brunei. Brooke inaugurated one hundred years of rule by a remarkable English family and a new form of imperial endeavor. At once traditional Bor-nean potentates, benevolent autocrats, and cautious modernizers, the Brookes viewed themselves as protectors of Sarawak's people; their enemies considered them unwelcome interlopers. The first raja spent his final years consolidating his control of surrounding districts and defending his government against various challenges. Although his political and financial position often seemed precarious, Brooke obtained for Sarawak the status of independent state under British protection. But its relations with Britain were often strained, partly owing to a consistent Brooke policy of incorporating territory at the expense of the declining Brunei sultanate. By 1905 the present boundaries of the state were achieved, but Brunei itself had also become a British protectorate.

James Brooke was succeeded as raja by his nephew Sir Charles Brooke, who ruled from 1868 to 1917, and who in turn passed the raj on to his son, Sir Charles Vyner Brooke (1917–1946). These men furthered the Brooke pattern of personal rule. Charles Brooke built on his uncle's foundation to develop a modern state and a sound economic base during his half-century of power. He mounted bloody military campaigns to suppress headhunting and at the same time incorporate autonomy-loving Dayak into the raj. His policies also created a plural society: Chinese immigrants, who came in response to economic incentives, accounted for 25 percent of the total state population of 490,585 by 1939. Chinese shops followed the building of Brooke forts, and Chinese-dominated towns developed throughout the state. Brooke involved the Malay elites in government and also allowed limited Dayak participation through the Council Negri, a consultative body formed in 1867. Hence, Sarawak society came to be characterized by a three-way division: most Malays were in government or fishing; most Chinese in trade, labor, or cash-crop farming; and most Dayak, especially Iban, in the police force or shifting cultivation.

The Brookes encouraged gambier and pepper planting, and Sarawak became the world's major supplier of pepper. Later, rubber became dominant, and an oil industry developed. Most cash-crop farmers remained smallholders rather than following the plantation pattern characteristic of Malaya or Sabah. Social change, especially the expansion of Christianity and mission schools, altered the nature of Dayak and Chinese society. Chinese and Malay schools also developed in urban areas. In the 1930s both the Chinese and Malay communities experienced a rise in ethnic consciousness. By this time personal rule had largely run its course, and Vyner

Brooke delegated authority to senior European civil servants and to the growing bureaucracy in Kuching.

The Japanese occupation of Sarawak (1941–1945) brought about major changes, including increasing politicization and conflict within and among ethnic groups owing to economic hardship and selective repression. Once it emerged from the war, Sarawak faced a turbulent political situation. Vyner Brooke's decision to cede the state to Britain as a crown colony had Chinese and some Dayak support, but it generated a powerful anticession movement among a section of the Malay community. The resulting sociopolitical divisions persisted for years. British colonial rule brought further bureaucratization and more rapid economic growth. By the late 1950s direct local elections were introduced, and political parties were formed in expectation of independence.

In 1963, Sarawak agreed to accept independence through federation with Malaysia, shifting from a Bornean to a peninsular orientation. But decisions had been made in haste, and some Sarawakians, including a small communist insurgency, opposed the development and continued to do so for years. During the early Malaysian period, political crises occurred frequently in the now elected and multiparty Council Negri. Since 1970 Sarawak politics have stabilized under the Malay-dominated profederal Sarawak Front, which represents the triumph of peninsular alliance-style, ethnic-based politics. The government has placed considerable emphasis on malaysianization of Sarawak's society and culture, including the spread of the Malay language, and on dramatically increasing exploitation of rich oil and timber resources, sometimes at the expense of interior peoples. Sarawak now flourishes economically but still retains a special flavor as befits a historical and sociocultural heritage rather different from that of the peninsular states.

[See also Iban; Dayak; Malays; Brooke, Sir James; Brooke, Sir Charles; Brooke, Sir Charles Vyner; and Malaya, Federation of.]

James Jackson, *Sarawak: A Geographical Survey of a Developing State* (1968). Michael Leigh, *The Rising Moon: Political Change in Sarawak* (1974). Robert Pringle, *Rajahs and Rebels: The Ibans of Sarawak under Brooke Rule, 1841–1941* (1967). R. H. W. Reece, *The Name of Brooke: The End of White Rajah Rule in Sarawak* (1982). Steven Runciman, *The White Rajahs: A History of Sarawak from 1841–1946* (1960).

CRAIG A. LOCKARD

SARBADARIDS (1336–1381), a militant Shi'ite group in western Khurasan centered in the city of Sabzavar. The dozen leaders of this polity, not strictly speaking a dynasty, adopted the name *Sarbadar*, that is, those prepared to put their "heads on the gallows" rather than accept injustice.

The state was one of several that arose in Iran during a time of weak central authority. It was founded by a local amir, Abd al-Razzaq Bashtini, as a protest against social and economic repression. His successor, Vajih al-Din Mas'ud, greatly expanded the movement and enhanced its legitimacy by allying with the leader of a local Sufi *tariqa*, Shaikh Hasan Juri.

Power sharing between the Sufi shaikhs and the local amirs was a hallmark of the Sarbadarid state, but it was ineffective and eventually contributed to the state's downfall. The followers of the shaikhs were an armed group recruited from urban workers; they expected the imminent arrival of the Mahdi and wanted to establish a theocracy. The "secular" Sarbadarid leaders, on the other hand, had less extreme religious ideas and were prepared to work within the framework of a larger state.

The last and longest-ruling of the Sarbadarids, Ali Mu'ayyad (r. 1364–1381), was opposed to establishing a theocracy and tried to destroy the Sufi organization. He planned to substitute a more moderate Imami (Twelver) Shi'ism for the radical variety they espoused. However, the state was put to an end before he could institute this.

Internal divisions combined with external enemies such as the (Sunni) Kart dynasty at Herat seriously weakened the Sarbadarid state. It surrendered to Timur in 1381, and the last of the Sarbadarids served as military commanders in other parts of Timur's empire. The Sarbadarid effort, while ultimately unsuccessful, foreshadowed the establishment of the Safavid empire by another militant Sufi group in western Iran in 1501.

[See also Kart Dynasty.]

John Mason Smith, Jr., *The History of the Sarbadār Dynasty 1336–1381 A.D. and Its Sources* (1970).

LAWRENCE POTTER

SAREKAT ISLAM. The Sarekat Islam, originally Sarekat Dagang Islam, the first large Indonesian nationalist party, was founded in 1911 by Raden Mas Tirtodisoerjo. It changed its name to Partai Sarekat Islam in 1923 and in 1929 to Partai Sarekat Islam Indonesia (PSII). Many people joined it, in particular in its early years, and even before 1920 the Sarekat Islam claimed a membership of more than one and a half million. In those years it also became involved in instances of local unrest, for example in West Java. Among its well-known leaders were Haji Umar Said Tjokroaminoto, Agus Salim, Abdul Muis, and Abikusno Tjokrosujoso. In its first years the Sarekat Islam also had a number of Communists among its leaders, including Semaoen and Alimin, who were also active in another party, the Indische Sociaal-Democratische Vereeniging (ISDV), the predecessor of the Partai Komunis Indonesia. At first they worked in uneasy cooperation with the Islamic leaders, but they were forced out of the Sarekat Islam in the early 1920s.

Originally an organization for all Muslims, Sarekat Islam became associated more and more with modernist Islam, in particular after traditionalists had established the Nahdatul Ulama in 1926. In the 1930s the Sarekat Islam experienced a number of conflicts, mainly over the question of cooperation or noncooperation with the colonial government. These resulted in a number of splinter groups. In 1933 Sukiman founded the Partai Islam Indonesia (PARII); in 1934 the later Darul Islam leader Kartosuwirjo established a second PSII, and in 1935 the Barisan Penjedar PSII of Agus Salim and Mohammad Rum was founded.

The PSII first entered the Masjumi after 1945 but broke away from it in 1947. As it turned out, the PSII continued to exist as a minor party, and in the national election of 1955 it received only 3 percent of the vote. In 1973 the PSII entered the new Islamic party Partai Persatuan Pembangunan, continuing its nonpolitical activities under the name of Syarekat Islam.

[*See also* Indonesia, Republic of; Semaoen; Alimin Prawirodirdjo; Partai Komunis Indonesia; Nahdatul Ulama; Darul Islam; Barisan Sosialis; *and* Masjumi.]

Deliar Noer, *The Modernist Muslim Movement in Indonesia, 1900–1942* (1973).   C. VAN DIJK

SARIT THANARAT

SARIT THANARAT (1908–1963), Thai military and political leader. Born in Bangkok, Sarit was the son of Major Luang Detanan, an army linguist who translated Cambodian chronicles into Thai. Through his maternal family, Sarit had prominent relatives on both sides of the Thai-Laos border (General Phoumi Nosavan, the Laotian defense minister who staged a coup d'état against the Phoui government in late December 1959, was Sarit's cousin).

Sarit studied in schools in Bangkok and Mukdahan and entered the Royal Thai Military Academy at the age of eleven. He graduated in 1929.

Sarit first experienced combat duty in the suppression of the Boworadet Rebellion of 1933. Later, in World War II, he distinguished himself as a popular battalion commander and an able military administrator of Lampang Province in the north. At the end of the war, many army officers were put on the inactive reserve rolls, but because of his outstanding record Sarit escaped this fate. Instead, he was given command of the prestigious First Regiment of the First Division, strategically stationed in Bangkok.

In 1947, when the army staged a coup against the Pridi-backed Thamrong government, Sarit's troops played a pivotal role in the power seizure. The following year, Sarit was promoted to commander of the First Military Circle (Bangkok). In 1949 he led his troops in the suppression of the Palace Rebellion, better known as the Free Thai coup attempt. From that time on, Sarit's career took a meteoric path— he was appointed commander of the first army, commander-in-chief of the army in 1954, and supreme commander of the armed forces in 1957.

The leaders of the 1947 coup did not assume full political leadership until 1951, when they forced the Khuang Aphaiwong government to resign. In the ensuing Luang Phibunsongkhram cabinet, Sarit became the deputy minister of defense, a position he kept until he became minister of defense in 1957.

The early 1950s marked Sarit's political education. He served as chairman of the National Lottery Organization and also sat on the boards of numerous banks and corporations. Using his government and business connections, Sarit was able to build up his political machinery through generous use of funds, particularly from the lottery organization.

Although he was the deputy leader of the ruling Serimanangkhasila Party, Sarit was able to escape public condemnation of strong-arm police tactics used in the elections of early 1957. But Phibun's courting of democratic legitimizing processes was to counteract Sarit's rising popularity. The "dirty" elections of 1957 brought forth public outrage. Sarit took the opportunity to express sympathy for the protesters and indirectly implicated Phibun and party secretary-general Phao Siyanon in election fraud. In September 1957, Sarit staged a coup d'état. His benefactor Phibun and his friend Phao were forced into exile.

Sarit did not become prime minister until 1958, when he returned from Walter Reed Hospital to stage a *coup de main* against General Thanom Kittikachorn, his trusted lieutenant. Sarit declared that his seizure of power was necessary to pave the way for a revolutionary regime advocating economic development, social and cultural conservatism, political authoritarianism, and anticommunism. He became the leader of the Revolutionary Council, and Thanom served as his deputy.

From 1959 until his death in 1963, Sarit ruled Thailand with an iron fist. He did not tolerate dissension, whether political, religious, or intellectual. His absolute power was reinforced by an interim constitution that gave the prime minister decisive authority whenever he deemed it necessary.

The Sarit regime promoted trade and emphasized the improvement of infrastructure. The suppression of communist expansion at home and abroad became a prominent regime policy, and such policies led to closer cooperation with the United States in the execution of the latter's foreign policy—through SEATO and later through military support of the American efforts in Indochina. Lastly, Sarit's rule also marked the rising popularity and status of King Bhumibol and the royal family, whose support gave the Sarit regime stability and legitimacy.

By the time Sarit died, he had amassed a personal fortune of over $120 million, most of which was confiscated by the Thanom government. Next to Phibun, Sarit is one of the best known, if not most notorious, Thai military dictators.

[See also Thailand; Pridi Phanomyong; Free Thai; Phibunsongkhram, Luang; Khuang Aphaiwong; and Thanom Kittikachorn.]

Thak Chaloemtiarana, *Thailand: The Politics of Despotic Paternalism* (1979).   THAK CHALOEMTIARANA

SARNATH, near Varanasi, India, ancient Rishipatana or Mrigadava, is where the Buddha preached his first sermon and is one of the four places where, after his death, a shrine was built. The emperor Ashoka erected a pillar and stupa there. The stupa was enlarged six times, the final enlargement in the eleventh century under the reign of Mahipala I. In the Gupta period, Sarnath, with thirty monasteries and thousands of monks, was a center of Buddhist art, producing hundreds of Buddha images. Another colossal brick and stone stupa, named Dhamekh, was constructed, as were temples and monasteries. In succeeding years images of Mahayana-Vajrayana deities were worshiped there. The latest buildings were commissioned by the Gahadavala queen Kumaradevi in the twelfth century.

[See also Buddhism: An Overview and Varanasi.]

J. M. Rosenfield, "On the Dated Carvings of Sārnāth," *Artibus Asiae* 26 (1963): 10–26. D. R. Sahni, *Catalogue of the Museum of Archaeology at Sarnath* (reprint, 1972).

GERI HOCKFIELD MALANDRA

SARRAUT, ALBERT-PIERRE (1872–1962), a high colonial official and administrator in early twentieth-century French Indochina. Sarraut entered politics as a member of the Radical Socialist Party and was elected as a deputy of the National Assembly in 1902. In 1911 he was appointed governor-general of French Indochina to succeed Antoni-Wladislas Klobukowski, who had been dismissed several months earlier. Sarraut was a firm believer in France's "civilizing mission" in Indochina, and he introduced a number of reforms that endeared him to much of the local population. Ultimately, however, the hopes aroused by his promises turned to disillusion. Stepping down from his post in late 1913, he returned for a second term from 1917 to 1919. He later became minister of colonies and premier of France during the 1930s.

[See also Klobukowski, Antoni-Wladislas.]

Joseph Buttinger, *Viet Nam: A Dragon Embattled* (1967).   WILLIAM J. DUIKER

SASANID DYNASTY. The Sasanids, the last dynasty of the pre-Islamic Iranian empire, reigned from 224 or 228 to 651 CE. The central administration of Iran appears to have been weakened in the last century of Parthian (Arsacid) rule, with the result that several western Iranian provinces, particularly Fars (Greek, Persis), the ancient homeland of the Achaemenids, enjoyed considerable autonomy. Around 213 the Persian Papak, son of Sasan (whose family were the hereditary priests of the Zoroastrian temple of Adur Anahid at Istakhr, near Persepolis), slew the Bazrangid satrap Gochihr. The Sasanids then took advantage of a battle for the Arsacid succession to seize the empire; Ardashir I, son of Papak, defeated the Parthian Ardavan V and appears to have been in full control by 228.

As the descendants of the Achaemenids and as restorers of their territory, glory, and orthodoxy, the Sasanids modeled themselves consciously on that earlier Persian dynasty; the *Karnamag-i Ardashir-i Papakan (Chronicle of Ardashir the Son of Papak)*, a fictional epic in Pahlavi, is a reshaping of the legend of the overthrow of the Medes by Cyrus. The official Sasanid propaganda, however, obscured the fact that many of the practices they claimed to revive were inherited from the Parthians. The Arsacids had wrested Iran from the Seleucids and held it for nearly half a millennium; perhaps by mistake rather than by design, Sasanid historiographers reduced this period by half and represented it as a time of chaos. The Parthians had also upheld Zoroastrianism; according to the *Denkard*, a text based on Sasanid learning, one of the kings named Ardavan had ordered the redaction of the Avesta. Yet the great Parthian fire temple of Adur Burzen Mihr near Nishapur was demoted to third place among Iranian shrines.

Zoroastrian Iran. The Islamic historian Mas'udi (d. 956) cites the advice of Ardashir I to his son and successor, Shapur I (r. 241–272): "Know that faith and kingship are brothers; one cannot survive without the other. Faith is the foundation of a kingdom, and the kingdom defends the faith." A newly centralized Zoroastrian priestly hierarchy under the zealous priest Tosar (or Tansar) assisted the "king of kings" at Ctesiphon in eliminating local resistance by suppressing shrines outside the new system. In response to the new policy, King Gushnasp of Tabaristan, a mountainous region south of the Caspian Sea that was slow to submit to Ardashir, complained to Tansar about the dousing of local sacred fires by Ardashir's priests.

The throne superimposed on the fire altar, an image found on coins, was to become an enduring symbol of the alliance of church and state in Sasanid Iran, and the seals of the Sasanid period indicate that the Magi fulfilled a variety of judicial, administrative, and commercial functions in the empire. Ardashir's defeat of the Parthians is depicted as a religious victory over evil in the bas-relief of his investiture at Naqsh-i Rustam, the *basilikon oros* where the Achaemenid kings were interred: the supreme God, Ohrmazd, hands the diadem of sovereignty to the Sasanid, and the mounts of the two trample underfoot the evil spirit Ahriman and the defeated Ardavan, respectively. [*See also* Ardashir I.]

Shapur I campaigned against Rome to recover lands to the Euphrates and beyond, capturing the emperor Valerian at Edessa in 260. His long inscription in Middle Persian, Parthian, and Greek on the Ka'ba-yi Zardusht at Persepolis records conquered lands and is thus a basic source for Iranian geography as well as for Sasanid administration, a system of offices hereditarily occupied, as under the Parthians, by the scions of the great noble houses.

Although Shapur I favored the Manichaeans, the Zoroastrian high priest Kartir (or Kirder), who

FIGURE 1. *Head of a King.* Iranian, Sasanid period, fourth century; silver with mercury gilding. The king is depicted wearing a necklace, pendant earrings, and a crown with a striated globe headdress. Height 40 cm.

served under six kings from Shapur to Narseh (r. 293–303), gradually accumulating honors and titles, records his own zealous persecutions of Buddhists, Jews, Christians, nonconformist Zoroastrians, and others in more inscriptions than have been left by any single Sasanid monarch. In one of these, at Sar Mashhad, Kartir describes a vision of heaven similar to that described in the Pahlavi *Book of the Righteous Viraz*: supernatural justification, perhaps for a doubting king, of his extremism. The latter part of the third century was a time of short reigns and turbulent battles for the succession, with consequent military reversals; the Roman emperor Carus reached Ctesiphon in 283, and Galerius defeated the army of Narseh in 297. [*See also* Shapur I *and* Kartir.]

Relations with the West. The fourth century is dominated by the figure of Shapur II (r. 309–379). Against Christian Constantine and apostate Julian alike, as chronicled by Ammianus Marcellinus the Iranian king is a grandiose and implacable foe, styling himself *particeps siderum . . . frater solis ac lunae* ("partner of the stars . . . brother of the sun and moon"). He responded to the proclamation of Christianity as the official Roman religion, and to the rapid spread of the faith in Iran itself, with punitive taxes and a campaign that came to be known as the Great Persecution. Iranian nobles and those who proselytized Christianity were the converts generally singled out for harshest treatment. In the fifth century, the Sasanids accorded official recognition to the Nestorian church, partly because the church was anathematized by Byzantium and thus owed the enemy no loyalty; the Nestorian patriarch resided at Ctesiphon and was appointed by the king. [See also Shapur II.]

Jews in Iran generally fared well. They did not proselytize, and Iran could count on their hostility to the increasingly anti-Semitic Byzantines. Some Jews also professed Zoroastrianism and were thus spared the poll tax. There are also, however, instances of severe Sasanid repression of Jewish mass messianic movements that had led to civil disturbances. In the fourth century, for instance, the emperor Julian had sought to win Jewish support against Iran by promising to rebuild the Temple at Jerusalem, but the exilarch supported the Persians.

Armenia in the fourth century was newly christianized, and its Arsacid royal family was hostile to the Sasanids; the country remained a bone of contention between Byzantium and Iran to the seventh century. The Armenian historian P'awstos Buzand has left an epic account of the wars of the fourth century. The last Armenian Arsacid, Artashes, opposed by the factious and independent-minded local dynasts, the naxarars, was replaced at the order of Bahram V (surnamed Gur, "the onager"; r. 420–438) in 428 by a Persian marzban (governor). Bahram's successor, Yazdigird II, encouraged by the Magi and by his able wuzurg framadar (prime minister), Mihrnarseh, sought to reimpose Zoroastrianism on the Armenians. Despite the apostasy of a number of naxarars and the defeat of the Armenian commander Vardan Mamikonean at the Battle of Avarayr (451), most Armenians held to their faith, which, because of its increasing doctrinal alienation from Byzantium, the Persians chose to tolerate. [See also Bahram Gur.]

Adurbad-i Mahraspandan, Zoroastrian high priest under Shapur II, must have faced internal challenges to orthodoxy, for he is said to have undergone and miraculously survived an ordeal in which molten bronze was poured over his breast. A number of collections of moral and didactic maxims, called andarz, are attributed to him, and later high priests of Fars traced their descent to him, but nei-

ther he nor any other single priest ever again amassed the power Kartir had held. Indeed, the later Sasanids tended rather to subdivide crucial offices and to widen their base of support. Thus, the single wuzurg framadar was replaced by four spahbads (commanders), one for each quadrant of the empire, and concessions were granted to the lesser nobility, the azadhah (free men), by Khusrau I. But the monarchy continued to be threatened, as the Arsacids had been, by a factious, powerful, centrifugal nobility.

The Parthians were themselves from Central Asia, but the eastern borders, subject to nomadic raids, were a source of trouble for both the Achaemenid and Sasanid dynasties from Fars. In the late third century, Shapur I had conquered the Kushan kingdom in Bactria and northern India, but new powers—Hephthalites, then Turks—were to threaten the empire. In the fifth and sixth centuries Iran and Byzantium vied for control of the trade routes across Central Asia to the Tarim Basin and China beyond.

Peroz (r. 459–484) was killed in battle against the Hephthalites, a warlike Indo-European people to whose kingdom Iran became tributary for nearly thirty years; his son, Kawad I (r. 488–497 and 499–531), who had lived two years as their hostage, had to rely on his former captors to return him to the throne when he was deposed and imprisoned in the Fortress of Oblivion by a hostile noble faction. Khusrau I (r. 531–579), in alliance with the Turks, at last defeated the Hephthalites in 558. [See also Huns.]

Khusrau had to contend with internal foes as well: his father Kawad, perhaps in a bid to strengthen the crown against nobles and clergy, had supported the communistic movement of Mazdak, who had sought to dismantle the latter and to annul the privileges of the former. The young king earned the grateful epithet Anushirvan ("of immortal soul") for his bloody suppression of the Mazdakites. His reign saw also the final redaction of the twenty-one nasks ("divisions") of the Avesta and the translation of many Indian works into Pahlavi. After the Muslim conquest of Iran, some of these, including the astrological table zig-i shahriyaran and tales from the Pancatantra, were translated into Arabic by Iranian converts from Zoroastrianism such as Ibn al-Muqaffa. Much of the Thousand and One Nights is Indian legend in Iranian garb. Khusrau I also invited to his court the Greek philosophers whose ancient school at Athens had been closed by Justinian, according to Agathias. [See also Khusrau Anushirvan and Mazdak.]

SASANID IRAN

SOGDIANA
ARMENIA
Artaxata
Caspian Sea
Araxes
GILAN
PARTHIA
Bukhara •Samarkand
Oxus (Amu Darya)
•Merv
TABARISTAN •Nisa
•Balkh
BACTRIA
MEDIA •Rayy Nishapur•
KHURASAN •Bamian
Hari Rud •Kabul
•Ecbatana
✗ Nihavend 642 •Herat
Tigris
Ctesiphon
Helmand
•Kandahar
✗ Qadisiyya 635 •Susa •Yazd SISTAN
Euphrates
KHUZISTAN Indus
•Istakhr •Kerman
Shiraz•
FARS KERMAN
ARABIA
Persian Gulf
MAKRAN

⬚ The Sasanid Empire ca. 610 CE
≡ Hephthalites (Huns) 5th–6th centuries CE
✗ Battle sites

0   200   400   600 km
0   200   400 miles

Decline of the Empire. Khusrau II Abarwez (New Persian, Parviz, "the victorious"; r. 591–628), whose reign is chronicled by the Armenian Sebeos and others, was assisted by the Byzantine Maurice in recovering his throne following the revolt of Bahram Chubin, a general from the powerful Parthian Mihran family who had apparently sought to restore the Arsacids. Khusrau pursued an ambitious policy of conquest, seizing Jerusalem in 614 and having the relics of the True Cross removed to Persia. This was no mere looting: Khusrau hoped to rule all the world's faiths and to subjugate Byzantium and China; for their rulers he kept empty thrones beneath his own at court. Heraclius counterattacked, invading Media in 622–626 and extinguishing the sacred fire of Adur Gushnasp; the Iranians then pursued the invader back to the gates of Constantinople.

The "victorious" king who had sought to rule the world was murdered by his sons, and his imperious policies and ruinously expensive wars had alienated the important Arab buffer state of the Lakhmids of Hira; the Christian and Jewish communities, too, were to welcome the invading Muslims. Neither Byzantium nor Iran had taken any account of Muhammad's conquest of Mecca in 630, and the last of the Sasanids, Yazdigird III, crowned a year later, was to behold the Arabs crossing the Tigris into Ctesiphon a decade into his reign. He and the Persian garrison are reported by Dinavari and Tabari to have exclaimed then that the *devs* ("demons") had arrived. Perhaps they were expected, for dire apocalyptic predictions were in the air. But the defense of Iran was impeded less by superstitious resignation than by economic exhaustion, and by rivalry and treachery among the Iranian generals. Yazdigird spent the second half of his reign like an Iranian Lear retreating across Iran ahead of the Arabs; he found little hospitality for his retinue among the nobles who grudgingly received him, and they denied him the taxes needed to raise an army. In 651 the fugitive king was slain by a miller at Merv with whom he had taken refuge from the city's treacherous governor. [See also Yazdigird III.]

Armed resistance continued sporadically throughout the empire; forty thousand defenders are said to have fallen in the long siege of Istakhr; the holy fire of Adur Anahid there seems to have been spirited off to a village near Yazd, where it still burns. Mountainous regions near the Caspian that had resisted Ardashir now held out against Islam for at least a century, and it was not until the ninth century that there were appreciable mass conversions to the religion of the Arab enemy. It was then, when the old culture of Iran appeared irretrievably doomed, that several Zoroastrian priests of Fars set down in writing some of their religious and epic lore, in the Pahlavi books, for posterity. But the Sasanid heritage survived also in Arabic and New Persian works, notably the *Shahnama* of Firdausi, and in the masterpieces of Sasanid architecture, textiles, and metalwork, with their many derivatives in Islamic and medieval European art.

[See also Denkard; Kushan Dynasty; Manichaeism; and Zoroastrianism.]

Mary Boyce, trans., *The Letter of Tansar* (1968). S. H. Taqizadeh, "The Early Sasanians," *Bulletin of the School of Oriental and African Studies* 11 (1943–1946). Ehsan Yarshater, ed., *The Seleucid, Parthian and Sasanian Periods* (1983), vol. 3 of the *Cambridge History of Iran*.

JAMES R. RUSSELL

SATAVAHANA DYNASTY,

also known as the Andhras, succeeded the Mauryas in the Deccan in India. The Puranas have conflicting accounts about their genealogy and chronology, and extant coins add some more names to the dynasty. The most powerful king was Gautamiputra Satakarni, who flourished early in the second century CE. The two other notable kings were Vasishthiputra Pulumavi and Yajna Sri Satakarni. Soon after the reigns of these two sovereigns, in the third century, the Satavahanas declined and lost power. Some of the kings fought wars against the Sakas of western India with mixed success. They were patrons of Brahmanism, but Buddhist activities also flourished.

[See also Maurya Empire.]

R. C. Majumdar, ed., *The Age of Imperial Unity* (4th ed., 1968). K. A. Nilkanta Sastri, ed., *A Comprehensive History of India*, vol. 2 (1957).   A. K. NARAIN

SATHING PHRA. See Satingpra.

SATI

(alternate spelling, *suttee*), the Hindu custom of a widow being cremated together with her husband on his funeral pyre as an expression of her devotion. The term also refers to the woman herself. *Sati* is a Sanskrit word meaning "virtuous woman," and earliest Indian texts refer to this meaning only; the sati ritual seems not to have belonged to the Vedic age. Travelers first reported satis in the fourth century BCE, and Indic references to the practice appear in texts as early as the *Mahabharata* (c. 300 BCE–300 CE). In the nineteenth century witnesses told of satis most frequently in Rajasthan, Central India, the Punjab, the Ganges River valley, and, in southern India, in Madura and Vijayanagar. The British at first refused to prohibit the custom, but in 1829 Lord William Cavendish Bentinck signed Regulation 17, which made the burning or burying alive of widows a criminal offense and the use of force or drugs an act punishable by death. Conservative Hindus in Calcutta appealed the Regulation to the Privy Council without success, but by 1860 the practice was illegal throughout the subcontinent. Nonetheless, satis occasionally continue to be reported even in the latter part of the twentieth century.

Ashis Nandy, "Sati: A Nineteenth Century Tale of Women, Violence and Protest," in *Rammohun Roy and the Process of Modernization in India*, edited by V. C. Joshi (1975). "Suttee," in *Hobson-Jobson*, edited by Henry Yule and A. C. Burnell (1886; reprint, 1968), pp. 878–883. Edward Thompson, *Suttee* (1928).

JUDITH E. WALSH

SATINGPRA

refers both to a small district town in south Thailand and to the long, narrow peninsula fronting the Gulf of Siam in which the town lies. Chance finds there of sculpture and pottery dating back a millennium or so, together with local legends that insist it was once a royal capital, have long hinted at Satingpra's importance in antiquity. Recent archaeological excavations at Satingpra have confirmed this impression. It appears that from the seventh through the thirteenth century a small urban center at Satingpra, supported by a sophisticated network of canals for drainage, irrigation, and navigation, was engaged in trade with China, India, and other areas in Southeast Asia.

Stanley J. O'Connor, "Satingphra: An Expanded Chronology," *Journal of the Malay Branch of the Royal Asiatic Society* 39.1 (1966): 137–144. LORRAINE M. GESICK

SATŌ NOBUHIRO

SATŌ NOBUHIRO (1769–1850), Japanese political economist and reformer of the late Edo (Tokugawa) period. Satō Nobuhiro was for a time advisor to Mizuno Tadakuni, who led the *bakufu*'s Tempō Reforms of the 1830s and 1840s. His thought represents a strange mixture of ideas drawn from Confucian, Shinto, and Western sources, but taken as a whole it may be characterized as "absolutist." He advocated a degree of centralized control over state affairs unprecendented in Japanese political thinking, arguing that one national government should maintain exclusive control over trade, commerce, industrial development, agriculture, military affairs, and education. Satō proposed policies that entailed abolishing the hereditary status system and instituting a system of advancement based on merit. He stressed the need for universal, state sponsored education and for a conscript army and navy. He urged that national isolation be rejected in favor of overseas expansion and colonization. The centralized rule he envisioned for Japan was to be conducted by a monarch "established in accordance with divine will," by which phrase he might have meant either the shogun or emperor. Thus, in many crucial ways he foreshadowed the political reforms of the Meiji Period.

[*See also* Tempō Reforms.]

BOB TADASHI WAKABAYASHI

SATRAP

SATRAP, the Median designation of a governor in the Achaemenid empire. The satraps probably existed under the Medes, since the Old Persian form for governor is *khshassapavan*. The satraps combined military and political leadership, emulating the imperial court. Under the Seleucids the title was given to governors of smaller regions than under the Achaemenids, and by Sasanid times the satrap had become the chief of a large city and surrounding countryside. In the late Achaemenid empire the satraps in Anatolia frequently revolted from central authority, but they preserved many Achaemenid institutions after the fall of the empire. The last satraps governed under the Sasanid king Shapur I.

J. M. Cook, *The Persian Empire* (1983), pp. 220–222. RICHARD N. FRYE

SATSUMA

SATSUMA, domain in southwestern Japan, corresponding roughly to present-day Kagoshima Prefecture, continuously ruled by the Shimazu family from 1196 from 1868. During the Tokugawa period the area included the provinces of Owari, Hyūga, and Satsuma and the island groups of Amami-Oshima, Kikai-shima, Tokuno-shima, Okinoerabeshima, and Yoron-shima. The Ryūkyū kingdom was a dependency of Satsuma.

A *tozama han* with the second largest *kokudaka* (officially registered productivity in terms of rice) among non-Tokugawa-clan domains, Satsuma was notorious for its tight social controls. A thorough security system along borders and highways kept out strangers, and detailed regulations imposed heavy social discipline upon local people. These controls were enforced by samurai whose numbers constituted a larger percentage of the total domain population than in any other *han*.

The distinguished lineage of the Shimazu family, the military strength and tradition of the domain, and its relative security from *bakufu* military attack made the Shimazu lord especially influential among his peers. Control over Ryūkyū gave him special access to China and to information about the activities of Western nations there in the first half of the nineteenth century. Satsuma's semitropical location was advantageous for the cultivation of sugar, production of which was made a state monopoly.

Satsuma leaders, particularly Saigō Takamori and Ōkubo Toshimichi, played a key role in orchestrating the downfall of the Tokugawa, and Satsuma troops maintained stability in the critical transition years of the Meiji government. But by 1877, in the Satsuma Rebellion, conservative and progressive factions of Satsuma were fighting on opposite sides. After the rebellion Satsuma men led by Matsukata Masayoshi and their counterparts from Chōshū alternated in dominating the central government for several decades.

Torao Haraguchi et al., trans., *The Status System and Social Organization of Satsuma* (1975). Robert K. Sakai, "The Consolidation of Power in Satsuma-han," in *Studies in the Institutional History of Early Modern Japan,* edited by John W. Hall and Marius B. Jansen (1968). Robert K.

Sakai, "The Satsuma-Ryūkyū Trade and the Tokugawa Seclusion Policy," *Journal of Asian Studies* 22.2 (May 1964).
ROBERT K. SAKAI

SATYAGRAHA, a term coined by Mohandas Gandhi to characterize his methods of nonviolent resistance. It has also been applied to nonviolent campaigns other than Gandhi's, and the term is used to describe the Gandhian theory of conflict resolution in general.

In 1906, when Gandhi was leading a protest in South Africa against a government ordinance requiring Indian immigrants to register and submit to being fingerprinted, he utilized techniques of noncooperation and public demonstration that he called "passive resistance." Seeking a better term for the approach, he sponsored a contest in his journal *Indian Opinion.* Modifying a suggestion submitted by his own cousin, Gandhi created the term *satyagraha* by joining two Sanskrit words, *satya* ("truth") and *agrah* ("to grasp firmly"). Gandhi himself translated the term as *truth force,* and he explained to a British committee of inquiry that the term applied to those political movements that "intended to replace methods of violence" with methods "based entirely upon truth."

Gandhi was involved in three *satyagraha* campaigns against the South African government from 1906 to 1914, and he gave the name Satyagraha Ashram to the headquarters he established near the city of Ahmadabad when he returned to India in 1915. His first *satyagraha* campaigns in India involved economic issues: a campaign for workers' rights in an indigo plantation in Champaran in 1917, a strike for higher wages for millworkers in Ahmadabad in 1918, and a protest against high taxes levied on the farmers of Kheda in the same year.

The first all-India *satyagraha* organized by Gandhi was a protest in 1919 against the Rowlatt Bills, an attempt by the British to contain the growing violence of the nationalist movement. When some of the Indians in this *satyagraha* resorted to violent means, Gandhi abruptly ended the campaign, claiming that it was "a Himalayan miscalculation" on his part to think that his followers were disciplined enough to conduct the protests entirely without violence. The second all-India *satyagraha* was begun in 1920, and again he called off his campaign in 1922 when violence erupted at Chauri Chaura, where a police station was set on fire. Perhaps Gandhi's most vividly remembered *satyagraha* was the third all-India campaign in 1930, which included a march to the sea, at Dandi, where Gandhi proceeded to extract salt from seawater to circumvent the government tax on salt from commercial sources. Gandhi's final all-India *satyagraha* was the Quit India movement launched in 1942. But even though Gandhi was arrested almost as soon as the campaign had begun, and although he waited out the campaign imprisoned in the Aga Khan palace near Pune, this final *satyagraha* is regarded by many Indians as having come to a crowning success in the creation of an independent India on 15 August 1947, a few months before Gandhi was assassinated on 30 January 1948.

The term *satyagraha* has been applied to campaigns waged by other nonviolent activists, including the Pakhtun (Pathan) leader Abdul Ghaffar Khan, and the American civil rights leader Martin Luther King, Jr. What unites these various movements of protest is primarily a commitment to the use of nonviolent techniques for social change. But the idea of *satyagraha* as Gandhi had developed it by the end of his life is considerably more elaborate; it constitutes a broad theory of conflict resolution that may be applied to a variety of situations.

At the heart of this theory is the notion that every conflict is essentially a fight between principles: two "angles of vision," as Gandhi put it, that illuminate the same truth. The goal of a *satyagrahi*—one who is committed to the *satyagraha* approach—is to find the deeper level of truth that unites the parties at odds, "hold firmly" to it, and ultimately convert the opponent to the truthful side. The search for the truth may require *satyagrahis* to abandon their own self-interest, and the fight on behalf of the truth may require them to shoulder whatever suffering occurs as a result of the conflict—a practice of self-sacrifice that Gandhi called *tapasya,* invoking the Sanskrit term for asceticism. They are constrained to use techniques that are consistent with their goals, for Gandhi regarded the ends and the means of the fight to be ultimately the same. And since a truthful goal would always be life-affirming rather than destructive, the techniques of *satyagraha* are necessarily nonviolent.

Satyagraha as a theory of conflict may be applied to domestic quarrels as well as political encounter; Gandhi credited his wife with special skills in this regard. One of Gandhi's successors, Jayaprakash Narayan, advocated *satyagraha* as the basic theory of political consensus and policy-making for a "communitarian society"—the ideal Gandhian society he envisioned in India's future.

[See also Gandhi, Mohandas Karamchand and Narayan, Jayaprakash.]

Joan Bondurant, *Conquest of Violence: The Gandhian Philosophy of Conflict* (1958). Judith Brown, *Gandhi and Civil Disobedience* (1976). Mohandas Gandhi, *Satyagraha in South Africa* (1928). Raghavan Iyer, *Moral and Political Thought of Gandhi* (1973). Mark Juergensmeyer, *Fighting with Gandhi* (1984). Gene Sharp, *The Politics of Nonviolent Action* (1973).

MARK JUERGENSMEYER

SAVAK is an acronym for the widely feared State Security and Intelligence Organization (Sazman-i Ettela'at va Amniyat-i Keshvar) started by the shah of Iran in 1957 to forestall challenges to his power such as that mounted by Mohammed Mossadegh in 1953. SAVAK received technical training and support from the United States and Israel and was part of an elaborate security apparatus with various organs competing with one another for influence and the shah's favor.

In the minds of most Iranians SAVAK was synonymous with terror. Its agents infiltrated virtually all sectors of public life and tried to deter opposition and criticism of the shah through arbitrary arrests, secret trials, imprisonment, torture, and even death. It has been argued that through SAVAK's extensive recruitment of part-time agents one in ten Iranians was an informant; this, however, cannot be verified. Nonetheless, many Iranians believed this to be the case, thus contributing mightily to the fear and intimidation that were SAVAK's stock-in-trade. The very existence of SAVAK was a major stimulus to the Islamic Revolution, and during the revolution most Iranians were made aware of the discovery of secret torture houses as well as the experiences of prisoners released from the shah's jails. After the revolution SAVAK was eliminated. It was soon replaced, however, by an organization named SAVAMA, the goals and methods of which differed little from those of its predecessor.

Ervand Abrahamian, *Iran between Two Revolutions* (1982). Marvin Zonis, *The Political Elite of Iran* (1971).

JERROLD D. GREEN

SAVANGVATTHANA (1907–c. 1979), king of Laos (r. 1959–1975). Born at Luang Prabang, Savangvatthana was the son of King Sisavangvong. He was educated in Hanoi and Paris and graduated with degrees in political science and law. In 1930 he was made secretary-general of his father's kingdom, and in 1941 he was recognized as crown prince. He supported his father in resisting Japanese pressure in March 1945 and the Lao Issara later in the year and in obtaining a new constitution when the French returned.

Savangvatthana succeeded his father on 1 November 1959, a time of political turmoil. If perhaps more philosopher than man of action, he was a man of civilized, regal charm and high intelligence, and he had a brilliant grasp of the basic problems of his country. In the long, sporadic civil war that followed a succession of military coups in 1959–1960, Savangvatthana was often called upon to mediate, conciliate, or advise, but he had no illusions about the likely outcome. "Alas," he is said to have remarked to Prince Sihanouk of Cambodia in 1961, "I am destined to be the last king of Laos." After the Communist takeover of Laos in 1975, he abdicated and was "elected" supreme adviser to the new government; he chose instead to retire, was removed for "reeducation" in 1977, and is thought to have died in the process in 1979 or 1980.

[See also Laos; Sisavangvong; and Lao Issara.]

A. J. Dommen, *Conflict in Laos* (1971). Brian Urquhart, *Hammarskjold* (1972).   HUGH TOYE

SAVARKAR, VINAYAK DAMODAR (1883–1966), Indian revolutionary. A Chitpavan brahman, Savarkar earned a bachelor's degree from Fergusson College, Pune, and formed a revolutionary society, Abhinava Bharat (1905). He went to study law in London, where he wrote *The First Indian War of Independence–1857* (1908). Involved in terrorist groups, he was sentenced to life imprisonment (1910) and wrote *Hindutva*, outlining the idea of "Hinduness" and a Hindu nation. Conditionally released (1924), he worked for the uplift of Hindu society and Untouchables before final release in 1937. As president of the Hindu Mahasabha (1937–1942), he opposed the partition of India and was tried but acquitted for complicity in the murder of Mohandas Gandhi (1948).

[See also Chitpavan Brahmans and Hindu Mahasabha.]

D. Keer, *Veer Savarkar* (1966).   JIM MASSELOS

SAW (U Saw; 1900–1948), a major Burmese nationalist politician during the late 1930s and 1940s. U Saw rose to prominence because of his championing of the Saya San peasants' rebellion of the early 1930s. Forming his own party within the House of Representatives in 1938, as well as a private army, the Galon Tat, he quickly gained a place in the cabinet. Soon thereafter he became premier, perhaps because of his ability to weld a coalition of Burmese economic interests. Following unsuccessful talks in London in 1941 to gain a promise of constitutional reforms after the war, U Saw was arrested and detained by the British in Uganda, allegedly for contacting the Japanese embassy in Lisbon to offer his assistance in an anti-British movement. After the war U Saw returned to Rangoon and sought to regain his prewar preeminence; finding this impossible, he organized a conspiracy to assassinate U Aung San and other members of the governor's Executive Council. For this he was tried and hanged.

[See also Saya San and Aung San.]

Robert H. Taylor, "Politics in Late Colonial Burma: The Case of U Saw," *Modern Asian Studies* 10.2 (April 1975): 161–194.   ROBERT H. TAYLOR

SAW, QUEEN, ruler of the Burmese kingdom of Pagan. She is best known for her admonition of King Narathihapade (r. 1255–1287), who was made the scapegoat for the destruction of the Pagan kingdom. Her speech, as retold by chroniclers, became the standard for all kings who needed some sort of reproach, and one finds it verbatim (or near verbatim) in predictable segments of the chronicles.

There were several Queen Saws in Pagan, one of whom did in fact live during Narathihapade's reign and was not his queen but his grandmother, who may in fact have admonished the king on occasion. In her inscription of 1271 CE, Queen Saw tells us that she had lived through the reigns of three kings: one was her husband, another her son, and the third (Narathihapade) her grandson.

Queen Saw's obviously influential presence as queen, dowager, and granddowager during the last sixty years of the dynasty must have been significant and reflects the extremely important role that women in general and queens in particular played in Burmese society. The queens and princesses of Pagan played a particularly important role in their patronage of the religion; well over half of the important donations made to the *sangha* (the Buddhist monastic order) during the Pagan period were made by women.

[See also Narathihapade.]

Michael Aung-Thwin, "Prophecies, Omens, and Dialogue: Tools of the Trade in Burmese Historiography," in *Moral Order and the Question of Change: Essays in Southeast Asian Thought,* edited by Alexander Woodside and David K. Wyatt (1983), pp. 78–103. Paul J. Bennett, *Conference under the Tamarind Tree: Three Essays in Burmese History* (1971).   MICHAEL AUNG-THWIN

SAWAH. Botanists believe that Southeast Asia was one of the original locales of sawah (wet rice) cultivation. The earliest evidence of sawah in Southeast Asia has been obtained from excavations at Non Nok Tha in northwestern Thailand and at Ulu Leang in Sulawesi that date to roughly 3500 BCE, some 2,500 years prior to the time that wet rice became a staple in central China. Surveys of archaeological evidence from Thailand indicate that wet-rice cultivation was extended into lowland areas after the advent of iron technology during the first millennium BCE. In this era farmers growing broadcast rice, watered by natural flooding, settled in the upper Mekong Delta and the Mun-Chi River basin in northeast Thailand. The process of growing rice in bunded fields and transplanting it from nursery beds—a method that is more labor intensive than broadcasting flood rice—became standard on the mainland in about the eighth century. The earliest epigraphic reference to water management in Southeast Asia occurs in a middle fifth-century inscription from West Java, but it appears that sawah was adopted earlier and grown more extensively on the mainland than in the island realm. In the early nineteenth century, sawah acreage in Java was still only one-third of what it is at present, and it was restricted to terrain especially suitable for irrigation.

Te-tzu Chang, "The Rice Culture," *Philosophical Transactions of the Royal Society of London,* series B, 275 (1976): 143–157.   KENNETH R. HALL

SAYA SAN (or Hsaya San), leader of a major rebellion against British rule in Burma (1930–1932), an event that fully galvanized Burmese nationalism.

Saya San spent his earlier years as a Buddhist monk, then as a country "doctor" and seller of folk medicines, and then as a second-echelon leader in one of the constituent parties that made up the General Council of Burmese Associations (GCBA), the umbrella group of nationalist associations in the 1920s. He led a survey of rural conditions and peasant grievances for the GCBA in 1927–1928. As the Great Depression hit Burma and peasant distress became dire, he seems to have lost faith in the ability of modern politics to mobilize Burmese peasants. Faced with insensitivity and outrageous provocations from British authorities, he prepared for rebellion, which broke out in Tharrawaddy District in December 1930.

Attacks were first mounted against village headmen, police posts, and the forest service. Over the next eighteen months, the rebellion sputtered and flamed in most of the districts of Lower Burma. The government committed as many as 10,000 troops to its suppression; 1,300 rebels were killed and 9,000 rebels taken into custody. The rebellion may only partly be dismissed as a retrogressive, backward-looking explosion of peasant anger. However, it must be seen as an early (and surely premature) expression not just of the traditional values and social patterns of the Burmese peasantry but also of the changes that peasant society had undergone in a half-century or more of British rule, changes that included some considerable degree of politicization. Saya San's appeal was moral and political, and through him desperate peasants could look ahead (and not just backward) to a new Burma ruled by an authority more legitimate than the British. Saya San's trial in 1932 brought to prominence both his cause and his defense lawyer, the fiery Dr. Ba Maw. Saya San was executed on 28 November 1937.

[*See also* Burma; General Council of Burmese Associations; *and* Ba Maw.]

M. Adas, *Prophets of Rebellion* (1979). J. F. Cady, *A History of Modern Burma* (1958). Patricia Herbert, *The Hsaya San Rebellion (1930–32) Reappraised* (1982). James C. Scott, *The Moral Economy of the Peasant* (1976).   DAVID K. WYATT

SAYYID AHMAD OF RAE BAREILLY (1786–1831), leader of a socioreligious reform movement in North India. In his preaching, Sayyid Ahmad stressed the affirmation of *tawhid* (monotheism) and rejection of *bid'at* (innovation in religious matters). He considered British India a *daru'l harb* (abode of war) and in 1826 he migrated to the independent North-West Frontier tribal area, where he established an operational base. His interest was in British India but he got entangled in local wars and died fighting at Balakote. His followers, the Ahl-i Hadis (Wahhabis), sustained and expanded the movement, which had the wide-ranging effect of sharpening the adherents' sense of religious identity and introducing significant social reforms.

[*See also* Ahl-i Hadis.]

Qeyamuddin Ahmad, *The Wahabi Movement in India* (1966). Peter Hardy, *Muslims of British India* (1972).

QEYAMUDDIN AHMAD

SAYYID DYNASTY, one of the dynasties of the Delhi sultanate that claimed descent from the prophet Muhammad. The Sayyids ruled from 1414 to 1451 and comprised four sultans—Khizr Khan, Mubarak Shah, Muhammad Shah, and Ala ud-Din Shah. During this period the process of the dissolution of the Delhi sultanate gathered momentum. The political vision of its rulers did not extend beyond a radius of less than two hundred miles around Delhi. For all practical purposes the Sayyid sultans were *iqtadars,* or local governors. Rebellions of governors, local chieftains, and landlords (*zamindars*) became the order of the day. The concept of a strong centralized monarchy disappeared. The amount of yearly revenue during this period depended upon the capacity of the state to chastize its defaulting chiefs. The Sayyid dynasty had emerged as a principality of Multan; it ended as a principality of Badaon. [*See also* Delhi *and* Multan.]

KHALIQ AHMAD NIZAMI

SCHALL VON BELL, JOHANN ADAM (known to the Chinese as Tang Ruowang; 1592–1666), Jesuit missionary to China. Schall was a monumental figure among Jesuits in China whose greatness stemmed from his mathematical and strategic brilliance. He has been called the second founder of the China mission for his success at reestablishing the mission with a new dynasty when the Manchus conquered China in 1644.

Born into a prominent Catholic family in Cologne, Schall studied at the German College in Rome and arrived at Macao in 1619. After a stay in Xi'an, Shaanxi Province, he was called to Rome in 1630 to continue the work of the late John Schreck in reforming the Chinese calendar. Although he had assisted the Ming dynasty by forging cannons in its defense, Schall's tactics during the transition were so successful that the leaders of the new Qing dynasty retained his eminent services and allowed the Christian mission in China to continue.

In 1645 Schall was named the president of the Chinese Bureau of Astronomy and was given high scholar-official status. It was during these years that he came perhaps the closest of any missionary to converting a Chinese emperor to Christianity, but the Shunzhi emperor died prematurely in 1661. During the consequent regency of the new child emperor Kangxi, accumulated anti-Christian resentments surfaced in the famous persecution led by the scholar-official Yang Guangxian. Schall was indicted and imprisoned and, during the course of the trial, suffered a debilitating series of strokes by which he lost the ability to defend himself. Although condemned, he and his Jesuit associates, including Ferdinand Verbiest, were pardoned and released. Schall died shortly thereafter on 15 August 1666 in Beijing.

[*See also* Jesuits: Jesuits in China *and* Verbiest, Ferdinand.]

Rachel Attwater, *Adam Schall* (1963). Joseph Needham, *Science and Civilisation in China*, vol. 3, *Mathematics and the Sciences of the Heavens and the Earth* (1959). Jonathan Spence, *The China Helpers: Western Advisers in China, 1620–1960* (1969), chap. 1.

DAVID E. MUNGELLO

SCHWARTZ, CHRISTIAN FREDERICK

(1726–1798). Born at Sonnenburg and educated at the University of Halle, Schwartz was assigned to the Tranquebar Mission in India in 1750. His ministry took him to Trichinopoly, Tinnevelly, Ramnad, and Tanjore, where he distinguished himself as Tamil scholar, educator, surgeon, preacher, chaplain, and diplomat. His assignment as chaplain to various British fort garrisons led to his wielding considerable power as mediator between the British and indigenous princes like Haidar Ali and the Marathas of Tanjore. As mentor and guardian of Prince Serfogee he played a pivotal role in stabilizing the prince's ascent to the throne.

[*See also* Tanjore.]

Jesse Page, *Schwartz of Tanjore* (1921).

PATRICK ROCHE

SCULPTURE

CHINESE SCULPTURE

The history of Chinese sculpture differs from that of most countries in that the names of sculptors are rarely recorded, even in historic times. This is in keeping with the traditional estimation of this art, which was often relegated to the status of a craft. The Chinese gentry who wrote the scholarly and critical treatises on art held a prejudicial attitude toward the subject matter of the innumerable Buddhistic images that constitute the bulk of Chinese sculpture. This attitude may be related in a more

subtle way to a deeper antipathy toward the depiction of the human body and a disregard for three-dimensional forms in general.

The most striking sculptural artifact of prehistoric times is the *bi*, a flat disk that was fashioned by laborious grinding from the hard stones that we call jade. Most often interpreted as a symbol of heaven, the *bi* is a purely abstract symbol, whatever its meaning may be (see figure 1). Significantly, figurative representation of any sort is rare in prehistoric China. Indeed, fertility images, common in other prehistoric cultures, are nearly unknown in China, as is any depiction of the naked human body.

Figural art becomes much more prevalent in the early Bronze Age. The tombs dating from the Shang dynasty (1766–1122 BCE) contain numerous small independent carvings of animals and humans done in a variety of hard stones and bone. However, the major increase in plasticity of design occurred on the ritual bronze vessels of the period. Their decoration also reveals a marked bias for symbolic forms, signs, or animal conceits, which are not attempts at imitating the appearance of real animals but rather are the metaphorical constructions of imagined ones. There are some provocative exceptions, representations of human beings or common animals, but these are both artistically and statistically exceptional. [*See* Bronze Age in China.]

Tomb figures, usually fashioned of wood, appear with increasing regularity in the later years of the Zhou dynasty (1122–256 BCE). The potential of this genre seems to have exploded into a full-fledged art

FIGURE 1. *Jade Bi.* Late Neolithic period(?). Diameter 179 cm.

form under the patronage of Qin Shihuangdi, China's first great unifier and the founder of its first empire, the short-lived Qin dynasty (221–206 BCE). The excavation of a peripheral section of his tomb has yielded thousands of life-sized figures of horses and imperial guardsmen. Although they are not true portraits, great attention is paid to the physical appearance, pose, and costume of these figures, which are fashioned in fired clay and then painted. There is as well some interest in characterization, a concern for departing from fixed stereotypes, which is equally obvious in other sculptures of the period whether executed in wood, bronze, or fired ceramic (see figure 2). Yet this spectacular tomb find does not presage any sudden flowering of independent sculpture. The tomb of General He Qubing (c. 17 BCE) is the single example of exterior monumental sculpture dating from before the common era. A few large monolithic images of chimeras produced in the next seven centuries illustrate the low priority given to monumental images of this kind.

Although the more elaborate tombs were decorated internally with narrative themes executed in shallow relief, these are more properly related to the art of painting. The tomb figures found in these tombs are usually small, either glazed, painted, or plain ceramic figures depicting attendants, entertainers, animals, house models, and so forth, not unlike those found in the tombs of ancient Egypt. Apparently, these figures represent a subterranean art, grave offerings that were never intended to be seen and appreciated by the living. They were rather the companions of the dead, a humane substitute for the human sacrifice that had accompanied the dead in the early centuries of the Bronze Age.

A major impetus to the development of the plastic arts was provided by Buddhism, which came to China shortly after the beginning of the common era. Because of official persecution that led to the destruction of religious sculpture, there is little more than a literary record of the earliest Buddhist sculpture in China. The few surviving works, dating from the fourth century, reveal a knowledge of, and dependence on, forms that originated in Indian domains, in either the subcontinent itself or the Central Asian kingdoms that were within the Buddhist cultural sphere.

The close relationship between Chinese sculpture of the fifth century and that of Central Asia is immediately apparent in the great Buddhist sanctuaries carved out of the living rock in central and far western China. These pilgrimage sites, situated along the old trade routes that linked East Asia, India, and

FIGURE 2. *Tomb Figure, Xi'an.* Terra-cotta statue unearthed at the tomb of Qin Shihuangdi (r. 221–210 BCE).

the Western world, were active over many centuries. They were occasionally refurbished, and sometimes provide dated documents that aid in the construction of a more exact history of Buddhist sculpture. This evidence is buttressed by the numerous surviving examples of independent stone or bronze images that bear dated dedicatory inscriptions. The picture that emerges is of a stylistic development that is not dissimilar from what is known in Western art. By the early sixth century Chinese Buddhist art became less like Indo-Central Asian styles; this more unique expression was established as the Chinese archaic style. By the eighth century, during the Tang dynasty, Chinese sculpture had attained a classic form that was exported to Japan and Korea and to those areas of Central Asia under Chinese cultural influence (see figure 3).

It is characteristic of earlier Buddhist forms that they stress the creation of ideal forms with a corresponding suppression of individual traits in depicting divine beings. An interest in the specific, the realm of the portrait, is reserved for images of the priests and founders who provided spiritual guidance and were therefore important in a personal and human way.

The enormous output of religious sculpture did not stimulate the production of secular works. Statues of emperors or important figures remained absent from the Chinese spectrum. Characteristically, the need to commemorate the leaders of the society was accomplished through the carving of large memorial stelae that record their biographies and accomplishments in finely chiseled calligraphy. These memorials were erected at the sites of their tombs and, in the case of imperial burials, statues of officials and symbolic animals were set up along the spirit way that led to the tomb itself. The Tang tombs near Xi'an or the Ming tombs at Nanjing and outside Beijing illustrate this type of tomb sculpture (see figure 4). Similar sculptures of fabulous animals appear within the precincts of the Forbidden City in Beijing, but these are the only sculptures found there and their function is as much decorative as symbolic. Even in modern times, sculpture does not play an important role in the arts of China. Recent works like the programmatic *Rent Collector's Courtyard*, statues of Mao Zedong, or the *Monument to the Heroes of the Revolution* erected in Tiananmen Square outside the Forbidden City depend on Western socialist art styles to illustrate their political themes if only because there was no logical sculptural precedent to be found within the historic repertoire of traditional Chinese art forms.

Throughout the centuries, numerous objects were carved from hard stones and other attractive materials to grace the homes and palaces of the wealthy. Although such items as elaborate brush holders, jade vessels, or elaborately constructed rocks for the decoration of gardens are usually classified as decorative or minor arts, they are in another sense better representatives of the Chinese sculptural instinct. Although these are not monumental public images they illustrate familiar themes or cherished shapes like the *bi*, which is not only the earliest Chinese sculptured form but also the most enduring motif in the history of Chinese sculpture.

FIGURE 3. *Longmen Caves, Luoyang.* Begun in 494 CE, Longmen is one of several sites associated with the Buddhist sculptural tradition in China.

FIGURE 4. *Lion Sculptures, Ming Tombs, Nanjing.*

R. Soame Jenyns and William Watson, *Chinese Arts: The Minor Arts* (1963). Max Loehr, assisted by Louisa G. F. Huber, *Ancient Chinese Jades from the Grenville L. Winthrop Collection in the Fogg Art Museum, Harvard University* (1975). Mizuno Seiichi, *Bronze and Stone Sculpture of China from the Yin to the T'ang Dynasty,* translated by Kajiyama Yuichi and Burton Watson (1960). Laurence Sickman and Alexander C. Soper, *The Art and Architecture of China* (3d ed., 1968). Osvald Sirén, *Chinese Sculpture from the Fifth to the Fourteenth Century* (1925). Alexander C. Soper, *Literary Evidence for Early Buddhist Art in China* (1959).

ROBERT POOR

JAPANESE SCULPTURE

Japanese sculpture prior to the Meiji period consists primarily of images of Buddhist and Shinto deities and of commemorative portraits of monks and laymen.

The continuous tradition of sculpture in Japan begins with the introduction of Buddhism from Korea in 552. The sculptural styles practiced during the Asuka era (552–645) were heavily influenced by those of the Korean kingdoms. Many of Japan's earliest sculptors were descendants of Korean or Chinese immigrants. Most renowned among these is Tori Busshi, creator in 623 of a gilt bronze triad representing the Buddha Shaka (Sanskrit, Shakyamuni) flanked by two *bosatsu* (Sanskrit, *bodhisattva*) in Hōryūji, Nara (see figure 1). The affinities between Japanese and Korean imagery during the Asuka era are so close that the provenance of many statues housed in Japanese temples is a matter of heated scholarly debate that remains unresolved.

In the sculpture of the Early Nara period (645–710, as dated by art historians), the rigid frontality, slender forms, and elaborately pleated drapery characteristic of that of the Asuka era gave way to increasing naturalism. The bodies of deities are more rounded and clothed in more fitted, revealing garments. While statuary of the Asuka was limited to

FIGURE 1. *Shaka Triad.* By Tori Busshi. Asuka period, 623 CE; Hōryūji, Nara. Bronze, height 176 cm.

gilt bronze and camphor wood, in the Nara period dry lacquer and clay were also used. Reflecting shifts in the political sphere, China became the chief source of cultural influence (see figure 2). The most representative monuments of this era include a gilt bronze triad of the Healing Buddha, Yakushi (Bhaisajyaguru), and a group of clay figurines in the Hōryūji pagoda. Both feature full forms, expressive facial features, and graceful, mobile poses.

Following the establishment of a permanent capital at Nara in 710, government-sponsored workshops in the major Nara temples assumed leadership of sculptural production. Tōdaiji, national headquarters of Buddhism during the Late Nara period (710–784), maintained workshops for the creation of lacquer, clay, and bronze statuary. The most ambitious project undertaken at Tōdaiji was the casting of a fifty-three-foot image of the cosmic Buddha Rocana (Vairocana). Dedicated in 752, it is a fitting symbol of the union of church and state so central

FIGURE 3. *Daibutsu, Tōdaiji, Nara.*

FIGURE 2. *Sculpture of the Buddhist Monk Ganjin.* Kaisandō, Tōshōdaiji, Nara, mid-eighth century. Dry lacquer, polychromed. The portrait of Ganjin reflects the more natural style of the period and the recognition of the importance of individual monks. Highly influential in later Japanese art, this statue provided inspiration for the Kei-school sculptors of the Kamakura period.

to the practice of Buddhism during the Nara period (see figure 3).

During the subsequent Heian period (784–1185) continental influences were assimilated and indigenous styles emerged. Esoteric Buddhism, introduced to Japan at the end of the eighth century, had a profound effect on both the subject and style of images produced during the first half of the period, while those of the second half were influenced by Pure Land Buddhism.

A group of statues arranged in the form of a mandala in Tōji, the Kyoto headquarters of the Shingon sect, are typical of the style and iconography associated with Esoteric imagery. Made of solid wood cores thinly covered with lacquer and paint, they reflect the shift away from the realism of the Nara toward a more abstract form of expression suited to the symbolic nature of Esoteric deities.

Outside the capital, large solid woodblocks were used to carve awesome images with heavy, often obese figures, somber expressions, and deeply chiseled surfaces. Statues carved in this single woodblock manner, reflecting a sensitivity toward wood that is a hallmark of the native sculptural style, include both Shinto and Buddhist deities.

With the patronage of the aristocratic Fujiwara

family, the workshop led by Kōshō and Jōchō dominated sculptural production in the eleventh and twelfth centuries. Their workshop perfected a technique whereby statues were assembled from many small wooden pieces and then coated with lacquer overlaid with paint or cut-gold designs. This new joined woodblock technique was economical and practical, and it facilitated mass production. Jōchō's masterpiece is the supremely elegant statue of the Buddha Amida (Amitabha) carved in 1053 for the Uji Byōdōin (see figure 4).

During the Kamakura period (1185–1333) aristocratic styles coexisted with new styles influenced by renewed contact with China and with a revival of the Nara manner stimulated by the restoration of the great Nara temples following a disastrous fire in 1180. The Kei, so called after the second character in the names of its members, is the dominant school of sculpture. Located in Nara, Kyoto, and Kamakura, the principal Kei workshops were founded by Unkei (1151–1223), Kaikei (fl. 1185–1220), and their followers. The highly versatile and prolific Kei masters created images of Buddhist and Shinto deities as well as uncompromisingly realistic portraits of monks and courtiers. The heritage of the Kei style endured through the Edo period (1600–1868).

J. Edward Kidder, *Masterpieces of Japanese Sculpture* (1961). Kyōtarō Nishikawa and Emily Sano, *The Great Age of Japanese Buddhist Sculpture, AD 600–1300* (1982). Langdon Warner, *The Craft of the Japanese Sculptor* (1936).   CHRISTINE M. E. GUTH

SOUTHEAST ASIAN SCULPTURE

Two traditions of monumental sculpture have persisted in Southeast Asia from prehistory into the twentieth century. The first of these are the bronze drums known as Dong Son from the site in northern Vietnam where they were first excavated in 1924. [*See* Dong Son.] The drums, classified by Franz Heger as Type 1, have a flat, circular tympanum on which design elements, often including birds, boats, and warriors, have been organized concentrically around a central star. The body has bulbous shoulders, a cylindrical midsection, and a splayed foot. They have been found in large numbers in Vietnam; scattered finds have also been recorded from Thailand, Cambodia, western Malaysia, Sumatra, and Java and other islands of the Indonesian archipelago. Their distribution may reflect trading contacts, but it is also probable that the drums were emblems of power and prestige integrated into local ritual contexts.

The dates for the earliest drums are unfixed, and the origin of metallurgy in Southeast Asia is itself a matter of controversy. There is, however, a developing body of evidence that indicates that bronze was being produced in northern Vietnam by at least the early second millennium BCE and that the drums are a product of the late Bronze period in Vietnam, the Go Mun, which began sometime after 1000 BCE. By this time village life had reached a level of sufficient complexity to sustain full-time craft specialists.

Nowhere is the persistence of the imagination demonstrated more remarkably in Southeast Asia than in the fact that a variant of these drums, classified as Heger Type 3, was still being produced in this century by the Karen people of Burma. These drums were also used by many other hill tribes scattered throughout southern China, Assam, Burma, Thailand, Vietnam, and Laos. According to Richard Cooler, the ensemble of design elements is a vision of water, fruitfulness, and prosperity in this life and the next.

FIGURE 4. *Amida Nyorai, Byōdōin, Kyoto.* By Jōcho, completed c. 1053.

FIGURE 1. *Head of Vishnu*. Cambodia, pre-Angkor period (seventh to eighth century). Gray sandstone; height 42.5 cm.

Megaliths of various kinds, including menhirs, (erect stones), dolmens (flat stones resting on two stone pillars), stone urns, large stone sarcophagi, stone seats, and massive stone sculptures, also offer a similar thread of continuity across a great temporal span. They are found widely throughout Southeast Asia and were still being erected in Nias, Sumba, and Borneo during the present century. The oldest of them do not appear to predate the introduction of metals into the region, although an earlier view, first put forward in 1928 by Robert Heine-Geldern, held that there were two megalithic traditions: one associated with the Neolithic period and the other a younger tradition reflecting stylistic motifs drawn from the art of the bronzes discussed above. More recent scholarship, however, tends to discount the view that megaliths in Southeast Asia are elements of a unified intraregional culture and instead sees them as independent efforts, scattered widely across space and time and in a variety of forms, to link the vagaries of human fate to the continuity and durable power of both nature and the revered ancestors.

While bronze and stone have withstood the rigors of tropical humidity and termites, the presumably much more abundant sculpture in wood has vanished from the archaeological record. It would be dangerous to assume that the rich representational and decorative carving on houses, boats, weapons, graves, masks, ceremonial posts, and objects of daily use with which tribal people in Southeast Asia surround themselves today are mirror images of vanished prehistoric traditions. Nevertheless, where subsistence patterns have changed little, the symbolic expression of those forms of life may very well offer elements of continuity with traditions and cultures of the past.

FIGURE 2. *Dancing Celestial Figure (Apsara)*. Cambodia, late eleventh century. Bronze, height 39.3 cm.

Sometime in the first centuries of the common era the dynamic world of late Metal Age Southeast Asia, bounded by village, family, tribe, ancestors, and tutelary deities, began to burst its confining order—certainly not everywhere or all at once, but at some strategic and exposed places it lay in fragments. The central themes of developing cities and towns were expressed in the only cultural patterns on hand that claimed to be universal: the classical tradition of the courts of India with their Hindu and Buddhist religions, temple architecture, and art. This marked a great shift in the content, styles, and social setting of sculpture in Southeast Asia, and, in fact, these developments follow rather closely those religious tendencies in India around the first century CE that led to a need for a human representation of the Buddha and personal devotion to the Hindu gods Shiva, Vishnu, and their feminine aspects, the great goddesses. In Southeast Asia, sculptural representations of these gods were frequently merged with portrait statues of kings, nobles, and other dignitaries.

Initially, Buddhist sculptors in India had represented the events of the Buddha's life in a symbolic, or aniconic, form. Thus, for example, a tree stood for his enlightenment at Bodh Gaya, a wheel for his teaching (dharma), an empty throne or footprints marked his presence, a tumulus or grave mound (stupa) indicated his entry into nirvana. All of these symbols have become familiar in the Buddhist art of Southeast Asia. [See also Buddhism: An Overview and Stupa.]

The first devotional images of the Buddha in Southeast Asia were imported from India or Sri Lanka in a style that was developed initially in the Andhradesha region of South India and flourished between the second and fourth century. By at least the sixth century, images in this style were being made in local workshops on the Southeast Asian mainland. Other Indian styles of Buddhist art, such as the Gupta, post-Gupta, and Pala, subsequently imprinted themselves on the imagination of Southeast Asian sculptors, but they transformed these influences into representations of a distinctive local flavor.

Hindu gods also enjoyed a considerable popularity in Southeast Asia. Shiva was most frequently encountered in his symbolic representation as a *lingam,* or phallus. The earliest *lingams* are quite realistic, but the tendency over time was to move toward a highly conventionalized emblem divided into three parts: a cylindrical top, octagonal midsection, and a cubic base. On the basis of epigraphy we know

FIGURE 3. *Seated Buddha.* Thailand, fifteenth century, Sukhothai type.

that the *lingam* was often associated with royal cults beginning at least from as early as about 400 CE. [See also Shaivism.]

Vishnu, the preserver of the universe, was also frequently represented in Southeast Asia. The earliest sculptures are of a four-armed god carrying a conch shell, a club, and a discus and wearing a tall crown. Some of these representations may date from as early as 400 CE. [See also Vaishnavism.]

Jean Boisselier, *The Heritage of Thai Sculpture* (1975). Jan Fontein, R. Soekmono, and Satyawati Suleiman, *Ancient Indonesian Art of the Central and Eastern Javanese Periods* (1971). Madeleine Giteau, *Khmer Sculpture and Angkor Civilization* (N.D.). J. Stephen Lansing, "Megalithic Religion: Historical Cultures," in *The Encyclopedia of Religion,* edited by Mircea Eliade (1987). Gordon Luce, *Old Burma—Early Pagan,* 3 vols. (1969). Urs Ramseyer, *The Art and Culture of Bali* (1977). Mubin Sheppard, *Taman Indera* (1972).   STANLEY J. O'CONNOR

IRANIAN AND CENTRAL ASIAN SCULPTURE

Monumental sculpture from ancient Iran is represented primarily by commemorative rock reliefs that mark major roads and stations along the arteries of communication in the rugged Zagros mountains of western Iran. The Victory of Anubanini, king of the Lullubi, carved in the early second millennium BCE at Sar-i Pul, west of Kermanshah, is the earliest in a series of reliefs from an important juncture of the main east-west Zagros artery. Anubanini's political statement, ratified by the presiding image of the goddess Ishtar, follows the familiar idiom of Mesopotamian art of the Ur III and Insin-Larsa periods.

Almost two and one-half millennia later, another native ruler of the Iranian plateau, Shapur II of the Persian Sasanid dynasty, recorded his celebrated victory of 363 CE over the Roman emperor Julian the Apostate, in a relief carved at Taq-i Bustan, along the same Zagros highway. In Shapur's relief, Iranian Zoroastrian deities confirm and proclaim the victory according to the prevailing artistic formulae of the world of late antiquity. The two cited examples of monumental sculpture are linked by a remarkable series of rock reliefs that span the reigns of pre-Islamic rulers of Elamite, Achaemenid, Parthian, and Sasanid dynasties. Whereas monumental sculpture in Iran is also found in architectural contexts, exemplified by the decoration of Achaemenid palaces of the sixth through the fourth century BCE, relatively few examples of such sculpture are known from western Iran from other periods of its history.

In eastern Iran and Central Asia, it is painted clay and stucco that served as the principal media in monumental sculpture. Hellenistic and Roman artistic conventions, later enriched by Indian and Chinese influences, were there adapted to the needs of new native dynasties that emerged in oases and towns that flourished along the Silk Route in the first millennium CE. The decline of monumental sculpture that followed the advent of Islam in Iran and Central Asia may be attributed to Muslim rejection of an art form that had functioned as a principal vehicle for the expression of the native values and religions of the pre-Islamic period in these lands.

Edith Porada, *Ancient Iran, the Art of Pre-Islamic Times* (1962). B. Rowland, *The Art of Central Asia* (1974). E. Yarshater, ed., *The Seleucid, Parthian and Sasanian Periods* (1983), vol. 3 of the *Cambridge History of Iran*.   GUITTY AZARPAY

SCYTHIANS. *See* Saka Dynasties.

SEBUKTIGIN, ABU MANSUR (942–977), founder of the Ghaznavid dynasty, which, under his son Mahmud, developed into a Turco-Persian em-

pire. His father, Juq, was the chieftain of a small principality in Turkestan that was liquidated by hostile neighbors; Sebuktigin, then twelve years of age, was taken prisoner. Subsequently, a certain Haji Nasr purchased him, and it was perhaps at this time that he embraced Islam. In 959 he was purchased by Alptigin, military leader of Khurasan, and was quickly promoted to high ranks. His talent facilitated his rise to the throne of Ghazna. In 979 and 988 he defeated Jaipal, the head of the Hindu Shahi dynasty in the Punjab, annexing the frontier towns of Jaipal's territory. His construction of roads in the frontier region facilitated Mahmud's Indian campaigns. Subuktigin died in August 977 in a village on the border of Balkh.

[*See also* Ghaznavid Dynasty; Mahmud of Ghazna; *and* Hindu Shahi Dynasty.]

C. E. Bosworth, *The Ghaznavids: Their Empire in Afghanistan and Eastern Iran* (1963), pp. 35–44. Muhammad Nazim, *The Life and Times of Sultan Mahmud of Ghazna* (1931), pp. 28–33.   KHALIQ AHMAD NIZAMI

SECLUSION (*sakoku*), the term usually applied to Japanese foreign policy in the Tokugawa period (1600–1868), particularly to the suppression of Christianity, the expulsion of Portuguese traders and Jesuit missionaries, the restriction of incoming foreign trade to the single port of Nagasaki, and the prohibition of Japanese overseas travel. Attempts by central political authority to assert control over foreign relations and external trade were part of the move toward reunification in the late sixteenth and early seventeenth centuries. Early evidence of such moves to control foreign relations were Toyotomi Hideyoshi's 1587 edict ordering expulsion of the Jesuit missionaries and his confiscation of Nagasaki, then the center of the Portuguese trade with Japan.

The Tokugawa *bakufu*, founded in 1603, also tried to control external relations. In 1604 Tokugawa Ieyasu began issuing vermilion-seal trading licenses (*shuin-jō*) to favored Japanese merchants and daimyos as well as to Chinese and European traders. The system was effective in promoting and protecting trade, but the problem of Christianity proved intractable, and it seemed subversive. In 1612 Ieyasu banished Japanese Christians from the country, and in 1614 ordered the Jesuit mission expelled, although the Portuguese and Spanish traders were allowed to remain, along with the Chinese, Dutch, and English. Meanwhile, Ieyasu sought improved relations with Japan's East Asian neighbors. He succeeded in reopening diplomatic relations with Chosŏn (Korea) in 1607, and in 1609, a Satsuma expedition conquered the kingdom of Ryūkyū, which was from thereafter both a Japanese and a Chinese tributary state, as well as a Satsuma semicolony.

Relations with the Iberian countries remained difficult because they were unwilling to trade without evangelizing. But as the Dutch (1609) and the English (1613) began trading in Hirado, as relations with Chosŏn improved, and as increasing numbers of Chinese merchants arrived there was less need to tolerate the Portuguese. This was true even after the collapse of the English trade in 1622 and of the Spanish trade in 1624. Edo's more severe attitude was seen in the execution of fifty-five Christian martyrs, nine of them Jesuits, in Nagasaki in 1622. A major economic problem affecting the *bakufu's* foreign policy was that Japan's main export items were silver, of which Japan was at the time the world's leading producer, and copper; both were also in great demand in the rapidly expanding Japanese domestic economy.

As relations with Chosŏn and Ryūkyū stabilized and the Dutch provided many of the same trading services as the Portuguese, the need to control foreign relations, to limit the access of Kyushu daimyo to the profits and the strategic advantages of trade, and to end the threat of Christian subversion prompted more vigorous restriction of external relations. In 1631 the *bakufu* began to require Japanese trading ships to be licensed not only by the shogun (the *shuin-jō*), but by the shogun's senior council as well. Starting in 1633 the *bakufu* issued a series of new, restrictive edicts, not only prohibiting Christianity, but restricting Japanese residence overseas and thus controlling trade more tightly. Five sets of edicts were issued between 1633 and 1639, known collectively, if anachronistically, as the "Seclusion Edicts." The edict of 1635 completely prohibited Japanese from voyaging overseas, although exceptions were made for specially licensed trading and diplomatic voyages to Chosŏn and Ryūkyū; Chinese traders were restricted to the single port of Nagasaki, and the export of Japanese weapons was prohibited.

The Shimabara Rebellion of 1637–1638 exacerbated the *bakufu's* fear of Christianity—the rebellion had economic causes, but the participants were mostly Christian converts—and the *bakufu* gave up on trade with the Portuguese. In the summer of 1639 Edo issued its final edict, expelling the Portuguese from trade with Japan. Thereafter, Japan's only contact with Europe was with the Netherlands East India Company's trading post, confined after 1641 to the small, man-made island of Deshima, in Nagasaki Harbor. [*See* Shimabara *and* Deshima.]

From 1639 until the opening of Japan to Western trade by Commodore Matthew C. Perry in 1853 to 1854 Japan had a restricted set of external relations, trading only with the Dutch and Chinese at Nagasaki, with Chosŏn at Pusan in southeastern Korea, with the kingdom of Ryūkyū at Naha, and with the Ezo (Ainu) at Matsumae. Edo had diplomatic relations only with the kings of Chosŏn and Ryūkyū, having no formal, state-to-state relations with the Ming and Qing governments in China.

This "system of national seclusion," as it is usually described, entailed a severely restricted flow of technical, scientific, and other knowledge from Europe. The diminished access to what would later become the "modern" world imposed some costs on Japan in terms of economic and scientific development. The "closure" of the country, however, is usually seen as having been an essential step in building the Tokugawa *bakufu,* cutting off its enemies from strategic resources, extirpating potentially subversive Christianity, and enabling the *bakufu* to control Japan's foreign trade.

Recent research has shown, however, that the diplomatic, economic, and strategic relationships that the *bakufu* continued to maintain, with the Dutch as well as Chosŏn, Ryūkyū, and Chinese traders, were important elements in the establishment and maintenance of *bakufu* legitimacy, and in the process of building the early modern Japanese state, as well as in constructing a sense of national identity. The trade, moreover, did not wither in 1639, nor was that the *bakufu's* intent, as the comments of shogunal advisers to both Japanese and foreign traders made clear at the time. Foreign trade remained a major element in the Tokugawa economy into the early eighteenth century, at least, with Japanese silver and copper the principal exports, and silks, medicines—especially Korean ginseng—and books the principal imports. As Japanese copper and silver production declined during the seventeenth century, the *bakufu* became increasingly concerned about the threat to its monetary system and tried to control it, restricting copper and silver exports and limiting the number of Chinese ships entering Nagasaki in 1688. The *bakufu* tried again, in 1715, to limit the number of Chinese ships coming in, this time by establishing a new licensing system. The principal causes of the decline in foreign trade, however, were the declining productivity of Japanese mines, the rising demand for money within the Japanese economy, and the emergence in the second quarter of the eighteenth century of domestic production in silk and ginseng, both in sufficient quantity and of sufficient quality to undercut the demand for imports. Largely as a result of these developments, Japan's foreign trade atrophied in the eighteenth century.

By the late eighteenth century this atrophied state of foreign relations had come to be regarded as normal, indeed as reflecting the *bakufu's* "ancestral law," which permitted *only* trade with Holland and China, and diplomacy with Chosŏn and Ryūkyū. The rising Western demand for trade with Japan in the nineteenth century thus became, in effect, a challenge to the *bakufu's* ability to uphold its own constitution. Indeed, in 1825 Aizawa Seishisai explicitly tied the shogun's performance in maintaining this "ancestral law" by "repelling the barbarians" to the shogun's duty to the emperor as his "barbarian-quelling generalissimo." *Bakufu* inability to control the foreigners and maintain "seclusion," therefore, increasingly challenged the legitimacy of the institution, and was a major factor in the *bakufu's* eventual demise.

[*See also* Kirishitan *and* Tokugawa Period.]

C. R. Boxer, *The Christian Center in Japan, 1549–1650* (1950) and *Jan Compagnie in Japan, 1600–1817* (2d rev. ed., 1950). George Elison, *Deus Destroyed: The Image of Christianity in Early Modern Japan* (1973). Engelbert Kaempfer, *A History of Japan Together with a Description of the Kingdom of Siam, 1690–1692*, 3 vols. (1906). Donald Keene, *The Japanese Discovery of Europe, 1720–1830* (rev. ed., 1969). George B. Sansom, *The Western World and Japan* (1950). Tashiro Kazui, "Foreign Relations during the Edo Period: *Sakoku* Reexamined," *Journal of Japanese Studies* 8.2 (1982): 283–306. Ronald P. Toby, *State and Diplomacy in Early Modern Japan: Asia in the Development of the Tokugawa Bakufu* (1984).

RONALD P. TOBY

SECOND OPIUM WAR. See Arrow War.

SECRET SOCIETIES. Traditionally there were two types of unlawful associations in China, the religious sectarian fraternities *(jiao)* and the sworn brotherhoods *(hui)*. While the religious groups worshiped their unorthodox gods, practiced healing, and pursued their salvation, the brotherhoods ran gambling, smuggling, and extortion operations. Both groups were ruthlessly persecuted by the government when discovered, particularly during the Qing dynasty (1644–1911), hence the need for maintaining some secrecy.

Numerous connections existed between the two groups in terms of origin, ritual, and even membership. Consequently, when the term *mimi shehui* (secret societies) was first adopted by the Chinese (from a Japanese rendition of the English original) at the turn of the twentieth century, it referred to both the sectarians and the brotherhoods. Increasingly, however, application of the term has been limited to the latter group. The Triads and, later, the Gelaohui (Elder Brother Society) are typical of secret societies in China, while various mutations of them still exist among Chinese communities in all parts of the world.

[*See also* Triads.]

RICHARD SHEK

SEISTAN. *See* Sistan.

SEIYŪKAI, more fully, Rikken Seiyūkai (Friends of Constitutional Government Association), one of the two major political parties in Japan before World War II. Organized in 1900 by the oligarch Itō Hirobumi, the Seiyūkai soon came under the leadership of the professional politician Hara Takashi (Kei). Hara parlayed his party's strength into securing for it key seats in oligarchic cabinets, from which he dispensed public works projects to increase Seiyūkai popularity at the local level. In 1918 the elder statesmen chose Hara to head the nation's first party cabinet. The Seiyūkai won an unprecedented majority in the 1920 elections, but Hara's assassination in 1921 left the party badly fragmented.

In 1924 the party divided into the Seiyūhontō and the rump Seiyūkai, which briefly participated in the Kenseikai-dominated coalition cabinet of Katō Takaaki. Despite the inclusion of the liberal Kakushin Kurabu in 1925, the Seiyūkai shifted strongly to the right under the new presidency of General Tanaka Giichi. Tanaka's cabinet (1927–1929) militarily intervened in China and suppressed left-wing activities at home. Riding the tide of popular nationalism, the Seiyūkai won its largest electoral victory in 1932, but young naval officers assassinated Premier Inukai Tsuyoshi that May. The Seiyūkai steadily lost influence in succeeding nonparty cabinets. In 1939 the party split into factions headed by Nakajima Chikuhei and Kuhara Fusanosuke. Both factions voluntarily dissolved in July 1940, most members joining the Imperial Rule Assistance Association (Taisei Yokusankai).

[*See also* Itō Hirobumi; Hara Takashi; Katō Takaaki; Tanaka Giichi; *and* Taishō Political Change.]

Gordon M. Berger, *Parties out of Power in Japan, 1931–1941* (1977). Peter Duus, *Party Rivalry and Political Change in Taishō Japan* (1968). Tetsuo Najita, *Hara Kei in the Politics of Compromise* (1967).

SHELDON M. GARON

SEKIGAHARA, BATTLE OF,

battle at Sekigahara, Mino Province, in the autumn of 1600, at which Tokugawa Ieyasu achieved military hegemony over Japan.

Shortly before his death in 1598 Toyotomi Hideyoshi settled his succession on his infant son Hideyori and named a board of regents *(gotairō)* who were sworn to maintain the peace and support the cause of Hideyoshi's heir until he could rule in his own right. Members of the regency, however, were driven by their own strong ambitions, and tension and conflict emerged almost immediately upon Hideyoshi's death. Soon Tokugawa Ieyasu, the most powerful of the regents, threatened the stability of the regency by accepting oaths of allegiance from nearly half of the daimyo who had been loyal to Hideyoshi. Against him, Ishida Mitsunari, a Toyotomi house vassal and an old and implacable foe of Ieyasu, drew together a Western Alliance that included forces contributed by the regents Mōri Terumoto, Ukita Hideie, and Uesugi Kagekatsu, as well as several other powerful daimyo of western and southern Japan.

The contest for national hegemony was fought out at Sekigahara in October 1600. The outcome was at first in doubt, but the Western Alliance was split by distrust among the great lords, and many never committed their full forces. At height of battle, Kobayashi Hideaki defected to the Tokugawa side and rolled up the flank of the Western Alliance.

This victory made Tokugawa Ieyasu the military master of Japan and enabled him to rearrange the political map of the country. He reduced the domains of four of his major opponents by 2,215,000 *koku* (a volumn measurement, based on rice productivity, used to rate the various domains) and confiscated ninety other domains with a total productive capacity of 4,300,000 *koku* for redistribution to his supporters. Victory also gave him control over the ecomonic wealth of the nation's most important mines, harbors, and commercial centers, and it opened the way for Ieyasu to acquire political domination through appointment as shogun.

[See also Tokugawa Period; Tokugawa Ieyasu; *and* Toyotomi Hideyoshi.]

JAMES L. MCCLAIN

SEKISHO,

barrier inspection stations established along traffic routes in Japan for either strategic or financial reasons. The Taika Reforms of 645 established the first *sekisho* in the vicinity of the capital. Of these, the *sekisho* at Fuwa in Mino Province (modern Gifu Prefecture), at Suzuka in Ise Province (modern Mie Prefecture), and at Arachi in Echizen Province (modern Fukui Prefecture) were of considerable importance because they were designed to protect the capital area. In the event of a potential crisis, officials were dispatched to see to the closing of these *sekisho*.

During the medieval period there were changes in control and function. The shogunates were joined by estate owners and feudal lords in building *sekisho* for financial as well as strategic purposes. Religious institutions also benefited from the *sekisho*: in the Kamakura Period, the *sekisho* at Hyōgo became a prime source of income for the Tōdaiji and Kōfukuji temples of Nara.

In the Tokugawa period *sekisho* were revived by the shogunate as protective devices against military threats from hostile daimyo, and were erected on the five principal highways connecting the shogunal capital of Edo with the rest of the archipelago. From the Tokugawa perspective, the strategically important *sekisho* were at Hakone on the Tōkaidō, Yokogawa and Fukushima on the Nakasendō, Kuribashi on the Nikko Kaidō, and Matsudo on the Mito Kaidō. All *sekisho* officials and guards were particularly concerned with the unauthorized movement of arms toward Edo and the departure from Edo of daimyo wives (who were forced to remain in Edo as guarantees of their husbands' loyalty), both of which could signal the beginning of an anti-Tokugawa plot. Commercially, however, the *sekisho* served to impede the efficient movement of goods throughout the country. The *sekisho* were abolished by the Meiji regime in 1869.

[See also Tōkaidō.]

RONALD J. DICENZO

SELANGOR,

Malay state on the west coast of the Malay Peninsula, site of Kuala Lumpur, the federal capital of Malaysia.

The Klang River basin was long involved in the political life of the region, but a sultanate was not established there until the eighteenth century, when the area's population began to grow with the arrival from Sumatra and Sulawesi of immigrants (the Bugis people) who had been drawn by Selangor's promising tin deposits. Bugis chiefs first obtained authority to rule in the area as agents of the sultan of Johor. In 1742, after twenty years of struggle with Malay rivals, the Bugis established Raja Lumu as Sultan Sallehuddin. Throughout the remainder of the century, Sallehuddin worked to obtain recognition from neighboring Malay sultans. Sultan Ibrahim (c. 1780–1826) was involved in frequent warfare to expand and then to maintain his dominion. Pressures on the state increased from the 1820s onward as the competition over the tin deposits of the west-coast states escalated, particularly when large numbers of Chinese laborers were imported to the mining districts, and many different interests—Malay chiefs as well as British authorities and Chinese investors in the Straits Settlements—came to have a stake in the competition.

In Selangor, where each of the five major river basins was under a different chief, each of whom had invited Chinese miners to his area to enhance its revenues, conflict grew, particularly when wars erupted among the rival Chinese secret societies (the Ghi Hin and Hai San) that had been formed by the miners. When a son-in-law (Sultan Abdul Samad), in preference to a son, succeeded to the sultanate in 1857, allowing the in-laws to profit at the expense of the sons in the division of tin revenues, the Selangor Civil War broke out. The Chinese were dragged into the conflict, forced to take one side or the other. This war, which was particularly intense from 1870 to 1873, led to British intervention in the area to restore peace and economic stability. The outcome of British involvement was the application to Selangor of the precedent established in the Pangkor Engagement (1873). A British resident, whose advice was to be asked and acted upon in all matters save those respecting Malay religion and custom, was posted at the court of the sultan of Selangor in 1874. Over the next half century, rapid economic development, involving first tin and then rubber, made Selangor modern and prosperous, but modernity and prosperity came at the expense of the Malays, who were to find themselves making up only one-third of the state's population (the other two-thirds of the people were Chinese and Indian immigrants). Klang, the old capital, was overshadowed by inland Kuala Lumpur, which became thoroughly modern and almost completely Chinese and European. As the hub of the administration for the Federated Malay States (1895) and then the Federation of Malaya and Malaysia (1963), Kuala Lumpur also became a center of Malay education, journalism, intellectual life, and nationalism. Selangor remains a constitutional sultanate, a constituent part of Malaysia.

[*See also* Malaysia; Kuala Lumpur; Ghi Hin; Hai San Society; Kapitan China; Pangkor Engagement; Federated Malay States; Swettenham, Sir Frank; *and* Yap Ah Loy.]

Barbara W. Andaya and Leonard Y. Andaya, *A History of Malaysia* (1982). J. M. Gullick, *A History of Selangor 1742–1957* (1960).
                                    DAVID K. WYATT

SELEUCID DYNASTY, founded by Seleucus I, who, by designating Antiochus I, his son by the Bactrian Apame, as his heir, made it the only successor dynasty of mixed Macedonian and Iranian blood. Its territory was nevertheless called "kingdom of the Macedonians," and it relied on Greeks and Macedonian soldier colonies throughout its territory.

Antiochus inherited what had been the Achaemenid empire, except for Ptolemaic Egypt, Syria-Phoenicia, and the Indian provinces given up by his father; he lost control of much of Asia Minor, however. Antiochus II regained parts of it and gained parts of Syria, but his attempt to reach a settlement with the Ptolemies through a marriage alliance failed, and after his death in 246 BCE the kingdom began to disintegrate because of succession troubles in the west and the rise of Parthian power in the east. Antiochus III temporarily regained all that Seleucus I had held and more, but was defeated by the Romans, dying a broken and humiliated man. His son Seleucus IV (r. 187–175) patiently rebuilt the economic, military, and diplomatic resources lost, and his brother Antiochus IV (r. 175–164) used them to conquer and annex most of the Ptolemaic kingdom. But he precipitately yielded to an unenforceable Roman ultimatum, abandoning his gains and thus becoming a de facto Roman client, humiliated and financially exhausted. His intervention with excessive force in a dispute in the Judaean province resulted in the Maccabaean rebellion, which later received Roman support and led to the independence of an enlarged Judaean kingdom. Antiochus IV died preparing to invade the Iranian provinces that had been lost after his predecessor's death. Succession troubles now became endemic in the kingdom, the eastern provinces were lost to the Parthians, and by 129 the kingdom was confined to an area around northern Syria. In 83 its remnants were taken over by Tigranes of Armenia. Briefly restored by the Roman commander Lucullus, it was finally annexed to Rome by Pompey in 64.

Seleucus I founded two capitals, Seleucia on the Tigris River for the eastern half of his kingdom and Antioch on the Orontes for the west. Seleucia, about thirty-five miles from Babylon, became a cosmopolitan center of commerce, flourishing even under the Parthians; its population was said to be 600,000 at one time. Seleucia was sometimes the residence of the heir apparent. Since the monarchs were mainly interested in the west, Antioch became the capital of the king himself and ultimately of Roman Syria.

Seleucid administration pragmatically adapted the Achaemenid system; the satrapies were subdivided into smaller units, which assumed increasing importance, and large areas such as Asia Minor and Iran were at times under a powerful viceroy who was always likely to rebel. Greek cities and numerous local dynasts and temples had varying degrees of autonomy. As under the Achaemenids, the royal army was small (perhaps 10,000); its core was the Greco-Macedonian phalanx, supplemented by mercenaries, who also served as garrisons. Native subjects served as cavalry and light-armed infantry.

The royal court increased in size, expense, and complexity as the kings' territories diminished, with the "relatives" and "friends" subdivided into grades; attendants multiplied. As etiquette also prescribed conspicuous generosity, it became increasingly difficult to maintain defense and administration; the population thus became increasingly dissatisfied, always ready to welcome change.

The Seleucids' most successful institution was the Seleucid era, reckoned from 312/311 BCE. It was superseded only by the Christian and Muslim eras and survived in some areas until modern times.

[See also Antiochus III; Antiochus VII Sidetes; and Seleucus I.]

E. R. Bevan, The House of Seleucus (1902).

ERNST BADIAN

SELEUCUS I (d. 281 BCE), known as Nikator ("the conqueror"), companion of Alexander the Great and the greatest of his successors. He organized the assassination of the regent Perdiccas in 320 BCE and received the satrapy of Babylonia. When Antigonus gained control of the Iranian satrapies Seleucus fled to Ptolemy and in 312 made a dash across the desert with one thousand men to capture Babylon. Over the next ten years he conquered the whole of the eastern satrapies and firmly established his rule. In 303, eager to join in the coalition against Antigonus, he ceded Alexander's Indian provinces (in part perhaps already lost) to Chandragupta Maurya in return for a corps of elephants, which in an astonishing march he took across Iran and Armenia to western Asia Minor. Antigonus's defeat and death involved Seleucus in a quarrel with Ptolemy over Syria, which left a fatal legacy to both dynasties.

With the east secure, he devoted his attention to the struggles of the successors, leaving Antiochus, his son by a Bactrian princess, to rule the east as joint king. In 281 he defeated and killed Lysimachus, then crossed to Europe and, aged nearly eighty, was within sight of reuniting most of Alexander's empire when he was assassinated in a conspiracy led by an exiled son of Ptolemy, who at once proclaimed himself king of Macedon. Antiochus succeeded to his provinces in Asia.

[See also Alexander III and Seleucid Dynasty.]

ERNST BADIAN

SELF-STRENGTHENING MOVEMENT. See Qing Dynasty.

SELJUK DYNASTY. The Seljuks (1038–1157), who began as a family of nomads leading a migration from Central Asia into Khurasan, became, arguably, the most important rulers in medieval Islam. Many of the political and administrative systems begun or refined during the Seljuks' reign lasted into the twentieth century; many of the events and institutions of the period set the stage for the universalizing of Islamic civilization.

In the first decade of the eleventh century, the descendants of Seljuk, a leader of the Qiniq tribe of Oghuz (Ghuzz) Turks, were active as mercenaries in Transoxiana. Forced to come to terms with the expanding Ghaznavid power, two of Seljuk's grandsons, Toghril and Chaghri, submitted to Mas'ud of Ghazna and crossed into Khurasan in 1035. They quickly gained influence over the cities and continually harassed the armies there until decisively defeating the Ghaznavid forces at Dandanqan in 1040.

Following Turkish and nomadic custom, the new territories were divided among the members of the leading family. Chaghri took over the administration of Khurasan, while Toghril (r. 1038–1063) moved continually farther west, eventually ousting the last of the Buyid dynasty from Baghdad in 1055. By 1058 he was accepted by the caliph as the supreme political authority within Iraq and Iran.

Under a son of Chaghri, Alp Arslan (r. 1063–1072), and his son, Malikshah (r. 1072–1092), the Seljuk empire reached new levels of both religious and secular achievement. The prestige of the caliphate was restored by the removal of the Shi'ite Buyids and by the Seljuks' support of Sunni causes; Nizam al-Mulk, vizier for both Alp Arslan and Ma-

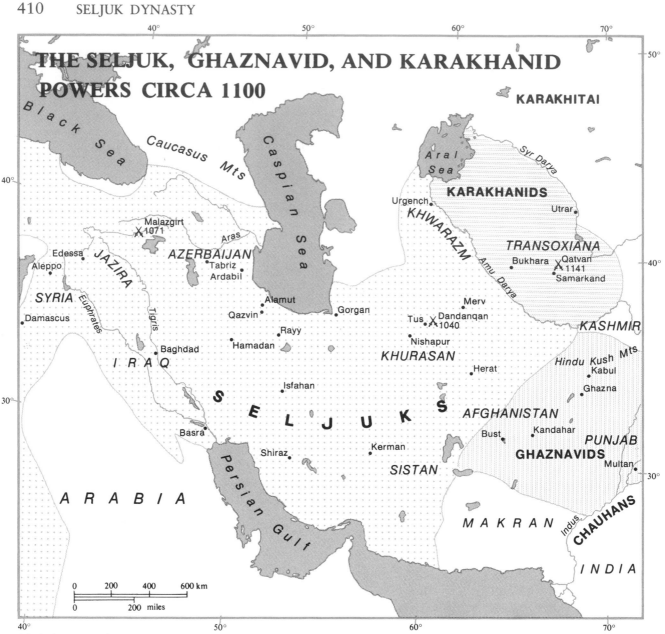

THE SELJUK, GHAZNAVID, AND KARAKHANID POWERS CIRCA 1100

likshah, set about rebuilding the bureaucratic structures of the classical Perso-Islamic heritage. Militarily, the Seljuks altered the course of world history by defeating the Byzantine armies at Manzikert in 1071 and thus sealing the fate of Anatolia.

Following the almost simultaneous deaths of Nizam al-Mulk and Malikshah, the reigns of the latter's sons, Berkyaruk (r. 1092–1105) and Muhammad (r. 1105–1118), were marked by an increase in the importance of other family members and favored tribal leaders, or *atabegs,* who were often the protectors of Seljuk heirs and beneficiaries of valuable land grants.

Muhammad's death signals the dissolution of the Seljuk state, the strength of which had been a function of the union of Persian administrative practice and Turkish military power. The accompanying partial persianization of the Turkish "most exalted sultans" had necessarily alienated large numbers of their followers. Thus the decentralizing forces of the ever present tribalism allowed the dynasty's rule to continue only locally, with Sanjar (r. 1097–1157), the last of the "Great Seljuks," in Khurasan, and with other lines in Rum (i.e., Anatolia, 1077–1307), Syria (1078–1117), Iraq (1118–1194), and Kerman (1041–1186).

Examples of the patronage of arts and letters in the Seljuk period are the establishment of numerous *madrasas* (institutes of higher learning), the philosophy of al-Ghazali, the political theory of Nizam al-Mulk, and the poetry of Anvari and Omar Khayyam.

[*See also* Buyid Dynasty; Ghazali, al-; Ghaznavid

Dynasty; Ghuzz; Iran; Khayyam, Omar; Khurasan; Nizam al-Mulk; *and* Toghril Beg.]

C. E. Bosworth, "The Political and Dynastic History of the Iranian World (A.D. 1000–1217)," in *The Cambridge History of Iran*, vol. 5, *The Saljuq and Mongol Periods*, edited by J. A. Boyle (1968). Marshall G. S. Hodgson, *The Venture of Islam* (1974), vol. 2. Ann K. S. Lambton, "The Internal Structure of the Saljuq Empire," in *The Saljuq and Mongol Periods,* already cited. Bertold Spuler, "The Age of the Caliphs," in *The Muslim World* (1960).   RUSSELL G. KEMPINERS, JR.

SEMANG. *See* Orang Asli.

SEMAOEN (1898–1971), Indonesian political activist. He was born in Gunang Gangsir, Pasuruan, East Java. In 1914 he became a member of the Sarekat Islam, the first large Indonesian nationalist party, and in 1915 of the Indische Sociaal-Democratische Vereeniging (ISDV).

In the Sarekat Islam, Semaoen was the leader of the Marxist-oriented faction. After clashing with the Islamic-oriented members, he and his supporters were forced to leave the party in the early 1920s. Apart from his political work in the Sarekat Islam, ISDV, and its successor the Partai Komunis Indonesia (Indonesian Communist Party), Semaoen played a very prominent role in the labor movement. In 1923 he was arrested, interned on the island of Timor, and, when given the choice, exiled from the Dutch East Indies. He went to Russia (where he attended the fifth congress of the Comintern in 1924) and to Holland. He returned to Indonesia in 1956.

[*See also* Sarekat Islam *and* Partai Komunis Indonesia.]

C. VAN DIJK

SEN, KESHUB CHANDRA (1838–1884), one of the leaders of the Brahmo Samaj, a Hindu reform organization. Sen was indefatigable in the pursuit of creative new ideologies to arrest what he considered to be India's backwardness. Theodore Parker's Unitarianism attracted him at first, but Debendranath Tagore converted him to Neo-Vedantism. In the 1860s Sen supported Bijoy Goswami's efforts to infuse Vaishnavism with modern values from the West: after meeting Ramakrishna, he sought to modernize Shaktism. In 1870 Sen initiated reforms for workers, peasants, and women, but several years later he repudiated social reform for the study of comparative religion, a process which ended in 1879

with the establishment of his New Dispensation, one of the most brilliant, but fruitless contemporary attempts at global religious synthesis.

[*See also* Brahmo Samaj; Tagore, Debendranath; *and* Ramakrishna.]

David Kopf, *The Brahmo Samaj and the Shaping of the Modern Indian Mind* (1979). Protap Chandra Mazoomdar, *The Life and Teachings of Keshub Chandra Sen* (1887).   DAVID KOPF

SENA DYNASTY. Originating in Karnataka, India, the Senas settled in Bengal and rose to prominence under Vijayasena (c. 1097–1160), who assumed authority over much of Bengal. A successor, Lakshmanasena (c. 1178–1206), made military excursions far into Bihar, but early in the twelfth century the dynasty's power was weakened by the invasions of Muhammad Khalji, and it survived only until the middle of the century.

[*See also* Bengal.]

A. M. Chowdhury, *Dynastic History of Bengal (c. 750–1200 A.D.)*(1967). R. C. Majumdar, ed., *The History of Bengal*, vol. 1 (1943).   FREDERICK M. ASHER

SENANAYAKE, DON STEPHEN (1884–1952), Sri Lanka's first prime minister (1947–1952). Involved in national politics since the 1920s, Senanayake became a leading figure in the state council which was established in 1931. By the early 1940s Senanayake emerged as the key Sri Lankan figure in the negotiations over independence. He had a decisive influence in the making of the new constitution and was primarily responsible for the smooth transfer of power in 1948. Leading the United National Party government that he formed in 1947, Senanayake committed himself to a united and multiethnic Sri Lanka. The disenfranchisement of the Indian Tamils in 1948–1949 revealed that Senanayake's concept of multiethnicity had decided limits. Further, he was unable to allay the fears of the Tamils in regard to the dominance of the majority Sinhalese and he was to witness the beginnings of Tamil ethnic parties. His consummate interest was agriculture and his major legacy was the program he began, as a minister in the state council in the 1930s, for the regeneration of the dry zone through irrigation and settlement of Sinhalese colonists. His foreign policy had as its basis a firm faith in the Commonwealth and a deep fear of India as an expansionist power, and while he entered into defense agreements with Britain at independence, Senanayake readily established both diplomatic and trade ties with communist countries.

[*See also* United National Party; Tamils in Sri Lanka; *and* Sri Lanka.]

Ceylon Historical Journal 5: The D. S. Senanayake Memorial Number (1955–1956).

VIJAYA SAMARAWEERA

SENANAYAKE, DUDLEY SHELTON (1911–1973), prime minister of Sri Lanka (1952–1953; March–July 1960; and 1965–1970). Senanayake first assumed the prime ministership as the successor to his father, Don Stephen Senanayake. Although in 1952 there was no agreement that he was the seniormost candidate for the office, the resounding victory of the United National Party at the 1952 polls under his leadership muted the controversy. However, Senanayake's decision to resign a year later in the face of public disturbances over unpopular governmental measures brought forth the image of an irresolute leader. Nonetheless, he remained a personally popular figure and was to make a comeback to lead the party to victory again in 1965. His most significant contribution to the party was the softening of its rightist image.

[*See also* United National Party; Senanayake, Don Stephen; *and* Sri Lanka.]

VIJAYA SAMARAWEERA

SENDAI, capital of Miyagi Prefecture and largest city (population, 664,799) in the Tōhoku region of northern Honshu, Japan. Although the Miyagi area was developed as early as the Heian period (794–1185) by the Fujiwara, Sendai itself gained prominence only during the Tokugawa period (1600–1868), as the castle town of the Date family. In return for his military services at the Battle of Sekigahara (1600), Date Masamune (1567–1636) received from Tokugawa Ieyasu a fief with an assessed productivity of 620,000 *koku* (measures of rice) in the Miyagi area. Masamune erected his castle at Sendai. Masamune's support of Catholicism resulted in a mission to Rome to encourage further proselytization and trade. Despite their *tozama* daimyo status (which meant exclusion from national politics), the Date nevertheless remained loyal to the Tokugawa until their fall in 1868.

Although largely destroyed by United States bombing during World War II, Sendai, which is 290 miles north of Tokyo, today stands as the political, cultural, economic, and educational center of northern Honshu. It is the location of Tōhoku University, one of Japan's major national universities. Nearby Matsushima continues to be as much of a major tourist attraction as it was in earlier times, when it won fame as one of the "three famous scenic places in Japan" *(nihon sankei)*. Sendai is also famous for its annual Tanabata Festival (6–8 August). Religiously, it is the northern Honshu center for Christian missionary activity.

[*See also* Tozama Daimyo *and* Sekigahara, Battle of.]

RONALD J. DiCENZO

SENGGERINCHIN (Chinese, Senggelinqin; d. 1865), Mongol general who demonstrated military prowess defending the Qing dynasty of China against its foreign and domestic enemies.

Born into a Mongol clan loyal to the Manchu rulers of China, Senggerinchin gained his first success leading imperial troops against the Taiping rebels in 1853, when he halted their northward sweep toward the capital near Tianjin. Further victories in Shandong in 1855 earned him the title of prince. During the Arrow War (the Second Opium War), he was assigned command of the Dagu Forts. He greatly strengthened the defenses (some say with Russian guns) and blockaded the waterway leading toward Beijing. Thus, when a combined Anglo-French fleet arrived and attempted to run the blockade on 25 June 1859, he masterfully repulsed the invaders, much to their surprise, and inflicted heavy losses.

In August of the following year, however, a much larger force returned and landed, skirting the defenses and seizing the forts from the rear. This time, Senggerinchin proved incapable of forestalling their march on the capital, which they entered on 13 October. Humiliated and demoted, Senggerinchin nevertheless went on to redeem himself by winning impressive victories against the Nian rebels in Shandong, where he was finally killed in 1865. Thereafter, the Manchus were forced to rely on such Chinese officials as Zeng Guofan to quell internal unrest.

[*See also* Arrow War; Dagu Forts; Qing Dynasty; *and* Zeng Guofan.]

ROLAND L. HIGGINS

SENGOKU PERIOD, the period in Japanese history from the middle of the fifteenth to the late sixteenth century CE. Most historians agree that the

Ōnin War of 1467–1477 marked the beginning of this epoch, but they are divided on a concluding date. Many choose 1573, when the last Ashikaga shogun fled Kyoto; others claim that the period came to an end only after Toyotomi Hideyoshi pacified Kyushu in 1587; still others point to Hideyoshi's victory over the Hōjō of Odawara in 1590; and some favor 1600, when Tokugawa Ieyasu assumed the mantle of national hegemony with his triumph at Sekigahara.

There is, however, more uniform agreement about the general characteristics of the era. It was an age when the country was at war with itself, just as the name *Sengoku* ("warring states") implies. During the early fifteenth century, the Ashikaga shogunate entered a long, debilitating decline and lost its ability to maintain control over the regional military governors *(shugo),* who were competing for power and authority in the provinces. A shogunal succession dispute in 1467 became the pretext for these military governors to enter Kyoto and to fall upon each other in battle, sparking the devastating Ōnin War. Within a decade, most had exhausted themselves in battle, and the shogun Yoshimasu had given up his office to become a religious aesthete. As centralized authority disintegrated fighting spread throughout the countryside. In the early sixteenth century, Japan was afire, as small groups of warriors, even peasants and religious adherents, banded together to contend for local power. No power of the country escaped this warfare, and the contemporary chronicles are suffused with portraits of chaos.

In this situation, the political and economic structures of the medieval period either collapsed or lost their meaning. After the 1470s no Ashikaga shogun could exercise effective power beyond the city limits of Kyoto. The military governors passed into history, and even most of the families from the old class of land stewards *(jitō),* who had wielded much power on the village and local level, did not survive these decades of combat. As local bands of warriors and peasants struggled for power, they seized control of agricultural surpluses and ignored the distribution of dues that had prevailed under the old *shōen* system. Consequently, the aristocrats and imperial family in Kyoto became impoverished. Their political offices had become bare structures, stripped of any real power, and they were gradually compelled to live on the largess of the warrior class, who supported the emperor and aristocrats out of respect for their traditional roles as the standard-bearers of an elite culture and the font of political sovereignty.

During the latter half of the Sengoku period, Japan was reunified. At first, this proceeded by military means as the daimyo, or local military commanders, forged control over local territorial holdings. On the national level, Oda Nobunaga, Toyotomi Hideyoshi, and then Tokugawa Ieyasu imposed their hegemony over the other daimyo, a process that was consummated in 1590 when Hideyoshi claimed military supremacy, and institutionalized in 1603 when Ieyasu had himself appointed shogun, a position that remained in his family for the next two and a half centuries.

In tandem with this military reunification, the national hegemons and local daimyo created new political and economic institutions in order to assert their authority over the people and resources of their respective domains. Hideyoshi, for example, claimed high status at the imperial court, had himself deified as a Shinto *kami,* and claimed the right to distribute all landed proprietorships in the country, permitting no daimyo, or even the court or religious institutions, to hold territory unless it came as an entrusted grant *(azukari mono)* over his vermilion seal *(shuin).*

On the regional level, the daimyo, who came increasingly to serve as chiefs or local administration within the Hideyoshi power structure, also moved to assert greater authority over their domains. The daimyo conducted cadastral surveys *(kenchi)* that defined villages as administrative units and advanced the right of the lord to levy dues and taxes on the peasantry. They conducted "sword hunts" to disarm villagers and issued codes that regulated rural life and forbade the cultivators from leaving their villages. The daimyo also compelled their vassal samurai to leave rural areas and to settle in the growing castle towns, a move that brought the samurai under more direct supervision and provided an opportunity to convert them from a class of landed vassals into a service bureaucracy.

The Sengoku period was an era of sharp contrasts. It was an age of collapse and destruction, as warfare flamed throughout the country, burning out the supports of the medieval political and economic institutions. But it was also an age of creation and remarkable energy, and out of the fire and storms of warfare came a new institutional structure, one in which the national hegemon and daimyo were the unassailable rulers, leaders of a state where power and wealth were more effectively concentrated than at any previous time in Japanese history.

[*See also* Muromachi Period; Ōnin War; Oda Nobunaga; *and* Toyotomi Hideyoshi.]

Mary E. Berry, *Hideyoshi* (1982). George Elison and Bardwell L. Smith, *Warlords, Artists, and Commoners* (1981). John W. Hall et al., eds., *Japan before Tokugawa* (1981).   JAMES L. McCLAIN

SENI PRAMOJ (b. 1905), Thai political leader. Born in Nakhon Sawan Province, Seni was the son of Prince Khamrop, the director general of the police department. Seni was educated at Oxford and studied for the bar at the Gray's Inn. As the Thai ambassador to the United States in 1941, Seni refused to submit Prime Minister Luang Phibunsong-khram's declaration of war to the American government. Instead, he helped organize and became a prominent member of the Free Thai movement, which collaborated with Pridi Phanomyong's Seri Thai organization in Thailand in an effort to resist the Japanese. After the end of World War II, Seni became prime minister and helped negotiate a fair settlement with the Allies, who had viewed Thailand as an enemy state because of its government's collaboration with Japan but treated it leniently in consideration of the Free Thai's anti-Japanese role.

A lawyer by profession, Seni continued to be active in politics. He eventually became head of the Democratic Party and was elected to Parliament. Seni became prime minister again in 1976, but his tenure was cut short by the 6 October 1976 coup d'état, which ended the three years of open democracy that had been brought about by the student uprisings of 14 October 1973.

[*See also* Thailand; Phibunsongkhram, Luang; Pridi Phanomyong; *and* Free Thai.]

Direk Jayanama, *Siam and World War II* (1976). Jayanta Ray, *Portraits of Thai Politics* (1972).

THAK CHALOEMTIARANA

SENKAKU. *See* Diaoyutai Islands.

SEN NO RIKYŪ (1522–1591), the founder of the most important traditions of *cha no yu*, the Japanese tea ceremony. Born in Sakai to a wealthy seafood merchant, Sen no Rikyū was the grandson of Tanaka Sen'ami, a *dōbōshū* member, one character of whose name Rikyū's father had adopted as a surname. With the childhood name Yoshirō, he studied *cha no yu* first with Kitamuki Dōchin of the elegant Nōami tradition and later with Takeno Jōō, who practiced *wabicha* ("poverty tea"). He also studied Zen at Daitokuji and took the adult name Sōeki.

Together with Imai Sōkyū and Tsuda Sōgyū Rikyū served first Oda Nobunaga and later Toyotomi Hideyoshi as tea master. In 1585 he served tea to Emperor Ōgimachi and received the name (Gō) Rikyū Koji. At the Great Kitano Tea Party in 1587, which Hideyoshi staged for all classes of society, Rikyū was in charge. For reasons still unclear Rikyū incurred Hideyoshi's wrath and in 1591 had to disembowel himself. One possible cause was that the placing of Rikyū's statue above the gate of Daitokuji may have affronted Hideyoshi or that Rikyū may have frustrated Hideyoshi's sexual advances toward his daughter. Rikyū was also accused of accepting improper gifts.

Rikyū promoted *wabicha*, which emphasized the simplest forms and utensils. He designed a mud-walled tearoom smaller than two mats, served tea without a shelf directly on the tatami, and promoted the use of rough utensils like raku ceramics. In this way he sought to heighten the spiritual basis of *cha no yu*. His heirs and disciples became the mainstream of the ceremony in the Edo period and in contemporary Japan.

[*See also* Tea Ceremony.]

V. DIXON MORRIS

SENOI. *See* Orang Asli.

SEOUL, capital of the Republic of Korea; its population in 1986 was 9.5 million. Seoul's historical gates and palaces, which memorialize the past, are overshadowed by the newly constructed skyscrapers and tall apartment blocks of this rapidly expanding, vibrant city.

In 1394 Seoul was established as the capital of the last Korean dynasty, the Yi or Chosŏn (1392–1910), in a well-protected and propitious geomantic site. The city wall, with four cardinal and five subsidiary gates, and the Yi palaces were built on the granite base of the surrounding mountains and the well-drained alluvial flood plains of the Seoul basin and the Han River to the south. The city suffered from Japanese and Manchu invasions in the sixteenth and seventeenth centuries, but remained the center of administration and culture.

Many changes took place in Seoul, particularly under the Japanese colonial regime (1910–1945). The railroad station for the north-south peninsular line and the western line to the port of Inch'ŏn was built outside the South Gate; the area between the old city and the Han River became the Japanese military, commercial, and residential center. Within the city an imposing granite government-general building was constructed on the site of an old palace. Streets were widened and large banking, governmental, and commercial buildings were constructed.

Seoul was severely damaged during the Korean War (1950–1953); only shells of the major buildings remained. The reconstruction and expansion of Seoul since 1953 has been phenomenal. Under a well-conceived master plan, new streets and elevated highways and tunnels were constructed. A subway system, also serving as an immense air-raid shelter, has been built to relieve the congestion of surface traffic of buses and taxis. Blocked by mountains to the north, Seoul has spread to the east and south with many bridges across the Han River; on an island in the Han a modernistic National Assembly and other buildings were constructed; Seoul National University was moved to a site far south of the city. Despite efforts to decentralize government and educational establishments, Seoul still has many schools, universities, museums, government offices, hospitals, churches, and hotels, as well as headquarters for large corporations, banks, and newspapers.

Despite its location near the Demilitarized Zone, Seoul is the cultural, economic, intellectual, political, and social center of the Republic of Korea. The selection of Seoul in 1982 as the site of the 1988 Olympic Games spurred a frenetic new round of construction. Seoul, having had a tumultous past, is preparing for an even more hectic future.

Donald N. Clark, *Seoul: Past and Present* (1959).

SHANNON MCCUNE

SEPOY. Derived from the Persian *sipahi* (horseman), the term *sepoy* from the mid-eighteenth century has come to mean an Indian foot soldier disciplined and dressed in the European style and usually under European command. Sepoy battalions, largely recruited from among high-caste brahmans and Rajputs, constituted the major component of the East India Company's army. After the so-called Sepoy Mutiny of 1857 recruits were drawn instead from the Sikhs, Gurkhas, and Muslims of the Northwest.

Sita Ram, *From Sepoy to Subedar* (1873, reprint, 1970).   THOMAS R. METCALF

SEPOY REBELLION. *See* Mutiny, Indian.

SEPPUKU ("disembowelment"), also known as *harakiri* ("stomach-slitting"), the unique form of suicide adopted by the samurai (warrior) class of Japan. The practice of suicide by disembowelment probably began among the samurai in the late eleventh or twelfth century. One of the first recorded cases is that of the famous warrior Minamoto no Tametomo, hero of the war tale *Hōgen Monogatari* (*Tale of Hōgen*), in 1170. In later centuries *seppuku*—the actual cutting of the stomach—became a preliminary form of self-torture, presumably intended to demonstrate the courage of the samurai. Death was inflicted by another samurai serving as a second (*kaishaku*), who beheaded his fellow warrior with a sword.

One possible reason for the evolution of *seppuku* among samurai was the Japanese belief that the soul is in the stomach (*hara*), and that by cutting the stomach one could penetrate to the essence of one's being. Reasons for committing *seppuku* included: to avoid capture in battle; to follow a lord in death; and to admonish a superior. During the Tokugawa period (1600–1868), *seppuku* was also an honorable method of capital punishment for samurai.

[*See also* Samurai.]

PAUL VARLEY

SERENDIB, one of the names by which Sri Lanka was known in ancient times. It was the Arabic form of the Sanskrit name *Sinhala-dvipa* and the Pali name *Sihala-dvipa*. The name had gained currency in the West by the time of the Roman emperor Julian. It formed the basis of the word *serendipity* coined by Horace Walpole (1754) after *The Three Princes of Serendip*, a fairy tale.   K. M. DE SILVA

SERINGAPATAM, a historical city about fifteen kilometers from Mysore city, India, is an island formed by the river Kaveri. It served as the capital of Mysore for more than 150 years and was a flourishing town during Chikkadevaraja's time (1672–1704). It came into greater prominence under Haidar Ali and Tipu Sultan, who endowed it with beautiful structures such as the Masjid Ala, the Darya Daulat, and the Gumbuz. After Tipu's fall in 1799 the British kept their troops there and Arthur Wellesley—later duke of Wellington—was in command of these troops until 1805. It began to decline rapidly after the British moved their troops to Bangalore in 1811 and leased the island to the raja for fifty thousand rupees a year.

[*See also* Haidar Ali Khan *and* Tipu Sultan.]

G. B. Malleson, *Seringapatam, Past and Present* (1876).

B. SHEIK ALI

SERVANTS OF INDIA SOCIETY. The Servants of India Society was founded by moderate nationalist Gopal Krishna Gokhale in 1905 to recruit young educated Indians into a secular monastic order serving the Indian nation. Members worked to develop public opinion in support of education, social reform, cooperative movements, communal harmony, and the rights of laborers, women, and Untouchables. The society published influential newspapers and instituted welfare activities and schools, including the Gokhale Institute of Politics and Economics. Well-known society members included, besides Gokhale, educators, reformers, and labor leaders such as V. K. Srinivasa Sastri, N. M. Joshi, H. N. Kunzru, and A. V. Thakkar.

[*See also* Gokhale, Gopal Krishna.]

D. G. Karve and D. V. Ambekar, eds., *Speeches and Writings of Gopal Krishna Gokhale*, vol. 2, *Political* (1966). B. R. Nanda, *Gokhale: The Indian Moderates and the British Raj* (1977). FRANK F. CONLON

SESSHŪ TŌYŌ (1420–1506), major Japanese ink painter of the Muromachi period (1392–1568), active during the second half of the fifteenth century. Born in Bitchū Province (today part of Okayama Prefecture), Sesshū Tōyō went to Kyoto as a young Zen monk, serving as attendant to Shunrin Shūtō (fl. 1430–1465) and studying painting with the painter-monk Shūbun at Shōkokuji monastery. Around 1462 he began to use the professional name Sesshū. In 1464 Sesshū moved to Yamaguchi (today's Yamaguchi Prefecture), which was the territory controlled by the powerful Ōuchi family, and there established a studio called Unkokuan.

In 1467 Sesshu traveled to Ming China with a trade mission sent by the Ōuchi family. The trip took him from Ningbo (Ningpo) to Beijing (Peking), offering the artist firsthand experience not only of the actual Chinese scenery but also of contemporary Ming paintings such as those of Li Zai, still unknown to Japan. Sesshu visited the monastery of Tiantongshan in Siming, where he attained the monastic rank of *shuzo*, or primate. In Beijing Sesshū painted a wall painting in the building of the Board of Rites. He made sketches of Chinese village life, some of which survive to this day through later copies. He returned to Japan in 1469. By 1476 he had opened a studio in Bungo Province (now part of Ōita Prefecture, Kyushu); he later moved back to Unkokuan in Yamaguchi. His reputation as painter was high among the leading Zen monks not only of Kyoto but also of the provinces.

Sesshū's paintings interpret Chinese paintings of the Ming, Yuan (1279–1368), and Song (960–1279) dynasties in unique ways. The Chinese paintings Sesshu was familiar with were those of Li Tang (fl. late twelfth century), Xia Gui (fl. c. 1195–1224), Muqi (Japanese, Mokkei; fl. thirteenth century), Mi Youren (1086–1165), and Yujian (mid-thirteenth century).

The style of Sesshū departs from the lyrical and contemplative mode of his teacher, Shūbun, especially in the dynamic brushwork and structured composition. *Autumn and Winter Landscapes,* a pair of hanging scrolls (Tokyo National Museum); *Landscape of the Four Seasons,* in a horizontal handscroll known as the *Long Landscape Scroll* (1486; Mōri Foundation, Hōfu, Yamaguchi Prefecture); and *Landscape* (c. 1505; Ōhara Collection, Okayama), are typical of his structured compositions. His best-known work, *Haboku Landscape* (1495; Tokyo National Museum), is done in the manner of Yujian and was given to his follower Josui Sōen. Sesshū himself wrote a colophon on it. Another well-known work by Sesshū done in a manner different from his usual style is a landscape sketch of Amanohashidate (c. 1501; Kyoto National Museum), a scenic spot on the Sea of Japan coast that he visited on a trip he took around Honshu.

Sesshū also painted portraits and other subjects. The portraits *Masuda Kanetaka* (1479; Masuda Collection) and *Bodhidharma and Huike Severing His Arm* (1496; Sainenji, Aichi Prefecture) are well-known examples. In the bird-and-flower genre he interpreted Ming academic paintings. Numerous screens, some of which are in Western collections, are attributed to Sesshū. The most certain attribution is a pair of screens in the Kosaka Collection in Tokyo.

The Sesshū tradition was continued well into the sixteenth and seventeenth centuries by his followers. Hasegawa Tōhaku and Unkoku Tōgan are two of the best-known names. Tōgan was the leading painter in Sesshū tradition in the early Edo period, identified with Unkoku school, so named after Sesshū's studio in Yamaguchi.

[*See also* Painting: Japanese Painting *and* Muromachi Period.]

YOSHIAKI SHIMIZU

SETTHATHIRAT, king of Lan Sang and Lan Na, a leading figure in sixteenth-century mainland Southeast Asia.

Born in 1534, Setthathirat was the son of King Phothisarat (r. 1520–1547) of Lan Sang, who ruled the Mekong Valley from Luang Prabang. In 1546, amid a succession crisis in Lan Na, the high dignitaries of Chiang Mai invited Phothisarat to be their king. He gave them his son instead, and Setthathirat, then only twelve years old, was led away to rule Lan Na, where he was given a local queen, Thao Mae Ku. He remained there only over a year, and then, hearing of the death of his father in Luang Prabang, left Chiang Mai in the hands of his queen and rushed back to Laos to contest his brothers for the throne of Lan Sang (1548).

He would have done better to remain in Chiang Mai: the Burmese, now preparing to conquer Ayudhya (Siam), soon evicted Thao Mae Ku, and Setthathirat not only lost that one hope of uniting the Lao world but also gave the Burmese an opportunity to gain resources and a strategic position that they would use against him. With the Burmese gaining power to the west, Setthathirat set about preparing his defense. He moved his capital south to Vientiane (1563) and fortified it, and he proposed a marriage alliance with Princess Thepkasatri, daughter of King Chakkraphat of Ayudhya. Chakkraphat bungled this promising diplomatic overture. He attempted to substitute Thepkasatri's younger sister and sent the poor girl to Laos poorly guarded. A Burmese force intercepted the Siamese party and captured her. Furious, Setthathirat attempted to send an army to rescue her (1565), only to fail and provoke a Burmese attack against Vientiane. Setthathirat fled the city and harassed the Burmese until they withdrew.

To rally his people, the king then desperately mobilized them to work on Buddhist monuments, the That Luang in Vientiane and the That Phanom near Nakhon Phanom. After the Burmese took Ayudhya in 1569, they sent another force against Vientiane. Again, Setthathirat withdrew and forced their withdrawal. Finally, he was drawn into a military campaign against mountain people in the extreme south of his kingdom, in the course of which he simply disappeared. The ensuing civil war over the throne made possible the Burmese capture and sack of Vi-

entiane in 1574 and the capture of Setthathirat's infant heir. For all his failures, Lao remember Setthathirat as a great king, perhaps not least because he was a full and equal participant in the greatest warfare the region had ever known.

[*See also* Lan Sang; Lan Na; Chakkraphat; *and* Ayudhya.]

David K. Wyatt, *Thailand: A Short History* (1984).

DAVID K. WYATT

SEVEN SAGES OF THE BAMBOO GROVE (Chinese, *zhulin qixian*), eccentric members of the second generation of the *qingtan* ("pure conversation") school of Neo-Daoism who were active in China during the chaotic Wei–Jin transition (c. 265). These included Ruan Ji (210–263), Xi Kang (223–262), Shan Tao (205–283), Liu Ling (d. after 265), Ruan Xian (234–305), Xiang Xiu (c. 221–300), and Wang Rong (234–305). Congregating at a bamboo grove in northern Henan Province, the Seven Sages expressed their individualism in philosophical debates, poetry, and unconventional behavior, including nudity and excessive drinking. Holmes Welch interprets such spontaneous tendencies as indicative of "lyrical" or "romantic" Daoism, while Étienne Balazs relates their "nihilism" to the political upheavals of their age.

The Seven Sages of the Bamboo Grove emphasized *ziran* ("spontaneity") as a way of behavior and rejected official state service. Their refusal to serve the Sima clan, who eventually overthrew the Wei and established the Jin in 265, may be explained as an ethical decision rather than an act of disloyalty. All of their actions were supposedly based on the teachings of Daoism, and they collected and studied anew the works of Laozi and Zhuangzi. Richard Mather concludes that the Seven Sages were Wei loyalists whose doctrine of spontaneity was opposed to the prevailing Confucian doctrine of *mingjiao* ("teaching of names") associated with the Sima clan. Indeed, in 262, after the execution of Xi Kang, the host of the Seven Sages, their activities came to an end.

[*See also* Daoism *and* Qingtan.]

Étienne Balazs, *Chinese Civilization and Bureaucracy* (1974). Liu I-ch'ing, *Shih-shuo Hsin-yü: A New Account of Tales of the World,* translated by Richard B. Mather (1976). Richard B. Mather, "The Controversy over Conformity and Naturalness During the Six Dynasties," *History of Religions* 9.2–3 (1969–1970): 160–180. Holmes Welch, *Taoism: The Parting of the Way* (1966).

ANITA M. ANDREW

SHAANGANNING, border region located in the remote area in northwest China at the borders of Shaanxi, Gansu, and Ningxia provinces, where the Chinese Communist Party (CCP) established an independent regime, or soviet, in the early 1930s.

After the Xi'an Incident of 1936, when the Communists joined the Guomindang (Kuomintang, KMT, or Nationalist Party) regime in a "united front" against the Japanese, the Shaanxi Soviet was renamed the Shaanganning Border Region, tacitly recognized by the KMT as a region of the central government administered by the CCP. In return for this recognition, along with an annual subsidy for the defense and administration of the region, the CCP renounced all attempts to overthrow the central government and placed the Red Army, renamed the Eighth Route Army, under the nominal command of the Nationalist forces. The CCP also agreed to end all attempts at radical land redistribution policies, substituting relatively moderate policies of rent reduction and rural cooperativization.

After 1939, following several military incidents that led to the breakdown of the United Front, the KMT attempted to impose a blockade on the region. As the KMT regime in Chongqing stagnated in corruption and inactivity, the CCP, headquartered in Yan'an, carried out guerrilla activities against the Japanese and inherited the mantle of nationalism, attracting people of all classes to its cause. By 1945 the border regions under CCP control expanded to nineteen areas with a population of 70 to 90 million. While scholars debate whether the CCP's success was merely the result of anti-Japanese "peasant nationalism" rather than the Party's social and land policies in the border regions, it is not disputed that these border regions provided the CCP with the popular support and administrative experience that enabled it to conquer all of the mainland by 1949.

[See also United Front; Yan'an; and World War II in China.]

Jerome Chen, *Mao and the Chinese Revolution* (1965). Hsu Yung-ying, *A Survey of Shensi-Kansu-Ninghsia Border Region*, 2 vols. (1945). Chalmers Johnson, *Peasant Nationalism and Communist Power: The Emergence of Revolutionary China, 1937–1945* (1962). Mark Selden, *The Yenan Way in Revolutionary China* (1971).

JOHN A. RAPP

SHAANXI, province in west-central China with a population of 28,904,423 in an area of 195,800 square kilometers (1982). The area around the pro-

vincial capital of Xi'an was the site of prehistoric cultures, as well as the homeland of the rulers of the Zhou dynasty (1122–1256 BCE) and the Qin state that founded the first Chinese empire in 221 BCE. Xi'an (then known as Chang'an) remained the political center of the empire until the tenth century, after which the province declined in importance. Shaanxi suffered serious unrest and disorder several times in the following centuries, including three famines in the early twentieth century. In the early Republican period (1912–1928), Shaanxi also suffered from warlordism and civil war. In 1936 the Communist armies of the Long March reached western Shaanxi and established a base area headquartered in Yan'an, from which they launched their operations against the Japanese and their conquest of China in the civil war (1945–1949).

Shaanxi is primarily an agricultural province, although the fertility of the soil and type of crops vary in different areas, including spring wheat, millet, and pastoral areas in the north; rice, winter wheat, and other crops in the irrigated Wei River valley; and subtropical forest and citrus crops in the south. Huge reserves of coal lie under the north Shaanxi plateau, some of which have been developed to fuel the light and heavy industries of Xi'an. Xi'an is also the leading cultural, educational, and administrative capital of northwest China, as well as a world-class tourist attraction.

JOHN A. RAPP

SHAFI'I, one of the four schools of law in orthodox Islam, named after Muhammad ibn Idris al-Shafi'i (d. 820), its founder and guiding influence. Disturbed by the confusing plethora of views, methods and practices that prevailed in the legal circles of his day, Shafi'i set out to develop a systematic theory of law on the basis of which legal thought and practice in Islam might be unified. His *Risala*, composed in Cairo near the end of his life, constitutes his most important work on juridical theory. In it he sets down what were to become the characteristic features of Shafi'i law. Although Shafi'i aimed at the elaboration of a comprehensive theory of law, his most important contribution to the history of Islamic jurisprudence lies in his insistence on the indispensability of the *sunna*, or tradition of the Prophet, as a substantive source of law. Over against Hanafis and Malikis, for whom the *sunna* was largely a function of local practice, Shafi'i not only linked it to the Prophet himself but declared it to be divinely inspired. In keeping with his position on the primacy of revelation (that is, the Qur'an and the *sunna*), he sought to limit personal judgment (*ijtihad/ra'y*) to analogical reason (*qiyas*), whose only function was to extend the application of those principles laid down in the revealed texts to problems not addressed by the latter.

Shafi'i's views, although not universally accepted at first, had a substantial impact on Islamic law in the long term. His views defined the essential elements of what was to become classical Shafi'i doctrine, and compelled Hanafis, Malikis, and others to undertake important revisions of their own legal systems. From Baghdad and Cairo, the chief centers of the early Shafi'i school, its influence spread throughout the central lands of Islam from Egypt to Khurasan and, by the late Mamluk period, had become the dominant school of law in this vast region. While the school found only limited acceptance in India and Central Asia, it became and remains the principal school of law in the Muslim lands of Southeast Asia.

[*See also* Hanafi; Maliki; Qur'an; *and* Sunni.]

N. J. Coulson, *A History of Islamic Law* (1964), pp. 53–73 and index. Majid Khadduri, *Islamic Jurisprudence* (1961), translation of the *Risala*. Joseph Schacht, *The Origins of Muhammadan Jurisprudence* (1950).

MERLIN SWARTZ

SHAHIYA DYNASTY. A Turkish Muslim dynasty ruling in what is now Afghanistan, the Shahiyas were overthrown in the ninth century by a brahman, the founder of the Hindu Shahi dynasty. The best-known of the Shahis, Jayapala, became king toward the end of the tenth century. His kingdom at one time included parts of Afghanistan and the Punjab. He fought several battles against Sebuktigin and Mahmud of Ghazna; the Turkish rulers of Ghazna were generally the victors. In 1001 Mahmud finally defeated Jayapala and later captured him. In 1020–1021 Mahmud inflicted a decisive defeat on the Shahi Trilochanapala, and Shahi rule ended soon after.

[*See also* Hindu Shahi Dynasty.]

H. M. Elliot and John Dowson, *The History of India As Told by Its Own Historians*, vol. 2 (reprint, 1952). R. C. Majumdar, ed., *The History and Culture of the Indian People*, vols. 3, 5 (1957).   MEERA ABRAHAM

SHAH JAHAN (1592–1666). The rule of the fifth Mughal emperor, Khurram Shihab al-Din Muhammad, better known as Shah Jahan, the third son of

Jahangir, is often considered the Mughal political and cultural apogee. As a prince he displayed great military talent; until 1622 he was favored as the heir apparent. Frustrated by attempts to designate Shahryar as Jahangir's successor, the prince Shah Jahan rebelled in 1623. Pardoned by Jahangir, Shah Jahan succeeded to the throne in 1628 and adopted titles that emphasized his Timurid ancestry. The initial years of Shah Jahan's reign were marked by regional rebellions, including renewed conflict in the Deccan. Most difficulties were quickly supressed, but the Deccan troubles persisted. In 1636 Shah Jahan appointed Prince Aurangzeb viceroy of the Deccan and pursued an increasingly aggressive policy against the Deccani rulers and the Maratha leader Shivaji, temporarily maintaining firm authority there. Less successful was Shah Jahan's attempt to regain territories in Afghanistan, including Qandahar and Balkh, regarded as the Mughal homeland, thus affecting Indian trade and fresh recuitment of Central Asian Muslims into the Mughal army.

When Shah Jahan became ill in 1657, his four sons vied for the throne. Although Shah Jahan recovered, Aurangzeb seized power, imprisoning his father in the Agra Red Fort until his death nine years later. Many feel that Shah Jahan was an extremely orthodox Muslim; however, his orthodoxy is more apparent in his state policy than in his personal belief, for he favored Dara Shikoh, his son with mystical leanings, and continued to recruit Hindus into the Mughal army. A keen patron of architecture, Shah Jahan built the Taj Mahal (a tomb for his wife) and a new city of Delhi, called Shahjahanabad, which included the Red Fort and the Jama Masjid.

[*See also* Jahangir; Aurangzeb; Taj Mahal; Red Fort; Delhi; *and* Marathas.]

B. P. Saksena, *History of Shah Jahan of Delhi* (1932).

CATHERINE B. ASHER

SHAHNAMA, perhaps the single most significant text in Iranian cultural history. Firdausi's *Shahnama (Book of Kings)* is an epic of some fifty thousand distichs tracing the mythological history of Iran from the creation of the first man/king to the downfall of the Sasanid dynasty in the seventh century CE. Drawing his material primarily from oral tradition and partially from fragments of previous *shahnamas*, Firdausi completed his monumental, if ill-received, work in 1009/1010, fully aware that he had revitalized the Persian language and literary tradition as well as the historical and cultural identity of Iran after the seventh-century Arab conquest.

While traditionally described as *tarikh-i asatiri* ("mythological history"), the text is interspersed with historical facts and characters, providing a good account of the social and cultural history of Iran before Islam as well as a valuable depiction of the Iranian concept of history in general. In the form of various wars between good and evil elements, most notably between Iran and its mythical enemy Turan, the dualism of opposing and mutually exclusive forces—a basic tenet of Zoroastrian morality—is reflected. Composed in a single meter, *mutaqarib*, the *Shahnama* is divided into some fifty parts consisting of such great tragedies as *Rustam u Suhrab* and *Syavush*, and romances such as *Zal u Rudaba* and *Bijan u Manija*; it is valued above and beyond its historical significance as a great work of art.

[*See also* Firdausi *and* Persian Literature.]

Ferdowsi, *The Epic of the Kings*, translated by R. Levy (1973). Theodor Nöldeke, *The Iranian National Epic*, translated by L. Bogdanov (1979).   MARIAM PIRNAZAR

SHAHR-I SUKHTA (lit., "burnt city"), site of a large prehistoric settlement near the Hamun delta in Sistan. Indicated by a series of light-colored mounds protected by a twenty-centimeter deposit of sand, salt, and clay, the occupational layers range from late Chalcolithic to around 1900 BCE. Excavations by Italians revealed a large number of houses with thick mud-brick walls that contained thousands of clay figurines, lapis lazuli beads, flint tools, blades, and pottery utensils. The settlement was also a center for the production of objects of sandstone, alabaster, and lapis lazuli, and it had commercial links with Mesopotamia, Central Asia, and the Indus Valley. Its substantial population is indicated by very extensive cemeteries lying on its edge.

Sylvia A. Matheson, *Persia: An Archaeological Guide* (2d ed., 1976), pp. 278–281, 304ff.

A. SHAHPUR SHAHBAZI

SHAHRUKH (1377–1447), the fourth son of Timur, ruler of Khurasan and Transoxiana shortly after his father's death from 1407 until 1447. The first Timurid ruler, he began the task of reconstruction necessitated by his father's devastating campaigns. Anxious to establish himself as a legitimate Muslim sovereign, he moved his capital from Samar-

kand to Herat, where he became a patron of Perso-Islamic culture, supporting poets and artists, encouraging historical writing, and providing for religious endowments. He established the institution of the *kitabkhana,* the royal library complete with artists' workshops for the production of illuminated manuscripts; he also exchanged embassies with China on several occasions. It was during his rule that Chagatai Turkish began to develop as a literary language. Through his patronage, Shahrukh laid the groundwork for the rebirth of Khurasani cultural life that was to continue throughout the fifteenth century. Of his five sons Ulug Beg alone survived to succeed him.

[*See also* Timurid Dynasty *and* Ulug Beg.]

René Grousset, *The Empire of the Steppes*, translated by Naomi Walford (1970). Gavin Hambly, ed., *Central Asia* (1969), pp. 150ff.   MARIA E. SUBTELNY

SHAIBANID DYNASTY, a tribal confederation of Uzbek Turks who traced their ancestry to Shiban, the youngest son of Genghis (Chinggis) Khan's eldest son Jochi. The Shaibanids ruled over Transoxiana from their capital at Bukhara between 1500 and 1598.

The conditions for the rise to political prominence of the Uzbek clans were set some half century before the Shaibanids' assertion of independent rule through their relationship to the Timurid ruler Abu Sa'id (1451–1479); his succession to the throne had been secured only by the help of a tribal coalition dominated by the Uzbek chief Abu al-Khair Khan, who ruled in Khwarazm between 1447 and 1468. Throughout the latter half of the fifteenth century the Timurids, while still controlling major cities such as Samarkand, Bukhara, and Herat, were forced to contend with a rising tide of Uzbek power, both in Transoxiana and in Khurasan, and were preoccupied with the necessity of warding off the continuous attacks launched by the Uzbeks from secure bases in the hinterland of Transoxiana. The end result of a half century of constant military interchange was the capture of Samarkand and Bukhara in 1500 by Muhammad Shaiban, thereby inaugurating a century of complete domination of Transoxiana by the Uzbek confederation. During the same fifty-year period when the Sunni Muslim Uzbeks were consolidating their power in eastern portions of the Timurid empire, the Shi'ite Muslim Safavids, benefiting from the preoccupation of the khans of Samarkand and Herat in their eastern territories, were building up a base of strength in western Iran. The

Safavid Ismail I clinched his victory over his Ak-koyunlu rivals at about the same time that Muhammad Shaiban marched into Samarkand and Bukhara.

In much the same way that military harassment by the Uzbek khans had prevented true unification of the Timurid realm from the mid-fifteenth century, Uzbek military pressure in the east, exerted primarily against Khurasan and particularly Herat, which changed hands many times, substantially weakened the effectiveness of Safavid rule. Throughout the sixteenth century the Uzbeks prevented a lasting consolidation of Safavid power over Iran, whose eastern and western portions were only securely and thoroughly united in the next century. In the latter-day age of Sunni internationalism, a revival of earlier Seljuk policy led by the Ottoman sultan Suleiman (1520–1566) and continued under his successors, the Shaibanids were formally approached with proposals for a mutual alliance aimed at dismantling Shi'ite Safavid control of Iran. These overtures were intensified during the reign of the Shaibanid khan Abdullah II (1583–1598), but no truly coordinated attack resulted, and soon afterward the Shaibanids were displaced from rule over their home territories in Transoxiana by a rival collateral branch of the Chinggisids.

[See also Uzbekistan.]

Wilhelm Barthold, *Four Studies on the History of Central Asia* (1956).

RHOADS MURPHEY, JR.

SHAIKH AL-ISLAM, important religious title used in several Muslim societies from the tenth century onward. The functions of the *shaikh al-Islams* varied, but their growing importance marks the absorption of religious roles into government bureaucracies. The title first appears in eastern Iran to designate a community's paramount religious scholar and educational official. In crisis, such officials, sometimes with the synonymous title *sadr al-sudur*, sought to become autonomous urban leaders. In the twelfth century the title spread widely and gradually gained the connotation of an imperial official with religious responsibilities. In the Delhi sultanate he distributed largesse to religious figures. Under the Ottomans he was the sultan's chief jurisconsult and headed a hierarchy of religious officials. Under the Safavids the *shaikh al-Islam* remained the paramount local official; the imperial official comparable to the Ottoman *shaikh al-Islam* was called the *sadr al-sudur*.

Richard W. Bulliet, "The Shaikh al-Islam and the Evolution of Islamic Society," *Studia Islamica* 35 (1972).

RICHARD W. BULLIET

SHAIKHI, a prominent school of Twelver Shi'ite theology founded by Shaikh Ahmad Ahsa'i (1753–1826). Ahsa'i, a Shi'ite Arab born in Bahrein, had studied in Najaf and Karbala before settling in Iran for a period of fifteen years. His teachings rapidly gained a large following from among the intellectually progressive *ulama* (religious scholars) and the ruling classes.

Ahsa'i borrowed from Muslim philosophers and mystics the idea of the Perfect Man and developed his own conception of the Perfect Shi'ite, a specially gifted being whose conscious knowledge of the divine is immune from error by virtue of his spiritual affinity to the Hidden Imam. "To each historical age its own Perfect Shi'ite," was the common Shaikhi belief.

Ahsa'i's successsor, the Iranian-born Kazim Rashti (d. 1844), further elaborated the Shaikhi view of evolutionary cycles of progressive revelation of esoteric truth; he argued that, although the prophet Muhammad's prophecy was the last and his law the most perfect, religion must undergo changes in order to fit mankind's needs and the exigencies of the time. When Rashti died, dispute over his succession split the school into two branches. The largest accepted the leadership of Muhammad Karim Khan Kirmani, a Qajar prince who further expanded the concept of the Perfect Shi'ite, or Fourth Pillar, as the ideal leader of the community, until he was forced to retreat behind outward profession of orthodoxy. A moderate, though minor, branch developed in Azerbaijan.

It is not known whether Ahsa'i's and Rashti's views were meant to be studied in the context of "existential time" and not "chronological time," as Henri Corbin suggested; as mere ideas, as Shaikhi apologists claimed in response to orthodox denunciation; or whether they were to be applied concretely, as the subsequent radical movement of the Babis proclaimed. Kirmani Shaikhism itself survived as a socially conservative, apolitical school of theory until it was closed down by the government of the Islamic Republic of Iran in 1979. But the Shaikhi allegorical interpretation of basic Shi'ite doctrines and, more importantly, the belief that religious laws have to undergo constant adjustment to the times and conditions of society, proved to be supremely attractive to future generations of lay secularist Iranians who were committed to social reforms and who played a major role in the Constitutional Revolution of 1905.

[*See also* Babi *and* Shi'a.]

Mangol Bayat, *Mysticism and Dissent: Socioreligious Thought in Qajar Iran* (1982).   MANGOL BAYAT

SHAILENDRA. *See* Sailendra.

SHAIVISM is an Indian religious sect dedicated to the Hindu god Shiva. The worship of Shiva is prevalent throughout the entire Indian peninsula, including Nepal, but in modern times the largest Shaivite communities are to be found mainly in the South. Shaivites worship their god most frequently in the form of the sacred linga, a phallic symbol of great antiquity.

It is an impossible task to trace with certainty the historical development of Shaivism from the earliest times. Based on archaeological evidence from the Indus Valley, several scholars have suggested the possibility of a pre-Aryan cult dedicated to an ancient form of Shiva, who is often termed "proto-Shiva." The speculation is based primarily on the existence of a seal depicting a three-faced deity wearing a horned headdress, seated cross-legged on a throne and surrounded by a buffalo, a tiger, an elephant, and other animals. John Marshall has identified this image, not without disputation, as Shiva, for in later times Shiva is represented as the "three-faced one," as Pashupati ("lord of animals"), and as Yogishvara ("lord of yogins").

During the Vedic age (c. 1500–500 BCE) Shiva was worshiped as Rudra, a dreadful, howling deity known especially for his destructive qualities. The ambiguous nature of the destructive and generative god is evidenced by Rudra's epithet, *Shiva,* a deprecatory Sanskrit euphemism meaning "gracious" or "auspicious." In later times Shiva was recognized as the destructive aspect of the Hindu *trimurti,* a trinity of gods representing the creative (Brahma), sustaining (Vishnu), and destructive (Shiva) energies of the universe. Near the end of the Vedic period Rudra-Shiva is proclaimed the supreme deity by the *Svetashvatara Upanishad* (c. sixth century BCE), a development that heralds the rise of exclusivity in worship and theism.

The earliest record of an actual Shaivite community occurs in the *Mahabharata* epic. There mention is made of the Pashupatas, devotees of Shiva

as he appears in the form of Pashupati. The Pashupata sect was especially concerned with ascetic practices and was frequently denounced for its non-Vedic conduct. Subsects of the Pashupatas (Kapalikas and Kalamukhas) were reported to engage in meat eating, drinking, and ritualized sex, and were particularly distinguished by the practices of frequenting cemeteries and drinking wine from human skulls. Members of these sects can still be found in regions of Nepal and West Bengal.

Philosophical Shaivism developed in three branches: The Shaiva Siddhanta of South India is characterized by its realism and dualism; its primary devotional literature is a collection of hymns known as the *Tirumurai,* written by Shaivite saints (c. fifth through ninth century CE). Kashmir Shaivism, traditionally said to have been revealed to Vasugupta in the eighth century, became the philosophic counterpart to the Shaiva Siddhanta, maintaining an idealistic and monistic view of the world and stressing the importance of devotion in worship. The Lingayats, founded in the twelfth century, rejected caste distinctions and denied the authority of the Vedas. Despite a generally anti-Brahmanical stand, the Lingayats remain devoted to Shiva and particularly worship him in the form of the *lingam.*

[*See also* Hinduism.]

Constantina Rhodes Bailly, trans., *Shaiva Devotional Songs of Kashmir: A Translation and Study of Utpaladeva's Shivastotravali* (1987). R. G. Bhandarkar, *Vaisnavism, Śaivism and Minor Religious Systems* (1913). J. C. Chatterji, *Kashmir Shaivism* (1914). F. Kingsbury and G. E. Philips, trans. *Hymns of the Tamil Śaivite Saints* (1921). John Marshall, *Mohenjodaro and the Indus Civilization,* 3 vols. (1931).   STUART W. SMITHERS

SHAKYAMUNI. *See* Buddhism: An Overview.

SHAMANISM. The term *shaman* is derived from the Manchu-Tunguz word *šaman* ("he who knows"). *Shamanism* describes primarily the religious traditions of the Siberian and Ural Altaic peoples but encompasses as well other religious traditions, such as those of the Inuit (Eskimo) and North American Indian, that employ shamanistic practices in conjunction with other, more central religious rites.

Shamans differ from priests in their preoccupation with ecstasy and ecstatic states. Through the medium of ecstasy the shaman brings about physical cures and escorts the souls of the dead to their abode in the world beyond. The ecstatic techniques of shamans are intimately linked with their manipulation of the spirit world. In a case of sickness, for example, it is presumed that the soul of the sick person has been lost or stolen by demons. While the shaman is in a state of ecstatic trance, his or her soul leaves the body and, with the aid of powerful spirits, finds and rescues the errant or captive soul of the afflicted person. The separation of the soul from the body and the soul's ascent into the spirit world are identifying marks of shamanic ecstasy.

A less common form of ecstasy involves the possession of the shaman by a spirit, with the result that the spirit speaks through the mouth of the shaman. Through both types of trance the shaman gains control over good and/or evil spirits, wresting from them secret knowledge and power to foretell future events, to solve both individual and communal crises, and to ensure prosperity.

In his ecstatic rites, the shaman dresses in ritual garments usually depicting an animal (e.g., a bird or a deer) and employs a variety of instruments, including drums, drumsticks, and metal rattlers. Song, dance, and sacrifices to appease or cajole spirits play a part as well in shamanic rites.

The shaman is usually identified by the community in early youth or adolescence. Certain physical abnormalities, but more often aberrant psychological manifestations such as seizures, hallucinations, and violent mood swings, are considered signs that someone has been chosen by the spirits. Generally, individuals do not accept voluntarily the shaman's vocation but must be coerced into submission by the spirits. Once the new shaman is singled out, he or she is initiated, instructed, and subjected to trials by older shamans. The deaths of shamans are brought about by the spirits, and their burial places are sacred. The spirits of dead shamans act as protectors of the community against hostile spiritual forces.

Mircea Eliade, *Shamanism: Archaic Techniques of Ecstasy* (1964).   PETER J. AWN

SHAMSHER, BIR

SHAMSHER, BIR (d. 1901), nephew of Jung Bahadur Rana and prime minister of Nepal from 1885 to 1901. In November 1885 Shamsher led a coup d'état against the regime of the last of Jung Bahadur's brothers, Pamodip Singh. This coup initiated the rule of the second generation of Rana family members, who would hold power until 1945. During his rule, Shamsher granted the British permission for the open recruitment of Nepalese hillmen for the Gurkha units of the Indian army.

[*See also* Jung Bahadur Rana *and* Nepal: History of Nepal.]

B. L. Joshi and L. Rose, *Democratic Innovations in Nepal* (1966).   RICHARD ENGLISH

SHAMSHER, CHANDRA

SHAMSHER, CHANDRA (1863–1929), fifth Rana prime minister of Nepal, ruled from 1901 to 1929. Shamsher was elevated to office after Bir Shamsher's immediate successor, Deva Shamsher, was forced to abdicate by his jealous Rana half brothers. Chandra Shamsher brought about the abolition of slavery in Nepal in 1925, and during his reign the British Government of India formally recognized Nepal's sovereign and independent status.

[*See also* Shamsher, Bir; Rana; *and* Nepal: History of Nepal.]

B. L. Joshi and L. Rose, *Democratic Innovations in Nepal* (1966).   RICHARD ENGLISH

SHAN

SHAN. The definition of *Shan* is somewhat variable, and the explication of that variability constitutes the framework of Shan history. *Shan* is cognate with *Siam*, itself from an ancient Khmer and Cham name for the Tai-speaking peoples from the twelfth century or earlier, and is the anglicization of the Burmese word for the people calling themselves *Tai Long* (Greater Tai; *Thai Yai* in Siamese) and called *Ngio* by the Northern Tai. Mainly, they live in the Shan State (originally a collection of large and small principalities) of eastern Burma, the valleys of the upper Irawaddy drainage, and the former Shan principalities of the upper Chindwin drainage in northwestern Burma. Since the eighteenth and nineteenth centuries, they include the Khamti and related groups living in the eastern corner of Assam and the Shan of the mid-nineteenth-century quasi-state of Mae Hongsorn in northwestern Thailand. The term also includes the so-called Chinese Shan (*Shan Tayok* in Burmese) of southwestern Yunnan, who acknowledge the name *Tai Long* but call themselves *Tai No* (Northern Tai). On both sides of the China-Burma border on the Shweli (Nam Maau) River are the Maw Shan (Tai Maau). Moreover, in the nineteenth century the British extended the term to the Northern Tai (also known then as Western Lao in the context of their vassal relationship to Bangkok) on the grounds that from early in the sixteenth century the Burmese kingdom often ruled, and always dominated, Chiang Mai and other northern Thai states. On related grounds, the term extends to the Khun of the Shan State of Kengtung, a Burmese dependency since at least the sixteenth century, and to much of the Sipsongpanna (Xishuangbanna) of southern Yunnam (Yunnan) on the Burma-Lao border, especially the state of Chiang Hung (Siamese, Chiang Rung), whose royal line was intimately connected with that of Kengtung.

Inclusion in the Shan category depended on two criteria. First, a principality must claim to derive its legitimacy from the somewhat shadowy ancient Tai kingdom of Mongmao (Mong Maau), originally a client state of Dali (formerly Nanzhao) in southwestern China, and then claiming to be a successor state to Dali. Second, the principality must be the successor—as is claimed by the Maw Shan, the Southern Shan of Burma's Shan State (Tai Tau), and to some extent the Tai No—to the Shan conquest of the old Burmese kingdom of Pagan in the late thirteenth century and must have ruled this major kingdom during the fourteenth and fifteenth centuries (especially at Ava). In either case the Shan call themselves Greater Shan because they consider themselves the successors to major Buddhist thrones of an antiquity greater than that of either Chiang Saen (from which the northern Tai states supposedly descend) or Sukhothai (the kingdom that ruled before the establishment of Siam). [See Dali; Pagan; and Sukhothai.]

However, while Dali may to some extent have been a Buddhist country, Mongmao cannot have been one since its early thirteenth-century offshoot, the Ahom kingdom of eastern Assam (founded before the fall of Dali, about 1229 CE), professed, according to its chronicles (especially the *Ahom buranji*), the pre-Indic animism currently found among the so-called tribal Tai (e.g., the Black Tai) of the China-Laos-Vietnam borderlands. In view of the dependency of inclusion in the Shan category upon a claim of successorship to major Buddhist monarchical traditions of antiquity, the case of Mongmao constitutes a major puzzle of Shan history. [See Mongmao *and* Ahom.]

In post-Pagan times, prior to the sixteenth-century conquest of Chiang Mai by Burma's Toungoo dynasty, the present Southern Shan States of Burma seem to have been attached to Chiang Mai rather than (or as well as) Burma. The Buddhism of the Shan, too, owes much to Northern Tai Buddhism, and monasteries in the Northern Tai ordination tradition (*kong yon*) using the Yuan script are common in southern Shan and standard in Kengtung. An equally old strand in Shan Buddhism goes back to

Pagan Burma, and the myriad Shan loanwords from Pali, the scriptural language of Theravada Buddhism, came through Burmese, which makes for much of the distinctiveness of the Shan languages.

Moreover, the system of official guardian spirits (*coa mong*) of Shan states and villages, while shared with the Northern Tai and distinct from the Burmese system of thirty-seven *nats*, is analogous to the *nats*. It is no doubt derived from the era of Burmese domination, when Chiang Mai adopted the Burmese style of *dhammarajika* kingship, of which the system of royally appointed guardian spirits is a proper component.

By the eighteenth century the Shan were firmly under Burmese suzerainty, and the tradition was established of playing off the Chiang Mai connection, and through it the Bangkok connection, against the Burmese; this was done by means of recurrent rebellions against excessive Burmese encroachments upon Shan political and cultural autonomy. This tradition has reemerged since Burma's post–World War II independence, especially after the abortive Shan-led Federalist movement of 1960–1962 and the revolution of 1962, as a secessionist rhetoric among many of the Shan insurgent movements now current. They are characterized by an ambivalent oscillation between pan-Tai irredentism and the perception of Burma as the context giving meaning and ideological viability to Shan ethnic, cultural, and linguistic particularity.

Charles Backus, *The Nan-Chao Kingdom and T'ang China's Southwestern Frontier* (1981). Sao Saimong Mangrai, *The Padaeng Chronicle and the Jengtung Chronicle Translated* (1981). B. J. Terwiel, *The Tai of Assam and Ancient Tai Ritual*, vol. 1 (1980). Constance M. Wilson and Lucien M. Hanks, *The Burma-Thailand Frontier over Sixteen Decades* (1985).   F. K. LEHMAN

SHANDONG, large Chinese province on northeast coast; its area is 153,300 square kilometers and its population is 74,945,200 (1982). Shandong may be divided into five major regions: (1) a long maritime border encompassing the Shandong Peninsula and several major ports, notably Qingdao; (2) a central mountain region that never has been prosperous but that contains major coal reserves; (3) a prosperous northern plain centered on the modern cities of Zibo and Weifang and corresponding to the territory of the ancient state of Qi; (4) a poor northwestern agricultural plain crossed by the Grand Canal; and (5) the southwestern plain, also along the Grand Canal, near the center of which lies the ancient state of Lu, home of the philosophers Confucius and Mencius. The provincial capital, Ji'nan, lies northwest of the center of the province. The Yellow River is Shandong's other main geographic feature. From 1342 to 1855, and again from 1938 to 1948, the river, often called "China's Sorrow," flowed southeastward across the Lu region into the East China Sea. Today, and for most of the time since 1855, the Yellow River has followed a channel north of the central mountains and Ji'nan to empty into the Bohai Gulf.

Since the first millennium BCE Shandong has been an important site of Chinese culture. In the 1860s the chief campaigns suppressing the Nian rebels were fought in Shandong. Afterward the province remained in the control of conservative political forces associated with the Tongzhi Restoration. Antimissionary killings led to a German leasehold at Jiaozhou Bay in 1898. Shandong was the cradle of the Boxer Uprising, with much of the activity occuring first in the Lu section, but shifting as the movement grew into the poor northwestern region and adjacent sections of Zhili. Yuan Shikai was made governor in December 1899 to control the Boxers and he effectively dominated the province until his death in 1916. From then until 1949 Shandong suffered from a series of inadequate and grasping military rulers, with a brief respite under Han Fuqu from 1930 to 1937.

Modern influences penetrated Shandong through Christian missions and then via German development of Qingdao, railroads, and mines. Japanese influence replaced that of the Germans in 1915. Modern rail and shipping facilities sped up the emigration of Shandong's impoverished peasantry, notably to the Northeast (Manchuria). After Japan occupied Shandong in late 1937, the Chinese Nationalists struggled for, but lost the leadership of, Shandong's anti-Japanese guerrilla movement to the Communists. After 1945 forces of the Republic of China occupied Shandong's major cities, but never regained control of the countryside. Since 1949 the Shandong government has closely followed the prevailing national policies.

Economically, the northern plain region around the ancient state of Qi has prospered since the late eighteenth century through successive development of salt processing, commercial farming, the export of agricultural products, and, eventually in the twentieth century, mining, industry, and modern transportation. In the 1970s the major Shengli (Victory) oilfield and associated industry brought increased prosperity to this region. Interior sections of the province have fallen behind the Qi region. These densely populated, largely rural portions of Shandong remain largely dependent upon agriculture, especially wheat, cotton, and sorghum cultivation. The central mountains adjacent to the southwestern Lu region possess huge coal mines at Yanzhou that produce high-quality coking and power coal. Huge projects involving the opening of coal mines, building railways to the coast, and construction of a coal port at Shijiusuo were major elements in China's Sixth Five-Year Plan (1981–1985).

David D. Buck, "The Provincial Elite in Shantung During the Republican Period," *Modern China* 1.4 (August 1975): 417–436. Ramon Myers, *The Chinese Peasant Economy: Agricultural Development in Hopei and Shantung, 1890–1949* (1970).   DAVID D. BUCK

SHANDONG INTERVENTION, collective term for a series of Japanese military occupations of China's Shandong Province from 1927 to 1929. Shandong had been a thorn in Sino-Japanese relations since the initial occupation of the peninsula by Japan in 1914. In 1927, when Chiang Kai-shek's Northern Expedition approached Shandong, the government of Prime Minister Tanaka Giichi sent a military force to the peninsula, ostensibly to protect Japanese lives and property there, but also to block any further Chinese movement north to Manchuria, where Japan had major economic interests. The temporary disruption of Chiang's reunification drive, as well as objections at home and abroad to the Japanese expeditionary efforts, led the Japanese government to withdraw its troops from Shandong that same year.

When the Northern Expedition was once more set in motion in April 1928, the Tanaka government dispatched even larger forces to the province and these occupied the principal rail line, as well as the city of Ji'nan. The entry of Japanese forces into that city provoked fierce clashes with Chinese troops already there, resulting in heavy civilian casualties. On the pretext that Japanese military prestige was involved, the General Staff in Tokyo, without regard to the views of the civilian government, dispatched additional units to Shandong from Manchuria, as well as from the home islands. These forces undertook an arbitrary and high-handed occupation of Shandong until withdrawn in the spring of 1929, thereby further inflaming relations between China and Japan.

[*See also* Ji'nan Incident; Northern Expedition; *and* Tanaka Giichi.]

MARK R. PEATTIE

SHANDONG QUESTION, dispute between China and Japan over the disposition of former German rights and interests consequent upon places and property that Japan had occupied in 1915. The Treaty of Versailles had confirmed Japan's claim to these rights, but China refused to sign the treaty and thus resisted Japan's claims. The United States supported the Japanese position. At stake were the ninety-nine-year leasehold at Jiaozhou Bay, improvements including Qingdao city and port, ownership of the Qingdao to Ji'nan railroad, and control of mines in Shandong. The Japanese agreed to return all of these to China in 1922 after negotiations following the Washington Naval Conference. China was required to repay Japan for all the improvements it had made to the German holdings after 1915. The question of the willingness of the Nationalist movement, which became the new government of the Republic of China in October 1928, to assume these obligations became an important question behind the Tanaka cabinet's policy toward China after 1927. Japan's attitude in the 1922 settlement of the Shandong question is associated with the moderate, conciliatory policies of Foreign Minister Shidehara Kijūrō and marks the end of the assertive, independent policy Japan followed in China after 1914.

[*See also* Versailles Treaty of 1918.]

Russell Fifield, *Woodrow Wilson and the Far East: The Diplomacy of the Shantung Question* (1952).

DAVID D. BUCK

SHANG DYNASTY. The kings of the Shang, or, as it was also known to later Chinese, the Yin, dynasty were the first Chinese rulers for whom we have historical records. Archaeological corroboration is still being sought in late Neolithic (Longshan) or early Bronze Age (Erlitou) sites for an antecedent Xia dynasty, referred to in traditional texts, but it is only with the Shang that we enter the realm of written history.

The Shang kings ruled over the first civilization to appear in East Asia, a civilization characterized by class stratification, a stable political-religious hierarchy administering a territorially organized polity, centralized management of natural and human resources, and a complex, deeply rooted, cultural tradition. Current research suggests that their dynasty probably lasted from the middle of the sixteenth to the middle of the eleventh century BCE, although some traditional sources give the dates as 1766–1122.

Early Shang settlements (Erligang phase) have been identified at such sites as Zhengzhou in modern Henan and Panlongcheng in Hubei. The Late Shang hegemony (c. 1200–1045) embraced large sections of modern Henan, northern Anhui, western Shandong, southern Hebei, and Shanxi. Other contemporary Bronze Age sites existed beyond this core area; they were culturally, but not dynastically, Shang.

The center of Late Shang power lay in northern Henan, where a significant range of settlements was focused around the modern village of Xiaotun, near Anyang, the administrative and mortuary center of at least the last eight or nine Shang kings, from Wu Ding to Di Xin. Each major settlement was inhabited by a bronze-using elite, including ritual and administrative specialists, warriors, and artisans, who ruled over a dependent peasantry that cultivated the main crop, millet, with stone hoes, spades, and sickles. The North China climate was somewhat wetter and warmer, and thus more favorable for agriculture, than it is today, but the wealth of the Shang kingdom appears to have derived more from efficient labor utilization and centralized coordination than from major advances in agricultural technique.

The power of the king depended upon his ability to mobilize conscripts in the thousands for either labor service or military duty. The most notable cultural legacy of the Shang, in fact, was a politico-religious worldview, centered on the worship of the ancestors, that emphasized hierarchical ties of dependency and obligation at all levels of society. The most notable products of the Shang genius for labor organization, the royal tombs and the ritual bronze vessels buried in them, expressed, as they legitimated, the authority of the ruling elite.

The last eight kings were buried at Xibeigang, across the Huan River to the northwest of Xiaotun, in cruciform pits as much as 12.8 meters deep, equipped with four sloping or stepped ramps. Some consorts and elites of nonroyal status appear to have been buried in tombs with one or two ramps. The royal dead were placed in ornately carved and decorated burial chambers furnished with large numbers of ritual bronze vessels, jades, and other ceremonial and personal artifacts. Tomb number 5, the first elite tomb excavated at Xiaotun (in 1976) that had not been looted by grave robbers, probably contained the body of a woman who belonged, either by ties of marriage or blood, to the royal Zi lineage. The presence of over 1,600 objects in the tomb, including more than 440 bronzes and over 750 jade carvings, indicates the wealth that the living, in a form of conspicuous mortuary consumption, were willing to bury with the dead of high status.

Powerful evidence of the obligations, tantamount to servitude, that the ruled owed the rulers, living or dead, is found in the custom of accompanying-in-death. Both animals and humans accompanied their masters in this way. Victims of widely differing status were buried with or near the Late Shang kings. Some were provided with coffins and bronze ritual vessels or weapons of their own, some (generally female) with no coffins but with personal ornaments; others were provided with no furnishings and were beheaded, cut in two, or mutilated and put to death in other ways. Tomb 1001, for example, which may have been the tomb of the powerful ruler Wu Ding (c. 1200–1180), has yielded the remains of ninety servitors who accompanied the king in death, plus seventy-four human sacrifices (with skulls and bodies generally buried in the tomb ramps), twelve horses, and eleven dogs; it is certain that more victims were originally present. The sacrifice of prisoners of war and others of low status appears to have been reserved for the elites; close to two thousand pits containing human sacrifices have been found near the royal tombs and in the temple-palace area at Xiaotun. The custom of the living accompanying the dead, however, was also practiced, on a reduced scale, at the middle levels of society; a small number of graves in the commoner cemetery to the west of Xiaotun, for example, contained one or two such victims accompanying their master.

These burial sacrifices suggest not only that violence and blood-letting played an important role in Shang religious life. They also indicate the degree to which status relations and obligations among the living—from which death provided no metaphysical alternative, no psychological escape—continued to be observed among the dead. These relations lay at the core of Shang political culture and were projected from this world into the next. The religious beliefs that validated such relations were stronger than life itself.

The ritual bronze vessels found in the Shang royal tombs provide further evidence of such an ethos. These vessels were decorated with a variety of abstract linear patterns, some of which formed stylized monster masks, equipped with eyes, curved horns, ears, and cruel upper jaws; more plastic representations of animals such as water buffalo, tigers, and birds, might also be present. The significance of this powerful iconography, which was generally symmetrical about a central axis, may never be fully understood, but it is assumed that it played some sacred role, mediating or apotropaic, depending upon the motif.

Most of the bronze vessels were for use in the cult of the ancestors—for offering wine libations, meat, and other comestibles, which were thought to please the spirits of the departed. In sociopolitical terms, these bronzes, like the tombs in which they have been found, are eloquent testimony to the way in which the Shang elites were able to mobilize the labor of peasants and craftsmen in the service of royal worship. The tombs themselves, deeply excavated, provided with a massive wooden burial chamber, and then filled in with layers of rammed earth, required thousands of man-days of labor to construct. The bronzes too—which could weigh as much as 875 kilograms—required formidable concentrations of labor on the dynasty's behalf: to mine, transport, and refine the copper, tin, and lead ores; to manufacture and tool the clay models, cores, and molds used in the casting process; and to run the foundries. To cast a vessel like the Si Mu Xin caldron, for example, which was found in Tomb 5 and which weighs 128 kilograms, would have required

FIGURE 1. *Yu (Wine Vessel)*. Covered bronze ritual vessel with *taotie* (animal mask) design. Shang dynasty, Anyang period (thirteenth to eleventh century BCE). Height 36 cm., width 23 cm.

the centrally planned and coordinated labor of hundreds of workers over a considerable period of time. Unlike the smithy tradition in the West, in which a single artisan could shape a bronze vessel to his own design in his own workshop, the piece-mold casting tradition of Shang China required, by its very nature, centralized planning, control, and social discipline. The masterpieces that resulted—and "masterpiece" is hardly apt, for they were, in fact, the product of many masters of ceramic modeling and bronze casting working in concert—were the highest products of Shang civilization. They symbolize both the religious beliefs of the time and the commitment of large sectors of the society to those beliefs and to the service of those who most benefited from them.

Details of the ancestral cult may be derived from the oracle-bone inscriptions of the Shang, which were first unearthed in 1899. The Late Shang diviner, who was increasingly the king himself, sought to foretell or influence the future by applying a glowing brand or similar heat source to the back of a cattle scapula or turtle plastron. The resulting heat-stress crack was interpreted as an auspicious, inauspicious, or neutral response to the "charge" that the diviner had proposed to the bone at the time the heat was applied. While such divinatory cracking of bones—which appeared in China about the middle of the fourth millennium BCE—is a venerable and widespread custom in Asia and North America, the Shang Chinese raised the system to a highly systematic art by (1) drilling the bones in patterned ways so that the cracks would themselves be regularly patterned; (2) cracking turtle plastrons as well as cattle scapulas; and (3) carving or incising into the bone, after the cracks had been interpreted, the date, the name of the presiding diviner (the names of some 120 are known), the subject of the charge, the king's prognostication, and the eventual result. Not all these elements may be present, but the large number of inscribed oracle bones that the Shang kings produced (well over one hundred thousand pieces have now been excavated at Xiaotun) provide us with a remarkably vivid sense of the Shang king's daily activities and decision making.

The inscriptions reveal that the king lived in a nontranscendental world in which the sacred and the secular were inextricably linked. A king such as Wu Ding divined virtually all aspects of life: rituals and sacrifices, military campaigns, hunting expeditions, excursions, the fortune of the coming ten-day week, the fortune of the coming day or night, the weather, the harvest, sickness, childbirth, dreams,

FIGURE 2. *Shang Ritual Implements*. Bone, Anyang period (thirteenth to eleventh century BCE).

settlement building, the issuing of orders, the arrival of tribute payments, divine assistance or approval, and requests addressed to ancestral or nature powers. Given the specialized labor required to prepare, crack, and incise the bones, it is clear that the Shang kings placed great value on the divinatory institution. Royal scapulimancy and plastromancy, in fact, validated the ancestral rituals and sacrifices in which the bronze vessels were employed. The timing of the sacrifice, its ancestral recipient, and the nature and quantity of the animal or human victims might all be divined beforehand. Further, the carving into the bone of the royal prognostications and eventual results served to confirm the king's special powers, for no inscription ever records that the king made a wrong forecast. The record, in short, is filtered and orthodox, designed to validate the king's status.

The inscriptions indicate that only the king had the ability to interpret the meaning of the pyromantic cracks, a fact that may explain the title by which he occasionally referred to himself: "I, the one man." He was the theocrat, the lineage chief, whose rituals, prayers, and divinations linked his people to the powers that controlled the world. Since the favor of the spirits was expressed through his person it is no surprise that special attention was paid to his own health and fortunes; the king himself, caught in a web of spiritual forces, was in a sense a human oracle bone.

The inscriptions also reveal the degree to which structure and order—prominent features of the social organization that produced the bronzes and of the symmetrical and abstract iconography that decorated their surfaces—were also central to religious conceptions. The ancestral sacrifices were performed according to an increasingly rigid cycle in which the royal ancestors of certain status received cult, according to generational seniority, on their name day. (The kings and queens were named by the same ten *gan,* "stems," used to name the days of the week.) Thus, Wu Ding, under the reforms inaugurated by the so-called "New School" diviners of Zu Jia (c. 1170–1151), would receive cult only on Ding days, Zu Jia only on Jia days, and so on. So systematic was the sacrificial schedule that it has permitted modern scholars to reconstruct the genealogy of the dynasty, stretching back some seventeen generations to the reign of the founder, Cheng Tang, whose sacrificial name was Da Yi.

The regular alternations of the various *gan*-named kings have also encouraged some modern scholars to propose that the Shang practiced a form of alternating succession in which the kingship passed from one *gan*-named lineage group to another and back again with the passage of generations. If this proves to be so, then the dynasty itself is best understood not as a tightly structured lineage in which descent passed from father to son or brother to brother (this is the traditional view) but as a looser confederation of sublineages in which kingship may have passed from uncle to nephew or nephew to nephew.

The Late Shang state is best understood as a patrimonial polity in which generational kin relations, true or fictious, and the obligations of filiality and concern they imply, played a major political role. The power of the king's ancestors—demonstrated by the king's ability, in divination and sacrifice, to satisfy their wishes or persuade them to intercede with Di, the high god, for fruitful rains, good harvests, and victories in battle—was essential to the power of the king. Just as he was subservient to their wishes in a context of ritual respect and filial duty, so were his dependents—who might, on occasion, be encouraged to participate in the royal rituals—incorporated into the politico-religious structure represented by the sacrificial cycle practiced at the Xiaotun cult center.

In such a polity, royal power was bound to be highly personal. The king traveled extensively, on campaign and in the large-scale royal hunts that served to replenish his larder, train his troops, and show his flag. The polity can best be conceived as a series of loose alliances among the members of the Zi lineage and its sublineages, and between the Zi lineage and the independent groups on the periphery. The kingdom was only strong when the king, "I, the one man," was present. For the rest, it depended upon ties of religion, kinship, divinatory prowess, force of arms, largesse and reciprocity, and self-interest. "L'état c'est moi" would not have been an inappropriate motto.

With the exception of the light spoke-wheeled chariot, which appears, apparently abruptly, in the archaeological record at Xiaotun (c. 1200) and whose presence suggests some contact, direct or indirect, with bearers of Indo-European culture, presumably a warrior elite, most significant aspects of Shang culture may be traced back, in either their origins or elaborations, to indigenous Neolithic roots. This generally unbroken evolution from Neolithic culture to Bronze Age civilization suggests that the Shang flowering, which is to be seen as an intensification of enduring cultural dispositions rather than as an abrupt or novel departure, represented a tradition of great attractiveness and strength. Shang forms of social and political organization served as models for, and constraints upon, the Zhou, who conquered them in the mid-eleventh century. The Shang may accordingly be seen as China's seminal dynasty.

[*See also* Bronze Age in China.]

Kwang-chih Chang, *Shang Civilization* (1980) and *Art, Myth, and Ritual: The Path to Political Authority in Ancient China* (1983). Wen Fong, ed., *The Great Bronze Age of China* (1980). David N. Keightley, *Sources of Shang History: The Oracle-Bone Inscriptions of Bronze Age China* (1978) and "The Religious Commitment: Shang Theology and the Genesis of Chinese Political Culture," *History of Religions* 17 (1978): 211–225. Paul Wheatley, *The Pivot of the Four Quarters: A Preliminary Study into the Origins and Character of the Ancient Chinese City* (1971).   DAVID N. KEIGHTLEY

SHANGHAI, China's largest, most dynamic, and most economically important city. Until opened as one of five ports for foreign trade and residence by the 1842 Treaty of Nanjing, Shanghai ("on the sea") had been a modest walled administrative city and port in a rich agricultural area noted for its cotton textile and handicraft production. Within twenty years Shanghai had become China's major port, for it is located at a natural breakpoint between riverine, intercoastal, and ocean shipping, at the edge of China's richest and most advanced economic region. The city is located on the Huangpu River, near the mouth of China's great inland river, the Yangtze, and linked to the inland through a vast network of canals and waterways. The Huangpu serves as Shanghai's port and roadstead.

Shanghai prospered under special foreign privileges contained in a welter of treaties, agreements, and customs that grew up after 1842. The city of Shanghai had three major administrative subdivisions: the International Settlement, the French Concession, and the Chinese city, each of which operated under separate administration and laws. Yet Shanghai itself grew as one city. Early in Shanghai's history as a treaty port a secret society uprising (1853–1854) led to the opening of the previously exclusive foreign concession to Chinese residence. Shanghai's prominence was enhanced in the 1860s when the fall of many nearby cities to the Taiping rebels led to a large inflow of refugees. Shanghai, under a combination of Qing and foreign military protection, remained secure during those years. Even after peace returned, many Chinese continued to maintain business or residential facilities in Shanghai.

Shanghai remained China's most important treaty port and in the twentieth century regularly handled more than 50 percent of China's foreign trade by value. A foreign culture developed with business establishments, houses, schools, churches, hospitals, shopping, and recreation all designed for Western tastes. The Japanese presence grew rapidly after 1900, and by the 1930s Shanghai became the most cosmopolitan and prosperous of all the various foreign-dominated entrepôts in Asia, such as Saigon, Manila, Bangkok, and Singapore. In 1935 there were 3.75 million people in Shanghai, of whom 58,000 were foreigners. The Japanese were the largest single group, with 20,000 residents.

By the 1870s Shanghai was the home of a new kind of Chinese culture that was innovative and receptive to Western ways, but still distinctly Chinese. Supported by Chinese businessmen involved in the foreign trade—the so-called comprador class—this culture was openly bourgeois. Its literature, housing, dress, and social practices all were identifiably Chinese, but strongly influenced by Western examples. The new ways included politics as well; after 1900 Shanghai produced efforts for local democracy and national political change of both a moderate reformist and more radical revolutionary type. [*See also* Compradors.]

Such a city obviously has been the site for many important events in modern Chinese history, rang-

FIGURE 1. *View along the Bund, Shanghai.* A reminder of Shanghai's former status as a center of European power in China, the Western architecture along the Huangpu River still dominates the city today.

ing from the exploits of Charles "Chinese" Gordon (1833–1885) against the Taipings in the 1860s through the efforts during the Cultural Revolution in 1967 to create a new form of city administration based on the Paris Commune. Yet Shanghai's importance derives mainly from its economic and cultural roles.

In 1895, under terms of the Treaty of Shimonoseki, foreigners for the first time could own and operate industrial facilities in China. Shanghai, already the commercial and financial center for foreigners and Chinese, became the primary beneficiary of this new industrial development. Shanghai's skilled workers, managers, and their plants were the most important modern resource the People's Republic of China (PRC) inherited in 1949. In 1955 the output per worker in Shanghai was more than three times the national average and Shanghai contributed a fifth of the state's revenues. Shanghai's quantitative role is matched by quality, for it is a center of national technological innovation. Since the 1950s millions of skilled people have been transferred from Shanghai or brought to the city for training in a planned effort to lessen the gap between Shanghai and China's other regions and their cities. Culturally, Shanghai's press, movies, literature, music, and other activities set the progressive styles in China prior to 1949, but not since that time.

In the PRC, Shanghai became a large municipality that reports directly to the central authorities in Beijing. Shanghai's present size of 6,186 square kilometers makes it larger than Connecticut; it has a population of 11,805,000 (1982). Administratively, Shanghai is divided into ten counties and a large central city, which in turn is subdivided into twelve urban districts. More than 6.2 million people live in the 223-square-kilometer central city. The counties contain satellite cities with populations from 50,000 to 300,000. First created in the 1950s following Soviet planning principles, these new towns have blossomed again since 1978 with new housing and amenities, as well as new factories.

When the Communist regime took over Shanghai in 1949 many of the city's talented bourgeoisie fled elsewhere, including Hong Kong and Taiwan, where their skills have contributed to modern development. Under the PRC, Shanghai's previous character as the fount of foreign and bourgeois culture has limited the leadership's willingness to trust Shanghai in cultural and political affairs. In a nation that is still largely peasant in character, the PRC leadership has never advocated urban proletarian culture as the national standard; thus Shanghai, the cradle of China's industrial proletariat, has not been in the forefront in that respect either.

Chinese priorities from 1958 to 1978 favored rural over urban development, small-scale over large-scale enterprises, production over commerce, and new cities over old treaty ports. Shanghai, although it remained China's most important port, fell behind world standards for berthing and cargo handling. Shanghai's downtown skyline remained practically unchanged from the 1930s until 1980 and the city took on a shabby, rundown, and overcrowded look. Beneath this unimpressive exterior, and especially at the edges in satellite towns, Shanghai's industry has continued to grow as a major source of China's material and human wealth. In the 1980s the signs of growth and change are penetrating to the old city center, but central Shanghai continues to lag behind the pace of change in Beijing, its only rival as China's premier city.

Christopher Howe, ed., *Shanghai: Revolution and Development in an Asian Metropolis* (1981). Rhoads Murphey, *Shanghai: Key to Modern China* (1953).

DAVID D. BUCK

SHANGHAI COMMUNIQUÉ, joint statement of the United States and the People's Republic of China issued on 28 February 1972 at the end of President Richard Nixon's first visit to China. The communiqué has been the official basis for the normalization of relations between the two countries. It was immediately followed by the establishment of liaison offices in Beijing and Washington, missions that achieved embassy status after full diplomatic relations were instituted in 1979. In the communiqué, the US officially acknowledged the position of both the Communists and the Nationalists that Taiwan island was part of China, and agreed in principle to withdraw all its military forces from the island.

U.S.-China Diplomatic Relations: Reference Materials, edited by U.S.-China People's Friendship Association (1977). United States Congress House Committee on International Relations, "Relations with China," in *Congress and Foreign Policy—1976* (1977); and *U.S.-China Relations: The Process of Normalization of Relations: Hearings . . . , November 18, December 8, 17, 1975 and February 2, 1976* (1976). JOHN A. RAPP

SHANGHAI INCIDENT, military collision between Chinese and Japanese forces in Shanghai between January and May 1932. The confrontation came at a time when Japan was completing its conquest of southern Manchuria. For more than a decade Japanese policies in China and Chinese responses to them (most recently in the form of a Chinese boycott of Japanese goods) had created tensions between the Japanese community in Shanghai and the vastly larger Chinese population in the city. These tensions were heightened in January 1932 by an attack on a group of Japanese Buddhist monks by a Chinese mob. This incident, apparently fomented by several Japanese officers in the city, led to a series of demonstrations and counterdemonstrations by both sides.

Late in January the senior Japanese naval commander in Shanghai ordered a contingent of marines into the old Chinese quarters, where they were turned back in fierce combat by the larger numbers of the Chinese 19th Route Army. In retaliation Japanese naval aircraft heavily bombed the Chinese section. Because its forces were greatly outnumbered, the high command in Tokyo dispatched two army divisions to Shanghai, which led to widespread fighting in and around the city throughout February. By March, however, the Chinese forces had been obliged to withdraw and on 5 May both sides signed a truce agreement that provided for an end to the Chinese boycott, the creation of a demilitarized zone around the international settlement, and the withdrawal of Japanese army forces. The machinations of Japanese *agents provocateurs*, in provoking the crisis within a major city where Western powers had important interests, tarnished the Japanese image abroad and helped turn international sympathies away from Japan.   MARK R. PEATTIE

SHANG KEXI (c. 1603–1676), Chinese military official of the Ming dynasty who changed his allegiance to the Manchus and aided in the pacification of China.

Born to a military family in Liaodong, Shang led troops against invading Manchus in his home province during the 1620s. Discouraged by Ming military mismanagement, by 1629 many discontented Chinese soldiers began defecting to the Manchus. In 1634 Shang made his move, and in return the Manchus made him a general heading his own Chinese force. Ten years later Shang joined the pursuit of Li Zicheng and two years later helped subdue a Ming army in Hunan. In 1649, as the "South-suppressing Prince," he drove Prince Gui of the Ming out of Guangdong. The next year, after a nine-month siege, Shang captured the city of Guangzhou (Canton) in a bloody massacre that cost the lives of an estimated seven hundred thousand inhabitants.

By 1660, after continued fighting, Shang was finally able to bring Ming loyalist resistance in Guangdong Province to an end. He ruled the province virtually independently until 1671, at which time his son, Shang Zhixin (d. 1680) took over. In 1676, against his father's wishes, Zhixin joined the Rebellion of the Three Feudatories *(sanfan)*, which ended in complete failure in 1681.

[*See also* Three Feudatories Rebellion.]

Lynn Struve, *Southern Ming, 1644–1662* (1984).

ROLAND L. HIGGINS

SHANHAIGUAN, literally, the "pass between the mountains," lies some 260 miles east of Beijing on the border between Hebei and Liaoning provinces, the narrow point of passage from North China to Manchuria and Korea. Earlier known as Yuguan and fortified by the Northern Qi (550–577) and Northern Zhou (557–581) dynasties, Shanhaiguan today contains many defensive works built by the rulers of the Ming dynasty (1368–1644). These include a central bastion (the easternmost gate-tower of which bears the famous inscription "Tianxia diyi guan"; "First Gate under Heaven"), an impressive wall extending to the sea, and numerous subsidiary watchtowers and forts. Shanhaiguan subsequently has been famous as the first city occupied by the Manchus and as the boundary between China and the Japanese client-state Manchukuo from 1932 to 1945.   ARTHUR N. WALDRON

SHANKARA (c. 788–820), Indian philosopher, theologian, and exegete. Shankara's is the most famous name in the Hindu philosophical tradition, and he is revered as the founder of Advaita Vedanta, the fundamental principle of which is that the only reality is *brahman* and that any perceived duality in the world is the result of illusion *(maya)* or ignorance *(avidya)*.

All of the eleven purported biographies of Shankara were composed several centuries after his death and are unreliable for an unbiased reconstruction of his life. However, current scholarship generally agrees on the following: Shankara was born in the South Indian region of Kerala; following the orders of his guru, Govinda, he went to Kashi (modern Varanasi), where he wrote a commentary *(bhasya)* on the *Brahma Sutras*, thereby establishing his reputation; his fame spread still further when he visited Mandanamishra, an exponent of the Mimamsa form of Vedic ritualism; the two engaged in public debate for several days until at last Mandanamishra accepted defeat, whereupon he became a *sannyasin* and, according to tradition, Shankara's most beloved disciple.

Shankara's renowned dialectical skills were displayed during a grand tour of India, during which he is said to have defeated in debate all those systems of thought that were opposed to his own form of nondualism, Advaita. He particularly engaged Buddhists, and although their long-established prestige and influence in the urban centers was already waning, he is considered by his biographers and Hindu historiographers to have been instrumental in the "defeat" of Buddhism in India and the reestablishment of the true Brahmanical religion. Both the debates and his written works seem to indicate that Shankara must have been well versed in Mahayana Buddhism, in addition to the systems of Hindu orthodoxy. Indeed, his knowledge of Buddhism was so profound that his critics labeled him a "Buddhist in disguise" and accused him of appropriating Buddhist concepts.

In his later years Shankara founded four seminaries *(mathas)*, their rule based most probably on the Buddhist monastic system of *viharas*. Located in the four principal directions, these centers were intended to propagate Advaita Vedanta and to exercise nominal regional control over their adherents. As Shankara's spiritual heirs, the heads of these institutions all bear the name *Shankaracharya*.

[See also Vedanta.]

S. N. Dasgupta, *A History of Indian Philosophy*, 5 vols. (1922–1955). T. M. P. Mahadevan, *Homage to Sankara* (1959). S. Radhakrishnan, *Indian Philosophy* (1958).

STUART W. SMITHERS

SHAN STATE INDEPENDENCE ARMY

(SSIA), formed in May 1958 by a group of Shan chiefs who were disillusioned with the relationship between the Shan State and the Burmese central government in Rangoon (established in 1947) and wished to secede from the union. The SSIA became one of many petty armies led by traditional leaders who sought to maintain political authority in their areas in the face of outside efforts to democratize the feudal basis of Shan government. Its founders wished to develop an independent Shan government, but like other such movements in the region, the SSIA was never able to gain either substantial foreign backing or internal support needed to defeat the military forces of the central government and as a result had to rely on smuggling to finance itself.

[See also Burma *and* Shan.]

Josef Silverstein, *Burmese Politics: The Dilemma of National Unity* (1980). ROBERT H. TAYLOR

SHANTOU (Swatow), Chinese seaport at the northeast corner of Guangdong Province. It first developed as a port city for Chaozhou Prefecture with the expansion of foreign trade and introduction of mechanized transport in the late nineteenth century. Today Shantou is mostly a market and shipping point for the agricultural produce of the surrounding regions of northeast Guangdong and has little industry. JOHN A. RAPP

SHANXI, northern Chinese province bordered by Hebei to the east, Henan to the south, Shaanxi to the west, and the Inner Mongolia Autonomous Region to the north. The province consists of a large mountainous plateau covered with loess and furrowed by deep ravines. As a result of its geographical location, Shanxi has served as a gateway to China for invaders from the north over the centuries, and whenever the unity of the Chinese empire has been weak, Shanxi has easily become a semiautonomous region.

Shanxi has been inhabited since the beginning of Chinese civilization during the Bronze Age. Legend has it that Yu the Great, one of China's mythical sage kings, released the waters of the Yellow River in Shanxi, and the town of Linfen, Shanxi, is given as the birthplace of the mythical Emperor Yao. Under the Zhou dynasty Shanxi was the fief of Jin, a powerful kingdom during the Spring and Autumn period. The Tuoba people, founders of the Wei dynasty in the fourth century CE, settled in Shanxi, and the Northern Qi capital was located at Taiyuan, the present-day provincial capital.

During the late Ming and Qing periods the inhabitants of Shanxi became prominent in trade, and Shanxi bankers set up a widespread banking system used for the government transfer of funds. At the end of the Ming the rebel Li Zicheng led his peasant armies from northern Shanxi to overthrow the Ming dynasty on the eve of the Manchu invasion. In the first half of the twentieth century Shanxi was a semiautonomous region under the warlord Yan Xishan.

At present Taiyuan is the provincial capital as well as an industrial and commercial center, although the city of Datong is of equal commercial and industrial importance. Shanxi's rich coal and iron deposits are currently being developed by the government.

Donald G. Gillin, *Warlord: Yen Hsi-shan in Shansi Province, 1911–1949* (1967). Andrea Lee McElderry, *Shanghai Old Style Banks (Ch'ien-chuang), 1800–1935* (1976). Yang Lien-sheng, *Money and Credit in China, a Short History* (1952).
SALLY HART

SHANYU, title of the chief of the Xiongnu, the northern barbarian adversaries of the Chinese Han dynasty (206 BCE–220 CE). The Xiongnu empire proved inherently unstable, and after 60 BCE, except for a brief period of unity from 20 to 47 CE, there were often two or more rival *shanyu*, a situation that allowed the Chinese court to control the Xiongnu through the tribute system. The *shanyu* headed a hereditary aristocracy of leading clans, delegating authority over the steppe lands to a hierarchy of vassals.

[*See also* Han Dynasty *and* Xiongnu.]

JOHN A. RAPP

SHAPUR I (r. 243–273), Iranian ruler. Shapur succeeded his father, Ardashir I, as Sasanid monarch after ruling jointly with him from 240. His mother, Mardut, was a second-rank wife of his father.

As prince, Shapur may have been governor of Khurasan. At the beginning of his reign he conquered Gilan and Khwarazm and then turned west, conquering and destroying Hatra. In 243 he lost Carrhae and Nisibis to Gordian III's Roman army, which then defeated him near Resaina. Shapur defeated and killed Gordian at Massice (Meshik) on the Euphrates, renaming it Peroz Shapur ("victorious is Shapur") in commemoration. Philip the Arab paid him an indemnity of 500,000 denarii and abandoned Armenia. When Shapur had the Armenian king, Khosrov, assassinated in 252, the latter's son, Tiridates II, fled to the Romans; Artavasd, son of Tiridates, ruled Armenia for Shapur. In 253 or 265 Shapur defeated the Romans at Barbalissus and invaded Syria, taking Dura Europos and Antioch; he resettled the captives in his new city of Veh Antiok Shapur ("Shapur's better Antioch," or Gundeshapur) in Khuzistan. When Valerian tried to raise Shapur's sieges of Carrhae and Edessa between 258 and 260, Shapur defeated and captured him and invaded Syria and Cappadocia, but he was harried out of Syria by Odenath of Palmyra. About 262 Shapur replaced Artavasd by his own son as king of Armenia and had client rulers in Iberia and Albania. He spent the last decade of his reign constructing massive irrigation works in Khuzistan and

building up his capital at Bishapur in Fars with captive labor. He commemorated his achievements in seven rock reliefs in Fars and a long inscription on the Ka'ba-yi Zardusht.

Shapur called himself king of Iran and Aniran ("non-Iran"). His empire included most of Mesopotamia and the Transcaucasus, Oman (Mazun), and former Kushan territory up to Peshawar and the borders of Kish (Kashgar), Sughd, and Shash (Tashkent). He increased the centralization begun by his father; ended the autonomy of Abrenag and Merv; and made his sons kings of Mesene, Armenia, Gilan, and the new provinces of Sakastan (Sistan) and Hind in former Kushan territory. He expanded crown territory by founding fifteen royal cities administered directly by *shahrabs* (governors) and appointed *shahrabs* to existing cities such as Rayy and Hamadan. His court was organized around two councils. The first consisted of the royal family. The second comprised the kings of Adiabene, Kerman, and Iberia; the heads of the Varaz, Suren, Andigan, and Karen clans; and the steward (*framadar*) of the royal estates. Other high officials at his court included the commander of the royal guard (*hazara-pat*), the chief secretary, and the chief judge.

Shapur encouraged Zoroastrianism by founding Varahran fires (sacred fires symbolizing goodness) in conquered territory, establishing fires and sacrifices for members of the royal family, providing benefices for priests, and collecting Avestan texts. But he also tolerated Jews, Christians, and Manicheans. Mani converted two of Shapur's brothers, joined his retinue, was permitted to preach freely throughout the empire, and dedicated his *Shahpuhrakan* to the king.

[*See also* Mani *and* Sasanid Dynasty.]

W. B. Henning, "The Great Inscription of Šāpūr I," *Bulletin of the School of Oriental Studies* 9 (1937–1939): 823–849. Ehsan Yarshater, ed., *The Seleucid, Parthian and Sasanian Periods* (1983), vol. 3 of the *Cambridge History of Iran*.
MICHAEL G. MORONY

SHAPUR II (309–379), son of Hormizd II, had the longest reign of any Sasanid monarch. Enthroned as an infant by rebellious nobles, he was controlled by nobles and priests during his minority. Whether Shapur supported or opposed Zurvanism, a form of Zoroastrianism, he founded a fire for Anahita, the tutelary deity of the Sasanids, and it was during his reign that the Zoroastrian priesthood began to be organized hierarchically and to be identified with the state. Zoroastrian priests subordinate to a high priest (Old Persian, *magupat*) were appointed in each province. This coincided with less tolerance for the members of other religions. With the sanction of the Mazdaean high priest, Adurbad Mahraspandan, Shapur confiscated the property of Manicheans. From 339 until the end of his reign he persecuted Christians and doubled their taxes. He is said to have favored rabbis but massacred thousands of messianic Jews in about 360.

Shapur's early campaigns were in eastern Arabia and against the Romans, whose frontier fortifications in Mesopotamia stopped him at first. In about 350 he destroyed Susa after suppressing a revolt there, but he had to lift his siege of Nisibis to drive Chionite invaders out of eastern Iran. He fought the Chionites until 358, when he concluded a peace with them and returned to attack the Romans with the Chionites as allies. Taking Amida (Diyarbakr) in 359 or 360, he deported its population and that of other Roman towns to Khuzistan. Roman captives built the city of Eran Khwarra Shapur ("Shapur's glory of Iran") near the site of Susa. Weavers from Amida who were settled there and elsewhere in Khuzistan introduced the manufacture of silk and gold brocades.

When Arabs from Bahrain raided Fars, Shapur occupied Bahrain, invaded the Yamama, and deported Arabs to Hormuz, Khuzistan, and Kerman. He strengthened his western defenses by building a trench and line of fortifications (the Khandaq Sabur) along the desert border of Iraq. He also established an arms and supply depot at Peroz Shapur (Anbar) and may have begun the creation of militarized frontier districts governed by *marzbans* (governors).

In 363 Julian's Roman army went down the Euphrates flanked by Armenian allies marching east from Carrhae. The Romans took Peroz Shapur and defeated Shapur at Ctesiphon, but after Julian was killed, Jovian secured the army's safe return by making peace, evacuating Nisibis and Singara, and abandoning Armenia. In 365 Shapur invaded Armenia, pillaged and destroyed the towns, and deported the population, many of whom were Jews.

[*See also* Chionites; Sasanid Dynasty; *and* Zoroastrianism.]

Ammianus Marcellinus, *Historiarum*, edited and translated by J. C. Rolfe (1935). Richard Frye, "The Persepolis Middle Persian Inscriptions from the Time of Shapur II," *Acta Orientalia* 30 (1960): 83–93. Ehsan Yarshater, ed., *The Seleucid, Parthian and Sasanian Periods* (1983), vol. 3 of the *Cambridge History of Iran*.

MICHAEL G. MORONY

SHARI'A, the revealed law of Islam, the sum of God's commandments relating to human conduct, as distinct from those relating to belief. These commandments are contained in the Qur'an and the accounts *(hadith)* of the Prophet's model behavior; other rules are inferred through analogy. In the idealistic attempt of the Muslims to create the perfect social order, based on God's will and justice, the *shari'a* is seen to cover the widest range of man's activities, including acts of religious worship, the law of contracts and obligations, personal status law, and public law. The science concerned with the study of the positive rules of law is called *fiqh*, although *shari'a* is sometimes used in this sense.

[*See also* Hadith *and* Qur'an.]

Joseph Schacht, *Introduction to Islamic Law* (1964).

JEANETTE A. WAKIN

SHARI'ATI, ALI (1933–1977), Iranian social and religious critic. Shari'ati's writings were extremely popular and influential among Iranian students of the seventies, including political groups such as the Mujahidin-i Khalq.

Shari'ati was born in Sabzevar, in the province of Khurasan. His father was an expert in Qur'anic exegesis *(tafsir)*, but Shari'ati did not pursue a formal Muslim education, choosing instead to work on a doctorate in sociology and religion at the Sorbonne. He was imprisoned briefly upon his return from Paris in 1964, and again from mid-1973 until 1975.

From 1967 until the summer of 1973 Shari'ati was active in the Husainiyya Irshad, a pious, scholarly institution that became a popular center of Islamic debate, especially along nontraditional lines. It was in his lectures at the Husainiyya Irshad that Shari'ati developed and elaborated his major ideological themes, using a blend of Western sociological and Islamic terms.

Shari'ati lashed out at the Shi'ite clergy *(ulama)* in Iran for shunning roles of leadership in social and political reforms. He further antagonized many *ulama* by arguing that one should study Islam outside of the *madrasas*, in a forum like the Husainiyya Irshad. Shi'ite Islam, Shari'ati said, was a religion of protest and purification and had been corrupted by the traditional *ulama* in conjunction with the state.

Two years after he was released from his last term in jail, Shari'ati went to England. In 1977 he was found dead there, in his brother's home; he is widely believed to have been killed by members of the Iranian secret police, SAVAK.

Ali Shari'ati, *On the Sociology of Islam*, translated by Hamid Algar (1979), and *Marxism and Other Western Fallacies: An Islamic Critique*, translated by R. Campbell (1980).   JAHAN SALEHI

SHASTRI, LAL BAHADUR (1904–1966), prime minister of India from 1964 to 1966. Shastri was the son of a schoolteacher and minor tax official who died when Lal Bahadur was eighteen months old. Taking his surname from his Shastri degree (roughly equivalent to a bachelor's degree), Lal Bahadur became first a follower of Mohandas Gandhi and then a loyal member of all of Jawaharlal Nehru's cabinets after 1952, eventually being acknowledged as one of Nehru's principal political lieutenants.

Shastri was elevated to the prime ministership after Nehru's death by the "Syndicate," a handful of party bosses who favored Shastri because he was from India's largest state (Uttar Pradesh), had the mantle of Nehru, and was a skilled compromiser loyal to party and political friends. Shastri proved a skillful prime minister and a surprisingly capable statesman in international affairs. He died of a heart attack at Tashkent the day after the completion of a successful treaty ending the Indo-Pakistan War of 1965.

[*See also* Gandhi, Mohandas Karamchand; Nehru, Jawaharlal; *and* Tashkent Agreement.]

Current Biography (1964), pp. 404–407. *New York Times Magazine* (14 June 1964), pp. 11 ff.

MARCUS FRANDA

SHATO TURKS, the easternmost tribe of the Western Turks. Early in the eighth century Tibetan attacks pushed the Shato north to a region near Lake Balkhash. In the mid-eighth century they became tributary to the Uighurs, sending troops with the Uighurs to assist the Tang against the An Lushan rebels. In the late eighth century they shifted their allegiance to the Tibetans, but early in the ninth century, when the Tibetan forces began to wane, they shifted their allegiance to the Tang. As a result, they were pursued by the Tibetans and lost many men. The Tang settled the remaining forces in central Guanzhong and the Ordos region in northern Shaanxi.

The Shato played a vital role in the Tang suppression of the Pangxun Rebellion in 869. Their leader

Zhuye Qinxin was rewarded with the imperial surname and became Li Guochang. Under his guidance they began to assert their independence from the Tang. Responding to this threat the Tang began to mount a buildup but were forced to stop in 875 when the Huang Chao Rebellion again required asking for Shato aid. With the collapse of the Tang the Shato established their own dynasty, the Later Tang (923–936), which succeeded in consolidating power in much of North China. After the collapse of the Later Tang in 937 the Shato maintained an independent existence in northern Shaanxi as the Later Han until 979.

[*See also* Five Dynasties.]

Wilhelm Barthold, *Four Studies on the History of Central Asia*, vol. 3, *Mír Ali-Shír, A History of the Turkmen People*, translated by Vladimir Minorsky and Tatiana Minorsky (1962). Wolfram Eberhard, *A History of China* (1960). Denis Twitchett, ed., *Sui and T'ang China, 589–906, Part 1*, vol. 3 of *The Cambridge History of China* (1979).   JOHN PHILIP NESS

SHEN BUHAI (d. 337 BCE), one of several prominent Chinese Legalist philosophers. A native of the state of Zheng, he was employed by Marquis Zhao of Han. He rose to become prime minister of Han, a position he probably held from 354 to 337 BCE, the year of his death. As prime minister he is credited with overcoming numerous internal struggles within the state, creating a highly organized bureaucratic government able to deal with its internal administration as well as delicate interstate relations. Because of his contributions the state of Han acted as an important model for later developments by other states.

Shen emphasized the concept of *xingming*, actualities and names, a concept common to several schools of philosophy. For Shen the teaching had primarily political implications. It stressed the correspondence of names and actual circumstances. For the Legalist this was the basis of the authority of the ruler as well as the foundation of the process of selection of officials. It is *shu*, methods or techniques, however, that distinctly identifies Shen Buhai's contribution to Legalism. It focused upon the position and authority of the ruler and equally the selection, maintenance, and examination of all officials and ministers. Such methods seemed imperative in an age that saw the decline of hereditary officialdom. Shen said little of common Legalist ideas such as law *(fa)* or rewards and punishments. For some this has excluded him from the Legalist school, but for most the methods he advocated placed him squarely in the Legalist focus upon the power and authority of the ruler and the state.

[*See also* Legalism.]

Herrlee G. Creel, *Shen Pu-hai: A Chinese Political Philosopher of the Fourth Century B.C.* (1974). K. C. Hsiao, *A History of Chinese Political Thought* (1979).

RODNEY L. TAYLOR

SHENG XUANHUAI (1844–1916), Chinese official, entrepreneur, and industrial promoter. Sheng first entered public service as a protégé of Li Hongzhang and achieved national prominence in developing new industries in late Qing-dynasty China. In order to meet China's urgent need for modernization, Sheng promoted the *guandu shangban* (government supervision and merchant management) system, in which new industrial undertakings were funded by both public and private sources and managed by merchants under the supervision of officials. Under his direction, a number of pioneering companies, notably the China Merchants' Steam Navigation Company (1872) and the Imperial Bank of China (1896), flourished in the last decades of Manchu rule.

[*See also* Li Hongzhang.]

Howard L. Boorman, ed., *Biographical Dictionary of Republican China* (1967–1971). Albert Feuerwerker, *China's Early Industrialization: Sheng Hsuan-huai (1844–1916) and Mandarin Enterprise* (1958).

CHANG-TAI HUNG

SHEN-KAN-NING BORDER REGION. *See* Shaanganning.

SHENYANG (Mukden), the capital and largest city of Liaoning Province, China. Historically the capital of the Manchus before their conquest of China, and the political and economic center of southern Manchuria during the Japanese occupation, by 1945 Shenyang had become a major industrial city. Today its industries include engineering, smelting, and chemical production, along with the manufacture of tires, textiles, and glass. It is also an educational, cultural, and administrative center. In 1982 the city proper contained an estimated population of more than four million.   JOHN A. RAPP

SHERPA, a Buddhist population numbering approximately twenty-four thousand concentrated in the Solu and Khumbu valleys of Nepal's Everest region and Darjeeling, India. The Sherpas migrated to Nepal from the Khams region of eastern Tibet in the sixteenth century to escape religious persecution by the Mongols. Although they have developed a distinct ethnic identity, the Sherpas maintain strong cultural, religious, and economic ties with Tibet. The prosperous Sherpa economy, based on high-altitude herding combined with settled agriculture and a lucrative transmontane trade in Tibetan salt, iron, wool, ghee, and rice, long supported an elaborate complex of Tibetan Buddhist ritual and institutions, including some of Nepal's finest monasteries. This virtual trade monopoly was undermined after the British established a direct route from Calcutta to Lhasa in 1904. As a result, Sherpas began migrating to Darjeeling to work as porters and guides for the early mountaineering expeditions in the eastern Himalayas.

The Chinese closing of the Tibetan border in 1959 nearly put an end to the Sherpa trading economy, but by that time Nepal had opened its borders to the West. With their firmly established reputation as mountaineers, the Sherpas have found ample employment with the growing number of climbing expeditions in the Nepal Himalayas. The infusion of cash into the Sherpa economy within recent decades has also enabled them to redirect their business skills into Nepal's expanding tourist industry.

[*See also* Himalayas.]

C. von Fürer-Haimendorf, *Himalayan Traders* (1975). S. Ortner, *Sherpas through Their Rituals* (1978).

RICHARD ENGLISH

SHER SHAH (c. 1486–1545), founder of the Afghan Suri dynasty. He was unique among Indian sultans, for he rose from the rank of petty landholder to ruler of North India. Establishing his power base in eastern India, the seat of his landholdings, Sher Shah temporarily supplanted Mughal authority in India. Impressing the sultan of Bihar with his administrative ability, Sher Shah was appointed the guardian of the next king, a minor, and eventually became the de facto ruler of Bihar. Capitalizing on the unstable political situation in North India, Sher Shah, with the consolidated support of the generally divided Indian Afghan tribes, assumed the title of sultan in 1538, acquiring the sultanate of Bengal and gaining victories against the Mughal emperor Humayun. [*See* Humayun.] In 1540 Sher Shah decisively defeated Humayun, expelling the Mughals from India. The next five years of his reign were spent in constant warfare, annexing new territories and consolidating his rule. By the time of his death, most of North India was under Suri control.

Sher Shah's fame rests not only on his military prowess but on his administrative ability and execution of justice. His reforms included the branding of cavalry horses and taxation based on measurement of land, measures adopted by the Mughals as well. In spite of Sher Shah's military preoccupations, he constructed roads, serais (inns or palaces), wells, mosques, forts, and imperial mausoleums, the most famous being his own tomb at Sasaram (Bihar). All of these, built between 1540 and his death, appear to be part of a planned propagandistic campaign aimed at projecting his image as a ideal Islamic ruler born with the preferred high-ranking qualifications for kingship.

[See also Suri Dynasty and Bihar.]

K. R. Qanungo, Sher Shah and His Times (1965). I. H. Siddiqi, History of Sher Shah Sur (1971).

CATHERINE B. ASHER

SHI'A, a term designating the branch of Islam that gives primary loyalty and allegiance to the person and religious authority of Ali ibn Abi Talib, cousin and son-in-law of the prophet Muhammad.

Originally the shi'at Ali (partisans of Ali) may have had only political motivations in their support of Ali's candidacy to succeed to the leadership of the Muslim community. Later, especially after Ali's own war with his Umayyad rivals and his subsequent martyrdom at the hands of a religious dissident, his followers appeared to find distinctly religious meaning in their attachment to his cause. This feeling intensified as it was transferred to Ali's sons, especially to Husain, the second son, whose own martyrdom at Karbala not only provided a genuine and widely recognized shock to Muslim piety but also stimulated the development of an elaborate spiritual interest in the "Family of the House [of Muhammad]" (Ahl al-bait).

Subsequent Shi'ite doctrine tended to exclude religious recognition of all other early figures and to rely solely on a tradition derived from a particular line of divinely inspired imams, all descended from Ali. According to Shi'ites, the prophet Muhammad had received a literal, scriptural text of the holy law whose correct interpretation was exclusively and secretly entrusted orally to Ali, who was said to have been proclaimed successor by the Prophet himself at Ghadir Khumm. From Ali, this teaching passed, in turn, by careful and explicit designation to each of his successors. Therefore, only by allegiance and devotion (walaya) to the proper imam of each subsequent generation could a Muslim have access to

the true content and meaning of the Islamic faith. The three principal branches of Shi'ism—Zaidi, Isma'ili, and Ithna Ashari (Imami)—differ most strikingly in the particular line of imams they accept as correct and genuine.

PAUL E. WALKER

SHIBA KŌKAN (1747?–1818), Japanese artist and polymath, an early disseminator of Western artistic practices and scientific knowledge. Shiba Kōkan's birthdate is in dispute: many standard sources indicate 1738, but his American biographer argues for 1747. Kōkan first achieved fame as a painter in the traditional Chinese bird-and-flower style and as a designer of ukiyo-e woodblock prints. He then became fascinated with Western art and became the first outstanding Japanese exponent of Western-style oil painting. In 1783 he revolutionized the graphic arts in Japan by producing copperplate engravings.

Kōkan also wrote widely on scientific subjects. Geography and astronomy were his primary interests, but he made contributions in botany, zoology, history, and medicine as well. He was also one of the early disseminators of Copernican ideas in Confucian-dominated eighteenth-century Japan.

Toward the end of his life, Kōkan turned from science to the mystical tenets of Zen and Daoism, but he remained to the end dedicated to expanding the dimensions of Japanese thought and society by absorbing new ideas and techniques from the outside world. He died in 1818, half a century before the Meiji government announced, in the Charter Oath of 1868, that it would seek knowledge throughout the world.

[See also Rangaku; Ukiyo-e; and Painting: Japanese Painting.]

C. R. Boxer, Jan Compagnie in Japan, 1600–1817 (2d rev. ed., 1950). Calvin L. French, Shiba Kōkan (1974).

RICHARD RUBINGER

SHIBLI NU'MANI, MUHAMMAD (1857–1916), Indian scholar of Persian literature and Islamic history. The son of a wealthy landholder of Azamgarh (eastern Uttar Pradesh), Shibli pursued a peripatetic Islamic education in a variety of North Indian centers of learning. In 1883 he was appointed professor of Persian in the newly founded Aligarh College, later shifting to the professorship of Arabic. At Aligarh his interests shifted from literature to Islamic history. Influenced by his British colleague

T. W. Arnold, Shibli set out to write a series of works in Urdu, particularly of the early history of Islam. In 1893 he traveled to Istanbul to be honored by the Ottoman sultan. Upon his return Shibli helped found the Nadwa't al-Ulama, first a voluntary association of Islamic scholars and later a theological academy in Lucknow. In 1898, following the death of Sir Sayyid Ahmad Khan, the founder of Aligarh College, Shibli resigned and devoted himself to his research and to establishing the leadership of the *ulama* in the political concerns of Indian Muslims.

[*See also* Ahmad Khan, Sir Sayyid.]

DAVID LELYVELD

SHIDEHARA KIJŪRŌ

SHIDEHARA KIJŪRŌ (1872–1951), Japanese diplomat and statesman. Shidehara's diplomacy in the 1920s is known for its internationalist cooperative orientation.

Upon entering the foreign service in 1896, Shidehara was first posted at Inch'ŏn, Korea, under Consul Ishii Kikujirō. In 1903 he married Iwasaki Masako, younger sister of Katō Takaaki's wife. By this marriage he was related to the Mitsubishi *zaibatsu*. In 1915 he became a vice-minister under Foreign Minister Ishii. Thereafter he served in that capacity under four more foreign ministers in the following four years. At the Washington Conference of 1921 to 1922, he played a positive role in concluding the Four-Power Treaty and resolving the Shandong question. [*See* Shandong Question.]

In 1924 he was made foreign minister in the cabinet of Katō Takaaki, and the first round of the so-called Shidehara Diplomacy began. He was against quick resort to military force in China but was eager to make economic advancement through international cooperation. Because of this attitude he was denounced as "weak-kneed" by those who demanded a "positive" policy. The showdown came with the Mukden Incident, which began Japan's conquest of Manchuria, in September 1931. [*See* Mukden Incident.] Shidehara could do nothing but recognize the fait accompli of the Kwantung Army, and in December the cabinet of Prime Minister Wakatsuki collapsed.

Shidehara then led a semiretired life, but, when the Pacific War ended with Japan's defeat, he became premier in October 1945. His utmost concern was to preserve the national polity, and it is said that the insertion of the pacifist Article 9 into the new constitution was his contribution. Although he played his part in postwar party politics, he was not adept at it. While serving as president of the House of Representatives, he died from a heart attack in March 1951.

KIMITADA MIWA

SHIGA NAOYA

SHIGA NAOYA (1883–1971), Japanese novelist, short story writer, and leading member of the literary circle that produced the journal *Shirakaba* from 1910 to 1923. In contrast to the previous generation and contemporaries such as Tayama Katai and Shimazaki Tōson, the *Shirakaba*-man was aristocratic, well-heeled, and supremely confident. Shiga's reputation is built on a handful of novellas, some short autobiographical pieces, and one long novel, *A Long Night's Passing (An'ya kōro)*, which was begun in 1912 and took the next twenty-five years to complete. Shiga's writing is marked by an interesting dissonance between theme and style: the burden of most of his autobiographical works is the struggle against a father figure, with self-realization as the goal and irresponsibility as a seemingly inevitable by-product; the style, however, is unruffled and at its worst can be overpoweringly smug. At its best the measured presentation of a series of intense moments of perception can also be a moving experience, and it is for this quiet confidence that his writing is prized. A combination of financial security and a realization that he had nothing more to say led to almost total silence during the last forty years of his life.

Francis Mathy, *Shiga Naoya* (1974). Shiga Naoya, *A Long Night's Passing,* translated by Edwin McClellan (1976). William F. Sibley, *The Shiga Hero* (1980).

RICHARD BOWRING

SHIGEMITSU MAMORU

SHIGEMITSU MAMORU (1887–1957), Japanese career diplomat and statesman. The son of a former samurai from Ōita Prefecture, Shigemitsu graduated from Tokyo Imperial University in 1911 and entered the foreign service. He participated in the Versailles Peace Conference as a member of the Japanese delegation. In April 1932, while his negotiations with the Chinese were in progress for the conclusion of a truce over the Shanghai Incident, he was a victim of a Korean nationalist's bomb, losing his lower right leg.

During the first cabinet of Konoe Fumimaro, Shigemitsu was made ambassador to the Court of Saint James, and shortly after the beginning of Japan's war against the United States he served as ambassador to the Wang Jingwei regime within Japanese-occupied China. In April 1943 Premier Tōjō Hideki made him his foreign minister. In his statements Shigemitsu took up the theme of the "liberation and reconstruction of Asia," which had been given secondary importance in Japan's war objectives, as of grave consequence. It was his way of preparing an end to the war for Japan. His idealistic concepts for a new world order were rather clearly expressed in the joint communiqué that was adopted at the Greater East Asia Conference in Tokyo on 6 November 1943.

When Japan was defeated and the cabinet of Higashi Kuni was formed, Shigemitsu returned as foreign minister and signed the surrender document on board the USS *Missouri* on 2 September 1945. He was found guilty at the International Military Tribunal and was imprisoned until 1950. He became the president of the Kaishintō (Reform Party) in 1952. He served as foreign minister in three consecutive cabinets of Hatoyama Ichirō for two years, until December 1956. During this period Soviet-Japanese relations were normalized and Japan was admitted into the United Nations.

Shigemitsu Mamoru, *Japan and Her Destiny: My Struggle for Peace,* translated by Oswald White and edited by F. S. G. Piggott (1958).   KIMITADA MIWA

SHIJIAZHUANG, Chinese city, capital of Hebei Province; population, 1,070,000 (1982). Shijiazhuang was a town of fewer than six hundred until key rail links were built in 1905 and 1939, transforming it into an important center of commerce and light industry. Since 1949 it has become a leader of the textile industry, especially in the production of Hebei cotton. Shijiazhuang also contains dyeing and printing factories, and in recent years has added petrochemical, fertilizer, and agricultural machinery industries.   JOHN A. RAPP

SHI KEFA (d. 1685), Chinese general and late Ming loyalist. A native of Henan Province, Shi obtained the *jinshi* degree in 1628 and displayed early talent as a military official. During the 1630s his career as an antibandit troop commander, especially in western Jiangnan, gained him a solid reputation as a loyal, brave, and admired leader.

In 1644, when the Manchus seized Beijing, Shi, now minister of war in the secondary capital of Nanjing, helped establish a new government there under the Ming prince of Fu. During the brief duration of the southern court, Shi acted as one of the few stabilizing influences, smoothing over personal and factional rivalries while attempting to build up the defense perimeter north of the Yangtze River. In spite of his efforts, an overwhelming Manchu force under Dodo surrounded his command at Yangzhou on 13 May 1645 and entered the city after a seven-day siege. Shi, failing at suicide, was killed sometime during the ten-day massacre that ensued.

Shi Kefa has long remained a symbol of Ming loyalty and resistance to the Manchus. In the 1890s Chinese revolutionaries exalted his heroic last stand and the infamous Yangzhou massacre to rekindle anti-Manchu sentiment.   ROLAND L. HIGGINS

SHIMABARA, a peninsula of western Kyushu, Japan, southeast of Nagasaki, the scene of a major peasant uprising (1637–1638) in which most of the rebels were Christian converts. The "Christian" rebellion on Shimabara and the nearby Amakusa Islands was the final stimulus for the Tokugawa *bakufu*'s expulsion of the Portuguese in 1639, its ruthless suppression of Christianity, and its comencement of a policy often called "seclusion" (*sakoku*).

Part of the Kirishitan (Christian) daimyo Arima's domain in the sixteenth century, the peninsula had been home of the Jesuit seminary and printing press. Its population was heavily Christian and remained so even after Tokugawa Ieyasu's expulsion of the missionaries in 1614. Many Christian *rōnin* (masterless samurai) had also taken refuge there in the early seventeenth century, as their lords were killed and as persecution of Christianity increased.

In 1616 the *bakufu* put a new daimyo in Shimabara, Matsukura Shigemasa, who was less eager to persecute the Christians in his domain than to bring it under his control and curry favor with the shogun. He built a new castle at Shimabara, in the northeastern part of the peninsula, far from the entrenched Christian holdovers from the Arima days, and tried to show loyalty to Edo by volunteering construction levies for Edo Castle that were two and one-half times what was expected. He generated new revenues through heavier levies on the peasantry, creating great economic suffering. Shigemasa's leniency with the Kirishitan brought Tokugawa Iemitsu's anger, and from 1627 he began actively persecuting local Kirishitan, employing a wide variety of tortures in a five-year reign of terror. Increased *bakufu* restrictions on foreign trade in the 1630s discontinued one source of revenue for Shigemasa's son Katsuie, further straining local finances and increasing the burden on the people in the domain, a distress made worse by a series of poor harvests beginning in 1634.

This economic and religious powder keg exploded on 11 December 1637, when a mob of seven or eight hundred peasants, outraged over the death of a village headman's wife who had been taken hostage for unpaid taxes, attacked the home of a Matsukura retainer. The news spread quickly to neighboring Amakusa, the home of the deceased hostage, and provoked a peasant outburst there also. The Shimabara Rebellion's immediate causes were overtaxation and governmental cruelty, but it rapidly took on religious overtones. The revolt was quickly put down in Amakusa, but survivors crossed to Shimabara to join the rebels there, and by the end of the year as many as 37,000 rebel peasants and *ronin* from Shimabara and Amakusa had taken refuge in Hara Castle, on the southeast coast. The Matsukura forces could not control the revolt, which they called a Christian uprising in relating the news to the *bakufu*. Shogunal bans on daimyo forces crossing domain lines slowed a more general military response. Edo got the news six days after the initial outbreak and sent Itakura Shigemune to quell the rebellion. Itakura found the rebels armed with muskets and entrenched in Hara Castle, nominally commanded by Masuda Shirō (also called Amakusa Shirō), a charismatic savior figure reputed to have performed miracles, even to have "descended from heaven." The first shogunal forces did not reach the castle until 20 January 1638, and soon afterward Itakura arrived with some 50,000 men, but he had little success against the well-fortified rebels. Hearing he was to be replaced, Itakura led a charge on the Japanese New Year's Day (14 February) that was a fiasco: he lost 3,928 men and was himself killed. His replacement, the *rōjū* Matsudaira Nobutsuna, decided to starve the rebels out rather than to attack again. He called on aid from the Dutch, whose ship *de Ryp* bombarded the castle on 24 February. This last tactic only provoked the rebel scorn for the shogunal forces' reliance on foreigners. Matsudaira dismissed the Dutch and waited for reinforcements. By late March he had over 125,000 men, and it became clear the rebels were at the brink of starvation. The final assault came on 12 April, and after three days of fighting the castle fell. All but one of the rebels were slaughtered, their numbers put at between 20,000 and 37,000, while *bakufu* forces lost as many as 13,000 men.

The Shimabara Rebellion confirmed the *bakufu*'s revulsion toward Christianity and its fears that it was impossible to deal with the Portuguese without risk of Christian infiltration. On 5 July 1639 the *bakufu* ordered the Portuguese out of Japan, ending a century of relations, because the traders financed missionaries, smuggled them into Japan, and "were responsible for fomenting the Shimabara Rebellion." Until the 1870s Christianity was strictly proscribed, surviving only as an underground cult. The Shimabara Rebellion was the last major military action in Japan until the eve of the Meiji Restoration in the 1860s.

[See also Amakusa; Seclusion; *and* Kirishitan.]

C. R. Boxer, *The Christian Century in Japan, 1549-1650* (1951). Otis Carey, *A History of Christianity in Japan*, vol. 1, *Roman Catholic and Greek Orthodox Missions* (1909). George Elison, *Deus Destroyed: The Image of Christianity in Early Modern Japan* (1973). Ivan Morris, "The Japanese Messiah," chap. 7 in his *The Nobility of Failure: Tragic Heroes in the History of Japan* (1975). James Murdoch, *A History of Japan*, vol. 2, *During the Century of Early Foreign Intercourse* (1903).

RONALD P. TOBY

SHIMAZU HISAMITSU

SHIMAZU HISAMITSU (1817–1887), Japanese leader who, as father of the daimyo Tadayoshi, assumed leadership of Satsuma in 1858 after the death of Shimazu Nariakira, his half brother. A political rival of Nariakira, Hisamitsu refused sanctuary to Saigō Takamori, Nariakira's protégé, and twice exiled him, first as a political prisoner and later as a criminal. In 1862 he brought a large military force to Kyoto, annihilated a group of radical imperial loyalists in what became known as the Teradaya Incident, and gained prestige as a proponent of *kōbu gattai* (the movement to increase imperial power at the expense of the *bakufu*) by escorting the imperial envoy, Ōhara Shigetomi, to Edo.

On the return trip Shimazu's samurai caused the Richardson, or Namamugi, Incident when they killed a British officer. Shimazu's refusal to apologize or pay indemnity resulted in the bombardment of Kagoshima by the British navy in 1863. In 1864 samurai opinion forced him to release Saigō from prison, and thereafter the initiative for directing Satsuma's policy in national affairs was seized by Saigō and Ōkubo Toshimichi. Although he was granted high titles in the new Meiji government of 1868, Shimazu opposed its social and economic reforms.

[See also Satsuma; Richardson Incident; Kagoshima Bombardment; Saigo Takamori; *and* Shimazu Nariakira.]

W. G. Beasley, *The Meiji Restoration* (1972). Conrad Totman, *The Collapse of the Tokugawa Bakufu, 1862–1868* (1980).   ROBERT K. SAKAI

SHIMAZU NARIAKIRA (1809–1858), lord of the *tozama han* of Satsuma, Japan (1851–1858); one of the most enlightened and influential leaders of his time. The *bakufu* minister Abe Masahiro valued his judgment, and the lord of Mito exchanged information and ideas with him on matters concerning national security. Nariakira advised Abe to allow trade with the West while building up Japan's defenses. He also pressed for *kōbu gattai*, a concept for bringing the imperial court and *bakufu* closer together, with influential daimyo given some voice in formulating national policy. To carry out his ideas Shimazu raised Saigō Takamori from obscurity to sudden national prominence by entrusting him as his personal spokesman and agent.

Nariakira ordered the collection and translation of Western technical books and the application of the acquired technology to practical use. Thus, Satsuma was one of the first domains to build the reverberatory furnace; it also built and navigated Japan's first steamship (1855). The Shuseikan was organized for the promotion of various new industries from tooling machinery and manufacturing weapons to producing alcohol and cut-glass. Nariakira also purchased machinery from England for textile manufacturing, and he personally experimented with gas lamps, telegraphy, and photography. On his death he was succeeded by his half brother, Shimazu Hisamitsu.

[*See also* Satsuma; Tokugawa Period; Saigō Takamori; *and* Shimazu Hisamitsu.]

Robert K. Sakai, "Shimazu Nariakira and the Emergence of National Leadership in Satsuma," in *Personality in Japanese History*, edited by Albert M. Craig and Donald H. Shively (1970).   ROBERT K. SAKAI

SHIMODA, a port about 100 miles southwest of Edo (Tokyo), Japan. Shimoda was opened to American ships in 1854 by Matthew C. Perry's Treaty of Kanagawa chiefly because of its potential value as a port of call. Perry surveyed the harbor. While there, he refused to give passage to the Japanese nationalist Yoshida Shōin, who was later imprisoned for trying to leave the country.

In December 1854 a Russian vice admiral, Putiatin, went to Shimoda to negotiate along the same lines as Perry. His flagship was destroyed by a tidal wave on 23 December, but Putiatin was nevertheless able to conclude a treaty on 7 February 1855.

In September 1856 Townsend Harris established the first American consulate in Japan, at the Gyokusenji in Shimoda, in accordance with the Kanagawa treaty. He quickly realized that Shimoda, having poor land communications, was of little value for trade. Hence, when he negotiated a commercial treaty in Edo early in 1858 he omitted Shimoda from the ports to be opened, substituting Kanagawa (Yokohama).

[*See* Kanagawa Treaty; Perry, Matthew C.; *and* Harris, Townsend.]

George A. Lensen, *The Russian Push toward Japan: Russo-Japanese Relations 1697–1875* (1959). Oliver Statler, *Shimoda Story* (1969). Payson J. Treat, *Diplomatic Relations between the United States and Japan, 1853–1895*, 2 vols. (1932; reprint 1963).
W. G. BEASLEY

SHIMONOSEKI, TREATY OF, treaty concluding the Sino-Japanese War of 1894 to 1895. Japan's original war objective was to supplant Chinese influence in Korea. As the war developed rapidly in their favor, the Japanese grew more ambitious. The army desired a territory in southern Manchuria to gain a foothold on the continent and to tighten Japanese control over the Korean peninsula. The navy sought Taiwan as a stepping stone for further advance toward the south. Japanese party politicians, journalists, intellectuals, and businessmen strongly endorsed these military and economic ambitions. The government leaders were aware that their excessive demands might cause the West to intervene, but driven by their imperialistic ambition and wanting to take full advantage of the increasingly certain victory, they were determined to require extensive concessions as terms for peace.

The peace conference was opened on 20 March 1895 at Shimonoseki between the Japanese plenipotentiaries, Premier Itō Hirobumi and Foreign Minister Mutsu Munemitsu, and their Chinese counterpart, Li Hongzhang. The seasoned Chinese statesman attempted to persuade the Japanese to restrain their demands, stressing the need of Sino-Japanese cooperation against the West. On 24 March a Japanese fanatic wounded Li. Fearful above all that the incident might cause sympathy among the Western powers with China, Japan conceded a truce, which Li had proposed earlier. Throughout the turbulent negotiations, Li waited in vain for the West to intervene against the extensive Japanese demands. With no direct Western intervention in sight, Li was compelled to capitulate. The Treaty of Shimonoseki was signed on 17 April, stipulating, *inter alia:* China's recognition of Korea as an independent state; cession of the Liaodong Peninsula, Taiwan, and the Pescadores Islands; payment of an indemnity of 200 million taels of silver; and conclusion of a commercial treaty similar to those China had with the Western powers, including the opening of additional ports and other facilities for Japanese and Western economic activities.

Although the Russian-German-French Triple Intervention was soon to deprive Japan of the major war prize, the Liaodong Peninsula, the Treaty of Shimonoseki established Japan as the dominant power in East Asia.

[*See also* Sino-Japanese War; Triple Intervention; *and the map accompanying* Meiji Period.]

Hilary Conroy, *The Japanese Seizure of Korea, 1868–1910* (1963). Mutsu Munemitsu, *Kenkenroku: A Diplomatic Record of the Sino-Japanese War, 1894–1895,* translated by Gordon M. Berger (1982).

SHUMPEI OKAMOTO

SHIMONOSEKI BOMBARDMENT, Japanese attack on Western ships in 1863. Fortified with the *bakufu's* expulsion decree, *jōi* ("expel the barbarians") sympathizers in Chōshū *han* arranged to shell Western shipping in the Shimonoseki straits. They attacked the American ship *Pembroke* and bombarded French and Dutch ships as well. These vessels were damaged but escaped. The American warship *Wyoming* was soon dispatched to Shimonoseki and destroyed Chōshū's Kameyama battery and sank three small Western-style craft Chōshū had in the vicinity. Four days later the French ships *Sémiramis* and *Tancrède* pounded the remaining batteries into submission, and French marines briefly occupied the battery at Maeda.

Chōshū's attacks ceased, but the episode continued to have repercussions. Deep apprehensions over the West's military power brought the Chōshū government to create its first Western-style rifle company, the Kiheitai. Besides this, the bombardments stirred Western powers to send a joint fleet to Shimonoseki in 1864 to chastise Chōshū further. The four-nation naval expedition provided the occasion for increased diplomatic contacts and a rapprochement between Chōshū and the English.

THOMAS M. HUBER

SHINGON ("true word"), the term used to refer to the teachings of one of the most influential schools of Japanese Buddhism, the Shingonshū. Established as an independent school by the monk Kūkai (774–835), Shingon is a branch of Esoteric, or Tantric *(mikkyō),* Mahayana Buddhism, which spread from India around the seventh century CE into China, Tibet, Korea, and Japan. Tantric Buddhism incorporated many elements—devotion to cosmic and procreative divinities, magical rituals and formulas, and yogic practices—from the ancient Vedic and Hindu traditions.

Kūkai studied the form of Tantric Buddhism known as Mantrayana, the "vehicle of mantras," in China between 804 and 806 under the master Huiguo (746–805). He further systematized this teaching in his own writings, establishing it as the Shingon school in Japan.

Shingon teaches that the secret, esoteric teachings of the cosmic Buddha Dainichi Nyorai (Sanskrit, Mahavairocana), conveyed to initiates in magical ceremonies and secret readings of particular sutras, reveal the path to salvation more directly than the exoteric teachings of Shakyamuni Buddha as transmitted overtly in the sutras. The central text of the Shingon school is the *Dainichikyō* (Sanskrit, *Mahavairocana Sutra),* which expounds the possibility of knowing that one's own mind is originally enlightened and that all sentient beings can attain the wisdom of Buddhahood. Mahavairocana, as revealed in the sutras and in Shingon mandalas, embodies both the "becoming" and "being" of this original enlightenment.

Kūkai, in his many commentaries on these sutras, argued vigorously that esoteric teachings embraced exoteric teachings and were the supreme expression of Buddhism. He stressed that his Shingon Buddhism was beneficial in "pacifying and defending the nation" *(chingo kokka)* and in enabling all individuals, who are "originally enlightened" *(hongaku),* to "attain enlightenment in this very existence" *(sokushin jōbutsu).* In Shingon practice great emphasis is placed on the transmission of hidden interpretations of the sutras and on initiation and other ceremonies, in which depictions of the Buddhist cosmos, mandalas, and ritual implements are used. Initiates utter and contemplate "true words" (mantras) and employ mystical hand gestures *(mudras)* as aids in the attainment of spiritual insight and salvation. Kūkai's powerful advocacy of Shingon, coupled with its magical and aesthetic appeal to monks and laypeople alike, made it a powerful force from the moment of its introduction to Japan. Its impressive ceremonies, elaborate arts, and promise of magical efficacy *(gensei riyaku)* appealed strongly to the Heian aristocracy.

Saichō, the founder of the Tendai school in Japan, had studied Tantric Buddhism, and thus Tantric influence was felt within Tendai as well. After Saichō's death what had been a trickle of Shingon practice within his school became a flood. A Tendai esotericism *(taimitsu)* was derived from Shingon esotericism *(tōmitsu)*, making Shingon the most powerful religious current in Heian Japan. The Shingon school has survived to the present and Shingon Buddhism, although less influential as a school, continued to have a profound effect on later Buddhist thought and practice. Japanese mountain devotion, Shugendō, was heavily influenced by esoteric practice. Shingon influences also found their way into Zen and Pure Land Buddhism. Moreover, the legend and cult of Kūkai, the founder, continued to grow over the centuries. Kūkai's reputation as both a religious and a culture hero guaranteed a measure of influence for the Shingon school. Today there are six main branches of Shingon, headed by the monasteries of Kongōbuji (Mount Kōya), Kyōōgokokuji (Kyoto), Daigoji (Kyoto), Ninnaji (Kyoto), Chishakuin (Kyoto), and Hasedera (Nara). There are more than ten thousand surviving Shingon temples, sixteen thousand priests, and three million adherents.

[*See also* Kūkai, Tendai, *and* Saichō.]

Joseph M. Kitagawa, *Religion in Japanese History* (1966). Kiyota Minoru, *Shingon Buddhism* (1967). E. Dale Saunders, *Buddhism in Japan* (1964).

MARTIN COLLCUTT

SHINJINKAI, or New Man Society, the leading organization of the Japanese left-wing student movement of the 1920s. Founded in December 1918 by three students in the Faculty of Law at Tokyo Imperial University, the Shinjinkai called for democratic political reform through its magazine *Demokurashii (Democracy)*; its members were also active in the labor movement.

As time passed, the ideology of the Shinjinkai became more radical, shifting from moderate liberalism to orthodox Marxist-Leninism, particularly after the discontinuation of the magazine in 1922. The group was the center of an active national Marxist student movement after 1923 and a leader of the national federation known as the Gakuren. Government suppression of the student left grew in intensity after 1925, forcing the formal dissolution of the Shinjinkai in 1929, although its activities continued underground for another five years. The total membership of the Shinjinkai over its eleven years of existence was more than four hundred, and many of the members went on to distinguished careers as politicians, writers, and academics. The historical significance of the Shinjinkai lies both in the precedents that it established for the much larger postwar student movement and in its role in establishing Marxism as a familiar and persuasive ideology among Japanese intellectuals.

Henry D. Smith II, *Japan's First Student Radicals* (1972).
HENRY D. SMITH II

SHINRAN (1173–1262), a leading disciple of the monk Hōnen and founder of the Japanese school of Pure Land Buddhism known as Jōdo Shinshū, the True Pure Land school. Shinran was one of the most important figures in the Kamakura-period popularization of Buddhism. Moreover, since his ideas and writings molded what was to become the most popular school of Japanese Buddhism, Shinran must be regarded as one of the most influential figures in the whole history of Buddhism in Japan.

Born into an aristocratic family, Shinran was orphaned in childhood. At the age of nine he entered the Tendai monastery of Enryakuji on Mount Hiei, where, like other Tendai monks, he studied the *Lotus Sutra* and other texts and practiced meditation and esoteric rites. He was also introduced to sutras describing the compassion of the Buddha Amida and the blessings of the Pure Land. In his late twenties Shinran had a dream in which the bodhisattva Kannon encouraged him to leave Mount Hiei and devote himself exclusively to the study of Pure Land teachings with Hōnen. Shinran stayed with Hōnen until the latter's exile. When Hōnen was exiled to Kyushu, Shinran went into exile in eastern Japan, where he made many followers among farmers and warriors and laid the basis for what later grew into the True Pure Land school.

Although the relations between Hōnen and Shinran were very close and although Shinran claimed to be nothing other than a "true follower" of Hōnen, in his writings, preaching, and practice Shinran pushed his teachings on Amida and the Pure Land to a more radical position than that of Hōnen. Where Hōnen's Pure Land school continued to stress celibacy and the monastic life, Shinran rejected monastic vows. He encouraged a married priesthood and Pure Land practice within ordinary family life. Shinran himself married the regent Kujō Kanezane's daughter, the nun Eshin. Where Hōnen had been tolerant of Buddhas other than Amida, Shinran stressed an exclusive trust in Amida. Where Hōnen had practiced multiple invocation of the *nembutsu*, Shinran argued that "one calling" was sufficient. Added invocations were deemed merely expressions of gratitude. Where Hōnen had expressed a quiet confidence in the attainment of the Pure Land, Shinran was stricken by a sense of his own sinfulness and helplessness. This led him to stress, more forcefully than Hōnen, the reach of Amida's compassion to the sinful as well as the righteous. In fact, sinners aware of their weaknesses might be closer to the welling of Amida's mercy: "If even the good can be reborn in the Pure Land, how much more so the wicked!"

After Shinran's death his followers broke into rival groups, *monto,* who were frequently at odds with each other and bitterly divided by accusations of heresy. The *monto* were reunited by the efforts of the monk Rennyo (1415–1499) into a powerful school under the leadership of the Honganji temple.

[*See also* Hōnen; Pure Land; *and* Amidism.]

Alfred Bloom, *Shinran's Gospel of Pure Grace* (1965). Joseph M. Kitigawa, *Religion in Japanese History* (1966).

MARTIN COLLCUTT

SHINSHŪ ("true school"), the abbreviated name of Jōdo Shinshū, the True Pure Land school, a branch of Japanese Buddhism. Shinshū was established by Shinran (1173–1262), the foremost disciple of Hōnen (1133–1212), who is credited with establishing Pure Land teaching, with its emphasis on devotion to Amida, as an independent branch of Japanese Buddhism.

For much of the medieval period Shinshū was popularly known as the Ikkōshū, which has been translated "single-minded school." This name, which only later came to imply militancy and rigid organization, was derived from the name of the monk Ikkō, a follower of Ippen, the founder of the Ji school. It was applied indiscriminately to Shinran's followers. Rennyo, who revived the fortunes of Shinshū in the fifteenth century, as well as other leaders of the school, disliked the title Ikkōshū. Appeals to the Tokugawa *bakufu* for official recognition of the title Jōdo Shinshū were rejected, largely because of opposition from members of the Jōdoshū, or Pure Land school, who were naturally reluctant to grant official recognition to a variant Pure Land teaching claiming greater "truth." The title Jōdo Shinshū was officially recognized by the Meiji government in 1872.

Although Shinran was a favored disciple of Hōnen and claimed to be no more than a sincere follower of his master, his teachings were more radical than Hōnen's, and Jōdo Shinshū included practices not seen in the established schools of Buddhism or in Hōnen's Pure Land school and its other offshoots.

Unlike most other Kamakura period reformers, Shinran rejected celibacy, the monastic rule, and religious hierarchy. He did not found temples, nor did he claim to be a leader. His disciples and followers formed local associations, *monto.* The *monto* developed on the basis of family relations, with ecclesiastical leadership inherited from generation to generation. After Shinran's death the *monto,* several of which were led by his offspring, squabbled among themselves, accusing each other of heretical interpretation of Shinran's teachings. They were eventually united by the efforts of the eighth-generation leader Rennyo (1415–1499), who revived Shinran's original teachings and asserted the primacy of the Honganji (a major Shinshū temple in Kyoto) among the *monto.* During the medieval period these Shinshū *monto* were known as the Ikkōshū. With their following of farmers and warriors in the provinces, the *monto* formed powerful religious and military organizations in many parts of the country. In bitter local uprisings (*ikkō-ikki*) they waged battle with the warlords of the Warring States (Sengoku) period. Shinshū *monto* took over Kaga province in 1488 and ruled it for more than ninety years, until they were defeated by Oda Nobunaga in 1580. *Monto* provided some of the stiffest resistance to Nobunaga in his attempt to conquer the country. He struggled with the Ikkōshū led by the Honganji for more than ten years, until 1580, when he was at last able to crush Honganji and put it to the torch.

Honganji's fortunes began to recover under Toyotomi Hideyoshi, who reestablished it in Kyoto. In 1602 Shinshū was divided by a succession dispute within Honganji between "western" (*nishi*) and "eastern" (*higashi*) factions. This division was recognized by the Tokugawa shogunate in the creation of two temples, Nishi Honganji and Higashi Honganji, in different parts of Kyoto. Both branches of Shinshū enjoyed the favor of the Tokugawa shoguns. Although suspect in some domains, True Pure Land teachings continued to spread through villages and towns. Following the purge of Buddhism in the early Meiji period, Jōdo Shinshū priests and believers have been active in the modern recovery of Buddhism in Japan. Jōdo Shinshū is today the largest branch of Japanese Buddhism, claiming more than thirteen million adherents.

[See also Shinran; Pure Land; Hōnen; Ikki; and Rennyo.]

David L. Davis, Ikki in Late Medieval Japan," in John W. Hall and Jeffrey P. Mass, eds., Medieval Japan: Essays in Institutional History (1974). Stanley Weinstein, "Rennyo and the Shinshū Revival," in John W. Hall and Toyoda Takeshi, eds., Japan in the Muromachi Age (1977).

MARTIN COLLCUTT

SHINTO is the indigenous religion of the Japanese people. The focus of Shinto is reverence for *kami*, a term used equally for deities and for an awesome, numinous quality perceived in such objects of nature as unusual trees, rocks, waters, and mountains. The spirits of departed emperors, heroes, and other famous persons are revered as *kami*, and it is popularly believed that ordinary persons become *kami* after death. *Kami* receive worship and tribute at shrines; these take the form of food offerings, music, dance *(kagura),* and the performance of such traditional skills as archery and sumo.

Founded by no single individual, codified in no single text, Shinto represents in part the formalization of communal rites and symbolic expressions of the Japanese people. Its practice shows great regional variation and includes rites of passage for birth and marriage as well as elaborate state ceremony. Shinto rites emphasize beauty, purity, and harmony, aesthetic as well as religious themes regarded as uniquely Japanese. The core of Shinto is its ritual; historically, doctrine has been a secondary concern.

In a syncretism lasting for centuries, Shinto had been submerged within Buddhism, largely dependent upon it for doctrinal formulation. As Shinto achieved independence in the modern period, sectarian founders with their own doctrines appeared, attracting a great lay following.

Ancient Period (300 BCE–645 CE). The Japanese islands were peopled by the migration of ethnic groups from the South Pacific, Southeast Asia, and Northeast Asia. Each group brought its myths, and these reveal two distinct cosmologies. The first, a horizontal cosmology, featured a world of the dead existing on the same plane as the human world and located far out to sea. The second is a vertical cosmology, a three-tiered universe with a realm of the gods, Takamahagara, above the human world and a world of the dead below. [See Takamagahara.]

These two cosmologies are preserved in the myths of the *Kojiki* (712) and the *Nihon shoki* (720). These works link the origins of important clans to the *kami;* the imperial clan is portrayed as descended from the sun goddess Amaterasu. Compiled so as to legitimate the rule of the imperial clan, the myths show the deities of the Izumo clan yielding the land to the Yamato pantheon, led by the legendary first emperor, Ninigi, grandchild of Amaterasu.

The religious practices of the ancient period can be known fragmentarily from the archaeological record and from Chinese chronicles. From these sources it appears that small principalities in Kyushu, which maintained tributary relations with China, were governed by leaders, often female, who in a state of possession, proclaimed oracles from the *kami;* these were relayed to the governed by a male figure in charge of the secular functions of government.

Early communal ritual, conducted by a clan head for a clan deity, was carried out at first at sacred places simply set off by a row of stones or rope, *(iwasaka).* These were later supplanted by shrines. Important ritual practices included the offering of food, prayer *(norito),* purification rites, dance, and shamanistic rites of possession *(kamigakari)* and revelation. Both myth and ritual developed at a local, communal level and a central, state level in the ancient period, and Shinto today retains this dual character.

The Ritsuryō State (645–1185). The myth and ritual complex that developed in ancient Japan was profoundly influenced by the introduction of Buddhism in the mid-sixth century. In fact, it was only after Buddhism's advent that the word *Shinto* was applied to the native cult, to distinguish it from Buddhism. Under Buddhism's influence, and with the benefit of state patronage, Shinto rites, doctrines, and shrines were systematized under the *ritsuryō* institution, a political, legal, and administrative system that was based on Chinese models. An initiative of the imperial court, *ritsuryō* structured Japanese society until the end of the Heian period. [See Ritsuryō State.]

The Urabe and Nakatomi clans emerged as specialists in Shinto matters, superintended by the Jingikan (Office of Shinto Worship), an official organ of government. There was an elaborate calendar of court ritual including Buddhist, Daoist, and Shinto rites. The priesthood was formalized, and shrines of national importance were constructed. The *Engi shiki* (927) sets out in detail the procedure for a variety of rites and gives 3,132 as the total number of shrines in the country. These are subdivided into numerous categories according to scale, character, and national significance.

It was inevitable that the simple cult of the ancient Japanese be overwhelmed by highly developed Chinese and Korean culture, and one result of this process was a syncretic theory called *honji suijaku,* which held that *kami* are phenomenal manifestations and guardians of Buddhist divinities, implying that the Buddhist figures are more original and powerful. A parallel development was the formulation within Buddhist schools of theories subordinating and assimilating Shinto. For example, Tendai's Sannō Ichijitsu Shinto (or Hie Shinto) held that the *kami* of Mount Hie (headquarters of the Tendai school), a deity called Sannō, is identical with both Amaterasu and Shakyamuni Buddha. Similarly, Ryōbu Shinto, developed in the Shingon school, connected the two mandalas sacred to that school with the Inner and Outer shrines of Ise. These theories, which probably were little known at a popular level, were nonetheless popularly supported at the *jingū-ji,* shrine-temple complexes in which a worshiper paid tribute both to *kami* and Buddhas for prosperity and well-being, with no exclusive allegiance implied to one or the other. These shrine-temples were built in great number, with construction continuing down to the Meiji period (1868–1912), and they fostered among the populace a religious orientation that did not distinguish between Buddhism and Shinto as distinct religions.

Whereas ancient ritual had been conducted by kinship groups, ritual groupings came to be defined increasingly by geography. The *miyaza,* or shrine confraternity, exemplified this trend. *Miyaza* membership was monopolized by the oldest and most powerful families of a village, who conducted rites for a territorial tutelary deity. The *miyaza* performed many secular functions as well. Great temples and shrines often became large landholders, as wealthy persons commended lands to them in order to escape taxation.

Medieval Period (1185–1600). The pervasive subordination of Shinto to Buddhism did not pass without protest. The desire to establish Shinto's supremacy has been the driving force behind much of Shinto scholarship, as exemplified by Watarai, Yuiitsu, and Suika Shinto. Established by Watarai Ieyuki (1256–1362), Watarai Shinto promoted the deities of the Outer Shrine at Ise and the virtues of honesty and purity. It emphasized as well the link

between Ise deities and the imperial family. Thus Watarai was closely associated with Kitabatake Chikafusa (1293–1354), author of the *Jinnō shōtōki* (1339–1343), which recounts the imperial lineage's descent from the *kami* and upholds the imperial regalia as sacred symbols of political legitimacy. Yuiitsu Shinto, also called Yoshida Shinto after the house that founded it (particularly Yoshida Kanetomo, 1435–1511), reversed *honji-suijaku* conceptions and proclaimed that Shinto is the origin of all religions, Buddhism and its divinities being only phenomenal derivations of *kami.* Nevertheless, Yuiitsu, as a syncretic system, was considerably influenced by Buddhism. Suika Shinto, founded by Yamazaki Ansai (1618–1682), emphasized patriotic loyalty to the emperor and the attitude of reverent exactitude (*tsutsushimi*) as the basis of Shinto.

Tokugawa Period (1600–1868). Shinto during the Tokugawa period was dominated by the Yoshida house, which was granted control over the majority of shrines by the government. The Shirakawa house controlled those shrines directly linked to the imperial court. The Yoshida had the authority to grant rank to shrines and priests, though in most cases Shinto priests at *jingu-ji* remained subordinate to their Buddhist counterparts. While Buddhist temples received support from parish organizations, Shinto parishes developed on a wide scale most conspicuously in the support of the Ise Shrine.

In connection with an increase in pilgrimage, shrines of large scale and national significance, such as Kanda Myōjin, staged splendid annual festivals, attracting people from a wide area. In addition, some shrines, such as Kasuga, Kotohira, Kumano, and Fushimi Inari, developed networks of confraternities for annual pilgrimage, and these groups became an important part of village life. People made pilgrimage to pray for a good harvest, personal safety, and general personal well-being.

Although Shinto was rarely distinguished thoroughly from Buddhism institutionally, doctrinally, or in popular consciousness, the desire to establish its independence finally emerged clearly in the Kokugaku ("national learning") movement. In its early period, as reflected in the work of Motoori Norinaga (1730–1801) and Kamo no Mabuchi (1697–1769), Kokugaku was largely a literary movement, and there was nothing inherently or exclusively "Shinto" about it. But it developed a decidedly nativist, utopian identification with Shinto late in the Tokugawa period, especially under the influence of Hirata Atsutane (1776–1843). Later Kokugaku writers proposed a return to direct imperial rule as a panacea for all Japan's fiscal, political, and social problems. They took the age of the gods as described in the *Kojiki* to be historical reality, and they regarded the acceptance of foreign culture as the cause of all national ills. The later Kokugaku movement profoundly influenced the character of Shinto and provided a catalytic doctrinal focus for the priesthood, which had for so many centuries been incapable of collective action or effective protest against Shinto's subordination to Buddhism.

Also in the late Tokugawa period appeared the first Shinto sects, that is, groups with historical founders who preached their own interpretation of Shinto doctrine. The first of the thirteen traditionally enumerated sects was Kurozumikyō. Founded in 1814 by an Okayama Shinto priest, Kurozumi Munetada (1780–1850), Kurozumikyō was able to advance itself by riding the wave of contemporary fervor for Ise pilgrimage. Early preachers practiced faith healing and advocated a daily rite of sun worship and recitation of an ancient *norito*, the Great Purification Prayer (*ōharai no norito*). This group and the other Shinto sects were able to escape persecution by cooperating with local officials in educational campaigns designed to secure the populace's allegiance to the status quo and thereby prevent peasant unrest. This early educational enterprise and its ideological orientation engendered an elitist, nationalist tendency that later spelled the stagnation of most of the thirteen sects. Only Kurozumikyō, Tenrikyō (founded 1838), and Konkōkyō (founded 1859) currently retain any significant following.

Meiji Restoration through 1945. In 1868 the state ordered the separation of Buddhism from Shinto (*shinbutsu bunri*) and began structuring Shinto as an independent religion. In part, the motivation for this epochal action was the desire to unite the people in a single creed so that they could undertake as one body the many tasks and sacrifices necessary in the creation of a modern nation. Also, the state feared expansion of the power of Buddhism and wished to prevent it from assuming a position like that of the Roman Catholic church in Europe. In the forced separation of the two, Buddhism suffered significant loss; priests were defrocked, precious statuary melted down, and hundreds of temples destroyed. The support of larger Shinto shrines was guaranteed, and the state issued its own creed as the official doctrine of Shinto.

From 1872–1885 the state undertook the so-called Great Proselytization Campaign (*daisenpu undō*) and with a corps of "national evangelists" (*kyōdōshoku*) attempted to make Shinto the religion of the state. Evangelists, drawn largely from the Shinto priesthood and ministers of the Shinto sects, preached and proselytized throughout the country, reporting directly to the state. However, the state-authored creed had no basis in popular thought, and dissension among the evangelists themselves led to the downfall of the initiative.

With the promulgation of the Meiji Constitution of 1889, limited freedom of religion was granted to all imperial subjects. Thereafter, the state withdrew from the promotion of Shinto doctrine and instead created rites defined as nonreligious and compulsory, often involving worship at Shinto shrines. In this sense Shinto continued to be the unofficial religion of the state, and one can speak of "State Shinto" during this period. Subjects were required to enshrine a talisman from Ise Shrine. National shrines were erected, such as the Yasukuni Shrine for the war dead (1869) and the Meiji Shrine (1915), constructed largely through nationwide voluntary labor. Worship at these and other shrines came to be regarded as an expression of patriotism, and the patriotism of persons resisting such worship, including Christians and members of the new religions, was suspect; such resistance might be used as a pretext for severe persecution, a tendency especially marked after 1925.

1945 to the Present. The Allied Occupation made the abolition of Shinto's state patronage a matter of high priority, and today Shinto's legal status is the same as that of any other religion. However, such widely practiced Shinto rites as worship for the souls of the war dead at the Yasukuni Shrine provide a focus for continuing debate on the proper interpretation of the constitutional separation of church and state. As a result of the constitution's guarantee of freedom of religion, many sectarian Shinto groups, suppressed before 1945, now operate freely. Older Shinto shrines, however, have suffered from the loss of state support. The removal of the coercive element of prewar State Shinto has left the priesthood ill-prepared to take the initiative in teaching and proselytizing. While many Japanese visit shrines at the New Year and on other occasions, they do so less from devotion to Shinto doctrine and deities than from simple cultural tradition. Nevertheless, as of 1983 there were 91,610 Shinto shrines, churches belonging to the Shinto sects, and proselytization stations. Shinto rites are treasured by the Japanese people as an expression of their cultural identity and of the harmony they idealize within society, between humanity and nature, and between humanity and the universe.

[*See also* Amaterasu Ōmikami; Ise; Ise Mairi;

Kamo no Mabuchi; Kojiki; Kokugaku; Motoori Norinaga; New Religions in Japan; Nihon Shoki; *and* Yasukuni Shrine.]

Hirai Naofusa, "Shintō," translated by Helen Hardacre, in *The Encyclopedia of Religion*, edited by Mircea Eliade (1987), vol. 13, pp. 280–294.

HELEN HARDACRE

SHIRAZ, capital city of the southwestern Iranian province of Fars. Shiraz first became important at the beginning of the Islamic period, when the Arabs selected it as an administrative center in preference to the nearby Sasanid city of Istakhr, which was also closer to the imposing Achaemenid ruins of Persepolis. Since it was removed from the primary caravan route linking Iraq with Central Asia, Shiraz seldom rose above the status of an important provincial city. It achieved cultural greatness in the thirteenth and fourteenth centuries, however, when the poets Sa'di and Hafiz glorified their hometown in verse. During the reign of Karim Khan Zand (r. 1751–1779) Shiraz was briefly the capital of the most important Iranian principality, but with the fall of the Zands the capital shifted to Tehran. Shiraz is located on a high plain ringed with mountains. Its population in 1978 was 450,000.

A. J. Arberry, *Shiraz: Persian City of Saints and Poets* (1960).

RICHARD W. BULLIET

SHIVAJI (1630–1680), known as the Grand Rebel, was the founder of the Maratha kingdom.

He was born to Shahaji, a leading Maratha, and Jijabai in 1630 (old date, 1627) at the fort of Shivner. He behaved like a born ruler, adopting his own seal at the age of sixteen. Shivaji fortified the Pune *jagir* (a grant of public revenues), which had been bequeathed to him by his father, by capturing forts in its vicinity. His first noteworthy political act was the capture of Javali (1656) from the Mores, vassals of the Adil Shahi. This secured his entrance into south Konkan (in Maharashtra) and gave him two forts, Pratapgad and Raigad. Raigad later became his capital.

Shivaji fought against the Adil Shahi of Bijapur and the Mughals to found the state of Maratha. The defeat of the Adil Shahi general Afzal Khan (1659) was a turning point in Shivaji's political career. It virtually silenced the Adil Shahi and made Shivaji the master of south Konkan. His threats to the Mughals began in 1657, when he looted Junnar and

captured Kalyan-Bhivandi. He attacked Shaista-khan, the viceroy of Deccan, and the commander in chief at Pune (1663); he raided Surat, the richest port of the Mughals on the west coast (1664, 1670, and 1672), and collected large booty. Aurangzeb then sent his Rajput general Mirza Raja Jaisingh, who subdued him and concluded a treaty at Purandar (1665) by which Shivaji surrendered twenty-three forts as well as territory, yielding a revenue of four lakh *hons* (gold coins), and retained only twelve forts and territory yielding one lakh *hon*. He visited Aurangzeb at Agra in May 1666 and got himself trapped, but he managed a miraculous escape and returned to his capital in November. He renewed his struggle against the Mughals, captured most of the forts, and remained unconquered and undisturbed until his death.

By 1674 he had subdued his opponents, brought a good deal of territory under his sway, and come to command great respect. On 6 June 1674 he became *chhatrapati* (chief), the sovereign ruler of the Marathas. To mark this event he started a *rajshaka* (royal era) and issued a gold coin, the *shivarai hon*. He strengthened his state by arranging an expedition to Karnataka (1677) that shut the gateway to the south for the Mughals, decimating the power of Bijapur in Karnataka and forging a wedge between Bijapur and Hyderabad, the two remaining sultanates of the Deccan. These conquests brought him both land and gold.

Shivaji could not, however, completely check the Siddis (originally from Abyssinia), who were supported by the Mughals and the Adil Shahi, holders of the fortified island of Janjira (Raigad District). He captured Phonda Fort and adjoining territories from the Portuguese at Goa and demanded *chauth* (a military cess) from them. He challenged the British by plundering their factory at Rajapur. To the British he was at first a Grand Rebel, but later they thought of him as the greatest diplomat in the East. His relations with the French and the Dutch were purely commercial and often used as a check on the British.

Shivaji's kingdom included the present-day Pune, Nasik, Raigad, Thane, Ratnagiri, Kolhapur, and Satara districts of Maharashtra and some pockets of land in Karnataka. An organizational genius, he instituted a system of civil and military administration. His army of more than two million men comprised cavalry and infantry, as well as a modest naval force of 400 vessels, and possessed nearly 240 strongholds. He promoted the economic interests of the state and was tolerant in religious matters. He died on 5 April 1680, leaving behind eight wives, two sons, and six daughters. Shivaji's memory is still cherished in Maharashtra.

[See also Marathas; Maharashtra; Deccan Sultanates; Mughal Empire; Surat; Aurangzeb; and Portuguese: Portuguese in India.]

A. R. Kulkarni, Maharashtra in the Age of Shivaji (1969). Jadunath Sarkar, Shivaji and His Times (1952).

A. R. KULKARNI

SHI XIE. See Si Nhiep.

SHŌEN was a private form of agricultural enterprise common in Japan between the eighth and sixteenth century. Usually translated "manor" or "estate," shōen were owned by a member of the capital aristocracy, a temple, or a shrine. The absentee proprietor appointed a local magnate as foreman to oversee the cultivators, who paid rent in rice and labor. Shōen were scattered throughout Japan, although most were concentrated near the capital in central and western Japan. Records survive from approximately four thousand shōen.

The Taihō Codes of 702 banned most private landholding, but as the Nara state attempted to open new fields, wealthy aristocrats and temples were granted rights to clear fields and organize shōen. Foremen gathered laborers from among vagrants; still, most early shōen could be maintained only until the early tenth century. From that time a new kind of shōen was created through a method called commendation. Local strongmen gave a set percentage of the yield of their fields to a court aristocrat or temple; in return the aristocrat or temple would use influence to remove the property from tax rolls (fuyuken) and to protect it from entry (funyūken). The government limited the number of tax-exempt estates by recording the shōen that had obtained these rights. By the mid-eleventh century the offices (shiki) of proprietor and foreman had become fixed and the cultivators were organized into units called myō. Shōen had come to cover about 40 percent of the arable land then opened in Japan.

In the late twelfth century war raged throughout the country as the Taira and Minamoto fought, and many shōen were pillaged. In 1185 Yoritomo rewarded his vassals with shōen revenues by establishing a new position called jitō. Conflicts over revenue between warriors and proprietors became commonplace. To resolve the problem, many shōen were divided in half (shitaji chūbun). During the wars of the fourteenth century more shōen were plundered, especially in eastern Japan. With the founding of the Muromachi government, local lords named shugo daimyo further intruded on the shōen holdings of the court. The civil wars of the Warring States (Sengoku) period and the land survey of Toyotomi Hideyoshi in the late sixteenth century finally put an end to all shōen.

Kan'ichi Asakawa, Land and Society in Medieval Japan (1965). Keiji Nagahara, "Landownership under the Shōen-kokugaryō System," Journal of Japanese Studies 1 (Spring 1975). Elizabeth Sato, "The Early Development of the Shōen," in Medieval Japan: Essays in Institutional History, edited by John Hall and Jeffrey Mass (1974).

WAYNE FARRIS

SHOGUN, term that in medieval Japan referred to a variety of military commanders, but that is now used almost exclusively to refer to the heads of the three warrior regimes that dominated Japan between 1192 and 1867. The current usage is derived from the title sei-i tai shōgun, or "generalissimo for the suppression of the eastern barbarians," adopted by the heads of all these regimes, beginning with Minamoto Yoritomo in 1192.

The first shogunal regime, or bakufu, was based in Kamakura and was officially in power from 1192 to 1333. But Minamoto Yoritomo had maintained a largely autonomous regime in Kamakura ever since defeating the Taira in the Gempei War (1180–1185), and his formal investiture as sei-i tai shōgun in 1192 added nothing to his power or prestige. It is quite common, therefore, to date the beginning of his regime as 1185, the year in which he was explicitly granted authority not only to maintain peace in the country but also to appoint his followers into landholding positions throughout Japan known as jitō, a sort of bailiffship. By the time Yoritomo's direct line of succession died out in 1219, this regime was so well consolidated that it would survive for more than a century under a series of puppet shoguns who were controlled by the Hōjō family of shogunal regents.

For all its strength, however, the shogunate only gradually displaced the imperial court as Japan's de facto government. Although Yoritomo may have toyed with the idea of becoming a dictator, he ultimately chose to leave most aspects of governance to the court. Even after elements at court had provoked a war with the shogunate during the Shōkyū Incident (1221), the Kamakura regime was extremely reluctant to seize court prerogatives. [*See also* Shōkyū Incident.*]

In fact, Kamakura's major concern was to protect the landed interests of the fairly small number of shogunal vassals *(gokenin)* who had received appointments as *jitō*. It insisted that it alone had jurisdiction over the *jitō* and their prerogatives, but it normally left the determination of other land rights entirely to the imperial court in Kyoto.

In 1333 the Kamakura shogunate was overthrown by warriors professing loyalty to the deposed emperor Go-Daigo. The latter reascended the throne and ruled the country himself for a time, but in 1336 he was driven from the capital by Ashikaga Takauji, a former supporter. Takauji was made *sei-i tai shōgun* in 1338, and his regime, which ultimately settled in the Muromachi section of Kyoto, survived until 1573. [*See also* Go-Daigo.]

The Muromachi shogunate differed from its Kamakura predecessor in at least two important ways. First, it came far closer to being Japan's de facto government. Whatever Takauji's intentions may have been in the 1330s, the fact is that the nearly sixty years of civil war that raged between Go-Daigo's successors and a branch of the imperial family that Takauji installed on the throne in 1336 all but ruined the imperial court as an effective political institution. By the end of the fourteenth century, it was the shogunate that performed all functions of national governance.

At the same time, however, the prolonged strife of the fourteenth century had forced the Ashikaga shoguns to delegate most of their authority over the provinces to a group of countlike officials known as *shugo*. *Shugo* had also been appointed by the Kamakura shogunate, but whereas the Kamakura *shugo* had been a closely circumscribed shogunal appointee, his Muromachi counterpart was a territorial magnate of baronial proportions. Indeed, the history of the Muromachi shogunate during the fifteenth century is as much the history of the baronial rivalries of the *shugo* as it is the history of the shogunal house and the bureaucracy that served it. [*See also* Shugo.]

This is particularly true of the period after 1441. In that year, Ashikaga Yoshinori, whose rule had been marked by a vigorous campaign to cut back on the *shugo*'s baronial pretensions, was assassinated, and the shogunate fell first to one, and then a second, of his very young sons. For the next quarter century, shogunal politics were dominated by the bitter wrangling of baronial factions, and in 1467 this wrangling erupted into an eleven-year war

that all but destroyed the Muromachi shogunate. For the next century, Japan lacked any central government worthy of that name.

Between 1568 and 1600, however, a series of climactic civil wars resulted in the reunification of the country under Tokugawa Ieyasu. The Muromachi shogunate had slipped into oblivion during the interim, and in 1603 Ieyasu had himself named *sei-i tai shōgun*. His dynasty, which was based in Edo, would continue to rule the country until 1867.

This last shogunate was a good deal more powerful than either of its predecessors, but a number of features make it seem something of an anomaly among early modern regimes. First, while roughly 25 percent of the country was set aside as the domain of the shogun and of his minor enfeoffed vassals, the rest was consigned to roughly 250 barons, or daimyo, with whose rule the shogun would not normally interfere. The Tokugawa shogunate has therefore seemed to many scholars to be less like the absolutist regimes of contemporary Europe than like a peculiar form of "centralized feudalism."

Second, the shogunate adopted a number of repressive, if not retrograde, policies that also seem in striking contrast to those of European regimes. These include the freezing of social status, the substantial isolation of the country from external contact, and a denigration of the nonagrarian sectors of the economy. Nevertheless, the Tokugawa shogunate presided over a period of prolonged peace, considerable prosperity, and sustained institutional development.

By the mid-nineteenth century, however, the shogunate had begun to seem incapable of responding to the problems of a rapidly changing social order and an increasingly threatening West. In 1867, therefore, it was overthrown by men professing to believe that the restoration of direct imperial rule would better serve the country.

[*Many of the Ashikaga and Tokugawa shoguns are the subject of independent entries. See also* Minamoto *and* Bakufu.]

Peter J. Arnesen, *The Medieval Japanese Daimyo* (1979). Harold Bolitho, *Treasures Among Men* (1974). John W. Hall, *Government and Local Power in Japan, 500–1700* (1966). John W. Hall and Toyoda Takeshi, eds., *Japan in the Muromachi Age* (1977). Jeffrey P. Mass, *Warrior Government in Early Medieval Japan* (1974). Jeffrey P. Mass, ed., *Court and Bakufu in Japan* (1982). Conrad Totman, *Politics in the Tokugawa Bakufu* (1967). H. Paul Varley, *The Ōnin War* (1967).

PETER J. ARNESEN

SHŌKYŪ INCIDENT, also called Jōkyū Incident, an attempt by the retired Japanese emperor Go-Toba to overthrow the Kamakura shogunate in 1221. While it is often suggested that this abortive coup represented an attempt by Japan's civil nobility to recapture control of the country, recent scholarship suggests that noble opposition to the shogunate was not very pronounced. Indeed, Go-Toba's principal support may have come from warriors who resented the degree to which the shogunate was dominated by the Hōjō family of shogunal regents.

The uprising was smashed in little more than a month. Go-Toba, his sons, and his infant grandson, who had just assumed the throne, were sent into exile; Go-Toba's nephew was installed as emperor; and the court was subjected to far closer warrior surveillance than it had been in the past. While the Shōkyū Incident clearly resulted in a significant increase in the power of the Kamakura shogunate, however, the court was not yet undone. It is true that the court's attempt to install one of Go-Toba's grandsons on the throne in 1242 was squelched, and that any warrior foolish enough to have supported Go-Toba suffered attainder, but most noble landholdings were left intact, and Kyoto's authority over civil affairs was confirmed. The real collapse of Kyoto's authority did not take place until the far lengthier and more disruptive civil wars of the fourteenth century.

[See also Kamakura Period.]

Jeffrey P. Mass, *The Development of Kamakura Rule, 1180–1250* (1979).   PETER J. ARNESEN

SHŌTOKU TAISHI (574–622). The son of the Japanese emperor Yōmei, Prince Umayado, as Shōtoku Taishi was known by his contemporaries, aided Soga no Umako in destroying the anti-Buddhist faction at court in 587. He was named heir apparent in 593 and appointed to a newly created post, the regency (sesshō). His elevation to this post, from which he could oversee the daily business of the government, began the trend of a strong regency that continued throughout the seventh century.

Shōtoku Taishi is credited with impressive accomplishments over the next thirty years, although official histories undoubtedly exaggerated them. In 603 he initiated a new way of ranking court bureaucrats. Unlike the previous system of titles (kabane), which had emphasized pedigree, Shōtoku Taishi's organization was based on individual merit and resembled both Chinese and Korean systems. It divided officials into twelve cap-ranks and served as a prototype for later institutions implemented under the emperors Tenji and Temmu. In 604, Shōtoku Taishi proclaimed his Seventeen Article Constitution. This work was essentially a series of Buddhist and Confucian proverbs exhorting officials to be loyal and industrious.

Shōtoku Taishi sponsored a resumption of relations with China, sending four missions to the Sui court. Shōtoku Taishi also continued the policy of attempting to reconquer Mimana, a former Japanese outpost on the Korean peninsula.

Shōtoku Taishi's greatest contribution may have been his sponsorship of Buddhism, which grew dramatically in influence and popularity in the early 600s. He is credited with founding temples, both Hōryūji in Nara and Shitennōji in Osaka, and is believed to have been one of the first Japanese to have understood the major precept of the religion: the perception of the world as illusion. His reputation as a scholar of Buddhism grew in later ages until he came to be regarded as a saint with superhuman powers.

[See also Yamato.]

W. G. Aston, trans., *Nihongi* (1896). Hanayama Shinshō, "Shōtoku Taishi," in *The Encyclopedia of Religion*, edited by Mircea Eliade (1987), vol. 13, pp. 298–299.

WAYNE FARRIS

SHŌWA EMPEROR. *See* Hirohito.

SHŌWA PERIOD, contemporary period of Japanese history, coinciding with the reign of the current emperor, Hirohito (b. 1901), who ascended the throne on 25 December 1926. The Shōwa period (1926–) follows the Taishō (1912–1926) and Meiji (1868–1912) periods, named after the reigns of Hirohito's father and grandfather, respectively. The year 1988 corresponds to the sixty-third year of Shōwa. The first year of Shōwa embraced only the last six days of 1926.

Shōwa literally means "enlightened peace." The appellation belies the period's character. Since 1926, Japan has experienced the extremes of success and catastrophe. The empire reached an apogee in 1942, only to be dismembered and dissolved three years later. Military triumphs in 1941–1942 that promised a new age in Asia and the Pacific instead brought Japan to the brink of destruction. From defeat and occupation, Japan rebounded and built the most dynamic economy in the world, second in scale only to that of the United States. One of the most chauvinistic and martial nations became the only country in the world to renounce the right of belligerency in its constitution. These vicissitudes are reflected in the contrasting moods and tones of Shōwa culture, which has exhibited a complex and unstable blend of xenophobia and cosmopolitanism, militarism and pacifism, asceticism and hedonism, pride and humility, self-confidence and self-doubt.

Historians have commonly divided the Shōwa period into prewar and postwar phases, with imperial Japan's unconditional surrender in 1945 as a watershed. Recently, scholars such as John Dower and Akira Iriye have questioned this periodization by pointing to continuities in both domestic and foreign affairs that span the years before and after the war. Opinions are divided on whether the militarism and expansionism of the early Shōwa period were fortuitous aberrations in the modernization process or whether they were a natural or inevitable heritage of the Meiji Restoration. A unifying theme for Shōwa Japan may well be the search of a dynamic nation, grappling with kaleidoscopic problems of modernity, to find not only national security and economic prosperity but a place in the world consonant with its own changing self-image.

Waning of "Taishō Democracy" (1926–1931). Repercussions of the world depression, aggravating political and social tensions within Japan, led to an erosion of what has been loosely called "Taishō Democracy," a phenomenon associated with the years from 1910 through the early 1920s, when political parties played an unprecedented role in government, when Marxism and various forms of avant-garde experimentation animated students and the intelligentsia, and when sections of the urban population (including women) tasted the ambivalent attractions of a secular, individualistic culture emanating from Europe and the United States. Suppression of communists in the late 1920s adumbrated growing state intervention in political dissidence. The Special Thought Police, operating within the framework of the Peace Preservation Law (passed in 1925), cooperated with other agencies in uncovering and cauterizing (by arrest if necessary) "dangerous thoughts." Centripetal forces gradually made themselves felt in economics and culture as a result of complex, contradictory developments: disillusionment with factionalism and venality in the political parties; indignation at big business, which seemed to flourish amid bankruptcies of small enterprises and (particularly in northern Japan) hardships among farmers; intolerance at perceived manifestations of "insincerity" or "Western decadence" in

society and in the arts. [*See also* Peace Preservation Law *and* Taishō Political Change.]

The international environment abetted the domestic malaise. Naval and patriotic circles chafed at the Washington treaties (1921–1922), which held Japan to inferior ratios of capital ships relative to the United States and Great Britain. The United States' Exclusion Act (1924), barring Japanese immigration, deeply wounded Japanese sensibilities. Japan's imperial possessions and economic interests on the Asian continent appeared to be threatened by a rising tide of Chinese and Korean nationalism, by subversive Comintern designs, and by Anglo-American reluctance to recognize Japan's "special interests" in China.

Tokyo's response to these challenges in the late 1920s fluctuated between unilateral action and gestures toward international accommodation. Some historians contrast the "active" policies of the Seiyūkai party's prime minister, General Tanaka Giichi (1863–1929), with the "accommodating" posture of the Minseitō party's foreign minister, Shidehara Kijūrō (1872–1951). Others maintain that "Tanaka diplomacy" and "Shidehara diplomacy" differed more in style than in substance, for both sought to expand Japan's position on the Asian mainland. [*See also* Tanaka Giichi *and* Shidehara Kijūrō.]

Toward the end of the 1920s, certain civilian nationalists and military officers (primarily from the middle ranks) grew increasingly impatient with the perceived irresoluteness of Japan's leaders. Patriotic societies multiplied and intensified their activities. Some espoused idealistic notions of domestic reform, inspired by the agrarian utopianism of Gondō Seikyō (1868–1937) or the state socialism of Kita Ikki (1883–1937). Others, following Ōkawa Shūmei (1886–1957), advocated overseas expansion. Most shared a rhetorical commitment to emperor worship and propounded Japan's messianic destiny.

Among staff officers of the Kwantung Army (created in 1905 to guard Japan's Kwantung leasehold on the Liaodong Peninsula of southern Manchuria), such impulses were translated into actions taken without formal consultation with military, not to mention civilian, authorities. The assassination of Manchurian warlord Zhang Zuolin (1873–1928) on 4 June 1928 foreshadowed further instances of *gekokujō* (literally, "lower overcoming upper"), in which field officers took unauthorized initiatives calculated to confront their superiors with a political or military *fait accompli*. Loss of control over and within the Imperial Army became both an initiation of and a diplomatic apology for Japanese expansion on the Asian continent during the early 1930s. [*See also* Kwantung Army *and* Zhang Zuolin.]

The "Dark Valley" (1931–1941). Plagued by political violence and regimentation at home and by international isolation resulting from aggression in China, Japan in the 1930s entered what has been called a "dark valley" *(kurai tanima)* of fateful developments that culminated in the events of 1945. Yet the decade also witnessed an economic recovery, undiminished vitality in the arts, and a greater degree of social cohesiveness, forged by an awareness (inculcated by schools and the media) that the national will was being tempered for the epochal task of East Asian reconstruction.

The Mukden Incident (18 September 1931), another example of *gekokujō* within the Kwantung Army, precipitated the Japanese occupation of Manchuria, where a puppet state called Manchukuo was established on 1 March 1932. The incident set in motion an escalating series of Sino-Japanese conflicts (e.g., in Shanghai and Inner Mongolia) that culminated in the outbreak of fighting near Beijing (Peking) at Marco Polo Bridge (7 July 1937), which quickly spread to become a general undeclared war. [*See also* Mukden Incident; Manchurian Incident; *and* Shanghai Incident.] Japan left the League of Nations following a near unanimous vote calling for Japan's withdrawal from Manchuria (23 February 1933). In the face of this isolation and growing friction with the United States and the Soviet Union, Tokyo associated itself with Germany (and subsequently with Italy) by signing the Anti-Comintern Pact (25 November 1936). Yet significant cooperation among the so-called fascist powers did not ensue. Despite a degree of pro-German sentiment within the army and the Foreign Ministry, Tokyo distrusted Berlin, and there was never extensive economic or strategic coordination between the two governments, especially after the Nazi-Soviet Nonaggression Pact (23 August 1939).

Political violence erupted inside Japan with such regularity from 1930 to 1936 that *New York Times* correspondent Hugh Byas wrote of "government by assassination." The murders of prime ministers Hamaguchi Osachi (1870–1931) and Inukai Tsuyoshi (1855–1932, leader of the last prewar cabinet), Finance Minister Inoue Junnosuke (1869–1932), and Mitsui chairman Dan Takuma (1858–1932) were committed by ultranationalists who regarded their victims as guilty of offenses against *kokutai* (national polity) through weakness, insincerity, and corruption.

Violence spread to within the Imperial Army, which in the early and middle 1930s was beset with tensions generated by factional struggles over strategy, training priorities (Japanese "spirit" versus "Western" mechanization), and the army's relationship to domestic socioeconomic reform. These tensions climaxed on 26 February 1936, when units of the Konoe Guards division mutinied and seized parts of Tokyo near the Imperial Palace. Leaders of the uprising were young officers influenced by the writings of Kita Ikki and sympathetic to General Araki Sadao (1877–1967), charismatic figure in the Kōdō ("imperial way") faction of the army and a fervent if opaque champion of Japanese spiritual values. The mutineers managed to kill the superintendent of military education and several members of the cabinet of Okada Keisuke (1868–1952), a retired admiral of moderate views. They failed, however, to attract support from the military or the imperial family. Within three days, the ringleaders had surrendered and their units had been disarmed. In a break with recent precedents, the authorities acted promptly and severely. A number of the officers and Kita Ikki were executed. [*See also* February Twenty-sixth Incident; Kita Ikki; Araki Sadao; *and* Okada Keisuke.]

The February Twenty-Sixth Incident lies at the heart of debates about Japan's slide into militarism and overseas aggression in the 1930s. Some historians call it a turning point—from "fascism from below" to "fascism from above." In this analysis, Army mainstream factions used suppression of the uprising as an opportunity to reestablish military discipline, to neutralize the Kōdō faction (with its links, however tenuous, to domestic reform), and to develop a program of national aggrandizement in coordination with the civil bureaucracy and big business. Other writers question the relevance of "fascism" to the Japanese experience. Still others express reservations about the explanatory force of the breakdown of central control *(gekokujō)* or the encroachment of military power on civilian governmental prerogatives as useful tools in understanding Japanese domestic and foreign policies in the 1930s. Some analysts, explicitly or implicitly adopting Marxist modes of analysis, explain the "dark valley" in terms of class relationships and economic forces. Some non-Marxists nonetheless see Japanese policies in the 1930s as the result of deep or structural causes, such as a broad consensus about vital national interests (security and autonomy) inherited directly from the Meiji leadership.

As the 1930s drew to a close, Japan, unable to obtain either a political settlement or a military victory in China, committed itself to increasingly ambitious foreign policy objectives, such as the desire of Prime Minister (Prince) Konoe Fumimaro (1891–1945) for the construction of a "new order" in East Asia (3 November 1938). The outbreak of war in Europe (1 September 1939) and German blitzkrieg successes in Scandinavia, the Low Countries, and France (April–June 1940) prompted Tokyo to seek a solution to the China impasse and to Japan's strategic vulnerability through southward expansion and closer association with the Axis powers. Pressure was put on Britain to close the Burma Road (a supply line to the Chinese Nationalists). With the agreement of Vichy authorities, the Imperial Army occupied northern Indochina (September 1940). Negotiations were begun with Dutch colonial authorities to grant Japan access to the petroleum-rich East Indies. Foreign Minister Matsuoka Yōsuke (1880–1946) sought to deter American intervention in Asia by concluding the Tripartite Pact with Germany and Italy (27 September 1940) and by signing the Neutrality Pact with the USSR (13 April 1941), which was effected despite Soviet-Japanese tensions resulting from border clashes around Manchukuo that culminated in pocket wars at Changgufeng (1938) and Nomonhan (1939). [*See also* Burma Road *and* Nomonhan, Battle of.]

These measures provoked a serious deterioration of relations with the United States during 1940 and 1941. The Roosevelt administration responded with a massive armaments program and economic sanctions: abrogation of the United States-Japan commercial treaty (26 July 1939), embargo on scrap metal exports to Japan (16 October 1940), and—in retaliation for the Imperial Army's occupation of southern Indochina in July 1941—the freezing of Japanese assets in the United States and a general embargo on all fuel exports to Japan. Great Britain and Holland joined the embargo against Japan.

During the summer of 1941 Prime Minister Konoe sought a diplomatic solution to the Japanese-American impasse, supporting negotiations in Washington that continued into the autumn. At the same time, however, Konoe accommodated the military, which prepared a timetable for war with the United States to be activated in the absence of a diplomatic solution. Konoe's relationship to the military was ambivalent, and the extent of his responsibility for Japan's hostilities against China and the United States has not been clearly established. Some see his creation (October 1940) of the Imperial Rule Assistance Association (Taisei Yokusankai), which absorbed many groups including the disbanded political parties, as an effort to restrain the Army. Oth-

ers call him a coordinator of Japan's quest for hegemony in Asia. [*See also* Konoe Fumimaro.]

Despite opportunities offered by Germany's invasion of the USSR (22 June 1941), Japan opted to move south rather than north in the summer of 1941, largely because of uncertainty about the Soviet-German conflict, respect for Soviet air and armored power gained during the border war at Nomonhan (1939), and a conviction that acquisition of Southeast Asia's natural resources would make the empire strategically invulnerable. As negotiations in Washington failed to break what Tokyo perceived as American-led economic strangulation of Japan, General Tōjō Hideki (1884–1948), who had succeeded Prince Konoe as prime minister in October, presided over final preparations for military action against "ABCD [American-British-Chinese-Dutch] encirclement." [*See also* Tōjō Hideki.]

Neither the army nor the navy gave careful thought to the consequences of a long war with antagonists whose collective human and material resources vastly exceeded those of Japan. A combination of interservice rivalry, faith in Japanese spirit, underestimation of American willpower, overestimation of Germany's war prospects, economic urgency (Japan was expending irreplaceable fuel stocks), and fatalism contributed to a series of decisions that culminated in the opening of hostilities on 8 December (Japan time).

Greater East Asia War (1941–1945). Tokyo's immediate war objective was to destroy Anglo-American-Dutch forces in Asia and the western Pacific and to seize Southeast Asia in preparation for exploiting its natural wealth. The Imperial Navy's surprise attack on Pearl Harbor, organized by Combined Fleet commander Yamamoto Isoroku (1884–1943), was designed to immobilize the United States Navy's Pacific Fleet long enough for Japan to consolidate its position in Southeast Asia and build an impenetrable perimeter through the central and southern Pacific. Long-term war aims were not clearly spelled out, but they involved a negotiated peace with an anticipated war-weary United States and the creation of a greater East Asia Co-Prosperity Sphere (Dai Tōa Kyōeiken), uniting under Japanese leadership an area stretching from India to Hawaii and from eastern Siberia to New Zealand into a self-sufficient, economically integrated community. [*See also* Pearl Harbor *and* Yamamoto Isoroku.]

From December 1941 until May 1942 imperial forces garnered stunning victories: a successful attack on the Pacific Fleet at Pearl Harbor; piecemeal destruction of the United States' Philippines-based Asiatic Fleet; the seizure of Hong Kong, Guam, Wake, Manila, Singapore, and Rangoon; and the capture, intact, of oil fields in the Dutch East Indies. By the summer of 1942, however, the tide had begun to turn against Japan as a result of overextension in the South Pacific; inadequate utilization of Southeast Asian resources; poor interservice cooperation; and an unexpectedly early American counteroffensive, which (with submarines) interdicted Japan's maritime supply lines and severely damaged the Imperial Navy's air forces (Battle of Midway, 5 June 1942). America's overwhelming material superiority became obvious in 1943, as its "island hopping" campaigns gathered momentum in New Guinea, the Solomons, the Gilberts, and the Aleutians. During 1944, despite Imperial Army offensives in China and Burma, the Americans invaded the Marshalls and Marianas, acquiring bases from which B-29 bombers made sorties over Japanese cities.

Despite desperate measures to compensate for material inferiority (including creation of the *tokkōtai,* or suicidal "special attack squadrons"), Japan's war effort by 1945 was approaching collapse. Nearly stripped of naval and air power, the empire's forces were isolated and unable to prevent enemy seizure of Iwo Jima (1 March) and Okinawa (21 June) or to halt the fire-bombing of Tokyo, Nagoya, Osaka and other major cities.

Military and diplomatic reverses underlay the fall of the Tōjō (18 July 1944) and Koiso (5 April 1945) cabinets, leaving Prime Minister Suzuki Kantarō (1867–1948) the difficult and delicate task of securing peace in the face of domestic diehards and Allied insistence on unconditional surrender (which put in doubt the future of the imperial institution). Tokyo's official disregard of the Potsdam Declaration of 26 July (outlining surrender terms for Japan) led to the dropping of atomic bombs on Hiroshima (6 August) and Nagasaki (9 August) and to Moscow's declaration of war (8 August), followed by a Soviet invasion of Manchuria, northern Korea, southern Sakhalin, and the Kurile Islands. On 14 August the Suzuki cabinet notified the Allies of its acceptance of the Potsdam Declaration, and on 15 August at noon Japan broadcast Emperor Hirohito's imperial rescript announcing the end of the war. [*See also* Suzuki Kantarō *and* World War II in Asia.]

Occupation (1945–1952). Officially an Allied undertaking, the Occupation was largely an American affair directed by Supreme Commander of the Allied Powers (SCAP) General Douglas MacArthur (1880–1964). Unlike that of occupied Germany, Japan's civil bureaucracy continued to function as a government, and the imperial institution was retained as an instrument serving American policy.

One of the Occupation's first priorities was to dismantle the Japanese empire and the ideology that supported it. Japan was stripped of its colonies and reduced to four main islands. The Imperial Army, Navy, and Special Thought Police were disbanded. Hirohito disavowed his divinity in a broadcast on New Year's Day, 1946. *Zaibatsu* (financial-industrial combines) were broken up. War crimes suspects, including General Tōjō, were arrested and put on trial.

Demilitarization and democratization were hallmarks of the reforms of the early Occupation period (1945–1947): release of political prisoners, encouragement of labor unions, a purge of "rightists," decentralization of educational administration, textbook revision, broadening of the electorate, support of women's rights, land reform, and the promulgation of a new constitution (3 May 1947) confirming popular sovereignty and renouncing the right to make war and maintain armed forces (Article 9).

In 1947–1948, the spread of the cold war to Asia propelled a shift in SCAP policies in the direction of economic reconstruction, political stabilization, and anticommunism. Some Americans began to favor limited Japanese rearmament. The Korean War (1950–1953) accelerated this reorientation.

The San Francisco Peace Treaty (8 September 1951) signaled Japan's partial (it was not signed by the Soviet Union, the People's Republic of China, the Republic of China, India, or others) return to the community of nations. In signing the treaty, Prime Minister Yoshida Shigeru (1878–1967), Japan's most influential postwar statesman, chose to pursue his country's interests within the framework of measured association with United States strategy in Asia. In exchange for American guarantees of Japan's security, Yoshida acquiesced to American bases in Japan, American administration of Okinawa and the Ogasawara Islands (returned to Japan in 1972 and 1968, respectively), recognition of the Nationalists in Taiwan as the government of China, and renunciation (with no beneficiary) of Japan's claims to southern Sakhalin and the Kurile Islands. [*See also* Occupation of Japan; San Francisco Treaty; MacArthur, Douglas A.; *and* Yoshida Shigeru.]

Reemergence As a World Power. The latter half of the Shōwa period has witnessed Japan's remarkable emergence as a world economic power and, less dramatically, Japan's increasingly active role in international relations. In the 1950s Tokyo established diplomatic ties with most noncommunist Asian nations and with the Soviet Union and its satellites, and entered the United Nations. Relations were normalized with the Republic of Korea only in 1965 and with the People's Republic of China in 1972 (a peace treaty being concluded in 1978). No peace treaty, however, has been signed with the Soviet Union because of an impasse over Japan's claims to the "northern territories," a group of islands at the southern end of the Kurile archipelago occupied by Soviet forces in 1945. [See Kurile Islands.]

Limited association with American Asian strategy coupled with a policy of *seikei bunri* (separation of politics from economics) enabled Japan during the 1960s and early 1970s to promote trade and investment without direct involvement in international rivalries or heavy defense expenditures. Japan's posture during this time contributed to the awarding of the Nobel Peace Prize to former prime minister Satō Eisaku (1901–1975) in 1974. However, the 1973 Arab oil shock, upheaval in Iran, and chronic crises in the Middle East, by exposing Japan's heavy dependence upon imported sources of energy, have revealed the fragility of its prosperity. Moreover, Japan has come under increasing pressure from Washington to cooperate with American global strategy and to assume greater responsibility for its own security. This pressure is not unrelated to growing protectionist sentiment in Europe and the United States regarding trade with Japan.

With a brief exception in 1947, a conservative party "dynasty" has dominated postwar Japanese politics; despite internal factionalism it has preserved its preeminence against a vociferous but divided opposition. Relatively low rates of unemployment and inflation have not, however, exempted Japan's political leaders from criticism for environmental pollution, problems associated with a high population density, and political corruption.

In the late Shōwa period, Japanese culture and aesthetic values enjoy unprecedented respect and influence throughout the world. Writers such as Kawabata Yasunari (1899–1972, a Nobel laureate in 1968) have given Shōwa literature international standing. At the same time, more and more Japanese are searching for the roots of their own cultural identity.

Japan is also searching for its identity in an international context, for a role consonant with its economic power, with constraints imposed by memories of the past and pressures emanating from a divided world. Interest in a greater Pacific community of nations reveals parallels with prewar idealism about East Asian reconstruction, and as such suggests that as the Shōwa period draws to a close its apparent contradictions may turn out to have an underlying unity.

[*See also* Hirohito.]

Gordon Mark Berger, *Parties Out of Power in Japan, 1931–1941* (1977). James B. Crowley, *Japan's Quest for Autonomy: National Security and Foreign Policy, 1930–1938* (1966). J. W. Dower, *Empire and Aftermath: Yoshida Shigeru and the Japanese Experience, 1878–1967* (1979). Akira Iriye, *Power and Culture: The Japanese-American War, 1941–1945* (1981). Masataka Kosaka, *A History of Postwar Japan* (1982). Mark R. Peattie, *Ishiwara Kanji and Japan's Confrontation with the West* (1975). Ben Ami Shillony, *Politics and Culture in Wartime Japan* (1981). J. A. A. Stockwin, *Japan: Divided Politics in a Growth Economy* (1975). Richard Storry, *A History of Modern Japan* (rev. ed., 1982).   JOHN J. STEPHAN

SHŌYA, one of the titles (another being *nanushi*) of the office of village headman in Japan during the Tokugawa period (1600–1868). Such officials, villagers themselves, had two different kinds of responsibility. On the one hand they represented the local feudal authority (shogun, daimyo, or samurai fiefholder) and in this capacity performed a variety of functions: collecting taxes from their fellow villagers, transmitting official instructions, and helping maintain law and order. On the other hand, and no less important, a *shōya* also represented his village, making its wishes known to the overlord when appropriate (and sometimes even when not), negotiating contentious issues with neighboring villages, and, within his own community, witnessing agreements and adjudicating disputes. In return for these services, a *shōya* received compensation—tax concessions, or sometimes rice or money—not from his overlord, but from his fellow villagers.

Selection of *shōya*, as with so much in Tokugawa Japan, was subject to considerable local variation. In some areas, they were simply chosen by the local feudal authority. In others they were elected at a meeting in which villagers or their representatives were allowed to participate, on the assumption that the decision would subsequently be ratified by the overlord. Appointments were sometimes for life; indeed, there were examples of villages where particular families were able to monopolize the position generation after generation. Elsewhere a group of leading villagers might rotate the office among themselves at regular intervals. Where *shōya* were elected by their fellow villagers (or a limited section of them), there was more possibility of varied representation, but it was always likely that the post would go to one of the richer families in the village. For this reason *shōya* were seldom entirely free of the suspicion of their poorer fellows, who not infrequently made them the subject of complaint and, particularly in the latter part of the Tokugawa period, the object of communal violence.

[*See also* Tokugawa Period.]

HAROLD BOLITHO

SHUDDHI is a Sanskrit term meaning purity, correctness, or purification. Swami Dayananda Saraswati introduced it in its present use in modern India as a term for a special purification ritual. Members of the Arya Samaj employed it to reconvert Hindus lost through conversion. Individual *shuddhis* were performed in the 1880s, and by the mid-1890s Aryas began group purifications. They also purified Untouchables through *shuddhi*, transforming them into clean-caste Hindus. During the 1920s the Arya Samaj organized *shuddhi* campaigns in Kerala to readmit Hindus converted during the Moplah uprising and in the North to reconvert the Malkana Rajputs from Islam. *Shuddhi* contributed to Hinduism a set of conversion rituals that can apply to anyone regardless of religious background.

[*See also* Untouchability *and* Arya Samaj.]

Kenneth W. Jones, *Arya Dharm: Hindu Consciousness in Nineteenth-Century Punjab* (1976). G. R. Thursby, *Hindu-Muslim Relations in British India: A Study of Controversy, Conflict and Communal Movements in Northern India, 1923–28* (1975).   KENNETH W. JONES

SHUDRA, lowest ranking of the four traditional Hindu *varna* categories outlined in ancient texts and continued in modern usage as components of an inexact pan-Indian hierarchy of interdependent groups. In myth, the *shudras* arose from the feet of primordial man and were charged with the duty of providing economic support for society. *Shudras* are considered ritually less pure than members of the upper three *varnas* (*brahmana, kshatriya,* and *vaishya*), and many may be descendants of indigenous peoples conquered by Aryan invaders of the subcontinent. Traditionally, *shudras* as well as Untouchables, who rank beneath *shudras*, were denied knowledge of sacred Hindu texts.

Included within the *shudra* category are many diverse groups of cultivators, carpenters, blacksmiths, barbers, potters, and the like. In South India, where few castes are unquestionably accepted as *kshatriya* or *vaishya,* many prominent martial, landowning, and trading groups, such as Nairs and Chettiars, are classed as *shudras*.

[*See also* Untouchability *and* Caste.]

Pauline Kolenda, *Caste in Contemporary India: Beyond Organic Solidarity* (1978). David G. Mandelbaum, *Society in India* (1970).   DORANNE JACOBSON

SHUGO, provincial officials appointed by the Kamakura and Muromachi shogunates of Japan. The term is often rendered in English as "constable" or "military governor," but "count" may do greater justice to the variety of nuances that *shugo* bore during the Kamakura and Muromachi periods.

Traditional accounts maintain that Minamoto Yoritomo established a nationwide network of *shugo* in 1185, but it is now suspected that *shugo* were not widely appointed until the 1190s. In any case, it is clear that the Kamakura period *shugo* had a fairly narrow range of functions. First, he was the commandant of the shogunal vassals (*gokenin*) living in his province, and was thus obliged to compile registers of all such men, to mobilize them for guard service in Kyoto, and occasionally to lead them in combat. Second, he bore at least some responsibility for criminal justice, although this duty might be severely circumscribed by the presence of immune estates within his province.

The *shugo* also performed a variety of other tasks on occasion, but he was normally not very powerful. This is particularly evident from the fact that *shugo* were explicitly forbidden to usurp the authority of the old civil provincial government, and were also prevented from assuming personal lordship of the shogun's vassals.

All this changed during the lengthy civil war that followed upon Ashikaga Takauji's creation of the Muromachi shogunate in the 1330s. Warfare was so widespread that the new shogunate had no choice but to allow individual *shugo* enormous powers of recruitment. In particular, *shugo* were permitted to make grants and confirmations of land title to whatever men would join their armies. The difficulty was that while grants of land were a powerful inducement to service, the fact that it was the *shugo* who made the grants allowed him to interpose himself between the shogun and men who, during the Kamakura period, would have been the shogun's own vassals. In addition, the civil war of 1336–1392 resulted in the almost total collapse of the old civil government. While this left the Muromachi shoguns as de facto rulers of the country, their regime lacked the capacity to administer the provinces directly. The shoguns had little choice, therefore, but to allow the *shugo* to assume most of the functions of provincial governance.

While the process of *shugo* aggrandizement was not without its reverses, by the second quarter of the fifteenth century the various *shugo* had become hereditary barons of such power that they could occasionally dictate shogunal policy. As it turned out, however, the *shugo* were themselves so closely tied to the shogunal order that few *shugo* dynasties survived the effective collapse of shogunal authority as the fifteenth century ended.

Peter J. Arnesen, *The Medieval Japanese Daimyo* (1979). John W. Hall, *Government and Local Power in Japan, 500–1700* (1966). Jeffrey P. Mass, *Warrior Government in Early Medieval Japan* (1974).

PETER J. ARNESEN

SHUJA UD-DAULAH (1732–1775), third nawab, or ruler, of Awadh (Oudh), India, from 1754 until his death. One of the most capable statesmen of eighteenth-century India, he made his realm into the major indigenous power in North India, fighting the British almost to a standstill at Baksar in 1764. Realizing his value as an ally, the East India Company reinstated him in 1765, and for the next decade a process of mutual testing and political experimentation occurred. Under the subsidiary alliance system, in which he paid for the use of British-officered troops, the way was opened for increasing company intervention during subsequent reigns. Shuja nonetheless modernized his army during this period, closed Awadh to the disruptive effects of European trade, secured the treasury in the custody of his chief wife Bahu Begam, and made large annexations in lands on his western borders.

[*See also* Awadh *and* Baksar, Battle of.]

A. L. Srivastava, *Shuja-ud-daulah*, vol. 1, *1754–1765* (1939); vol. 2, *1765–1775* (1945). R. B. Barnett, *North India between Empires* (1980). RICHARD B. BARNETT

SHU MAUNG, THAKIN. *See* Ne Win.

SHUNGA DYNASTY. The Shunga dynasty was founded by the brahman army chief Pushyamitra, who overthrew the Mauryas in 184 BCE and ruled most of the northern and central parts of India. He succeeded in warding off the attack of the Indo-

Greeks in the Ganges Valley. According to the Puranas, the dynasty included ten kings, who ruled for a total of 112 years; Pushyamitra's reign was for 36 years. Although the Shungas revived the Vedic ritual of sacrifice and restored Brahmanical preeminence, Buddhist activities and monuments continued to flourish during this time.

[*See also* Maurya Empire.]

K. A. Nilakanta Sastri, ed. *A Comprehensive History of India*, vol. 2 (1957). A. K. NARAIN

SHUSTER, WILLIAM MORGAN (1877–1961), American lawyer hired by the government of Iran to serve as treasurer-general in 1911. Shuster had earned a reputation as an astute fiscal administrator on account of his financial work for the United States civil governments in Cuba and the Philippines from 1898 to 1908. He was among several American advisers with whom the Iranian government contracted for services after the Majles (parliament) had approved the hiring of American advisors as a counter to the influence of British and Russian officials. During his seven-month tenure, Shuster was in constant conflict with representatives of tsarist Russia who resented his attempts to keep Iran's tax revenues free of foreign interference. The Russian government, with the support of the British government, finally issued an ultimatum to Iran demanding Shuster's dismissal, and in December 1911 the Majles reluctantly complied. After departing Iran, Shuster wrote *The Strangling of Persia* (1912), which Iranian nationalists regard as a classic study of the impact of European imperialist policies upon their country.

[*See also* Constitutional Revolution.]

Robert McDaniel, *The Shuster Mission and the Persian Constitutional Revolution* (1974). William M. Shuster, *The Strangling of Persia* (1912). ERIC HOOGLUND

SHWEDAGON PAGODA. The Shwedagon Pagoda has grown in size and importance over the passing centuries as a revered Buddhist *chedi* to become a symbolic center of Burmese national identity. Rising 326 feet from a prominent hill in the capital of Rangoon, the gold-covered monument in honor of the Buddha is a source of deep Burmese pride.

Its history includes an account of how supranormal events accompanied the enshrining of eight hairs of the Buddha during his lifetime. Rebuilt and elaborated after numerous earthquakes and enlarged by

FIGURE 1. *Shwedagon Pagoda, Rangoon.* Lesser shrines surrounding the stupa.

many merit-seeking kings and queens, the *chedi* reached its full height during the reign of King Hsinhpyushin in 1774. After the British conquered Lower Burma, King Mindon made the replacement of its sacred umbrella at the top a gesture of his concern for lost national unity. Still later, as political power eventually shifted from northern to southern Burma, twentieth-century nationalist movements protesting British rule and seeking independence used the Shwedagon as a rallying point for national consciousness. Once ransacked for treasure by British troops billeted there, the Shwedagon is now an inviolable, stately, and sacred national shrine honored by the Burmese as well as pilgrims from the international community.   JOHN P. FERGUSON

SIAM. *See* Thailand.

SIANG KHWANG (Xieng Khouang, Xiangkhoang), ancient principality of northeastern Laos, center of the Plain of Jars.

Although at the center of a prehistoric culture that left monumental stone "jars" strewn across the Plain

of Jars, Siang Khwang's written history begins with the arrival of Tai peoples in the area, perhaps in the seventh century CE. Lao legend includes Siang Khwang among those places ruled by the sons of the first Lao ruler, Khun Borom. Throughout the many centuries that followed, Siang Khwang was never more than a regional center, though it had separate, local traditions and history. The list of its early rulers is much like a similar list from Luang Prabang. The city was an early conquest of Fa Ngum as he sought to unite the first Lao kingdom, Lan Sang, and its history thereafter is closely linked with that of Lan Sang. Lao kings regularly looked to Siang Khwang for men for their armies, as did dissident claimants of the Lao throne; when forced by invading armies to flee their capital, Lao kings often fled to Siang Khwang, as Anu did in 1827. The strategic position of the state contributed to its importance in the eyes of the capital, as it controlled an important transit route to the coast of Vietnam at Vinh. Its rulers have proudly maintained their local traditions and history down almost to the present, but their independence (and, indeed, their existence) has been snuffed out since 1975.

[*See also* Laos; Khun Borom; Fa Ngum; Lan Sang; Luang Prabang; Tai Peoples; *and* Anu.]

DAVID K. WYATT

SIBERIA covers roughly one-third of the surface area of Asia but is home to only a minute fraction of Asia's population. The cultures of its inhabitants are largely homogeneous and thus contrast with the dramatic diversity of cultures in the rest of Asia. Siberia stretches from Kamchatka Peninsula, the Maritime Territory of the Russian SFSR, and the Chukchi Peninsula in the east, along the Arctic Ocean in the north, to the Ural Mountains in the west. It merges into the Asian heartland in the south through the basins of the Ob, Irtysh, Yenisei, and Lena rivers (going from west to east), the Lake Baikal area, and the mountain ranges of eastern Siberia.

It is also in the south that Siberia shares the steppe zone with Central Asia. The northern fringe of this steppe gradually becomes the typical Siberian taiga, an almost impenetrably thick forest belt, extremely rich in fauna, ranging in width from 600 to 1,500 miles. As the climate changes going farther north, the taiga turns into the tundra, a flat area hospitable mostly to lichens and mosses. Siberia's climate can range from $-92°F$ to $+90°F$. The weather is more clement in the south; thus, most of the more recent immigrants have settled there. With these new immigrants have come the introduction of agriculture. The traditional occupations of the native population have been, and to some extent still are, hunting for game and fur, fishing, and reindeer breeding.

There are about forty languages (and therefore ethnic groups) in Siberia. The Tunguz languages, the most prominent of which is Manchu (the language of the original Qing rulers of China), are spoken from northeasternmost Siberia westward as far as the Yenisei River. Manchu and Jurchen (an extinct Tunguz language) are written languages. The other Tunguz languages only acquired writing systems during the twentieth century. The only Mongol language of Siberia is Buriat. The best-known Siberian Turkic languages are Yakut (with more than 300,000 speakers), Khakas, Altai, Shor, and Siberian Tatar. All of these are closely related to each other as well as to the many other Turkic languages of Eurasia and to the language of the Orkhon Inscriptions. Many scholars believe that the Turkic, Mongol, and Tunguz groups are related; these they designate the Altaic language family.

The Uralic family is represented in Siberia only by the four living Samoyed languages (the best known of which is Nenets or Yurak-Samoyed, spoken east of the Ob River and on the Taimyr Peninsula) and the two Ob-Ugric languages, Khanty and Mansi (Ostiak and Vogul), which, as a pair, are most closely related to Hungarian. It is generally believed that Hungarian split off from the other two some two thousand years ago.

The four remaining linguistic units are classified as Paleo-Siberian because they are thought to be vestiges of earlier languages spoken by populations that were spread over much wider areas. They are the Luorawetlan family (Chukchi, Koriak, and Kamchadal) along the far northeastern coast facing Alaska, Yukagir along the Lena River, Giliak in the Amur Basin and on Sakhalin Island, and Ket (or Yenisei-Ostiak) in the Turukhansk Region.

[*See also* Ainu; Huns; Jurchen; Language Families; Manchu Language; Manchus; Mongols; *and* Orkhon Inscriptions.]

ROBERT AUSTERLITZ

SICHUAN, province in southwest China with an area of 569,000 square kilometers. The province consists of two parts: the rugged and sparsely populated Khams Plateau to the west and the fertile and densely populated Red Basin in the east. The Yangtze River flows through the province. Sichuan's population in 1983 was 99.7 million. The Han Chinese, who make up about 96 percent of the population, live primarily in the Red Basin. The ethnic minorities, of whom the Yi, Tibetans, Qiang, and Miao are the most numerous, live in the western and southwestern parts of Sichuan.

Because of the diversity of climate and terrain, Sichuan produces a wide variety of crops. Terraced hills characterize the eastern part of the Red Basin. Sichuan leads China in agricultural production. Unlike the rest of China, the rural population of Sichuan is typically dispersed rather than concentrated in villages. The major cities of the province are Chongqing, Chengdu (the provincial capital), Luzhou, Yibin, and Zigong.

Sichuan has been a part of China for more than two thousand years. The ancient kingdoms of Shu and Ba, centered on the Chengdu plain and Chongqing area, respectively, were conquered by Qin in 316 BCE. During the Han dynasty (206 BCE–220 CE) the productivity of the Chengdu plain, the development of trade, and large-scale mining made Sichuan one of the richest regions in China. In the centuries that followed Sichuan often was the seat of regional governments during periods of disunity.

During the Three Kingdoms era, for example, Sichuan constituted the state of Shu (221–264).

The twenty-year Mongol conquest devastated the province in the thirteenth century. A separate regime was established in Sichuan by Zhang Xianzhong at the end of the Ming (1368–1644). Zhang's brutalities, coupled with the depradations of Ming and Qing armies and the destruction of crops, nearly depopulated the province. During the Qing dynasty (1644–1911) Sichuan was resettled by immigrants, mostly from Hubei, Hunan, and Guangdong. Social pressures and millenarian sects sparked the White Lotus Rebellion (1796–1805) in Sichuan and neighboring provinces.

During World War II the Japanese invasion forced the Nationalist government to relocate in Chongqing, and refugees came to Sichuan in large numbers. Since World War II Sichuan has become a major industrial area.

Cheng Te-k'un, *An Early History of Szechwan* (1945). Robert A. Kapp, *Szechwan and the Chinese Republic: Provincial Militarism and Central Power, 1911–1938* (1973). Sun Ching-chih, *Economic Geography of Southwest China* (1962).   ROBERT ENTENMANN

SIDDHARTHA GAUTAMA. See Buddhism: An Overview.

SIDOTTI, GIOVANNI BATTISTA (1668–1715), Italian priest, born in Palermo (Sicily); the last missionary in Tokugawa Japan after the closing of the country through the Expulsion Edict of 1639. In 1703, Sidotti embarked in Genoa with Monsignor Charles Thomas de Tournon, who went to China to promulgate the papal decree on the Rites Controversy. Sidotti learned Japanese in Manila before landing secretly in 1708 at Yakushima, near Ōsumi (in Kagoshima, Kyushu). He was arrested at once and taken first to Nagasaki, then to Edo's prison for Christians, where he died.

Sidotti was interrogated by Arai Hakuseki, Confucian scholar and shogunal adviser. During his long inquiries about Christianity, history, geography, and astronomy, Hakuseki developed respect for Sidotti's determination and factual knowledge (and intervened against his execution). Hakuseki worked this new knowledge into the first works of *rangaku* ("Dutch learning"), his *Sairan igen (Lexicography of Foreign Place Names)* and *Seiyō kibun (Notes on the Western Ocean)*, in which he also chronicles his interviews with Sidotti. Sidotti maintained that he

was (like de Tournon) on a diplomatic mission to explore the Japanese situation with the hope of once again opening Japan to Christianity, as had occurred in recent years in China (1669) and Siam.

[*See also* Christianity: Christianity in Japan.]

HERMAN OOMS

SIEBOLD, PHILIPP FRANZ VON (1796–1866), one of a handful of residents of the Dutch trading station on the island of Deshima in Nagasaki harbor. Siebold provided the West with its best accounts of Japan during the period of self-imposed isolation (1639–1854). Siebold was born 17 February 1796 in Wurzburg, Germany. After obtaining a medical degree in 1820, he entered Dutch government service. He was appointed physician to the Dutch factory in Japan and arrived on Deshima in August 1823.

Siebold became the first foreign resident permitted to leave the confines of Deshima to treat patients in Nagasaki and to lecture at his own school in the suburbs. In return for his services he encouraged contributions to his collection of Japanese scientific specimens and cultural artifacts. His avid curiosity about Japan was, however, both his greatest asset and the cause of his undoing. In 1829 he was banished from Japan for life for possessing forbidden information.

Siebold spent the next thirty years in Europe writing, advising governments on Japanese affairs, and overseeing his collection. The Siebold collection, consisting of some five thousand items from Japan, was purchased by the Dutch government in 1837 and became the foundation of the National Ethnology Museum at Leiden.

Following the repeal of his banishment in 1857, Siebold returned to Japan and from 1859 to 1862 was active in trade negotiations and diplomacy. Ill-suited to these tasks, he returned to Europe and died in Munich in 1866.

[*See also* Deshima; Rangaku; *and* Seclusion.]

John Z. Bowers, *Western Medical Pioneers in Feudal Japan* (1970). Richard Rubinger, *Private Academies of Tokugawa Japan* (1982). Philipp Franz von Siebold, *Manners and Customs of the Japanese* (1973).

RICHARD RUBINGER

SIEM REAP, city in northwestern Cambodia near the ruins of Angkor and Tonle Sap, or the Great Lake. The name of the town, which means "Siam

defeat," probably commemorates a battle in the sixteenth century. In 1794 the surrounding province, including the temples of Angkor, was placed under Thai administration. This lasted until 1907 and resumed in 1941–1946. Under the French and in the early years of Cambodian independence, Siem Reap was an important tourist center. The town has often been the scene of savage fighting during the civil wars that have plagued Cambodia since 1970.

DAVID P. CHANDLER

SIGIRIYA, an architectural *tour de force* in Sri Lanka constructed by the parricide Kassapa (473–491), who imaginatively converted a solitary sheer monolith of granite rising five hundred feet from the plains into an elegant palace surrounded by superbly designed ornamental gardens. It served as the capital during his brief reign.

Sigiriya is remembered today for its exquisite frescoes in a rock pocket some forty feet above the access pathway. The identity of these female figures has always been a matter of debate among scholars. These paintings are the earliest surviving specimens of the pictorial art in Sri Lanka that can be dated: they are approximately the same age as those of Ajanta in India, with which they bear comparison.

[*See also* Ajanta *and* Sri Lanka.]

K. M. de Silva, *A History of Sri Lanka* (1981).

K. M. DE SILVA

SIHANOUK. *See* Norodom Sihanouk.

SIJO, the most popular, elastic, and mnemonic classical Korean poetic form, which dates from the fifteenth century. The *sijo* is a three-line poem, each line consisting of four rhythmic groups, a minor pause occurring at the end of the second and a major one at the end of the fourth. An emphatic syntactic division is usually introduced in the third line, often in the form of an exclamation, presenting a leap in logic and development. Some interjections postulate a dialogue, attesting to the poet's openness to the world and his ability to ask. With a total of about forty-five syllables, the *sijo* is longer than the Japanese *waka* (thirty-one syllables) and the Chinese penta- and heptasyllabic *jueju* ("broken-off lines").

A useful example for analysis is the fourth poem in the spring cycle from Yun Sŏn-do's *The Angler's*

Calendar, written in the year 1651. (In translation I have used a six-line stanza.)

> Is it a cuckoo that cries?
> Is it the willow that is blue?
> Several roofs in a far fishing village
> Swim in the mist, magnificent.
> Boy, fetch an old net!
> Fish are climbing against the stream.

The poem opens with two questions that suggest uncertainty of the senses of hearing and sight. In the next two lines the narrator sees something, but it is far away, dim, unsteady in the mist. The last two lines are brief, forceful, and speak of a practical and immediate connection with nature. The poem thus presents nature's mystery, beauty, and bounty in terms of illusory loveliness, real visual loveliness, and life-sustaining matter-of-factness in the form of food from the stream. The poem not only suggests the felt transcendence of the vision but also reveals a consciousness of the transience of earthly joy and beauty.

The *sijo* was sung and orally transmitted until the texts were written down about the beginning of the eighteenth century. The recent variorum edition contains 3,335 poems, but more examples are being unearthed. In addition to the standard form described above, there are two variant forms. It is an oral art even today for both the lettered and unlettered, and modern examples, like modern *haiku* in Japan, are written in free-verse style exceeding three lines.

Peter H. Lee, *Celebration of Continuity* (1979) and *Anthology of Korean Literature: From Early Times to the Nineteenth Century* (1981).   PETER H. LEE

SIKANDAR HAYAT KHAN. *See* Khan, Sir Sikandar Hayat.

SIKHISM. The Sikh community originated with the teachings of Nanak (1469–1539) and in the group of disciples whom he attracted. Nanak was a Punjabi, and it was in the Punjab that his followers, known thereafter as Sikhs ("learners, disciples"), gathered. The message that he preached was the doctrine of freedom from transmigration by means of *nam simran* (meditation on the divine name of God). Mistakenly regarded as a syncretic mixture of Hindu and Muslim ideals, the teachings of Nanak are more accurately associated with the devotional Sant tradition of northern India. Like the other Sants (such as Kabir and Namdev), Nanak put forth his message in simple hymns of great beauty.

Nanak was known to his followers as guru ("preceptor"), and the successors who formed his spiritual lineage received the same title. The lineage comprised ten gurus, extending over two centuries and concluding with the death of Guru Gobind Singh in 1708. During the period of the third guru, Amar Das, the expanding Sikh community, known as the Panth, was organized more effectively with the introduction of a system of overseeing the community's religious and social life. The fourth guru, Ram Das, established the holy city of Amritsar, in which his son Guru Arjan compiled the sacred scripture known as the *Adi Granth*. This substantial collection includes the compositions of the first five gurus supplemented by the works of Kabir and other Sants. The temple erected to house the new scripture was the Harimandir Sahib, eventually to become known simply as the Harimandir, the celebrated Golden Temple.

The period of Guru Arjan's leadership was particularly important for several reasons. The office of guru, now established within the family of the fourth guru, was disputed by rival claimants. From outside the community, the growing Panth was attracting unsympathetic attention from the Mughal authorities in Lahore. Guru Arjan died in Mughal custody and mutual hostility thereafter became endemic. The sixth guru, Hargobind, is traditionally believed to have armed his Sikhs and to have built the majestic Akal Takht (adjacent to the Harimandir Sahib) as a symbol of the Panth's involvement in worldly affairs. The lengthy incumbency of the seventh guru was peaceful, but Mughal hostility revived under Aurangzeb and eventually led to the execution of the eighth guru, Tegh Bahadur, in 1675.

This execution significantly strengthened the tradition of martyrdom within the Panth and contributed directly to the climactic event in Sikh history, the founding of the Khalsa order in 1699, a decision by Guru Gobind Singh that conferred on the Panth a clear identity and a specific discipline. All who accepted initiation into the Khalsa vowed to observe thereafter a pattern of belief and conduct that combined traditional piety with loyalty to a militant ideal. Sikhs of the Khalsa were to adopt distinctive emblems (the "five *k*s," including uncut hair, a comb, a steel bangle, a sword or dagger, and military-style breeches). They were to be unshakable in their loyalty to the guru and resolute in the defense of righteousness. The numerous regulations that together make up their Khalsa duty are known as

the Rahit, subsequently recorded in documents called Rahitnamas.

Fierce conflict between the Sikhs and the Mughals followed soon after the founding of the Khalsa, initiating a pattern which was to characterize much of the eighteenth century. The enemy was to change, with Afghan succeeding Mughal as chief opponent, and later still the Sikhs were to engage in internecine warfare as the various chieftains sought to establish their authority in the Punjab. It was, however, a consistent pattern in that it involved a frequent recourse to arms and progressively strengthened the martial traditions of the Panth. The eighteenth century has ever since been perceived as a time of struggle, heroism, martyrdom, and ultimately triumph. The tradition is conspicuously expressed in popular views of Baba Dip Singh, slain in an attempt to evict Muslim invaders from the Harimandir Sahib.

Meanwhile other important developments had been taking place within the Panth. With the death of Guru Gobind Singh the line of personal gurus came to an end. The guru's authority passed thereafter to the sacred scripture (the *Guru Granth*) and to the corporate community (the Guru Panth). The words recorded in the *Adi Granth* have ever since been accorded the full weight of that authority and as such are binding to all Sikhs. Corporate decisions have proved virtually impossible to secure under modern conditions, but during the struggles of the eighteenth century, formal resolutions of the Khalsa Panth carried the sanction of the guru's authority.

From the struggles of the eighteenth century there eventually emerged an acknowledged victor. This was Ranjit Singh, ruler of the Punjab from the turn of the century until his death in 1839. Traditionally viewed as a supreme exemplar of the Khalsa ideal, Ranjit Singh remains a particularly popular folk hero. His death, however, was followed by a rapid decline into chaos, by two wars against the British, and by the British annexation of the Punjab in 1849. To the new rulers it seemed that the Khalsa tradition was undergoing rapid decay and that the Panth soon had to "merge back into Hinduism."

Any such process was arrested and reversed during the late nineteenth and early twentieth century. The British themselves contributed to the change by enlisting Sikhs and favoring Khalsa observance in the Indian Army. Much more influential, however, was the Singh Sabha movement. Led by intellectuals and supported by some prominent members of the Sikh aristocracy, this movement summoned Sikhs to a renewed loyalty. Through literature, journalism, education, and preaching, its exponents stressed loyalty to the gurus and to the Rahit, emphasizing the unique nature of Sikhism and the distinct identity of its adherents.

From World War I onward the elitist Singh Sabha was progressively overtaken by political activists, known as the Akali movement, and by advocates of armed insurrection, known as the Ghadr Party. Proponents of the Akali movement set their sights on securing control of the Punjab's principal *gurdwaras* (Sikh temples). Initially the British authorities upheld the claims of the hereditary incumbents who had controlled the gurdwaras for several generations, but these claims soon gave way. In 1925 the gurdwaras, with their substantial assets and patronage, were entrusted to the Shiromani Gurdwara Parbandhak Committee (SGPC). Elected at regular intervals by registered adult Sikhs, this body still retains its authority and as such exercises a major influence in Sikh affairs.

Indian politics have continued to play a primary role in Sikh affairs to the present day, the principal contenders being the Akali Party (almost exclusively Sikh) and the Congress Party. Neither can be clearly or consistently defined in terms of its policies toward Sikh affairs, although the latter has obviously been constrained by larger all-India interests. Questions of Sikh identity have continued to jostle with economic concerns. The boundary between the two major parties has normally been blurred, with abundant scope for movement across party lines. In the recent past, however, the division has become much more distinct, leading eventually to open conflict and to the Indian Army's assault on the Golden Temple complex in June 1984.

A recurrent issue raised by these troubles is the question of precisely who is a Sikh. A strict view includes only those men and women who undergo Khalsa initiation *(amrit sanskar)* and obey the precepts of the Rahit. A more relaxed view extends the Panth's boundaries to embrace the so-called Sahajdhari Sikhs (those who affirm reverence for the gurus but who neither enter the Khalsa nor observe the Rahit in its full rigor). Amrit-dhari and Sahajdhari unite in their devout reverence for the gurus, for the sacred scripture, and for the *gurdwara*. Although *gurdwaras* have been extensively used for political activity they retain their sanctity as repositories of the sacred scripture and as visible expressions of the Sikh ideal of service.

One feature of the Panth that sometimes attracts comment is the persistence of caste within it. Although the gurus denounced caste distinctions, the institution is still generally observed by their followers. It is, however, observed in a significantly diminished form. A majority of Sikhs belong to the rural Jat caste.

The numerical dominance of Jats within the Panth helps to explain other features of the contemporary community. Jats have been conspicuous participants in agrarian development and contribute significantly to the Sikhs' reputation for economic enterprise. Their commitment to the martial traditions of the Panth also serves to nourish and sustain this feature of the Sikh inheritance. Although the total Sikh population is impossible to compute accurately it is probably close to fifteen million worldwide. A substantial majority (9.4 million) of Sikhs still live in the Punjab, where they constitute 52 percent of the state's total population. Significant numbers have migrated to other countries, particularly to England and North America.

[*See also* Nanak; Singh, Ranjit; *and* Punjab.]

W. O. Cole and Piara Singh Sambhi, *The Sikhs: Their Religious Beliefs and Practices* (1978). J. S. Grewel, *From Guru Nanak to Maharaja Ranjit Singh* (1982). Harbans Singh, *The Heritage of the Sikhs* (1983). Khushwant Singh, *A History of the Sikhs,* 2 vols. (1963, 1966). M. A. Macauliffe, *The Sikh Religion,* 6 vols. (1909). W. H. McLeod, *The Evolution of the Sikh Community* (1975), *Guru Nanak and the Sikh Religion* (1976), and *Textual Sources for the Study of Sikhism* (1984). Teja Singh, *Sikhism: Its Ideals and Institutions* (1970).

W. H. McLeod

SIKKIM, a formerly independent Buddhist kingdom located on the southern border of Tibet between Nepal and Bhutan in the eastern Himalayas. Sikkim was settled by Tibetan herdsmen and swidden-cultivating Lepchas from at least the thirteenth century, but it was not until the early seventeenth century that a scion of the east Tibetan Mingyang dynasty came to power with the support of the Nyingmapa Buddhist clergy.

In Sikkim, unlike Tibet, monastic orders did not gain control of the government. Rather, political power was retained by the hereditary secular ruler, or *chogyal,* and a limited number of Bhutia and Lepcha noble families. Nevertheless, Buddhist monasteries played a prominent role in the consolidation of the kingdom, and the stability of reign of successive *chogyals* was dependent on the support of the ecclesiastical hierarchy. During the nineteenth century, rivalries over endowments of land and bonded labor as well as over favor at court developed among the powerful monasteries and eventually erupted into armed disputes over concessions to the British and settlement of Nepalese immigrants within the country.

Sikkim's domain once extended from Tibet's Chumbi Valley westward to the Arun River in Nepal, but successive incursions by the Bhutanese during the seventeenth century and the eastward expansion of the Gorkha raja during the last quarter of that century greatly diminished the land area of Sikkim, which now covers less than 3,000 square miles. The British restored Sikkim's Tarai holdings after the Anglo-Nepal War but ceded much of that territory in 1850 as a punitive measure for the detention of two British officials. Subsequent civil and ecclesiastical friction, an invasion by Tibetan forces, and claims of Chinese suzerainty over Sikkim prompted the British to annex the entire kingdom as a protectorate in 1889.

In 1947 India succeeded to the protectorship over Sikkim and gradually assumed a greater role in the country's affairs, especially from 1962, when India and China went to war over the Himalayan borders on Sikkim's northern frontier. During the early 1970s political opposition parties representing the Nepalese majority (nearly 75 percent of the total population) pressed the government of the twelfth *chogyal*, Palden Thondup Namgyal, for constitutional reforms and closer ties with India. A popular referendum called in the spring of 1974 resulted in a landslide victory for the National Congress Party. However, the *chogyal* attempted to obstruct the proposed reforms of the new constituent assembly, and his Bhutia and Lepcha supporters staged anti-Indian demonstrations around Gangtok, the Sikkimese capital. In an effort to protect its government, the assembly sought military assistance from New Delhi and subsequently voted to abolish the monarchy and seek statehood with India. On 16 May 1975 Sikkim became the twenty-second state of the Indian Union.

[*See also* Namgyal, Palden Thondup.]

Government Secretariat of Bengal, *The Gazeteer of Sikkim* (1894). Karen P. Jenkins and W. Jenkins, *The Himalayan Kingdoms: Bhutan, Sikkim and Nepal* (1967).

RICHARD ENGLISH

SILANG, DIEGO

SILANG, DIEGO (1730–1763), Filipino leader of the Ilocos Revolt (1762–1763) against the maladministration and oppressive practices of Alcalde Mayor Antonio Zabala. Silang, who served the parish priest of Vigan as mail courier to Manila, launched the revolt on 14 December 1762. After Silang had declared himself *alcalde mayor,* the acting governor-general, Simon de Anda, forbade him to function as such. Silang ignored Anda and thereafter aligned himself with the British, who had just captured Manila. Silang was assassinated on 28 May 1763 with the blessings of the bishop of Vigan, Bernardo Ustariz. Silang's place was taken by his wife, Gabriela, and uncle, Nicholas Carino. Gabriela was captured and was hanged on 29 September 1763.

BERNARDITA REYES CHURCHILL

SILK ROUTE

SILK ROUTE, or Silk Road, a popular term for the premodern system of transcontinental trade routes connecting eastern and western Eurasia via central Eurasia. More specifically, the term refers to a route running from the capitals of North China to the Jade Gate in Gansu, whence it divided into a northern route that passed north of the Tian Shan into Semirechie and a pair of southern routes that passed south of the Tian Shan through the Tarim Basin—one to the north of the Taklamakan desert, one to its south. These latter either crossed the western Tian Shan near Kashgar, passing into Ferghana, or the Pamirs via the Wakhan, passing into Tocharistan (Bactria). The northernmost route went either west to Khwarazm and on to eastern Europe, or southwest via Sogdiana and Merv to northeastern Iran. Of the two southerly routes, one went from Ferghana to Sogdiana, Merv, and northeastern Iran, the other from Tocharistan to northeastern Iran. From the cities of the latter area, the reunited route crossed northern Iran and then split, one route going south and southwest, one continuing west to the Black Sea, Constantinople, and western Europe.

The trade goods involved actually reached as far as Britain and Japan, but the commerce was normally one of multiple resale; except in the Mongol period, individuals rarely traversed more than a short portion of the route. The profit was lucrative enough to bring exceptional prosperity to the medieval cities of Central Asia, and also apparently to cause numerous wars for control of the region. The most important conquests are those of Alexander the Great, Han China, the Sasanids, Tang China, the Tibetan empire, the Uighurs, the Mongols, and the Manchus. The opening of the direct sea route to China by western Europeans, coupled with the Manchu conquest of eastern Turkestan, brought isolation and economic decline all along the Silk Route. After the Russian conquest of Western Turkestan in the nineteenth century, east-west trade along the Silk Route came to an end.

[*See also* Caravan; Camel; Central Asia; *and the map accompanying* Islam.]

H. Härtel, et al., *Along the Ancient Silk Routes* (1982). Guy Le Strange, *The Lands of the Eastern Caliphate* (1905; reprint, 1976). J. I. Miller, *The Spice Trade of the Roman Empire* (1969).   CHRISTOPHER I. BECKWITH

SILLA, southern Korean kingdom that originated among the Han tribes; with Koguryŏ and Paekche, one of the Three Kingdoms of Korean history. According to the Chinese history *Sanguozhi,* which gives a detailed description of Korea dating from the middle of the third century CE, the Han tribes were then divided into numerous autonomous communities, each in its own mountain valley, and had not yet reached the stage of state formation. There were three major geographical divisions of the tribes: Mahan in the southwest with more than fifty autonomous communities; Chinhan in the southeast with twelve, and Pyŏnhan or Pyŏnchin in between, also with twelve. Among the communities of Chinhan one is named Silu, probably an early Chinese equivalent of the name Silla. If so, we should see in this particular community, at this period no more than an undifferentiated name in a list, the nucleus of the future kingdom of Silla. It is clear, however, that no Silla kingdom as such existed in the mid-third century, in spite of the claim made in Sino-Korean texts of the twelfth and thirteenth centuries that Silla's first king came to the throne in 57 BCE. That particular year is a "magical" date, the first year of a sixty-year cycle and exactly twelve such cyles before the final elimination of the state of Paekche, which later was Silla's main rival.

In the third century there was an official called "the Chin(han) king," but this king, according to the *Sanguozhi,* was always a man of Mahan, and indeed resided in Mahan and not in Chinhan. It has been conjectured by modern scholars that the so-called "Chin king" was no more than a Mahan chieftain who served as intermediary for the Chinese officials in Korea in their dealings with the Chinhan tribes. Since Mahan was adjacent to the Chinese commandery of Daifang, while Chinhan was far away in southeastern Korea, it was convenient for the Chinese to make a Mahan chieftain responsible for the more remote Han communities. [*See* Three Hans.]

Such a system can hardly have survived the collapse of the Chinese empire in the early fourth century, when various nomad states occupied North China, isolating the Chinese commanderies in Korea. As the governors of the commanderies lost their position of authority a group of warrior princes from the northern kingdom of Puyŏ moved into Mahan and established the kingdom of Paekche, which rapidly absorbed both Mahan and the former Chinese commandery of Daifang; at the same time the kingdom of Koguryŏ centered on the upper Yalu River advanced southward into Korea and occupied the former commandery of Lelang. [*See* Commanderies in Korea, Chinese.] Koguryŏ seems to have attempted to outflank Paekche by extending its control over the Chinhan tribes, a development that seems to be closely connected with the final emergence of Silla as an organized state unit in the late fourth century. This is suggested by the fact that several Silla court titles appear to be derived from Koguryŏ usage and by the fact that Silla envoys first appeared in China in company with envoys from Koguryŏ.

Paekche countered the Koguryŏ move by entering into an alliance with the Yamato state in Japan, in furtherance of which various Japanese expeditions crossed into Korea from Kyushu to secure a sphere of Yamato influence. In 399 Japanese forces besieged Kŭmsŏng ("the walled town of the Kim," i.e., of the ruling family in Silla), and Koguryŏ dispatched troops to its rescue. At this time Silla was clearly dependent on Koguryŏ, and the Silla king was obliged to send his crown prince to Koguryŏ as a hostage.

By the late fifth century, however, the situation had changed. For reasons that are unclear—perhaps no more than resentment over Koguryŏ's continuing control—Silla turned against the northern state and made an alliance with Paekche. At this time and indeed throughout its history the Silla kingdom was basically an alliance of clans, yet until the end of the kingdom in the tenth century the primacy of the Kim clan was never questioned. The Silla elite were divided into five "bone ranks" that were closely connected with lineage. Thus, the main line of the royal house constituted the first bone rank, or *sŏnggol,* while the cadet lines of the same house lapsed into the second rank, or *chin'gol.* The various offices at the royal court were affiliated with particular bone ranks and could only be held by members of that rank. It is possible that this system came about through some sort of alliance of tribes that brought the kingdom itself into existence.

The furthest from contact with China, Silla was also the last of the Korean kingdoms to develop, and until the early sixth century was something of a cultural backwater. Buddhism, which had entered both Koguryŏ and Paekche in the fourth century, did not reach Silla until very much later, and only became firmly entrenched as the result of the patronage of King Pŏphŭng (r. 514–540). In the reign of the succeeding king, Chinhŭng (r. 540–576), a Koguryŏ monk, Hyeyong, was made head of all the monasteries in Silla. About the same time Silla began to keep its own historical records—of which, unfortunately, not even fragments remain today.

An outward sign of the new strength and confidence of the developing state was the rupture with Paekche when, in 552, Silla seized the Hansŏng area that the two allies had just won back from the enfeebled kingdom of Koguryŏ. During the same reign Silla annexed much of the Kaya (Mimana) area between itself and Paekche, a district that had retained the old clan structure but had failed to evolve into a major state. Silla also occupied most of the east coast of Korea, taking over the lands of the Okchŏ formerly ruled by Koguryŏ.

By the beginning of the seventh century Koguryŏ was again strong enough to begin winning back its lost territory, but at this point its energies were diverted by the need to face the series of invasions from the Sui and Tang dynasties of China. It was thus clearly in Silla's interest to remain in close alliance with China until the final elimination of Koguryŏ by the latter in 668.

The seventh century was a crucial period in the development of Silla, since the death of King Chinp'yŏng (r. 579–632) ended the direct sŏnggol male line, and the throne passed first to his daughter, Queen Sŏndŏk (r. 632–647), then to his sister Chindŏk (r. 647–654), and finally to the cadet chin'gol lineage. This uncertainty in the succession coincided with the series of wars between the Korean states that culminated in the Tang invasions, and perhaps created a feeling of crisis in Silla. Certainly the same period saw a complete reorganization of the Silla military system, as well as the emergence of the "knights" known as hwarang ("flower boys"). The hwarang were boys, sons of men of noble lineage, who were given special military and religious training to become the leaders of bands often several hundred strong. The band members were bound together by strict discipline and a code of chivalry, and played an important part in the wars of the period. The practice was also closely connected with the cult of Maitreya, the coming Buddha, which was especially popular in Silla. [See Hwarang.]

The destruction of the kingdoms of Paekche and Koguryŏ by the Tang armies led naturally to a change in the policy of Silla. The Silla court had no desire to see the restoration of direct Chinese rule in Korea and, from soon after the fall of Koguryŏ, began to take over outlying districts of the old Paekche kingdom and also to support rebel movements against the Tang further north. From 671 to 683 Silla supported a Koguryŏ puppet who seems to have sent embassies to Japan on his own account but who resided in Silla territory. Tang attempts to coerce Silla were somewhat spasmodic, owing to China's difficulties in other areas, and by 673 Silla had occupied most of Paekche and parts of southern Koguryŏ. In 679 Silla dispatched officials to govern the former kingdom of T'amna on Cheju Island, once tributary to Paekche. By this time the Chinese had abandoned P'yŏngyang. Their attempt to halt the Silla advance by restoring the former king of Koguryŏ had also come to nothing. In the end, however, Silla failed to extend its control north of the Taedong River, perhaps because of difficulties that were experienced in holding the new conquests. King Munmu (r. 661–680) resettled hundred of Koguryŏ families in the former Paekche lands and appointed members of the chin'gol to reside in the conquered areas and control them; however, these nobles were demoted to the third bone rank and therefore excluded from holding office at court, a feature of the system that led to frustration and eventual political instability. By the end of the seventh century another state had emerged in the former territory of Koguryŏ, the kingdom of Parhae, which remained a rival of Silla for the next two hundred years.

In spite of these failures, the period from 668 to 780 was the golden age of Silla. At this time much of the carrying trade between China, Korea, and Japan seems to have passed into Silla's hands, and the country seems to have grown both in wealth and sophistication. By the eighth century the capital, now called Kyŏngju, contained more than seven hundred thousand people and thirty-five vast private estates. On the surrounding mountains were wealthy monasteries, most of which sent a stream of monks to study in China or even further afield. Several Silla monks are known to have visited India, and one of them, Hyech'o (commonly known by his Chinese name, Huichao), left a record of that country preserved in China. Buddhism is also associated with the earliest known block-printing in Korea, dating from the mid-eighth century and predating by a century any similar printing in China. It was also during the eighth century that the Silla court attempted to introduce the Chinese examination system and the Tang system of land tenure, although it is not clear how far these attempts were successful. In the Royal Academy at Kyŏngju students studied the Chinese classics; others went to China itself for study and even remained there to enter the Chinese bureaucracy. Of these the most celebrated was Ch'oe Ch'i-wŏn, born in 857, who went to China at the age of twelve, and after success in the examinations received a provincial post in southern China, returning to Silla in 885. [See Ch'oe Ch'i-wŏn.]

By this time the Silla kingdom was entering its final period of decline. The origins of this crisis go back to 780 when the young king Hyegong was murdered in a palace coup; from this time on the kings came from various rival collateral lines, and were not infrequently murdered or killed in civil wars. In the remaining century and a half of the state's existence there were no fewer than twenty rulers, without including rebel regimes that flourished briefly in the provinces, such as the Ch'angan kingdom that a certain Kim Hon-ch'ang attempted to establish in Ungjin, the old Paekche capital, in 822. In the disorders of the times the great landed families of the provinces became virtually independent, a development that disrupted the tribute system by which grain was brought to the overgrown capital, and caused a series of famines around Kyŏngju. At this time Parhae was at the height of its power, and this frontier threat led the Silla court to undertake the construction of a wall across the peninsula from the Taedong River, an attempt that added to the general unrest. Because piracy was rampant along the coast, in 828 King Hŭngdŏk (r. 826–837) appointed the commoner Chang Po-go as commissioner for Ch'ŏnghae off the southwestern coast.

Chang Po-go seems to have succeeded in temporarily putting down piracy, but in doing so he became virtually an independent warlord, as well as gaining such control over the China trade that he was able to endow temples built by Korean communities in the Chinese province of Shandong. Official envoys traveling from Silla to China were obliged to proceed in Chang's ships. In 837, when bitter civil wars broke out after the death of King Hŭngdŏk, Chang Po-go was able to intervene and, eventually, to install his own protégé as king. In 839 Chang alientated the aristocracy of the capital by attempting to force King Munsŏng (r. 839–857) to name Chang's daughter as queen. As a result, Chang rose against the court but was murdered in 841 or 842 by a hired bravo whom the Silla court rewarded with the rank of general. [See Chang Po-go.]

The career of Chang Po-go suggests that behind the political turmoil of the late Silla was an underlying frustration with the rigidity of Silla social structure. This is equally indicated by the various risings that, following a period of partial recovery in mid-century, broke out on the accession of another reigning queen, Chinsŏng, in 887. Within a few years the government's writ could no longer be enforced outside the capital district, and the court was threatened by the revolt of the farmer's son Kyŏn Hwŏn in the southwest and the former Buddhist priest Songjŏng in central Korea. Ch'oe Ch'i-wŏn, summoned from a provincial post to take up office at court in 894, was unable to make the journey to the capital because of the disorders. For another forty years rulers of Silla continued to be enthroned, but this final phase of Silla history is more naturally considered as an aspect of the so-called Later Three Kingdoms.

In its attempts to import Chinese administrative structures and educational systems into Korea, Silla laid a foundation upon which it was possible for the later Korean dynasties, Koryŏ and Yi, to build after the collapse of the bone-rank system in the civil wars. Silla also left behind a legacy of literature now largely lost, the beginnings of a system of writing Korean language in Chinese characters, and a quantity of fine sculpture, of which the Buddha and bas-reliefs at Sŏkkuram are perhaps the finest examples.

[See also Paekche; Koguryŏ; Parhae; and Later Three Kingdoms.]

W. E. Henthorn, A History of Korea (1971). Richard Rutt, "The Flower Boys of Silla," Transactions of the Korea Branch of the Royal Asiatic Society 38 (1961): 1–66.   KENNETH H. J. GARDINER

SIMA GUANG (1019–1086), Chinese literatus; leading Northern Song statesman and historian; author of the Zizhi tongjian (Comprehensive Mirror for Aid in Government), an annalistic history of China from 403 BCE to 959 CE. Sima held influential positions at court in the 1060s and led the opposition to Wang Anshi (1021–1086) and his so-called New Policies. Forced out of service in 1070, he retired to Luoyang, where he finished the history in 1084. Sima was recalled in 1085 to lead a government bent on restoring traditional institutions and limiting the state's interference in the economy and society. A political history that set new standards of critical historiography, the Comprehensive Mirror also explores the key problem of relations between the ruler and the bureaucracy. Some have viewed the work as a justification for monarchical absolutism, but it has also been read as an attempt to limit the ruler and to strengthen the authority of the literati staffing the bureaucracy.

[See also Wang Anshi.]

E. G. Pulleyblank, "Chinese Historical Criticism: Liu Chih-chi and Ssu-ma Kuang," in *Historians of China and Japan,* edited by W. G. Beasley and E. G. Pulleyblank (1961), pp. 135–166. Anthony Sariti, "Monarchy, Bureaucracy, and Absolutism in the Political Thought of Ssu-ma Kuang," *Journal of Asian Studies* 32.1 (1972): 53–76.   PETER K. BOL

SIMA QIAN (c. 145–93 BCE), author of China's most famous history, the *Shiji*. In 108 BCE Sima Tan, Qian's ailing father, had his son promise to finish the history the father had begun. When his father died, Sima Qian took his position as *taishiling,* or grand historian. In 98 BCE Sima Qian angered Emperor Wu by defending the loyalty of a general who had been captured by the enemy; as a result, Sima was sentenced to be castrated. Others would have committed suicide to avoid the punishment, but Sima defended his choice as the only one that would allow him to finish the history begun by his father.

Sima Tan's contribution to the *Shiji* is not known; the work is generally taken to be by Sima Qian. Tan is renowned for offering the first comparative appraisal of the various philosophical traditions (e.g., Confucianism and Daoism), making clear his own preference for Daoism.

The *Shiji* is a history of China from earliest times to Sima Qian's era. Its 130 chapters are divided into five parts. The first consists of chronicles *(benji)* of ruling houses and of the reigns of individual emperors, providing a terse chronology of Chinese history. The second part contains chronological tables *(biao)* of appointments and ennoblements. Part three is made up of essays *(shu)* on such topics as rituals, the calendar, and economics. Records of hereditary households *(shijia),* the fourth part, provides annals of lesser ruling houses in the preimperial period. The fifth part, 70 of the 130 chapters, is devoted to biographies *(liezhuan).* The biographical chapters recount the lives of people and are arranged by periods or by topics. The format developed by Sima Qian was to have a profound impact on subsequent history writing in China. Later histories were usually dynastic in scope and therefore lacked Sima's broad historical coverage and failed to include his fourth part. However, the structure of all later dynastic histories can be traced to

his creative genius. The *Shiji*, much praised for its style, is also esteemed as a great work of literature.

Sima disapproved of the growing power of the emperor and the extent to which the bureaucracy dominated Chinese life. He praised those who were honestly successful, such as businessmen, even though entreprenurial activities were anathema to Confucians. His history has a spirit of toleration that is not found in later bureaucratically compiled dynastic histories.

Burton Watson, *Ssu-ma Ch'ien: Grand Historian of China* (1958).   JACK L. DULL

SIMLA, capital of the state of Himachal Pradesh in northwestern India. This town of fifty thousand is dramatically situated on a ridge of the Himalayan foothills at approximately 7,200 feet above sea level. Its cool climate and beautiful setting make it a popular retreat from the summer heat of the plains, a feature appreciated by the British, who used it as the summer capital of India from 1865 to 1939. Simla was also the site of the fruitless Simla conferences of June 1945 and May 1946, two historic efforts to resolve differences between the ruling factions of what would later become India and Pakistan. [See also Himachal Pradesh.]

                                    BRUCE MCCOY OWENS

SIMON COMMISSION. In 1919 the Indian Statutory Commission, appointed under the Government of India Act, was required to report on India's political progress and indicate whether "responsible government" should be extended. The chairman, Sir John Simon, was an eminent Liberal lawyer. Among the other six members only Clement Attlee was to become well known. The commission encountered outright hostility from almost every element in Indian politics when they visited India and Burma in 1928–1929. They reported in 1930, recommending that full ministerial government be introduced at the provincial level; they also recommended the separation of Burma from India. However, their proposals for federal government at the center were too restricted even to satisfy British political opinion. The report was set aside by the decision to hold a round table conference with Indian political leaders in November 1930.

[See also Government of India Acts.]

R. J. Moore, *The Crisis of Indian Unity, 1917–1940* (1974). *Report of the Indian Statutory Commission,* vol.

1, *Survey*, Cmd. 3568; vol. 2, *Recommendations*, Cmd. 3569, His Majesty's Stationery Office (1930).

HUGH TINKER

SIN CH'AE-HO

SIN CH'AE-HO (1880–1936), Korean journalist, historian, and independence movement activist who is best known for his published essays that present a nationalistic reinterpretation of Korean history.

Born into a learned family of *yangban* status in Ch'ungch'ŏng Province, Sin became a junior scholar at a state Confucian academy in Seoul in 1905. He quickly decided on a career in journalism, writing news articles, editorials, and historical essays for the *Hwangsŏng sinmun* and the *Taehan maeil sinbo*, two newspapers known for their nationalistic stance. He also joined the Sinminhoe, a secret society of young nationalists inspired by An Ch'ang-ho, and a few other associations that advocated education and reform. In these closing years of the Yi dynasty (1392–1910), Sin thought that the spiritual development of the people was more important than material improvements. [*See also* An Ch'ang-ho.]

Shortly after Japan's annexation of Korea in 1910, Sin left his homeland, and traveled in Manchuria, the Russian Maritime Province, and China; he eventually settled in Beijing in 1915. His travels included visits to historical and archaeological sites in Manchuria.

In the wake of the March First Movement protesting Japanese rule in 1919, Sin formed a patriotic youth group in Beijing before going to Shanghai, where he occupied a seat in the Legislative Council of the Korean Provisional Government. Before long Sin became disenchanted with many of his colleagues, especially Syngman Rhee (Yi Sŭng-man), the first president of the government in exile; Sin resigned his post and left Shanghai. For the next several years Sin devoted himself to historical research, exploring linguistic and geographical explanations for the names and events recorded in old histories of Korea; a few of his writings, such as *Chosŏnsa yŏn'guch'o* (*Research Notes on Korean History*) and *Chosŏn sanggosa* (*Ancient History of Korea*), were later published in Korea and are considered landmarks of nationalistic historiography.

As a political activist Sin became more radical, joining an Asian anarchist league in 1926. The Japanese consular police arrested him in 1928 in Beijing; Sin died in Lüshun (Port Arthur) while serving a ten-year prison term.

[*See also* Korea, Japanese Government-General of.]

Han-Kyo Kim, ed., *Studies on Korea: A Scholar's Guide* (1980), see especially chapter 3, part 1. Ki-baik Lee, *A New History of Korea*, translated by Edward W. Wagner (1984).

HAN-KYO KIM

SIND

SIND, or Sindh, area that takes its name from the Arabic word for the Indus River and extends over the lower portion of that river valley. The Sind contains numerous archaeological sites associated with the Indus Valley civilization (c. 2250–1750 BCE), the most important of which is Mohenjo-Daro. The earliest historical references to the Sind are found in Persian sources dating from the reign of Darius, who conquered the region around 515 BCE.

Owing to its relative isolation from the centers of both India and West Asia, the history of the Sind has been marked by successive conquests from both the east and west, followed by periods in which local dynasties governed with a high degree of autonomy in the name of the imperial authority and asserted their independence whenever its power weakened.

Alexander fought his way through the Sind in 326–325 BCE. Thereafter the Sind was annexed by various empires from the Seleucids and Mauryas to the Kushans and Sasanids. There is also substantial archaeological evidence of the influence of Buddhism from at least the first century CE.

Muhammad bin Qasim's conquest of the Sind in 711–713 marked the first successful intrusion of Muslim power into the Indian subcontinent. The region was ruled by Arab governors in the name of the Umayyads and Abbasids until the eleventh century, when it was conquered by Mahmud of Ghazna. The Delhi sultans exercised a loose suzerainty over the Sind, but effective power during most of the sultanate was held by two regional dynasties—the Samras (c. 1053–1330) and the Sammas (c. 1351–1521).

In 1521 the Sind was conquered by the Arghuns and in 1554 by the Tarkhans. The Mughals annexed the region in 1591 but governed it through powerful local dynasties—the Tarkhans (1591–1612), Daudpotras (1612–1700), and Kalhoras (1701–1782). In the eighteenth century first Nadir Shah and then the Durranis invaded the Sind. While acknowledging their suzerainty, the Kalhoras continued to rule the region until they were displaced by another local dynasty, the Talpurs (1783–1843).

The British conquered the Sind in 1843 and administered it as part of the Bombay Presidency until 1936, when it was made into a separate province. In 1947 the Sind was incorporated into Pakistan and in 1954 merged into the province of West Pakistan. In 1969 it was once more made a separate province within Pakistan.

[*See also* Indus River; Indus Valley Civilization; *and* Alexander III.]

H. T. Lambrick, *Sind: A General Introduction* (1964).

STEPHEN RITTENBERG

SINDHIA. The Sindhia family, also known as the Shindes (derived from Sendrak), are Maratha by caste and were the *patils* (headmen) of Kanherkhed in Satara district, Maharashtra, India. Ranoji (d. 1745), the son of Jankoji and the founder of the house, joined the *peshwa*'s service in 1716 and became *jagirdar* (noble) of 65 lakhs of rupees. He had five sons: Jayappa, who was murdered; Dattaji, who died fighting; Jotiba; Tukoji; and Mahadji, the successor to Jayappa's son Jankoji, who was killed at Panipat. Mahadji's claim was recognized in 1767, and Gwalior became the capital of the Shindes. Mahadji was a great warrior and administrator. He restored the Mughal emperor to his position (1772) and received the title *vakil*-i *mutlaq* ("regent plenipotentiary"). He was also responsible for the English defeat at Wadgaon (1781) and the Treaty of Salbai (1782). With the help of De Boigne, a Frenchman, he built a model army. Mahadji died at Wanawadi, near Pune, in 1794. His grandnephew and successor, Daulatrao (c. 1780–1827), lost heavily to the English and finally joined them in 1817, losing his independence.

[*See also* Gwalior *and* Marathas.]

A. R. KULKARNI

SINGAPORE (also Singapura, the "lion city," formerly Temasek), island located off the southern tip of the Malay Peninsula and the site of the Republic of Singapore. Very little is known about the island's early history. Although it commands three of the most convenient channels linking the Straits of Melaka with the South China Sea, there was no major settlement on the island prior to the nineteenth century. Aside from a period in the fourteenth century when the founder of Melaka, Sri Tri Buana (Parameswara), resided there, the island was occupied only on a temporary basis by Orang Laut or by small groups of tribal peoples.

In 1818, following the Dutch reoccupation of Melaka and Riau, Thomas Stamford Raffles and Major William Farquhar sought to establish an English settlement in the Straits to provide a secure base for the British East India Company's trade with China. On 29 January 1819 they met Temenggong Abdul Rahman on Singapore Island. The *temenggong* signed a provisional treaty with Raffles and sent for Tunku (Prince) Hussein, the eldest son of Sultan Mahmud III (d. 1812). Hussein had been passed over when Raja Ja'afar and the other Bugis chiefs at Riau had recognized his younger brother, Tunku Abdul Rahman, as sultan. Raffles recognized Hussein as sultan of Johor and then signed a treaty by which the British were permitted to found a settlement on Singapore and the sultan and the *temenggong* were given pensions. Although the Dutch in Riau and Batavia objected, the British presence was a *fait accompli* and was eventually recognized in the Anglo-Dutch Treaty of 1824. It was also in 1824 that the then-resident, John Crawfurd, persuaded the two Malay chiefs to cede the entire island to the East India Company. By that time, Singapore had already attracted a substantial population and was rapidly becoming the major entrepôt in the western part of the Indonesian archipelago.

Raffles's initial aim was to make Singapore a free port. There were thus no import or export duties, wharf fees, marine or port dues, or any charges at all on shipping, nor was there any regulation of the movement of goods and people in and out of the port. The settlement remained a free port until the second half of the twentieth century, with only minor concessions made to the necessities of government, and probably came close to representing the ideal of free trade as expressed by the classical economists.

At first the economy of the port was essentially an updated version of the trading pattern that had supported earlier entrepôts in the Straits (e.g., Riau, Melaka, Srivijaya). Singapore functioned as a staging area for merchants involved in the long-distance east-west trade and as the major collecting point for the produce of Southeast Asia, namely, spices, gold, rare gums, resins, and other goods collected from the tropical rain forests and the produce of the mines and nearby plantations. The port thus drew private European merchants from India and Britain, who established agency houses that sold European and Indian products and purchased Asian goods on behalf of European and Asian customers. The agency houses sold British textiles, iron and steel, and Indian opium and bought and sold Asian goods.

The port rapidly attracted settlers from the surrounding areas. Malays and Bugis from Riau, Melaka, and other nearby states, along with many other

Southeast Asians, flocked to Singapore with goods to trade. Chinese merchants, planters, and craftsmen also quickly appeared, many of them from nearby Riau, Melaka, and Penang, while others from southern China soon followed. Population growth was sustained throughout the next century, with the Chinese gradually coming to form a larger and larger majority.

Until 1867 Singapore was ruled by the East India Company and the Indian government. Together with the other British possessions of Penang and Melaka, it made up the Straits Settlements. By the 1830s Singapore had become the headquarters of the settlements. In 1867, however, the Straits Settlements became a crown colony, and authority was transferred to the colonial office. Singapore retained this status (except during the Japanese occupation, 1942–1945) until 1959, when it was granted local self-government. It gained independence within the Federation of Malaysia in 1963 but seceded from the federation in May 1965 and became fully independent. Initially, local government was in the hands of a European resident councillor and later a governor. After 1867, the crown appointed a governor, who ruled with an Executive Council (made up of officials) and the advice of a Legislative Council, comprising both officials and unofficials. In 1948, as Singapore moved toward self-government, the Legislative Council became elective.

Economically, Singapore functioned as an entrepôt during the first part of the nineteenth century. Its economy, dependent largely on the prosperity of distant markets and relative ease of communications, tended to be volatile and speculative. In the 1860s, however, shifts in the global economy made reliance on the long-distance trade less attractive. Singapore merchants became more exclusively involved in handling products of the immediate hinterland, especially pepper and gambier, which were grown in Singapore and in nearby Johor and Riau. Likewise, production of commodities (e.g., tin, sugar, sago, tapioca, and indigo) was encouraged in the other nearby states. By the 1870s these commodities had come to be the staples of Singapore's economy. The port thus played an important role in integrating local economies into the world system.

Production was largely accomplished by Chinese coolies, who flocked to Singapore in increasing numbers, most only passing through on their way to the jungles of Sumatra or the peninsula. Within Singapore, the economy was divided among various Chinese-speaking groups. At the top of the economic pyramid were the Baba merchants (Straits-born Chinese, of Hokkien origin, but usually from Melaka), who spoke some English and thus had immediate access to the Europeans. They loaned capital to the wealthier of the two major Chinese-speaking groups settled in the colony, the Hokkiens and the Teochius. The latter, in turn, dominated debtor networks among their own countrymen. Among these, a variety of specialized pursuits were represented. Occupations were usually determined by kinship, speech group, and place of origin.

The secret societies, or triads, were another major element of Chinese society in Singapore. They mainly served to protect the economic preserves of the various Chinese groups and to impose sanctions on those identified as opposed to the interests of the leaders. The major societies, the Ghi Hin and the Ghee Hok, tended to be associated with the Teochiu and Hokkien groups, but the changing nature of Chinese society in Singapore and the clandestine operations of the secret societies offer little firm evidence about their internal workings.

Throughout the nineteenth century, a number of major secret-society wars erupted in the Malay world. In Singapore, major secret-society conflicts occurred in 1846, 1854, 1862, 1871, and 1883. In most cases, the causes of these disputes can be traced to economic dislocations, such as serious fluctuations in the prices of major commodities and shifts in the markets, or to demographic changes.

By the 1870s the function of governing the Chinese, both in Singapore and the other Malay colonies, came to be the business of the Chinese Protectorate, which registered the societies, regulated labor, and attempted to curb prostitution. By the beginning of the twentieth century, Chinese society began to stabilize: more and more women began to settle in Singapore, families were established, and schools were founded.

Between 1900 and 1960 the political life of the Singapore Chinese was influenced largely by developments in China itself. Thus, the years prior to 1911 were marked by the activities of Sun Yat-sen to overthrow the Qing dynasty, while the 1920s and 1930s saw the Chinese divided between the Guomindang (Kuomintang) and the Communist Party. These developments naturally influenced the growth of Chinese schools, labor unions, and commercial organizations. In the late 1930s the Singapore Chinese rose in opposition to the Japanese invasion of their homeland.

By contrast, the Straits-born Chinese, who received English-language educations, took their status as British subjects seriously. While individuals such as Song Ong Siang and Lim Boon Keng promoted interest in Chinese culture and language study, they were also active in demonstrating their loyalty to the crown. They formed the Straits Chinese British Association, solicited funds to purchase fighter planes for Britain when World War I began, and formed a rifle company to support the Allied cause. The presence of a prominent group of English-speaking Chinese in Singapore would be the basis for a significant social group in the years after independence.

From Singapore and the other Straits Settlements, British political influence expanded into the South China Sea and the Malay Peninsula. In the 1830s and 1840s antipiracy campaigns to secure Singapore's trade swept the Orang Laut from the seas. The support among Singapore's governors and mercantile elite for the *temenggongs* of Johor was a fundamental element in the long-term success of the *temenggongs* in fully displacing the descendants of Sultan Hussein. Under Temenggong (later Maharaja and finally Sultan) Abu Bakar, Johor came to be intimately tied to the British economic and political presence.

Singapore and Penang were the staging areas for British economic penetration of the Malay Peninsula. Chinese miners and planters, moving in from the Straits Settlements, pioneered the economic development of the peninsula. In the 1870s, when conflicts between different groups of miners arose, the British government intervened and extended its political hegemony over the Malay states of the peninsula.

By the beginning of the twentieth century, Singapore had been displaced by Kuala Lumpur as the administrative center of the British colonies in the federated and unfederated Malay states. But as the terminus for the Malay railroad system and as the banking and commercial center of the region, Singapore retained its primary role as the economic capital of the British empire in the Malay world.

The ease with which Singapore was taken by the Japanese in 1942 demonstrated the uselessness of trying to maintain such a colony if the state did not already control the surrounding air and sea routes. Following the war, the British began the process of decolonization. With its overwhelming Chinese population, Singapore was seen as incompatible with the political aspirations of the Malays. Thus, the Federation of Malaya remained administratively separate from Singapore, and each began to develop its own political structure. The 1950s were marked by outbreaks of communal violence between Malays and Chinese as well as by British moves to destroy communist or socialist movements in both Singapore and the Federation of Malaya.

As Singapore moved toward independence in the 1950s, a number of political parties emerged, among them the Socialist Front (Barisan Sosalis) and the People's Action Party (PAP). The latter was led by Lee Kuan Yew, a London-trained lawyer who by the early 1960s had emerged as the clear victor in the power struggle to dominate the new state. Following a one-year attempt to rejoin Singapore to the rest of former British Malaya in the Federation of Malaysia, Lee led Singapore to full independence in 1965. The PAP and Lee then dominated Singapore into the 1980s. During these years the island republic made the transition from entrepôt to an export-oriented manufacturing center and attained an impressive degree of economic progress.

[*See also* Melaka; Riau; Raffles, Sir Thomas Stamford; Farquhar, William; Temenggong; Mahmud Riayat Syah III; Bugis; Abdul Rahman; Anglo-Dutch Treaty; Crawfurd, John; Agency House System; Straits Settlements; Malaya, Federation of; Pepper; Gambier; Coolie Trade; Overseas Chinese; Ghi Hin; Abu Bakar; Barisan Sosalis; People's Action Party; *and the map accompanying* Malaysia.]

Charles B. Buckley, *An Anecdotal History of Old Times in Singapore* (1902). Lee Poh-ping, *Chinese Society in Nineteenth and Early Twentieth Century Singapore; A Socioeconomic Analysis* (1977). Song Ong-sian, *One Hundred Years' History of the Chinese in Singapore* (1923). Carl A. Trocki, *Prince of Pirates: The Temenggongs and the Development of Johor and Singapore 1784–1885* (1979). C. M. Turnbull, *A History of Singapore 1819–1975* (1977).   CARL A. TROCKI

SINGH, BHAGAT (1907–1931), an Indian revolutionary who became a national hero when he was arrested and hanged for throwing a bomb in the Central Legislative Council in Delhi in 1929 and for the murder of a police constable. As a college student, he had joined the Indian National Congress, but left it because of its lack of militancy. He was associated with various groups that used the slogan "Inquilab zindabad" ("Long live revolution"), believing that a Russian-style revolution could be brought about against British rule. Despite Bhagat Singh's espousal of violence as necessary for gaining independence, his popularity was so great that Mohandas Gandhi and Jawaharlal Nehru both praised him as an inspiration for Indian youth.

AINSLIE T. EMBREE

SINGH, FATEH (d. 1972), Sikh leader who achieved Punjabi Suba (i.e., a separate Punjabi-speaking state). Strictly raised, he devoted the greater part of his life to preaching and social service, and earned the title of Sant. His work among rural Sikhs drew him into the Akali Dal and in 1960 he was appointed "dictator" of the Punjabi Suba campaign by Tara Singh. In 1962 Fateh Singh displaced his leader, a change that signaled rural ascendancy within the movement. His emphasis on linguistic rather than sectarian claims made Punjabi Suba acceptable in New Delhi and it was finally conceded in 1966.

[*See also* Akali Dal; Punjab; *and* Sikhism.]

Dalip Singh, *Dynamics of Punjab Politics* (1981). P. Wallace and Surendra Chopra, eds., *Political Dynamics of Punjab* (1981).   W. H. McLeod

SINGH, K. I. (1906–1982), one of the founding members of the Nepali National Congress Party (NNC) and prominent figure in Nepal's political opposition. He was a guerrilla leader in the revolution that overthrew Nepal's Rana oligarchy in 1951. In 1957 Singh was asked by King Mahendra to form an interim government that would set the stage for general elections, but his independent thinking so exacerbated tensions among prominent political leaders that he was quickly dismissed by the king. During his brief term as prime minister, Singh advocated close ties with India and more cautious relations with the Soviets and the Chinese—a policy that secured lasting ties of economic cooperation with New Delhi. Singh was again briefly appointed to the prime ministry in 1967 and continued to serve on the Council of Ministers until 1980, when he resigned to campaign for a multiparty democracy in Nepal's national referendum.

[*See also* Rana *and* Nepal: History of Nepal.]

B. L. Joshi and L. Rose. *Democratic Innovations in Nepal* (1966).   Richard English

SINGH, RANJIT (1780–1839), son of a Sikh chieftain, born during a confused period in Punjab history. Using his inherited Gujranwala domain as a base, he was able to assert his authority over Afghans and rival Sikh chieftains by means of pacts, marriage alliances, and warfare. Lahore fell to him in 1799 and Amritsar in 1805. With these cities and much of the plains firmly in his grasp he was effectively maharaja of the Punjab. During the remaining years of his reign Ranjit Singh consolidated what he already held while substantially enlarging his boundaries. Kangra fell in 1809, Multan and Peshawar in 1818, and Kashmir in 1819. Only in the southeast, where his ambitions clashed with British fears, were his intentions frustrated. In 1809 it was agreed by both sides that the Sutlej River should mark his boundary.

Passionately interested in scientific warfare, Ranjit Singh added to his irregular troops a strong army organized on western lines. Considerable attention was also directed to creating an orderly administration. Although the state thus established was strongly centralized, Singh earned a considerable reputation for justice and benevolence. Soon after his death the kingdom disintegrated and was finally annexed by the British in 1849.

[*See also* Punjab; Lahore; Amritsar; *and* Kashmir.]

J. S. Grewal and Indu Banga, eds., *Maharaja Ranjit Singh and His Times* (1980). Khushwant Singh, *Ranjit Singh: Maharajah of the Punjab* (1962).

W. H. McLeod

SINGH, TARA (1885–1967), the most prominent Sikh politician of modern times, having emerged as a leader soon after the founding of the Akali Dal in 1920. For the next four decades he remained the dominant figure in the party. Following the partition disaster of 1947 he promoted the cause of Punjabi Suba (statehood), insisting that the Sikhs were entitled to their own homeland. He was disadvantaged, however, by his Khatri caste, urban identity, and separatist inclinations. In 1962 he was displaced by his former lieutenant Fateh Singh, a rival supported by the rural Jats. Originally trained as a teacher, he was invariably known as Master Tara Singh.

[*See also* Akali Dal; Singh, Fateh; *and* Punjab.]

Baldev Raj Nayar, *Minority Politics in the Punjab* (1966). Dalip Singh, *Dynamics of Punjab Politics* (1981).

W. H. McLeod

SINGLE WHIP REFORM. *See* Yitiaobianfa.

SINGOSARI, East Javanese kingdom (1222–1292). The *Pararaton*, the Javanese *Book of Kings*, relates that Singosari was founded by Ken Angrok (Rajasa), who capped his career in crime by dethroning the king of Kediri in 1222 and establishing a new dynasty in Janggala, east of the Brantas River. Little is known of the Singosari realm until the reign of the last ruler, Kertanagara (1268–1292), who attempted to expand his kingdom throughout the archipelago. While a large expedition from Singosari was on its way to subdue Sumatra, discontented vassals led by the Kediri prince Jayakatwang seized the capital and killed Kertanagara in 1292.

The Singosari period is known for the great significance of its art and architecture. It witnessed the final emergence of Javanese artistic elements within a unique Hindu-Javanese style, exemplified by the bas-reliefs decorating Candi Jago. A similar, interrelated blending also took place in religion; Shaivism, Buddhism, and folk beliefs were merged into an integrated whole. Kertanagara, for example, practiced the cult of Shiva and Buddha.

[*See also* Pararaton; Ken Angrok; Kertanagara; *and* Majapahit.]

M. C. HOADLEY

SINGU (1756–1782), fourth ruler of Burma's Konbaung dynasty (r. 1776–1782). Eldest son of Hsinhpyushin (1763–1776), Singu ascended the throne at age twenty on the death of his father. He initiated no foreign or domestic policies and summarily ended the aggressive policy of his predecessors on the eastern frontier. His political position was initially strong but eroded quickly because of his dissolute behavior and mistreatment of his royal uncles and father-in-law, the minister and general Maha Thiha Thura. In February 1782 Singu's cousin Maung Maung (only son of Naungdawgyi, r. 1760–1763) seized the palace in Singu's absence. With strong official and gentry support, Singu's uncle, the future Bodawhpaya (1782–1819), took the throne a week later and executed both Maung Maung and Singu.

[*See also* Konbaung Dynasty; Hsinhpyushin; Maha Thiha Thura; *and* Bodawhpaya.]

WILLIAM J. KOENIG

SINHALA. The predominant cultural heritage of the Sinhala people of Sri Lanka has its roots in two ancient traditions that have joined together and produced a distinctive development of its own. The first tradition has Indian sources of inspiration—particularly Buddhism and the Sinhala language. Buddhism, said to have been brought to Sri Lanka by the Indian missionary Mahinda (son or brother of the emperor Ashoka) in the third century BCE, has been both a philosophic wellspring and a source of cultural inspiration; much traditional literature, art, and intellectual development is centered on Buddhism or Buddhist motifs. The Sinhala language, originally written in Brahmi characters, has developed its own syllabic script and is of the Indo-Aryan group. Its early structure was largely influenced by the Pali and Sanskrit languages. Both religion and language have developed distinctive forms after more than twenty centuries in Sri Lanka.

The second tradition in which Sinhala culture is lodged is a complex of indigenous cultural expressions—music, sculpture, dance, art, architecture, dress, poetry, and others. These are rooted in the local village ways and folklore of the people. The local tradition has exerted a strong influence on the cultural cores transplanted from India, resulting in the development of a strong and unique Sinhala culture. Thus, for example, the literary language had attained its present form by about 1200 CE and has varied little since. In the twentieth century modern secular forms of culture have become popular—theater, film, literature, music, and the like. Although purists complain that Western cultural influences currently have an impact on the Sinhala tradition, the integrity of this tradition remains evident in festivals such as the Kandy Perahera, in Kandyan dance, and in the spiritual practices of the Sinhala people.

[*See also* Sri Lanka.]

Ananda Coomaraswamy, *The Arts and Crafts of India and Ceylon* (1964). S. D. de Laverolle, *Origins of Sinhala Culture* (1976). W. Rahula, *History of Buddhism in Ceylon* (1966). Martin Wicksamasinghe, *Aspects of Sinhalese Culture* (1973). N. D. Wijesekera, *The People of Ceylon* (1965).

RALPH BUULTJENS

SI NHIEP (Chinese, Shi Xie) was born in 137 at Cangwu (modern Wuchou), then the seat of Jiaozhi (Giao Chi); his ancestors had immigrated from Shandong during the Wang Mang disorders. He received the *maocai* degree and served briefly at the Han court. In the 180s he was appointed prefect of Jiaozhi in northern Vietnam. As Han collapsed, Si Nhiep gained control of northern Vietnam and parts of southern China. He formally submitted to the Wu dynasty when it was proclaimed. His rule in Vietnam was remembered as a time of peace and prosperity and as marking the beginnings of Vietnamese Buddhism. He died in 226.

[*See also* Jiaozhi.]

Keith W. Taylor, *The Birth of Vietnam* (1983).

KEITH W. TAYLOR

SINO-JAPANESE WAR (1894–1895), war between China and Japan, initially for the control of Korea, marking the culmination of complex developments in nineteenth-century international politics in East Asia. Traditionally, China treated Korea as its tributary. Japan, on the other hand, asserted that its national security could not tolerate the domination of Korea—"a dagger pointing at Japan's heart"—by any foreign power. Given that the East Asian nations had struggled against continuous Western encroachment throughout the century, in many ways the contest over Korea would determine which of these nations had most successfully assimilated Western military skills and would emerge as the leader in the East Asian resistance against the West.

Soon after the establishment of the Meiji government in 1868, the Japanese began to meddle in Korean internal affairs. In 1882 an anti-Japanese riot broke out in Seoul. China sent troops to Korea, suppressed the riot, and came to supervise the Korean government closely. In 1884, however, a Korean faction, encouraged by the Japanese, attempted a coup against Chinese dominance. The Chinese forces again prevailed, and China's influence in Korea grew. Although some Japanese demanded an immediate war with China, the Japanese government, lacking military preparations, averted the confrontation and instead concluded the Treaty of Tianjin with China in 1885. [See also 1882 Uprising and 1884 Coup d'État.]

During the following years, the Japanese government stepped up war preparations and imposed steadily higher taxes, displeasing the opposition forces in the new Imperial Diet. By 1894 Japan's political situation had reached a critical point. In May of that year the anticourt and antiforeign Tonghak Uprising in Korea brought the Sino-Japanese tension over the kingdom to war. As the uprising spread rapidly, the Korean regime sought Chinese assistance. In accordance with the Treaty of Tianjin, China informed Japan of its troop deployment. Japan's domestic political differences were quickly forgotten. Enthusiastically supported by political and military leaders as well as intellectuals, the Japanese government dispatched troops to Korea. By the time the Japanese troops arrived in Korea, the uprising had been suppressed, and, according to the Treaty of Tianjin, all foreign troops were to withdraw immediately. Japan ignored the treaty and replaced the pro-Chinese Korean regime with a collaborator, who proceeded to repudiate all the treaties with China and requested Japan to expel the Chinese forces. Having thus established the justification for war, the Japanese navy at once attacked a Chinese fleet near the Korean coast. On 1 August 1894, after considerable fighting had already taken place, the two nations officially declared war.

The war proved to be a contest between Japan's well-organized state army and China's disorganized, often ill-equipped provincial troops. Moreover, while the Chinese common people often seemed unaware of, or unconcerned with, the war, the Japanese masses supported it enthusiastically and willingly contributed to the war effort. Japan was victorious on both land and sea, winning the Battle of P'yŏngyang on 16 September, the Battle of the Yellow Sea on the next day, conquering Port Arthur on 21 November, and demolishing the Chinese fleet at Weihaiwei on 12 February 1895. After the fall of Port Arthur, China began to seek peace, but all segments of the Japanese population, seeing the war develop decisively in their country's favor, wanted increasingly greater fruits of war. Japanese leaders, seeking to solidify their bargaining position, rejected an early Chinese overture for peace and continued military operations. As Japan seemed invincible, China proposed formal peace negotiations and sent its leading statesman, Li Hongzhang, to Shimonoseki. From 20 March 1895 a turbulent peace conference was held between Li and the Japanese plenipotentiaries, Premier Itō Hirobumi and Foreign Minister Mutsu Munemitsu. Li strenuously resisted severe Japanese demands, hoping, in vain, that the Western powers would intervene and force Japan to reduce its demands. Finally, on 17 April, the Treaty of Shimonoseki was concluded. The treaty stipulated China's recognition of Korean independence; payment of an indemnity of 200 million taels; cession of Taiwan, the Pescadores Islands, and the Liaodong Peninsula; and conclusion of a commercial treaty, opening several ports and other places for Japanese as well as Western economic activities. [See also Shimonoseki, Treaty of.]

Fighting, however, did not end with the signing of the treaty. Resisting the Japanese takeover, Taiwanese islanders fiercely fought the Japanese occupation forces. Finally, on 21 October 1895, after having sent some 50,000 troops to Taiwan and losing more than 4,600 men, Japan conquered the island. Meanwhile, barely one week after the conclusion of the Treaty of Shimonoseki, Russia, Germany, and France "advised" Japan, in the name of permanent peace in East Asia, to retrocede the Liaodong Peninsula. With no recourse but to succumb to the Triple Intervention, as it came to be known, Japan gave up the newly acquired territory in exchange for an additional indemnity from China.

This profoundly humiliated the Japanese, who resolved to avenge the bitter experience. [*See also* Triple Intervention.]

The Sino-Japanese War established Japan as the dominant power in East Asia. Internally, the victory enhanced the prestige of the emperor and his soldiers. Wartime and postwar arms buildup and the huge indemnity greatly advanced Japanese industrialization. Externally, contempt replaced the traditional Japanese respect toward the Chinese. Toward Korea, Japan grew more insolent, culminating its ambition in 1910 with the colonization of the kingdom. Thus, the Sino-Japanese War was the precursor of Japanese imperialism, which was to trouble Japan and the world for the next fifty years.

[*For the extent of Japan's acquisitions resulting from this war, see the map accompanying* Meiji Period.]

Hilary Conroy, *The Japanese Seizure of Korea, 1868–1910* (1963). Marius B. Jansen, *Japan and China: From War to Peace, 1894–1972* (1975). Mutsu Munemitsu, *Kenkenroku: A Diplomatic Record of the Sino-Japanese War, 1894–1895*, translated by Gordon M. Berger (1982).   SHUMPEI OKAMOTO

SINO-TIBETAN LANGUAGES.

The Sino-Tibetan language family consists of two major branches, Sinitic and Tibeto-Burman. All the historical stages and dialectal variants of Chinese are classified under the Sinitic branch. Tibeto-Burman is a very diverse subgrouping containing hundreds of languages and dialects. Sino-Tibetan languages are spoken in most of China, including the Tibetan Plateau, and in Burma, northeastern India, Nepal, Bhutan, and parts of Southeast Asia. The major written languages of the Sino-Tibetan family include Chinese (written since the second millennium BCE), Tibetan (written since the seventh century CE), and Burmese (written since the twelfth century CE). Chinese is written in a logographic script in which the graphic units represent individual words or morphemes; both Tibetan and Burmese are written in alphabets derived from Indian prototypes.

A relationship between Tibetan and Chinese has been recognized for more than a century. This relationship is evident from a number of striking lexical resemblances that include pronouns, numerals, and a small but important stock of basic words. Despite these almost universally recognized similarities, however, the relationship between Chinese and Tibeto-Burman is viewed by most scholars as a distant one.

Some linguists (including many in China) include the Tai and Miao-Yao languages in the Sino-Tibetan family. Such a view, once widely accepted in the West also, has by and large been abandoned by American and European scholars. Whether Tai and Miao-Yao should be classified with Austronesian (or Malayo-Polynesian) in an Austro-Tai family, as proposed by Paul Benedict, is, however, still open to question.

Sino-Tibetan includes many different linguistic types. Many Tibeto-Burman languages, like Chinese, are monosyllabic and tonal, but a significant number are not. Some modern Tibetan dialects, for example, are tonal, like that of Lhasa; others, like Amdo, lack tones altogether. Tibeto-Burman word order is predominantly of the subject-object-verb type, whereas Chinese generally places the object after the verb. Modifiers come before the word modified in Chinese, but in Tibeto-Burman the opposite order is much more common. These and other structural differences between Chinese and Tibeto-Burman have suggested to some linguists the possibility of Chinese having undergone the influence of some structurally unrelated language at an early point in its history.

[*See also* Chinese Language.]

Paul K. Benedict, *Sino-Tibetan: A Conspectus* (1972). Nicholas C. Bodman, "Proto-Chinese and Sino-Tibetan: Data Toward Establishing the Nature of the Relationship," in *Contributions to Historical Linguistics, Issues and Materials*, edited by Frans Van Coetsem and Linda R. Waugh (1980).   JERRY NORMAN

SINO-VIETNAMESE RELATIONS.

Chinese relations with Vietnam began about 200 BCE. The area near modern Hanoi first came under the control of Nan Yue (a semi-Chinese state formed during the breakup of the Qin empire), and then in 111 BCE it was taken over by the Han dynasty. The Han attempted serious sinification only after the rebellion led by Trung Trac (39–42 CE).

Chinese authority faded during the decline of the Tang dynasty, and after Ngo Quyen defeated a Chinese force in 938, he proclaimed himself an independent king. Sinicization of Vietnamese society was still shallow at this time; it was deepened by later Vietnamese rulers, especially in the fifteenth and nineteenth centuries.

Tributary relations between China and the state the Chinese called Annam ("pacified south"), or Jiaozhi, were established in 973. However, the presentation of tribute and acceptance of Chinese titles by Vietnamese rulers did not imply Chinese control. When Chinese armies tried to impose actual rule (980–981, 1076, 1406–1428, 1788–1789), the Vietnamese always succeeded in expelling them. Vietnam's nominal tributary status achieved its greatest real expression between 1883 and 1885, when Chinese armies attempted to defend Vietnam against French conquest.

During World War II Japan occupied Vietnam. From late 1945 to mid-1946 troops of the Yunnan militarist Lu Han, sent to disarm the Japanese, occupied Vietnam down to the sixteenth parallel. The Chinese troops did considerable looting.

The People's Republic of China (PRC) provided weapons, supplies, and economic aid to the Democratic Republic of Vietnam starting in 1950. In late 1965 and early 1966 the PRC put about fifty thousand military personnel in the northern section of North Vietnam to deter a possible US invasion. However, Sino-Vietnamese relations deteriorated in the 1970s. China objected to Vietnam's friendship with the USSR and to the Vietnamese invasion of Kampuchea in 1978. China briefly invaded the northernmost section of Vietnam in 1979 in an effort to draw off Vietnamese troops from Kampuchea.

Keith W. Taylor, *The Birth of Vietnam* (1983). Allen Whiting, *The Chinese Calculus of Deterrence* (1975).

EDWIN E. MOISE

SINYETHA PARTY (Burmese, "poor man's" or "proletarian" party), name given by Dr. Ba Maw to a political party he formed in 1936 that contested the general election held to select the members of the first House of Representatives under the 1935 Burma constitution. The party's manifesto was notable for its explicit policies to aid the peasantry by instituting such measures as land reform, a reduction in taxes and rent, a policy of electing village headmen as well as other administrative reforms, and the establishment of free compulsory education. The party gained only 16 of the 132 seats in the legislature, and Ba Maw was forced to abandon his program in order to gain the support of British and Indian commercial interests. He managed then to form a coalition cabinet with the support of a legislative majority. This government fell two years later in the face of peasant and worker protests.

[*See also* Ba Maw *and* Burma.]

John F. Cady, *A History of Modern Burma* (1958).

ROBERT H. TAYLOR

SIPAHI. *See* Sepoy.

SIRAJ UD-DAULAH (1733–1757), successor to Alivardi Khan, his maternal grandfather, as nawab of Bengal on 15 April 1756. The East India Company desired his favor and protection, which Siraj promised. From the very beginning Siraj was beset with conspiracy from close relatives and high officials of the domain—a circumstance that did not improve his weak character. Jean Law, chief of the French factory at Kasimbazar, observed that the English gave Siraj reasons for complaint against them by building "strong fortifications" and digging a "large ditch" in the nawab's domain contrary to established laws of the country, abusing the privilege of free passage for the company's trade, and giving shelter to the nawab's recalcitrant subjects.

A determined nawab decided to punish the English for disgracefully expelling his messenger from Calcutta. He captured Calcutta on 20 June 1756; it was at this time that the incident of the Black Hole took place. The English retreated to a riverside shelter nearby. The nawab, however, made no attempt to consolidate his victory. Calcutta was easily recovered by Colonel Robert Clive and Admiral Watson on 2 January 1757. The nawab accepted British terms in the Treaty of Alinagar on 9 February 1757. In the next months a series of events began that led to the Battle of Plassey, where Siraj ud-Daulah met his death.

[*See also* Bengal; Black Hole; *and* Plassey, Battle of.]

K. K. Dutta, *Siraj-ud-daulah* (1971). Brijen K. Gupta, *Siraj-ud-daulah and the East India Company* (1962).

PRADIP SINHA

SIRHAK ("practical learning"), an intellectual trend or movement of the latter half of Korea's Yi dynasty (1392–1910). The term *sir* (Chinese, *shi*) means "practical" or "real," and the compound *sirhak*, "practical, real learning," has a long Confucian and Buddhist history; its meaning or content varies as often as views change concerning what is real or practical as opposed to what is empty and impractical. A group of nationalistic Korean scholars in the 1930s began using the term to designate a movement among scholars during the latter half of the Yi dynasty to pursue studies in areas such as law, administration, economic institutions, and Korean geography, language, and literature.

One sometimes hears of a *sirhakp'a,* or "school of Practical Learning." Strictly speaking this is a misnomer: there were a number of groups that shared traits that now earn them the label *sirhak,* but there is no evidence that this broadly based trend achieved the status of a self-conscious school of thought. The traits that distinguished *sirhak* scholars from their ordinary Neo-Confucian contemporaries include: (1) a spirit of criticism toward the establishment and the doctrinaire Neo-Confucianism of the Zhu Xi school, which had become its rigid orthodoxy; (2) a spirit of seeking evidence to establish facts, as opposed to more speculative modes of thought; and (3) a spirit of practicality.

Two social factors made this caste of mind common enough to be identified as a movement. Factional conflict forced certain groups to the periphery; all were upper-class and educated, but without hope of a significant career in government. Many *sirhak* scholars belonged to one such faction, the Namin (Southerners). Further, many of them lived in or near Seoul; with neither government stipend nor rural estates for support, they came in intimate contact with the economic problems and hardships of the common people and voiced these concerns in their writings. The abiding social, political, and economic concerns of *sirhak* distinguish it from the contemporaneous school of Han Learning in China, with which it has a number of affinities.

Sirhak was, then, an outsider's intellectuality. For one period, however, factionalism abated and *sirhak* moved to the center: the reigns of Yŏngjo (r. 1725–1776) and Chŏngjo (r. 1777–1800). This was the period of large-scale compilation projects, the advocacy of industrial and mercantile development, the birth of a new, truly Korean literary movement, and the most sophisticated application of the new methodology of "seeking evidence." The greatest genius of the *sirhak* movement, Chŏng Yag-yong (Tasan; 1762–1836) held office at the close of this period and in the aftermath lived the remainder of his life in exile, tainted, as were many other Namin, for association with Christianity (*sŏhak,* "Western learning"). Political upheaval and repression seems to have stifled this premodern "modern" learning at a critical point, and attempts to link *sirhak* to the modernization movement of the late nineteenth century are unconvincing.

[*See also* Yi Dynasty *and* Chŏng Yag-yong.]

Michael C. Kalton, "An Introduction to Silhak," *Korea Journal* 15.5 (1975): 29–46. Hugh H. W. Kang, ed., *The Traditional Culture and Society of Korea: Thought and Institutions* (1975). Ki-baik Lee, *A New History of Korea,* translated by Edward W. Wagner (1984).

MICHAEL C. KALTON

SIRHINDI, AHMAD (1564–1624), a Sufi saint of the Naqshbandi order who, on account of his scholarship, reformist views, and piety, came to be regarded as the "renewer of the second millennium." His family claimed descent from Caliph Umar I. Shaikh Ahmad received his early education at his birthplace, Sirhind (in the Punjab), from his father, Shaikh Abdul Ahad, and later moved to Sialkot for further studies. The emperor Akbar invited him to Agra, where he came into contact with Abu'l Fazl and Faizi. At the age of twenty-eight he joined the Naqshbandi order at Delhi and became a disciple of Khwaja Baqi Billah. Shaikh Ahmad soon gained great popularity and his disciples were spread over large parts of India and Central and West Asia. The three-volume collection of his letters is an important source of information about his teachings and activities. It has been translated from Persian into Arabic, Turkish, and Urdu. His views raised opposition in certain quarters, leading to his imprisonment for a year at Gwalior by Jahangir.

Shaikh Ahmad criticized the religious experiments of Akbar. He rejected Ibn Arabi's doctrine of *wahdat-ul-wujud* ("unity of being") and put forward his own theory of *wahdat-ul-shuhud* ("unity of vision"). He preached adherence to the laws of Islam and the traditions of the Prophet. Shaikh Ahmad was opposed to mystic music and preferred a life of sobriety to a life of ecstasy. Some of his ideas seem to have influenced Aurangzeb, who was deeply attached to the saint's descendants. Shaikh Ahmad's tomb at Sirhind is visited by a large number of people even today.

[*See also* Naqshbandi; Aurangzeb; *and* Sufism.]

Burhan Ahmad Faruqi, *The Mujaddid's Conception of Tawhid* (1940). Y. Freidmann, *Shaykh Ahmad Sirhindi: An Outline of His Thought and a Study of His Image in the Eyes of Posterity* (1971).   FARHAN AHMAD NIZAMI

SIRIBUNYASAN (r. circa 1760–1781), the last independent king of Vientiane in Laos. His father, King Setthathirat II, had seen the partition of Laos into three kingdoms, and in addition to these interregional rivalries Siribunyasan now further suffered, first, Burmese invasions through the 1760s, and then a massive Siamese invasion in 1778–1779.

Having fled toward Vietnam, Siribunyasan returned to Vientiane and submitted to Siam as a vassal. For all his descendants' efforts, Vientiane was not to be independent again until after World War II. On his death in 1781, Siribunyasan was succeeded, as vassal king, by his son Nanthasen.

[*See also* Vientiane; Lan Sang; *and* Anu.]

David K. Wyatt, "Siam and Laos, 1767–1827," *Journal of Southeast Asian History* 4.2 (1963): 13–32.

DAVID K. WYATT

SISAVANGVONG (1885–1959), king of Laos (r. 1904–1959). The son of Zakharine, king of the French-protected kingdom of Luang Prabang in northern Laos, Sisavangvong was educated in Saigon and Paris and succeeded his father on 28 April 1904. His powers were restricted under French protection, and his reign was uneventful until 1941 when the Japanese forced France to cede the royal province of Sayaboury, immediately across the Mekong River from Luang Prabang, to Thailand. Greatly perturbed, Sisavangvong threatened abdication, but the French compensated Luang Prabang by adding to its three remaining provinces three other provinces hitherto under colonial rule and by modifying the protectorate.

After the Japanese evicted the French in March 1945, Sisavangvong maintained his kingdom's loyalty to France until Japan forced cooperation. When Japan capitulated, he proclaimed the continuance of the French protectorate and welcomed the returning French. This led to conflict with his prime minister, Prince Phetsarath, and with the nationalist Lao Issara, who, backed by Vietnamese troops and by the Chinese occupying northern Laos in the Allied interest, set up a rebel government and in November 1945 forced Sisavangvong to abdicate. In April 1946 the Lao Issara asked him to resume the throne, and three years later, when the French returned in force, he asked for and obtained new constitutional arrangements. A new constitution for a united democratic kingdom followed in May 1947, and in 1949 Laos achieved independence. King Sisavangvong steadfastly refused to leave his capital when it was threatened by Vietnamese forces fighting the French in 1953 and 1954. He died, respected and well loved, after a reign of fifty-five years, on 29 October 1959.

[*See also* Laos; Luang Prabang; Phetsarath; *and* Lao Issara.]

A. J. Dommen, *Conflict in Laos* (1971). HUGH TOYE

SISODIYA DYNASTY. The Sisodiyas of Chitor, Udaipur, and Mewar in Rajasthan, India, were the premier Rajput dynasty from 1326 to 1948 and were renowned for their centuries-long struggle for independence against the Muslims. They achieved political supremacy in western and central India under Rana Kumbha (r. 1433–1468) and competed for the North Indian empire under Rana Sanga (r. 1509–1528), whose defeat by Babur in 1527 was a crucial step in the founding of the Mughal empire. Maharana Pratap Singh (r. 1572–1597), popularly remembered as Rana Pratap, became a national hero on account of his resistance to the Mughal conquest under the Emperor Akbar. Submitting to the Mughals in 1606, the Sisodiyas played a crucial role in the history of the Mughal empire. They gained independence in the eighteenth century, but were unable to defend themselves against the Marathas and other invaders. After 1818 the Sisodiyas were ruled under British protection until their native state of Mewar became part of the Republic of India in 1947.

[*See also* Mewar; Chitor; Udaipur; Rajput; *and* Rajasthan.]

G. N. Sharma, *Mewar and the Mughal Emperors (1526–1707 A.D.)* (1954). SHIVA BAJPAI

SISOWATH (1840–1927), king of Cambodia (r. 1904–1927) under the French protectorate, succeeding his brother, Norodom (r. 1860–1904). In the 1860s and 1870s, Sisowath ingratiated himself with the French by helping to put down several rebellions against them and his brother. He also helped suppress a more serious uprising in 1885–1886. In the 1890s, the French secretly promised him the throne. He served their interests throughout his reign, which was marked by the commercialization of Cambodian agriculture, expanded public works, and successful French negotiations with Siam to regain the Cambodian provinces of Battambang and Siem Reap. [*See also* Cambodia.]

DAVID P. CHANDLER

SISOWATH MONIVONG (1876–1941), king of Cambodia (r. 1927–1941) under the French protectorate, succeeding his father, King Sisowath (r. 1904–1927). As the first Cambodian monarch to be educated even partly in France, Monivong served as an officer in the French army for two years before World War I. Like his father, Monivong was pro-

French, but the colonial regime gave him little authority and few substantial tasks. His reign encompassed the Great Depression and the Franco-Siamese War of 1940–1941. Monivong wrote commendable classical Cambodian verse and was given the honorary rank of brigadier-general in the French army in 1934. [See also Franco-Siamese War.]

DAVID P. CHANDLER

SISTAN. Medieval Sistan (or Sijistan), with its capital at Zaranj, lay directly south of Khurasan and was bordered by Kuhistan and by the desert of Kerman. *Sistan,* which derives from a term meaning the land of the Sakas, or Scythians, figures in Iranian myth as the home of the epic hero Rustam. The Arab invasion of the region began in 643–644. The most important local dynasty was that of the Saffarids, founded by Ya'qub ibn Laith, whose real and pretended descendants influenced regional politics until Nadir Shah's time (eighteenth century). Rival claims for Sistan led to the formation of a British border commission, which in 1872 established the frontier between Iranian and Afghan Sistan along the ancient course of the Helmand River, the principal water source for the area.

[See also Saffarid Dynasty and Saka Dynasties.]

Wilhelm Barthold, *An Historical Geography of Iran* (1984), pp. 64–71. V. F. Buchner, "Sistan," in *The Encyclopaedia of Islam* (new ed., 1960–).

ARIEL SALZMANN

SISURIYAWONG (Chuang Bunnag; 1808–1883), also known as Suriyawong, *somdet chaophraya,* the most powerful minister at the court of Siam in the reigns of Mongkut and Chulalongkorn; regent for Chulalongkorn.

Sisuriyawong was one of the ablest and certainly the most powerful of the members of the Bunnag family, a family of Arabo-Persian descent that had served the Siamese kings since the early seventeenth century. He was born in Bangkok in 1808 and named Chuang. His father, Dit Bunnag, was then a junior official in the Phrakhlang (Treasury); his mother, Lady Chan, was the daughter of Chaophraya Phonlathep (Thong-in), the minister of lands. As Chuang's father rose in the bureaucracy, so did he, and by the later years of the reign of Rama III (r. 1824–1851) he held the title Phraya Sisuriyawong, one of the four heads of the Royal Pages Department.

In the 1840s, Chuang was one of the small group of Thai who dabbled in things Western and took both delight and profit in building Western-style, square-rigged ships. With his father, now Chaophraya Phrakhlang, and his uncle, Chaophraya Siphiphat (That Bunnag), Chuang manipulated Mongkut's accession to the throne in 1851. The Bunnags were rewarded with the lion's share of posts in the new government. With the death of his father and uncle in 1855–1856, Chuang, now retitled Chaophraya Sisuriyawong, became Kalahom, or minister governing the southern provinces, and was the most powerful figure in the government. He worked closely with Mongkut, securing the court's agreement to treaties forced upon Siam by the Western powers and making such changes in the state's administration as seemed necessary. On the death of Mongkut in 1868, he became regent for fifteen-year-old King Chulalongkorn and was retitled Somdet Chaophraya Borommaha Sisuriyawong. When Chulalongkorn was freed of the regency in 1873 and began considering radical reforms, Sisuriyawong resisted, not because he blindly opposed change, but because he underestimated the urgency of reform. The two remained at loggerheads until Sisuriyawong's death on 19 January 1883. He, his father, and his uncle are the only nonroyal officials ever to have been honored with the semiroyal designation *somdet.*

[See also Bunnag Family; Chakri Dynasty; Mongkut; Kalahom; Phrakhlang; Phrakhlang Dit Bunnag; Chulalongkorn; Phra Nang Klao; *and* Thiphakorawong Kham Bannag.]

David K. Wyatt, *The Politics of Reform in Thailand* (1969) and *Thailand: A Short History* (1984).

DAVID K. WYATT

SIX DYNASTIES. A generic term for the three and one-half centuries of divided rule in China between the fall of the Eastern Han dynasty in 220 and the reunification by the Sui in 589, *Six Dynasties (liuchao)* applies specifically to the six regimes whose capitals were located in Jiankang (modern Nanjing) during that period: Wu (222–280), Eastern Jin (317–420), Liu-Song (420–479), Southern Qi (479–502), Liang (502–557), and Chen (557–589). Since this listing implies the legitimacy of these particular "Chinese" states in the South, while ignoring the claims of the "non-Chinese" states that existed in the North at the same time, some historians prefer the more inclusive term Southern and Northern Dynasties *(nanbei chao).* Strictly speaking, however, the latter designation refers only to those regimes that arose after the fall of Western Jin in 316, when China became divided at about the thirty-third parallel into competing northern and southern states.

The large number and often short duration of some of these "dynasties" and "kingdoms" have undoubtedly complicated the study of the period as a whole and obscured some of the social, economic, and cultural trends that continued to develop more or less normally despite the kaleidoscopic shifts in the centers of power. These developments were influenced by the influx of large numbers of pastoral and nomadic peoples from the steppe land north of the Great Wall into the arid plains of North China and the simultaneous migration of many northern Chinese gentry families into the previously less-populated but well-watered valleys of the Yangtze River system in the South. The result was that after the division the social and cultural changes in the North and South began to assume different characters.

Chronology. In order to find some direction or pattern in the chaotic events of the period it may be helpful to break it down into five successive stages, viewing each as a phase in the long struggle to recover the lost unity of the Han empire.

During the first phase, which lasted nearly one hundred years (220–316), the idealized image of a unified empire that had somehow survived four centuries of steady erosion during the Han was by now totally shattered, but as yet no viable alternative presented itself. The tripartite division into the Three Kingdoms—Wei (220–265) in the north, Shu-Han (221–263) in the southwest, and Wu (222–280) in the southeast—was not accepted by anyone as a solution. Each state claimed legitimate succession to the whole of the Han empire and viewed the others as rebels. The brief interlude of the fourteen years from 280 to 304 in which Western Jin managed to reclaim most of the old Han territory bolstered the illusion that unity could indeed be restored. But the same forces that had destroyed the Han—the growth of powerful families with their semiautonomous estates and the increasing military power of the pastoral-nomadic tribes of Xiongnu and Xianbei who had settled south of the Great Wall, against the simultaneous disarmament of the central forces—also destroyed the Jin. Taking advantage of an unguarded moment during the fratricidal power struggle among the Jin princes to seize the throne from the imbecile Emperor Hui (r. 290–306), the Xiongnu general Liu Yuan (r. 304–310) declared himself king of Han, in what is now Shanxi Province. His successor, Liu Cong (r. 310–318), sacked the Jin capital in Luoyang in 311. Facing the unknown peril of alien rule, many of the powerful gentry families picked up what movable property and slaves they could and fled southward across the Yangtze River, where they set up a government in exile—the Eastern Jin (317–420)—with its capital in Jiankang. There the remainder of the Southern Dynasties maintained a precarious control of South China until 589.

In the second phase, from 317 to 383, there was a rapid proliferation of small kingdoms in the North, ruled mostly by chieftains of the non-Chinese minorities who had settled in particular areas. Since there were a total of sixteen altogether between 304 and 439, they are known collectively as the Sixteen Kingdoms (*shiliu guo*). In reality, the division was never into more than four or five at any one time. Two Xiongnu kingdoms known afterward as Former and Later Zhao made their capitals in Pingcheng (in Shanxi) and Ye (in Henan) between the years 304 and 352. Three others known respectively as Former, Later, and Western Qin occupied the area of modern Shaanxi between 351 and 417. Two of these were ruled by Di (Tibetans) and one by Xianbei. The first, Former Qin (351–394), under the forceful leadership of Fu Jian (r. 359–385), swept all the others before it and by 376 had conquered the whole of North China. Realization of the dream of a single empire seemed once more to be within reach. Acting with great deliberation and circumspection, Fu Jian carefully weighed his chances, then gathered an invading force of one million men, including 270,000 cavalry. In the autumn of 383 he set out to conquer the vastly smaller army of footsoldiers of Eastern Jin. Mired in the swamps surrounding the Fei River (a tributary of the Huai), Fu Jian's hosts suffered a disastrous rout, and once more the dream of reunion faded. [*See also* Fei River, Battle of.]

In the third phase, from 383 to 439, the spawning of separate kingdoms, momentarily halted by Fu Jian's bid for empire, resumed. Fu's erstwhile lieutenants scrambled to pick up the fragments of his lost domain. The Qiang (another Tibetan group) founded the Later Qin (384–417) in Fu Jian's old capital at Chang'an. A Xianbei group in Jincheng (southeast Gansu) set up the Western Qin (385–431). Five separate Xianbei kingdoms bearing the name Yan occupied various parts of the northeast (modern Hebei) between 352 and 436, and another five named Liang (two Chinese, the others Tibetan, Xiongnu, and Xianbei) ruled the northwest (modern

Gansu) between 313 and 439. A Xiongnu group that had preserved its pastoral way of life in the Ordos region within the loop of the Yellow River declared a kingdom of Xia (407–431).

In the fourth phase, from 439 to 534, a new contender for supremacy appeared—the Northern Wei (385–534). Although previously known as Dai, this branch of the Xianbei, under the leadership of the Tuoba, assumed the name of Wei at the time of Fu Jian's downfall. Their first capital was located in Pingcheng, just south of the Great Wall in Shanxi. By the year 439 they had conquered the last of the Sixteen Kingdoms and held hegemony over all of North China. Yielding to pressure from Chinese officials in the court who had also urged the enactment of sweeping land reforms known as the "equalized fields" *(juntian)*, they moved the capital south to the old Eastern Han capital in Luoyang, where they enacted further laws, banished the Xianbei language, and otherwise became thoroughly Chinese. This further alienated the conservative Tuoba nobility, who had never been able to adapt to the sedentary life of the North China Plain and had become more and more impoverished and resentful. A rift eventually occurred in 534, when a Chinese official, Gao Huan, placed a puppet on the throne whose reign (534–550) is known as Eastern Wei. His predecessor fled with other Tuoba loyalists to Chang'an, where they set up a purely Tuoba regime, the Western Wei (535–557). For the third time the fleeting vision of reunion had faded away unfulfilled. [*See also* Northern Wei Dynasty.]

The fifth and last phase, from 534 to 589, saw the steady increase in strength of Western Wei and its successor, Northern Zhou (557–581), at the expense of Eastern Wei, whose single puppet ruler was deposed in 550 and replaced by Gao Huan's son Yang. Gao Yang promptly declared a "Chinese" dynasty, the Northern Qi (550–577), but it was no match militarily for the Northern Zhou, who succeeded once more in reuniting all of North China and even part of the South in the form of the protectorate, Later Liang (555–587). But Northern Zhou in its turn was overthrown by one of its Chinese officials, Yang Jian, who founded the Sui Dynasty (581–618), with its capital still in Chang'an. Eight years later Yang Jian took advantage of the almost universal longing for reunification to conquer the last of the Southern Dynasties. [*See also* Northern Qi Dynasty *and* Sui Dynasty.]

In the case of the Southern Dynasties (Eastern Jin, Liu-Song, Qi, Liang, and Chen) during the period of division (317–589), there is little in the political realm to report other than the miracle of their survival in the face of Fu Jian's massive debacle of 383 and the halfhearted forays by the Northern Wei around the time of their southward move in 494. Various of the Southern Dynasties themselves made a few (largely symbolic) attempts to "recover the North" in 354, 369, and 417, but no one was really deluded into trying to make these temporary footholds permanent. The natural defenses of the Huai and Yangtze rivers, together with the fragmentation of the northern powers and their own harassment by the non-Chinese Ruanruan from the rear, were the South's only real external bulwarks. The greatest danger they faced came from within.

The northern émigré families who controlled all the important court positions or were dispatched to the provinces as civil and military governors settled for the most part in or near the capital in Jiankang or in other metropolitan centers like Xiangyang and Wuchang (in Hubei). Some reclusive types rusticated on their country estates in the hilly region around Guiji (in Zhejiang). The older local Wu aristocratic families, whose vast estates occupied the rich agricultural zones of the Yangtze Valley, tolerated the refugees and accepted minor posts in their government but spoke a different dialect and maintained a social distance. The emperors were at the mercy of the northern families and their cliques at court, who tried to maneuver their way into positions of power through intermarriage with the royal line or otherwise to manipulate the legitimate succession. Such intrigues posed a constant threat of rebellions and coups d'état, which indeed often occurred. As a precaution, especially during the final years of Southern Qi, some emperors like the marquis of Donghun (r. 498–501) resorted to wholesale slaughter of all rival contenders and their families.

An interlude of calm followed the founding of Liang (502–557) by Xiao Yan (Liang Wudi; r. 502–549), who achieved the longest and most stable reign of any southern emperor. Even he became so deeply involved in his support for the Buddhist clergy as he grew older, however, that he lost touch with reality. His last days were devastated by the rebellion of Hou Jing, a renegade Tuoba general to whom he had entrusted great power in the hope of recovering the North after the breakup of Northern Wei in 535. Although Liang rallied again and survived in truncated form until 557, the days of the Southern Dynasties were numbered. Chen Baxian, the suppressor of Hou Jing, established a precarious successor to Liang, the Chen, which was finally absorbed into the Sui empire in 589.

Cultural and Religious Developments. From the cultural point of view the Six Dynasties present a picture of far greater stability and continuity than the violent vicissitudes of the North and South would lead one to expect. There were of course significant differences in the social organization and economy of the seminomadic northern tribesmen and the agriculturally oriented Chinese majority in both North and South. These differences also affected the culture of both areas, especially in the realm of classical studies in the North, and limited the creation of "refined" literature even while stimulating new departures in the realm of fantastic tales and popular ballads.

Buddhism. By far the most striking contrast, however, may be seen in the way the Buddhist religion was assimilated in each area after its introduction from India and Central Asia toward the end of the Han. Dramatic inroads were made in northern metropolitan centers like Chang'an and Luoyang as well as in the border outposts of Dunhuang in the northwest and Yungang in the northeast, but the pattern was different in the South. The non-Chinese rulers of the North relied on Buddhist monks for numinous support and used them as diviners and magicians, while at the same time subordinating the *sangha* (the monastic community) to state control. Some Northern Wei rulers sponsored huge building projects such as the cave temples in Yungang, Longmen, and Dunhuang.

In the South, which was farther from the Central Asian ports of entry and consequently had less direct contact with missionaries, there was less popular piety and less evidence of state support, with the possible exception of the reign of Emperor Wu of Liang. Southern Buddhism on the whole seemed to be more elitist and theoretical—a subject for debate and philosophical conversations among dilettante intellectuals. Religious fads often sprang up following the translation of a new sutra (scripture). During the fourth century, for example, the Prajnaparamita sutras, which preached a doctrine of "emptiness" *(shunyata)* similar to Laozi's notion of "nonbeing" *(wu),* held center stage along with the *Vimalakirtinirdesa,* which exalted the role of the wealthy layman. In the fifth century a veritable revolution erupted following the translation of the *Nirvana Sutra,* which proclaimed the universal presence of the Buddha nature *(foxing)* in all beings, with the potential for instantaneous enlightenment and the blissful survival of the "true self" *(zhenwo)* in nirvana. This was followed in the late fifth and early sixth centuries by the backlash of pious sobriety when eloquent monks like Baoliang and Sengsong popularized the scholastic theories of the (Hinayana) Sarvastivada school in India as found in Harivarman's treatise, *Perfection of Truth (Chengshi lun).* This sober phase of southern Buddhism is referred to as the Chengshi school. It was eventually replaced by a return to the old doctrine of Emptiness, much refined by the monk Jizang (549–623) through his commentaries on three important treatises of the Madhyamika school. This in turn is referred to as the "Three Treatise" (Sanlun) school. [*See also* Buddhism: Buddhism in China.]

Daoism. Simultaneous with the development of this foreign religion on Chinese soil the great indigenous religion of Daoism was also coming to maturity, both at the popular level and among certain gentry families such as the Wang family of Langye and the Chi family of Gaoping. The Way of the Celestial Masters (Tianshi Dao) was the dominant sect in the North and experienced its greatest political influence under the Northern Wei emperor Taiwu (r. 424–452), when, as Celestial Master, Kou Qianzhi (d. 448) served as a special adviser to the throne. When northern Daoists fled south early in the fourth century they found learned exponents of this sect like Ge Hong (284–363) advocating a mixture of Confucian morality and Daoist alchemy. But a new, distinctively southern variety of Daoism was developing in the Zhejiang area with greater attention to new revelations of scripture that stressed "inner alchemy" and transcendence. These new scriptures were gathered and edited by Tao Hongjing (456–536), who became the first patriarch of the Maoshan sect, named for his hermitage near Jiankang. It was this form of Daoism that became dominant in the Tang period that followed. [*See also* Daoism.]

Philosophical discussion in this period, which has been characterized by the term *xuanxue* ("study of the mysterious"), began with a reassessment of the discredited Confucian orthodoxy of the Han. People like Wang Bi (226–249) and Guo Xiang (d. 312) reinterpreted the Sage in the more mystical framework of the *Book of Changes (Yijing)* and the late Zhou philosophical texts *Laozi* and *Zhuangzi.* Arguments swirled about the question whether "nonbeing" *(wu)* was, as Wang Bi claimed, pure potentiality out of which "being" *(yu)* emerged, or whether, as the more hard-headed Guo Xiang insisted, it was simply "nothing." Being itself belonged to the realm of the uncaused and "self-existent" *(ziran).* With increased interest in Buddhism and Daoism many discussions devolved into attempts to harmonize apparent contradictions between these doctrines and those of Confucius.

The Arts and Literature. Great strides were made in the arts in this period, especially under the impact of Buddhist sculpture and painting. There was a steady growth from the rather stiff, frontal, and attenuated figures of the late fifth and early sixth centuries to a greater freedom of movement and fullness of form toward the end of the sixth, as may be seen in the cave temples of Dunhuang, Yungang, Longmen, and in certain Buddhist stelae. Secular paintings have not survived as well, but copies from the ninth and thirteenth centuries of scrolls attributed to Gu Kaizhi (345?–406) preserve a fair approximation of Six Dynasties style, with its cellular composition and disproportionate scale. In the lush mountain settings of the South a new interest in landscape developed, to which the poems of Xie Lingyun and Tao Qian bear ample testimony. It was natural that attempts would be made to paint landscape as well. Technical problems of scale, atmosphere, and space, however, were not addressed until much later. [*See also* Painting: Chinese Painting.]

In the realm of literature, especially poetry, the five-syllable verse inherited from the Latter Han was refined and perfected by poets like Cao Zhi (192–232), until by the late fifth century Shen Yue (441–513) and others of his circle had devised tonal and other euphonic prescriptions that laid the foundation for the highly sophisticated and craftsmanlike "regulated poems" *(lüshi)* of the great Tang masters. Six Dynasties prose became notorious in later periods because of the intricacy of its balanced parallel couplets *(pianti wen)*. The antiquarian movement *(guwen)* fostered by Han Yu (768–824) and others was a self-conscious protest against the presumed artificiality of this style. No one has ever contested, however, the quintessential "Chineseness" of the binary principle on which it was founded. [*See also* Guwen *and* Han Yu.]

Notable advances in material culture in this period are the development of the draw loom for weaving complex patterns, the watermill for pounding and grinding grain, the wheelbarrow, and the use of tea as a beverage. Because of closer contact with India and Central Asia there were also some significant imports, including Indian medical practice and dicing games and Central Asian music. From the nomadic peoples of the steppes came riding pants and the stirrup—advances of great consequence in warfare.

In the light of such developments, which continued without interruption throughout this troubled period, it is possible to view the age as the matrix out of which a new and unified empire was emerging. All the justly acclaimed cultural achievements of the Tang were present here in embryo.

[*See also* Three Kingdoms; Jin Dynasty; Sixteen Kingdoms; *and* Southern and Northern Dynasties.]

Étienne Balazs, *Chinese Civilization and Bureaucracy* (1964). Wolfram Eberhard, *A History of China* (rev. ed., 1960). L. Carrington Goodrich, *A Short History of the Chinese People* (3d ed., 1959). Richard Mather, *Shih-shuo hsin-yü, A New Account of Tales of the World* (1976). Michael Rogers, *The Chronicle of Fu Chien* (1968). Holmes Welch and Anna Seidel, eds., *Facets of Taoism* (1979). Erik Zürcher, *The Buddhist Conquest of China* (1959).

RICHARD MATHER

SIXTEEN KINGDOMS, short-lived regimes (actually nineteen in number) established in North China during the period 304 to 439, mostly by invading nomads. The Sixteen Kingdoms era was the first time in history in which a part of China was ruled by foreigners. The name derives from a chronological account of the period, *Annals of the Sixteen Kingdoms (Shiliuguo chunqiu)*. Although a few of the rulers of these kingdoms may have been Chinese, most belonged to one of five peoples: Xiongnu and Jie (ancestors of the Turks), Xianbei (ancestors of the Mongols), and Di and Qiang (ancestors of the Tibetans). These peoples before their rise to power had all been influenced by Chinese civilization during the Latter Han (25–220) and Three Kingdoms (220–280) periods. Conquering China, they established semi-sinicized states out of which, beginning in the fifth century, a more unified Northern Dynasties society was born.

The Sixteen Kingdoms period was characterized by endemic warfare and strong racial tensions between the rulers and their Chinese subjects; large-scale social dislocations in which the great Chinese houses fled to havens south of the Yangtze River; the return of a natural economy in which cloth and agricultural produce temporarily replaced money; the ascendancy of a feudal nobility and the renascence of the privileges of birth; and oppression of the common people in the form of increased taxes and more onerous military and labor service obligations. Such conditions paved the way for the rise of Buddhism, perhaps the most important cultural development of the period. Among its many doctrines, those promising salvation based on faith proved particularly appealing on the popular level. On a different level, the foreign rulers of the kingdoms became ardent patrons of this foreign faith, supporting the construction of Buddhist temples, the fashioning of Buddhist images, and the translation of Buddhist scriptures. Buddhist monks, allowed free access to the palace, became their close advisers on political and military matters.

[See also Six Dynasties and Southern and Northern Dynasties.]

HOWARD J. WECHSLER

SIXTH DALAI LAMA. See Tsangyang Gyatso.

SJAFRUDDIN PRAWIRANEGARA (b. 1911),

Indonesian politician. Born in Anjar Kidul, West Java, he was educated as a lawyer under the Dutch colonial administration. He was a principal economic figure in the independent Republican government, serving as minister of finance (1946–1947) and minister of welfare (1948). He became president and acting prime minister of the Emergency government formed on Sumatra after the Dutch captured Yogyakarta in December 1948. He was appointed minister of finance in 1950. Increasingly opposed to Sukarno's policies, he joined the Pemerintah Revolusioner Republik Indonesia (PRRI) rebellion in 1958, becoming prime minister in the rebel government. He surrendered in 1961 and was kept in close confinement until 1966. Under Suharto's New Order, he returned to the private sector and, though barred from an active political role, became an outspoken critic of the government on behalf of Muslim interests.

[See also Sukarno; Pemerintah Revolusioner Republik Indonesia/Perdjuangan Semesta; and Suharto.]

AUDREY R. KAHIN

SJAHRIR, SUTAN (1909–1966), Indonesian so-

cialist leader; prime minister (1945–1947). A Dutch-educated (in Medan, Bandung, and the Netherlands) Minangkabau, Sjahrir in 1931 helped found the Pendidikan Nasional Indonesia to educate a socialist leadership for Indonesia's nationalist movement. He was arrested in 1934 and exiled. During the Japanese occupation of Indonesia he remained underground. In 1945, as prime minister, he conducted negotiations with the Dutch. In 1948 he formed the Indonesian Socialist Party (PSI). Although lacking electoral strength and regarded as the intellectuals' party, the PSI was influential in Parliament and civil service until banned in 1960.

After 1950 Sjahrir withdrew from active politics. His last years were spent under house arrest.

[See also Partai Nasional Indonesia and Partai Sosialis Indonesia.]

JOHN D. LEGGE

SLAVE DYNASTY OF DELHI. See Mamluks.

SLAVERY AND SERFDOM

SLAVERY IN CHINA

A slave is a person who is owned by another and who can be sold by that person, hence the term *chattel slave*. Generally, the slave is also a person who is powerless. Although there is no problem about the applicability of the first criterion, ownership, to slaves in China, not all Chinese slaves were powerless; indeed, some enjoyed great power. An additional characteristic of slavery in China is that slavery was but one of many dependent categories throughout Chinese social history. Thus, before commenting directly on slavery it is necessary to place that institution within the broader framework of dependency relationships.

"Good" people *(liangmin)* and "inferior" people *(jianmin)*—also rendered as "base" or "mean" people—are two common categories into which the population of China was customarily and legally divided. Inferior people included slaves as well as those who were less servile but still not free. In the Tang dynasty (618–907), for example, the law code specified different punishments for the same crime committed by official slaves *(guan nubei)*, official bondsmen *(guanhu)*, and general bondsmen *(zahu)*—all three are categories of government-owned slaves or near-slaves. Whereas the slave had to labor year-round for the government unit that owned him, the general bondsman was required to serve only a set number of days per year. Furthermore, the general bondsmen, like commoners, were eligible to receive allocations of land under the state land system *(juntian)*. Thus, instead of a sharp distinction between free and slave in this society, there were gradations of servitude among those in the "inferior" people category. These social shadings were not limited to this category, however; both officials and commoners were subjected to different legal treatment depending upon the nature of the relevant relationships in which they were involved.

The early history of slavery in China is far from clear. Marxist historians, bound by the Marxist unilinear interpretation of all human history, assert that slavery was the dominant mode of production beginning in the Xia dynasty. Such historians disagree on when the slavery stage ended. Some put it as early as the beginning of the Zhou dynasty (c. 1122–256 BCE); others place the transition from slave to feudal society as late as the end of the Later Han dynasty in 220 CE. There are no archaeologically attested documents from the Xia dynasty, and those from the Shang dynasty (c. 1766–1122 BCE) contain no evidence of the sale of humans. Hence, although there is firm evidence that Shang society was strongly patrimonial and that everyone lived in a dependency relationship vis-à-vis the Shang ruler, there is no conclusive evidence of slavery in that period. By the Zhou dynasty there are references to chattel slavery, but the historian is hard-pressed to say more than that it existed. The documentation on slavery beginning in the Han period (206 BCE–220 CE) is sufficiently full that a more confident analysis of slavery can be made. Because of the continuities involved, the following discussion is topical; some historical variations are noted under the topical headings.

Sources of Slaves. There were two major sources of government-owned slaves: criminals and war captives. Under the Chinese legal system, the relatives of a person convicted of a heinous crime might be enslaved. If a slave owner were convicted of a crime, his property, including his slaves, might be confiscated, adding to the number of government-owned slaves. The other principal source of government-owned slaves, war captives, were not all non-Chinese. When the Mongols conquered China in the thirteenth century many Chinese were enslaved. As the Manchu founders of the Qing dynasty (1644–1911) moved south into China, they also enslaved large numbers of Chinese.

Privately owned slaves came from a variety of sources. First, government-owned slaves were sometimes given to officials and others. Second, sale of self or family members was the most common source of privately owned slaves. In times of famine or comparable disasters, children or other family members were sold into slavery as part of the survival strategy. Commendation of land and family was a third route to permanent servitude. In times of large-scale civil disorders, such as the Period of Disunion (220–589), commendation was fairly common. Such people might become either slaves or personal retainers (*bugu*). Personal retainers technically were not slaves, for they could not be sold, but they could be given away. In transferring control to a third party, the master of a personal retainer could charge

for the food and clothing he had provided for the retainer; in other words, there was an ill-concealed sale of the personal retainer. On the other hand, the personal retainer was juridically superior to a slave but inferior to a commoner. In the Ming dynasty (1368–1644) many commoners and even some men trained for the bureaucracy commended themselves to others.

Inheritance was the fourth category under which people became slaves. In parts of South China it was not uncommon for whole lineages to be in permanent servitude to other lineages. Finally, people were kidnapped or in other illegal ways seized and sold into slavery. Hired laborers were "inferior" people, and although they were legally distinguished from slaves, in practice they were little different from them. Late in the Ming period the state, in recognition of the growing number of laborers in commerce and industry and the increasing complexity of the labor market, decreed that short-term laborers were to enjoy the legal status of "good" people although long-term laborers were to continue as "inferior" people. Poverty pushed people into slavery or near-slavery and the promise of protection by a powerful family encouraged others to commend themselves into a servile status not markedly different from slavery.

The Labor of Slaves. Government-owned slaves worked at a variety of tasks. Those who were literate (and some who were not) served in government offices. Others worked in government-operated factories and workshops and on imperial stud farms and in imperial parks. The Manchus enslaved some Chinese in order to make them the personal servants of the Manchu emperors. These hereditary "bond-servants" were often assigned tasks that in earlier regimes would have been performed by eunuchs. As trusted political servants of the emperor they often enjoyed immense wealth and power. Slave status under such circumstances was much less important than proximity to the great power of the throne.

Privately owned slaves were also directed into many activities. Slaves worked the land at least as early as the Han dynasty and continued to do so into the twentieth century. Slaves provided part of the labor force in small-scale industries and, on behalf of their owners, engaged in commerce and trade. In many such cases slaves worked side by side with their owners or with personal retainers, tenants, and long-term laborers whose status was only one or two steps above that of the slave but definitely lower than that of the commoner. Privately owned slaves were frequently used as household servants. Finally, the wealthy owner of a large number of slaves, particularly if he was an absentee landlord, might use one or more of his slaves as an overseer. By the latter part of the Ming dynasty, such master slaves had become a social anomaly. Some were very wealthy, owning property and even slaves themselves. They developed close ties with local government officials and were able to dominate local "good" people. When peasant and slave uprisings began, master slaves and their homes were among the first to be attacked. By early Qing times, the number of agricultural slaves had declined in favor of tenancy, and the rent bursary system had emerged as a means of overseeing the income from landlord properties. The master slave thus became rather rare.

Manumission and Abolition. As early as the Han dynasty there had been demands to abolish or to limit slavery, but the first attempt to eliminate it, by Wang Mang in 9 CE, had ended in failure. There were occasional imperial orders to remove specific individuals from slave status. The founders of the Han and the Ming dynasties both decreed that those who had been forced into slavery by the chaos of the civil wars leading to the founding of their regimes were to be returned to commoner status. Ming Taizu (Hongwu; r. 1368–1398) also decreed that commoners were not to own slaves, but that decree led only to a change in name of such privately owned slaves to adopted sons. After the attempt by Wang Mang there was no major effort to abolish slavery. In 1909, as part of a major modernization effort, the Qing throne decreed the abolition of slavery, but even that did not end the institution; slavery persisted in parts of China until the founding of the People's Republic of China in 1949.

Slavery thus existed for more than two thousand years in China. Instead of being seen as an isolated institution, however, it should probably be viewed as but one dependency relationship among many that existed at all levels of Chinese society. There is not sufficient evidence to indicate how many slaves existed at any one time during this long period, but, since the limited evidence suggests that slaves never provided the major work force, China should be conceived of as a slave-owning society but at no time as having a slave society.

T'ung-tsu Ch'ü, *Han Social Structure*, edited by Jack L. Dull (1972). M. I. Finley, "Slavery," in *International Encyclopedia of the Social Sciences*, edited by David L. Sills, vol. 14 (1968), pp. 307–313. Wallace Johnson, *The T'ang Code*, vol. 1, *General Principles* (1979). Jonathan D. Spence, *Ts'ao-yin and the K'ang-hsi Emperor: Bondservant and Master* (1965). Yi-t'ung Wang, "Slaves and Other Comparable Social Groups during the Northern Dynasties (386–618)," *Harvard Journal of Asiatic Studies* 16.3–4 (December 1953): 293–364. J. L. Watson, ed., *Asian and African Systems of Slavery* (1980).

JACK L. DULL

SLAVERY AND SERFDOM IN SOUTH ASIA

The terms *slave* and *serf* are frequently found in historical works on South Asia, but slavery and serfdom, as specific forms of unfree labor, were never significant features of South Asian economies and societies. *Slavery* is usually understood to combine the notion of involuntary servitude with the practice of trade in humans whose labor provides profit to the slave owner; *serfdom* refers to the obligation of those who work upon the land and of others who live in peasant communities to provide unpaid labor to those with local political dominance, a hereditary gentry or aristocracy.

The literatures of India do contain references to the word *slave,* as, for example, in Vedic usage where those conquered by Aryans are called *dasa;* in the thirteenth century words meaning "slave" were used to refer to a succession of Muslim rulers in Delhi (the "Slave Dynasty") and to devotees of the god Shiva among Tamil-speakers in South India.

In addition to such figures of speech, there is continuous evidence of some domestic slavery in certain parts of the subcontinent from Buddhist times until the middle of the nineteenth century, when the holding and sale of slaves was declared illegal in India and other parts of the British empire. However, in no part of India has it been carefully and critically established that either slavery or serfdom was the basis of field agriculture in the ways that were found in the American South or in medieval Europe. Nevertheless, the condition of Untouchable field laborers in most parts of India for the last thousand years has been as degraded as that of slaves in the American South and as exploited as that of European serfs, and this degradation and exploitation persist in many parts of South Asia to this day.

Among contemporary scholars of South Asia there are some who speak of an Indian feudalism and serfdom that existed anywhere between the third and seventeenth centuries. However, most historians of the classical Gupta age to the time of British colonial rule have not critically considered whether either slavery or serfdom were features of the organization of labor. Most would probably accept the idea that peasants in India—those living in village communities—owned such means of production as bullocks and plows and depended upon family members for most of their labor needs, that is, the idea that the Indian peasantry was free of servile or feudal obligations.

That said, most scholars would also agree that historically, and at present, a sizable proportion of rural families who derive their entitlements to food and shelter from their labor in the fields of others have suffered disabilities as severe as "slaves" in other places. Perhaps one-fifth of rural households in South Asia have long been stigmatized as Untouchable, and most have owned neither land nor the means of producing upon the land, thus adding poverty and total economic dependence to deep social abasement. Another section of rural families have suffered from similar, though less severe, pollution stigmatization, which, when added to the limitations on their entitlement to land, has subjected them to the rigors of coerced labor (usually debt bondage to wealthier peasants) that made their condition similar to that of serfs elsewhere.

The reason that the terms *slavery* and *serfdom* are problematic when discussing unfree labor in South Asia is not that actual conditions of labor have been very different from those of the American South, feudal Europe, or places like Latin America. Rather, it is that the political and economic relations in which labor—such as that in agriculture—is embedded have been different, and the ideologies justifying the degraded and exploited conditions of many agrestic workers in South Asian societies have also been different. South Asia had few urban patriciates supported by slavery in the pattern of the classical Greco-Roman world; it knew little of the capitalism of the antebellum South; nor was South Asia, in the judgment and usage of most historians, ruled by landed aristocracies upon whose local dominance feudalism of the sort found in medieval Europe or Japan could be sustained.

[*See also* Untouchability *and* Land Tenure and Reform: Land Tenure, Revenue, and Reform in South Asia.]

T. J. Byers and Harbans Mukhia, eds., *Feudalism in Non-European Societies* (1985). *The Cambridge Economic History of India*, vol. 1, edited by Tapan Raychaudhuri and Irfan Habib (1982); vol. 2, edited by Dharma Kumar and Meghnad Desai (1983).

BURTON STEIN

SLAVERY AND SERFDOM IN SOUTHEAST ASIA

Unlike other, more densely populated regions of Asia, Southeast Asia was short of labor resources throughout its history, and this fact has much to do with the area's labor conditions and states of servitude. On the one hand, chattel slavery was geographically—if not demographically—widespread. Most Southeast Asian societies recognized a category of hereditary, transferable slaves, in most cases outsiders such as prisoners of war or those captured from upland ethnic minorities. There was some trade, for example, in slaves taken from the interior highlands of Laos, southern Vietnam, Malaya, and the Philippines through the nineteenth century. Over time these slaves were assimilated, and thus they constantly had to be replaced. They appear to have been employed mainly in domestic service.

Much more pervasive were social arrangements under which those of higher rank had claim to the labor service of commoners, who might be required to work for their masters from three to six months out of the year. Such masters included government officials, Buddhist monasteries, and, in some sense, even governments themselves, which required labor service as a form of payment. In Thailand and Burma, for example, all able-bodied adult males were required to work for the crown for several months each year—perhaps digging canals or in domestic service at the court—while others rendered service to their personal patrons, and the labor of still others went to the support of religious institutions. In general, commoners preferred service to monasteries and personal patrons over service to the crown, as it was more personal and they could form enduring relationships to use, when necessary, to their own advantage. Throughout the region, the onerous government administration of corvée (forced labor) was commonly associated with a practice termed, for lack of a better word, debt slavery. This refers to arrangements by which individuals might borrow money from a patron and render him labor service by way of interest; thus, the usual security for loans was labor rather than land, which was useless without the labor to cultivate it. Similarly, those of high rank counted their wealth far less in terms of durable goods and property than they did in terms of the amount of labor they controlled.

While slavery as such was relatively uncommon and disappearing from Southeast Asia about 1870, other forms of labor control persisted into the early twentieth century.

Bruno Lasker, *Human Bondage in Southeast Asia* (1950). Akin Rabibhadana, *The Organization of Thai Society in the Early Bangkok Period, 1782–1873* (1969).

DAVID K. WYATT

SMEDLEY, AGNES (1892–1950), an American journalist who reported on the Chinese Communist movement. Agnes Smedley arrived in China for the first time in 1929, after a decade of work with the Indian independence movement in the United States and Germany. From Shanghai, Xi'an, Yan'an, and while living with Communist-led guerrilla units during the initial stages of the Sino-Japanese War, she wrote passionately about the plight of the downtrodden in China. Of her China books (five in number), the most influential was *Battle Hymn of China* (1943) and the most important was probably *The Great Road* (1956). The latter was a biography based on extended personal interviews with Marshal Zhu De, a peasant who became the leading military figure of the Chinese revolution. Zhu De reminded Smedley of her father and her own humble origins on a tenant "dirt farm" in northern Missouri. Smedley, who was never a communist, died in 1950 under attack as a Soviet spy because of charges originating from General MacArthur's Tokyo headquarters.

STEPHEN R. MacKINNON

SNEEVLIET, HENDRICUS J. F. M. (alias Maring; 1883–1942), Dutch revolutionary Marxist dispatched by the Comintern to China in 1921. Sneevliet applied to China his early experience in building revolutionary alliances in the Dutch East Indies. He is credited with developing the Comintern's China policy of the united front from below and its theoretical analysis of the Guomindang (Kuomintang, Nationalist Party) as a "bloc of various classes."

Sneevliet attended the first meeting of the Chinese Communist Party (CCP) in July 1921 and advised alignment with the Comintern. He urged the Guomindang to allow individual CCP members to join the Nationalist Party. Sneevliet's purpose was to provide the Communists with the opportunity to build a worker base under the Goumindang umbrella. At the appropriate time the workers would unite with the Communist Party, overthrow the Nationalists, and establish a Soviet revolutionary government. Because the Communists had followed his strategy of building up their own separate party apparatus, they were able to survive the break with the Guomindang of 1928. In 1923 Sneevliet was recalled to the Soviet Union and replaced by Michael Borodin.

[See also Partai Komunis Indonesia; Comintern; Communism: Chinese Communist Party; United Front; and Borodin, Michael.]

Dou Bing, "Sneevliet and the Early Years of the CCP," *China Quarterly* 48 (October–December 1971): 677–697. A. C. Muntjewert, "Was There a Sneevlietian Strategy?" *China Quarterly* 53 (January–March 1973): 677–697. Dou Bing, "Reply," *China Quarterly* 54 (April–June 1973): 345–354.   RICHARD C. KAGAN

SNOUCK HURGRONJE, CHRISTIAN (1857–1936), Leiden-trained Arabist and adviser on Islam and indigenous affairs to the government of Netherlands India from 1889 to 1906. He was subsequently appointed professor at the University of Leiden and became the preeminent figure of late colonial Indies scholarship. Snouck Hurgronje's timely analysis of Acehnese society helped quell *ulama*-led resistance to Dutch rule in North Sumatra and became the basis for Holland's Islamic policy: among subject peoples, tolerate Islamic doctrine but eliminate Islam as a political force. He advocated Western education as a means of assimilating Indonesian elites to Dutch culture and interests and promoted other policies associated with the early twentieth-century Ethical school in Dutch colonial thinking.

[*See also* Aceh; Nahdatul Ulama; *and* Ethical Colonial Policy.]

Christian Snouck Hurgronje, *The Acehnese*, translated by A. W. S. O'Sullivan, 2 vols. (1906), and *Mekka in the Latter Part of the Nineteenth Century*, translated by J. H. Monahan (1931).   JAMES R. RUSH

SNOW, EDGAR (1906–1972), American journalist who reported on the Chinese Communists' Long March. Snow arrived in China in 1928, fresh from the University of Missouri's School of Journalism and in search of adventure. After serving an apprenticeship with J. B. Powell's *China Weekly Review* in Shanghai, Snow moved to Beijing where he married Helen Foster Snow (also known by the pen name Nym Wales) and taught journalism at Yanjing (Yenching) University. By then deeply interested in Chinese affairs, he began to participate in Chinese politics vicariously through his students. He met Song Qingling (wife of Sun Yat-sen), Lu Xun, Mao Dun, and other major intellectual and political figures who opposed Chiang Kai-shek's Guomindang government.

Snow's big break came in 1936 when he was able to reach the Communist guerrilla stronghold of Baoan via Xi'an in the mountains of northwest China. Snow arrived at just the right moment, becoming the first foreign correspondent to interview the Communists as they emerged from their epic Long March. The resulting book, *Red Star over China* (1937), had a profound impact. Although the book was never a best-seller in the West, it was widely read as the first objective and generally positive account about conditions and leadership in Communist-controlled areas. Even more important was the influence that the book had in translation within China, where it was eagerly devoured by Chinese intellectuals. Today, because of the exclusive biographical interviews with Mao Zedong, Zhou Enlai, Zhu De, and others, the book still has a unique place.

During World War II Snow became a roving reporter worldwide. He did not return to China until 1960, when once again his reports broke a long embargo on accurate information about China. From the appearance of *Other Side of the River* in 1961, one can trace the thaw in Sino-US relations that led to the Kissinger-Nixon volte-face of 1972. In 1970 Snow appeared on the gates of Tiananmen Square with Mao Zedong—a clear signal from the Chinese side that a change was in the air. Ironically, Snow died in Switzerland in 1972 on the same week that Nixon made his historic trip to Beijing.

[*See also* Long March.]

STEPHEN R. MACKINNON

SŎ CHAE-P'IL. *See* Jaisohn, Philip.

SOE, THAKIN (b. 1905), first Burmese interpreter of Marxism and a founder of the Burma Communist Party. From 1946 until 1969 Soe remained the leader of the smallest faction of the underground Communist movement. During the 1930s he compiled books expressing Marxist ideas in Burmese Buddhist idiom. In 1942 he organized an anti-Japanese underground movement, and in 1944 he was made president of the national front of the Anti-Fascist People's Freedom League. His style and dogmatism lessened his influence in nationalist politics after World War II. Because he was unable to compromise with other Communist leaders, Soe's political influence waned, but his reputation as a theorist grew. Released from prison in 1980, he wrote unpublished memoirs and critiques of his earlier interpretations.

[*See also* Anti-Fascist People's Freedom League.]

Frank N. Trager, *Burma: From Kingdom to Republic* (1966).

ROBERT H. TAYLOR

SOEDIRMAN (1912–1950), the first Indonesian military commander. General Soedirman taught at a Muhammadiyah primary school in Cilacap (1935–1943) until trained by the Japanese (1943–1945) as *daidan-cho* (battalion commander) of the PETA army in Banyumas. After the Japanese surrender Soedirman was more successful than most PETA officers in equipping a local division of the new Indonesian army with weapons obtained from the Japanese. He was elected supreme army commander by his former PETA peers on 11 November 1945, though many civilian leaders, particularly those of the left, continued to distrust his emphasis on the autonomy and mystique of the army. Soedirman's primary importance was as a symbol of military unity and heroism, particularly after the Dutch captured the entire civilian leadership (December 1948). Weakened by tuberculosis, he was carried about in a litter by the resistance. He accepted the settlement with the Dutch with obvious reluctance (July 1949) but died six months later.

[*See also* Indonesia, Republic of; Muhammadiyah; PETA; *and* Indonesian Revolution.]

ANTHONY REID

SOGA, aristocratic lineage prominent in Japanese court politics from about 530 to 645. The Soga were originally famous as traders, and they supervised several communities of Korean technicians from their base in the southwestern part of the Nara basin.

In 534 Soga no Iname became a close adviser to the emperor and subsequently came into conflict with Mononobe no Okoshi over court support of Buddhism. Iname supported the new religion, while Mononobe rejected Buddhism in favor of the indigenous Shinto gods. In 587 Iname's son Soga no Umako defeated the anti-Buddhist forces in battle and later had a recalcitrant Emperor Sushun murdered and replaced with his niece, the empress Suiko.

For the next thirty years Suiko, Umako, and Shōtoku Taishi (also a Soga kinsman) dominated the court. Their rule saw the rapid advance of Buddhism, the systematization of the court bureaucracy, the extension of government control to new areas, and the dispatch of diplomatic missions to the Sui court of China.

Umako's sons Emishi and Iruka inherited power after their father's death in 626, but in 645 they were murdered in the Taika coup d'état. Despite this setback, descendants of the Soga continued to play an important role in court politics until well into the Nara period of 710 to 784.

[*See also* Yamato *and* Shōtoku Taishi.]

W. G. Aston., trans., *Nihongi* (1896). John W. Hall, *Japan from Prehistory to Modern Times* (1970).

WAYNE FARRIS

SOGDIAN was a Middle Iranian language formerly spoken by scattered groups in Central Asia from the second through the tenth century. These groups originated in the region of the Zeravshan River in Soviet Uzbekistan, in the vicinity of the cities of Bukhara and Samarkand. With the passage of time, Sogdian-speaking communities spread eastward into Utrushana, Ferghana, and the oases of the Tarim Basin and Gansu Corridor (especially in the Turfan Depression). Mercantile colonies existed even in major commercial centers in China such as Chang'an. A descendant of Sogdian (Yaghnobi) is still spoken by the inhabitants of the Yaghnob River valley in the northern Pamirs, east of Samarkand.

Although a number of scripts, including Syriac and Manichaean, were eventually employed to write Sogdian, the Aramaic script of the Achaemenid chancellery, as it developed in the Sogdian homeland of Transoxiana, provided the basis for the development of "literary Sogdian" and Sogdian literature. The Sogdian script and scribal style was to form the basis for the craft of writing among the pre-Islamic Turks, Mongols, and Manchus, and, consequently, Sogdian was to have a permanent historical influence upon these Central and East Asian peoples. Sogdian was also an important literary medium of exchange between China and the Near East (but not India). This was particularly the case for the Buddhist, Manichaean, and Nestorian Christian communities.

[*See also* Sogdiana.]

M. J. Dresden, "Introductory Note," in Guitty Azarpay, *Sogdian Painting: The Pictorial Epic in Oriental Art* (1981), pp. 1–10.   DAVID A. UTZ

SOGDIANA, the area centering on the cities of Samarkand and Bukhara, now in Uzbekistan, between the middle and upper courses of the Amu Darya (Oxus) and Syr Darya (Jaxartes) rivers. Sogdiana also includes part of the Ferghana Valley (in the present-day Uzbek, Tadzhik, and Kirghiz republics of the Soviet Union) and Merv (in the Turkmen SSR), where a civilization flourished from about

the sixth century BCE until the Mongol conquest. The Sogdians were ancestors of today's Tajik and Uzbek peoples, and a descendant of the Sogdian language (related to Middle Persian) is still spoken in the Yaghnob valley, north of the Pamirs.

Part of the Achaemenid empire, Sogdiana was conquered in the fourth century BCE by Alexander the Great, who destroyed its principal city, Maracanda (Samarkand). After the conquest many Sogdians left home and settled in oasis cities across Central Asia, as far as China, as is shown by the Sogdian documents, apparently dating to the fourth century CE, discovered in a watchtower west of Dunhuang in China. In the third century BCE Sogdiana may have been included in an independent Greco-Bactrian kingdom. Little is known of the Parthian period, but Sogdiana was ruled by a Sasanid royal governor for a little more than a century after 260 CE. Subjugated by the Hephthalite Huns in the late fourth and fifth centuries and by the Turks in the sixth and seventh, Sogdiana fell to the Arabs in the late seventh and early eighth centuries. During this period the Sogdian language was receding, but in the cities Sogdian communities continued to exist, dominating much of the carrying trade (especially silk) between east and west. Extant documents show these Sogdians to have been Christian, Buddhist, and Manichaean in religion. Known in China as the "barbarians of the nine surnames" *(jiuxinghu)*, Sogdians played an important role particularly in Tang times (the rebel general An Lushan was of part-Sogdian ancestry).

[*See also* Sogdian; Silk Route; *and* Samarkand.]

Guitty Azarpay, *Sogdian Painting* (1981). Richard N. Frye, *The Heritage of Persia* (1963). Edwin G. Pulleyblank, *The Background of the Rebellion of An Lu-shan* (1955).   ARTHUR N. WALDRON

SŌHAK, "Western learning," the term in Yi-dynasty Korea for the combination of Roman Catholicism and Western science that was introduced in the early eighteenth century through the Chinese writings of the Jesuit missionary Matteo Ricci (1552–1610). The more controversial and problematic aspect, Catholicism, greatly overshadowed the scientific aspect. The new learning gained its most attentive hearing from a group of scholars belonging to the Namin (Southerner) faction, which had long been excluded from positions of power in the faction-ridden political world of the late Yi dynasty. Ricci's catechetical tract, *Tianzhu shiyi (The True Lord of Heaven)*, was especially effective.

In 1779 a small group of Namin scholars spent ten days in a Buddhist temple discussing Sŏhak. One of their number, Yi Sŭng-hun, was baptized in 1784 by a European missionary in Beijing while accompanying his father on a tribute mission. He brought back more Western books and soon baptized a number of his friends. The new faith spread through a network of marriage, blood, and friendship ties, especially but not exclusively within the Namin faction. Among the early group was Chŏng Yag-yong (Tasan; 1762–1836) and his two brothers; Chŏng, now recognized as the outstanding genius of the *sirhak* ("practical learning") movement, later withdrew when negative ramifications such as the prohibition of ancestor rites became known. [*See* Chŏng Yag-yong *and* Sirhak.]

Many remained firm, however, and the group grew rapidly, appointing its own priests and carrying out Catholic rituals. They willingly stopped this activity when better informed and awaited the arrival of an officially ordained priest. When a priest from China, Zhou Wenmo, finally arrived in 1794, he found to his surprise there were already some four thousand Catholics in Korea.

There were also problems: by 1786 the new doctrine and the importation of books related to it had already been proscribed. The first active persecution took place on a very limited scale in 1791, when Confucian sensibilities were outraged by the destruction of ancestral tablets by several Catholics. In 1800 King Chŏngjo died, and his policy of toleration died with him; by December of that year the dowager queen had mounted a strong persecution. Political motives played a part; during the reigns of Chŏngjo and his predecessor factional politics had abated and the Namin again participated in government. Now Christianity provided the queen and her party a convenient excuse for purging her Namin political rivals.

In response to this purge a Catholic, Hwang Sa-yŏng, wrote to the French bishop of Beijing describing events and requesting the dispatch of French warships. The letter was intercepted and Hwang executed, but the government now saw Sŏhak as a potentially subversive force. This fear occasioned harsh suppression, particularly in the latter half of the nineteenth century as the threat from Western powers became increasingly evident. During lax periods the proscribed religion spread rapidly, however, especially among the lower classes. By 1860 French missionaries ministered secretly to more than twenty thousand Korean Catholics.

[*See also* Ricci, Matteo *and* Christianity: Christianity in Korea.]

Don Baker, "A Confucian Confronts Catholicism," *Korean Studies Forum* 6 (1979–1980): 1–44. Woo-keun Han, *The History of Korea*, translated by Kyung-shik Lee (1970). Ki-baik Lee, *A New History of Korea*, translated by Edward W. Wagner (1984). James B. Palais, *Politics and Policy in Traditional Korea* (1975).

MICHAEL C. KALTON

SOISISAMUT, king of Champassak (r. 1713–1737), semilegendary first ruler of the kingdom of Champassak in southern Laos. Local annals say that Champassak was ruled by a queen in the late seventeenth century until she handed the government over to a Buddhist monk, who in turn enthroned Soisisamut, allegedly a posthumous son of Surinya-vongsa, the last king of Lan Sang, who had died about 1694. Soisisamut established a dynasty and a persistent tradition of southern Lao independence of Vientiane and the north.

[*See also* Champassak *and* Surinyavongsa.]

C. Archaimbault, *The New Year Ceremony at Basak (South Laos)* (1971). Sila Viravong, *History of Laos* (1964).

DAVID K. WYATT

SŌKA GAKKAI. *See* New Religions in Japan.

SOLO. *See* Sala.

SOMA. *See* Haoma.

SOMANATH, an ancient pan-India pilgrimage place, also known as Somnath, Somanathapattan, Prabhasa, Prabhasapattan, or Prabhasatirtha. It is situated on the southwestern coast of modern Kathiawar, Gujarat state, India. It is sacred to all Hindus because it marks the place of the god Krishna's passing away and is one of the twelve major Shaivite shrines. Somanath Temple, dedicated to Shiva, occupies an elevated site on the western corner of the city overlooking the sea. As the dynastic shrine of the Chalukyas of Gujarat, Somanath grew into an enormous temple complex, supported by the revenue of 10,000 villages and served by 1,000 priests performing daily rituals and 350 dancers and musicians entertaining the deity and devotees alike, all year round. Between 1025 and 1026 Mahmud of Ghazna sacked the city, demolishing the temple, slaying its 50,000 Hindu defenders, and looting its fabulous wealth. Although rebuilt under King Kumarapala (1143–1172), the temple was depredated again by the Muslims in 1298.

M. S. Commissariat, *A History of Gujarat*, vol. 1 (1938).   SHIVA BAJPAI

SONG DYNASTY.

The Song dynasty (960–1279) was a period of great social, cultural, and economic change that culminated in a major transformation of Chinese civilization. The dynasty was founded by Zhao Kuangyin (927–976), titled Taizu (r. 960–976), a military leader proclaimed emperor by his troops. Unifying the country after nearly a century of strife, Taizu proved a talented administrator and set a high standard of modesty, generosity, and thoughtfulness for his successors to emulate. The first half of the dynasty (960–1126) is known as the Northern Song because the capital was in the Yellow River valley at Kaifeng. The second half (1127–1279) is called the Southern Song because after Kaifeng and the rest of the North were conquered by the alien Jin dynasty, a reconstituted Song government was established at Hangzhou, well south of the Yangtze River.

Political and Military History. The desire to regain all of the land once held by the Tang dynasty (618–907) shaped much of early Song history. Taizu reorganized the armed forces to prevent the rise of regional warlords, the bane of the late Tang period. He created a professional army of career soldiers whose officers were regularly rotated and were under civilian control. Between 963 and 975 he subjugated one southern regime after another, the last surrendering to his brother and successor Taizong (r. 976–997) in 979. But such military successes were not to be had on the northern borders of the empire. In the north and northeast the Khitan state of Liao held sixteen prefectures that had been part of the Tang realm, including the Beijing area. In the northwest a confederation of Tangut tribes had established the Xixia state, centered in Gansu. Taizong's two attempts to regain the northeast were failures, and peace with Liao was achieved in 1004 only when the Song court agreed to make substantial tribute payments in silver and silk each year. After a four-year war with the Xixia from 1040 to 1044 a similar agreement was reached with them, providing some measure of security for the Song thereafter.

The state established by the early Song emperors was probably the most centralized in Chinese history, at least with respect to court control of local administration. To supervise and coordinate the work of prefects, the court assigned judicial intendants, fiscal intendants, military intendants, and intendants of transportation and monopolies, each assigned to a different set of overlapping prefectures.

The central administration was divided into three organs: Finance, Army, and the Secretariat. In general, emphasis was placed on checks and balances, so that these organs of government often had overlapping responsibilities.

The Song was an era when the scholar-official took center stage in government, when men of the highest talents were recruited into government service and allowed to set policy, challenged neither by empresses, eunuchs, nor generals. It became customary for emperors to listen to a range of opinion before making decisions and usually to defer to their leading officials. Factionalism among officials themselves, however, marred their age of glory. The major issue dividing officials was how to make the Song state strong enough to overcome the foreign threat. The Song inability to regain all of North China did not result from lack of effort. The size of the army was more than tripled between 979 and 1041 to about 1.25 million men, and military expenses came to absorb more than three-quarters of state revenues. Paying for defense, however, posed fiscal difficulties, which in turn led to disputes among bureaucrats.

By the mid-eleventh century inadequate government revenue made reform of some sort critical. The first great reformer was Fan Zhongyan (989–1052), who attempted in 1043 and 1044 to institute a reform of personnel recruitment and local administration. A man of unimpeachable character and motivations, his policies were nevertheless opposed by conservatives and soon were abandoned. As the fiscal situation worsened and retrenchment of government activities proved inadequate, a new reform movement was started. It was led by Wang Anshi (1021–1086), a brilliant writer and experienced local official who gained the support of Emperor Shenzong (r. 1067–1085).

During the period 1069 to 1085 Wang reorganized the budget, had the basis for land tax assessments changed, introduced new schemes for collecting and transporting special tribute taxes, instituted interest-bearing loans to peasants to keep them from becoming dependent on landlords, converted labor service obligations to money taxes, reformed the local clerical service, and set up government pawnshops. He hoped both to increase total production, thus making the country richer, and to bring more of these riches into state coffers. He also revised the examinations for entry to office, increased the number of government schools, and introduced a local militia to aid in national defense. These new policies—the most thoroughgoing to be introduced in a thousand years—caused massive re-

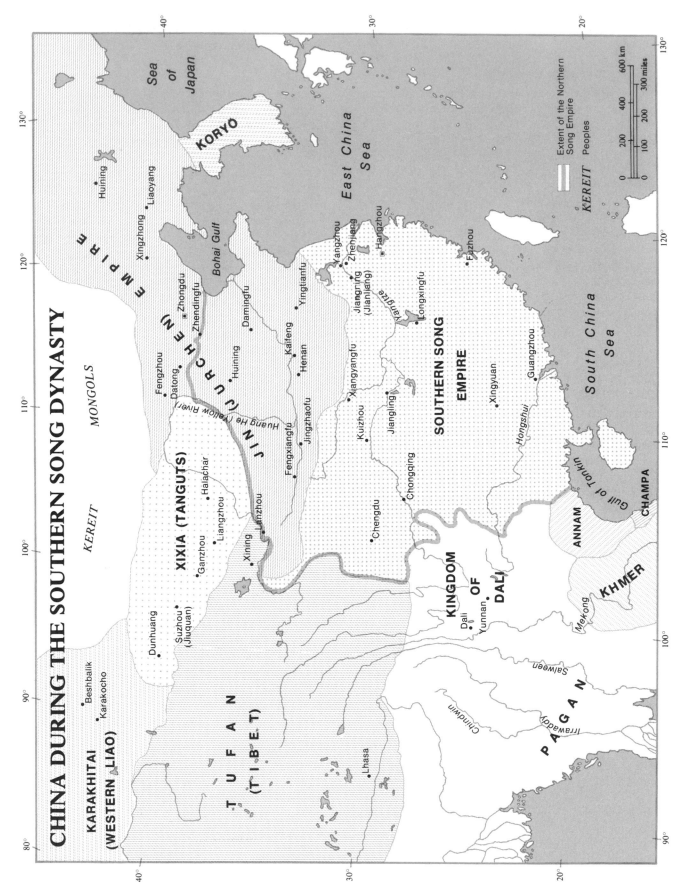

CHINA DURING THE SOUTHERN SONG DYNASTY

KARAKHITAI
(WESTERN LIAO)

MONGOLS

KEREIT

JIN (JURCHEN) EMPIRE

XIXIA (TANGUTS)

TUFAN (TIBET)

KINGDOM OF DALI

SOUTHERN SONG EMPIRE

KORYO

Sea of Japan

East China Sea

South China Sea

Bohai Gulf

Gulf of Tonkin

ANNAM

CHAMPA

KHMER

PAGAN

Extent of the Northern Song Empire

KEREIT Peoples

600 km
300 miles
400
200
200
100
0   0

Huining
Xingzhong
Liaoyang
Zhongdu
Datong
Zhendingfu
Fengzhou
Huining
Damingfu
Yingtianfu
Kaifeng
Henan
Jingzhaofu
Fengxiangfu
Yangzhou
Zhenjiang
Hangzhou
Jiangning (Jianjiang)
Longxingfu
Fuzhou
Guangzhou
Xiangyangfu
Kuizhou
Jiangling
Chongqing
Xingyuan
Hongshui
Chengdu
Dunhuang
Suzhou (Jiuquan)
Ganzhou
Liangzhou
Halachar
Xining
Lanzhou
Beshbalik
Karakocho
Lhasa
Dali
Yunnan

Huang He (Yellow River)
Yangtze
Yangtze
Mekong
Salween
Chindwin
Irrawaddy

sistance and protest on the part of men in office. Personal antagonism, differences of regional and class interest, and opposing philosophies all contributed to an intense factionalism; Wang Anshi ousted from office those who opposed him, and when conservatives such as Ouyang Xiu (1007–1072) and Sima Guang (1018–1086) later gained control they responded in like fashion. Nevertheless there is also a positive side to these factional disputes: men of education and wealth were made to worry about issues of public welfare, and some diverted their frustrated energies into local efforts at establishing charitable institutions. [See also Wang Anshi; Ouyang Xiu; and Sima Guang.]

The early twelfth century was ruled by one of China's most cultivated emperors, the painter and calligrapher Huizong (r. 1100–1125). He left much of the job of governing to his chief councillor Cai Jing (1046–1126). The only great rebellion of the Song occurred during his reign; between 1120 and 1122 Fang La and his followers killed officials and upper-class families in a wide area of inland South China before being suppressed. [See also Fang La.] More critical to Huizong's reign was the mistake of treating the enemy of his enemy as a friend. In 1115 a Jurchen state to the north of the Liao declared itself the Jin dynasty and began a war against the Liao. The Chinese responded by attacking the Liao from the south, in 1122 concluding an alliance with the Jin that called for a division of Liao territory. In 1125 this alliance collapsed, and between 1126 and 1127 Kaifeng was besieged, then sacked, and Huizong and his heir were both taken north into captivity.

Chinese loyalists, regrouping in the South, proclaimed a younger son of Huizong as emperor (Gaozong; r. 1127–1162), and by 1138 the situation had stabilized, with Gaozong's court at Hangzhou, far from the Jin court at Beijing. For the rest of the twelfth century the overriding concern of officials and intellectuals was regaining the North. Later historians have nearly uniformly condemned the various peace parties as appeasers and have found a hero in Yue Fei (1103–1141), a general who tried to regain the North and who in fact reached the Luoyang area before being recalled and executed. After a treaty in 1142 the Song government made annual tributary payments to the Jin, much as it earlier had to the Liao.

During the Southern Song dynasty, factional strife continued to mar life at court, especially during periods having strong chief councillors such as Han Tuozhou (1151–1202), Shi Miyuan (1164–1233), and Jia Sidao (1213–1275). The problem of the northern border only grew worse as the Mongols took Beijing in 1215, then destroyed both the Jin and Xixia states from 1232 to 1234. For forty years the Song state resisted the Mongols, who in a short time conquered much of Asia. Cities in key places along Song defense lines held out against sieges for as long as four years. Finally, Song resistance collapsed between 1273 and 1279, and Kublai Khan became emperor of China from his capital in Beijing. [See also Kublai Khan.]

Agriculture and Population. Agricultural productivity greatly increased during the Song, owing in large part to the growth of wet-field rice cultivation, one of the most labor-intensive but also most productive forms of agriculture. Several advances contributed to this growth. Technical improvements in damming methods and water pumps made it easier to maintain fields that could be flooded as needed. The discovery and selection of new seed strains—aided by the introduction of a variety of early-ripening, drought-resistant rice from Southeast Asia in the early eleventh century—made it possible to grow wet-field rice in a much wider range of terrains and climates than before. To take advantage of the great productivity of wet-field rice, reclamation of land at the edge of lakes and marshes was undertaken on a large scale.

As rice gained in importance, so did the whole southern half of the country, now experiencing a major expansion in population. The Yangtze Valley and southeast coast, areas that had accounted for one-fourth of the Tang population, had half the population of the Song in 1080. Moreover, the densities of the core areas of the lower Yangtze reached over twenty households per square kilometer. Overall, the population of China seems to have reached about 100 million people by 1100.

The majority of this population were, as always, engaged in agricultural work. Modern scholars have extensively debated the prevalence of various kinds of tenancy and serfdom in the Song. Some have argued that a manorial system with extensive use of unfree labor (peasants attached to the land they tenanted) was widespread in South China during the Song. Others see the agricultural economy of the Song as more "modern" than previously, with tenants seldom obliged to do more for their masters than pay rent. The evidence does seem strong that by the twelfth century tenancy was very common, but the nature of this tenancy seems to have been governed by local custom and to have varied considerably from one region to the other, depending on how scarce labor was, the type of agriculture practiced, the distance from large cities, and so on.

Technical, Industrial, and Commercial Advances.

The Song witnessed an economic revolution of major proportions. Cities grew at an astonishing rate, responding to the needs of commerce. The circulation of money reached levels more than twenty times that of the Tang. Water transportation became highly developed, and major industries, such as iron manufacture and textile production, made remarkable advances.

The material civilization of China in the Song was higher than anywhere else in the world. Much of the credit for this must go to the inventiveness of Chinese craftsmen and entrepreneurs. Traditional industries such as silk, lacquer, and porcelain reached their highest levels of technical perfection. Cotton became widespread for use in clothing. The production of ceramic utensils also reached new heights, even becoming a major item in overseas trade. Major advances were made in metallurgy, so that iron production grew to around 125,000 tons per year in 1078, a sixfold increase since the year

FIGURE 1. *Song-dynasty Meiping Jar.* Cuzhou ware, probably from Xiuwu or Cuzhou, twelfth century. Light gray stoneware with sgraffito designs in black slip on white slip under transparent glaze. Height 31.8 cm., diameter 21.6 cm.

800. This was made possible by improvements in technology: bituminous coke took the place of charcoal, hydraulic machinery was used to drive the bellows, and explosives were used in the mines. The iron produced was used in industrial processes (production of salt and copper, for instance), for tools, weapons, and ships.

The general prosperity of the Chinese population in the Song and the quality of its manufactured products together created an enormous internal and external demand for goods. Interregional trade developed rapidly, aided by the perfection of an immense network of waterways, including navigable rivers and canals, estimated to have been over 50,000 kilometers long. Specialization of all sorts increased. Regions became famous for particular products: iron, tea, sugar cane, paper, books, rice, and so on. Merchants also became highly specialized and organized; large commercial ventures were organized with a separation of owners (shareholders) and managers. Credit was commonly employed and brokers of many kinds appeared. In the large cities merchants were organized into guilds, under guild heads, who would deal with the government as a unit in matters of taxation or requisitions.

Foreign trade also grew rapidly during the Song. Along their northern borders Chinese goods were traded for horses, continuing a long tradition. A new development was a great maritime trade based on the seaports of the southeast coast and directly or indirectly reaching most of Asia. This maritime trade was made possible by development of huge ships powered by both oars and sails and capable of holding several hundred men. Also important to ocean-going travel was the invention of the compass, first reported in Chinese sources in 1119.

The evident prosperity of merchants in the Song also led to a restructuring of the tax system by a government chronically short of funds. By Southern Song times the government was deriving more revenue from its direct and indirect taxes on commerce than from its land tax.

Urbanization developed in two ways during the Song period: old cities, such as county and prefectural seats, grew to many times their previous size, outgrowing old city walls, and new towns grew up at the sites of markets. In either case, the relative importance of administrative functions in city organization declined as "natural," relatively unregulated economic activities took over. In the Song there were dozens of cities with populations over fifty thousand people, and the two capitals, Kaifeng and Hangzhou, each had populations of a million or more inhabitants. In the great cities crafts of all sorts were practiced and all manner of luxuries were available. Entertainment quarters stayed open until dawn, providing amusements ranging from jugglers and acrobats to storytellers, musicians, and fortune-tellers. Wine shops and restaurants were located throughout cities, catering both to local residents and itinerant merchants. However, population density also caused sanitation and safety hazards. Communicable diseases spread more rapidly than before, and fire posed problems so serious that commoners living in multistory houses were not allowed fires to cook their food but had to buy cooked food from street vendors.

The volume of commercial activity in the Song dynasty was so great that it strained the currency system. The copper coin had long been the standard currency of China and remained so in the early Song. What was new was the volume of its production; during the Northern Song it is estimated that 200 million strings of 1,000 cash each were issued by the government, an annual rate twenty times higher than in the Tang. Yet even this did not meet all the needs of the economy. The use of unminted silver gained some favor, especially for foreign trade, but the development of paper money is what really saved the situation. Paper currency had a history going back to the late ninth century, when private financiers had issued redeemable certificates of deposit so that merchants would not have to carry large quantities of money with them. Beginning in 1024 the government began to issue its own notes, which became the major form of currency in the twelfth and thirteenth centuries. Under the Southern Song notes equivalent to 400 million strings of cash were issued.

The Scholar-Gentry Class and Cultural Life. Among the many transformations of the Song period the best documented is a transformation of the ruling class. In the very broadest terms this transformation was a departure from the aristocratic system of the Tang and earlier, toward the "scholar-gentry" of the Ming (1368–1644) and later. Pedigree lost most of its former importance as passing government examinations for entry to office became a central concern of the upper class. Moreover, distinctions of status within the upper class came to have less social significance than formerly. During the Northern Song one can still recognize an upper level of the elite, whose members overwhelmingly became officials and who treated each other as equals, preferring to have their children marry each other. Gradually, however, this upper elite seems to

have merged with the broader- and locally based upper class, so that by 1200 even the highest officials were coming from families with strong local roots, families whose men pursued diverse careers as landlords, merchants, teachers, and officials.

This transformation of the ruling class was brought about in part by government policies and political events. The examination system, especially the examination for the *jinshi,* which tested knowledge of the classics, history, and literary skills, became the predominant means of gaining office. While it probably did not create as much social mobility as formerly believed, it did open more opportunities for government service for local gentry families and reached high levels in objectivity and rationality, reducing the importance of connections to high court officials.

The educated class was of course also very much affected by the increased prosperity of their society, the quickening of commerce and transportation, and improvements in material life. The advance that may have had the greatest long-term effect on them was the perfection of printing. Using a carved wooden block for each page, Chinese printing was based on the principle of the seal imprint. The first full-scale printing projects date from the late Tang. In the middle of the tenth century both the Chinese classics and the Buddhist canon were published in their entirety. During the Song, printed books of all kinds became extremely common. Not only were serious "important" works printed, but also a great variety of miscellaneous writings, scholarly notes, ghost stories, practical guides, gazetteers, and so on. Movable-type printing was also developed during the Song, using pottery type, but it never gained the popularity of woodblock printing. The greater availability of books after the spread of printing allowed an expansion of the size of the educated class; access to knowledge was no longer restricted to those whose families had long collected books.

Whatever causal force should be attributed to economics, politics, and technology, a shift in the attitudes of the educated class is clearly noticeable during the Song. This shift was in the direction of civilian over military values, secular over religious goals, urban over rural orientations, maturity and refinement over daring and ebullience, and the native over the foreign and exotic. This shift in goals and attitudes is generally associated with the intellectual movement called Neo-Confucianism, but it extended also into other pursuits of the educated class, such as poetry, painting, scholarship, and connoisseurship.

Neo-Confucianism is the Western term for a group of schools of thought called in Chinese *daoxue* ("study of the way"), *lixue* ("study of principle"), or *xinli xue* ("study of heart-and-mind and principle"). Confucianism had never died out during the Age of Division or the Tang dynasty; there had always been scholars who studied the classics, and Confucian virtues and ceremonies never lost importance in political and social life. As a philosophy concerned with ultimate issues, however, Confucianism had long been eclipsed by Buddhism. Thus, a basic contribution of the Neo-Confucianism of the Song was a philosophically based denial of the Buddhist belief that the world is empty or illusory; these Confucians asserted that the world as experienced was real and that action in it was valid.

In the early stages of the Neo-Confucian movement emphasis was placed on the student-teacher relationship and the attempt to reattain the sage-directed government of ancient times. Early leaders included Hu Yuan (993–1059), Fan Zhongyan, and Ouyang Xiu. After the factional fights over Wang Anshi's reforms, Neo-Confucianism produced fewer activist reformers; instead, a more inward-looking orientation, which stressed perfecting oneself before reforming the world, gained followers. Key early teachers in this school were Zhou Dunyi (1012–1073), Zhang Zai (1020–1077), Cheng Hao (1031–1085), and Cheng Yi (1032–1107). Particularly important was the attention they devoted to the *Classic of Changes (Yijing)* as a basis for cosmology and metaphysics. The synthesizer of this school was Zhu Xi (1130–1200), a prodigious scholar who wrote commentaries to many of the classics as well as hundreds of letters and essays. His synthesis of Neo-Confucianism later became the orthodox standard for the examination system. [*See also* Neo-Confucianism; Cheng Brothers; Zhang Zai; Zhou Dunyi; *and* Zhu Xi.]

In terms of its effects on men in the educated class, the most important features of Song Neo-Confucianism are probably its emphasis on seriousness and reverence; the importance it accorded study, especially of history and the classics; its support for academies and for studying with teachers well into adulthood; its rejection of Buddhism; and its preference for solving small, close-at-hand problems, including the problems of one's own character and motivations, rather than tackling the biggest ones, generally beyond any individual's capacity.

Another major cultural achievement of the Song was in the field of historiography. Sima Guang wrote a history of China from ancient times through the Tang, the first such comprehensive chronological account attempted since the first century BCE. His sophistication in the scrutinizing of sources is especially notable. Discrepancies between sources were noted and reasons for choosing one version over another presented. Comprehensive encyclopedias were also compiled and printed in great number in the Song; a good example is the *Tongzhi* of Zheng Qiao (1104–1162), which included material not only on government and ritual but such topics as surnames, phonetics, flowers and insects, and archaeology.

Part of the turn "inward" mentioned earlier was a renewed interest in antiquity. Scholars began to collect and study all sorts of ancient artifacts, especially bronze vessels and mirrors and inscribed stones (or rubbings made from them). The catalog of one private collection records two thousand inscriptions.

The Song is also the first great age of scholarly painters, men whose refined sensibilities and understated monochrome landscapes seem much in tune with the philosophy and upper-class culture of the age. Great painters of the age include Fan Kuan, Xu Daoning, Mi Fei, Guo Xi, Xia Gui, and Ma Yuan. Later artists were to look back to these Song masters for inspiration, often imitating and copying their styles.

[*See also* Jurchen Jin Dynasty *and* Liao Dynasty.]

Carson Chang, *The Development of Neo-Confucian Thought* (1957). Herbert Franke, ed., *Sung Biographies*, 4 vols. (1976). Jacques Gernet, *Daily Life in China on the Eve of the Mongol Invasion, 1250–1286* (1970). Robert M. Hartwell, "Demographic, Political, and Social Transformations of China, 750–1550," *Harvard Journal of Asiatic Studies* 42 (1982): 365–422. Yves Hervout, ed., *A Sung Bibliography* (1978). E. A. Kracke, Jr., *Civil Service in Early Sung China, 960–1067* (1953). James T. C. Liu, *Reform in Sung China: Wang An-shih (1021–1086) and His New Policies* (1959). Yoshinobu Shiba, *Commerce and Society in Sung China*, translated by Mark Elvin (1970). John Winthrop, ed., *Crisis and Prosperity in Sung China* (1975). PATRICIA EBREY

SONG QINGLING (Soong Ch'ing-ling; 1890–1981), second wife of Sun Yat-sen and in her later years a prominent figure in the People's Republic of China. Born in Shanghai, daughter of the wealthy Christian Charles Jones Soong, she attended Wesleyan College for Women in Macon, Georgia. After graduating in 1913 Song became secretary to Sun Yat-sen and then arranged her own marriage to him in 1914. Following Sun's death in 1925 and Chiang

Kai-shek's right-wing coup during the Northern Expedition of 1927, Song Qingling went to Moscow, siding with the left wing and the Communists. After the founding of the People's Republic of China in 1949 she held a number of honorary posts including, in 1959, that of deputy chairman of the People's Republic. Her sister, Soong Mei-ling, was married to Chiang Kai-shek, and a brother, T. V. Soong, held high ministerial posts in the Guomindang-governed Republic of China.

[See also Guomindang; Chiang Kai-shek; Soong Mei-ling; Soong, T. V.; and Sun Yat-sen.]

Sterling Seagrave, *The Soong Dynasty* (1985).

EDWARD L. FARMER

SONG THAM, king of Ayudhya (r. 1610 or 1611–1628), was the first to increase aggressively Siam's contacts with the West. His claim to the throne and even the date of his accession as King Intharacha III are uncertain; foreign contemporaries insisted he was Ekathotsarot's son by a concubine and first noticed him in 1611. He made extensive use of immigrants in his army and government and worked to turn trade with the newly arrived Dutch and British East India companies to his advantage. On his death in December 1628, with no heir appointed, a yearlong succession struggle erupted.

[See also Ayudhya; Ekathotsarot; and Prasat Thong.]

E. W. Hutchinson, *Adventurers in Siam in the Seventeenth Century* (1940). George Vinal Smith, *The Dutch in Seventeenth-Century Thailand* (1977). David K. Wyatt, *Thailand: A Short History* (1984). DAVID K. WYATT

SON NGOC THANH (1907–c. 1976), Cambodian political figure, was born in Vietnam of a Cambodian father and a Vietnamese mother. He was educated largely in France, returning to Cambodia in 1936 and becoming associated with the Cambodian-language newspaper *Nagara Vatta* (1936–1942) and with anti-French intellectuals in Phnom Penh. In 1942 he was implicated in an anti-French demonstration and fled to Japan, returning to Cambodia in 1945 after the Japanese had imprisoned French authorities throughout Indochina. Thanh served as foreign minister in a pro-Japanese Cambodian government from May to August 1945 and then as prime minister as well, following a coup staged by his supporters. He was arrested by the French in October 1945 and exiled to France. Many

of his followers formed the nucleus of the anti-French Democratic Party.

Thanh returned to Cambodia in 1951 and founded an anti-French newspaper. He fled into the northwest in early 1952, overestimating the support he would receive from the primarily Communist-oriented anti-French guerrilla forces. This tactical blunder enabled his rival, Prince Norodom Sihanouk, to claim credit for obtaining Cambodia's independence from France in 1953. Thanh and the Democrats were outmaneuvered by Sihanouk in 1955. Thanh sought asylum in Thailand and South Vietnam, obtaining financial support from these anti-Sihanouk regimes as well as from the United States. He was indirectly involved in the coup that overthrew Prince Sihanouk in 1970 and served briefly as prime minister of the Khmer Republic (1970–1975). However, he failed to attract significant support and was seen largely as a symbolic representative of an older generation. Thanh's absences from Cambodia during crucial periods in its history prevented him from establishing strong political roots. With the collapse of the Khmer Republic, he fled to Saigon, where he was arrested. He died of natural causes after his release.

[See also Cambodia; Norodom Sihanouk; and Khmer Republic.]

DAVID P. CHANDLER

SON PYŎNG-HŬI (1861–1922), third leader of the Tonghak ("Eastern learning") religious movement of Korea, independence activist, and chairman of the thirty-three signers of the Declaration of Independence that figured in the March First Movement of 1919.

Son was born in 1861 in Ch'ŏngju, Ch'ungch'ŏng Province, the son of a concubine. As a victim of the discrimination associated with this status, Son joined the egalitarian Tonghak movement in 1882 and soon became the chief disciple of Ch'oe Si-hyŏng, the second leader of the religion. He participated in the last stages of the Tonghak rebellion in the 1890s. With most of the Tonghak leadership dead or imprisoned after the rebellion, he inherited the leadership from Ch'oe Si-hyŏng in 1898.

For a time Son resided in Japan and adopted a pro-Japanese attitude, thinking that Japan offered the best chances for the Tonghak movement and for Korean independence. Disappointed when Japan made Korea a protectorate in 1905, he reversed his attitude and expelled Yi Yong-gu and other pro-Japanese members from Tonghak. Convinced of the need for a redirection and redefinition of the movement, he renamed the religion Ch'ŏndogyo ("religion of the Heavenly Way") and reformulated the doctrine. Some of the major elements of this reformulation include the unity of mind and matter, the unity of religion and politics, uniformity of discipline, and the unity of faith. Son introduced disciplinary and devotional practices and emphasized continuous engagement in political and religious activities. Under his direction, Ch'ŏndogyo founded the Tongdŏk Girls' High School, the Posŏng Boys' High School, and a center to train youths in the Ch'ŏndogyo faith; he also established a publishing house. To stress the self-reliance of the faithful, he transferred control to local units.

Under Son's leadership Ch'ŏndogyo emerged as an active force in the Korean independence movement and Korean intellectual life. Son Pyŏng-hŭi headed the thirty-three representatives of the Korean people who signed the Declaration of Independence in the 1919 movement to protest Japanese rule. He was imprisoned for his activities and died of illness in 1922.

[See also Tonghak; March First Independence Movement; and Korea, Japanese Government-General of.]

Benjamin Weems, *Reform, Rebellion and the Heavenly Way* (1964).   JaHyun Kim Haboush

SOONG, T. V. (Song Ziwen; 1894–1971), eldest son of the westernized and politically prominent Charles Jones Soong family of Shanghai. His father was a close associate of Sun Yat-sen; an older sister married Sun in 1914; his youngest married Chiang Kai-shek in 1927. By dint of these family ties and his own excellent training in Western economics and business (at Harvard and Columbia universities), Soong became a prominent official within the Guomindang (Kuomintang, or Nationalist Party) in Sun's provisional government in Canton (Guangzhou) in 1923. During the Chiang Kai-shek years he served as minister of finance (1928–1933), head of the Bank of China (after 1935), minister of foreign affairs (during much of World War II), and president of the Executive Yuan (1945–1947). In 1949, when the Communists came to power, he moved to the United States.

[See also China, Republic Period; Chiang Kai-shek; Sun Yat-sen; Song Qingling; and Soong Mei-ling.]

Parks M. Coble, Jr., *The Shanghai Capitalists and the Nationalist Government, 1927–1937* (1980). Sterling Seagrave, *The Soong Dynasty* (1985). Y. C. Wang, *Chinese Intellectuals and the West, 1872–1949* (1966).

Parks M. Coble, Jr.

SOONG CH'ING-LING. *See* Song Qingling.

SOONG MEI-LING (b. 1897), youngest daughter of the westernized and politically prominent Charles Jones Soong of Shanghai and wife of Chiang Kai-shek. Mei-ling spent much of her youth in the United States studying in Georgia as a teenager, graduating from Wellesley College in Massachusetts in 1917. The Soong family was prominent in Guomindang (Kuomintang) circles; Mei-ling's father was a supporter of Sun Yat-sen, and an older sister, Song Qingling (Soong Ching-ling), had married Sun in 1914. In December 1927 Mei-ling married Chiang Kai-shek and began a prominent career as the wife of China's dominant leader. The Chiang-Soong marriage has been the subject of extensive historical gossip and disagreement; some writers speculate that it was a purely political alliance while others find evidence of strong romantic links between the partners. Commentators have shown equal diversity in evaluating Madame Chiang's political influence on her husband. She is credited by most for Chiang's conversion to Christianity in October 1930 and by some for the peaceful solution to the Xi'an Incident (along with her brother T. V. Soong and brother-in-law H. H. Kung). Her influence may have extended into Chiang's personnel and policy decisions but the evidence is uncertain.

Madame Chiang found greater favor with Westerners, especially Americans, than among Chinese. Fluent in English and a devoted Christian, she was Chiang's personal envoy and frequent translator when dealing with Americans. Her role thus became especially prominent after the outbreak of the Sino-Japanese War in July 1937, when Chiang needed support from the United States. She wrote books and articles, made speeches, and received foreign guests, urging them to support China's cause. From 1942 to 1943 she barnstormed America, staying in the White House and addressing a joint session of Congress. In the Civil War and Taiwan years, Madame Chiang promoted the anticommunist cause among her American allies, particularly the pro-Chiang "China lobby," and continued to play the prominent public role of a first lady. After the death of her husband in April 1975 she moved to the United States, but she continues to be influential in Taiwanese politics, particularly in opposing the democratic reforms of her stepson, Chiang Ching-kuo, the leader of Taiwan since 1978.

[See also Chiang Kai-shek and Chiang Ching-kuo.]

Howard L. Boorman, ed., *Biographical Dictionary of Republican China* (1967–1971). Emily Hahn, *The Soong Sisters* (1941). Sterling Seagrave, *The Soong Dynasty* (1985). Soong Meiling, *Selected Speeches* (1957). Barbara Tuchman, *Stilwell and the American Experience in China, 1911–45* (1971).   PARKS M. COBLE, JR.

SORGE INCIDENT, spying incident of World War II in which Richard Sorge, a German national, was able to supply Russia with information obtained in Japan. Richard Sorge (1895–1944) was one of the most successful spies of World War II. The son of a German oil technician and his Russian wife, he became a leftist while serving in the German army in World War I and joined the German Communist Party in 1919. A highly educated and intelligent geopolitician, he wrote for German periodicals, entered the Russian intelligence service, and served as German correspondent in Tokyo after 1933. There he posed as an ardent Nazi and won the confidence of the German military attaché and later ambassador to Japan Eugen Ott, thereby gaining free entry to the embassy and employment as press attaché.

Sorge also became a close associate of a leading Japanese intellectual, Ozaki Hotsumi, a sometime member of the Shōwa Research Association with ready access to the group of intellectuals around Prince Konoe Fumimaro, who would later become prime minister. Through such channels of information, Sorge was able to transmit, via Shanghai, information to Moscow about German plans to invade Russia, Japanese decisions to strike south instead of against Siberia, and other intelligence, in remarkable detail and volume. Japanese police arrested the ring in 1941 and Sorge and Ozaki were executed in 1944.

In postsurrender Japan the incident became a sensation when revealed. The Japanese government had played down the incident, both out of embarrassment because of the success Sorge had enjoyed in high quarters and because of the need to preserve Soviet relations, then served by a nonaggression pact. Japanese police and Occupation authorities implied that Sorge had been unmasked through treachery within the Japan Communist Party, thereby creating deep rifts in Party leadership. A sympathetic Japanese left lionized Ozaki as a martyr for the cause of international understanding and peace. The Soviet government kept its distance from the affair until 1964, when *Pravda*, in the new readiness to admit high-level errors under Stalin, hailed Sorge as a "man whose name will be for future generations a symbol of devotion to the great cause of the fight for peace, a symbol of courage and heroism."

F. W. Deakin and Richard Storry, *The Case of Richard Sorge* (1966). Chalmers Johnson, *An Instance of Treason: Ozaki Hotsumi and the Sorge Spy Ring* (1964).
MARIUS B. JANSEN

SOULBURY COMMISSION. Although the State Council of Ceylon imposed a boycott on it, the Soulbury Commission (22 December 1944–7 April 1945) used a draft constitution produced by the State Council and the advice of D. S. Senanayake and Oliver Goonetilleke to produce the white paper of 31 October 1945. This went well beyond the reforms promised in 1943 and was accepted by the State Council on 9 November 1945.

[See also Sri Lanka.]

K. M. de Silva, ed., *Universal Franchise, 1931–1981: The Sri Lankan Experience* (1981).   PATRICK PEEBLES

SOUPHANOUVONG (b. 1909), Laotian prince and politician. Born in Luang Prabang, Souphanouvong is the son of Prince Boun Khong, viceroy or "second king" of the protected kingdom of Luang Prabang in the French colony of Laos, by Mom Kham Ouane, a nonroyal wife. He was educated at Hanoi and Paris and graduated as a civil engineer in 1937. He proved to be a student of vigor, brilliance, and ambition. On his return home he asked for an appointment in Vietnam, considering Laos "a country without a future," and was posted to Nha Trang, where he later married the Vietnamese Le Ty Ky Nam, daughter of a postal official, whose ambition matched or surpassed his own. His position in Vietnam was much inferior to that of his half brother Prince Souvannaphouma in Laos and well below the standard for French engineers with similar qualifications. This may have been one of the reasons for his hatred of the French.

Souphanouvong was quick to see the opportunities presented by the Japanese capitulation in August 1945, which the Vietnamese quickly exploited for themselves. In early September, US agents flew him from his post at Vinh to Hanoi, where he was welcomed by Ho Chi Minh, who gave him arms, a body of "advisers," and money for the liberation of Laos. In mid-September he reached Thakhek in middle Laos and found the Lao Issara already active. At the end of October he was in Vientiane, the Laotian capital, with his Vietnamese entourage, and was made foreign minister in the Lao Issara government. Having signed a mutual military aid agreement with the Vietnamese and written a spiteful letter of repudiation to the French, he returned to military duty at Thakhek, where, as chief of the largely Vietnamese Lao Issara force, he was present when the returning French routed his troops on 21 March 1946. He was badly wounded when crossing the Mekong River to Thailand on Vietnamese "advice" at an early stage in the battle.

Souphanouvong's alliance with the Vietnamese went to the very heart of Lao nationalism. In origin, the Lao Issara itself had been as much anti-Vietnamese as anti-French, and the many Lao who opposed the Lao Issara did so because they preferred the French to the Vietnamese, their traditional enemies. Souphanouvong took the opposite view. His impenetrable vanity, his identification of Laotian with Vietnamese interests, and his arrogant insistence on military collaboration with the Vietnamese in 1946–1948 alienated his colleagues in exile and caused his expulsion from the Lao Issara before it was disbanded in 1949.

Prince Souphanouvong then went to North Vietnam at the invitation of Vo Nguyen Giap. In September 1950 he became head of the Lao front organization created by the Vietnamese, the Neo Lao Issara, in which capacity he accompanied the Vietnamese invasion of Laos in 1953 and 1954. The Geneva Agreement of 1954 confirmed his forces, now known as the Pathet Lao and numbering some six thousand men, in occupation of the two northern provinces of Sam Neua and Phongsaly, pending integration into the Laotian state. Souphanouvong's price for integration, however, turned out to be Pathet Lao entry into the government. Many Laotian leaders found this hard to swallow. There were difficult, much-interrupted negotiations, brought to fruition only in 1957, when Souphanouvong and one of his aides entered the government of Prince Souvannaphouma under the Vientiane Agreements. The Pathet Lao prince proved a vigorous, innovative minister. In the ensuing supplementary elections called to implement integration, he became a deputy for Vientiane with a sweeping majority. But anti-Communist and anti-Vietnamese fears again took over; the fall of the government in 1958 robbed him of office, and in 1959 disagreements about the integration of his troops, which the new government tried to force, led to his imprisonment and to the resumption of Pathet Lao insurgency.

Prince Souphanouvong and his comrades escaped from prison in May 1960. They were still walking through the monsoon-soaked country when the Neutralist coup of August 1960 brought Prince Souvannaphouma back to office and to new negotiations with his half brother. Expelled by the military countercoup of December 1960, Souvannaphouma and his Neutralists allied themselves with the Pathet Lao, and before the ensuing civil war was halted by international action in May 1961, the alliance had taken over nearly all the hill country of Laos. In the process the Pathet Lao became a disciplined force encadred and supported by the Vietnamese. His military strength enabled Souphanouvong to take a strong line in the negotiations that followed and to secure a full one-third share in the tripartite coalition government of 1962. But despite the continued optimism of Prince Souvannaphouma, integration was no longer possible. The stresses of the mounting Vietnam War led to renewed fighting in 1963. Souphanouvong and his Pathet Lao colleagues left for the hills, and Laos, split by its own civil war, became a theater of the Vietnam War as well.

The sudden North Vietnamese victory of 1975 brought the Pathet Lao to power in Laos just as suddenly. When the revolution was complete and the king deposed, Souphanouvong became president of the People's Democratic Republic. Laos became a Vietnamese colony.

[*See also* Laos; Souvannaphouma; Lao Issara; Vo Nguyen Giap; Vientiane Agreements; *and* Pathet Lao.]

Arthur J. Dommen, *Conflict in Laos* (1971). Paul Langer and Joseph Zasloff, *North Vietnam and the Pathet Lao* (1970).   HUGH TOYE

SOUTH ASIA. This regional designation, now widely accepted in academic circles, still enjoys little popular vogue. Its usage derives from the inapplicability of "India" or "Indian subcontinent" as regional names following the partition of 1947. "Indo-Pakistan subcontinent," which briefly obtained limited currency, similarly became outdated with the establishment of Bangladesh in 1971. Presently, South Asia is normally taken to include India, Pakistan, Bangladesh, Nepal, Bhutan, Sri Lanka, and the Republic of the Maldives. Some texts extend its coverage to Afghanistan, which may also be regarded as part of "Southwest Asia," "the Middle East," "Central Asia," or "Inner Asia."

The first of many multidisciplinary units focusing on the region in North American universities was the Department of South Asia Regional Studies, founded in 1947 at the University of Pennsylvania. In Europe, similar pioneer entities were established at Heidelberg (Südasien Institut) and Cambridge (Centre for South Asian Studies) in 1962 and 1964, respectively. The scholarly journal *South Asia* was launched in Australia in 1971.

The foreign ministers of the region's seven core countries have met regularly since 1980, and in August 1983 they established a permanent Committee for South Asia Regional Cooperation (SARC).

[*See also independent entries for the countries mentioned herein.*]

Richard D. Lambert, *Language and Area Studies Review* (1973). Joseph E. Schwartzberg, ed., *A Historical Atlas of South Asia* (1978).   JOSEPH E. SCHWARTZBERG

SOUTHEAST ASIA, the southeastern corner of the Asian landmass, encompassing all that lies between India, China, Australia, and New Guinea. The countries of Southeast Asia include Burma, Thailand, Laos, Cambodia, Vietnam, Malaysia, Singapore, Brunei, Indonesia, and the Philippines. It is often said that Southeast Asia acquired identity as a

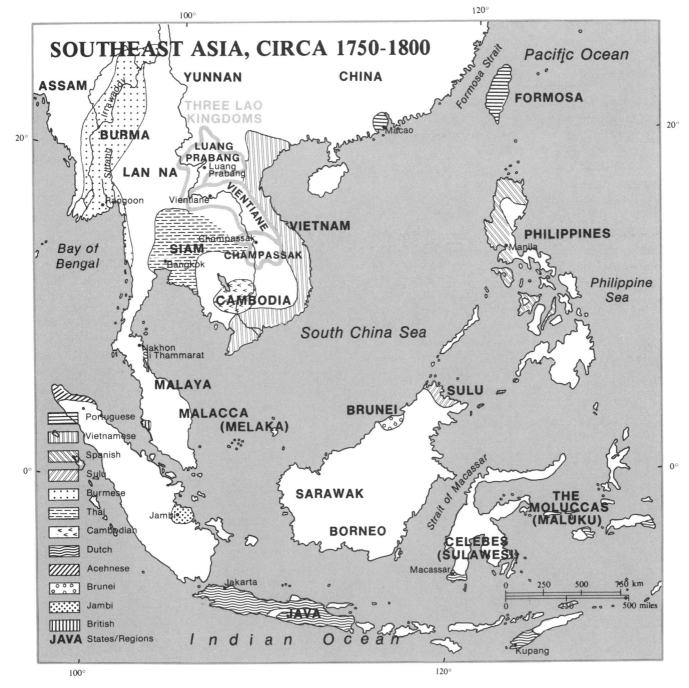

region only during World War II, when it gained the name as the theater of operations under the responsibility of British admiral Lord Louis Mountbatten (1900–1979). But the region existed and had a distinctive cultural and historical identity long before Westerners found it necessary to find a name for it.

Southeast Asia's cultural and linguistic identity is complex. The peoples of the region are classified into many different ethnolinguistic families—Tibeto-Burman, Miao-Yao, Tai, Austroasiatic, and Austronesian (Malayo-Polynesian) are the chief ones—but the relations between them are unclear. They share many cultural traits that distinguish them from their neighbors (e.g., bilateral kinship and the relatively high social position accorded women), and their physical appearance is distinctive. Most of all, however, they have lived for millennia in relatively closer contact with each other than with their Indian and Chinese neighbors in a unique environment in which, to the present, the ratio of population to resources has been much lower than elsewhere in Asia.

Social development begins as early in Southeast Asia as anywhere in Europe, with early advanced metallurgy and urbanism, as in the Dong Son and Ban Chiang civilizations. [See Dong Son and Ban Chiang.] A major stimulus to state formation came in the early centuries of the common era, when Southeast Asia gained in importance as part of the inter-Asian trade between India and China. Trade stimulated contacts with India and the adoption of many features of Indian civilization, including Buddhism and aspects of Hinduism (but not the Indian caste system) in such states as Dvaravati and Srivijaya, while Vietnam underwent many centuries of colonization by China. [See Dvaravati and Srivijaya.] Indianization thus affected the cultures of all the region except Vietnam, most notably the Cambodian empire of Angkor. [See Indianization and Angkor.]

After the collapse of the indianized states about 1300, what might be called a classical or vernacular age ensued, in which the distinctive cultures and polities of the region took shape and flourished—cultures that in the long run would form the basis for the modern states of the region. Development in many cases was interrupted by the arrival of Western powers, the Portuguese and Spaniards in the sixteenth century and the Dutch and English in the seventeenth. While a few areas quickly came under European control, most of the region did not fully fall under imperial regimes until the nineteenth century, though Siam (Thailand) remained independent (see map 1).

During the colonial period the states of the region were isolated from one another, their contacts and concentration focused primarily on the metropolitan colonial powers. Japanese occupation of all the region during World War II invigorated a nationalism that prevented the full reinstitution of colonial rule after the war, and all the region gained independence by 1957. But independence itself solved few of the region's political and economic problems, and much conflict (notably the Indochina wars of 1946–1954 and 1960–1975) has worked to slow political, social, and economic development.

[For the geopolitical situation in Southeast Asia around 1300 and 1540, see the maps accompanying Sukhothai and Ayudhya, respectively.]

G. Coedès, The Indianized States of Southeast Asia, translated by Susan B. Cowing (1968). C. A. Fisher, Southeast Asia: A Social, Economic, and Political Geography (1964). D. G. E. Hall, A History of Southeast Asia (4th ed., 1981). David Joel Steinberg, ed., In Search of Southeast Asia: A Modernized History (1985).

DAVID K. WYATT

SOUTHEAST ASIA TREATY ORGANIZATION. The Southeast Asia Treaty Organization (SEATO) was created to implement the goals of the Manila Pact and the Pacific Charter, which were signed on 8 September 1954 by representatives from Australia, France, New Zealand, Pakistan, the Philippines, Thailand, the United Kingdom, and the United States. The Manila Pact, officially known as the Southeast Asia Collective Defense Treaty, was a military alliance intended to prevent or counter any Communist attempt to subvert the freedom or to destroy the sovereignty or territorial integrity of nations in the treaty area. The Pacific Charter was a declaration in which the signatories pledged themselves to uphold the principles of self-determination and self-government and to promote higher living standards, economic progress, and social well-being. These social objectives notwithstanding, the primary purpose of SEATO was to implement the Manila Pact and to ensure the security of the member states through a policy of collective defense.

Despite the initial enthusiasm of the participating nations, SEATO soon encountered operational difficulties because of disagreements over the proper means of dealing with Communist activities, and a long trend of organizational decline began. Because the organization insisted upon unanimous policy decisions, these disagreements prevented SEATO from acting in such places as Laos and Vietnam. Its inability to reach important decisions, plus charges that it was a neocolonialist creation, caused SEATO to be increasingly perceived as moribund and irrelevant. As a result of these difficulties, and because of the Communist victory at the end of the Indochina wars in 1975, a general agreement was reached to disband SEATO effective 30 June 1977.

Astri Goldstein, *SEATO: Rethinking Regionalism* (1969). Corrine Phuangkasem, *Thailand and SEATO* (1973). SEATO, *Collective Security: Shield of Freedom* (2d ed., 1963). Justus M. Van der Kroef, *The Lives of SEATO* (1976).   WILLIAM A. KINSEL

SOUTHERN AND NORTHERN DYNASTIES

(420–589), traditional Chinese nomenclature for the greater part of the early medieval period, often used by extension for the entire period from the loss of unity under the Western Jin dynasty in the early fourth century to its reestablishment under the Sui dynasty in 589. The nearest common English-language term in this broader sense is *Age of Disunion.*

Strictly speaking, the designation refers to the period occupied by the dynasties that are recorded in the *Southern History (Nanshi)* and the *Northern History (Beishi).* For South China, this includes the Southern Dynasties (narrowly defined): (Liu) Song (420–479), Southern Qi (479–502), Liang (502–557), and Chen (557–589). For North China, the dynasties concerned are the Northern Wei (386–534/535), with its successor states the Eastern Wei (534–550) and the Western Wei (535–556); the Northern Qi (550–577); and the Northern Zhou (557–581). It will be observed that the Northern Dynasties do not fit the traditional chronology for the period at either end. For the beginning of the period, 420 must be regarded as a rough compromise between 386 (when the Northern Wei established its independence from the crumbling Former Qin dynasty) and 439 (when it reunified North China). The end of the period is dated not from Yang Jian's usurpation of the Northern Zhou throne in 581, but from the Sui conquest of the Chen, the last remaining dynasty in the South, in 589.

As shorthand for the period during which no single dynasty could make a convincing claim to the dominion of all of China, *Southern and Northern Dynasties* has the serious drawback of ignoring the fourth century, during which South China saw the rise of the Eastern Jin dynasty (318–420) and North China was divided among the alien regimes known collectively as the Sixteen Kingdoms. Both the dismissal of the fourth century and the keying of the chronology to events in the South can be understood as legacies of the Neo-Confucian theory of political legitimacy, in terms of which there could only be one valid Chinese government at any given time. The weak but native Southern Dynasties were considered to possess a truer claim to the Chinese throne than did the alien Northern Wei dynasty, despite the latter's vastly greater significance for the subsequent political history of China. *Southern and Northern Dynasties* is marginally superior as a label for early medieval China to the often-seen *Six Dynasties,* in that there is historically no agreement as to which six regimes of the period are meant. It is worth discussing at such length the confused terminology for the period because it reflects the difficulties that early medieval Chinese history posed for traditional historiography, with its imperial and metropolitan biases, and the subsequent tendency by scholars to ignore the period in general.

The Southern Dynasties. The historiographical cliché applied to the Southern Dynasties is that they were "aristocratic" in comparison to the tribal soldiery in the North. In truth, some of the northern tribes, especially those dominated by Turkic elements, were very strictly aristocratic, whereas the southern governments conspicuously found their origins, one after another, in military headquarters. The pattern was set by the preceding Eastern Jin dynasty, which grew out of an attempt on the part of a Western Jin military dictator to construct a fortified refuge on the south bank of the Yangtze River. By the time Liu Yu began the Southern Dynasties proper by founding the (Liu) Song dynasty in 420, that retreat had grown into an uneasy blend of recent refugees from fighting in the North China Plain, Chinese settlers whose ancestors had moved south during the Eastern (Latter) Han and Three Kingdoms periods, and an increasingly repressed non-Chinese indigenous population spread out along the middle and lower course of the Yangtze.

Definitions of the southern aristocracy have traditionally emphasized the persistent autonomy of certain leading families, but there has been a tendency in recent scholarship to cast doubt on the antiquity and influence of even the most elite families and to revise upward our estimates of the freedom of action of the southern emperors. However, the Southern Dynasties have probably been studied less than any portion of Chinese history except the tenth century, so any conclusions one comes to must be tentative.

The military threat from the North dictated much of the political evolution of the Southern Dynasties. Liu Yu gained the prestige that validated his usurpation through victories over Northern Wei forces, and his less martial descendants were finally overthrown by another general spawned by the endless conflict, Xiao Daocheng. Xiao's Southern Qi regime seems to have been particularly unstable, with savage conflict both within the imperial family and also between the preexisting elite and military men of lower origins. It is likely that this murderous situation was consciously promoted by northern scheming. An imperial relative, Xiao Yan, who had survived in the shelter of a peripheral princely court, finally forced his way to the throne in violation of the legitimate succession. Making a ceremonial break as well, he named his government the Liang dynasty.

Known as Liang Wudi, Martial Emperor of Liang, Xiao Yan would be famous for his durability if nothing else, reigning from 502 to 549, longer than any other southern ruler. His lack of interest in military conquest, combined with the internal disorders of the Northern Wei, allowed the South a brief respite from the interminable fighting. Ultimately, however, the troubles in the North proved fatal to the Liang when it attempted to play off a non-Chinese northern commander, Hou Jing, against his Western Wei ruler. Hou Jing destroyed the capital, the dynasty, and most of the civilian elite in an attempt to enthrone himself in Jiankang (modern Nanjing) in 549, but was unable to establish a government in the face of universal opposition.

From this time on, Chinese rule in the South crumbled away into a puppet regime to the west known as the Northern Liang (555–587), which was subordinated to whatever power ruled in the northwest, and a miserable remnant in the east known as the Chen dynasty. Set up by the Liang general Chen Baxian, it was the logical end of the evolution of the southern governments from cliques of refugees from the northern court to rough native soldiery. Disorganized and impoverished, the South offered little opposition to the highly organized and well-executed invasion of the Sui that reunited China in 589.

Classical treatments of the contribution of the Southern Dynasties to Chinese civilization emphasize their literary output, which in the ensuing period had a delicious reputation for decadence. Unfortunately, their most significant contribution, their role in the opening up of the economic potential of South China and their incorporation of the Chinese into the trade routes of Southeast Asia, is much more difficult to document. The extraordinary wealth of the southern area, and its emergence as the center of gravity of Chinese economic life, are develop-

ments that become clear only during the Song dynasty, but there are signs that this course was well under way by the Sui conquest.

The southern trade routes provided one of the avenues of Buddhism's entry into China, and its development in the South was along lines very different from those taken by Buddhism in the North. Maintaining a polite distance from the centers of political power, elite Buddhism in the South participated in the development of monastic institutions and philosophical debates strongly marked with features of the religious Daoist thought that represented the native alternative to mainstream Confucian orthodoxy.

The Northern Dynasties. The most astonishing aspect of North China during the early medieval period is that government after government made no pretense of being Chinese in its origins or fundamental impulse. (Some would argue that the major difference between early and late medieval China in this regard is that the rulers of the late medieval empire, for example, the Tang dynasty, had learned to make such a pretense.) Although many questions remain unanswered about the identities of the peoples involved, there is no doubt that they were radically different in language, culture, and ethnicity from the Han Chinese whose territory they entered during the early centuries of the first millennium CE. As in the case of the Roman empire, it is fair to assume that the aliens were numerically inferior to the indigenous population, but it is worth remembering that they, too, made their contribution to the human mixture that inhabits northeast Asia today.

The foreign peoples of this period were very different from the Mongols of the Yuan dynasty (1279–1368), in that they did not enter China as irresistible conquerors or represent a drastically lower level of cultural development. While it has been argued that the Yuan dealt a staggering blow to the Chinese society and economy, establishing the basis for the stagnant kingdom of Malthusian necessity encountered by the West, it is plain that the aliens of the Northern Dynasties had a creative and galvanizing effect on Chinese political institutions. Their own techniques of rule blended with those of the native elite in a powerful hybrid that conclusively demonstrated its superiority to the more traditional political culture of the Southern Dynasties. Such a constructive blend was made more possible by the gradual and relatively peaceful penetration of the foreign tribes, which often entered North China at the invitation of Chinese regimes, and which had decades or even centuries to absorb useful elements of the culture of their Chinese neighbors before becoming decisive elements of that culture themselves.

Buddhism, which swept East Asia during the first millennium CE, underwent a distinctive evolution as a part of the hybridization of Chinese and foreign cultures occurring in North China. From the first, Buddhism was attractive to the alien rulers in the North as being the most refined cultural instrument available to them that was not the particular property of their Chinese subjects. Buddhism was a sophisticated form of cultural expression that Chinese and foreigner alike could share, leading those in authority to see it as a tool for welding together their ethnic patchwork kingdoms. Initially, the attraction was probably at the level of spells and magical compulsion, but as the Sino-foreign hybrid regimes grew in political sophistication, their rulers made more and more subtle use of Buddhism's philosophical resources and of the education of its clergy. During the Northern Dynasties, emperors routinely characterized their authority in terms of their being living Buddhas, an attitude that found its apotheosis later under the Tang dynasty (618–907), when Wu Zetian (Wu Zhao) justified her position as China's only female emperor on the basis that she was Maitreya, Buddha of the future.

This politicization of Buddhism had major consequences for the history of northeast Asia. When Buddhism entered the Korean peninsula in the fourth century, its ties with politics were already strong, and it was passed on to the Japanese in the sixth century as the highest level of political technology available. A number of features of Japanese Buddhism, including the link between Zen and militarism, make better sense when one sees them in the light of the uses to which the religion was put by the Northern Dynasties.

Overall, the political legacy of the northern regimes was one of increased central executive power and enhanced social prestige for the emperor. This was carefully retained even by dynasties whose personnel and culture were much more southern and Chinese in derivation, such as the Northern and Southern Song (960–1127 and 1127–1279, respectively). One social legacy that did not endure was an improved position for women, a temporary gain that was reversed by the end of the tenth century.

Traditional historians have often presented aliens on Chinese soil as unpleasant but peripheral, possessing only nuisance value rather than historical significance. One lesson of the Northern Dynasties is that an important part of China's being has been defined in contact with non-Chinese peoples, and that its history should always be understood as occurring within a multistate system encompassing Central Asia.

[See also Jin Dynasty; Northern Wei Dynasty; Six Dynasties; and Sixteen Kingdoms.]

Wolfram Eberhard, *A History of China* (1969). Patricia Buckley Ebrey, *The Aristocratic Families of Early Imperial China* (1978). J. D. Frodsham, *An Anthology of Chinese Verse: Han, Wei, Chin, and the Northern and Southern Dynasties* (1967). Dennis Grafflin, "The Great Family in Medieval South China," *Harvard Journal of Asiatic Studies* 41 (1981): 65–74. James Robert Hightower, *The Poetry of T'ao Ch'ien* (1970). Arthur F. Wright, *Buddhism in Chinese History* (1959) and *The Sui Dynasty* (1978), chapters 1–3.   DENNIS GRAFFLIN

SOUTH PERSIA RIFLES, British-controlled military force in Iran from 1916 to 1921. The South Persia Rifles were organized to protect British interests in southern and eastern Iran during World War I, when German agents were successfully cultivating strong anti-British sentiments among the Iranians. Under the command of Sir Percy Sykes, the South Persia Rifles was comprised of British and Indian officers and local Iranian recruits. By 1918 the force had retaken Kerman and Shiraz as well as smaller towns that had fallen under the control of tribal groups hostile to Great Britain.

[See also Sykes, Sir Percy Molesworth.]

Percy Sykes, *A History of Persia,* 2 vols. (2d ed., 1921), pp. 451–517.   ERIC HOOGLUND

SOUTHWARD ADVANCE. *See* Nam Tien.

SOUVANNAPHOUMA (b. 1901), Laotian prince and political leader. Born in Luang Prabang, Souvannaphouma was the son of Prince Boun Khong, viceroy or "second king" of the kingdom of Luang Prabang in Laos, nephew of King Sisavangvong, and full brother of Prince Phetsarath. After some schooling in Hanoi, he continued his education in France, where he earned degrees in architectural engineering (Paris, 1928) and electrical engineering (Grenoble, 1930). He had a distinguished career as civil engineer in Laos, restoring important ancient monuments in Vientiane and constructing a key hill-section of the Vientiane–Luang Prabang road in 1940. In 1933 he married Aline-Claire Allard, a Frenchwoman whose mother was Lao. He became a minister in the rebel Lao Issara government in October 1945, fled to Thailand when the French returned to Laos in 1946, and took the lead in the return home of the moderate majority of his colleagues after the grant of substantial Laotian independence in 1949. He was minister of public works in 1950 and became prime minister of Laos in November 1951.

For the next twenty-four years the career of Prince Souvannaphouma closely paralleled the story of Laos. As prime minister when the Vietnamese invaded in 1953, when final independence from France was negotiated, and when the Geneva Agreement ended the First Indochina War in 1954, it fell to him to establish and preserve his country's neutrality between Thailand and North Vietnam, ancient enemies now on opposite sides of the Cold War. But the war had left a mortgage on Laotian neutrality—the rebel Pathet Lao movement, which reflected ethnic, regional, and class differences but was supported and politically colored by the Vietnamese Communists and headed by the prince's brilliant half-brother, Prince Souphanouvong. In 1954 Prince Souvannaphouma started negotiations that, despite interruptions, resulted in the Vientiane Agreements of 1957, which called for the integration of Prince Souphanouvong and the Pathet Lao into the body politic. Domestic jealousies, which had always been in the background, and the anticommunist stance of the United States, on whose financial generosity Laos depended, reversed the process in 1958. An anticommunist government took over, Prince Souvannaphouma went to Paris as ambassador, and the Pathet Lao returned to insurgency.

A Neutralist military coup against the resumed civil war ousted an even more reactionary government in August 1960 and recalled the prince to power. With US military help (at first unofficial), a military countercoup was prepared at once. But for a few weeks Prince Souvannaphouma, a man of moderation and compromise, seemed to have captured American confidence. With avuncular patience he held the eager Neutralists in check, negotiated a truce with the Pathet Lao, and opened diplomatic relations with the Soviet Union. Once the Thai closed the border, however, US confidence did not hold. In December 1960, after the most serious fighting seen in the capital in modern times, the countercoup forces and their backers drove the Neutralists from Vientiane.

Now receiving aid from the Soviets, the Neutralists retreated to a safe military base and forged an alliance with the Pathet Lao. Prince Souvanna-phouma had done his best to prevent fighting and was distressed beyond measure when it became inevitable. He and most of his ministers fled to Cambodia, where it was soon clear that the Soviets continued to recognize his government. Bitter at his betrayal by the United States, the prince decided that national reconciliation was still attainable under these circumstances, and he moved his government to Neutralist territory.

In June 1962—after a civil war, a painfully slow negotiation of internal interests with the counter-coup government and the Pathet Lao, the calming of Thai fears by the United States, and another Geneva conference—Prince Souvannaphouma was back in Vientiane as prime minister of a tripartite coalition supported by international guarantees. It was too late. Passage through Laos was now indispensable to the North Vietnamese for their war in the south—a development unacceptable to the United States, which was already engaged on the other side. These external strains broke up the internal compromise. In 1963 the Pathet Lao ministers in the coalition returned to the areas they controlled, and in 1964 the Neutralist forces split under Pathet Lao attack, the majority merging with those of the right. They were soon supported by Thai troops and US aircraft. Laos became a subsidiary theater of the Vietnam War, whose sudden end with a North Vietnamese victory in 1975 accordingly signaled the victory of the Pathet Lao in Laos.

To the last, Prince Souvannaphouma seemed as if he had not entirely given up hope. His government had been shuffled and reshuffled, and there had been coups and attempted coups; in one of these, he himself had suffered imprisonment. In 1968 and 1973 he had brought negotiations with the Pathet Lao close to success but was defeated each time by domestic reaction. There was no room for compromise after the fall of Saigon, however. "Dear comrades," he said on 11 May 1975, Constitution Day in Laos, "Important changes have taken place which some had not expected so suddenly, but they are here. . . . It is necessary to look at the facts and prepare to arrive at an accord with history." Still sometimes seen in Paris, he lives in retirement in Vientiane.

[See also Laos; Luang Prabang; Sisavangvong; Phetsarath; Lao Issara; Pathet Lao; Souphanouvong; Vientiane Agreements; and Geneva Conference on the Laotian Question.]

Arthur J. Dommen, *Conflict in Laos* (1971). Bernard B. Fall, *Anatomy of a Crisis* (1969). Charles A. Stevenson, *The End of Nowhere* (1972).   HUGH TOYE

SŎWŎN (Chinese, *shuyuan*), Korean Neo-Confucian private academies. Such academies were championed by early Neo-Confucians in both China and Korea as retreats for learning and moral cultivation. Each academy was also dedicated to the memory of one or several exemplary earlier Confucians, and ritual sacrifices were conducted twice yearly to honor these men. The first *sŏwŏn* in Korea was founded by Chu Se-bung in 1542. The institution spread rapidly, until there were more than eight hundred by the early eighteenth century, more than double the number in China during the Ming dynasty (1368–1644).

In addition to the functions for which they were initially instituted, Korean private academies became important local power bases for political factions and elite clans associated with them. They were a symbol of prestige for the wealthy families that instituted and supported them, and a means by which such families could glorify illustrious forebears by publishing their writings or making them the object of semipublic veneration in the *sŏwŏn's* ritual activities. They were also social centers that served to cement relationships and maintain the ties by which such families perpetuated their power and authority in local communities.

Such academies were often strongly criticized for their factional ties and their use to promote particular families or clans. In the mid-eighteenth century the government had some three hundred *sŏwŏn* destroyed, and in 1871 it was finally decreed that all but forty-seven be demolished; most of these remain in existence.

[See also Neo-Confucianism in Korea.]

Woo-Keun Han, *The History of Korea*, translated by Kyung-shik Lee (1970). Ki-baik Lee, *A New History of Korea*, translated by Edward W. Wagner (1984). James B. Palais, *Politics and Policy in Traditional Korea* (1975).

MICHAEL C. KALTON

SPAIN AND THE PHILIPPINES. The Philippines was part of the Spanish empire from 1565 to 1898. During this period Spain exercised political and economic control of the archipelago and tried to use the islands as a stepping stone for the conquest of other Asian territories. The Philippines were the westernmost possession of Spain, and thus King Philip II could say that he possessed an empire over which the sun never set.

A mixture of economic and political motives—the desire for spices and control of the Pacific—dominated initial Spanish control of the islands, but by the nineteenth century the possessions were a liability to the Spanish crown. Thereafter, the islands were retained primarily for religious motives.

Following Magellan's discovery of the Philippines in 1521, a series of unsuccessful attempts to colonize the islands took place. It was not until 1565, however, that the first permanent Spanish settlement was founded. On 13 February of that year an expedition that set out from New Spain under a minor Spanish official, Miguel Lopez de Legazpi, successfully reached Gamay Bay off Samar Island, then proceeded to touch at Leyte, Camiguin, Bohol, and finally Cebu on 27 April, where the first settlement was made. [See Legazpi, Miguel Lopez de.] In May 1571 the tiny group of settlers moved to Manila. Thereupon, Juan de Salcedo conducted an expedition of conquest around Laguna de Bay and down the Cagayan River, and Martin de Goiti and one hundred soldiers penetrated the center of the island of Luzon, demanding the submission of the local peoples of Bulacan, Pampanga, and Pangasinan. After 1571 the Spanish occupation centered on Manila and Luzon.

The number of Spanish settlers in the Philippines was never large, fluctuating between two hundred in the seventeenth century and two thousand in the late eighteenth. These low numbers are explained by the remoteness of the islands from Mexico, a lack of economic incentives, and the Philippines' hot, uncomfortable climate.

A large mestizo population (offspring of Spaniards and natives) such as grew up in Mexico and other parts of the Spanish empire never developed in the Philippines. [See Mestizo.] In the Philippines a mestizo was the offspring of a native Filipino and a Chinese. (The Chinese were attracted to the archipelago by the opportunity to trade with the Spaniards and by the commercial activity that had been conducted for centuries between China and the islands of Southeast Asia.)

The highest Spanish official in the islands was the governor-general, who was under the jurisdiction of the viceroy of New Spain. Assisting him was the Audiencia of Manila, a board of six or seven crown-appointed officials who acted as advisers to the governor-general and as court judges in major civil cases. [See Audiencia.] As a major capital city, Manila was governed by a *cabildo*, or town council, which saw to the services that a city was obliged to provide. The *cabildo* made sure that food supplies were available, market prices were just, garbage was collected, the streets swept, and criminals punished. In the provinces (*alcaldias*), an *alcalde mayor*, or provincial governor, held authority. [See Alcalde Mayor.] His primary responsibility was to enforce directives coming from Manila. On the local, municipal level was the *gobernadorcillo*, who heard minor cases in the first instance. These offices, from governor-general to *gobernadorcillo*, constituted a centralizing force in Philippine society.

Of equal importance as a centralizing force was the Catholic church. [*See* Catholicism in the Philippines.] From the time of the reconquest of Spain from the Muslims in the twelfth century, the church and state in Spain were united. The conquest of America was likewise a joint undertaking, with the cost of sending missionaries to America and building churches borne by the Spanish crown. In return, the crown received certain privileges when it came time to appoint bishops and parish priests. The mutual privileges and concessions were part of what was called the *patronato real* ("royal patronage").

In the early days of Spanish rule, missionary work was undertaken by Augustinians, Dominicans, Franciscans, and Jesuits. Secular priests (those not bound by vows) came after. [*See* Friars.] The archipelago was divided into dioceses and into parishes. From the parish the priests would try to visit the towns of the surrounding area. The further one was removed from the parish, the weaker were the institutional ties to the church. A type of folk Catholicism developed. Both pre-Hispanic beliefs and the new Christian rituals were placed side by side and honored as equals. The concrete, rather than the abstract, was followed, so the use of *santos* (statues of saints) and public demonstrations of religious belief through processions, public prayer (novenas), and membership in *cofradías* ("sodalities") became popular.

In the first two hundred years of colonial rule a vigorous missionary effort achieved enormous success in conversions to Catholicism. By the end of the Spanish colonial period, only a few pockets of non-Christians existed in the archipelago.

Both the religious and political structure in the Philippines was constructed on a shaky economic foundation. The crown was in the main a poor paymaster, and local income from taxes was so low that a yearly subsidy called the *situado* had to be sent from Mexico to the Philippines to pay the costs of civil administration. The costs of colonization were partly covered by a head tax, called the *tributo*, that was paid by males between the ages of eighteen and fifty. Exempt from tribute were those over fifty, the sick, native officials, and the *principalia*, who were not obliged to pay in view of their pre-Hispanic social status and the role they played in colonial

administration. [*See* Principalia.] The tax was payable in coin or in kind, but most often natives were able to use only the latter.

Closely connected with the payment of tribute was the exaction of labor services. Spanish jurists argued that the mother country's right to both taxes and work was derived from the same source, the nature of vassalage. As in America, labor became a controversy par excellence. The colonists sought to use natives as slaves; on the other hand, the crown sought to respect the liberty of its vassals. The result was an uneasy compromise that created colonial labor institutions such as the *repartimiento* and *servicios personales*. In the Philippines forced labor was required for the shipyards of Cavite, and even in the nineteenth century every able-bodied man was obliged to render forty days service (called the *polo*) to the state or in lieu of this service to pay three pesos. The cruelty associated with labor service was a major complaint of those seeking reform.

While tribute and labor were important aspects of the Philippine economy, the economic history of the islands during the Spanish period was largely shaped by the Manila galleon trade. [*See* Manila Galleon.] This was a simple arrangement whereby Manila merchants acted as middlemen in shipping Asian merchandise to Mexico. Each year, usually in April, a large galleon would be loaded in Manila with luxury items such as silk, pearls, sapphires, ivory, and fabrics from China, Macao, India, and Cambodia and begin the six-month crossing to Acapulco, catching the Japan Current down the Pacific coast of America. Once in Acapulco, the goods would be sold to waiting merchants, who paid in silver pesos that were then shipped back to Manila. The value of the cargo sent to Mexico was limited to 250,000 pesos and the silver return to 500,000, but actual shipments were in excess. When the Englishman George Anson captured the Manila galleon *Covadonga* in 1746, he found over a million pesos on board, much of it hidden to escape customs payments.

Most of the Spanish business activity in the Philippines was limited to the galleon trade until the late eighteenth century, when a group of government officials and entrepreneurs attempted to develop agriculture and mining and integrate these new industries into the external trade of the islands. The eighteenth century was a great colonial century for Spain, marked by capital growth, the large-scale import of raw materials, and a rising population. The Philippines participated in this resurgence.

In the nineteenth century the Philippines maintained a lively trade in export crops. English and American vessels unloaded wines, copper, nails, oil, and other manufactured goods and in return carried off hemp, sugar, tobacco, and rice. Nathaniel Bowditch, who sailed the *Astrea* out of Salem, Massachusetts, was the first American to leave a detailed account of the incipient Asian trade (1796), and by 1816 so many American ships were stopping in Manila that the US government decided to appoint a permanent consul for the Philippines. In 1848 the colonial government declared Manila a free port for American whaling vessels, and by this time the great merchant houses of Peele Hubbell and Company, Richard Tucker of Salem, and Russell Sturgis were established. British trade, however, still far exceeded American.

The social and economic changes brought about in the nineteenth-century Philippines by the influx of foreign capital and foreign commerce were deeply significant. Prices in Manila rose almost 500 percent between 1846 and 1870. The development of large landed estates *(haciendas)* and the conversion of rice land to the exportable yields of sugar, abaca, and tobacco were instrumental in producing sharply defined social classes: a landed aristocracy; a middle class formed of businessmen, white-collar workers, and fairly affluent tenant farmers; and a landless peasant class. [*See* Hacienda.] From the middle class arose a desire for reform that eventually led to the revolution of 1896. [*See* Philippine Revolution.]

Spain's long colonial rule in the Philippines produced deep-rooted changes in society. The islanders were greatly affected by the introduction to their country of a new religion, new economic relations, and new political realities. Moreover, the mix of Spanish, Chinese, and native Filipinos produced new ethnic types. New concepts of land use and land distribution affected the farmer's relation to the soil. Social groups that wielded influence, not because of physical might, but because they possessed land and wealth, emerged. The Spaniards introduced a different value system that was by and large accepted, although it was adjusted to fit local realities.

In the Philippines today the only visible reminders of Spain's former presence are a few colonial buildings and a few street names. The more subtle influence on attitudes and social conventions, however, remains part of the fabric of Philippine society.

H. de la Costa, *The Jesuits in the Philippines, 1581–1768* (1961). Nicholas Cushner, *Spain in the Philippines: From Conquest to Revolution* (1971). John Leddy Phelan, *The Hispanization of the Philippines* (1959). William Lytle Schurz, *The Manila Galleon* (1939). Edgar Wickberg, *The Chinese in Philippine Life, 1850–1898* (1965).
NICHOLAS P. CUSHNER

SPECIAL ECONOMIC ZONES. In 1979 the government of the People's Republic of China (PRC) established special economic zones (SEZs) in four areas—Shenzhen, Zhuhai, and Shantou (Swatow) in Guangdong Province, and Xiamen (Amoy) in Fujian Province. Hainan Island was later given the status of a special SEZ. This type of zone is common throughout the capitalist world, particularly in Taiwan, where such zones have been successfully developed for more than two decades. The use of SEZs in the PRC is unique to a socialist state, and is a sign of pragmatic economic policy planning in China.

China's SEZs rank among the largest in total area in the world. Their main purposes are to promote foreign commerce, investment, and technology transfers. The liberalized trading regulations that prevail there are designed to attract foreign capital. The Chinese government has enhanced profitability for foreign companies by means of exemptions on customs duties, low income taxes, easy terms for remittance of profits to home offices, permission to establish wholly foreign-owned enterprises in China, and autonomy in management issues, including hiring, firing, and quality control.

Rather than creating a national agency, China has permitted local provincial units to administer the zones. This policy has led to greater flexibility and accessibility. The SEZs have been successful in their goal of attracting foreign capital. Within three years more than two billion dollars has been invested. In 1981 annual revenue for Shenzhen had increased five times the amount generated in 1978, a year before the SEZ was introduced. Investments concentrate on real estate construction, heavy and light industry, transportation, and energy. As the SEZ scope enlarges, investment opportunities diversify. Recent negotiations even include plans for a university complex.

The SEZs have not been entirely successful. Primary among their problems are the lack of clear and detailed regulations, insufficient attention to consumer satisfaction, hazardous levels of pollution, and political squabbles among government and Chinese managers. Without an efficient auditing system in China, the SEZs' economic planning and profitability will suffer from mismanagement and even corruption. The most marked failure of the SEZs is their inability to filter foreign capital, technology, and equipment to other regions in China. Despite these problems, the SEZs stand out as China's most significant effort to modernize and liberalize its socialist economic policies.

Clyde D. Stoltenberg, "China's Special Economic Zones: Their Development and Prospects," *Asian Survey* 24.6 (June 1984): 637–654.   RICHARD C. KAGAN

SPEELMAN, CORNELIS JANSZOON (1628–1684), conqueror of Makassar. Born in Rotterdam, Speelman served the Dutch East India Company (VOC) in Asia from his sixteenth year. An exceptionally able diplomat, soldier, and writer, he left voluminous records of his missions. After long service in Batavia, he was secretary of a Dutch mission to Persia (1651–1652) and governor of Coromandel (1663–1665). He organized the overthrow of the VOC's most important rival in the spice trade, Makassar, by skillfully exploiting internal divisions and expecially Bugis resentment of the dominant Makassarese (1666–1669). In 1677 he inaugurated a more interventionist policy in Javanese affairs, taking Surabaya from the rebel Trunajaya. He ended his career as governor-general (1681–1684) and was again able to intervene successfully in an internal conflict in Banten (1682).

[*See also* Makassar; Bugis; Trunajaya; *and* Banten.]   ANTHONY REID

SPICE TRADE commonly refers to the European trade in spices from islands of the eastern Indonesian archipelago, established in the beginning of the sixteenth century. The spices were principally nutmeg and mace from the Banda Islands and Amboina and cloves from the northern Moluccas (Maluku), notably Ternate and Tidore, and later cinnamon and black pepper. Beginning in late medieval times these commodities were in great demand in Europe, where they were used to preserve meat following the annual slaughter of cattle that could not be fed through the European winter.

Prior to the European intrusion, however, the cultivation of spices in the eastern archipelago and long-distance trade in spices had been well established for many centuries. Malay and Javanese had long traded in the eastern islands, exchanging textiles and basic foodstuffs for spices; Chinese traders exchanged luxury items such as porcelain; and Arab merchants, working through the Malacca (Melaka)

entrepôt, had long brought the spices of the archipelago into the Middle East and, through Venice, into Europe itself. Therefore, when they first sought out the Spice Islands at the end of the fifteenth century, the Portuguese were intruding on a long-established and sophisticated network of long-distance Asian trade.

To secure a major position for themselves in this trade, the Portuguese captured Melaka, the main regional entrepôt, in 1511. But to avoid the threatened Portuguese monopoly, the Asian traders who had earlier made Melaka the archipelago's unrivaled commercial center now moved to other ports in the region. Consequently, to secure their trading ambitions, the Portuguese were forced to establish a physical presence in the Spice Islands themselves. In 1522 they began construction of a fortress on Ternate, and in 1578 they built a garrison on Tidore; toward the end of the century their presence came to be centered on Amboina. But the Portuguese were unable to dominate the lucrative spice trade. Weaknesses in their commercial organization and the inadequacy of their military and financial resources, as well as the continued strength of the Asian trade network, limited Portugal's commercial achievements in the archipelago. In any case, by the midsixteenth century Portuguese trading ambitions were being redirected toward East Asia.

Portuguese ambitions were finally extinguished by the Dutch. The latter had long been involved in retailing spices received in Portugal through northern Europe. But the outbreak of the Dutch war of independence against Spain in the 1560s, and the union of the crowns of Spain and Portugal in 1580, severely hindered this trade and forced Dutch merchants to seek direct access to the spice producers in the east. Dutch traders began arriving in the Indonesian archipelago in the last years of the sixteenth century. Competition among Dutch merchants in the spice trade was so severe in these early years that prices rose steeply, thus diminishing European profits. Consequently, in 1602 the Dutch commercial interests were amalgamated to form the Dutch East India Company (VOC), which was given a monoply of Dutch trade with Asia.

In the following century the VOC came close to achieving a monopoly over the spice trade of the Indonesian archipelago. Dutch commercial organization and military and financial resources were far superior to those of the Portuguese, and the Dutch were prepared to use their physical might not only to drive their Portuguese predecessors from the archipelago and repel emerging competition from English merchants but also to ruthlessly restrict the cultivation of, and local trade in, spices in an attempt to secure their monopoly and force up prices.

In the 1620s the population of the Banda Islands was practically exterminated by Dutch measures designed to secure their monopoly of the trade in nutmeg, and throughout the seventeenth century the Dutch embarked on periodic raids in the eastern archipelago to destroy spice cultivation that was taking place beyond their authority. Dutch domination of the spice trade during this period extended far beyond the produce of the Spice Islands themselves. Within the Indonesian archipelago, the Dutch secured a virtual monopoly over the Sumatran sources of pepper (notably Palembang, Jambi, and Padang) by the 1660s; beyond the archipelago, the VOC seized Colombo from the Portuguese in 1656 and thus captured the supply of cinnamon in Ceylon (Sri Lanka). Cochin, an important source of black pepper, fell to the Dutch in 1663.

Although the spice trade made fortunes for many of the early Portuguese and Dutch traders in the archipelago, it is not clear whether the VOC made a sustained profit from this trade. It may be argued, however, that the financial costs of imposing and then maintaining a near-monopoly of the archipelago's supply of spices at the very least severely diminished Dutch net returns. In any event, by the early eighteenth century, changes in agricultural practices had curtailed the demand for spices in Europe (which had been the main consuming area in the previous century). Moreover, the relative importance of the spice trade to European merchants in Asia was severely diminished by the dramatic growth in the tea and coffee trades that took place in the East in the eighteenth century.

[See also Melaka and Dutch East India Company.]

K. N. Chaudhuri, *Trade and Civilization in the Indian Ocean. An Economic History from the Rise of Islam to 1750* (1985). J. C. van Leur, *Indonesian Trade and Society: Essays in Asian Social and Economic History* (1955). M. A. P. Meilink-Roelofsz, *Asian Trade and European Influence in the Indonesian Archipelago between 1500 and about 1630* (1962).   IAN BROWN

SPIRITUAL POLLUTION refers to a campaign against pornographic literature and bourgeois tendencies in intellectual circles launched by the Chinese Communist Party in October 1983 and ended in February 1984. Specific targets of criticism included Party democrats who had raised the issue of Marxist humanism and the possibility that "alien-

ation" might exist in socialist society. Because of passive resistance among intellectuals afraid of a repeat of the restrictions and purges of the Cultural Revolution, as well as concern over potentially harmful economic results and negative world reaction, the campaign was restrained and eventually reined in. Some observers speculate that Deng Xiaoping began the campaign in an attempt to gather Party support for the Party rectification campaign simultaneously in progress. On the other hand, Deng may have genuinely believed that the theories of socialist humanism threatened the stability of the Party and state, and thus perhaps he ended the drive against spiritual pollution only when it became an even greater threat.

[See also April Fifth Movement; Democracy Wall; Deng Xiaoping; and Marxism and Socialism: Marxism in China.]

Christopher Wren, "China is Said to End a Campaign to Stop 'Spritual Pollution,'" *New York Times*, 24 January 1984. Wu An-chia, "The Movement to 'Eliminate Ideological Pollution,'" *Issues and Studies* 20.3 (March 1984): 11–24.   JOHN A. RAPP

SPRATLY ISLANDS, a group of several small islands, shoals, and sandbars in the South China Sea. Scattered over a wide area between the Philippines, the island of Borneo, and the eastern coast of Vietnam, the Spratlys had little economic value and were rarely occupied prior to the twentieth century. In the 1970s, however, the islands became the focus of international attention with the search for oil reserves in the South China Sea. Today, some or all of the Spratlys are claimed by several nations, including China, Malaysia, Vietnam, and the Philippines. Malaysia, Vietnam, the Philippines, and the Republic of China on Taiwan have occupation forces on several of the islands.

Lim Joo-Jack, *Geo-Strategy and the South China Sea: Regional Balance, Maritime Issues, Future Patterns* (1979). Justus M. van der Kroef, "The South China Sea: Competing Claims and Strategic Conflicts," in *International Security Review* 7 (1982): 305–329.

WILLIAM J. DUIKER

SPRING AND AUTUMN PERIOD. In Chinese history the Eastern Zhou period (770–256 BCE) is subdivided into the Spring and Autumn and the Warring States periods. The former period takes its name from a book, the *Spring and Autumn Annals (Chunqiu),* purportedly compiled by Confucius. The work, a terse chronicle of the state of Lu, covers the years 722 to 481. To avoid creating a historical gap between 770 and 722 the period is generally construed to begin in 770. Although the *Spring and Autumn Annals* ends with events in 481, many feel that a far more significant date is 403, when the states of Han, Zhao, and Wei became legitimate political entities, having supplanted the state of Jin.

[*See also* Confucius *and* Zhou Period.]

JACK L. DULL